A complete index to Minnesota History magazine
can be found at
http://www.mnhs.org/market/mhspress/MinnesotaHistory/index.html
It covers v. 1 (1915) – to the present

(www.mnhs.org - Look under "products and services" and click on Minnesota History
Quarterly – then on "Index"
6/08

April 1, 2009

Minnesota History Magazine Launches New Website

Minnesota History, the quarterly of the Minnesota Historical Society launched a brand new user-focused website April 1. The site, www.mnhs.org/mnhistory<http://www.mnhs.org/mnhistory>, features nearly one hundred years of previously unavailable archival material with easy-to-use navigation, including fully searchable PDFs of the magazine's articles through 2003. The popular online index now includes live links to these PDF articles. The new interface also makes it easier to order issues and subscribe to the magazine. Future plans for the website include teacher pages.

Anne R. Kaplan, longtime editor of Minnesota History, notes , "We developed this enhanced website to serve history lovers throughout the state and beyond. It gives instant, easy, and free access to a wealth of valuable information previously unavailable online."

"Since the index to Minnesota History has been posted on our website for several years, many, many researchers have called, written, and emailed the MHS library for more information. Now we can send them directly to the citations," said Minnesota History Center archivist Ruth Bauer Anderson. Anderson recently received an email with requests for 96 citations to terms or names found in the index. She was happy to be able to tell the writer about the new ability to link from the index directly to the PDF files.

Minnesota History is a lively, richly illustrated magazine about the history of the state and the Upper Midwest. Published quarterly by the Minnesota Historical Society Press<http://www.mhspress.org>, Minnesota History features engaging articles on fresh topics ranging from the hayloft hoopsters who almost won the 1946 state basketball tournament to the birth of civil rights in Minnesota and the plight of the Dakota people at the Crow Creek Reservation. Whatever the topic, Minnesota History articles are original, soundly researched, and intriguingly written.

Minnesota History's wealth of illustrations includes many rarely seen images from the Historical Society's archives of some 250,000 historical photos, art, objects, posters, and fine-art photographs. These illustrate Minnesotans, their lives, landscapes, leisure, and occupations from the pre-territorial period to the present.

In addition to articles selected by expert referees, Minnesota History features regular departments that:

Publications of the

Minnesota Historical Society

RUSSELL W. FRIDLEY, Director

JEAN A. BROOKINS, Assistant Director
For Publications and Research

Consolidated Index
to *Minnesota History*
Volumes 11-40 (1930-67)

HELEN T. KATZ, Editor

MINNESOTA HISTORICAL SOCIETY PRESS • St. Paul • 1983

5/04

Copyright © 1983 by the Minnesota Historical Society

Library of Congress Catalog Card Number: 15-11185

International Standard Book Number: 0-87351-163-8

Introduction

The first multivolume index to
Minnesota History covered volumes 1
through 10 (1915-29) and appeared in
1931 under the editorship of Theodore C.
Blegen and Bertha L. Heilbron. The
present index of volumes 11 through 40
(1930-67) encompasses the single volume
indexes prepared principally by Miss
Heilbron and Ilse Levi. Helen T. Katz
consolidated the 30 separate indexes
with major assistance from Sarah P.
Rubinstein. Research and editorial help
was provided at various times by Mary D.
Cannon, Carolyn Gilman, Anne R. Kaplan,
Virginia L. Martin, Deborah L. Miller,
Ann Regan, and Bruce M. White.

In a serial publication spanning 37
years, both text and index evolve in
content and format. Thus, while this
compilation is based on individual
volume indexes, it differs in several
ways from them, due primarily to the
systematizing and guidance of June D.
Holmquist. A notable change is that the
editors reduced the total number of
entries and employed cross references to
cut the length of others -- a procedure
adopted in the interest of attaining
coherence and avoiding unwieldiness.

Generally the editors omitted page
references to facts or incidents that
were repeated throughout the separate
volumes, the names of donors to the
collections of the Minnesota Historical
Society, and the names of speakers whose
speeches are neither abstracted in the
text nor extant elsewhere. The con-
solidators retained all place names when-
ever the text furnished information
about them. They added county locations
to entries for geographical designa-
tions, such as townships, that are not
found on highway maps, and identified by
state or country places outside Minnesota, other than well-known cities.

In the original volume indexes,
individual churches were grouped under
headings representing their denominations. They now appear in separate
entries by name of the church and again
under their locations. For example,
Wesley Methodist Church in Minneapolis
is indexed by the name of the church and
under Minneapolis: Methodist churches,
but not under Methodist church.

Entries for women whose husbands are
also included in this compilation appear
in conventional fashion -- for example,
Smith, Mrs. John, rather than Smith,
Ruth. Otherwise a woman is listed under
whatever name she herself used, as in
Gág, Wanda. If she married during the
course of the years covered by the text,
the entry for her original name carries
a cross reference to her married name.

In referring to Minnesota's Indian
people, current usage favors Dakota and
Ojibway in preference to Sioux and
Chippewa. The change is not reflected
in this index because in most instances
the earlier terms were used in the text
of the volumes covered. Similarly, what
has been variously labeled the Sioux

War, the Sioux Uprising, or the Sioux Outbreak is now often designated as the Dakota War of 1862. In this work, however, it is referred to as the Sioux Outbreak.

Authors of articles or book reviews published in the magazine formerly were indexed by a double entry system -- one referring to the articles and reviews that appeared and a second to list all other references to that person. Here they appear in a single entry organized according to the following sequence: name and page references, titles of works in the magazine, works reviewed, reviews by, and other necessary subheads.

In an index that covers 30 volumes, a few entries will become quite long; therefore, in the interest of clarity, they have been paragraphed. See, for example, the entry for Minnesota Historical Society, which carries six separate paragaphs, each with its own heading and subheadings. The remaining differences between this compilation and the original volume indexes are primarily typographical and need no explanation.

An index under preparation has the vicious attribute of revealing inconsistencies and inaccuracies in the original text. Researchers checked all available sources in their efforts to correct recognized errors of logic, of dates, and in spelling of proper names. A list of errata, some of which appeared in the individual, published indexes, is included at the end of this work.

Consolidated Index

Adams, Elmer E., 13:120, 16:124, 18:
465, 20:353, 445; work reviewed,
31:51; speaker, 13:452, 14:122,
21:337, 23:103; author, 14:460,
15:360, 480, 16:118, 17:488, 20:
103; papers, 34:360
Adams, Mrs. Frank, speaker, 11:286
Adams, Franklin P., author, 17:226
Adams, G. J., 20:460
Adams, Mrs. Harriet, Sioux captive,
38:109n
Adams, Henry, 37:83; author, 12:85,
40:313; career, 17:73, 19:435, 39:
260
Adams, Herbert B., historian, 19:433,
24:336
Adams, James T., works reviewed, 13:
415, 14:202, 16:86, 21:180–182,
401, 30:53–55; author, 11:99, 13:
293, 14:77, 90, 28:357; editor,
19:60, 24:252, 26:358, 28:69, 30:
386
Adams, John, 19:311, 20:9; President,
17:10, 25:268; biography, 32:187
Adams, John Quincy, President, 22:70,
29:340; quoted, 22:75; secretary
of state, 25:182
Adams, Mary A., work reviewed, 27:333
Adams, Moses N., 35:171; missionary,
11:316, 13:195, 16:137; Indian
agent, 16:73, 35:167–177
Adams, Ramon F., author, 39:262
Adams, Randolph G., 23:134; editor,
28:173
Adams, Raymond W., author, 17:226
Adams, Sam E., legislator, 26:201n
Adams, Samuel, in Revolutionary War,
28:54
Adams, Wilbur B., author, 20:355
Adams, William F., author, 35:193
Adams, Lutheran church, 11:464; Nor-
wegian settlement, 12:269, 40:357
Adams High School, Minneapolis, news-
paper, 28:90
Adams School, St. Paul, 19:168, 211
Adamson, Hans C., work reviewed, 34:
351
Addams, Jane, reformer, 14:201
Addington, Hugh M., compiler, 25:309
Adelmann, Clara, 19:32
Adhémar, Jacques, trader, 11:261, 24:
179
Adkins, Mrs. Katherine N., author,
15:253
Adler, Dankmar, architect, 35:71
Adler, Otto, 29:89
Adney, Edwin T., work reviewed, 39:
256
Adoption, see Child welfare
Adrian, Charles R., "Minnesota's Non-
partisan Legislature," 33:155–163
Adrian, Catholic settlement, 21:210,
31:22, 35:139; history, 35:335
"Adriatic," steamboat, 25:72
Adshead, ———, vice-consul, 14:225
Advent Christian Church, Independence
Township, 21:85
Advertising, historical aspect, 12:
441, 28:382; to promote settlement, 13:32–35, 14:395, 17:107,
115, 276, 19:126, 20:245, 21:64,
22:93, 31:222, 225, 226, 230, 32:
163; of patent medicines, 14:413;
in frontier newspapers, 27:18–20;
for railroad travel, 30:234, 235,
237, 239; of resort areas, 36:92;
catalogs, 37:256

Aeronautics, see Aviation, Balloons,
Unite States Air Corps
Aeschliman, Mrs. Gertrude, author,
16:359
AFL-CIO, Minnesota, 40:362. See also
American Federation of Labor
Afton, (city and township), architec-
ture, 15:468, 21:211, 27:231, 34:
129, 38:343, 348; academy, 17:389;
flour milling, 18:208; agricul-
ture, 22:336, 361, 27:138, 30:195;
Germans, 23:404; Methodist church,
34:129; post office, 36:211
Agard, Walter R., author, 35:44
Agassiz, Louis, naturalist, 11:318,
32:85, 33:271; travels, 25:273,
29:267, 30:223; educator, 32:82,
33:279
Agassiz Club, St. Paul, science
group, 24:167
Agassiz Literary Club, Battle Lake,
17:488
Agate Bay, see Two Harbors
Aged, see Welfare
Ager, Waldemar, author, 13:324
"Agnes," steamboat, 13:238
Agnew, Alyes N., 23:155
Agnew, Dwight L., author, 23:86
Agnew, Mrs. Mabel, 14:439
Agralite Cooperative, Benson, his-
tory, 40:315
Agrarian movement, development, 11:
79, 32:181–183, 35:284, 36:101;
leaders, 16:365, 35:284; source
material, 29:102; Canada, 29:341;
Illinois, 38:235. See also Farm-
er-Labor party, Farmers' Alliance,
Farmers' Union, Granger movement,
Nonpartisan League, People's par-
ty
Agre, M. W., speaker, 28:85
Agrelius, Carl P., Swedish settler,
17:398
Ågren, P. G., author, 18:73
Agricultural and Mechanics' Club of
the Legislature of Minnesota, 22:
253
Agricultural Council, organized, 18:
323
Agricultural History Society, 15:119,
19:148n, 22:428, 24:255; objec-
tives, 26:82, 27:60
Agricultural Museum, first agricultural journal, 18:407
Agricultural societies, see Agriculture, individual state and county
societies
Agriculture, in fiction, 11:63–74,
185, 16:106, 107, 20:183, 23:113–
125, 156–158, 31:135–137, 36:80,
39:293; pioneer, 11:83, 96, 12:
137, 14:99, 15:209, 347, 18:286,
19:226, 322–324, 20:448, 32:49,
38:204, 40:272, 303; co-operative,
11:100, 17:474, 24:73, 29:76, 30:
405, 35:334; Minnesota communities, 11:114, 116, 12:337, 15:487,
16:233, 17:117, 358, 487, 24:91,
35:245; at trading posts, 11:175,
18:238, 23:244, 339; implements
and machinery, 11:186, 457, 12:
100, 141, 182, 13:204, 14:458, 15:
123, 238, 251, 464, 16:106, 277,
474, 17:190, 343, 18:289–291, 20:
232, 341, 432, 464, 21:341, 441,
22:201, 326, 23:316–327, 24:75,
92, 287–306, 352, 26:87, 90, 181,

287, 28:85, 29:22, 85, 30:371,
395, 31:55, 34:36, 348, 37:143,
151; at missions, 11:216, 15:110,
275, 16:107, 138–140, 19:142, 143–
145, 20:90, 21:23, 28, 163, 39:
306, 307, 308; periodicals, 11:
326, 12:325, 16:338, 17:234, 327,
18:195, 407–414, 21:328, 22:201,
23:86, 179, 283; Iowa, 11:326, 25:
71; economic aspects, 12:14, 334,
13:12, 332, 16:71, 190, 18:291–
293, 299, 21:449, 22:320, 23:179,
26:360–362, 28:38–44, 35:375, 36:
123, 37:220, 38:177–185, 334, 40:
296; U.S., 12:90, 16:221, 18:449,
19:347, 21:91, 22:92, 23:180, 24:
255, 34:251, 263, 35:45, 37:178;
methods, 12:147, 14:353, 18:341,
20:359, 36:28, 39:260; soil, effect on migration, 12:172–174;
Scandinavians in, 12:247, 17:402,
18:74, 19:200, 211, 29:278, 34:
173; relation to railroads, 12:
329, 13:111, 15:333, 18:106, 23:
54, 30:393, 33:33, 61, 36:68;
bonanza farms, 13:205, 16:129, 18:
79, 20:404, 21:448, 451, 25:300,
29:14, 15, 31:122, 33:61, 68, 70,
36:68, 37:259, 265–268, 39:206,
40:263; among Indians, 13:330, 15:
111, 122, 123, 263–269, 301, 305,
16:472, 25:154, 35:24, 28, 37:
273, 275, 276, 279, 280, 38:93,
94, 132, 40:158; Wisconsin, 13:
438, 29:86, 33:224, 36:235, 38:
194; history, 14:11, 22:110, 23:
378, 30:264, 370, 36:105, 150,
195; organizations, 14:137, 16:
478, 17:326, 18:294, 21:342, 22:
111, 249–269, 328, 23:91, 24:260,
28:37–44, 377; New York, 15:123,
17:111, 327; education, 15:243,
487, 16:352, 17:227, 19:113, 474,
22:412, 32:118, 33:224, 37:19–29,
134, 221, 39:83; at military
posts, 15:311, 16:351, 19:448, 21:
99; Middle West, 15:353, 19:102;
Red River Valley, 17:128, 20:207,
21:212, 448, 31:56, 32:119, 33:
314, 36:69, 281; relation to climate, 17:254, 18:285; atlas, 18:
102; New France, 18:395; research,
18:449; diversification, 19:148,
20:62, 27:115, 29:13, 25, 26, 335,
30:370; strip cropping, 20:359;
Irish in, 22:220, 35:205–213, 325;
itinerant labor, 25:221–223, 37:
265–270; Kansas, 25:375; Canada,
28:64, 366; New Jersey, 28:80;
veterans' colonies, 39:241–251;
tradition, 40:293; bibliography,
40:360; historic sites, 40:404.
See also Agrarian movement, Dairy
industry, Farmers, Fairs, Grasshopper plagues, Horticulture,
Livestock industry, United States
Department of Agriculture, various
farm products
Aguar, Jyring and Whiteman, 39:131
Aguinaldo, Emilio, Filipino insurgent, 23:171
Ahern, George P., author, 15:482; report on veterans' colonies, 39:
245–250
Ahern, Patrick H., author, 34:214;
compiler, 34:311; editor, 39:299
Ahlquist, Emma M., 21:85

Ahlstrom, Rev. L. J., author, 16:340
Ahrendt, Karl, actor, 32:103, 104
Ahrens, Mrs. Albert E., 28:302; speaker, 29:265
Ahsahivaince, Chippewa Indian, 24:262
Aiken, George L., 33:174
Aiken, Dr. Samuel C., speaker, 28:140
Aikens, Dr. George E., speaker, 12:292
Ainse, Sally, trader, 20:338
Ainsworth, D. W., flutist, 23:310
Ainsworth, Peter, author, 11:326
Air Line Pilots Association, 33:242
Air Corps, see United States Air Corps
Air mail, see Mail service
Aird, James, trader, 18:193
Airplanes, see Aviation
Airports, Minnesota, 19:99, 24:184
Aitken, David, trader, 20:71, 22:277
Aitken, John, trader, 22:357
Aitken, William A., trader, 11:359, 367, 16:358, 18:194, 19:342, 20:71, 78, 21:349, 23:24, 24:22n, 26:342, 36:248, 249, 39:303; posts, 11:374, 21:346, 22:277n, 36:40, 41, 47, 327
Aitken, Mrs. William A., 36:40
Aitkin, pageant, 11:111; schools, 16:245; Methodist church, 16:356; name, 21:349; pioneer life, 21:447; river port, 33:7-19; bridge, 33:15
Aitkin County, history, 11:111, 14:233, 22:109, 220, 23:105, 288, 35:50; trading post, 11:371; lumber industry, 12:428, 37:41; place names, 21:286, 346, 349, 350; schools, 21:448, 22:220; steamboating, 22:108, 33:8, 16, 40:263; wildlife, 30:127; veterans' colonies, 39:243, 245
Aitkin County Historical Society, 19:468, 29:273, 360, 30:77, 40:411; centennial program, 30:87, 164, 398; building, 30:275
Aitkin County War History Committee, 24:268
Aitkin Investment Co., 12:428
Aitkin Lake, Aitkin County, name, 21:349
Aitkin Volunteer fire Department, history, 15:132
Aitkinville, Morrison County, ghost town, 36:327. See also Swan River
Aiton, George B., missionary, 14:454; author, 12:418
Aiton, John F., missionary, 11:316, 12:98, 13:99, 195, 18:375, 19:448, 20:34
Akeley, Healy C., lumberman, 29:139, 140, 142
Akeley, history, 18:469, 23:401; railroad, 29:139; lumbering, 29:140, 31:75, 34:149-153; Methodist church, 31:75
Akeley Township, Hubbard County, history, 18:469
Akepa (Akeepa, Akipa), Sioux leader, 12:121, 127, 130n
Akerman, John D., airplane designer, 33:236, 243, 34:44
Akers, Berry H., author, 30:264
Akers, Mrs. Charles N., author, 12:105
Akers, Mrs. Cyrus W., author, 11:97
Akers, Dwight, author, 20:201

Akers, Peter, circuit rider, 21:203
Akers family, papers, 21:203
Akin, D. F., 19:235
Akiwense family, Chippewa Indians, 39:305n
Alabama, franchise law, 12:9; census records, 26:382
"Alabama," steamship, 15:307
Alabama State Department of Archives and History, 26:382
Alango, St. Louis County, Finnish settlement, 25:161, 320
Alaska, source material, 23:273; roads, 24:2, 84, 291, 26:9; exploration, 24:344; boundary, 25:172; sealing, 25:290, 40:217, 218; air service, 26:9; Russians in, 26:56, 37:56; place names, 30:67; gold mining, 32:60, 174, 33:43, 35:52; Indians, 35:141; acquired by U.S., 37:57; religion in, 39:128
Alaska Commercial Co., 40:217, 218
Alaska Township, Beltrami County, history, 15:132
Alavus, St. Louis County, Finnish settlement, 22:291n, 25:320
Albachten, Mrs. J. H., author, 27:81
Albany, N.Y., fur trade center, 11:234, 236, 259, 40:163; city hall, 40:99; Wyandot conference, 40:204
Albany Congress, 15:258
Albany House, Ont., Hudson's Bay Co. post, 34:254
Albany River, Ont., explored, 16:418n
Albaugh, D. W., G.A.R. commander, 16:434, 439
Albemarle, George Monk, Duke of, 16:391, 399, 419, 423, 425n
Albers family, 28:388
Albert, Rev. John H., 29:323
Albert Lea, historical meeting, 11:199, 291; history, 11:289, 30:271; mail service, 11:400, 28:83; stage lines, 11:402; ethnic settlements, 12:269, 15:136, 31:126; pioneer cabin, 14:304; county seat, 14:314, 15:346, 20:357; Fourth of July celebration, 14:353; Masonic lodge, 15:136; churches, 15:242, 16:335; folk arts museum, 16:364, 17:68; mayor, 18:114; library, 19:122, 27:175; oil co-operative, 20:103; wholesale grocery, 21:221; industry, 23:106, 301; first newspaper, 23:300; planning survey, 25:94; schools, 25:94; government, 30:144; rail center, 30:233, 236, 240, 33:43; county centennial, 35:335
Albert Lea Co-operative Creamery, history, 23:301
Albert Lea Insurance Co., 24:109
Albert Lea Lake, name, 16:478
Albert Lea War History Committee, 23:390
Alberta, Canada, wheat farming, 35:48; government, 35:148; Hutterite colony, 40:44; organizations, 40:262
Alberti, Dr. Rudolph, 34:19n
Alberts, Robert C., author, 33:351
Albertson, John, 22:221
Albinson, Dewey, artist, 13:307, 17:229, 19:461, 27:48; speaker, 23:36
Albinson, Elmer, 23:36
Albion Academy, Albion, Wis., 273

Alborn Township, St. Louis County, history, 23:302; railroad, 34:180
Albrecht, C. W., 17:469
Albrecht, Fred, 16:497
Albrecht, Harold, author, 34:128
Albrecht, Father Joseph, 19:124
Albrecht, William, 14:455
Albrecht Co., furriers, 17:337, 40:149
Albright, S. J., 14:268, 15:476
Alcan Highway, 24:84, 25:291, 26:9
Alcock, F. J., author, 34:132
Alcock, Merle, singer, 39:62
Alcorn, Edward, 17:235
Alden, Berry, artist, 28:281
Alden, Freeborn County, Baptist church, 17:118; history, 30:405
Alden Advance, anniversary, 22:344
Alden Lake, St. Louis County, railroad station, 34:181
Alder, Elise, 13:117
Aldrich, B. B., 25:21
Aldrich, Bess S., author, 20:116, 23:156
Aldrich, Mrs. Chilson D. (Darragh), 12:207; work reviewed, 32:120; author, 11:215, 16:18, 24:75, 31, 31:129, 134, 145; speaker, 18:66
Aldrich, Cyrus, Congressman, 25:22, 245, 29:283, 32:24, 30, 36:174n, 37:325-332, 38:56, 217, 218, 220
Aldrich, Leonard, pioneer farmer, 23:324
Aldrich, Philip, mail carrier, 36:207
Aldrich, Thomas B., 18:32
Aldrich-Vreeland Act, 12:12
Alere, Girar, French soldier, 13:203
Alexander, Charles, editor, 30:203
Alexander, Col. E. B., 12:61n
Alexander, Edward P., 24:70, 27:258; reviews by, 22:410, 23:65, 24:336, 26:62; author, 22:418, 23:74, 376, 24:337, 353, 26:65, 163, 271, 27:164, 34:213, 35:150, 36:150; editor, 23:90; speaker, 26:74, 27:66
Alexander, Gerard L., author, 33:139
Alexander, Guy, speaker, 25:407
Alexander, Hartley B., 19:218
Alexander, Jack, author, 21:204
Alexander, Jean H., author, 11:329, 12:418, 18:105
Alexander, Norman, author, 26:389
Alexander, Thomas B., work reviewed, 40:407
"Alexander McDougall," whaleback, 34:13
Alexandria, Norwegian settlement, 12:277; frontier post, 12:302, 38:66, 67, 283, 286; historical meeting 13:277-279; diamond jubilee, 15:135; history, 15:246, 18:355, 30:161, 271, 31:184, 36:106, 37:206; pageant, 19:256; roads, 21:235, 240-243, 35:258, 38:64, 209; depicted, 23:273
Alexandria, Va., First Minnesota at, 25:38, 117n
Alexandria Citizen-News, anniversary, 18:467
Alexandria Woman's Club, 15:135
Alexia, Sister, Benedictine nun, 27:99
Alexis, Joseph, author, 29:278
Alfalfa raising, history, 16:122, 364, 19:21-33, 69, 38:378
Alford, E. F., speaker, 12:283
Alfred, Mother, career, 37:186

Alfsborg Township, Sibley County, Norwegian settlement, 12:275; history, 13:122

Alger, Lake County, railroad station, 34:181

Alger, Smith and Co., logging firm, 13:351n, 361, 27:301n, 302, 34:181, 36:132; railroad, 34:179

Alger Line, see Duluth and Northern Minnesota Railroad

"Algoma," steamboat, 34:39, 35:281

Algona, Iowa, in Sioux Outbreak, 11:210

Algonquian Indians, 14:368; relations with French, 15:257, 19:271; in Wisconsin, 15:471; pottery, 16:15; Brothertown band, 27:69

Algonquin Club, publications, 20:338

Alice, St. Louis County, transportation service, 21:291, 27:272, 36:190

Alida, Clearwater County, ghost town, 16:493

Aliferis, James, composer, 30:280

Alink, Derk, Dutch pioneer, 28:121, 122

Alink, Mrs. Derk, 28:124

Alis, Karel, publisher, 13:269

Allamakee County, Iowa, mounds, 16:112

Allan, George W., 21:186

Allan Line, promotes emigration, 20:249, 251

Alland, Helene, "A High School Survey at St. Cloud," 26:234-238; author, 26:258

Allanson, Mrs. Ellen B., see Brown, Ellen

Allanson, George G., 12:112, 428, 22:205; author, 11:456, 12:456, 13:340, 16:248, 18:461, 19:465, 20:99, 103, 27:365, 28:191, 29:366

Allanson, John S., 35:171

Allanson, Mrs. John S., house, 39:274, 275

Allanson, M. Ethel, 12:120n

Allar, Helen, 28:250, 251, 253

Allard, Mrs. Dora, 20:454, 21:443

Alleine, Joseph, author, 22:355

Allen, Mrs. ---, Stillwater pioneer, 24:203

Allen, Albert H., author, 12:439; bibliographer, 26:72; editor, 29:173

Allen, Azlene, actress, 23:314

Allen, Benjamin F., banker, 40:127

Allen, Byron G., speaker, 25:312

Allen, Claudia M., speaker, 13:121

Allen, E. A., speaker, 11:460

Allen, Mrs. E. D., 11:334

Allen, George W., art patron, 36:314

Allen, Guerdon S., 26:285; author, 22:218, 35:323n; speaker, 27:364, 28:88, 29:276

Allen, Harold B., "Hunting for Minnesota Proverbs," 27:33-36; author, 27:55, 34:127, 37:42; speaker, 28:75, 280

Allen, Henry E., work reviewed, 40:41

Allen, Hervey, author, 25:191

Allen, Howard W., author, 38:238

Allen, James, army officer, explorations, 12:217, 226, 13:173, 288, 18:180, 182, 183, 25:396, 33:316; journal, 36:184

Allen, James Lane, 20:82; author, 20:110

Allen, Capt. James P., papers, 12:319, 13:100

Allen, Max P., author, 27:352

Allen, Paul, hardware merchant, 23:88

Allen, Phyllis, author, 29:77

Allen, Robert, 11:238n

Allen, Robert E. B., 25:305; speaker, 306, 397

Allen, Dr. S. A., author, 21:437

Allen, Rev. S. T., author, 12:445

Allen, Dr. W. A., Rochester physician, 11:465

Allen, W. B., author, 16:229

Allen, Willard, 12:340

Allen, William F., historian, 19:433, 24:336

Allen, William Q., postmaster, 34:186

Allen and Chase, stage company, 38:64

Allen Junction, St. Louis County, railroad station, 34:180

Alley, John B., attorney, 19:193, 194

Alliance party, 34:221; history, 32:129, 138-146, 36:113, 114, 118, 122, 183. See also Farmers' Alliance, People's party

Allis, Mary Lou, 27:147

Allison, John H., Sr., work reviewed, 37:258; author, 30:267, 39:132

Allison, Joy, author, 23:156

Allison, William B., politician, 35:246

Allison piano, 39:323n

Allouez, Father Claude J., explorer, 12:282, 283, 349, 353, 14:339, 18:388, 19:198; journal, 13:254; missionary activities, 13:400, 14:215, 19:275

Allston, Washington, artist, 31:102

Allyn, Robert, 19:129

Alman, Miriam, work reviewed, 38:198

Almanacs, as source material, 15:444-449

Almelund, depicted, 33:315

Almer, A. T., author, 30:158

Almond, Wis., settled, 34:127

Alnes, Stephen, author, 36:283, 37:263

"Alpha," steamboat, 21:254, 259n, 261

Alphabet Road, history, 13:342

Alsatians, colonies, 21:74; St. Paul, 38:251

Alsop, Henry W., author, 11:104

Alsop, Stewart, author, 40:299

Alsop and Mahlum, boatbuilders, 33:10

Alsop Brothers, papers, 30:40, 91

Alter, J. Cecil, author, 20:204

Altgeld, John P., politician, 15:338, 22:80, 39:106; Illinois governor, 36:121, 122

Altnow, Randall D., author, 14:360

Altnow family, genealogy, 14:360

Alto, Wis., Dutch settlement, 28:121-124, 128

Alton, Ill., river port, 17:435, 22:16; thresher factory, 23:324

Alvarado, Lutheran church, 22:441

Alvord, Clarence W., historian, 16:453, 21:183, 29:337, 30:316, 32:6, 39:166; papers, 11:319, 12:26; biography, 17:462. See also Alvord Memorial Commission

Alvord, Thomas G., Jr., author, 16:236

Alvord Memorial Commission, 11:93, 12:31, 13:317, 22:44, 23:38, 366, 35:52; fund, 11:41, 35:52; publications, 13:436, 17:61, 21:311,

23:37, 366, 24:33, 41-43, 60, 26:36, 28:48, 32:56, 243

Alyea, Hubert N., speaker, 34:176

Alwin, Edward L., author, 14:353

Amahami Indians, 15:232

Amana, Iowa, Utopian colony, 33:228

Amberg, Gustav, theater director, 32:103, 104, 166, 171, 33:315, 34:241

Ambler, Charles H., 24:162

Ambler, T. A., speaker, 40:61

Amboy, history, 25:211

Amboy Township, Cottonwood County, history, 19:473

"Ambrosius," emigrant ship, 37:262

Amdur, Dr. M. K., author, 23:387

Amelia Lake, Pope County, mills, 21:218; garrison, 38:285

Amenia and Sharon Land Co., bonanza farm, 20:405, 39:206

"America," steamboat, 25:412, 35:280, 281

America books, Ole M. Raeder, 11:82, 20:293; Ole Rynning, 16:108, 18:74; anthology, 29:154

America First Committee, 33:306, 38:332

America letters, 18:455; Norwegian, 11:89, 103, 13:206, 15:473, 16:108, 17:343, 18:316, 19:49, 97, 210, 20:35, 21:85, 24:258, 32:121, 35:31-33, 36:236, 40:357; influence, 12:181, 260, 305; English, 12:339; German, 17:79, 26:66, 39:65-74; Swedish, 17:400, 19:331, 20:249-258, 30:157, 34:353, 35:31-33, 36:195, 38:386; value, 20:334; Dutch, 35:90; Welsh, 37:256

American Academy of Fine Arts, history, 34:120

American Agriculturist, on frontier, 22:336

American Airlines, army contract, 26:7

American Alumni Council, 14:434

American Anthropological Association, 12:31; meetings, 11:313, 21:82; publications, 19:111

American Antiquarian Society, collections, 18:448, 21:95

American Art-Union, 13:301, 33:113; history, 34:120

American Association for the Advancement of Science, 15:229, 39:121, 122n

American Association of Farmers' Institute Managers, 37:25

American Association of Museums, 16:58, 59; meetings, 15:66, 342, 23:278, 27:266, 30:257. See also Midwest Museums Conference

American Association for State and Local History, 24:70, 377, 25:73, 26:63, 28:369, 29:94, 30:368; organized, 22:428; publications, 23:376, 24:254, 362, 25:204, 310, 379, 403, 26:36, 62, 163, 278, 27:160, 252, 28:71, 73, 175, 180, 29:81, 30:257, 386, 31:54, 33:311, 37:37, 38:240, 387, 39:209, 40:361; meetings, 25:84, 26:74, 27:49, 30:149, 32:123, 36:84n, 328, 37:85, 136, 348, 40:35; awards, 31:11, 34:176, 353, 360, 35:336, 36:69, 103, 104, 105, 108, 327, 37:182, 188, 38:92, 39:173, 40:264, 364

American Association of University

Women, 14:222; Minnesota branch, 14:217, 33:209. See also St. Paul College Club

American Automobile Association, Glidden tours, 38:205-215; founded, 38:244

American Bible Society, 18:351

American Board of Commissioners for Foreign Missions, Lac qui Parle mission, 12:245, 15:129, 16:133-151, 303, 23:398, 39:300; publications, 12:246, 19:448, 21:278; Leech Lake mission, 15:43; Minnesota survey, 15:126, 275; centennial, 16:354; archives, 20:452, 22:353, 24:44; at Yellow Lake, 28:3; among Sioux, 35:29, 38:357; nominates Indian agents, 35:167, 168, 170, 175

American Bridge Co., Minneapolis, 33:333; history, 28:189

American Catholic Historical Association, 19:209, 22:428

American Cedar Co., lumber camp, 34:59

American Church Temperance Society, Minnesota branch, 23:76

American Council of Agriculture, 38:182

American Council of Learned Societies, 11:93, 12:31, 442, 13:47, 105, 210, 15:352, 357, 16:349, 18:91, 217, 20:44, 76, 294, 325; survey, 13:184; publications, 14:230, 348, 17:114, 225, 476, 25:304; advisory board, 19:91

American Dialect Society, collects Minnesota proverbs, 27:33-36

American Ethnological Society, publication, 25:194

American Exchange Bank, Duluth, 37:123. See also First and American National Bank

American Expeditionary Forces, records, 40:361

American Farm Bureau Federation, 21:212, 28:37, 38, 39, 42, 43, 32:182, 35:334, 38:183

American Federation of Labor, 13:19, 22:370, 380, 37:383, 40:341, 353; Minnesota, 18:191, 20:433, 22:389, 35:59. See also AFL-CIO, Minnesota State Federation of Labor

American Folklore Society, 25:306, 28:280

American Forest Fire Medal Foundation, 24:346

American Forest History Foundation, see Forest History Society

American Forestry Association, 17:220. See also Forestry

American Friends Service Committee, 18:265

American Fur Co., 16:454; graduate theses, 11:98; trade goods, 11:101, 33:89, 35:196; posts, 11:354-356, 359-361, 366, 368-374, 376-382, 384, 13:222, 23:24, 33:350; traders, 12:236;238, 426, 14:223, 15:427, 19:95, 20:119n, 262, 263, 21:24n, 32n, 22:355, 30:72; competitors, 12:236, 13:237, 19:306, 22:191, 206, 277, 278, 280n, 310, 29:58, 32:68, 36:241-249, 38:328, 40:43, 144; banking activities, 13:108, 16:23; use of steamboats, 13:232, 233, 234, 243, 18:161n,

38:236; partners, 14:196, 21:95, 22:4, 205, 39:254; development, 15:120, 19:305; employees, 15:425, 430, 19:348, 23:233, 243n, 247, 27:97; medals, 16:322; papers, 17:61, 18:439, 27:129-131, 30:259; failure, 19:307; relations with Indians, 20:120, 21:163, 39:255; absorbed by Chouteau and Co., 22:156n, 36:38n; fisheries, 34:245, 248, 39:303; in politics, 35:107, 39:43, 148; policies and characteristics, 37:262, 40:178-187; relations with army sutlers, 40:22-31; Upper Missouri Outfit, 40:155, 186; trade agreement, 40:170; prices and production, 40:211n, 212-214, 215n, 216, 218, 220. See also Astor, John J.; Fur trade; Voyageurs; individual posts

American Geologist, 32:222, 224

American Heritage Foundation, 28:369

American Historical Association, 16:452, 17:14, 19:329, 38:200; meetings, 11:93, 12:31, 81, 315, 13:64, 105, 14:316, 15:118, 228, 16:196, 17:73, 94, 105, 385n, 19:101, 148n, 347, 20:43, 76, 85, 21:82, 22:44, 428, 23:82, 377, 30:24n, 46, 149, 39:220; Pacific coast branch, 13:328, 37:85; committees, 14:88-90, 193, 20:294, 25:168; officers, 16:60, 17:90, 18:92, 127n, 21:68; publications, 17:216, 19:433, 23:178, 26:63, 255, 278, 27:129-131, 28:362, 30:259; historical service board, 24:351, 25:205, 26:37, 278; radio program, 24:362; Beveridge memorial, 27:60

American Hoist and Derrick Co., St. Paul, anniversary, 15:140

American Home Missionary Society, archives, 15:62, 223, 16:52, 56, 313-318, 17:329, 393, 20:35, 22:55n, 34:338; Minnesota, 17:335, 19:247; on frontier, 21:71, 22:58, 30:202, 40:1-11

American House, Galena, Ill., 17:301

American House, Renville, 18:211

American House, Northfield, 35:112, 113

American House, St. Paul: 34:98; 12:392, 16:37, 30:197, 200, 36:264, 266, 39:145, 40:331; built, 22:57n, 39:144; described, 34:96, 97; pictured, 34:101, 36:265, 39:149; court session, 39:146

American Imprints Inventory, WPA project, 24:361

American Institute of Architects, 22:303, 23:272

American Institute of Graphic Arts, 21:95, 31:254, 33:35

American Jewish Archives, 29:283, 33:195n

American Jewish Committee, war activities, 23:292

American Land and Colonization Company of Scotland, 17:54, 99

American Legion, 16:305, 23:292, 27:231; Minnesota, 12:194, 212, 339, 430, 14:105, 457, 16:245, 367, 427, 17:127; Indianapolis headquarters, 23:393; educational program, 15:120; history, 26:166; supports disabled veterans, 39:241, 244, 245, 247, 249

American Legion Auxiliary, Minnesota, 11:445, 12:422, 13:197, 14:106, 438, 16:101, 127, 214, 369, 472, 23:292

American Library Association, meetings, 12:315, 15:66, 16:330, 18:57, 20:74, 325, 506, 21:82, 24:267; war work, 14:320; newspaper list, 18:16; committee, 20:294

American Medical Association, 16:29, 21:359; activities, 28:371

American Missionary Association, 17:229, 35:175

American Monthly, 30:204

American Museum of Natural History, 21:154, 22:133, 134, 141; publication, 21:325; Catlin collection, 23:181, 27:254

American Name Society, 33:186, 311

American National Bank, Little Falls, anniversary, 14:356

American Newspaper Publishers Association, 31:119, 37:168, 169

American Numismatic Society, 16:322

American Philosophical Society, 19:39, 36:222, 223, 224, 225, 37:188, 39:264, 40:409; publications, 18:323, 26:85

American Point, Lake of the Woods, 18:279, 34:2, 3, 4; post office, 34:7n

American Protective Association, Minnesota, 19:219, 26:373

American Public Health Association, 21:362

American Railway Express, in Minnesota, 18:220

American Railway Union, 36:120, 121, 39:101

American Red Cross, 23:21; in World War I, 11:418, 14:320, 16:370, 23:151, 28:349; Rice County, 16:242; in World War II, 28:82

American Reform Tract and Book Society, 19:142, 143

American Revolution, see Revolutionary War

American Slav Congress, Pittsburgh, 23:393

American Society of Equity, 18:323; history, 19:104, 21:202, 32:181, 35:334

American Soldier (Manila, P.I.), 17:469, 26:157

American Steel and Wire Division, United States Steel Corp., 36:103; museum, 19:345

American Swedish Historical Foundation, archives, 29:350

American Swedish Historical Museum, Philadelphia, 19:106

American Swedish Institute, Minneapolis, 40:48; museum, 23:190, 24:256; publications, 26:364, 30:391; history, 34:172, 36:106, 37:135

American Temperance Union, 22:124

American Turf Register and Sporting Magazine, 15:221; Rindisbacher illustrations, 14:286; history, 14:421-424

American Woman Suffrage Association, Boston, 39:4; Minnesota, 39:10

American Wright Co., Dayton, Ohio, organized, 22:302

American Yugoslav Association, 30:178

American Youth Commission, Washington, D.C., 23:393

Amerland, William H., autograph col-
    lection, 25:181, 286, 287, 26:32,
    256, 33:298
Amerman, P. S., diary, 11:96
Ames, Gen. Adelbert, in Northfield
    robbery, 11:117; letters, 36:281
Ames, Dr. Albert A., politician, 12:
    332, 35:60; Minneapolis mayor, 20:
    403, 35:344, 345
Ames, Dr. Alfred E., pioneer physi-
    cian, 21:101, 437, 39:112, 114;
    house, 12:402, 14:268, 272, 279,
    15:185, 25:5
Ames, Alonzo A., 22:379, 386
Ames, Blanche B., compiler, 36:281
Ames, Carlton C., "Paul Bunyan," 21:
    55-58; review by, 33:265; author,
    21:80, 176, 178, 187, 296, 24:176,
    33:91, 35:392
Ames, Rev. Charles G., 14:132, 19:
    214; lecturer, 12:400
Ames, Dr. Clair E., speaker, 15:316
Ames, Bishop Edward R., 18:350
Ames, Capt. Jesse, miller, 11:280
Ames, John T., 16:361
Ames, Michael E., politician, 39:43;
    lawyer, 40:222
Ames, Oakes, manufacturer, 19:193,
    194, 195
Amherst, Sir Jeffrey, governor gener-
    al, 11:235, 239, 267; Indian poli-
    cy, 29:65, 33:37
Amherst Township, Fillmore County,
    Norwegian settlement, 12:268
Amherstburg, Ont., trading post, 18:
    37, 38
Amick, Harry C., lawyer, 21:195
Amidon, Mrs. Perry, 22:216
Amikwa Indians, in fur trade, 40:208
Amor Township, Otter Tail County,
    pioneer life, 11:337, 12:340, 18:
    110, 335
Amos, Leola, 21:215
Ampato Sapa, Sioux woman, 20:136
Ampersand Club, 20:325
Amrine, Michael, work reviewed, 37:84
Amrud, Dr. Anna, 23:390, 25:96, 406,
    26:89, 283, 392, 27:265, 28:85,
    30:78; author, 22:445, 23:398, 30:
    282; speaker, 29:273, 30:276, 399
Amundsen, Mrs. A. E., 17:483
Amusements, see Social life
Anatole (Chrysler), St. Louis County,
    pioneer settlement, 34:184
Anawangmani, Simon, Sioux Indian, 38:
    149n
Ance Keweena, Mich., trading post,
    13:181
Anchor Line, lake freighters, 34:13
Ancient Arabic Order of Nobles of the
    Mystic Shrine, papers, 12:193
Ancient Order of United Workmen, Min-
    nesota, 21:383
Andeer, Carl, author, 18:69
Ander, O. Fritiof, reviews by, 14:94,
    30:377, 33:85, 309; works re-
    viewed, 13:308-310, 34:263, 35:
    290, 38:381; speaker, 15:227; edi-
    tor, 15:361; author, 15:473, 16:
    107, 18:213, 19:219, 26:274, 27:
    257, 30:153, 412, 37:40, 38:386
Anders, J. Olson, review by, 16:207;
    work reviewed, 14:94
Andersen, A. H., farmer, 24:180
Andersen, Arlow W., works reviewed,
    33:348, 38:332; author, 25:385

Andersen, Elmer L., review by, 34:
    257; governor, 39:257
Andersen, Fred C., author, 34:44
Andersen, H. Carl, speaker, 25:406
Andersen, Jens J., 28:244, 245
Andersen, Mrs. Jens J. (Petrine J.),
    28:244, 249
Andersen, John M., photographer, 38:
    352n
Andersen, Mads, Mormon missionary,
    36:290, 292
Andersen, Per S., work reviewed, 35:
    329
Andersen, R., author, 13:324
Andersen, Theodore A., work reviewed,
    34:165
Andersen Corporation, Bayport, 34:
    129; anniversary, 34:44
Anderson, A. C., trader, 40:167n,
    168n
Anderson, A. E., Mormon missionary,
    36:288
Anderson, A. G. W., translator, 14:
    235
Anderson, A. H., author, 17:231, 20:
    95, 101
Anderson, A. H., farmer, 25:334
Anderson, A. O., author, 24:190;
    speaker, 26:89
Anderson, Alexander C., 15:345
Anderson, Alexander P., 17:160n, au-
    thor, 22:333
Anderson, Alfred, author, 12:337
Anderson, Andrew G., bus operator,
    21:291, 36:190
Anderson, Anton, gold miner, 29:308,
    309
Anderson, Antone A., author, 34:218
Anderson, Arvid, author, 20:467
Anderson, Astrid, author, 29:278
Anderson, Avis, "My Scandinavian-Ger-
    man Heritage," 28:243-250
Anderson, Bergit I., work reviewed,
    22:415; author, 22:345
Anderson, Betsy, 37:87
Anderson, C. O., author, 13:119
Anderson, Campie, author, 35:294
Anderson, Carolus G., 28:389
Anderson, Charles, 24:87
Anderson, Charles, author, 24:258
Anderson, Charles, Gibbon pioneer,
    30:275
Anderson, Charles A., author, 30:160
Anderson, Dr. Charles L., naturalist,
    16:38, 19:267, 22:292, 433, 34:
    333n, 35:253, 261, 262; pioneer
    physician, 21:101
Anderson, Clarence N., author, 28:294
Anderson, Curtis, scuba diver, 38:24-
    34
Anderson, Bishop David, career, 30:
    387; in St. Paul, 37:53-57
Anderson, Ebba, author, 35:294
Anderson, Einar J., author, 11:103
Anderson, Rev. Ernest G., speaker,
    29:371
Anderson, Evan H., memorial, 15:467
Anderson, Fannie, work reviewed, 33:
    87
Anderson, Frank M., work reviewed,
    30:59; historian, 32:7
Anderson, Dr. Gaylord, 29:53
Anderson, George L., essay reviewed,
    36:150; author, 34:354
Anderson, H. E., author, 14:346
Anderson, Halvor, pioneer, 29:362,
    37:87

Anderson, Mrs. Halvor, 29:362
Anderson, Hannah, 37:87
Anderson, Harry A., 23:390
Anderson, Henry M., 18:110
Anderson, Hjalmar, 23:398
Anderson, Hogan, farmer, 29:14
Anderson, J., trader, 40:167n, 168n
Anderson, J. E., speaker, 15:365
Anderson, Jens, farmer, 29:14
Anderson, John, missionary, 15:235
Anderson, John, Publishing Co., 15:
    448
Anderson, John Tracy, 36:284
Anderson, John W., 14:428
Anderson, Jöns, Swedish immigrant,
    20:258
Anderson, Capt. Joseph, in Sioux Out-
    break, 12:297, 298, 300, 38:138
Anderson, K. W., author, 12:340
Anderson, Magdaline, author, 34:172
Anderson, Mary, actress, 28:101, 117,
    33:175
Anderson, Mary, labor leader, autobi-
    ography, 33:42
Anderson, Mary, Sioux captive, 38:
    109n
Anderson, Mrs. Mary J. H., autobiog-
    raphy, 14:330, 16:209
Anderson, Maxwell, author, 36:102
Anderson, Moppy, 28:86, 29:91
Anderson, Myrtle, author, 30:75
Anderson, Ole, 12:136
Anderson, Dr. Ole W., pharmacist,
    35:381
Anderson, Oliver, 25:313
Anderson, Oscar, trapper, 34:281
Anderson, Oscar A., college presi-
    dent, 40:383
Anderson, P. H., missionary, 33:43
Anderson, Parker O., author, 17:352
Anderson, Paul A., cholera victim,
    14:301
Anderson, Phil L., author, 15:364,
    31:145
Anderson, Rev. R. W., author, 22:343
Anderson, Rasmus B., 25:86; author,
    12:304, 328, 22:68, 26:288; speak-
    er, 14:448; education, 15:235;
    professor, 18:432, 433, 31:252;
    relations with Hamsun, 20:398,
    401, 408; biography, 40:351
Anderson, Robert, 16:209
Anderson, Robert, cavalry leader,
    25:242
Anderson, Robert D., author, 18:445,
    19:214
Anderson, Robert L., author, 29:169
Anderson, Russell H., author, 11:100,
    24:255
Anderson, Sam G., 19:343
Anderson, Mrs. Sam G., see Hutchin-
    son, Abby
Anderson, Sam G., Jr., 16:496
Anderson, Sara, 14:428
Anderson, Sherwood, author, 16:482
Anderson, Sydney, Congressman, 40:
    321, 323-329; portrait, 40:322
Anderson, Capt. Thomas G., trader,
    11:376, 25:267; at Prairie du
    Chien, Wis., 18:193, 20:259
Anderson, Torgny, editor, 39:130
Anderson, Veggo, 28:243, 244, 246
Anderson, Mrs. Veggo (Agnes H.), 28:
    243, 245, 246
Anderson, Mrs. Victor C., speaker,
    22:106
Anderson, Mrs. W. H., speaker, 14:461

Anderson, William, professor, 18:44, 23:389, 28:285, 29:35; "Minnesota Frames a Constitution," 36:1-12; reviews by, 17:194, 24:52, 27:337, 38:195; works reviewed, 17:201-204, 34:258; author, 16:233, 17:206, 24:60, 27:343, 28:329, 35:336, 37:347; speaker, 35:248, 339
Anderson, William A., 21:110
Andersonville, Ga., prison, 17:98, 25:148n, 38:291
Andersson, Axel, author, 18:69
Andersson, Dan, in Minnesota, 26:365
Andert, F. A., speaker, 11:460, 12:287
Andre, Anthony, 11:238n
Andreani, Count Paolo, 17:197; American travels, 19:34-42, 69, 104
Andreas, Alfred T., atlas publisher, 40:120-129
Andreas, B. M., author, 36:103
Andreas, Lyter & Co., map publishers, 40:124
Andreas, Sophia Lyter, 40:123
Andresen, August H., Congressman, 12:104, 13:122, 38:181, 40:368
Andrews, Lt. ---, at Fort Snelling, 18:400
Andrews, A. C., 12:291
Andrews, Alice, musician, 28:114, 33:321, 323
Andrews, Amasa, family, 26:68; house, 38:341, 342
Andrews, Mrs. Amasa, family, 26:68
Andrews, Ammah, house, 38:341, 342
Andrews, Caddie, singer, 33:323
Andrews, Charles, opera manager, 28:114, 33:318, 319, 321, 323
Andrews, Charles McLean, author, 25:295
Andrews, Gen. Christopher C., 21:412, 35:255, 265, 40:282; author, 12:434, 26:297n, 28:26, 31:105, 36:159, 39:174; forester, 14:104, 17:477, 23:99, 26:238, 240, 39:260, 40:145, 361; papers, 15:223, 16:332, 20:81, 25:289, 33:350, 34:339; in Civil War, 17:217, 468, 40:281-292; editor, 17:365; minister to Sweden, 20:192, 39:260; Minnesota travels, 22:85, 26:109; civic leader, 29:272; in politics, 36:183, 307, 308
Andrews, Mrs. Christopher C., 25:289
Andrews, Ed, singer, 33:317n, 320-322, 324, 325
Andrews, Florence, see Clayton, Florence A.
Andrews, Frances, 12:207; speaker, 12:291; author, 20:205
Andrews, George, musician, 28:114, 33:320, 321, 322, 323, 324, 325
Andrews, J. Cutler, work reviewed, 34:343
Andrews, Dr. J. W., 33:317n
Andrews, James, 21:430, 22:207
Andrews, James A., author, 12:94; surveyor, 22:86, 24:165; papers, 25:185, 29:49
Andrews, James C., 19:184n
Andrews, Jessie, singer, 33:323
Andrews, John, author, 20:444
Andrews, Rev. John R., 33:317n, 318, 319
Andrews, Laura, singer, 33:317n, 318, 320-322
Andrews, Lydia B., author, 13:115

Andrews, Mrs. Martha F., 28:81
Andrews, Mrs. Mary C., 22:207
Andrews, Nannie, singer, 33:323
Andrews, Nellie, see Hazelrigg, Nellie A.
Andrews, Roy Chapman, author, 28:180
Andrews, Ruth, 22:207
Andrews, S. Holmes, artist, 34:27, 85 (cover), 35:368, 37:308
Andrews, Sarah A., letters, 21:430, 22:207, 35:48
Andrews, Sarah E., 26:68
Andrews, Mr. and Mrs. Thomas, 33:318
Andrews, William H., 12:291; career, 13:115
Andrews family, musicians, 22:431, 30:174, 33:317-325
Andrews and Comstock, Hudson, Wis., real-estate firm, 24:165, 26:68
Andrews Opera Co., 28:99, 113; in Minneapolis, 33:176; tours, 33:317-325
Andrew's Sharpshooters, Civil War unit, 25:122, 123n
Andrist, Godfrey, 12:449
Andrist, Ralph K., author, 38:384, 39:342
Andros, Dr. Frederic, career, 11:316
Andrus, Percy H., author, 12:329
Andrus, W. P., author, 30:127
Andrus-Juneau, Isura, author, 22:327
"Andy Gibson," steamboat, 33:12, 13, 14, 40:411
AnDyke, F. M., pioneer, 16:361, 19:238
Andyke, Henry, miller, 11:280
Angel, John, sculptor, 39:160
Angell, William P., Quaker minister, 18:260, 261n
Angle, Paul M., 26:265; "The Clark Papers," 36:227-229; reviews by, 22:73, 30:59; works reviewed, 27:335, 28:171, 34:251, 35:147; author, 11:328, 22:82, 25:85, 389, 26:377, 30:95, 36:217, 40:313; editor, 28:186, 40:313; speaker, 28:393, 30:366, 36:196
Anglemyer, A. F., speaker, 12:206, 22:338
Angus, R. B., railroad builder, 17:218
Angus, rail center, 30:234
Animals, imaginary, 21:353-356. See also Wildlife, various animals
Anisansel, Henry, 14:216
Ann River Logging Co., Mora, 34:62
Ann Township, Cottonwood County, history, 39:130
Annan, Charles L., papers, 11:206
Annan, Gertrude L., author, 28:173
Annandale, founded, 17:492
Anne, queen of England, medals, 25:266
"Annie Johnston," steamboat, 38:291
Anoka, trading post, 11:375; flour mill, 14:234; lumbering, 15:244; schools, 16:123; pioneer life, 17:225, 18:112, 19:114, 145, 21:415, 26:286, 28:290, 30:112; churches, 17:229, 230, 350, 466, 21:415, 40:10; history, 17:234; described, 19:96, 30:91; fishing, 24:139; community study, 25:362-367, 28:164, 359; name, 25:366, 26:93; post office, 26:93, 40:89; centennial, 28:379; depot, 28:396; ferry, 35:255; Mormon mission, 36:

288; Halloween celebrations, 37:348
Anoka County, pioneer life, 11:459, 16:245, 492, 18:318, 22:220, 24:189, 28:380, 40:47; oxcart trail, 12:447; courthouse, 13:214, 447; anniversary, 13:341; history, 13:446, 40:47; mills, 14:234, 454; mythical towns, 15:194; archaeology, 15:483, 22:210, 24:180; district court, 18:108; farmers' club, 18:224; Quakers, 18:258; schools, 19:233, 29:90; roads, 21:448, 40:247n; fair, 22:257; archives, 23:188; wildlife, 30:228; politics, 36:306; balloon landing, 38:175
Anoka County Historical Society, 15:71, 364, 483, 16:63, 240, 245, 28:379; meetings, 16:123, 489, 17:119, 354, 481, 18:108, 221, 333, 463, 19:114, 229, 20:210, 349, 21:333, 22:104, 338, 23:99, 25:405, 26:178, 29:90, 178, 360; library, 23:100
Anoka County Union, history, 24:381, 40:47
Anoka County War History Committee, 24:81
Anoka Electric Cooperative, history, 38:204
Anoka Herald, politics, 38:305
Anoka Library Association, 38:53
Anonsen, Andrew E., autobiography, 21:112
Anonsen, Stanley H., 12:38, 13:71; "A School Pageant," 12:169-171; work reviewed, 11:434-436; author, 11:98; 12:39, 21:112; speaker, 11:119
Anselma, Sister, anesthetist, 33:294
Ansgarius College, Knoxville, Ill., 11:103
"Anson Northup," steamboat, 13:242, 335, 14:154, 16:334, 17:128, 217, 18:271, 275, 357, 19:110, 385, 386, 21:252n, 265, 23:110, 32:60, 260, 38:200; built, 11:308, 14:154; described, 18:356, 21:249; launched, 21:235, 38:65; first trip, 21:248; names, 21:250, 33:9, 271n; depicted, 33:273, 35:250
Antelope, Minnesota, 30:125; in fur trade, 40:210
"Antelope," steamboat, 11:138, 139, 12:113, 18:161, 27:296
Anthony, Irvin, author, 11:323
Anthony, Susan B., feminist, 37:86, 39:4, 10
Anthony Township, Norman County, history, 14:357
"Anthony Wayne," steamboat, 11:123, 37:311; excursions, 11:126, 127, 135
Anthropology, history, 36:148
Antietam, Md., battle, 20:277, 23:115
Anti-Horse Thief Association, 21:425; Waseca County, 19:350; Fergus Falls, 26:121
Anti-Monopolist (St. Paul), 15:345
Anti-Monopoly party, 16:455, 35:53, 57-59; organized, 21:384, 35:56, 98
Anti-Poverty Society, 22:379
Antiquarian and Historical Society of Illinois, 23:89
Antique Automobile Club of America, Minnesota Region, 38:205, 40:147

Anti-Saloon League, 15:120, 22:397

Anti-Semitism, Minneapolis, 31:44, 37:166; relation to Populism, 35: 378, 39:260, 343

Antislavery movement, see Abolition movement

Antitrust laws, supported by Populists, 12:17

Anti-Tuberculosis League, 27:82

Antonia, Sister, see McHugh, Mother Antonia

Antonine, Sister, see O'Brien, Sister Antonine

Apiculture, see Beekeeping

Apollo Club, Minneapolis, 14:345, 33: 95

Apostle Islands, 21:153; described, 23:243, 34:265; geology, 32:89; fisheries, 34:247; lighthouses, 34:351; history, 35:152

Appel, Livia, 11:46, 18:311; reviews by, 12:174-176, 17:88; work reviewed, 14:318-322; author, 11:40, 13:192, 14:61, 23:390, 28:332

Appelgate, Carl, speaker, 19:316

Appelman, Roy E., author, 20:441

Apple raising, varieties, 16:494, 23: 91, 26:170, 27:87, 36:327; growers, 19:357, 21:440, 31:162

Appleby, John, inventor, 20:62

Appleby, William R., professor of mining, 23:190; dean, 34:269, 271, 273

Applegarth, William, pioneer, 24:320

Applehagen, Emil, labor leader,22:380

Appler, A. C., author, 35:97

Appleseed, Johnny, see Chapman, John

Appleton, Norwegian settlement, 12: 275n

Appleton Press, history, 21:344

Appleton, Wis., Catholic church, 25: 193

Appolonia, Sister, teacher, 30:2, 12, 13

Aquipaguetin, Mille Lacs County, Sioux archaeological site, 25:330-333, 26:313, 314, 322, 325, 327, 328

"Arago," steamboat, 40:278

Arapaho Indians, 15:232, 35:377, 40: 358

Arbeiter Verein, New Ulm, organized, 21:381

Arbman, Holger, author, 39:170

Arbor Day, celebrated, 29:264

Arbre Croche, Mich., mission, 13:187, 15:110, 122, 222, 16:225, 19:457, 33:185, 39:306, 308

Arcadia, Watonwan County, history, 11:320

Archaeology, artifacts, 12:201, 15: 367, 16:1-21, 20:339, 21:424, 24: 78, 25:153-156, 304, 329-341, 26: 275, 280, 312-316, 319-323, 387, 28:76, 193, 29:83, 34:268, 35:244, 36:326, 39:262, 297, 40:339; Anoka County, 15:364, 483, 22:210, 24: 180; Iowa, 16:112, 39:339; Red River Valley, 16:128, 38:157-165; Lake Pepin, 16:152-165; Minnesota, 16:252, 358, 22:332, 28:373, 374, 29:165, 32:222, 34:354, 37:87, 39: 262, 264, 344; fossils, 18:104, 33:131; Brown house site, 19:354, 465; Fort Ridgely, 20:146-155, 21: 327; legal controls, 20:205; maps, 20:343, 25:304; Lac qui Parle, 21:

207, 434, 443, 27:360; relation to history, 23:280, 28:270-272, 33: 311, 37:30, 39:340; Wisconsin, 24: 371, 38:197; Canada, 24:371, 29: 165; Missouri Valley, 25:297; Mille Lacs aspect, 25:329, 330, 339-341; Headwaters Lakes aspect, 26:312-319; methods, 27:258, 39: 340; Ohio, 29:161; Rainy River aspect, 31:163-171, 231-237; in Dakotas, 34:354, 38:164, 39:212, 40:145; Fort Snelling, 35:192, 365-367, 36:152, 196, 230, 240; Spring Lake, 35:199, 36:282; Isle Royale, 35:339; Great Lakes area, 37:86, 174; Prairie Island, 37:86, 136, 282; underwater, 38:24-34, 39:123, 130, 171, 40:263, 306; pictographs, 38:87, 40:263; Newfoundland, 39:170, 342, 40:94; Norway, 40:49-58. See also Indian mounds, Kensington rune stone

Archer, Mrs. Frank, speaker, 20:211

Archer, John C., author, 11:217

Archer, William, 15:451

Archer-Burton, Sally, author, 14:232

Archer-Daniels-Midland Co., Minneapolis, history, 34:173

Archibald, Adams G., 19:412

Archibald, Cyril, miller, 12:453, 18: 342

Archibald, E. T., miller, 12:453, 18: 342

Archibald, George N., miller, 11:275, 277, 279

Archibald, John S., miller, 11:275, 277, 278, 279, 12:453

Archibald, Kate M., author, 29:261

Architects Small Home Service Bureau, papers, 23:273

Architecture, pictorial archives, 11: 450, 24:261, 28:349; St. Paul, 15: 50, 51, 52, 53, 55, 360, 23:221, 25:1-3, 5, 6, 9, 10, 26:289, 28: 293, 396, 29:114, 115, 37:192, 38: 187, 39:35, 40:101; Wisconsin, 16: 113, 22:99, 38:341, 343, 344, 345, 346, 40:101; Indiana, 16:228; source material, 19:452, 25:384; skyscrapers, 19:458, 23:229, 37: 38; Mississippi Valley, 21:324, 39:337, 40:103, 104, 107; South, 23:260, 37:185; Minneapolis, 23: 220, 222-226, 227-229, 231, 25:3, 4, 5, 37:192, 39:35, 40:104; early American, 25:298, 32:109, 34:347; Minnesota, 26:172, 36:147; Minnesota communities, 27:137, 37:188, 264, 39:130, 40:359; preservation, 27:228-232, 31:249, 35:150, 37: 263, 40:135; Canada, 28:179, 283; city planning, 33:331-339; guide, 34:314, 36:106; Owatonna, 35:242, 37:38, 344, 38:91; Collegeville, 36:100, 37:38, 187; Gothic influence, 37:189-203, 38:343-345; St. Croix Valley, 37:43, 38:186-189, 337-352; Greek revival, 38:338-343. See also Houses, University of Minnesota, various architects. Illustrated, 33:31, 34:101, 180, 37:111; mills, 12:65, 33:64, 65, 133, 35:1 (cover), 299, 36: 154, 39:287, 40:126; government buildings, 14:386, 30:317, 34:98, 35:232, 37:137, 145, 147, 149, 202, 38:187, 189, 349, 365, 39:

116, 40:97 (cover), 102, 103; churches, 18:250, 29:209, 211, 33: 49, 53, 55, 56, 57, 59, 191, 34: 92, 35:267, 38:231-233, 39:57, 133 (cover), 153-161, 225, 301 (cover), 309, 40:1; military posts, 20:150, 28:212, 213, 33:279, 34: 326, 35:260, 36:44, 253, 38:67, 145, 278, 39:238; schools and colleges, 27:98, 30:207, 33:59, 34: 90, 35:19, 137, 36:141, 39:213, 217, 40:383; theaters and halls, 28:98, 100, 32:170, 33:169, 170, 174, 178, 33:322, 35:227, 36:306; state capitol, 30:316, 33:162, 35: 297 (cover), 308, 311, 36:9; Fort Snelling, 32:12, 33:119, 189 (cover), 34:141, 35:22, 179, 182, 183, 365, 37:189 (cover), 40:29; trading posts, 32:93, 34:318, 321, 36: 38, 52, 243, 40:188-196; hotels, 33:2, 62, 323, 35:113, 214, 36:81, 93, 210, 265, 34:61, 37:117, 39: 283, 40:14, 15; post offices, 33: 22, 258, 34:6, 185, 35:277, 36: 209, 214, 215, 37:114, 39:253, 40: 89; railroad stations, 33:29, 34: 23, 37:96, 101; hospitals and rest homes, 33:56, 292, 295-297, 35: 217, 38:23, 79, 80, 85, 376, 39: 15, 16; industry, 33:66, 232, 36: 153 (cover), 155, 158, 160, 161, 37:14, 17, 99; clubs, 33:196, 36: 90, 91, 40:15; street scenes, 33: 197, 203, 34:33, 71, 88, 34:330, 35:53 (cover), 108, 117, 265, 361, 36:43, 197 (cover), 291, 37:206, 40:62; Minneapolis planning, 33: 331, 333-338; business buildings 34:31, 106, 334, 35:123, 36:127, 37:123, 125, 155, 192, 39:54, 330, 333, 40:100, 101, 107, 127; farms, 34:60, 62, 37:21; Duluth, 37:91, 92

Archives, defined, 25:287. See also various repositories

Arciniegas, German, author, 23:377

Arcola, Washington County, mills, 17: 278; architecture, 38:338; roads, 40:237

Arctander, John W., speaker, 27:105

Arctic, explored, 27:16, 29:262, 35: 227, 240, 294

"Arctic," steamboat, 22:437

Arcturus Mine, Mesabi Range, 25:411

Arden, G. Everett, work reviewed, 40: 353; author, 39:81

Arendahl Township, Fillmore County, Norwegian settlement, 12:268

Arends, Fridrich, author, 14:334

Arese, Count Francesco, explorer, 15: 121, 478, 31:196n

Arestad, Sverre, compiler, 24:257

Aretz, J. M., 24:224n; speaker, 21: 334, 27:74, 28:85

Arfwedson, C. D., author, 18:70

Argenson, Vicomte d', governor of New France, 15:174, 323

Argentines, Mesabi Range, 27:214

Argetsinger, O. G., 21:106; author, 17:125

Argo, Winona County, name, 34:280n

"Argo," steamboat, 18:374, 24:128, 28:136, 36:208

Argo Township, St. Louis County, map, 34:279; name, 34:280n

Argonne Farms, Dakota County, veterans' colony, 39:243, 245, 247-250
Argyle, history, 12:452, 20:360; churches, 14:452, 20:217; schools, 35:337; politics, 39:101
"Ariel," steamboat, 13:233, 236
Arikara Indians, Dakota Territory, 27:97, 35:339; agriculture, 34:255; described, 37:336
"Aristook," gunboat, 25:129
Arkansas, Irish colonies, 13:419; Whipple's visit, 19:75; history, 23:284, 26:382; geological survey, 25:175; in Civil War, 40:281-292
"Arkansas," Confederate vessel, 25:144, 147
Arkansas Historical Association, 23:285
Arkansas River, fort, 25:243
Arkins, Capt. William, papers, 19:211, 25:384
Arlberg, Max, author, 24:222
Arlington, Lord, 16:425n
Arlington, fire department, 11:119; harvest ball, 11:467; history, 13:122; pageant, 14:346; German-Russian settlement, 16:344
Arlington Club, Winona, 21:224
Arlington Township, Sibley County, politics, 28:36
Armajani, Yahya, 40:48
Armenians, 22:96
Armory Hall, St. Paul, 36:305
Armour, David A., editor, 40:145
Armsby, L., 16:317n
Armstrong, Augustus, 14:314
Armstrong, George W., territorial treasurer, 13:429, 17:211
Armstrong, Hart R., author, 40:363
Armstrong, Mrs. I. H., artist, 15:45
Armstrong, James D., 11:54, 14:78
Armstrong, Mrs. Jane C., 14:295
Armstrong, Dr. John M., 20:187, 23:50, 24:212n, 26:45, 27:46, 28:46; "The History of Medicine in Minnesota," 11:56-58; "The Asiatic Cholera in St. Paul," 14:288-301; "The Numerals on the Kensington Rune Stone," 18:185-188; review by, 24:238; author, 15:353, 16:353, 18:203, 20:91, 206, 344, 446, 21:437; 24:79, 182, 245, 25:399, 26:173, 28:335; speaker, 16:353, 17:350; editor, 19:225
Armstrong, Moses K., author, 11:324; railway interests, 19:108; career, 38:202
Armstrong, Nellie C., author, 15:124
Armstrong, Solon, 35:129
Armstrong, Spencer, letter, 18:298-301
Armstrong, T. H., lieutenant governor, 33:172
Armstrong, Vesta M. C., author, 29:83
Armstrong, Wallace, archaeologist, 38:160
Armstrong, William, artist, 15:357, 36:318
Armstrong family, house, 25:384
Armstrong Bay, Vermilion Lake, iron mining, 34:180
Armstrong Trading Co., Oak Point, 35:275
Army Air Force, see United States Air Corps
Army of the Cumberland, 26:205
Army of the Mississippi, 26:205

Army of the Potomac, 25:228; defeated, 20:275; officers, 25:36, 232, 244n, 246, 343, 349; transportation, 25:39n; infantry badges, 25:352; soldier vote, 26:200; reviewed, 29:124. See also First Minnesota Volunteer Infantry
Army of the Tennessee, reviewed, 29:124; takes Vicksburg, 33:211
Arndt, Armin, author, 17:115
Arndt, Karl J., compiler, 38:91
Arnesen, Barney, pioneer, 23:108, 27:272
Arnesen, Lake of the Woods County, fisheries, 35:275
Arneson, Dr. A. I., author, 36:327
Arnold, Henry V., 27:345
Arnold, Howard W., artist, 15:484
Arnold, Lincoln, 20:97
Arnold, Matthew, author, 29:154, 33:299
Arnold, Mrs. W. J., editor, 14:140, 26:293n
Arnold, St. Louis County, post office, 34:186
Arnquist, Judge Otto W., 24:165; letters, 25:185
Arpke, C. A., banker, 11:219
Arragon, R. F., author, 21:322
Arredondo, Eliseo, 17:165
Arrington, Joseph E., "Stockwell's Panorama," 33:284-290; author, 36:101, 190, 324, 37:38
Arrowhead country, history, 19:335, 31:58; wildlife, 21:287, 35:295; guide, 23:67; claimed by British, 24:343; ghost towns, 34:177-184; map, 34:179; natural resources, 36:69; forest fires, 36:131-138
Arrowsmith, John, map maker, 24:45, 29:259
Arscott, George, reminiscences, 24:383
Art, Indians depicted, 15:262, 17:475, 21:84, 22:201, 26:138, 150, 29:78, 350, 34:168, 35:287, 288, 36:75, 37:132, 38:40; Indian, 17:115, 22:189, 24:262, 30:392, 31:46, 199, 35:380, 36:74, 151, 38:87, 91, 39:259, 261, 40:407; Wisconsin, 17:455, 27:164; Canada, 18:216, 28:282, 36:317; Baltimore, 19:459; Twin Cities, 20:88, 22:332, 24:181, 26:156, 387, 32:62; American life, 17:107, 20:334, 21:402, 431, 24:257, 31:46, 55, 250, 33:133, 34:120, 253; relation to history, 21:322, 29:369, 31:248, 32:123, 33:208-210, 36:147; Slovenian, 22:200; North Shore, 22:341; frontier, 26:378, 27:159, 28:266, 278, 350, 30:74, 31:58, 32:61, 244, 33:263, 35:153, 379, 36:236, 37:31, 308, 38:201, 40:403; Minnesota communities, 27:137, 34:267, 35:51; centennial exhibits, 28:389, 30:176, 283; folk, 31:46, 32:110, 40:357; sculpture, 32:55, 33:86, 35:370, 40:408; Stenstrom primitives, 34:59-66; Montana, 35:295; dictionary, 35:369; New York, 35:381; Sioux Outbreak, 38:242. See also Architecture, Panoramas, Photography, Pottery, individual artists
Art History Club, Mankato, 19:358

Arthur, Chester A., President, 13:445, 18:30
Arthur, Hugh, speaker, 15:83, 16:67, 17:69
Arthur, Rev. L. A., 18:399
Arthur, Stanley C., author, 26:383
Arthurs, Stanley M., artist, 17:217, 40:287
Arthyde, Aitkin County, name, 21:350
Arvilla, N.D., archaeology, 16:11, 38:164; academy, 16:359
Asbury Methodist Church, St. Paul, 17:118
Ascension Church (Catholic), Norwood, 15:480
Ascension Church (Episcopal), St. Paul, 15:481
Ascension Church (Lutheran), St. Paul, 13:323
Ashburton, Lord, 23:60, 204, 205, 208. See also Webster-Ashburton Treaty
Ashby, Charlotte M., compiler, 36:278, 39:210
Ashby, Mrs. Harriet C., author, 12:212, 454
Ashby, Col. Turner, cavalry leader, 25:34
Ashby, stage route, 38:63
Ashby's Gap, Va., battle, 40:271
Ashdowne, J. H., and Co., 21:268
Asher, Louis E., author, 24:372
Ashland, Wis., history, 14:342, 19:122, 34:129; roads, 16:298; ski club, 17:228
Ashley, A. C., pioneer, 40:69
Ashley, Lord, 16:425n
Ashley, Porter W., 14:120, 16:240
Ashley, Gen. William H., expedition, 15:426, 429, 29:61, 38:199; trader, 39:261, 40:152, 102, 196, 201; grave, 40:192
Ashley River, Stearns County, 40:69, 70
Ashmun, Samuel, trader, 23:249, 329, 26:362; letters, 19:348, 20:77
Askeland, Halvard, journalist, 16:219, 20:408
Askeland, Rev. Nels K., in Roseau Valley, 24:323
Askin, John, trader, 16:224, 19:295, 299, 300n, 305, 21:134n; at Grand Portage, 21:119
Askov, history, 17:239, 20:466, 29:271, 39:130; Danish settlement, 23:387, 30:76, 31:28; newspaper, 29:375, 38:305
Askov Co-operative Association, organized, 17:239
Askov Creamery Association, 17:239
Aspden, H. H., speaker, 21:334
Aspden, Mrs. Henry, 15:133
Asseln, Henry, pioneer, 11:336
Assembly of God, in lumber camps, 34:61
Assiniboia, Man., 40:164; settlement, 22:3; in Sioux Outbreak, 34:317-324; fur trade, 36:247. See also Red River Settlements; Selkirk, Lord
Assiniboin Indians, North Dakota, 11:209, 19:379, 35:339; in fur trade, 11:265n, 14:223, 18:237; depicted, 23:94, 154, 36:312, 37:336; migrations, 26:328; burial customs, 26:329; Minnesota, 28:343, 29:165; Manitoba, 29:165

Assiniboine River, Can., explored, 19:412, 35:249, 261; steamboating, 21:260; trading post, 40:163
"Assiniboine," flood relief boat, 21:327
Associated Charities, 25:212, 377
Associated Western Literary Societies of Chicago, 21:326
Association of American Geographers, 19:367, 20:207, 23:169
Association of American Railroads, Washington, D.C., 23:393, 28:185, 351, 369
Assumption Church (Catholic), St. Paul, 13:123, 16:274n, 24:90, 25:9, 30:7, 9; Barnesville, 14:452; Richfield, 24:90
Astley, J. W., speaker, 18:223
Astor, George, piano builder, 39:313, 314
Astor, John J., 28:371, 36:248; relations with Selkirk, 12:91; letters, 12:82, 429; career, 13:179-181, 439, 440, 14:98, 19:305, 20:16, 29:61, 30:248, 35:243, 40:178, 187, 295; relations with rivals, 16:201, 17:476, 19:306; memorial tablet, 16:498; in fiction, 16:343; music merchant, 39:313; in fur trade, 40:152, 164, 214. See also American Fur Co., Astoria
Astor, William B., trader, 36:248, 40:183, 184
Astor House, Mackinac, Mich., American Fur Co. post, 11:451, 12:327
Astoria, Ore., founded, 13:180; expedition to, 15:352, 422, 428, 531; pictured, 26:56; trading post, 40:152, 164, 170, 180n, 181, 196, 197, 404
Astorians, 40:196; 1812 expedition, 40:197; in Black Hills, 40:355
Astronautics, chronology, 38:334
Astronomy, eclipses, 34:132
Atchison, George W., steamboat captain, 11:124n, 13:231
Atchison, John, steamboat captain, 11:124n, 13:231, 232, 233, 239, 31:212
Atchison, Kan., Benedictine school, 35:271
Ath, Belgium, Hennepin's birthplace, 11:3-6, 340, 343, 345, 18:446, 24:275; history, 19:47
"Athabasca," lake vessel, 20:326
Athabasca, see Lake Athabasca
Athearn, Robert G., reviews by, 38:237, 40:138; works reviewed, 31:241, 34:38, 35:291; author, 34:262
Athenaeum, St. Paul, 28:29, 32:166; dedicated, 27:329, 32:102; performances, 32:102-105, 172; burned, 32:105; built, 34:99n
Athenaeum Library Association, Minneapolis, 11:147
Atherton, Lewis, work reviewed, 34:200; speaker, 15:227; author, 17:219, 20:335, 33:226
Atherton, Phineas, trader, 16:224
Atkins, Albert H., sculptor, 39:160
Atkins, Capt. D., steamboat agent, 22:437
Atkins, John D., Indian commissioner, 18:305
Atkinson, Frederick G., 23:192, 34:204; autobiography reviewed, 22:186

Atkinson, Mrs. Frederick G., speaker, 21:51; author, 21:184
Atkinson, Gen. Henry, 18:154, 401, 22:28; expedition, 15:427; biography, 39:338
Atkinson, Samuel C., editor, 30:203
Atlanta, Ga., in Civil War, 18:453, 21:204, 38:267, 273
"Atlanta," steamboat, 11:143
"Atlantic," lake steamer, 11:103
Atlantic cable, opened, 26:67, 36:279, 38:55
Atlantic Charter, 23:217
Atlantic Monthly, on frontier, 22:336
"Atlas," steamboat, 22:15n, 33:17
Atlases, 14:91, 24:252, 25:374, 390; publication, 40:120-129
Atsina Indians, 15:232
Atwater, Caleb, 13:222, 20:55, 173, 36:280; historian, 13:225, 30:295; treaty commissioner, 36:280
Atwater, Isaac, 35:230; lecturer, 12:400; printer, 15:23; surveyor, 18:356; judge, 35:7; lawyer, 35:105, 106, 108, 110; businessman, 37:320; house, 40:375
Atwater, creamery, 22:346; depicted, 40:33
Atwood, Mrs. C. L., 12:429
Atwood, Edwin H., papers, 29:101
Atwood, Wallace W., author, 30:262
Aubert, Father Pierre, Oblate missionary, 36:48n, 51n
Auchagah (Ochagach), Assiniboin Indian, map maker, 12:362, 13:297, 18:234, 38:26
Auchampaugh, Philip G., review by, 12:178; author, 12:441, 13:434, 437, 17:106, 111; speaker, 13:216
Audubon, John J., author, 14:423, 30:227, 34:203; artist, 21:316; traveler, 23:281, 40:144
Audubon, stockade, 11:71; Dutch settlement, 38:121
Audubon Society, 37:223
Auerbach, Laura K., author, 40:362
Auerbach, Maurice, letters, 11:319; house, 23:221
Auerbach, Mrs. Maurice, 13:273
Augé, Sister Bernarda, 35:271
Auge, James, scout, 39:237
Augsburg College, Marshall, Wis., and Minneapolis, beginnings, 11:226, 34:131, 40:375; presidents, 17:225, 29:294, 40:377, 382, 383; in synod controversy, 29:296; character, 34:91, 40:377, 383; archives, 39:35; benefactors, 40:375, 376, 378; students, 40:376-378; buildings, 40:376, 377, 383; sports, 40:377; relocation plan, 40:378-382
Augsburg Park, Richfield, prospective college site, 40:378; plat, 40:381
Augsburg Publishing House, Minneapolis, 15:448
Auguelle, Antoine, 12:435, 15:100
Augusta Lake, see Lake Abigail
Augustadt, Walter W., author, 35:45
Augustana College, Rock Island, Ill., history, 17:110, 38:381; library, 17:329; American studies program, 26:274
Augustana Historical Society, 17:329; publications, 13:308-310, 17:328
Augustana Synod, 18:69; history, 13:305, 306, 308, 17:328, 28:75; pol-

icies, 22:381; Minnesota conference, 28:76
Aulneau, Father Jean-Pierre, Jesuit missionary, 38:193; at Lake of the Woods, 17:224, 473, 18:239, 279, 28:77, 31:52, 34:130, 35:140, 37:37, 39:302; letters, 18:244; skeleton found, 18:246
Ault, Thaddeus, 39:90
Aultman, C., and Co., thresher manufacturers, 24:301
"Aunt Betsey," steamboat, 31:86, 36:129
Aura, Beltrami County, Finnish settlement, 25:320
Aurand, A. Monroe, compiler, 16:220
Aurora, history, 21:456, 36:107, 37:41; mining, 28:251, 33:355; bus line, 35:338
Aurora, Ill., railroad, 22:94
Aurora (Duluth), school paper, 24:166
Aurora Ski Club, Red Wing, 17:228, 29:169
Aus der Ohe, Adèle, pianist, 39:53, 63
Austin, Cpl. Edward A., 25:253
Austin, G. S., author, 39:132
Austin, H. Russell, work reviewed, 29:334; author, 29:356
Austin, Helen, 22:296
Austin, Herbert, 22:296; papers, 35:340
Austin, Horace, papers, 11:445, 35:340; land officer, 12:389; governor, 16:454, 19:414, 21:359, 22:295, 296, 26:125, 29:7, 8, 13, 37:145, 146, 204, 205, 206, 207; career, 26:298; hunter, 33:154n
Austin, Mrs. Minnie, speaker, 23:102
Austin, motion-picture industry, 11:116; churches, 13:452, 14:218, 236, 20:431, 21:330; clubs, 15:243, 20:463, 24:94, 26:95; county seat, 15:250, 21:223; history, 16:368, 18:470, 25:101, 30:401, 33:353, 35:203, 36:107; incorporated, 17:237; library, 18:470; pioneer life, 21:222; name, 21:349; unions, 21:382, 393, 22:380; schools, 21:453, 26:183; fire department, 21:453; bank, 40:111; theater, 40:363. See also Hormel, George & Co.
Austin Daily Herald, anniversary, 23:108
Austin Dental Society, 16:368
Austin Floral Club, history, 18:470
Austin War History Committee, 23:390
"Australasian," steamship, 40:268
Australia, German settlement, 14:54; development, 37:182
Australian ballot, in Minnesota, 35:309, 310, 342
Austrian, Julius, trader, 30:405, 32:186
Austrian, Marx, trader, 32:186
Austro-Hungarians, Lester Prairie, 18:470; iron ranges, 21:290, 27:208, 210, 212, 32:196, 201, 40:60, 343; Chatfield, 24:98; in lumber industry, 36:162; dwellings, 37:75; Hastings, 37:199
Autographs, MHS collections, 33:185, 298-300
Automobiles, clubs, 20:463, 36:89; early use, 22:213, 26:19-28, 45; licensing, 26:25, 87; history, 27:

64, 34:354; 35:97; commercial, 27:174; Wisconsin, 27:356; in farm life, 30:264; Glidden tours, 38:205-215; steam-driven, 39:273, 274; manufacture in Minnesota, 40:148. See also Minnesota State Automobile Association

"Auxoticiat" voyage, Radisson's experiences, 13:257-263, 396

Avaloz, Karen H., review by, 39:297

Avard, Robert, pseud., see Beveridge, Robert

Avaugour, Baron d', governor of New France, 15:323

Averell, William W., cavalry leader, 25:253

Averill, James, steamboat captain, 34:10

Averill, John, Union officer, 33:4, 38:104

Avery, Carlos, 16:496, 21:452; speaker, 11:334; game commissioner, 18:451, 40:145

Avery, Percy, 21:452

Avery, Richard, pioneer, 24:320

Aviation, Garrard's experiments, 21:216, 22:222; Wright interview, 22:302-305; Minnesota, 24:184, 33:236-246, 34:44, 217; commercial, 25:195, 33:239-242; technology, 33:242-246; history, 34:42, 38:334; mail service, 34:175. See also Ballooning, United States Air Corps

Avila, Fray Pedro de, 35:241

Avoca, Catholic colony, 20:331, 21:210, 31:22, 35:136, 137, 138

Aydelotte, William O., author, 39:34

Ayer, Edward E., 14:426, 19:423n; collector, 17:109. See also Newberry Library

Ayer, Frederick, missionary, 14:454, 16:28, 19:342, 25:290; letters, 13:195; educator, 14:143, 19:132n, 29:270; marriage, 25:13; at La Pointe, 32:186

Ayer, Mrs. Frederick, I, missionary, 15:20n; educator, 16:318; portrait, 17:215; letters, 18:210, 25:289; marriage, 25:13

Ayer, Mrs. Frederick (Ellen Banning), II, 29:118, 33:4

Ayer, Mr. and Mrs. Harry D., 37:68, 69, 136, 188; collectors, 36:284, 328

Ayer, I. Winslow, author, 24:36

Ayer, Lyman W., letters, 18:210

Ayer Collection, see Newberry Library

Aylard, Carlton C., educator, 37:151

Ayres, George V., author, 11:212

Azilum, Pa., French colony, 18:87

Baardsson, Ivar, 17:175

Baasen, Francis, 14:245, 246, 25:343; politician, 28:27, 36; letter, 33:126

Babbett, Col. A. W., 27:6

Babbitt, Franc E., 16:1

Babbitt, Judge Kurnal R., 34:280

Babbitt, mining town, 19:464, 36:192, 38:204; taconite plant, 33:283, 355, 34:269-283, 37:42, 39:163. See also Mesabi Range

Babcock, Amy, 23:104

Babcock, C. Merton, author, 31:53; 37:88

Babcock, Charles M., highway commissioner, 12:84, 13:380, 25:379, 26:1, 42, 44; career, 11:215; author, 13:115; memorial, 26:43, 29:85

Babcock, Mrs. Charles M., author, 17:241

Babcock, Mrs. Emily A., translator, 14:15

Babcock, Frank, speaker, 20:210

Babcock, Mrs. George, speaker, 20:355

Babcock, Col. James F., "Rails West," 34:133-143; journalist, 14:440, 15:62, 417

Babcock, Joseph W., lumberman, Kasota mill, 11:171, 181, 182, 12:104

Babcock, Kendric C., 12:304; speaker, 11:213

Babcock, L. W., career, 28:73

Babcock, Laura, 22:107

Babcock, Lorenzo A., author, 14:164, 183n, 186, 188n; MHS founder, 20:367; lawyer, 35:363; editor, 39:45

Babcock, Stephen M., 19:152; career, 12:99; invents cream tester, 19:227, 27:118, 121, 30:248, 371

Babcock, Willoughby M., 11:47, 314, 12:188, 13:293, 16:60, 17:347, 20:189, 21:229n, 27:140, 30:42, 323, 37:43; "Historic Markers and Monuments in Minnesota," 11:25-35; ed., "To Fort Ridgely in 1853," 11:161-184; "Highways and History," 13:377-384; "Minnesota Local Historical Activity in 1933," 15:69-74; MHS reports, 15:75-85, 16:63-69; "Pictorial Source Material," 15:439-444; "Hunting History by Automobile," 16:192-195; "The St. Croix Valley," 17:276-287; "Louis Provençalle," 20:259-268; "Gateway to the Northwest," 35:249-262; "With Ramsey to Pembina," 38:1-10; "Minnesota's Indian War," 38:93-98; "Minnesota's Frontier," 38:274-286; reviews by, 12:75, 13:190, 24:159, 34:205, 36:234, 40:139; speaker, 11:93, 13:345, 14:211, 213, 344, 15:107, 310, 342, 16:63, 17:64, 18:61, 274, 464, 21:47, 82, 217, 22:47, 291, 23:47, 24:349, 29:178; author, 11:202, 214, 13:317, 14:98, 434, 15:462, 16:331, 484, 17:61, 18:459, 20:43, 430, 21:44, 182, 22:83, 432, 23:367, 24:163, 242, 25:43, 26:38, 27:142, 28:77, 30:156, 175, 34:316, 35:22n, 204, 340, 40:42; editor, 12:316; quoted, 13:73; interview, 20:189

Bach, Cile M., author, 39:342

Bache, Alexander D., 19:96

Bache, Søren, Norwegian pioneer, 24:348; diary reviewed, 33:85

Bachmann, Charles W., musician, 34:242

Bachmann, E. Theodore, author, 24:373

Bachmann, Elizabeth M., "Minnesota Log Marks," 26:126-137; reviews by, 34:308, 36:235; author, 25:92, 26:153, 28:331, 29:264, 30:157, 31:191, 36:151, 193, 37:86, 223, 40:361

Bachmann, Karl (Charles), Carver County pioneer, 25:184, 26:66

Bachmann, Mrs. Karl, 26:66

Bachner Brothers, Minneapolis, gun manufacturers, 33:307

Bachtle, Mrs. Carrie A., 23:390

Backland, Jonas W., 29:324

Backlund, Jonas Oscar, work reviewed, 37:177; author, 15:235, 34:43, 172; translator, 32:49

Backstrom, Charles H., review by, 37:84; work reviewed, 39:257

Backus, Capt. Electus, Fort Snelling commandant, 21:170, 32:97

Backus, Edward W., lumberman, 24:247, 26:136, 27:300n, 302, 31:183; log mark, 26:135

Backus, Elizabeth, teacher, 35:102, 104

Backus, Mrs. George J., sculptor, 20:413-415

Backus-Brooks Co., lumber firm, 24:247, 29:140

Backus Line, logging railroad, 27:300n

Bacon, Don H., mining interests, 35:338, 40:412

Bacon, Emma, 35:101

Bacon, Jerome A., mill owner, 39:5

Bacon, Gen. John M., 24:146

Bacon, Myrtle, author, 28:384

Bacon, William, 12:339

Bad Axe River, Wis., battle, 12:160, 17:296, 33:116, 39:339

Bad Hail, Sioux leader, 28:312, 30:215n

Bad Heart Buffalo, Amos, Sioux artist, 19:218

Bad River, Ashland County, Wis., 23:242; Chippewa reservation, 35:235

Bad Track, Lyon County, election precinct, 14:250, 251

Badboy, Mrs. Ella, 16:321

Bader, Arno, author, 18:215

Badger, Sioux Indian, murdered, 24:21

Badger, Lutheran churches, 22:349, 350; townsite, 24:326

"Badger," steamboat, 34:14

Badham, James, Cutlerite, 13:387

Badlands, S.D., archaeology, 33:131

Badoura Township, Hubbard County, history, 18:469

Baekkestad, Erling, 21:86

Baensch, Emil, author, 15:355

Baer, Frank W., career, 12:322

Baer, Jerome, 20:314

Baer, John, cartoonist, 38:304, 306

Baeton & Corinsky, Olmsted County, mill, 40:126

Bagby, Albert M., musician, 23:281

Bagley, E. R., author, 24:262

Bagley, Marion M., author, 31:59

Bagley, Sarah G., telegrapher, 38:242

Bagley, Sumner C., logger, 29:144

Bagley, Dr. William, speaker, 19:316

Bagley, William C., author, 12:418

Bagley, Lutheran church, 17:235; incorporated, 20:101; land office, 22:109; stage station, 23:29; newspaper, 29:356

Bahmer, Robert H., 12:425, 29:259, 36:218; "The Clark Papers," 36:219-227; review by, 22:78-80; author, 21:202, 22:82, 24:361, 35:51, 36:217, 219, 227, 228; speaker, 34:360, 36:196; archivist, 40:360

Bähr, Charles, actor, 32:166

Bailer, C. H., 19:232, 20:214

Bailey, A. C., 12:106

Bailey, Bernadine, work reviewed, 34:41
Bailey, C. H., author, 19:227; speaker, 27:80
Bailey, Mrs. Caroline P., 20:58
Bailey, Clyde M., educator, 38:385
Bailey, Esther Z., compiler, 35:334
Bailey, Everett H., MHS treasurer, 11:54, 55, 14:78, 16:68, 17:70, 18:67, 19:69; characterized, 20:44; career, 20:58-60; portrait, 21:96
Bailey, Mrs. Everett H., 20:58
Bailey, Frances, 21:45
Bailey, Francis P., 20:58
Bailey, George R., author, 11:328, 31:134, 36:81
Bailey, Mrs. Henry J., 26:93, 395, 28:380; speaker, 19:119
Bailey, Capt. Hiram S., in Sioux Outbreak, 38:110n
Bailey, Joel, surveyor, 15:223
Bailey, L. H., lawyer, 29:356
Bailey, Liberty H., botanist, 35:244
Bailey, Mrs. Mary, 23:104; speaker, 16:125, 21:110, 339, 23:399, 27:78, 146
Bailey, Richard, 23:371
Bailey and Primrose, St. Paul, mattress makers, 15:190
Baillair, Louis, trader, 22:281
Baille, James, Jr., 31:238
Bailleul, Jan, sculptor, 18:238
Baillif, J. O., papers, 26:156
Baillif, Matilda Pepin, 26:156
Baillif, Matilda V., 15:37, 26:156; author, 11:110, 13:116
Baillif family, genealogy, 11:110; papers, 26:156
Bailly, Alexis, trader, 11:225, 383, 13:224, 21;24, 119n, 23:94, 29:1, 36:264, 37:191, 40:262; papers, 11:444, 16:70, 73, 20:263, 264, 265, 23:272, 25:182, 383; farmer, 14:387; slaveholder, 25:202; justice of the peace, 32:72; treaty commissioner, 32:74. See also Bailly family
Bailly, Edward C., author, 31:59, 32:59, 34:131, 313
Bailly, H. G., trader, 17:278; townsite owner, 37:191
Bailly, Honoré-Gratien-Joseph, 12:431
Bailly, Joseph, trader, 11:324, 21:118n, 22:76, 31:59; in legal case, 21:117-148; genealogy, 32:59
Bailly, Joseph P., 25:383
Bailly, Marie, 11:324, 22:76
Bailly family, 14:438; genealogy, 11:324, 12:86, 431, 25:383, 31:59, 32:59, 34:313; in fiction, 22:76
Bailly de Messein, Charles-François, 12:431
Bailly de Messein, Michel, 12:431
Bailly de Messein, Nicholas, 12:431
Bailly de Messien family, see Bailly family
Baily, Mrs. Henry J., 20:99
Bainbridge, Alexander G., labor leader, 39:97
Bainbridge, John, author, 27:353
Baird, Gen. Absalom, Union officer, 38:272
Baird, Duncan H., author, 21:416
Baird, Julian B., 20:50; MHS treasurer, 20:51, 23:50, 24:57, 25:55, 26:45, 29:97, 98, 30:88; author,

34:42
Baird, P. D., author, 26:274
Baird, Mrs. Sarah G., diary, 17:467, 18:47; Granger, 30:254
Bajus, Rev. John, 24:73
Bakeless, John, reviews by, 32:45, 33:301; work reviewed, 32:111; author, 32:64, 35:291
Baker, Elder ---, 19:133
Baker, Alexander, pioneer, 17:364, 30:407, 31:184
Baker, Amanda, house, 38:344, 345
Baker, Ben, trader, 28:283
Baker, Benjamin F., trader, 11:372, 373, 17:210, 20:122, 127, 21:83, 168n, 35:24, 25, 40:30; mill owner, 17:283; house, 21:167
Baker, C. C., 29:275; speaker, 29:362
Baker, C. D., 14:357
Baker, Charles E., author, 34:120
Baker, Charles H., "Lake Itasca," 13:164-166
Baker, Clara, actress, 28:113
Baker, Edward, Oregon Senator, 35:94
Baker, F. D., 27:361
Baker, George L., railroad executive, 35:35
Baker, Helen M., speaker, 16:306
Baker, Howard, murdered, 38:134
Baker, Isaac P., steamboat owner, 38:236
Baker, Gen. James H., speaker, 12:226; newspaper publisher, 15:89, 18:337; poet, 16:81; politician, 28:27, 32:140, 145, 36:114, 115, 37:326, 328, 329; in Sioux Outbreak, 38:280
Baker, Jennie, 15:372, author, 13:454; speaker, 17:124
Baker, Jocelyn, author, 17:345
Baker, Joseph Stannard, 38:345; land agent, 23:164, 25:396
Baker, Lewis, 21:335, 29:361; editor, 39:330, 331, 332
Baker, O. E., author, 18:102
Baker, Ray S., work reviewed, 23:164; reformer, 14:200; quoted, 39:271
Baker, Robert O., 39:173
Baker, Roy A., 14:358; author, 16:369, 497
Baker, S. M., letters, 22:192
Baker, Theodore, anthropologist, 34:161
Baker, Virginia, 22:340
Baker, William E., author, 24:356
Baker, Willis, horse breeder, 26:120n
Baker family, musicians, 22:114, 118, 119, 120, 26:53, 29:265
Bakers Union No. 21, 21:387
Bakke, S., 14:54
Bakken, Henry H., editor, 24:258
Bakken, Ole, log cabin, 37:64
Balaton, Methodist church, 12:103
Balcomb, A., 11:453
Balcombe, St. Andre, 14:158; Winnebago agent, 37:327, 38:360, 362, 39:229, 230, 233, 239, 240
Balcombe, Dr. John L., 21:329
Bald, F. Clever, review by, 35:199; works reviewed, 34:206, 207; author, 18:325, 34:355, 35:154; speaker, 36:36
Bald Eagle Lake, acreage, 40:226n
Bald Hill, N.D., trading post, 11:380
Bald Island, see Prairie Island
Baldinger, Wallace S., author, 26:73
Baldwin, Benjamin C., papers, 16:71

Baldwin, Cameron L., author, 27:69
Baldwin, Clara F., author, 23:386, 27:71
Baldwin, Leland D., work reviewed, 23:61
Baldwin, M. W., politician, 39:105n
Baldwin, Judge Mathias, 37:166, 167
Baldwin, Munson, work reviewed, 40:314
Baldwin, Mr. and Mrs. Roger S., 34:139
Baldwin, Rufus J., legislator, 26:192, 199, 35:3, 36:168, 37:318
Baldwin, Samuel A., musician, 13:273, 39:54
Baldwin Locomotive Works, Philadelphia, 18:452, 38:313, 314, 318
Baldwin School, St. Paul, founded, 14:147, 16:274n, 27:167; evaluated, 16:275; depicted, 30:207. See also Macalester College
Balfour, Dr. Donald C., author, 23:289
Balke, Julius, industrialist, 29:67
Ball, Carleton R., author, 11:323
Ball, Capt. John, Union officer, 38:254
Ball, Joseph, speaker, 20:301; author, 21:436
Ball, Sen. Joseph H., speaker, 23:403
Ball, Thomas, artist, 31:100, 102
Ballantyne, Robert M., artist, 18:216, 36:127; trader, 23:92
Ballard, Dr. Charles W., cattleman, 26:121, 123
Ballenden, J., trader, 40:168n
Ballet, see Dance
Ballinger, Richard A., 22:79, 27:133
Ballinger-Pinchot controversy, 29:155
Ballooning, Minnesota, 12:202, 24:264, 38:166-176, 334, 39:278-285, 40:265-280; in Civil War, 25:22, 23n, 119, 120, 126n, 229, 242, 246, 345, 354, 35:184, 333; pictured, 33:243, 245, 38:157 (cover), 40:313. See also Aviation
Balls Bluff, Va., battle, 25:16, 22
Balmer, Frank E., 11:109, 441; author, 12:430; speaker, 11:289
Balmoral, Otter Tail County, grist mill, 20:353
Balsam Township, Itasca County, schools, 22:223
Baltimore, 13:408, 19:459
"Baltimore," steamboat, 34:10, 11
Baltimore and Ohio Railroad, 19:196; in Civil War, 25:356n; finances, 34:169
Baltrusch, Franz, musician, 33:100
Balzer, Jacob F., speaker, 11:199, 294, 17:357
Bancroft, Estelle B., author, 29:368
Bancroft, George, excursionist, 12:392, 393, 15:406, 411, 415, 419, 33:139, 140; Minnesota visit, 14:280, 16:27, 20:384, 386, 25:103, 114n; historian, 18:128, 145, 38:200, 39:335, 336, 40:313
Bancroft, Mrs. George V., author, 27:368
Bancroft, Hubert H., historian, 40:152
Bancroft, John E., publisher, 16:72; papers, 11:95
Bancroft Library, Berkeley, Calif., guide to manuscripts, 39:128

Bancroft Township, Freeborn County, Norwegian settlement, 12:269; townsite, 14:306; county seat controversy, 15:346, 20:357
Bandas, Rev. Rudolph G., 15:37
Bandon Township, Renville County, Norwegian settlement, 12:275n
Banér, Skulda V., author, 25:302
Banfield, N. F., Jr., 25:101
Banfil, John, 15:426
Bangs, Tracy R., 18:227
"Banjo," showboat, 32:59
Bank of Minneapolis, 35:225
Bank of Minnesota, St. Paul, 40:111, 114, 115, 116
Bankers Association of Minnesota, see Minnesota Mutual Life Insurance Co.
Banks, Nathaniel P., Union general, 25:32, 36, 134, 147, 226, 239, 343, 40:288; evaluated, 35:316
Banks and banking, Minnesota communities, 11:219, 220, 467, 12:451, 456, 13:122, 346, 14:356, 16:364, 19:465, 25:101, 211, 28:203, 40:110; Duluth, 13:78, 37:119-125; state, 13:108; private, 15:112, 18:76, 77; frontier, 16:24, 29:223-230, 32:44, 60; Wisconsin, 16:91, 30:71, 34:165; New York, 17:111; Twin Cities, 19:96, 113, 21:114, 25:212, 279, 29:88, 34:42, 99n, 166, 169, 204, 205, 35:49, 40:109-119; history, 20:345; Canada, 27:70; Intermediate Credit Banks, 38:179. See also Depressions, Economic conditions, individual banks
Bannerman, ---, Red River settler, 31:108
Banning, Ellen, see Ayer, Mrs. Frederick
Banning, Mrs. Margaret C., 12:207, 15:100; reviews by, 26:250, 30:142, 32:120; speaker, 19:312, 20:30, 30:287, 366; author, 20:117, 22:365, 23:67, 25:90, 26:258, 30:184, 31:129, 145, 191, 32:128
Banning, William L., 18:315, 33:4; land commissioner, 13:37; house, 15:53, 185; legislator, 34:332; gubernatorial candidate, 35:58; banker, 37:89, 91, 93, 97, 98
Banning, Mrs. William L., 29:121, 33:4
Banning, William L., Jr., 39:52n
Banning, Pine County, ghost town, 35:295
Bannister, Maj. ---, Union officer, 25:25
Bannister, Henry M., diary, 24:344
Bannon, William, merchant, 24:375
Banta, R. E., author, 19:458
Banter, Phil, author, 26:294
Banvard, John, panoramist, 17:134-136, 140n, 456, 19:458, 20:380, 382, 383, 24:63, 25:275, 26:53, 30:15, 153, 260, 393, 31:46, 32:188, 33:287, 35:379, 36:190, 233; influence, 20:200, 25:300; author, 24:64, 30:154; autobiography, 26:260; portrait, 27:155; papers, 29:187
Banvard family, genealogy, 26:260
Baptism River, Lake County, name, 12:287
Baptism River Club, records, 27:242

Baptism River State Park, established, 27:359
Baptist church, ethnic branches, 11:113, 12:343, 13:207, 305, 14:451, 15:235, 16:340, 17:403, 18:71, 21:76, 22:350, 23:381, 25:324, 27:68, 33:138; educational program, 14:147, 148, 20:62, 28:83, 34:91; Sunday schools, 15:234, 18:118; Minnesota, 16:235; Iowa, 16:340; Wisconsin, 27:68. See also individual churches and communities
Baptist Home Missionary Society, 28:135
Baptist missions, Minnesota, 11:217, 15:235; frontier, 21:71; Nebraska and Dakotas, 35:380; Nagasaki, Japan, 38:317
Baptiste, John, cholera victim, 14:290
Baraboo, Wis., circus town, 23:185
Baraga, Frederic, missionary, 11:205, 14:339, 15:446, 19:348, 21:102, 25:193, 26:146, 39:128; at Lake Superior, 12:207, 24:354, 28:62, 30:392, 32:186, 39:304, 308, 309; biographies, 13:187, 333, 15:122, 33:185, 36:32; papers, 14:98, 15:222, 17:95, 210, 342, 22:356; memorial, 14:456; Ojibway studies, 17:53, 25:194, 35:248, 39:303; mission posts, 19:457, 22:200; career, 34:174
Barbé-Marbois, François, career, 23:258
Barbeau, Emil, 20:332
Barbeau, Marius, 29:167; works reviewed, 17:204, 20:72, 38:238; author, 20:341, 22:93, 204, 433, 23:281, 24:77, 25:397, 30:261, 33:351, 34:126, 214, 37:345; editor, 25:393
Barbeau, Mrs. Rose, 14:216
Barbee, David R., 17:108
Barber, Albert, cholera victim, 14:290
Barber, Mary Jane, cholera victim, 14:290
Barber, Dr. R. D., 16:433
Barberg, Vernon G., 21:110
Barbour, Edwin, theater manager, 33:176
Barck, Dorothy C., speaker, 22:429
Barck, H. A., speaker, 13:342
Barclay, Isabel, author, 35:379
Barclay, Robert G., author, 40:313
Bardo, Gerald, 20:428
Bardon, John A., "Early Logging Methods," 15:203-206; author, 13:114, 196, 26:83, 33:355; pioneer, 14:233, 20:340, 21:152, 153, 154, 156, 157, 34:129; papers, 24:354
Bardon, Dr. Richard, 13:114, 24:380, 25:99, 26:92, 27:145, 28:89, 385, 29:94; ed., "A Winter in the St. Croix Valley," 28:1-14, 142-159, 225-240; review by, 31:246; author, 19:226, 357, 28:204, 307, 31:256; speaker, 25:405, 27:77, 146, 268, 37:41; editor, 28:95, 29:99
Bardwell, Elmer, speaker, 28:296
Bardwell, J. P., missionary, 15:20n, 38:9
Bargen, Frank, speaker, 16:491
Bargen, Isaac I., 14:119, 15:134; speaker, 20:95

Bargen, Mary, author, 12:101
Barges, Mississippi River, 12:159, 16:79, 17:430, 23:61, 62, 334, 335, 31:246, 39:167; in lumber industry, 24:136, 139; whalebacks, 36:33
Barincou, F., lithographer, 33:20
Baring-Gould, Sabine, author, 27:182
Barker, Mrs. Blaine B., 23:391
Barker, Burt B., 20:327; work reviewed, 36:315; author, 32:249
Barker, David, hotelkeeper, 17:279
Barker, Earle A., 14:450
Barker, Eugene C., author, 11:428, 25:391
Barker, Harold, politician, 34:192
Barker, Joseph, editor, 39:212
Barker family, musicians, 22:124
Barland, Rev. Thomas, letters, 19:210
Barley raising, Paynesville, 19:324; yield, 24:334
Barloon, Marvin J., author, 36:280
Barnard, Charles, 20:82
Barnard, E. T., 13:120, 279, 280, 14:358, 16:124, 17:484, 18:335, 465, 471, 20:97, 353, 22:107, 23:103, 25:408; speaker, 11:117, 14:237, 19:117, 120, 21:340; author, 19:231, 21:109, 218, 446, 24:87, 380, 26:91
Barnard, Ethel, 12:282
Barnard, Harry, work reviewed, 35:150
Barnard, Newell H., author, 29:263, 271
Barn Bluff, Red Wing landmark, 16:44, 476, 17:148n, 290, 33:118
Barnes, A. S., historian, 27:100
Barnes, Albert, Presbyterian minister, 40:1, 2, 4-6, 11
Barnes, Charles, 16:491
Barnes, Eugene, 23:368
Barnes, Fred, genealogist, 27:56
Barnes, Henry, boatbuilder, 11:128
Barnes, Irene, see Taeuber, Irene B.
Barnes, James, 13:425; author, 15:471
Barnes, Julius, 37:260
Barnes, Mrs. M. F., letter, 28:133n
Barnes, O. L., in Sioux Outbreak, 18:461
Barnes, Russell F., librarian, 27:140, 29:187, 281, 30:39, 410
Barnes family, genealogy, 27:56
Barnesville, anniversaries, 13:448, 35:382; newspaper, 21:448; churches, 14:452, 21:112; unions, 21:393
Barnesville Ladies Literary League, 29:269
Barnett, Claribel R., author, 14:349
Barnett, James H., work reviewed, 34:167
Barney, Fred E., real-estate dealer, 24:139, 140
Barney, Sheldon F., 24:272
Barnhart, J. S., editor, 21:416
Barnhart, John D., review by, 12:411-413; work reviewed, 34:82; speaker, 15:119; author, 25:402, 34:354
Barnhart, Thomas F., author, 22:212, 27:270
Barnitz, David G., 13:145, 146
Barns, Dr. Cass G., author, 12:440
Barns, Comfort, 11:169, 20:457
Barnum, Charles E., author, 17:112
Barnum, George G., 12:207, 34:204; in Civil War, 11:318, 20:195; speaker, 13:216; reminiscences, 17:98

Barnum, Phineas T., 12:400; speaker, 21:326; circus, 28:246, 266; museum, 38:287

Barnum, name, 11:318; history, 20:215, 31:67, 35:382; veterans, 39:243, 244

Barr, Alfred H., Jr., editor, 16:110, 17:107

Barr, Rev. J. T., author, 33:341

Barr, Will, author, 12:337

Barret, P., author, 16:221

Barrett, B. C., 17:241

Barrett, Mr. and Mrs. Giles L., actors, 33:284

Barrett, Lawrence, actor, 28:101, 117, 118, 33:175

Barrett, Peter, trial, 18:124n, 125

Barrett, S. A., author, 15:453

Barrett, Tim, trial, 18:124n, 125, 128

Barrick, Nimrod, diary, 19:344, 20:34

Barriger, John W., III, author, 21:97

Barringer, John, letter, 34:169

Barrington, Lewis, author, 23:192

Barrow, W. J., author, 24:361

Barrows, Morton, author, 17:129

Barrows, Mrs. S., speaker, 15:369

Barrows, ghost town, 19:464; name, 21:349

Barry, Father Colman J., 37:88, 38:335; reviews by, 33:304, 34:123, 37:221; works reviewed, 33:305, 35:145, 37:299, 38:193; author, 26:275, 31:187, 35:46, 37:133; speaker, 37:40

Barry, David F., photographer, 34:174

Barry, Mrs. Edith L., 16:542

Barry, Edward L., diary, 16:336

Barry, Elizabeth, 18:59

Barry, J. Neilson, compiler, 26:273

Barry, Louise, editor, 29:175

Barry, R. T., 26:180, 27:174, 28:196

Barry, Irish settlement, 31:22

Barsness, Dr. Nellie N., author, 20:466

Barsness, Olive, 25:209, 26:391, 29:181

Barsness Township, Pope County, Lutheran church, 24:92

Barstow, Mrs. Nelson, 15:483

Bartch, A. P., 23:200

Bartelt, Harry, 28:375

Barth, Carl, engineer, 29:157

Barth, G. W. O., author, 14:234

Barthelemy, C. R., 16:302

Bartholomew, Charles L. ("Bart"), cartoonist, 22:320, 29:50, 102, 30:179, 234, 240, 35:300, 305, 306, 312n, 36:120, 121, 123, 125, 126n; papers, 23:40

Bartholomew, Paige, papers, 28:279, 29:284

Bartke, Frank, farmer, 25:336

Bartlett, Herbert R., artist, 16:113

Bartlett, Joseph, descendants, 15:343

Bartlett, R. C., 21:108, 22:106, 23:104

Bartlett, S. M., 22:23n

Bartlett, William W., author, 11:326, 12:434

Bartlett, Winifred, 14:461, 31:207; speaker, 14:450

Bartlett family, genealogy, 15:343

Barton, Albert O., author, 19:107

Barton, Arah, politician, 39:49

Barton, Benjamin, editor, 36:224, 225

Barton, Bruce, author, 13:337

Barton, Clara, in Minnesota, 18:208, 35:215; lecturer, 21:326

Barton, Elijah, lawyer, 21:196

Barton, George A., author, 20:358, 36:103

Barton, Mrs. John A., speaker, 11:460

Barton, William E., author, 28:64, 361

Barton, Mrs. Winifred W., 16:301

Bartram, John, pioneer archaeologist, 16:152

Bartram, William, pioneer archaeologist, 16:152

Baruch, Bernard M., author, 36:68

Barzun, Jacques, author, 26:161, 36:32

Bas de la Rivière, Man., trading post, 11:363, 28:1-3

Bascom, John, educator, 30:381

Bascomb, D. J., merchant, 21:214

Baseball, amateur clubs, 13:148, 19:162-181, 472, 20:358, 468, 21:340, 23:31, 40:61; Minnesota, 15:489, 17:87, 18:343, 30:406; equipment, 17:491; frontier, 20:441, 444; history, 21:426; depicted, 30:54, 36:94, 40:33; Twin Cities, 36:93, 39:331

Basilica of St. Mary, Minneapolis, 13:312

Baskin, Forster, and Co., atlas publishers, 40:128

Basler, Roy P., author, 35:147

Bass, George F., archaeologist, 38:244, 39:124; work reviewed, 40:260

Bass, Jacob W., hotelkeeper, 35:355, 356; letter, 36:261; postmaster, 40:88

Bass, Mrs. Jacob W. (M. D. Brunson), 39:321

Bass, William, 24:116

Bass Lake, Faribault County, pioneer settlement, 24:382

Bass Lake, Ramsey County, acreage, 40:226n

Bass Lake, St. Louis County, disappearance, 23:99

Basset, Francis, I, pewterer, 40:204

Basset, Francis, II, pewterer, 40:204

Bassett, Edward, family, 26:90

Bassett, Joel B., 18:97, 26:135; businessman, 35:341, 37:319

Bassett, Mrs. Joel B., 22:255

Bassett, John, farm, 13:133, 17:266, 268, 22:100

Bassett, Mrs. M. H., 25:408; author, 28:296

Bassett, T. C. Seymour, author, 27:256

Bassett, Wayne R., author, 31:61

Bassett, William, 25:130

Bassett, St. Louis County, Finnish settlement, 25:160

Bassett, J. B., and Co., log mark, 26:135

Basswood Grove, Washington County, church, 26:286

Basswood Lake, border lake, 29:130, 34:178, 37:225 (cover); fur trade, 11:358, 12:82, 22:274, 275, 309, 310, 29:134, 35:282; trade route, 37:243, 245, 248, 250, 253

Basswood River, boundary river, archaeology, 38:29, 30, 39:130

Bastian, Huber, artist, 34:267

Batavia, Todd County, history, 15:371

Batchelder, Mrs. Charles, 20:363; author, 23:103

Batchelder, Ernest, art teacher, 26:79

Batchelder, George A., author, 11:324

Batchelder, George W., career, 30:82

Batchelder, Josiah Q., boatbuilder, 20:364

Batchelder, Loren H., dean, 39:220, 221

Batchelder and Buckham, Faribault, law firm, 16:241, 19:467

Bateaux, racing, 17:367; described, 20:340

Bateman, Walter, author, 36:326

Bates, C. Francis, trader, 34:326, 327

Bates, David G., steamboat captain, 11:124, 13:224, 225, 231; trader, 13:221

Bates, Edward, 15:406, 411

Bates, Mrs. Kate S., 21:96

Bates, Katherine L., poet, 26:301

Bates, Lehmen, farmer, 31:80

Bates, Phyllis, author, 15:245

Bates, William J., sheriff, 40:344

Bath Township, Freeborn County, Norwegian settlement, 12:269

Battle Creek Park, Ramsey County, 17:311

Battle Hollow, Stillwater, 11:225; prison site, 37:138, 142, 151

Battle Island, Mississippi River, 11:452

Battle Lake (lake), see West Battle Lake

Battle Lake (town), literary clubs, 17:488; Baptist church, 17:488; Scandinavian settlement, 24:240

Battle River, Beltrami County, log drives, 29:146

Battle Township, Beltrami County, history, 15:32

Batty, Mrs. Eliza, 11:321

Bauder House, Winona, 12:47

Baudry, Toussaint, trader, 19:274

Bauer, Aleck, 24:106

Bauer, Arnold J., author, 16:130, 252

Bauer, Edwin F., artist, 29:269

Bauer, Harold, pianist, 33:104, 39:63

Bauer, Harold C., author, 20:356

Bauer, Harry C., speaker, 32:123

Bauer, Levi, butcher, 24:106

Bauer, Philip, essay reviewed, 36:150

Baughman, Mrs. Blanche K., 27:148

Bauk, Rev. J. S., 31:82n

Baum, Arthur W., author, 27:272

Bauman, Catherine, 22:45, 23:367, 24:31, 34

Baumann, Rev. B., 13:100

Baumann, Frederick, review by, 34:251

Baumgartner, George, 29:303

Baumhofer, Rev. Earl, speaker, 16:124, 19:117

Baumhofer, Mrs. Hermine Munz, "A New Tool for a New History," 28:345-352; review by, 32:184; author, 28:399, 31:188, 32:192, 33:351

Baur, John E., author, 36:277; compiler, 38:385

Baur, John I. H., author, 21:150, 156, 157

Bavarians, see Germans

Baxby, Lt. ---, Fort Snelling officer, 18:405, 40:79

Baxter, Alexander, trader, 11:258, 264n; mining interests, 11:263

Baxter, H. G., letter, 13:197
Baxter, Judge Luther L., papers, 11:
205, 445, 12:319, 13:197, 14:100,
17:212
Baxter, Maurice G., author, 31:125
Baxter, Capt. William R., letter, 26:
197n
Baxter Township, Lac qui Parle County, Norwegian settlement, 12:275n
Baxter's Fire Zouaves, Pennsylvania
regiment, 25:137
Bay, J. Christian, 17:131; author, 19:
217, 23:379, 33:314; quoted, 32:
125; editor, 32:204, 33:90
Bay City, Mich., lumber town, 23:356
Bay Lake, Crow Wing County, history,
16:490; name, 21:348
Bay State Milling Co., Winona, 20:470
Bayard, James A., Delaware Senator,
37:48
Bayfield, Henry W., naval officer,
17:345, 35:152
Bayfield, Wis., railroad, 34:67, 69,
70, 73, 37:113n; fishing, 34:247,
249; history, 35:152
Bayliss, Joseph E., works reviewed,
19:198, 35:199
Bayliss, Mrs. Joseph E. (Estelle L.),
works reviewed, 19:198, 35:199
Bayly, Billy, author, 29:344
Bayly, Charles, career, 26:273
Bayport (Baytown), Lutheran church,
11:468, 14:52, 53; German settle-
ment, 14:52; history, 16:337, 23:
299; shipyards, 20:364; clamming
industry, 28:285. See also Minnesota State Prison
Bayport Improvement Club, 23:299
Baytown Township, Washington County,
Germans, 23:404
Bazille, Charles, donor of capitol
site, 14:330
Bazille, Edmund W., 39:154n
Beach, Joseph W., 15:83, 21:70; poet,
16:81, 26:308
Beach, Moses Y., journalist, 11:164,
166; compiler, 40:295
Beach, Rex, author, 31:58
Beach, S. S., 16:488, 18:116, 20:96,
212, 349, 21:108, 444, 22:50, 106,
23:102, 391; speaker, 16:306, 20:
48, 464, 21:445, 22:217, 23:48;
author, 17:237
Beach, Sylvia, author, 37:184
Beach, Walter B., 22:105
Beadle, B. V., speaker, 22:440
Beads, as ornaments, 36:101; in fur
trade, 40:198, 203, 205-209
Beagle, Mrs. C. D., author, 15:475
Beal, A. H., photographer, 33:175,
178n
Beal, Barney, folk hero, 40:391
Beales, H. L., work reviewed, 38:198
Beals, Mrs. Katherine M., 11:321
Beals, Walter B., 11:321
Beaman, Samuel, speaker, 12:400
Bean, Frank A., miller, 14:103, 23:
388, 32:13n
Bean, Jacob, lumber dealer, 38:349
Bean, Mrs. Jacob, playhouse, 38:349,
352
Bean, James, 18:250
Bean, Maj. John L., 18:207
Bean, Mrs. Nancy K., 19:221
Bean, Judge Roy, folk hero, 26:166
Bean, Mrs. W. E., author, 19:233
Bear, Henry, papers, 21:214

Bear, in fur trade, 23:330, 30:131,
40:210, 212, 219; Black Hills, 32:
220; Minnesota, 33:354, 35:48, 38:
4. See also Wildlife
Bear Creek, Clearwater County, history, 35:203
Bear Creek, Fillmore County, archaeology, 28:373
Bear Creek, McLeod County, Catholic
church, 15:30
Bear Creek, Mower County, Norwegian
settlement, 12:269
Bear Head, Todd County, history, 15:
371
Bear Island, Leech Lake, 24:143
Bear Lake Sunshine Club, history, 20:
102
Bear River, Koochiching County, history, 20:102
Bear River, Northwest Angle, 34:8
Bear River Journal (St. Louis County), established, 20:216
Bear River Valley, St. Louis County,
lumbering, 21:344
Beard, Charles A., historian, 14:201,
20:197, 420, 21:14, 34:81, 39:335;
work reviewed, 20:317-319; speaker, 15:119, 228; isolationist, 40:
410
Beard, Mrs. Charles A. (Mary R.),
work reviewed, 20:317-319; editor,
15:230
Beard, Dr. Richard O., author, 12:
204; quoted, 14:329; speaker, 15:
219
Beardmore, Ont., archaeology, 20:199,
34:215, 40:95
Beardsley, Arthur, educator, 16:184
Beardsley, Methodist church, 16:355
Beargrease, Henry, Chippewa Indian,
33:26, 105-109, 111
Beargrease, John, Chippewa Indian,
33:26, 105-109, 111
Beargrease, Mary, Chippewa Indian,
33:105-109, 111
Bearss, Edwin C., archaeologist, 38:
244; work reviewed, 40:306
Beasley, J. L., author, 16:226
Beasley, Norman, work reviewed, 12:
178
Beath, Paul R., author, 29:267
Beaton, Kendall, work reviewed, 36:27
Beattie, Lt. A., Union officer, 12:
196
Beattie, Margaret R., author, 31:58
Beatty, George H., speaker, 20:99
Beatty, Mrs. Laura E., reminiscences,
12:335
Beatty, Leslie R., forest ranger, 38:
336
Beatty, Robert T., author, 12:449
Beatty, W. Donald, review by, 33:306
Beatty Portage, Lac la Croix, 13:
298
Beaty, George, speaker, 16:362
Beauford Township, Blue Earth County,
history, 18:338; United Brethren
church, 15:362
Beaufort Hotel, Minneapolis, 35:73
Beauharnois, Charles de la Boische,
Marquis de, governor of New
France, 12:362, 363, 16:323, 18:
234, 236, 243, 32:227, 238n, 38:
27, 39:302
Beaulieu, Arthur, author, 12:223
Beaulieu, Bazil, trader, 36:242, 244,
245

Beaulieu, Clement H., trader, 11:372,
16:380, 18:209, 24:354, 28:209,
30:259, 32:91n, 95; land claim,
28:222
Beaulieu, E., artist, 30:204, 207,
215, 218
Beaulieu, Paul, trader, 36:242, 244,
245
Beaulieu, Theodore H., editor, 21:415
Beaulieu family, 14:233
Beaumont, Mr. and Mrs. Ethan A., 20:
337
Beaumont, Dr. William, surgeon, 20:
202, 26:271, 30:259; at Fort Crawford, 14:223, 36:324; centennial,
14:445, 15:234; in St. Louis, 17:
474, 21:428; career, 19:105, 21:
429, 26:170, 30:248; papers, 20:
337, 27:236; experiments, 21:95,
26:366; author, 21:366, 367; memorial, 33:316, 36:324
Beaumont and Gordon, St. Paul, grocers, 38:173n
Beaupre, Bruno, 16:268, 20:185
Beauregard, Gen. Pierre G. T. de,
Confederate officer, 25:120, 121,
133, 246
Beaver, Lt. Frederick J. H., with
Sibley expedition, 20:328
Beaver, Rhoda M., 12:407
Beaver, Scott County, located, 12:61n
Beaver, Winona County, history, 35:
245, 39:36
Beaver, in fur trade, 11:245, 15:157,
23:330, 27:63, 30:132, 38:190, 39:
207, 40:154, 155, 158, 179, 205,
206, 212, 219, 220; living habits,
11:323; Michigan, 18:451; Minnesota, 22:103, 194, 214; in Canadian
art, 22:433; disease, 30:123; pictured, 40:38, 187; hats, 40:187,
208, 215; prices and production,
40:212-215, 218
Beaver Bay, name, 12:287; roads, 16:
296, 298, 19:309, 310, 34:178,
181; history, 17:359, 30:407; depicted, 20:453; sawmill, 22:346;
fur trade, 26:384; taconite project, 33:355; described, 35:49
Beaver Bay Club, North Shore, history, 27:73
Beaver Club, Montreal, 21:136n; history, 11:327, 17:222
Beaver Creek, Ill., Norwegian settlement, 12:181
Beaver Creek, village and township,
Rock County, Norwegian settlement,
12:274; Presbyterian church, 28:
395
Beaver Crossing, Lake County, rail-
road, 34:181
Beaver Dam, Wis., history, 24:369
Beaver Falls, Renville County, Norwe-
gian settlement, 12:275n; newspa-
per, 17:102; history, 36:107
Beaver Island, Mich., Mormon colony,
23:356
Beaver Islands, Mississippi River,
monument, 31:62
Beazell, William F., 12:434
Beccue, A. C., 11:119
Bechdolt, Adolf F., speaker, 39:115
Becht, John K., saloonkeeper, 39:175
Bechhoefer, Charles, career, 13:324
Bechyn, Renville County, name, 13:199
Beck, E. C., author, 35:243
Beck, Garrard, 14:43

Beck, Lewis C., author, 33:132, 34:360

Beck, Richard, translator, 13:209; author, 17:344; speaker, 26:397

Becker, C. W., 17:183

Becker, Carl L., work reviewed, 17:73; speaker, 13:105; historian, 14:10, 90, 26:356, 34:199, 250, 30:158, 36:97, 39:335, 336; reviewer, 26:306, 307

Becker, Eugene D., 33:314; reviews by, 34:345, 36:99, 39:294; photographer, 33:45, 213, 34:317 (cover), 37:44, 335, 38:85n, 154-156, 165n, 189n, 231n, 337 (cover), 352n, 388, 39:124, 133 (cover), 153-161, 190n, 310n, 326n, 40:58n, 97 (cover), 108n, 338n, 412

Becker, George L., railroad president, 13:42, 37:154, 155, 158n, 160; politician, 14:164, 165, 254n, 28:33, 35:47, 62, 312, 36:124, 37:45, 46, 47, 48, 50, 39:101, 148, 151, 332; railroad land commissioner, 31:225, 226; water company director, 40:224

Becker, Mrs. George L., 37:160

Becker, John, diaries, 18:445, 19:48

Becker, Kenneth, artist, 27:141

Becker, Otto, artist, 28:79

Becker, Victoria M., family, 27:30

Becker, W. W., 19:235; author, 16:249

Becker, Walter F., author, 35:338

Becker County, history, 11:332, 16:363, 23:29; ethnic settlements, 12:277, 25:318, 28:121, 36:34; county seat fight, 12:444; archives, 15:196; forts, 15:244; pageants, 16:237, 26:396; township histories, 18:112; school, 21:219; church, 22:343; Red River trails, 24:167; food production, 25:312; newspapers, 26:282; pioneer life, 27:58; physicians, 36:70; grasshopper plague, 37:208; poorhouse, 38:274; nursing home, 38:377; Finnish place names, 40:358

Becker County Drivers' Association, 19:229

Becker County Historical Society, organized, 11:13; reorganized, 17:355; meetings, 18:108, 221, 19:115, 229, 20:95, 21:215, 333, 22:104, 24:85, 186, 25:208, 312, 29:361, 30:78; collecting activities, 18:333, 26:282; exhibit, 18:463; museum, 22:215, 23:397, 24:379, 26:392, 27:170, 265, 361; appropriation, 25:406

Beckford, William, 38:343

Beckman, Dr. Emil H., 24:347

Beckman, Oscar, 23:101

Beckwourth, James P., fur trader, 15:427, 428

Bedal, Lafayette, 18:118

Beddie, Ruth D., author, 19:98

Bede, J. Adam, speaker, 12:35

Bede's Budget (Pine City), 17:469

Bedwell, Harry, career, 36:322

Bee, Capt. Barnard E., pursues Inkpaduta, 12:116n, 38:123

Beebe, Burr, 13:176

Beebe, Dr. Loran W., author, 22:330

Beebe, Lucius, author, 33:314

Beebe, Ward, house, 40:359

Beebe, Dr. Warren L., St. Cloud physician, 33:282, 294

Beecher, Catharine E., 28:132, 133; feminist, 30:251

Beecher, Mrs. H. L., speaker, 23:109

Beecher, Henry W., abolitionist, 11:156, 32:15, 21, 25; career, 26:300, 35:195; author, 27:16

Beecher, Mrs. Mary R., 13:175n

Beede, Aaron M., author, 23:287

Beede, Cyrus, banker, 18:251

Beef Slough, Chippewa River, 30:243; trading post, 11:383; booms, 26:132, 27:191-196, 200, 201, 30:71

Beekeeping, Excelsior, 20:81; Big Woods, 35:78, 85

Beeler, Madison S., author, 33:311

Beer, James R., author, 33:354

Beers, Henry P., 20:199; works reviewed, 17:321, 36:29, 38:382, 39:165; compiler, 24:173

Beers, Lorna D., author, 16:106, 23:156, 31:137, 145

Beers, Dr. W. G., 35:151

Beeson, Lewis, 17:385n, 18:231n, 21:312, 22:317, 24:351, 26:63, 186, 27:49, 140, 31:113; "Collecting War Records," 23:19-23; "The Minnesota War History Committee," 23:149-153; MHS reports, 24:26-40, 25:40-52, 26:29-41; reviews by, 17:458, 21:180-182, 401, 22:330, 23:89, 24:337; works reviewed, 17:81-83, 18:83, 21:78; author, 17:60, 464, 22:45, 419, 24:58; newspaper librarian, 21:81; speaker, 22:447, 25:95; acting superintendent, 23:366, 24:30, 32, 57, 59, 242, 378, 27:46, 30:327; editor, 24:33, 31:57, 34:219, 355; career, 27:243

Beet raising, 24:126, 259, 27:87, 35:201

Beethoven Musical Association, Owatonna, 16:255

Begg, Alexander, journal reviewed, 35:282

Beggin, Margaret, author, 26:396

Behling, David J., author, 29:171

Behncke, David L., aviator, 33:242

Behrens, Oscar, speaker, 15:115

Beil & Herment, Chicago and New York, construction firm, 39:158

Beinhauer, Myrtle, author, 16:478, 36:238

Beinhorn, Frederick, New Ulm pioneer, 19:472, 27:268, 30:28, 30, 31:24

Beise, Dr. H. C., 26:283, 27:75

Bekivetang family, Chippewa Indians, 39:305n

Belanger, Louis, 13:133

Belanger (Bellanger) family, Chippewa Indians, 14:216, 39:305n

Belanski, Mrs. Stanislaus (Ann), 16:174

Belchertown, Mass., emigration from, 19:133, 140, 141, 321, 337, 341

Belcourt, Father George A., missionary, 12:83, 318, 19:379n, 20:327, 430, 21:432, 22:149, 26:75, 29:101, 31:240, 34:84, 35:282; letters, 12:82, 22:280n; Ojibway dictionary, 18:46, 21:36, 205; memorial, 23:287; biography, 34:305

Belde, Walter, 29:289n

Belden, Rev. C. D., author, 14:237

Beldon, W. D., author, 11:114

Belgian Information Center, New York, 23:393

Belgians, 12:255, 21:74; Martin County, 12:103; Lyon County, 14:356, 24:79, 177, 35:325, 38:243; Wisconsin, 14:447, 20:86, 24:176, 27:134; Canada, 20:342

Belgium, in World War I, 11:349

Belgrade, bank, 33:54

Belknap, Jeremy, career, 39:336

Bell, Dr. ---, frontier physician, 11:58

Bell, A. J., letter, 11:331

Bell, Charles N., author, 13:209, 337, 14:342, 15:239

Bell, E. and H. Y., St. Paul, meat packers, 26:115

Bell, Dr. E. T., author, 31:124

Bell, Edwin, trader, 18:209

Bell, Edwin, steamboat captain, 21:265, 37:227

Bell, G. W. H., 23:273

Bell, Gordon L., author, 39:171

Bell, Harriet C., author, 19:345

Bell, Henry H., and Co., Duluth, bankers, 37:121, 122

Bell, Ida P., "A Pioneer Family of the Middle Border," 14:303-315; author, 14:79

Bell, Mrs. Ivie, author, 16:368

Bell, J., trader, 40:167n, 168n

Bell, J. E., 19:267n

Bell, James Ford, 16:20n, 21:208, 25:154n, 32:13n, 34:204; work reviewed, 34:257; author, 12:203; collector, 19:69, 31:105-109, 188, 33:352, 34:310, 35:151, 36:70, 37:222; papers, 30:63

Bell, James H., diary, 17:212, 18:47

Bell, James S., 34:204

Bell, John, novelist, 31:145

Bell, John, presidential candidate, 24:309; Senator, 39:143, 144

Bell, John E., pioneer, 24:115

Bell, Capt. John R., journal, 35:292

Bell, Laird, author, 22:95, 39:131

Bell, Marguerite N., author, 34:217

Bell, N. J., 19:116

Bell, R. C., 11:206

Bell, R. J., journalist, 24:326

Bell, Solomon, pseud., see Snelling, William J.

Bell, W. W., author, 18:220

Bell, Whitfield J., Jr., author, 30:149, 34:212

Bell, Dr. William, trader, 13:195

Bell, Rev. William, 15:469

Bell, Rev. William J., speaker, 11:112

Bell family, 22:193

Bell Foundation, 40:149

Bella Coola Valley, B.C., Norwegian colony, 17:110

Bellair (Bellain), Louis, trader, 22:281

Bellaire family, 14:216

Bellamy, Edward, radical leader, 27:334

Belland, Henry, Sr., voyageur, 14:426, 22:144, 145n

Bellar, William, author, 38:334

Belle Isle, Va., prison camp, 25:145-151, 224, 225

"Belle of Bellevue," steamboat, 37:285

"Belle of Minnetonka," steamboat, 12:433, 18:374, 29:292

"Belle P. Cross," steamboat, 35:279

Belle Plaine, history, 11:118; rail-road, 11:467, 12:59, 61n; trading post, 12:210, 14:238; historic sites, 12:342; postal service, 13:454; economic conditions, 14:463; industries, 15:138; pioneer life, 15:252, 492, 17:364, 28:266, 36:196; schools, 15:371, 28:267; hunting, 16:253; churches, 16:255, 20:218, 28:395; elections, 16:367, 28:36; British settlement, 28:260; centennial, 34:128; river port, 36:257; in Sioux Outbreak, 38:101

Belle Plaine, Iowa, townsites, 27:355

Belle Plaine City, Scott County, ghost town, 28:260

Bell Plaine Foundry and Machine Shop, 15:252

Belle Plaine Herald, founded, 28:265

Belle Prairie, schools 14:143, 16:318, 17:465, 19:132n, 20:446, 25:12, 13, 29:270; mission, 25:290; German settlement, 31:25, 32:36; salt springs, 32:217

Belle Prairie Seminary, 14:143, 19:132n, 25:13

Belleau, Father J. M., author, 21:432

Bellevue, Iowa, described, 17:421

Bellevue, Neb., historic site, 40:193

Bellevue Seminary, Bellevue, Nicollet County, 14:146

Bellevue Township, Morrison County, settled, 11:220; schools, 25:12

Bellevue War, outlaw raids, 17:421n

Bellin, Nicolas, map maker, 27:66

Bellman, Minneapolis weekly, evaluated, 26:304-310

Bello, Dr. Edoardo, author, 21:437

Bellot, H. Hale, 15:118; reviews by, 16:196, 17:199, 19:432-434; work reviewed, 33:214; author, 17:50, 206, 19:444

Bellows, Curtis, trader, 29:218

Bellows, Henry A., author, 18:192, 26:306, 308

Bells, early Minnesota, 18:371-380; Rush Lake church, 19:124; Red River mission, 20:204

"Bellview," steamboat, 13:227, 228

Belmont, Wis., first capital, 15:16

Belmont Township, Jackson County, Norwegian settlement, 12:274; roads, 23:402

Beloit Co., emigrant group, 13:111

Belthuis, Lyda, author, 29:266

Belting, Natalia M., review by, 30:249; work reviewed, 29:337; author, 30:292

Belton, George R., author, 23:93

Beltrami, Giacomo C., explorer, 16:453, 29:351; evaluated, 11:452; search for Mississippi source, 12:225, 13:277, 15:101, 16:118, 21:79, 29:83; author, 12:238, 13:222, 369, 436, 30:220, 31:105, 35:200, 242, 378; portrait, 13:60, 83, 84, 27:241; passenger on "Virginia," 20:378, 30:212n, 40:411; markers, 26:388, 29:168, 279, 352

Beltrami County, lumber industry, 13:366, 29:137-149; township histories, 15:132, 244, 365, 483, 16:125; archives, 15:197, 23:93; pioneer life, 18:112, 26:93; agriculture, 19:364; Cass Lake mission, 19:120; frontier area, 23:24; growth, 23:29, 32; county seat,

23:30; archaeology, 26:321; newspapers, 29:356; schools, 36:104; history, 38:388; electric service, 40:315

Beltrami County Historical Society, 18:221, 33:313, 356, 34:131, 36:104; organized, 30:398; meeting, 35:50; publications, 35:202, 380, 38:388

Beltrami County War History Committee, 23:390

Beltrami Eagle (Bemidji), 29:356

Beltrami Island State Forest, 20:66

Beltrami Lake, Beltrami County, name, 21:352

Beltrami Park, Minneapolis, 29:352

Beltrami State Park, Beltrami County, dedicated, 29:279, 351

Belview, Norwegian settlement, 23:290

Belview Independent, history, 35:50

Bemidji, Chippewa leader, 23:25, 28:189, 33:313

Bemidji, newspapers, 16:125, 29:356; early trails, 16:492; historical session, 18:205, 280-282; winter carnival, 19:234; name, 20:343, 23:27; lumber industry, 21:177, 23:33, 29:138-148, 31:68, 75, 35:202; pioneer community, 23:24-34, 33:313; hotels, 23:25; population, 23:26, 33; churches, 23:27, 32, 31:68, 70, 71; railroads, 23:28, 33, 29:138, 147; county seat, 23:29, 30, 68; resort center, 23:31, 28:93, 34:65; described, 25:278; history, 28:78; parks, 28:189; trade center, 29:137; local government, 30:144; disabled veterans, 39:243

Bemidji Daily Pioneer, 16:125; anniversary, 33:313

Bemidji Eagle, first issue, 16:126

Bemidji House, hotel, 23:25

Bemidji Lumber Co., 27:302

Bemidji State Teachers College, history, 19:233, 25:210, 34:93, 131

Bemidji Township, Beltrami County, history, 15:365

Bemidji Townsite and Improvement Co., 23:27, 30

Bemis, Mrs. F. C., author, 14:236

Bemis, Dr. Joseph G., letters, 13:438

Bemis, Dr. N. M., case book, 16:242

Bemis, Samuel F., speaker, 13:106

"Ben Bolt," steamboat, 14:297

"Ben Campbell," steamboat, 17:278, 29:203

"Ben Coursin," steamboat, 36:252

"Ben Hersey," towboat, 18:177

Bena, Cass County, Chippewa settlement, 26:81; boatbuilding, 33:14

Bendikson, L., 22:92

Benedict, Mrs. Jay E., 22:340; speaker, 21:217

Benedict, Mary D., author, 15:483, 16:233

Benedict, Catholic church, 17:117

Benedicta, Maine, Catholic colony, 21:74

Benedictine Order, St. Cloud and Stearns County, 11:205, 20:364, 32:39-42, 33:188, 34:171; Minnesota communities, 14:120, 21:457, 22:111, 26:275, 27:269, 28:84, 32:34-43; women religious, 12:456, 17:219, 33:58, 59, 36:24; Czech, 15:446; schools and colleges, 17:

84, 219, 20:104, 23:111, 27:169, 34:91, 92, 131, 35:263-271, 338, 39:321; U.S., 19:219; Northwest, 27:170, 33:53-60; Pennsylvania, 32:37, 33:53; missions, 33:57-60, 34:123, 131, 36:192, 38:335; hospitals, 33:291-297. See also College of St. Benedict, St. Benedict's Academy, St. John's Abbey and University

Beneš, Václav L., essay reviewed, 36:185

Beneš, Vojta, at Silver Lake, 15:41

Benevolent and Protective Order of Elks, Crookston, 17:362; records, 34:340; St. Paul, 37:308

Bengtson, Bennie, author, 29:94

Bengston, John R., review by, 35:42

Benham, Mrs. Erma, 16:361

Benham, Roy H., 39:245; speaker, 29:274, 362

Benisovich, Michel, "Peter Rindisbacher," 32:155; author, 32:191

Benit, William A., speaker, 17:358, 26:181

Benjamin, Darius C., publisher, 20:215

Benjamin, Harold, educator, 35:371

Benjamin, Dr. John, 38:151; career, 11:115

Benjamin, Joseph, blacksmith, 20:217

"Benjamin Noble," steamboat, 35:280

Benner, Franklin, letters, 27:248

Bennett, ---, music teacher, 39:320

Bennett, A. C., author, 20:203

Bennett, A. C., aviator, 34:44

Bennett, C. A., G.A.R. commander, 16:438, 439

Bennett, C. H., founder of Pipestone, 31:205

Bennett, E., letter, 15:221

Bennett, Edward H., architect, 33:334, 338, 339

Bennett, Estelline, author, 26:307

Bennett, Henry H., photographer, 20:203

Bennett, James Gordon, journalist, 25:249, 27:1

Bennett, John, author, 27:275

Bennett, L. G., map maker, 40:125n

Bennett, R. H., sheep raiser, 26:113

Bennett, Richard, author, 33:132

Bennett, Russell H., 33:333; work reviewed, 39:78; author, 13:115

Bennett, Mrs. Russell M., author, 27:176

Bennett, W. J., speaker, 23:396

Bennett Law, opposed, 18:381, 383

Bennion, Dr. S. E., 23:102

Bennyhoff, Donald C., speaker, 24:187

Benoit, Eugene, missionary, 39:309

Benshoof, L. M., 18:269; speaker, 18:271

Bensley, Dr. Edward H., author, 36:324

Benson, A. F., speaker, 15:138

Benson, Adolph B., work reviewed, 31:111; author, 19:216, 20:442, 30:391; editor, 30:148

Benson, Rev. C. E., speaker, 22:108

Benson, Charles, 11:146

Benson, Elmer A., 19:427; speaker, 16:483; governor, 19:315, 34:188, 40:368, 374; politician, 34:190-192, 38:41, 40:91; Senator, 40:366; depicted, 40:373

Benson, Esther, "A Community Study," 25:362-367; author, 25:382
Benson, Ezra Taft, quoted, 40:294
Benson, Fred, seaman, 35:279
Benson, Mrs. G. A., 20:456
Benson, Henry N., attorney general, 12:36, 38, 15:78, 80, 490, 16:241, 300, 17:70, 19:470, 20:50, 353, 21:217, 22:50, 293, 295, 296, 23:48, 50, 25:98, 209, 26:45, 150, 27:76, 28:200, 29:97; speaker, 12:104, 452, 15:80, 123, 16:122, 301, 491, 17:67, 18:329, 19:465, 21:53, 438, 22:47, 215, 29:276; career, 39:299
Benson, Mrs. Henry N., 16:301
Benson, Jared, politician, 37:329
Benson, Lillian R., author, 26:266
Benson, Lyman L., stage owner, 29:206, 222
Benson, Marty, athlete, 39:20
Benson, Ramsey, author, 18:221, 31:132, 145
Benson, Tony, speaker, 17:484; mine inspector, 34:274
Benson, William C., work reviewed, 31:50
Benson, history, 11:338, 339, 17:366, 19:408; Norwegian settlement, 12:277, 23:290, 40:357; immigrant house, 13:41; Lutheran church, 15:481; railroad, 21:241; library, 26:290; in World War II, 26:389; Catholic colony, 35:139
Benson County, N.D., place names, 38:385
Benson Grove, Iowa, convention riot, 18:432
Benson House, Benson, hotel register, 20:364
Bent, Charles, 15:430
Bent, George P., author, 13:114
Bent, Silas, author, 27:253
Bent, William, 15:430
Benteen, Frederick W., letters, 34:40
Bentley, Frances, author, 12:208
Bentley, Dr. J. W., 21:329
Bentley, Will, author, 35:336
Benton, Charles W., 18:150
Benton, Thomas H., Missouri Senator, 19:306, 33:304, 39:31, 40:185
Benton, Thomas H., artist, 21:402
Benton, Ward H., 26:284; speaker, 24:86
Benton and Roberts, Mankato, law firm, 26:259
Benton County, history, 13:447, 36:106; pioneer life, 15:483; Germans, 21:98; archives, 21:327; schools, 24:88; wheat raising, 29:19; described, 29:204, 217; district court, 29:219; historical map, 31:62
Benton County Agricultural Society, organized, 14:137, 22:251, 40:334
Benton County War History Committee, 23:390
Benton Township, Carver County, history, 35:50; Dutch settlement, 37:160
Bent's Fort, Colo., post, 15:430, 40:195
Benville Township, Beltrami County, history, 15:483
Benz, George, 15:347
Benzie, W. A., banker, 39:246
Bercaw, Louise O., compiler, 16:235

Berdahl, Christian O., author, 26:284
Berens, H. H., Hudson's Bay Co. governor, 34:319
Berg, Carl, speaker, 17:483
Berg, Ernest L., author, 26:275
Berg, John, 15:488; author, 15:489, 17:361
Berg, Lillie C., author, 37:187
Berg, M. H., 19:355
Berge, Henrietta, 22:191, 421, 23:44
Bergen, Louis, trader, 20:264
Bergen, McLeod County, Lutheran church, 14:452
Bergen, Norway, runes, 40:49-58, 59
Bergendoff, Rev. Conrad, author, 17:329, 27:256, 29:278; speaker, 29:258; bibliography, 38:381
Berger, Dorothy, work reviewed, 36:62
Berger, Josef, work reviewed, 36:62
Berger, Victor, reformer, 40:140
Bergeson, A. P., 21:336, 444
Berggren, Alfred, 12:321
Berghold, Father Alexander, 15:484, 26:181, 32:172
Berghult, C. R., speaker, 19:315
Bergin, Alfred, speaker, 13:450, 18:329; author, 16:493, 38:92
Berglund, Emil, author, 37:135
Berglund, Hilma, artist, 12:306
Bergman, Austin I., lawyer, 21:196
Bergman, Rev. F. H., speaker, 16:130
Bergman, Solomon, 35:293
Bergmann, Leola N., works reviewed, 26:59, 32:51; author, 29:174
Bergqvist, Leonard, interpreter, 20:253, 254
Bergsma, Peter A., 33:129
Bering Sea, seal hunts, 40:217, 220
Berkey, Dr. Charles, 11:113
Berkey, Hiram, lumberman, 18:167
Berkey, Peter, businessman, 40:225
Berkhofer, Robert F., Jr., review by, 38:191; work reviewed, 39:292
Berkleo, Samuel, pioneer, 24:160
Berks County (Pa.) Historical Society, 25:197, 26:78, 168, 383
Berkshire County, Mass., Stockbridge mission, 22:150n
Berland, Pascal, mixed-blood, 36:48
Berlie, Rev. E., speaker, 14:122
Berlin Township, Steele County, Norwegian settlement, 12:269
Berman, Hyman, historian, 40:410
Bern, Dodge County, Swiss settlement, 28:333
Bernadotte Township, Nicollet County, Scandinavian settlements, 12:275, 36:201
Bernard, Belva D. M., author, 38:42
Bernard, John T., Congressman, 40:369, 371, 373
Bernard, L. L., author, 23:289
Bernard, Lionel, troupe manager, 23:312n
Bernard, Sister M., author, 11:209
Bernard, Mrs. Otto, speaker, 26:284
Berneche, Zephirin, lumberman, 32:151n, 152, 33:22
Bernhardson, Lars, pioneer, 12:337
Berning, T. J., author, 18:105, 219, 36:105
Bernou, Abbé Claude, 12:410, 16:449, 23:57; editor, 20:67
Beroun, Pine County, name, 13:199
Berrum, Mrs. Agnes, 36:140
Berry, Charles A., 25:238

Berry, Charles H., papers, 24:61, 30:90
Berry, Daniel E., cholera victim, 14:297
Berry, Don, work reviewed, 38:199
Berry, Edward, postmaster, 13:454
Berry, Justice John M., 35:116
Berryville (Va.) Conservator, 25:33
Bersell, Eunice, author, 12:102
Bersell, P. O., author, 32:54
Bersie, Hiram, steamboat captain, 13:231, 15:409, 416, 417, 34:142, 143
Bertaut, Bartholemy, 16:418n
Berthel, Mary W., 17:61, 30:343n; "Hunting in Minnesota," 16:259-271; "Place Names," 21:345-352; MHS report, 23:46-51; ed., "Goodhue's Minnesota," 29:193-222; "The Minnesota Historical Society," 30:293-330; reviews by, 14:91, 16:199, 206, 22:413-415, 24:236, 341-343, 26:149, 248-250, 29:74, 35:95; work reviewed, 30:50-52; speaker, 15:107, 19:63, 21:286; career, 16:304, 23:366, 24:33, 29:287, 30:44, 35:52, 100; author, 16:467, 20:207, 27:61, 129, 28:276, 29:51, 372, 30:274, 406, 39:132; geographic board activities, 26:37; death, 38:204
Berthel, Dr. and Mrs. R. W., 26:31
Berthold family, in fur trade, 15:421
Bertil, Prince, visits Twin Cities, 29:183, 277
Bertram, George M., 20:141
Bertrand, C. J., historian, 11:5, 6, 10, 18:446
Bertrand, J. P., 24:186, 26:178; work reviewed, 37:86; speaker, 19:353, 22:442, 23:295, 24:56, 86, 378; author, 20:188, 25:96, 26:88
Bertsch, Carl W., artist, 13:87
Bessesen, Mrs. William A. (Beatrice G.), opera singer, 19:344; papers, 20:34
Bessette, Fred W., author, 17:364, 21:211
Best, St. George, poet, 26:301
Bestick, Mrs. E. J., 17:355, 22:104
Beston, Caleb, boatbuilder, 13:224
Bestor, Arthur E., Jr., review by, 33:82; work reviewed, 31:112; author, 36:185
Beta, pseud., see Adams, Chandler B.
Bethany Covenant Church, Cloquet, 16:121
Bethany Home for the Friendless, Minneapolis, 39:14
Bethel, W. N., author, 14:361
Bethel, history, 21:415, 24:189, 28:78, 129
Bethel College and Seminary, St. Paul, established, 15:235, 33:138; described, 31:112; anniversary, 28:83
Bethel Deaconess Hospital, Mountain Lake, 20:459
Bethlehem Academy, Faribault, 21:115; anniversaries, 16:371, 21:455
Bethlehem English Lutheran Church, St. Paul, anniversary, 16:235
Betten, Francis S., author, 15:355
Betten, Neil, "Strike on the Mesabi," 40:340-347
Bettenburg, P. C., author, 17:480
Better Business Bureau, Minneapolis, 14:437, 15:61

Betts, H. H., artist, 27:363
Betz, Andreas, 20:459
Bevaness, Chippewa Indian, 19:387n
Bevans, Corydon D., 11:169
Bevans, Henry L., 11:169n
Bevans, Henry T., 16:99
Bevans, John D., editor, 37:164
Bevans, Sgt. Milton L., disciplined, 25:246
Bevans Landing, Carver County, 11:169
Bevear Gold Mining and Milling Co., 15:489
Beveridge, Albert J., politician, 22: 79, 27:133; author, 28:361, 29:62, 39:220
Beveridge, Robert, 17:208, 35:14; author, 19:93; speaker, 21:83
Beveridge, Mrs. Robert, 17:385n, 18: 59
Beyea, Andrew S., letters, 14:436
Beyea family, genealogy, 14:436
Beyer, Carlyle, author, 18:446
Beyer, Richard L., author, 23:278, 25:85
Beyer, Thomas, author, 21:185
Beyers, H., Dutch pioneer, 28:128
Bibbins, Arthur, 13:408
Bible, translated into Dakota, 12: 244, 15:275, 16:142, 21:278
Bibliographical Society of America, 15:120, 341, 16:55, 65, 18:322, 24:361
Bicha, Karel D., author, 40:360
Bickford, A. E., speaker, 12:454
Bickford, "Bunk," 14:308, 309, 314
Bickford, Mrs. Maria C., 14:308, 313, 314
Bicycling, early machines, 23:290, 27:64; depicted, 27:65, 30:54, 40:1 (cover), 34; clubs, 33:315, 36:89
Bidamon, Maj. Lewis C., 17:430n
Bidamon, Mrs. Lewis C. (Emma H.), 17:429, 430n
Biddle, Nicholas, 39:165; editor, 36: 224; author, 40:304
Bidwell and Waldby, St. Paul, bankers, 40:113, 114
Bienville, sieur de, 13:85, 19:396, 24:53
Bierer, B. W., author, 35:243
Bierlein, S. W., author, 17:488
Bierman, Mrs. A. C., 12:106
Bierman, Bernard W., coach, 19:427, 35:335, 36:94; athlete, 39:18
Bierman, James M., lumberman, 24:201
Biermann, Adolph, state auditor, 35: 297
Biersach, Paul C., author, 11:330
Bierstadt, Mrs. ———, 13:410n
Bierstadt, Albert, artist, 33:264
Bierwirth, Leopold, consul, 40:277, 278
Biever, Lawrence, author, 18:340
Big Bend Dam, Missouri River, 39:213 (cover)
Big Bend Township, Chippewa County, Norwegian settlement, 12:275n, 13: 116
Big Bog, Beltrami County, wildlife, 30:128
Big Cobb River, Waseca County, 18: 298n
Big Eagle, Sioux leader, 12:121, 38: 126-128, 144, 146-149; describes Sioux Outbreak, 38:129-143

Big Eddy Hill, Mille Lacs County, Indian camps, 11:335, 25:58
Big Falls, history, 23:107; logging, 34:59
Big Fork River, Itasca County, lumbering, 24:93, 265; mounds, 31:163
Big Fork Valley, settled, 22:345, 415
Big Grove Norwegian Lutheran Church, Brooten, 24:93
Big Horn River, Mont., Wyo., 27:161
Big Iron, Sioux Indian, 15:274, 21:23
Big Island, Mississippi River, trading post, 11:375
Big Lake, Sherburne County, Swedish settlement, 20:243, 257, 258; railroad, 37:155, 156n, 158, 159
Big Pine River, Crow Wing County, mounds, 25:340
Big Sandy Lake, see Sandy Lake
Big Sioux River, N.D., Iowa, boundary, 24:368; road, 40:233
Big Stone County, pioneer life, 19: 234, 20:215; archives, 22:434; Norwegian settlements, 23:290; Catholic colony, 35:134, 138, 205-213, 325; history, 37:87; mounds, 37:347; Hutterite colony, 40:44; electric service, 40:315
Big Stone County War History Committee, 23:390
Big Stone Lake, border lake, 36:297; posts, 11:379, 18:278, 19:108, 383, 22:282, 33:274, 276; navigation, 14:351, 16:42, 17:304-306, 307, 21:250, 26:272; boundary, 19: 424, 425; engineering projects, 20:448; trails, 21:229; source of Minnesota River, 33:122n; resorts, 37:87; railroad, 37:156, 157, 38: 46; mounds, 37:347; Sioux villages, 38:145; prehistoric farming, 38:165
Big Thunder, Sioux leader, see Little Crow (Big Thunder)
Big Woods, settled, 11:132, 144, 15: 251, 20:449, 22:111, 30:401, 33: 250, 318, 35:77-86; transportation, 11:133, 21:234; Norwegian settlement, 12:247, 276, 31:27; hunting, 16:263, 38:134; botanical studies, 18:332, 22:292, 32:220; geography, 19:367, 30:117; remnants, 21:440, 22:103, 290, 23: 191; log cabins, 37:71; in Sioux Outbreak, 38:147, 148, 284
Big Woods Landing, Marshall County, history, 35:47
Bigelow, Dr. Charles E., author, 24: 182, 263, 382, 25:100, 307
Bigelow, Mrs. Charles H. (Florence Fairchild), 39:52n
Bigelow, Mrs. Frederic R., 25:409; speaker, 24:161, 25:41, 313, 27: 268; author, 28:71
Bigelow, Herbert H., career, 35:245
Bigelow, Horace, pioneer, 33:4
Bigelow Township, Nobles County, school, 18:227, 27:76
Bigflow, Murdock and Co., St. Paul, 24:301
Bigfork, school, 20:359; settled, 22: 415; cemetery, 24:383; anniversary, 35:203; logging area, 37:88
Biggert, Elizabeth C., work reviewed, 34:40
Bigsby, Dr. John J., explorer, 22:

179, 276, 23:203, 205, 25:273, 29: 132, 134, 267, 34:285
Bigsby and Gardner, St. Peter, merchants, 11:135
Bijou Opera House (Bijou Theater), Minneapolis, 18:212, 33:101
Bikuben (Salt Lake City), Mormon newspaper, 36:286, 287, 290, 292
Bilansky, see Belanski, Mrs. Stanislaus (Ann)
Bill, ———, photographer, 21:95
Bill, Alfred H., author, 35:293
Bill, Dyer, speaker, 19:120
Bill, Capt. Fred A., 14:224, 20:194; "The Wabasha County Herald-Standard," 15:86-88; work reviewed, 29: 73; author, 11:211, 14:362, 15: 125, 130, 360, 481, 21:261n, 23: 186; editor, 16:345
Bill, Ledyard, author, 35:217, 218
Billberg, Eddy E., 13:345, 16:241, 492, 17:96; work reviewed, 11:436; speaker, 11:223, 18:204, 273; author, 31:145
Billberg, Inga, author, 17:129, 130
Billigheim, J., theater director, 34: 239, 241
Billings, Frederick, 25:277
Billings, John S., sheriff, 11:319, 15:251, 38:12, 16-19
Billings, Josh, humorist, 33:327
Billings, Sheldon J., 15:251
Billington, Ray A., works reviewed, 30:250, 38:237, 40:303; author, 36:185, 37:261, 38:201, 39:33
Billy the Kid, outlaw, 34:209
Biloxi, Miss., founded, 18:389
Bilsborrow, H. J., author, 11:111
Biltmore Forest School, N.C., history, 34:176, 256
Bimetallism, see Free silver
Bimson, Rev. William C., author, 13: 343
Binder, Carroll, author, 30:406
Bingham, Mrs. ———, pioneer, 20:144
Bingham, Rev. Abel, career, 35:199
Bingham, Edwin R., editor, 38:42
Bingham, George C., artist, 25:278, 26:359, 33:264; biography, 21:402
Binisibi (Allen Junction), railroad station, 34:180
Binkley, Robert C., 18:44; "History for a Democracy," 18:1-27; review by, 17:448-450; author, 16:342, 17:459, 18:91; speaker, 18:68, 19: 43; papers, 30:258
Binkley, William C., author, 23:377
Binns, Jonathan, Quaker minister, 18: 253, 254, 255
Birbeck, M., author, 18:73
Birch Cooley (Coulee), Renville County, monument, 11:29, 31, 12:297-301, 13:340, 23:291; battle, 11: 299-304, 457, 12:84, 297, 298, 444, 13:453, 18:461, 20:454, 21: 182, 36:234, 38:97, 103, 105, 106, 107n, 138, 139, 140, 148, 156, 274, 358, 39:33; mission, 11:455, 16:119, 20:344; Norwegian colony, 12:275n; in fiction, 35:288; name, 37:42; store, 38:135n
Birch Cooley Memorial State Park, 19: 468, 37:59, 39:82
Birch Island Township, Beltrami County, history, 15:132
Birch Lake, St. Louis and Lake coun-

ties, map, 34:279; taconite findings, 39:163
Birchdale Township, Todd County, history, 16:131
Bircher, William, Civil War diary, 38:262, 265
Bird, Donald, author, 12:337, 15:134
Bird, Dr. J. P., speaker, 13:121
Bird, Walter D., 18:108, 20:95, 22:104, 24:85, 27:265
Bird Island, Catholic church, 11:117; history, 13:453, 16:131, 218, 19:126; newspapers, 17:102; garrison, 38:285
Birds, varieties, 16:38, 30:124; Minnesota, 15:349, 20:171, 22:213, 30:220-231, 36:103; banding, 22:214; North America, 30:221. See also Conservation, Wildlife
Birdsall, Amy, 28:88
Birge, Edward A., educator, 30:381
Birkeland, Knute B., 40:378, 379, 380
Birmingham, George, author, 29:154
Birney, James G., abolitionist, 32:15, 33:218
Biron, Michael, speaker, 24:219; author, 24:222
Biron, Pierre, voyageur, 32:235
Birr, Kendall, author, 31:250
Bisbee, Lewis C., diaries, 17:98
Biscay, creamery, 11:290, 12:335, 19:157n, 20:360; history, 21:452
Bischof, F., artist, 27:30
Biscoe, Rev. George S., missionary, 15:346, 16:28, 17:394, 26:114; papers, 15:465, 16:52, 349, 17:395n, 29:12, 39:270
Biscoe, T. C., 15:347
Bishoff, William N., speaker, 32:123
Bishop, Carl, speaker, 19:362
Bishop, Frances, author, 11:337
Bishop, Harriet E., (Mrs. John McConkey), 15:187, 29:359, 38:74; author, 11:168n, 14:140, 22:9, 40:147; teacher, 14:142, 144, 145, 15:254, 17:478, 18:372, 28:191, 30:198; career, 28:132-141; portrait, 38:75
Bishop, Mrs. J. M., 20:97
Bishop, Mrs. J. W., speaker, 14:229
Bishop, Jesse, 28:135
Bishop, Sgt. John F., in Sioux Outbreak, 34:235, 238
Bishop, John P., author, 32:115
Bishop, Judson W., Union officer, 12:445, 38:258, 261, 263, 266-273; author, 11:13; surveyor, 21:436
Bishop, Miranda, 28:134
Bishop, Putnam, 28:134
Bishop Hill, Ill., Swedish colony, 17:402, 24:256, 29:278, 31:27, 54
Bismarck, N.D., capital, 14:113, 36:3; newspapers, 15:201; railroads, 18:78, 28:396; Catholic church, 33:56, 39:299; hospital, 33:56, 58, 60, 294
Bismarck Tribune, established, 22:175
Bismark Township, Sibley County, history, 13:122
Bison, see Buffalo
Bispham, David S., singer, 39:56
Bissell, Richard, review by, 39:167; work reviewed, 31:246; author, 38:384
Bisson, George W., editor, 36:201-205
Bitter, Karl, sculptor, 40:408

Bittle, Rev. Celestine N., author, 16:346
Bittrich, George, composer, 23:172
Bivot, Zoe, cholera victim, 14:290
Biwabik, ethnic settlements, 13:108, 22:391n, 25:186, 319; founded, 21:290; mining town, 32:194; bus terminal, 35:338. See also Mesabi Range
Bixby, Dr. A. L., speaker, 11:297
Bixby, Horace, steamboat captain, 17:384, 25:72, 31:246
Bixby, Mrs. Lydia, 28:63
Bixby, Tams, 17:160n; publisher, 13:449, 23:94; townsite promoter, 23:27
Bjerkeng, Paul B., translator, 13:205
Bjoin, T. H., 20:466
Bjorgan, G. Rudolph, review by, 38:382
Bjork, Kenneth O., 35:296; "The Alexander Faribault Home," 35:320-324; "Mormon Missionaries," 36:285-293; reviews by, 32:49, 177-179, 33:80, 266, 35:31-33, 320-324, 374, 37:177, 299, 38:37, 381; works reviewed, 29:156-158, 36:98; author, 21:426, 23:381, 30:391, 32:64, 192, 40:351; speaker, 24:270, 30:279
Bjorklund, Lorence F., artist, 40:145
Bjorkman, Edwin, 20:397n
Bjorlee, Dr. Ignatius, 21:449; author, 22:221
Bjørnson, Bjørnstjerne, 20:398; author, 18:199; in Minnesota, 25:85, 33:169
Bjornson, G. B., legislator, 33:159
Bjornson, Hjalmar, author, 26:288
Bjornson, Valdimar, reviews by, 34:164, 35:325; speaker, 35:99
Black, Chauncey, author, 28:361
Black, Eleanor, editor, 24:260
Black, George, diary, 21:326
Black, Hugo, 20:318
Black, J., trader, 40:167n, 168n
Black, Jean, 26:39
Black, Jeremiah, speaker, 36:323
Black, Rev. John, 38:2
Black, John D., economist, 13:333, 39:245, 246, 247, 249, 250
Black, Capt. Mahlon, papers, 12:428
Black, Martha M., author, 15:356
Black, Oz, cartoonist, 30:406
Black, Samuel, work reviewed, 35:141; explorer, 17:75; trader, 28:6, 12, 40:177
Black, William P., 18:140
Black, Winifred, 17:474
Black Ball Line, shipping company, 30:187
Black Day Woman, Sioux Indian, legend, 13:367, 375
Black Dog, Sioux leader, 13:374, 38:129n; village, 11:184, 33:122, 35:29
Black Hammer Township, Houston County, Norwegian settlement, 12:268
Black Hawk, Sauk leader, 11:81, 431, 452, 12:160n, 17:296, 19:330, 351, 25:275, 30:270, 34:41; career, 13:95, 330; autobiography reviewed, 35:87
"Black Hawk," steamboat, 11:131, 142, 143, 15:409, 34:135n
Black Hawk Purchase, centennial, 14:226, 15:125

Black Hawk War, battle, 12:160, 17:296, 33:116, 39:339; Taylor's participation, 22:206, 27:253, 28:177
Black Hills, gold mining, 11:106, 12:175, 177, 200, 13:438, 439, 14:113, 205, 445, 15:200, 201, 16:106, 32:219, 35:52, 37:222, 40:255, 354, 410; newspapers, 16:465; explored, 18:242; in Stevens panorama, 30:21; geology, 32:220; hunting, 32:220; map, 38:386
Black Hills and Fort Pierre Railroad Co., established, 39:298
Black Hoof, Carlton County, inn, 37:107
Black River, Kittson County, trading post, 11:367, 22:282
Black River, Mich., 23:139, 242
Black River, Wis., 17:295, 19:382, 30:162; lumbering, 15:475, 16:479, 27:191, 194, 30:71, 32:253, 34:35, 39:211; settled, 30:162
Black River Falls, Wis., frontier road, 40:387, 389
Blackburn, ———, tombstone, 25:355
Blackburn, Glen A., compiler, 24:343
Blackduck, library, 21:448; history, 23:105, 26:93; logging, 29:147
Blackduck American, 29:356
Blackduck Co-operative Creamery, 21:448
Blackduck Lake, Beltrami County, prehistoric village, 12:331, 26:312, 39:262; archaeology, 16:14, 15, 26:313-316, 320, 321, 322, 325, 327, 328, 31:164, 167
Blackduck River, Beltrami County, log drives, 29:146
Blackfeet Indians, 32:249, 38:214; living conditions, 15:232, 35:377; in fur trade, 29:59, 38:199, 40:201; legends, 38:201
Blackhoof River, Carlton County, stage station, 40:244
Blackjack, Joe, trapper, 37:236, 254
Blackmer, Frank, 14:307
Blackorby, Edward C., work reviewed, 39:79
Blacks, 27:40; franchise, 12:8, 36:8, 11, 174, 175n; Minnesota, 14:460, 19:98, 20:447, 21:192, 30:265, 36:72, 38:87; in fur trade, 15:352, 423-433; education, 18:264; religion, 23:110, 24:92, 39:128; in Civil War, 23:170, 25:353, 357, 39:187, 188; Iowa, 29:174; history, 31:244, 39:260, 299; in the South, 33:188; folklore, 35:95; Indiana, 36:101; segregation problem, 39:63, 82, 172; Twin Cities, 40:146. See also Abolition movement; Scott, Dred; Slavery
Blacksmithing, on frontier, 20:21, 23:320, 35:382
Blackwell, Dr. Elizabeth, 39:9
Blackwell, George, 16:471
Blackwell, Henry B., 39:5, 6, 10
Blackwell, John, 16:471
Blackwood, Garfield, speaker, 11:118; author, 25:102
Blad, Louise H., catalogue typist, 13:425, 15:67, 16:61; museum assistant, 20:44, 22:190
Blain, Father J., draftsman, 18:245, 247
Blaine, Harold A., 19:436

Blaine, James G., in Minnesota, 22:
262; presidential candidate, 32:
146, 35:67, 73, 75, 39:330; Congressman, 34:68, 69, 36:183, 37:
333
Blaine, James V., FBI agent, 36:218
Blaine (Watonwan), Blue Earth County,
milling center, 27:365
Blair, Charles, 12:125
Blair, Eddie, lumberjack, 34:149
Blair, Francis P., 15:406; career,
15:330
Blair, Francis P., Jr., politician,
36:303; career, 15:330; Minnesota
visits, 15:331, 406, 16:27, 19:456
Blair, Mary, author, 24:382
Blair, Montgomery, 20:284; career,
15:330; papers, 15:331
Blair, Thomas, pioneer, 24:382
Blair, Walter A., work reviewed, 11:
83-85; author, 11:212
Blair family, in politics, 15:330-332
Blaisdell, Humphrey M., 24:270
Blaisdell, Mr. and Mrs. John T.,
Christmas party, 16:384
Blaisdell and Cartwright, minstrel
show, 28:111
Blaisdell Addition, Minneapolis, 16:
385
Blake, Harrison, 16:35
Blake, Henry, 38:242
Blake, John P., and Co., Rochester,
29:8
Blake, Robert, author, 18:112
Blakeley, Mrs. ---, at Red Rock, 31:
84
Blakeley, Mrs. Cecilia, Chippewa In-
dian, 26:81
Blakeley, Dr. Robert, 13:132
Blakeley, Russell, 34:357; steamboat
captain, 18:230, 34:31n, 37:55;
stage line operator, 19:385, 33:
277, 38:64; businessman, 22:420,
30:70, 37:316; in fiction, 37:10
Blakeley, Scott County, brickmaking,
11:467
Blakeley and Lewis sawmill, Nininger,
13:150
Blakely, Charles, 29:146n
Blakely, David, editor, 14:306, 406;
career, 37:306
Blakely, Manzer, 29:143n, 146n
Blakely and Farley Co., Beltrami
County, logging firm, 29:145
Blakey, Roy G., review by, 34:308;
works reviewed, 14:207, 21:300-
302, 24:52, 25:280; author, 16:82,
357, 20:91
Blakey, Mrs. Roy G. (Gladys C.), re-
views by, 23:265, 25:279, 34:308;
works reviewed, 16:82, 21:300-302;
speaker, 15:219; author, 16:357,
20:91, 23:271, 25:288
Blakkestad, Julius, 33:101
Blanch, Arnold, artist, 17:229
Blanch, Lucile, artist, 17:229
Blanchar, C. L., speaker, 13:343
Blanchard, J. B., 20:444
Blanchard, R. E., 17:368
Blanchard Beach, geology, 38:158
Blanchet, Guy, author, 35:240
Blandin, Charles K., 16:497, 21:286
Blandin Paper Co., Grand Rapids, 22:
446
Blanding's Department Store, Detroit
Lakes, 29:86
Blane, Charles, pioneer, 20:454

Blaschko, Leonard J., author, 39:275
Blashfield, Edwin H., artist, 19:114,
35:318
Blathwayt, William, 19:394; career,
19:393
Blatnik, John, Congressman, 36:151,
38:241, 40:407
Blau, Joseph L., author, 36:185
Blauvelt, Lillian, singer, 39:53
Blease, Cole, 12:10, 26:308
Blecker, Paulin M., author, 36:35
Bleecker, Ann E., author, 28:90
Bleedorn, William, bell manufacturer,
16:364, 18:376
Blegen, Anne H., 11:46, 443
Blegen, Rev. John H., 23:77; at Lake
Minnetonka, 29:289-299, 40:375
Blegen, Julius P., author, 16:249
Blegen, Theodore C., 19:224, 24:162,
254, 25:169, 27:184, 30:36, 366;
"Local History Work," 11:24; MHS
reports, 13:55-67, 14:59-71, 15:
56-68, 16:47-62, 17:49-63, 18:42-
60, 19:43-62, 20:29-45; "That Name
Itasca," 13:163-174; "The Day of
the Pioneer," 14:134-142; "The
Pond Brothers," 15:273-281; "Henry
H. Sibley," 15:382-385; "St. Croix
Valley History," 17:385-395; "Fort
St. Charles," 18:231-248; "The
'Fashionable Tour,'" 20:377-396;
"The Pond Narrative," 21:15-32,
158-175, 272-283; "Pioneer Book-
shelves," 22:351-366; "The Minnesota Historical Society and the
University," 23:1-10; ed., "Armistice and War on the Minnesota
Frontier," 24:11-25; "The Saga of
Saga Hill," 29:289-299; "A Worker
in the House of History," 34:114;
"Manuscript Collecting," 34:337-
340; "Frederick J. Turner," 39:
133-140; "Schiller's Indian Thren-
ody," 39:198-200; reviews by, 11:
89, 13:184, 304-307, 15:98-102,
16:452-460, 22:404-408, 34:199,
203, 298, 35:233, 36:145, 37:174,
40:256; works reviewed, 12:304-
306, 308-310, 14:195-197, 17:81-
83, 18:83, 198-201, 19:427-430,
22:68-70, 29:57, 160, 30:372, 31:
41, 32:114, 121, 34:257, 35:31-33,
37:83, 176, 300, 38:76; MHS assistant superintendent, 11:46;
professor, 11:47, 19:60, 20:294,
21:187, 39:215; speaker, 11:288,
12:36, 206, 13:194, 278, 282, 286,
341, 14:76, 213, 15:107, 16:65,
304, 17:66, 105, 18:64, 182, 272,
282, 20:297, 353, 428, 21:456, 28:
392, 30:161, 168, 365, 34:268;
editor, 12:31, 14:69, 16:59, 108,
17:62, 221, 463, 19:93, 459, 462,
20:293, 21:39, 26:252, 32:53, 33:
139, 349, 36:236, 39:259; author,
12:95, 201, 284, 444, 13:64, 290,
295, 14:434, 15:127, 221, 462, 16:
77, 115, 233, 239, 350, 481, 484,
17:60, 18:56, 93, 214, 218, 19:81,
101, 340, 446, 20:293, 417, 21:68,
82, 182, 23:289, 24:258, 372, 25:
294, 305, 393, 27:254, 277, 28:
332, 29:164, 375, 30:91, 264, 286,
370, 31:11, 33:228, 354, 34:126,
35:44, 36:105, 38:333, 40:412; MHS
superintendent, 12:311; honorary
degrees, 17:94, 19:208; resigna-

tion, 20:287; tributes, 20:287-
295, 427, 29:370, 30:171, 32:9,
37:40, 299; fellowships, 21:46,
30:326, 37:136; dean of graduate
school, 21:187; career, 23:72, 30:
323, 324-326, 37:88; translator,
24:260, 26:167, 28:281; historical
service board director, 24:351,
25:205, 26:37, 278; quoted, 32:
163n, 39:266
Blenker, Louis, 25:36
Blessed Sacrament Catholic Church,
Hibbing, 26:96
Blessing, Fred K., author, 26:81, 35:
44, 244, 37:307, 347, 39:84
Bleyer, Willard G., author, 13:210
Blichfeldt, John, 29:298
Blied, Rev. Benjamin J., works re-
viewed, 26:146, 27:43; author, 26:
272, 29:354, 34:313
Bliefernicht, E. R., author, 15:361
Blikstad, Bersvend J., author, 19:366
Bliss, J. S., author, 26:298
Bliss, Maj. John H., Fort Snelling
commandant, 15:274, 16:135, 21:20,
22-24, 35:25
Bliss, Mrs. John H., 21:23, 24
Bliss, Lafayette, speaker, 15:138
Bliss, Mrs. Olive I. H., author, 17:
129
Bliss, Paul S., author, 16:111
Bliss, Mrs. William W. S. (Mary Elizabeth Taylor), 30:97, 98
Blizzards and storms, prairies, 11:
65-67, 71, 145, 187, 220; 1880s,
12:101, 14:460, 18:138, 141, 220,
30:146; 1870s, 12:201, 16:246, 18:
229, 30:372, 36:195; southern Minnesota, 12:428, 17:235, 37:204;
1865, 13:387; St. Paul tornado,
16:116; St. Cloud, 17:365; 1940,
30:383; Dakota, 32:244; 1857, 34:
21. See also Climate
Bloch, E. Maurice, reviews by, 31:45,
32:110, 35:370; author, 31:64, 32:
128
Block, Julius H., letter, 13:197
Blocker, Mrs. Elizabeth, 26:368, 27:
46
Blodget, Lorin, climatologist, 38:54
Blodgett, George, 22:112
Bloemendaal, Rev. G. I., 28:123
Blomfield, A. L., engineer, 34:277
Blomfield, Edward A., 19:360, 20:96,
209, 26:179, 28:86, 30:166; inter-
viewed, 20:212; speaker, 20:352,
23:47, 24:270; author, 20:455, 23:
187, 27:266; editor, 22:216; let-
ter, 23:194; tribute, 30:277
Blomgren, Edwin A., 24:162, 25:40
Blomkest, name, 31:253
Blondeau, ---, Jr., trader, 11:259,
264n
Blondeau, Maurice, trader, 11:261,
264n, 13:222; testimony, 21:134
Blondell, Sam, author, 12:208
Bloom, Howard E., author, 12:193
Bloom, John P., speaker, 40:411
Bloom, Olaf, 28:298
Bloom, Sol, Congressman, 17:15
Bloomer, Amelia, feminist, 30:251
Bloomer, Samuel, diary, 25:117n; let-
ter, 37:334
Bloomer, Mrs. Samuel, pioneer, 24:
204n
Bloomer Township, Marshall County,
"petrified" man, 12:421

Bloomfield, Wis., frontier life, 27:
55, 94, 28:188; Methodist church,
27:84
Blooming Grove, Waseca County,
church, 14:123
Blooming Prairie, churches, 16:254;
creamery, 23:199
Blooming Prairie Times, anniversary,
16:254
Bloomingdale, Wis., frontier life,
27:153
Bloomington, Pond homestead, 15:242,
21:273, 39:344; mission, 15:280,
16:314, 21:168, 282; Presbyterian
church, 16:484; cemetery, 17:336;
agriculture, 18:408, 36:104; ferry, 30:119, 121; schools, 36:35;
shopping center, 36:283; history,
39:212; pictured, 39:271; government, 39:299
Bloomington, Iowa, see Muscatine
Bloomquist, A. A. C., 20:212
Bloomquist, Edward E., 15:372, 16:362
Blostad, Helen, author, 20:211
Blouet, Leon P., humorist, 40:12-20
Blount, Gov. William, 15:14, 17:452
Blow family, 29:351
Blu, Elmer F., 26:45, 28:51, 395, 29:
97
Blucker, George M., career, 18:211
Blue Cross Hospitalization Plan, 27:
160; history, 40:47
Blue Earth, first hotel, 11:111;
newspaper, 11:218; historical
meeting, 11:292; stage lines, 11:
403, 12:51n; history, 12:449, 25:
410, 35:77, 152; pageant, 12:450;
churches, 15:480, 16:335, 23:106,
25:100, 410; volunteer guards, 16:
172; schools, 22:344; mill, 23:
388; implement trade, 24:302n;
townsite, 27:355
Blue Earth County, pioneer life, 11:
445, 14:277, 16:126, 27:155, 30:
396; ethnic groups, 12:273, 448,
18:465, 19:211, 464, 31:27, 32:62;
churches, 12:448, 18:466; county
seat, 13:116; agriculture, 13:176,
26:181; history, 13:342, 17:234,
18:337, 20:356, 23:187, 25:99, 35:
293; schools, 14:353, 454, 15:244,
365; fairs, 16:489, 17:125, 18:
337, 22:257; archives, 19:52, 66,
88; pioneer house, 24:88; livestock industry, 26:125; milling,
27:365; politics, 28:31, 32, 35:
308, 38:121; marriage records, 29:
284, 30:156; library, 31:61; government agencies, 35:201; grasshopper plagues, 36:56, 57, 58, 37:
204, 207; Winnebago reservation,
36:257, 38:253; Mormon mission,
36:292; troops in Civil War, 38:
259; in Sioux Outbreak, 38:281,
283, 285; poor farm, 38:368
Blue Earth County Agricultural Society, 16:489, 18:227, 22:258
Blue Earth County Enterprise (Mankato), 21:312; anniversary, 19:364
Blue Earth County Historical Society,
12:38, 16:240, 21:312; organized,
11:12, 21:105; museum, 11:16, 13:
447, 14:454, 17:120, 18:334, 19:
229, 358, 468, 20:47, 350, 453,
21:49, 104-107, 22:105, 338, 23:
12, 14, 15, 193, 24:187, 26:49,
27:170, 361, 29:92, 33:210, 34:

315, 35:293, 38:43; activities,
11:17, 15:72, 75, 484; members,
11:19; fees, 11:20, 12:39; meetings, 13:341, 14:234, 15:130, 16:
360, 20:210, 21:106, 215, 442, 22:
215, 27:265, 29:273; essay contest, 14:353, 454, 15:244, 365;
manuscript collection, 16:489, 26:
282; centennial celebration, 30:
399
Blue Earth County Old Settlers Association, 13:116
Blue Earth County War History Committee, 24:81
Blue Earth River, Faribault and Blue
Earth counties, 11:172; trading
post, 11:377; ferry, 12:52; prairie surveyed, 30:392; Winnebago
reservation, 31:211, 40:332; settled, 35:77, 78; pictured, 35:79;
fishing, 35:79, 80, 81
Blue Earth Settlement Claim Associa-
tion, 12:202
Blue Mounds, Wis., museum, 24:364
Blueberry War, 11:454, 35:235
Bluestein, Gene, musician, 36:152,
194
Blum, Fred H., author, 34:266
Blum, Grace C., 34:131
Blum, Louis, 15:113
Blum, N. H., storekeeper, 15:113
Blume, H., author, 32:167
Blumenthal, Walter H., work reviewed,
34:162; author, 34:311
Blumer, A. and W., Allentown, Pa.,
printers, 27:31
Bly, Eber H., 21:220
Bly, Nellie, journalist, 17:474
B'nai Brith, Independent Order of,
12:193, 14:104
Boal, James McC., artist, 35:22,
182, 369, 36:16, 17n
Board of National Popular Education,
program, 14:144, 145, 15:223, 17:
335, 28:132, 135, 138, 139, 140
Boardman, Charles W., author, 26:279
Boardman, Frances, review by, 33:222;
author, 21:101, 39:59, 60, 61, 63
Boardman, Lawrence, author, 13:346,
28:74
Boardman, Mrs. Lawrence (Kathryn F.
Gorman), author, 11:455, 459, 465,
12:102, 446, 16:353, 27:366, 34:
174, 218, 37:308
Boardman, Neil, novelist, 31:129,
139, 145
Boardman, Thayer M., compiler, 32:189
Boas, Franz, author, 23:181
Boatfield, Helen C., author, 16:239
Boats, see Barges, Canoes, Keelboats,
Mackinac boats, Steamboats and
steamboating
Bobbitt, John T., author, 29:77
Bobcat, in fur trade, 30:134
Bobleter, Col. Joseph, 19:234
Bobodosh, Chippewa leader, 11:448
Bochart, Jean, 19:396
Bock, Frederick W., 40:249
Bodde, Derk, author, 39:34
Bode, Carl, work reviewed, 35:194;
author, 30:65
Bodfish, Rev. J. P., colonizer, 31:22
Bodholdt, K. C., author, 13:324
Bodin, John, artist, 38:286n
Bodmer, Karl, artist, 19:458, 22:
154n, 155n, 26:359, 29:58-61, 31:
54, 55, 32:155, 33:264, 34:117,

255, 35:144, 151, 200, 242, 380,
36:236, 37:78, 133, 38:385, 39:
261, 40:314, 403
Bøe, A. Sophie, author, 20:331
Boe, Lars W., 31:51; speaker, 16:365,
17:484; biography, 30:377
Bøe, Rev. N. E., biography, 20:331
Boeck, Charles, newspaper assistant,
18:58
Boeckeler, A., lumberman, 18:174
Boeckmann, Dr. Eduard, 20:466; inven-
tor, 17:69; career, 12:446
Boeckmann, Dr. Egil, author, 12:446
Boedeker, Harold S., translator, 33:
89
Boen, H. E., author, 34:359
Boen, Haldor E., politician, 39:104
Boer, Ellen, author, 14:123
Boerger, William, speaker, 17:22
Boerhaave, Hermann, author, 21:363
Boesch, Mr. and Mrs. Werner, pio-
neers, 20:449
Boese, Albert, 14:52
Boettcher, Rev. N. P. Christopher,
13:114
Bogan, Ralph, taxi driver, 27:272
Bogardus, Capt. A. H., marksman, 16:
271
Bogardus, Emory S., author, 11:99
Bogart, Ernest L., author, 17:226
Bogen, Ludwig, journalist, 33:180,
188
Boggiss, Dorothy L., author, 34:174
Boggs, S. Whittemore, author, 20:207,
24:175
Bogstad, Mrs. R. R., teacher, 23:298;
speaker, 23:103
Bohemia, immigration from, 15:26-30;
religious situation, 15:32n
Bohemian Catholic Church of St. Jo-
seph, Silver Lake, 15:38
Bohemian Flats, Minneapolis, 23:68
Bohemian language, in Czech settle-
ments, 15:38
Bohemian National Alliance, Silver
Lake, 15:41
Bohemian Reading and Educational So-
ciety, McLeod County, activities,
15:40; history, 17:237, 22:224
Bohemians, see Czechs
Bohmbach, Emil, 20:353, 21:108, 216,
22:106, 23:104
Bohn, H. G., 27:34
Boie, W. E., speaker, 15:115
Boies, William J., author, 26:306
Boiling Springs, Redwood County, 38:
243
Boilvin, Nicholas, Indian agent, 17:
96, 19:303, 23:145n, 25:89, 272
Bois Blanc Island, Lake Huron, 23:142
Bois Blanc Lake, Lake County, post,
36:244. See also Basswood Lake
Bois Brulé River, see Brule River
Bois brûlés, see Mixed-bloods
Bois des Sioux River, log drive, 17:
116; boundary, 19:424; trails, 21:
229; pictured, 38:5
Bois Fort Indian Reservation, see
Nett Lake Indian Reservation
Bois Plumé (Bois Plaine), Cannon Riv-
er, trading post, 11:382
Boissy, Tancred, author, 18:71
Boisverd, Joseph, trader, 28:145,
148, 156, 225, 233
Bojer, Johan, author, 20:180, 32:250
Boland, Mr. and Mrs. Hendrik, Dutch
pioneers, 28:122

Boland, Jan, Dutch pioneer, 28:122
Boland, Mr. and Mrs. Willem, Dutch pioneers, 28:121, 122, 124
Bolek, Franciszek, author, 13:108
Boleyn, Dr. E. Sydney, prison physician, 24:181
Bolin, Eva, speaker, 20:99
Bolino, August C., author, 37:38
Bolivar Heights, W. Va., army camp, 25:31, 35, 36, 228, 26:196
Boller, Henry A., journal, 40:314
Bolles, Erastus, miller, 40:235, 236; house, 38:337, 338
Bolles, Lemuel, miller, 24:201, 202; settler, 38:337
Bolles, Sias, Methodist minister, 26:243
Bolley, H. L., agriculturist, 34:173
Bollum, Mrs. O. M., speaker, 23:386
Bolstad, Helen C., 12:320; author, 12:339
Bolstad, Rev. O. L., 15:245; speaker, 11:218
Bolt, Ewe, Dutch pioneer, 28:125
Bolton, Charles K., 12:197
Bolton, Herbert E., 14:11, 333, 18:456, 22:67; author, 11:428, 14:336
Bolton, N. G., author, 11:222
Bolz, J. Arnold, work reviewed, 37:216
Bomb Shell (Fort Ripley), 15:24
Bombard, Owen W., author, 33:313
Bon Homme County, S.D., Hutterite colony, 23:183
Bonanza farms, 16:190, 20:404, 31:253; Red River Valley, 13:205, 20:404, 25:300, 29:14, 31:122, 32:112, 33:70, 36:68, 281, 37:259, 265-270, 39:206; Minnesota, 21:448, 451
Bond, Beverly W., Jr., work reviewed, 15:208, speaker, 13:326
Bond, J. Harman, journal, 13:334
Bond, John C., author, 21:199
Bond, John Wesley, 35:282; author, 34:49, 38:46-49, 51, 52; treaty clerk, 38:2-10; in Sioux Outbreak, 38:151
Bond, Samuel R., journalist, 38:58, 60, 218
Bond, Dr. Scipio, 15:483, 16:240, 17:119, 18:463, 19:114
Bond, Capt. William, 19:396
Bonde, Peter, reminiscences, 21:451
Bone Lake, Washington County, lumber camp, 36:158
Bonfadini, Romualdo, author, 15:478
Bonga, George, trader, 15:352, 425, 20:80, 30:265, 31:125, 32:128, 36:72; papers, 15:194
Bonga, Jack, 15:426
Bonga, Jean, 15:425
Bonga, Marie J., 15:425
Bonga, Pierre, interpreter, 15:425
Bonga, Stephen, mixed-blood, 13:196, 18:209; land claim, 17:335; trader, 20:71, 24:18n, 354; guide, 21:152, 153
Bonga family, in fur trade, 15:352, 20:447, 21:128
Bonhus, Emma A., author, 30:162
Bonn, Henry, coppersmith, 26:20
Bonnell, Carl E., author, 29:90; speaker, 29:178, 361
Bonness, Fred W., steamboat captain, 33:12, 14

Bonness, Frederick W., lumberman, 12:428, 16:73, 74
Bonneville, Capt. Benjamin L. E. de, trader, 29:59, 36:317
Bonnier, Tora Nordstrom-, "In Fredrika Bremer's Footsteps," 32:106-108
Bonniwell, ---, Hutchinson visitor, 23:298
Bonniwell, Mrs. H. H., speaker, 22:217
"Bonny Boat," steamboat, 27:12
Bonrepaus, Dusson de, letters, 19:394, 395
Boobar, Frank H., author, 18:229
Boody, Henry P., author, 15:474
Book, Bill, pioneer, 24:321
Boom companies, 28:306, 379; functions, 24:134-137, 26:130, 132, 133, 27:193, 28:182, 188; tow depicted, 34:45 (cover)
Boomhower, ---, farmer, 24:299, 301
Boone, Daniel, folk hero, 22:313, 40:403; anniversary, 15:476
Boorstin, Daniel J., historian, 39:335, 336
Boose, Arthur, labor organizer, 27:352
Booth, Bradford A., editor, 33:90
Booth, Cameron, artist, 17:229, 25:80
Booth, Edwin, actor, 28:101, 117, 32:103
Booth, Frank W., lawyer, 21:196
Booth, Franklin, artist, 33:309
Booth, Josie, drama troupe manager, 28:110
Booth Fisheries (Booth Packing Co.), 34:245-247, 249, 35:275
Boothby, Dr. Walter M., editor, 35:155
Boquet, Col. Henry, 29:65
Borah, William E., 17:160n
Borak, Arthur M., author, 12:93
Boratko, Andre, artist, 19:366
Borchert, John R., reviews by, 34:306, 35:331; author, 36:192, 38:42; speaker, 36:284
Borchsenius, George V., in Alaska, 31:58, 32:175, 191
Borden, Gail, dairyman, 12:99
Border lakes, 36:151, 37:249; fur trade, 37:37, 188, 216, 235-254, 264, 345, 346, 38:24-34; map, 37:244; geology, 38:158; described, 39:34, 212; canoe route, 40:145, 358; explored, 40:316. See also individual lakes
Bordin, Mrs. Ruth B., "Three Historic Buildings," 27:228-232; author, 27:247
Bordwell, Constance, author, 37:183
Borger, Herman, author, 35:90
Borgerding, Christopher, 33:54
Borgerding, Father Thomas, missionary, 18:331, 23:402, 33:60, 34:131
Borgers, Rev. Herman, "The Hollanders in Minnesota, 1856-97," 28:121-131; career, 28:120
Borglum, George P., speaker, 12:96
Borglum, Gutzon, sculptor, 33:86
Borhegyi, Stephan F., archaeologist, 38:244
Bori, Lucrezia, singer, 39:62
Borland, Hal, author, 19:220
Born, Wolfgang, author, 29:261
Bornet, Vaughn, D., work reviewed, 40:91

Borrett, George T., 20:390
Bort, Clyde F., lawyer, 17:213
Borup, Dr. Charles W. W., 36:70; frontier physician, 11:58, 28:335; trader, 11:374, 384, 19:226, 20:134, 22:4, 273, 274, 355, 26:362, 29:58, 32:88, 89, 97, 36:262, 264, 269; MHS founder, 20:367, 368; library, 22:356; music lover, 28:320, 29:119, 39:51, 321; pioneer merchant, 31:157; politician, 36:265, 268, 39:148
Borup, Elizabeth, mixed-blood, 17:335, 18:209
Borup, Theodore, mixed-blood, 17:335, 18:209, 19:172
Bosanquet, Fatio, 11:238n
Bosanquet, Richard, 11:238n
Bosard, Florence, music critic, 33:96
Boscawen, Edward, 22:64
Boss, Andrew, 20:206, 26:285; work reviewed, 22:412; author, 16:352, 20:448, 21:328; alfalfa promotion, 19:25, 32; papers, 29:285; biography, 32:118; influence, 33:224
Bosshard, Gottfried, 17:96
Bosshard, Gustav, 17:96
Bossing, Nelson L., author, 26:279
Boston, slave case, 15:412; social life, 17:464; immigrant home, 18:69; fur market, 40:312; climate, 40:312; financial center, 40:406
Boston and Albany Railroad, route, 15:256
Boston and New York Central Railroad, 17:335
Boston Antislavery Society, 22:128
Boston Block, Minneapolis, 23:220, 222
Boston Ideal Opera Co., 16:238, 28:114, 33:325
Boston Public Library, 17:97, 18:208
Boston University, medical school, 39:6-9
Bostonians, Battle Lake literary club, 17:488
Bostwick, Henry, trader, 11:239, 261, 19:291; mining interests, 11:263
Boswell, John S., journalist, 34:140
Bosworth, C. H., 19:167
Botany, Minnesota, 32:218, 220, 34:172, 333n, 35:244; upper Midwest, 34:308, 35:241; prairies, 34:310; North America, 35:204
Bothne, Gisle, runologist, 36:33, 39:135, 136, 137, 138; papers, 18:48, 98, 34:339
Botkin, B. A., 25:306; work reviewed, 35:39; author, 23:179, 25:392, 26:166, 27:275; editor, 33:91, 34:214
Botsford, Isaac, journalist, 14:307, 314
Botsford-Marble family, genealogy, 14:439
Bottineau, Charles, treaty negotiator, 15:288, 292
Bottineau, Pierre, 14:391, 20:209, 38:243; trader, 11:118, 15:253, 292; honored, 12:331; guide, 14:435, 15:336, 19:342, 20:193, 328, 432, 21:96, 28:286, 30:395, 38:1 (cover), 3, 4, 6, 58; founder of Osseo, 15:487; career, 35:197; scout, 40:313
Bottineau County, N.D., explored, 21:99; history, 29:85
Botz, Neil J., author, 29:280

Bouché, J. M., 12:375
Bouchea, Peter F., guide, 17:388
Boucher, François, trader, 21:119n,
    125, 126, 129, 132, 133, 140-144
Boucher, Pierre, 12:307, 18:234
Boucher family, genealogy, 34:313
Boucherville, René Thomas Verchères
    de, reminiscences, 23:181
Boucicault, Dion, dramatist, 23:313;
    actor, 28:111
Bouck, C. W., trader, 22:275, 310
Boudinot, Elias, 18:397
Boudrye, Mason, speaker, 36:284
Bougainville, Louis A. de, 13:203;
    author, 13:202
Boughton, Charles E., Sr., author,
    21:223
Boulic, Marcel, speaker, 36:284
Boullé, Pierre H., author, 39:337
Boundaries, international (northern),
    11:108, 331, 12:443, 13:296-298,
    14:109, 15:239, 16:225, 230, 480,
    18:231, 277, 279, 19:223, 20:207,
    441, 21:204, 328, 22:62-65, 92,
    177, 179, 306, 439, 23:202-208,
    255, 357, 24:45-48, 72, 175, 256,
    276-286, 341-343, 25:182, 26:385,
    33:181, 315, 35:378, 36:32, 242,
    247, 37:183, 39:32, 128, 40:356,
    359; Wisconsin, 11:211, 339, 25:
    396; Indiana, 15:124; Illinois,
    15:474; Iowa, 16:478, 24:368, 28:
    184, 30:392; Anglo-French dis-
    putes, 18:428-430; Michigan, 22:
    74, 75, 24:234, 27:129; Maine, 23:
    205, 209; treaties, 24:252; North
    Dakota, 29:85; Washington-Oregon,
    38:219. See also Webster-Ash-
    burton Treaty
    Minnesota, 12:198, 14:157, 27:
    128, 29:195n, 30:272, 36:2, 5, 6;
    western, 19:424-426; Polk County,
    20:207; southern, 24:368, 30:392;
    Ramsey County, 30:397; Lake Coun-
    ty, 30:407
Bound Grove, Olmsted County, camp
    meeting, 31:82
Bouquillon, Thomas, 25:373
Bourgeois, in fur trade, defined, 40:
    162
Bourget, Paul, author, 24:242, 29:
    154, 30:268
Bourgoyne, Zella, speaker, 20:455
Bourier, Louis (Pierre Bourrier, Pe-
    ter Boyer), Renville Ranger, 38:
    139
Bourinot, Arthur, 29:167
Bourke, John P., trader, 22:282-285,
    27:67, 36:38, 41, 42, 47, 51-53
Bourns, Frank, scientist, 39:116-120
Boury, L. J., 22:146
Boutell family, in Minnesota, 25:80
Boutwell, George S., speaker, 35:227
Boutwell, Rev. William T., on name
    "Itasca," 12:218, 219, 225, 226,
    13:166, 172, 173, 292, 18:180,
    181; honored, 12:331; papers, 13:
    195, 320, 22:353; journal, 13:288,
    36:184; missionary, 14:342, 454,
    15:344, 32:186, 36:192; at Leech
    Lake, 15:366, 16:375, 21:21, 40:
    146; at Stillwater, 17:97, 18:375,
    24:160; at Sault Ste. Marie, 18:
    94, 34:219; marriage, 22:206, 29:
    355; grave, 24:385; portrait, 27:
    241
Boutwell, Mrs. William T., (Hester

Crooks), 14:381, 22:306; at Yellow
    Lake, 29:355; wedding, 29:367
Bouvais, Antoine, cholera victim, 14:
    290
Bouvette, Clifford W., 27:172; speak-
    er, 19:469
Bovey, Charles A., I, lumberman, 37:
    41, 39:106
Bovey, Charles A., II, 26:80; pub-
    lisher, 25:385
Bovey, Charles C., 34:204
Bovey, Mrs. Charles C., 16:20n, 20:
    50, 25:154n
Bovey, Kate K., author, 20:346
Bovey, William H., 18:282, 20:187,
    21:410, 23:50, 25:44; career, 25:
    54
Bovey family, genealogy, 20:346
Bovey, iron mines, 22:346; in World
    War II, 26:280; strike, 40:345
Bovey and De Laittre Lumber Co., 36:
    160
Bowdish, Rev. C. L., Methodist minis-
    ter, 31:82
Bowdoin, James, 18:397
Bowell, William D., 30:290, 410, 31:
    123; speaker, 30:364
Bowen, A. E., politician, 38:305
Bowen, Catherine D., author, 32:187
Bowen, Dana T., "Great Lakes Ships
    and Shipping," 34:9-16; work re-
    viewed, 34:39; author, 22:202;
    speaker, 33:356
Bowen, Jessie M., work reviewed, 19:
    335
Bower, Thomas, 40:126
Bowerman, Sarah G., author, 11:216,
    15:128
Bowers, Claude G., 14:90
Bowers, Capt. James M., 14:332
Bowers, John O., author, 11:324
Bowery, New York City, origin, 24:157
Bowing, Mrs. H. C., conservationist,
    24:182
Bowler, Burton H., 11:446, 16:131;
    speaker, 25:80
Bowler, Capt. James M., Union offi-
    cer, 40:282, 284
Bowler, Sister Mary M., 16:483
Bowles, Samuel, excursionist, 12:392,
    15:406, 20:384
Bowman, A. W., 19:359
Bowman, C. V., author, 11:103
Bowman, Frank J., publisher, 21:451
Bowman, George D., 17:276, 279
Bowman, Hank W., author, 34:127
Bowman, Isaiah, author, 12:198
Bowman, James C., author, 23:379
Bowman, John B., Ursuline benefactor,
    14:40
Bowman, John C., author, 22:204
Bowman, Rowland C., artist, 29:102
Bowmaster, William, 38:15
Bowron, Joseph, 24:160
Bowsfield, Hartwell, review by, 37:
    257; speaker, 40:362
Bowstring Lake, Itasca County, post,
    11:370; settled, 26:289
Bowstring River, Itasca County,
    mounds, 26:316; archaeology, 26:
    322
Boy Scouts of America, cleanup proj-
    ects, 21:328, 22:438, 23:251n, 27:
    358, 28:375, 30:76; educational
    program, 15:120; Rice County, 15:
    252; Cottonwood County, 30:165;
    anniversary, 37:43

Boyce, ---, trader, 19:77
Boyce, A. E., author, 20:469
Boyce, Mrs. Hannah E., letters, 20:81
Boyce, James, 20:469
Boyce, John, lumberman, 13:353
Boyce, Mrs. John, letters, 19:474
Boyce, Mrs. Sara D., 18:55, 19:57;
    speaker, 18:64
Boyce, William R., 19:474
Boyd, Cyrus F., diary, 33:228
Boyd, George, Indian agent, 20:263,
    264, 23:347
Boyd, Lt. George, Jr., in Civil War,
    15:465, 25:249
Boyd, James, author, 20:116
Boyd, James, letter writer, 34:329
Boyd, Julian P., works reviewed, 31:
    179, 32:248, 33:260, 34:118, 252,
    35:144, 285, 36:231, 38:90, 39:
    295; author, 16:104, 18:325, 21:
    321, 22:200, 36:217, 219; editor,
    25:295
Boyd, Robert K., "How the Indians
    Fought," 11:299-304; "The Birch
    Cooley Monument," 12:297-301; au-
    thor, 12:84, 200, 13:340
Boyd, Thomas A., career, 25:305
Boyd family, genealogy, 17:230
Boyer, René, 13:85
Boyesen, Alf E., biography, 16:337
Boyeson, Hjalmar H., 18:431, 432, 31:
    130, 36:79
Boylan, Ferman, boatbuilder, 26:398
Boylan, Rose J., work reviewed, 30:
    249
Boyle, Robert, 16:414
Boyles, Kate and Virgil D., authors,
    23:156
Boynton, Clifford, speaker, 20:100
Boynton, George R., artist, 35:381
Boynton, Percy H., author, 11:100,
    428
Boynton, Ruth E., author, 27:365
Bozeman Trail, Indian battles, 39:
    342
Brace, Rev. Charles L., welfare work,
    39:125, 126
Bracken, Dr. Henry M., career, 19:
    111, 34:35; papers, 19:213, 20:33
Brackenridge, H. H., lawyer, 15:8
Brackenridge, Henry M., author, 38:
    198
Brackenridge, W. L., speaker, 22:267
Brackett, Alfred B., Union officer,
    21:417, 33:280, 281. See also
    Brackett's Battalion
Brackett, George A., 19:268n, 390;
    papers, 16:71; railroad survey,
    23:54; politician, 29:85, 35:66,
    70, 72, 73, 76; road builder, 29:
    313
Brackett, Winslow M., journal, 13:
    346; fireman, 25:313
Brackett's Battalion of Minnesota
    Cavalry, in Sioux Outbreak, 16:
    349, 18:68, 19:389-392, 26:261,
    33:281; in Civil War, 33:278; Com-
    pany C, 33:280
Bradbury, John, author, 33:181, 35:
    241
Braddock, Gen. Edward, 18:195; char-
    acterized, 29:65
Braden, Mrs. Alice, 20:95, 22:104;
    speaker, 22:105
Braden, William W., auditor, 23:173,
    189
Bradford, Andrew, printer, 15:6, 13

Bradford, Fielding, printer, 15:10
Bradford, John, printer, 15:10
Bradford, Lee C., author, 15:240, 28:285
Bradford, William, printer, 15:4, 13
Bradish, Alva, artist, 18:147
Bradley, Chester D., curator, 40:267, 268
Bradley, Maj. George, in Sioux Outbreak, 38:110n
Bradley, George H., 14:450, author, 15:241
Bradley, Henry C., 25:141
Bradley, Mrs. Mary E., pioneer, 22:448
Bradley, Newton, publisher, 34:336; banker, 40:114-118
Bradley, Gen. Omar N., quoted, 37:70, 40:131
Bradley, Rev. Preston, speaker, 24:378
Bradley, R., 21:375
Bradshaw, Dawson, house, 38:338
Bradstreet, Col. John, 33:37
Brady, Gen. Hugh, 18:184n, 32:86n, 35:199
Brady, James A., author, 30:271
Brady, Mathew B., photographer, 34:212, 35:247; portrait work, 25:17, 28:348, 35:130-132, 36:183n, 37:215n; methodology, 33:216; career, 35:92
Brady, Michael C., 18:149
Brady, Thomas F., municipal judge, 20:468
Bragdon, Claude F., art critic, 40:98, 104-106
Bragdon, Earl D., review by, 40:254
Bragg, Gen. Braxton, Confederate officer, 25:241, 38:266, 267, 269, 271, 272
Braham, name, 31:253; electric co-operative, 37:347
Brainard, Dudley S., 13:211, 17:64, 104, 123, 233, 19:119, 22:108, 29:94; "Nininger," 13:127-151; reviews by, 12:308-310, 17:85; speaker, 13:16, 17:357, 20:355; author, 13:448, 16:117, 26:83
Brainard, H. J., dairy farmer, 27:110
Brainard, Homer W., author, 14:233
Brainard, John G. C., author, 27:238
Brainard, Leverett, diary, 35:201
Brainard, Virginia, see Kunz, Virginia B.
Brainerd, Ben R., author, 16:472
Brainerd, "Bluenose," storyteller, 24:367
Brainerd, Charles E., 12:407
Brainerd, Chauncey N., 12:405; "My Diary," 12:45-64; travels, 12:43, 13:194; career, 12:407-409
Brainerd, Mrs. Chauncey N., 12:407, 408
Brainerd, Ethalind, 12:407
Brainerd, George M., 12:407
Brainerd, J. C., 16:255
Brainerd, William C., 12:407
Brainerd, fire department, 12:101; Indian scare, 12:310; immigrant house, 13:41; history, 13:115, 18:452, 27:269, 338, 31:126, 36:195; hunting center, 16:267-269; hotel, 16:268; roads, 16:299; Paul Bunyan pageant, 16:487; WPA conference, 17:346; government, 21:220; museum, 21:330-333, 35:201; labor

groups, 21:383, 394, 22:368, 380; telephone directories, 22:344; cooperatives, 22:374; Finnish settlement, 22:392n, 25:318; hospital, 24:142, 30:405; railroads, 24:142, 29:138, 139, 31:122, 33:66, 67, 323, 35:337; in Leech Lake uprising, 24:145-147; churches, 28:190, 31:126; minstrel show, 28:107; Masonic lodge, 28:381; sawmill, 29:139, 140; name, 30:70; river port, 33:10, 13; election, 1902, 35:350; disabled veterans, 39:243
Brainerd and Northern Minnesota Railway, 29:138
Brainerd and Northern Railroad, 24:142
Brainerd Daily Dispatch, anniversary 12:337; contest, 14:348
Brainerd Lumber Co., 29:139, 140, 142, 146, 148
Brainerd Tribune, anniversary, 18:167
Brainerd War History Committee, 23:390
Brake, Hezekiah, author, 19:217
Bramble, St. Louis County, 27:82
Branch, David, 25:347
Branch, E. Douglas, review by, 11:422-424; works reviewed, 11:421, 16:87; author, 12:70, 38:201
Branch, Mrs. S. F. W., 25:352
Brand, Charles J., agriculturist, 19:26, 27, 32; author, 16:121
Brand, George, house, 37:75
Brandborg, Charles W., papers, 20:194
Brandeis, Justice Louis D., letter, 18:314; quoted, 37:161
Brandel, Walter, farmer, 37:75
Brandenstein-Zeppelin, Count Alexander von, 40:268-270
Brandenstein-Zeppelin, Countess von, 40:270
Brandes, Frederic, author, 35:155
Brandl, Cecilia, author, 19:225
Brandon, Cpl. John C., 25:149
Brandon, William, author, 38:40
Brandon, roads, 21:235
Brandrup, J. R., autobiography, 19:356
Brandt, Albrecht, lay preacher, 14:50
Brandt, John, speaker, 11:458, 25:407
Brandt, Nils, 11:89
Brandt family, genealogy, 11:89
Brangdon, J. W., 18:471
Branham, Jesse, in Sioux Outbreak, 24:86
Braniff International, airline, 33:240
Brannon, Lt. Col. Francis M., 24:5
Brannon, Gen. John M., Union officer, 38:267-269
Brant, Harry G., 16:340
Brant, Joseph, Mohawk leader, 11:80, 90, 19:298, 330, 39:338
Brant, game bird, in Minnesota, 16:189n
Branton, Dr. A. F., speaker, 16:305
Braslan, Charles P., seed merchant, 27:79
Braslau, Sophie, singer, 39:59
Brass, manufacture, 35:154; trade item, 40:200, 204-207, 209
Brasted, Col. Alva J., speaker, 15:108
Bratrud, Rev. Milton T., speaker, 16:490

Brattland, Judge M. A., speaker, 20:456
Bratton, Howard, author, 21:115
Bratton, Mrs. Howard, 15:138, 22:107, 23:104
Brauer, Theodor, educator, 33:187
Braun, Dr. E. E., 33:300
Braun, Frank X., author, 31:243
Braun, Sister Lioba, missionary, 18:269, 26:275, 33:60
Brawley, D. F., 15:51
Bray, Mrs. Alice, 29:282
Bray, Edmund C., author, 38:242
Bray, Mrs. Edmund C. (Martha C.), "The Minnesota Academy of Natural Science," 39:111-122
Bray, Newton J., author, 11:217, 12:342, 16:101; speaker,15:492, 22:443
Bray, Rosetta, murdered, 38:11-20
Brayer, Herbert O., author, 25:310, 27:252; compiler, 27:349
Brazeau, John, career, 15:430
Brazeau, Joseph, trader, 22:279
Brazie, Dr. Henry, 19:97
"Brazil," steamboat, 13:223, 20:87
Breasted, Charles, author, 34:126, 37:1, 3
Brébeuf, Father Jean de, missionary, 18:386
Brebner, John B., works reviewed, 15:93, 22:70, 26:363; author, 13:328, 23:201, 25:199
Breck, Rev. James L., career, 11:109, 36:35; educator, 11:329, 14:111, 16:371, 17:232, 18:326, 25:102; missionary, 14:55, 56, 16:97, 24:72, 27:368, 28:190, 210, 213, 32:50, 37:177
Breck Missionary Society, accounts, 21:86
Breckenridge, W. J., "Minnesota Wild Life," 30:123-124, 220-231; review by, 34:259; speaker, 22:290, 30:176; author, 30:184, 292, 36:72
Breckenridge, industries, 11:111; railroad, 12:254, 13:41, 24:333, 29:13, 36:7; Baptist church, 14:124; history, 15:372, 18:271, 354, 355, 35:245, 336, 382; named, 16:111; schools, 18:224; junior historical society, 19:64; convention, 21:267; union activities, 36:121
Breckinridge, John C., biography, 16:111; land speculator, 20:336, 21:429, 36:237, 37:113; presidential candidate, 23:372, 24:309, 28:34, 37:51, 54; Confederate general, 38:269
Breda, Olaus J., linguist, 39:133, 134, 135
Breda, St. Louis County, railroad station, 34:180
Breed, D. R., pioneer, 33:4
Breen's Opera House, Moorhead, 28:99
Breese, Marshall County, post office, 13:119
Breihan, Carl W., work reviewed, 34:124
Brekke, Mrs. Leonard, author, 34:171
Bremer, Fredrika, "New Scandinavia," 31:148-157; quoted, 12:247, 16:33, 20:129, 130, 388; traveler, 20:129-139, 28:317, 318, 29:182, 32:106-108, 33:351, 35:95, 105, 39:317; interest in Indians, 20:134-

138; artist, 20:135; author, 20:
137, 25:114n, 30:159, 198, 31:121,
39:81; described, 35:106
Bremer School, Minneapolis, name, 32:
108
Bremicker, Charles, editor, 14:105
Bren, Rev. Hugo, 17:96; author, 15:
122; editor, 15:233, 354, 472, 16:
106
Bren, Joseph, pioneer, 25:410
Brendal, J. P., compiler, 29:179
Brenden, G. J., 19:362
Bresnahan, P. W., 11:119
Brett, Judge Bernard B., 15:137, 16:
124, 241, 17:122, 18:110, 19:116,
20:96, 21:108
Brettingen, Betty, author, 24:273
Breuer, Marcel, architect, 36:100,
37:38
Brevator, St. Louis County, history,
21:456, 23:302
Brevig, Tollef L., missionary, 33:43
Brewer, Nicholas R., artist, 36:112;
autobiography, 20:184
Brewster, Charles G., surveyor, 17:
335, 18:47
Brewster, Mr. and Mrs. James, 34:139
Brewster, Joseph, lumberman, 24:201
Brewster, William, 18:401
Brewster, G.A.R. post, 16:434; his-
tory, 20:465, 36:107
Brewster's Hotel, Stillwater, 16:377
Brezler, Anne, 25:201; work reviewed,
18:307-309; author, 28:357
Briand, Aristide, 18:427, 23:372
Bricelyn, Baptist church, 15:128;
Norwegian settlement, 23:290
Bricelyn Sentinel, history, 20:460
Bricher, Thomas, 26:53
Bricklayers Benevolent Union, St.
Paul, 21:386
Brickley, M. H., 19:308; speaker, 12:
284
Brickner, Joseph, game warden, 38:336
Bridger, James, frontiersman, 12:175,
20:328, 35:243, 38:199
Bridgers, Frank E., work reviewed,
39:170
Bridges, Frank W., author, 40:363
Bridges, Hal, work reviewed, 33:220
Bridges, Leonard H., author, 31:58
Bridges, S. G., 13:286, 18:334, 19:
359
Bridges, drawbridge, 12:455, 16:257;
St. Paul, 13:178, 15:140; Rum River, 16:72; Bemidji, 16:126, 23:31,
33; cantilever, 16:183; Monticello, 16:257; disasters, 16:257, 18:
120; Fort Snelling, 16:279n, 35:
185, 189, 39:328; covered, 16:486;
opposed, 16:499; Mississippi River, 17:343; East Grand Forks, 18:
341; suspension, 18:468, 21:450,
27:79, 288, 28:70, 29:30, 32-34,
34:30, 35:101 (cover); spiral, 20:
460, 27:175, 269, 345; pontoon,
22:98, 23:286, 25:198, 236, 345,
346, 358, 27:258; Minneapolis, 23:
68; Minnesota, 23:290, 36:278; ae-
rial, 24:62; Winona, 24:80; railroad, 24:177, 33:18, 34:83, 37:
187; Wisconsin, 28:290; Rock Island, Ill., 30:160; swing, 33:15;
pedestrian, 34:140; Great Lakes
cities, 39:82
Bridgewater Township, Rice County,

wheat raising, 11:278; earthworks,
16:308
Bridgit, Miss ---, cholera victim,
14:294
Bridgman, Donald E., 16:348
Bridgman, Elizabeth K., work re-
viewed, 22:186
Bridgman, George H., interviewed, 12:
457; career, 21:51, 184, 23:192;
memorial, 33:354
Bridgman, Mrs. George H., memorial,
33:354
Bridport, Hugh, artist, 36:294
Brietweiser, Dr. J. V., speaker, 22:
441
Briggs, ---, lead miner, 22:24
Briggs, Charles H., 18:468
Briggs, Ernestine, author, 30:388
Briggs, Harold E., author, 11:324,
12:200, 329, 13:205, 435, 16:229,
28:276, 30:338; speaker, 13:105
Briggs, John DeQ., author, 20:362
Briggs, John E., author, 13:208, 20:
338, 21:425; speaker, 22:329
Briggs, Margaret, 18:460, 30:70
Briggs, R. R., 17:379
Briggs, Dr. Vernon L., author, 14:439
Briggs, Mrs. Warren S., 39:56, 58,
59, 61, 62
Brigham, Albert P., author, 15:240
Brigham, Dr. George S., 33:294, 295
Brigham, Johnson, publisher, 26:302,
28:185
Brigham, Lillian R., author, 14:114
Bright, Jesse D., Indiana Senator,
37:48
Brighton Township, Nicollet County,
history, 15:114; mission, 20:90;
Norwegian settlement, 25:411;
Methodist church, 25:412
Brignoli's Italian Opera Troupe, 28:
110
Brill, Alice C., author, 25:212, 377
Brill, Ethel C., 12:196; reviews by,
12:422, 13:95, 420-422; author,
11:101, 12:331
Brill, Judge Hascal R., 19:441; papers, 24:62, 34:339
Brill, Judge Kenneth G., 17:70, 20:
50, 21:410, 23:50, 25:55, 26:42,
151, 30:37, 287; speaker, 25:54,
26:43, 285, 27:143, 144, 28:197,
391; MHS president, 26:45, 185,
27:27, 45, 58, 28:200, 29:36, 97,
30:330; papers, 27:249, 34:339;
career, 30:171, 34:114, 115
Brill, William H., 12:196
Brimlow, George F., author, 25:405,
26:77
Brimson, Finnish settlement, 25:160,
161, 319, 323
Brin, Mrs. Arthur, speaker, 13:341;
author, 13:428
Brings, Lawrence M., editor, 34:165,
35:196
Bring's Quarry, Stearns County, 14:
361
Brink, Carol, works reviewed, 28:274,
37:300
Brinkman Apartments, St. Peter, 17:
487
Brinsmade, Gen. Peter N., 21:22
Brioschi, Charles, sculptor, 13:83
Brisbane, Arthur, 23:195
Brisbin, John H., 26:203
Brisbine, Dr. A. G., 14:295, 298, 299

Brisbois, B. W., 13:234, 15:464;
trader, 20:79
Brisbois, Charles, characterized, 36:
44
Brisbois, Michel, house, 37:40
Brisbois, William, trader, 36:260
Brisbois and Rice, traders, 14:215
Brissette, E., 26:106
Bristow, Benjamin H., 13:130
Bristow, J. L., Kansas Senator, 22:79
B'rith Abram, fraternal order, 13:323
British, travelers' accounts, 15:353,
29:154, 34:38, 42, 45-53; Mormon
converts, 36:286. See also Cor-
nish, English, Great Britain,
Manxmen, Scots, Welsh
British American Magazine, 14:334
British Columbia, fur trade, 31:1,
40:178; explored, 35:141, 240;
gold mining, 35:249, 251; source
material, 39:128; historic sites,
40:191
British North American Boundary Com-
mission, 37:86
British North American Exploring Ex-
pedition, 39:211
Britt, Albert, work reviewed, 19:330;
speaker, 19:361
Brittin, Col. L. H., 19:184n; avia-
tion pioneer, 25:195, 33:241, 242
Britton, Lake County, railroad sta-
tion, 34:180
Broadhead, Sallie, diary, 29:344
Broadwater, John W., speaker, 13:449
Broch, Theodor, author, 24:74
Brock, Emma, author, 22:365
Brockington, Leonard W., author, 35:
240
Brockman, George, 20:102
Brockway, W. H., missionary, 16:333,
17:210
Brockway, Stearns County, Slovene
settlement, 25:194
Brockway Brothers, Eyota, livestock
raisers, 26:117, 121
Brodbelt, Ben S., auditor, 34:333
Broderick, Francis L., work reviewed,
39:26
Broderick, T. M., geologist, 34:276
Brodhead, John R., collector, 36:30
Brodie, Col. Alexander O., 22:164
Brodin, Knut, compiler, 40:45
Brodt, Mrs. H. W., 11:298, 17:21, 20:
97
Broestl, John A., librarian, 38:244
Brogan, D. W., author, 16:474
Brogan, Dan, author, 35:155
Brogan, Denis W., author, 29:154, 34:
168
Brokaw, E. W., educator, 13:216
Broma, Frank, 13:274
Bromenshenkel, Father Fintan, author,
26:275
Bromenshenkel, Father Sylvan, author,
26:388
Bromfield, Louis, author, 20:116, 23:
117, 156, 29:167, 40:299
Bromley, Carlisle A., mail carrier,
36:210
Bromley, Edward A., photograph col-
lector, 20:209, 27:358, 33:200n,
253, 35:98
Bromley, Henry, fur dealer, 34:103
Bromme, T., author, 18:73
Brøndsted, Johannes, author, 33:88,
34:215, 39:170
Brongniart, Adolphe, 13:418

Bronson, Charles A., 37:200
Bronson, Edgar B., author, 38:201
Bronson, Rev. Edward H., 17:363
Bronson, Elizabeth, will, 37:199n
Bronson, James D., 11:225; house, 38: 351
Bronson, Mrs. Martha A., 11:218
Brook, Michael, reviews by, 38:198, 39:170, 40:44, 313, 353; librarian, 38:244; author, 39:212
Brook Lake Township, Beltrami County, history, 15:132
Brook Park, visited, 39:264
Brooke, Gen. George M., establishes Fort Ripley, 28:206
Brooke, Col. John R., 25:228
Brookhart, Smith W., Iowa Senator, 24:240
Brookins, Jean A., reviews by, 36: 318, 37:180, 40:255; work reviewed, 38:379; editor, 37:44
Brooklyn, N.Y., museum, 21:149, 150, 157
Brooklyn Center, MHS meeting, 23:296
Brooklyn Township, Hennepin County, archives, 18:95
Brooks, ---, steamboat clerk, 31:212
Brooks, Asa P., author, 20:195
Brooks, Rev. Cyrus, 18:367
Brooks, Edmund D., bookseller, 27:40; publisher, 27:41
Brooks, Fern E., speaker, 17:357, 18: 465
Brooks, Rev. Jabez, 31:80; professor, 15:247, 16:180; Hamline president, 16:30, 21:184
Brooks, John W., railroad executive, 33:308
Brooks, Margaret, 18:110
Brooks, Philip C., author, 24:361
Brooks, Phillips, letters, 29:189
Brooks, Preston S., Congressman, 16: 280, 281n, 28:325
Brooks, Spencer, teacher, 30:271
Brooks, Van Wyck, author, 14:201, 21: 13
Brooks, history, 38:204
Brooks Scanlon Lumber Co., Duluth, 27:302
Brooksbank, James J., house, 38:352
Brookston, history, 21:455, 23:302, 25:160; railroad, 32:151; fire, 33:46
Brooten, Lutheran church, 24:93
Brosnan, T. W., labor leader, 22:371
Bross, William, diary, 28:172
Broste, Ole K., pioneer, 23:105, 400
"Brother Jonathan," steamboat, 38:348
Brotherhood of Carpenters and Joiners of America, Morris branch, 21:394
Brotherhood of Locomotive Engineers, Minnesota branches, 21:382
Brotherhood of Locomotive Firemen and Enginemen No. 126, Austin, 21:393
Brotherton, R. A., author, 25:95, 34: 311
Brothertown (Brotherton) Indians, Algonquian band, 27:69
Brott, George F., 15:139; publisher, 17:365; speculator, 35:245
Broughton, C. A., editor, 11:26n
Brouillet, Father Jean-Baptiste, missionary, 34:123
Brouillette, Benoit, work reviewed, 20:422; author, 24:179
Brousseau family, pioneers, 32:153,

154, 33:25-27, 72, 74, 75, 106, 111
Brouwer, Father Theodorus, 29:67
Browder, Earl, isolationist, 40:410
Brower, Charles, 15:396
Brower, David, editor, 38:91
Brower, Jacob V., 12:449, 18:182, 26: 238, 34:173; archaeologist, 11: 109, 13:245-247, 16:1, 309, 312, 25:330, 332, 340, 26:321; author, 12:226, 228, 13:173, 253, 26:303; topographer, 13:287, 24:372, 25: 401, 30:313; memorial, 20:344; park superintendent, 36:93, 235, 37:60
Brower, James S., in Civil War, 25: 237, 250
Brower, Leone Ingram, cataloguer, 12: 316, 13:425, 24:243; review by, 16:209; author, 17:61
Brower, Philip P., author, 30:389
Brower, Ripley B., legislator, 35:349
Brown, Mr. and Mrs. ---, innkeepers, 40:390
Brown, Capt. A. L., diary, 22:340
Brown, Albert, speaker, 17:121
Brown, Albert G., Mississippi Senator, 18:453
Brown, Alice, 20:110
Brown, Mrs. Alva I., speaker, 17:121
Brown, Amanda, 12:118, 119, 125, 128, 129, 132
Brown, Andrew H., author, 36:280
Brown, Angus, 12:125, 35:171, 174
Brown, Anna T., author, 15:367, 35:90
Brown, Anne, singer, 39:63
Brown, Augusta, 12:133
Brown, Benson, speaker, 25:99; contractor, 27:267
Brown, C. O., 15:89
Brown, Carleton, 21:70
Brown, Charles E., author, 15:471, 474, 24:367, 28:363; editor, 26: 170, 381
Brown, Charles T., speculator, 39:91
Brown, Charles W., 18:321
Brown, Mrs. Charlotte, 18:298
Brown, Clara M., author, 26:279
Brown, Corydon P., career, 28:65
Brown, Mr. and Mrs. Cyrus, 38:83
Brown, D. Alexander, work reviewed, 39:77
Brown, Dee, works reviewed, 33:86, 34:385; author, 30:66
Brown, Dorothy, 27:46
Brown, E. A., author, 15:252
Brown, E. L., hunter, 30:128n, 132
Brown, Earle, 25:378, 26:43; letters, 16:242; farm, 23:297; museum, 25: 302, 26:36
Brown, Ed, jeweler, 33:2
Brown, Edward H., blacksmith, 24:64
Brown, Edwin H., papers, 19:452, 20: 33
Brown, Eliza, 18:321
Brown, Ellen, 12:118, 120, 125, 126, 128, 129, 132; in Sioux Outbreak, 11:456, 28:191
Brown, Emily, daughter of Joseph R., 12:124, 126, 128
Brown, Emily, of Traverse des Sioux, 26:282
Brown, Ernest L., taxidermist, 24: 246, 26:255; diaries, 25:379, 28: 179; naturalist, 31:183; picture collection, 37:38
Brown, Florence, author, 20:92

Brown, Frances, author, 15:485
Brown, Francis H., song writer, 26:52
Brown, Francis J., editor, 19:459; author, 27:262
Brown, Frank, 18:126
Brown, Rev. Frederick T., 38:75
Brown, Garfield W., papers, 15:348; legislator, 33:157, 159
Brown, George W., author, 16:230, 23: 377, 25:199; editor, 26:80, 40:145
Brown, Gerald S., work reviewed, 37: 305
Brown, Glenn, 22:303
Brown, H. F., cattleman, 26:121
Brown, H. H., balloon flight, 38:171, 173, 174
Brown, Henry D., author, 32:187, 33: 351; speaker, 37:88
Brown, Hiram D., biography, 35:245
Brown, Homer C., author, 12:443
Brown, J. L., author, 11:455
Brown, Jacob, 25:272, 28:18, 19n
Brown, James H., 29:300
Brown, John, abolitionist, 11:207, 25:30, 31, 32:20, 33:218, 37:46; trial, 25:32
Brown, John, author, 21:364
Brown, Joseph R., 14:352; townsite owner, 11:170, 12:128, 24:160, 274; characterized, 11:331, 12: 114, 37:10; trader, 11:375, 376, 379, 380, 381, 12:116, 237, 428, 21:162, 24:195; houses, 11:448, 456, 12:118-133, 456, 19:354, 465, 20:51, 103, 24:196, 29:185, 34: 267, 36:283, 38:243, 39:272-277; steam wagon, 11:454, 12:115, 13: 95, 21:86, 22:204, 34:306, 35:155; family, 11:456, 12:112, 118, 120, 121, 126, 132, 133n, 14:245n, 28: 191; founder of Henderson, 12:113, 15:480, 23:404; Indian agent, 12: 121-123, 21:171, 23:85, 29:237, 32:72, 38:94, 131, 147, 149, 356, 39:92, 261; army major, 12:124, 300; editor, 12:128, 398, 22:211; marriage, 12:128; in Sioux Outbreak, 12:297-299, 38:97, 103, 139, 280; politician, 14:129, 163, 249, 252, 262, 36:265, 266, 39:41; pioneer, 14:238, 15:358, 16:454, 17:490, 21:458, 24:193, 195; election judge, 14:251; explorer, 14: 352, 40:313; lumberman, 17:313, 24:198; park memorial, 18:472, 23: 291; career, 21:99, 26:288, 27: 259; actor, 23:305-307, 30:388; letters, 25:183, 31:60; farmer, 29:1; in fiction, 37:5, 111; portrait, 38:104
Brown, Mrs. Joseph R. (Susan Frenière), 12:121, 132, 19:354, 20:51, 39:275, 276; career, 12:126-129; Sioux captive, 38:103n, 39:274
Brown, Joseph R., Jr., 12:126, 132
Brown, Julian E., memorial, 15:467
Brown, Mrs. Laura, 19:471
Brown, Rev. Leonard, traveler, 15: 406, 34:139
Brown, Lydia, 12:125
Brown, Margaret L., author, 37:306
Brown, Mary, secretary, 14:461
Brown, Mary, student, 35:268
Brown, Mattie A., 21:221
Brown, N. B., excursionist, 37:102
Brown, N. R., convention delegate,

14:245; census taker, 14:258, 259, 261
Brown, Nellie, 18:321
Brown, Nina, 23:392
Brown, Orlando E., Indian commissioner, 36:267, 268, 39:41
Brown, Orville, editorial policies, 20:269-286, 32:19, 21, 23, 27, 30
Brown, Col. Paul H., 24:5
Brown, Philip E., supreme court justice, 13:82
Brown, Ralph Adams, author, 29:77, 34:311
Brown, Ralph D., 17:56, 332, 347, 18: 50, 51, 94, 19:53; "Minnesota Prehistory," 15:148-156; "Excavations at Grand Portage," 18:456-458; speaker, 15:220, 17:346, 460, 18: 43, 63; author, 17:115, 346, 18: 328, 464
Brown, Ralph H., "Early Accounts of Minnesota's Climate," 17:243-261; ed., "The Journal of Charles C. Trowbridge," 23:126-148, 233-252, 328-348; reviews by, 25:174, 374, 27:128; works reviewed, 29:248-250, 344; author, 17:331, 19:456, 21:435, 22:438, 23:369, 24:364, 25:181, 383, 27:152, 28:337; geographer, 23:169; editor, 23:271, 33:346
Brown, Robert M., 28:300; "A Territorial Delegate," 31:172-178; "The Great Seal of the State of Minnesota," 33:126-129; reviews by, 32: 183, 33:303; speaker, 29:184; author, 31:192, 32:192, 39:35; archivist, 33:227, 35:100
Brown, Robert R., biography, 18:211
Brown, Rollin, 21:29n
Brown, Rollo W., author, 20:438
Brown, Rome G., politician, 34:226
Brown, Samuel J., interpreter, 12: 121; described, 12:126; park memorial, 12:456, 23:291; befriends Sisseton, 35:170, 171; Sioux captive, 38:128; scout, 40:313
Brown, Seth A., 23:77
Brown, Sibley, 12:126
Brown, Mrs. T. D., speaker, 20:352
Brown, W. B., diary, 17:119
Brown, W. Burlie, author, 35:291
Brown, W. E., convention delegate, 14:245
Brown, W. P., miller, 35:14
Brown, W. Russell, speaker, 34:314
Brown, W. W., theater owner, 28:99
Brown, Gen. William C., work reviewed, 11:87-89; author, 12:103; speaker, 12:452; biography, 25: 405, 26:77
Brown, William R., pioneer farmer, 18:47, 23:316, 27:61; diary, 17: 465, 20:323, 417, 26:106
Brown family, genealogy, 16:102
Brown and Allen, Boston, piano makers, 39:319
Brown & Bigelow, St. Paul, publishers, 25:374; history, 27:178, 34: 129, 312, 35:245, 36:101; site, 37:43
Brown-Blodgett Co., St. Paul, records, 27:56
Brown County, ethnic settlements, 12: 261, 273, 21:97, 22:335, 26:94; agriculture, 13:176, 37:208; census records, 13:426, 20:93, 21:

339; pioneers, 13:447, 14:234, 16: 126, 22:109; politics, 14:262, 16: 246, 17:125, 28:31, 32, 29:49, 38: 121; schools, 16:458; history, 16: 493, 17:235, 20:94, 23:105, 187, 31:24, 36:70, 37:348, 40:263; boundaries, 21:333; medicine in, 22:212, 334; poor relief, 22:343, 38:369, 374; ghost towns, 23:195; horse racing, 26:287; historic markers, 30:164, 276, 399; grasshopper bounty, 36:57; in Sioux Outbreak, 36:168, 38:283; mills, 36:193; Mormon mission, 36:288, 292; Civil War troops, 38:259
Brown County, S.D., irrigation system, 23:86
Brown County, Wis., pioneers, 21:428
Brown County Farm Bureau, history, 23:300
Brown County Historical Society, officers, 11:332, 16:240, 302, 19: 338, 24:190; museum, 12:37, 18: 221, 463, 19:230, 359, 469, 20:47, 92-95, 323, 454, 21:107, 215, 23: 11, 12, 14, 193, 27:171, 35:50; meetings, 12:206, 335, 14:234, 16: 364, 17:120, 20:350, 21:333, 22: 338, 23:295, 30:164; membership campaign, 19:115; tour, 19:468; collections, 19:472, 20:350, 24: 379, 25:312, 26:88, 282; activities, 30:276, 34:170, 314, 36:70, 327; publications, 37:307, 38:86, 39:132
Brown County War History Committee, 23:390
Brown-Martin Lumber Co., Northfield, records, 16:242, 19:467
Browne, Charles A., author, 17:226, 26:75
Browne, Henry R., work reviewed, 30: 254
Browne, J. Ross, secret agent, 13:434
Brownell, Joseph W., author, 37:85
Brownell, William C., author, 16:339
Browning, Orville H., 39:88
Browns Creek, Stillwater, 24:196, 197, 200
Brown's Falls, see Minnehaha Falls
Brown's Hotel, Lake City, 15:467, 16: 257
Brown's Point, Sandy Lake, post, 23: 249n, 34:268
Browns Valley, Brown house, 12:456; described, 19:227; land rush, 24: 207, 208, 261, 27:365; archaeology, 28:181, 38:160, 161, 39:262; post, 33:274n
Browns Valley Man, 16:3, 7, 8, 117, 19:111, 21:100, 35:201, 244
Brownsville, Jackson County, Norwegian settlement, 25:411
Brownsdale, history, 16:367; convention, 21:384
Brownson, Orestes, 25:373
Brownsville, stage station, 11:403; grain depot, 14:387; pioneer life, 17:361; settlement, 17:486, 487; archaeology, 28:285
Brownton, history, 21:452; garrison, 38:281
Bruccoli, Matthew J., author, 40:95
Bruce, Amos J., Indian agent, 15:343, 16:96, 21:167, 168, 173-175; letters, 15:463
Bruce, Kenyon, poet, 26:302

Bruce, Robert, author, 17:226
Bruce, William, trader, 33:130
Bruce, William G., author, 25:299
Bruce family, 35:282; genealogy, 12: 335
Bruce Township, Todd County, history, 16:131
Brué, A. H., cartographer, 34:219
Brueckner, Leo J., author, 26:279
Brulé, Etienne, explorer, 11:110, 12: 283, 19:198, 272, 25:273, 28:234, 32:90n, 39:81; at Lake Superior, 12:348; biography, 31:54
Brule Lake, Cook County, railroad, 34:181; forest fire, 36:131-134, 136
Brule River, Cook County, explored, 11:452, 22:327; stage line, 16: 298; route, 20:10; name, 23:244, 32:90n; fur trade, 28:147n; described, 28:234; fishing, 33:254; history, 34:167, 35:202
Brumbaugh, G. Edwin, author, 31:249
Brumley, John D., army surgeon, 25: 141
Brummond, Kathryn S., author, 12:335
Brunaw, F., lumberman, 24:201, 202
Brune, Ruth E., 27:34
Brunet, E. M., artist, 18:239
Brunet, Francis, trader, 24:22n
Bruno, Frank J., 39:26
Bruns, H. A., miller, 15:134
Bruns, Harvey, 12:165
Bruns, Henry A., farmer, 29:14
Brunskill, Frank W., police chief, 18:320, 37:165
Brunson, Alfred, Indian agent, 12: 190; missionary, 14:363, 17:230, 20:123, 443, 19:99, 21:23n, 430, 25:212, 29:354, 33:90; at Prairie du Chien, Wis., 18:193
Brunson, Lewis, and White, St. Paul, steamboat agents, 11:139
Brunson Seminary, Hamilton, Fillmore County, 14:147
Brunswick Town, N.C., archaeological site, 40:207
Brunswick Township, Kanabec County, Baptist church, 15:481; history, 18:340, 34:62; agriculture, 22:110
Brunswick Hotel, Minneapolis, 35:73
Brunswick-Balke-Collender Co., Chicago, history, 26:269
Brush, Charles R., 18:155
Brush Creek Township, Faribault County, Norwegian settlement, 12:270
Brush Electric Co., 36:99
Brust, William, 11:332, 17:120, 23: 296
Brusven, Anton, speaker, 21:447
Bruzek, John F., journalist, 20:462
Bryan, Enoch A., work reviewed, 18: 306
Bryan, Henry S., 34:266, 35:38
Bryan, Dr. Herman, speaker, 23:397, 24:378; author, 25:200
Bryan, Jerry, diary, 37:222
Bryan, John A., author, 29:351
Bryan, Kirk, author, 21:100
Bryan, Mina R., work reviewed, 31:179
Bryan, William J., 15:338, 17:165, 22:313, 26:357; politician, 12: 412, 15:337, 35:62, 63, 36:125, 205, 37:181, 39:29, 93-96, 102-107, 169, 332; papers, 16:456; pacifist, 18:265
Bryant, Margaret M., 27:34

Bryant, William Cullen, poet, 20:109, 27:16, 36:76; letter, 14:340; antislavery leader, 20:271; traveler, 25:273

Bryce, George, author, 13:298, 18:81

Bryce, James, 12:85; Duluth visit, 13:81; letter, 16:218; author, 29:154

Bryenton, Charles, log mark, 26:135

Bryer, Jackson R., author, 40:411

Brymner, Douglas, 22:429, 39:166; translator, 24:152

Bryn-Jones, David, work reviewed, 18:423-428

Bryn-Jones, Mrs. David, speaker, 26:285

Bryn Mawr Golf Course, Minneapolis, 40:32

Bryngelsson, Lennart G., author, 24:174

Bryton, Frederic, actor, 28:113, 33:175, 176, 178

Buchan, John (Lord Tweedsmuir), author, 29:154

Buchan, Susan C. (Lady Tweedsmuir), author, 20:197

Buchanan, James, 12:441; presidential candidate, 13:434, 27:14, 37:307; feud with Douglas, 13:437; letters, 17:106; memorial, 17:417; President, 20:272, 32:20, 117, 118, 37:54, 55, 38:121, 147; policies, 22:240, 243, 246, 247, 37:46; biography, 38:202

Buchanan, St. Louis County, townsite, 12:382, 385-387, 15:370, 37:112; lake port, 16:298; settled, 21:151, 34:177, 178; ghost town, 26:276

Bucher, Isaac, 28:318

Buchser, Frank, artist, 35:242

Buck, A. E., author, 21:329

Buck, Daniel, author, 40:147

Buck, E. D., merchant, 21:214

Buck, Elizabeth H., see Buck, Mrs. Solon J.

Buck, Frank, author, 14:121

Buck, G. A., 22:108, 23:104; editor, 23:404

Buck, H. R., author, 29:271

Buck, Judge Harry L., speaker, 20:304; politician, 40:321, 323, 326

Buck, Herbert L., 12:106, 13:121, 15:138, 16:125, 17:232; author, 16:100; speaker, 16:125, 497

Buck, L. Talbert, author, 13:432

Buck, Solon J., 13:184, 25:281, 27:49; MHS reports, 11:37-50, 12:21-33; reviews by, 11:77, 189-191, 30:50-52; works reviewed, 14:318-324, 21:179; speaker, 11:52, 287, 12:35, 39, 292, 23:366, 27:144, 30:365; author, 11:92, 312, 340, 428, 12:200, 289, 442, 443, 13:441, 14:230, 336, 15:357, 16:239, 17:114, 394n, 19:102, 21:91, 22:200, 26:265, 39:172; editor, 11:457, 13:64, 14:61, 35:233; MHS superintendent, 12:184, 23:5, 32:7, 8, 34:339, 39:220; career, 12:311-314, 30:316-322, 34:175, 37:136; portraits, 12:312, 37:88, 39:221; quoted, 13:47, 17:332, 460; at National Archives, 16:329, 19:347, 22:419; professor, 19:218; at Library of Congress, 29:259; memorial award, 34:175, 220, 35:51, 296,

36:71, 240, 37:264, 38:92, 336, 39:84, 264, 40:96, 316

Buck, Mrs. Solon J. (Elizabeth Hawthorn), 32:183; reviews by, 11:83-85, 436, 30:50-52; works reviewed, 19:442, 21:179; author, 11:196, 30:95

Buck, William, 18:116; homestead, 16:368

Buckbee, John C., 29:270

Buckeye drill, use in Minnesota, 24:304

Buckham, Mrs. Anna, 11:466

Buckham, Judge Thomas S., 11:466, 19:467; reminiscences, 23:103; mayor, 40:300

Buckham, Mrs. Thomas S. (Anna Mallory), reminiscences, 23:103

Buckham Memorial Library, Faribault, 11:52, 466; 12:105, 19:466, 21:115

Buckingham, J. S., 19:74

Buckingham, Joseph T., editor, 17:438

Buckingham, William, publisher, 16:113

Buckler, Richard T., quoted, 38:181; Congressman, 40:374

Buckley, Frank, "Chautauqua in the Minnesota State Prison," 29:321-333; review by, 37:340; author, 29:376, 31:57

Buckley, Mr. and Mrs. George W., 22:342

Buckman, Catholic church, 13:119

Buckner, Gen. Simon B., 25:28; biography, 22:205

Buckton, Rev. T. J., speaker, 17:231

Budapest String Quartet, Budapest, Hungary, 39:63

Budd, Mrs. Charles, speaker, 25:313

Budd, Edward G., industrialist, 39:30

Budd, Elizabeth, author, 29:357

Budd, George E., career, 12:322

Budd, J. Danley, 34:266, 35:38

Budd, J. L., horticulturist, 23:91

Budd, Ralph, 11:54, 14:78, 17:70, 19:50, 20:50, 23:50, 26:45, 29:97; "The Historical Society and the Community," 20:365-376; author, 11:104, 20:426, 26:162; speaker, 20:427, 21:97; railroad president, 24:253, 39:30; transportation commissioner, 35:45

Buechner, Louis, lithographer, 33:127

Buel, Jesse, agrarian, 40:295

Buell, C. J., quoted, 33:163

Buell, Gen. Don C., Union officer, 25:32n, 120, 242, 38:260, 261, 265, 266, 39:182, 195

Buell, Lake County, railroad station, 34:181

Buena Vista, Beltrami County, in county-seat fight, 23:30; business, 29:141; Beltrami plaque, 29:168

Buena Vista, Mexico, battle, 23:75

Buena Vista, Wis., see Hudson

Buenger, Theodore, 24:264

Buerger, Capt. Emil, in Sioux Outbreak, 38:278

Buetow, Herbert P., career, 35:38

Buffalo, Minn., schools, 18:120; architecture, 40:100

Buffalo, N.Y., ethnic groups, 14:54, 25:394, 27:213; flour milling, 14:206; transportation center, 40:272, 273

Buffalo (N.Y.) Historical Society, 20:424

Buffalo (bison), 16:42, 21:201, 37:191, 228; hunts, 11:102, 15:357, 385-394, 17:151, 441, 18:275, 417, 19:379, 381, 385, 388, 20:55, 23:154, 336, 339, 26:75, 27:63, 29:59, 32:59, 33:93 (cover), 277, 35:258, 260-262, 36:309-314, 37:78, 38:201, 39:239, 40:144, 163, 183; food item, 14:385, 33:200, 35:97; depleted, 15:238, 17:476, 30:124, 125, 37:134, 38:385; in art, 19:423, 27:254, 32:157, 161, 33:264; in fur trade, 20:144, 21:141, 36:260, 38:70, 190, 40:155, 211, 213, 214, 219, 220; Red River Valley, 28:281, 30:126, 38:1, 6, 7, 10, 70; history, 33:138, 34:345; robes, 33:198, 34:327, 40:210; prehistoric, 38:162. See also Pemmican

Buffalo Bay, Man., Lake of the Woods, 18:231

Buffalo County, Wis., settled, 20:443

Buffalo Creek, Renville and McLeod counties, garrison, 38:283

Buffalo Lake, Renville County, history, 13:453; in Sioux Outbreak, 38:279n

Buffalo Lake News, anniversary, 23:403

Buffalo Prairie, Clay County, pioneer life, 11:70-74

Buffalo River, Clay County, settlement, 19:234, 25:262

Buffalo Wool Co., 31:106n

Buffington, LeRoy S., architect, 22:425, 23:219-232, 271, 31:55, 40:100, 104, 105, 107, 108; building designs, 16:110, 19:458, 27:230, 37:187; author, 25:75

Buffington, Mrs. LeRoy S., 23:221

Bufford, J. H., music publisher, 26:53

Buford, Gen. Abram, Confederate officer, 39:188

Bugbee, Emily H., poet, 26:294

Bugbie (Bugbee), Albert E., letters, 18:444, 19:321-327

Buggy, Horace N., author, 26:184

Bugonaygeshig, Chippewa Indian, 24:143, 144, 146, 148

Buh, Father Joseph F., missionary, 14:454, 18:331, 23:402, 25:194; speaker, 40:61

Buhl, history, 36:196

Buhl Foundation, 12:93, 184

Buhler, Ernest O., land agent, 39:245

Buick automobile, 26:23

Buley, R. Carlyle, reviews by, 26:356-358, 34:34; works reviewed, 26:143, 32:44; author, 18:213, 26:370, 28:276, 33:308, 350, 36:100, 37:261

Bulgars, Detroit, Mich., 20:202; Minnesota, 22:180, 27:204, 211, 212, 214, 215, 40:341; bibliography, 25:299, 26:167; reverse migration, 27:214

Bulger, Capt. Andrew, governor of Assiniboia, 32:161

Bulkley, Col. C. S., engineer, 27:260

Bull, Benjamin, 34:204

Bull, Coates P., 20:82

Bull, Ephraim, horticulturist, 28:54

Bull (H. C.) Memorial Library, Cokato, 21:440
Bull, Ole, 18:199, 33:178n; colonizer, 12:304, 20:428, 21:98, 25:393,
26:167, 29:267; concerts, 14:140,
16:32, 20:223, 28:110, 30:15, 33:
169, 175, 39:321, 322; American
tours, 23:88, 25:86; statue, 27:
270; reformer, 36:80
Bull, Mrs. Ole, 25:86
Bull Moose party, organized, 29:156
Bull Run, Va., battle, 20:271, 25:16;
144, 356, 38:248, 259, 39:174,
176, 177, 181, 190, 191
Bullard, F. Lauriston, work reviewed,
28:63
Bullard, John S., builder, 38:341;
house, 38:342
Bullard, L. E., author, 20:359
Bullard, Lenord, builder, 38:341;
house, 38:342
Bullard, Polly, "Iron Range School-
marm," 32:193-201; author, 32:255
Bullard, W. H., 32:193
Bullard Brothers, St. Paul, jewelers,
32:193, 255
Bullard House, Reads Landing, regis-
ter, 12:191
Bullis, Franklin H., author, 17:351
Bullis, Harry A., 34:204; speaker,
33:186; career, 35:44
Bullo, ---, scout, 39:237
Bumstead, Rev. Horace, career, 11:110
"Bun Hersey," steamboat, 31:36
Bunde (Bundi), Chippewa County, Fri-
sian settlement, 28:126
Bundlie, Gerhard, 14:105; speaker,
16:115, 29:367
Bundy, Henry, steamboat captain, 26:
266
Bundy, Isaac, pioneer farmer, 28:85
Bunker, Mrs. Alice S., 15:459
Bunkersberg, Derk, Dutch pioneer, 28:
125
Bunn, Helen, 29:53
Bunn, Dr. John, 20:88
Bunnell, Dr. Lafayette H., career,
15:233, 237, 20:340, 22:98
Bunnell, Milie, career, 14:360
Bunnell, Willard, house, 36:139, 140,
144
Bunnell's Landing, Winona County,
road, 21:233
Bunyan, Paul, folk character, 15:241,
18:452, 23:378, 25:275, 27:351,
29:107, 108, 113, 32:55; legends,
13:333, 16:236, 487, 20:117, 21:
55-59, 176-178, 296-298, 353, 429,
22:180, 204, 207, 24:176, 265,
367, 25:392, 26:73, 170, 380, 381,
27:165, 255, 269, 278, 280, 28:92-
94, 177, 306, 362-364, 372, 29:
261, 30:248, 31:39, 32:126, 151n,
187, 253, 33:90, 265, 35:200, 243,
36:73, 77, 78, 96, 37:39, 40:391,
392, 402; bibliography, 23:379,
24:261; glossary, 24:74; museums,
24:363, 364; monument, 26:166, 28:
189; in Illinois, 28:287
Burbank, Henry C., 16:24, 225, 341,
38:71; house, 16:71, 98; legislator, 34:93. See also Burbank companies
Burbank, Rev. J. E., abolitionist,
32:27
Burbank, James C., 35:154; stage op-

erator, 14:351; house, 38:347n.
See also Burbank companies
Burbank, John A., Dakota governor,
27:67
Burbank Township, Kandiyohi County,
Mormon mission, 36:290
Burbank companies, stage operators,
11:405-407, 13:241, 14:154, 292,
16:225, 18:275, 353, 25:183, 32:
63, 34:18n, 37:53, 56, 38:63-71,
39:232-234, 236; steamboat owners,
19:386, 21:249-251, 23:321, 29:
177, 35:154
Burch, Dr. Frank E., author, 31:124
Burch, Franklin W., compiler, 40:361
Burch, L. D., author, 19:125
Burch, Leslie, speaker, 29:274
Burch, Newell, diary, 39:132
Burch, Robert, log mark, 26:136
Burchard, H. M., dairyman, 27:120
Burchard, John E., biography, 16:337
Burcher, William M., author, 26:168
Burda, Mrs. Mary Dunkl, 23:168, 24:
31, 162, 25:41
Burdick, Mr. and Mrs. Jesse, Cutler-
ites, 13:387
Burdick, Kary, Cutlerite, 13:387
Burdick, R. C., insurance agent, 22:
99
Burdick, Usher L., 18:109; work re-
viewed, 21:68; author, 26:170, 29:
73, 30:160
Bureau of American Ethnology, 15:232,
16:476, 19:105, 26:275
Bureau of Engraving, history, 29:269
Burfening, William, 18:97, 24:134n
Burg, Capt. Frank, 24:379
Burgan, John M., 25:121
Burger, Lt. Emil A., 25:246
Burges Hall, Hastings, 15:349, 16:
383
Burgesse, J. A., translator, 26:75
Burghardt, Andrew F., author, 36:326
Burg's Battery, in Sioux Outbreak,
24:379
Burgum, Jessamine S., work reviewed,
19:205
Burke, Catherine, author, 26:288, 28:
291
Burke, Evelyn, author, 25:93, 204,
314, 28:82
Burke, Redmond A., author, 38:91
Burke, W. J., author, 24:173
Burkhalter, Lois, author, 38:36
Burkhard, William, gunmaker, 33:307
Burkhart, J. A., author, 28:379
Burkleo, Samuel, 21:458
Burleene Township, Todd County, his-
tory, 16:131
Burleigh, Walter A., Indian agent,
39:229
Burleigh County, N.D., place names,
36:325
Burleson, Hugh L., missionary, 25:305
Burleson, Rev. Solomon, 36:319
Burlingame, Merrill G., reviews by,
35:31, 37:78; work reviewed, 24:
158; author, 28:204
Burlingame, Roger, author, 38:334
Burlington, Iowa, Wisconsin territo-
rial capital, 15:16, 475; Baptist
church, 16:340; depicted, 17:425,
427; lumber market, 26:132, 29:
146; exodus of gold seekers, 30:
393
Burlington, Lake County, road, 16:298
"Burlington," steamboat, 13:223, 236,

446, 18:154, 455, 20:379; described, 13:233
Burlington and Missouri River Railroad, 23:64
Burlington Bay, Lake County, sawmill,
22:346; settled, 34:177
Burlington, Cedar Rapids & Northern
Railroad, route, 30:232, 233
Burlington Lines (Chicago, Burlington
& Quincy Railroad), 36:322, 39:
298; colonization activities, 16:
344, 23:63-65, 34:68; built, 17:
345, 24:114; archives, 19:50, 20:
374, 24:253, 25:392, 31:111; excursion, 20:76; anniversaries, 20:
365, 21:305, 22:94, 30:151; route,
20:373; control, 22:202; pictorial
record, 30:379; agricultural program, 30:393, 31:58; in Civil War,
33:219; innovations, 35:45; rates,
35:241; origin, 36:105; mail service, 36:278; converts to diesels,
39:30; history, 40:356
Burlington University, Burlington,
Iowa, 25:12
Burman, Ben L., work reviewed, 21:403
Burn, James D., author, 29:154
Burnaby, Andrew, 24:158
Burnand, Eugene, immigration agent,
12:255
Burnes, Robert L., author, 30:154
Burnett, Edmund C., work reviewed,
23:257
Burnett, Kathryn, author, 25:102
Burnett, William, trader, 19:298, 304
Burnett, railroad, 32:151, 33:106,
107, 110, 111; pioneer life, 32:
152-154, 33:22-28, 72-76, 105-111;
post office, 33:25-28; map, 33:
107; school, 33:108
Burnett County, Wis., pioneer life,
28:2, 29:355
Burnette, O. Lawrence, Jr., editor,
38:198; compiler, 38:201
Burnham, Dr. Alfred, 14:313, 314
Burnham, Daniel H., architect, 33:334
Burnham, Guy M., author, 13:110, 14:
342
Burnham, Mrs. Harry M., 12:339
Burnham, Hiram, 25:346
Burnham, Mrs. Mabelle E., 14:120
Burnham, Mrs. Rushia, 14:311
Burnham's Novelty and Dramatic Co.,
28:111
Burnhamville, Todd County, history,
15:371
Burnley, Charles T., 21:334
Burnley, Mrs. Charles T., 21:439
Burnquist, Joseph A. A., 11:444, 30:
171; governor, 14:416, 34:227,
230, 231, 232; letters, 16:218;
speaker, 30:400; lieutenant gover-
nor, 33:156, 160; author, 34:222
Burns, David, hotelkeeper, 38:71
Burns, Fitzhugh, memorial, 15:467
Burns, George H., 13:145, 148, 17:
273, 19:162; speaker, 13:146
Burns, Dr. J. H., speaker, 12:208
Burns, John, author, 20:340
Burns, Lee, author, 16:228
Burns, Margery, author, 40:47
Burns, Mark L., 12:223n; speaker, 12:
292, 14:350
Burns, Ned J., author, 24:172, 30:257
Burns, Lt. Robert, letter book, 29:
374

Burns, Robert I., work reviewed, 40: 143

Burns, William W., Union officer, 25: 34, 35, 37, 122, 123, 137

Burnside, Gen. Ambrose E., Union officer, 20:279, 25:24, 35, 150, 232, 233, 238, 243, 244, 251, 343, 350

Burnside Farm Club, 11:16

Burnside Township, Goodhue County, school, 37:282; poor farm, 38:367

Burnstown Farm Bureau, 16:364

Burntside Lake, St. Louis County, fishing, 33:258, 259

Burntwood River, see Brule River

Burpee, Lawrence J., 14:84, 27:241; "Grand Portage," 12:359-377; "A Hundred Years of North America," 23:201-210; reviews by, 22:62-65, 177-181, 23:253-256, 24:45-48, 25: 272-274; speaker, 12:293, 13:56, 16:211, 17:49, 23:297; editor, 12: 316, 18:244; author, 12:330, 14: 444, 15:238, 16:480, 19:223, 20: 341, 438, 22:82, 187, 23:270, 384, 24:60, 25:288, 26:268, 27:70, 28: 71, 35:140, 36:30, 39:81; translator, 24:152

Burr, A. G., author, 29:85

Burr, Aaron, 35:291

Burr, Mrs. Aaron, house, 38:343

Burr, David H., map maker, 34:219, 40:120

Burr, William, artist, 33:290, 36:324

Burrill, Robert, author, 30:75

Burris, Evadene A., see Swanson, Mrs. Gustav

Burroughs, Clyde H., author, 17:475

Burroughs, Ira, lumberman, 24:127

Burrows, John M. D., reminiscences, 24:77

Burrows, George, author, 21:368

Burrus, Ernest J., author, 35:43

Burt, Alfred L., 25:67, 295; "Our Dynamic Society," 13:3-23; reviews by, 15:93, 16:83-85, 17:453-455, 18:81-83, 194, 21:395, 36:63, 39: 338; works reviewed, 15:94-98, 22: 306-308, 23:253-256; author, 12: 330, 13:328, 14:62, 17:459, 18:91, 203, 21:408, 22:63, 23:270, 26: 171; speaker, 13:75, 14:59; compiler, 37:342

Burt, Harold S., author, 26:265

Burt, Mrs. J. W., 23:41

Burt, Roy F., politician, 34:194n

Burt, W. H., legislator, 35:2

Burt, William A., geologist, 25:197; author, 40:141

Burtness, Osten, 12:264

Burton, Clarence M., 23:134; historian, 39:166

Burton, Florence, author, 18:332

Burton, J., 19:135, 137

Burton, Marion L., educator, 11:110, 22:101, 31:52, 32:176, 36:186

Burton, Richard, professor, 22:158, 163, 164, 27:41; author, 15:451, 16:81, 26:306, 307, 310

Burton, Rev. S. S., 31:82n

Burton, Ward C., 19:365; editor, 14: 351

Burton Historical Collection, 15:462, 19:448; publications, 20:333

Burwell, Louise, 25:208, 29:91; author, 27:176

Burwell, William D., 17:338

Bus transportation, Mesabi Range, 22: 102, 28:384, 35:338; St. Paul, 34: 44. See also Greyhound Bus Lines

Busbey, Hamilton, 17:217

Busch, Bishop Joseph F., 20:446; anniversary, 16:371; speaker, 34:229

Busch, Rev. William, 11:54, 14:78, 17:70, 19:209, 20:50, 23:50; review by, 14:325; speaker, 14:229, 15:76, 217; author, 15:104, 17:84, 18:89

Buscher, Dr. Julius, author, 33:356

Bush, Alfred L., work reviewed, 38:90

Bush, Archibald G., career, 35:38, 36:283

Bush, J. Clark, 13:175

Bush, John, pioneer, 13:370n

Bush-Brown, Albert, author, 37:344, 38:91

Bush Valley, Houston County, strip cropping, 20:359

Bushman Ferry, Minnesota River, 20: 100

Bushnell, David I., Jr., 14:287, 19: 423; works reviewed, 13:301, 21: 185; author, 21:201, 25:330, 26: 328

Bushnell, David P., Indian agent, 39: 306

Bushnell, Rev. Horace, in Minnesota, 19:266, 267, 35:219

Bushnell, Rev. John E., author, 20: 101

Business, importance of history, 11: 99, 26:264, 27:174; progress, 13: 14-17, 34:169; advertising, 14: 413, 37:256; records, 14:437, 20: 84, 165-168, 302, 375, 20:166, 22: 40, 83, 23:86, 24:173, 25:83, 391, 392, 26:163, 278, 384; pioneer, 20:19-21, 335, 464, 22:205, 23: 198, 24:191, 27:309-318, 28:211, 29:374, 34:121, 35:200, 39:65-74; Twin Cities, 20:98, 34:17-27, 50, 51, 102-104, 128; mail order, 21: 103, 24:372; Minnesota, 22:437, 23:31, 32, 24:98, 273; leaders, 22:420; wholesale, 23:88, 24:64, 33:226, 34:106-113; interstate, 33:335; moguls, 34:38, 35:36; in fiction, 35:44; lists of firms, 35:241, 36:278; relation to politics, 39:98, 100, 109, 110. See also Banks and Banking, Economic conditions, Industry, Meat packing, various business firms

Business and Professional Women's Club, Rochester, 17:362, 18:334

Business Historical Society, 22:326, 428; publications, 23:87, 26:72, 27:64

Business Men's Union, Minneapolis, 35:66

Business Women's Club, Minneapolis, 22:423

Business Women's Holding Co., Minneapolis, 22:423, 23:40

Buslett, O. A., author, 13:324

Busse, August F., house, 39:274, 275

Busse, Fred A., 23:392

Bustitown, Itasca County, settled, 22:415

Busy West, history, 26:296-299, 310

Butchers Benefit Society, St. Paul, 21:382

Butler, Andrew P., Senator, 31:178

Butler, Gen. Benjamin F., Union officer, 20:278, 284, 25:239, 240, 32: 26, 27, 33:217

Butler, Blanche, letters, 36:281

Butler, Charles, excursionist, 25: 104n

Butler, Rev. Colvin G., speaker, 18: 110, 27:363

Butler, Cooley, 24:93

Butler, Ellis P., 20:114

Butler, Emmett, 24:93

Butler, Fanny K., 29:124

Butler, Henry S., 19:453

Butler, John, 24:93

Butler, Dr. Levi, in Civil War, 16: 334, 39:196

Butler, Mamie R., author, 30:265

Butler, Nathan, papers, 11:42, 21: 315, 24:167

Butler, Ovid, editor, 17:220, 34:256

Butler, Justice Pierce, 17:160n, 213, 19:441, 20:185, 372, 25:204, 27: 262, 28:199, 29:55; quoted, 37: 171, 172; career, 39:205

Butler, Robert, 27:27

Butler, Ruth L., review by, 26:148; work reviewed, 18:438, 28:272; author, 24:71, 26:154, 376

Butler, Steve, author, 12:340

Butler, Walter, 24:93

Butler, William, 24:93

Butler, Mrs. William, 18:207

Butler Brothers, St. Paul, building projects, 25:204; incorporated, 26:173, 174

Butler Brothers-Hoff Co., 29:294

Butler family, genealogy, 25:204

Butler, Otter Tail County, Dutch settlement, 16:251

Butler vs. Chambers, legal case, 27: 120

Butte Pelée, N.D., trading post, 11: 380

Butterfield, Alec, author, 34:357

Butterfield, Charles F., miller, 27: 365

Butterfield, Gen. and Mrs. Daniel, 37:203

Butterfield, Herbert, work reviewed, 35:87

Butterfield, Kenyon L., educator, 37: 25

Butterfield, Lyman H., work reviewed, 31:179; author, 35:147; compiler, 36:30

Butterfield family, at Lake Minnetonka, 36:327

Butterfield, Watonwan County, history, 20:214

Buttermaking, see Dairy industry

Butternut Valley Township, Blue Earth County, Norwegian settlement, 12: 273; garrison, 38:280

Butters, Frederic K., papers, 27:23, 153, 34:339

Butters, I. H., stationer, 27:153

Butters, Mr. and Mrs. William, papers, 27:153

Button, George H., letters, 21:193

Buttons, historical value, 39:297

Butts, Porter, 17:332; work reviewed, 17:455

Butz, Casper, poet, 24:222

Buxton, Mrs. Charles I., 11:287

Buyck, settled, 34:178

Buzzle Township, Beltrami County, history, 15:365

Bydgelagenes Faellesraad, Inc., 17: 213
Byers, Erastus, log marks, 26:135, 137
Byers, John F., 18:126
Byers, R. T., author, 23:281
Bygland, Polk County, Lutheran church, 31:126
Byman, V. T., speaker, 18:464
Byram, R. F., editor, 13:344
Byrd, Cecil K., work reviewed, 34:350
Byrd, Richard E., explorer, 28:362
Byrd, Mrs. Thomas B., 23:134
Byrne, James C., author, 23:191
Byrnes, Hazel W., 14:114
Byrnes, Timothy E., 18:128n
Byron, Norwegian settlement, 19:211

"C. D. Dorr," steamboat, 24:139
"C. W. Moore," steamboat, 34:1 (cover)
Cabanné family, in fur trade, 15:421
Cabeen, Richard M., author, 26:174
Cabell, James B., author, 21:3, 4
Cable, Field S., editor, visits St. Croix Valley, 17:276, 284-286
Cable, George W., 17:375, 40:12; lecture tour, 18:28-35; author, 20:110
Cable, H. W., businessman, 34:266, 35:38
Cable, Ransom (Richard) R., railroad official, 34:83, 39:31
Cabot, John, 18:383
Cabot family, genealogy, 14:439
Cabrera, Luis, 17:165
Cabrillo, Juan Rodríguez, explorer, 32:112
Cadden, Rev. John P., author, 26:266
Caddy, Alice, artist, 21:404
Cadieux, ——, voyageur, 28:9n
Cadieux, Lorenzo, author, 34:174
Cadillac, Antoine de la Mothe, sieur de, 16:199, 18:389, 19:279, 33:87; founds Detroit, Mich., 19:284, 32:184; at Michilimackinac, 26:268, 27:63
Cadle, Richard F., missionary, 18:326
Cadman, Charles W., composer, 26:52, 36:190
Cadotte, ——, interpreter, 25:297
Cadotte, Jean Baptiste, posts, 11:209, 241, 368; trader, 11:245, 261, 18:325, 20:469, 22:206, 23:243n, 24:179, 32:186, 34:207, 352, 357; expelled from North West Co., 16:201; explorer, 28:233n
Cadotte, Joseph, trader, 36:242, 243
Cadotte, Michael, trader, 23:243, 25:372
Cadotte family, in fur trade, 11:326, 385, 14:342
Cadwallader, Sylvanus, journalist, 34:344
Cadwell, C. E., author, 25:211
Cadwell, M. N., diary, 12:101
Cady, E. T., publisher, 22:123
Cady, George L., author, 17:229
Cady, Capt. John S., 16:306
Cady, U. A., 26:261
Cahalane, Victor H., speaker, 40:149
Cahenslyism, 15:105, 27:161, 28:72, 33:305, 37:133

itor, 16:110, 17:107; author, 32:110
Cahokia, Ill., French settlement, 18:389, 394, 19:293, 30:73, 249
Cahoon's seed sower, 24:304
Caillet, Father Louis E., 15:31, 26:303
Cain, Nick, pioneer, 24:320
Cain, Rev. W. L., speaker, 16:305
Caird, Sir James, author, 15:353
"Cairo," warship, 40:306
Cairo Township, Renville County, Norwegian settlement, 12:275n
Cakepoint, Mich., located, 23:238
Calderwood, Willis J., 25:63
Caldwell, Chester L., biography, 16:337
Caldwell, Erskine, author, 20:116, 23:124; editor, 25:287
Caldwell, John, 18:81
Caldwell, Rev. John C., prison chaplain, 37:142
Caldwell, Norman W., work reviewed, 23:160
Caldwell, Russell L., author, 35:151
Caldwell, Samuel, 35:31
Caldwell, Taylor, novelist, 21:9
Caldwell and Co., St. Paul, 40:112, 113
Caledonia, pioneer life, 11:114, 14:331, 17:486, 25:183; anniversary, 34:128
Caledonia, Wis., Bohemian settlement, 15:27, 28
Calef family, in Minnesota, 25:292
Caleff, Henry, 13:133, 140, 146
Caleff, Peter, 17:266, 268, 22:100
Calhoun, Donald C., editor, 33:312
Calhoun, John C., 12:436, 13:221, 18:450, 23:7, 74, 24:3; secretary of war, 23:126-132, 33:345, 36:294; papers, 37:37
Calhoun, Rev. Thomas, 32:18
California, acquired, 11:189, 431, 30:191; gold rush, 11:429, 17:323, 22:125-127, 27:16, 30:152, 190, 33:266, 35:251; Norwegians in, 12:304; county boundaries, 13:108; settlement promoted, 13:331, 35:116, 36:68; bibliography, 14:448; Quakers, 18:259; diaries, 20:349, 23:8; board of health, 21:358; trade, 27:111, 39:70; railroad, 30:234, 237; frontier, 30:251; panorama, 33:290; fur trade, 35:48, 38:199
California Historical Survey Commission, 15:124
California Indian Hobbyist Association, 40:411
Calkin, Homer L., compiler, 32:189
Calkins, Elisha, 34:263
Calkins, Franklin W., author, 37:306
Callahan, Daniel, 28:267
Callahan, Jeremiah G., career, 19:214
Callahan, John, speaker, 27:356
Callahan, Patrick H., author, 15:235
Callender, John M., archaeologist, 35:384, 36:152, 39:212; "An Archaeologist Explores the Site of Old Fort Snelling," 35:365-367; work reviewed, 36:230; author, 36:196
Callières, Louis H. de, 19:395
Callihan, ——, cholera victim, 14:301
Calmar, Iowa, history, 19:460
Calof, Mrs. A., 13:429

Calthrop, Samuel R., 19:212
Calumet County, Wis., history, 18:326
Calumet Iron and Steel Co., Chicago, 18:139, 149
Calumets, see Pipes
Calvary, Wis., Capuchin monastery, 16:346
Calvary Baptist Church, Albert Lea, 15:242; Minneapolis, 17:337
Calvary Cemetery, Mankato, chapel bell, 18:374
Calvé, Emma, singer, 39:55
Calvin, Arthur M., author, 24:356
Cambria, history, 16:493; prehistoric village, 26:387
Cambridge, pageant, 13:450; pioneer life, 19:210; newspaper, 27:344; name, 30:332; Swedish setttlement, 34:61
Cambridge Community Library Club, 27:366
Camden State Park, 16:481; pageants, 18:333, 30:281, 407; museum, 30:277
Cameron, Daniel, 25:211
Cameron, Donald R., boundary commissioner, 39:32
Cameron, Duncan, author, 29:66
Cameron, John, trader, 11:367, 368
Cameron, John D., trader, 20:71, 21:399, 22:309, 36:245, 246
Cameron, Murdock, trader, 11:179
Cameron, Simon, secretary of war, 25:11, 32:22, 37:212, 213
Cameron, W. Bleasdell, author, 24:370
Cameron Dam, Wis., battle, 23:98
Camp, Charles L., 18:451, 34:303
Camp, Maj. and Mrs. George A., 30:291
Camp, Dr. James L., 12:449, 24:142; in Indian battle, 24:144-146
Camp Burns, Renville County, garrison, 38:283
Camp Coldwater, Hennepin County, 21:167, 171, 35:24, 185, 187, 192; Kearny expedition at, 12:439; importance, 20:122; white inhabitants, 20:123; school, 20:127; established, 23:338n. See also Fort Snelling
Camp Croft, S.C., newspaper, 23:393
Camp Fire Girls, St. Paul, 11:214
Camp McClellan, Iowa, Sioux prison, 38:356
"Camp Misery," Yorktown, Pa., 25:120n
Camp Oglethorpe, Ga., in World War I, 40:362
Camp Parker, N.D., in Sibley expedition, 18:209
Camp Parole, Annapolis, Md., in Civil War, 25:152, 224, 238
Camp Pope, Redwood County, in Sioux Outbreak, 14:331, 38:114, 285
Camp Porter, Blue Earth County, Winnebago prison, 38:361, 362
Camp Release, Lac qui Parle County, 18:317, 444; wayside and monument, 23:291, 27:359, 37:59, 38:154; in Sioux Outbreak, 38:100, 108-111
Camp Ripley, Morrison County, National Guard training center, 12:101, 202, 13:340, 38:244; history, 17:480, 24:167, 25:94. See also Fort Ripley
Camp Savage, Scott County, language school, 27:261

Camp Slaughter, Dak. Ter., in Sibley
expedition, 18:209
Camp Smith, Dak. Ter., in Sibley ex-
pedition, 18:209
Camp Stone, Md., in Civil War, 25:15-
17, 20-30, 353
Camp Township, Renville County, Nor-
wegian settlement, 12:274, 275n
"Camp Wilkin," Brown County, 38:283
Campbell, ---, fur trader, 36:46
Campbell, Col. ---, at Fort Snelling,
18:455
Campbell, Alex, railroad conductor,
30:237
Campbell, Rev. Alexander, 24:339
Campbell, Antoine J. (Joe), 38:357;
agency clerk, 27:264; interpreter,
38:106n; Sioux captive, 38:141
Campbell, Archibald, fur trader, 16:
96
Campbell, Archibald, boundary commis-
sioner, 39:32
Campbell, Bernie, author, 34:130
Campbell, Clifford W., author, 26:
291, 27:72
Campbell, Colin, 18:193; voyageur,
20:259
Campbell, Capt. Donald, 29:65
Campbell, Duncan, 18:193; trader, 20:
262, 263
Campbell, Rev. E. V., pioneer pastor,
12:456
Campbell, Gabriel, 16:184
Campbell, George M., author, 21:424
Campbell, Rev. George P., compiler,
29:176
Campbell, Henry C., author, 13:247,
396
Campbell, J. Duncan, author, 39:297
Campbell, Col. John W., 24:6
Campbell, Marjorie W., work reviewed,
36:64, 38:327; author, 34:174
Campbell, Marvin R., letter, 39:271
Campbell, Murray, author, 33:89
Campbell, Norman R., translator, 37:
274n
Campbell, Patrick, author, 19:103
Campbell, Robert, trader, in Minneso-
ta, 12:326, 26:171; diary, 13:336;
explorer, 17:75
Campbell, Mrs. Robert, 13:336
Campbell, Robert, and Co., St. Louis,
steamboat firm, 38:355
Campbell, Scott, 18:193, 20:78, 21:
169; interpreter, 21:26, 27
Campbell, Vance, author, 40:186
Campbell, Walter S., reviews by, 16:
89, 17:200, 19:330, 30:374, 33:
344, 35:235; works reviewed, 22:
60, 35:333; author, 11:428, 16:
105, 17:50, 206, 19:337, 26:165,
30:412, 32:114, 40:154; speaker,
13:328, 20:52, 21:38
Campbell family, traders, 35:282
Campbell, railroad, 13:41
Campbell and Williams, logging firm,
27:302
Campbell Beach, Lake Agassiz, geolo-
gy, 38:158, 162, 163
Campbellites (Disciples of Christ),
15:237, 36:290
Campion, ---, trader, 11:264n
Campion, William F., author, 36:107
Campton, Charles E., 19:308, 310
Canada, William W., 17:160n
Canada, under French, 11:78, 15:97,
23:161, 34:305; frontier, 11:107;

relations with U.S., 11:191-194,
13:9, 209, 18:443, 20:319-321, 22:
70, 306-308, 23:58-60, 201-210,
24:45-48, 57, 152-154, 179, 25:
171, 199, 26:363, 29:165, 30:387,
34:317-324, 35:35, 283, 36:191,
324, 325, 37:257; politics, 12:88;
ethnic groups, 12:25, 16:102, 18:
71, 20:342, 26:57, 27:166, 35:33;
history, 12:330, 16:83-85, 231,
23:83, 253-256, 25:66, 26:80, 28:
60-62, 65, 29:78, 37:86, 38:328;
annexation question, 13:113, 15:
334, 16:103, 332, 33:139, 315, 35:
34, 47, 151, 202, 282, 37:52-57,
126, 38:56; historical societies,
13:431; historical dictionary, 13:
439; source material, 15:125, 18:
216, 37:80; immigration and emigration, 15:239, 16:339, 24:328-
335, 27:207, 34:144; pioneer life,
15:356, 22:204; discovery, 15:476;
biographies, 16:113, 40:145; explored, 16:416-423, 26:274, 34:
174, 35:140, 142, 38:380, 39:211;
encyclopedia, 16:480; bibliographies, 17:223, 35:295, 334, 36:280,
39:128; Indian department, 18:37,
40; Mennonites, 18:456; lumber industry, 20:341, 35:237; railroads,
21:63, 406, 23:53, 35:237, 37:38;
museums, 21:421, 28:282; historic
sites, 22:99, 40:188-191; Indians,
24:371, 34:355, 37:40, 38:284;
art, 26:386, 36:102, 317; banking,
27:70; architecture, 28:283; folk
songs, 29:167, 39:128; agrarian
movement, 29:341, 30:151; place
names, 30:67; wildlife, 30:125,
128, 221, 230; compared to U.S.,
30:261; government, 31:117; maps,
34:132, 40:173, 189, 355; rivers,
38:386; roads, 40:358. See also
Border lakes, Boundaries (international), Fur trade, Red River Settlement
"Canada," steamboat, 35:102, 38:362;
cholera victims, 14:301
Canada Committee, 11:249, 254
Canada Steamship Lines, Ltd., 35:281
Canadian archives, see Public Archives of Canada
Canadian Churchman (Kingston, Ont.),
file, 24:330n
Canadian Geographical Society, 12:
293, 23:385, 443
Canadian Historical Association, 12:
293, 35:47
Canadian Journal of Industry, Science, and Art, file, 14:334
Canadian National Railway, at Bau-
dette, 24:278n; Roseau County, 24:
327
Canadian Pacific Railway, built, 16:
463, 21:260, 24:277, 328, 329, 31:
119, 120, 38:241, 311; history,
17:217, 21:406, 40:142
Canadian Pacific Railway Co., 35:39;
colonization policies, 11:327, 21:
63, 23:53; financed, 25:200, 39:
31; steamer line, 34:14, 35:281
Canadian party, in Ontario, 24:329
"Canadiana," steamboat, 34:15
Canadians, in lumber industry, 13:
357, 365, 21:56, 27:201; Minnesota, 19:191, 20:121, 22:104, 27:
212, 215; U.S., 23:201, 25:199;

folklore, 33:184; in politics, 36:
237. See also French Canadians
Canals, Erie, 13:8, 15:14, 26:359,
40:184; Duluth, 20:463, 24:62, 26:
291, 27:72, 30:397, 37:100n;
Stillwater, 24:199; Great Lakes,
34:263, 39:82; St. Lawrence Sea-
way, 35:292; government subsi-
dized, 37:82. See also Sault
Ste. Marie
Canby, E. R. S., 35:241
Canby, Henry S., author, 17:226, 21:
14
Canby, museum project, 17:233
Canby News, anniversary, 19:476
Cane, Melville H., editor, 34:42
Canfield, E. H., 12:106, 16:241; au-
thor, 16:367
Canfield, Ethel, author, 23:84
Canfield, Polly, editor, 30:290;
speaker, 30:364
Canisteo District, Mesabi Range,
mines, 22:345
Canisteo Township, Dodge County, Nor-
wegian settlement, 12:270
Canney, Joseph H., 18:250
Cannon, Carl L., editor, 13:331
Cannon, Cornelia, novelist, 23:117,
156, 31:135, 145, 36:80
Cannon, James P., author, 36:326
Cannon, Mrs. Jennie V., work re-
viewed, 24:240
Cannon, Joseph G., 16:460, 22:79;
Congressman, 40:317, 318, 321,
322, 324, 325
Cannon, Mary A., author, 20:103
Cannon, Mary D., see Nagle, Mary D.
Cannon, Ralph, author, 21:427
Cannon, Walter, editor, 39:298
Cannon City, Rice County, mills, 11:
271, 280; frontier life, 19:238;
plow factory, 23:324; Eggleston's
stay, 26:242, 33:192, 39:267;
ghost town, 35:12, 21
Cannon Falls, roads, 11:394, 17:268;
stage line, 11:402, 30:70; mill,
12:338; churches, 13:118, 15:481;
frontier life, 15:486, 19:114;
baseball club, 19:169; commercial
club, 20:83; business, 34:127
Cannon Falls Lyceum, minutes, 23:301
Cannon Lake, Rice County, trading
post, 11:382
Cannon River, Rice, Goodhue counties,
14:220, 29:210; steamboating, 17:
262
Cannon River Valley, settled, 11:171,
22:111, 170-172, 26:332, 31:20,
35:110-112; milling, 11:271-282,
12:80, 338, 16:253, 28:331, 35:13;
fur trade, 11:382, 16:100; mounds,
16:307, 27:261
Cannonball River, see Cannon River
Canoes and canoe travel, cottonwood,
11:182; routes, 11:233, 14:85, 17:
307, 20:79, 22:271, 439, 23:251n,
28:11n, 29:133, 31:23, 32:242, 34:
46, 36:295, 38:26, 27; in fur
trade, 11:258, 426, 15:160, 28:6,
10, 58, 148, 33:130, 261, 39:256,
40:158, 162, 165, 359; Mississippi
River, 16:78, 29:217, 36:43;
races, 16:480, 33:91; Henry Lewis' journey, 17:150-158, 288-301,
421-436; construction and maintenance, 21:93, 22:88, 23:127, 137,
139, 143, 246, 281, 385, 31:94,

36:238; birch-bark, 23:61, 32:84,
88, 33:105, 106, 107, 40:158; described, 23:135; depicted, 33:
187, 34:45, 49, 52, 40:275; recreational, 34:46, 48, 132, 36:43; in
underwater exploration, 38:25, 29,
30, 32, 33; in mail transporta-
tion, 40:78, 275. See also Cass,
Lewis: expedition; Le Conte,
Joseph
Canosia, St. Louis County, post of-
fice, 34:186
Cansu Paha, Yellow Medicine County,
mission, 11:94
Canton, Thomas, 21:334
Canton Mine, St. Louis County, de-
veloped, 34:44
Canton Presbyterian Church, anniver-
sary, 15:481
Cantwell, Frank ("Jumbo"), 11:104
Cantwell, Robert, author, 20:116
Canty, Thomas, 18:321
Cap au Gris, Lincoln County, Mo., 17:
434n
Cape, Wilson, author, 13:435
Capecchi, Joseph A., sculptor, 30:91
"Capital," steamboat, 37:296
Capital Publishing Co., St. Paul, 29:
107
Capitol Airlines, in Minnesota, 33:
240
Caplazi, Paul, pioneer, 25:314
Cappel, Jeanne L., author, 13:331
Cappon, Lester J., 26:85; review by,
25:281; work reviewed, 36:150; au-
thor, 24:70, 81, 375, 25:288, 310,
402, 28:370, 36:236, 38:333; ar-
chivist, 25:73, 84, 391, 26:278;
editor, 25:204; compiler, 25:401,
38:388
Capser, A. J., 14:219
Capser, Sister Gertrude, 35:264, 271
Capser, Leo, establishes museum, 35:
154; house, 38:352
Capser, Joseph, 20:364
Capuchin Order, 16:346
Card, Nelson, 25:139
Cárdenas, Gen. Lázaro, 15:258
Cardinal, Mrs. Clarence, author, 18:
224
Cardinal, Jean M., career, 12:76
Cardinal family, at Prairie du Chien,
Wis., 18:193
Cardle, Rev. Archibald, speaker, 14:
456; author, 15:112
Cardozo, Isaac N., 35:293
Carey, Deloris, speaker, 18:462
Carey, Edward, translator, 21:370
Carey, John R., 22:351
Carey, Richard E., 17:123; author,
17:233, 20:363
Cargill, Inc., Wayzata, history, 40:
315
Carheil, Father Etienne de, Jesuit,
19:278, 285, 287
Caribou, in Minnesota, 21:212, 23:
330n, 30:125, 128
Carimona, Fillmore County, roads, 11:
394, 396n; stage lines, 11:402;
county seat fight, 16:127; his-
tory, 21:220; ghost town, 35:12
Carimona House, register, 20:302
Carlander, Harriet B., work reviewed,
34:260
Carlander, Kenneth, 35:276
Carle, Warren, teacher, 13:140, 146

Carle, Mrs. Warren (J. L. Matherson),
13:140, 146
Carleton, Sir Guy, 19:292, 35:35;
governor of Quebec, 11:253, 256,
15:95, 96
Carleton, Mark A., 31:55
Carleton College, Northfield, founded, 15:251, 347, 24:182, 31:181;
depicted, 15:252; fire, 15:346;
student life, 17:129, 28:278;
characterized, 20:438; history,
21:115, 35:379, 40:256; source material, 25:289; building, 35:112;
athletics, 39:21
Carley, Kenneth, "The Sioux Campaign
of 1862," 38:99-114; "As Red Men
Viewed It," 38:126-149; "The Second Minnesota in the West," 38:
258-273; reviews by, 33:267, 346,
34:81, 165, 304, 343, 35:93, 37:
126, 255, 38:86, 39:77, 40:92;
works reviewed, 37:335, 38:35; author, 37:264, 308
Carli, Dr. Christopher, pioneer physician, 17:393, 19:463, 21:437,
23:95, 24:202, 36:193
Carli, Joseph, 24:203
Carli, Mrs. Lydia, 29:367
Carli, Dr. Paul, 34:174
Carli, Mrs. Paul, 24:196, 203, 349
Carlin, Lt. William P., at Fort Rip-
ley, 28:344
Carlisle Indian School, Carlisle,
Pa., 17:200
Carlisle Township, Otter Tail County,
history, 11:116
Carlsen, Clarence J., author, 13:428,
24:366
Carlson, Dr. Anton J., speaker, 21:
101
Carlson, Mrs. C. B., reminiscences,
21:451
Carlson, C. Emanuel, essay reviewed,
38:381
Carlson, C. J., 28:189
Carlson, Carl E., author, 36:35
Carlson, Carl J., author, 22:436
Carlson, Charles E., career, 25:307
Carlson, Charles G., storekeeper, 36:
201
Carlson, E. J., author, 16:225
Carlson, Edgar M., author, 28:286
Carlson, Judge Eskil, author, 29:278
Carlson, H. J., 28:189
Carlson, Helen, 25:41, 26:256
Carlson, John, speaker, 20:455
Carlson, John A., author, 19:236
Carlson, Leland H., work reviewed,
33:43
Carlson, Louis, 14:42
Carlson, Mrs. Louis, 14:31n
Carlson, Stan W., author, 20:206
Carlson, Walter, speaker, 29:363; au-
thor, 34:131; compiler, 36:239
Carlsson, Rev. Erland, 13:307, 17:
396, 30:263; letters, 15:361, 17:
329; at Chisago Lake, 24:190, 25:
314, 443, 28:76
Carlstedt, Ellworth T., "When Fond du
Lac Was British," 20:7-18; author,
15:114, 224, 17:468, 20:74, 26:
386, 27:71; speaker, 19:313
Carlstedt, P. G., author, 39:212
Carlston Township, Freeborn County,
history, 30:405
Carlton, C. C., author, 17:117
Carlton, Dr. E. C., speaker, 21:217

Carlton, Mrs. E. C., speaker, 23:109
Carlton, R. B., 24:354
Carlton, Richard P., career, 35:38
Carlton, Presbyterian church, 11:112;
railroads, 26:387, 30:70; history,
35:382; lumber camp, 36:78; bank,
39:246
Carlton County, history, 11:112, 18:
338, 35:382; population, 11:414;
Finnish settlements, 16:246, 25:
318, 319, 28:82, 35:333; county
seat, 16:287, 37:108n, 40:244;
newspaper, 19:120; mill, 22:220;
railroad lands, 37:96, 97, 99
Carlton County Agricultural Society,
19:364
Carlton County Farm Bureau, 20:100
Carlton County Historical Society,
organized, 30:164, 276; publication, 38:243
Carlton County Old Settlers Association, 23:300
Carlton County Vidette (Carlton), established, 19:120
Carlton House, Sask., post, 36:51
Carlyle, Thomas, 17:450, 19:6, 7
Carman, Harry J., author, 12:434, 15:
353, 19:347, 22:326
Carmer, Carl, author, 34:358, 35:39
Carmichael, Oliver C., "Higher Educa-
tion in Minnesota," 34:90-95
Carmichael, Thomas, log mark, 26:135,
136
Carmony, Donald F., author, 28:78
Carnegie, Andrew, 39:95; mining in-
terests, 16:26, 23:361, 362; let-
ter, 18:316; library sponsor, 22:
363
Carnegie Endowment for International
Peace, 18:12, 20:319, 23:201, 26:
363; publications, 22:62-65, 24:
45, 152-154
Carnegie Steel Co., Minnesota hold-
ings, 23:362. See also U.S. Steel
Corp.
Carney, Jim, author, 37:43
Carney, Mary V., author, 12:309
Carney, Thomas, colonizer, 34:132
Caroline, queen of England, medal,
40:204
Caroline, Blue Earth County, railroad
village, 18:469; post office, 22:
444
Caron, Henry, translator, 21:205
Carondelet, Baron de, 19:295, 33:302
Carp Lake, Lake County, fur trade
route, 37:247
Carp River, Mich., 23:242
Carpatho-Russians, Mesabi Range, 27:
212, 213
Carpenter, Sgt. Alfred P., letter,
38:251, 253, 255, 256
Carpenter, C. P., publisher, 15:245,
35:302, 303
Carpenter, Cephas W., 16:71; biogra-
phy, 22:104
Carpenter, Charles W., 16:445
Carpenter, Mrs. E. A., 13:122
Carpenter, Elbert L., 33:99, 333, 334
Carpenter, Mrs. Elbert L., 33:334
Carpenter, F. H., politician, 34:226
Carpenter, Horace T., publisher, 26:
301
Carpenter, Laura H., author, 31:92
Carpenter, Leonard G., 32:57
Carpenter, Matthew H., career, 34:209
Carpenter, Ruth H., speaker, 22:218

Carpenter, Samuel B., 16:445
Carpenter, William B., author, 21:364
Carpenter family, genealogy, 35:248
Carr, "Jim," 12:178
Carr, "Maggie," 12:178
Carr, Mrs. O. M., speaker, 13:120
Carr, R. D. V., pioneer journalist, 13:119; speaker, 17:483
Carr, Robert, pioneer, 23:25
Carr Lake, Beltrami County, history, 26:396
Carr Lake Community Club, 26:396
Carr Lake Farmers Club, 19:364
Carranza, Venustiano, 17:165
Carrel, Alexis, correspondence, 25:64
Carrière, Joseph M., author, 28:177
Carroll, Gladys Hasty, novelist, 23:120n
Carroll, Horace B., author, 28:175
Carroll, John A., work reviewed, 38:237
Carroll, Joseph, ticket agent, 34:174
Carroll, Walter N., biography, 19:214
Carrollton Township, Fillmore County, Norwegian settlement, 12:268
Carson, G. E., merchant, 23:24, 25
Carson, G. M., pioneer, 23:25
Carson, Gerald, works reviewed, 34:121, 38:39
Carson, M. E., merchant, 23:24; post-master, 23:25
Carson, P. S., sheep raiser, 26:111
Carson, William G. B., work reviewed, 31:116; author, 14:114
Carson Pirie Scott, Chicago, depart-ment store, 40:107
Carstenson, Vernon, reviews by, 30:57-59, 31:41, 32:117, 176, 33:261, 34:124; works reviewed, 30:380-382, 36:235, 38:329; author, 30:95, 31:64, 32:128, 192, 37:134
Carsteson, Casper, 14:41, 42
Carte, D'Oyly, 17:325
Carter, Charlotte I., 37:20
Carter, Clarence E., 17:4; reviews by, 22:73-76, 23:258, 24:343; works reviewed, 16:202-205, 17:452, 24:234, 25:271, 26:362, 30:57-59, 31:48, 240; author, 22:82, 24:353, 26:264, 36:236; editor, 14:336, 19:217, 21:423, 36:85, 323
Carter, Gulielmus, 21:443
Carter, Harvey L., author, 35:200
Carter, Hodding, work reviewed, 24:53
Carter, John, author, 29:331
Carter, Lepha A., diary, 21:443
Carter, Marjory D., 18:336; speaker, 17:358, 18:62, 64, 111
Carter, Perry J., author, 20:217, 361, 465; speaker, 22:442
Carter, Sibyl, Episcopal deaconess, 20:310, 344, 36:35
Carter, Theodore G., papers, 18:210, 26:67
Carter family, theatrical troupe, 40:363
Carteret, Sir George, 16:393-395, 399, 422n, 423, 17:75; career, 16:396
Carteret, Philip, governor of New Jersey, 16:422, 425n
Cartier, Sir George E., in Riel Re-bellion, 33:183
Cartier, Jacques, 13:395, 18:383, 385, 36:70; explorer, 15:94, 32:112, 35:151, 379; monument, 15:476; portraits, 16:480

Cartland, Grace, actress, 28:113, 115, 33:175
Cartwright, David W., author, 22:194, 23:40
Cartwright, Col. George, 16:393, 395, 404, 410, 414n, 17:75
Cartwright, William, 25:191
Cartwright, William H., Jr., author, 23:400, 24:89, 191
Caruso, Enrico, 33:322
Caruso, John A., review by, 40:141; works reviewed, 37:301, 40:259
Caruthers, W. A., 14:262
Carver, Clifford N., author, 17:216
Carver, Helen, pioneer, 33:4
Carver, Capt. Henry, pioneer, 33:4
Carver, Mrs. Henry L., 38:77n
Carver, Jonathan, 13:109; grant, 11:94, 13:99, 14:216, 17:95, 18:439, 19:95, 22:101, 26:32, 154, 27:71, 31:241; career, 11:110, 325, 17:216, 26:164; in Northwest, 11:265, 266, 377, 14:374, 375, 15:479, 16:453, 17:196, 18:193, 194, 22:206, 31:196, 36:274, 279, 40:314; on Mississippi, 11:383, 16:152-165, 30:217; at Grand Portage, 12:365-367, 20:10; papers, 13:320, 25:267, 34:338; author, 14:334, 23:239n, 24:231, 34:154-159, 268, 35:97, 248, 36:100, 39:198; portrait, 26:283, 34:156; cave, 30:208; cen-tennial, 30:301, 305; map maker, 36:277
Carver, Rufus, 34:157
Carver, W. F., biography, 35:377
Carver brothers, logging operations, 29:139, 146
Carver family, genealogy, 17:216
Carver, pioneer life, 12:449; flour mill, 15:28; Germans, 28:24, 36, 32:100, 34:242; described, 30:112; platted, 34:264
Carver County, churches, 11:459, 13:447, 14:451, 24:214; history, 12:201, 14:235, 15:245, 16:364, 32:76, 34:264, 36:106; ethnic groups, 15:114, 16:493, 18:338, 22:335, 28:25, 33:180, 251; frontier life, 15:133, 37:72, 73, 77; agricul-ture, 18:408, 19:21-31, 27:175; first school, 20:143n; horticul-ture, 21:85; literary societies, 24:214, 219; politics, 28:31-35, 34:227, 35:306; medicine, 29:265, 353; name, 34:158; poor farm, 38:368, 369
Carver County German Reading Society, library, 23:294, 397, 24:220-223; history, 24:214-225
Carver County Historical Society, 25:208, 26:283, 28:295; organized, 21:333, 443; museum, 22:105, 338, 23:100, 293-295, 24:214, 25:95, 312, 406, 26:88, 392, 27:74, 29:90, 30:78, 399; collections, 23:397, 27:171; meetings, 24:85, 28:85; publications, 30:276
Carver County Telephone Co., 20:356
Carver County War History Committee, 23:390
Carver Grays, volunteer guards, 16:171
Carver's Cave, St. Paul, 20:124, 28:317, 33:122; described, 21:84, 23:340, 30:208
Carwell Mill, Kingston, 11:116
Cary, Mary, author, 31:61

Cary, Robert, author, 12:100, 19:225
Cary, William, artist, 37:262, 40:150n
Casadesus, Robert, pianist, 39:63
Casagrande, Joseph B., author, 35:244
Cascade, Cook County, railroad, 34:181; settled, 34:184; forest fire, 36:133-136
Cascade Junction, St. Louis County, railroad station, 34:184
Cascade Lake, Cook County, logging railroad, 36:132
Cascade Township, Olmsted County, frontier life, 11:185
Casco, Wis., Belgian settlement, 24:176
Case, Benton J., 16:93
Case, Charles M., 16:93
Case, Charles M., Jr., 16:93
Case, Clifford, Senator, 40:134
Case, J. Mrs. George P., 19:84, 27:73
Case, J. I., Co., Racine, Wis., thresher manufacturers, 23:324, 24:302; history, 34:348
Case, James R., sawmill owner, 13:132, 150
Case, Jerome I., manufacturer, 34:348
Case, John H., author, 14:438
Case, Lynn M., editor, 15:121
Case, S. L., author, 16:364
Casey, C. H., 12:454
Casey, Lyman R., politician, 35:68
Casey, P. J., author, 35:156
Casey, R. E., speaker, 20:214
Casey, Ralph D., review by, 40:302
Casey, Robert J., work reviewed, 30:146
Casey, Silas, 25:36
Casey, W. J., author, 20:218, 432
Casket, literary magazine, 30:203
Casper, Henry W., work reviewed, 40:352
Cass, Andrew R., 16:186
Cass, Lewis, 25:89, 33:20, 34:207, 35:290, 291, 37:302; explorer, 11:81, 12:317, 16:349, 453, 18:184, 26:276, 33:263, 37:62; career, 11:110, 12:440, 14:342, 32:117; Indi-an commissioner, 11:208, 28:277, 31:96; governor, 11:431, 25:371, 36:247, 37:79; expedition, 12:216, 15:425, 17:95, 19:349, 20:78, 21:93, 23:40, 75, 126-148, 233-252, 271, 328-348, 24:371, 372, 25:272, 26:363, 380, 31:93-97, 190, 33:345, 36:184; secretary of state, 28:21; presidential candidate, 30:104, 189, 35:354, 39:143; papers, 34:212, 35:383; secretary of war, 36:323, 40:23-26
Cass County, lumber industry, 12:428; records, 21:111, 22:211; historic sites, 22:220; museum, 22:343, 444; archaeology, 26:321; name, 30:189, 31:97
Cass County Development Association, 19:98
Cass County Historical Society, or-ganized, 30:276
Cass Lake (village), museum, 18:222, 281, 19:115, 230, 359, 22:343, 444, 23:13, 28:193, 295
Cass (Upper Red Cedar) Lake, Cass and Beltrami counties, post, 11:369, 14:231, 20:14, 22:357, 24:230; land office, 11:447, 12:387; Schoolcraft's visit, 12:216, 13:

287, 18:180, 184, 185n, 23:333n; name, 12:219, 30:189, 31:97; fort, 13:99; printing press, 15:20, 22, 23, 18:450, 20:78; missions, 19: 120, 20:80, 90; historic sites, 22:220; Indian agency, 23:93; lumber industry, 29:146, 148; history, 30:394, 35:338

Cass Lake Junior Chamber of Commerce, 22:343

Cassel, H., author, 18:71

Cassel, Peter, colonizer, 12:415, 17: 401, 31:27

Casselton, N.D., bonanza farming, 20: 404, 33:69, 70

Casserly, Eugene, California Senator, 37:99, 100

Cassidy, George W., artist, 33:287

Cassidy, Sgt. Hugh, 25:142, 143

Cassidy, Mrs. Thomas J., 11:439

Cassina Lake, see Cass Lake

Cassville, Wis., pictured, 17:134n; pioneer life, 18:326; historic house, 30:270; described, 33:116

Castle, Henry A., 35:220, 221, 37: 204; journalist, 14:394, 16:364; G.A.R. leader, 16:433, 440, 443, 38:78; letters, 17:337; author, 36:82

Castle, Lewis G., 37:260

Castle Garden, New York City, 20:255

Castle Rock, mounds, 16:309; baseball, 21:340

Castruccio, Giuseppe, speaker, 13:83

Caswell, Irving A., author, 12:447, 13:214, 340, 447, 14:118, 22:220

Caswell, Mrs. Irving A., speaker, 16: 489, 17:354

Cataract Fire Engine Co., St. Anthony, 35:123

Cataract Flour Mill, Minneapolis, built, 24:133

Cataract Hotel, Minneapolis, 12:402

Cataract Island, Falls of St. Anthony, 33:124, 125

Cataract Street, Minneapolis, 16:182

Cataraqui, Ont., post, 12:350

Catawba Indians, in fur trade, 40:208

Cate, James L., works reviewed, 29: 345, 30:255, 31:247

Cater, Harold D., MHS reports, 30:36-49, 293-330; "Sky Pilot Primitive," 34:59-66; reviews by, 29: 344, 32:109, 33:35, 216; MHS director, 29:281; speaker, 30:88, 363, 34:43; resignation, 34:175

Cater, Mrs. Harold D. (Virginia H.), pianist, 30:289

Caterpillar Tractor Co., Peoria, Ill., history, 34:312

Catfish Creek, Iowa, lead mines, 12: 77

Cathcart, Mrs. Alexander H., (Rebecca Marshall), 28:317; author, 39:51, 317

Cathcart, J. S., 22:170, 173

Cathedral High School, St. Cloud, 16: 372

Cathedral of Our Merciful Saviour (Episcopal), Faribault, 15:129, 16:119, 380

Cathedral of St. Paul (Catholic), history, 20:446; depicted, 26:173, 39:133 (cover); architecture, 39: 153-162

Cather, Willa, 16:106, 20:438, 26: 356, 32:116, 250, 34:307; author,

20:111, 23:116, 125, 157, 40:305

Catherine, Mother M., essay reviewed, 38:193

Catholic Aid Association of Minnesota, 20:460, 22:335

Catholic Bulletin (St. Paul), founded, 17:129

Catholic church, Iowa, 11:210, 20: 338, 28:184, 33:356, 35:136, 137; Canada, 11:306, 16:461, 17:454, 18:376, 22:287, 24:41, 39:309; educational program, 12:205, 13:313, 14:361, 16:333, 363, 372, 483, 17: 83, 219, 349, 473, 20:62, 23:96, 191, 24:366, 25:372-374, 27:161, 271, 28:72, 29:81, 353, 30:154, 33:305, 34:105n, 154, 214, 35:133-139, 243, 36:24, 39:128; colonization work, 13:333, 14:355, 20:331, 463, 21:73-76, 191, 192, 210, 23: 191, 31:21, 35:133-139, 205-213, 325, 339, 37:184; Northwest, 14: 230, 15:104, 455, 16:114, 119, 17: 83-85, 18:89, 436, 38:302, 39:128; French regime, 14:338; ethnic groups, 16:344, 17:85, 27:213, 31: 29, 32:15, 33:187, 305, 327, 34: 171, 343, 35:33, 51, 61, 155, 193, 36:35, 198, 37:133, 184, 39:210; Minnesota dioceses, 16:371, 20: 446, 21:102, 33:54, 185, 188, 35: 137, 39:35, 188, 299; St. Paul diocese and archdiocese, 17:102, 33:223, 34:313, 39:35, 299; opposed, 19:219, 34:343, 37:164; archives, 20:423, 27:252, 29:79, 39: 35; Eucharistic Congress, 22:334, 23:97; relations with Knights of Labor, 22:382, 30:254; Wisconsin, 23:286, 26:272, 29:354, 35:152; centennials, 25:88; architecture, 26:173; in Civil War, 26:304, 27: 43, 34:129; in politics, 28:34, 36, 32:15, 33:305, 34:229, 35:61, 243, 39:96; policies, 28:257; chaplains, 34:129; liturgical movement, 35:372; historic sites, 36:105; publications, 36:325; Middle West, 38:203; ecumenical movement, 38:335; welfare activities, 39:26, 40:359; Nebraska, 40:352. See also various churchmen, orders, individual parishes and communities

Catholic Church of the Incarnation, Minneapolis, 16:121

Catholic City Federation of St. Paul, 17:85

Catholic Colonization Bureau, 11:436, 31:21, 35:206, 211

Catholic Colonization Society, organized, 15:236

Catholic Historical Society of St. Paul, reorganized, 14:229, 15:65, 72, 26:266; activities, 15:76, 218, 361, 16:59, 18:57; publications, 15:104, 455, 17:61, 83-85, 18:89; manuscript collections, 15: 217, 16:54, 17:102; meetings, 16: 234, 17:229

Catholic Indian Bureau, history, 34: 123

Catholic Industrial School of Minnesota, St. Paul, Clontarf, 13:100, 17:83, 21:78, 35:134, 135, 136

Catholic missions, Red River settlements, 11:94, 13:426, 21:432, 22:

286, 27:166, 31:240; among Chippewa, 11:205, 13:187, 18:268, 331, 23:402, 24:262, 26:275, 28:191, 29:168, 31:54, 34:305; Northwest, 11:305-307, 325, 442, 14:339, 17: 84, 113, 18:89, 437, 20:79, 23: 366, 26:56, 30:290, 31:239, 35: 380; among Sioux, 11:316, 345, 13: 339; schools, 12:205, 13:339, 19: 379; Dakota Territory, 12:437, 23: 383, 29:173; French, 15:455, 17: 473, 20:327, 28:61, 30:249, 34: 216; Wisconsin, 16:347, 23:285, 29:355; Minnesota, 17:473, 25:193, 28:277, 38:193; Slovenian, 22:200, 25:194, 30:392, 33:185; Austrian, 26:146; U.S., 34:123. See also Benedictine Order, Jesuits, individual missions and missionaries

Catholic Order of Foresters, St. Agnes Court, archives, 20:35, 82

Catholic Orphan Asylum, St. Paul, 16: 369

Catholic University of America, Washington, D.C., history, 31:187, 35: 243

Catlin, Francis, letters, 40:311

Catlin, Frederick M., memorial, 12: 194

Catlin, George, career, 11:110, 15: 471, 27:254, 29:349, 350, 30:139-141, 34:215, 36:322, 37:32, 40: 144; explorer, 11:216, 17:224, 347, 18:458, 22:333, 28:184, 31: 193, 35:97, 36:277; in Minnesota, 13:375, 15:156, 454, 16:232, 18: 156, 20:308, 378, 391, 31:196, 198-200, 202, 207, 36:18-21, 37: 62; author, 14:424, 16:33, 351, 22:13, 154, 155n, 215, 31:178, 35: 180, 38:385; artist, 17:456, 21: 151, 431, 24:365, 26:214n, 359, 27:63, 29:60, 31:54-56, 197, 32: 188, 33:92 (cover), 187, 264, 350, 34:117, 126, 346, 35:88, 200, 334, 379, 380, 36:236, 37:133, 306, 39: 261, 40:199; collector, 18:158, 30:260; exhibits, 23:181, 29:61, 78, 30:176, 34:121, 35:246; in Britain, 25:297

Catlin, Dr. Hiram W., diary, 23:75

Catlin, John C., politician, 14:129, 36:261

Catlin, Putnam, letters, 40:311

Catlinite (pipestone), geology, 15: 143; analyzed, 21:424; used by Indians, 26:280, 40:206, 209; described, 29:262; quarrying methods, 34:314; legend, 37:62. See also Pipestone National Monument

Cats, Jacques, 20:423, 424

Catt, Carrie C., feminist, 39:12

Cattle industry, range, 12:176, 13: 93, 33:86; shipping, 31:122, 40: 232; historic sites, 40:404. See also Dairy industry, Livestock industry

Catton, Bruce, 39:266; work reviewed, 33:87; editor, 34:168; author, 35: 153

Cattron, Lawrence H., author, 16:121

Caughey, John W., author, 24:172, 28: 172

Caulfield, John, businessman, 40:228, 230

Cavalier County, N.D., place names, 38:385

Cavanaugh, James M., Congressman, 14:
164, 191, 254n; convention dele-
gate, 37:47, 48, 49
Cavelier, Jean, journal, 20:67, 439,
24:365
Cavert, W. L., author, 12:100, 35:97
Cavileer, Charles T., 15:370, 16:486;
at Pembina, 13:241, 40:83; papers,
22:336, 27:165, 36:262
Cavileer, Lulu, author, 40:83
Cavill, J. C., Indian agent, 16:321
Cavin, Brooks, 38:352; review by, 40:
408
Cawein, Madison, poet, 26:308
Caxton Printers, Caldwell, Idaho,
publications, 20:115
Cay, Edwin S., speaker, 19:310; au-
thor, 19:452
"Cayuga," steamboat, 34:15
Cayuga Indians, in fur trade, 40:208
Cayuse Indians, 11:81
Cazeaux, Pierre, author, 21:370
Cazneau, William L., colonizer, 34:
75n
"Cecilia," steamboat, 13:233, 234,
238
Cedar City, Mower County, ghost town,
16:367
Cedar Falls, Iowa, museum, 11:106;
lecture series, 21:326; history,
25:71
Cedar Grove, Wis., Dutch settlement,
28:120, 368
Cedar Island Lake, Hennepin County,
19:138
Cedar Lake, Man., fur trade, 11:264,
40:172
Cedar Lake, Minneapolis, described,
30:117; map, 35:24, 27
Cedar (Lower Red Cedar) Lake, Aitkin
County, trading post, 11:372, 20:
14
Cedar Lake Township, Scott County,
church, 12:451; settled, 20:218,
432; elections, 28:34, 35:350
Cedar Mills Township, Meeker County,
school, 11:220
Cedar Rapids, Iowa, Czech settlement,
25:300
Cedar Rapids, Iowa Falls and North-
western Land and Town Lot Co., 15:
491
Cedar River Valley, Dodge and Mower
counties, roads, 21:233
Cedar Township, Martin County, Norwegian settlement, 12:274
Cedar Valley Seminary, Osage, Iowa,
22:159
Cedarville, Martin County, ghost
town, 14:459, 15:71
Cederstam, Pehr A., at Chisago Lake,
17:402, 403, 24:190
Celtic World (Minneapolis), 16:338
Cemeteries, Woodlawn, Winona, 11:446;
Jamptland, Goodhue County, 12:450;
Chippewa, 13:442, 16:321; Vasa
Township, Washington County, 14:
426-428; Grant County, 14:457;
Winsted, 16:488; Mankato, 16:493,
17:234; Oakland, St. Paul, 17:54,
57; survey, 17:55, 65; abandoned,
17:234, 24:181; Oak Hill, Excel-
sior, 17:336; Quaker, 18:254;
Traverse des Sioux, 20:464; military, Fort Ridgely, 21:438; Lay-
man's, Minneapolis, 22:222
Censorship, legal cases, 24:373; in

Civil War, 25:132. See also Minnesota Commission of Public Safety
Census, Minnesota, 1857, 12:191, 13:
59, 426, 14:179n, 243, 253-261,
436, 17:359, 22:101, 29:172, 30:
162; 1850, 16:64, 17:393, 18:55;
Red River Valley, 16:230; 1865,
16:427; 1860, 17:57, 28:20, 33;
Illinois, 17:221; use, 18:64, 23:
39, 167, 367; Wisconsin Territory,
19:350; 1840, 20:452, 21:326; Twin
Cities recount, 21:329; 1820 and
1830, 21:428; agriculture, 23:326;
Minnesota, 1875, 28:303; Texas,
31:116; guides, 33:44, 39:210; microfilm, 34:212, 40:360
Centennial Exposition, Philadelphia,
1876, 40:353
Centennial Society, Elk River, his-
tory, 17:241
Center, Mrs. Amelia H., 13:445
Center City, 37:88; Swedish settle-
ment, 35:337, 38:243
Center Creek Township, Martin County,
history, 11:463
Center Grove, Otter Tail County, camp
meeting, 31:82
Centerville Township, Anoka County,
Sioux village, 13:248, 401; ar-
chaeology, 22:210
Central Baptist Church, Minneapolis,
17:337
Central Conference of Teamsters, 37:
185
Central Cooperative Exchange, 38:203
Central Cooperative Oil Association,
Steele County, 23:200
Central Cooperative Wholesale, Supe-
rior, Wis., 25:301; history, 17:
348, 22:315
Central High School, Minneapolis, 38:
22; athletics, 39:19, 20
Central High School, St. Paul, 24:
209, 40:146; history, 16:369; lab-
oratory, 24:211, 239
Central House, St. Cloud, 24:332
Central House, St. Paul, 16:377, 19:
134, 29:35; legislative meeting,
18:106, 22:100, 30:196
Central Labor Union, Chicago, 22:383
Central Livestock Association, South
St. Paul, 35:334
Central Pacific Railroad, 11:190, 21:
313
Central Park, St. Paul, 12:458
Central Park Methodist Church, St.
Paul, 14:363
Central Point, Goodhue County, saw-
mill, 16:256
Central Railroad Co., history, 34:328
Central Republican (Faribault) poli-
cies, 20:270-286
Central University, Hastings, 18:409
Central Verein, meeting, 22:335
Century Gazette (Morrison, Ill.), 37:
39
Century of Progress Exposition, Chi-
cago, 12:188, 26:252
Čermák, Rev. Jaroslav, 15:31
Cerny, George, author, 39:129
Cerro Gordo County, Iowa, townsites,
27:355
Cerro Gordo Township, Lac qui Parle
County, Norwegian settlement, 12:
275n
Chaboillez, ---, trader, 40:145
Chaboillez, Charles J. B., 13:439;

trader, 11:366, 367, 12:438, 23:
272; journals, 36:324, 37:37
Chadbourn, C. H. dairyman, 27:120
Chadbourn, Charles N., 17:320
Chadbourne, R. W., 19:184n
Chadron, Neb., museum, 34:353
Chadwick, Ransom A., diary, 17:98
Chafee, Zechariah, Jr., author, 24:
373
Chafetz, Henry, author, 37:345
Chaffee, James F., Methodist minis-
ter, 26:243
Chaffee, Samuel, 22:221
Chahinkapa Park, Wahpeton, N.D., 18:
104
Chaillu, P. B. du, lecturer, 11:158
Chalkley, Katherine F., work re-
viewed, 23:80
Chalmers, J. H., speaker, 29:275
Chalmers, J. W., author, 37:134
Chalmers automobile, 38:207
Chalybeate Springs, St. Anthony, 18:
409, 25:91, 35:219
Chamber of Commerce Building, Minne-
apolis, 22:385
Chamberlain, ---, 18:131
Chamberlain, A. T., 16:176
Chamberlain, Dora, 14:305
Chamberlain, Ella, 14:305
Chamberlain, Mrs. Emily, 14:305, 306,
310, 311
Chamberlain, George, author, 24:78
Chamberlain, George, Freeborn County
pioneer, 14:305, 306
Chamberlain, John, 38:387; work re-
viewed, 14:200-202
Chamberlain, Luther, author, 11:74
Chamberlain, Paul F., speaker, 15:138
Chamberlain, Selah, 24:96, 40:110,
112
Chamberlain, Thomas C., educator, 30:
381
Chamberlin, Mrs. M. E., 17:231
Chamberlin, W. H., author, 25:67
Chambers, Alex, 19:239
Chambers, Clarke A., 39:300, 40:316,
410; reviews by, 34:342, 35:89;
work reviewed, 39:26; author, 38:
203
Chambers, John S., author, 26:145
Chambers, Julius J., 11:110, 12:226;
author, 12:228
Chambers, William, ferry operator,
30:121n
Chambliss, Charles E., author, 23:180
Chamlee, Mario, singer, 39:59, 60
Champagne, Rev. Antoine P., author,
27:260, 35:242, 36:190
Champigny, marquis de, 19:287, 396
Champion Township, Wilkin County,
settled, 18:224
Champion, Winona baseball club, 19:
165
Champion reaper, 24:292
Champlain, Samuel de, 13:395, 19:69,
31:239, 35:151, 379; explorer, 12:
347, 25:273, 32:112, 215, 36:70;
cartographer, 12:348, 27:219, 40:
356; in fur trade, 18:386; author,
36:30
Champlain Society, 15:477, 16:475,
18:244, 19:109; publications, 16:
105, 200, 19:104, 20:71
Champlin, Ezra T., legislator, 35:
302, 303
Champlin, history, 11:227, 17:125,
26:178; mill, 16:492

Champlin Township, Hennepin County, archives, 17:466
Champney, Stella M., author, 13:209
Chanarambie Township, Murray County, Sioux ceremonials, 34:355
Chancellorsville, Va., battle, 25: 345-347, 38:246, 250n
Chandesota, Sioux woman, 12:126
Chandler, Dr. Benjamin, 27:236
Chandler, Clayborne, pioneer, 23:319
Chandler Mine, Vermilion Range, 18: 473, 35:338
Chandonnet, Charles, trader, 21:147
Chaney, Clarence R., MHS president, 33:236, 242; artist, 33:310
Chanhassen (village and township), Carver County, settled, 19:141, 22:173, 28:333, 31:20; history, 20:140-145; records, 20:329, 506
Chankaska Creek, Le Sueur County, 11: 171n
Channer, Rev. Elwyn, 31:78
Channing, Edward, historian, 19:82, 435, 21:302, 34:81
Channing, Ellery, 16:35
Channing, William Ellery, 23:261
Chanute, Octave, aeronaut, 40:268n
Chapel, Charles E., work reviewed, 38:197
Chapel of St. Paul, 37:154n; established, 11:108, 22:51, 23:97, 30: 5, 206, 34:131n, 39:153; history, 12:397, 26:173, 30:2; depicted, 21:84, 25:10, 56, 27:271, 29:209, 39:162; hospital, 33:268, 312
Chapelle, Howard I., work reviewed, 39:256
Chapin, Earl V., 23:104; "History of the Roseau Valley," 24:318-327; author, 24:353, 25:90, 26:150, 290, 28:178, 375, 383, 29:83, 89, 270, 30:70, 76, 82, 34:217
Chapin, F. Stuart, author, 26:279
Chapin, Harold C., 18:138
Chapin, Jane L., editor, 17:111, 445, 18:103
Chapin Hall House, Hudson, Wis., 21: 430
Chapman, A. H., diary, 27:247
Chapman, Bela, trader, 11:370, 17: 210, 26:362
Chapman, David F., author, 24:263
Chapman, E. P. J., speaker, 18:462
Chapman, Edward G., 21:195
Chapman, George H., 20:196
Chapman, H. H., author, 11:215
Chapman, John (Johnny Appleseed), folk hero, 18:452, 22:313, 26:166, 28:56; biography, 28:281, 34:201
Chapman, Louise, speaker, 15:241; author, 16:238
Chapman, Timothy, 23:322n
Chapman, William, actor, 33:39
Chapman, William M., work reviewed, 40:46
Chapman, William W., 19:351, 460
Chapman family, 26:357
Chapple, W. W., composer, 23:172
Charbonneau, Toussaint, 14:204, 40: 193
Chardon, François A., trader, 15:430; journal, 12:316
Chardon, Ohio, land deeds, 15:223
Charity Islands, Lake Huron, 23:140n
Charles II, king of England, 16:395, 396, 415, 418; letter, 16:419; medals, 25:266; portraits, 26:274

Charles, John, trader, 20:72
Charles Lake, Ramsey County, 40:230
"Charles W. Wetmore," steamer, 22:349
Charless, Joseph, 15:13
Charleston, S.C., in Civil War, 25: 228, 245, 256, 40:278; Democratic convention, 37:46-51, 54
Charlestown, Redwood County, grasshopper plague, 37:210
Charlesworth, Hector, 14:449
Charlevoix, Pierre F. X. de, explorer, 23:239n, 243, 31:195
Charlottenburg, Washington County, German settlement, 24:271
Charlton, David, surveyor, 40:67
Charlton, Kandiyohi County, name, 40: 68
Charnwood, Godfrey R. B., author, 28: 360
Charpentier, Celine, artist, 38:20n, 43, 52n, 62n, 85n, 215n, 39:23n, 64n
Charter, Mrs. Chester, 22:105; speaker, 25:313
Charter Oak Mining Co., Detroit, Mich., 27:153
Charters, W. W., author, 25:392
Chartres, Duc de, 25:138
Chase, Alexander R., with Cass expedition, 23:135, 239, 248, 328, 347; maps Sandy Lake, 334
Chase, Mrs. C. E., 17:119, 19:114
Chase, Carlo, speaker, 17:484
Chase, Carroll, author, 26:174
Chase, Charles L., territorial secretary, 14:162, 163, 249, 36:9
Chase, Harold W., editor, 39:210
Chase, Heber, author, 21:369
Chase, Lt. John, 25:29
Chase, Jonathan, log mark, 26:135
Chase, Josiah, 19:184n
Chase, L. A., author, 25:95
Chase, Rev. M., 29:215
Chase, Mary Ellen, work reviewed, 21: 70; author, 20:116
Chase, Milan M., diaries, 20:195
Chase, Ray P., 11:31
Chase, Roe G., editor, 38:305
Chase, Salmon P., secretary of treasury, 20:281, 284, 22:129, 23:135n, 37:330, 40:270n, 271; Supreme Court justice, 20:285; politician, 23:261, 32:28
Chase, Stuart, author, 12:418
Chase, Warren, steamboat captain, 33: 15
Chase, Wayland J., author, 16:115
Chase, Zina W., diary, 16:217, 17:54
Chase's Landing, Wis., road, 40:245
Chaska, Sioux Indian, 38:133, 135, 39:261
Chaska, river port, 11:132, 138; townsites, 14:435, 40:74; Moravians, 14:451, 20:100, 330, 24:84; newspapers, 16:127, 493, 18:113, 27:327; G.A.R. post, 16:431; ferry, 17:241; Germans, 24:214, 32: 100, 34:240-242; log cabins, 37: 71; railroad, 39:92
Chaska Thalbote, German paper, 35:328
Chaska Township, Carver County, election, 28:33
Chatelain, Verne E., 13:383, 14:329, 18:281, 22:316, 25:76; "The Public Land Officer," 12:379-389; "Federal Land Policy," 22:227-248; reviews by, 11:432-434, 23:161-163,

357-359, 25:69-71; assistant superintendent, 12:426; speaker, 13: 280, 15:229; author, 23:85
Chatfield, Judge Andrew G., 28:190, 37:333; letters, 12:192, 38:52; founds Belle Plaine, 15:252, 28: 260, 34:128; speaker, 22:254
Chatfield, Frank, 28:190
Chatfield, history, 11:113, 25:183, 30:52; roads, 11:394, 399, 23:401; stage lines, 11:398, 402, 406; banks, 13:117, 15:112, 16:364, 19: 465, 29:203, 40:110, 112, 116, 118; county seat fight, 15:136, 16:127; Lutheran church, 15:481; in Civil War, 16:176, 38:67, 258, 273; creamery, 19:157n, 24:104; records, 21:214, 24:89, 191, 383, 25:383; economic aspect, 24:95-110, 29:229; name, 28:190; wheat market, 29:31; centennial, 33:353; iron mining, 36:253; anti-abolition sentiment, 39:260; politics, 40:327n
Chatfield Academy, history, 11:113, 14:147, 24:191; curriculum, 14:148
Chatfield Commercial Club, 23:401, 24:96n
Chatfield Co-operative Creamery Association, 24:105
Chatfield Co-operative Livestock Association, 24:106n
Chatfield Democrat, pioneer newspaper, 14:403, 27:4-20
Chatfield Electric Light and Power Co., organized, 24:108
Chatfield Historical Society, 13:448, 16:240; meetings, 14:235, 456, 16: 242
Chatfield News, established, 14:397, 404; history, 18:114
Chatfield Railway Co., incorporated, 24:96
Chatfield Republican, 14:183
Chatham, see Lacy House
Chattanooga, Tenn., newspaper, 22: 422; in Civil War, 38:266-273
Chattanooga, Winona County, 20:364
Chaudière Falls, Ottawa River, 28:7, 10
Chautauqua Literary and Scientific Circle, history, 16:30, 29:321, 32:177, 37:340; in state prison, 29:321-333, 37:150; in Middle West, 31:57
Cheadle, Dr. Walter B., 16:113, 21: 204
Checkered Cloud (Mock-pe-en-dag-a-win), Sioux woman, 13:370, 372
Cheese making, see Dairy industry
Cheever, Harrison, letters, 14:216
Cheever, William A., mills, 15:350, 17:139, 147, 392, 29:265, 39:287; St. Anthony pioneer, 19:141, 145, 24:127, 130, 27:312; tower, 27: 287, 40:63, 64
Cheever family, at St. Anthony, 14: 216
Cheneaux Islands, Lake Huron, 23:143n
Chenevert, Mrs. Charles, 14:435
Cheney, Charles B., author, 25:202, 28:73, 183, 33:158n, 162
Cheney, E. G., 12:204; work reviewed, 22:183; author, 15:358, 28:376, 30:68
Cheney, William, meteorologist, 39: 112

Cheney family, musicians, 22:114, 124
Chengwatana Township, Pine County, German settlement, 31:224; ghost town, 34:358; Indian village, 37: 104, 105, 40:241, 243. See also Pine City
Chequamegon Bay, Wis., Lake Superior, post, 11:233, 244, 245, 12:352, 13:203, 19:287, 32:236; mission, 12:353; explored, 14:342, 15:176, 317, 321, 324, 19:273, 23:242, 34: 357
Cheritree and Farwell, St. Paul, 36: 283
Chermak, John, speaker, 13:118
Chernick, Jack, author, 23:388
Cherokee Indians, removal, 15:121, 37:271; Prairie Island, 37:281; in fur trade, 40:205, 208
Cherokee Lake, Cook County, forest fire, 36:134-136
Cherokee Strip, Kansas, opened, 12: 420
Cherry Grove, Fillmore County, post office, 12:433, 497
"Chesapeake," captured frigate, 40: 348-350
"Chesapeake," steamboat, 28:135
Chesapeake and Ohio Railroad, Lake Michigan ferry, 38:237
Chesley, Dr. Albert J., 19:111, 34: 35; author, 33:312
Chesley, Mrs. Dora, 14:461
Chessman, G. Wallace, author, 34:265
Chester, Job, family, 28:88
Chester, Joseph L., 22:34; career, 22:14
Chester, railroad stop, 12:49; baseball club, 19:180
Chester, Pa., mapped, 12:441
Chester Township, Red Lake County, history, 38:204
Chesterson, Thomas, cabin, 21:450
Chesterton, G. K., 14:448; author, 29:154
Chetanwekechetah, Sioux leader, 38: 149
Chevalier, Cadet, trader, 15:432
Chevalier, Paul, voyageur, 18:240
Chevallier, Charles, trader, 11:259
Chevallier family, traders, 11:258
Chew, Mrs. Anne C., editor, 24:157
"Cheyenne," steamboat, 21:254, 259n, 261, 269, 271
Cheyenne American Fur Co., 13:222
Cheyenne-Fort Laramie-Deadwood Trail, Wyo., S.D., map, 12:93
Cheyenne Indians, 11:209, 15:232, 16: 89, 27:6, 39:342, 40:358; portraits, 24:365; culture, 34:255, 39:259; North Dakota, 35:339
Chibiabos, Chippewa leader, 15:315
Chicago, exposition, 12:188, 26:252; immigrant agents, 13:40; name, 14: 376; visitors' accounts, 14:448; early printing, 15:14, 16:111; frontier fort, 15:380, 40:184; fur trade, 15:423, 17:335, 19:299, 34: 104, 40:219; rail center, 15:474, 21:239; described, 16:36, 17:41, 20:130, 23:348, 25:369, 30:141, 40:76; frontier era, 16:90; pictured, 17:221, 19:421; Haymarket riot, 18:140n; in 19th century, 20:403, 21:18, 23:87, 165, 24:128, 25:106, 27:281, 36:295, 37:178, 40:129, 273, 275, 277, 278; indus-

tries, 23:324, 40:125, 127; ethnic groups, 23:381, 25:394, 26:251, 27:210, 30:28, 189, 32:104, 168, 34:353; fire, 24:116, 28:186, 35: 153; war records, 25:93; auto race, 26:20; market center, 26: 115, 118, 125, 29:2, 7, 34:17, 24, 25, 39:68, 69, 40:232; cultural center, 26:73, 28:107; rivalry with Duluth, 33:65-67, 37:92, 93, 100, 112, 116, 117, 38:386, 39:66; city plan, 33:333; political conventions, 35:64, 66, 67, 75, 39: 102-104; port, 36:69; Pullman strike, 36:121, 122; mail route, 40:85, 87
Chicago Academy of Sciences, 23:370
Chicago and Northwestern Railroad, 11:181n, 17:345, 22:267, 24:97, 35:15n, 21; museum, 18:472; land sales, 24:177, 27:355; history, 25:196, 28:303, 29:170, 30:146, 33:219, 36:105
Chicago and Rock Island Railroad, see Rock Island Lines
Chicago Bay, Cook County, Lake Superior, fishing, 33:256
Chicago Board of Trade, 39:99, 100
Chicago, Burlington, and Northern Railway Co., records, 29:189. See also Burlington Lines
Chicago, Burlington & Quincy Railroad, see Burlington Lines
Chicago Choir Opera Co., 33:321
Chicago, Fulton and Iowa Railroad, 36:256
Chicago Great Western Railroad, 25: 92, 27:352, 35:21; history, 33: 356, 34:214, 35:45, 36:33, 105; built, 33:226, 36:321
Chicago Historical Society, 26:265; collections, 17:221, 464, 36:280; anniversaries, 27:354, 35:147
Chicago Landverein (Chicago Land Society), 16:363, 19:472, 21:111, 31:24; activities, 27:268, 36:327
Chicago, Milwaukee, and St. Paul Railroad, see Milwaukee Road
Chicago, Milwaukee, St. Paul and Pacific Railroad Co., history, 31: 120. See also Milwaukee Road
Chicago, Rock Island and Pacific Railroad, see Rock Island Lines
Chicago, St. Paul, Minneapolis, and Omaha Railroad, 19:113, 24:134n; anniversary, 12:327; mergers, 18: 220, 36:71; locomotives, 36:321; Russian corps, 38:311, 313, 315n
Chicago Theological Seminary, 11:94, 15:223, 16:313
Chicago Tyre Spring Co., 18:149
Chickamauga, Ga., battle, 38:258, 267-273
Chickasaw Indians, 15:121
Chidester, Ann, author, 31:129, 139, 145, 37:3n
"Chieftain of Winnipeg," steamboat, voyage described, 24:278-286
Child, James E., author, 23:303
Child, Lydia M., feminist, 30:251
Child, Sargent B., editor, 24:361
Child Psychology Study Circle, St. Paul, 15:140
Child welfare, New York, 17:111, 39: 125; labor regulations, 18:332, 21:374; Minnesota, 20:88, 30:245,

39:11, 15-17; reform struggle, 39: 26
Children's Aid Society, New York City, history, 39:125
Children's Home Society of Minnesota, 38:82, 83n
Children's Hospital, Minneapolis, 39: 17n
Children's Hospital, St. Paul, history, 34:314
Children's Service, St. Paul, history, 21:343, 455
Childress, A. B., speaker, 14:461
Childs, B. F., photographer, 21:317, 34:177 (cover)
Childs, Clarence H., 18:128n, 146
Childs, Dudley R., 33:290n
Childs, Mrs. Dudley R. (Missouri Stockwell), 33:285, 290n
Childs, George E., career, 18:211
Childs, Dr. George F., 21:329
Childs, Marquis, author, 34:84
Childs, Nellie, 21:219
Chilson, Herman P., author, 40:313
Chimney Rock, Neb., 40:195
China, ginseng market, 34:146n; fur market, 40:157, 179, 182n, 208, 217; trade, 40:406
"China," steamship, 40:278
China National Aviation Corp., 26:6
Chinard, Gilbert, 20:67; work reviewed, 18:86; editor, 14:221
Chinese, in horticulture, 24:259; in Nagasaki, 38:321, 324
Chinese Eastern Railway, 38:321
Chinese War Relief, 23:21
"Chinook," language, 13:91
Chipewyan Indians, 40:160
Chipman, Frederick J., author, 30:55
"Chippewa," steamboat, 13:234, 238
Chippewa City, Chippewa County, county seat fight, 17:235, 26:392
Chippewa County, ethnic settlements, 12:261, 275n, 13:427, 18:338, 28: 121, 124, 126, 29:87, 35:33, 90, 36:104; agriculture, 14:353; Lutheran church, 14:451; history, 16:127, 40:47; county seat, 17: 235, 26:392; fair, 18:466; archives, 22:100; war history committee, 23:390, 25:96; Mormons, 36:292, 293; Farmer-Labor club, 38:303
Chippewa County Historical Society, 22:445, 30:399, 39:300; organized, 17:231, 18:62; exhibits, 17:355, 481, 22:215, 30:165; museum, 18: 222, 334, 463, 19:230, 359, 20: 210, 26:89, 178, 283, 392, 27:75, 171, 263-265, 359, 28:295, 386; meetings, 19:115, 20:95, 21:107, 22:105, 339, 23:193, 24:85, 25:96, 208, 312, 406, 28:85, 29:178, 273, 361, 30:78, 276; tour, 20:351; archives, 20:455; excavation projects, 21:207, 334, 435, 443, 22: 210, 23:50, 27:360
Chippewa County, Mich., territorial boundaries, 26:362
Chippewa County (Mich.) Historical Society, 24:377, 379
Chippewa County, Wis., trial courts, 36:275
Chippewa County Pioneer Association, 18:222
Chippewa Falls, Pope County, history, 16:305, 468

Chippewa Falls, Wis., river port, 11:
211; Indian agency, 11:326; lumbering, 27:194, 196, 197; power
company, 35:381
"Chippewa Falls," steamboat, 12:210,
19:391n
Chippewa Indian Co-operative Marketing Association, 17:472
Chippewa (Ojibway) Indians, medicine,
11:58, 15:121, 16:343, 475, 17:
392, 21:416, 27:341, 351, 28:375,
33:91, 35:44, 244, 37:182, 39:84;
missions, 11:94, 305, 12:205, 14:
55-58, 15:354, 466, 16:97, 216,
469, 18:197, 268, 19:379, 457, 20:
78, 310-313, 431, 21:414, 22:200,
23:402, 24:262, 26:275, 388, 31:
54, 33:60, 185, 34:131, 305, 36:
192, 319, 39:301-310, 40:146; census, 11:206, 12:26, 15:196, 16:97,
23:329-331; customs, 11:209, 13:
107, 17:109, 19:457, 22:334, 24:
54, 262, 29:131, 35:244, 37:79,
86, 347, 38:191, 40:358; reservations, 11:320, 332, 12:205, 13:
114, 20:442, 22:220, 23:13, 27:
358, 28:374, 29:169, 35:235, 380,
38:335, 40:42, 148; lands, 11:445,
18:306, 20:83, 24:262, 34:311, 35:
49; crafts, 11:447, 18:323, 333,
22:59, 23:288, 25:87, 28:193, 30:
392, 39:171; history, 12:68, 16:
452, 28:77, 29:66, 37:174, 40:42,
47; agencies, 12:84, 17:336, 18:
48, 20:193, 32:88, 35:23; music,
12:199, 326, 24:71, 26:275, 27:65,
161, 29:86, 32:58, 124, 33:312,
35:244; hostilities, 12:202, 14:
332, 17:154, 22:88, 24:143-148,
180, 27:8, 28:77, 212-214, 29:238,
30:387, 33:278, 38:131, 132n, 275;
legends, 12:215-225, 13:331, 27:
254, 357, 32:126, 35:143, 36:75,
37:235-254, 38:192, 40:358; annuities, 13:101, 16:296, 17:338, 21:
315, 24:18-20, 29:198; pictured,
14:330, 15:117, 20:54, 57, 445,
21:156, 23:94, 154, 26:174, 27:77,
32:161, 33:20, 74, 75, 105, 108,
35:277, 37:263, 348; of Canada,
14:337, 17:345, 35:377; wild-rice
harvest, 14:381, 17:472, 21:100,
325, 22:438, 23:181, 34:172, 35:
155, 37:183; maple-sugar making,
14:383, 30:261; schools, 16:333,
19:132n, 33:73, 74, 105-111, 35:
138, 338; games, 17:115, 37:347;
clothing, 20:199, 33:227; leaders,
21:285; place names, 21:346, 348,
25:304, 28:374, 30:331; artifacts,
23:188, 36:284, 37:307; food, 23:
330-332; characterized, 24:282-
284, 27:289-291, 32:84, 33:274,
37:106; source material, 25:183,
29:101, 38:335, 40:409; in Britain, 25:297; poetry, 33:90; North
Dakota, 35:339; Illinois, 36:191.
See also Chippewa-Sioux warfare,
Chippewa treaties, Mixed-bloods,
Ojibway language
Chippewa-Lac qui Parle State Park,
16:192; historical meeting, 16:
302; archaeology, 21:207, 334, 434
Chippewa Land District, surveyed, 26:
78, 224
Chippewa National Forest, 23:67; described, 11:215; history, 16:101,

24:81, 30:389, 34:264, 35:245, 338
Chippewa Region Historical Society,
18:222, 441, 25:406; organized,
18:62, 109. See also Cass Lake
(village), museum
Chippewa River, Minn., 14:362, 21:162
Chippewa River, Wis., 12:200; steamboating, 11:211, 15:125, 26:272,
28:92; lumbering, 16:479, 21:55,
22:95, 26:132, 27:191-202, 30:71,
243, 34:35, 39:211. See also
Chippewa Valley
Chippewa-Sioux boundary line, in
Wisconsin, 12:434; surveyed, 13:
426, 14:93, 18:207; mapped, 21:83
Chippewa-Sioux warfare, battles, 11:
225, 12:454, 13:100, 443, 14:116,
18:404, 20:457, 24:11-25, 25:160,
27:296, 30:214, 396, 35:269, 337,
384, 37:68, 88, 138; Lake Superior
area, 12:353, 18:237; source material, 14:215, 20:327, 21:31, 35:
335, 40:262; Stillwater, 15:280,
21:167n; Rum River, 15:280, 479,
19:105, 21:167n; St. Paul, 15:
306n, 16:280, 19:140n, 28:138, 29:
35; history, 16:251, 18:184, 21:
325, 401, 28:77; legends, 17:440;
effect on fur trade, 19:276, 20:7;
Fort Snelling, 21:79, 24:11, 25:
272, 30:213n, 31:216; Morrison
County, 21:337; peace negotiations, 23:328, 334, 337, 339, 25:
396, 31:96, 32:231, 35:105, 39:
302; Roseau Valley, 24:324-326
Chippewa Station, Douglas County, re-
lay station, 38:64, 66, 67; garrison, 38:280
Chippewa treaties, 20:80, 21:315, 27:
289, 29:233, 34:355, 35:49; 1863,
11:216, 12:203, 14:350, 438, 15:
84, 282-300, 18:209, 38:70; 1854,
12:384, 29:233, 34:177, 39:309;
1837, 14:352, 15:426, 16:454, 18:
161n, 20:120, 23:85, 24:16, 29:
232; 1851, 15:282-300, 23:85, 38:
1-10; 1861, 15:294; 1864, 15:295-
297, 299; 1847, 16:333; 1855, 19:
384n, 25:315, 28:205, 29:35n, 233,
39:309; 1820, 23:145-147; 1826,
31:96, 97; 1862, 39:259
Chippewa Valley, Wis., 12:191; history, 22:206; lumbering, 24:261, 27:
197-199, 28:182, 32:188, 252, 37:
185. See also Chippewa River
Chisago City, townsite, 22:99; Swedish settlement, 23:88, 34:164, 39:
131; history, 27:175
Chisago County, Swedish settlement,
17:399, 400, 404, 24:79, 31:27,
35:337, 36:240; pioneer physicians, 19:463; history, 23:187,
400, 24:190, 29:178, 36:195; war
history committee, 24:268; politics, 36:308; poor farm, 38:369n,
374; nursing home, 38:377; frontier road, 40:239, 242
Chisago County Historical Society,
18:334, 23:398, 24:85, 25:96;
meetings, 28:196, 29:178
Chisago County Press (Lindstrom), 16:
246, 29:175
Chisago House, Taylors Falls, 17:283
Chisago Lake, Swedish settlement, 17:
329, 397-399, 402, 403, 24:190,
40:65; described, 17:400, 31:27;

Lutheran church, 24:190, 25:314;
history, 36:195
Chisholm, railroad, 11:467; ethnic
groups, 12:436, 19:112, 25:186,
30:156; forest fire, 14:462, 27:
367, 36:196; mining museum, 34:43,
35:99; strike, 40:345. See also
Mesabi Range
Chisholm Children's Museum, Duluth,
39:323n
Chittenden, Hiram M., author, 16:475,
34:215, 40:151-153, 155, 156, 201
Chivington, Col. John M., letter, 38:
223
Chmelar, Julia, author, 12:205
Choate, Rufus, 25:396
Choctaw Indians, 40:358; removal, 15:
121
Cholera, epidemics, 14:288-302, 20:
230, 21:17, 18, 19, 24:79, 182,
36:17; on steamboats, 16:209, 19:
343, 30:9, 39:67; Reed's study,
24:210
Choné, Father Pierre, missionary, 39:
308, 309
Chorley, E. Clowes, author, 25:305
Chorley, Kenneth, author, 35:150
Chouart, Jean Baptiste, 16:418n;
trader, 29:153, 36:150
Chouart, Médard, see Groseilliers,
sieur de
Chouteau, Auguste, 12:77, 17:219;
trader, 16:113, 19:293; library,
20:203; author, 33:132
Chouteau, E. F., 13:226
Chouteau, Pierre, 17:219; trader, 16:
113
Chouteau, Pierre, Jr., pioneer, 17:
96, 30:266; steamboat operator,
13:233; trader, 35:357n, 40:183,
184, 214
Chouteau family, in fur trade, 15:
421, 24:179; genealogy, 15:473
Chouteau, Pierre, Jr., and Co., St.
Louis, posts, 13:278; traders, 22:
156, 278, 34:325-327, 36:15n, 38,
260-264, 40:155, 212, 213, 218;
1851 Sioux treaties, 32:66, 74,
76, 78, 79; steamboat firm, 38:
236, 355, 358, 362; history, 39:
255
Chowen, W. S., agricultural leader,
20:448
Chrislock, Carl H., 37:88; "The Alliance Party," 35:297-312; "Sidney
M. Owens," 36:109-126; "Minnesota
Republicanism," 39:93-110; reviews
by, 36:31, 187, 37:131, 38:235,
39:29, 79, 169, 293, 40:139;
awards, 36:71, 240, 39:36, 212;
author, 36:237, 40:362
Christ, Hans, farmer, 39:81
Christ Church Hospital and Orphans
Home, see St. Luke's Hospital, Duluth
Christ Episcopal Church, St. Paul,
11:340, 12:105, 33:5, 38:75, 39:53
Christ Lutheran Church, St. Paul, 25:
213
Christ-Janer, Albert, work reviewed,
21:402
Christensen, Alex, author, 30:395
Christensen, Bernhard, college president, 40:382, 383
Christensen, Chris L., portrait, 25:
278

Christensen, Erwin O., work reviewed, 32:110
Christensen, Mrs. Henry, author, 22:441
Christensen, Norman, author, 18:226
Christensen, Rhoda, 22:421, 26:39
Christensen, Thomas P., author, 11:324, 13:435, 15:355, 471, 18:102, 27:163, 34:313
Christenson, E. A., 17:231
Christenson, Lars, artist, 40:357
Christgau, R. J., author, 17:227
Christian, George C., 17:104, 30:175
Christian, George H., miller, 11:278, 281, 30:204
Christian, Sarah B., author, 14:448
Christian Brothers, in Minnesota, 29:354, 30:154
Christian Church, Garden City, 14:353, 455
Christian Commission, in Civil War, 25:351
Christian Front movement, 40:360
Christian Hill, Anoka, 25:364
Christian Missionary Alliance, 34:61
Christian Reformed church, Nobles County, 28:130; Prinsburg, 28:126; Pine County, 28:131
Christian Union Church, Anoka County, 18:224
Christiania, Norwegian settlement, 11:286, 12:271
Christiania, Norway, see Oslo, Norway
Christiansen, F. Melius, choir leader, 24:258, 25:86, 192, 26:59
Christianson, C. N., 28:194
Christianson, J. O., 26:151, 28:75, 390; speaker, 25:201, 28:298, 35:99, 36:104
Christianson, John, trans., Hamsun's "On the Prairie," 37:265-270
Christianson, Theodore, work reviewed, 16:452-456; governor, 11:213, 333, 461, 12:96, 104, 35:371, 37:161, 40:148; papers, 15:98; Congressman, 15:490, 40:369; speaker, 29:85
Christianson, William C., review by, 35:198
Christie, Alexander, trader, 36:49, 53
Christie, Mrs. George W. (Eva Lindbergh), 17:59, 18:207, 35:293
Christino Indians, Radisson's visit, 13:260. See also Cree Indians
Christison, Dr. J. T., speaker, 19:112
Christison, Muriel B., "LeRoy S. Buffington," 23:219-232; author, 23:270, 26:150
Christmas, Charles W., 22:223; monument, 23:296; surveyor, 24:187, 270, 33:331
Christmas, George, author, 22:225
Christmas, pioneer celebrations, 11:118, 16:95, 130, 132, 373-390, 18:107, 20:339, 363, 21:109, 152, 22:10, 223, 226, 336, 23:26, 102, 200, 24:182, 26:93, 27:47, 90, 91, 94, 28:78, 80, 81, 186, 337, 30:67, 396, 31:221, 32:198, 36:127-130, 38:385; menus, 14:391, 16:378, 17:126; amusements, 15:349, 16:377, 383, 17:48n, 125; Fort Snelling, 16:373; church services, 16:380, 19:191; gifts, 16:381-383, 389, 17:242, 34:107; among Chippe-

wa, 17:109; music, 21:101; in army, 22:319, 25:239, 37:334; seals, 27:48, 30:175; among Mennonites, 30:161; cards, 33:351; U.S., 34:167
Christmas Lake, Hennepin County, 16:129
"Christopher Columbus," steamboat, 15:123
Christopher Columbus Memorial Association, 13:60, 83
Christy, Howard Chandler, artist, 26:384
Christy, J. C., letter, 11:162
Chrysler, St. Louis County, railroad station, 34:184
Chubb, John, 11:462
Church, Randolph W., author, 24:361
Church Club, St. Paul, 30:23
Church of Christ, Pleasant Grove, 16:355; Minnesota, 33:354
Church of the Redeemer (Lutheran), St. Paul, 21:223, 22:88
Church of the Redeemer (Universalist), Minneapolis, 16:120
Churchill, John, 29:154
Churchill, Harry P., biography, 16:337
Churchill, Levi, lumberman, 18:176
Churchill, Winston, 14:201, 23:217
Churchill, Man., founded, 13:300
Churchill and Nelson, Stillwater, lumber firm, 38:187
Churchill River, Man., post, 40:190
Churchville, Pipestone County, Dutch settlement, 28:128
Chute, Charles R., reminiscences, 11:215
Chute, Mary G., author, 31:145
Chute, Richard, 14:132; letters, 15:464, 36:269; papers, 21:411, 23:40; in fur trade, 22:191, 32:71, 74, 76, 77; in politics, 36:4n; businessman, 37:312, 313, 319
Chute, Mrs. Richard, 32:71, 74
Chute, Dr. Samuel H., 35:124
Chute, William Y., career, 21:411
Chute family, genealogy, 21:411; papers, 22:40
Cigar Makers' Union, St. Paul, 21:379, 387; records, 17:338, 18:47, 20:432
Cincinnati, Ohio, cholera epidemic, 14:300; first printing, 15:12, 14; cultural center, 17:142, 23:63, 28:107; relief committee, 18:251; Germans, 30:25, 32, 188, 32:168; history, 31:185, 32:44; river port, 36:251, 252, 253, 255; balloon flight, 40:314
"Cincinnati," naval vessel, 25:131
Circle of Industry, St. Paul, women's club, 30:198
Circuses, Minnesota, 15:252, 16:32, 19:120, 23:199, 28:101, 266; early U.S., 16:110, 28:246, 32:59; Wisconsin, 17:427, 24:76
Citizens Alliance, Minneapolis, 18:191, 192
City and County Hospital, St. Paul, 17:69
"City Belle," steamboat, 21:98
City College of New York, local history teaching, 30:63
City Guard, St. Paul, 16:172; Wright County, 16:175

"City of Aitkin," steamboat, 33:11, 12, 17
"City of Alma," steamboat, 37:285
"City of St. Louis," steamboat, 12:433, 14:351, 29:292
Civil service, reform, 23:264
Civil War, papers and diaries, 11:95, 96, 205, 318, 12:191, 319, 13:198, 318-320, 427, 445, 14:63, 15:111, 112, 347, 19:343, 387-389, 20:192, 195, 21:192, 204, 215, 22:86, 192, 422, 23:170, 25:20-39, 117-152, 224-257, 342-361, 385, 28:304, 326, 29:374, 30:91, 33:228, 35:313-319, 39:132, 263; currency, 11:98, 26:157; participation of ethnic groups, 11:103, 17:222, 20:244, 246, 22:319, 23:371, 24:157, 27:328, 29:86, 32:169, 33:180, 34:200, 35:193; accounts, 12:74, 14:203, 15:328, 16:86, 454, 17:112, 21:414, 22:408, 27:161, 29:63, 33:214, 34:81, 304, 37:255, 257, 38:35; Minnesota in, 12:84, 15:99, 16:332, 17:207, 212, 19:44, 32:20, 39:173-197, 40:281-292; effects, 12:248, 262, 21:237, 22:71, 26:111, 39:72, 73; causes, 13:205, 23:260-263, 31:243; public opinion, 14:108, 20:273-286, 24:307-317, 27:345, 28:20n, 31:60, 243, 35:93; veterans, 14:117, 15:196, 16:367, 19:452, 33:82, 35:245, 37:345, 38:287-297, see also Grand Army of the Republic; photographs, 14:440, 28:348, 33:216, 35:92, 36:169, 40:410; volunteers, 16:175-177, 22:174-176, 25:384, 26:258, 36:174, 175, 37:191, 193, 39:129, 40:123; medical services, 16:334, 21:358; prisoners, 17:98, 20:81, 25:141-152, 224-227, 238; in art, 17:136, 25:186, 30:393, 35:35, 153, 37:38, 308, 38:298-300, 40:410; financing, 18:77, 21:300; army life, 18:444, 19:338, 36:279, 37:33, 188, 39:78, see also Taylor, Isaac L.; draft, 21:222, 25:249, 250, 36:156; Copperheads, 24:154-156, 31:244, 37:126, 262; sutlers, 25:122, 129, 225; soldier vote, 25:202, 229, 26:167, 187-210, 257, 36:167-172, 37:330, 331; army manuals, 26:157; Catholic attitude, 27:43; politics, 29:342, 30:382, 33:346, 38:202, 40:277; wallpaper newspapers, 33:211-213; transportation facilities, 33:218, 37:185, 38:42, 45, 46, 55; chaplain, 34:129; journalists, 34:343; rebellion act, 35:1-10; Fort Snelling in, 35:184, 185, 39:278, 279; centennial, 36:240, 284, 37:223, 224, 264; archives guide, 38:382, 39:210; Wisconsin in, 38:384, 40:96; maps, 39:127, 210; forts, 40:43; in Arkansas, 40:281-292; "Cairo" torpedoed, 40:306. See also various battles and military units
Civil Works Administration, 15:72, 109, 137; MHS projects, 15:64, 73, 198, 217, 441, 443, 461, 16:54, 65; buildings survey, 15:127, 359; archives survey, 15:198, 346. See also Federal Emergency Relief Ad-

ministration, Minnesota State
Board of Control
Civilian Conservation Corps, 20:146,
40:373; in Superior National Forest, 36:134, 136-138
Claffy, Lawrence, 19:308
Clague, Frank, Congressman, 31:207,
33:157
Clague, Mr. and Mrs. John, 26:285
Clam Lake, Burnett County, Wis., 28:
159n, 225, 227
Clamming industry, Mississippi Valley, 28:285
Clapesattle, Helen, "Health in Rochester," 20:221-242; "Florida's Rival," 35:214-221; reviews by, 18:
307-309, 19:439-441, 20:181-183,
21:308, 23:159, 24:240, 25:67-69,
26:143, 27:330; works reviewed,
22:404-408, 34:203; author, 19:
445, 20:187, 322, 21:310, 23:9,
96, 169, 364, 24:245, 25:76, 91,
26:154, 27:147, 343, 28:335, 30:
358, 36:277, 39:172; speaker, 20:
187, 298, 23:299, 24:192, 35:99
Clapham, Sir John, author, 24:340
Clapp, Alice B., author, 16:227, 21:
93
Clapp, Benjamin, 40:184; letter, 32:
12, 13
Clapp, George C., diary, 26:258
Clapp, Moses E., papers, 16:242, 17:
213, 337, 19:48; Senator, 18:316,
424, 20:83, 22:79, 34:328; career,
28:74; attorney general, 38:14
Clara City, founded, 18:338, 36:104;
churches, 20:447, 28:126
Clare, Peter, Methodist minister, 26:
68
Claremont, Congregational church, 17:
468; windmill, 18:467; history,
19:335
Clarendon Hotel, St. Paul, records,
16:72
"Clarion," steamboat, 11:136, 163n,
164, 179, 181, 184, 13:241
Clarissa, incorporated, 18:343; fire
department, 22:448
Clark, ---, steamboat captain, 18:405
Clark, A. C., 17:100
Clark, Alan R., author, 37:42
Clark, Alden H., speaker, 16:354
Clark, Andrew J., journalist, 24:326
Clark, C. F., druggist, 12:185
Clark, C. W., autobiography, 16:217
Clark, Champ, 15:338
Clark, Charles, 14:279
Clark, Lt. Charles A., 13:60; in
Philippines, 12:192
Clark, Capt. Charles P., 12:323, 13:
60; papers, 12:193
Clark, Charles U., work reviewed, 16:
199
Clark, Mrs. Clifton, author, 18:224
Clark, Dan E., review by, 24:235;
work reviewed, 18:303-305; author,
24:245, 28:362
Clark, Dwight F., author, 23:281
Clark, E. W., and Co., Philadelphia,
banking house, 13:330, 37:91-93,
119, 120
Clark, Edwin, 11:444; Indian agent,
12:84, 15:114
Clark, Edwin, pioneer association
secretary, 20:413
Clark, Frank H., 18:315, 37:93
Clark, G. N., author, 28:169, 29:153

Clark, George Rogers, 15:473, 19:311,
40:142; expedition, 19:295; in
Revolutionary War, 33:346
Clark, Glenn, author, 31:63
Clark, Greenleaf, 40:225; biography,
11:216
Clark, Dr. H. B., speaker, 29:181
Clark, Maj. Harold M., 12:193, 323,
13:60, 14:106
Clark, Harold W., diaries, 24:167
Clark, Harry H., speaker, 29:348
Clark, Homer P., 11:54, 14:78, 17:70,
20:50, 51, 23:50, 26:45, 29:97;
"Everett Hoskins Bailey," 20:58-
60; author, 20:74
Clark, Mrs. Irving, 32:62
Clark, J. C., hotelkeeper, 20:393
Clark, J. Hinckley, banker, 37:102
Clark, J. V. H., explorer, 34:213
Clark, J. W., diary, 16:100
Clark, James I., author, 35:202
Clark, James W., review by, 35:41;
author, 24:78, 28:357, 31:191, 36:
105, 39:263
Clark, John, missionary, 32:95
Clark, Maj. John B., at Fort Snel-
ling, 36:42, 47
Clark, Mrs. John B., at Fort Snel-
ling, 36:42
Clark, John C., politician, 30:104,
39:38
Clark, John S., professor, 18:146,
150
Clark, Mrs. John S., 18:146
Clark, Jonathan, 39:165
Clark, Joseph S., Senator, 40:134
Clark, Malcolm, murdered, 20:432
Clark, Marion G., author, 13:331
Clark, Martha M. F., house, 39:276
Clark, Mrs. Mary S., notebooks, 24:
167
Clark, Mary W., author, 12:341
Clark, Matt, lumberman, 31:38
Clark, Lt. Nathan, 18:405
Clark, Neil M., author, 19:113
Clark, Olive, museum assistant, 20:44
Clark, Robert C., author, 14:222, 19:
216
Clark, S. N., Indian agent, 20:193
Clark, Samuel, 12:382
Clark, Thomas D., work reviewed, 36:
275; author, 25:391, 27:64, 159,
275
Clark, Victor S., author, 11:216
Clark, W. F., letter, 16:217
Clark, William, 15:424, 473, 25:269,
39:169; explorer, 14:430, 17:432n,
20:84, 26:165, 28:184, 29:61, 34:
303, 40:152, 192; author, 14:423,
38:386, 39:164, 267; papers, 15:
462, 33:268, 312, 34:315, 360, 35:
51, 100, 204, 248, 340, 36:36,
101, 196, 216-229, 37:88; diary,
29:175; museum, 29:260; Indian
agent, 35:22, 25, 26, 28, 36:247.
See also Lewis and Clark expedition
Clark, William A., industrialist, 39:
170
Clark, William H., author, 21:96, 27:
255, 35:44
Clark, Lake County, railroad station,
34:181
Clark House, Duluth, 12:107, 37:110n,
117
Clarke, Charles E., 13:132, 140, 141
Clarke, Dwight L., author, 38:201

Clarke, Freeman, 40:117, 118
Clarke, James, 17:427n
Clarke, James F., feminist, 39:4
Clarke, Jeannette, 11:146n
Clarke, Miles P., journal, 12:455
Clarke, Nehemiah P., logging opera-
tions, 18:332; cattleman, 26:121
Clarke, Thomas, papers, 35:384
Clarke, William, 22:154
Clarkfield, fire department, 15:373;
anniversary, 17:492; Norwegian
settlement, 23:290
Clarks Grove, Baptist church, 11:
113, 13:207, 15:128, 21:341; co-
operative creamery, 11:289, 19:
155, 157n, 21:340; history, 12:
430, 15:348, 486; Danish settle-
ment, 27:256, 31:27
Clarkson, James S., politician, 35:74
Clarkson, Mrs. Mabel H., 22:216
"Clarksville," steamboat, 33:286, 288
Clary, Anna L., author, 19:114
Clary, Ernest S., biography, 18:211
Claude, Anne J., see Lavocat-Martin,
Anne C. J.
Clause, ---, trader, 11:262
Clausen, A. C., 23:27
Clausen, Clarence A., work reviewed,
33:85; translator, 24:258
Clausen, Claus L., pioneer minister,
11:216, 446, 12:257, 14:54, 22:68,
24:348, 33:85, 37:184, 38:233;
colonizer, 12:264, 13:206, 27:164,
31:157, 174; biography, 31:126
Clausen, Hans, 12:148
Clausen, Martin, 29:308, 309
Clausen, Peter G., artist, 13:197,
19:215, 20:35, 22:333, 28:113, 33:
178
Claussen, Hans R., settler, 25:298
Clay, Cassius, speaker, 22:257
Clay, Charles, author, 15:478
Clay, E. W., artist, 14:423n
Clay, Grady, author, 36:283
Clay, Ham, Sr., author, 15:245
Clay, Henry, politician, 22:66, 37:
37, 39:38, 47, 143; secretary of
state, 25:182; letter, 33:299;
agrarian, 40:295
Clay, John, quoted, 40:308
Clay, M. W., obtains telephone franchise, 24:192
Clay, Capt. Mark W., Union officer,
39:195n
Clay, W. S., 20:96, 21:108, 24:192
Clay County, settlement, 11:42, 21:
448; Norwegians, 12:278, 336, 17:
359; courthouse, 12:337; Catholic
church, 14:452; agriculture, 21:
212, 29:14, 357; history, 23:187,
28:190; buffalo herds, 30:126; library, 31:61; nursing home, 38:377
Clay County Historical Society, 16:
240, 19:234, 20:46; organized, 14:
119; museum, 17:355, 482, 18:222,
463, 20:454, 21:334, 23:11, 193,
25:258-264; membership, 18:109;
meetings, 16:242, 17:231, 18:334,
19:359
Clay County War History Committee,
24:82
Clayton, Florence A., singer, 33:
317-322, 324, 325
Clayton, Fred, comedian, 33:323
Clayton, James L., "Growth of the
American Fur Trade," 40:210-220;

review by, 40:403; historian, 40: 155, 316

Clayton, John M., Senator, 35:354; secretary of state, 39:38, 40, 143, 144

Clayton, Mr. and Mrs. L. J., pioneers, 21:454

Clayton, Walter P., recollections, 21:454

Clayton Antitrust Act, 12:18

Clayton, Iowa, river town, 12:165

Clayton County, Iowa, politics, 20:78

Clayton County, Wis., 1838 census, 19:350, 20:78

Clear Lake, Sherburne County, Swedish settlement, 20:257

Clear Lake, Waseca County, resort, 36:194

Clearwater, Baptist church, 30:156; camp meeting, 31:82; octagonal house, 38:348

Clearwater County, archives, 15:197; newspapers, 15:484, 29:356, 38: 305; pageant, 16:237; history, 16: 247, 35:203, 36:195; townsites, 16:493, 22:109; Lutheran church, 17:235; archaeology, 26:321, pioneer life, 35:200

Clearwater County Agricultural Society, 18:467

Clearwater County Historical Society, organized, 19:468, 20:46; meetings, 20:95; reorganized, 30:399

Clearwater Guard, 16:176

Clearwater Lake, Carver County, see Waconia Lake

Clearwater River, Beltrami County, logging, 29:137, 145

Clearwater Township, Wright County, politics, 26:205n

Cleary, Father James M., interview, 12:457; author, 26:304

Cleaveland, Arba, pioneer, 19:140, 141, 20:141-143; death, 19:268; legislator, 20:144

Cleaveland, Mrs. Arba, 19:140, 268; letters, 20:141, 144

Cleaveland, Clarissa, 20:141n

Cleaveland, Moses, 31:181

Cleaver, Charles G., "Frank B. Kellogg's View of History," 35:157-166; reviews by, 35:234, 327, 36: 97, 185, 37:83, 339, 38:35, 39:335

Clegg, Charles, author, 33:314

Cleland, Charles S., author, 21:457

Cleland, J. H., author, 17:360

Cleland, M. Goodwin, author, 31:134, 146, 36:81

Clemans, Rev. E. C., 23:77

Clemen, Rudolf A., author, 12:177

Clemens, Clara, 17:375, 377, 379, 381, 383

Clemens, Jean, 17:375

Clemens, Orion, 17:375

Clemens, Samuel L. (Mark Twain), 20: 82, 377, 386, 33:327; in Minnesota, 17:369-384, 20:65; lecture tour, 18:28-35; author, 20:116, 21:404, 23:113, 26:73, 36:75, 37: 284, 38:384, 40:304; career, 29: 61; river pilot, 31:246; speaker, 40:12, 20

Clemens, Mrs. Samuel L., 17:379, 381, 383

Clemens, Susie, 17:375

Clement, Mrs. Winifred S., speaker, 27:362

Clements, Roger V., author, 37:184

Clements, William L., historian, 39: 166

Clements Library, Ann Arbor, Mich., 18:455

Clementson, M., 18:340

Clementz, John, author, 35:154

Clemmer, Mary, biography, 11:216

Clendenin, Mary, 32:334

Clerihew, Alex E., 19:184n

Clevedon, Wis., English colony, 35: 202

Cleveland, Elijah, 31:10; diary, 31:9

Cleveland, Grover, 18:145, 22:382; President, 14:203, 18:30, 32:148, 35:312, 36:121, 39:29, 327, 330, 332; in Minnesota, 22:375; election, 35:76, 39:102

Cleveland, Mrs. Grover, 22:375

Cleveland, Guy K., 13:214; legislator, 35:2

Cleveland, Horace W. S., biography, 11:216; memorial, 30:77, 168

Cleveland, J. R., 26:68

Cleveland, John, 38:362

Cleveland, county seat fight, 12:444; history, 21:103

Cleveland, Ohio, first press, 15:14; transportation center, 27:136, 34: 11, 12, 40:272, 273n; Slavs, 27: 210, 213

Cleveland-Cliffs Iron Co., history, 32:46

Cleveland Co., in fur trade, 22:277n

Cleveland Plain Dealer, 37:168, 173

Cleworth, Marc M., author, 23:86

Clifford, Frederic W., 33:333

Clift, G. Glenn, author, 34:357

Clifton, St. Louis County, 16:298; post office, 34:186; townsite, 35: 49, 37:112

Climate, Twin Cities, 11:109, 14:268, 18:128-130, 132, 136, 138, 141, 145, 22:5, 438, 33:195-200; Minnesota, 11:148, 12:163, 13:355, 14: 376, 15:305, 16:387, 17:212, 243-261, 19:235, 20:245, 395, 24:321, 29:166, 197, 31:229, 32:35, 34: 141, 216, 36:91, 38:54, 204; relation to health, 13:32, 15:302, 16: 29, 238, 17:255-260, 396, 412, 18: 300, 22:135, 169, 25:91, 28:16, 31:19, 33:32, 35:214-221, 38:74, 40:74; droughts, 15:463, 18:324, 40:409; dust storms, 16:474, 28: 79; Lake Traverse, 17:309; St. Croix Valley, 17:386, 39:287; Iowa, 17:401, 19:195, 20:161n; Red River Valley, 18:107; Northwest, 18:155; effect on agriculture, 18: 285, 287-289, 20:158, 161; meteorological records, 20:349, 452, 21:313, 435, 22:93, 38:2; Fort Snelling, 22:93, 36:15; Great Lakes area, 23:234, 235, 238, 245, 249, 332; border lakes, 24:285; hailstorms, 37:204; eastern winters, 40:312. See also Blizzards and storms, Floods

Climax, site of fire-steel find, 18: 41, 188-190

Clinch, William J., 12:287; speaker, 11:460, 12:283

Cline, Howard F., work reviewed, 38: 238

Clinton, De Witt, 40:179

Clinton, Mr. and Mrs. Oliver P., pioneers, 22:223

Clinton, Iowa, sawmill, 27:190; lumber center, 27:195

Clinton County, Iowa, English settlement, 28:78

Clinton Falls, Steele County, farming, 17:467; statistics, 28:305; ghost town, 35:13

Clinton House, Nininger, removed, 13: 151

Clintonville, Wis., history, 19:222

Clio Club, Minneapolis, 13:197

Clitherall, Maj. George B., 13:132; speaker, 13:145; career, 13:385n

Clitherall, Mormon settlement, 11: 222, 13:280, 281, 385-394, 36: 289n; history, 13:344, 20:457; farming, 23:317, 318

Cloeter, Rev. Ottmar, missionary, 19: 50, 96; career, 14:55-58

Cloman, Flora, author, 22:436

Clontarf, school, 17:84; Catholic colony, 35:134-136, 138

Cloquet, ethnic groups, 12:436, 22: 392, 398, 24:174, 25:326, 36:237; lumber industry, 13:358, 21:212, 25:211, 31:71, 162, 34:184, 40: 361; forest fire, 15:225, 17:360, 24:346, 33:45, 46, 92, 37:223; co-operatives, 22:315; Covenant church, 34:61; in fiction, 35:196, 36:75; history, 35:382; architecture, 37:264

Cloquet Cooperative Society, 18:324, 24:174

Cloquet Lumber Co., 27:302, 29:177

Cloquet River, St. Louis County, geology, 13:404, 406

Closway, Gordon R., author, 36:327

Clotho, Todd County, history, 15:371

Clotworthy, Samuel, 14:274

Cloud, Josephine, speaker, 11:120

Cloudman (Marpewecapta), Sioux leader, 12:124n, 15:274, 316, 21:168n, 172n, 24:20n, 35:28, 38:147n; village, 12:98, 443, 18:157

Clough, David M.; letters, 19:96; governor, 23:27, 36:118n, 39:98, 101-104, 106-110, 35:63

Clough, John E., biography, 11:217

Clough, Shepard B., author, 26:388

Clough, Solon H., 16:290

Clough, William P., biography, 11:217

Clough, Wilson O., work reviewed, 34: 300

Clouston, Edward, 36:37n

Clouston, Robert, trader, 36:37-53, 37:85, 40:167n, 168n; letters, 38: 199

Clouston, William, trader, 22:310

Cloutier, ---, trader, at Grand Portage, 12:369

Cloutier, Alex, 17:471

Cloutier, Bernard, 17:471

Cloutier, Philip R., author, 36:237

Clover Valley, St. Louis County, railroad station, 34:181

Cloverleaf Co-operative, creamery, 23:197

Cluff brothers, boatbuilders, 33:14

Clyde Iron Works, Duluth, 35:156

Coad, Oral S., author, 11:100

Coal, 29:213; Cottonwood County, 22: 109; monopoly, 39:97; Redwood County, 40:336

Coan, John R., 29185

Coates, John, 33:294
Coats, R. H., author, 25:199
Coatsworth, Elizabeth, author, 32:56
Coatsworth, Emerson S., work reviewed, 35:377
Cobb, Albert C., lawyer, 17:213
Cobb, Rev. Daniel, 31:90
Cobb, Mrs. Daniel, 38:76n
Cobb, E. D., 38:220, 221, 222
Cobbett, William, author, 29:154
Coburn, Frederick W., author, 17:115
Cochran, G. R., agricultural leader, 34:350
Cochran, Mrs. Harrison H., speaker, 12:284
Cochran, Thomas C., author, 27:253, 39:34
Cochrane, John, 15:96; letters, 30:91
Cochrane, John C., author, 26:83; speaker, 19:119
Cochrane, Mrs. John C., 25:316
Cochrane, W. S., editor, 29:100
Cochrane, William, author, 31:58
Cocking, Mary, 20:119
Cocking, Matthew, trader, 16:200; explorer, 20:119
Cockran, William, trader, 20:71
Codde, Pierre de, 20:423, 424
Codere, Charles F., 39:36
Codman, William, 16:363, 22:444, 24:272; author, 16:492, 20:219, 364, 470, 22:100, 226, 23:187, 200; speaker, 25:286
Cody, James, recollections, 14:297
Cody, Margaret, cholera victim, 14:297
Cody, William F. ("Buffalo Bill"), 12:175, 22:313, 34:345; show, 34:169; pictured, 34:174
Coe, Alvan, missionary, 17:210, 18:197, 20:443, 21:28n, 73
Coe, Charles H., 18:129, 136, 138, 146
Coe, Ralph, editor, 39:35
Coeur d'Alene, Idaho, Indian agency, 27:97; miners' strike, 40:340, 341
Coffey, Walter C., 19:32, 23:51; speaker, 15:115, 241, 16:487, 23:301, 24:265, 26:82; author, 23:287, 32:118; university president, 32:176, 36:186
Coffin, Charles C., journalist, 17:228, 34:244
Coffin, Robert P. Tristram, author, 27:238
Coffin, Roscoe C., 18:249n, 264n
Coffin, Victor, 21:67
Coffman, Lotus D., 22:101, 404, 35:371; author, 11:108, 12:418, 13:428; speaker, 11:213, 13:341, 19:107; university president, 12:87, 18:101, 32:176, 34:95, 35:371, 36:186, 318, 38:385
Cogshall, Eri, carpenter, 37:194-197
Cogswell, C. C., 25:349, 356
Cogswell, T. M., field agent, 34:243
Cogswell, Theodore, house, 38:340
"Coharbor," steamboat, 25:151
Cohasset, sawmill, 29:146
Cohen, Dr. A. K., 17:20, 18:222, 20:95; speaker, 17:346
Cohen, Henry I., 11:218, 13:74, 294
Cohen, Isadore, author, 34:129, 171
Cohen, J. G., 21:188
Cohen, Nathan, author, 19:355, 20:468, 21:116, 22:349, 24:384, 25:213; speaker, 21:292

Cohoe, Cheyenne Indian, artist, 39:259
Coit, Anna N., author, 35:149
Cokato, pioneer life, 17:367; products, 17:482; Finnish element, 20:214, 21:110, 24:226, 384, 25:318, 324; canning factory, 20:470; museum, 21:344, 440-442, 22:83, 23:11, 14, 15, 190, 26:256; churches, 22:350, 24:376, 26:398
Cokato Elevator Co., records, 17:339, 18:47
Colaneri, Father A. M., 35:136
Colbert, Edouard-Charles-Victurnien, work reviewed, 18:86
Colbert, Jean Baptiste, 13:418, 18:388, 19:279
Colbrath, Corah L., 26:180; author, 28:88; speaker, 26:92
Colburn, Mary J., author, 17:251n, 256
Colby, Charles, 14:306, 313
Colby, Clara, 14:305
Colby, Maj. Elbridge, author, 18:333
Colby, Libby, 14:305, 307
Colby, Maggie, 14:305
Colby, Pauline, missionary, 20:310-313, 23:373, 24:142-144
Colby, Sarah Jane, 14:313
Colby family, at Itasca, 14:304, 313
Colcord, Lincoln, translator, 20:180; author, 37:184
Cold Spring, mill, 13:391, 21:242n; pioneer life, 18:229; in Sioux Outbreak, 28:192
Cole, Arthur C., work reviewed, 15:328-330; speaker, 13:326
Cole, Carl, 27:147
Cole, Cyrenus, work reviewed, 21:307; author, 19:351
Cole, Edward, trader, 16:224
Cole, Emerson, papers, 18:210, 19:48, 22:83, 25:184
Cole, Mrs. George, pioneer teacher, 22:442
Cole, George B., steamboat captain, 11:124
Cole, George R., speaker, 20:352
Cole, Gordon E., attorney general, 26:199, 28:27, 33:128
Cole, Harry E., work reviewed, 11:309
Cole, Col. Haydn S., 20:196; work reviewed, 17:88
Cole, Henry L., 19:389
Cole, Dr. James M., 21:330, 36:60
Cole, John, trader, 33:130
Cole, Mary, author, 25:412
Cole, Moses, 18:118
Cole, Wayne S., works reviewed, 33:306, 38:331
Cole, Dr. William H., 17:88
Cole, W. T., and Co., printers, 18:135
Cole and Hammond, Minneapolis, lumber firm, 18:211
Colehour, James A., pioneer, 20:457
Coleman, A. S., politician, 14:261
Coleman, Sister Bernard, review by, 39:34; work reviewed, 38:192; author, 30:392, 34:172, 40:223
Coleman, Christopher B., 15:124, 24:344, 26:169; author, 16:346, 17:327, 18:214; speaker, 17:105
Coleman, D'Alton C., author, 31:120
Coleman, Jane C., 14:295
Coleman, Dr. John B., house, 38:352

Coleman, Laurence V., author, 15:229, 24:362
Coleman, R. V., works reviewed, 21:180-182, 401, 26:358, 29:152, 30:53-55, 32:247; editor, 28:69
Coleraine, Methodist church, 16:235; iron mining, 22:346, 36:35; strike, 40:345
Coles, Edward, letters, 16:111
Coles and Winans, butchers, 16:242
Cole's Circus, 28:101
Coles County, Ill., probate records, 17:189
Colfax, Schuyler, in Minnesota, 16:27; politician, 19:456, 23:314, 36:304; biography, 33:267
Colfax, Kandiyohi County, Methodist church, 20:35
Colgrave, G. H., 31:84
Colhoun, James Edward, with Long expedition, 16:156, 35:242; diary, 19:447, 22:282n, 23:7, 36:295, 38:41; scientist, 36:295, 37:31
Colin, Victor, author, 35:155
Colket, Meredith B., Jr., work reviewed, 39:170
College of St. Benedict, St. Joseph, history, 16:372, 20:446, 30:265, 34:131, 35:271; convent, 32:42, 33:58-60, 35:263-271, 36:24, 39:321. See also Benedictine Order, St. Benedict's Academy
College of St. Catherine, St. Paul, 15:309, 21:70, 39:128; founded, 17:349, 32:61; family history project, 27:319-326, 28:164, 242n, 303; centennial, 29:370, 30:177, 184; history, 34:131
College of St. Paul, founded, 14:147, 148, 16:275n, 30:202. See also Macalester College
College of St. Scholastica, Duluth, history, 20:104, 34:131
College of St. Thomas, St. Paul, history, 17:29, 349; military academy, 27:271; centennial, 30:69
Collegeville, university campus, 26:388. See also Benedictine Order, St. John's Abbey and University
Coller, Julius A., 16:253; Senator, 35:349
Coller, Julius A., II, works reviewed, 14:325, 37:180; speaker, 14:77, 229; author, 14:238, 17:229
Colleton, Sir John, 16:398
Colleton, Sir Peter, 16:398, 399; grants, 16:423-426
Collett, Felix, miller, 11:275
Collier, Charles A., 21:191
Collier, Donald, work reviewed, 28:270-272
Collier, John, 15:258
Collins, F. E., businessman, 34:50, 51
Collins, John, surveyor, 23:203, 40:356
Collins, Rev. L. C., 22:170, 171
Collins, Loren W., 19:164; letters, 16:218
Collins, Maria A., 14:428
Collins, P. M., 27:260
Collins, Paul V., editor, 20:336
Collins, William ("Captain Mosby"), 25:148n
Collins, Dr. William T., 16:442
Collins Township, McLeod County, records, 20:349

Collinwood, Meeker County, mill, 11: 116; history, 18:345, 530, 19:117; literary society, 24:383

Collis, Traverse County, Irish settlement, 31:22

Collyer, Rev. Robert, lecturer, 11: 158

Colman, Charles L., 16:347

Colman, Norman J., agricultural leader, 33:307

Colmer, H. C., 17:355

Cologne, platted, 34:264; history, 35:50; log buildings, 37:73, 74

Coloney, Myron, author, 15:246

Colonial Dames of America, 40:45; Minnesota, 11:315, 448, 13:60, 104, 14:223, 432, 15:67, 16:99, 215, 471, 22:39, 23:41, 30:185n, 411, 37:44; history, 17:230; publications, 15:90-92, 16:221, 20: 66, 23:57

Colonization Society of North America, 30:28

Colorado, history, 14:114, 449, 16: 217; lumber market, 18:175; war records, 26:278; historic sites, 27:158; pictured, 27:159

Colorado State Historical Society, 27:158

Colston, John, English farmer, 33:321

Colt, Samuel, inventor, 28:54, 36:68

Colter, Charles, meat packer, 33:195, 198, 200; building, 33:196, 197n, 34:99

Colter, George, cattle dealer, 33: 195n

Colter, John, explorer, 24:158, 33: 180

Coltman, William B., 14:98

Colton, J. H., author, 20:203, 35:181

Colton, Kenneth E., author, 19:351, 21:326, 431, 24:70; speaker, 22: 329

Colton, Roy E., author, 15:485, 16: 252

Columbe, Corinne, 33:73, 109, 110

Columbe, Helene, 33:73, 109, 110

"Columbia," brig, 34:11

"Columbia," excursion boat, 34:15

"Columbia," river boat, 37:296

Columbia Broadcasting System, 17:354, 20:362

Columbia College, Dubuque, Iowa, founded, 15:213

Columbia County, proposed, 19:118

Columbia Fur Co., 22:283, 40:186; posts, 11:124, 373, 375, 377-379, 13:222, 224; organized, 12:235, 40:155; absorbed by American Fur Co., 12:236

Columbia Junction, St. Louis County, school, 33:74; railroad, 33:108, 111

Columbia River, fur trade, 16:202, 17:476, 29:339-341, 39:261, 40: 152, 164, 170, 179, 181, 182, 26:56; floods, 34:307; explored, 40:180

Columbia University, New York City, history, 14:443; college of dentistry, 17:100, 19:67, 71, 72; archivist program, 19:218

Columbian Club, Minneapolis, archives, 19:345, 20:35

Columbus, Christopher, 40:198; statue, 13:83-85

Columbus, John, estate, 15:344

Columbus, William, Sioux Indian, 38: 149

Columbus, Anoka County, townsite, 40: 247n

"Columbus," steamship, 15:307

Colvile, Eden, 28:317; letters reviewed, 35:282

Colvill, William, honored, 12:331; Union officer, 13:114, 449, 18:96, 25:247, 269, 358-360, 26:281, 29: 345, 38:246-248, 252, 253; homestead, 17:482; editor, 28:381; congressional candidate, 33:330

Colville, Andrew W., 21:399

Colvin, Esther M., compiler, 16:235

Colvin, Mrs. Sarah T., work reviewed, 25:376

Comanche Indians, 13:92, 16:89

Combe, George, author, 21:364

Combs, Albert B., 25:230

Combs, W. S., J. R. Brown's executor, 39:275

Combs, William S., St. Paul school board president, 13:270, 272

Combs and Brother, St. Paul, bookstore, 19:382n

Comfort, Benjamin F., author, 11:208

Comfort, Mildred H., work reviewed, 27:138

Comfort, Thomas M., 35:203

Comfort, William H., 25:143

Comfrey, Congregational Church, 12: 336

Comines, Philippe de, author, 19:5

Coming, John, trader, 22:288

Commager, Henry S., 30:49; works reviewed, 12:74, 16:450, 29:154, 37:299; author, 19:102, 435, 39: 172; speaker, 37:40

Commercial Bank, Duluth, 37:124

Commercial Club, Minneapolis, 17:382

Commercial Club, St. Paul, 39:55

Commercial West, characterized, 26: 311; politics, 39:110

Commission to Study the Organization of Peace of New York, 23:393

Committee of 48, papers, 11:446, 12: 321

Committee of Twenty-Two, 38:183

Committee on Conservation of Cultural Resources, 23:48, 152, 279

Committee on Public Information, Washington, D.C., in World War I, 19:329, 21:200, 29:82

Committee on Records of War Administration, 23:389

Committee on the Control of Social Data, 23:152

Committee to Defend America by Aiding the Allies, 40:366n

Common Council for American Unity, 22:95

Commonwealth Homestead Association, 21:313

Communism, principles, 18:2, 4, 23: 216

Communist party, 37:172; Minnesota, 18:191, 25:325, 34:188, 191, 192; platforms, 35:291

Community League of Oxboro Heath, archives, 19:452, 20:35

Comnick, Mr. and Mrs. Charles, house, 39:275, 276

Como Park, St. Paul, history, 12:458; concerts, 23:403; statues, 26:388; centennial programs, 30:404

Complin, Margaret, author, 15:477

Comstock, Ada, 16:184, 25:68; author, 22:101

Comstock, Benjamin, papers, 21:106

Comstock, Elting H., author, 23:189

Comstock, Harlow B., papers, 14:101

Comstock, John, banker, 30:71; papers, 24:165

Comstock, Marshall, 14:280

Comstock, Mary, 26:68

Comstock, Solomon G., 25:68; speaker, 13:285; papers, 20:81, 34:339

Comte, Ernest, author, 34:174

Conant, Edward M., speaker, 25:208, 26:68, 89

Conard, William J., missionary, 21: 438

Concord, Dodge County, ghost town, 35:12

Concordia College, Moorhead, history, 15:134, 20:337, 23:95, 196

Concordia College, Red Wing, 27:271

Concordia College, St. Paul, history, 24:264, 27:270, 35:98

Condit, Carl W., author, 37:187

Cone, Frank A., author, 21:185

Conestoga wagons, see Covered wagons

"Conewago," steamboat, 11:143

Confederacy, history, 13:318; currency, 25:232; Minnesota's countermeasures, 35:1-10. See also Civil War

Confederate army, records, 13:318; Swedes in, 24:157; history, 33:83; prisoners, 38:285; in Arkansas, 40:281-292. See also Civil War

Conference of Historical Societies, 13:65, 106

Congden, Harry P., speaker, 26:399

Conger, Charles L., 16:336

Conger, George P., author, 11:459

Conger, Mr. and Mrs. John, descendants, 16:336

Conger family, genealogy, 15:469

Conger, history, 30:405

Congregational Association of Minnesota, organized, 19:144, 265, 20: 141n

Congregational church, Minnesota, 13: 343, 449, 15:223, 16:469, 20:81; Bradford, Iowa, 14:227; Czech, 15: 35, 36; records, 16:466; Minneapolis, 17:338; school, 22:445. See also American Home Missionary Society, individual cities and church bodies

Congregational Conference of Minnesota, 15:111

Congregational Home Missionary Society, see American Home Missionary Society

Congregational Library, Boston, 17:97

Congregational missions, to Chippewa, 11:94; to Sioux, 16:133-151, 303, 354, 483, 23:97; Minnesota, 20:90, 21:15-32, 158-175, 272-283, 438, 40:1-11; frontier, 21:71-73; Missouri River, 35:380; Pembina, 38: 9. See also American Home Missionary Society

Congress, see Continental Congress, U.S. Congress

Congress of Industrial Organizations, see AFL-CIO

Conklin, J. F., theater manager, 28: 103

Conklin, Mrs. Nora, speaker, 18:465

Conley, Mrs. Boyd, 29:182

Conley, Dr. H. H., author, 23:199
Conley, Lewis, 13:114
Conlon, Arthur, 27:297n
Connecticut, public printer, 15:6;
    climate, 17:254n; emigration from,
    19:84, 20:314, 31:181, 34:85;
    proxy voting, 26:209; fur indus-
    try, 40:219
Connelly, Brendan J., author, 34:171,
    314, 356
Connelly, John M., author, 36:328
Connemara, Ireland, emigration from,
    35:205-213
Connick, Charles J., artist, 39:161
Connolly, Alonzo P., newspaperman,
    37:147
Connolly, Bishop James L., 20:50, 21:
    410, 23:50, 25:73, 26:45; reviews
    by, 15:212-214, 16:90, 18:436, 21:
    77, 396, 25:372-374, 26:146, 28:
    62, 33:37, 223; speaker, 14:229,
    15:81, 122, 16:115, 18:320; au-
    thor, 16:362, 498, 18:440, 21:80,
    408, 25:383, 26:154, 28:96
Connor, Lawrence, speaker, 17:121
Connor, Ralph, author, 31:77
Connor, Robert D. W., 22:419; "Our
    National Archives," 17:1-19; na-
    tional archivist, 16:104; speaker,
    17:71, 18:42, 22:326; author, 17:
    90, 21:322
Connor, Thomas, trader, 11:374; al-
    leged diary, 14:223, 15:90-92
Connors, Annie, 15:372, 493, 17:124,
    19:119, 20:99, 21:110, 23:396
Connors, J., labor leader, 40:344
Connors, Joseph B., "The Elusive Hero
    of Redwood Ferry," 34:233-238; au-
    thor, 38:243
Connor's Point, Superior, Wis., fur
    post, 20:12, 13
Conover, Sarah F. D. (Sarah Fair-
    child), portrait, 21:156, 429
Conover Hall, St. Paul, 39:53n
Conrad, Timothy A., scientist, 18:314
Conservation, land, 12:18, 16:207,
    17:220; timber, 16:236, 237, 29:
    68, 155, 373, 30:389, 31:158-162,
    33:92, 180, 34:294, 35:98, 36:134,
    235, 38:329, 39:97, 98n; Minneso-
    ta, 17:480, 18:415, 19:239, 21:
    287, 440, 22:103, 213, 337, 23:
    99, 24:78, 80, 182, 356, 25:92,
    30:75, 274, 32:63, 36:69, 193;
    U.S., 21:200, 22:183, 36:68, 40:
    319, 322; textbook, 35:204; impor-
    tance, 40:131-136. See also For-
    estry, Wildlife
Considine, Bob, author, 38:91
Considine, Thomas, postmaster, 34:185
Consolidated Vermilion and Extension
    Co., 34:180
Constable, A. C., 21:446, 22:441
Constans, Henry P., 11:111, 292
Constans, Mrs. Henry P., 11:111
Constans, William, 23:322n, 34:97;
    papers, 11:42
Constans Hotel, Blue Earth, 11:111
Consumers Power Co., Minneapolis, 36:
    99
Continental Congress, history, 17:9,
    23:257
Conway, Alan, work reviewed, 37:256
Conway, Rev. John J., editor, 26:301
Conway, Margaret, 15:113; author, 11:
    446

Conwell, F. A., chaplain, 25:234,
    254, 343
Conwell, Russell H., 20:101; biog-
    raphy, 11:217; journalist, 14:394
Cook, A. D., 26:126, 133, 134
Cook, Arthur P., postmaster, 34:185
Cook, Charles, pioneer, 40:69
Cook, Elisia, 18:321
Cook, Fannie, author, 23:157
Cook, Franklin, engineer, 37:315
Cook, George S., photographer, 33:217
Cook, H. C., author, 22:326
Cook, J. B., and Son, St. Paul, liv-
    ery service, 33:3
Cook, Dr. J. F. D., author, 12:204
Cook, James, cartographer, 40:356
Cook, Jonathan, 13:120
Cook, Nancy, 20:119
Cook, William H., trader, 20:119
Cook, Mrs. William H., 20:119
Cook family, massacred, 11:71
Cook County, history, 11:217, 414,
    12:283, 17:359, 38:381, 386, 34:
    177, 267, 35:280; economic condi-
    tions, 21:449; forest fire, 36:
    132; geology, 36:320; schools, 39:
    310
Cook County Historical Society, 11:
    17, 13:74, 16:240, 489, 29:274,
    30:288; organized, 11:13; meet-
    ings, 11:15, 115, 217, 460, 12:
    186, 288, 13:56, 337, 442, 14:346,
    455, 456, 15:492, 16:488, 17:120,
    482, 18:462, 464, 19:359, 468, 20:
    454, 21:443, 22:339, 442, 23:396,
    25:96, 28:386, 29:91, 178, 30:78,
    34:314, 35:246; museum, 11:16, 13:
    71, 15:131; members, 11:19; dues,
    11:20; restoration project, 12:
    207, 292, 21:207; markers, 16:489
Cook County War History Committee,
    24:268
Cook Gold Mining and Milling Co.,
    stock certificate, 34:328
Cook Hotel, Rochester, history, 30:
    278
Cooke, Alistair, work reviewed, 33:
    184
Cooke, Dwight, radio commentator, 33:
    186
Cooke, Henry, financier, 37:97, 98
Cooke, Jay, 15:358, 19:104, 34:216;
    railroad activities, 11:191, 217,
    17:111, 218, 21:97, 28:284, 35:
    150, 36:179, 39:31; financier, 13:
    17, 18:76-79, 19:404, 20:336, 23:
    53, 34:68, 37:38, 89-100, 113,
    120, 39:211, 40:356; papers, 18:
    315, 20:168, 21:86, 33:220, 34:40,
    338; in Duluth, 18:473, 20:363,
    26:96, 28:303; failure, 25:102;
    autobiography, 30:182; expansion-
    ist, 33:315, 35:47
Cooke, Jay, and Co., Philadephia,
    failure, 12:253; Duluth activi-
    ties, 37:91-93, 97, 98, 100, 102,
    119-121
Cooke, Capt. L. W., Indian agent, 23:
    76
Cooke, Pitt, 37:102
Cooke and O'Brien, logging firm, 27:
    302
Cook's Creek, Man., 21:250, 252n
Cooks, Pastry Cooks, and Confection-
    ers Association, 21:387
Cooley, Mrs. H. M., 11:321
Cooley, Jerome E., biography, 22:323

Cooley, Rev. Myron, reminiscences,
    17:488; fisherman, 33:254-259
Cooley family, in Minnesota, 22:89
Cooley's Portable Creamery, 27:118n
Coolidge, Calvin, President, 17:15,
    314, 425, 20:317, 22:80, 423, 28:
    41n, 30:146, 35:159, 166, 38:182-
    184, 40:293
Coolidge, Mrs. Calvin, 35:159
Coolidge, Mrs. Marshall, memorial,
    15:343, 16:51, 102, 336, 18:46,
    21:194, 24:36, 25:41
Coon, Galen H., papers, 11:42
Coon, Dr. George, pioneer, 33:1
Coon Creek, Anoka County, pioneer
    life, 22:220, 35:254
Coon Rapids, government, 39:299
Cooney, Thomas, work reviewed, 27:
    138; speaker, 16:125, 27:78, 364
Coons, William S., author, 20:346
Cooper, David, MHS founder, 20:367;
    judge, 28:313, 30:109, 35:357,
    363, 39:39, 44, 144-146, 148, 151,
    268; lawyer, 35:5-7, 10
Cooper, Mrs. David, 28:313
Cooper, Edward A., biography, 14:333
Cooper, Emma, teacher, 21:458
Cooper, F. H., businessman, 29:67
Cooper, James, Senator, 30:104, 109,
    39:144
Cooper, James F., portrayal of Indi-
    ans, 16:105, 26:215, 33:304; au-
    thor, 17:451, 19:437, 20:107, 109,
    23:113, 40:275
Cooper, Rev. Leland R., 20:76, 25:55,
    26:64, 29:162; speaker, 20:188,
    21:39; author, 34:44, 37:86, 183,
    40:363, 412
Cooper, Paul L., author, 34:354
Cooper, Peter, presidential candi-
    date, 35:58
Cooper, William J., author, 12:418
Cooper, William S., author, 17:226
Cooper and Bailey, circus, 28:246
Co-operative Barrel Manufacturing
    Co., Minneapolis, 22:372
Cooperative Commonwealth Federation,
    29:341
Co-operative Land Association, Minne-
    sota, 22:375
Cooperative League of the U.S., his-
    tory, 38:203
Cooperative Light and Power Associa-
    tion, Two Harbors, history, 37:347
Co-operative movement, in agricul-
    ture, 11:100, 12:90, 17:474, 24:
    73, 26:381, 28:37-44, 304, 29:76,
    35:334; Minnesota, 17:239, 348,
    473, 18:410, 460, 19:154, 155,
    157n, 20:459, 21:103, 202, 340,
    22:314, 371-375, 24:78, 106, 27:
    365, 30:66, 264, 405, 33:188, 36:
    274; history, 18:106, 26:361; con-
    sumers, 18:323, 22:314, 25:301,
    38:203; among Finns, 18:324, 22:
    96, 25:325; Wisconsin, 19:151, 21:
    326; oil associations, 23:98, 200;
    Northwest, 24:174, 26:171, 27:165,
    168; Denmark, 27:119; Middle West,
    29:158, 35:203, 39:129; power as-
    sociations, 34:84, 37:347; U.S.,
    38:179, 180, 182. See also Dairy
    industry, individual organizations
Cooper-Cole, Dr. Fay, 19:340
Coopers, labor activities, 21:380,
    385, 388

Cooperstown, N.Y., baseball centennial, 19:338
Copas, Frank, speaker, 17:124
Copas, Washington County, frontier road, 40:238
Copeland, Mr. and Mrs. John, 38:313
Copeland, Joseph T., 25:357
Copeland, Perry, 38:313
Copeland, Peter W., in Russian railway corps, 38:310-325
Copeland, Mrs. Peter W., 38:313
Copland, James, author, 21:368
Copper mining, Lake Superior region, 11:263, 14:445, 15:154, 16:110, 21:424, 23:128, 239, 240, 26:260, 31:190, 32:215, 34:179, 35:241, 40:141; Michigan, 25:272, 28:251, 30:269, 32:86, 34:207, 35:339, 40:358; Minnesota, 29:212, 35:338; St. Croix Valley, 32:217; Wisconsin, 35:202; Red River Valley, 38:162
Copperheads, in Civil War, 24:154-156, 31:244, 37:126, 262
Copway, George, Chippewa Indian, 12:222, 19:450; missionary, 11:217, 17:404, 18:443, 20:81, 29:131
Coquart, Father Claude-Godefoy, missionary, 37:37, 39:302
"Cora," steamboat, 13:233, 234, 22:58n, 29:265, 39:144, 265 (cover)
Corbeau family, Chippewa Indians, 39:305n
Corbett, Cecilia, 35:268
Corbett, Sophia, 35:268
Corbett, W. A., 16:334
Corcoran, ———, Red River settler, 31:108
Corcoran, John, diary, 35:335
Corcoran, Col. Michael, 25:147
Corcoran, T., trader, 40:167n, 168n
Corcoran, William W., 20:336, 21:429
Corcoran Gallery, Washington, D.C., 31:248
Corcoran Township, Hennepin County, plat, 23:171, 36:36
Corey, Albert B., work reviewed, 23:58-60; author, 26:168, 265, 38:240; speaker, 29:368
Corey, Paul, author, 23:119, 121, 157
Corinth, Miss., in Civil War, 38:265
Corkran, William, author, 35:147
Corlett, William T., author, 16:475
Corley, Lt. James L., 38:2
Corlies, Chapman, & Drake, St. Paul, 38:81
Corliss, Carlton J., author, 15:474
Corliss, E. E., 13:393
Corliss, William, 13:393
Cormack, John, raft pilot, 23:324
Cormican, James, biography, 13:324
Cormick, Cezar, trader, 16:224
Cormie, J. A., author, 21:433
Cormorant Lake, Becker County, in rune-stone story, 13:183, 17:29, 28:59
Corn Belt Committee, 38:183
Corn raising, methods, 18:341, 24:303; increase, 20:62; Meeker County, 22:446; Middle West, 28:273, 33:64, 35:291, 36:278; history, 30:64, 34:160; by Indians, 34:174, 40:158. See also Agriculture
Cornelius, Jack, author, 36:195
Cornell, A. B., pioneer, 20:61
Cornell, Charles C., potter, 33:230
Cornell, Cyrus, potter, 33:230

Cornell, Ezra, 25:71
Cornell University, Ithaca, N.Y., regional history collection, 24:364, 26:243n, 27:61, 153, 29:384; Wisconsin pine lands, 25:69-71, 27:196, 199, 39:298
Corniea family, genealogy, 11:110
Corning, Judith, author, 21:343
Cornish, in mining, 14:448, 25:370, 410, 27:135, 204-206, 208, 212, 32:86, 40:341; language, 25:219, 27:56; Wisconsin, 27:134, 258; folklore, 33:184
Cornish Township, Sibley County, history, 13:122
"Cornstalk War," 12:202
Cornwell, C. C., and Son Hardware Co., Plainview, papers, 13:122
Cornwell, F. J., merchant, 13:122
"Corona," steamboat, 29:314
Coronado, Francisco de, explorer, 32:112
Corpe, Maj. Austin, 23:41
Correll, Ernst, editor, 29:166
Correll, Big Stone County, Baptist church, 19:234
Corrigan, Agnes, speaker, 17:346
Corrigan, Rev. Joseph A., work reviewed, 21:77; author, 17:83
Corruth, Fred H., career, 25:305
Corry, Thomas, trader, 14:229, 33:130
Corse, Gen. John M., 40:123
Cort and Murphy, theatrical troupe, 33:176
Cortissoz, Royal, author, 19:114
Cortot, Alfred, pianist, 39:60
Corvuso, McLeod County, history, 21:452
Corwin, Thomas, 26:357; Senator, 30:104; treasury secretary, 39:40
Corwith Brothers, Galena, Ill., steamboat owners, 22:17n
Cory, Ellery, letter, 39:320
Cosgrave, John O'Hara, artist, 23:356
Cosmopolitan Club, University of Minnesota, 20:325
Cosmos, history, 19:470, 21:452
Costain, E. B., steamboat captain, 36:128
Costain, Thomas B., work reviewed, 34:305
Costigan, Edward P., papers, 23:263-265
Costello, Mrs. Daniel, author, 17:236
Cosulich, Bernice, author, 11:458
Coté, Henry, children baptized, 39:304; builds chapel, 39:305, 306
Coté, Margareth, mission teacher, 39:303, 304, 305n
Coté (Cotté), Pierre, trader, 15:105, 22:276, 23:244-246, 26:362, 36:245; at Grand Portage, 39:306-309
Coteau des Prairies, forests, 26:66; name, 31:193; explored, 33:352; quarry, 36:18, 19, 69
Coterie Club, Benson, 26:290
Cottage Grove, agriculture, 14:386, 17:358, 394, 18:408, 24:290, 29:5, 12, 204; Congregational church, 15:346, 466, 17:394; in 1860s, 15:466, 16:349, 39:270; G.A.R. post, 16:430; described, 17:287; Severance farm, 22:164; dairy, 27:113; settled, 34:18n, 40:8, 9; post office, 40:83; frontier road, 40:233, 235

Cottage Grove Academy, projected school, 14:146
Cottage Hospital (St. Barnabas Hospital), Minneapolis, 24:372, 26:94
Cotter, H. M. S., author, 22:432
Cotter, Bishop Joseph, 33:54
Cotter High School, Winona, 29:354
Cottman, William B., editor, 34:311
Cotton, Austin D., 18:123n
Cotton, production, 40:296
Cottonwood, history, 39:130
Cottonwood County, ethnic settlements, 12:274, 14:444, 32:62; census, 13:426, 14:254, 255, 258, 259, 261; history, 14:244, 17:485, 19:116, 21:219, 24:65, 36:106, 195; politics, 14:247-251, 262; courthouse square, 16:247; land company, 16:470; roads, 19:121, 234; Mennonite community, 20:181, 459, 23:88; insurance company, 20:357; coal beds, 22:109; grasshopper plagues, 24:382, 25:100, 37:209; medicine, 29:353; historic sites, 29:361, 30:400; Methodist organizations, 30:395; loan companies, 35:307; petroglyphs, 40:263
Cottonwood County Historical and Old Settlers Association, 11:14, 16:240, 26:283, 30:78; collections, 11:18, 17:231; members, 11:19; dues, 11:20; meetings, 11:112, 12:101, 14:346, 15:134, 16:123, 17:120, 19:116, 20:95, 23:100, 27:75, 28:86, 295, 29:361; museum, 12:37, 14:119, 30:165
Cottonwood County War History Committee, 23:390
Cottonwood Oil Co., co-operative, 17:348, 21:103
Cottonwood (Waraju) River, Cottonwood and Redwood counties, described, 11:173; trading post, 11:377; Norwegian settlement, 12:272; garrison, 38:283, 286
Cottrell, W. F., compiler, 25:83
Couch, Gen. Darius N., Union officer, 25:36, 228, 232n, 245, 246, 351, 354
Coues, Elliott, 16:157; editor, 15:353, 37:175, 38:199; ornithologist, 22:92, 24:255; author, 33:182, 40:147
Cougar (mountain lion), in Minnesota, 30:130, 33:354
Coughlin, Brigid, speaker, 34:218
Coughlin, Father Charles E., 37:5, 39:210; biography, 40:359
Coughlin, J. P., 23:195, 24:188
Couillard, Cornelious, 12:197
Couldock, C. W., actor, 23:310
Coulter, M. R., 23:391
Coulter, W. J., 19:164
Coulter, William, butcher, 14:272
Council Bluffs, Iowa, early press, 12:439, 13:111; lumber market, 18:175; Mormon mission, 36:289
Council for Democracy, 23:292
Council of National Defense, 23:389; Minneapolis child welfare work, 16:336
Council of Underwater Archaeology, 39:171
Counselman, Ted B., engineer, 34:274, 277, 280, 281, 283

"Countess of Dufferin," locomotive, 21:260
Countryman, Gratia, 19:67, 20:50; speaker, 11:120, 19:66, 21:83, 113; librarian, 17:209, 20:39, 39: 122, 270; author, 23:386
Countryman, Levi N., farmer, 13:142, 150; diary, 28:92, 39:269, 270
Country Press (Moorhead), history, 21:448
Coupanger, Matilda, 20:435
Courcelles, sieur de, 16:404
Coureurs de bois, in fur trade, 19: 277; as explorers, 20:341
Courserole, Joseph, 38:2
Court, Frank A., 23:390
Courtland Township, Nicollet County, Lutheran church, 15:480; politics, 28:36; log houses, 37:76n
Courtnay, T. E., author, 33:316
Courts, 18:122; district, 15:348, 23: 387, 35:4-7; probate, 17:189193; justice of the peace, 17:339, 467; juvenile, 17:363; Montreal, Que., 21:117-148; Wisconsin, 27:238, 36: 275. See also Minnesota Supreme Court, individual cities and counties
Courtwright, John, at Fort Snelling, 30:103
Courville, Cyril B., author, 35:241
"Cousin Jacks," see Cornish
Cove, Mrs. William, pioneer, 24:203
Covenant church, 34:61; Cloquet, 16: 121
Coventry, Charles B., author, 21:365
Coverdale, William H., author, 23: 385; Canadiana collection, 25:302
Covered wagons, trains, 11:212, 336; journeys, 11:325, 333, 14:303-305, 16:126, 247, 367, 17:488, 19:234, 20:469, 21:210, 223, 453, 22:222, 436, 34:22; centennial, 11:452; depicted, 12:50, 14:303, 30:116
"Covington," gunboat, 40:288
Cowan, Ann M., author, 16:480
Cowan, Eugene, speaker, 19:316
Cowan, Granniss, author, 14:448
Cowan, Robert E., author, 14:448
Cowan, Dr. William, 16:480
Cowden, Elizabeth, 19:469
Cowden, Fred, memorial, 19:469
Cowdrey, Mary B., works reviewed, 19: 203-205, 34:120
Cowell, Mrs. Sidney R., compiler, 24: 367
Cowgill, Rev. F. B., 31:82n
Cowing, Cedric B., work reviewed, 39: 293
Cowing, Phillip, speaker, 12:105
Cowles, Florence C., author, 11:210
Cowles, John, publisher, 35:384
Cowles, Walter C., 19:163, 176
Cowles, William P., architect, 33:334
Cowley, Augustus M. P., banker, 24: 375
Cowley, Mrs. A. T., author, 15:477
Cowley, Malcolm, 39:266; author, 32: 115
Cowling, Donald J., speaker, 13:121, 23:299; college president, 40:256
Cox, Bill, author, 30:264
Cox, E. St. Julien, impeachment, 15: 224, 16:246; in Sioux Outbreak, 28:294
Cox, Hanford F., author, 19:358

Cox, Sister Ignatius L., letters, 30: 1, 10
Cox, Isaac J., speaker, 13:327
Cox, William S., career, 26:173; naval record, 40:348-350
Cox, William T., author, 21:212, 253; conservationist, 32:180, 37:223
Coxe, Dr. Daniel, 19:393, 396
Coxey, Jacob S., politician, 36:120, 122
Coxey's Army, history, 11:104; in Minnesota, 11:319
Coy, Owen C., author, 13:108, 15:124
Coyne, James H., author, 13:253
Cozzens, James G., author, 20:116
Crabb, A. Richard, author, 30:64
Craddick, Harry L., author, 34:165
Craemer, Henry, interpreter, 14:56
Cragg, Mrs. Arthur, author, 16:372, 18:320
Cragun, Merrill K., 29:369; author, 30:39, 174; speaker, 30:83
Craig, Charles P., 37:260
Craig, Gerald M., work reviewed, 35: 142
Craig, Hardin, 26:306, 307
Craig, Marion J., author, 26:302
Craigie, James G., miller, 20:353
Craigville (Craig), Koochiching County, settled, 22:415; logging railroad, 28:376
Craik, Andrew, 16:248
Craine, Mrs. ---, diary, 29:266
Crainge, John, 11:238n
Cram, Ralph Adams, architect, 26:173, 39:155
Cramahé, Hector, lieutenant governor, 11:256, 15:96
Cramer, Julian, pseud., see Chester, Joseph L.
Cramer, Zadok, author, 28:377
Cramer, Lake County, Finnish settlement, 18:324; ghost town, 34:182
Crampton, John A., author, 40:95
Cramsie, Jennie, 35:268
Cramsie, Mary, 35:268, 269
Cramton, Louis C., author, 14:225
Cranberries, early use, 14:382, 16: 378, 17:415, 22:59, 34:146, 36: 257, 39:70; Wisconsin, 25:198, 26: 69, 170; trade item, 38:71
Crandall, A. W., author, 17:126
Crandall, Ethan, papers, 20:348
Crandall, Prudence, abolitionist, 33: 218
Crane, Edgar, author, 28:372, 374
Crane, Hart, poet, 20:108
Crane, Neil T., author, 36:282
Crane, Ralph E., legislator, 34:222
Crane, Richard T., 12:107, 21:154, 37:264
Crane, Verner, 15:455
Crane, Warren B., letters, 21:344
Crane, Mrs. William H., 14:429
Crane Lake, St. Louis County, trading post, 11:360, 28:285, 33:261, 36: 242-244; stage station, 16:297; archaeology, 28:373; portage road, 34:178
Cranston, J. Herbert, author, 31:54
Cranstone, Lefevre J., artist, 32:45
Crapsey, Lura A., author, 25:100
Crary, N.D., Scandinavian settlement, 28:268
Craven, Avery, 16:327; works reviewed, 23:260-263, 36:100; speaker, 15:119, 17:105, 23:82; author,

16:196, 325, 19:435, 23:377, 34:81
Craven, Joseph W., publisher, 21:339; legislator, 35:306
Craven, Wesley F., works reviewed, 29:345, 30:255, 31:247
Craven, William, earl of, 16:399, 419, 423, 425n
Crawford, Andrew W., 33:338
Crawford, Charles, 12:130
Crawford, Charly, 35:174
Crawford, Helen, author, 14:204
Crawford, James R., speaker, 23:399
Crawford, Kenneth, author, 17:216
Crawford, Thomas, sculptor, 25:227n
Crawford, W. L., livestock dealer, 24:106
Crawford, William S., balloonist, 38: 171, 172
Crawford, Winona, mixed-blood, 12: 127, 130n
Crawford County, Mich., boundaries, 18:165, 21:428, 26:362
Crawford County, Wis., boundaries, 16:347, 17:224, 21:428, 23:384, 25:198
Crawley, F. Radford, 23:385
Cray, Judge Lorin, 15:76; bequest, 11:20, 20:350, 21:49, 104, 33:210
Cray, Willard R., lawyer, 21:196; papers, 21:194
Crazy Horse, Sioux leader, 34:355
Credit River (Elk Creek), Scott County, 21:167n, 168
Cree (Kilistinon) Indians, 15:170, 176; in fur trade, 11:265, 18:237, 32:236-238; North Dakota, 19:379, 35:339; in art, 23:154; language, 21:433, 31:238; conjuring, 24:54; relations with Sioux, 24:318, 32: 230, 231, 234-236; in Seven Years' War, 32:233; Manitoba, 34:77n; hunts, 35:240; described, 37:336, 40:158
Creek Indians, removal, 15:121
Creel, George, author, 29:82, 34:222
Creele, Herrlee G., editor, 38:304, 305
Creighton, Donald G., editor, 26:80; author, 35:153, 36:65, 191
"Cremona," steamboat, 15:86, 88
Crepeau, Henry J., 24:274
Crépeuil, François de, Jesuit, 16:199
Crescent baseball club, Red Wing, 19: 166, 168, 170, 178
Crescent Grange, Anoka County, history, 17:481
Cresco, Iowa, crop failure, 20:159
Cressey, Rev. Alfred, 31:82n
Cressey, Rev. T. K., speaker, 12:397
Cressy, C., teacher, 13:141
Cressy, Rev. E. W., 13:148
Cretin, Bishop Joseph, 11:105, 12: 337, 13:339, 17:475, 20:85, 460, 24:72, 28:321, 30:3, 7, 11, 13, 31:25, 32:37, 39, 39:154; career, 11:217, 13:215, 14:110, 121, 293, 15:81, 354, 16:119, 18:436, 22: 334, 29:354, 33:223, 38:193; author, 11:324; papers, 15:122, 17: 102; educator, 16:333, 483, 17: 349, 25:373, 374, 30:5, 6, 10; colonizer, 35:46
Cretin High School, St. Paul, history, 29:354
Crèvecoeur, Michel G. J. de (J. Hector St. John), map maker, 12:82;

author, 29:154, 33:304, 40:312, 402
Crever, B. H., 18:471
Crever, Willard G., author, 27:76, 362
Crevier, Joseph, missionary, 11:306; letters, 12:82
Crick, B. R., work reviewed, 38:198
Crile, Lucinda, author, 28:70
Crime, 16:128, 34:209, 39:262; homicide, 11:213, 12:97, 14:93, 16:97, 116, 174, 175, 17:154, 430n, 18: 124n, 240, 19:379, 23:98, 26:288, 28:209, 213, 32:98, 33:52, 34:344, 37:115, 38:11-20, 39, 133, 134n, 234; horse theft, 13:153-157, 17: 235, 421, 26:120; smuggling, 22: 280; arson, 28:209; lynching, 28: 213; swindles, 29:84, 33:89, 34: 358; assault, 37:165; kidnaping, 37:343. See also James brothers, Younger brothers
Crinkley, Mrs. M. A., author, 22:102, 438, 25:399
Crippen, Harlan R., author, 23:283
Crippen, Raymond, author, 35:245
Crispus Attucks Home for the Aged, St. Paul, 38:80
Criterion Theater, see Pence Opera House
Crittenden, Christopher C, 22:428; author, 23:279, 376, 25:310, 401; speaker, 24:70; editor, 24:377, 25:403
Crittenden, Gen. George B., Confederate officer, 12:319, 38:262, 264, 39:179, 181
Crittenden, John J., politician, 14: 190, 24:312, 314, 39:143, 150, 151
Crittenden, Gen. Thomas T., Union officer, 39:192, 193
Croatians, Mesabi Range, 21:290, 23: 387, 27:204, 210-213, 40:341, 347; Minnesota, 22:96, 180, 30:282; U.S., 38:241
Crocker, ---, 18:138, 139
Crocker, Mrs. H. P., author, 16:132
Crocker, William, 34:204
Crockett, Davy, folk hero, 21:95, 22: 313, 26:166, 33:265, 40:391, 403
Croffut, William A., author, 12:327; journalist, 14:406
Croffut and Clark, St. Anthony, publishers, 11:444, 12:85
Croft, Rev. Fred, 20:352
Crofton, Maj. R. E. A., at Fort Wadsworth, 35:173
Croghan, George, 29:65
Croghan, Col. George, 29:65; reports from frontier, 36:148
Crokatt, Charles, merchant, 11:238
Crokatt, James, merchant, 11:238
Croly, Herbert, philosopoher, 36:97
Crommelin, Claude A., diary, 37:154-160
Crommelin, Henri, quoted, 37:152, 153
Crompton, F. C. B., author, 14:221
Cromwell, history, 38:243
Cronau, Rudolf, author, 24:222; artist, 36:21
Cronk, Iva G., author, 24:385, 25:313
Cronlund, Martin H., author, 27:162
Cronsioe, Svante, editor, 17:403, 31: 27
Crook, Gen. George, 19:389, 33:280; autobiography, 27:161
Crooked Lake, border lake, history,

19:233, 29:282; fur trade, 29:133; pictographs, 36:102, 38:91. See also Picture Rock
Crooks, Mr. and Mrs. George, 21:108
Crooks, Hester, see Boutwell, Mrs. William T.
Crooks, John S., biography, 14:333
Crooks, Mrs. Margaret R., 11:322
Cooks, Ramsay, family, 11:205; trader, 11:217, 15:421, 422, 473, 17: 95, 210, 343, 18:193, 19:95, 306, 20:262, 21:95, 22:205, 277, 23: 234, 347, 30:259, 32:186, 34:245, 35:282, 39:254, 303, 316, 40:22-31, 141, 178, 179n, 182-186, 214; American Fur Co. president, 13: 226, 235, 14:93, 196, 421; letters, 14:98, 21:93, 27:130
Crooks, Mrs. Ramsay, portrait, 12:324
Crooks, Richard, singer, 39:62
Crooks, William, 15:473; papers, 15: 223; legislator, 36:58; railroad promoter, 38:46; in Sioux Outbreak, 38:110, 280, 357, 39:236
Crookston, religious groups, 11:117, 16:251, 17:219; history, 11:223, 12:135, 17:128, 18:116, 34:171, 39:271; incorporated, 15:491; pageant, 16:237; newspapers, 17:103; flood, 17:230; Elks lodge, 17:362; band, 19:474; drama, 20:466, 28: 105; unions, 21:393; agricultural school, 22:413, 32:119; land office, 23:30, 34:1, 5;railroad, 28: 383; sawmill, 29:137, 138, 145; hospital, 35:381; museum, 37:135, 38:92; archaeology, 38:162, 164
Crookston Daily Times, founded, 17: 128
Crookston Lumber Co., 31:75; railroad logging, 27:302, 304; mill, 29:148
Crookston War History Committee, 23: 390
Cropley, Carrie, compiler, 29:356
Croquet game, in Atwater, 40:33
Crosby, Francis M., pioneer lawyer, 21:413
Crosby, Franklin M., 25:154n
Crosby, Fred, author, 15:140
Crosby, George C., 26:45, 29:97
Crosby, George H., biography, 13:213
Crosby, Henry W., Lakeland pioneer, 27:154, 34:132, 36:207
Crosby, Howard W., photographer, 33: 52n
Crosby, John, I, 34:204
Crosby, John, II, 34:204
Crosby, Thomas, horse breeder, 26:118
Crosby family, genealogy, 25:315
Crosby, name, 21:349; balloon flight, 38:335
Crosier Order (Order of the Holy Cross), mission, 14:239; history, 37:221
Cross, Dr. Edwin C., 19:169; in Rochester, 20:238-240; speaker, 27:115
Cross, Dr. Elisha W., in Rochester, 20:238-240
Cross, Henry H., artist, 19:123
Cross, Jules, speaker, 23:397
Cross, Marion E., review by, 34:204; works reviewed, 20:66-68, 31:114; translator, 23:57; author, 34:173
Cross, Whitney R., author, 24:364, 27:61
Cross, William, diaries, 17:212, 18: 47

Cross Lake, see Lake Bemidji
Cross River, Cook County, 19:457; name, 12:207, 13:187
Crossen, Henry, 28:262
Crossing Sky, Chippewa leader, 29:35
Crothers, Samuel M., author, 26:301
Crouse, Kenneth, author, 29:170
Crouse, Nellis M., work reviewed, 35: 140
Crow Creek, S.D., Sioux at, 37:272. See also Fort Thompson
Crow Feather, Chippewa leader, 29:35
Crow Flies High Butte, N.D., 40:193
Crow (Eokoros) Indians, described, 14:375, 37:336; in Red River area, 15:232, 35:339; at Fort Snelling, 28:349; in fur trade, 34:326, 40: 201; dwellings, 35:377
Crow Island, Mississippi River, trading post, 11:372, 13:222
Crow River, Hennepin and Wright counties, pioneer life, 16:132; historic site, 29:87; located, 29: 216n; Winnebago settlement, 40: 332; archaeology, 40:339
Crow River Valley Medical Society, 16:471
Crow Wing, trading post, 11:218, 26: 227, 28:208, 209, 218, 35:337, 36: 40; missions, 12:84, 332, 14:56, 57, 20:90, 431, 27:289, 28:190, 210, 291, 29:168, 33:185, 36:40n, 39:305, 308n; agency, 12:202, 27: 296, 297n, 28:214; treaty, 13:389; mail service, 16:294, 33:89, 40: 83; roads, 16:296, 21:234; Christmas celebration, 16:379; described, 17:225, 22:85, 40:274, 275, 277; battle, 21:182; logging, 24:130; river port, 33:10, 271n; Indian reservation, 36:267, 269, 38:353; council, 39:259
Crow Wing County, "Blueberry War," 11:454; lumbering, 12:428; Indian mounds, 15:485, 25:340, 28:193; pioneers, 18:212; forestry, 19: 121; place names, 21:286, 346, 350; steamboating, 22:108; history, 22:344, 36:195; Finns, 25: 318; nursing home, 38:377
Crow Wing County Historical Society, 16:240, 20:46, 30:399; organized, 11:13; bequest, 11:20; meetings, 11:217, 12:208, 14:346, 348, 15: 245, 485, 16:489, 17:120, 355, 18: 464, 19:116, 20:95, 21:107, 22: 439, 29:361; tours, 12:449, 30: 275; museum, 13:74, 214, 294, 357, 14:235, 15:366, 16:242, 360, 17: 491, 18:222, 333, 19:469, 20:357, 455, 21:330-333, 22:216, 23:11, 12, 13, 26:89, 27:361, 28:86, 295, 386; WPA project, 17:346, 355; archaeological survey, 35:340
Crow Wing County War History Committee, 23:390
Crow Wing Land Association, 14:435
Crow Wing River, Crow Wing County, 32:189; fur trade, 11:372, 20:12, 13, 32:230, 233, 234, 236; hunting, 20:50; trail, 21:229; name, 21:346; described, 23:335; logging, 29:137; German settlement, 31:25
Crow Wing State Park, 36:240, 37:88
Crowe, Harry S., work reviewed, 37:80
Crowe, Isaac, papers, 18:315, 19:48

Crowe, Robert, author, 14:239
Crowe, William H., diary, 35:336
Crowley, C. J., speaker, 18:465
Crowley, Cornelius, speaker, 14:229
Crown Point, N.Y., military post, 15:
110, 18:390
Crown Point Roller Mill, Faribault,
11:274
Crowson, Mrs. Altie, 29:266
Croy, Homer, work reviewed, 28:273;
author, 26:308, 28:186, 31:62, 34:
125, 35:202
Crozier, ———, baseball player, 19:174
Cruger, Lt. William E., 18:402
Cruikshank, E. A., editor, 12:199,
14:228
Crum, Rufus K., 13:449
Crump, Rev. E. J., 22:170, 172
Crump, J. L., editor, 19:125
Crust, Edward, 12:101
Cruveilhier, Jean, author, 21:364
Crystal Bay, Lake Minnetonka, 29:295
Crystal City, N.D., settled, 33:315
Crystal Lake, Blue Earth County, in
Sioux Outbreak, 38:279
Crystal Lake Township, Hennepin Coun-
ty, town board, 16:248
Crystal Palace Exhibition, New York,
15:413, 17:143n, 26:358; Minnesota
displays, 11:174n, 12:445, 16:256,
26:66, 34:287
Cubberley, Ellwood P., educator, 35:
198
Culbertson, Alexander, frontiersman,
20:328, 33:131
Culbertson, John B., slaveholder, 25:
202; settler, 40:26n
Culbertson, Thaddeus A., work reviewed, 33:131; explorer, 34:304
Culkin, Dorothy B., 12:283
Culkin, William E., 11:315, 12:187,
322, 16:241, 19:312, 20:453; "William Albert McGonagle," 11:413-
420; work reviewed, 12:422; local
history work, 11:14, 16:244, 18:
223, 19:64, 20:451; author, 11:22,
438, 14:462, 15:244, 17:123, 357;
speaker, 11:51, 52, 118, 224, 338,
12:210, 281, 287, 454, 13:121,
216, 286, 14:75, 238, 455, 495,
15:138, 492, 16:371, 488, 18:465,
19:119; tributes, 18:462, 19:118,
30:288; legislator, 35:342, 343
Culkin Lake, Lake County, name, 18:
462
Cullen, Elaine P., 20:44
Cullen, Orland, pioneer, 33:1
Cullen, Maj. William J., politician,
26:195, 197, 198, 201n; Sioux
agent, 38:131
Culligan, John M., author, 15:456
Culliton, John T., author, 11:327
Culp, Julia, singer, 39:59
Culver, Dr. C. A., speaker, 13:345
Culver, J. B., 12:384; banker, 37:120
Culver, J. M., labor official, 21:376
Culver, Joshua, postmaster, 34:185
Culver, Dr. N. S., 20:238
Culver, Norman K., millwright, 24:101
Culver, history, 21:456, 23:302
Culver and Farrington, St. Paul firm,
37:213n
Cumberland, Duke of, papers, 18:194
"Cumberland," steamboat, 24:166
Cumberland, Wis., community survey,
25:61

Cumberland City, Hennepin County,
townsite, 26:397
Cumberland Gap, Tenn., in westward
movement, 15:257
Cumberland House, Sask., trading
post, 18:82, 28:2, 33:130, 261,
40:191
Cummings, A. P., journalist, 34:139
Cummings, Albert B., insurgent, 22:
79
Cummings, Maj. Alexander, 23:137
Cummings, Mrs. D. S., 19:232
Cummings (Coming), John, 22:288
Cummings, R. W., real-estate agent,
24:133
Cummings, Richard O., author, 23:284
Cummings, Robert, at Redwood agency,
11:177, 183
Cummings, Robert W., alderman, 35:120
Cummings, N.D., farming, 15:238
Cummins, Albert B., reformer, 33:41
Cummins, John R., pioneer farmer, 16:
71, 18:285, 288, 290, 295, 23:
325n, 29:8n, 10, 24
Cunard Line, steamships, 30:188
Cundy, Ernest, trader, 11:464
Cundy, William E., 25:238
Cuneo, Mrs. Andrew, pioneer motorist,
26:24
Cuneo, Cyrus, artist, 36:249n
Cuneo, John R., work reviewed, 36:273
Cunningham, Ann Pamela, biography,
39:336
Cunningham, H. D., missionary, 11:316
Cunningham, Mary E., review by, 36:
62; author, 27:66, 353, 28:187,
29:163, 370; editor, 28:71, 30:
286; speaker, 29:348
Cunningham, Russell N., work re-
viewed, 37:258
Cunningham, William J., author, 13:
441, 23:87
Cunnington, Henry, musician, 33:100
Cunnion, T. C., lumberjack, 33:184
Cupperud, Roy H., author, 20:363
Curling, described, 29:169; Missis-
sippi River, 40:386
Curme, George O., linguist, 39:133,
134, 139
Curot, Michel, trader, 20:14, 28:3,
145n; diary, 28:155n
Curran, Hugh A., work reviewed, 15:
214-216
Curran, James W., author, 20:85, 21:
91
Currelly, C. T., author, 20:199
Current, Richard N., review by, 31:
240; work reviewed, 31:113; au-
thor, 30:26, 31, 31:256
Current Events Club, Crookston, 13:
323
Current News Club, Marshall, 15:363
Currie, Irish colony, 19:92, 31:22,
35:139
Currier, F. D., 26:107
Currier, Frederick M., legislator,
35:308, 309
Currier, Gilman, speculator, 39:90
Currier, Granville, 25:225
Currier, Merrill, speculator, 39:90
Currier, Nathaniel, lithographer, 19:
458
Curry, Henry B., music critic, 33:103
Curry, John S., career, 25:278
Curry, Thomas, trader, 11:258, 264
Curti, Margaret W., author, 36:230
Curti, Merle, 26:161; review by, 29:

57; works reviewed, 30:380-382,
36:230; author, 25:294, 29:103,
31:250, 32:192, 33:262, 34:211,
38:201
Curtin, Andrew G., governor of Penn-
sylvania, 25:359
Curtis, Amanda, 13:117
Curtis, Carolyn, work reviewed, 31:
111
Curtis, Chauncy W., labor leader, 21:
389, 22:372
Curtis, Elsie, 12:449
Curtis, Gold T., lawyer, 40:222
Curtis, Harley, postmaster, 36:210
Curtis, Mrs. J. L., 12:449
Curtis, Lucile H., 39:225
Curtis, Gen. Samuel R., 25:34
Curtis, Will, publisher, 39:225
Curtis, Mrs. Will, 17:124, 18:111,
20:100, 22:219; speaker, 19:362
Curtis and Eaton, St. Anthony, bank-
ing firm, 35:129
Curtiss, Glen H., airplane builder,
27:168
Curtiss-Wedge, Franklin, author, 20:
218
Cushing, Caleb, land operations, 17:
404, 23:164, 24:127, 130, 25:395,
27:312; water-power interests, 18:
444, 38:242
Cushing, John P., papers, 13:180
Cushing, Mary W., author, 34:214
Cushman, Charlotte, actress, 18:153
Cushman, Harvey B., 23:62
Cushman, Robert E., author, 33:161n
Cussons, James M., miller, 24:89,
100, 102, 27:80
Custer, Edgar A., autobiography, 18:
452
Custer, Gen. George A., 34:245, 35:
241; Black Hills expedition, 11:
106, 12:175, 32:219, 40:254, 410;
1876 campaign, 12:302, 13:331, 22:
175, 27:97, 28:79, 169, 35:333;
career, 16:226, 31:251; explorer,
34:303
Custer, Big Stone County, post office, 17:485
Customhouse and Federal Courts Building, St. Paul, 25:3, 38:187, 40:
135
Cut Foot Sioux Lake, Itasca County,
name, 16:101
Cut Nose, Sioux Indian, 11:285, 13:
443, 15:470, 23:365, 38:128
Cuthbertson, G. A., author, 16:348
Cuthbertson, Stuart, author, 21:423
Cutler, Alpheus, Mormon leader, 13:
386, 36:289
Cutler, Dr. C. W., speaker, 16:361
Cutler, Erastus, Culterite, 13:387
Cutler, F. Sanford, reviews by, 33:
307, 346, 34:116, 255, 346, 35:89,
195, 199, 235, 333, 377, 36:32,
33, 319; author, 34:220, 35:156,
36:35; museum curator, 36:108
Cutler, Rev. Manasseh, 31:181; land
operator, 16:204
Cutler, William W., 11:54, 55, 12:
207, 14:78, 16:53, 20:50, 427, 23:
50, 26:45, 28:47; speaker, 13:291,
14:343, 432, 25:54; MHS president,
14:79, 15:83, 85, 310, 457, 458,
16:68, 69, 211, 301, 306, 466, 17:
62, 70
Cutlerites, Mormon group, Minnesota
colony, 13:385-394

Cuyuna Range, 11:461, 19:464, 22:103, 32:46; explored, 13:213; geology, 15:131, 34:358; name, 21:350; history, 22:43, 103; discovered, 27:160, 263, 338, 30:267, 409; in fiction, 36:81; manganese, 39:79. See also Iron mining
"Cyclone," steamboat, 37:285, 292
Cyphers, John T., house, 38:344, 345
Cyriax, R. J., author, 34:80
Czech Central West Presbytery, 15:32n
Czechoslovakia, established, 15:41; bibliography, 27:242; in World War I, 38:323-325
Czechs, immigration, 11:113, 318, 24:259; McLeod County, 11:334, 15:26-42, 85, 342, 16:331, 488, 17:128, 237, 21:452, 22:224, 23:297, 398, 34:356; Steele County, 12:343, 13:216, 14:123, 20:63, 21:457; Le Sueur County, 12:451, 13:450, 14:120; Minnesota, 13:114, 269-276, 19:345, 21:203, 22:320, 23:40, 381, 24:98, 101, 25:410, 28:75, 266, 333, 31:28, 35:152, 38:243, 39:72; Ramsey County, 13:270n; Iowa, 14:341, 15:33, 25:299, 26:273; in Sioux Outbreak, 15:28; religious affiliations, 15:30-36; language, 15:38; social life, 15:38-40; sokols, 15:40, 25:300, 36:91; in World War I, 15:40; U.S., 15:67, 17:61; almanacs, 15:445; South Dakota, 19:222; contributions, 22:96; Twin Cities, 23:68, 33:6; Northwest, 23:286; bibliography, 26:167; Mesabi Range, 27:204, 207, 208, 211; Michigan, 27:205; Morrison County, 29:358; Milwaukee, 30:139; sports, 36:91

Daaes family, 21:65
Dablon, Father Claude, 13:254; author, 25:296, 26:75, 37:128, 40:141
Dabney, Virginius, author, 17:477
Dacotah House, New Ulm, 24:190, 27:328, 32:173; history, 15:365, 20:356, 25:314
Daggett, Francis E., G.A.R. commander, 16:430, 439, 441; journalist, 25:307
Daggett, Paul, author, 15:105; speaker, 16:235
Daggett Brook Township, Crow Wing County, organized, 26:259
Dagobert, Father, 24:53
Daguerre, Louis J. M., photographer, 33:288, 34:28, 29
Daguerreotypes, history, 21:95, 26:170, 29:164, 34:28-33, 35:182
Dahl, Borghild, 29:298; author, 25:309, 30:93, 36:90
Dahl, James, speaker, 18:334
Dahl, John F., lawyer, 21:196
Dahl, Lucile, 36:239
Dahl, Myrtle H., teacher, 35:371
Dahl, Theodor H., 16:471; biography, 11:328
Dahlberg, Jean C., "Laura A. Linton," 38:21-23
Dahlen, Andrew, biography, 16:337
Dahlen, Knute T., lawyer, 21:196
Dahlgren, Frank, speaker, 22:441

Dahlhielm, Erik, author, 22:112
Dahlhjelm, A. M., Swedish pioneer, 17:400-402; letters, 31:27
Dahlin, Georg L., author, 18:71
Dahlquist, C. B., 19:362, 22:341
Daigneau, Don V., author, 11:116, 23:109
Daigneau, F. E., 13:427
Daily Bee (Duluth), 18:473
Daily Journal (International Falls), historical editions, 16:366, 17:361
Dairy industry, co-operatives, 11:100, 289, 457, 12:335, 430, 13:216, 15:115, 251, 348, 482, 486, 17:236, 239, 480, 486, 18:470, 19:151, 155-157, 239, 20:82, 360, 21:340, 452, 22:221, 224, 226, 265-268, 346, 420, 23:106, 197, 199, 301, 24:175, 190, 273, 25:58, 27:365, 29:158; economic aspect, 11:117; pioneer, 11:336, 24:104, 33:31; Minnesota communities, 12:337, 451, 13:449, 16:128, 251, 17:492, 20:357, 466, 26:272, 37:20, 21, 108; development, 17:101, 18:411, 27:107-121, 33:326; Wisconsin, 19:149-152, 157, 29:268, 335, 39:31; education, 19:152-161; university farm, 22:413; cattle breeds, 26:123, 28:371; Ontario, 28:366; extent, 30:154; periodicals, 36:190; protected, 40:147, 320, 323, 324. See also Agriculture
"Dakota," stern-wheeler, 21:254, 259n, 261n
Dakota City, Nicollet County, plat, 17:238
Dakota City Guards, volunteer unit, 16:173n
Dakota County, Norwegian settlements, 11:286, 12:271; politics, 13:141, 26:201, 35:98, 301, 36:173, 39:49; pioneers, 14:438; archives, 15:195-197, 345, 21:327, 449; pageant, 16:493; medical history, 21:102, 213; windmill, 24:190; farming, 24:293, 302, 26:371, 29:2n, 13, 26; surveyed, 28:395; mail service, 36:193; courthouse, 37:202; Indians, 37:274, 275; poor farm, 38:369n
Dakota County Agricultural Society, 13:147, 150, 22:253; fairs, 15:246; meeting, 23:324; constitution, 28:92
Dakota County Guard, volunteer unit, 16:173n, 177
Dakota County Historical and Archeological Society, organized, 20:351; meetings, 21:107, 334, 23:100, 29:91, 178, 274; activities, 22:440, 30:87, 37:264; museum, 34:267, 35:99, 338; publication, 39:132, 40:148
Dakota County Tribune (Farmington), history, 15:245
Dakota County War History Committee, 23:390
Dakota House, New Ulm, see Dacotah House
Dakota House, St. Paul, 14:300
Dakota Indians, see Sioux Indians
Dakota Institute, Hastings, 15:349, 16:383
Dakota Land Co., 14:244, 245, 246,

250, 251, 259, 261, 21:220, 35:238, 38:57, 217
Dakota Landing, Dakota County, townsite, 17:278
Dakota (Sioux) language, 33:273, 275, 37:277, 281; used by missionaries, 11:317, 15:222, 275-278, 16:140-145, 333, 354, 21:16, 21, 25-28, 30, 31, 158, 160, 272, 276, 278, 279, 282, 413, 27:264; textbooks, 12:316; publications, 17:224, 21:26, 280; used in fur trade, 18:439, 20:261; vocabulary, 19:95, 30:216, 331; dictionaries, 19:448, 21:161, 277, 25:390, 30:298, 33:57, 351, 36:68, 280, 39:150; described, 21:325, 23:181; bibliography, 24:71. See also Sioux Indians
Dakota missions, 16:133, 335; publications, 16:143; history, 16:345, 354, 25:399
Dakota Sentinel (Nininger), established, 13:150
Dakota Southern Railway, 19:108
Dakota Territory, missions, 11:212, 36:291, 292, 38:385; stock raising, 11:324; settled, 13:435, 22:160, 161, 23:115, 33:56-58, 34:124, 313; gold rush, 14:113, 32:219, 40:410; pioneer life, 14:205, 19:203-206, 20:341, 28:289, 38:202; Mennonite colonies, 14:225, 16:344, 18:99, 20:181; newspapers, 15:200-202, 17:103; governors, 16:115, 26:79; mail service, 17:465, 30:174; boundaries, 19:426, 24:368; wheat raising, 20:404, 405, 33:64-67, 69, 37:121, 265; in fiction, 23:116, 119, 122, 123, politics, 27:67, 97, 35:238; imprints, 29:173; Indians, 34:174, 319, 35:135, 138, 289, 36:279, 38:69, 98, 114, 279, 281, 284, 287, 288, 354, 356, 363, 364, 39:85, 227-240; fur trade, 34:325-329; travel in, 35:246, 260; in Civil War, 37:255; archives, 39:35; atlas, 40:129. See also North Dakota, South Dakota
Dakotah, Washington County, townsite, 12:128n, 15:464, 24:196, 274; records, 21:458, 24:160
"Dakotah," side-wheeler, 11:128
Dale, Edward E., 26:161; work reviewed, 12:176; speaker, 13:326, 27:66; author, 25:85, 26:378, 27:159, 28:174, 371, 29:260
Dale, Harrison C., author, 14:348
Dale, O. G., speaker, 16:129
Dalen, Dennis L., scuba diver, 38:24-34
Daline, Gordon, author, 17:360
Dallas, Alexander, governor of Rupert's Land, 34:317-319, 321, 323
Dallas, J., artist, 32:190
Dalles of the St. Croix, described, 17:391; resort, 36:92. See also Interstate Park, Taylors Falls
Dally, Capt. "Nate," work reviewed, 12:310
Dally family, Stearns County pioneers, 12:310
Dalrymple, Dana G., author, 39:260
Dalrymple, John S., work reviewed, 37:259
Dalrymple, Oliver, 26:361; farms, 13:

205, 20:404, 25:300, 29:14, 31: 122, 32:112, 33:70, 36:68, 281, 37:265, 266, 39:206; biography, 37:259

Dalton, John E., author, 26:270

Daly, Judge Charles P., 31:224; papers, 28:202

Daly, J. C., lumberjack, 13:362n, 365n

Daly, M. J., 13:120, 23:103, 38:14, 16

Daly, Marcus, industrialist, 39:170

Daly, Mrs. Nora, speaker, 29:90

Dalyell, Capt. James, 29:65

Daly's Stock Co., 28:117

Dalzell, A. Hugh, author, 22:432

Dalzell, John, 18:140, 142

Dame, Katherine, author, 12:212

Dampier, William, 19:397n

Damrosch, Walter J., speaker, 39:53

Dams, Mississippi River, 11:118, 220, 18:452, 19:103, 182, 24:93, 130, 27:63, 28:293, 37:275, 286, 288, 290-295, 321, 322; Cameron, Wis., 23:98; Shell Rock River, 23:106; Nicollet Island, 24:130; Chippewa River, 27:197; Pokegama Lake, 33: 11; Sandy Lake, 33:14, 15; Sulphur Creek, 34:279, 280; Minnesota, 38: 203; Missouri River, 39:213 (cover); Pine County, 39:264; St. Croix River, 40:240, 357. See also Water power

"Damsel," steamboat, 34:240

Dan Patch, race horse, 12:421, 20: 201, 21:425, 28:192, 36:65, 93, 103

Dan Patch Airline, 22:349

Dan Patch Railroad, 40:378

Dana, Charles A., 19:406; in Minnesota, 12:392, 25:103, 35:181; excursionist, 15:406, 409, 411, 413, 414, 417, 20:384, 386

Dana, Napoleon J. T., army officer, at Fort Ridgely, 11:163, 165, 168, 174, 177, 14:459, 15:137, 29:319n, 33:263; biography, 11:328; in Civil War, 25:21-23, 25, 29, 35, 122-124, 125, 142, 347, 37:328, 334; politician, 39:195

Dana, Mrs. Napoleon J. T., 29:319

Dana, Samuel T., work reviewed, 37: 258; author, 30:389

Danbury, Wis., fur trade, 28:149n; Sioux trail, 28:158n

Dance, contemporary, 21:58-62

Dane County, Wis., history, 22:192, 26:397

Dane, R. S., speaker, 16:115

Danelski, David J., work reviewed, 39:205

Danes, South Dakota, 11:324, 19:222, 28:300; Minnesota communities, 11: 334, 20:63, 23:387, 29:271, 30:76, 38:42, 243, 39:130; Iowa, 13:435; U.S., 15:355, 20:442; almanacs, 15:447; in dairy industry, 17:239, 19:155, 21:340, 27:119; publications, 27:256; songs, 36:194. See also Scandinavians

Dangremond, Rev. Gerrit, 28:128

Daniel, Robert, author, 36:230

Daniel, Will H., author, 28:69

Daniells, Lorna M., compiler, 36:278

Daniels, Dr. A. W., pioneer physician, 18:209, 25:404

Daniels, Dr. Jared W., 12:300, 35: 235; Indian agent, 35:168, 170

Daniels, John K., sculptor, 19:365, 26:388, 27:250, 29:96, 34:353

Daniels, John W., businessman, 34:173

Daniels, Jonathan, author, 39:209

Daniels, Thomas L., 32:13n

Daniels and Co., Rochester, druggists, 20:235

Danielson, Andrew, 13:345

Danielson, H., author, 18:71

Danielson, Ole, author, 22:443

Danielson Township, Meeker County, creamery, 11:457; history, 19:470

Danish Evangelical Lutheran Church in America, 27:256

Danish Lutheran Publishing House, Blair, Neb., 15:447

Danish People's Society (Danish Folk Society), colonizing activities, 17:239, 23:387, 29:271, 30:76, 31: 28

Danner, Effa M., author, 19:221

Dansk Folkesamfund, see Danish People's Society

Danube, history, 13:153, 19:126

Danz, Frank, musician, 33:93, 95, 97-101, 104, 36:106

Danzig, Allison, author, 35:335

Dardenne, John, 32:102, 165

Dardenne, Mrs. John, actress, 32:102

Dare, L. A., 12:106

Darec, Louis, 13:86

Dargan, Marion, 17:462

Darkey Lake, Ont., picture rock, 29: 130

Darling, Edwin, author, 26:294

Darling, Frederick L., house, 38:340, 341

Darling, Jay N., author, 22:183

Darling, R. A., author, 17:238

Darling, W. L., author, 13:115

Darling, William F., biography, 22: 104

Darling, Morrison County, Lutheran church, 24:90

Dart, Anson, pioneer, 40:312

Dart, Eliza C., pioneer, 40:312

Dart, Joseph, miller, 16:226

D'Artaguette, ---, 13:85

Dartt, Edward H. S., diaries, 20:34, 79

Darwin, Charles, letter, 37:231, 232; naturalist, 39:113, 115

Darwin, history, 19:117; land speculation, 24:57, 114n; farming, 24: 115, 116

Dash, Victor A., postmaster, 34:186

Dasovich, Thomas, "My Yugoslav Background," 28:250-253; author, 29:99

Dasovich family, 28:250-253

Dassel, transportation, 12:339; history, 19:117, 24:273; agriculture, 22:446, 23:171

Daubenmire, Rexford F., author, 18: 332

Dauffenbach, Christian, potter, 33: 231

Dauffenbach, Mrs. Roy, author, 36:195

Daugherty, Cora, 17:364

Daugherty, James, 18:452

Daugherty, Susie, 17:364

Daughters of the American Colonists, Minnesota society, 12:98, 443, 14: 350, 26:31, 151

Daughters of the American Revolution, 18:214; markers, 11:28, 51, 111,

330, 335, 13:214, 14:97, 350, 453, 15:359, 362, 16:485, 20:464, 21: 434, 22:208, 40:245; chapters, 12: 321, 429, 14:335, 16:256, 336, 360, 494, 17:208, 488, 18:46, 55, 342, 19:47, 21:194, 22:342, 23:41, 25:41, 206, 316, 26:31, 27:249, 28:305, 30:22, 36:140; Minnesota, 12:429, 13:311, 16:64, 117, 20:33, 21:218, 24:36, 25:9, 78, 29:96, 34:340, 35:190; publications, 14: 110, 114, 228, 15:349, 483, 16: 232, 18:108; genealogical program, 14:214, 439, 15:59, 343, 349, 16: 51, 102, 20:33, 194, 21:34, 22:39, 27:156, 30:156, 182; radio presentations, 15:66, 108, 127, 221, 241, 348, 456, 466, 16:57, 115, 27:180; educational program, 15: 120; Mendota restorations, 15:195, 313, 16:487, 19:235, 20:342, 23: 192, 27:231, 30:282, 32:107, 33: 209, 37:60, 39:316; Michigan, 15: 475; history, 35:197, 36:186

Daughters of the Founders and Patriots of America, 20:33, 37:224

Daunais, Oliver, 23:397

Davenport, Ambrose, trader, 11:372

Davenport, E. L., actor, 33:175

Davenport, Fanny, actress, 28:117

Davenport, F. Garvin, "Newton H. Winchell," 32:214-225; author, 32: 255

Davenport, Col. George, trader, 13: 222; murdered, 17:421, 423, 22:22n

Davenport, Col. Henry, 27:253

Davenport, Ida, 17:341

Davenport, Thomas, 35:283

Davenport, Iowa, history, 13:111; schools, 16:275; river port, 17: 424, 25:114, 26:381, 36:46, 38: 356; museum, 20:90; Catholic church, 20:338; art gallery, 21: 202; described, 22:22; German settlement, 25:298, 27:163

"Davenport," steamboat, 24:331, 37: 296, 38:357-359, 362

David, C. W., 14:194

David, Lester, author, 34:310

"David Tipton," steamboat, 37:296, 297

Davidow, Alexander, diplomat, 40:265 (cover), 268, 270, 273

Davids, W. B., author, 33:226

Davidson, Andrew A., author, 13:453, 14:359, 17:487, 30:274; speaker, 21:447, 23:403

Davidson, Daniel S., author, 18:323

Davidson, Donald, poet, 20:113

Davidson, Gordon, 14:81; author, 13: 439

Davidson, John F., 27:65

Davidson, Gen. John W., Union officer, 40:282-286

Davidson, Katherine H., compiler, 39: 210

Davidson, Levette J., author, 33:91

Davidson, Lorenzo D., author, 19:461

Davidson, Margaret G., work reviewed, 40:405

Davidson, Martha, author, 24:181

Davidson, Mrs. Martha, 17:183

Davidson, Peyton S., steamboat captain, 26:272, 36:251, 254

Davidson, Sarah A., 21:15n; "St. Paul in 1849," 22:55-59; review by, 22: 94; work reviewed, 32:114; author,

22:82, 23:98, 33:139; editor, 26:278

Davidson, T., flatboatman, 21:259

Davidson, William F., steamboat owner, 11:139, 16:470, 19:195, 26:272, 33:198, 34:26, 27, 36:26, 250-258, 37:185, 227, 38:236, 39:129, 210, 298; papers, 13:321, 14:64, 66, 16:73, 23:7, 34:268, 35:340; speculator, 39:90

Davidson, William M., author, 34:356

Davie, Maurice R., work reviewed, 17:328

Davies, A. P., letters, 13:427

Davies, Ayres, author, 23:184

Davies, Blodwen, author, 15:238

Davies, Cecil, 19:61

Davies, Ffrangcom, singer, 39:55, 56

Davies, James, 15:83

Davies, Kenneth G., "From Competition to Union," 40:166-177; work reviewed, 38:199; author, 36:150; speaker, 40:149

Davies, Pearl J., work reviewed, 36:189

Davies, Wallace E., work reviewed, 35:197

Davis, Alexander J., architect, 38:189

Davis, Lt. C. Edward, 25:255

Davis, Charles, railroad builder, 21:439

Davis, Charles H., Union officer, 25:130

Davis, Charles R., Senator, 35:306; Congressman, 40:321, 350

Davis, Clyde B., author, 22:204

Davis, Cushman K., 12:196, 197; papers, 11:318, 14:102, 15:223, 17:160n, 337, 20:81, 445, 21:35, 414, 34:339; biography, 11:328; lawyer, 12:175, 38:79; Senator, 24:373, 28:72, 35:76; governor, 27:250, 35:57, 36:55, 56, 37:147, 207, 208, 211; author, 30:372

Davis, Darrell H., author, 16:357, 18:218, 21:449

Davis, E. Page, emigrant agent, 13:28-30

Davis, Edward W., 34:271, 36:35; "Taconite," 33:282; "Pioneering with Taconite," 34:269-283; "Seegwin," 37:235-254; review by, 32:244-246; work reviewed, 39:163; author, 13:115, 32:256, 33:355, 40:364; exploring activities, 37:188, 38:24-34

Davis, Mrs. Edward W., 34:280

Davis, Edwin H., 29:162

Davis, Ellabelle, singer, 39:63

Davis, Elmer, work reviewed, 32:254

Davis, Elrick B., author, 24:74

Davis, F. A. W., lawsuit, 35:4-10

Davis, Dr. F. W., speaker, 26:91

Davis, Frank F., county attorney, 18:124

Davis, Garrett, Senator, 25:27, 37

Davis, Hallie, 16:213

Davis, Sgt. Henry L., 26:279, 27:48

Davis, J. H., surveyor, 27:263

Davis, James, printer, 15:7

Davis, James S., farmer, 23:316

Davis, Jefferson, 12:10; military career, 22:98, 29:335, 35:178; Confederate president, 25:150, 239, 243; secretary of war, 27:315, 36:17n; author, 29:64; marriage, 30:97, 189

Davis, Mrs. Jefferson (Sarah K. Taylor), 25:15n, 29:335, 30:97

Davis, John, author, 12:208

Davis, John W., author, 15:221, 19:213

Davis, John W., Union soldier, 25:226, 241

Davis, Kenneth S., work reviewed, 37:81; author, 31:134, 145, 36:77

Davis, LeRoy G., "A Diphtheria Epidemic," 15:434-438; "Some Frontier Words and Phrases," 19:241-246; "Frontier Home Remedies," 19:369-376; "Some Frontier Institutions," 20:19-28; author, 11:63, 71, 185, 186, 19:105, 337, 444, 445, 20:74, 353, 360, 21:210, 22:109, 23:195, 28:335, 31:13, 36:327; speaker, 20:49

Davis, Mary, 14:307

Davis, Ralph R., legislator, 37:169, 170

Davis, Richard S., author, 36:194

Davis, Robert D., author, 22:213, 36:70

Davis, Robert R., prison official, 37:146

Davis, Rose M., author, 35:380

Davis, Ruth E., author, 24:259

Davis, Susan B., author, 13:208, 15:474, 16:113, 20:339

Davis, Timothy, 11:393

Davis, Tom, politician, 34:232

Davis, Dr. William, author, 16:353

Davis, William M., pioneer farmer, 35:245

Davis Lake, Aitkin County, 33:10

Davison, C. B., author, 11:463

Davison, Philip G., editor, 26:162

Davison, Sol, work reviewed, 17:322-324

Davison and Connelly, St. Paul, plow factory, 24:297

Davy, Capt. Peter B., expedition, 12:200, 13:436, 23:84, 31:253, 38:62

Dawes, Charles, 22:423; reparations plan, 18:425

Dawes Severalty Act, 23:163, 35:289

Dawison, Bogumil, actor, 32:104

Dawley, ——, steamboat clerk, 15:417

Dawley, Allen W., farmer, 18:285, 286, 293

Dawley, Charlotte, author, 28:285

Dawson, Kenneth, speaker, 40:149

Dawson, Marcella, 27:49

Dawson, Robert M., work reviewed, 31:117

Dawson, Simon J., explorer, 21:433, 28:178, 32:242, 36:191. See also Dawson Trail

Dawson, William, 18:363, 39:332; mayor, 39:329

Dawson, flood, 11:69; Lutheran church, 11:114; history, 21:222; newspaper, 21:342

Dawson, Yukon Ter., in gold rush, 29:313, 314

Dawson Trail, Man.-Ont., 21:328, 23:404, 24:285, 33:187, 40:145; route, 18:247, 21:245, 433, 26:290, 28:178, 34:213; history, 24:328, 32:242, 40:359

Day, A. Grove, author, 33:90

Day, Alfred, 12:206, 21:159n

Day, Burt W., journalist, 21:452

Day, Charles, speaker, 17:121

Day, Dr. David, 37:182; scrapbook, 35:340; relief commissioner, 36:56

Day, Ditus, letter, 20:80

Day, Mrs. Ditus, letter, 20:80

Day, Mrs. F. T., 25:210

Day, Frank A., 17:160n, 20:82; legislator, 35:307, 310, 36:121, 122

Day, Mrs. Fred, speaker, 20:99

Day, Genevieve C., author, 15:237, 21:430, 39:83

Day, Henry E., author, 19:365

Day, J. C., papers, 15:466

Day, June S., catalog typist, 21:45, 23:44; library assistant, 23:367

Day, Len, lumberman, 26:381

Day, Leonard R., murdered, 26:288

Day, Levi E., author, 12:206

Day, Matthew, printer, 15:4

Day, Pauline, work reviewed, 30:385

Day, Robert, 12:206

Day, Stephen, printer, 15:4

Day, Judge Vince A., speaker, 21:335, 25:80; papers, 27:155; war activities, 40:366n

Day, William A., author, 19:366

Day family, in Minnesota, 22:89

Day County, S.D., Indian scout camps, 40:313

Daylight, Todd County, history, 15:371

Day Lumber Co., Minneapolis, 25:385

Daynard, Shirley, 29:283

Dayspring, mission magazine, 14:330

Dayton, Edson C., author, 19:108

Dayton, G. Nelson, 16:20n, 25:154

Dayton, George D., 16:20n, 25:154n; autobiography, 16:121; career, 29:88

Dayton, Lyman, railroad director, 35:359

Dayton, "Sonny," 23:309

Dayton family, genealogy, 13:197; history, 39:131

Dayton, G.A.R. post, 16:431; Catholic church, 16:484; court, 17:467; archives, 20:209; settled, 35:258; excavations, 40:339

Dayton, Iowa, Swedish settlement, 23:184

Dayton Hollow, townsite, 18:117

Dayton Co., Minneapolis, art exhibit, 29:369, 30:282; history, 39:131

Deaconess Hospital, Minneapolis, 19:459, 29:296

"Dead Man," pseud., letters, 22:15-34

Dead River, Marquette County, Mich., 23:237

Deadwood, S.D., frontier medicine, 11:108; history, 11:212, 14:113, 37:222; newspapers, 15:201

Deadwood Central Railroad, history, 39:298

Deahl, Thomas F., reviews by, 37:180, 38:89, 39:168; newspaper curator, 37:43; author, 37:264

Dean, Dr. Edwin B., speaker, 13:121; author, 15:252

Dean, Mrs. Edwin B., speaker, 13:121

Dean, Eliab B., 21:429

Dean, Mrs. Eliab B., see Conover, Sarah F. D.

Dean, Flavia, pioneer teacher, 22:344

Dean, George, architect, 40:107

Dean, George W., in Civil War, 22:422

Dean, John, 19:238

Dean, Rebecca P., career, 38:242

Dean, William B., pioneer merchant, 22:422; papers, 23:40, 371
Dear, Hubert, 22:218, 341
Dearborn, Betty F., biography, 12:446
Dearborn, Col. Greenleaf, 11:125
Dearborn, Gen. Henry, 40:180n
Dearstyne, Ruth, 22:52
Deas, Charles, artist, 32:61, 33:264, 35:182
Debel, Neils H., speaker, 11:291
DeBoer, Maude, 27:147
De Bonne, Capt. Louis, 18:325
Debs, Eugene V., socialist leader, 27:334, 36:120-122
De Cailly, Rev. Louis, author, 15:213
De Camp, Joseph, mill operator, 34: 236, 38:107n
De Camp, Mrs. Joseph, 34:236, 38:107n
De Camp, Ralph E., artist, 35:295
De Canop, ---, boatbuilder, 21:262
Decatur, Stephen, naval officer, 40: 348n
Decker, Edward W., author, 18:462; banker, 19:113
Decker, Leslie E., work reviewed, 39: 257
Decker, Maud K., author, 18:327
Decker, Wilbur F., 19:184n; "Action on the Upper Mississippi," 19:182-189; author, 19:207
Deckert, Charles, pioneer, 17:491
Deckman, Mrs. J. H., editor, 24:383
Declaration of Independence, history, 34:199
Decora, William, Winnebago Indian, 18:474
Decorah, Iowa, museums, 12:328, 18: 452; English colony, 13:110; post office, 40:87
Decorah-Posten (Decorah, Iowa), Norwegian paper, 11:207
Decoration Day, see Memorial Day
Decorri, Benton County, settled, 16: 315; post office, 26:93, 40:89
DeCoster, Mrs. Donald W., Jr. (Georgia), 37:263
De Coteau, William, 40:313
Decouteaux, Marguerite, mixed-blood, 11:431
Deen, Lucile, speaker, 29:164; quoted, 30:333
Deen, Tilla R. D., author, 30:396
Deener, David R., author, 39:128
Deep Lake, Ramsey County, 40:230
Deephaven, schools, 22:345
Deer, hunts, 14:422, 423, 16:189, 32: 220, 37:347; depicted, 18:451, 40: 209; in fur trade, 23:330, 38:190, 40:158, 180, 212, 213; protected, 28:290; Minnesota, 30:125, 128, 35:48
Deer Creek, history, 11:222; hunting, 16:262; cemetery, 24:91
"Deer Lodge," steamboat, 32:244
Deer Park Township, Red Lake County, history, 38:204
Deer River, history, 15:348, 27:172, 30:272; railroad, 23:33, 29:138; archaeology, 26:322
Deere, John, plow manufacturer, 23: 323, 31:55; biography, 24:75
Deere, Lydia S., author, 18:224, 313, 530
Deering, Charles C., author, 23:285
Deering, Charles W., steamboat captain, 29:292
Deering, ---, actress, 23:306

Deering, Samuel, dairyman, 27:120
Defenbach, Byron, author, 14:204
Defenbacher, D. D., speaker, 21:216, 30:66
De Ford, Miriam, author, 25:176
Defour, ---, guide, 23:247
De Gannes, ---, memoir, 16:450
De Gardeur, Ens. Louis, 18:325
De Gogorza, Emilio, singer, 39:59
De Gonnor, Father Nicholas, missionary, 13:339
De Graaf, Derk, 28:129
De Graff, Charles, livestock raiser, 26:117, 121
De Graff, railroad, 13:41; Irish settlement, 31:23
De Graw, John, lumberman, 21:324
Degree of Honor, St. Paul, 12:321, 39:53n
De Haas, Carl, author, 25:301
Dehn, Adolf, artist, 17:229, 26:165, 31:55
Deinard, Amos, 13:323
Deinard, Mrs. Amos, 26:372
De Jonge, Rev. Jacob B., 28:123
De Kay, ---, baseball player, 19:164
De la Barre, William, 18:184n, 34: 204; milling engineer, 17:352
Delacroix, Ferdinand V. E., artist, 30:268
Delafield, Maj. Joseph, diary reviewed, 24:341-343; boundary commissioner, 25:182, 26:32, 29:131, 132, 38:191, 40:359
Delafield, Wis., Episcopal church, 38:167
DeLaittre, C. P., steamboat captain, 33:12
DeLaittre, Calvin, author, 37:41
DeLaittre, Howard M., lumberman, 37: 41
DeLaittre, John, lumberman, 23:273, 33:333, 337, 37:41; speaker, 37: 135
DeLaittre, John, Jr., 23:273
DeLaittre, Joseph A., lumberman, 37: 41
De Lambert, R. W., timber agent, 31: 160
De Land, Charles E., translator, 24: 152
Delaney, A., steamboat agent, 31:85
Delaney, J. Lyman, grain merchant, 24:103
Delanglez, Father Jean, works reviewed, 21:396, 23:57, 30:56; translator, 20:439; author, 22:63, 92, 327, 25:296, 26:74, 164, 268, 27:62, 350, 28:362; editor, 24: 365, 25:87
Delano, Columbus, secretary of the interior, 35:172
Delano, Col. Francis R., prison warden, 35:360, 362, 364, 37:139-141, 143; builder, 37:138; in Sioux Outbreak, 38:276
Delano, Presbyterian church, 27:344; name, 37:141n
Delano Eagle, history, 29:90
De Laurier, Joseph, voyageur, 18:241
DeLaurier, O. B., author, 11:224, 15: 371, 16:131, 372, 498, 18:474, 23: 111, 296, 24:94; speaker, 18:343
De Laval, Carl G. P., dairyman, 12:99
De Laval separator, 27:118, 121
Delavan, Norwegian settlement, 12:

270; first teacher, 25:211; history, 30:285
Delavan, Wis., circus town, 23:66, 185
Delaware, Swedish settlements, 24: 156, 26:57, 28:280; military service records, 26:278; atlas, 40:22
Delaware County (Pa.) Historical Society, 12:441
Delaware Indians, history, 34:160; Illinois, 36:191; sites, 40:209
Delaware Township, Grant County, county fairs, 15:487
De Lestry, Edmond L., 11:207; author, 11:196, 324, 339, 12:344, 435; editor, 26:303
De Lestry's Western Magazine, history, 26:303
Del Fiacco, Don, author, 36:240
Delgado, David J., compiler, 40:96
Delisle, Claude, cartographer, 25:87
Delisle, Guillaume, cartographer, 22: 274, 25:87
Delisle, William, cartographer, 27: 66
Delles, Mrs. Caroline H., 22:440
Dellwood, summer colony, 17:490
Delmont, James J., author, 18:327
Delmore, Dr. J. L., career, 34:173
Delo, David M., author, 25:196
De Long, A. H. (Al), in Sioux Outbreak, 11:334, 12:335
De Long, Mrs. Scott H. (Julia), 22: 104, 23:99; author, 17:234
Deloria, Ella C., 40:409
De Lorme, ---, trader, 21:120n
Del Otero Hotel, Spring Park, 20:352, 29:293
Delsing, Mr. and Mrs. Franz, pioneers, 30:135
Delta Lawn Tennis Club, St. Paul, 40: 32
Delta Sigma, University of Minnesota, literary society, 16:182
Delton Township, Cottonwood County, pioneer life, 17:126
Demaree, Albert L., author, 23:86
Demerest, Lt. David B., 25:344
De Meules, Donald H., "Ignatius Donnelly," 37:229-234
De Meurons, professional soldiers, at Red River Settlement, 24:77, 31: 108
Deming, John, horticulturist, 31:174
Deming, U. S., letter, 11:467
Deming, Wilbur S., author, 23:97
Demmon, J. S., 14:261
Democratic-Farmer-Labor Association, 34:190, 191, 38:301
Democratic-Farmer-Labor party, factions, 34:187-194, 39:210; beginnings, 34:232, 348; history, 35: 53-63, 304, 38:41, 309, 40:91, 362. See also Farmer-Labor party
Democratic party, territorial period, 13:433, 14:132, 133, 156-159, 244, 246, 259, 30:197, 35:107, 38:121, 39:38-48, 148, 150; state conventions, 14:161, 162, 245, 261, 19: 441, 27:338, 36:307, 37:54, 39:49, 104; newspapers, 14:247, 17:386, 427, 20:279, 27:4, 6, 8-11, 13-15, 19, 33:329, 35:363, 36:308, 37: 330, 39:327-334; relation to third-party groups, 15:337, 32: 130-134, 140-142, 34:187, 188, 189, 221, 35:56-63, 98, 297-312,

36:117; platforms and policies, 16:441, 17:416, 22:240, 241, 243-247, 386, 23:381, 24:309, 310, 312, 26:188, 191-198, 200, 202, 205, 209, 27:132-134, 28:26, 30:105, 32:15-33, 35:94, 291, 37:181, 39:29, 82, 260; Pennsylvania, 17:106, 28:319; in Civil War, 20:273, 277, 279; national conventions, 20:281, 36:303; campaigns: 1910, 22:86, 40:317-329, 1860, 22:242, 37:45-51, 1848, 30:189, 1916, 34:231, 1892, 35:76, 39:96, 1902, 35:350, 1898, 39:108; 1890, 36:113, 1894, 36:124, 39:101, 1896, 39:102, 107; Minnesota, 23:314, 28:74, 31:42, 34:37, 36:259, 271, 37:84, 343; donkey symbol, 25:395; immigrants in, 28:21, 23, 25, 27, 29, 34, 31:31, 243, 32:15; in legislature, 33:155-163, 36:168-172, 37:333; patronage, 33:314, 40:26; Iowa, 34:41; Wisconsin, 34:166; Tennessee, 39:143. See also Minnesota constitution, Minnesota constitutional conventions, Politics

"Demoine," steamboat, 13:238
De Monts, Pierre Du Gua, 40:188
Demorest, Rose, author, 26:175
Dempster, C. L., speaker, 17:123
Dempster, Dr. James H., author, 30:268
De Muth, Mrs. W. F., 12:339
Denfeld, Fred, 29:49
Dengler, Paul, author, 12:418
Denham, Methodist church, 14:452
Denig, Edwin T., work reviewed, 37:336; author, 14:223; trader, 32:124, 37:262, 38:385
Denin, Susan, actress, 33:174
Denis, Keith, speaker, 23:397
Denison, Merrill, author, 14:115, 35:97
Denkmann, F. C. A., lumberman, 27:190, 194, 195, 32:188
Denkmann family, philanthropies, 30:90, 329
Denler, Arnold, speaker, 18:223
Denley, William, missionary, 20:90
Denley, Mrs. William, missionary, 20:90
Denmark, 20:250; co-operative movement, 27:119
"Denmark," steamer, 16:173
Denmark Township, Washington County, history, 16:125; road, 40:235
Denna, Lewis, Cutlerite, 13:387, 390
Denney, Reuel, work reviewed, 37:84
Dennis, James M., work reviewed, 40:408
Dennis, Col. John S., 35:283
Dennis, Judge Samuel K., speaker, 25:197
Dennison, Eleanor E., author, 24:373
Dennison, Methodist church, 14:354; mounds, 16:307, 310; history, 34:127
Denniston, Helene, house, 38:350
Denny, Lt. St. Clair, at Fort Snelling, 18:401, 25:386
Denonville, Marquis de, 19:280, 281, 40:208
De Noyon, Jacques, 13:439; explorer, 16:230, 22:178, 23:280, 31:183
Densford, Katharine J., career, 37:301

Densmore, Benjamin, pioneer, 12:86; builder, 14:100, 15:47, 48, 49; papers, 15:60, 464, 16:52, 469, 17:53, 19:343, 21:192; in Civil War, 15:112, 21:87; house, 15:350
Densmore, Frances, 12:27, 102, 205, 223n, 13:107, 14:123, 15:347, 465, 20:309; "The Garrard Family," 14:31-43; "A Minnesota Missionary Journey," 20:310-313; review by, 15:453; author, 12:199, 326, 15:59, 16:468, 476, 20:322, 344, 24:71, 26:275, 307, 28:176, 32:123, 33:90, 91, 312, 34:129, 213, 35:244; speaker, 15:242, 17:346, 21:285, 39:53; ethnologist, 24:54, 27:161, 32:58, 34:176, 312; bibliography, 27:253; editor, 34:161
Densmore, Mabel, 20:173, 27:171, 35:50
Densmore, Margaret, speaker, 12:102
Densmore, Orrin, 12:86
Densmore Bros., Red Wing, foundry, 33:234, 34:127
Dentan, Samuel, missionary, 17:224, 18:225, 21:27n, 160, 167, 22:30n
Dentan, Mrs. Samuel, missionary, 21:160
Dentistry, college, 17:100; relation to medicine, 19:66; Owre's contribution, 19:71-73; on frontier, 19:371, 21:437, 22:354, 37:348
Denton, Daniel, account of New York, 16:411-413
Denver and Rio Grande Western Railroad Co., records, 25:310
Depew, Chauncey M., politician, 12:192, 35:73-75
Depew, Mary Eleanor, 23:221
De Peyster, Arent S., poet, 40:21
De Peyster, J. Watts, editor, 40:21
Depressions, 14:238; 1873, 12:248, 262, 278, 18:79, 21:384, 22:261; 1857, 12:387, 13:127, 138, 149, 174, 14:155, 390, 15:114, 135, 346, 16:25, 316, 17:416, 417, 18:65, 291, 21:153, 235, 22:8, 232, 236, 239, 23:313, 27:5, 28:220, 322, 29:227-229, 30:302, 34:100n, 35:215, 36:173, 174, 39:68-70, 40:75; 1930s, 14:12, 21:2, 5, 29:167; 1837, 14:199; 1893, 27:206, 34:110; 1914-15, 27:214; 1883-85, 34:109. See also Economic conditions
Deputy, Manfred W., 19:233
De Rainville family, 12:232
Derby, Elias H., 11:126n
Derby, Lily B., author, 12:102
Derleth, August, work reviewed, 29:251; author, 22:205, 24:76, 25:176, 29:251
Dern, George H., 16:57
Derrynane, Le Sueur County, Catholic church, 28:84
Des Barres, Joseph F. W., cartographer, 40:356
Des Brissay, George, engineer, 34:280
Deschaillons, Jean-Baptiste, 35:140
D'Eschambault, Father Antoine, review by, 35:140; speaker, 13:345; author, 14:237, 18:272n, 23:286, 27:62
D'Eschambault, Georges, trader, 27:62
Description and travel, Minnesota, 11:161-184, 12:43-64, 157-168, 14:99, 15:478, 16:35-46, 272-281, 19:217, 404-413, 20:79, 119-128, 22:

157-168, 433, 28:309-328, 336, 339-344, 29:195-222, 349, 351, 30:11, 111-121, 390, 32:81-99, 33:112-125, 350, 34:45-53, 35:335, 37:101-118, 134, 40:12-20, 387-390; by stagecoach, 11:401-407; by automobile, 14:116; Mississippi River, 14:333, 19:95, 104, 351, 458, 20:439, 21:94, 22:13-34, 327, 23:183, 281, 25:274, 26:155, 27:63, 30:4, 62, 158, 31:246, 250, 32:202-213, 33:30-33, 134-143, 35:200, 36:237, 38:384, 39:167; visitors' accounts, 14:448, 15:353, 16:338, 19:73-76, 28:276, 29:335-337, 32:185, 34:38, 42; Midwest, 16:102, 19:449, 20:462, 26:74, 34:169, 216, 35:43, 239, 38:41; Red River Valley, 17:304-306, 20:432, 24:330-335, 27:165, 28:80, 29:73, 30:259, 31:122; Swedish, 18:70-72, 19:216, 27:72, 39:81; see also Bremer, Fredrika; Northwest, 18:451; Great Lakes, 19:34-42, 103, 113, 216, 349, 20:10, 438, 22:319, 431, 26:76, 83, 171, 35:153, 292, 37:79; Minnesota River, 19:84, 37:225-228; emigrant journeys, 19:123, 133-147, 234, 20:208, 210, 249-258, 331, 345, 469, 21:211, 22:192, 343, 27:72; Canada, 19:223, 21:204, 29:167, 33:186, 34:132, 35:142, 240, 37:183, 305, 306; St. Paul, 19:400, 22:55-59, 30:202-219, 31:109; guides, 19:463, 20:64-66, 23:65, 67, 89, 29:87, 167, 30:73, 384; missionary journeys, 20:310-313, 331, 21:17-32, 158-175, 273-283, 33:90; "Fashionable Tours," 20:377-396, 28:272; westward journeys, 20:430, 21:443, 22:99, 222, 336, 436, 24:91, 27:166, 247, 281-299, 28:135-137, 29:188, 31:253, 39:261, 316, 40:271-278; Iowa, 21:431, 22:19, 410, 29:253; by covered wagon, 21:453; border country, 22:177-181, 276-286, 439, 23:182, 24:341, 26:171, 29:130-136, 30:69, 262, 34:1-8; Rock and Wisconsin rivers, 24:76; eastern journeys, 24:77, 29:116, 150; railroad excursion, 25:103-116; Watonwan River, 26:394; Missouri River, 29:58-61; Fort Snelling area, 30:101, 31:209-221; Alaska, 31:56; U.S., 33:184, 34:163, 35:95; Fort Garry to St. Louis, 36:37-53, 37:85. See also Exploration and discovery, Roads and highways, Transportation
Deseret, Mormon state, 13:111. See also Utah
Desloge, Joseph, 28:79
De Smet, Father Pierre-Jean, missionary, 11:350, 16:90, 35:380, 38:385, 39:128; explorer, 29:61, 34:304; shrine, 40:197
De Smet, S.D., ranch, 21:425
Des Moines, Iowa, climate, 20:161n; history, 24:369
Des Moines (Lower) Rapids, Mississippi River, 22:15, 17, 18, 20; surveys, 17:430n
Des Moines River, Iowa, 14:220, 16:478; fur trade, 11:381, 14:85, 32:230; mills, 22:185; army post, 38:286, 40:23-26

Des Moines River Valley, Norwegian
settlements, 12:272, 274
Des Moines & Fort Dodge Railroad,
route, 30:234
Desmond, M., teamster, 20:340
Desnoyer, Stephen, innkeeper, 33:200n
De Soto, Hernando, explorer, 14:371,
442, 21:201, 24:53, 32:112, 37:62
Desrosiers, Léo-Paul, author, 21:93
Destler, Chester M., work reviewed,
27:334; letter, 28:94; author, 28:
172
Detamore, W. H., speaker, 15:365
Determan, Anna O., 40:366
Determan, S. B., 21:218
Detje, Harold C., cartographer, 29:
344
Detroit, Mich., fur trade, 11:234,
250, 19:287, 290, 291, 295, 299,
306, 20:7, 40:164, 180, 182, 219;
fort, 13:203, 15:379, 19:280, 284,
297, 20:14; ethnic groups, 18:394,
20:202, 27:257, 36:14, 17; pioneer life, 19:218, 21:182; siege,
19:288, 29:65; treaty, 23:145n;
transportation center, 24:330, 34:
11, 40:271, 272; historic sites,
27:158; history, 32:184, 33:36,
87; climate, 40:312
Detroit (Mich.) Historical Society,
32:187, 33:351
Detroit (Mich.) Institute of Arts,
30:176
Detroit (Mich.) Public Library, auto-
motive records, 27:64; copying projects, 39:165
Detroit Lakes, G.A.R. post, 16:431;
settled, 16:432; historical meeting, 18:204, 269-271; band, 19:
229; road, 20:310; mission, 20:
431; county seat, 23:29; centen-
nial exhibit, 29:369; wildlife,
30:130; pioneer life, 30:160;
Baptist church, 33:254
Detroit Lakes Civic and Commerce
Association, 17:228
De Turk, Ernest E., author, 13:441
Detwiler, Mrs. J. E., author, 18:470
Detzer, Rev. J. A., editor, 22:88
Detzer, Col. Karl, 26:166
Deuel, Thorne, author, 24:236
Deutsch, Abbot Alcuin, 35:372
Deutsch, Babette, author, 16:115
Deutsch, Dorothy, 23:168, 24:31
Deutsch, Harold C., speaker, 23:399,
30:66, 264
Deutsch, Herman J., 12:200
Deutsch Amerikanischer Farmer (Lin-
coln, Neb.), 16:338
Deutsche Musikzeitung (Philadelphia),
32:239
De Valls Bluff, Ark., military hospi-
tal, 40:283, 288, 291
De Vaya, Monsig. Count Vay, author,
29:154
Devereaux, J. C., editor, 14:394
Devier, William, 40:224
Devil's Lake, Kanabec County, island,
34:61
Devil's Lake, N.D., trading post, 19:
385, 34:327; buffalo hunt, 26:76;
settled, 30:160; reservation, 35:
170, 172; Sioux encampment, 38:
151, 281; Glidden tour, 38:212;
Jewish colony, 40:4
Devlin, Mr. and Mrs. Hoyt, pioneers,
21:317

Devlin, John, sheriff, 39:49
Devol, George, 24:53
DeVoto, Bernard, 33:182, 40:154;
works reviewed, 29:58-61, 33:301,
34:79; quoted, 17:372, 29:78, 40:
151; author, 18:214, 19:347, 25:
389, 27:254, 33:263, 40:152, 305;
editor, 28:173
Dewar, Frank, speaker, 18:224
De Warville, Brissot, 18:396
Dewdney, Selwyn, works reviewed, 38:87
40:407; author, 36:102, 151; editor
40:358
Dewey, Dr. James J., 21:437
Dewey, Mr. and Mrs. Jerome, pioneers,
22:222
Dewey, John, 25:68
Dewey, Dr. John J., pioneer, 20:91
Dewey, Melvil, 17:448
Dewey, Nelson, house, 30:270, 31:249
Dewitt, Mr. and Mrs. Andrus, pioneers
34:54-58
De Witt, C. H., 24:256
De Witt, F. J., 14:245
"Dexter," steamboat, 25:72
DeYoannes, A. M., 23:392
DeYoung, M. H., politician, 35:68, 69
"Diamond Jo," steamboat, 24:369, 38:293
Diamond Jo Line, 37:265 (cover); his-
tory, 24:369; in lumber industry,
26:132
Diamond Lake, Hennepin County, 35:24
Diaz, Albert J., editor, 40:313
Dibb, Dr. William D., gold seeker,
40:307
Dibble, ---, cholera victim, 14:291
Dibble, Edwy O., 23:392
Dibble, Leonard W., letters, 17:211,
253n, 18:48
Dicey, Edward, author, 29:154
Dichter, Harry, author, 22:431
Dick, Everett N., 19:446, 26:161;
reviews by, 24:158, 28:57; works
reviewed, 19:78-80, 22:311; au-
thor, 24:164, 255, 28:96; com-
piler, 39:82
Dick, Helen D., "A Newly Discovered
Diary," 18:399-406; author, 18:
440; speaker, 19:92
Dick, Maximilian, violinist, 19:333
Dickens, Charles, 27:233, 28:275, 29:
187; author, 27:16, 29:124, 154,
30:200; traveler, 39:167
Dickenson, George W., interviews, 16:
101
Dickenson, H. D., 18:150n
Dickeson, Dr. Montroville W., 23:369,
29:261; panorama, 23:349-354, 31:
56
Dickey, Earl C., storekeeper, 35:17
Dickey, Joel M., memorial, 15:467
Dickey, William Bruce, miller, 35:14,
16, 18
Dickey, Mrs. W. L., speaker, 20:352;
author, 34:170
Dickinson, Anna, lecturer, 11:157,
158
Dickinson, Charles D. ("Pop"), pio-
neer aviator, 19:237, 25:195, 33:
241
Dickinson, Daniel S., politician, 37:
50
Dickinson, Horace D., biography, 18:
211
Dickinson, J. C., 34:234, 235
Dickinson, John, composer, 22:130

Dickinson, Leonard R., legislator,
34:60
Dickinson, N.D., pioneer life, 19:108
Dickson, Albert J., diary, 11:325,
12:428, 13:60
Dickson, Anna, 26:31; author, 27:167
Dickson, Arthur J., editor, 11:325
Dickson, Don, archaeologist, 27:163
Dickson, James, expedition, 11:454,
15:336, 17:444-447, 26:55, 27:38,
31:131, 35:202, 36:216
Dickson, James R., 25:182
Dickson, Robert, trader, 11:179, 379,
12:199, 232, 233, 13:99, 190, 14:
98, 15:473, 17:196, 18:193, 194,
19:302, 304, 20:16, 18, 21:99, 22:
271, 282-288, 23:272, 27:62, 31:
189, 36:67, 39:255, 40:181n; biog-
raphy, 11:328; post, 11:375; in
War of 1812, 12:234, 16:223; fam-
ily, 22:287
Dickson, Sam T., railroad builder,
24:96; miller, 24:100-102
Dickson, Thomas H., 12:432; papers,
25:182
Dickson, William, 18:193
Dickson family, genealogy, 25:182
Dickson Mounds State Park, Lewiston,
Ill., 27:163
Diedrich, Nicholas D., author, 19:222
Diehl, Dr. Harold S., speaker, 21:
101; author, 26:173, 33:312
Diekema, Gerrit J., 29:175
Dies, Edward J., author, 31:55
Dieson-Hegland, Georgina, author, 32:
127
Diethelm, Ray, 21:333
Dietrich, John H., biography review-
ed, 23:362-364
Dietrich, Mrs. John H., see Winston,
Carleton
Dietrichson, Rev. Gustav F., 36:287
Dietrichson, Rev. J. W. C., 37:184
Dietz, Mrs. Alice, 15:242
Dietz, John, 23:98
Dight, Dr. Charles F., author, 17:
116; papers, 24:34, 356, 25:62-64;
biographies, 25:91, 38:243
Dignan, John P., 35:252
Dike, William H., in Civil War, 28:
325
Dilg, Will, 19:239
Dillan, William A., author, 36:281
Dilley, Minnie M., speaker, 15:242;
author, 17:118
Dilley, S. B., 16:265, 267; hunter,
33:143n, 146-148, 154
Dilliard, Irving, work reviewed, 30:
249; author, 25:305
Dillman, Daisy E., author, 34:43
Dillman, Jacob, pioneer, 17:87
Dillman, Willard F., work reviewed,
17:86; poet, 16:81
Dillon, John, comedian, 28:111
Dillon, Michael J., speaker, 26:179
Dills, Charles, 14:309
Dills, Daniel, 14:309
Dills, Mrs. E. L., 22:216
Dilworth, unions, 21:393
Dimond, Alfred S., journalist, 36:25
Dingan, Patrick, 25:142
Dingley, Daniel, trader, 17:391
Dingwall, Iva A., "Pioneers' Dinner
Table," 34:54-58; "Some Frontier
Remedies," 34:195-198
Dinse, Jean M., author, 26:383
Dion, Maurine, 27:144

Dionne, Narcisse E., author, 13:253
Diphtheria, epidemics, 15:434-438, 19:333, 36:70, 37:186, 39:3; diagnosis, 24:212
Dirnberger, Ethel, author, 36:194
Dirt Lodge, Iowa, trading post, 13:222
Disciples of Christ (Campbellites), 15:237, 36:290
Di Stefano, N., labor leader, 40:344
Ditson, Oliver, music publisher, 26:53
Dittemore, Paul L., author, 25:308
Diven, Robert J., author, 13:441
Divine, Robert A., work reviewed, 35:373
Dix, Dorothea, 28:54, 39:3; memorial, 16:451
Dix, Gen. John A., excursionist, 15:406; politician, 20:282, 284; Union officer, 25:143, 144n
Dix-Hill cartel, 25:151n
"Dixie," song, 15:482, 23:198, 310, 24:384, 27:177, 30:152, 39:84
Dixon, John, 21:18
Dixon, Marge, author, 26:255, 27:82
Dixon, Ill., founded, 21:18n
"Dixon," steamboat, 33:256
Dixon School, St. Paul, 19:168
Djurberg, G. J., Swedish immigrant, 20:258
Doane, A. Sidney, author, 21:365
Doane, Gilbert H., work reviewed, 37:181; editor, 36:35
Doane, H., 16:317n
Dobbin, Archibald S., Confederate officer, 40:285
Dobbs, Mary H., author, 15:133
Dobbs, Mattiwilda, singer, 39:63
Dobbs, W. C., author, 20:356
Dobbyn, Rev. William R., editor, 29:100, 36:119, 39:103, 104
Dobell, Isabel B., review by, 36:64
Dobert, Eitel W., author, 31:242
Dobie, ———, trader, 11:261
Dobie, J. Frank, review by, 36:65; work reviewed, 33:225; author, 19:437, 35:331, 37:262, 38:201; editor, 28:173
Dobie, John, "Commercial Fishing," 35:272-277; work reviewed, 36:235; author, 27:272, 35:98, 36:193; photographer, 33:229 (cover)
Doble, Thomas L., in Civil War, 25:247, 343, 349, 350, 354
Dobner, Katherine, 20:457
Dobratz, H. A., 16:240
Dobrick, Edward G., Jr., author, 20:216
Dobson, Eleanor R., author, 16:239
Dockstader, Mrs. Carrie, 22:322
Dockstader, Frederick J., author, 35:380, 39:129
"Dr. Franklin No. 1," steamboat, 11:128, 136, 12:164n, 17:293n, 301, 18:230, 19:139, 140, 20:383, 22:58n, 29:203, 31:211, 217, 33:112, 35:102, 37:10
"Dr. Franklin No. 2," steamboat, 13:233, 18:373, 22:156, 29:204, 30:196, 201, 35:355, 37:311
Dr. Martin Luther College, New Ulm, 34:170
Dodd, James E., 20:85
Dodd, William B., 22:348, 27:155; biography, 12:104; in Sioux Outbreak, 13:322, 21:313, 22:323;

account book, 14:64; road builder, 20:456, 40:148
Dodd, Mrs. William B., portrait, 12:104; diary, 13:322
Dodd Road (Mendota-Big Sioux Road), 12:317; surveyed, 11:390; route, 11:392; built, 20:456, 21:233, 22:323, 40:148
Dodds, J. S., editor, 24:368
Dodge, Bion A., memorial, 15:467
Dodge, Capt. Chester W., diary, 25:289
Dodge, Dorothy, author, 38:41
Dodge, Fred B., lawyer, 17:213
Dodge, Henry, 15:355, 17:344, 31:178; treaty commissioner, 20:120, 24:16, 17
Dodge, Mrs. Liva, speaker, 18:465
Dodge, Louis L., 14:103
Dodge, Lulu, 16:103
Dodge, Norman L., author, 32:125
Dodge, Ossian, speaker, 33:169
Dodge, W. C., letter, 32:28n
Dodge family, genealogy, 14:103
Dodge Center, Christmas masquerade, 16:384; businesses, 22:109; settled, 30:19
Dodge Center Star-Record, anniversary, 22:109
Dodge County, Norwegian settlements, 12:265, 270, 14:444, 31:27, 35:32; frontier life, 15:367; road, 16:496; pioneer Christmas, 17:126; Baptist churches, 19:122; history, 19:335; archives, 22:434; medicine, 24:182, 263, 382, 25:100, 307; population, 1857, 27:7; wildlife, 30:224; farming, 35:52; courthouse, 38:189n; in Civil War, 38:259; poor farm, 38:367; politics, 40:327, 328
Dodge County, Wis., history, 18:326
Dodge County Agricultural Society, 22:253
Dodge County Brewery, Mantorville, 40:126
Dodge County Historical Society, 16:240; proposed, 11:218, 461; established, 12:449, 13:71, 30:276; officers, 13:117; meetings, 13:424, 30:400; museum, 35:246
Dodge County Medical Society, history, 24:382
Dodge County Republican, history, 22:344
Dodge County War History Committee, 24:268
Dodgeville, Wis., pioneer life, 27:55, 83, 84; road, 27:85; churches, 27:94, 28:188
Doe, Hilton, house, 38:346
Doell, Charles, speaker, 24:269
Doerfler, Father Bruno, author, 35:339
Doermann, Humphrey, author, 37:307
Dogs, as pets, 14:281; hunting, 16:265-267; for travel, 22:346, 23:251, 33:121n, 36:285 (cover); in mail service, 23:199, 29:133, 30:196, 40:83, 85
Doherty, Michael J., 28:200
Doherty, Mrs. Ruth, 15:488, 16:240
Dolan, Mrs. Lois, 27:340, 28:47
Dole, Nathan H., author, 26:306
Dole, William P., Indian commissioner, 15:285, 295, 38:230, 354-356, 360, 364, 39:229, 230, 233

Doll, Frank G., 29:308
Dollier de Casson, François, explorer, 30:57
Dolliver, Jonathan P., politician, 21:68, 22:79, 27:133
Dolven, Mabel, author, 29:354
Dolven, O. E., author, 29:354
Dome Club, St. Paul, 30:179
Dominican Order, Faribault school, 16:371, 19:475, 21:455
Dominion City, Man., history, 34:132
Doms, W. E., 12:203
Donahower, Jeremiah C., in Civil War, 38:263, 268
Donahue, Mrs. John H., speaker, 14:229
Donald, David, reviews by, 34:250, 341; work reviewed, 33:216
Donaldson, Aris B., 16:181
Donaldson, H. S., merchant, 21:265
Donaldson, L. S., 19:184n
Donaldson, L. S., Co., Minneapolis, history, 12:457
Donaldson, Capt. Robert S., at Vicksburg, 33:213
Donaldson, Scott, author, 39:212
Donaldson, Thomas, author, 23:161, 26:376
Donaldson, William, and Co., Minneapolis, 35:67
Donavan, R. L., author, 15:487
Dondore, Dorothy, author, 20:200
Doneghy, Virginia, bibliographer, 31:188
Donehogawa (Gen. Ely S. Parker), 25:267
Doner, Mary F., author, 36:237
Donery, J. A., author, 29:169
Dongan, Thomas, 19:280, 281
Donna, Magdelin, cholera victim, 14:290
Donnelley, R. R., and Sons, Chicago, publishers, 15:353; building, 40:125, 127, 129
Donnelly, Ignatius, 15:338, 16:379, 17:477, 19:96, 441, 20:432, 22:382, 23:96, 26:361, 33:1, 350, 35:132, 36:83, 37:37, 38; works reviewed, 31:49, 37:81; career, 11:328, 12:201, 16:116, 21:44, 416, 28:54, 73, 279, 29:84, 36:31, 151, 204, 37:307, 39:132, 220; founder of Nininger, 11:454, 13:69, 127-150, 14:135, 403, 15:195, 16:481, 17:262-275, 18:368, 25:275, 32:19; biographies, 13:114, 30:290, 38:235; third-party leader, 14:169, 16:455, 21:383, 389, 22:386, 388, 25:298, 26:77, 170, 32:131-146, 34:37, 187, 35:56-62, 97, 98, 284, 291, 298-312, 36:109-111, 113-116, 119, 125, 37:19, 181, 38:236, 387, 39:96, 100, 103, 104, 260, 328, 329, 40:140, 360; papers, 14:331, 15:345, 16:52, 70, 94, 456, 17:100, 164, 269, 394, 18:444, 19:47, 20:370, 433, 21:86, 323, 22:99, 23:171, 25:193, 29:49, 283, 30:320, 31:99, 33:220, 34:312, 37:135, 39:96; publisher, 14:405, 27:2; in Shakespeare-Bacon controversy, 15:221; legislator, 15:224, 36:58, 60, 39:97; attitudes and policies, 15:297, 298, 28:175, 35:378, 36:178, 37:130, 39:343; lieutenant governor, 16:176, 24:308, 25:11, 13, 26:191, 28:30, 31, 32:

19, 33:128, 34:333, 37:213, 327–
329; senatorial candidate, 17:212,
26:195; speaker, 17:265, 271, 26:
304, 33:169, 38:72, 40:300, 363;
author, 17:275, 19:432, 25:398,
26:301, 28:24, 26, 270, 29:264,
30:62, 351, 372, 33:47, 48, 37:
261, 39:83; poet, 22:201, 26:294n;
Congressman, 26:195, 197, 201n,
36:173–183, 213, 300–308, 37:90,
97, 98, 100, 312, 314, 315, 330–
333, 38:61, 220, 221, 227, 39:87,
88, 40:38; patronage struggle, 33:
314; humorist, 33:326–330; scientific theories, 37:229–234. See
also Donnelly House
Donnelly, Mrs. Ignatius (Katherine),
37:327; singer, 29:119, 39:321,
324; letter, 38:72
Donnelly, Bishop James, 37:231
Donnelly, Rev. Joseph P., works reviewed, 30:249, 40:312
Donnelly, Philip, 33:327n
Donnelly family, in Hastings, 22:89;
genealogy, 33:327n
Donnelly House, Nininger, 13:142,
151, 14:135, 15:53, 55, 22:99,
100, 23:100, 37:65, 233; park
site, 16:127, 20:92; proposed
restoration, 19:111, 20:343, 450,
21:108; razed, 37:64
Donnelly Memorial Association, 20:
450, 21:82, 108, 329, 23:100
Donner, George, 29:61
Donoghue, James R., compiler, 35:295
Donohue, George, author, 40:363
Donohue, John K., probation officer,
35:290
Donohue, John R., memorial, 12:194
Donovan, Frank P., Jr., "Passenger
Trains of Yesteryear," 30:232–241;
reviews by, 30:146, 151, 31:111,
33:42, 34:83, 35:237, 283, 36:66,
150, 232, 321, 37:131, 341, 38:
237, 39:30; works reviewed, 30:
378, 32:47, 34:204, 36:322; au-
thor, 21:423, 30:184, 292, 31:128,
33:226, 316, 356, 34:99n, 130,
172, 216, 35:49, 203, 36:33, 40:
410
"Dooley, Mr." (Finley P. Dunne), 20:
421
Dooley, D. J., author, 40:411
Dooley, John, author, 29:344
Doolittle, James R., Senator, 16:99
Door County, Wis., ethnic settle-
ments, 12:180, 14:447; Potawatomi
Indians, 15:171, 172, 174
Doran, Michael, politician, 39:102,
331, 332
Dorati, Antal, symphony conductor,
33:222
Dorf, A. T., author, 19:459
Dorf, Philip, author, 35:244
Dorfflinger, Carl, author, 24:218
Dorfman, Joseph, author, 14:437, 37:
39
Dorman, O. B., banker, 26:157
Dorn, Helen P., author, 25:198
Dornbusch, C. E., compiler, 38:202
Dorr, Albert H., 24:133
Dorr, Caleb D., career, 24:125–141,
255; alderman, 35:120
Dorr, Mrs. Caleb D., described, 24:
132
Dorr, Charles M., 24:125
Dorr, Mrs. Charles M., 24:125

Dorr, Harold M., work reviewed, 22:
73–76
Dorr, J. V. N., engineer, 34:277
Dorr, Mrs. Russell R., 39:55, 56
Dorr, William G., 15:73, 79, 127,
359, 531
Dorrilites, religious sect, 36:278
Dorsey, Florence L., author, 23:183
Dorsey reaper, 24:288
Dorson, Richard M., reviews by, 33:
225, 34:261, 35:39; works reviewed, 27:237, 33:183, 346, 35:95;
author, 21:95, 27:159, 28:186,
378, 35:154, 200, 37:39, 38:333;
speaker, 28:75
Dorweiler, Louis C., author, 27:261
Dos Passos, John, author, 20:107,
116
Dostal, W. A., author, 14:341
Doty, James D., papers, 13:99, 23:
132, 329n, 33:345; explorer, 13:
369, 23:131, 135, 248, 328, 347,
348n, 31:94; career, 15:355, 34:
208; treaty negotiator, 16:149,
332, 542; territorial judge, 25:
271
Doty, James H., pioneer, 13:119, 16:
491
Douay, Father Anastasius, 11:348
Doud, Freeman, pioneer, 23:25
Dougan, Henry K., author, 15:140
Dougherty, John, explorer, 34:285
Dougherty, Richard, author, 40:315
Dougherty, Mrs. Wallace, 23:390
Doughty, Arthur C., editor, 13:300
Doughty, Howard, author, 38:200
Doughty, Col. Sam, hunter, 33:154
Douglas, Mrs. ——, trial, 16:451
Douglas, Charles A., 17:165
Douglas, Edward M., author, 12:199
Douglas, Frederic H., author, 22:189
Douglas, George B., translator, 17:
140, 145, 32:189, 202, 208, 210,
212
Douglas, George P., 12:207
Douglas, Henry F., 33:333, 337
Douglas, James, trader, 20:72, 40:
168n
Douglas, Jesse, photographer, 15:181n
Douglas, Jesse S., review by, 22:409,
31:241; author, 22:418, 24:70,
253, 31:256
Douglas, John B., 13:92
Douglas, Stephen A., 21:429, 26:357,
37:113n; Senator, 14:128, 130,
164, 23:261, 262, 30:196, 272, 31:
178, 35:242; Minnesota visit, 16:
27, 98; papers, 16:224; presidential candidate, 24:166, 309, 27:
14, 28:34–36, 32:19, 20, 34:333,
37:45–51, 54, 39:175; author, 36:
323, 38:202
Douglas, Thomas, see Selkirk, Earl of
Douglas, W. H. S., work reviewed, 30:
146
Douglas, Wallace B., career, 12:322
Douglas, William, author, 27:166
Douglas, Justice William O., conservationist, 38:91, 40:136
Douglas County, politics, 12:194, 36:
306, 39:95, 96; ethnic groups, 12:
277, 21:102, 25:318, 39:133, 134;
Lutheran church, 14:451; history,
15:246, 30:161, 271, 36:106; pioneer life, 18:225; first newspaper, 18:467; agriculture, 19:107;
archives, 22:211; organized, 22:

344; emigration from, 23:26;
schools, 35:149. See also Kensington rune stone
Douglas County, Wis., road, 16:289
Douglas County Historical Society,
16:240, 21:334; organized, 13:73,
14:456, 15:71, 72, 108, 135, 29:
361; meetings, 15:246, 17:120,
231, 21:443, 23:296; essay contest, 17:121; pageant, 17:356
Douglas County (Wis.) Historical
Society, 24:377; museum, 20:340,
24:378; history, 29:273; exhibit,
34:174
Douglas County Medical Society, organized, 22:330
Douglas County Old Settlers and Pioneers Union, 14:456
Douglas County War History Committee,
23:390
Douglass, Capt. David B., explorer,
23:129–131, 135, 240, 334, 340,
347, 348, 31:94, 33:345, 35:241
Douglass, Frederick, speaker, 11:157,
158, 40:12
Douglass, Harl R., author, 12:418;
speaker, 15:219
Dousman, Hercules L., 25:272, 27:164,
32:72; trader, 11:384, 13:225, 226
229, 231, 237, 15:384, 18:193, 19:
95, 22:205, 206, 278, 30:72, 259,
32:79, 80, 36:260, 40:23–25, 29,
30, 81; papers, 12:426, 16:73, 18:
439, 20:337, 21:412, 26:363; career, 13:223, 15:383; steamboating
interests, 13:233–235, 239; in Indian affairs, 16:97; house, 17:
344, 20:76, 339, 443, 24:242, 25:
314, 409, 26:359, 28:71, 31:57,
37:40; portrait, 17:345
Dousman, Mrs. Hercules L., 20:79;
portrait, 17:345
Dousman, Hercules L., Jr., 12:426
Dousman, Louis, speaker, 17:344
Dousman, Michael, trader, 40:186
Dousman family, at Prairie du Chien,
Wis., 24:161
Douthit, Davis, author, 30:66
Douville, James, 16:257
Douville, Raymond, author, 28:370
Dow, L. U., 25:26
Dow, Lorenzo, revivalist, 24:113
Dowd, Pearl, 13:390
Dowd, Zinah, 25:147
Dowdey, Clifford, author, 28:173
Dowell, A. A., speaker, 14:122, 21:
436, 27:80; author, 17:227
Dowie, James Iverne, work reviewed,
38:381; author, 37:39
Dowling, Archbishop Austin, 20:92,
25:305, 39:159, 160; portrait,
12:433; educator, 33:223; career,
35:155
Dowling, Edward J., author, 36:32
Dowling, Michael J., 12:421, 14:117,
24:181; papers, 27:56; teacher,
34:173
Dowling School, St. Paul, 14:117
Downer, Harry, author, 13:111
Downer, John B., land officer, 39:86,
91
Downes, P. G., author, 36:151
Downey, Fairfax, work reviewed, 22:
409
Downie, Capt. Mark W., 25:249
Downing, Andrew J., 20:130, 138, 25:
111, 31:148; architect, 27:125,

37:192, 38:343; house, 37:193
Downing, Margaret D., 27:147
Downing, William, speaker, 27:365
Downs, Lynwood G., 27:187; "The Sol-
dier Vote," 26:187-210; "The Writ-
ings of Albert Wolff," 27:327-329;
"Music Moves West," 32:239-242;
reviews by, 26:364, 35:328; au-
thor, 26:370, 27:343, 32:255;
speaker, 28:178
Downs, Mrs. Lynwood G., 27:240
Downs, Winfield S., editor, 22:104
Dowsing (water witching), in U.S.,
36:324
Doyle, John J., probation officer,
35:289
Doyle, Thomas H, author, 13:336
Drache, Hiram M., review by, 40:303;
work reviewed, 39:206
Draeger, Earl, 25:41
Drago, Harry S., work reviewed, 40:
307
Drake, ---, murdered, 17:154
Drake, A. J., lumberman, 24:201
Drake, Benjamin, 13:428; speaker, 13:
341; papers, 29:49
Drake, Carl B., author, 33:312, 36:
70, 38:92
Drake, Dr. Daniel, work reviewed, 29:
338; author, 26:143
Drake, Hiram, 25:254
Drake, J. R., 29:24
Drake, Marian, 30:79, 165; speaker,
30:277
Drake, Thomas E., "Quakers in Minne-
sota," 18:249-266
Drake family, in Rice County, 20:355
Drama, see Theater
Draper, Lyman C., manuscript collec-
tion, 15:355, 26:148, 385, 30:269,
35:335; historian, 20:173, 27:164,
33:311, 38:200; editor, 23:132;
biography, 34:119; papers, 35:146
Draxten, Nina, author, 40:357
"Dreadnaught," steamboat, 30:187
Dreher, Otto, actor, 32:103, 104
Dreiser, Theodore, 14:201; author,
19:437
Drenning, June, see Holmquist, Mrs.
Donald C.
Drepperd, Carl W., author, 31:53
Dresbach, Michael R., letters, 17:
466, 18:48
Dreuillettes, Father Gabriel, mis-
sionary, 15:163, 168, 170n
Drew, Benjamin, diary, 19:211, 20:34
Drew, Carter, 12:125
Drew, Edward B., pioneer, 14:264,
280, 16:71, 20:159, 23:318, 320
Drew, Rev. S. J., pioneer, 13:343
Drew, Rev. Theophilus, 26:243
Drewes, Elsye M., author, 20:102
Drewry, Elizabeth B., author, 23:389
Drier, Roy, author, 35:247
Drifter, The (Kahboka), Sioux leader,
21:169, 38:147
Driggs, Howard R., work reviewed, 35:
290
Drimmer, Frederick, compiler, 38:384
Drips, J. H., author, 37:224
Drivewell patent, lawsuit, 23:180
Drought, Dr. W. W., author, 20:103
Drouillard, Nelson, carpenter, 18:
209
Droulers, Charles, author, 22:207
Druid Horn Players, 22:115
Drumm, Stella M., editor, 39:261

Drummond, Lake County, on map, 34:
179; railroad, 34:180
Drummond Island, Lake Huron, Indian
rendezvous, 17:81; British post,
18:184n, 23:143
Drury, Charles F., 16:355
Drury, John, 25:201; works reviewed,
29:72, 30:141
Drury, Newton B., author, 31:249
Dryden, Hugh L., 33:245
Dryden Township, Sibley County, 1860
vote, 28:36; settled, 34:219
Drywood, Todd County, history, 15:371
Dubach, Mrs. Ana King, 25:17
DuBay, Jean Baptiste, trial, 27:238
Dube, Mrs. Vivien G., 24:378; author,
29:273
DuBois, Ben, speaker, 37:40
DuBois, Cornelia A., "Operatic Pio-
neers," 33:317-325
DuBois, Dr. Julian F., author, 17:220
Du Bois, W. E. B., Black leader, 31:
244
Dubois, Ind., German settlement, 28:
246
Dubos, Jean-Baptiste, letters, 19:
396, 397
Dubourg, Bishop L. William, 11:306
Dubuque, Julien, 28:184; biographies,
12:76, 13:439; grave, 17:152, 300;
miner, 23:344n
Dubuque, Iowa, river port, 11:130,
143, 12:159, 17:152, 413, 26:132,
272, 29:318, 30:5, 33:116, 39:298;
stage lines, 11:401, 402, 12:166,
30:69; lead mines, 12:76, 18:434,
23:344n; land office, 12:383, 28:
284; trade center, 12:240, 27:19,
34:17, 18, 22, 23; archdiocese,
15:212, 19:460; pictured, 17:148n,
25:110, 34:21, 136; newspapers,
17:300; bishopric, 18:436; climate, 20:161n; beginnings, 22:97,
98; theater, 23:313; sawmill, 27:
190; railroad, 36:5; post office,
40:87
"Dubuque," steamboat, 11:104, 17:151,
295, 37:296
Du Buque Visitor, established, 14:447
Ducatel, J. T., 12:83
Duchesneau, Jacques, 22:60
Duchouquette, François, 15:428
Duckett, Kenneth W., author, 34:313
Duddles, R. E., 14:119
Duddy, Edward A., author, 12:201, 16:
350
Dudevant, Amentine L. A. (George
Sand), 20:137
Due, John F., work reviewed, 37:131
Duerk, Hilarion, author, 21:456, 22:
333
Duerr, Joseph, 32:41
Duesenberg automobile, 40:148
Duesterhoeft, Mrs. William, 12:339
Dufaut, ---, trader, 11:359, 20:10,
28:147n
Duff, Louis B., author, 13:431
Duff, Philip, author, 35:382
Dufferin, Frederick T. Blackwood,
Marquis of, in Manitoba, 21:261;
letters, 34:357
Duffield, Lt. Henry M., 39:194
Duffield, Col. William W., 39:193,
194
Duffus, R. L., author, 15:476
Duffus, Mrs. William, author, 12:211
Duffy, W. F., map maker, 40:125n

Duford, J., 15:425
Dugan, James E., work reviewed, 25:
280
Duin, Edgar C., "Settlers' Periodical," 33:29-34
Dugré, Alexandre, author, 19:348
Du Gua de Monts, Pierre, trader, 40:
188
Dukinfield, A. S., editor, 21:450
Duley, William J., scout, 39:234, 237
Dulles, Foster R., author, 21:422
Dulles, John Foster, 38:240
Du Lhut, Daniel Greysolon, sieur, explorer, 11:204, 12:307, 354, 361,
435, 14:215, 15:100, 16:193, 349,
418n, 449, 453, 18:193, 233, 19:
276, 278, 286, 313, 20:68, 21:348,
22:327, 352, 23:58, 25:372, 30:
224, 375, 32:186, 35:292, 36:70,
37:68, 114; career, 11:328, 13:
439, 15:238; trader, 11:357, 385;
rescues Hennepin, 14:371, 21:92;
fort, 19:280; will, 20:452, 26:
262; in fiction, 36:76, 77
Duluth, Catholic churches, 11:118,
14:452, 16:299, 39:299; founded,
11:433, 14:232, 32:90n, 186, 37:
89-100, 112n; economic conditions,
11:466, 14:103, 17:214, 218, 19:
405, 20:83, 336, 345, 22:374, 25:
102, 33:67, 34:358, 35:152, 36:
189, 37:119-125; pioneer life, 12:
107, 20:363, 21:195, 414, 25:313,
28:78, 38:42; hotel, 12:107, 37:
110n, 117; historical meetings,
12:281-284, 19:308-317; land office, 12:384, 387, 16:360; ethnic
groups, 12:436, 18:453, 24:226,
25:186, 319, 325, 327, 30:156, 31:
29, 36:320, 39:131; port, 12:442,
13:40, 41, 14:232, 233, 16:288,
19:113, 405, 21:422, 22:437, 24:
62, 26:77, 27:353, 28:69, 252, 31:
58, 229, 32:126, 33:66, 34:1 (cover), 12-14, 75, 35:294, 37:39, 89
(cover), 91, 94-100, 115, 38:386,
39:211, 40:359; chronology, 12:
454; history, 13:77-80, 22:111,
26:276, 27:252, 31:246, 34:177,
37:347; newspapers, 14:359, 18:
472, 25:327; Methodist churches,
14:452, 17:378, 379, 26:96, 28:83;
geology, 15:131, 39:132; Baptist
churches, 15:243, 27:82; lighthouse, 15:360; post office, 15:
467, 34:185, 37:114; roads, 16:
282-299, 19:103, 28:381; mail service, 16:285, 287; G.A.R. encamp-
ments, 16:431, 441; Benedictines
in, 17:219, 33:58-60, 294; climate, 17:260, 20:452, 30:154; Mark
Twain's visits, 17:375, 378-380;
schools, 17:469; railroads, 18:78,
21:239, 22:379, 25:412, 28:284,
29:13, 17, 33:15, 61-63, 69, 35:
21, 364, 37:38, 96, 101-118, 40:
247; industries, 18:343, 36:103;
Lutheran churches, 19:106, 20:468,
25:102, 27:82, 28:294; medicine,
19:226, 22:330; described, 20:64,
193, 28:279, 29:167, 30:142, 32:
150, 194, 33:65, 67, 68, 37:3, 4,
109-118; historic sites, 20:217,
34:314, 37:64; pictured, 20:453,
21:154, 157, 28:350, 30:55, 34:71;
transportation, 20:468, 21:291,
30:267; music, 21:116, 39:323;

mills, 21:150, 25:78, 30:242; recruiting station, 21:207; labor unions, 21:393, 22:376, 377, 380, 27:352, 40:342, 347; land platting, 22:349; name, 22:351, 26:250, 28:78; libraries, 22:361-365; temperance society, 22:391, 392n; bridges, 23:290, 24:62; in World War II, 25:94, 26:175; utilities, 25:315; Unitarian church, 25:324; Episcopal church, 26:96, 37:110n; ship canal, 26:291, 27:72, 30:397; theaters, 26:291, 28:109, 32:100, 33:41, 242; fisheries, 28:349, 34:245, 246, 249; logging center, 29:141, 36:158, 162, 163; city government, 30:144; in fiction, 31:134, 37:5, 9; politics, 34:229, 38:303, 39:105, 344; taconite plant, 34:277-279, 283, 39:163; sports club, 36:89; horticulture, 36:327; elevators, 37:17, 18, 99; athletics, 39:19; mongoose controversy, 39:297

Duluth and Iron Range Railroad, built, 11:415, 12:285, 33:258, 40:412; first locomotive, 12:284, 19:336; history, 19:113, 26:174; route, 27:203, 34:178-180, 184, 276; sold, 33:221; dock, 34:266

Duluth and Northeastern Railroad, logging road, 19:113, 24:264, 27:300, 308, 34:181, 184, 40:361

Duluth and Northern Minnesota Railroad, logging road, 27:301, 307, 34:179, 181-184

Duluth and Superior Railroad, 12:182

Duluth and Winnipeg Railroad, incorporated, 24:278n; built, 34:14, 15. See also Great Northern Railroad

Duluth Automobile Club, 38:208

Duluth Board of Trade, history, 35:99

Duluth Building and Loan Association, 37:123

Duluth Chamber of Commerce, 28:390, 34:69

Duluth Children's Home, built, 34:44

Duluth Clearing House Association, 37:122

Duluth Evening Herald, history, 14:359

Duluth Gas and Water Co., franchise, 25:315

Duluth Grand Opera House, 28:98

Duluth Ladies Library Association, 22:362

Duluth Library Association, 20:363, 26:386

Duluth, Missabe and Iron Range Railroad, 27:300; ore hauler, 25:307, 26:77, 36:281; surveyed, 27:263; described, 30:378; history, 35:152, 40:48

Duluth, Missabe and Northern Railroad, 11:416, 32:150, ore hauler, 32:151; financed, 37:124

Duluth, Mississippi River and Northern Railroad ("Wooden Shoe"), built, 21:439

Duluth National Bank, 37:122

Duluth Posten, file acquired, 15:468

Duluth Public Library, 18:95, 22:362, 364; history, 21:456; anniversary, 22:351

Duluth, Red Wing and Southern Railroad, 35:17, 21

Duluth, St. Cloud, Glencoe and Mankato Railroad, history, 13:342

Duluth Savings Bank, 13:78, 37:120, 121

Duluth Skandinav, history, 19:106

Duluth Ski Club, 17:228, 34:218

Duluth Skin-Divers Club, history, 35:278-281

Duluth, South Shore and Atlantic Railway Co., history, 39:263

Duluth State Normal School, 13:79, 28:76

Duluth Symphony Orchestra, founded, 26:276, 27:367

Duluth Typographical Union, history, 17:363

Duluth Union National Bank, 37:122

Duluth War History Committee, 23:390, 24:84, 186, 376, 25:94

Duluth, Winnipeg and Pacific Railroad, 40:392

Duluth Woman's Club, 17:357

Dumond, Dwight L., work reviewed, 18:302

Dumoulin, Father Sévère, 14:284, 21:432, 24:42

Dumphy, Charles, 11:459

Dunbar, ---, 19:136, 137

Dunbar, John B., 20:174

Dunbar, Henry W., composer, 22:131

Dunbar, Ralph, 33:325

Dunbar, W. F., 34:333

Duncan, Kenneth, author, 40:412

Duncan, Matthew, pioneer printer, 15:13

Duncan, Todd, singer, 39:63

Duncanson, Charles A., author, 17:488, 18:116, 228, 341, 21:454, 27:80

Dundas, mills, 11:274, 275, 278, 279, 12:453, 18:118, 342; name, 11:275n; churches, 12:453, 17:212, 18:118; mounds, 16:308; baseball club, 19:169, 170; history, 21:115; cooperage business, 22:373; camp meeting, 31:82

Dungan, Samuel, letters, 34:310

Dungay, Dr. N. S., speaker, 27:363

Dunham, R. S., author, 17:227, 18:107

Duniway, Clyde A., 11:15, 117, 13:121, 15:138, 16:67, 124, 241, 17:70, 123, 312, 18:111, 335, 19:64, 118; review by, 15:102; speaker, 11:52, 53, 13:73, 292, 344, 15:80, 16:66; author, 11:337, 15:109, 17:226

Dunkards, in Minnesota, 13:448, 31:119

Dunkl, Mary, see Burda, Mrs. Mary

Dunlap, Alexander, 25:356

Dunlap, Leslie W., author, 25:390

Dunlap, Roy J., speaker, 16:67, 17:69; author, 30:69, 273, 33:313, 37:43

Dunlap, William, 25:356

Dunleith, Ill., railroad, 17:413, 34:18, 23

Dunlevy, Sister Ursula, author, 23:186, 287

Dunlop, "Tiger," explorer, 25:273

Dunn, ---, trader, 11:261

Dunn, Alice M., "People and Places in Old St. Paul," 33:1-6

Dunn, Andrew C., 26:203, 205

Dunn, E. S., 13:342

Dunn, H. H., legislator, 33:157, 160

Dunn, Irene, author, 14:360

Dunn, James T., 23:75; "The St. Croix Valley Welcomes the Iron Horse," 35:358-364; "Mail for Pioneers," 36:206-215; "The Minnesota State Prison," 37:137-151; "Minnesota's Oldest Courthouse," 38:186-189; "St. Paul's Schubert Club," 39:51-64; reviews by, 31:245, 34:350, 36:100, 322, 38:39, 39:207, 40:310, 406; works reviewed, 31:185, 36:62, 38:333, 39:290; author, 30:387, 31:56, 256, 34:316, 35:204, 36:72, 106, 37:44, 348, 38:336; librarian, 31:11, 32:58, 34:220, 40:269, 270; editor, 33:1-6; speaker, 35:52, 36:152; compiler, 36:194

Dunn, Mrs. James T. (Mária Bach), translator, 40:265-278

Dunn, Dr. John B., St. Cloud physician, 33:295

Dunn, John W. G., photographer, 36:215n, 37:137 (cover)

Dunn, Marshall B., pioneer, 11:333

Dunn, Robert, gubernatorial candidate, 16:99

Dunn, Robert C., legislator, 33:159, 36:117, 120

Dunn, Roy E., speaker, 24:385, 27:363, 30:278

Dunn, Samuel, brakeman, 30:239

Dunn, Thomas, 15:96

Dunn, W. W., author,, 20:445

Dunn, Winslow W., legislator, 35:346, 347, 348

Dunn Township, Otter Tail County, history, 11:116

Dunne, Finley P. ("Mr. Dooley"), 20:421

Dunne, Vince, labor leader, 18:191, 192

Dunne, William H., author, 34:132

Dunne brothers, labor leaders, 23:197

Dunnell, Mark L., 28:349; Congressman, 37:319

Dunning, Alice, actress, 28:110

Dunning, William A., 25:68

Dunphy, James, author, 18:338, 19:364

Dunwoody, William H., 33:333, 336, 337, 34:204; career, 11:328, 29:88

Dunwoody Institute, Minneapolis, in World War I, 28:349

Du Parque, F., author, 21:370

Du Plessis, ---, trader, 11:259

Dupre, J. Huntley, 39:264; "E. D. Neill's Gospel of Minnesota," 30:202-219; reviews by, 29:65, 35:87, 39:337; work reviewed, 30:244; author, 29:103, 30:291; speaker, 30:264, 36:72

Dupree, A. Hunter, work reviewed, 36:26

Duprez and Benedict, minstrel troupe, 28:110

Du Priest, Gladys H., "The Waseca County Horse Thief Detectives," 13:153-157; author, 15:253

Du Puis, Hypolite, house, 19:235, 20:343, 23:192, 37:60, 61

Duquesne, Michel Ange, governor of New France, 19:289, 32:229, 230, 234-237

Durand, ---, trader, 21:123, 126, 127, 130, 132; at Grand Portage, 21:145

Durand, Rev. Arthur, speaker, 19:232, 20:458

Durand, Asher B., see Durang
Durand, Loyal, Jr., author, 30:154
Durand Township, Beltrami County, history, 15:133
Durang [Asher B. Durand?], artist, 17:142
Du Ranquet, Dominique, missionary, 39:309, 310
Durant, Edward W., lumberman, 18:175, 177, 31:34-36, 39
Durant, Mrs. Kate, speaker, 30:77
Durant, Will, 17:92
Durant, Wheeler, and Co., Stillwater, 18:178
Duratschek, Sister Mary C., author, 29:173
Durey, Mary, centennial queen, 30:177
Durfee, Waite D., Jr., author, 35:336
Durfee, W. R., pioneer, 24:354
Durfee and Peck, traders, 34:325
Durgan, Michael, tavernkeeper, 11:459
Durham, J. W., pioneer, 16:492, 18:273, 22:349, 24:320, 324
Durham boat, 22:144n
Durocher, Aurele A., author, 39:263
Durrie, George H., artist, 14:440, 15:62, 34:134, 135
Duscha, Julius, author, 27:366, 28:76
Düsseldorf, Germany, Henry Lewis' residence, 17:143-146
Dustin, Col. Daniel H., cholera victim, 14:294
Dustin, Fred, author, 28:72, 34:39, 35:339
Dustin family, murdered, 21:182, 35:337
Dutch, U.S., 11:77, 16:403, 29:67, 79; Minnesota, 11:77, 13:427, 14:239, 356, 15:367, 16:251, 21:203, 27:214, 28:120-131, 37:152-160; Wisconsin, 12:158n, 20:86, 27:134, 135, 28:379; war with British, 16:391, 392, 395; colonization projects, 18:338, 21:74, 25:299; immigration, 27:40, 28:367, 35:33, 90, 292, 36:104, 37:222; Michigan, 29:174; in Civil War, 33:84; cookery, 40:47. See also Reformed Church in America
Dutch West Indies Co., 15:208
Dutcher, Flora, author, 31:57
Du Toit, Frederick E., pioneer journalist, 14:394, 18:113
Du Toit, George, 19:22
Dutton, Carl E., work reviewed, 17:85
Dutton, Dr. Charles E., 38:208, 209
Duus, Olaus F., work reviewed, 29:160
Duval, William P., 36:323
Duvall, Dr. William P., career, 20:235
Duvall, Mrs. William P., 20:236
Duxbury, Francis A., 39:26; legislator, 33:156, 157
Dvořák, Antonín, in Middle West, 14:341, 28:302, 36:190
Dvořák, Josef, 15:35
Dwan, Dennis, 16:240; speaker, 14:456; author, 16:101
Dwan, John, 35:38; career, 34:266
Dwelle, Abner, pioneer, 17:366
Dwelle, Glenn M., 15:371, 16:240, 17:367, 18:344, 19:116, 20:99, 25:208; speaker, 16:256
Dwight, Edmund, traveler, 36:44, 45
Dwight, Timothy, educator, 22:66
Dwinnel, William S., legislator, 35:343

Dwinnell, Mrs. Nora, 23:298
Dworschak, Rev. Baldwin, 33:114n
Dworschak, J., theater director, 34:242
Dworschak, Therese, actress, 34:242
Dyck, Henry D., author, 33:187
Dyer, Brainerd, author, 28:177, 33:82
Dyer, Francis L., Indian agent, 39:233
Dyer, Mr. and Mrs. William J., 33:129
Dykema, Simon, Dutch pioneer, 28:125
Dykstra, Clarence A., speaker, 20:206
Dymock, Atkinson, 26:358
Dziuk, Claudia, author, 36:106

Eachus, G. H., 23:94
Eades, Harry, 33:320
Eads, James B., 24:54, 35:40
Eagle Bakery, St. Paul, 14:391
Eagle Bend, history, 30:397
Eagle Head, Sioux leader, 21:162
Eagle Help, Sioux Indian, 21:164, 165
Eagle Lake, history, 11:116, 36:195
Eagle Roller Mill Co., New Ulm, history, 12:449, 16:127, 27:78
Eagle sawmill, Nininger, 13:150
Eagle Township, Carlton County, history, 38:243
"Eaglet," ketch, 16:399, 400, 417n, 419-421, 425n
Eakins, G. E., speaker, 13:337
Eames, Henry H., geologist, 19:309, 24:166, 32:217, 37:42
Eames, Paul, 28:51
Eames, Richard, mining engineer, 24:34, 166
Eames, Richard, Jr., author, 24:166
Eames, Wilberforce, bibliographer, 20:198, 26:140; editor, 26:140
Earhart, Joseph, 17:230
Earhart, Lida B., author, 17:230
Earhart, Margaret, 17:230
Earhart, Mary, author, 26:77
Earhart family, genealogy, 17:230
Early, C. G., 16:338
Early, James S., speaker, 21:287
Early American Glass Club, 27:240
Earthquakes, Mississippi Valley, 12:98; Minnesota, 14:110
East Central Electric Association, Braham, 37:347
East Chain Township, Martin County, settled, 18:341, 20:462; post office, 24:380
East Grand Forks, history, 18:341, 20:207
East High School, Minneapolis, athletics, 39:20
East India Co., 16:182n, 202
East Main, Que., post, 40:171
East Moe, Douglas County, Lutheran church, 20:460
East Prairieville, Rice County, ghost town, 20:355
East St. Olaf, Olmsted County, Norwegian settlement, 12:270
East Savanna River, geology, 13:406; canoe route, 23:251n, 31:95, 32:95, 34:46
East Side Commerical Club, St. Paul, 27:249
East Side Cornet Band, Minneapolis, 32:167

East Side Dramatic Society (Cäcilienverein), Minneapolis, 32:167
East Union, Carver County, Lutheran church, 14:451; literary society, 24:214; school, 26:167; log houses, 37:72, 76n
Easter, celebrated, 15:39, 30:161
Eastern States Archaeological Federation, 23:349
Eastin, Roy B., compiler, 38:42
"Eastland," steamboat, 34:39
Eastlick, Mrs. Lavina, Sioux captive, 29:364, 30:16, 38:242, 385, 40:147
Eastlick, Merton, portrait, 34:267; in Sioux Outbreak, 30:15, 16, 20
Eastlick family, in Minnesota, 22:89
Eastman House, Que., 34:255
Eastman, Alvah, 17:233, 20:98; journalist, 17:365
Eastman, Dr. Charles A., 12:123n, 15:100, 19:348, 21:168n; career, 11:110; speaker, 11:348n, 438, 12:97
Eastman, Mrs. Elaine G., review by, 18:305; work reviewed, 17:200; author, 19:348, 26:302, 378
Eastman, Jason C., papers, 34:339
Eastman, John (Many Lightnings), Sioux Indian, 12:123n
Eastman, Rev. John, interpreter, 38:127
Eastman, Jonathan O., author, 16:255
Eastman, Karin, 14:428
Eastman, Mary F., feminist, 39:5
Eastman, Gen. Seth, artist, 12:215, 13:169, 290, 301, 369n, 14:335, 382, 383, 15:470, 17:134n, 155n, 345, 456, 19:419-423, 20:334, 21:151, 196, 209, 22:333, 25:304, 26:359, 27:167, 29:185, 30:157, 176, 261, 284, 406, 31:46, 54-56, 210n, 219, 32:188, 190, 211, 33:45 (cover), 264, 34:121, 129, 35:182, 197, 288, 379, 36:20-23, 148, 277, 328, 37:38, 38:149, 201, 39:315; at Fort Snelling, 17:68, 153, 154n, 156, 288, 25:289, 30:152, 31:210, 211, 213, 214, 216, 218; suppresses Winnebago, 17:155-157; career, 19:419-423, 38:36; surveyor, 27:316, 28:219-222
Eastman, Mrs. Seth (Mary H.), 13:166, 31:219; author, 12:215, 227, 13:169, 292, 370, 372, 373, 18:180, 448, 19:421, 31:210, 220, 34:129, 35:380, 36:21-23, 74-76, 38:201, 39:315; poet, 12:220
Eastman, W. W., Co., Minneapolis, 24:290
Eastman, Welles, speaker, 28:391
Eastman, William W., miller, 23:225, 37:319; lumberman, 37:41
Eastman, Bovey and DeLaittre, Pokegama Lake, lumber firm, 16:101
Eastman Block, Minneapolis, 23:225
Easton, A. B., journalist, 24:201
Easton, J., hotelkeeper, 12:401
Easton, J. H., hotelkeeper, 12:401
Easton, Jason C., banker, 13:117, 15:60, 111, 16:364, 20:302, 22:350, 24:107, 28:203, 29:223-230; papers, 16:73, 20:288, 21:324; commission merchant, 24:100; miller, 24:101; livestock raiser, 24:105, 26:124; horse trader, 24:383; career, 30:53
Easton, Lorraine, 30:276
Easton, William E., 17:341, 19:476;

pioneer journalist, 11:468, 17:
313, 530; speaker, 16:244; author,
17:491
Easton family, newspaper publishers,
26:399
Easton, Pa., shipbuilding, 26:66
Eastvold, Rev. C. J., career, 15:235
Eastwood, Carl, author, 14:457
Eaton, Allen H., author, 14:111, 28:
70; speaker, 25:397
Eaton, Burt W., 11:54, 283, 12:35,
14:78, 16:241, 17:70, 19:46, 66,
20:50, 297, 301, 21:48, 213, 22:
188, 340, 23:35, 24:180, 27:362;
speaker, 11:461, 12:209, 13:344,
15:485, 16:66, 256, 18:335, 20:96,
299, 21:217; lawyer, 24:375
Eaton, Edward D., author, 15:358
Eaton, G. D., author, 23:117, 157
Eaton, Guy A., postmaster, 34:185
Eaton, Joel, 25:183, 383
Eaton, John H., secretary of war, 35:
28
Eaton, Quaintance, editor, 31:61; author, 36:33
Eaton, S. S., 13:140
Eaton, Samuel S., balloon passenger,
38:171, 173–175
Eatonville, Hennepin County, Sioux
village, 35:28
Eau Claire, Wis., logging museum, 24:
364; French-Canadian settlement,
27:135; lumbering, 27:194, 196,
197, 200; power company, 35:381;
road, 40:387
Eau Claire Lumber Co., 27:194n
Eau Claire State College, 34:131
Eberhart, Adolph A., 22:104; papers,
11:319, 34:339; autobiography, 25:
184, 26:167, 30:391; governor, 33:
155, 40:148
Eberhart, Nell R., song writer, 26:52
Eberly, Mrs. Katherine, museum assis-
tant, 24:31
Eberstadt, Lindley E., 36:218
Ebersviller, Lorraine, author, 11:221
Ebert, Isabel J., compiler, 35:335
Eberts, Dr. Herman, career, 33:87
Eble, Kenneth, author, 39:35
Eby, Esther E., author, 18:454
Eccles, W. J., author, 34:310
Echo Lake, St. Louis County, lumber-
ing, 34:183, 36:153 (cover)
Echols, Watonwan County, farmers'
club, 20:218
Echota, Otter Tail County, townsite,
15:465
Eck, Charles A., career, 19:214
Eck, Aimee H. (Mrs. Lester J.), 30:
156; letter, 30:92; author, 31:124
Eckel, Edmond J., architect, 40:103
Eckel, Mrs. Edward H. (Emily P.), 11:
96, 40:350
Eckener, Hugo, author, 40:267
Eckert, E. K., 20:86
Eckholm, Gordon, archaeologist, 25:
333
Eckland, Halvor, in Civil War, 14:
427, 428
Eckland, Henry C., 19:471
Eckles, Clarence H., career, 12:99;
papers, 17:53, 101, 34:339
Eckles Township, Beltrami County,
history, 15:365
Ecklund, Carl A., postmaster, 36:215
Eckman, Dr. James, 34:218; reviews
by, 24:347, 30:143, 31:43; author,

21:209, 22:334, 434, 23:96, 24:
182, 263, 353, 382, 25:100, 307,
29:353, 30:184, 31:64, 33:91, 34:
358, 37:135
Eckman, Jeannette, work reviewed, 31:
184
Eckstrom, Rev. Carl A., author, 20:
468
Eclipses, 34:132
Ecology, see Conservation, Pollution
Economic conditions, among immigrants, 11:83, 12:305, 31:28, 31;
frontier, 13:7, 9, 355, 14:463,
15:52, 198, 329, 16:23–25, 209,
316, 17:416–420, 18:421, 19:323,
325–327, 21:87, 24:191, 25:183,
26:288, 27:9, 28:190, 202, 203,
321–323, 30:150, 33:251, 301, 34:
96–105, 310; South, 23:259, 26:
155; Southwest, 26:168; Minnesota,
26:172; price fixing, 28:38–44;
after Civil War, 37:130; Prairie
Island Sioux, 37:278; after World
War I, 38:334; Wisconsin, 40:111.
See also Agriculture, Banks and
banking, Business, Depressions,
Labor, various industries
Economic history, American, 11:79,
19:90, 26:162, 27:64, 33:92, 40:
353; bibliography, 11:100; source
material, 16:70–75, 37:256; meat
packing, 18:470, 23:108, 388;
Northwest, 26:166; local, 28:174;
Midwest, 37:133
Economic History Association, 26:264,
27:64, 29:257
Economics Laboratory, Inc., St. Paul,
history, 39:211
Eddy, Edward B., surveyor, 24:97n
Eddy, Edward D., Jr., author, 35:379
Eddy, Ezra B., 26:68
Eddy, George W., 24:132, 140
Eddy, Henry T., 14:231, 452; biog-
raphy, 12:200
Eddy, Josephine, author, 36:327
Eddy, Mary Baker, 28:55
Eddy, Samuel, 23:330n; author, 25:
298, 28:285; review by, 34:260
Eddy Hall, University of Minnesota,
23:231
Edelbrock, Abbot Alexius, 18:473, 27:
105, 32:41, 33:53, 55, 57–59
Edelbrock, Anton, pioneer, 32:37, 35:
268
Edelbrock, Barney, 35:268
Edelbrock, Joseph, storekeeper, 35:
265, 268
Edelbrock, Mary, 35:268
Eden Township, Brown County, Metho-
dist church, 15:481
Eden Prairie, Presbyterian church,
14:330; pioneer life, 14:330, 16:
209; flour mill, 18:315; govern-
ment, 39:299
Eden Publishing House, St. Louis, 15:
446
Eden Valley, history, 17:487
Ederer, Bernard F., work reviewed,
35:288; author, 34:131
Edgar, Beatrice, manuscript assist-
ant, 22:191, 421, 23:44, 168, 24:
31
Edgar, Grace W., 14:351
Edgar, John, farmer, 29:8n
Edgar, Marjorie, 19:92, 30:84; "Fin-
nish Folk Songs," 16:319–321;
"Finnish Charms and Folk Songs,"

17:406–410; "Imaginary Animals,"
21:353–356; "Finnish Proverbs,"
24:226–228; review by, 22:96; author, 16:344, 467, 485, 17:459,
21:408, 22:83, 317, 24:244, 25:74,
30:156, 31:13, 36:78; recital, 19:
43
Edgar, Randolph, 12:432, 13:60; author, 11:206, 14:351, 26:308
Edgar, William C., 13:60, 14:352, 17:
160n; author, 11:329, 12:80; Belgian relief work, 11:349, 14:233,
27:154; editor, 14:118, 26:303,
304–310, 311; papers, 19:213, 20:
82
Edgerly, Parker M., 19:265
Edgerly, Lt. Winfield S., 34:131
Edgerly, Mrs. Winfield S., papers,
34:131
Edgerton, Capt. Alonzo J., 26:197n,
37:47, 48, 50, 54, 38:275, 362;
Senator, 22:425
Edgerton, D. Priscilla, author, 19:
466
Edgerton, E. S., banker, 37:154
Edgerton, Erastus J., banker, 13:
178n, 34:97, 99n, 40:110, 116,
117
Edgerton, Jay, reviews by, 34:125,
160, 345, 35:88; author, 13:314,
16:483, 27:242, 34:312, 353, 355,
35:99, 196, 242, 36:219
Edgerton, Mary J., 13:178
Edgerton, Dutch settlement, 28:129;
history, 34:171
Edina, mills, 16:248; Grange unit,
17:467, 30:75
Edinburgh, Scotland, General Register
House, 17:7
Edison, Thomas A., 22:313
Edison Electric Light Co., Wisconsin,
36:99
"Editor," steamboat, 34:25
Edman, Edwin, speaker, 29:363
Edmonds, Mrs. Frank, 14:223
Edmonds, Walter, author, 20:116, 506,
21:8
Edmunds, Newton, Indian agent, 39:229
Edstrom, Milton, speaker, 12:38
Education, secondary, 11:42; normal
schools, 11:225, 14:148, 231, 18:
105, 28:132, 36:327, 39:171; Minnesota system, 11:329, 12:68, 320,
398–400, 14:416–420, 15:466, 16:
275, 18:105, 219, 19:68, 333, 446,
23:189, 25:306, 30:6, 244, 34:90–
95; independent, 11:438, 12:158,
398, 16:275, 17:478; frontier, 11:
454, 12:148, 204, 13:216, 14:121,
142–149, 18:219, 293, 22:22–27,
24:323, 370, 28:334, 30:372, 32:
45, 33:72–76, 105–111, 35:137,
156, 36:35, 104, 141, 193, 37:43,
344; medical, 12:204, 17:220, 18:
459, 27:135, 33:312; Indian, 12:
242, 434, 16:145–147, 17:84, 95,
201, 224, 18:197, 269, 375, 21:
30n, 412, 22:430, 25:13, 30:2, 31:
206, 33:74, 36:24, 37:282; history, 12:417–419, 14:333; correc-
tional schools, 12:456, 27:56, 36:
238; religious, 15:130, 32:223;
agricultural, 16:30, 352, 18:411,
21:91, 33:224, 39:83; Middle West,
16:275, 276, 21:65–67; kinder-
gartens, 19:110, 20:340, 34:217,
219; commercial, 19:356; Twin

Cities, 20:88; land-grant colleges, 24:174, 35:379, 38:385; pharmaceutical, 24:175; intercultural, 24:259; physical, 24:367, 39:18-23; methods, 25:57-61, 68, 84, 258-264, 367, 26:47-51, 164, 267, 27:147, 319-326, 333; on iron ranges, 32:47; garrison schools, 33:263; academic freedom, 35:30; classical, 35:44; nursing, 37:300; historical, 38:196. See also individual educational institutions
Educational Film Library Association, 25:84
Edwards, D. C., Chicago, printers, 40:128
Edwards, David, 11:74
Edwards, Deane, author, 30:274
Edwards, E. E., librarian, 18:364
Edwards, E. G., miller, 24:101, 102
Edwards, Eugene O., author, 27:69
Edwards, Everett E., 19:93, 432, 27: 60;"American Indian Contributions," 15:255-272; "Agricultural Periodicals," 18:407-414; "Wendelin Grimm," 19:21-33; "T. L. Haecker," 19:148-161; reviews by, 16:327, 17:326, 18:195, 20:417, 22:412, 25:71, 29:158, 341, 32: 118; work reviewed, 17:198; author, 12:90, 15:122, 16:221, 474, 17:331, 18:102, 203, 440, 19:69, 91, 102, 207, 20:75, 333, 426, 21: 91, 22:418, 23:180, 378, 24:255, 25:76, 26:82, 29:192, 278, 376, 32:128; compiler, 13:330, 24:337, 25:84, 40:360; speaker, 14:213, 15:314; editor, 24:157
Edwards, John N., author, 40:308
Edwards, John P., pioneer, 14:118
Edwards, Jonathan, author, 21:418
Edwards, Ninian, Illinois governor, 15:13, 20:18; excursionist, 15:405
Edwards Ferry, Md.-Va., First Minnesota encampment, 25:16, 28:326; balloon flight, 40:276
Edwardsville, Big Stone County, stagecoach station, 14:118
Eenyangmanee, Sioux leader, 11:178n
Eernisse, Ab., 28:129
Effie, history, 21:341, 24:325n
Effigy Mounds National Monument, Allamakee County, Iowa, 37:307
Effington, Otter Tail County, Lutheran church, 15:481
Efshen, Oluf, scout, 24:325n
Egan, Howard E., author, 11:110
Egan, I. J. (John J.), artist, 23: 349, 353, 29:261, 31:56, 32:188
Egan, Maurice F., author, 26:301
Egeli, Bjorn, artist, 37:88, 136
Egelston, Alvord C., career, 21:196
Eggan, Fred, work reviewed, 34:301; author, 23:403
Eggert, Albert L., author, 23:403
Eggleston, Cordelia, see Pond, Mrs. Samuel W., I
Eggleston, Edward, "The-Man-That-Draws-the-Handcart," 33:270-281; speaker, 11:157; author, 12:201, 16:106, 349, 19:9, 386, 437, 22: 157, 23:113, 26:74, 30:62, 373, 31:130, 33:92, 34:311, 36:74n, 37: 11, 39:267, 40:71; in Minnesota, 18:268, 347-370, 19:221, 22:160, 328, 25:91, 26:77, 27:167, 33:189-193, 269, 34:139, 35:215; cen-

tenary, 18:454; pastor, 21:314, 34:132; papers, 24:364, 27:61, 28: 303; library, 26:242-247, 28:337; biography, 28:167
Eggleston, Mrs. Edward, 18:351, 360, 26:243
Eggleston, George, 18:348, 349
Eggleston, Walter A., 12:207
Ehlen, H. F., author, 17:118
Eich, Estelle, work reviewed, 38:192
Eide, B. M., author, 22:343
Eide, Richard B., "Minnesota Pioneer Life," 12:391-403; reviews by, 31: 186, 33:348, 34:202; work reviewed, 26:149; author, 12:321, 13:48, 22:211, 27:49, 28:334, 31: 192
Eielsen, Elling, 12:180; Lutheran leader, 12:201, 13:428, 37:184, 38:233; bibliography, 24:74
Eifert, Virginia S., author, 36:278
Eighth Air Force, in England, 26:279
Eighth Illinois Cavalry, in Civil War, 26:67
Eighth Minnesota Volunteer Infantry, in Sioux Outbreak, 12:102, 302, 20:192, 23:75, 38:66, 280, 281, 283, 284; in Civil War, 20:192, 38:287, 291, 39:183
Eighth Missouri Cavalry Regiment, in Civil War, 40:288
Eighth New York Heavy Artillery, in Civil War, 20:81
Eighty-fifth New York Volunteer Infantry, in Civil War, 17:98
Eighty-second Illinois Volunteer Infantry, in Civil War, 20:244
Eighty-seventh College Training Detachment, history, 25:312
Eikman, Martin, 28:131
Einarsson, Stefan, runic studies, 17: 31, 32, 177-179, 181
Eiselmeier, John, author, 23:286
Eisenbarth, E. E., showboat captain, 33:39
Eisendrath, William N., Jr., editor, 34:254
Eisenhower, Dwight D., President, 40: 297
Eisenschiml, Otto, work reviewed, 29: 63
Ekman, John S., 23:374
Ekstrand, Mrs. George W., speaker, 16:115; author, 16:233
"El Paso," steamboat, 33:131
Eland Township, Beltrami County, history, 15:132
Elazar, Daniel J., work reviewed, 38: 195; author, 39:209, 344
Elbow Lake, county seat, 15:486, 23: 371; fair, 21:113; roads, 21:235, 38:63; history, 33:353; museum, 37:87, 38:162
Elder, Lucius W., 17:332; author, 19: 458
Eldot, Walter, author, 34:44
Elections, returns, 11:435, 14:247-252, 24:309, 30:272, 34:188, 194, 231, 232, 35:58, 61-63, 76, 295, 36:124, 125, 308, 37:51, 333, 40: 223, 325-327; direct, 12:5, 6, 23: 264; ethnic vote, 13:434, 28:20, 33, 34, 31:31, 33:180, 36:237, 326, 40:328; territorial, 14:133, 138, 162, 163, 246, 20:144, 35: 105, 36:7-9, 70, 261, 266, 270, 39:40-43; gubernatorial, 16:459,

17:162, 26:67, 31:42, 61, 36:113, 173, 37:328, 38:297, 39:96, 101, 107, 108, 257, 40:90; county, 18: 110, 21:402, 37:20, 39:231n; influence of labor, 22:385, 386, 35: 332, 40:91; primaries, 23:285, 28: 74, 35:341-351, 36:34, 40:328; soldier vote, 26:187-210, 36:168-172; third-party tactics, 31:124, 32:130-134, 140, 35:57, 60, 97, 241, 291, 298-300, 312; nonpartisan, 33:155-163; presidential, 36: 151, 37:343, 39:47; congressional, 36:183, 38:177, 178, 39:107, 40:79, 324; legislation, 37:132; senatorial, 39:95
Electric power, Wisconsin, 36:98; Twin Cities, 37:320, 321, 323; cooperatives, 37:347
Eleventh Illinois Cavalry, in Civil War, 25:18
Eleventh Judicial District, history, 23:387
Eleventh Minnesota Volunteer Infantry, in Civil War, 19:450, 31:99, 38:287, 290
Elgin, Lord, in Canada, 34:45
Elgin Township, Wabasha County, Yankee settlement, 39:201, 202; Methodist church, 39:202
Eliot, Charles W., 16:30
Eliot, Rev. Frederick M., speaker, 28:293
Eliot, Samuel A., 15:211
Eliot, T. S., 20:107
Elizabeth Marie, Sister, work reviewed, 33:38
Elk, hunted, 16:189; in fur trade, 21:141, 144, 40:210; Minnesota, 22:103, 194, 30:125, 127, 31:191, 35:48
Elk Creek (Credit River), Scott County, 21:167n, 168
Elk Island (Isle aux Cerfs?), Mich., 23:137
Elk Lake (Goldschmidt Lake, Schutz Lake), Carver County, 33:248
Elk River, trading post, 11:119, 375; jubilee celebration, 12:448; history, 15:252, 19:367, 34:54; map, 15:464; G.A.R. post, 16:432n; Episcopal church, 17:98; flood, 17:230; Hungarian settlement, 17: 364; Babcock marker, 26:43; pioneer life, 34:195-198, 38:92
Elkader, Iowa, described, 12:165, 166
Elke, Estella L., author, 15:114
Elkins, Frank, author, 29:169
Elkins Act, 12:16
Elks, see Benevolent and Protective Order of Elks
Elkton, Carlton County, stage station, 40:244
Eller, Col. Floyd E., 25:311; "A Soldier Looks at History," 24:1-10; speaker, 24:56; author, 24:59
Eller, Mrs. Max, author, 35:248
Ellet, Mrs. W. H. (Elizabeth F.), Minnesota tour, 20:393, 28:317, 35:180, 181
Ellice, Edward, merchant, 14:338, 40: 168n, 169, 170, 177
Ellicott, Andrew, surveyor, 24:53
Ellingboe, John, 22:70
Ellinger, Walter A., 12:193
Ellingsen, Agnes E., author, 13:322, 14:438

Ellington Township, Dodge County, history, 12:337
Ellingwood, Ralph, author, 34:170
Elliot, Adolphus F., physician, 39:112n; Union officer, 39:195n
Elliot, Mrs. D. S., 14:218
Elliot, Mrs. M. M., poet, 26:298
Elliot, Col. Washington L., 25:136
Elliot, Wyman, 22:257, 31:162
Elliott, Bruce, speaker, 23:397
Elliott, Charles B., "Diary of Charles Burke Elliott," 18:123-151; career, 17:213, 18:121, 25:304; portrait, 18:124; author, 18:129n; diaries, 18:203, 317, 19:49
Elliott, Mrs. Charles B. (Edith Winslow), 18:121, 127, 134-143, 147, 149, 150
Elliott, Maj. Charles W., 18:123n, 134, 135, 137, 141-143, 149, 150; "The University of Minnesota's First Doctor of Philosophy," 18:121-151; speaker, 18:121n, 205; author, 18:203, 449
Elliott, Clarkson R., career, 18:137n
Elliott, Henry W., author, 18:131
Elliott, Jesse T., 18:126
Elliott, Mathilde R., review by, 34:347
Elliott, Mrs. R. B., author, 11:115
Elliott, T. C., author, 13:109, 16:477, 17:225, 18:103
Elliott, William G., author, 13:210
Elliotta, Fillmore County, ghost town, 30:70, 35:12
Ellis, A. V., cattleman, 26:124, 30:81
Ellis, Mrs. A. V., 30:81
Ellis, Albert G., pioneer printer, 15:16
Ellis, Charles, architect, 40:105
Ellis, Elmer, author, 13:205; speaker, 13:327
Ellis, Frederick E., review by, 35:198
Ellis, Harvey, architect, 23:227n, 231; career, 40:97-108
Ellis, J. D., 19:468
Ellis, L. Ethan, work reviewed, 38:35; author, 20:336, 38:240
Ellison, Augustus, 25:138
Ellison, Elizabeth, author, 25:95
Ellison, Smith, 27:127
Ells, S. C., author, 20:342, 32:124
Ellsworth, Benjamin, house, 40:122
Ellsworth, Clayton S., author, 26:164
Ellsworth, E. H., song writer, 26:53
Ellsworth, Col. Elmer E., 16:166; in Civil War, 11:95; career, 25:38n
Ellsworth, Ernest O., 15:491
Ellsworth, Eugene S., 15:491
Ellsworth, Franklin F., papers, 28:304, 29:49; author, 31:45
Ellsworth, H. H., speaker, 12:341
Ellsworth, Henry L., 17:326, 34:292; expedition, 35:239
Ellsworth, Margaretta, 38:336
Ellsworth, founded, 15:490, 20:361; Catholic church, 16:485
Ellsworth House, Lake City hotel, 26:177
Ellsworth Township, Meeker County, history, 19:117
Elm, Mrs. Anna R., compiler, 30:268
Elm Creek, Hennepin County, history, 18:463

Elm Creek Cemetery Association, Martin County, 18:340
Elmer, history, 21:456
Elmer Township, St. Louis County, settled, 23:302
Elmhurst Cemetery, St. Paul, 34:356
Elmira, Olmsted County, mill, 24:89, 102
Elmore, Lutheran church, 15:481; history, 36:104
Elmslie, George G., architect, 40:98, 107, 108, 359
Elmwood, Hennepin County, pottery works, 33:231
Elsbury, George K., artist, 20:435, 38:286n
Elsinger, Joseph, 38:83
Elsmith, Dorothy O., author, 38:42
Elson, M. B., 27:267
Elston, Hattie P., author, 28:288
Elston, Wilbur, reviews by, 39:28, 40:140
Elsworth, R. H., author, 17:473
Elton, John, author, 33:132
Elviken, Andreas, work reviewed, 33:85
Elwell, J. Ambrose, author, 12:343
Elwood, ---, show manager, 28:111
Elwood, Charles B., 22:83
Ely, Edmund F., missionary, 11:307, 12:107, 14:123, 16:337, 483, 17:351, 22:352-354, 23:14, 28:83; papers, 16:360, 20:452, 40:146; postmaster, 34:186
Ely, Mrs. Edmund F., 22:353
Ely, Rev. Edward, diary, 12:108, 18:230; author, 15:136
Ely, Mrs. Edward, artist, 34:174
Ely, Richard T., historian, 24:336; papers, 36:29; philosopher, 36:97
Ely, ethnic groups, 12:436, 22:392n, 24:174, 226, 25:186, 319, 30:156; lakes, 24:93; newspaper, 25:327; post office, 26:251; mining town, 28:251, 35:338; pictured, 35:51; chronology, 36:107; fire fighters, 36:133, 135; July 4 celebration, 40:60; churches, 40:61; strike, 40:345
Emancipation, see Abolition movement
Emanuel Academy, Minneapolis, history, 38:382
Embargo Act, 1807, 40:179-182, 213
Embarrass, Finnish settlement, 18:324, 22:392n
Embarrass River, see Zumbro River
Emch, Lucille B., "An Indian Tale," 26:211-221; editor, 26:257
Emden, Renville County, Dutch settlement, 28:126, 127
Emerald Township, Faribault County, Norwegian settlement, 12:270
Emergency Conservation Work, 15:131
Emergency Relief Administration, see Minnesota State Board of Control
Emerick, Mrs. Maria H., author, 13:344
Emerson, C. L., civil engineer, 13:133, 17:266; surveyor general, 16:174
Emerson, Charles L., author, 17:112
Emerson, George H., railway manager, 38:312-314, 316, 318, 321, 325
Emerson, Isaac, 12:449
Emerson, Dr. John, owner of Dred Scott, 16:350, 20:420, 21:165n,

25:202, 27:167, 29:351, 33:138; letters, 20:89
Emerson, Mrs. Ralph, 25:2
Emerson, Ralph W., 12:85, 326, 20:65, 109, 135, 406, 29:49, 100; lecture tours, 11:145-159, 16:31, 21:326, 23:285, 35:226; speaker, 24:118, 40:12
Emerson, Man., port, 21:261; history, 34:132
Emerson and Manning, minstrel troupe, 28:110
Emery, Edwin, works reviewed, 34:83, 202; author, 31:119
Emery, Jacob, pioneer, 23:302
Emery, R. C., author, 16:367
Emery, Bishop Richard, 36:319
Emigrant agents, 11:103, 13:28, 15:488, 17:403-405, 20:256; Sweden, 17:404, 18:74, 20:192, 36:237, 37:134, 262
Emigrant Aid Journal (Nininger), 19:162, 28:31; established, 13:130, 132, 135, 138, 144, 14:403, 27:2; discontinued, 13:150; file, 17:272, 18:323, 29:84
Emigrant houses, provided by railroads, 13:40; Minneapolis, 16:368; Port Huron, Mich., 20:256; Clear Lake, 20:257; St. Paul, 38:74
Emigrant journey, changing aspect, 11:103; from England, 11:107, 27:85; overland, 11:429, 17:413, 23:105, 30:199; from Norway, 12:336, 19:123, 22:343, 23:105, 25:262, 28:292; from Ireland, 14:330; from Sweden, 16:365, 20:249-258, 359, 26:259, 27:72
Emigrant ships, 20:402; from Sweden, 20:250, 37:262; from Denmark, 20:250, 251; from Liverpool, 20:252-254; from Germany, 23:88
Emigranten (Inmansville and Madison, Wis.), Norwegian newspaper, 16:108, 27:13, 36:287
Emigration, see Immigration and emigration
Emigration societies, New England, 17:323; Sweden, 17:403-405. See also Immigration and emigration
Emily Township, Crow Wing County, resort, 13:115
Emmanuel Mission, St. Paul, 27:81
Emmanuel's Lutheran Church, Inver Grove, 14:53
Emme, Eugene M., author, 38:334
Emmel, Henry, 32:41
Emmel, Louis, 35:268
Emmet, Thomas A., author, 21:369
Emmet County, Iowa, trading post, 11:381
Emmet Township, Renville County, Norwegian settlement, 12:275n
Emmett, Daniel D., musician, 15:482, 23:198, 310, 24:384, 27:177, 28:397, 30:152, 39:84
Emmett, Lafayette, judge, 15:482, 26:382, 28:397, 35:7-10; house, 23:198, 24:384, 25:1, 2n, 56, 27:271; convention delegate, 39:272
Emmons, Betsy, poet, 16:81
Emmons, Ebenezer, geologist, 33:282
Emmons, Harold, airline executive, 33:242
Emmons, William H., 14:117; author, 16:407, 17:477; editor, 25:308

Empire (City), Dakota County, politics, 13:141; church, 27:344
Empire Block, St. Paul, theater, 23:311
Emporium, St. Paul, store, 37:263
Emrich, Duncan, speaker, 29:349
Emty, Rev. Fridrich, 15:32
Encampment, Lake County, settled, 34:177
Encampment Forest, Lake County, history, 27:72, 35:294, 37:348
Enchanted Island, Lake Minnetonka, 34:128
Enderle, H. J., author, 34:171
Endicott Building, St. Paul, 28:396
Endreson, Guri, in Sioux Outbreak, 11:92, 12:261n, 30:272; monument, 13:450
Enesvedt, Odean, speaker, 30:87
Enestvedt, Ole O., 20:449, 21:223; author, 25:213
Engberg, George B., 28:48, 29:98; "Rise of Organized Labor," 21:372-394; "The Knights of Labor," 22:367-390; "Lumber and Labor in the Lake States," 36:153-166; reviews by, 27:334, 29:252, 30:147, 31:111, 185, 32:252, 36:274, 34:81, 35:194, 326, 37:127, 38:329, 379, 40:91; author, 21:195, 408, 22:418, 25:380, 27:343, 28:94, 95, 29:288, 30:73, 184, 31:128, 192, 32:256, 37:88; research fellow, 27:340; speaker, 29:257
Engberg, Jonas, letters, 11:453
Engberg, Peter, 13:28
Engdahl, Anna, pioneer, 34:7, 8
Engdahl, Axel, logger, 34:7, 8
Engdahl, Walfrid, author, 40:147
Engebretson, Betty L., "Books for Pioneers," 35:222-232
Engebretson, William H., 14:237; speaker, 11:223
Engelhardt, Fred, author, 12:418, 419, 16:118, 18:105, 219
Engelhart, Peter, miller, 35:18
Engelmann, George, 17:96, 26:154
Engelstad, Eivind J., 18:189
Engemoen, Joe, 20:459
Engen, Nels M., 23:102, 25:402; speaker, 21:445
Enger, Mrs. Karen, pioneer, 24:321
"Engineer," steamboat, 18:433
Engineering, history, 29:156
Engineers' Club, Minneapolis, 15:140
Engineers' Club of Minnesota, 30:158
Engineers' Society, St. Paul, 15:140
England, see Great Britain
Engle, Paul, 23:122; author, 23:157
Engleman, Rose, compiler, 35:334
English, Emory H., author, 27:163
English, W. Francis, editor, 26:384
English, Minnesota, 11:295, 12:103, 13:138, 14:232, 16:216, 271, 496, 17:199, 18:309, 21:112, 448, 22:262, 27:204, 207, 209, 210, 215, 281-299, 28:258-268; Wisconsin, 12:158n, 18:193, 20:86, 27:83, 30:248, 35:202; Iowa, 13:110, 28:78; Northwest, 19:218; immigration, 22:72, 27:85, 30:263; Red River Valley, 25:260, 261, 31:18; place

names, 26:248; folkways, 28:177; eastern U.S., 32:112. See also British
English and Classical School, St. Paul, 11:438
English Compromise, 14:175n
English language, in U.S., 17:319; on frontier, 19:241-246, 445; use by immigrants, 20:462; Upper Midwest dialects, 34:127, 37:42; in fiction, 34:311, 37:88; logging terms, 36:278
English River, Iowa, mills, 22:185
English River, Ont., 40:172
Englund, Pearl, author, 29:278
Engstrom, Carl G., author, 18:466
Enmegahbowh, John Johnson, Ottawa Indian, 13:393, 15:114, 20:91, 329, 431, 36:35, 319
Ennis, ———, steamship agent, 20:252
Enoch (Hanoch), Sioux Indian, 22:145
Ensign, Mary E., speaker, 15:227
Enstrom, Louis, 22:341, 24:271, 324, 25:409, 27:364, 28:298
"Enterprise," steamboat, 13:242, 14:151, 279, 36:212
Enz, Mrs. J. E., 12:102, 13:118
"Eolian," steamboat, 16:470, 36:252-258, 38:361
Epidemics, see individual diseases
Episcopal church, Minnesota, 11:319, 338, 12:318, 13:311, 312, 427, 14:102, 16:97, 477, 18:46, 19:47, 20:433, 21:86, 24:73, 26:286, 34:339, 35:321, 322, 36:35; archives, 11:450, 14:64, 16:52, 217, 470, 17:54, 98, 18:445; schools, 12:398, 16:371, 17:232, 18:331, 23:95; growth, 24:72; South Dakota, 35:248; army chaplains, 36:230; North Dakota, 36:319; Wisconsin, 38:167. See also individual Minnesota communities
Episcopal Church Hospital, see St. Luke's Hospital
Episcopal missions, Minnesota, 11:332, 455, 12:118, 14:55, 57, 359, 15:111, 363, 16:97, 119, 376, 477, 17:240, 20:344, 21:35, 24:142, 27:81, 28:190, 210, 30:391, 37:42, 38:136n, 144n; Winnipeg River, 12:318; Wisconsin, 14:111, 18:326, 32:50; among Chippewa, 15:466, 20:90, 431, 23:26; U.S., 21:71; New York, 24:13; Nebraska and Dakotas, 35:380; Northwest, 37:177; among Sioux captives, 38:357
Epler, William, postmaster, 34:185
Epstein, Leon D., work reviewed, 36:188
Epworth League, 17:467
Equality Township, Red Lake County, history, 38:204
"Equator," steamboat, 11:134, 135, 140, 12:94, 113n, 36:212
Equity Cooperative Exchange, 21:69, 202, 28:37, 43, 44; history, 26:381, 29:76; papers, 28:304
Ercilla, Alonzo de, poet, 15:261
Erck, Edward, musician, 33:100
Erd, Frank, 25:314
Erd, Marie G., 39:56

Eric-Jansonists, in Illinois, 17:401
Ericksen, Theresa, 11:448, 18:48; speaker, 18:92; papers, 19:97; establishes nurses' registry, 35:46
Erickson, A. M., author, 25:185
Erickson, Arnold B., author, 37:347
Erickson, Carl R., 38:308
Erickson, Charlotte, work reviewed, 35:326
Erickson, Mrs. Constance, author, 16:369
Erickson, Edward, pioneer, 24:325n
Erickson, Erick, grave, 14:428
Erickson, Erick P., pioneer, 25:394
Erickson, Gordon, 27:147
Erickson, Henrietta B., museum assistant, 23:367, 24:31
Erickson, J. E., 26:394, 27:362
Erickson, M. L., 15:372, 19:116, 20:99, 21:108, 22:106; speaker, 16:244
Erickson, Minnie, 14:428
Erickson, Ole, 14:428
Erickson, R. E., house, 38:344, 345
Erickson, Col. Sidney, speaker, 23:267, 268
Erickson, Theodore A., youth leader, 22:438, 24:80; work reviewed, 35:149; author, 28:377
Erickson, Wallace H., speaker, 36:108
Ericson, Roland, guide, 22:439
Ericson Township, Renville County, Norwegian settlement, 12:275n
Ericsson, John, career, 30:148, 34:200
Ericsson, Rev. Robert W., author, 14:452
Erie, Pa., transportation center, 40:272
"Erie," steamboat, 34:39
Erie Canal, trade route, 15:14, 40:184; opened, 26:359
Erie Indians, 13:397, 400
Erie Mining Co., 34:216, 37:42
Erie Railway Co., aids immigration, 13:30; in Civil War, 33:218
Erikson, Hjalmer, 18:110
Erikson, John, missionary, 15:235
Erikson, Leif, explorer, 25:193, 33:216, 39:170, 342; monument, 29:96
Erikson, Stanley, 24:183; author, 25:93, 311, 401
Eriksson, Erik M., author, 14:112
Eriksson, Leonard, author, 17:102
Erkkila, Mrs. Milma L., speaker, 26:392
Erlandson, Erland, explorer, 17:75
Erlanger, Abraham, troupe manager, 28:104
Ermatinger, Edward, trader, song collection, 34:126, 38:239
Ermatinger, F., trader, 40:167n
Ermatinger, James, 22:206
Ermatinger family, in fur trade, 11:326, 35:382
Ermine, in fur trade, 40:202
Ermoyan, Souren, 31:254
Ernst, Rev. A. C., speaker, 15:372, 24:271
Ernst, Dorothy J., "Wildcats and

Patriots," 40:109-119; author, 37:
87, 39:210
Ernst, Emil C., author, 18:469
Ernst, Robert, review by, 33:179
Errembault, Louis, papers, 33:352
Erreson's Hall, Crookston, 28:99
Erskine, ---, see Askin, John
Erskine, David M., 18:134
Erskine, history, 14:358
Erwin, Guy B., 29:303, 304, 308, 315
Erwin, Marie H., author, 24:365
Erwin, William W., lawyer, 18:124,
125; politician, 32:145
Esabaneweia family, Chippewa Indians,
39:305n
Esarey, Logan, work reviewed, 33:308;
speaker, 15:119; author, 28:174,
36:86
Esbjörn, Rev. Lars P., 13:305, 306,
308, 32:53; diary, 17:329
Esbjornson, Robert, work reviewed,
35:96
Eschambault, Joseph Fleury, sieur de,
32:237n
Eskimos, 14:376; folklore and folk
songs, 39:129; artifacts, 39:129
Esko, Finnish settlement, 25:318,
320; history, 35:382
Espagnol, François, 39:305
Espelie, Ernest M., work reviewed,
38:381
Espenshade, Edward B., Jr., author,
26:381
Espy, John, speaker, 32:213
Esquagama Lake, St. Louis County,
mounds, 27:267
Essen, Paul A., 25:405
Esser, Harold, 21:105
Estabrook, Joseph T., author, 19:452
Estabrook, Theodore, 17:232, 19:118,
20:98, 21:109; author, 18:223
Estenson, E. A., 23:103
Estenson, E. O., 28:59
Esterly, George, biography, 12:201;
inventor, 23:322, 24:288
Estes, Dr. David C., 16:163n
Estherville, Iowa, blizzard, 11:187n;
stockade, 11:210
Estonians, U.S., 20:442
Estrem, Andrew, author, 23:92
Ethelbert, Sister M., author, 26:275
Ether, Vere, farmer, 29:14
Etheridge, ---, baseball player, 19:
174
Ethiopia, crisis with Italy, 40:369,
371
Ethnography, North America, 37:346
Ethno-history, 40:149, 156, 199; bib-
liography, 36:30
Ethnology, methods, 40:156
Etzell, George A., 18:344
Eucharista, Mother, 27:319n, 343;
author, 30:69; speaker, 30:177
Eugenics movement, Minnesota, 17:115,
24:356, 25:63, 64, 91
Eureka, Nicollet County, ghost town,
17:238
Eureka Township, Dakota County,
Norwegian settlement, 12:271
Eurich, Alvin C., work reviewed, 12:
417-419
European-American Emigration Land
Co., 17:404
Eustis, W. H., boatbuilder, 33:13
Eustis, Warren C., 16:183
Eustis, William H., 18:126, 24:181,
33:334; autobiography, 11:213, 17:

353; politician, 16:459, 19:303,
35:63, 39:108; lawyer, 35:66, 67,
70, 75
Eustrom, Hans, 37:262
Evander, Hulda, speaker, 11:116
Evangelical Free Church, 34:61;
Minnesota, 37:42
Evangelical Lutheran Zion Church,
Madison, 15:481
Evangelical Synod of North America,
Minnesota conference, 18:326, 23:
387
Evangelical United Brethren Church,
Kiester, 29:176
Evans, A. P., medievalist, 14:194
Evans, Andrew, translator, 15:478
Evans, Mrs. Anne C., 12:87
Evans, Arja D., lawyer, 17:213
Evans, Charles, author, 28:81
Evans, Clarence, author, 31:189
Evans, D. C., 26:195
Evans, David H., politician, 34:232
Evans, E. P., 13:116
Evans, E. W., author, 18:470
Evans, Francis A., author, 16:339
Evans, Harold C., author, 21:426
Evans, Mrs. Helen M., 14:104
Evans, Henry O., work reviewed, 23:
361
Evans, Hubert, author, 31:125
Evans, James, missionary, 12:427, 13:
60, 14:115, 15:240, 463, 18:459,
20:72, 21:433
Evans, John, archaeologist, 26:227,
33:131
Evans, John C., pioneer farmer, 17:27
Evans, Luther H., 17:332, 18:50, 19:
51, 28:15; speaker, 18:322, 27:
349; author, 19:455, 20:198
Evans, M. Tedd, speaker, 14:450
Evans, Maurice V., lawyer, 21:196
Evans, Dr. O. O., horse breeder, 26:
120
Evans, Oliver, inventor, 11:272n,
274, 16:226, 33:132, 35:200
Evans, Paul H., speaker, 14:124
Evans, Robert G., politician, 35:68,
69, 70
Evans, Walter P., author, 19:213
Evansville, Methodist church, 20:35
Evansville, Ind., French settlement,
28:254
Evarts, Dr. Arrah B., speaker, 28:88
Eve, Dr. Duncan, 26:68
Eveleth, ethnic groups, 12:436, 19:
112, 22:392n, 25:319; churches,
16:355, 485; mining town, 16:486,
17:240, 19:118, 334, 21:289, 290,
28:251, 32:245; history, 28:383,
32:193-201. See also Mesabi Range
Evenson, Eliza, author, 17:235
Everest, Kate A., 18:382n
Everest, W. H., author, 28:372
Everett, E. A., auto driver, 38:208
Everett, Edward, letters, 29:187
Everett, J. R., author, 16:219
Everett, Mrs. Nellie, speaker, 16:244
Everett, Willis H., postmaster, 34:
186
Evergreen, Itasca County, history,
22:345, 415
Evergreen Stock Farm, Austin, 26:124
Everitt, J. A., agrarian leader, 21:
202, 32:181
Everts, E. A., pioneer, 20:457
Everts, Louis H., map publisher,
40:124, 128

Eves, J. W., 18:257n
Evesmith, Hansen, 13:197, 428
Evinrude, Ole, inventor, 23:381
Evjen, Mrs. C., speaker, 11:116
Evjen, John O., author, 14:231, 16:
350, 17:225; biography, 15:358
Ewald, Chris, 29:362
Ewan, Joseph, author, 38:333
Ewart, Theodore, journal, 40:255
Ewarts, James T., 25:230
Ewbank, Louis B., editor, 16:346;
author, 25:395
Ewell, Richard S., 25:143
Ewens, Robert, speaker, 27:356
Ewers, John C., reviews by, 35:287,
376, 36:30, 316, 40:259; works
reviewed, 36:317, 37:132, 336, 38:
238, 40:144, 403; author, 21:423,
34:213, 35:151, 380, 36:101, 38:
41, 40:201; speaker, 40:149, 411
Ewing, Charles, Indian commissioner,
34:123
Ewing, Frank H., memorial, 15:467
Ewing, George W., trader, 11:376, 32:
68, 69, 74, 76-79, 36:263, 269,
270, 40:214, 216; papers, 32:128
Ewing, Ruth G., author, 39:263
Ewing, William G., trader, 11:376,
32:68, 69, 74, 76-79, 36:263, 269,
270, 40:214, 216; papers, 32:128
Ewing, W. G. and G. W., Co., fur
traders, 21:411; papers, 22:191
Ewing House, St. Peter, 17:488
Excelsior, history, 11:95, 14:352,
19:341, 20:352, 23:196, 27:176,
30:407, 34:43, 36:36; schools, 12:
398, 14:146, 18:374, 26:396;
churches, 16:314, 17:465, 18:47,
20:81, 141n, 27:232, 28:392, 34:
43, 40:11; colonized, 16:315, 469,
18:225, 20:141n; historical meeting, 28:386, 392; fishing, 30:118,
120, 40:73; railroad, 30:236, 237;
trolley line, 36:150
"Excelsior," steamboat, 11:130, 136,
19:249, 22:147, 28:314, 29:204,
32:71
Excelsior baseball club, Fort Snelling, 19:163
Excelsior Brewery, see Hamm, Theodore, Co.
Excelsior College, Excelsior, 12:398,
14:146
Excelsior Pioneer Association, colonization company, 16:315, 469, 18:
225, 20:140, 40:10
Exchange Hotel, Ely, history, 14:360
Exchange State Bank, Grand Meadow,
architecture, 40:359
Exel, Lt. Christian, 28:23; diary,
36:239
Exploration and discovery, North
America, 11:189, 452, 15:93, 28:
170, 362, 32:111, 35:379; in fur
trade, 11:262, 265, 12:326, 28:1-
14, 142-159, 225-240, 35:243;
French, 12:350-358, 16:199, 448-
450, 18:385-390, 20:341, 22:429,
23:280, 28:61, 32:226-238, 34:305,
35:151, 40:145, 259; Northwest,
14:220, 16:349, 19:461, 22:181-
183, 25:96, 29:58-61, 33:316, 34:
154-159, 303, 35:97, 39:169; Minnesota, 14:221, 367-377, 16:453,
19:385, 21:340, 23:401, 24:318-
320, 25:77, 211, 30:267, 273, 375,
392, 31:41; Far West, 14:430, 15:

234, 28:68, 29:61, 37:34; Canada, 15:238, 16:418n, 17:476, 19:103, 28:176, 29:78, 166, 167, 259, 339-341, 31:238, 33:187, 35:47, 142, 36:191, 37:86; trails, 15:255, 21:433, 28:178, 32:242; Bell collection, 19:69, 31:105-109, 188, 33:352, 34:310, 35:151, 36:70, 37:222; Great Lakes, 19:272, 273, 274, 276, 280, 20:438, 25:272-274, 368-370, 29:266, 31:54, 35:151, 39:81; Red River country, 20:88, 21:432, 22:92, 193, 27:62, 35:378; Norse, 21:92, 23:378, 24:176, 27:350, 28:59, 176, 271, 33:216, 34:199, 214, 302, 35:294, 39:170, 342, 40:59, 94; Mississippi Valley, 21:403, 22:97, 24:372, 26:379, 27:62, 253, 28:70, 32:216, 33:186; relation to art, 23:183; Grand Canyon, 24:62; Alaska, 24:344; border country, 25:182, 27:70, 35:378; lumber areas, 25:211; western hemisphere, 28:57; Picture Rock, 29:130-136; railroad survey, 29:165; Fort Snelling area, 29:316-320; Pipestone, 31:193-208, 37:62. See also Description and travel, individual expeditions and explorers

Exposition Building, Minneapolis, 39:93; design, 23:220, 227; automobile exhibit, 26:21; concerts, 33:100, 101, 104; convention, 35:64-76; opera season, 36:33

Eyota, Lutheran church, 14:48; pioneer life, 23:401, 24:299n; architecture, 38:348

Eyre, Col. William, 18:195

Eyrich, Martin L. F., 19:472

Eyster, William C., banker, 37:121

Fabel, E., account book, 15:347

Faber, James F., 21:333, 28:295; author, 15:245; speaker, 26:89

Facsimile Text Society, 14:443

Fadden, Charles, 12:126, 132

Fagre, Theodore, editor, 16:254

Faherty, Mrs. Mary, 20:210; speaker, 25:405

Faherty, William B., author, 22:98

Fahlstrom, Jacob, Swedish pioneer, 29:182, 278, 354, 30:145, 272; memorial, 29:183, 277, 40:48, 147; trader, 36:326, 40:65

Fahlun Township, Kandiyohi County, lake depicted, 33:250

Fahrney, Ralph R., author, 19:435

Fahrni, Margaret M., work reviewed, 28:64

Fair Oaks, Va., in Civil War, 11:462, 25:134-140, 351, 29:64

Fairall, Rev. P. H., 15:33

Fairbairn, Mabel, author, 19:473

Fairbanks, Avard, sculptor, 35:245

Fairbanks, Charles W., letter, 18:316

Fairbanks, John H., trader, 16:31, 19:348, 23:249, 251n; recollections, 19:349; letters, 20:77

Fairbanks, Robert, trader, 15:292, 18:209

Fairbanks, Vernon E., 29:96

Fairbanks, W. N., 34:132

Fairbanks, St. Louis County, Finnish settlement, 25:160

Fairchild, Florence, 39:52n

Fairchild, Henry S., 22:263, 38:82

Fairchild, Mrs. Henry S., 38:77n, 81, 83

Fairchild, Lucius, letters, 12:440

Fairchild, Sarah (Conover), portrait, 21:156, 429

Fairfax, history, 13:453, 454; churches, 15:129, 243, 20:345; band, 15:370; schools, 20:467, 36:204

Fairfax Township, Polk County, pioneer life, 12:136

Fairfield, G. A., author, 14:457

Fairfield, Freeborn County, county seat fight, 15:346, 20:357

Fairfield, Martin County, mythical city, 14:256

Fairfield Guards, volunteer unit, 16:173n

Fairfield Township, Swift County, Norwegian settlement, 12:275n

Fairhaven, history, 18:229

Fairmont, English settlement, 14:232, 31:30, 131, 37:185; election precinct, 14:250; county seat, 14:256; churches, 14:452, 16:336, 380; parks, 21:222; pictured, 22:225; business history, 24:270; antihorsethief society, 25:97; school, 25:411; ration board, 26:175; name, 27:172; Rotary Club, 28:292; museum, 35:155; in Sioux Outbreak, 38:277, 279, 280, 283, 284, 286

Fairmont Railway Motors, history, 22:224

Fairs, Chicago, 12:188, 24:102, 26:252; agricultural, 12:445, 15:135, 246, 251, 16:33, 327, 18:467, 22:249-269; territorial, 14:137, 22:9, 38:173, 175; county, 14:458, 460, 461, 15:485, 491, 16:251, 496, 18:117, 337, 466, 21:450, 458, 22:442, 446, 23:75, 106, 402, 403, 30:408, 34:359; Mankato, 17:125; Philadelphia, 40:353. See also Crystal Palace Exhibition, Minnesota State Fair

Fairvale Farm, Minneapolis, 27:113

Fairview Hospital, Minneapolis, 40:383

Fairy Lake, Todd County, 40:75; Baptist church, 24:94; depicted, 40:68, 70; described, 40:69, 74, 77

Faith, John, letters, 23:75

Faiver, Louis, Nininger resident, 13:132, 148, 26:191

Falcon, Pierre, ballad writer, 35:202

Falconer, Gilbert, postmaster, 34:185

Falconer, James W., book collector, 27:41

Falconer, W. A., author, 15:125

Falk, Karen, speaker, 27:356

Falkenberg, P. J., 15:447

Fall, Albert B., politician, 27:134

Fallon, John P., farmer, 16:71

Fallon brothers, Hutchinson pioneers, 11:334

"Falls City," steamboat, 39:68n

Falls City Light Guards, 16:169

Falls Evening News (St. Anthony), 16:72; mailing list, 11:444; estab-

lished, 14:401; carriers' greeting, 16:386

Falls of St. Anthony, discovered, 11:7, 340, 343, 348, 468, 12:96, 13:210, 14:371, 15:100, 16:350, 19:99, 21:92, 23:372, 30:216; visited by travelers, 11:124, 15:405, 414, 16:33, 18:156, 23:170, 24:369, 25:104-116, 28:272, 278, 317, 29:170, 174, 31:209, 34:156, 35:180, 181, 37:53, 160, 40:411; name, 11:349, 30:216, 33:124, 352; pictured, 12:84, 15:211, 350, 17:147, 20:59, 25:166n, 26:288, 27:270, 30:112, 157, 218, 32:12, 61, 33:65, 113, 116, 124, 178, 284, 34:28, 31, 33, 138, 155, 159, 35:64, 108, 117, 205 (cover), 246, 341 (cover), 36:20, 23, 276, 37:309 (cover), 310, 313, 316, 40:63, 64, 75; described, 12:162, 14:84, 330, 16:281, 20:125, 23:338, 24:230, 27:287, 288, 28:17, 29:214, 253, 30:205, 217, 31:154, 32:96, 98, 216, 221, 34:48, 49, 139-141, 35:95, 36:41, 43, 37:64, 39:68, 40:359; water power, 13:32, 15:303, 467, 17:477, 19:407, 20:193, 24:128-131, 200, 27:310, 311, 30:197, 32:34, 33:63, 35:98, 118, 37:309-323, 40:137; legends, 13:250, 367, 376, 15:278, 17:440, 19:422, 25:165-167, 27:357, 36:22, 76, 77; portage, 14:350; postmark, 15:487; head of navigation, 17:154n, 19:182; sawmills, 20:126, 21:211, 450, 23:290, 24:126, 127, 129, 130, 27:312-314, 28:376, 29:100, 208, 231, 30:197, 35:1 (cover), 28, 39:316, 317; history, 21:401, 25:306, 396, 26:398, 27:281, 36:71, 38:296, 40:315; Chippewa encampment, 24:20; ferry, 30:195, 197, 210; mapped, 35:23, 24; bird life, 35:342. See also Flour milling

Falls of the St. Croix, water power, 25:396, 27:310, 29:205, 38:242. See also St. Croix Falls, Wis.; Taylors Falls

Falquist, Andrew, 18:313

Falstrom, Jacob, see Fahlstrom, Jacob

Family Herald (Minneapolis), 17:469

Family Service of St. Paul, history, 25:377

Faneuil, Peter, 18:397

Fanning, John T., career, 12:201

Fanning, M. E., 17:123

Fant, Handy B., compiler, 36:278

Fantini, Louis, speaker, 34:174

Far West, explored, 14:430, 15:234, 28:68, 29:61, 37:34; frontier, 18:304; health conditions, 36:277

Farestad, Orville J., author, 16:131

Fargo, N.D., river port, 21:260n, 29:73, 31:253; printers' union, 21:393; social life, 26:207; railroad, 31:122; visited, 33:69, 70, 38:212; history, 34:357; power company, 35:381; Bryan speech, 39:95; diocese, 39:299

Faribault, Alexander, 16:55, 147, 213, 17:229, 20:78, 35:335; miller, 11:274-277, 281; trader, 11:382, 388, 394, 395, 16:25, 497, 20:123, 264, 265, 29:267; family, 14:438; property, 15:345, 35:110,

37:191; hunter, 15:386, 387, 390, 391, 393, 394; translator, 21:279, 280; career, 30:408, 35:320-322; marriage, 35:321; in Sioux Outbreak, 38:139. See also Faribault House: Faribault
Faribault, Mrs. Alexander (Mary Elizabeth Graham), 35:321
Faribault, David, trader, 11:375, 15:253; wedding, 32:72, 73; in Sioux Outbreak, 34:235, 238, 38:127n
Faribault, Mrs. David (Nancy McClure), 13:413, 32:71; wedding, 13:296, 32:72, 73; in Sioux Outbreak, 34:235, 238, 38:127n. See also Huggan, Mrs. Charles G.
Faribault, Elizabeth, 14:32
Faribault, Fred, family, 18:342
Faribault, Jean B., 13:439, 15:383; trader, 11:274, 376, 12:201, 15:386n, 18:193, 20:259, 263, 22:285, 24:179, 35:321, 38:139n; claim to Pike Island, 12:190, 317, 21:182; farmer, 29:1; cattle merchant, 29:158; artist, 35:324. See also Faribault House: Mendota
Faribault, Oliver, trader, 15:315, 21:173n, 174, 175
Faribault, Richard, letters, 16:242
Faribault, Rodolphe E., 18:211
Faribault family, 17:229; genealogy, 18:211, 27:155
Faribault, libraries, 11:52, 466, 12:105, 19:466, 467, 21:115; visiting lecturers, 11:146, 149, 154, 16:31, 19:416; mills, 11:271, 274-277, 280, 12:80; trading post, 11:382, 16:497; roads, 11:395, 398; mail service, 11:400; churches, 12:341, 453, 15:129, 16:119, 380, 17:117, 363, 18:118, 19:475, 20:431, 27:271, 35:321; hotel, 13:213; name, 15:386n; insurance agencies, 16:242, 20:308; growth, 16:243, 21:343, 35:110; holiday celebrations, 16:380, 40:300; G.A.R. post, 16:431; schools, 17:363, 19:367, 20:200, 23:191, 24:366, 25:373, 28:72, 34:104, 105n, 214, 35:323, 39:131; described, 19:96; baseball club, 19:169, 170, 176; history, 19:466, 21:233, 30:408; industrial center, 20:217; newspaper, 20:270-286; railroads, 21:343, 35:14, 18, 21, 37:157; construction strike, 21:379; street names, 24:193; circus, 28:101; incorporated, 28:191, 294; wildlife, 30:223; German theater, 32:100, 34:242; power company, 35:381; in fiction, 37:3, 39:267; Sioux settlement, 37:272; anti-abolition sentiment, 39:260; livery stable, 40:127. See also Faribault House: Faribault
Faribault City Flouring Mill, 11:280
Faribault County, Norwegian settlements, 11:286, 12:269, 270, 23:290, 31:27; history, 12:102, 14:456, 18:298-301, 19:364; Indians, 14:453; archives, 20:205; fair, 22:259; pioneer life, 25:100; physicians, 25:307, 399; Catholic church, 25:410; wheat raising, 29:19; name, 30:332; in Sioux Outbreak, 38:281; poor relief, 38:368

Faribault County Agricultural Society, 22:253, 258
Faribault County Historical Society, organized, 30:79; museum, 30:165; activities, 30:276, 34:314
Faribault County War History Committee, 23:390, 24:185
Faribault Daily News, history, 21:115
Faribault Foundation, 26:285, 395, 35:322
Faribault Grange Flouring Mill, 11:280
Faribault Guard, 16:177
Faribault House, Faribault, 19:475; purchase, 26:180, 285; restored, 26:395, 27:77, 146, 231, 267, 28:88, 196, 29:365, 30:169, 33:210, 35:50, 37:67, 69; history, 35:320-324
Faribault House, Mendota, 29:206n, 30:271, 36:95, 37:58, 60, 61; restored, 15:443, 20:343; history, 15:467; described, 16:233, 19:235, 21:211, 23:192; guide, 20:342
Faribault House, Shakopee, history, 12:97
Faribault Island, see Pike Island
Faribault Lecture and Library Association, 11:146
Faribault Mill, built, 11:275
Faribault Old Settlers Association, 35:322
Faribault Public Library, history, 11:466; newspaper files, 19:467
Faribault Republican, politics, 28:29
Faribault Woolen Mills, 22:107, 348
Faricy, Austin, poet, 16:81
Faricy, Roland J., 20:427; speaker, 20:426
Faricy, William T., speaker, 35:153
Faries, Hugh, trader, 11:363, 14:223; diary, 15:90-92, 34:254
Farley, James A., postmaster general, 18:472, 28:305
Farley, Jesse K., Jr., author, 25:187
Farley, Jesse P., career, 25:187
Farley, Beltrami County, logging town, 29:145, 31:70; newspaper, 29:356; Presbyterian church, 31:70
Farley Telegram, 29:356
Farm and Labor party, organized, 22:388, 32:133, 146
Farm Bloc, in Congress, 32:182
Farm Boy Cavaliers of America, 28:396
Farm Bureau, 18:323
Farm Credit Administration, publications, 17:473, 18:323; Minnesota archives, 20:205
Farm Island Lake, Aitkin County, name, 21:347
Farm Loan Banks, function, 12:14
Farm Market Guide, Alliance paper, 28:40
Farm, Stock, and Home (Minneapolis), history, 18:410, 411, 20:85, 36:109-126
Farmer, E. C., 17:124, 18:111, 19:362
Farmer, Emanuel D., 37:141
Farmer, J. Q., speaker, 15:249
Farmer, Marion, 18:465, 19:471
Farmer (Fargo, N.D., and St. Paul), agricultural paper, 18:410
Farmer-Labor Advocate (St. Paul), history, 38:304
Farmer-Labor Association, history, 38:301-309, 40:371

Farmer-Labor Leader (St. Paul), history, 38:304-309
Farmer-Labor party, significance, 14:339, 18:192, 21:93; Minnesota, 15:99, 17:161, 18:424, 20:194, 198, 21:323, 25:193, 202, 325, 28:73, 183, 37:39, 39:334, 40:147; history, 16:456, 482, 17:164, 478, 18:218, 459, 23:284, 28:44, 32:246, 35:155, 36:101, 103, 105, 151, 38:177-185, 301-309; convention, 28:372; organized, 30:66, 31:124, 36:282; ideology, 33:42, 40:360; South Dakota, 36:88; foreign policy, 40:365-374. See also Agrarian movement, Democratic-Farmer-Labor party, Labor, Nonpartisan League
Farmer-Labor Press Association, 38:305
Farmer Seed and Nursery Co., Faribault, 19:238
Farmers, William P., 16:241
Farmers, diaries, 11:457, 15:463, 16:52, 474, 17:99, 212, 465-467, 18:284-297, 445, 19:95, 344, 20:31, 34, 74, 81, 166, 288, 291, 334, 417, 21:85, 22:41, 24:354, 26:256, 281, 27:61, 28:92, 172, 29:357, 30:326, 327, 33:91; pioneer life, 13:4, 22:336, 361, 27:83-95, 28:174, 37:204-211; characterized, 16:106; in politics, 16:455, 29:101; songs, 36:194. See also Agriculture, Farmer-Labor party
Farmers' Alliance (Northern Alliance), 21:91, 33:307; co-operative aspect, 11:100, 18:323; policies, 12:7, 412, 15:338; Minnesota, 12:194, 430, 14:169, 15:99, 17:162, 20:194, 21:342, 29:101, 32:62, 129-146, 35:53, 58-60, 297-312, 36:71, 109-114, 117, 119, 40:362; history, 12:326, 26:171, 361, 30:151, 33:224, 34:354, 35:334, 36:101; relations with labor, 22:384, 386, 388; Iowa, 31:190; Middle West, 35:65; attacks university, 37:22; Illinois, 38:236; influence, 39:332. See also Agrarian movement, Alliance party, People's party
Farmers' Alliance and Industrial Union (Southern Alliance), 12:412. See also People's party
Farmers and Mechanics Savings Bank, Minneapolis, history, 23:197, 31:114, 34:205
Farmers' Board of Trade, 29:10
Farmers' Club, organized, 22:260
Farmers Club of Meeker County, 18:97
Farmers Community Park, Winona County, 36:144
Farmer's Co-op Creamery, Mora, 36:195
Farmers Co-operative Elevator Co., Mountain Lake, 20:459
Farmers' Cooperative Marketing Act, history, 29:102
Farmers Education and Cooperative Union of America, 29:267
Farmers' Holiday Association, 35:284, 285; history, 40:91
Farmers' Home, Gibbon, 36:197-199
Farmers Independent (Bagley), 15:484, 38:305
Farmer's institutes, 28:377; educational program, 37:22-29

Farmers' Museum, Cooperstown, N.Y., 31:14; described, 26:266, 27:353, 31:15-17

Farmers' National Bank, Waseca, 13: 122

Farmers Protective Union, organized, 22:374

Farmers Union, co-operative purchasing, 17:348, 18:323; Wright County, 22:112; history, 23:91, 26:171, 28:37, 38, 43n, 29:76, 30:151, 32:181, 35:334, 36:101; purpose, 27:352; leaders, 28:44; North Dakota, 29:267; Iowa, 31: 190; Montana, 35:203

Farmers Union Central Exchange, St. Paul, 24:174, 30:67, 35:203

Farmers Union Grain Terminal Association, St. Paul, 21:202, 35:203

Farming, see Agriculture

Farmington, schools, 11:113; railroad, 16:247; history, 16:470, 28: 190; churches, 17:98, 27:344, 28: 395; weather station, 19:235; unions, 21:380; bank, 25:211; mail service, 28:83, 36:193; camp meetings, 31:82

Farmington Reporter, history, 15:245

Farmington Telegraph, history, 15:245

Farms and farmers, see Agriculture

Farnam, Henry, railroad builder, 25: 105, 107, 116, 34:133, 138, 142

Farnam, Henry W., 15:416, 34:138n, 143

Farnell, W. C. F., author, 18:102

Farnham, Charles W., biography, 13: 324

Farnham, Daniel R., 22:319

Farnham, Russell, trader, 13:221, 40: 185n

Farnham, S. W., and Co., banking firm, 35:129

Farnham, Sumner W., lumberman, 13: 354, 26:135, 136, 37:319

Farnham and Lovejoy, lumber firm, 26: 135, 136

Farnsworth, John F., Congressman, 34: 72

Farnsworth, William, trader, 40:186

Farnum, Emily, author, 18:311

Farr, Isabelle, 13:120

Farrand, Max, 14:316

Farrar, Amos, trader, 13:221

Farrel, Maggie, student, 27:104

Farrell, Charles F., 24:106n

Farrell, James, author, 20:116

Farrell, John T., author, 29:79

Farrington, George W., St. Paul pioneer, 14:292, 23:321, 322

Farrington, Col. John, 28:320; horse breeder, 26:118; railroad executive, 34:83

Farrington, S. Kip, Jr., author, 24: 175, 26:77

Farrington, Samuel P., 18:134n

Farseth, Pauline, work reviewed, 32: 121

Farther-and-Gay Castle, Joseph R. Brown's house, 12:111-133

Farwell, Methodist church, 20:35

Farwell, Ozmun, Kirk and Co., St. Paul, history, 36:283

Fascism, interpretation of history, 18:2, 4; dangers, 23:216; effect in U.S., 40:371-374

Fassett, Irene, author, 37:348

Fassett, J. Sloat, politician, 35:74

Fast, Mrs. Hermann J., 18:445; diaries, 19:48, 29:189

Faster, John, 27:293n

Fatio, F. P., 11:238n

Faulkner, William, author, 20:116

Fauteux, Aegidius, "D'Eraque, Darrac, or Darec?" 13:85

"Favorite," steamboat, 15:130, 16:40, 36:252-258, 37:227, 38:289, 356, 361

Fawcett, Gilbert G., author, 26:276, 28:78; speaker, 29:94

Fawcett, James W., author, 17:115

Fawcett, Lois M., reference librarian, 11:46, 16:95, 29:372, 30:41; "Minnesota Stories in the 'Fireside Henty Series,'" 14:86; "Frontier Education," 14:142-149; "Some Early Minnesota Bells," 18:371-380; "Marking Minnesota's Western Boundary," 19:424-426; genealogical notes, 22:89-91, 322-325, 425-427, 23:78-81, 173-177, 374, 24: 65-67, 169-171, 357-359, 25:80-82, 187-189, 292, 386-388, 26:70, 158-160, 261-263, 374, 27:58, 155-157, 346, 28:200, 305; reviews by, 30: 145, 33:84, 36:186; speaker, 13: 194, 14:328; author, 17:61, 209, 18:440, 19:444, 446, 20:43, 28: 334, 30:184; career, 38:244

Fawcett, Wilford H., publisher, 36:32

Fawcett (Faucette), William, 11:174

Fawell, Robert S., biography, 19:214

Fawkes, Bohn, auto driver, 38:207, 211, 213

Fawkes, Leslie H., auto driver, 38: 207, 208

Fawkes Automobile Co., Minneapolis, 38:207

"Fawn," steamboat, 33:9, 11-14

Faxon (Walker's Landing), Sibley County, site, 11:169, 170n

Fay, Celinda (Mrs. Aaron Goodrich, I), 39:143, 152

Fay, Sidney B., author, 40:366

Faye, Helen, editor, 37:37

"Fayette," steamboat, 18:168

Fayolle, Father Jean, 21:454

Fayram, Frederick, 33:96, 99

Fazekas, Andrew, 17:364

Fearing, Jerome W., author, 39:211

Feather Cloudwoman, Indian woman, 20: 136

Featherstone, J. W., 11:119; author, 19:367

Featherstone Church, Red Wing, 39:223

Featherstonhaugh, George W., characterized, 12:240, 18:163; author, 15:124, 18:455, 30:210, 31:105; geologist, 15:128, 16:159-162, 164, 232, 17:305, 307, 308, 21: 164n, 33:352

Feboldson, Febold, legends, 29:267, 37:39

Feda, Ben, speaker, 20:300

Feder, Norman, author, 39:261

Federal Barge Line, 20:304

Federal Cartridge Corp., Anoka, 25: 365

Federal Communications Commission, archives, 22:211

Federal Courts Building, St. Paul, 40:253

Federal Emergency Relief Administration, MHS projects, 15:443, 461, 16:54, 65, 330, 17:55-59; Freeborn

County, 16:490. See also Civil Works Administration, Works Progress Administration

Federal Farm Board, 12:15, 32:182

Federal Farm Loan Board, established, 29:167

Federal Home Loan Bank Board, archives, 22:211

Federal Housing Administration, archives, 22:211

Federal Intermediate Credit Bureau, 12:14

Federal Land Bank, 39:247

Federal Reserve Bank, Minneapolis, 33:332

Federal Reserve System, adopted, 12: 12, 13; archives, 22:211

Federal School of Illustrating and Cartooning, Minneapolis, 22:320

Federal Steel Co., see United States Steel Corp.

Federal Trade Commission, 12:18, 28: 304

Federal Writers' Project, Minnesota, 19:59, 463, 475; work reviewed, 20:64-66; publications, 20:356

Federated Press Service, 38:305

Federated Trades Assembly, Duluth, 22:380

Federated Women's Clubs, Jackson County, 12:338

Federation of Organized Trades and Labor Unions, 22:383

Fee, Timothy, house, 19:235, 20:343

Feely, Mrs. William F., 23:390

Feig, H. C., 29:363; author, 19:366

Feikema, Feike, see Manfred, Frederick F.

Felch, Mr. and Mrs. Charles J., pioneers, 27:153

Felch, Daniel F. M., in Civil War, 27:153

Felch, J. H., engraver, 33:128

Felch family, genealogy, 27:153

Felders, Catherine, 35:268

Feldmeir, Daryle, author, 34:266

Fell, Dr. V., 20:141n

Fellers, R. E., speaker, 30:170

Fellow, A. Rochester, pseud., see Scudder, Samuel

Felstet, Nels, pioneer, 22:345

Felt, Lorene M., author, 12:211

Felt-Raabet (Minneapolis), file acquired, 16:219

Felton, Edgar, 37:105n

Felton, Harold W., work reviewed, 28: 362-364; author, 33:265

Felton, Samuel M., railroad official, 37:102, 105n, 38:312

Felton family, 35:336

Felton, history, 21:448

Feminism, see Woman's rights

Fenaroli, Luigi, author, 35:200

Fences, frontier types, 18:230, 22: 448, 27:86; stump, 21:429; for livestock, 26:124, 125

Fenger, Dr. Christian, 22:405

Fenian raids, 15:239, 356, 33:315, 35:282

Fenne, John, 16:425n

Fenner, Mildred S., author, 27:61, 35:98

Fenske, Theodore, speaker, 26:396; author, 28:385

Fenske, Walt, author, 19:364

Fenton, Benjamin, 25:238

Fenton, John H., work reviewed, 40:90

Fenton, William N., work reviewed,
36:30
Ferber, Edna, author, 16:105, 106,
347, 20:116, 23:157, 36:77
Fergstad, Mrs. Anna Q., 15:364
Fergus, James, 19:124, 23:282, 30:
273; letter, 40:38
Fergus Falls, history, 11:117, 16:
369, 497, 17:488, 18:117, 19:413,
20:103, 23:289, 34:360, 35:384;
state hospital, 12:105; historical
meeting, 13:280-283; golden jubilee, 13:452; picture exhibit, 14:
357; Blacks, 14:460; rebuilt, 16:
194; Lutheran church, 17:102; log
drives, 17:238; German settlement,
18:453; pioneer life, 19:124, 22:
225; founded, 20:103, 23:171, 29:
358, 30:273, 40:38; depicted, 22:
107; antihorsethief association,
26:121; school, 26:166; name, 30:
273; in fiction, 36:80; murder
case, 38:11-20
Fergus Falls Journal, history, 29:358
Fergus Falls Public Library, history,
27:270
Ferguson, Clarence, speaker, 14:235
Ferguson, Frank, speaker, 12:342
Ferguson, Franklin T., "The Cathedral
of St. Paul," 39:153-162
Ferguson, George, speaker, 23:380
Ferguson, James, surveyor, 24:342
Ferguson, Robert, pioneer printer,
15:14
Ferguson and Clark, Minneapolis, 24:
297
Fern, Fanny, 17:474
Fernald, S., lumberman, 24:127
Ferrant's Hall, Minneapolis, 19:266n
Ferrel, William, scientist, 18:352,
33:191, 271
Ferrell, Robert H., author, 39:80
Ferrier, Kathleen, singer, 39:64
Ferries, Lower Sioux (Redwood), 11:
29, 34:233-238, 38:154, 156; Le
Sueur River, 12:51; Blue Earth
River, 12:52; McGregor, Iowa, 14:
304; Mendota, 16:72; Great Lakes,
16:288, 38:237; Minnesota River,
16:279, 20:100, 30:119, 121, 34:
233-238; Mississippi River, 17:
215, 20:413, 415, 21:229, 24:80,
27:79, 28:286, 29:30, 208, 35:187,
255, 39:328; Chaska, 17:241; Nininger, 17:269-271, 274; East Grand
Forks, 18:341; Rock River, 21:18n;
La Crosse, Wis., 21:211, 24:177;
Reads Landing, 21:232; Montrose,
Iowa, 22:18, 20; licenses, 22:447;
charters, 28:342n; Bloomington,
30:119, 121; Verdon Township, 33:
19; Rum River, 35:255; Henderson,
39:274
Ferris, Mrs. Gratia F., 15:492
Ferris, Joseph A., author, 12:343
Ferris, Robert G., work reviewed, 40:
404
Ferry, Hawkins, author, 24:261
Ferslev, Helen L., work reviewed, 30:
247
Fertile, county fair, 14:358; history, 28:383; archaeology, 38:162
Fesler, Judge Bert, 12:207, 18:205,
19:310, 20:50, 21:289, 292, 23:50,
28:394; speaker, 11:460, 12:342,
17:482; author, 19:355, 34:177n,
35:49

Fessenden, Thomas G., agrarian, 40:
295
Festival of Nations, St. Paul, 22:
336, 23:95, 25:306, 27:39, 30:282,
31:58, 33:91, 36:107
Fever (Galena) River, Wis., Ill.,
trading post, 13:221; steamboating, 13:437, 15:411, 33:115; Henry
Lewis' camp, 17:297, 300, 421;
lead trade, 23:183
Fevold, Eugene L., work reviewed, 37:
183
Fick, Mrs. William C., Jr., speaker,
16:256
Fiction, agricultural, 11:63-74, 185,
16:106, 20:183, 23:113-125, 156-
158, 31:135-137, 36:80, 39:293;
Minnesota settings, 12:309, 15:
364, 450, 457, 461, 18:368, 20:
117, 21:209, 22:166, 23:118, 24:
173, 25:90, 30:142, 246, 287, 31:
129-147, 32:33, 122, 33:45-52, 92,
192, 350, 356, 34:309, 35:196,
234, 37:1-13, 39:267; about immigrants, 16:107, 30:391, 32:250,
34:163, 35:333, 38:38, 39:126,
341; historical, 18:66, 19:312,
21:6-10, 25:191, 192, 28:287, 34:
123; about Indians, 25:165, 33:
190, 35:288, 38:88, 191, 39:208;
regional, 25:175, 33:191, 34:175,
210, 219, 36:237; rune-stone
story, 34:353; business, 35:44;
railroad stories, 36:322. See
also Literature
Fiddes, J. S., 12:339, 14:120
Fidler, Peter, trader, 16:106, 24:
262, 27:67, 31:183, 34:352; surveyor, 33:139, 36:324
Fidler, Vera, author, 36:324
Fidler's Fort, Winnipeg, Man., his-
tory, 21:432
Fiegel, Lester J., 22:340; speaker,
34:359
Field, A. M., educator, 34:350
Field, H. H., author, 24:175
Field, Henry Martyn, author, 25:184
Field, Iduna B., author, 18:452
Field, Marshall, capitalist, 33:221
Field, N. F., speaker, 13:452
Field, Oliver P., author, 26:82
Field, Rachel, author, 21:10
Field, Thaddeus C., businessman, 35:
98
Field Museum of Natural History,
Chicago, 39:120
Field-Schlick, Inc., St. Paul, his-
tory, 11:227, 35:98
Fielder, Mildred, author, 39:298
Fielding, Capt. ---, 19:391
Fields, Elmer F., author, 24:91
Fields, Emily, 18:301
Fifteenth Massachusetts Volunteer
Infantry, 25:236
Fifteenth Minnesota Volunteer Infan-
try, 12:324, 429, 16:340, 17:215,
341, 23:212
Fifteenth Wisconsin Volunteer Infan-
try, 15:235, 17:222, 19:459, 24:
348. See also Heg, Col. Hans C.
Fifth Avenue Baptist Church, Minnea-
polis, 17:337
Fifth Iowa Cavalry, 19:388
Fifth Minnesota Volunteer Infantry,
in Civil War, 12:446, 28:326, 29:
101, 31:35, 34:129, 35:313-319,
38:245 (cover), 287; officers, 14:

335, 17:336, 19:211, 25:384; sol-
dier vote, 26:196, 197, 201, 205,
206; in Sioux Outbreak, 28:214,
33:356, 34:236, 38:96; homecoming,
38:292
Fifth U.S. Infantry, at Fort Snelling
21:83, 23:213, 307, 338n, 40:78
Fiftieth New York Volunteer Engineers
21:358
Fiftieth New York Volunteer Infantry,
14:323
Fikkan, A. H., 28:298, 29:181, 365
Filharmonix clubs, Minneapolis, 33:93
97
Filler, Louis, author, 37:344
Filley, H. Clyde, author, 11:100
Fillmore, Charles D., cholera victim,
14:294
Fillmore, Mary, 15:412
Fillmore, Millard, 37:307; excursionist, 12:392, 393, 14:280, 15:405,
410, 411, 415, 419, 16:27, 20:384,
386, 25:103, 114n, 34:135, 142,
143, 38:49; President, 28:321, 30:
10, 32:190, 36:271, 39:44-46, 147-
151, 174; Vice-president, 30:104,
39:38, 143
Fillmore County, pageant, 11:333;
ethnic groups, 12:265, 266, 17:
102, 19:464, 21:98, 28:32, 121-
124, 31:27, 35:90; churches, 13:
448, 14:236, 15:136; agriculture,
14:119, 23:323, 326, 24:99, 103,
29:2n, 13; archives, 15:197, 198,
23:188; fair, 15:485; history, 16:
127, 21:443; Christmas celebration, 16:379; Quakers, 18:256,
257; schools, 18:316; ghost towns,
21:220; population, 24:97; dairying, 24:104; medicine, 27:168,
269, 28:84; politics, 28:32, 40:
327, 328; iron mining, 36:70, 283;
poor farm, 38:369n, 373
Fillmore County Agricultural Society,
15:486, 22:253
Fillmore County Historical Society,
16:240, 20:75, 21:443, 25:406, 27:
75, 30:365; organized, 15:80, 485,
16:63, 123; meetings, 16:360, 18:
109, 223, 20:96, 300, 25:97, 27:
342, 361, 28:86; museum, 21:335,
26:89, 163, 179, 283, 393, 28:194,
386, 29:91, 274, 30:79, 165; exhibit, 23:398
Fillmore County Medical Society, 27:
270
Fillmore County War History Committee, 23:391, 25:94
Filsinger, Catherine, editor, 34:254
Fimon, Frank, 22:448
Finance and Commerce (Minneapolis),
file acquired, 15:225
Finberg, Earl, author, 26:387, 27:263
Finch, Dr. William W., 11:395
Fine, Sidney, work reviewed, 37:305
Finger, Charles J., author, 13:333
Fingerson, Carrie, 25:337
Fingerson, Fingar, farmer, 25:337
Fink, Frederick, career, 30:271
Fink, Mike, keelboatman, 18:452, 20:
202, 26:166, 33:265
Finland, emigration from, 22:393, 431
25:320, 27:205, 207, 32:185, 40:
399-401; newspapers, 22:399
Finland, Carlton County, see Kettle
River
Finland, Lake County, history, 16:

357, 34:182, 38:42; Finnish set-
tlement, 18:324, 25:320
Finland Swedes, Minnesota, 12:436,
27:206, 213, 39:131; defined, 13:
108, 27:207; immigration, 26:57;
Michigan, 27:205
Finlay, George E., artist, 38:200
Finlay, James, trader, 11:258, 261,
264, 12:368, 14:229, 18:82, 37:
241-254
Finlay, John, 21:122
Finlayson, Duncan, trader, 20:71
Finlayson, R., trader, 40:167n, 168n
Finlayson Township, Pine County,
quarries, 35:295
Finley, David E., author, 35:370
Finley, John H., editor, 12:434, 14:
408
Finley, M. I., author, 39:34
Finley Collection, Knox College,
Galesburg, Ill., 19:216
Finn, Wadena County, Finnish settle-
ment, 25:320
Finner, Roland W., photographer, 39:
271n
Finneran, Helen T., author, 39:83
Finney, Mrs. Grover, 23:102
Finnish American Historical Library,
29:347
Finnish-American Historical Society,
Minnesota, 26:31, 27:142; activities, 20:214, 21:110, 25:317, 378,
26:39, 29:185, 273, 30:77, 164,
401, 404
Finnish Colonization Co., 33:16, 17
Finnish Temperance League, 22:392
Finns, immigration, 11:221, 18:72,
22:431, 27:65; in lumber industry,
13:365; Minnesota, 16:246, 339,
21:102, 203, 22:220, 23:300, 24:
384, 25:317-328, 28:82, 32:185,
34:184, 35:292, 36:192, 38:42,
243; folklore, 16:319-321, 344,
467, 485, 17:406-410, 459, 22:97,
180, 225, 24:73, 226-228, 25:74,
30:156, 31:32, 32:188, 196, 33:
184, 36:74, 194, 39:129, 40:391-
402; Michigan, 16:339, 20:202, 27:
205, 28:378, 32:185; place names,
16:350, 40:358; agriculture, 16:
357, 18:324, 22:96, 31:122; medical practice, 18:338; tercentenary, 19:220; iron range, 19:334,
23:387, 27:204, 206-213, 215, 31:
28, 32:126, 195-200, 36:107, 40:
48, 60, 61, 341-347; North America, 20:442, 25:393, 29:347, 34:
163, 37:129; language, 21:116, 24:
226, 25:160; monuments, 21:342,
30:401; co-operatives, 22:96, 315,
23:98, 24:174, 36:34, 38:203; temperance societies, 22:391-403, 40:
344; in fiction, 23:118, 35:333;
Wisconsin, 25:301, 27:134, 32:184;
in fishing industry, 25:370;
poetry, 27:42; library, 27:162;
pioneer celebration, 30:404. See
also Finland Swedes
Finn's artillery, Winona, 14:182
Finntown, Carlton County, Finnish
settlement, 25:320
Finseth, Ole A., author, 36:103
Finstad, O. J., speaker, 14:119
Finstrom, Ernest A., author, 18:331
"Fire Canoe," steamboat, 11:137
Fire fighting, 35:123; Twin Cities,

13:346, 20:88, 30:163; Red Wing,
18:468; St. Anthony, 35:124
Fire steels, in Indian trade, 18:36-
40, 188; at Climax, 18:188-190
Firearms, in fur trade, 33:89, 35:
151, 195, 281, 35:196, 376, 36:
316, 37:254, 40:207, 208; manufacture, 33:134, 267, 307, 35:45;
antique, 34:127; rifles, 35:89,
279, 280; revolvers, 36:68; history, 37:35, 38:197
Fireside Henty Series, Minnesota
stories, 14:86
Firestone, Allan, papers, 11:42, 97
Firkins, Chester, poet, 16:81; papers, 16:100
Firkins, Ina T. E., 15:452, 16:100;
review by, 14:322-324; author, 37:
187
Firkins, Oscar W., work reviewed, 15:
451; author, 15:358, 18:106, 330,
26:308; papers, 16:52, 100, 17:58,
34:339; teacher, 21:2, 70
First American National Bank of Duluth, 37:120, 121
First and American National Bank, Duluth, 37:122, 125
First Baptist Church, Danish, Clarks
Grove, 11:113, 13:207, 15:128, 21:
341; St. Cloud, 12:107; Minneapolis, 12:343, 16:335; Faribault,
12:453; Breckenridge, 14:124;
Austin, 14:236; Morristown, 14:
359; Bricelyn, 15:128; Mankato,
16:120; St. Paul, 16:120, 38:75;
Willmar, 16:355; Eveleth, 16:356;
Alden, 17:118; Anoka, 17:230, 350;
Waseca, 18:316, 19:49; Long
Prairie, 24:94; Hudson, Wis.,
24:165; Duluth, 27:82
First Bank Stock Corporation, 19:113,
25:280, 34:166, 205
First Battery, Minnesota Light Artil-
lery, 38:287, 289
First Company, Massachusetts Sharp-
shooters, 25:21n, 122, 123n
First Congressional District, Demo-
cratic convention, 26:203
First Heavy Artillery, in Civil War,
26:157, 258
First Lutheran Church, Newburg, 14:
119; Scandia Grove, 14:356; Litch-
field, 14:451
First Methodist Church, Crookston,
11:117; Chatfield, 13:117; St.
Cloud, 14:239; New Ulm, 14:353;
Worthington, 14:357; Taylors
Falls, 15:468; Ortonville, 16:337,
355, 356; Eveleth, 16:485; Duluth,
17:378, 379
First Minnesota (Berryville, Va.),
Civil War newspaper, 25:33
First Minnesota Association, 38:296
First Minnesota Heavy Artillery, 12:
319, 13:100, 445, 38:289, 292, 295
First Minnesota Light Artillery, 33:
84, 37:307
First Minnesota Mounted Rangers, in
Sioux Outbreak, 12:318, 22:86, 38:
276, 280, 281
First Minnesota Volunteer Infantry,
33:217, 38:78, 226; in Civil War,
11:42, 95, 15:128, 479, 16:472,
18:95, 25:117-152, 342-361, 28:
325, 29:344, 33:83, 38:245-257,
39:83; officers, 15:465, 16:99,
26:157, 258, 30:91, 33:281n, 37:

189 (cover), 328, 329, 38:259, 39:
173-180, 191-197; absorbs Pioneer
Guard, 16:176; personnel, 16:177,
18:96, 20:329, 22:87, 24:354, 36:
328; chaplain, 16:215, 24:27, 30:
202, 303, 38:52; in camp, 19:467,
23:212, 25:11-39, 224-257, 26:158,
28:214, 326, 37:226n, 39:204;
vote, 25:229, 26:196-198, 200,
201, 36:170; uniforms, 26:281, 33:
87, 37:213n; Germans in, 33:84;
Christmas, 1861, 37:334; honored,
38:243; monument, 38:245; homecoming, 38:287, 291, 296; history,
38:330; Gorman case, 39:129
First Minnesota Volunteer Infantry
Association, 18:316
First National Bank, Goodhue, 11:219;
Wabasha, 15:492; Minneapolis, 18:
141, 21:114, 34:205; St. Paul, 20:
58, 346, 33:268, 313, 34:42, 99n,
169, 204, 40:116, 119, 231, 335;
Windom, 22:343; Owatonna, 22:350;
Red Wing, 26:287; Stillwater, 31:
35; Mankato, 34:325. See also
First and American National Bank,
Duluth
First Nebraska Volunteer Infantry,
12:432
First Presbyterian Church, Blue
Earth, 15:480; Hallock, 15:481
First State Bank, Chatfield, see
Root River State Bank
First State Bank, Le Roy, 40:359
First Swedish Baptist Church, St.
Paul, 29:359
First Trust Co., St. Paul, 40:231
First Unitarian Church, Minneapolis,
23:228, 363
First U.S. Artillery, Ricketts' Bat-
tery, 25:30n
First U.S. Infantry, at Fort Snel-
ling, 13:301, 28:15, 17, 30:99
First U.S. Volunteer Infantry, 21:
416, 38:285
First Universalist Society, Anoka,
17:466
First Vermont Heavy Artillery, 17:
337, 25:289
Fisch, Max H., author, 30:258
Fischer, Anna, actress, 32:172
Fischer, Carlo, musician, 33:101
Fischer, Charles S., piano maker, 19:
318
Fischer, Earl B., 14:109
Fischer, F., author, 16:130
Fischer, Hilke, Dutch pioneer, 28:125
Fischer, Richard, actor, 32:173
Fish, Arthur M., compiler, 35:383
Fish, Carl R., historian, 12:328, 13:
291, 24:337, 39:220
Fish, Judge Daniel, 19:217
Fish, Dr. Everett W., editor, 19:125,
32:135, 136, 139, 36:116, 118,
119, 39:99, 100
Fish, Hamilton, 18:125, 20:320, 40:
410; papers, 14:103
Fish, Col. John B., 11:415
Fish, P. I., 13:134
Fish and fishing, conservation efforts, 14:384, 22:214; sport, 14:
421, 423, 16:188, 189, 358, 17:
392, 22:337, 23:404, 24:139, 25:
237, 309, 29:202, 292, 297, 30:
118-120, 32:87, 33:237, 251-259,
35:50, 79-81, 36:92, 195, 39:287,
40:34, 73; Northeast, 18:121, 135,

137, 139n, 25:172; by Indians, 20:
334, 23:144, 240, 242, 330, 40:
158; hatchery system, 21:84; commercial, 21:449, 24:47, 79, 25:
185, 316, 26:174, 27:262, 272, 28:
176, 349, 32:186, 33:66, 34:1, 3,
221 (cover), 243-249, 260, 265,
35:46, 49, 272-277, 36:69, 38:336,
39:303, 310; Canada, 22:64, 40:
191; legends, 23:403; depicted,
30:118

Fish Hook Lake, Hubbard County, ar-
chaeology, 26:321
Fish Lake, Kanabec County, 34:62, 63
Fishbaugher, Harvey, speaker, 13:449
Fishbein, Dr. Morris, author, 28:371
Fishblatt, ---, 18:124
Fishburn, Jesse J., author, 29:85
Fishel, Leslie H., Jr., review by,
38:87
Fisher, Alexander, 20:72
Fisher, David, 18:222, 19:115, 20:95
Fisher, Dorothy Canfield, author, 25:
175
Fisher, Elijah L., postmaster, 34:185
Fisher, Fred W., author, 32:63
Fisher, George, 23:391
Fisher, Harold L., author, 34:170
Fisher, Harriet L., 22:85
Fisher, Henry M., trader, 11:379, 18:
193, 22:278-280, 288, 35:82; pa-
pers, 20:79
Fisher, Jacob, 40:236; millwright,
24:128, 193, 201, 202; lumberman,
24:196-198; builder, 37:138
Fisher, Dr. James, 16:478
Fisher, John, 25:360
Fisher, Kate, 28:110
Fisher, Louis A., 13:204
Fisher, Rex G., editor, 37:307
Fisher, Seth, author, 33:188
Fisher, Vardis, 20:115
Fisher, in fur trade, 13:237, 23:330,
30:134, 40:212
"Fisherman John," bodyfinder, 39:262
Fisher's Landing (Fisher), Polk Coun-
ty, river port, 21:262, 263, 23:
110, 25:187
Fishlow, Albert, historian, 40:406
Fishwick, Marshall W., work reviewed,
34:261; author, 33:90
Fisk, Andrew J., diary, 18:270
Fisk, Dan, townsite promoter, 38:229
Fisk, David H., farmer, 40:236
Fisk, Mrs. Eleanor M., research assistant, 27:340, 28:47
Fisk, Capt. James L., 36:176n; papers, 13:322, 18:270; emigrant
guide, 38:216-218; army career,
38:216-230. See also Fisk expeditions
Fisk, Robert C., 15:117
Fisk, Robert E., diary, 18:270
Fisk, Robert F., politician, 37:326,
327
Fisk expeditions, 12:191, 13:436, 16:
332, 334, 18:270, 23:184, 28:187,
31:253, 36:191; 1862, 11:453, 15:
465, 34:304, 36:280, 38:56-62,
218, 220, 40:262; 1866, 21:95, 38:
71, 39:262; 1863, 21:315, 23:282,
38:218-220; 1864, 26:261, 38:220,
227, 40:307; mapped, 38:386. See
also Fisk, Capt. James L.
Fiske, Rev. A. S., 19:268
Fiske, Douglas A., 19:184
Fiske, John, 18:148, 29:189

Fiske, Timothy, archaeologist, 40:263
Fitch, Allan, speaker, 29:91
Fitch, Charles, livestock dealer, 29:
91
Fite, Gilbert C., "Some Farmers' Accounts," 37:204-211; "The Agrarian
Tradition," 40:293-299; reviews
by, 37:178, 259, 39:206; works reviewed, 30:60, 33:86, 35:368, 38:
238, 40:303; author, 27:356, 29:
77, 35:45, 38:203, 40:409; speaker, 37:136
Fittler, Theodore, potter, 33:230
Fitz, E. Howard, 11:298, 19:116, 20:
97; speaker, 18:229; papers, 29:
363
Fitz, Mrs. Rudolph H., papers, 29:188
Fitzgerald, Lord Edward, 19:104
Fitzgerald, F. Scott, 15:100, 26:251,
37:345; author, 18:330, 21:3, 4,
29:173, 30:62, 31:133, 142, 145,
35:235, 36:74, 237, 325, 37:184;
career, 28:279, 32:115-117, 37:
133, 307, 38:203, 39:35, 263;
birthplace, 37:66; evaluated, 39:
210, 40:95, 411
Fitzgerald, Mrs. F. Scott, 32:116
Fitzgerald, Sister Mary C., author,
23:383
Fitzgerald, Nancy, author, 30:397
Fitzgerald, Robert L., speaker, 28:
385
Fitzgerald brothers, bus operators,
28:384
Fitz Gibbon, Mary (Mary F. Knopp),
18:59, 22:45
Fitzhugh's Woods, Ark., battle, 40:
289, 290
Fitzjohn and Melaney, Hastings, contractors, 37:194
Fitzpatrick, John C., editor, 14:108
Fitzpatrick, Mark, author, 16:488,
17:129, 26:184, 27:177, 271, 29:89
Fitzpatrick, Thomas, architect, 39:
154n, 155
Fitzsimons, Richard W., "The Expan-
ding Role of History," 40:35-38
Fitzwilliam, William, 16:113
Five Civilized Tribes, 23:95; mis-
sions, 15:211
Five million loan, 14:183n, 15:243,
34:147; established, 11:397, 14:
155, 22:232; debt repudiated, 16:
356, 22:233, 34:148
Fix, Calvin R., 19:449, 20:34
Fjelbroten, Rosie, 28:247-249
Fjeld, Marvin, speaker, 16:490
Fjelde, Jacob, sculptor, 15:100, 20:
192, 415, 21:294, 22:104
Fjelde, Lillian, 23:391
Fjelde, Paul, sculptor, 12:447, 21:
294, 295, 34:228, 230n
Fjelde, Pauline, artist, 14:111
Fjelde family, artists, 12:447
Fjoseide, Mrs. N. N., author, 11:115
Fladvad, Even O., skier, 17:228
Flag Day, celebrated, 23:167, 211,
267, 268
Flagg, Mr. and Mrs. A. C., 34:139
Flagg, Charles N., 20:185
Flagg, Dr. Samuel D., 14:301
Flagstad, Albert E., biography, 15:
480
Flaherty, Amos, author, 36:105
Flaherty, Robert, 31:184
Flamand, Joseph, voyageur, 11:451
Flanagan, John T., 19:436; "Thoreau

in Minnesota," 16:35-46; "Oscar
Wilde's Twin City Appearances,"
17:38-48; "Mark Twain on the Upper
Mississippi," 17:369-384; "William
Joseph Snelling's Western Narratives," 17:437-443; "Captain Marryat at Old St. Peter's," 18:152-
164; "The Hoosier Schoolmaster,"
18:347-370; "Bayard Taylor's Minnesota Visits," 19:399-418; "Fredrika Bremer," 20:129-139; "Knut
Hamsun in the Northwest," 20:397-
412; "Hamlin Garland," 22:157-168;
"The Middle Western Farm Novel,"
23:113-125; "A Bibliography of
Middle Western Farm Novels," 23:
156-158; "An Early Tale of the
Falls of St. Anthony," 25:165-167;
"Early Literary Periodicals," 26:
293-311; "Thirty Years of Minnesota Fiction," 31:129-144; "Some
Minnesota Novels, 1920-50," 31:
145-147; "Folklore in Minnesota
Literature," 36:73-83; "The Minnesota Backgrounds of Sinclair
Lewis' Fiction," 37:1-13; "A
French Humorist Visits Minnesota,"
40:12-20; reviews by, 17:319, 324-
326, 19:80, 20:183, 21:403, 23:68,
355, 24:237, 25:175, 274, 26:358-
360, 27:40, 233, 28:54, 360, 30:
53-55, 246, 372, 31:246, 32:115-
117, 250, 33:39, 221, 34:123, 163,
210, 35:87, 196, 239, 36:185, 237,
37:129, 218, 335, 38:38, 333, 39:
291; works reviewed, 17:450-452,
23:62, 26:356-358, 36:95, 37:299,
339; speaker, 16:68, 18:204, 268,
25:397, 36:323, 37:40, 40:411; author, 16:329, 17:90, 226, 331,
459, 18:28n, 203, 326, 440, 454,
19:91, 104, 221, 444, 20:186, 202,
426, 442, 21:96, 189, 209, 408,
431, 22:187, 201, 23:74, 89, 168,
370, 24:245, 25:181, 192, 288, 26:
211n, 370, 27:55, 175, 177, 247,
28:96, 276, 337, 369, 370, 399,
30:95, 149, 292, 412, 31:192, 256,
32:128, 256, 36:101, 185, 190,
237, 37:263, 306, 39:131, 40:146
Flanders, Walter, author, 25:196
Flandrau, Charles E., 18:317, 22:113,
164; judge, 12:201, 14:247, 35:7,
37:140; honored, 12:331; house,
12:340, 34:218; pioneer, 12:444,
14:238, 22:295, 27:259, 31:237,
34:357; in Sioux Outbreak, 13:440,
38:86, 97, 116-125, 275-277, 279,
284; author, 14:141, 16:386, 36:
74, 39:196, 40:147; Indian agent,
14:248, 22:422, 38:89, 122; papers, 23:40; editor, 39:332
Flandrau, Charles M., 13:325; review
by, 15:450; author, 13:316, 18:
330, 26:306, 307, 39:58, 59;
career, 36:325
Flandrau, Grace, 23:50, 26:45, 28:82,
29:97; "St. Paul: The Personality
of a City," 22:1-12; author, 17:
217, 18:330, 20:117, 22:82, 24:
384, 31:129, 133, 143, 145, 34:
357; speaker, 22:52, 295, 23:36,
25:55
Flandreau, S.D., Sioux colony, 37:
274; settled, 38:126
Flanigan, John, politician, 39:49
Flann, A., artist, 39:289n

Flaskerd, George, 25:270; author, 21: 424, 22:93, 24:180, 25:398, 26: 275, 37:347

Flat Mouth, Chippewa leader, 20:80, 21:285, 24:147, 28:315

Flat Stone Point, Lake Huron, fossils, 23:141

Flatboats, Red River, 16:100, 33:277; function, 21:259, 260n

Flaten, O. E., photographer, 35:295

Flathead Indians, in fur trade, 24: 74; missions, 29:59

Flax raising, 20:469, 34:172

Fleck, Byron Y., author, 31:58

Fleckenstein, Ernst, 14:237

Fleckenstein Brewery, Faribault, 14: 237

Fleetwood, Mary, author, 38:202

Fleischer, Frederick S., 17:302, 303

Fleisher, Eric W., work reviewed, 34: 199

Fleming, Elizabeth, author, 26:383

Fleming, Mrs. Florence, 11:218

Fleming, James, lawyer, 17:213

Fleming, John F., author, 36:219, 37: 222

Fleming, R. Harvey, works reviewed, 21:398, 22:309-311; author, 14:228

Fleming, Roy F., author, 17:345, 26: 380; editor, 34:355

Fleming, Mother Stanislaus, work reviewed, 15:212-214

Fleming and Wood, theater troupe, 33: 176

Flenley, R., author, 34:262

Fletcher, Andrew, quoted, 39:266

Fletcher, Benjamin, governor of New York, 15:6

Fletcher, Mr. and Mrs. Calvin, Cutlerites, 13:387

Fletcher, Daniel O., author, 38:386

Fletcher, Gilbert, artist, 21:104, 27:171, 33:310

Fletcher, Henry J., lawyer, 21:196

Fletcher, Henry P., ambassador, 35: 163

Fletcher, Dr. Hezikiah, 37:314, 316

Fletcher, John, Cutlerite, 13:387

Fletcher, John G., author, 31:251

Fletcher, Jonathan E., Indian agent, 11:224, 17:156, 22:191, 31:211

Fletcher, Loren, politician, 36:125

Fletcher, Mary, Cutlerite, 13:387

Fletcher, May, author, 23:193

Fletcher, Robert H., author, 12:177, 20:203

Flett, William, trader, 15:477

Fleurimond, Pierre, trader, 19:78

Fleury, Louis, ferryman, 34:235

Flexner, Eleanor, author, 37:39

Flexner, James T., author, 19:105, 22:406, 34:120

Flick, Alexander C., author, 11:33, 14:442; editor, 14:341, 17:111

Fling, Paul V., speaker, 24:88

Flinn, Charles A., speaker, 21:446

Flinn, George A., author, 16:348

Flinspach, Catherine, 26:256, 27:140, 28:47

Flint, Austin, author, 21:365

Flint, C. Cather, excursionist, 15: 406

Flint, Lt. Franklin F., 28:344

Flint, Schuyler, 11:96

Flint, Timothy, author, 40:304

Flint Hills, Iowa, trading post, 13: 222

Flogstad family, pioneers, 22:443

Flom, Floyd O., review by, 36:188; work reviewed, 34:308

Flom, George T., author, 12:201, 304, 305, 13:441, 21:304, 22:68, 28:60; rune-stone studies, 17:21, 34, 169; linguist, 17:319, 39:135, 136

Flonzaley Quartet, in St. Paul, 39: 57, 63

Floods, on prairies, 11:67-69; Zumbro River, 11:186; Minnesota River, 12:210, 17:230, 21:344, 39: 251; Red River, 14:286, 16:469, 17:305, 21:205, 326, 28:190, 34: 306; Otter Tail County, 16:250; Minnesota, 17:230, 20:449; Roseau Valley, 24:322; effect on lumbering, 27:197; control, 34:306

Floodwood, logging, 25:102; co-operative, 25:326

Flor, Albert D., author, 18:466; speaker, 19:359

Flor, James H., author, 20:432

Flora, Snowden D., author, 34:216

Flora Township, Renville County, Norwegian settlement, 12:275n

Floral, Ralph, author, 27:269

Floral Culture Association of Minnesota, 20:81

Florence, Lutheran church, 11:115

"Florence," steamboat, 38:359, 363

"Florence Deering," steamboat, 29:292

Florian, Marshall County, Polish settlement, 13:108

Florida, land boom, 14:198; Indians, 15:379; Bishop Whipple's visit, 19:74, 75; colonization, 23:85; centennial, 27:348; rival of Minnesota, 35:214-221; territorial papers, 36:323

Florida State Historical Society, 14:442

Florissant, Mo., Jesuits at, 20:84

Florist business, Minneapolis, 18:252

Flour and Cereal Workers' Union, 18: 445

Flour Lake, Cook County, logging, 36: 133

Flour milling, Iowa, 11:106, 22:184; Minnesota, 11:216, 17:214, 268, 21:373, 22:102, 24:89, 28:331, 30: 55, 372, 406, 34:265, 35:11-21, 36:257, 281; Cannon River Valley, 11:271-282, 12:80, 453, 15:251, 16:253, 18:342; Minneapolis, 11: 277-279, 329, 12:90, 99, 203, 333, 13:204, 14:102, 15:131, 17:352, 18:208, 468, 21:314, 427, 22:186, 336, 23:223, 225, 28:73, 31:252, 33:63-65, 332, 37:14, 15, 18; machinery, 11:278, 330, 33:132; Belgian relief project, 11:349; explosion, 11:455, 15:99, 17:352, 27:270, 35:155; pioneer, 11:465, 13:150, 16:305, 492, 18:208, 467, 21:218, 242, 27:357, 28:383, 29:4, 34:129, 35:28, 36:104, 38:71; out state, 12:52, 65-67, 206, 449, 451, 14:124, 234, 15:134, 16:127, 128, 18:173, 341, 23:88, 24:101-103, 25:101, 27:365, 28:266, 30: 271, 34:287, 36:193, 215, 37:191; methods, 12:89, 25:308, 35:200; St. Anthony, 12:393, 24:133; history, 13:204, 17:343, 26:366, 33: 132, 39:127; Northwest, 14:206; Rochester, N.Y., 14:227; Dakota

County, 18:114, 24:190; miller's union, 21:381; packaging, 22:373; St. Paul, 37:263; relation to politics, 39:98-100, 103, 106, 109, 110. See also Grain marketing, Wheat raising

Flower, B. O., publisher, 22:161

Flower, Mark D., 16:443

Flower, Dr. Ward Z., 36:198

Floyd, John B., secretary of war, 27: 315, 28:220, 222, 29:239, 38:202

Floyd Iron Works, Duluth, 26:129n

FluiDyne Engineering Corp., Minneapolis, 33:244

Flygare, E. R., 11:298, 23:291; speaker, 11:463, 13:451, 16:491, 22:441

Flygare, William, author, 30:407

Flying, see Aviation

Flynn, Dorothy D., author, 25:311, 26:279

Flynn, Edward F., speaker, 13:344, 28:86

Flynn, H. E., work reviewed, 18:201

Flynn, John, Duluth pioneer, 28:125, 34:185

Flynn, John F., 21:446

Flynn, Michael, 20:218

Flynn, Rev. Vincent J., 29:97, 30: 171; speaker, 30:170

Fobes, Lt. F. B., at Fort Ripley, 28:214

Foffa, Father Chrysostom, 33:57

Fogdall, S. P., author, 21:341

Fogel, Robert W., author, 39:343, 40: 406

Fogelson's Fancy Goods Shop, Duluth, 34:44

Fogerty, Robert P., review by, 34: 209; author, 30:292

Fogg, Frederic A., MHS president, 11: 200, 439; bequest, 11:200, 12:33; career, 11:438; educator, 13:271

Fogg, Mrs. Frederic A. (Louise Miller), 11:439

Fogg, Frederic M., 11:439

Fogg, Sumner, 11:438

Fogg, Mrs. Sumner (Caroline Golding), 11:438

Fogliardi, Gen. ---, 25:343

Foley, Rev. J. P., 26:395

Foley, Louis G., inspector of institutions, 38:374

Foley, Timothy, 39:154n

Foley, William T., author, 30:264

Foley, history, 13:447

Foley Brothers, St. Paul, history, 28:376

Foley Independent, history, 13:447

Folger, Henry C., 27:41

Folk Arts Foundation of America, 28: 286, 30:328, 31:32; influence, 27: 280; meetings, 28:75, 186, 29:83, 30:24n, 35:52; publications, 28: 183, 199, 30:180

Folk music and songs, Norwegian, 12: 305, 18:198-201, 20:428, 24:260; French and Canadian, 13:88, 17: 204, 20:72, 29:167, 34:126, 214, 35:339, 37:345, 38:200; lumberjacks, 13:362; Finnish, 16:319-321, 344, 467, 17:406-410, 25:321, 28:379, 30:156; Indian, 22:138, 27:65, 29:86, 32:58, 123, 33:311, 34:161, 213, 35:244; Minnesota, 23:98, 27:72, 179-199, 28:199, 302, 32:163; 19th century, 23:159;

gold rush, 24:260; immigrant, 24:261, 30:135-137; bibliographies, 26:267, 32:126, 39:128; Mississippi Valley, 28:281; collections, 29:98; chimney sweeps, 33:188; Slavic, 34:296. See also Folklore

Folkebladet (Minneapolis), file acquired, 14:105

Folkets Röst (St. Paul), established, 14:402

Folklore, Itasca legend, 12:215-225, 227, 13:169, 18:180; Indian, 12:366, 14:86, 15:261-263, 453, 23:181, 24:54, 26:170, 35:142, 153, 339, 36:18-23; Czech, 15:39; Hiawatha legend, 16:280n, 24:237, 35:380, 36:75; Finnish, 16:485, 24:226-228, 32:188, 40:391-402; ghost story, 20:328; of loggers, 21:55; in ballet, 21:58-62; imaginary creatures, 21:353-356, 22:83, 23:379, 27:263, 31:191; Mississippi River, 21:404, 25:72, 35:39; French, 22:139, 28:177; historical aspect, 23:178, 27:273-280, 30:263, 31:11-17, 251, 34:213, 36:278; bibliographies, 24:367, 26:267; societies, 25:84, 26:153, 28:280; U.S., 25:215-223, 392, 27:65, 238, 28:186, 187, 29:269, 30:248, 33:91, 183, 34:316, 39:76, 262; Minnesota, 26:97-105, 253, 32:62, 126; heroes, 26:166; Pennsylvania German, 27:29-32; frontier, 27:159, 28:339; British, 28:177; Scandinavian, 28:280, 29:105-113, 267, 37:39; Mennonite, 30:161; Slovenian, 33:355; railroads, 34:214; Mexican, 34:266; Blacks, 35:95; in literature, 36:73-83, 95, 190; in newspapers, 36:101; water witching, 36:324; fur trade, 37:235-254. See also Folk music and songs

Folle Avoine, Chippewa Indians, 28:144n, 233. See also Menominee Indians

Follett family, in Hastings, 22:89

Folsom, David E., explorer, 40:262

Folsom, George, settler, 40:242

Folsom, Simeon P., 16:469, 35:356n

Folsom, Mrs. Stanley, 23:398

Folsom, William H. C., lumberman, 18:176; house, 27:232, 38:338, 339, 352, 40:239

Folsom-Cook expedition, to Yellowstone, 14:225

Foltz, Margaret, teacher, 39:275

Folwell, Russell H., diaries, 24:167

Folwell, Capt. William B., 19:453, 20:36, 435, 21:37

Folwell, William W., 11:61, 207, 16:248, 17:92, 160n, 469, 18:48, 105, 446, 19:50, 23:225, 386, 24:174, 25:64, 68, 28:76, 30:349, 34:238, 35:116, 36:318; "A Visit to Farther-and-Gay Castle," 12:111-133; works reviewed, 12:68-70, 14:322-324, 35:233; MHS president, 11:56, 30:330; memorials, 11:39, 55, 212, 329; papers, 11:42, 441, 12:26, 28, 312, 20:370, 27:248, 32:11, 35:299; career, 11:108, 12:200, 14:452, 15:480, 16:122, 186, 18:462, 28:66, 32:3-5; author, 11:201, 217, 297, 323, 443, 12:23, 25, 35, 36, 81, 111, 309, 13:64,

249, 14:14, 62, 220, 409, 16:452, 453, 17:207, 308, 19:427, 465, 23:5, 24:28, 195, 27:254, 28:172, 328, 330, 336, 357, 30:322, 35:21, 204, 248, 36:6, 37:135, 188, 264; university president, 11:215, 12:191, 16:30, 178, 180, 182, 542, 18:219, 22:101, 23:1-4, 30:357, 31:41, 52, 32:9, 176, 215, 36:186; diary, 12:318, 13:59; educator, 13:197, 16:184, 470, 18:150, 35:371; centenary, 14:78, 231; quoted, 14:195, 15:294, 16:34, 20:373, 21:357, 24:195, 30:197, 302, 316, 35:139, 36:12, 38:370, 39:13, 188, 272; in Civil War, 16:179; portraits, 17:470, 23:274, 27:346; speaker, 18:138, 316, 20:29, 39:114

Folwell, Mrs. William W., 14:323, 17:469, 18:48, 446, 19:50; portrait, 23:274

Folwell family, papers, 12:429

Folwick, Orlin, author, 18:105

Fond du Lac, Minn., fur trade area, 11:191, 359, 360, 12:92, 281, 13:433, 14:360, 15:224, 16:193, 498, 19:41, 314, 349, 20:15, 77, 327, 23:244, 330, 26:387, 28:146, 147n, 150, 233n, 277, 30:132, 31:94, 96, 32:93, 36:246, 248, 39:82, 303, 40:363; treaty, 1826, 11:208, 13:426, 14:98, 16:472, 17:55, 95, 475, 26:380, 28:277, 31:96, 97, 33:20, 37:79; missions, 11:307, 13:187, 16:333, 483, 17:96, 22:352-354, 39:308n; name, 12:422; cemetery, 12:430, 21:456; Indian settlement, 16:214, 23:244, 329, 32:91; roads, 16:282, 283, 290, 291, 293, 298, 37:103n, 109n; mail service, 16:287, 34:186; port, 16:292, 34:24, 47; pageant, 17:347; historical meeting, 19:313; British regime, 20:7-18; population, 1840, 20:452; history, 21:151, 31:246; boundary question, 23:208, 24:342; climate, 23:332; Finland Swedes, 39:131. See also Fort St. Louis

Fond du Lac, Wis., history, 18:326; electric service, 36:99

Fond du Lac County, Wis., history, 18:326

Fond du Lac Indian Reservation (Chippewa), 16:295, 33:26, 35:293; lumbering, 11:445; surveyed, 12:384; smallpox outbreak, 27:351; school, 33:73, 74, 105, 108-111; history, 40:363

Fond du Lac River, routes, 12:362, 23:233, 244-248, 251. See also St. Louis River

Foner, Philip S., author, 35:97

Fontanna, Stanley G., author, 30-389

Fontenelle, Lucien, trader, 29:59

Food, frontier, 12:142, 14:141, 378-392, 15:134, 16:378-380, 389, 499, 17:414, 18:296, 19:474, 23:182, 284, 401, 24:117, 261, 25:88, 26:108, 27:69, 87, 88, 90, 91, 95, 28:174, 248, 313, 321, 337, 30:284, 34:19, 20, 24, 54-58, 35:267, 38:7, 73; of ethnic groups, 15:39, 269-271, 24:259, 28:148, 245, 252, 30:161, 32:72, 36:197, 198, 203, 37:240, 249; at Fort Snelling, 15:

401; on river boats, 15:417, 25:112; ice cream manufacture, 17:116; American customs, 23:284, 30:265, 40:47; in lumber camps, 24:383, 34:151; of Civil War troops, 25:121-123, 126, 129, 233, 234, 236, 239, 240, 251, 353, 359; in Confederate prisons, 25:142, 144-151; of fur traders, 28:145, 151, 229, 233, 281, 32:94, 37:236, 237; early St. Paul, 29:114, 120, 121, 33:1, 4, 5, 195, 198, 200, 34:52, 97, 98, 37:188; game, 32:87, 94, 97, 37:43, 238, 38:4, 39:70, 40:389, 390; of overland emigrants, 34:263; at Minneapolis convention, 35:72; Minnesota products, 36:278. See also Maple sugar, Pemmican, Wild rice

Foot Lake, Kandiyohi County, Norwegian settlement, 11:219

Football, University of Minnesota, 17:228, 20:206, 441, 30:154, 36:94, 39:333; high school, 20:104; Minnesota, 30:406, 36:93, 103; history, 34:358, 35:335

Foote, Andrew H., 25:26

Foote family, genealogy, 13:198

Foraker, Joseph B., biography, 30:147

Forbes, Edwin, artist, 33:217, 38:257n, 286n, 39:190n

Forbes, Esther, author, 30:247

Forbes, John M., railroad builder, 30:151, 39:31, 40:356, 406

Forbes, Maury, 25:241

Forbes, Thomas R., 22:320

Forbes, W. A., cholera victim, 14:290

Forbes, William H., 31:173; trader, 11:444, 12:119, 130, 18:209, 38:135n; Indian agent, 16:73, 22:320; MHS founder, 20:368; papers, 21:85

Forbes Avenue, St. Paul, name, 20:369

Forbes Library, Northampton, Mass., 22:169

Ford, Alice, work reviewed, 31:46

Ford, Allyn K., 29:100, 164

Ford, Antoinette E., works reviewed, 13:420-422; author, 13:338, 20:89, 38:204

Ford, Charles, farmer, 29:20

Ford, Edwin H., "Southern Minnesota Pioneer Journalism," 27:1-20; reviews by, 29:62, 30:383; work reviewed, 34:83; author, 19:456, 27:54, 142, 28:333, 29:103

Ford, Guy S., 11:54, 13:106, 16:60, 17:70, 106, 18:68, 92, 19:226, 237, 20:50, 85, 206, 289, 23:5, 50, 24:266, 25:169, 26:45, 29:97, 32:9, 35:371, 39:226; Columbus Day address, 13:83-85; reviews by, 15:207, 17:73, 18:191; work reviewed, 19:328-330; MHS president, 11:55, 200, 315, 438, 12:40, 424, 13:69, 74, 75, 83, 423, 14:77, 78; speaker, 12:282, 286, 13:65, 14:211, 344, 15:56, 458, 19:101, 21:101, 113, 26:367, 29:372; quoted, 17:51, 23:4; author, 18:115, 203, 19:73, 223, 21:182, 23:289, 26:307; dean, 19:340; editor, 20:437; World War II work, 21:200, 29:82; career, 32:5-8; university president, 32:176, 36:186

Ford, Henry, quoted, 14:10; career, 22:313; papers, 33:313

Ford, Mrs. Henry, papers, 33:313

Ford, J. A., 17:286
Ford, Dr. John D., 14:148, 18:219, 19:446, 35:221
Ford, L. M., 18:407, 19:357
Ford, L. M., and Co., St. Paul, 14:278
Ford, Nathan, 39:53
Ford, Orville D., papers, 24:354
Ford, Paul L., editor, 34:156
Ford, R. Clyde, work reviewed, 13:190; author, 12:440
Ford Motor Co., interest in aviation, 33:241; St. Paul plant, 33:313
Ford Music Hall, St. Paul, 39:53-55
Foreign policy, role of fur trade, 40:149; of Farmer-Labor party, 40:365-374. See also Isolationism
Foreign Policy Association, St. Paul, 23:270
Foreman, Carolyn T., author, 25:297
Foreman, Grant, author, 15:121, 28:78
Forepaugh, Joseph L., pioneer, 33:4
Forepaugh, Mrs. Joseph L., 27:250
Forest and Stream, history, 16:187
Forest City, Meeker County, in Sioux Outbreak, 11:335, 20:192, 26:196, 35:156, 38:137n, 276, 279-281, 283, 286; history, 19:117
Forest fires, 1910, 1:417; 1918, 11:417, 15:99, 131, 225, 17:117, 360, 20:452, 30:74, 33:92, 37:223; Wisconsin, 12:328; Chisholm, 14:462; 1894, 15:99, 18:97, 19:465, 33:92; prevention, 17:220; history, 24:345, 374; North Shore, 25:185, 36:131-138; relation to lumbering, 27:307, 30:243; effect on wildlife, 30:129, 226; in fiction, 33:45-47
Forest History Society, Inc., (Forest Products History Foundation), 30:47, 33:91, 36:69, 39:84; established, 27:340, 28:49-51; staff, 28:47, 48, 30:180, 329, 37:41, 187; activities, 28:92, 331, 29:52, 98, 186, 257, 266, 30:46, 71, 89, 90, 151, 31:190, 34:115, 176, 220, 316, 37:41, 187, 40:405; publications, 28:393, 29:70, 373, 30:47, 153, 33:219, 35:48, 237, 243; library, 33:227
Forest Lake, Anoka County, Indian village, 15:483
Forest Lake, Hennepin County, settled, 29:294
Forest Lake, Washington County, history, 22:350, 27:174, 30:398; railroad, 37:103
Forest Mills, Goodhue County, history, 35:11-21
Forest Prairie, Meeker County, history, 19:117
Forests Products Laboratory, Madison, Wis., 30:159
Forest Township, Rice County, Norwegian settlement, 12:272
Forester, Frank, pseud., see Herbert, Henry W.
Foresters, Minnesota Catholic Order of, 14:352
Foreston, history, 19:236; name, 21:347
Forestry, Minnesota, 17:17, 220, 352, 24:246, 29:169, 264, 30:68, 35:98, 37:26, 40:361; Middle West, 17:110, 33:227; pioneer, 23:191, 29:373; U.S., 29:155, 33:219, 34:264,

40:405; tree farm movement, 30:151; legislation, 30:267; education, 30:389, 33:353, 34:176, 256; Wisconsin, 36:235. See also Conservation; Forest History Society, Inc.; Lumber industry
Forests, depletion, 15:482, 16:236, 40:132; protection, 30:389; U.S., 32:112; border, 36:69, 151; importance, 36:181; Michigan, 37:132; Minnesota, 37:159, 39:132. See also Conservation, Forestry, Lumber industry, individual state and national forests
Forestville, Fillmore County, county seat fight, 16:127; flour mill, 16:128; store, 16:367, 20:302, 21:36, 220, 324; ghost town, 35:12
Forgan, James B., career, 12:201
Forgard, Mrs. Dan, author, 12:340
Forgeron, Amiot, 32:229
Fork Township, Marshall County, history, 12:452
Forman, Henry J., critic, 26:308
Forman, Jonathan, review by, 33:44
Forrest, Edwin, actor, 23:313
Forrest, James T., author, 37:262
Forrest, Gen. Nathan B., Confederate officer, 38:269, 39:185, 186, 188, 189, 191-194, 196, 197
Forrest, Robert B., reminiscences, 24:263, 34:355
Forrest, Robert J., "The American Fur Company's Post," 14:84-86; "Mythical Cities," 14:243-262; author, 14:329, 15:194, 29:172
Forrest, William S., actor, 23:313
Forrestal, Ann, author, 24:264
Forrester, Marjorie, author, 37:86, 183
Forsbeck, Filip A., author, 16:479
Forsberg, A. O., 21:336, 444
Forschler, H. G., author, 17:361
Forsee, Frances A., author, 13:204
Forshael, Axel F., Swedish immigrant, 20:258
Forside, Mr. and Mrs. Ole, 39:324
Forslof, Alice, 28:268
Forslof, Andrew, 28:268
Forslof, Mrs. Andrew, 28:268
Forslof, Ara, 28:268
Forslof, Pearl, 28:268
Forslund, Mrs. Eric W., author, 24:369
Forstall family, in Stillwater, 25:210
Forster, Ada L., author, 33:354
Forsyth, Robert A., with Cass expedition, 23:135, 239, 336, 347, 348n
Forsyth, Thomas, Indian agent, 13:221, 24:71; trader, 19:299, 21:129, 133, 40:171
Forsyth, Richardson and Co., fur traders, 21:129, 40:181
Forsythe, George, 22:348
Forsythe, John, 22:348
Fort Abercrombie, N.D., stage station, 11:308, 32:277n, 38:63; trail, 12:118, 28:80; history, 14:205, 18:104; frontier post, 15:285, 287, 288, 20:191, 27:259, 29:236, 238, 245, 246, 33:272, 39:129, 40:130; emigrant station, 15:465, 31:253, 38:57-59, 71, 217, 227; fur trade, 18:271, 37:158; river port, 18:275, 21:251, 32:126, 34:324; proposed restoration,

19:64; mail service, 19:387, 33:278; described, 19:409; pictured, 20:435, 21:37, 33:279, 35:259, 37:348, 38:278; roads, 21:235, 241; soldier vote, 26:196, 201; located, 32:253, 35:260n; in Sioux Outbreak, 33:356, 35:337, 339, 38:66, 275, 277, 278, 280, 283, 286; anniversary, 35:382; archaeology, 38:165
Fort Abercrombie Park, N.D., 18:104
Fort Abraham Lincoln, N.D., 22:175; history, 28:187
Fort Adams, Lac qui Parle County, trading post, 11:378
Fort Albany, Ont., 40:188
Fort Alexander, Man., trading post, 11:364; port, 21:263
Fort Ancient, Ohio, archaeological site, 40:206, 207
Fort Armstrong, Ill., 15:410; built, 13:111; pictured, 15:349, 17:147, 424; located, 17:81
Fort Atkinson, Iowa, history, 19:460; Winnebago council, 31:211; settled, 39:2, 3
Fort Atkinson, Neb., built, 15:380, 17:81; frontier post, 17:322; evaluated, 36:149; fur trade, 40:314
Fort Barbour, Wis., trading post, 11:375
Fort Beauharnois, Lake Pepin, trading post, 11:382, 40:146; site, 11:452, 16:64, 256, 20:187; mission, 13:339, 16:498, 17:473, 23:97; history, 16:234, 19:456, 21:182; name, 16:323, 18:236; established, 16:489, 18:233, 20:306, 25:96, 30:122n; garrison withdrawn, 18:240, 19:208
Fort Benton, Mont., Blackfoot agency, 20:328; military road, 38:58, 61; fur trade, 38:199, 40:194
Fort Berthold, N.D., trading post, 27:97, 32:244, 34:326; site, 40:193
Fort Berthold Indian Reservation, 33:56
Fort Biddle, Crow Wing River, trading post, 11:372
"Fort Blunder," N.Y., 23:203, 204
Fort Bolivar, Otter Tail County, trading post, 11:373
Fort Bourbon, Man., trading post, 11:264, 18:236
Fort Bowman, Ill., history, 30:249
Fort Brady, Mich., established, 18:184n, 32:86n
Fort Buford, N.D., massacre, 34:262; fur trade, 34:327
Fort Chanyaska, Martin County, located, 38:284
Fort Charlotte, Pigeon River, site, 11:217, 358, 460, 15:240, 20:205, 24:342, 28:143n, 36:151; trading post, 37:63, 40:146
Fort Chipewyan, Alta., history, 19:223
Fort Clark, N.D., history, 12:316, 15:429; pictured, 27:255
Fort Colvile, Wash., trading post, 27:341
Fort Coulonge, Que., located, 28:10
Fort Cox, Watonwan County, described, 28:294
Fort Crawford, Wis., Eastman at, 13:

301, 19:419, 37:38; sports, 14:
423; Beaumont monument, 14:446,
15:234; pictured, 15:349, 16:53,
17:147, 296, 345, 36:44; history,
17:344, 27:253, 28:177, 40:78; Indians at, 18:404, 38:201; excavations, 20:188, 339; described, 23:
343, 36:324; post office, 40:79.
See also Prairie du Chien, Wis.
Fort Cumberland, Sask., trading post,
11:264
Fort Custer, Mont., 17:88
Fort Daer, N.D., located, 11:309,
367; trading post, 22:277; settled, 22:287
Fort Dauphin, Man., located, 18:235,
236, 35:141, 40:173; trading post,
40:174
Fort Dearborn, Ill., hunting, 14:422;
trading post, 19:299, 300; massacre, 31:240
Fort de Chartres, Ill., restored, 29:
338
Fort Defiance, Iowa, built, 11:210
Fort Defiance, N.D., trading post,
22:279
Fort Des Moines, Iowa, history, 17:
322, 24:239, 368
Fort des Prairies, Sask., trading
post, 11:265
Fort Detroit, see Fort Ponchartrain
Fort Dodge, Iowa, road, 21:233; fron-
tier post, 28:212
Fort Donelson, Tenn., captured, 25:
27, 28
Fort Douglas, Man., located, 11:355,
365; history, 13:337, 22:99
Fort Duquesne, Mille Lacs Lake,
French post, 32:227, 233, 236
Fort Edmonton, Alta., 21:186; trading
post, 36:51n; Christmas celebra-
tion, 38:386
Fort Edwards, Ill., frontier post,
15:379; U.S. factory, 17:335
Fort Ellice, Man., trading post, 22:
278, 279; located, 35:253, 261,
36:51n
Fort Ellis, Mont., 17:88
Fort Ellsworth, Va., located, 25:39n
Fort Espérance, Sask., built, 12:369
Fort Fairmont, Martin County, marker,
11:296; history, 15:489
Fort Fisher, N.C., in Civil War, 19:
338
Fort Frances, Ont., name, 11:361, 22:
273, 34:132; trading post, 16:223,
18:277, 20:72, 23:203, 24:284n,
285, 28:283; lumbering, 16:366,
31:162; pictured, 21:204, 24:284;
newspapers, 21:451; located, 22:
272, 26:230; history, 23:107, 30:
407; railroad, 31:183; paper industry, 32:61
Fort Frontenac, Ont., trading post,
18:389, 19:276, 286
Fort Gaines, see Fort Ripley
Fort Garry (Upper), Man., trading
post, 11:365, 15:120, 357, 16:480,
21:432, 33:70, 37:158n, 38:71;
port, 13:242, 18:357, 19:410, 412,
21:235, 248, 253, 270, 24:329, 32:
126, 35:261, 38:64; printing
press, 15:22; history, 15:239, 23:
186, 28:283, 33:186; pictured, 15:
240, 19:110, 21:317, 432, 31:253,
33:186, 227, 35:240, 262, 36:38,
309, 40:190; Christmas celebra-

tion, 16:382; newspaper, 16:465;
social life, 16:480; St. Boniface
bells, 20:204; garrison, 27:70;
demolished, 30:261; during Sioux
Outbreak, 34:317-324. See also
Lower Fort Garry, Red River Set-
tlements, Winnipeg
Fort George, Ore., pictured, 26:56.
See also Astoria
Fort George H. Thomas, see Fort Pem-
bina
Fort Gibraltar, Man., trading post,
11:365, 13:209; pictured, 21:432;
history, 22:99. See also Fort
Garry
Fort Gibson, Okla., frontier post,
17:322
Fort Goodhue, Sibley County, garri-
son, 38:281, 283
Fort Gratiot, Mich., located, 23:136,
137. See also Fort St. Joseph
Fort Greely, Alaska, newspaper, 23:
393
Fort Greene, Lac qui Parle County,
trading post, 11:379
Fort Hanska, Brown County, described,
36:193
Fort Harrison, Ind., treaty, 23:145n
Fort Hays Kansas State College, pub-
lication, 19:457
Fort Henry, Ont., restored, 31:118
Fort Henry, Tenn., captured, 25:26n
Fort Hill, Brown County, history, 14:
455
Fort Holes, Stearns County, built,
38:204
Fort Holmes, Mich., located, 17:81,
23:142
Fort Howard, Wis., frontier post, 11:
105, 211, 13:99, 203, 15:379, 16:
112, 33:263, 36:149; sports, 14:
421; located, 23:346
Fort Jesup, La., frontier post, 17:
322
Fort Judson, Blue Earth County,
Christmas celebration, 17:125
Fort Kaministiquia, Ont., trading
post, 11:357
Fort La Baye, Wis., 23:346n
Fort Lacorne, Sask., trading post,
11:264
Fort La Jonquière, Red Wing, French
post, 32:227-229, 233-236
Fort Langley, B.C., reconstructed,
40:191
Fort La Pointe, Goodhue County, trading post, 11:382
Fort Laramie, Wyo., history, 19:219;
pictured, 26:165, 40:196; archi-
tecture, 34:247
Fort La Reine, Man., trading post,
11:265, 18:236, 242, 22:429, 35:
141, 37:37
Fort la Traite, Sask., trading post,
11:264
Fort Leavenworth, Kan., military
road, 19:103; army post, 24:2, 28:
16n
Fort Le Sueur, Prairie Island, French
post, 11:381, 19:456
Fort Lewis, Carver County, trading
post, 11:376
Fort L'Huillier, Blue Earth County,
French post, 11:377, 13:85, 18:
233, 19:214
Fort Lincoln State Park, N.D., 22:207

Fort McKay (Fort Shelby), Wis., 17:
344, 23:343n
Fort Mackinac, Mich., 13:99; de-
scribed, 20:202, 23:142, 32:84;
restored, 23:89. See also Macki-
nac
Fort McKenzie, Mont., 35:241
Fort McLeod, N.W.T., 35:34
Fort Macon, N.C., surrender, 25:125
Fort Madison, Iowa, factory, 17:335;
described, 17:429; battles, 34:41
Fort Maitland, Fla., history, 18:325
Fort Mandan, N.D., history, 36:217,
220, 222, 224; site, 40:193; cli-
mate, 40:312
Fort Marcy, Morrison County, 36:14.
See also Fort Ripley
Fort Marin, Iowa, located, 11:384;
trading post, 19:456
Fort Maurepas, Man., trading post,
11:364, 18:236, 19:461
Fort Meigs, Ohio, siege, 12:234
Fort Michilimackinac, see Fort Macki-
nac
Fort Montgomery, N.Y., history, 23:
203, 204
Fort Necessity, Pa., markers, 14:111
Fort Niagara, N.Y., 19:297; history,
34:156
Fort Nipawee, Sask., trading post,
11:264
Fort Norman, N.W.T., history, 19:223
Fort Osage, Mo., 40:192; architec-
ture, 34:347
Fort Owen, Mont., trading post, 35:31
Fort Pembina, N.D., history, 12:438,
22:280, 27:259; depicted, 35:260
Fort Pierre, S.D., 15:357, 27:255,
40:193; flood, 11:68; trading
post, 32:124
Fort Pomme de Terre, Grant County,
history, 38:63-71; garrison, 38:
286
Fort Ponchartrain, Mich., established, 19:284; Indian hostilities, 19:288; transferred to British, 29:65
Fort Prince of Wales, Man., history,
19:223
Fort Providence, N.W.T., built, 12:
368
Fort Pulaski, Ga., captured, 25:122
Fort Randall, S.D., 27:255; Indian
resettlement area, 38:98, 354,
355, 360, 39:227, 228, 230, 238;
frontier post, 38:199, 39:129
Fort Renville, Chippewa County, described, 12:231; historic site,
23:50
Fort Resolution, N.W.T., history, 19:
223
Fort Rice, N.D., 19:205, 206; post,
34:326, 38:228
Fort Ridgely, Nicollet County, frontier post, 11:133, 163n, 12:115n,
212, 14:110, 18:311, 29:234, 237,
238, 243, 246, 30:25, 36:13, 95,
38:118; river port, 11:136, 137,
164-180, 36:252, 256, 258, 37:227;
maps, 11:167, 20:148, 34:236, 38:
282, 39:127; name, 11:177n; roads,
11:393, 19:103, 21:234, 27:344,
35:251, 38:217; archives, 11:444,
18:208, 20:327, 22:297-301; in Indian wars, 12:100, 116n, 303, 15:
224, 17:337, 18:209, 23:403, 25:
383, 33:191, 38:95-97, 101, 128,

131n, 136-139, 144-146, 148, 280,
283; pictured, 12:117, 14:234,
357, 15:137, 20:150, 454, 22:333,
33:264, 36:253, 37:74, 348, 38:
102, 145; history, 14:459, 16:493,
20:94, 191, 208, 22:447, 27:343,
29:317n; pageants, 15:359, 16:359,
487, 20:449; excavations, 15:490,
18:51, 66, 107, 328, 458, 19:53,
225, 345, 20:146-155, 208, 361,
21:327, 23:280; cemetery, 21:438;
hospital, 24:372; soldier vote,
26:196, 201, 208; Sioux reservation, 28:212, 344n, 29:233, 235,
244, 245, 34:328; in fiction, 35:
288; historic site, 39:33, 40:146.
See also Fort Ridgely Memorial
State Park
Fort Ridgely Choral Festival Association, 15:490
Fort Ridgely Historical Association,
15:490
Fort Ridgely Memorial State Park,
pageant, 11:456; battle commemo-
rated, 13:443; established, 20:
147, 37:59, 39:299; publication,
20:208; museum, 21:445; described,
23:192. See also Fort Ridgely
Fort Ridgely State Park and Historical Association, 19:465, 20:464
Fort Ripley (Fort Gaines), Morrison
County, mail service, 11:308, 40:
83, 87; maps, 11:372, 28:217, 38:
282; history, 11:444, 12:202, 317,
13:340, 14:435, 17:225, 18:208,
333, 19:50, 96, 23:298, 28:205-
224, 339-344, 29:270, 34:42, 35:
337, 40:146; historic site, 12:
101, 15:366, 28:293; frontier
post, 14:110, 19:353, 20:191, 29:
233-235, 238, 243, 246, 30:109,
36:13, 14, 39:175; depicted, 14:
335, 28:212, 36:15, 37:348, 40:
146; publication, 15:23; buildings, 15:116, 24:132; in Sioux
Outbreak, 15:396, 20:192, 33:281n,
38:275, 280, 39:175; Christmas
celebration, 16:380; roads, 19:
103, 21:231, 40:233; mission, 20:
431, 24:13n; soldier vote, 26:196;
churches, 28:219, 36:238; name,
35:182; historical meeting, 35:340
Fort Robinson, Neb., 24:208
Fort Rouge, Man., history, 11:365,
13:209, 22:99; map, 18:235; located, 18:236
Fort Rouillé, Ont., 22:64
Fort St. Anthony, see Fort Snelling
Fort St. Antoine, Wis., 11:452, 15:
100; history, 11:383, 16:114, 19:
456, 33:352
Fort St. Charles, Northwest Angle,
trading post, 11:362, 12:307, 364,
17:224, 18:276, 19:461, 29:133,
31:52, 40:146; historic site, 11:
448, 37:61, 62, 308; history, 18:
231-248, 272, 21:401, 39:302;
maps, 18:235, 19:214, 32:228;
name, 18:236; proposed state park,
20:42, 343, 21:408, 22:214; mission, 23:97; markers, 23:404, 32:
62; located, 24:318, 27:70; chapel, 37:37
Fort St. Croix, Wis., trading post,
11:385
Fort St. James, B.C., 40:191

Fort St. Joseph, Mich., British post,
19:198; French post, 23:137n
Fort St. Louis, Wis., trading post,
11:359, 19:314, 20:13-17, 28:147n.
See also Fond du Lac, Minn.
Fort St. Nicolas, Wis., trading post,
11:384, 19:456
Fort St. Pierre, Ont., trading post,
11:361, 12:364, 14:231, 19:456,
27:97, 29:133; name, 18:236; maps,
19:214, 32:228
Fort Shelby (Fort McKay), Wis., 17:
344, 23:343n
Fort Sheridan, Ill., 23:268
Fort Simpson, N.W.T., history, 19:223
Fort Sisseton (Fort Wadsworth), S.D.,
trail, 16:485, 19:227; history,
19:107, 22:297, 25:100
Fort Slocum, Watonwan County, history, 29:272
Fort Smith, Ark., in Civil War, 40:
286, 291
Fort Snelling (Fort St. Anthony),
Hennepin County, river port, 11:
165, 210, 12:164, 13:224, 230-232,
330, 16:26, 478, 18:372, 433, 20:
378, 379, 22:13, 27:355, 29:198,
31:209, 33:353, 36:252, 40:411;
visitors, 11:208, 15:473, 18:156,
159, 23:170; markers, 11:330, 15:
359, 26:388, 29:352; trading post,
11:376, 13:222, 240, 14:231, 15:
222, 303, 40:184, 358; schools,
11:431, 14:143, 17:478, 25:19n,
26:232, 35:290; archives, 11:444,
12:190, 317, 16:97, 21:207, 314,
22:297, 23:271, 25:289, 398, 26:
32, 27:130; location, 12:61, 16:
192, 22:32, 23:213, 25:114, 30:
211n, 31:155; troops, 12:61, 17:
155n, 20:122, 21:227, 24:126, 144,
28:78, 208, 33:87, 118n, 316, 36:
13-17, 38:2; churches, 12:397, 16:
231, 354; established, 12:437, 14:
166, 338, 15:380, 479, 16:454, 17:
81, 354, 22:287, 23:128n, 213,
338n, 33:263; fairs, 12:445, 17:
72, 22:256, 259; history, 13:212,
16:351, 18:108, 399-406, 19:354,
21:309, 401, 27:130, 261, 29:100,
30:372, 35:178-192, 340, 36:69,
105, 40:138; pictured, 13:301, 14:
335, 15:469, 16:53, 17:147, 154,
155n, 19:419, 20:191, 334, 453,
21:186, 22:333, 434, 25:304, 26:
142, 171, 359, 27:167, 271, 28:
349, 29:286, 318, 30:157, 32:12-
14, 61, 125, 33:113, 114, 119, 34:
30, 141, 35:22, 157 (cover), 178-
188, 191, 365, 36:16, 37:37, 38:
37, 39:173 (cover); officers, 13:
301, 15:311, 395, 17:67, 153,
154n, 156, 225, 464, 18:159, 399,
19:448, 20:419, 22:287, 24:56, 27:
67, 253, 28:15-19, 177, 29:100,
30:98-103, 189, 33:263, 36:42n,
40:262; name, 14:110, 17:450, 18:
450, 26:212, 18:450; refugee haven, 14:286, 20:56, 23:94, 29:232;
health conditions, 14:289, 15:302,
16:353, 20:91, 33:91, 39:260; Indian treaties, 14:352, 18:339, 20:
120; wildlife, 14:423, 18:159, 32:
97, 35:242; agriculture, 15:222,
311, 16:351, 31:96, 33:263, 39:
251; missionaries, 15:242, 16:134,
18:197, 21:21-23, 24:4, 12, 33:90;

historical meetings, 15:309-312,
23:167, 267, 24:30; buildings, 15:
360, 397, 16:39, 249, 17:88, 18:
338, 37:189 (cover); frontier
life, 15:395-404, 16:22, 373, 18:
399-406, 455, 21:79, 22:312, 28:
177, 29:100, 158, 316-320, 30:98-
103, 189, 31:96, 237, 32:97, 33:
197, 36:14-17, 315, 38:385, 39:
312, 313; military post, 15:478,
16:22, 17:154n, 464, 18:159, 455,
19:388, 447, 448, 20:90, 21:227,
22:57, 206, 434, 24:1-3, 355, 27:
67, 288, 29:231, 239, 317-320, 33:
316, 34:42, 35:357, 36:149, 39:
129, 254; post office, 15:487, 40:
78-82; described, 16:39, 279, 18:
156, 30:210-215, 372, 31:155, 33:
122, 40:146; ferry, 16:72, 279n,
29:208n, 39:328; diorama, 16:213,
17:56, 72, 207, 463; Dred Scott's
residence, 16:350, 19:354, 20:89,
420, 21:165, 25:202, 27:167, 29:
351, 30:265, 33:138, 39:299; Civil
War days, 17:112, 23:212, 25:13-
15, 26:195, 197, 201, 205, 206,
27:317, 28:325, 33:87, 37:
213n, 215, 38:246, 273, 292, 39:
175, 204, 40:292; climate, 17:244,
21:435, 22:93; cemetery, 17:480,
18:108, 400, 19:95, 30:212; Indian
battles, 18:404, 20:90, 24:12, 15-
25, 25:272; Indian settlement, 18:
448, 21:163n; sutler, 18:468, 19:
95, 23:288, 24:127, 26:362, 27:
311, 40:25-31; roads, 19:103, 29:
116, 126; census, 19:350, 20:123;
chaplain, 19:355, 24:13, 36:238;
library, 19:448, 21:19; land
sales, 20:336, 25:289, 27:314-318,
29:206, 243, 30:181, 34:145, 312,
38:202; museum, 20:342, 21:316,
22:207-209; squatters, 22:51, 29:
241, 242; in World Wars, 23:212,
24:4-10; theatrical performances,
23:306, 307, 30:388; Indian agency, 24:11-13, 26:362, 31:211, 38:
362, 39:314, 40:261; mills, 24:
126, 29:100, 208n, 30:195, 34:49;
hospital, 24:209, 372; historic
site, 27:166, 30:258, 35:339, 365-
367, 384, 36:152, 230, 240, 37:44,
59, 67, 68, 224, 39:33, 82, 264,
40:36, 37, 48, 92; abandoned, 28:
52, 77, 37:67; band, 28:320; Sioux
prisoners, 29:239, 37:272, 38:110,
113, 142, 353, 355-357, 361, 39:
228; surveyed, 29:316; in fiction,
30:246, 36:76; in Sioux Outbreak,
34:319, 38:97, 98, 275, 280; balloon experiment, 39:278, 279. See
also Camp Coldwater, Round Tower
Fort Snelling State Park, 40:316
Fort Snelling State Park Association,
37:223
Fort Stevenson, N.D., established,
32:243; fur trade, 34:325; archaeology, 34:354; Christmas at, 38:
386
Fort Stewart, Mont., 27:255
Fort Stikine, B.C., 17:446
Fort Sully, S.D., frontier post, 34:
131, 39:129; fur trade, 34:326,
327
Fort Sumter, S.C., in Civil War, 20:
270, 28:325, 29:64
Fort Sweney, Goodhue County, 16:309

Fort Tekamamiouen, Ont., trading post, 11:361

Fort Thompson, S.D., Sioux reservation, 34:328, 38:360, 363, 364, 39:227-240; dam, 39:213 (cover)

Fort Three Rivers, Ont., trading post, 11:357

Fort Totten, N.D., Indian agency, 16:73; military post, 21:99, 22:320; trail, 28:80

Fort Towson, Okla., frontier post, 17:322

Fort Union, N.D., 15:357, 27:255; trading post, 11:377, 14:223, 20:119n, 38:199, 385

Fort Vancouver, Wash., schools, 25:191; trading post, 26:55, 27:37, 29:340, 36:315

Fort Vaudreuil, Iowa, French post, 32:227, 235, 236; name, 32:232

Fort Vermilion, Sask., 37:175

Fort Vincennes, Ind., 18:390

Fort Wadsworth, see Fort Sisseton

Fort Walla Walla, Wash., 38:217

Fort Washington, Lake Traverse, trading post, 11:379

Fort Washington, Md., 25:117

Fort Wayne, Ind., frontier post, 15:379, 380; Indian agency, 24:343

Fort William (Thunder Bay), Ont., fur trade, 11:357, 12:91, 294, 376, 423, 16:23, 201, 223, 17:111, 18:215, 328, 19:109, 20:13, 14, 21:118, 120, 121, 22:277n, 278, 432, 23:92, 28:14n, 29:132, 31:56, 34:345, 36:315, 39:302, 40:169, 181; missions, 12:82, 427, 13:187, 29:168, 37:37, 39:303, 309; attacked, 12:287, 20:17, 40:166; name, 12:369, 23:272, 29:166; located, 12:372; port, 16:478, 18:216, 34:14; climate, 17:245n; pictured, 17:345; map, 22:272; historical meeting, 23:270, 396; grain center, 25:54, 28:283, 35:48; bird life, 35:242; history, 37:86; Catholic church, 39:309

Fort Winnebago, Wis., 18:154; frontier post, 11:452, 36:149, 159

Fort Yellowstone, Wyo., 17:88

Fort York, see York Factory

Fortier, Cyrille, author, 18:473

Fortier, Joseph, papers, 19:450

Fortieth Iowa Volunteer Infantry, 40:285

Fortieth New York Volunteer Infantry, 25:384

Fortschrift, Der (New Ulm), German paper, 27:343

Fortuna, Pine County, platted, 40:244

"Fortune," steamboat, 22:18

Forty-Eighters, see Germans

Forty-fifth U.S. Volunteer Infantry, 16:336

Forty-ninth parallel, see Boundaries

Forty Siding, Lake County, railroad station, 34:181

Fosdick, Raymond B., letter, 18:314

Foshay, Wilbur B., 25:279, 38:243

Fosnes, C. A., 17:355

Foss, Arthur, publisher, 30:273

Foss, Bishop C. D., 31:88

Foss, Rev. Claude W., 17:329

Foss, Dorothy, 28:300, 30:79; speaker, 29:184; author, 29:369, 30:86

Foss, Hans A., editor, 29:302; author, 31:130

Fosston, history, 14:358, 15:251, 23:198, 25:212, 34:359; creamery, 20:466; railroad, 23:25, 33, 29:137, 138; market, 23:28; newspaper, 30:273; logging, 33:356

Fossum, Alvira T., 34:63

Fossum, Andrew, 39:135; author, 13:197

Fossum, Paul R., "Early Milling," 11:271-282; speaker, 11:291; author, 12:80, 28:331

Foster, Dr.---, 24:116

Foster, Arthur P., speaker, 18:334; author, 18:463

Foster, Mrs. Burnside, house, 36:216, 217

Foster, Mrs. Daisy, 18:95, 111; speaker, 16:244

Foster, Charles H., work reviewed, 37:84

Foster, Everett W., reminiscences, 15:223, 16:52

Foster, Mrs. Fred, 17:124; speaker, 17:315

Foster, Gil, author, 24:92

Foster, James S., author, 11:324

Foster, John A., 39:18, 20

Foster, John B., speaker, 40:364

Foster, Mary S., 16:334

Foster, Mrs. Nancy, 24:116

Foster, Neva, author, 18:118

Foster, Robert O., author, 13:114

Foster, Stephen C., composer, 15:115

Foster, Suel, horticulturist, 23:91

Foster, Dr. Thomas, 17:278, 35:336, 355; physician to Sioux, 11:182; speaker, 13:146, 22:349; publisher, 14:179n, 188n, 360, 18:472, 24:384, 27:72, 32:27, 33:329, 34:70; author, 17:250n, 39:49; portrait, 26:142; treaty commissioner, 32:71, 38:2; postmaster, 34:155; Ramsey's secretary, 35:355n, 37:326, 327, 39:43

Foster-Harris (William F. Harris), work reviewed, 35:146

Foster Township, Faribault County, history, 39:212

Fotheringham, Janet, author, 16:468

Fountain Cave, St. Paul, described, 16:278, 20:124, 30:210, 33:121

Fountain City, Wis., population, 12:63; founded, 14:232; trading post, 20:443; pictured, 33:117n, 37:296, 40:63; theater, 34:239; river port, 37:283, 292

Four-H clubs, 18:340, 24:80; activities, 17:124, 227, 18:467, 473, 20:464, 22:111, 446; origins, 22:328, 438; publication, 22:424; history, 28:377, 35:149

Four Mile Lake, Cook County, logging railroad, 36:132

Four Minute Men, 12:193, 26:157

Four-Town Farm Bureau, 16:132

Fourierist movement, 31:112

Fournie, Mrs. Fred, 22:54

Fournier, Alexis, artist, 14:38, 20:185, 30:86

Fournier, Mother St. John, 30:3, 4, 8

Fourth Michigan Cavalry, 29:374

Fourth Minnesota Volunteer Infantry, in Civil War, 15:224, 19:343, 450, 28:326, 33:211-213, 35:245, 39:179; votes, 26:196, 201, 36:170; Germans in, 33:84; homecoming, 38:287, 289, 291

Fourth of July, early celebrations, 12:392, 13:145, 14:353, 16:127, 168, 173, 498, 17:273, 19:254, 20:102, 208, 351, 362, 23:26, 24:12, 224, 384, 26:287, 29:359, 30:200, 31:92, 34:101, 102, 35:50, 84, 85, 105, 38:72, 73, 40:60, 61, 300, 331; baseball games, 19:180; Wisconsin, 20:339; Marine, 26:253, 36:197 (cover); Stillwater prison, 37:146; Indian participation, 37:276

Fourth Wisconsin Volunteer Infantry, in Civil War, 22:319, 23:371

Fowler, ---, real-estate dealer, 24:134

Fowler, Arthur B., 14:331

Fowler, C. N., politician, 22:79

Fowler, Bishop Charles H., career, 12:201

Fowler, Charles R., 12:454

Fowler, Edith, 14:436

Fowler, Harold, 18:473

Fowler, Norman, in Civil War, 25:229, 247, 248, 250, 346, 349, 360

Fowler, Orson S., architect, 38:348, 349

Fowler, William, 22:265, 26:109

Fowler family, genealogy, 14:436

Fowler settlement, Martin County, history, 11:463

Fox, Dixon R., 11:93, 14:429, 31:112; author-editor, 11:99, 323, 13:431, 14:341, 16:196, 17:199; memorial, 27:162

Fox, Edith M., review by, 33:37

Fox, George R., author, 35:43

Fox, H. Clifford, author, 24:366

Fox, Lawrence K., 20:427; author, 17:220; speaker, 19:424n, 21:425

Fox, Patrick, house, 38:341

Fox, William, outlaw, 17:421

Fox, 22:194; hunts, 14:421, 422; in fur trade, 23:330, 30:133, 134, 35:295, 40:212. See also Wildlife

Fox Indians, massacred, 11:431; relations with French, 12:76, 19:274, 288, 32:227, 232, 238n; pictured, 20:56, 33:20; lead miners, 23:344; history, 36:191; culture, 37:174

Fox Lake Island, Martin County, legend, 34:315

Fox Lake Township, Martin County, school, 20:102; history, 34:315

Fox Prairie, Mo., river town, 17:431n

Fox River, Ill., Norwegian settlement, 12:181, 15:473, 19:200

Fox River, Wis., travel on, 13:225, 20:68, 23:345-347

Fox-Wisconsin portage, 11:246, 17:299n, 18:154, 20:68, 23:345

Foy, Eddie, actor, 28:106

Fracastorius (Fracastoro), Girolamo, author, 21:367

Fradenburg, Mrs. A. G., author, 12:207

Fraigger, A., 14:261

France, colonization projects, 11:77, 78, 16:448-450, 18:233, 383-398, 19:393-398, 20:439, 22:62-65, 29:164, 32:184, 33:36, 34:117, 299, 39:337; archives, 11:204, 15:61, 36:29; currency in Canada, 11:237; flour milling, 11:272-277; sale of Louisiana, 15:472, 18:384, 23:258; boundary disputes, 18:428-430; relations with U.S., 23:145n, 36:30;

relations with English, 24:150;
royal medals, 25:265; gifts to
U.S., 30:179. See also French,
French Canadians

Franchère, Gabriel, trader, 34:207;
work reviewed, 34:215; career, 12:
201, 13:439; author, 19:109, 29:
267, 31:56, 34:215

Franchère, Hoyt C., translator, 40:
404

Francis, David R., ambassador, 38:313

Francis, E. K., author, 35:247

Francis, William T., memorial, 12:194

Francis Joseph, Sister, 30:13; journey to Minnesota, 30:2-8

Franciscan order, Slovenian, 15:446;
Minnesota, 17:84, 118, 20:218,
446, 21:457, 35:135, 136, 39:
307. See also Recollect Order

Francisco, Oliver P., diary, 26:282

Franciscus, Frank, author, 15:484,
17:125, 234, 22:444, 24:88, 272,
381, 382, 27:174, 365, 28:294

Francois, ---, voyageur, 17:291;
trader, 19:78

Franconia, Chisago County, history,
23:400, 28:196, 380, 36:106; architecture, 38:343, 352

Frank, John, pioneer, 11:185

Frank, Mrs. John, 21:416

Frank, Joseph, musician, 33:104

Frank, Rev. Melvin, speaker, 14:237

"Frank Pargoud," steamboat, 25:72

"Frank Steele," steamboat, 11:126,
139, 16:40, 41, 44, 33:198n, 34:
26n, 36:252-258, 37:225, 227, 38:
173

Frankel, Hiram D., papers, 12:193,
14:104, 15:225, 22:87, 36:319

Frankford, Mower County, Norwegian
settlement, 12:269; in county seat
fight, 15:250, 21:223; school, 37:
64

Franklin, Benjamin, 15:7, 19:311, 22:
313, 359, 34:203, 40:294; biography, 21:10-12; printer, 33:300;
author, 34:212; inventor, 35:92

Franklin, Don, scuba diver, 38:24-34

Franklin, James, printer and publisher, 15:6, 34:203

Franklin, Sir John, explorer, 25:273,
28:341, 29:248, 34:80

Franklin, Mr. and Mrs. William, 18:
321

Franklin, Gen. William B., 25:36,
129, 132, 234, 235, 244, 245n

Franklin, Renville County, history,
13:453; newspapers, 17:103, 36:
205, 283; flour mill, 22:348; Finnish settlement, 25:318

Franklin Avenue, Minneapolis, name,
24:127

Franklin School, St. Paul, 16:370

Franklin Steele Square, Minneapolis,
name, 20:369

Franklin Tribune, 36:284

Frankson, Thomas, legislator, 33:159

Frantz, Joe B., work reviewed, 40:403

Frantzen, Jens, Mormon missionary,
36:289

Franzen, Anders, archaeologist, 38:
244

Franzmann, Carl A., work reviewed,
22:412

Fraser, A. D., author, 19:105

Fraser, Alexander, 17:111

Fraser, Donald M., legislator, 40:362

Fraser, Duncan, 31:162

Fraser, Jack, see Frazer, Joseph Jack

Fraser, John, 17:445; letter, 17:446

Fraser, John, Jr., trader, 40:177

Fraser, P., 11:238n

Fraser, Simon, I, trader, 12:294,
372, 13:432, 20:327, 34:344

Fraser, Simon, II, explorer, 13:432,
29:340, 31:1, 35:35, 36:64, 40:191

Fraser, Dr. Simon, 18:103, 36:315

Fraser family, correspondence, 17:
444, 446

Fraser River, B.C., 38:386; gold mining, 13:177, 15:357, 35:249, 251,
38:65; travel on, 29:340; trading
post, 40:191

Fratzke, Mrs. Erick, speaker, 23:398

Frazee, Mrs. C. P., 22:442; speaker,
18:110

Frazer, James W., 14:441

Frazer (Fraser, Frazier), Joseph
Jack, mixed-blood, 11:181; scout,
12:209, 38:101, 139; career, 15:
383, 32:114, 33:139, 37:186; hunter, 15:386-394; pictured, 16:473,
38:148; language teacher, 21:277;
characterized, 22:29, 30

Frazer, Robert W., work reviewed, 40:
42

Frazier, E. Franklin, author, 31:245

Frazier, Jack, see Frazer, Joseph
Jack

Frazier, Lynn J., 18:314, 34:222, 37:
39

Frazier, Philip, speaker, 16:303; author, 16:484

Freaney, Mrs. W. J., author, 26:300

Frear, Dana W., 19:360, 20:96, 22:50,
26:284, 27:145, 146, 172; speaker,
20:49, 22:48, 339, 28:386, 391,
29:91; author, 23:101, 27:176, 29:
179

Frear, Mrs. Dana W., speaker, 29:91

Fredeen, H. E., author, 22:431

Fredensburg, Nels, speaker, 20:95

Frederick, Francis, 28:192

Frederick, John H., author, 14:230,
349

Frederick, John T., 25:175; author,
11:208, 23:117, 157, 25:297, 31:
138, 146, 34:175, 37:339

Fredericks, Morris, author, 15:134

Fredericksburg, Va., in Civil War,
20:278, 25:233-238, 242-244, 344-
347, 349

Frederiksen, N. C., 20:408

Fredine, Gordon, author, 22:214

Free silver, political issue, 16:499,
39:29, 93, 94, 102-107, 327, 332

Free Soil party, 30:26, 189

Freeberg, Ron, author, 38:43

Freeborn, platted, 13:342; Congregational church, 13:449

Freeborn County, history, 11:289, 14:
303-315, 21:340, 23:301, 30:271,
35:335; pageant, 11:461; ethnic
groups, 12:265, 269, 21:98, 449,
31:27; railroad, 13:342; churches,
13:449, 21:449, 22:221; county
seat, 14:306, 15:346, 20:357; Masonic lodge, 15:136; sheriff, 17:
336; agriculture, 18:408; first
house, 18:467; archives, 19:52,
66, 88, 110; Grange organizations,
19:364; newspapers, 24:272; in
World War II, 26:389, 27:175;

medicine, 29:353; poorhouse, 38:
369; politics, 40:328

Freeborn County Agricultural Society,
22:258

Freeborn County Cooperative Oil Co.,
24:174

Freeborn County Historical Society,
16:365, 490, 29:178, 30:166, 35:50

Freedman's Bureau, in Civil War, 14:
101

Freedom, Lake County, railroad station, 34:181

Freedom (Manila, P.I.), file acquired, 17:469

"Freedom Train," Minnesota itinerary,
28:369

Freeland, George E., author, 24:78,
28:357

Freeman, Daniel H., 33:294

Freeman, Douglas, author, 21:10, 51

Freeman, E. M., "A Scientist Looks at
History," 20:1-6; speaker, 20:49;
author, 20:74

Freeman, Judge Edward, speaker, 14:
463; author, 23:387

Freeman, Edward A., historian, 18:3,
19:6

Freeman, Helga, author, 27:368

Freeman, John F., compiler, 40:409

Freeman, John H., author, 12:340

Freeman, Larry, work reviewed, 33:133

Freeman, Mary W., 20:110

Freeman, Orville L., governor, 34:
191, 35:191, 40:148, 297; speaker,
35:384, 37:135, 343

Freeman, Larpenteur and Co., St.
Paul, merchants, 14:380

Freeman Township, Freeborn County,
Norwegian settlement, 12:269

Freemasons, Duluth, 11:417, 21:223,
27:81; Minnesota lodges, 13:215,
217, 15:136, 366, 16:368, 17:389,
19:236, 20:102, 21:115, 23:171,
24:94, 28:381, 33:268, 310, 40:
331, 337; welfare work, 14:298;
women's affiliate, 16:370; St.
Paul, 19:431, 33:196, 197n; Canada, 21:247; grand masters, 23:48;
library, 26:82

Free-thought movement, Carver County,
24:215, 218, 219

Freewill Baptist Society, 14:147

Freier Sängerbund, male chorus, 32:
240

"Freighter," steamboat, 19:386, 21:
250, 36:252, 254, 256

Freiligrath, Ferdinand, 19:416

Freimuth's Store, Duluth, 26:276, 28:
78, 182

Freistatt, Wis., Lutheran church, 14:
54

Freman, John Finley, author, 36:323

Frémiot, Nicholas, Jesuit missionary,
39:308, 309

Frémont, John C., 18:156, 26:154; explorer, 12:442, 15:110, 16:349,
18:314, 19:192, 27:38, 350, 29:61,
30:209, 31:196, 200, 207, 33:290,
34:212, 219, 303, 35:97, 36:277,
37:35, 62, 38:201, 40:96; career,
13:439; author, 18:160, 22:154,
155n, 29:187; general, 20:272,
278, 25:138, 32:23, 24; presidential candidate, 20:282-284, 32:28,
37:307

Fremont, see Silver Lake, McLeod
County

Fremont City, Wright County, townsite, 18:210
Fremont Club, St. Anthony, 24:139, 32:164
Fremont County, Iowa, history, 25:300
Fremont, Elkhorn and Missouri Valley Railroad, 39:298
Fremstad, Olive, singer, 16:238, 22: 104, 33:100, 102, 104, 34:214, 35: 74; career, 18:450, 36:106, 37:262
French, Alice, 20:82
French, Anne W., biography, 17:477
French, Bella, editor, 26:297-299
French, Benjamin F., author, 25:193; translator, 34:118
French, C. A., author, 16:257, 17: 130, 242; publisher, 20:216, 28: 385
French, Daniel C., sculptor, 28:396
French, Rev. Horton I., speaker, 28: 392
French, Katharine, see Wheelock, Mrs. Joseph A.
French, Lynn, 19:115, 22:104, 23:99
French, Mrs. Lynn, 18:463; author, 19:233
French, Parker H., frontier journalist, 27:2
French, Mrs. Peggy L., 27:341
French, Theodore, 26:155, 34:331, 333; author, 26:67
French, explorations, 11:204, 211, 348, 12:107, 282, 306, 347-358, 14:214, 15:93, 157-180, 475, 16: 453, 18:233, 22:60, 178, 429, 24: 318, 26:379, 29:153, 32:112, 248, 34:216, 37:86, 39:81; Canadian regime, 15:94-98, 18:439, 19:198, 21:397, 34:305, 310, 35:151, 40: 145; place names, 16:350, 21:346, 26:248; relations with British, 16:404-406, 417, 418n, 18:194, 19: 296, 21:395, 23:160, 29:65, 30: 375, 36:272; social life, 19:218; libraries, 20:202; pioneers, 28: 253-255, 29:337, 30:249; in Civil War, 33:84; bibliography, 39:165, 40:312. See also French Canadians, Fur trade, Voyageurs
French and Indian War, results, 12: 357; history, 15:109, 36:273, 275; source material, 18:195; causes, 21:395; Indian activity, 32:233
French Canadians, in lumber industry, 13:351, 36:162; pioneers, 14:216, 356, 15:252, 18:228, 470, 19:232, 21:454, 22:51, 25:315, 27:134, 135, 28:380, 30:395, 34:313, 35: 221, 222; St. Croix Valley, 15: 238, 17:389; characterized, 15: 303, 20:341, 23:254, 343; St. Lawrence area, 16:477, 23:385; folklore, 17:204, 20:72, 22:139, 24: 367, 28:177, 34:126, 214, 35:339, 37:345, 38:200; westward movement, 20:422; in fiction, 22:76; described, 2 :145, 147; missions, 23:97, 24:41, 179, 31:239, 39:301-310; politics, 24:46; in mining, 27:204, 207-209, 215, 40:341; architecture, 28:283, 32:109; agriculture, 28:366. See also French, Fur trade, Voyageurs
French Lake, Wright County, Finnish settlement, 20:214, 22:392n
French language, in Mississippi Valley, 23:84; among Indians, 23:236

French Revolution, 18:396, 23:259
French River, Ont., trade route, 11: 233, 25:274, 40:208
French River, St. Louis County, settled, 34:177; post office, 34:186
French Roller Mill, Faribault, 11:280
Freneau, Philip, 18:397
Frenière, François, trader, 11:379, 22:285
Frenière, Narcisse, 12:127, 18:209; trader, 22:285
Frenière, Susan, see Brown, Mrs. Joseph R.
Frenkel, Albert W., 33:112n
Frenz, Horst, author, 23:286
Frenzeny, Paul, artist, 27:159
Fresenius, Karl R., author, 21:371
Fretheim, S. J., author, 25:195
Fretz, J. Winfield, author, 20:459
Freuchen, Peter, in Arctic, 17:171; author, 35:240
Freudenreich, Frederick de, house, 15:55; papers, 16:71
Freund, Josie, 27:99
Frey, J. William, 26:168
Frey, John R., editor, 39:198
Frick, A. H., author, 15:487
Friday Study Club, Stillwater, 24:194
Fridley, Abram M., Indian agent, 12: 83, 13:447, 30:5; house, 30:74; politician, 37:47, 48, 50
Fridley, Russell W., "The Writings of Jonathan Carver," 34:154-159; "Fort Snelling," 35:178-192; "Minnesota's Historic Sites," 37:58-70; "Charles E. Flandrau," 38:116-125; "Preserving Our Green Legacy," 40:131-136; reviews by, 34: 40, 166, 206, 35:42, 147, 285, 36: 33, 95, 273, 37:81, 305, 38:239, 331, 39:75, 254, 336, 40:42; work reviewed, 38:86; MHS director, 34: 175, 315, 36:284; author, 34:220, 35:156, 233, 340, 36:69, 105, 152, 230, 37:42, 44, 38:193, 40:92, 148, 316, 364; honored, 35:383
Fridley Township, Anoka County, history, 13:446; name, 24:332n
Friedl, Ernestine, author, 35:244
Friedmann, Franklin, potter, 33:231
Friedrich, Anton, 18:471
Friedrich, Carl J., author, 31:242
Friedrich, George W., conservationist, 32:63
Friedrich, Otto, author, 37:184
Friedrichs, Mrs. George W., 23:392
Friend, Andrew, diary, 16:489
Friend, Charles, portrait, 25:187
Friends of Democracy, war activities, 23:292
Friends of Temperance, history, 22: 393
Friends of the University of Minnesota Library, 28:393
Fries, Mrs. C., 14:106
Fries, Robert F., review by, 36:28; work reviewed, 32:252; author, 30: 71, 32:253, 34:263
Friesland, Pine County, Dutch settlement, 13:427, 28:130, 131
Frigid Frogs, see Duluth Skin-Divers Club
Friis, Herman R., review by, 34:302; work reviewed, 40:403; author, 34: 215; speaker, 40:411
Frink, George W., 17:235

Frisbys Grove, Stevens County, described, 19:227
Frisians, Minnesota, 28:121, 126, 127; Wisconsin, 28:379
Fritsch, Charles T., archaeologist, 38:244
Fritsche, Dr. Carl, author, 23:295
Fritsche, Dr. Louis A., career, 36: 282
Fritschel, Gottfried, journalist, 12: 195
Fritschel, Sigmund, journalist, 12: 195
Fritschel, Werner, author, 11:320
Fritz, Henry E., reviews by, 39:292, 40:261; work reviewed, 38:329
Fritz, Ruth, 21:45, 22:45
Fritzen, John, speaker, 15:138, 492; author, 16:101, 472, 17:233, 25: 185
Fritzner, Johan, 17:178
Frivold, Hjalmer E., author, 14:333
Frizell, Joseph P., 40:229
Frobisher, Benjamin, trader, 11:251-253, 258, 261, 263-265, 267, 269, 14:229, 16:201, 23:256, 28:5, 143, 37:254
Frobisher, John, trader, 20:326
Frobisher, Joseph, trader, 11:261-264, 364, 14:229, 16:200, 20:327, 28:5, 143n, 37:254
Frobisher, Thomas, trader, 11:264
Frog Point, Traill County, N.D., river port, 19:410, 20:207, 24:333
Frog Portage, Sask., fur trade route, 12:361
Frog Town, Anoka, 25:364
Frogner, Ellen, work reviewed, 38:192
Frohn Township, Beltrami County, history, 15:244
Frohsinn Singing Society, Minneapolis, 32:167
Froidevaux, Henri, author, 22:39
Froiseth, James E., 13:199
Fröisland, Nils, 20:397
Fröisland, Mrs. Nils, 20:398
Frontenac, Louis de Buade, comte de, 20:68, governor of New France, 12: 353, 18:388, 19:278, 281-283, 286, 34:310; relations with Jesuits, 14:229, 19:279, 21:396; author, 16:199; military activities, 18: 391, 392
Frontenac, resort, 11:318, 16:33, 19: 451, 20:307, 394, 27:368, 36:37 (cover), 92, 93, 37:64; French post, 11:382, 452, 32:227; marker, 13:339; history, 14:31-43, 22:83, 420, 33:188, 35:245; historical tours, 20:187, 306, 36:240; cemetery, 20:309; school, 29:87; camp meetings, 31:79, 92; mission, 38: 193
Frontenac Inn, 19:451, 20:306, 307
Frontenac State Park, 16:256, 20:42, 343, 35:245, 292
Frontier, Canada, 11:107; development, 11:189, 428-430, 39:129; cultural aspects, 12:198, 15:381, 382, 16:30-32, 17:411, 20:269, 22: 173, 23:62; significance, 13:3-23, 21:91, 29:258; in fur trade, 13: 334; defined, 15:378; economic aspect, 16:23-26, 17:322, 33:215, 35:213; political influence, 17: 106; Middle Western, 18:304, 35: 42; word usages, 19:241-246; in-

stitutions, 20:19-28; in art, 33:
263. See also Turner, Frederick
J.; Westward movement
Frontier Business (Morris), history,
12:202
Frontier Guardian (Kanesville, Iowa),
12:439
Frontier Monthly (Hastings), literary
magazine, 13:429, 26:294
Frontier Scout (Fort Rice, N.D.), 21:
416
Fronts, Mary Ann, clerk typist, 25:41
Frost, ---, pioneer, 20:311
Frost, A. B., artist, 33:142
Frost, Mrs. Bessie G., speaker, 14:
122
Frost, Harry J., author, 39:300
Frost, J., furniture dealer, 15:185
Frost, Jake, 14:308, 314
Frost, Mrs. Margaret, 14:314
Frost, Mary, 14:307
Frost, Robert, poet, 20:116, 32:187,
33:265, 36:78
Frost, Norwegian settlement, 23:290
Fruechte, Henry C., pioneer farmer,
22:223
Fruen, W. H., 25:410
Fruit, Lucretia, 12:167
Fruth, Rev. Alban, author, 36:192
Fry, Elizabeth, evangelist, 18:255
Fry, Smith D., author, 17:217
Fry, Col. Speed S., 38:263
Fryckberg, Marjorie, author, 25:202
Fryklund, P. O., 18:274, 336, 21:109,
25:409, 26:180, 30:82
Fuchs, Alphonse, speaker, 29:277
Fuess, Claude M., author, 13:46
Fugina, Frank J., steamboat captain,
27:63
Fugitive Slave Law, 16:87, 24:307,
312, 314, 32:16
Fuglie, Andrew, author, 15:493
Fuhrman, F. E., 38:315
Fulda, Catholic settlement, 20:463,
31:22, 35:139, 325
Fuller, Alpheus G., pioneer, 12:83,
29:29; house, 15:52, 54, 25:2n, 56
Fuller, Buckminster, architect, 38:
348
Fuller, David L., trader, 14:436
Fuller, Edmund, work reviewed, 35:92
Fuller, Elizabeth, account books, 14:
26, 269n
Fuller, Francis, 15:304n
Fuller, George E., 18:97
Fuller, George F., engineer, 20:190,
25:289; artist, 21:37, 29:318, 31:
100, 101, 35:182; at Fort Snel-
ling, 29:317-320
Fuller, George N., 27:140
Fuller, Harlin M., editor, 35:292
Fuller, Harrison, 11:115
Fuller, Hiram, 29:30n; excursionist,
15:406, 29:29
Fuller, Iola, author, 36:76
Fuller, Jane G., 29:29; letter, 29:
31-35
Fuller, Jerome, judge, 39:151
Fuller, Margaret, journalist, 17:474,
22:431, 24:48, 76, 25:273, 28:54
Fuller, Mrs. Mary I., 13:427, 14:298
Fuller, Melville W., 18:145
Fuller, Sara, quoted, 23:311
Fuller, Timothy P., 15:302
Fuller House, St. Paul, 12:403, 16:
272, 34:99n, 333, 38:176
Fullerton, George, 37:15n

Fullerton, Sam F., conservationist,
22:337
Fullerton, Thomas M., 17:465
Fullerton, William E., 14:217, 25:27
Fullerton Lumber Co., 37:18
Fulton, D. E., author, 11:336
Fulton, David C., house, 38:348, 350
Fulton, Mrs. J. C., 16:243
Fulton, Dr. John F., 24:210
Fulton, Dr. John F., Jr., 11:443, 12:
85; author, 14:230, 29:170; speak-
er, 34:176
Fulton, Mrs. Nellie, 17:358, 18:336
Fulton, Robert, inventor, 22:303,
305, 25:88, 35:92
Fulton, Ill., river port, 17:423, 36:
256
Fundin, Halvor, 14:428
Fundin, Marit, 14:428
Funk, John F., letter, 37:184
Fur, defined, 40:210
Fur trade, history, 11:216, 12:71,
36:323, 38:42, 190, 39:81, 40:151-
156; Michilimackinac, 11:231-270;
monopolies, 11:234, 244-247, 268,
12:236, 13:237, 15:157, 18:387,
393, 19:271, 289; economic aspects, 11:258, 265, 268-270, 12:
237, 13:228, 14:339, 19:40-42, 20:
265, 27:63, 32:124, 40:155, 159,
161, 163, 165-170, 176-186, 210-
220; licenses, 11:259-265, 13:221,
18:276, 19:278, 285, 287, 20:263,
21:123, 32:227, 36:50n, 38:200;
posts, 11:353-385, 13:107, 202,
433, 18:235, 19:456, 22:270-289,
23:137n, 26:76, 28:285, 30:122n,
35:320, 37:62, 40:188-197, 263;
locations mapped, 11:355; Canada,
11:424-428, 13:112, 14:229, 15:
120, 157, 16:106, 421-423, 18:430,
19:290, 24:149-151, 26:88, 28:61,
176, 282, 35:45, 140, 36:32, 37:
86, 346, 38:199, 386, 40:144, 157-
177, 188-191, 202; factory system,
13:221, 19:300, 34:310, 40:184,
185, 202; use of steamboats, 13:
221-243, 18:434, 26:276; prices,
13:237, 21:125, 139, 142, 146,
148, 23:333; Northwest, 13:334,
20:84, 326, 26:55, 56, 165, 27:66,
34:215; account books, 14:233, 16:
73, 20:263, 265-268, 452, 23:94,
24:353, 35:31; influence on settlement, 14:434; Missouri Valley,
15:353, 24:71, 33:301, 38:199, 40:
155; racial aspects, 15:421-423;
Cannon River, 16:100, 125; impact
of foreign wars, 18:391-394; medical history, 19:226; women in, 19:
304; use of canoes, 21:93, 28:6,
10, 148, 33:130, 187, 261, 34:174,
38:26, 39:256, 40:158, 162, 164,
165, 208; archaeology, 21:206, 23:
188, 25:398, 28:285, 35:141, 155,
365-367, 38:24-34, 39:130, 40:150,
195, 203-209, 259, 260, 263, 412;
bibliographies, 21:423, 24:235,
34:215; cultural aspects, 22:4,
10, 355-358, 24:262; in fiction,
22:76, 32:33, 34:210, 219, 36:77,
37:174, 235-254, 38:191; terminol-
ogy, 22:432, 23:84, 32:122; spe-
cies taken, 30:131-134, 38:190,
39:207, see also individual animals; museums, 34:353, 40:196,
197; conference, 40:149; rendez-

vous, 40:149, 152, 155, 157, 184,
197, 201, 202; coastal, 40:157,
204; picture packets, 40:364. See
also Red River carts, Trade goods,
Voyaeurs, various fur companies,
posts, and traders
Furber, Mrs. Lucy, diaries, 13:100,
196
Furlan, Brother Lewis F., author, 28:
181
Furlan, Rev. William P., essay reviewed, 38:193
Furman, Lt. John G., 14:422
Furnas, J. C., author, 22:338, 36:325
Furner, Edward W., 18:143
Furness, Anna E. R. (Anita), 18:45,
20:427, 21:39, 27:48, 28:309, 29:
114n, 37:308; grant, 37:224; bequest, 39:36
Furness, Mrs. Charles E. (Marion Ramsey), 11:54, 55, 205, 315, 14:78,
291n, 17:62, 33:4, 37:44, 39:36,
52, 56n, 284, 321, 326; "Governor
Ramsey," 28:309-328; "Childhood
Recollections," 29:114-129; speaker, 11:294, 12:344; author, 28:
399, 29:99, 191; balloon ride, 39:
279-281
Furness, Laura, 18:45, 20:427, 21:39,
289, 410, 22:46, 296, 23:35, 50,
25:51, 26:45, 151, 27:48, 28:309,
29:97, 114n, 39:36; death, 37:44
Furness colony, Wadena, records, 23:
371
Furniture, see Houses
Furst, Sidney, editor, 40:47
Furuseth, Andrew, labor leader, 32:
51, 36:98
Fussell, Edwin, work reviewed, 39:291
Future Farmers of America, Minnesota,
34:349
Fyema, K., 28:131
Fyffe, David M., reminiscences, 17:
54, 99

G.A.R., see Grand Army of the Repub-
lic
"G. B. Knapp," steamboat, 36:213, 214
"G. W. Spar-Hawk," steamboat, 15:409,
413
Gaard, Richard, speaker, 20:213
Gabitaweegama, Crow Wing County, mis-
sion station, 14:57
Gable, Joseph, miller, 36:215
Gable, Margaret, curator, 19:468, 21:
105
Gabriel, Brother Angelus, author, 30:
154
Gabriel, Ralph H., work reviewed, 11:
189-191; editor, 11:100; author,
19:347, 38:46, 48
Gabrielson, Peter, 32:102n
Gabrilowitsch, Ossip, pianist, 39:59
Gadski, Johanna, singer, 39:55, 62
Gaebler, Emil, musician, 34:219
Gág, Anton, artist, 22:77, 26:282,
31:46, 36:240, 38:105, 125n; pho-
tographer, 20:215
Gág, Wanda, work reviewed, 22:77;
artist, 17:229, 25:201, 26:165,
30:283; biography, 31:45
Gage, Dr. and Mrs. Homer, 21:95
Gage, Gen. Thomas, 11:239, 247, 251,
253, 256, 262, 263, 268, 19:291;

report on fur trade, 11:232-234
Gager's Station, Stevens County, described, 19:227; post office, 19:239
Gagnon, Ernest, author, 29:77
Gagnon, Peter, career, 13:114; fisherman, 33:258
Gaillard, David D., career, 12:442
Gaines, Gen. Edmund P., 18:405, 28:19
Gaines, Paul, 14:236
Gaines, William H., Jr., editor, 36:231
Gainey, Daniel C., career, 39:217
Gakidina, Lake County, railroad, 34:180
Galarneau, Edward J., author, 30:407
Galaxy Mill, Minneapolis, 12:333
Galbraith, John P., lawyer, 14:333
Galbraith, John S., "British-American Competition in the Border Fur Trade," 36:241-249; author, 35:48, 36:102
Galbraith, Maj. Thomas J., Indian agent, 12:123n, 130, 132, 13:444, 18:209, 23:295, 25:183, 37:228n, 38:94-96, 106, 131, 39:229; at Birch Cooley, 12:297; politician, 14:249, 36:9, 37:324
Galbraith, Mrs. Thomas J., 12:130, 133n
Gale, A. H., and Co., New York, 39:317
Gale, Edward C., 11:54, 12:82, 96, 207, 289, 405, 13:65, 14:64, 78, 98, 99, 333, 15:81, 225, 16:302, 466, 19:269n, 20:96, 427, 23:50, 219, 25:208, 33:333, 334, 335; "On the Hennepin Trail," 11:3-10; "The Legend of Lake Itasca," 12:215-225; "Up the Rainy Lake River," 24:276-286; reviews by, 14:195-197, 19:83-85, 430-432, 20:418-420, 23:57; speaker, 11:53, 55, 13:69, 291, 15:313, 18:65, 204, 275, 19:308, 309, 316, 470; author, 11:340, 12:24, 290, 13:118, 19:91, 444, 20:426, 23:74, 24:352, 26:302; MHS president, 17:70, 208, 312, 313, 460, 18:67, 267, 320, 19:67, 20:49, 50, 427; interview, 21:410; career, 24:275, 25:54, 204; memorial, 24:276, 25:186, 26:284, 27:75; death, 25:44; papers, 26:155, 27:23
Gale, Mrs. Edward C., 24:279n
Gale, Harlow C., 23:228; author, 21:440; speaker, 39:121
Gale, Dr. John, army surgeon, 28:16
Gale, Marian, 24:279n
Gale, Richard P., speaker, 25:385
Gale, Robert G., critic, 26:306
Gale, Samuel C., 39:116; diary, 18:65, 19:269, 449, 20:34; pioneer, 21:410; house, 23:228, 40:99, 100
Gale, Zona, author, 20:438, 31:137
Gale Island, Lake Minnetonka, history, 21:440
"Galena," gunboat, 25:129, 152
"Galena," steamboat, 12:393, 14:293, 295, 15:409, 18:208, 34:135; race, 11:143, 27:8; burned, 17:207
Galena and Chicago Union Railroad, 25:196, 35:358
Galena, Ill., trade center, 11:126, 129, 144, 13:240, 17:389, 18:454, 25:110, 34:17; river port, 11:126n, 12:159, 13:223, 437, 20:383,

27:186, 187, 30:4, 205, 34:33, 36:46n; stage lines, 11:403, 405, 20:131, 35:355; cholera epidemic, 14:291, 21:18, 19; lead mines, 15:411, 18:406, 434, 22:23-26, 23:344n, 24:128, 32:99, 34:135; pictured, 17:221, 301, 32:162, 33:115, 285, 34:33, 40:63, 64; settled, 22:98; plow factory, 23:323; railroad, 27:182, 283, 34:18n, 35:109; historic sites, 33:137; telegraph, 36:264, 39:42; mail route, 40:81, 85-87
Galena (Ill.) Gazette 15:467
Galena Packet Line, 11:165, 25:88; transports mail, 36:208, 211; history, 39:298
Galena plow, use in Minnesota, 24:296
Galena River, see Fever River
Galenson, Walter, author, 37:185
Galer, Roger S., author, 25:199
Galesburg, Ill., founded, 24:113; college, 24:114
Galicians, St. Louis County, 27:82; Mesabi Range, 27:208, 212
Galinée, René Brehan de, explorer, 30:57
Gallagher, C. B., 40:224
Gallagher, Mrs. Delia, speaker, 21:333
Gallagher, Henry M., speaker, 22:108
Gallagher, Katharine J., 13:408; author, 14:230
Gallagher, L. P., 16:296
Gallagher, Mary, speaker, 11:224
Gallagher, Thomas, speaker, 20:343, 27:77
Gallaher, Ruth A., author, 12:439, 14:226, 15:125, 16:228, 478, 17:222, 19:106, 27:69
Galland, Dr. Isaac, work reviewed, 31:115; author, 20:203
Gallatin, Albert, 18:397, 40:180n; map maker, 34:219
Gallaudet, Rev. T. H., 16:143
Galligan, Mrs. John, 15:485, 18:109, 19:447, 20:96
Gallipolis, Ohio, French settlement, 16:204
Galloway, Dr. Hector, speaker, 20:242
Gallup, George, author, 21:401
Gallup, Milton N., editor, 39:82
Galpin, Rev. Charles A., 16:314n, 18:226, 19:144, 20:141; career, 34:43, 40:11
Galpin, Charles J., editor, 12:91
Galpin, Rev. George, 20:141
Galpin, Semantha, author, 34:43
Galpin, W. Freeman, 39:215, 216
Galt, John, 25:273
Galtier, Father Lucien, missionary, 11:210, 13:313, 17:475, 18:437, 21:102, 409, 24:4, 25:56, 26:173, 29:206n, 30:5, 206n; career, 11:105, 22:334; grave, 11:108, 22:436, 25:409, 37:40; builds chapel, 19:190, 237, 22:2, 51, 25:10, 37:154n, 39:153; letters, 19:191; memorial, 22:346, 39:162; in fiction, 30:247
Galusha, Hugh D., Jr., review by, 40:308; author, 36:279
Galusha, Reuben B., 39:329
"Galvanized Yankees," history, 39:77
Galveston, Tex., captured, 25:242
Galvez, Bernardo de, 19:294
Galvin, Sister Eucharista, reviews

by, 21:73-76, 33:185; author, 11:42, 21:80; speaker, 19:68
Galvin, M. J., speaker, 20:303, 28:200
Gamber, William K., curator, 36:152, 284
Gamble, Richard D., author, 36:238
Gambling, history, 37:345
Gambrill, J. Montgomery, editor, 20:440
Game, see Wildlife
Games, see Sports
Gandrud, Sam G., speaker, 28:382
Gandsey, Mrs. Susan, author, 14:462
Gannett, William C., career, 12:442
Gannon, Mrs. Joseph, 19:118, 20:98, 21:109; speaker, 18:335
Ganoe, William A., author, 17:477
Gans, Rudolph, pianist, 39:59
Gapter, Andrew, 33:230
Gara, Larry, works reviewed, 35:287, 38:196; editor, 35:335
Garard, Peter, 14:32
Gard, Robert E., author, 29:269
Gard, Wayne, work reviewed, 37:78
Garden City, stage line, 12:51n; described, 12:52; mills, 12:52n; Christian church, 14:353, 455; history, 20:450, 26:394, 34:127; garrison, 38:280
Garden City Sharpshooters, volunteer unit, 16:171, 172, 173n
Garden Club of America, publication, 28:377
Garden Valley Telephone Co., Polk County, history, 14:358
Gardiner, C. Harvey, editor, 40:313
Gardiner, Capt. John W. T., 29:317
Gardiner, Robert H., 29:318
Gardner, Abbie, Sioux captive, 38:123
Gardner, Alexander, photographer, 33:217, 39:281, 40:271n
Gardner, Augustine V., 12:197, 37:200-202; account books, 21:87; author, 39:78
Gardner, Mrs. Augustine V. (Mary Le Duc), 21:87, 37:192, 198, 200, 202; diary, 11:95
Gardner, Charles G., Union soldier, 25:128
Gardner, Charles M., work reviewed, 30:252-254
Gardner, Chastina, compiler, 17:474
Gardner, Mrs. James A., 16:491, 19:470, 20:456; speaker, 14:460
Gardner, Mrs. James S., career, 15:366
Gardner, Rachel D., author, 16:368
Gardner, S. S., 22:265
Gardner, Stephen, miller, 37:199
Gardner mill, Hastings, 18:114
Garfield, James A., President, 25:290, 35:58; Congressman, 36:173
Garland, Hamlin, author, 16:105, 106, 20:183, 22:201, 23:115, 122, 157, 26:302, 28:287, 34:87, 200, 37:2; Minnesota contacts, 22:157-168, 33:1; biographies, 37:129, 344
Garland, John, postmaster, 40:79, 82
Garland, Lucy, 13:101
Garland, Richard, 22:160, 167
Garlic River, Mich., located, 23:237
Garlid, George W., "The Antiwar Dilemma of the Farmer-Labor Party," 40:365-374
Garnes Township, Red Lake County, history, 38:204

Garraghan, Gilbert J., work reviewed, 16:90; author, 14:338, 20:84, 23:82
Garrard, Beulah M., 14:43
Garrard, Catherine W., 14:43
Garrard, Evelyn S., 14:43
Garrard, George W., 14:35; career, 14:42
Garrard, Mrs. George W., 14:35, 42, 43
Garrard, Gen. Israel, 16:372, 22:222, 445, 29:87; house, 11:452, 14:34, 37:64; at Frontenac, 14:31-42, 20:307, 309, 27:368
Garrard, James G., 14:32
Garrard, Col. Jeptha D., 14:42, at Frontenac, 14:33, 39; in Civil War, 14:37; aviator, 22:222
Garrard, Kenner, at Frontenac, 14:33; career, 14:34
Garrard, Lewis H., at Frontenac, 14:31, 32, 20:307; career, 14:33; house, 14:35; author, 40:305
Garrard, Margaret, 14:35
Garrard family, at Frontenac, 14:31-43, 16:468, 20:306, 33:188, 35:245
Garreau, Father Leonard, missionary, 15:163, 175, 531
Garrett, Pat, biography, 34:210
Garretty, Lt. Frank, 35:173
Garrioch, Rev. A. C., work reviewed, 16:462
Garrioch, Peter, 12:204, 35:282; teacher, 14:143; diary, 20:119-128; papers, 22:280, 34:352
Garrioch, Mrs. Peter (Margaret M.), 20:119n
Garrison, ———, Big Lake pioneer, 19:135
Garrison, Curtis W., author, 16:111; editor, 25:379, 26:150
Garrison, John B., 29:100
Garrison, Mabel, singer, 39:58
Garrison, Oscar E., 21:349
Garrison, William L., abolitionist, 19:436, 22:127, 32:15, 25, 33:218
Garrison, Crow Wing County, historical meeting, 21:284, 286; name, 21:349
Garry, Nicholas, diary, 21:93
Gartenberg, Max, author, 31:39, 32:126
Garver, Dr. J. A., 12:196
Garvie, Stuart B., hunter, 38:119
Garvin, ———, trader, 12:130
Garvin, Albert, prison official, 29:323, 37:150
Garvin, H. C., 20:470; papers, 24:194, 271
Garvin Heights State Park, 20:305, 332
Garwood, Darrell, author, 26:79
Gasco, Anthony, settler, 34:183
Gaskill, John L., 26:208
Gaskill mill, Marine-on-St. Croix, 36:215
Gaskins, John, 25:241
Gasmann, Hans, 18:199
Gaspé, Quebec, Norwegian settlement, 12:95, 180; Cartier celebration, 15:476
Gaston family, 12:321
Gates, Charles M., "Bridges Facing East," 16:22-34; "Account Books," 16:70-75; "The Lac qui Parle Mission," 16:133-151; "The Tourist Traffic of Pioneer Minnesota," 16:272-281; "Probate Records," 17:189-193; reviews by, 13:181, 16:87, 200-202, 18:435, 19:352, 22:306-308, 23:357, 25:271, 38:190; work reviewed, 15:90-92; editor, 14:223, 15:67, 218, 531, 16:348, 22:330, 40:313; manuscript curator, 16:61, 330, 17:62; speaker, 16:68, 303; author, 16:484, 17:61, 206, 18:440, 19:216, 21:189, 22:316, 23:8, 84, 370, 25:288, 28:336, 34:211; professor, 18:440
Gates, Donald S., author, 15:124
Gates, Frederick T., career, 12:442
Gates, Dr. G. L., 11:321
Gates, J. H., teacher, 18:221
Gates, James L. ("Stumpland"), career, 38:195
Gates, Mavis, author, 15:369
Gates, Paul W., 26:161; review by, 39:31; works reviewed, 15:332, 25:69-71, 37:222; author, 13:111, 206, 15:239, 20:336, 22:326, 24:343, 28:330, 34:263, 39:298
Gates, Judge Vernon, 11:283
Gateway Arch, St. Louis, 40:192
Gateway district, Minneapolis, 25:219, 221n
Gatzke, Polish settlement, 13:108
Gaultier, François, see La Vérendrye, Sieur de
Gaultier de Varennes family, genealogy, 35:242
Gaustad, Edwin S., author, 39:128
Gaustad, Ingrid, see Semmingsen, Ingrid Gaustad
Gauthier, Julie C., author, 20:207
Gautier, Antoine, trader, 13:222
Gautier, René, 12:307
Gavin, Daniel, missionary, 16:141, 142, 17:224, 19:95, 21:27, 159, 165, 277, 282, 22:30n; centennial, 18:225; marriage, 21:167
Gavin, Mrs. Daniel (Cornelia Stevens), missionary, 21:160, 276; marriage, 21:167
Gay, Edwin F., author, 24:68
Gay, Leon S., author, 28:174
Gayarré, Charles C. A., 36:30
Gayler, Charles, author, 18:319, 31:209n
Gaylord, history, 12:97, 13:122, 26:260, 332; Lutheran church, 14:360; German-Russian settlement, 16:344
Gazetteers, Illinois and Missouri, 34:360; value, 40:146
Gear, Rev. Ezekiel G., 20:431, 21:450, 28:190, 31:173; "Sioux and Chippeways," 24:15-25; chaplain, 11:96, 19:355, 28:211, 29:320n, 30:213n, 36:238, 37:56; missionary, 16:97, 24:4; career, 24:13, 36:35; in fiction, 37:5
Gear, Mrs. Ezekiel G., 29:320
Gear, Capt. Hezekiah H., 24:14, 15
Gear, John H., career, 12:442
Gebhard, David S., author, 40:108, 359
Geck, L. H. A., author, 33:188
Geer, Silas, house, 38:337
Gehl, John B., author, 19:222
Geiger, Louis G., work reviewed, 36:318
"Geiser," emigrant ship, 20:402
Geismar, Maxwell, author, 29:172
Geisse, P. F., boatbuilder, 17:269, 270
Gelb, George H., piano maker, 39:320
Gelb, Phillip S., author, 25:90
Gelber, Leonard, work reviewed, 33:261
Gemmell, W. H., 15:245, 16:240
Gene, Thomas P., 33:212
Genealogy, study methods, 11:454, 21:421, 26:235, 27:29, 319, 28:69, 29:337, 31:59, 36:236, 37:181; DAR contributions, 13:311, 14:214, 439, 15:59, 349, 18:214, 20:194, 30:156; sources, 23:242n, 38:42, 39:170; periodicals, 38:338
"General Barnard," steamboat, 37:297
"General Brooke," steamboat, 13:233-235, 237
General Company of Lake Superior and the South, 19:299
"General John Newton," showboat, 36:106
General Logging Co., railroad, 27:308, 34:183, 184, 36:131, 133, 136; in Sawbill area, 36:132-134
General Mills, Inc., history, 33:132, 34:203, 35:45; balloon research, 33:244, 38:334; publications, 35:150
General Motors Corporation, 13:337
General Register House, Edinburgh, Scot., 17:7
General Tractor and Equipment Co., 38:308
General Trading Co., Minneapolis, 34:355
Genet, Arthur S., speaker, 36:190
Genin, Father J. Baptiste, missionary, 20:79, 24:94
Genoa Mine, Gilbert, 36:240
Gens du Lac Indians, see Sioux Indians: Kaposia band
Gentry, Merideth P., Congressman, 39:144, 149
Genzmer, George H., author, 11:217
Geographic names, Scandinavian, 11:102, 21:203; Indian, 11:214, 15:259n, 465, 16:476, 20:343, 25:304, 27:65, 28:374, 30:331, 33:186, 38:136; Great Lakes area, 12:287, 349, 422; Minnesota, 12:430, 16:122, 350, 19:110, 20:42, 21:286, 345-352, 22:337, 441, 446, 26:37, 29:75, 264, 30:67, 271, 314, 34:181-184, 35:23, 24; Colorado, 13:439; Missouri, 16:227; origins, 17:320, 26:248-250, 33:311; Iowa, 19:222; South Dakota, 24:178; Finnish, 25:320, 40:358; Isle Royale, Mich., 28:72; North Dakota, 28:80, 33:325, 37:40, 38:385; nicknames, 30:157, 267, 33:139
Geography, historical, 11:428, 430, 14:317, 19:456, 24:364, 25:196, 26:57, 29:248-250; Minnesota, 15:240, 18:208, 30:155, 36:192, 39:263; early textbooks, 24:229-233; relation to settlement, 25:319; globes, 26:164; Northwest, 34:353; Great Plains, 35:148. See also Atlases, Maps
Geological and Natural History Survey of Minnesota, 18:219
Geological Society of Minnesota, 34:314
Geology, Minnesota, 11:97, 14:117, 15:106, 141-147, 340, 16:117, 17:85, 126, 226, 18:104, 21:288, 25:175, 26:222-233, 30:331, 32:81-99,

215-225, 33:138, 282, 34:116, 269-
283, 36:295, 296, 320, 37:263,
307, 38:242, 39:132; Savanna Portage, 13:403-407; bibliographies,
16:467, 19:217; stone industry,
17:85; Lake Superior region, 17:
108, 32:216, 36:188, 38:22; St.
Croix Valley, 17:115; Red River
Valley, 38:158. See also Minnesota Geological Survey
George I, king of England, Indian
medals, 25:266
George II, king of England, Indian
medals, 25:266, 40:204
George III, king of England, 40:176,
294; Indian medals, 25:266
George, Alice M., 14:276, 15:45
George, C. L., land dealer, 12:336
George, Esther A. (Mrs. Francis Rog-
ers), 39:1, 3; house, 39:2
George, Frederick, author, 30:163
George, Gen. Harold L., 26:8
George, Harrison B., reminiscences,
25:289
George, Harry E., 39:56
George, Henry, political economist,
14:201, 22:158, 161, 379
George, Immogene L., 15:304n
George, James, Union officer, 16:443,
38:258, 264, 266, 271
George, Walter L., author, 29:154
"George H. Houghton," steamboat, 33:
13, 14
"George M. Cox," steamboat, 34:39,
35:281
Georgetown, described, 13:303; his-
tory, 18:104, 34:357; river port,
18:355, 356, 21:250, 33:89, 277;
stage line, 19:110, 385; post, 21:
449, 29:176, 357, 33:278
Georgia, politics, 12:10; printing,
13:336, 15:7; Bishop Whipple's
visit, 19:75
Georgian Bay, Lake Huron, 25:274
Geraghty, P. J., 34:264
Gerard, Frederick, trader, 27:97
Gerber, Robert F., author, 28:381
Gerboth, Fred, 15:436
Gerdsen, Henry, 19:22
Gere, Capt. Thomas P., 18:209; diary,
12:100
Gere, William B., U.S. marshal, 14:
253n, 254, 259-261; house, 25:383
Geringer, August, publisher, 15:445
Gerlach, George N., 39:154n
Gerling, Ruby, author, 29:269
German-American Bank, St. Paul, 28:
182
German-American Centennial Committee
of Minnesota, 36:239
German American Insurance Co., 18:145
German-American Typographia, 21:386
German Evangelical Church Society of
the West, 21:427
German Farmers' Mutual Fire Insurance
Co., 23:404
German Land Association, New Ulm, 21:
111, 28:202, 30:31, 32, 34, 31:24,
32:169, 40:263, 310
German Opera Co., Chicago, 32:167
German Reading Society, St. Paul, 32:
100, 101, 104, 240, 34:99n
German Russians, immigration, 16:344;
South Dakota, 19:219, 222. See
also Mennonites
German Society, St. Paul, 16:74, 32:
104

Germania (Johnsburg), Mower County,
history, 15:490
Germania, St. Paul, choral society,
32:240
Germania Bank, St. Paul, 40:100, 101
Germans, literature, 11:102, 23:122,
27:327-329, 35:327, 36:80; Wisconsin, 11:105, 23:286, 30:139, 33:
117, 34:219; New Ulm, 11:174n, 16:
363, 21:111, 203, 27:268, 28:202,
30:29-35, 188, 33:91, 231, 34:170,
38:120, 243, 40:263, 309; Minnesota, 11:205, 13:449, 14:45, 15:136,
18:453, 20:181-183, 22:224, 23:
294, 24:381, 27:210, 31:23-26,
222-230; McLeod County, 11:334,
21:452, 23:102, 194; Stearns County, 12:106, 15:139, 18:89, 26:235,
27:169, 32:35-37, 39, 33:185, 34:
85, 171, 35:263-271, 36:24, 35,
39:321; immigration, 12:194, 428,
14:100, 334, 15:60, 447, 21:203,
299, 26:147, 27:40, 29:350, 31:
222-230, 33:179, 351; Twin Cities,
12:322, 15:224, 18:117, 19:203,
23:68; clubs, 13:116, 17:85, 338,
18:112, 22:335, 23:294, 24:214-
225, 244, 25:207, 26:79, 35:203,
294, 36:91, 239; Catholic groups,
13:117, 14:120, 15:490, 19:124,
21:74, 75, 453, 25:315, 27:176,
269, 28:84, 33:305, 34:171, 35:46,
37:133; almanacs, 15:446; in Sioux
Outbreak, 16:170, 36:239, 38:116-
118, 125; geographic names, 16:
350; periodicals, 17:52, 342, 386,
19:219, 22:424, 23:373, 24:35, 25:
197, 27:327, 343, 28:202, 303, 32:
239, 33:180, 187, 34:130, 35:328,
37:87, 38:91; Indiana, 17:79;
U.S., 18:398; in agriculture, 19:
21, 20:75, 21:91; educational activities, 19:68; customs, 20:86,
23:92, 24:366, 25:88, 27:322, 36:
202, 37:75, 40:47; unions, 21:379,
381, 385, 22:376; Washington County, 23:404, 24:271; Forty-Eighters, 24:220, 27:163, 31:222-230,
242, 33:179, 351; contributions,
24:259, 339, 29:80, 31:342, 34:42,
35:327; in politics, 25:298, 26:
373, 28:30-36, 32:15, 22, 36:237,
303, 308, 40:328; guidebook, 25:
301; Pennsylvania, 26:168, 177,
27:29-32, 141; intermarriage, 27:
167; overland journey, 31:253;
theaters, 32:100-105, 127, 164-
173, 33:188, 315, 34:239-242;
music, 32:239-242, 39:51, 321; in
Civil War, 33:84, 38:260; Sibley
County, 36:197-205; St. Anthony,
39:65-74. See also Germany, Hutterian Brethren
Germany, revolution of 1848, 24:220,
31:222, 223, 242, 33:179; emigration from, 27:324, 31:222-230,
250, 33:187; remigration, 34:219;
fur market, 40:216, 219
Germond, Garth, author, 34:129, 174
Gerolt, Baron von, 37:160n
Gerot, Paul S., author, 40:47
Geroy, Joseph, 21:107, 22:105, 24:85
Gerretson, Maud, 13:117
Gerry, Elbridge, excursionist, 15:406
Gerstenhauer, Eugen, 34:130
Gervais, Pierre, cholera victim, 14:
290

Gervais Lake, Ramsey County, acreage,
40:226n
Geselius, August, pioneer, 17:487
Geske, Norman A., 21:444, 22:216, 28:
302; "A Pioneer Minnesota Artist,"
31:99-104; review by, 30:139-141;
speaker, 28:390; author, 30:184,
31:127
Gesner, Rev. A. T., arrowhead collec-
tion, 26:280
Gessner, Robert, author, 12:434
Gestie, Bernice D., review by, 35:
371; author, 37:186
Getting, Mrs. A. F., author, 11:111
Getty, George F., 23:388
Getty, J. G., 26:112
Getty, J. Paul, author, 23:388
Getty, Sumner J., author, 18:338
Gettysburg, Pa., battle, 11:447, 15:
221, 20:279, 25:342, 360, 29:344,
38:245-257, 271, 273, 39:83; panorama, 23:198; historic site, 39:83
Getz, John, and Co., St. Paul, 39:319
Gewalt, Chester A., 16:362, 18:112,
19:120, 20:458; author, 18:104,
35:245
Geyer, Charles A. (Karl), botanist,
24:371, 26:153, 154, 27:38, 341,
35:241
Gheen, history, 21:116
Ghent, William J., author, 11:217,
13:441, 14:338, 349, 16:239, 350,
17:115, 477, 18:218
Ghent, Belgium, treaty, 17:197, 20:
16, 23:203, 208, 24:72, 341, 25:
182, 29:132
Ghent, Catholic colony, 14:355, 31:
22, 35:139; Belgians, 24:79, 38:
243
Ghormley, James, diary, 26:67
Ghost Dance War, 25:87, 26:378
Ghost towns, Iowa, 12:95; Cedarville,
Martin County, 14:459, 15:71;
Clearwater County, 16:493; Nicollet County, 17:238; Hennepin, Hennepin County, 19:464; on iron
ranges, 19:464, 20:468; Minnesota
Valley, 19:465; East Prairieville,
Rice County, 20:355; Grand Rapids,
Stevens County, 22:447; Iberia,
Brown County, 23:195; in 1857 cen-
sus, 29:172; Itasca, Anoka County,
29:216n; Maudada, Traverse County,
29:366; Elliotta, Fillmore County,
30:70; Koochiching County, 30:162,
272; Arrowhead region, 34:177-184;
Granite City, Morrison County, 34:
359; types, 35:11-13; Forest
Mills, Goodhue County, 35:11-21;
Marshall County, 35:47; Pine Coun-
ty, 35:338
Ghostly, Henry, 38:188
Giasson, Charles, trader, 22:276
Giasson, François, trader, 11:375
Gibault, Father Pierre, 16:90
Gibb, George S., work reviewed, 35:
286
Gibbon, Gen. John, 25:255, 345, 350,
360; author, 29:344
Gibbon, John M., 13:89; author, 17:
217, 33:187
Gibbon, settled, 13:122, 30:275, 35:
336; newspaper, 36:197-205, 284;
Catholic church, 36:198
Gibbon Gazette, editors, 36:197, 201-
205
Gibbons, Emma, author, 21:100

Gibbons, Floyd, journalist, 23:98
Gibbons, Cardinal James, 22:382, 33:305, 39:210
Gibbons, Lillian, author, 28:179
Gibbons, Thomas J., 39:154n
Gibbs, Charles, author, 34:170
Gibbs, George, artist, 23:183; map, 34:219
Gibbs, Heman R., 25:290; house, 27:228-230, 29:364, 30:168, 33:210, 34:130, 172; family, 34:172, 39:132
Gibbs, Janie B., 25:77
Gibbs, Thomas, druggist, 17:241, 20:461
Gibson, Capt. A. A., 29:237; artist, 19:420
Gibson, A. J., 11:224, 15:253, 371
Gibson, Andrew, engineer, 17:102
Gibson, Frederick M., letters, 26:68
Gibson, Col. George, 39:251
Gibson, Isabel, author, 22:334
Gibson, Paris, miller, 12:442
Gibson, W. S., hotel owner, 13:150
Gibson, Warren, 17:483, 19:117
Gibson, Mrs. Warren, 19:117
Gibson, William S., 15:108; speaker, 14:328; editor, 17:228
Giddens, Paul H., 33:354; work reviewed, 35:91; author, 38:241
Giddings, A. E., speaker, 16:489
Giddings, Dr. Aurora W., 21:415
Giddings, John I., 21:415
Giddings, Joshua, papers, 21:415
Giddings, Louisa, 21:415
Gideon, Peter, 20:141, 30:266; career, 12:442, 20:448, 21:440, 30:407; horticulturist, 16:194, 494, 19:357, 23:91, 30:371, 31:162, 33:224; marker, 20:352
Gidney, Rev. Joseph B., 14:436
Gidney, Margaret D., author, 29:163
Giere, Arthur F., author, 11:454
Gieseker, Brenda R., work reviewed, 30:249
Gieske, Millard L., reviews by, 39:205, 257, 40:90
Giffard family, genealogy, 34:313
Giffen, R. L., speaker, 11:338
Gilbert, Arlan K., editor, 35:200
Gilbert, Cass, 15:100, 17:160n, 22:302; "Memorandum," 22:303-305; architect, 16:110, 359, 20:207, 25:305, 29:264, 37:38, 41, 185, 186, 39:35, 155; reminiscences, 17:342; papers, 28:396, 29:49, 36:328
Gilbert, Mrs. Cass, 22:303
Gilbert, Clara, speaker, 23:102
Gilbert, E. W., work reviewed, 14:430; author, 15:234
Gilbert, G. K., 23:102
Gilbert, Heather, work reviewed, 40:142; author, 40:316
Gilbert, Henry C., Indian agent, 39:309
Gilbert, Joseph, trial, 15:338, 24:373, 35:368; biography, 30:66
Gilbert, Julia F., author, 17:342
Gilbert, L. W., speaker, 11:116
Gilbert, Lourentia, 40:390
Gilbert, Bishop Mahlon N., 15:466; portraits, 13:325, 17:471, 21:88
Gilbert, Newington, house, 38:343
Gilbert, Oliver, innkeeper, 40:390
Gilbert, Russell C., house, 38:339
Gilbert, William A., banker, 29:223-228

Gilbert, Sir William S., librettist, 17:40
Gilbert, Yugoslav settlement, 25:186, 30:392; mining town, 32:194, 36:240; bus line, 35:338
Gilbert and Easton, bankers, see Root River State Bank
Gilbertsen, Victor, author, 37:223
Gilbertson, A. T., speaker, 17:346
Gilbertson, Gena L., author, 24:93
Gilbertson, George, author, 15:246, 367, 17:236, 20:357
Gilchrist, Marie E., author, 24:256, 26:266
Gilcrease, Thomas, 30:20
Gilder, Richard W., 20:82
Gildersleeve, William, 34:3, 4, 8
Giles, Brother, missionary, 33:57
Gilfillan, Archer B., work reviewed, 35:331
Gilfillan, Charles D., 11:328, 23:78; memorial, 20:98; career, 20:354, 40:221-232
Gilfillan, Charles O., 20:98
Gilfillan, Emma Waage, 40:222
Gilfillan, Fannie Waage, 40:222
Gilfillan, James, I, 40:222
Gilfillan, Mrs. James, I (Janet Agnes), 40:222
Gilfillan, Judge James, II, 40:222, 225, 226, 228, 230, 33:4; career, 26:382
Gilfillan, Rev. Joseph A., 11:96, 20:431, 26:96, 36:319; author, 11:332, 15:466, 20:195; Ojibway scholar, 12:228, 422; missionary, 16:120, 20:91, 312, 313, 21:414, 22:40, 23:26
Gilfillan, Mrs. Joseph A. (Harriet Woodbridge), 16:120
Gilfillan, S. Colum, 21:414
Gilfillan Block, St. Paul, 40:231
Gilfillan Memorial Community Building, Morgan, 20:98, 354, 466
Gilfillan Siding, Redwood County, 40:232
Gilgal (Gilgas), Ill., townsite, 17:432
Gilkey, George R., review by, 34:210
Gillam, Dr. C. G., author, 16:368
Gillam, Edward E., reminiscences, 17:231; speaker, 19:116, 26:283; author, 22:109, 30:395
Gillam, Capt. Zachariah, 18:82, 24:340; Hudson Bay expedition, 16:400, 419-423, 425n
Gillam family, in fur trade, 18:82, 29:153
Gillard, Charlotte, author, 24:259
Gillese, John P., author, 37:38
Gillespie, Anna, speaker, 11:112
Gillespie, Mabel, social worker, 12:442
Gillespie, Vera W., author, 27:345
Gillette, Dr. Arthur J., 12:204, 20:445, 24:181, 30:405
Gillette, Guy M., Iowa Senator, 24:240
Gillette, J. M., author, 13:335, 23:287, 26:79
Gillette, Lewis S., 33:332, 333
Gillette State Hospital for Crippled Children, St. Paul, 12:204, 20:445
Gillian, Rev. J. W., see Gilfillan, Rev. Joseph A.
Gillingham, Fred, 18:337, 21:447
Gillmor, Frank H., papers, 29:375

Gillnaught, James, log mark, 26:136
Gilman, Dr. Albert O., 33:294, 295
Gilman, Chandler R., author, 15:468
Gilman, David, trader, 11:374, 19:143
Gilman, Francis, 16:71
Gilman, John M., letter, 26:195n
Gilman, Rhoda R., 39:84, 264, 40:96; "Ramsey, Donnelly, and the Congressional Campaign," 36:300-308; "Railroad Route from St. Paul to Duluth," 37:101-118; "Pioneer Aeronaut," 38:166-176; "Zeppelin in Minnesota," 39:278-285, 40:265-278; "Oliver Hudson Kelley," 40:330-338; reviews by, 37:130, 216, 39:26, 78, 341, 40:46, 146, 313, 316; work reviewed, 39:335; editor, 37:188, 224, 38:92, 336; artist, 40:150n; author, 40:412
Gilman family, papers, 39:26, 212
Gilman and Seager, St. Paul, farm equipment, 24:300
Gilmore, Rev. Arthur H., speaker, 18:204, 270, 315, 28:297; author, 32:118
Gilmore, James, author, 35:292
Gilmore, Patrick S., 37:306
Gilpin, Alec R., work reviewed, 36:67
Gilpin, William, explorer, 14:430
Ging, Kitty, murdered, 23:98, 26:288, 33:52
Gingerich, Melvin, work reviewed, 20:424; author, 37:184
Gingras, Antoine, legislator, 33:121n
Gingrich, Dr. C. H., author, 12:341
Ginsberg, Charles, brewer, 40:126
Ginseng, harvested by pioneers, 16:97, 17:415, 19:238, 21:235, 413, 22:111, 34:146
Ginster, Ria, singer, 39:60
Gippe, Louise, 19:115
Gipson, Lawrence H., author, 24:256
"Gipsy," steamboat, 24:13
Girard, James W., autobiography, 30:153
Giraud, Marcel, 17:462; work reviewed, 28:60-62; author, 28:362, 29:78, 32:60, 33:89
Girl Scouts of America, 22:345, 27:48
Giscome Portage, B.C., 12:361
Given, N. E., author, 28:189
Givins, James, at Grand Portage, 12:369
Gjelhaug, Anne, pioneer, 20:346
Gjerde, O. J., speaker, 29:363
Gjerdrum, Jørgen, letters, 21:426
Gjerset, Knut, author, 12:306, 328, 13:206, 14:444
Gjertsen, Rev. M. Falk, 20:408, 29:294
Glaab, Charles N., review by, 40:137; author, 36:34
Glacier National Park, 17:88, 19:223, 22:178
Glacier Park Hotel, 38:215
Glad, Paul W., works reviewed, 37:181, 39:169
Gladden, Elijah, cholera victim, 14:290
Gladding, Nathaniel, 26:154
Gladman, J., trader, 40:168n
Gladoski, Helen, 26:39; cataloger, 24:243; manuscript assistant, 25:40
Gladstone, William E., 37:231
Gladstone, Man., agricultural settlement, 28:64

Gladstone beach, N.D., geology, 38: 158
Gladwin, Maj. Henry, 29:65
Glantz, Charles, 23:392
Glase, Paul E., author, 26:168
Glaser, Alvin E. F., 28:86, 29:92; speaker, 29:275; author, 36:104
Glaser, Emma, "How Stillwater Came to Be," 24:195-206; author, 24:193, 244; speaker, 24:242, 349, 25:210, 27:78
Glasgow, Ellen, novelist, 16:106, 20: 116, 23:124
Glasoe, Paul M., 29:96; author, 24: 258
Glaspell, Kate E., author, 25:300
Glasrud, Clarence A., review by, 40: 351
Glass, Herb, 37:35
Glass, Hugh, trader, 28:273, 34:210
Glass, Phoebe, cholera victim, 14:290
Glass, Remley J., author, 27:355
Glass, Mrs. T. A., author, 28:384
Glatzel, Rose, 29:283
Glazebrook, G. P. de T., work reviewed, 20:69-72; author, 14:338, 20:87, 34:254
Glazer, Sidney, review by, 34:207
Glazier, Willard, 13:287
Glencoe, churches, 11:116, 13:216, 17:98; townsite, 11:132, 316, 334, 34:146, 40:65, 66, 75; stage route, 11:133, 134, 12:97; pageants, 11:219, 16:306; schools, 13:215, 14:121, 16:317, 18:409, 22:412, 32:119; claim shanty, 14: 270; settled, 15:28, 16:344, 21: 452, 35:47; district court, 15: 348; in Sioux Outbreak, 18:315, 38:275, 276, 280; power plant, 35: 381; railroad, 39:92
Glencoe Farmers' Club, 27:110
Glencoe Historical Society, 16:240; organized, 14:236, 15:71; pageant, 16:306; tour, 16:488, 17:64
Glendale, Scott County, Presbyterian church, 18:96
Glendorado Lutheran Church, Benton County, 14:451
Glenn, Laura, 28:395
Glenn, Perry, papers, 28:395
Glennon, Gertrude, 15:372, 25:314
Glennon, John S., 29:323
Glenville, railroad, 33:43
Glenwood, pageant, 11:337; parsonage, 16:316; schools, 18:342, 26:166; mounds, 19:361, 25:336-338; board of trade, 20:213; hospital, 21: 109; milling, 21:218; fire department, 21:338; museum, 26:389-391; history, 28:82; courthouse, 38: 189n; pictured, 40:123
Glenwood Academy, 20:458
Glenwood Civic Club, 11:223
Glenwood Herald, 19:125, 26:390
Glenwood-Inglewood Springs, Minneapolis, 25:410
Glidden, Carlos, 16:445
Glidden, Charles J., 38:205
Glidden tour, 1913, 38:205-215
"Glidiator," ice train, 25:299
"Globe," steamboat, 11:137, 141
Globe Building, St. Paul, razed, 40: 135
Globe Mills Co., New Ulm, records, 28:202
Globokan, Frank, artist, 33:28

Glorvigen, Adolph, speaker, 21:337
Glory, Aitkin County, name, 21:350
Glover, Jose, pioneer printer, 15:3
Glover, Lucille, author, 31:61
Glover, Richard, author, 30:150, 33: 130, 261; editor, 39:171
Glover, Wilbur H., 30:77; reviews by, 30:370, 33:307, 37:221; work reviewed, 33:224; author, 29:268, 30:412
Gluckman, Arcadi, work reviewed, 33: 307
Gluek, Alvin C., "The Sioux Uprising," 34:317-324; reviews by, 35:34, 282, 36:272, 37:217, 40:93; work reviewed, 40:43; author, 35: 47, 154, 202, 36:102, 191
Gluek Brewing Co., Minneapolis, founded, 28:291
Glyndon, immigrant house, 13:41; Christmas drama, 16:383; newspaper, 21:448, 25:261; founded, 25: 260, 29:87
Gmeiner, Father John, career, 12:442; author, 26:302, 28:72
Gnat Lake, Beltrami County, 21:352
Gnesen, St. Louis County, Polish settlement, 13:108
Gobeaux, Jules, potter, 33:230
Godard, Doris, editor, 25:403
Godard, Eugene, aeronaut, 39:283, 40: 314
Godbout, Alfonzo, pioneer, 23:25
Godbout, Rev. Archange, author, 17: 114
Godcharles, Frederic A., author, 15: 471
Goddard, Abner S., pioneer, 12:157, 167, 13:196; letters, 16:333
Goddard, Catherine, pioneer, 12:157, 167, 159n, 13:196; letters, 16:333
Goddard, Charles E., letters, 25:16n, 38:247, 248
Goddard family, 12:158n
Godé, Dominique, trader, 12:82, 18: 276
Godey's Lady's Book, 30:193
Godfert, Father ---, priest, 19:191
Godfrey, ---, sentenced, 38:110n
Godfrey, Ard, 14:99; postmaster, 12: 343, 40:83; house, 15:229, 360, 20:413, 24:128, 25:208, 27:231, 40:48; sawmill, 24:127; real-estate owner, 35:104
Godfrey, George, poet, 26:298
Godfrey, William S., author, 34:214
Godin, ---, trader, 22:276
Godowsky, Leopold, 39:56
Goetz, E. A., author, 15:140
Goetzinger, William H., 17:482, 19: 360, 23:296; "Pomme de Terre," 38: 63-71; speaker, 13:278, 17:356, 20:47, 23:103, 24:272; author, 16: 128, 247, 17:356, 359, 20:211, 24: 86, 29:362
Goetzmann, William H., work reviewed, 37:34
Goff, Al, editor, 36:104
Goff, Hiram S., author, 18:337
Gogebic Range, Mich., iron mines, 36: 276
Goggin, Mrs. George, 23:104; speaker, 17:124, 19:232
Goggin, John M., archaeologist, 38: 244
Gohdes, Clarence, work reviewed, 40: 311

Goheen, Adelbert, murderer, 38:11-20
Goheen, Anderson, in murder trial, 38:13, 16-20
Goheen family, 38:12, 13, 16-20; house, 38:17
Gohrke, Charles, 14:42
Goiffon, Father Joseph, missionary, 16:231, 20:79, 21:432, 454, 25: 187, 35:270; career, 16:235, 17: 113; diary, 20:34
Gold, trade item, 40:198
Gold Medal Flour, name, 11:329
Gold mining, California, 12:440, 23: 273, 30:152, 393, 33:266, 39:70; Pike's Peak, 13:114; Zumbro River, 13:176; Fraser River, 13:177, 302, 35:249, 251, 38:65; Black Hills, 14:445, 32:219, 35:52, 37:222, 40: 254, 354, 410; Rainy Lake, 15:489, 16:366, 17:361, 30:272, 34:178; Vermilion Range, 16:295, 19:355, 442, 450, 20:193, 24:166, 32:217, 34:178, 36:282; Montana, 23:184, 24:159, 34:328, 38:53-62, 39:261, 40:94, 254; Klondike, 29:300-315, 32:60, 35:199, 39:341; Lake County, 30:407; Alaska, 32:60, 174, 33:43, 35:52; routes, 38:58, 224, 386; Idaho, 38:220, 40:94; lost mines, 40:307
"Golden Eagle," steamboat, 21:403, 22:94
"Golden Era," steamboat, 12:393, 15: 409, 410, 416, 417, 19:249, 34: 134-136, 142, 143
Golden Gate, Brown County, ghost town, 19:465, 23:195, 36:327
"Golden Gate," steamboat, 25:117, 118
Golden Gate International Exposition, San Francisco, 21:324
"Golden Rod," showboat, 33:39
Golden Rule, St. Paul, store, 36:129
"Golden Star," steamboat, 28:92
"Golden State," steamboat, 11:143
Goldenstein, H., editor, 24:157
Goldhurst, William, author, 39:35
Goldich, Samuel S., author, 37:263
Goldin, Theodore W., letters, 34:40
Goldman, Eric F., editor, 22:328; author, 34:250
Goldmann, Freimund, author, 14:334
Goldschmidt Lake, Carver County, 33: 248
Golf, clubs, 11:101, 29:89, 36:89; on frontier, 20:441; depicted, 30:54, 36:90, 40:32, 385; Minnesota, 36: 103
Gollop, Lou, author, 35:153
Gompers, Samuel, labor leader, 13:19, 22:380, 34:189, 40:341
"Gondola," steamboat, 36:251
Gondos, Victor, Jr., author, 25:391
Gonneville, ---, farmer, 18:276
Good, Carl, 21:344, 441
Good Road, Sioux leader, 13:373, 21: 166n, 172n, 24:24n, 28:315, 38: 137; village, 11:166, 32:74, 35:29
Good Star Woman, Sioux Indian, 15:347
Good Templars, 22:394n, 31:90; Minnesota, 11:95, 13:142, 40:363; publications, 15:468; history, 22: 436, 36:35; records, 26:371, 34: 340
Good Thunder, Sioux leader, 11:455, 35:246, 38:136, 137, 148
Good Thunder (town), history, 16:126;

Grange, 32:62; medical center, 35:246

Good Will, S.D., mission, 35:169, 177

Goode, J. Paul, geographer, 25:305

Goodenough, Nelson, lumberman, 24:201

Goodhue, Horace, 31:122

Goodhue, James M., journalist, 11:393, 13:45, 211, 14:154, 15:467, 16:370, 17:276, 477, 18:44, 22:140, 182, 211, 225, 347, 414, 24:177, 26:95, 27:2, 28:197, 342n, 29:58, 30:273, 372, 31:181, 32:71, 35:44, 36:270, 38:46, 39:45; "Minnesota," 29:195-222; promotes Minnesota, 11:161, 12:391, 17:249, 20:395, 29:2, 31:19, 32:34, 34:50, 40:3, 302; quoted, 12:396, 399, 14:289, 403, 17:277, 18:371, 377, 378, 22:141, 23:308, 30:296, 345, 32:72, 35:183, 352, 39:44, 145, 40:4, 86, 224; career and writings, 12:442, 14:63, 29:372, 30:50-52, 197, 31:62, 34:52, 39:268; pictured, 13:296, 24:351, 26:141; characterized, 14:139, 400, 405, 22:6, 29:193; press, 14:447, 15:16, 18, 476, 20:348, 28:84, 30:42; Freemason, 33:310; public printer, 35:106, 39:46

Goodhue, James M., Jr., death, 14:290

Goodhue, history, 11:219, 20:357, 34:127; farming, 26:281; clay pits, 28:291

Goodhue County, Scandinavian settlements, 12:264-266, 270, 271, 320, 450, 14:354, 17:399, 29:177, 31:27, 34:167, 172, 38:172; courthouse, 12:338; dairying, 13:449; archives, 15:248, 22:434; crime, 16:128; archaeology, 15:367, 26:280, 29:83; history, 17:126, 20:211, 24:272, 25:314, 34:127, 35:203; pioneer life, 19:473; pictured, 22:333; fair, 23:106; medicine, 26:173, 287, 27:365; in World War II, 26:281; wheat raising, 29:2n, 13, 35:13, 16; politics, 36:306; in Civil War, 38:259; geology, 39:132; social conditions, 40:363. See also Prairie Island

Goodhue County Bible Society, 15:247

Goodhue County Historical Society, 11:17, 26, 312, 13:339, 14:346, 15:372, 470, 16:240, 20:352, 29:83, 36:240; organized, 11:14; museum, 11:16, 13:71, 15:367, 19:360, 22:440, 23:194, 296, 24:269, 379, 26:280-282, 35:50; membership, 11:19; meetings, 11:113, 12:102, 338, 13:118, 449, 14:120, 15:136, 16:125, 242, 489, 17:121, 22:216, 27:181; essay contest, 12:208

Goodhue County Home, 38:365, 367, 373, 377

Goodhue County Medical Society, 17:100

Goodhue County Rural Electrification Association, 23:107

Goodhue County War History Committee, 23:391

Goodland, Walter S., speaker, 27:356, 30:72

Goodland Township, Itasca County, name, 11:114

Goodnow, James, log mark, 26:136

Goodnow family, genealogy, 29:187

Goodrich, Judge Aaron, 19:256, 427, 30:310, 35:357, 363, 39:39, 44, 45; MHS founder, 20:367; speaker, 29:203n; career, 30:108, 39:141-152; papers, 35:204, 38:243; marriages, 39:143, 152

Goodrich, Mrs. Aaron, I (Celinda Fay), 39:143, 152

Goodrich, Mrs. Aaron, II, 39:152

Goodrich, Albert M., "The Radisson Problem," 13:245-255; "The Prairie Island Case Again," 13:395-402

Goodrich, Mrs. Alice P., 20:427

Goodrich, Allen L., 21:18

Goodrich, Mrs. Allen L., 21:9n

Goodrich, Carter, works reviewed, 17:322-324, 37:82

Goodrich, Earle S., journalist, 14:405, 22:211, 26:95, 37:46

Goodrich, Eliza, 39:141, 142

Goodrich, Enos, 39:142

Goodrich, Harry C., 23:391

Goodrich, Dr. James D., 14:292, 293, 297, 35:252, 253, 261

Goodrich, Levi H., 39:141, 142

Goodrich, Levi W., 39:141

Goodrich, Margaret, 19:320

Goodrich, Moses, 39:141, 143

Goodrich, Reuben, 39:142, 150

Goodrich, S. G., 17:437

Goodrich, W. F., author, 20:340

Goodrich Avenue, St. Paul, name, 20:369

Goodrich Avenue Presbyterian Church, St. Paul, 15:481

Goodrich Drug Store, Anoka, 25:365

Goodrich Line, Lake Michigan steamers, 26:266

Goodsell, Charles, 35:113, 114

Goodsmith, William, 33:190

Goodwill Industries, Minnesota, 17:227

Goodwin, Dorothy C., author, 23:180

Goodyear, Charles, inventor, 35:92

Goodykoontz, Colin B., works reviewed, 11:428-430, 21:71, 23:263-265; author, 11:429

Goose Prairie Township, Clay County, pioneer life, 12:336

Goose Rapids, Red River, 21:265, 267, 33:277

Gooseberry, see Groseilliers, sieur de

Gooseberry Falls State Park, historical meeting, 19:308-310; history, 19:452, 28:292

Gooseberry Island, Lake Huron, 23:143

Gooseberry River, Lake County, name, 12:287, 423; history, 28:292

Gopher, described, 16:38, 23:340

Gopher baseball club, Owatonna, 19:170

Gopher Campfire Club, Hutchinson, 16:496

Gopher Historian, 32:10, 62, 36:31, 62, 71, 108; established, 29:51, 30:328; promoted, 29:373

Gopher Historians, name, 29:373; publications, 30:38, 290, 367; chapters, 30:79, 86, 87, 162. See also Junior Historians

Gopher Mining and Trading Co., 29:303n

Gopher Ordinance Works, Rosemount, 33:243

Gopher State, nickname, 27:183, 30:157

Gopher State Amateur Press Association, 28:396

Gopher State baseball club, Rochester, 19:168, 169, 178, 179

Gopher State plow, 24:297

Gopher truck, 40:148

Goplen, Arnold O., author, 27:357, 28:187

Gorden, Peter J., author, 13:118

Gordhammern, Clarence, 23:392

Gordon, Rabbi Albert I., work reviewed, 31:44; speaker, 15:241; author, 15:467, 37:87

Gordon, C. H. M., author, 12:326

Gordon, Charles W., papers, 21:193

Gordon, Dudley J., 19:469, 21:331

Gordon, Lord Gordon, swindler, 12:327, 29:84, 33:89, 34:217, 352, 358

Gordon, Hanford L., poet, 26:294n, 298, 302, 36:76, 77

Gordon, Capt. Harry, 18:195

Gordon, Helen, author, 16:247

Gordon, Hermoine, author, 21:440

Gordon, John B., in Civil War, 29:64

Gordon, John H., 19:468

Gordon, Katherine R., 39:56

Gordon, Marjorie G., "British Trade at Michilimackinac," 11:231-270

Gordon, Otis H., pioneer, 22:346

Gordon, Rev. Philip, career, 25:194

Gordon, Richards, papers, 21:193

Gordon, Thomas C., artist, 37:38

Gordon, Thomas J., pioneer, 23:106

Gordon, W. A., author, 12:99

Gordon Lake, Cook County, forest fire, 36:134, 137

Gordon Stockade, S.D., architecture, 34:347

Gordon Township, Todd County, history, 16:131

Gordonsville, Freeborn County, history, 23:106

Gore, Sir St. George, buffalo hunter, 37:79

Gore Hall, Harvard University, 16:275, 276n

Gorgas, Adam B., banker, 35:363

Gorman, E. Stone, 19:164, 33:1

Gorman, Kathryn F., see Boardman, Mrs. Lawrence

Gorman, William P., steamboat captain, 13:226, 238

Gorman, Willis A., territorial governor, 11:95, 12:116, 14:132, 158, 159, 161-163, 16:174, 22:252, 254, 295, 23:309, 25:114n, 27:167, 28:183, 321, 29:318n, 32:41, 35:119, 357n, 360, 36:3, 6, 8, 9, 11, 283, 38:118, 119, 39:47, 48, 322, 40:62, 322; career, 12:442, 18:96, 26:303; activities, 13:433, 16:224, 454, 17:246; letters, 16:224, 20:328, 21:313, 30:91; speaker, 22:230, 26:67, 33:192, 34:143; in Civil War, 25:21, 25, 27, 29, 30, 35-38, 117, 120, 122-125, 129, 130, 133, 136, 229, 230, 249, 28:325, 326, 37:328, 38:175, 178; politician, 37:46-48, 50

Gorman, Mrs. Willis A., 14:295

Gorst, Thomas, 16:420, 421

Gortner, Ross A., author, 13:210, 18:107; career, 26:84

Gorton, Mr. and Mrs. Leander, 16:341

Gorton Township, Grant County, railroad, 13:41

Gospel Tabernacle, Duluth, 16:121
Goss, Caroline M., 19:320; author,
21:430
Goss, Homer, 18:112, 23:392, 24:88;
speaker, 20:304
Goss, Mrs. James, 15:483
Goss, Joshua, 34:158
Gossett, Thomas, review by, 31:115;
author, 31:128
Gossler, David, printer, 18:226
Gotshall, C. F., 19:184n
Gott, Benjamin, 11:101
Gottlieb, Paul, criminal suspect, 37:
165
Gottry, Lucille, 31:245
Gottschalk, Louis, work reviewed, 39:
34
Goucher College, Baltimore, Mayer
collection, 13:408-414, 26:140
Gough, John B., speaker, 11:157, 158,
22:124, 35:195, 40:12
Gould, Charles, gold seeker, 29:188
Gould, Charles D., 19:184n; career,
17:213
Gould, Clarence P., author, 27:59
Gould, Edwina, speaker, 18:463, 19:
115, 20:95, 22:339; author, 21:
107, 22:343
Gould, Dr. H. W., pioneer dentist,
21:437
Gould, Hallie M., author, 11:222, 13:
344
Gould, Jay, 29:84, 34:217, 358; rail-
road builder, 39:31, 40:356
Gould, Joseph E., work reviewed, 37:
340
Gould, Kenneth M., author, 16:114
Gould, Laurence M., "Minnesota Today
and Tomorrow," 30:331-342; speaker, 15:370, 30:286, 369; author,
30:412; college president, 40:256
Goulding, George W., 25:237, 256
Gournsey, ---, pioneer farmer, 24:290
Gove, E. J., 19:116
Gove, E. L., speaker, 21:445
Gove, Gertrude B., 17:123, 233, 26:
234, 258, 27:146, 29:94; "Depart-
mental Co-operation in the St.
Cloud Survey," 26:239-241; review
by, 34:41; author, 14:239, 15:139,
245, 16:247, 306n, 371, 17:464,
485, 489, 18:119, 282n, 23:110,
24:93, 28:384, 36:107, 195, 38:
204; speaker, 15:314, 19:119, 26:
235; editor, 35:152, 38:43
Gove, Mrs. Lucy R., teacher, 12:192
Government, Minnesota, 11:214, 12:98,
14:348, 15:99, 214-216, 243, 479,
17:201-204, 21:329, 23:187, 26:81,
29:83, 352, 30:144, 155, 36:106,
37:135, 347, 39:210; township in-
corporation, 39:299
"Governor Ramsey," steamboat, 12:
164n, 14:151, 19:143, 144, 24:138,
28:342, 29:204, 213, 215, 35:104,
105, 40:332
Governor's Island, N.Y., air field,
22:302, 305
Govorchin, Gerald G., author, 38:241
Goward, Mrs. E. J., reminiscences,
21:447
Gowdy, A. C., 16:471
Gowdy, Lillian M., 29:322
Gower, R. H. G. Leveson, author, 15:
231, 356, 477, 16:348, 479
Goyens, Father Jérome, author, 15:455
Graber, Albert, 13:198

Graber, Anna E., author, 35:202
Grace, Bishop Thomas L., 13:215, 15:
195, 345, 16:119, 18:352, 20:85,
34:313, 35:134, 270; implements
treaty, 15:297; educator, 16:483,
17:84; career, 18:89, 22:334, 33:
223; house, 25:5; colonizer, 31:
21; quoted, 38:64
Grace Methodist Church, St. Paul, 17:
467
Graceville, Catholic colony, 19:450,
24:79, 31:22, 35:138, 139, 205-
213; hotel, 23:300
Graebner, Norman A., editor, 38:240
Graebner, Theodore, author, 25:397
Graf, Herbert, work reviewed, 33:135
"Graf Zeppelin," airship, 39:280
Graff, Ella, 22:340
Graff, Henry F., author, 36:32
Graff, Mrs. Sophia, author, 17:491
Grafthen, Martin, 22:341
Graham, ---, pioneer farmer, 11:186
Graham, A. B., author, 22:328
Graham, Alexander, guide, 19:95
Graham, Andrew, North West Co. ped-
lar, 16:200
Graham, Andrew J., Episcopal rector,
18:141
Graham, Dr. Archibald, 20:336, 27:315
Graham, Dr. Christopher, 11:186, 22:
407
Graham, Christopher C., land officer,
22:246
Graham, Sister Clara, author, 32:61
Graham, David, 22:341
Graham, Mrs. David, author, 23:110
Graham, Duncan, trader, 18:193, 22:
282, 283, 285, 27:67, 29:267, 35:
321
Graham, Felix, trader, 19:95
Graham, Frederick U., traveler, 37:
134; diary, 17:67, 32:59
Graham, G. S., author, 15:239
Graham, George R., editor, 30:203
Graham, Harrison H., 37:191, 192
Graham, Hugh, author, 11:42, 329, 12:
205
Graham, Margaret J., 14:416
Graham, Martha, dancer, 21:59
Graham, Mary Elizabeth, 35:321
Graham, Philip, work reviewed, 33:39
Graham, W. A., work reviewed, 34:39
"Graham Bell," steamboat, 28:262
Graham Lakes Township, Nobles County,
pioneer life, 16:361, 20:361
Graham's Island, N.D., pioneer life,
30:160
Graham's Magazine, history, 30:203
Graham's Point, Wilkin County, townsite, 13:321, 29:236
Grahn, Arch, MHS field director, 29:
187, 360, 30:363, 34:359; speaker,
30:82; author, 37:44
Grain marketing, 39:328; elevators,
12:107, 37:14-18, 99; Minnesota
communities, 12:108, 13:212, 21:
238, 24:100, 272; foreign, 16:344,
37:261; statistics, 24:103, 37:
118; regulation, 25:201, 39:93,
94, 96, 97; co-operative, 26:381,
29:76; Milwaukee, 30:138; Duluth,
33:66, 37:118; river towns, 37:87;
grading, 37:159; during Civil War,
39:210; Minneapolis, 40:147. See
also Agriculture, Corn raising,
Flour milling, Wheat raising

Grainger, Percy, pianist, 17:101, 39:
59
Gran, Frank, pioneer, 25:411
Granahan, David, 19:81, 25:275
Granahan, Lolita, 19:81, 25:275
Granby Township, Nicollet County,
Norwegian settlement, 12:275
Grand Army of the Republic, 33:82;
posts, 11:321, 15:347, 464, 16:
127, 360, 430, 432-434, 437, 438,
440, 17:119, 121, 22:217, 343, 27:
57, 76, 30:35, 38:78, 39:190; records, 12:191, 13:319, 16:242, 22:
184; South Dakota, 13:439; encamp-
ments, 14:460, 15:117, 18:138, 30:
398; Minnesota, 16:427-447, 35:
314, 37:42; in politics, 23:165;
history, 35:197
Grand Calumet, Ottawa River, Ont.,
Que., portage, 28:9
Grand Encampment, Lake Pepin, trading
site, 16:155-159, 163, 164
Grand Fabri Mulders, opera troupe,
28:110
Grand Forks, N.D., trading post, 11:
368, 22:276, 286, 288; history,
16:229, 21:99; river port, 21:263;
railroad station, 28:396; sawmill,
29:137, 138, 140, 145; power company, 35:381
Grand Forks and Pembina Stage Line,
20:444
Grand Haven, Mich., history, 12:440
Grand Island, Lake Superior, described, 23:236, 237
Grand Lake, St. Louis County, history, 21:456, 23:302
Grand Lisière, see Great Oasis
Grand Marais, trading post, 11:358,
22:274; historical meeting, 12:
187, 286-288; name, 12:287; harbor, 14:119, 19:113; history, 21:
449, 28:381, 31:191, 34:177, 178,
181, 35:49; churches, 30:270, 39:
310; post office, 35:246; ranger
station, 36:133, 135
Grand Meadow, Norwegian settlement,
12:269; museum, 37:42; bank, 40:
359
Grand Medicine Society (Midewiwin),
Chippewa ceremonial, 21:285, 35:
44, 244, 38:193
Grand Mound, see Smith Mounds
Grand Opera House, Minneapolis, 18:
28, 33, 138, 33:176, 177
Grand Opera House, St. Paul, 25:102,
26:184, 32:104; records, 13:321;
Oscar Wilde's appearance, 17:43,
45; built, 23:312; depicted, 28:
103; performances, 28:109; frontier theater, 30:388
"Grand Pacific," steamboat, 31:85
Grand Portage, Pigeon River, in fiction, 11:102, 21:93, 32:33, 122;
trail, 11:217, 358, 12:283, 14:
229, 15:92, 131, 240, 16:489, 19:
463, 22:213, 24:342, 27:358, 28:
375, 38:25-29; trading posts, 11:
261, 262, 264n, 265, 308, 357, 12:
294, 423, 13:433, 14:166, 16:23,
348, 18:94, 457, 19:40, 95, 292,
20:14, 16, 87, 104, 21:119, 126,
133, 136-138, 147, 22:274, 24:364,
28:6, 13, 14n, 29:132, 351, 30:
132, 31:125, 33:131, 261, 37:236,
40:145, 162; historical meetings,
12:186, 288-296, 13:56, 30:287;

mission, 12:205, 15:110, 19:457, 23:97, 28:181, 29:168, 33:185, 39:301-310; excavation and restoration, 12:207, 13:71, 17:347, 461, 18:51, 328, 456-458, 19:53, 20:42, 444, 21:206, 22:83, 432, 40:150, 412; described, 12:289, 290, 373, 16:107, 20:205, 23:67, 28:142, 35:49, 37:175; history, 12:359-377, 21:182, 449, 27:340, 28:78, 34:177, 36:95, 38:193; forest, 16:237; highway, 17:117, 25:91; harbor, 19:113; Catholic church, 19:464, 23:196, 39:301 (cover), 308, 309, 310; census, 20:452; trade license case, 21:117-148; pictured, 21:152, 156, 26:174, 359, 39:308; museum, 22:215, 339, 38:34; Indian agency, 23:93; in poetry, 25:371; mail service, 26:83, 35:246; fisheries, 32:186, 33:256; national monument, 36:151, 37:61, 63, 186, 39:310

Grand Portage, St. Louis River, crossing, 23:245, 246, 31:94
Grand Portage Indian Reservation (Chippewa), 11:447, 12:326, 384, 18:209, 24:54, 40:42n, 146; smallpox outbreak, 27:351
Grand Rapids, Itasca County, churches, 11:219, 22:345; history, 15:487, 18:339, 22:345, 445, 25:315, 26:94, 289; band, 16:249; parent-teacher association, 17:236; paper mill, 21:286; agricultural school, 22:413, 27:358; logging, 22:416, 24:383, 30:68; Junior Historians, 27:147; river port, 33:7-9, 11-16, 40:263; railroad, 33:15; disabled veterans, 39:243
Grand Rapids, Stearns County, ghost town, 22:447
Grand Rapids Business Men's Association, 28:191
Grand Rapids Herald-Review, anniversary, 15:487
Grand River, Mich., mission, 15:122, 19:457; fur trade, 19:299
Grand Sable, Lake Superior, described, 23:234, 235
Grand Teton National Park, 40:197
Grand Theater, St. Paul, 23:199
Grand Trunk Railroad, immigrant route, 13:36, 24:330, 32:126; ferry, 38:237
Grande, Broder, author, 11:115
Grandelmyer, C., storekeeper, 35:270
Grandin family, farm, 39:206
Grandjean, A., author, 14:341
Grange, Mrs. John, author, 20:104
Granger, Dr. Charles T., author, 16:250
Granger, Gen. Gordon, Union officer, 38:271
Granger, John A., excursionist, 15:406
Granger movement, co-operative aspect, 11:100, 17:348, 18:323, 410, 19:151, 39:129; history, 12:326, 15:99, 17:478, 21:91, 436, 24:120, 26:171, 361, 30:252-254, 33:41, 35:298, 36:101; records, 15:61, 17:54, 98, 18:316, 19:49, 97, 22:41, 23:40; activities, 15:113, 243, 29:9, 101, 33:50, 224, 35:56, 58, 241, 334, 39:298, 40:297; op-

posed by Lutheran church, 16:107; local units, 17:467, 481, 18:316, 19:49, 364, 30:75, 32:62, 35:55, 40:333; in fiction, 23:119; publication, 26:295; Iowa, 36:238. See also Agrarian movement; Donnelly, Ignatius; Farmers' Alliance; Kelley, Oliver H.; National Grange
Granite City, Morrison County, ghost town, 34:359
Granite Falls, historical meeting, 16:302; Scandinavian settlements, 23:290, 27:72; archaeology, 27:261, 28:76; museum, 30:402; history, 38:243; railroad, 39:92
Granite Falls Township, Chippewa County, Norwegian settlement, 12:275n
Granite industry, St. Cloud, 12:456, 26:235, 35:152, 37:263; Minnesota, 29:171
Granite River, border river, archaeology, 38:33, 39:130
Grannis, A. B., 16:256
Grannis, Henry J., autobiography, 14:64, 103
Granquist, Reuben, 18:344
Granskou, Clemens M., author, 26:95; college president, 31:51
Grandstrand, Ruth, 23:104
Grant, ---, Morrison County farmer, 28:211
Grant, Bruce, author, 40:145
Grant, Charles, trader, 11:261, 16:200, 201, 38:28
Grant, Cuthbert J., trader, 11:371; career, 15:477, 21:206
Grant, David, trader, 11:357
Grant, Frederick C., author, 18:331
Grant, George, 21:297
Grant, Helen, 29:93
Grant, Capt. Hiram P., in Sioux Outbreak, 12:297-300, 38:103n, 110n, 138n, 139
Grant, Irvin, letters, 19:343, 20:33
Grant, Capt. J. Colfax, 14:440
Grant, James, trader, 11:369, 12:91, 92
Grant, Mrs. Jay M., house, 38:337
Grant, John, 11:238n
Grant, Maj. Lewis A., 12:442, 14:440
Grant, Madison, 34:343
Grant, Mary L., letter, 28:306
Grant, Maud, speaker, 17:481
Grant, Nellie, 29:128
Grant, Peter, trader, 11:357, 366, 367; author, 29:66
Grant, R. E., 19:170
Grant, Richard, trader, 20:71
Grant, Robert, trader, 11:238n, 12:369
Grant, Thomson, miller, 14:124
Grant, Ulysses S., 20:281-284, 22:313, 36:301, 303, 38:318; President, 13:17, 29:128, 33:267, 39:152; Minnesota visit, 15:403, 38:293-295; Indian policy, 18:268, 34:123, 35:167-177, 37:273; in Illinois, 22:73, 27:283; general, 25:23, 120, 350, 33:211, 212, 36:228, 38:271, 39:182, 185, 188, 40:281, 283; biography, 32:58
Grant, Mrs. Ulysses S., 29:128, 38:295
Grant, William, trader, 11:245-247, 268, 19:290, 20:326
Grant family, genealogy, 14:440

Grant and Dakota Railway Co., records, 23:171
Grant and Wood, stock company, 33:176
Grant County, railroad, 12:254; history, 12:259, 14:457, 16:247, 365, 24:273, 33:353; Norwegian settlement, 12:277; county seat, 12:444, 15:486, 23:371; trails, 16:128, 17:359, 20:47; archives, 21:101; in World War II, 24:185; Lutheran church, 29:179; stage route, 38:63-71
Grant County, N.D., place names, 36:325
Grant County Agricultural Association, fairs, 15:486; history, 21:113
Grant County Herald (Elbow Lake), history, 33:353
Grant County Herald (Lancaster, Wis.), history, 24:177
Grant County Historical Society, 19:360, 20:46; museum, 17:356, 482, 20:47, 211, 23:296, 29:179, 362, 37:87, 38:162; picture collection, 24:86, 187
Grant County Old Settlers Association, 12:450, 16:365
Grant County War History Committee, 24:82, 185
Grant House, Winona, 22:448
Grant Township, Boone County, Iowa, school, 23:184
Grant Township, Washington County, history, 17:490; Germans, 23:404
Grant Valley Township, Beltrami County, history, 15:365
Grantown, Man., founded, 21:206
Grantsburg, Wis., ethnic groups, 27:135; press, 28:84
Granville, Marshall County, ghost town, 35:47
Grape Island, see Pike Island
Graphic History Society of America, 33:351
Gras, Norman S. B., 14:194, 18:76; author, 11:99, 26:72; editor, 30:64
Grass Lake, Hennepin County, 17:304, 35:23n, 24
Grasshopper plagues, described, 11:65, 72, 13:119, 16:247, 18:288, 27:225, 29:21n; effects, 11:335, 12:262, 24:91, 29:16, 20, 271, 33:352, 38:70, 369; 1870s, 11:435, 455, 12:248, 262, 445, 13:42, 16:264, 432, 433, 17:98, 29:354, 357, 30:372, 33:143, 36:54-61, 104, 37:183, 204, 207-210; 1850s, 12:456, 17:364, 32:40, 35:266, 39:70; Minnesota, 15:245, 20:156, 329, 24:382, 25:100, 26:366, 29:16, 20, 21n, 30:35; Dakotas, 16:229, 32:244; Nebraska, 40:409
Grassick, Dr. J., author, 12:204
Grasty, Charles H., career, 12:442
Gratiot, Mrs. Adele, 29:175
Gratiot, Charles H., businessman, 30:249, 32:86, 87; army engineer, 40:24, 27, 28
Grattan, Thomas C., author, 29:154
Graves, C. E., 19:172
Graves, Col. Charles H., 19:406; career, 25:384, 38:299
Graves, Mrs. Charles H., 26:31, 38:299
Graves, Edward B., career, 12:322

Graves, Ethel G., 27:77; author, 16:234

Graves, Peter, career, 35:380

Graves, Randall B., papers, 18:210

Graves, Rose, author, 35:380

Graves, Gen. William S., 38:325

Gravesbacken, Vasa Township, Goodhue County, cemetery, 14:426-428

Gravier, Father Jacques, 16:449

Gray, C. W., author, 22:112

Gray, Carl R., Sr., 19:51n

Gray, Gen. Carl R., Jr., 19:50, 23:293; speaker, 18:320

Gray, George, newspaperman, 22:112

Gray, Mrs. Ina G., 19:321

Gray, Isaac, steamboat captain, 36:212

Gray, James, I, 28:73; papers, 22:86, 34:339, 37:44

Gray, James, II, 20:105, 306, 39:59; "A Literary Critic Looks at History," 21:1-14; "The University and the Historical Society," 32:1-11; reviews by, 19:328-330, 30:52, 380-382; works reviewed, 22:73, 26:250, 32:176, 34:203, 36:185, 37:300, 39:208; author, 12:290, 13:314, 18:330, 19:337, 20:117, 323, 363, 21:80, 22:36, 365, 437, 26:253, 378, 27:164, 30:95, 181, 412, 31:129, 133, 135, 138, 146, 32:63, 34:355, 39:131; speaker, 21:51, 27:67; editor, 28:69

Gray, John, merchant, 11:238n

Gray, John M., work reviewed 39:166

Gray, Margaret, 17:190

Gray, Ralph, author, 33:312

Gray, Capt. Robert, explorer, 29:61

Gray, Royal C., house, 38:350

Gray, T. K., Drug Co., Minneapolis, 18:211

Gray, Thomas K., druggist, 18:211

Gray, Col. W. F., emigrant agent, 13:29

Gray, William C., author, 40:310

Gray, Wood, work reviewed, 24:154-156; author, 35:243, 36:277

Gray Bird, Sioux leader, 38:138

Gray Cloud, Sioux woman, 20:351

Gray Cloud Female Seminary, 14:146

Gray Cloud Island, see Grey Cloud Island

Grayson, David, pseud., see Baker, Ray S.

Grease, Miss ---, 20:310, 311

Great Britain, American colonies, 11:78, 242, 15:94-97, 17:196-198, 216, 18:303, 384, 19:311, 353, 21:182, 22:98, 24:149, 234, 28:176, 32:109, 248, 33:87; relations with Indians, 11:78, 80, 240, 15:257, 19:280, 21:395, 29:65, 33:37, 40:162, 180; in fur trade, 11:243-270, 368, 375, 19:290-307, 20:7-18, 21:117-148, 29:351, 35:144, 36:241-249, 38:190, 199, 39:81, 40:163, 180, 182, 211-220; relations with U.S., 12:74, 22:306-308; consuls' reports, 14:225; relations with France, 16:403-406, 18:391-394, 428-430, 19:280-290, 393-398, 23:161, 24:150; explorations, 16:453, 38:380; source material, 18:195, 20:439, 39:165; boundary dispute, 18:428-430, 19:198, 353, 22:62-65, 24:341-343, 30:375; emigration, 21:299, 33:85,

35:374, 37:44; Mormon converts, 36:286; U.S. investments, 37:185, 39:98. See also British, Revolutionary War, War of 1812

Great European-American Emigration Land Co., 17:405, 18:74, 25:396

Great Lakes, shipping, 12:178, 14:232, 15:122, 16:348, 18:217, 20:438, 25:77, 29:165, 34:9-16, 36:276, 37:39, 38:386; explored, 12:282, 347-349, 17:345, 34:285, 35:151, 36:70, 37:302, 39:81, 40:314; names, 12:282, 349, 23:58; maps, 12:351, 13:186, 19:214; steamboating, 13:196, 15:123, 19:349, 22:202, 437, 23:355, 356, 24:166, 26:266, 276, 28:56, 310, 32:46, 84, 33:316, 356, 34:9-16, 35:278-281, 292, 36:296, 37:39, 102, 115, 118, 40:266, 272, 273; geology, 13:320, 21:325, 36:188; travel on, 15:14, 356, 18:154, 384, 19:199, 21:93, 234, 25:412, 26:266, 380, 28:56, 37:79, 39:211, 40:266, 272-275, 313, 316, 359; fur trade, 19:271-307, 21:423, 40:155, 213, 215, 216, 220, 259; Norse relics, 21:92; history, 22:431, 23:355, 24:175, 256, 26:76, 39:82, 40:141; fisheries, 24:165, 25:401; lighthouses, 24:175, 39:82; geography, 25:385, 26:384, 40:356; lumbering, 26:166; shipbuilding, 27:353; Indians, 33:344, 37:174, 40:358; shipwrecks, 34:39, 35:292, 36:237, 37:179; car ferries, 38:237. See also St. Lawrence Seaway, individual lakes

Great Lakes Exposition, 17:347

Great Lakes Historical Society, 25:296, 26:152, 265, 29:165

Great Lakes-St. Lawrence Tidewater Association, 37:41, 260, 303

Great Lakes Shoreline Recreation Area Survey, 37:182

"Great Manito," sandstone formation, 39:288

Great Metropolitan Theatre Co., Minneapolis, 33:175

Great Northern Iron Ore Properties, history, 32:46

Great Northern Railroad, stations, 11:338, 13:119, 14:122, 357, 15:41, 17:492, 18:338, 21:450, 23:33, 24:327, 28:383, 29:148, 33:144n, 256, 339, 35:275; locomotives, 11:338, 18:274, 379, 36:321, 37:159; history, 13:365, 21:96, 26:371, 28:70, 375, 34:214, 35:153, 337, 338, 382, 36:71, 102; completed to Pacific, 16:224, 343, 463, 34:216; Wisconsin, 17:345; bridge, 37:187; ore hauling, 26:77; logging, 28:138, 140; route, 33:55; hotel train, 38:206, 207

Great Northern Railway Co., history, 11:104, 17:218, 19:113, 20:336, 28:372, 30:373, 31:55, 35:39, 45, 39:31; surveys, 21:109, 29:165; colonization program, 26:372, 36:68; in World War II, 27:57, 38:310-325; archives, 30:55; Minnetonka resort, 34:173; strike, 36:105, 120-122; in politics, 39:101, 109; proposed merger, 39:333. See also St. Paul, Minneapolis, and Manitoba Railway Co.

Great Oasis (Tibbetts) Lake, Murray County, trading post, 11:380, 14:84-86, 329, 31:198; townsite, 14:250; archaeological site, 26:387

Great Plains, fur trade, 11:189, 40:192-197; history, 13:92-94, 327, 28:276, 40:409; conference, 23:380; periodical literature, 24:235; interpretation, 29:70, 35:148; farming, 29:260, 36:28

Great Salt Lake, Utah, levels, 17:304

Great Slave Lake, see Slave Lake

Great West (St. Paul), Alliance newspaper, 32:135-141, 36:116, 117

Great Western Band, St. Paul, 16:40, 19:175, 34:240, 242, 38:290, 294; history, 16:497, 20:356, 23:403

Greater America Exposition, Omaha, 39:120

Greater St. Paul Committee, activities, 37:323

Greaves, Mrs. H. A., speaker, 11:223

Greaves, William, 38:172

Grebstein, Sheldon, "Sinclair Lewis' Minnesota Boyhood," 34:85-89; author, 34:176, 38:387

Greek Orthodox church, Minneapolis, 19:123; Mesabi Range, 27:213

"Greek Slave," steamboat, 11:180, 181n, 12:393, 398, 19:249

Greeks, Detroit, Mich., 20:202; contributions, 22:96, 27:40; Mesabi Range, 27:204, 211, 212, 215, 40:341, 347; reverse migration, 27:214

Greeley, Elam, lumberman, 18:169, 24:197, 198, 202; postmaster, 24:203, 36:208, 40:87

Greeley, Mrs. Elam (Hannah Hinman), 24:203, 349

Greeley, Horace, journalist, 11:150, 14:339, 16:441, 17:327, 411, 25:91, 27:1, 30:192, 31:120, 33:300, 34:203, 217, 358, 39:152; quoted, 20:230; abolitionist, 20:271, 32:21, 25, 28; speaker, 22:86, 261, 34:148; papers, 34:212

Greeley, Phoebe, 24:203

Greeley, William B., author, 33:92

Green, Andrew, servant, 15:430

Green, Bartholomew, pioneer printer, 15:6

Green, Charles L., author, 11:323, 23:382

Green, Constance M., author, 23:178

Green, Dick, servant, 15:430

Green, Fletcher M., author, 14:338

Green, Frank, 17:491

Green, George, 17:300n

Green, Horace, author, 21:369

Green, James, cholera victim, 14:290

Green, James, Little Falls pioneer, 29:270

Green, John, locomotive engineer, 16:249

Green, John, Stillwater pioneer, 17:491

Green, John E., speaker, 11:112

Green, John R., British historian, 19:9

Green, Montreville, steamboat captain, 15:409

Green, Paul, author, 20:116

Green, Lt. Platt R., 18:402, 405

Green, Samuel, pioneer printer, 15:4

Green, Samuel B., horticulturist, 12:442

Green, Timothy, pioneer printer, 15:6
Green, W. J., 18:339
Green family, 16:492
Green Bay, Wis., fur trade, 11:246,
13:202, 17:196, 335, 18:390, 20:
205, 32:227, 229, 232, 235–238,
40:186; newspaper, 11:326, 15:16;
history, 11:452, 25:271, 272, 29:
173; Norwegian settlement, 12:180;
forest fires, 12:329; discovered
and explored, 12:348, 13:260, 397,
398, 15:171, 172, 175, 236, 18:
387, 23:240, 27:216–220, 34:156;
Indians, 13:260, 15:171, 172,
175, 18:387, 22:150, 27:218, 33:
20; historical celebration, 15:
474; name, 19:272; missions, 20:
443, 24:178. See also Fort Howard, Wis.
Green Bay and Winona Railroad, organized, 36:105
Green Bay colony, Martin County, history, 12:103
Green Bay Intelligencer, first Wisconsin newspaper, 11:327, 15:16
Green County, Wis., Swiss settlement,
28:188
Green Giant Co., Le Sueur, anniversary, 33:353
Green Island, S.D., flood, 11:68
Green Isle, Sibley County, history,
13:122; frontier farm, 37:205
Green River, Wyo., Union Pass, 40:197
Greenaway, Kate, artist, 33:340, 342
Greenback party, 36:183; Minnesota,
32:129, 35:58, 59, 298; accom-
plishments, 35:378
Greenbie, Marjorie B., author, 20:335
Greenbush, growth, 14:458; band, 21:
455; railroads, 24:327
Greene, Dr. Charles L., 24:347
Greene, Rev. David G., 16:135, 138,
140, 142, 145, 147, 148, 21:28,
169
Greene, Donald J., author, 34:126;
editor, 37:40
Greene, Evarts B., 12:312; author,
24:366
Greene, Lt. F. V., surveyor, 35:379
Greene, George B., 19:321
Greene, Howard, author, 18:326
Greene, Mrs. Maurice, 35:208n
Greene, Plunket, singer, 39:53
Greene, Theodore M., author, 26:72
Greener, S. N., baseball player, 19:
174, 175, 179
Greenfield, Ohio, Indian school, 18:
197
Greening, Burton O., 32:195
Greening, John, diary, 22:192
Greenland, Vinland voyages, 39:170
Greenleaf, A. W., and Co., brokers,
40:111, 112
Greenleaf, Anna, 28:123
Greenleaf, Damon, 19:172
Greenleaf, Rev. Eleazer A., mission-
ary, 17:350, 27:368
Greenleaf Township, Meeker County,
school, 11:220; farming, 19:344;
in Sioux Outbreak, 38:279
Greenleaf and Chappell, St. Paul,
jewelers, 14:267
Greenleafton, Fillmore County, Dutch
settlement, 28:120–124, 35:90;
name, 28:123
Greenless, Stephen, author, 34:174

Greenly, Albert H., compiler, 34:216,
36:100
Greenman, Emerson K., author, 35:154
Greenslit, Ethel M., author, 36:107
Greenvale Township, Dakota County,
Norwegian settlement, 12:271;
mounds, 16:308; pioneer life, 21:
340; schools, 22:445
Greenville, Ohio, treaty, 23:145, 25:
268, 26:384
Greenville, Wabasha County, settled,
16:315
Greenville Township, Rice County,
Manx settlement, 26:285, 27:173
Greenwald, L. J., 22:104
Greenwald, Mrs. L. J., 23:100, 29:90;
speaker, 22:338
Greenway, John C., 22:346
Greenway, Thomas, colonizer, 33:315
Greenway Township, Itasca County,
school district, 17:127
Greenwood, Grace, 30:251
Greenwood, William, 11:238n
Greenwood family, genealogy, 16:102
Greenwood, plat, 23:171; settled, 36:
36; post office, 40:88
Greenwood, Wis., history, 15:475
Greenwood Mill, River Falls, Wis.,
razed, 16:229
Greenwood Prairie Old Settlers, 16:
256
Greer, Allen J., legislator, 35:349
Greer, John N., educator, 35:371
Greever, William S., review by, 36:28
Gregg, Arthur B., author, 18:215
Gregg, David A., architect, 37:19
Gregg, Oren C., agriculturist, 27:
120, 121, 33:224, 39:83; career,
13:450, 20:448, 30:371, 37:19–29
Gregg, Mrs. Oren C., 37:20, 29
Gregg, Thomas, author, 14:352
Gregorich, Joseph, work reviewed, 13:
187; author, 22:200, 30:392
Gregory, Rev. Casper R., papers, 25:
182
Gregory, Rev. Daniel S., career, 12:
443
Gregory, Harriet, author, 14:123
Gregory, John, trader, 11:261, 12:
368, 20:326
Gregory, John G., editor, 16:347
Gregory, Samuel, feminist, 39:8
Gregory, Mrs. V. J., speaker, 15:241
Gregory, Walter, 19:184n
Gregory, Winifred, 15:120, 16:331;
editor, 18:322
Gregory, Morrison County, trading
post, 11:374, 36:40n
Greil, Patrick, missionary, 32:38
Grenier, Judson A., "A Minnesota
Railroad Man," 38:310–325
Greninger, A. B., author, 21:303
Grenoble, ——, French explorer, 12:
348
Gresham, Judge ——, 18:139
Gresham, Hugh C., author, 19:350
Gressel, Amalia, 15:222
Gretchtown, Nobles County, mythical
city, 14:250, 26:90
Grettum, May, teacher, 33:74, 75,
108–111
Greve, Edward, author, 30:407
Greve, Fred, 25:99
Greve, Sigmund, author, 25:92
Grevstad, Nicolay A., editor, 29:314n
Grew, Joseph C., ambassador, 40:48

Grey Cloud, David, Sisseton Indian,
35:173
Grey Cloud Island, Mississippi River,
19:466; history, 11:218, 17:311;
trading posts, 11:381; located,
12:128; described, 36:239; in fic-
tion, 37:10
"Grey Eagle," steamboat, 11:126, 323,
14:178, 15:187, 464, 17:207, 20:
387, 36:279, 40:411
Grey Eagle Township, Todd County,
history, 16:131
Grey Iron, Sioux leader, 38:129
Grey Leg, Sioux Indian, 22:135
Greyhound Bus Lines, Mesabi Range,
18:220, 27:272, 367, 33:353, 35:
338, 36:190; history, 21:291, 26:
270, 38:378
Gridley, Marion E., author, 22:201
Griebie, C. H., journal, 28:190
Grier, Harry, 28:302
Grier, Justice Robert C., 25:354
Grierson, Benjamin H., 25:350, 39:187
Grierson, Francis, author, 31:80
Grieve, Robert, 25:142
Griffin, Burt, author, 36:101
Griffin, Grace G., compiler, 24:173;
author, 28:68
Griffin, James B., author, 39:262
Griffin, James E., pioneer, 30:290
Griffin, Orro B., author, 18:229
Griffin, Thomas H., diary, 17:467
Griffith, Charles F., author, 11:210
Griffith, Edwin M., forester, 36:235
Griffith, Sir John, 16:425n
Griffith, Martha E., author, 25:299
Griffith, Thomas H., steamboat cap-
tain, 32:12n
Griffith, Winthrop, work reviewed,
39:258
Griffiths, L., 20:142
Griffiths, Richard, labor leader, 22:
368, 372
"Griffon," sailing vessel, 12:178,
19:276, 23:356, 25:274, 34:39, 35:
43, 153, 292, 40:141
Grignut, Paul, editor, 33:36
Griggs, Alexander, steamboat captain,
21:99, 264, 266
Griggs, Col. Chauncey W., family, 25:
204
Griggs, Edward H., autobiography, 16:
226
Griggs, Mrs. Theodore, house, 38:347n
Griggs, Cooper and Co., 25:204, 206
Griggs County, N.D., Sibley expedi-
tion camps, 39:36
Grignon, Charles, trader, 20:14
Grignon, Pierre, trader, 15:421
Grignon Tract, Wis., history, 24:255
Grim, George, author, 28:192, 30:406
Grimes, Alan P., author, 34:352
Grimes, James W., career, 34:41
Grimes, Jonathan T., 19:357, 28:201
Grimke, Francis J., 17:108
Grimké, Sarah, 19:436
Grimm, Joseph, 19:22, 23
Grimm, Wendelin, pioneer farmer, 20:
448, 25:386; develops alfalfa, 16:
122, 364, 19:21–33, 20:75, 38:378
Grimm Alfalfa Growers Associations,
19:32
Grimmestad, L. M., author, 23:290
Grimstad, Carl M., reminiscences, 24:
258
Grinager, Mons, 17:222

Grindstone River, Kanabec and Pine counties, crossing, 37:106n
Grinnell, George B., naturalist, 30:125, 32:220; author, 38:202
Grinnell College, Grinnell, Iowa, history, 33:356
Gripenberg, Alexandra, work reviewed, 34:163
Grist mill, defined, 11:275n
Griswold, Burr F., author, 21:204, 22:329
Griswold, Franklin C., lawyer, 23:196
Griswold, H. B., 18:446
Griswold, Mrs. Harriet, letters, 19:210
Griswold family, genealogy, 35:248
Grk, Risto, folk singer, 34:296
Groat, Hannibal, 20:349
Grob, Gerald N., author, 36:34
Groce, George C., work reviewed, 35:369
Grode, John S., 39:154n
Grodinsky, Julius, work reviewed, 39:30
Grondahl, R. L., 17:228
Groningen, Pine County, Dutch settlement, 13:427, 28:130, 131
Gronvald, Dr. J. C., 26:287, 31:190
Grooms, Horatio, agent, 21:22
Gros Ventres Indians, customs, 32:244. See also Hidatsa Indians
Grosbeck (Groesbek, Groesbeke), Stephen, trader, 11:258, 264n, 16:224
Grose, I. F., author, 19:473; speaker, 14:346
Groseilliers, Médard Chouart, sieur de, explorer and trader, 11:204, 385, 452, 12:77, 91, 283, 287, 350, 361, 13:247, 250, 251, 253-255, 262, 263, 396, 399, 400, 15:61, 158, 160, 162-165, 172-177, 180, 317-327, 368, 16:449, 453, 17:75, 94, 114, 223, 342, 18:312, 388, 19:273, 22:60, 181, 24:340, 26:171, 255, 273, 274, 28:170, 177, 29:153, 30:375, 32:124, 186, 33:187, 35:243, 36:150, 37:86; house, 13:110; biographies, 13:210, 439, 22:44, 24:149-151, 28:362; in New England, 13:418, 15:322, 16:440, 410; in England, 14:435, 15:177, 322, 16:393, 395-399, 415; at Washington Island, 15:166-170; title, 15:174; trip to Hudson Bay, 15:322, 16:399, 419-423; education, 16:412n; contribution to geography, 16:414-426; pictured, 29:79
Gross, Francis A., 33:54; speaker, 26:284
Gross, Mrs. Lizetta, 21:340
Gross, Samuel D., author, 21:368
Gross's Hall, New Ulm, 32:169
Grosvenor Library, Buffalo, N.Y., song collection, 26:379
Grotten, John, author, 17:359
Groundhouse City, see Ogilvie, Kanabec County
Groundhouse River, Kanabec County, post, 11:374; logging, 18:172, 24:273
Groundmaster, Alexander, trader, 22:288
Grout, Frank F., work reviewed, 36:320; author, 15:131, 34:358;

speaker, 24:269; editor, 25:308; geologist, 34:276
Grout, Jane M., diary, 13:213, 16:302, 17:363
Grove, Mrs. John, pioneer motorist, 26:24
Grove, Lee E., work reviewed, 27:40
Grove, Philip F., author, 23:157
Grove City, history, 19:470; located, 33:144n
Grove Lake Township, Pope County, Methodist church, 17:118; schools, 26:183, 398
Groveland Nursery, St. Paul, 14:278
Groveland Seminary, Wasioja, 14:147
Grover, A. J., 35:14
Grover, Ezra J., lawyer, 17:213
Grover, Wayne C., archivist, 29:259; author, 36:219, 236
Grow, Galusha A., Congressman, 16:27, 23:314; sponsors homestead bill, 12:382, 22:246
Grow & Christopher, New York, piano makers, 30:319
Grund, Francis J., author, 29:154
Grundysen, Tellef, author, 16:107, 18:432, 31:130
Gruner, J. W., author, 15:131
Grünewald, Anna, actress, 32:171
Grussendorf, D. T., speaker, 20:213
Grytbak, M. S., author, 15:140
Guardian Angels Church (Catholic), Hastings, 11:332; Chaska, 24:84
Guards of Temperance, Nininger, 13:147
Gudde, Erwin G., author, 33:311
Gudehus, Jonas H., author, 14:334
Guerin, Jules, artist, 33:334, 336
Guerin, Vital, cabin, 15:182; career, 34:266; in fiction, 37:10
Guerney Lumber Co., Wis., labor problem, 36:164
Guggenheim Memorial Foundation, fellowships, 15:218, 340, 16:60, 330, 391n, 17:62, 20:287
Gugisburg, Henry, banker, 36:201, 205
Guiche, Count de la, traveler, 28:317
Guidinger, Luella, 16:363, 18:112
Guignas, Michel, missionary, 13:210, 339, 17:473, 21:102, 26:173
Guilder, Adolphus, inventor, 15:131
Guilford, Howard A., newspaper editor, 37:163-169, 172, 173
Guillaid, ---, trader, 11:262n
Guillam, Capt. Zachariah, see Gillam, Capt. Zachariah
Guillet, Edwin C., author, 15:356, 40:358
Guillet, Father Urban, 16:90; letters, 30:249
Guinand, Hen., 11:238n
Guion, ---, St. Peter pioneer, 28:263
Guise, C. H., author, 21:200
Gulbrandson, Ole, pioneer, 17:486, 18:467
Gulbranson, Andrew W., author, 35:336
Gull Lake, Crow Wing County, trading post, 11:372; mission, 15:111, 20:431, 28:210, 213; fire tower, 19:121; Chippewa band, 28:214, 38:275
Gull River, Crow Wing County, lumbering, 20:455
Gullingsrud, Frank, 26:291
Gullixson, Dr. Andrew, author, 29:353
Gullixson, Rev. T. F., author, 25:195
Gulsvig, Milton, author, 12:211
Gundersen, James N., author, 38:204

Gunderson, John, 29:303, 309
Gunderson, Harvey L., author, 33:354
Gunderson, Lars, Klondike leader, 29:301-315, 376, 30:93, 31:58, 32:60, 39:341
Gunderson, Lars, Jr., 29:308
Gunderson, Robert G., author, 38:202
Gunderson, Russell O., work reviewed, 19:441
Gunflint Lake, border lake, wildlife, 18:451; iron mining, 34:179; forest fires, 36:136
Gunflint Trail, Cook County, constructed, 35:294
Gunn, Donald, historian, 20:186
Gunn, George H., 12:205; "Peter Garrioch at St. Peter's," 20:119-128; author, 20:186
Gunn, J. J., author, 12:331
Gunning, Frank W., 15:89
Guns, see Firearms
Gunther, Erna, author, 26:164
Gunther, John, author, 28:279
Gunzburg, M. Lowell, author, 17:474
Gurko, Leo, author, 34:261
Gurley, Judge George P., speaker, 14:450, 460, 17:483
Gurnee, Capt. Clinton, Union officer, 39:195n
Gurney, Joseph J., Quaker, 18:255
Gurowski, Adam G. de, author, 29:154
Gusler, Gilbert, author, 30:265
Gustaf Adolph, crown prince of Sweden, 19:356
Gustafson, A. F., author, 21:200
Gustafson, Alrik, author, 26:364
Gustafson, Genevieve, speaker, 20:213
Gustafson, Gust, author, 29:273
Gustafson, Hugo, printer, 36:204, 205
Gustavson, F. T., 13:293, 15:485, 18:222, 19:359, 22:343, 28:193, 295; speaker, 12:207, 16:66, 117, 490, 18:205, 281, 26:89; author, 16:358, 18:333
Gustavus Adolphus College, St. Peter, 39:81; history, 11:116, 12:104, 14:356, 24:55, 26:167, 28:286, 30:263, 33:309, 34:131, 172, 38:382; anniversaries, 18:329, 23:301; described, 31:112; student life, 35:245, 39:299; library, 39:35
Gut and Liver Line, see Minneapolis and Rainy River Railroad
Guth, Alexander C., author, 16:113
Guthe, Carl E., author, 13:431, 16:221, 30:257; speaker, 29:348
Guthrey, Nora H., 29:276, 364; author, 26:397, 27:80, 168, 269, 28:83, 29:93, 33:355
Guthrie, Tyrone, author, 39:263
Guthrie Theater, Minneapolis, history, 39:263
Gutterson, A. C., 16:255
Guttormsson, Rev. G., author, 18:469
Guyer, Mrs. Charles A., author, 13:444, 35:382, 39:51
Guyor, Edith L., author, 19:452
Guyot, Arnold, 17:252
Gvale, Gudrun H., work reviewed, 39:126
Gyde, E. A., boatbuilder, 33:17, 19

"H. M. Rice," steamboat, 24:138
"H. S. Allen," steamboat, 36:212
"H. T. Yeatman," steamboat, 11:140

"H. W. Alsop," steamboat, 11:104
Haakon, king of Norway, 17:177
Haan, Pieter, land agent, 28:125, 128
Haarstad mound, Marshall County, 38:
   163, 164
Haas, Mr. and Mrs. William L., house,
   39:275
Haas family, Scott County pioneers,
   11:118
Haberly, Loyd, work reviewed, 30:139-
   141
Habig, Marion A., author, 15:472
Hack, John, merchant, 33:233
Hacker, Louis M., works reviewed, 14:
   429, 19:90, 28:269; author, 12:
   201, 29:258
Hackett, Charles W., 15:372; por-
   trait, 12:433
Hackett, Francis, 14:90
Hackman, Richard, office assistant,
   25:41
Hader, Goodhue County, settled, 15:
   136, 17:486, 23:106
Hadfield, Dr. George, 20:206, 22:435
Hady, Thomas F., author, 39:299
Haecker, Theophilus L., dairying expert, 19:65, 20:31, 75, 29:268,
   33:224; career, 12:99, 19:148-161,
   22:420; author, 12:430, 18:411,
   29:158; papers, 20:33, 82, 34:339
Haecker Hall, University of Minneso-
   ta, dedicated, 19:160
Haefner, John H., author, 24:260
Haefner, Marie, author, 19:350
Hafen, Ann W., compiler, 28:371
Hafen, LeRoy R., review by, 14:430;
   work reviewed, 22:181-183; author,
   11:429, 13:439, 14:449, 15:234,
   16:115, 19:219, 27:158; editor,
   13:331, 35:292, 40:145; speaker,
   15:227, 40:149
Häfner, Gottlieb, 36:13n
Hagadorn, Henry J., diary, 12:200
Hagan, Ole, 40:47
Hagan, William T., author, 30:270,
   31:58, 35:151, 38:238
"Hagan Axe," Norse artifact, 40:47
Hagberg, Gust ("Jockmock"), settler,
   34:183, 184
Hage, George S., 17:124, 18:111, 19:
   362, 20:100, 214, 21:110, 22:219,
   443, 23:392, 26:395; "The Rail-
   road," 38:45-52; review by, 40:
   257; work reviewed, 40:302; speak-
   er, 19:120, 20:99, 21:219, 442,
   445, 24:88; author, 23:295, 24:
   271, 29:272; receives grant, 40:48
Hage, Mrs. George S. (Anne A.), "The
   Battle of Gettysburg," 38:245-257
Hagedorn, Father Eugene, translator,
   28:277, 29:168, 349
Hageman, Harry A., career, 14:333
Hagen, Everett, author, 15:479
Hagen, Lois D., author, 20:90
Hagen, Nellie, 28:386
Hagen, O. E., quoted, 17:168
Hagen, Oskar F. L., 17:455
Hagen, Dr. Paul, 22:107, 23:103, 24:
   188, 25:209, 26:91, 27:173
Hagen, S. N., author, 31:249, 33:314
Hagen, Thor, pioneer, 25:412
Hagerstown, Md., in Civil War, 25:
   355, 356n
Hagertz, Mary A., poet, 38:288
Hagerty, Mary L., speaker, 20:458;
   author, 22:348
Hagg, Harold T., 23:390; "Bemidji,"

23:24-34; "The Beltrami County
   Logging Frontier," 29:137-149;
   "The Lumberjacks' Sky Pilot," 31:
   65-78; reviews by, 22:416, 23:67,
   29:254, 33:345, 34:207, 35:142,
   36:184; work reviewed, 36:189; au-
   thor, 22:418, 23:73, 25:380, 29:
   192, 282, 288, 31:127; speaker,
   23:49
Haggberg, Otto, author, 28:292
Haggerty, Melvin E., 20:61, 22:166;
   author, 12:419, 18:105
Hagie, Dr. C. E., 17:484
Hagland, August, 11:464
Hagler, Mrs. Irvin, 12:449
Haglin, Charles F., architect, 37:14-
   18
Haglin, Eddie, 37:15, 17
Haglund, Louis, pioneer, 24:323
Hagman, Pelle, 14:428
Hagstrom, Dr. G. Arvid, 19:106;
   speaker, 13:107
Hahnemann, Dr. Samuel C. F., 39:8, 9
Hahnemann Medical Society, Hennepin
   County, 17:260n, 21:210
Haight, Floyd L., author, 28:72
Haight, Dr. G. G., author, 36:70
Hail, Susan O., 28:273
Haiman, Mieczyslaw, author, 25:86
Haime, Edward, 14:428
Haime, Maria, 14:428
Haime, Ole, 14:427
Haines, Aubrey L., editor, 40:262
Haines, Dora B., 11:443, 18:313, 21:
   416; work reviewed, 13:188-190;
   author, 12:447
Haines, Francis, work reviewed, 34:
   346
Haines, Jansen, 14:215
Haines, Lynn, 17:213; work reviewed,
   13:188-190; author, 12:447, 34:
   229; career, 13:210; papers, 18:
   313, 19:47, 48, 21:416, 22:40,
   423, 23:40, 372, 34:339
Haines, Richard, artist, 21:328, 22:
   208, 317, 23:268, 30:289, 35:189,
   197
Haines, Robert B., 26:232, 233; let-
   ters, 14:215, 15:61
Haines Brothers, piano makers, 39:318
Haining, Mr. and Mrs. John A., poets,
   16:81
Hair, H. Adams, letters, 12:102, 38:
   67
Hair Hills, N.D., post, 11:366
Haislet, Sam S., author, 14:457
Hal -- a Dacotah, pseud., see Sibley,
   Henry H.
Haldeman-Julius, E., author, 23:117,
   157
Haldeman-Julius, Mrs. E., author, 23:
   117, 157
Haldimand, Frederick, 18:430; gover-
   nor of Canada, 15:95, 97, 16:201,
   19:298, 25:266
Hale, Andrew T., 19:84
Hale, Charles, excursionist, 15:406,
   413, 25:103
Hale, Draton S., pioneer, 19:476
Hale, Edward E., letters, 11:318, 12:
   85, 20:82, 29:189
Hale, Judge and Mrs. Henry, 12:429
Hale, John P., politician, 16:27, 19:
   132, 35:115
Hale, Katherine, author, 15:238
Hale, Mary T., work reviewed, 19:83-
   85; speaker, 16:122; author, 21:79

Hale, Nathaniel C., author, 36:323
Hale, Richard W., Jr., work reviewed,
   38:89
Hale, Sarah Josepha, reformer, 25:65
Hale, William Bayard, 17:160n
Hale, William Dinsmore, papers, 12:
   89; in Civil War, 39:196
Hale, William Harlan, author, 34:211
Haley, J. Evetts, author, 26:168
Haley, Nelson C., in Minnesota, 29:
   352
Half-breeds, see Mixed-bloods
Halfway Creek, Wis., academy, 15:235,
   17:457
Half-way House, Robbinsdale, 23:297
Halfway House, St. Paul, 33:200
Halich, Wasyl, author, 19:112
Halkett, John, 21:399, 40:169; ca-
   reer, 21:433; author, 37:224
Hall, A. G., author, 29:169
Hall, Alfred S., 12:85
Hall, Mrs. Amos W., 38:77n
Hall, Barbara, author, 18:459
Hall, Capt. Basil, author, 26:215;
   artist, 26:359, 32:45
Hall, Caroline, 30:254, 40:337, 338
Hall, Charles F., author, 18:120
Hall, Judge Charles P. 12:102, 13:118
Hall, Christopher W., 18:150, 23:189;
   geologist, 38:22, 39:113, 115,
   117, 118, 120
Hall, Lt. Cyrus, 31:214
Hall, Darwin S., 25:102; journalist,
   13:453, 19:126
Hall, E. George, papers, 20:432, 21:
   36
Hall, Edward S., 20:309
Hall, Francis, career, 18:114, 21:340
Hall, Frank, career, 30:271
Hall, Frank E., reminiscences, 24:92
Hall, G. Stanley, 12:85
Hall, Grace C., speaker, 16:485; au-
   thor, 19:227, 26:291, 36:327
Hall, H. P., journalist, 24:273, 28:
   197, 39:327-329, 331; quoted, 39:
   101, 197
Hall, Herbert J., poet, 26:308
Hall, Mrs. Howard L., speaker, 26:89
Hall, J. O., editor, 12:108
Hall, James, 20:174, 23:89, 155; au-
   thor, 16:105, 20:442, 29:61, 40:
   304; biography, 23:62; editor, 26:
   293
Hall, Lelia, author, 39:61
Hall, Marshall, author, 21:367
Hall, Nathan K., politician, 39:38
Hall, Nathaniel, 40:335
Hall, R. J., politician, 32:136, 138,
   35:60, 300, 36:113, 117, 118
Hall, Richard, missionary, 16:28,
   314, 315, 17:335, 393, 19:144,
   249, 40:8, 9, 11
Hall, Maj. Robert H., at Fort Snell-
   ing, 24:355
Hall, Robert L., work reviewed, 38:
   197
Hall, Rollin J., 19:227
Hall, Sarah, author, 37:188
Hall, Sherman, missionary, 13:195,
   210, 15:47, 16:22, 316, 17:210,
   464, 19:144, 342, 21:73, 22:353,
   354, 356, 32:186; career, 14:342
Hall, Smith B., early motorist, 26:21
Hall, Walter P., work reviewed, 27:
   234-236
Hall, William S., 26:195n

Hall Brothers and Co., Duluth bank, 37:122
Hallam, Alfred, 27:85
Hallam, John, 27:85
Hallam, Joseph, English immigrant, 27:83–85; houses, 27:85, 89–92
Hallam, Mrs. Joseph (Mary Wood), 27:84, 85, 88
Hallam, Lizzie, 27:85, 89
Hallam, Louis, 27:86
Hallam, Mary, 27:86, 88
Hallam, Oscar, 27:83, 86; "Bloomfield and Number Five," 27:84–95; author, 27:55, 151, 28:188
Hallam, William, 27:86
Hallberg, Irene, 27:268
Hallbrook, ---, 28:264
Halleck, Gen. Henry W., Union officer, 25:133, 136, 137, 347, 28:326, 38:279, 39:182
Hallem, David, potter, 33:232, 234
Hallet, Davis and Co., piano makers, 39:318, 324
Halley, Patrick L., author, 31:58
Halliday, Bernard, 17:96
Hallidie, Andrew S., 35:283
Hallock, Charles, town founder, 13:210, 16:495, 29:270; sportsman-journalist, 16:187, 188, 190, 260, 268, 358, 23:186, 25:92, 33:142, 254
Hallock, founded, 13:210, 16:188, 358, 495, 25:92, 29:270, 33:142n; Presbyterian church, 15:481; census, 21:341; history, 21:415; hunting lodge, 36:89, 91
Halloran, M. W., 28:74; speaker, 20:99
Halloween, Anoka celebrations, 37:348
Hallowell, A. Irving, work reviewed, 24:54; author, 27:254, 35:334
Hallowell, James, trader, 20:327
Hall's Library Co., publishers, 26:301
Halltown, W.Va., battle, 25:228
Halonen, Mrs. Arne, 25:378
Halper, Albert, author, 20:116, 25:176
Halpern, Charles H., lawyer, 17:213
Halpert, Herbert, author, 24:261, 28:280
Halpin, James, 40:80
Halseth, Lloyd A., author, 19:120
Halstad, settled, 14:357; railroad, 28:383
Halstead, Murat, author, 26:357, 37:307; papers, 30:147
Halverson, F. Douglas, author, 21:422
Halverson, Leila, author, 35:46
Halverson, Lynn H., author, 34:265
Halvor, Marshall County, ghost town, 35:47
Halvorson, Kittel, politician, 32:140, 141, 35:298
Halvorson, Lars, motorist, 26:26
Ham, F. Gerald, compiler, 40:409
Ham, George H., journalist, 16:113
Hamann, Rosabelle, author, 14:354
Hambleton, Frank, 18:126
Hambleton, Josephine, translator, 38:328
Hambleton, Taylor, 18:126
Hambro, C. J., author, 19:459
Hamburg, churches, 13:447, 14:451; German settlement, 18:453, 28:36
Hamburg, Ill., located, 17:434

"Hamburg," steamboat, 11:143, 27:283–285
Hamel, A. G., forest supervisor, 36:133
Hamer, Philip M., 17:460, 18:49; work reviewed, 37:340; speaker, 18:322
Hamil, Fred C., author, 20:338
Hamilton, Alexander, 18:397, 21:10; publisher, 34:203; author, 34:352
Hamilton, Dr. Arthur S., author, 21:101, 210, 22:102, 23:190, 289, 387
Hamilton, C., and Co., St. Paul, bookstore, 19:382n
Hamilton, Charles, fur dealer, 34:103
Hamilton, Charles S., Union officer, 25:36
Hamilton, Elizabeth S., Minnesota tour, 13:446, 18:455, 20:379
Hamilton, Frank, murderer, 26:288
Hamilton, Mrs. George W., 38:76n
Hamilton, Henry, governor of Canada, 15:95
Hamilton, Holman, "Zachary Taylor and Minnesota," 30:97–110; work reviewed, 33:82; author, 22:206, 30:183, 406
Hamilton, Jake, minstrel, 28:111
Hamilton, Maj. John C., G.A.R. commander, 16:440
Hamilton, John W., with Nobles expedition, 35:253, 261
Hamilton, Laura M., "Stem Rust in the Spring Wheat Area in 1878," 20:156–164; author, 20:186
Hamilton, Lucy T., 25:13
Hamilton, Milton W., work reviewed, 33:37; author, 25:197, 26:78; editor, 26:383
Hamilton, Raphael N., author, 12:198
Hamilton, Samuel, 25:13
Hamilton, Maj. Thomas, 18:401, 403
Hamilton, W. J., Jr., author, 21:200
Hamilton, William J., reminiscence, 36:71
Hamilton, William S., 20:379; career, 15:355
Hamilton, Fillmore County, Methodist meetings, 21:86; Congregational church, 21:413
Hamilton, Mo., steam mill, 24:114, 116
Hamilton, Scott County, see Savage
Hamilton County, Iowa, history, 28:398
"Hamiltonian," steamboat, 34:39
Hamlin, ---, parade marshal, 40:300
Hamlin, Hannibal, politician, 28:24, 324, 35:115
Hamlin, P. L., author, 20:466
Hamlin, Sgt. Philip, at Gettysburg, 38:254, 256
Hamlin, Talbot, work reviewed, 25:173
Hamline, Bishop Leonidas L., 13:210, 19:131, 34:92
Hamline Methodist Church, St. Paul, 39:214, 217, 225, 226
Hamline University, St. Paul, Red Wing period, 12:399, 14:148, 224, 15:247, 361, 16:30, 318, 472, 19:343, 20:344, 25:203, 29:354, 34:92, 93; essay contests, 16:348, 17:359, 18:459, 19:357; growth, 18:208, 21:51, 184; choir, 22:52, 53; campaign against state schools, 32:223; Bridgman memorial, 33:354; athletics, 39:20, 21;

student life, 39:213–226; first piano, 39:317
Hamm, Russell L., author, 38:388
Hamm, Theodore, career, 37:263
Hamm, Theodore, Co., growth, 37:263
Hamm, William, career, 37:263
Hamm, William, Jr., career, 37:263
Hamm Foundation, activities, 37:263
Hamm Realty Co., founded, 37:263
Hammang, Francis H., author, 17:102
Hammar, Russell, 22:52
Hammarberg, Agnes E., author, 18:71
Hammergren, Shirley, 22:52
Hammes, Dr. E. M., author, 30:405
Hammon, Lt. S. L., letters, 30:91
Hammond, Charles, 26:357
Hammond, George, British minister, 18:134, 19:303
Hammond, George P., editor, 39:128
Hammond, Harriet K., 36:218
Hammond, Gen. John H., 33:4, 36:228; papers, 33:268, 34:315, 35:51, 204, 36:36, 196, 216–218, 37:88
Hammond, Mrs. John H., 36:218
Hammond, Margaret, 36:218
Hammond, Nellie, speaker, 17:124
Hammond, Thomas, speaker, 11:112
Hammond, Winfield S., governor, letters, 11:319, 14:437
Hamp, Mrs. Thomas, author, 17:234
Hampton, Catholic church, 20:460; described, 32:241
Hampton, Va., in Civil War, 25:118
Hampton Township, Dakota County, Germans, 28:33
Hamry, Effie, 27:346
Hamry, Orban J., 27:346
Hamsun, Knut, "On the Prairie," 37:265–270; author, 16:219; farm laborer, 20:337; in Northwest, 20:397–412, 25:85, 26:288, 301; letter, 21:189
Hanchett, August H., geologist, 11:433, 434, 32:217
Hancke, Gustav, violinist, 32:240
Hancock, Mrs. F. A., 28:385, 29:366
Hancock, Hilary B., 13:133, 37:315
Hancock, Joseph W., missionary, 11:316, 13:320, 15:248, 16:318n
Hancock, L. A., 19:167
Hancock, Maria H., 13:320
Hancock, Gen. Winfield S., Union officer, 25:229, 351, 354, 360, 29:345, 38:246, 251, 252; presidential candidate, 35:58
Hancock, Stevens County, schools, 14:361, 15:348; literary society, 24:214
Hancock Township, Carver County, Irish, 12:210
Hand, Daniel W., army surgeon, 12:324, 25:136; quoted, 17:258, 39:197
Hand, Wayland D., compiler, 25:84
Handevidt, Nels, farmer, 22:338
Handlin, Oscar, work reviewed, 33:80; author, 31:242, 37:299, 38:387, 39:343; speaker, 37:40, 40:364; editor, 37:184
Handy, Levin C., photographer, 35:131
Handy, Ray D., cartoonist, 40:317 (cover)
Handyside, Hugh, at Nininger, 13:132, 138, 147; speaker, 13:146
Handyside and Henderson, steamship company, 13:138

Handyside House, Nininger, 13:145, 148, 150
Haney, Avery F., 18:465
Haney, Capt. D., horse breeder, 26:118
Haney, Gladys J., author, 23:378, 24:261
Haney, J. C., and Co., 19:175
Hanford Airlines, 33:240
Hanging Kettle Lake, Aitkin County, name, 21:348
Hankenson, May (Mae), speaker, 16:488, 23:102
Hankinson, Richard H., 27:169
Hanks, George L., bell manufacturer, 18:377, 378
Hanks, Stephen B., lumberman, 13:350, 355, 18:177; river pilot, 16:116, 24:202
Hanley, Lee, photographer, 37:13n
Hanley, Thomas W., 18:136
Hanley Falls, growth, 36:194
Hanna, Archibald, speaker, 40:411
Hanna, Charles, author, 37:187
Hanna, R. A., author, 18:112
Hanna, Wyo., Finnish settlement, 40:395
Hannaford, J. M., Jr., 33:242
Hannaford, Koochiching County, founded, 23:107
Hannah Rutledge Home, Chippewa Falls, Wis., 38:83
Hannay, A. M., compiler, 16:235
Hannay, Capt. John W., 24:207
Hannegan, Ned, orator, 26:357
Hannemann, Max, author, 18:453
Hannenburg, G., 28:131
Hannibal, Mo., Mark Twain's home, 17:370, 371, 381; lumber market, 24:137
Hannikainen, Tauno, musician, 27:367
Hanover, Evangelical church, 16:485
Hanover Court House, Va., battle, 25:133n
Hansbrough, Henry C., Senator, 32:175
Hanse, L. L., speaker, 16:256
Hanseatic League, 40:49, 50
Hansen, Alvin H., author, 14:12, 26
Hansen, Mrs. C. J., speaker, 27:174
Hansen, Carl, 18:108, 20:95
Hansen, Carl G. O., speaker, 25:79; author, 26:269
Hansen, G. Armauer, author, 21:365, 367
Hansen, H. P., 17:356
Hansen, Janet, author, 14:358
Hansen, John, 20:408
Hansen, Marcus L., review by, 17:80; works reviewed, 21:299, 22:70-72; speaker, 13:105; author, 16:196, 23:201, 25:199, 31:23, 36:24, 37:346
Hansen, N. M., biography, 13:324
Hansen, Nels B., 17:484, 18:110, 19:117, 22:107
Hansen, Niels E., biography, 25:300
Hansen, Olga W., editor, 19:331
Hansen, Paul Hjelm, see Hjelm-Hansen, Paul
Hansen-Taylor, Marie, author, 19:400
Hanska, settled, 13:108, 23:400, 38:243; band, 24:190; Lutheran church, 34:64. See also Lake Hanska
Hansmeyer, Stephen, 29:366
Hanson, A., 14:54
Hanson, Rev. Allyn, 22:216

Hanson, Mrs. C. A., author, 19:123
Hanson, Charles E., work reviewed, 35:195
Hanson, Christine, author, 22:448
Hanson, Daniel, grave, 14:427
Hanson, Elizabeth, 29:325
Hanson, Gene K., author, 38:388
Hanson, Glenn, artist, 33:310, 317 (cover); editor, 30:67
Hanson, H. E., 14:119, 16:240, 19:116
Hanson, Herbert, house, 38:345
Hanson, J. C. M., librarian, 15:235
Hanson, J. H., author, 26:298
Hanson, J. P. and C. A., grocery firm, 15:246
Hanson, Johannes, Alexandria pioneer, 19:107
Hanson, John R., trader, 16:224
Hanson, Lars, Brown County pioneer, 20:459
Hanson, Louis, Brown County pioneer, 15:437
Hanson, Mary, Vasa pioneer, 14:428
Hanson, Ole, Vasa pioneer, 14:427
Hanson, Paul O., 20:96; speaker, 23:297
Hanson, Pearl C., author, 20:460
Hanson, Peggy, 26:368
Hanson, Peter E., secretary of state, 33:129
Hansonville Township, Lincoln County, history, 18:340
Hantho Township, Lac qui Parle County, school, 16:366
Harbach, Capt. A. A., 12:438
Harbison, Winfred A., "President Lincoln and the Faribault Fire-Eater," 20:269-286; author, 20:322
Harcourt, Alfred, publisher, 33:221
Hardie, James A., 38:223
Hardin, Rev. Rob R., author, 17:125
Harding, J. H., 40:127
Harding, Margaret S., 28:184, 36:190; speaker, 12:284
Harding, Simeon, diary, 11:96
Harding, T. Swann, author, 23:283
Harding, Walter, "Thoreau and Mann on the Minnesota River," 37:225-228; editor, 38:335
Harding, Warren G., source material, 22:423
Harding, St. Louis County, settled, 16:297, 34:178
Hardisty, R., trader, 40:167n, 168n
Hardman, William, traveler, 36:66
Hardware Mutual Insurance Company of Minnesota, 22:332
Hardy, Edward R., Jr., author, 16:477
Hardy, Nellie E., author, 25:313
Hardy, Capt. W. H., naval officer, 38:322, 323
Hare, F. Kenneth, speaker, 34:265
Hare, Samuel, author, 21:369
Hare Lake, Lake County, lumbering, 34:183
Hargrave, James, letters, 20:69-72; trader, 29:247, 40:168n
Hargrave, Joseph J., author, 21:249
Hargrave, Letitia, 31:238; letters, 29:247
Hargrave, Rae, author, 26:291, 387
Hargreaves, Mary W. M., work reviewed, 36:28
Harker, Mary A., 21:446
Harker, Richard, reminiscences, 26:169

Harkin, Alexander, storekeeper, 18:471, 20:464, 23:109, 36:193
Harkins, Wesley R., author, 34:216
Harkness, Edward, 13:342, 29:8n
Harlan, Gilbert D., editor, 39:261
Harlan, James, 14:190, 37:99
Harlan, Mrs. James, 25:140
Harlan, Wilson B., diary, 39:261
Harlow, Alvin F., editor, 34:214
Harma, Peter, 31:164
Harmon, Allen, election commissioner, 26:205, 206, 36:171, 172
Harmon, Almina A., 31:7
Harmon, Argalus, 31:4-6, 9
Harmon, Artemas C., editor, 31:9
Harmon, Calvin, 31:4-6, 8-10
Harmon, Clara, 31:5
Harmon, Daniel, the elder, 31:4, 5
Harmon, Mrs. Daniel (Lucretia), 31:5, 9, 10
Harmon, Daniel W., trader, 22:432, 31:1-10, 34:174, 39:267, 40:161; in fiction, 32:33, 122, 36:77
Harmon, Mrs. Daniel W. (Elizabeth), 31:1, 2, 9
Harmon, E. M., author, 12:99
Harmon, George, 31:1, 6
Harmon, George D., author, 23:85
Harmon, John, 31:1, 7
Harmon, Louis F., lumberman, 24:192
Harmon, Lucretia, 31:4-6
Harmon, Martin, 31:4-6
Harmon, Polly, 31:1, 7
Harmon, Ralph L., "Ignatius Donnelly and His Faded Metropolis," 17:262-275; speaker, 17:312; author, 17:331
Harmon, Raymond, forester, 36:133, 137
Harmon, Reuben, 31:6
Harmon, Sally, 31:1, 7
Harmon, Stephen, 31:1, 4, 6
Harmon, William, 31:7
Harmon, Sgt. William, in Civil War, 25:22
Harmon family, genealogy, 31:9
Harmonia Singing Society, Minneapolis, 32:165-167
Harmony, Fillmore County, Lutheran church, 12:337; historical society, 24:379
Harmony, Hennepin County, name, 40:89. See also Richfield
Harmony Island, B.C., Finnish settlement, 22:431
Harn, Hugh V., career, 19:214
Harney, Benjamin F., army surgeon, 28:16
Harnish, Mrs. E. F., 16:242
Harnoncourt, Rene d', author, 22:189
Harnsberger, John L., "Land, Lobbies, Railroads," 37:89-100; review by, 39:30; author, 37:38, 38:241, 39:211
Harper, Irene, author, 12:91
Harper, Josephine L., works reviewed, 36:29, 40:258
Harper, Lathrop C., author, 20:199
Harper, Lawrence A., author, 28:68
Harper, Robert S., author, 37:262
Harper, William R., career, 37:341
Harper's Ferry, W.Va., in Civil War, 25:30, 227, 355
Harper's Monthly, on frontier, 30:200, 204
Harpole, Patricia C., artist, 40:402n

Harriet Island, St. Paul, bridge, 40: 221 (cover)
Harriet Lake, Lake County, settled, 34:183
"Harriet Lane," steamboat, 25:242
Harrigan, Mrs. Robert, 15:372; speaker, 17:233
Harriman, Averell, politician, 40:293
Harriman, Edward H., 18:424; contest with Hill, 11:104, 22:202, 31:55, 34:216, 35:295, 36:68, 102, 40: 356; railroad magnate, 39:110
Harriman, Mrs. J. Borden, 25:64
Harrington, Betsey, 26:154
Harrington, Ellen P., 19:341
Harrington, J. C., work reviewed, 39: 340; author, 33:311
Harrington, John, diary, 19:342
Harrington, John, Union soldier, 25: 26
Harrington, John P., author, 35:48
Harrington, Lewis, papers, 11:115, 330, 19:341, 20:348; settler, 14: 270, 15:47, 22:224
Harrington, Lyn, work reviewed, 33: 186; author, 32:242
Harrington, Richard, photographer, 33:186
Harrington, W. E., of Hastings, author, 18:114
Harrington, W. E., of Hutchinson, banker, 11:220
Harrington, W. E., of Minneapolis, letter, 24:265
Harrington, William H., letters, 19: 341
Harrington family, papers, 19:341, 20:33
Harrington Farms, Hennepin County, settled, 27:176
Harriott, Dr. Isaac H., 15:247; townsite promoter, 13:335
Harriott, J. E., trader, 40:168n
Harris, August W., author, 37:185
Harris, Belle, trader, 20:12
Harris, Burton, work reviewed, 33:180
Harris, Carey A., Indian commissioner, 35:27
Harris, Dale B., author, 18:105
Harris, Daniel S., steamboat captain, 11:136, 165, 174n, 210, 13:231, 232, 235, 237, 15:409, 410, 464, 20:387, 25:88, 29:204; career, 12: 92, 18:434; portrait, 13:234
Harris, Mrs. Daniel S., 11:166
Harris, Edward, journal, 40:144
Harris, Sgt. Frank, band leader, 12: 432
Harris, Frank, ornithologist, diaries, 19:96
Harris, Fred, 26:31
Harris, H. L., author, 19:357
Harris, Harold, 11:54, 55, 14:78, 15: 217, 16:60; speaker, 11:291; memorial, 15:467
Harris, Harold R., "Commercial Aviation," 33:239-242
Harris, J. Arthur, career, 13:210, 18:107
Harris, Joel C., 17:370
Harris, John S., horticulturist, 20: 301, 448; diaries, 19:48, 96
Harris, Martin K., steamboat captain, 11:127, 29:203
Harris, Nelson, with Nobles expedition, 35:252
Harris, Phyllis P., author, 27:365

Harris, S., 17:301
Harris, Thomas, career, 35:31
Harris, W. L., furniture dealer, 18: 226, 33:95
Harris, William, farmer, 22:161
Harris, William F., see Foster-Harris
Harris family, genealogy, 35:248
Harris, Whitford and Bentley, shippers, 21:252
Harrisburg, Pa., in Civil War, 25:356
Harrisburgh, Hennepin County, post office, 40:88
Harrison, ---, pioneer farmer, 23:316
Harrison, ---, church trustee, 19: 267n
Harrison, Benjamin, President, 17: 162, 35:67, 73, 300, 39:95, 107; candidate, 35:64, 74-76
Harrison, C. E., letter, 25:185
Harrison, Carter, 37:234
Harrison, Frederick G., author, 40: 361
Harrison, Hugh, 18:134n
Harrison, James G., author, 26:379
Harrison, Joseph H., Jr., editor, 36: 231
Harrison, Samuel, 34:157, 158
Harrison, T. Glenn, author, 25:102
Harrison, William H., 28:56, 377, 39: 38; Indiana governor, 19:302, 20: 18
Harrison and Co., St. Anthony, plow factory, 24:297
Harrison, Farrington and Co., grocery firm, 18:134
Harrison Hall, Minneapolis, 22:371, 35:226
Harrison's Bay, Lake Minnetonka, fishing, 29:292
Harrisson, ---, at Grand Portage, 12: 371
Harrow, Gen. William, 25:354, 360
Harsen's Island, Mich., St. Clair River, 23:137
Harshman, Gladys, author, 12:320
Harstad, Bjug A., author, 12:100
Harstad, Peter T., author, 37:182
Harstad families, genealogy, 12:100
Hart, Albert B., letters, 26:69
Hart, Alex L., work reviewed, 25:280
Hart, Charles G., author, 12:108
Hart, Daniel L., druggist, 20:442
Hart, E., storekeeper, 20:399
Hart, Evan A., historic site supervisor, 33:19n; author, 35:382, 36: 327, 39:81; death, 39:132
Hart, Francis B., house, 23:229
Hart, Gardner E., reminiscences, 20: 362
Hart, Harman V., trader, 16:155
Hart, Rev. Hastings H., corrections board member, 19:112, 37:151, 275, 38:370-374, 39:126
Hart, Irving H., 14:116, 23:251n, 34: 268; "Origin of the Name 'Itasca,'" 12:225-229; "The Savanna and Prairie River Portages," 13:403-407; "Steamboating on Mississippi Headwaters," 33:7-19; author, 13: 69, 118, 173, 339, 443, 35:155
Hart, Isaac L., career, 20:362
Hart, Capt. William H., 20:196
Hart, William S., autobiography, 11: 110
Hart Township, Winona County, German settlement, 14:50
Harte, Bret, 20:110

Hartelt, August, blacksmith, 18:466
Hartford, Stearns County, platted, 22:447
Hartford Township, Todd County, history, 15:371, 16:256, 372
Hartin, Anna, 12:84
Hartland Township, Freeborn County, Norwegian settlement, 12:269
Hartle, John, Sr., speaker, 19:239
Hartley, Dr. E. C., author, 11:458
Hartley, Heber L., livestock breeder, 24:375
Hartley, I. E., 29:308, 309
Hartley, Irma, 24:145
Hartman, Sister Ardis, author, 18:89
Hartman, George B., author, 23:184
Hartman, W. A., author, 13:333
Hartman, Mr. and Mrs. William, house, 39:275
Hartmann, John E., 37:264; "The Minnesota Gag Law," 37:161-173; review by, 37:185
Hartshorn, William E., pioneer, 16: 377, 25:412
Hartshorne, Richard, author, 11:215, 13:441
Hartsough, Mildred L., work reviewed, 16:78-80; speaker, 15:219; author, 23:8, 28:331
Hartt, Mary B., author, 12:442
Hartt, Thomas, pioneer, 19:226
Hartwick Pines State Park, Mich., logging museum, 16:486
Hartwig, John R., author, 20:218
Harty, Julia, 28:266
Hartz, Louis, author, 34:250
Hartzog, George B., Jr., author, 40: 404
Harvard Club of Minnesota, activities, 12:428
Harvard University, Cambridge, Mass., founded, 15:4; business records, 20:302
Harvey, Col. A. J., aviator, 26:5, 15
Harvey, Charles T., career, 28:54, 35:199; canal builder, 34:10, 263
Harvey, D. C., author, 12:89, 13:431
Harvey, George, 18:425
Harvey, John H., author, 20:346, 27: 357, 30:274, 39:63, 64
Harvey, Rodney B., runic studies, 21: 202; speaker, 26:286
Harvey, Ruth, author, 31:120
Harvey, Samuel C., author, 25:305
Harvieux, Paul, trader, 21:118, 119, 127-130, 132, 133, 135, 139-141, 144, 145; testimony, 21:122-127
Harwick, Harry J., author, 36:34
Hasberg, K., immigrant agent, 12:256
Haskel, Rev. Daniel, editor, 31:7
Haskell, Burnette G., letter, 27:334
Haskell, C. F. B., letters, 29:165
Haskell, Daniel C., work reviewed, 15:210; editor, 29:165
Haskell, Frank A., author, 29:344
Haskell, Dr. Hiram A., author, 22:335
Haskell, Joseph, pioneer, 22:336, 361, 425, 23:321, 26:109, 27:78, 40:235
Haskell, Mrs. Joseph, 27:78
Haskin, Leslie L., author, 24:77
Haskins, Charles H., author, 21:67
Haskins, George L., author, 30:64
Haskins, Jessie, 12:204
Haslam, John, author, 21:368
Hassan, Alexander B., army surgeon, 28:209, 222

Hassan Rapids, Hennepin County, post office, 40:88
Hasselmo, Nils, work reviewed, 38: 381; author, 39:36
Hasselquist, Rev. Tuve N., 13:307, 17:329; biography, 13:308-311
Hassler, Ferdinand R., surveyor, 18: 314, 23:203, 36:224, 225
Hastings, dam, 11:218; churches, 11: 332, 12:208, 13:443, 15:197, 19: 49, 121, 20:460, 27:269; trading post, 11:381, 17:278; roads, 11: 389, 394, 13:128, 26:28; stage line, 11:402; river port, 13:139, 17:269, 273, 28:290, 34:26, 27, 96, 37:87, 38:72, 172, 292; county seat, 13:141; rival of Nininger, 13:143, 17:264, 267; mills, 13: 214, 18:114, 23:105, 27:190, 34: 287, 35:336; marketing center, 14: 387, 18:409, 26:332, 34:146n, 37: 87, 94; courthouse records, 15: 195; fair, 15:246; hospital, 15: 485; G.A.R. post, 16:127; rail- road, 16:247; Christmas celebra- tion, 16:383; historical meeting, 17:312, 18:42; described, 17:394; Vermillion baseball club, 19:163, 168, 169, 173, 175-177, 179; banks, 19:465, 22:89; bridge, 20: 460, 23:290, 27:175, 269, 345, 35: 336; winter sports, 23:105; maga- zine, 26:294; theater, 28:99, 32: 100, 34:242; wheat raising, 29:1, 2; wildlife, 30:223, 228; showboat performances, 33:39; architecture, 38:348; antiabolition sentiment, 39:260. See also Le Duc, William G.: house
Hastings and Dakota Railway Co., 35: 338; built, 16:247, 18:444, 26:66; first locomotive, 19:193-196; land grant, 39:88n, 92
Hastings Gazette, established, 13: 448, 14:397, 35:336; politics, 36: 301
Hastings, Minnesota River, and Red River of the North Railroad, 37: 191
Hasty, Frank, composer, 13:362
Hasty, Robert, lumberman, 24:200
Hatch, Edwin A. C., papers, 18:209, 20:79, 328, 21:35; battalion com- mander, 34:319-324, 38:70, 71, 284, 286; politician, 36:4n; Win- nebago agent, 38:362, 363
Hatch, Elizabeth, author, 34:129
Hatch, Dr. Philo L., physician, 22: 435; ornithologist, 36:103, 39: 112, 114, 115, 117, 120
Hatch, Rufus, sponsors railroad ex- cursion, 28:90, 33:61-64, 71
Hatch family, papers, 25:184
Hatch and Roberts, Mankato, plow manufacturers, 24:297
Hatch's Independent Battalion of Cav- alry, 14:217, 15:465, 16:359, 26: 208, 35:337. See also Hatch, Edwin A. C.
Hatcher, Harlan, work reviewed, 32: 46; author, 25:273, 26:76, 39:82
Hatcher, James R., steamboat captain, 36:254, 37:227
Hatcher, Sadie B., author, 13:432
Hatfield, Ruth, choreographer, 21:59, 61
Hathaway, Clarence, author, 36:105

Hathaway, Esse V., author, 17:342
Hats, 40:216; beaver, 40:187, 208, 215
"Hattie May," steamboat, 12:433
Hatzfeld, Herta, compiler, 36:325
Hauberg, John H., 34:263
Hauck, H. F., 12:185
Hauenstein, John, 20:459
Hauenstein Brewery, New Ulm, founded, 20:459
Haug, Lars O., career, 19:214
Haugan, A. E., 19:308
Hauge, G. S., speaker, 28:380
Haugen, Rev. C., 17:233; author, 11: 115
Haugen, Einar, review by, 18:198-201; work reviewed, 33:349; author, 14: 444, 16:109, 349, 18:203, 31:251; translator, 23:378, 24:176, 40:95
Haugen, S. O., 23:106
Haugen, Serena, 21:447
Haugen, Thelma, speaker, 26:284
Haugland, J. O., speaker, 25:208
Haugland, John C., "Politics and Ram- sey's Rise to Power," 37:324-334; "Alexander Ramsey and Party Poli- tics," 39:37-48
Haukebo, Clarice, author, 21:219
Haun, Julius W., author, 18:228
Haupers, Clement, 20:299
Haupt, Herman, railroad builder, 33: 218
Hauser, Rev. F. W., speaker, 16:491
Hauser, Heinrich, author, 14:116
Hauswolff, Carl U. von, traveler, 32: 49
Havana, Steele County, cheese fac- tory, 19:239
Havelock Township, Chippewa County, Norwegian settlement, 12:275n
Haven, Augustus, merchant, 24:100, 107
Haven, G. H., banker, 16:364
Haven, Mrs. G. H., 24:105
Haven, George A., 11:333, 13:448, 14: 100, 456, 16:240, 242, 23:391, 24: 96n
Haven, George H., banker, 16:364, 24: 96, 107
Havighurst, Walter, reviews by, 23: 63, 25:368-370; work reviewed, 19: 80, 23:355, 25:274, 28:55-57, 33: 137, 36:276, 37:218, 39:167, 40: 141; author, 23:74, 25:297, 383, 26:266, 34:169, 263, 35:291
Havighurst, Mrs. Walter (Marion), work reviewed, 33:137
Haviland, Benjamin F., quoted, 16:316
Havill, Edward, author, 31:131, 146
Havlis, Jošef, 15:34
Hawaii, in World War II, 28:73; Nor- wegians, 36:98; religion, 39:128
Hawaii War Records Depository, Hono- lulu, 26:85
Hawes, Dr. G. H., 35:175
Hawk Creek Township, Renville County, Norwegian settlement, 12:275n; flood, 25:213
"Hawk Eye State," steamboat, 28:326
Hawkesworth, George, postmaster, 34: 186
Hawgood, John A., author, 38:238
Hawkins, John H. W., 22:124
Hawkins, Oscar F., letters, 39:299
Hawkins, William G., author, 35:337
Hawkins Mine, Nashwauk, 28:251
Hawkins Zouaves, in Civil War, 21:414

Hawkinson, Carl, 20:100
Hawkinson, Ella A., 12:315, 16:242, 17:231, 18:334, 19:359, 445, 21: 52; "The Old Crossing Chippewa Treaty," 15:282-300; "The Clay County Historical Museum," 25:258- 264; reviews by, 19:437-439, 23: 360; author, 14:438, 16:210, 23: 187, 370, 25:288; speaker, 15:83
Hawks, Alvin A., 18:256n
Hawks, Emma B., editor, 23:86
Hawks, Maj. John, letter, 34:156n
Hawley, ---, steamboat captain, 33:12
Hawley, Alpheus F., trader, 34:325- 327, 39:230, 231n, 255
Hawley, Dr. Augustine B., diary, 27: 344
Hawley, Charles A., author, 20:338
Hawley, Helen, 21:358
Hawley, Dr. J. E., 21:358
Hawley, Clay County, ethnic settle- ments, 12:278, 25:266; Yeovil col- ony, 12:336, 28:190; history, 21: 448, 28:190, 380; politics, 38:178
Hawley Lumber Co., 38:177
Hawlish, Mrs. Henry, 23:298
Haworth, Samuel L., Quaker minister, 18:261, 265
Hawthorn, Elizabeth, see Buck, Mrs. Solon J.
Hawthorne, Nathaniel, 17:437, 20:106, 109, 23:113
Haxo, Henry E., work reviewed, 24: 152; translator, 22:429
Hay, J. H., speaker, 15:115
Hay, Jehu, career, 11:108
Hay, John, author, 19:437, 28:361, 40:313; statesman, 28:64, 38:40
Hay, John, trader, 11:107, 365
Hay, K. C., Press and Machinery Co., Minneapolis, 26:23
Hay, Thomas R., editor, 26:358
Hay, William, steamboat captain, 33: 12
Hay Creek, Roseau County, explored, 24:319
Hay Creek Township, Goodhue County, German settlement, 28:33
Hay Lake, Chisago County, Swedish settlement, 36:195
Hay raising, 18:341, 19:322
Haycraft, I. G., author, 26:156, 28: 85
Haycraft, Judge Julius E., 11:51, 52, 291, 445, 12:406, 13:194, 14:73, 79, 16:241, 17:70, 121, 19:116, 20:50, 52, 97, 21:50, 284, 445, 23:46, 50, 24:56, 25:53, 26:45, 29:92, 97, 363, 30:80; "A Type- written Letter of 1846," 16:445- 447; "Jane Grey Swisshelm and C. A. Lounsberry," 22:174-176; re- view by, 27:335; speaker, 11:199, 296, 12:39, 338, 13:451, 453, 14: 77, 459, 15:83, 493, 16:67, 491, 17:66, 69, 124, 18:64, 19:63, 359, 424n, 20:462, 21:53, 409, 22:295, 23:100, 397, 24:380, 28:194; au- thor, 13:343, 17:91, 210, 20:450, 22:187, 190, 441, 26:394, 27:343, 29:74, 272, 30:162, 272, 408; MHS president, 25:378, 407, 26:40, 42, 28:87, 387, 30:336; legislator, 33:156-160, 163n
Hayden, Charles, colonist, 22:170
Hayden, Charles, investor, 34:273, 280, 283

Hayden, Capt. Elijah, 25:345
Hayden, F. V., explorer, 23:282, 27:253
Hayden, Mary, in Sioux Outbreak, 34:238
Hayden, Peter, trader, 13:241, 20:71, 31:217
Haydnet, Joyce, author, 24:273
Hayes, Carlton J. H., 14:90
Hayes, Frank, author, 15:123
Hayes, Rev. Gordon, 21:158, 159n
Hayes, H. S., compiler, 17:340
Hayes, Herbert K., agriculturist, 30:64; author, 32:118
Hayes, Hiram, 19:250n
Hayes, Isaac I., lecturer, 11:157, 35:227
Hayes, Mrs. J. M., 15:245, 17:120, 18:222, 19:116, 21:107, 22:216
Hayes, Sir James, 16:394, 397, 399, 400, 29:154; awarded trade grants, 16:423-426
Hayes, Montrose W., author, 15:234
Hayes, Moses P., papers, 16:71
Hayes, Rutherford B., President, 16:271, 17:11, 34:287, 288, 35:58, 177, 357, 37:191; papers, 21:414, 28:203; Minnesota visit, 22:262, 29:128, 31:253, 34:293, 35:150, 377, 37:200-202; memorial library, 31:252
Hayes, Mrs. Rutherford B., Minnesota visit, 29:128, 37:200-202
Hayes, Warren H., architect, 35:71
Hayes, William E., work reviewed, 34:83
Hayes Foundation, publications, 25:379, 26:150
Hayes River, Man., fur trade route, 31:238, 32:161, 37:345, 40:189
Hayes Township, Swift County, history, 12:170, 211
Hayfield, founded, 17:236
Haymarket, Va., in Civil War, 25:357, 358
Haynes, Col. Caleb V., aviator, 26:4
Haynes, Edward, 28:387, 29:91
Haynes, Frank J., photographer, 21:95, 23:282, 36:279; biography, 39:294
Haynes, Jack E., author, 23:282; photographer, 36:279
Haynes, Maurice, editor, 36:72
Haynes, Theresa G., "Augsburg Park," 40:375-383; review by, 38:88; artist, 37:254n
Hays, Alexander, 25:356
Hays, H. R., work reviewed, 36:148
Hays, Isaac, letter, 13:418
Hays, Lambert, 13:199
Hays, W. J., artist, 27:254
Hays, Willet M., agronomist, 19:25, 26, 29, 32, 33:224
Haystead, Ladd, author, 35:45
Hayter, Earl W., author, 23:180
Hayward, Harry, murderer, 11:213, 16:116, 23:98
Hayward, J. E., 25:411
Hayward, creamery, 23:106
Hayward, Wis., Chippewa festival, 37:347
Haywood, Charles, compiler, 32:126, 39:128
Hazard, Ebenezer, career, 34:212
Hazard, Lucy L., author, 11:428
Hazard, Rev. T. H., 17:231
Hazel, Grant, 21:442

Hazel Run, store, 30:280
Hazelhurst, Charles, piano builder, 39:322, 323
Hazelhurst, Doris, 39:322
Hazelrigg, Charles, musician, 33:323
Hazelrigg, Nellie A., singer, 33:317n, 322, 324, 325
Hazeltine, George C., reminiscences, 17:99
Hazeltine, Susan, 20:143n
Hazeltine Lake, Carver County, name, 20:143n
Hazelton, Alice K., author, 23:105
Hazelton, Cutler J., 21:349
Hazelton Township, Aitkin County, name, 21:349; settled, 23:105
Hazelwood, Yellow Medicine County, mission, 13:429, 16:15, 18:444, 19:345, 20:351, 21:182, 23:272, 27:264; publications, 11:94, 205, 12:427
Hazen, Nellie, 27:361, 28:86, 29:361
Hazen Wakute Red Wing, Sioux leader, 12:317
Hazlett, Isaac, 13:346
Hazzard, George H., 31:88
Heaberlin, Fred S., author, 11:332, 12:204, 205, 18:311, 20:189
Head, George, portrait, 21:214
Head, J. Frazier, army surgeon, 28:207n, 344
Head Quarters Hotel, Brainerd, 16:268
Headingley, Man., farming, 24:334
Headley, Albert, speaker, 11:460
Headley, Charles W., author, 18:114, 22:445
Headley, D. W., author, 22:445
Headley, Leal A., work reviewed, 40:256
Headley, Louis, 40:256
Headley, Sherman K., 35:340
Headline, Clarissa, editor, 39:82
Headwaters Lakes aspect, archaeology, 26:312-329, 29:78, 31:164, 166, 169, 171, 235
Heal, Edith, author, 24:372
Heald, A. A., house, 38:346
Heald, Sarah T., 12:433, 15:245, 17:120, 356, 18:222, 19:116, 20:95, 21:332; speaker, 11:218, 17:346, 357; author, 15:366, 18:333
Heald, Weldon F., author, 37:134
Healey, W. B., 19:195
Health conditions, Minnesota advantages, 12:334, 13:446, 16:29, 36, 216, 238, 329, 353, 17:97, 214, 255-261, 367, 387, 412, 18:300, 348, 20:395, 22:135, 169, 25:91, 26:146, 27:248, 30:6, 33:32, 189, 34:100n, 35:214-221, 36:91; on frontier, 19:369-376, 20:224-242, 28:335, 35:241; Twin Cities, 20:88; among immigrants, 35:97, 38:74; Red River Settlement, 36:46n, 53; Far West, 36:277; Wisconsin, 37:182; in Civil War, 39:184, 40:282, 283, 291; pollution problem, 40:132. See also Hospitals, Medicine, Nursing, Public health, individual diseases
Healy, George, surveyor, 34:359
Healy, George P. A, artist, 34:100n
Healy, Mrs. O. W., author, 35:381
Healy, Richard, sheep breeder, 26:111
Healy, Thomas C, artist, 34:96, 100
Healy, W. J., author, 30:261

Heard, Isaac V. D., 20:82; historian, 34:233-238
Heard, Paul C., 22:104, 23:99
Heard, Mrs. Paul C., speaker, 26:178
Hearding, John H., speaker, 13:121, 17:484, 19:118; author, 16:479, 29:375
Hearne, Samuel, journal, 16:105; trader, 18:81, 82, 33:130, 35:243, 40:160, 190
Hearst, William Randolph, publisher, 34:203
Heartman, Martha E., compiler, 13:436
Heath, Frederic, author, 25:198, 29:86
Heaton, David, letters, 15:224
Heaton, Herbert, 29:164; "Business Records," 20:165-168; reviews by, 11:191-194, 18:76-79; author, 11:101, 18:91, 20:186, 24:360; speaker, 16:225, 27:172
Heatwole, Joel P., career, 28:73
Hebard, Grace B., work reviewed, 14:204
Hebbard, S. S., author, 13:253
Hebberd, Mrs. Arthur E., author, 24:177, 27:69
Hebberd, E. S., author, 27:69
Heberden, William, author, 21:365
Hebrew Ladies' Benevolent Society, St. Paul, 17:99
Hechler, Kenneth W., work reviewed, 22:78-80
Hecht, Arthur, "The Duluth Post Office," 34:185
Heck, Frank H., "The Grand Army of the Republic," 16:427-444; reviews by, 21:305, 23:63-65, 30:382, 31:242, 33:83; work reviewed, 23:165; author, 18:318, 19:452, 21:310, 23:74, 30:412, 31:256
Heck, N. H., author, 14:110
Hecker, Friedrich, German immigrant, 30:25
Hecker, Thad. C., author, 25:297
"Hecla," steamboat, 34:266
Hector, Lutheran churches, 12:105, 20:467; history, 13:453, 19:126; Swedish settlement, 18:70
Hedberg, C. H., school superintendent, 20:101
Hedberg, C. Harry, 21:337
Hedberg, J. P., letter, 39:133n
Hedberg, Louise, see Blad, Louise H.
Hedenstrom, E., translator, 38:92
Hedge, Alice, poet, 26:298
Hedges, Cornelius, explorer, 23:383
Hedges, James B., review by, 15:332; works reviewed, 12:72, 21:63, 30:250; author, 17:477, 21:407, 23:53
Hedges, Marie, 25:206
Hedin, Naboth, work reviewed, 31:111
Hedlin, Ralph, author, 37:134
Hedrick, Ulysses P., author, 15:123, 31:162
Hedstrom, Alma, speaker, 11:217
Heed, Arvid, bus operator, 21:291
Heed, Mique, author, 20:470
Heerman, Edward E., steamboat captain, 28:92
Heffelfinger, C. H., author, 16:224
Heffelfinger, Maj. Christopher B., 11:207, 26:157, 258; letters, 30:91
Heffelfinger, Frank T., 11:207, 16:20n, 25:154n, 32:13n; diary, 37:14n; grain merchant, 37:15-18

Heffelfinger, George W. P., 37:14n
Heffelfinger, Ruth J., "Experiment in Concrete," 37:14-18
Heffelfinger, Walter ("Pudge"), career, 34:358, 35:335
Heffelfinger family, 25:93
Heffron, Patrick R., 39:154n
Heg, Even, Wisconsin pioneer, 14:54, 24:348
Heg, Hans C., in Civil War, 15:235, 17:221, 24:348; career, 15:355, 19:459, 26:170
Hegeman, Jeannette, author, 20:339
Heggen, Thomas, novelist, 31:129, 191
Hegger, Grace, see Lewis, Grace Hegger
Hegman Lake, St. Louis County, picture rock, 29:130
Hegney, Timothy, schoolteacher, 39:309
Hegstrom, Rev. V. H., author, 18:329
Hegstrom farm, St. Louis County, Finnish settlement, 34:184
Hehr, Gottlieb, potter, 28:291
Heiber, O. C., 17:340
Heiberg, J. F., pioneer, 17:361
Heiberg, Kristen, speaker, 11:120
Heidal, C. O., author, 36:71
Heidelberg, Catholic church, 14:120
Heidelberg man, 16:8
Heier, Christian, Mormon missionary, 36:287
Heifetz, Jascha, violinist, 39:59
Height of Land Portage, Cook County, 22:439, 37:242
Heilbron, Bertha L., "A New Yorker in the Great West," 12:43-64, 405-407; "The Goucher College Collection," 13:408-414; "Minnesota Statehood Editorials," 14:173-191; "The American Turf Register," 14:421-424; "A Ramsey Portrait," 14:425; "A Mayer Item," 15:206; "Christmas and New Year's on the Frontier," 16:373-390; "Making a Motion Picture in 1848," 17:131-149, 288-301, 421-436; MHS reports, 18:267-283, 19:63-70, 308-317, 20:46-53, 296-309, 21:47-54, 284-293, 22:47-54, 290-296, 25:53-56, 26:42-46; "Supplies for the Nicollet Expedition," 19:192; "Pioneering in Stearns County," 19:321-327; "Seth Eastman's Water Colors," 19:419-423; "Theodore C. Blegen," 20:287-295; "A Pioneer Artist," 21:149-157; "Frank B. Mayer," 22:133-156; "Local Historical Museums," 23:10-16; "Mississippi Panorama," 23:349-352; "Walter Reed in Minnesota," 24:207-213; "From Kenora to Fort Frances," 24:275-286; "By Rail and River to Minnesota," 25:103-116; "Mayer's Album," 26:140; "Pennsylvania German Baptismal Certificates," 27:29-32; "A 'Craven Lad,'" 27:281-299; "Zachary Taylor and Old Fort Snelling," 28:15-19; "Bridging the Mississippi," 29:29-35; "Fort Snelling and Minnesota Territory," 29:316-320; "Documentary Panorama," 30:14-23; "Lewis Cass," 31:93-97; "Lewis' 'Mississippithal,'" 32:202-213; "Edwin Whitefield's Minnesota Lakes," 33:247-251; "Mathew Brady's Portraits," 35:130-132; "Some Sioux Legends in Pictures," 36:18-23; "Minnesotans at Play," 36:89-94; "Artist as Buffalo Hunter," 36:309-314; "Manifest Destiny in Minnesota's Republican Campaign," 37:52-57; "Where to Settle?" 39:286-289; "Edwin Whitefield," 40:62-77; reviews by, 11:307-309, 13:301, 14:205, 15:210, 17:455, 19:332-334, 335, 20:184, 21:185, 402, 22:415, 25:278, 30:141, 31:46, 32:55, 114, 33:263, 34:120, 253, 35:369, 36:233, 317, 37:32, 176, 38:36, 40:144, 311; works reviewed, 13:295, 26:62, 36:145; research assistant, 11:46, 16:59; editor, 13:192, 14:434, 17:332, 25:49, 30:43, 44, 37:188; speaker, 14:328, 15:107, 20:46; author, 16:95, 25:379, 26:36, 150, 27:49, 55, 30:180, 388, 393, 406, 31:58, 249, 250, 36:152, 328, 38:386, 388; compiler, 32:62
Heilbron, Julius, diary, 11:319
Heilbrun, Capt. Robert M., author, 25:94
Heilmaier, Anna M., "Peter Rindisbacher," 32:156-162; translator, 32:191; author, 36:326
Heim, Harry, artist, 38:297n
Heim, Moritz, career, 14:333
Heimes, Gladys, see Upham, Gladys
Heimlich, Herbert H., author, 20:442
Hein, Clarence J., "Minnesota's Direct Primary Law," 35:341-351; author, 39:299
Heine, Alex T., aviator, 34:44
Heinola, Otter Tail County, Finnish settlement, 25:320
Heins, George L., artist, 14:38
Heintzelman, Gen. Samuel P., Union officer, 25:27, 36, 119, 126, 39:176, 178
Heinzelmann, Martin, pioneer, 36:235
Heiskanen, Aate, labor leader, 40:344
Heiskell, William K., 27:316
Heiss, Archbishop Michael, career, 34:313
Heitmann, John, author, 23:381
Hektoen, Ludwig, author, 12:306
Helderman, Leonard C., author, 13:108
"Helen," steamboat, 36:45
Helen Angela, Sister, speaker, 15:313, 17:229
"Helen Blair," steamboat, 37:296
"Helen Mac," towboat, 18:177
Helena, Ark., in Civil War, 40:281-283
Helena, Mont., history, 39:262
Helena Township, Scott County, election, 28:34
"Helene Schulenberg," towboat, 18:175
Helgeson, Arlan, work reviewed, 38:194
Helgeson, Thor, pioneer, 21:223
Helinski, Theodore M., postmaster, 34:185
Hella, U. W., 35:191; speaker, 35:384; author, 37:87
Helland, Andreas, author, 11:227, 29:295
Helleberg, N.Y., history, 18:215
Heller, Mrs. Charles, speaker, 23:194, 24:86
Heller, Christian, artist, 36:240, 38:105, 125n
Heller, Walter W., politician, 37:343

Hellickson, Mrs. George C., 33:163n
Hellström, Carl F., consul, 25:79, 26:42
Helmes, Winifred G., work reviewed, 31:42
Helmholtz, Hermann L. F. von, physicist, 39:326n
Helper, Hinton, career, 28:54
Helsingborg, Sweden, emigration from, 20:248-250
Helvetia, Carver County, Swiss settlement, 21:202
Hemingway, Ernest, author, 39:35
Hemiup, Norton H., 18:144
Hemmestvedt, Mikkel, skier, 17:228, 29:169
Hemmestvedt, Torjus, skier, 17:228, 29:169
Hemnes Norwegian Evangelical Lutheran Church, Lyon County, 14:121
Hemp, trade item, 40:204, 206
Hempel, Rev. Wilhelm F., author, 26:83
Hemphill, W. Edwin, 26:85
Hempstead, ---, mining interests, 32:86, 87
Hempstead, William, steamboat owner, 22:17n
Hempstead and Beebe, St. Louis, steamboat owners, 11:124n
Henday, Anthony, explorer, 35:47, 243
Henderson, Margaret G., work reviewed, 30:247
Henderson, Dr. Melvin S., author, 24:181
Henderson, roads, 21:234; bridge, 23:290; history, 23:404; politics, 28:36; in Sioux Outbreak, 28:263, 38:113, 280; architecture, 37:71, 39:272-277; described, 37:226; ferry, 39:274; Brown monument, 39:276
Henderson, Glencoe, and St. Cloud Line of Stages, 11:133
Henderson Transportation Co., 11:133
Hendricks, Thomas A., 19:425
Hendricks, history, 13:340, 18:340
Hendricks School, St. Paul, history, 18:118
Hendrickson, A. H., speaker, 18:343
Hendrickson, Alf, speaker, 16:361
Hendrickson, H. N., 29:295
Hendrickson, John, scout, 24:325n
Hendrickson, Martin, labor leader, 25:324
Hendrickson, Roy, speaker, 23:297
Hendrickson, W. B., Grange member, 24:119, 120n
Hendrickson, Walter B., "Owen's Geological Survey," 26:222-233; work reviewed, 25:174; author, 23:382, 26:257, 28:330
Hendrickx, Jacques, author, 16:251
Hendriksen, Nils, Mormon missionary, 36:288
Hendrikson, H. O., author, 21:219, 24:382, 25:100, 34:358; editor, 36:327
Hendrum (township and village), history, 14:357, 18:97
Hendry, William, explorer, 17:75
Hendryx, Schuyler V. R., papers, 15:223
Heney, Francis J., lawyer, 40:322, 325
Henimger, Rev. Albert, speaker, 23:398

Henly, Mrs. Harold, 28:302
Hennemann, Carl, author, 25:412, 35:46
Hennepin, Gaspard, 11:5, 345
Hennepin, Father Louis, work reviewed, 20:66-68; birthplace, 11:3-7, 343-345, 18:446, 24:275, 25:208; monuments, 11:3, 4, 351, 12:443, 14:350; author, 11:7-10, 204, 347, 12:26, 410, 13:417, 15:455, 19:46, 99, 444, 22:327, 23:57, 372, 24:36, 26:157, 356, 27:242, 28:276, 29:99, 30:216, 32:215, 33:352, 35:153, 245, 248, 36:100, 38:41; career, 11:216, 345-349, 13:210, 439, 15:104, 19:393-398, 38:243; explorer, 11:340, 12:76, 435, 14:339, 15:100, 479, 16:199, 231, 449, 453, 17:342, 354, 473, 18:233, 22:56, 206, 23:85, 25:273, 329, 364, 28:184, 200, 30:141, 372, 33:124, 35:334, 36:70; portrait, 11:343, 16:350; anniversary, 11:468, 12:80, 96; map, 12:282, 349, 351, 32:190, 36:277; captured by Sioux, 14:371, 16:18, 193, 19:277, 21:92; bibliography, 20:423; colonizer, 20:439; artist, 33:264
Hennepin, Robertine L., 11:5, 345
Hennepin, Hennepin County, ghost town, 19:464
Hennepin, Ill., name, 30:218
Hennepin Avenue, Minneapolis, Indian trail, 15:256
Hennepin Avenue Methodist Church, Minneapolis, 12:191; anniversary, 17:230
Hennepin County, territorial postmarks, 15:487; pageant, 17:361; Indian scare, 18:66; antislavery society, 21:36; medicine, 21:101, 210; fairs, 22:252, 255, 256, 261; history, 23:196, 36:36; courthouse, 23:220, 26:288; archaeology, 24:78, 40:338; Finnish settlement, 25:319; churches, 26:393; boys' home school, 27:56; district court, 27:155; summer resorts, 27:176; politics, 28:31, 32, 34, 35:301, 343-347, 349, 36:305; agriculture, 29:2n; historic sites, 29:87; established, 29:208n, 30:219n; library, 31:61; in fiction, 31:130; potteries, 33:231; county seat, 35:107; boundaries, 35:119; jail, 35:122; poor farms, 35:124, 38:367; map, 40:125n
Hennepin County Agricultural Society, fairs, 14:137, 22:252, 256, 261; meeting, 22:254
Hennepin County Antislavery Society, 20:329
Hennepin County Bar Association, 17:213, 18:211, 19:214, 21:195, 25:185, 26:156
Hennepin County Grocery Association, 22:374
Hennepin County Historical Committee, 11:14, 339, 12:37, 15:242, 315
Hennepin County Historical Society, 20:75, 26:176, 27:266, 30:77, 365; organized, 19:231, 20:46; museum, 19:360, 469, 20:96, 209, 21:108, 444, 23:11, 15, 194, 25:313, 407, 26:89, 393, 27:172, 28:86, 31:99, 101-104, 36:104; meetings, 20:211,

21:216, 335, 22:105, 188, 339, 23:36, 246, 24:86, 187, 25:208, 313, 26:68, 179, 284, 27:75, 361, 28:194, 296, 386, 29:55, 91, 274, 362, 30:74, 166; tours, 20:352, 28:380; activities, 20:455; special exhibits, 20:461, 36:239; publications, 22:216, 440, 23:47, 68, 101, 28:87, 29:91, 179, 30:277, 36:70; incorporated, 24:269, 25:97; building project, 34:258, 35:99, 338
Hennepin County Medical Society, 12:197; history, 12:204, 21:102
Hennepin County Registered Nurses' Association, 26:94
Hennepin County Territorial Pioneer Association, 25:208
Hennepin County War Finance Committee, 26:372
Hennepin County War History Committee, 23:391
Hennepin Island, Hennepin County, Mississippi River, name, 21:349; sawmills, 27:288; described, 30:218
Hennesey, Walter H., career, 18:211
Hennessey, P. M., Contruction Co., 39:158
Henni, Bishop John M., 19:190, 39:307; career, 26:272
Henning, Lutheran church, 12:340; anniversary, 14:358; dairying, 15:251; railroad, 22:340
Henninger, Capt. Paul E., 18:320, 20:332
Henningsen, Dorothy, author, 14:239
Henningson, C. J., 23:391
Hennis, Charles J., editor, 39:45
Henrichsen, S. P., Mormon missionary, 36:288
Henriksen, N., author, 36:293
Henriksson, Henrik, 17:177
Henry, Alexander, I, 20:202; trader, 11:236, 239-242, 258, 261, 265, 268, 13:432, 17:222, 19:291, 20:9, 326, 22:432, 29:267, 34:254, 37:253; at Chequamegon Bay, Wis., 11:244, 245, 248; at Michipicoten, Ont., 11:262; mining interests, 11:263, 35:247; author, 11:267, 12:367, 26:329, 356, 38:385, 40:145; career, 12:440, 13:439, 35:199; explorer, 15:238, 16:230, 453, 24:364, 32:250
Henry, Alexander, II, trader, 11:366-368, 12:375, 13:432, 15:356, 424, 22:275, 29:133, 30:126, 131, 31:183, 38:28, 40:154, 160, 161, 178; journal, 12:437, 17:245n, 22:331, 37:174; career, 13:439; explorer, 16:453, 21:99, 22:110, 23:180, 239n, 28:64, 32:186, 250, 34:174
Henry, Andrew, trader, 38:199, 40:194
Henry, Frank, 34:204
Henry, George, author, 15:126
Henry, John, folk hero, 26:166
Henry, Joseph, scientist, 39:112
Henry, Patrick, house, 26:268
Henry, Ralph L., 40:256; author, 11:327
Henry, Mrs. S. M. I., 29:324
Henry, Thomas R., author, 34:310
Henry, William A., dairyman, 12:99, 19:152, 20:82
Henry, William F., postmaster, 34:185

"Henry Clay," steamboat, 11:143, 20:386
"Henry M. Rice," steamboat, 14:151
"Henry W. Longfellow," steamboat, 11:206
Hensel, Robert, pioneer, 22:345
Hensley, Clinton B., 15:89
Henson, Ray D., editor, 38:92
Henthorne, Sister Mary E., work reviewed, 13:418
Henton, Robert B., Indian agent, 37:275
Hepburn Act, effects, 12:16
Hepworth, Rev. G. H., lecturer, 11:158
Herberg Township, Traill County, N. D., history, 14:357
Herbert, Benjamin B., 18:451
Herbert, Henry W. (Frank Forester), 33:153; author, 14:424, 18:419, 33:151n
Herbert, J. D., "Fur Trade Sites," 40:188-191; compiler, 35:45
Herbert, O. C., speaker, 12:338
Herder, Herman, 12:454
Hereford, Robert A., work reviewed, 25:72
Hergesheimer, Joseph, author, 20:116
Herjulfsson, Bjarni, explorer, 33:216, 39:342
Herlinger, Mrs. ---, 20:60
Herman, county seat fight, 15:486, 23:371; fairs, 15:487; first school, 16:247; history, 17:236; Methodist church, 20:358
Herman Beach, Grant County, geology, 38:158, 159, 162
Hermann, Paul, author, 33:314
Hermanns Sohn im Westen (Stillwater), German paper, 17:386
Hermant, Leon, sculptor, 39:160
Hermanutz, Father Aloysius, missionary, 18:269, 331, 24:263, 26:275, 388, 33:60
Hermes, Rev. Wallace K., essay reviewed, 38:193
Herndon, William H., author, 28:361; papers, 36:229
Herndon House, Hastings, 19:163
Hernlem, A. F., 14:31n
Heron Lake, schools, 14:416, 18:116; history, 14:457, 36:104; Catholic church, 16:121; wildlife, 22:213, 30:221
Herrick, Charles J., author, 24:80, 35:154
Herrick, Clarence, naturalist, 24:80, 35:154
Herrick, U. G., speaker, 17:119, 354, 18:221
Herriman, D. B., Indian agent, 27:296n
Herring, Frank, 11:226
Herring, H. M., 11:226
Herring, John, butcher, 12:336
Herriott, F. I., author, 13:335, 438, 14:113, 342, 15:356; speaker, 14:77
Herriott, Marion H., "Steamboat Transportation on the Red River," 21:245-271; "Through Minnesota to the Canadian West," 24:328-335; author, 21:310, 22:105; editor, 24:353
Herriott, Mrs. William B., 38:77n
Herrmann, Paul, work reviewed, 34:302

Herrold, George H., author, 13:115, 15:140, 36:328
Herron, George D., biography, 13:210
Hersey, ---, baseball player, 19:178
Hersey, Harry C., jockey, 36:66
Hersey, Samuel F., lumberman, 18:170, 173, 174
Hersey, Nobles County, see Brewster
Hersey, Bean, and Brown, Stillwater, lumber firm, 18:175
Hersey, Staples and Co., Stillwater, lumber firm, 18:170-173, 24:205, 30:242, 31:62, 33:226
Hershey, Ben, lumberman, 29:85
Hertl Coal Co., St. Paul, 38:308
Hertz, Emanuel, author, 13:204
Hertz, Richard O., author, 26:272
Hertz, Rudolf, author, 12:331
Hertz, Will, author, 34:173
Hervieux, Paul, see Harvieux, Paul
Herwig, Aletha M., author, 13:102
Herwin, O. S., 21:426
Herzegovinians, see Yugoslavs
Hesard, J. B., 25:241
Hesler, Alex, photographer, 21:95, 34:30-33, 35:182
Hesper, Iowa, Quaker Meeting, 18:256n; history, 21:204, 22:329
Hess, Emanuel, 35:293
Hess, Stephen, author, 37:186, 40:359
Hess Opera Co., 20:466
Hesseltine, William B., review by, 23:259; works reviewed, 29:342, 34:119, 36:149; author, 23:271, 377, 29:257, 33:311, 36:187; speaker, 27:356; editor, 35:335, 37:307
Hestenes, Joseph R., author, 25:195
Hetherington, Sue, author, 23:382
Hetherwold, William, pseud., see Schoolcraft, Henry R.
Hetle, Erik, work reviewed, 30:377
Heurtebize, Louis, 12:307
Hewett, Edgar L., author, 16:4
Hewitt, Alpheus, 39:90
Hewitt, Dr. Charles N., 30:175, 405, 31:190; health department head, 11:458, 17:69, 29:84, 170, 39:114; career, 12:204, 19:111, 21:330, 357-362, 26:287, 34:34; medical library, 21:362-371, 23:167; army surgeon, 27:250
Hewitt, Mrs. Charles N., 21:358
Hewitt, Edwin H., 19:365
Hewitt, Girart, author, 17:256
Hewitt, Dr. Henry, 21:364
Hewitt, J. N. B., editor, 14:223, 19:105
Hewitt, Sister Liguori, 14:40
Hewitt, Stephen, steamboat captain, 12:61n
Hewitt, William E., career, 19:214
Hews, Robert, farmer, 29:23
Heyer, John C. F., 15:361; biography, 24:373
Heyne, Rev. E. T., author, 14:124
Heyne, Rev. Robert G., speaker, 28:85
Heyward, Du Bose, author, 20:113
Heywood, John, 27:34
Heywood, Russell H., 23:274
Heywood, Sarah, see Folwell, Mrs. William W.
Heywood, Silas L., 15:347
Heywood family, 17:470
Heywood's Minstrels, 28:111
Hiawatha, Iroquois leader, 24:237, 34:310, 35:380. See also "Song of Hiawatha"

Hibbard, E. L., 23:392
Hibbard, John J., pioneer, 22:346
Hibbard, Julia K. S., author, 13:213; house, 15:46, 182
Hibben, Frank C., author, 28:77
Hibbing, Frank, 34:218; mining interests, 14:462, 23:110, 34:216
Hibbing, ethnic groups, 12:436, 19:112, 30:156; history, 14:462, 23:199, 27:366, 36:196, 37:347; mining town, 16:486, 18:332, 19:334, 21:290, 23:110, 208, 28:251, 29:89, 32:245, 246, 36:81, 40:345-347; ski club, 17:228; bus line, 18:220, 21:291, 27:272, 33:353, 36:190; theater, 19:126; court, 20:468; removal, 21:103, 25:213, 28:279; historical meetings, 21:286-289, 34:218; temperance societies, 22:392n, 394, 395, 397, 399, 400; workers' society, 25:324, 325; Catholic church, 26:96; library, 27:178; described, 29:167; geological marker, 34:314. See also Mesabi Range
Hibbing Historical Society, 22:214, 218, 341, 23:14
Hibbing War History Committee, 23:391
Hibner, Aldis E., author, 15:343
Hickenlooper, Bourke B., Senator, 29:174
Hickerson, Harold, author, 35:244, 40:146; editor, 36:324, 37:37
Hickman, James, lumberman, 24:201
Hickman, Rev. Robert T., Black leader, 23:110, 30:266
Hickok, James B. ("Wild Bill"), 34:305, 345, 35:241
Hickory Township, Red Lake County, history, 38:204
Hicks, Granville, author, 25:305
Hicks, Hattie, 39:218, 223
Hicks, Henry G., 21:316; papers, 15:465; G.A.R. commander, 16:434, 439; legislator, 35:343
Hicks, Mr. and Mrs. John, 39:218, 223-225
Hicks, John D., "The Persistence of Populism," 12:3-20; "My Six Years at Hamline," 39:213-226; review by, 11:194; works reviewed, 12:411-413, 18:438, 25:170, 32:181-183; author, 11:328, 12:3n, 14:339, 16:196, 18:214, 23:83, 31:61, 34:354, 35:150, 36:185, 37:135, 262, 38:235, 387, 40:360; speaker, 12:40, 13:55, 15:119, 16:225, 23:380, 38:334
Hicks, Mrs. John D., 39:225, 226
Hicks, William E., 18:467
Hidatsa Indians, 13:60; customs, 13:102, 15:232, 29:263, 34:255, 35:339; name, 24:152; songs, 34:161, 35:244; villages, 40:193
Hides, defined, 40:210
Hidy, Ralph W., review by, 35:37; works reviewed, 35:91, 38:379
Hidy, Mrs. Ralph W. (Muriel E.), "A Dutch Investor in Minnesota, 1866," 37:152-160; reviews by, 35:38, 36:27, 39:257; work reviewed, 35:91
Hiebert, Mrs. B. N., author, 21:220
Hiebert, Gareth, author, 27:269, 28:77, 29:172, 33:312, 34:266, 36:152, 238, 239, 37:40, 42, 263, 38:243

Hielm, Pavels, 18:199
Hielscher, Dr. Helen H., author, 16:219
Hielscher, Julius, county commissioner, 38:367
Hielscher, Theodor, freethinker, 24:219
Higbee, Isabel D., clubwoman, 11:97, 15:243
Higgins, Frank E., lumberjacks' missionary, 13:323, 31:65-78, 184, 34:60
Higgins, Mrs. Frank E., 31:68, 77
Higgins, Dr. George W., speaker, 29:92
Higgins, Rev. William, diary, 25:77
Higgins, Lake County, railroad station, 34:181
Higginson, T. W., author, 26:302
High Forest, Olmsted County, hotel, 16:367, 18:227, 21:213; in Sioux Outbreak, 18:116; agriculture, 18:314; camp meetings, 21:86, 31:82; store, 21:214; justices' dockets, 21:215; ghost town, 35:12; history, 35:336
High Island Lake, Sibley County, 33:249
Higham, John, work reviewed, 34:343; author, 35:378
Highby, Paul R., author, 22:103
Highland, Lake County, iron mining, 34:180
Highland, Wright County, Quakers, 18:254n, 256
"Highland Mary," steamboat, 13:233, 17:152, 277, 278, 18:372, 31:209, 212
Highwater Township, Cottonwood County, history, 34:358
Highways, see Roads and highways
Highwood, St. Paul neighborhood, described, 36:239
Hildreth, Richard, 19:436
Hilger, Sister M. Inez, "A 'Peace and Friendship' Medal," 16:321-323; review by, 38:192; author, 16:476, 20:442, 24:262
Hill, Gen. A. H., 25:144n
Hill, Alberta K., "Out with the Fleet," 37:283-297
Hill, Alfred J., archaeologist, 11:326, 368, 13:163, 167, 15:109, 148, 16:21, 162, 21:315, 22:210, 25:336; map, 11:359; survey, 22:332; in Civil War, 24:27
Hill, Edward E., work reviewed, 39:296; compiler, 40:361
Hill, Evan, author, 36:236
Hill, Forest G., work reviewed, 36:96
Hill, Frank E., work reviewed, 38:379
Hill, George, diary, 26:177
Hill, George W., work reviewed, 32:184
Hill, Harry C., editor, 25:87
Hill, Henry, 16:137
Hill, James J., 11:351, 13:207, 14:205, 18:191, 21:451, 32:125, 35:45, 207, 36:151, 38:243; railroad magnate, 11:104, 13:33, 14:113, 16:224, 343, 463, 17:217, 19:110, 20:88, 336, 441, 21:64, 97, 439, 22:202, 23:87, 93, 24:278n, 28:376, 396, 29:165, 30:373, 31:55, 34:130, 35:152, 153, 295, 38:31, 100, 110, 40:356; steamboat interests, 11:308, 12:175, 30:262, 32:

60; honored, 12:331, 34:84; agricultural interests, 12:432, 13:111, 26:124, 36:68, 37:26, 39:334, 40:231n; career, 13:95, 440, 16:226, 20:75, 22:104, 28:169, 371, 34:38, 216, 35:38, 203, 36:102; papers, 15:223, 17:160n, 20:209; art collector, 19:420, 20:185, 24:242, 26:302, 30:268, 36:22, 194; religious interests, 22:347, 27:271; author, 23:322, 324, 38:241; legends, 26:73, 379; speaker, 26:307; house, 29:73, 34:314, 36:95; portraits, 30:40, 37:37; family, 30:60; fireman, 30:163; death, 30:383; in fiction, 31:132, 36:83; characterized, 33:51; in politics, 34:37; resort owner, 34:173; banking interests, 34:205; newspaper owner, 39:102, 332, 333
Hill, Mrs. James J. (Mary), biography, 30:60
Hill, Jim Dan, reviews by, 19:73-76, 20:420-422; author, 14:109, 19:91, 20:426; speaker, 28:198, 29:55
Hill, Joe (Joseph Hillstrom), itinerant singer, 25:221n, 26:166, 36:83
Hill, John, artist, 25:166n
Hill, Jonas R., 25:121, 237
Hill, Louis W., 14:64, 98, 24:242, 39:154n; automobile enthusiast, 38:206, 208, 214, 215
Hill, Mrs. Louis W. (Maud T.), 25:42, 39:58
Hill, Louis W., Jr., 17:70, 20:50, 23:50, 26:45, 29:97
Hill, Dr. Nathan B., 18:252
Hill, S. T., 14:219
Hill, Mrs. Sally Brown, pioneer, 21:453
Hill, Thomas B., author, 12:108
Hill, Will, composer, 32:163n
Hill, Rev. William B., author, 22:94
Hill City, name, 21:347
Hill family, genealogy, 30:60
Hill Family Foundation, marker project, 34:314; grants, 35:199, 339, 37:187, 264, 40:142; publication, 38:241
Hill, Griggs and Co., in Red River trade, 21:253, 254, 270
Hill Point, Clearwater County, archaeology, 36:326
Hill Reference Library, St. Paul, 18:210, 27:242; Eastman Collection, 19:419-423; centennial, 29:370, 30:284
Hill River Township, Red Lake County, history, 38:204
Hillbrand, Percie V., author, 39:263
Hiller, Wesley R., author, 20:335, 22:93, 210, 29:262; compiler, 26:81
Hillhouse, ---, steamboat captain, 13:145
Hilligoss, William J., 13:32n, 15:251
Hillman, George N., 13:445; author, 13:332; court reporter, 15:224
Hillman, William O., career, 13:324
Hillmond, Henry, legislator, 35:346
Hills, Leon C., author, 19:222
Hills, Margaret, 14:35
Hills, Lutheran church, 13:428; library, 19:239; anniversary, 21:455
Hillsboro, Iowa, buildings, 25:199
Hillsborough, Lord, in fur trade, 11:255, 256

Hillstrom, Joseph, see Hill, Joe
Hilly, Harry, settler, 34:183
Hilton, B. F., 12:158
Hilton, Judge Clifford L., speaker, 13:452
Hilton, Constance, author, 16:245
Hilton, E. P., theater manager, 33:177
Hilton, Edward F., lawyer, 17:213
Hilton, George W., works reviewed, 37:131, 38:237
Hilton, Rev. J. B., 13:148
Hilts, Theodore, Union soldier, 25:128
Hiltunen, Tom, editor, 30:404
Hime, Humphrey L., photographer, 36:191, 249n
Himmelman family, in Mankato, 17:234
Himrod, Anna, author, 22:103, 344, 36:195
Hinck, Rev. John H., 23:391
Hinckley, H. L., 30:312
Hinckley, Ira W., author, 26:397, 27:176, 33:315
Hinckley, Isaac, railroad president, 37:102
Hinckley, creamery, 13:216; fire, 23:99, 24:346, 374, 25:58, 275, 384, 412, 30:372, 383, 33:46, 92, 34:171, 218, 39:82, 300; school, 28:131; county seat fight, 34:217; railroad, 37:90
Hind, E. Cora, author, 35:295
Hind, Henry Y., author, 14:334, 33:183; explorer, 33:187, 36:191; papers, 34:352
Hind, W. G. R., artist, 36:40
Hindermann, Jacob, steamboat captain, 26:181
"Hindoo," steamboat, 19:144
Hine, Robert V., essay reviewed, 38:238; author, 38:201
Hineline, George C., 19:342
Hines Township, Beltrami County, prehistoric village, 26:312
Hinman, George W., work reviewed, 15:211
Hinman, Hannah (Mrs. Elam Greeley), 24:203, 349
Hinman, Robert H., career, 38:144n
Hinman, Samuel D., missionary to Sioux, 12:130-133, 14:359, 16:358, 38:144n, 357, 358, 364
Hinman, Col. Wilbur F., author, 33:82
Hinsch, Dr. A. D., theater director, 32:166, 167
Hinsdale, William B., author, 13:207, 14:112
Hinsman, Keith A., author, 34:313
Hintze, F. F., Mormon missionary, 36:289, 290, 293
Hipel, N. O., author, 23:385
"Hiram R. Dixon," steamboat, 34:245, 246, 35:49
Hirschfeld, Charles, work reviewed, 33:308; author, 22:328
Hirschheimer, H. J., 18:223; work reviewed, 32:253; author, 20:340, 24:177, 26:272, 27:69
Hirschy, C. C., 13:217
His Thunder, Sioux Indian, 38:135
Hispanics, Catholic, 37:133
Historic American Buildings Survey, Minnesota, 15:73, 79, 127, 250, 359, 443, 467, 16:55, 249, 257, 27:231; publication, 21:324
Historic buildings, Minnesota, 27:

125, 228-232, 266, 28:389, 29:54, 30:157; Middle West, 29:72; Wisconsin, 29:86; restoration, 31:249. See also National Council for Historic Sites and Buildings
Historic sites, marking, 11:25-30, 51, 202, 313, 314, 12:37, 102, 189, 313, 16:58, 194, 22:209, 23:46, 33:314, 35:296; administration, 11:30-35, 15:229, 18:281, 39:209, 337; surveys, 11:314, 12:30, 188, 13:63, 14:73, 228, 17:55, 65, 28:389; tours, 12:335, 443, 29:87, 36:240; mapped, 12:441, 17:112, 38:44; Minnesota, 12:449, 16:114, 20:343, 23:192, 28:292, 30:274, 35:338, 36:106, 283, 37:44, 58-70, 308, 38:43, 231-233, 243, 379, 388, 39:131, 274, 300, 40:48, 148, 263, 314; Iowa, 15:475; toured by automobile, 16:192-195; legislation, 17:105, 24:181, 253, 33:137, 40:35-38, 135; preservation, 25:381, 31:249, 35:150; Montana, 25:385; Ohio, 27:354; Wisconsin, 30:73, 35:151; Twin Cities area, 34:220, 36:240, 39:124, 40:255; Saskatchewan, 35:45; U.S., 36:95, 37:85, 186, 39:33, 40:45, 404; Catholic, 36:105; Presbyterian, 36:192; Sioux Outbreak, 38:154-156, 242, 39:130, 40:232; Midwest, 39:82; in Black history, 39:299; fur trade, 40:188-197; North Dakota, 40:316. See also Archaeology, Monuments and markers, individual sites
Historical and Archaeological Research Survey project, 23:43
Historical and Scientific Society of Manitoba, 17:476, 29:80
Historical museums, agricultural, 11:100, 18:102, 24:363, 26:266, 29:262, 38:204; ethnic, 13:206, 18:452, 19:460, 23:190, 26:364, 36:284, 328, 37:44, 45 (cover), 66, 68, 70, 188, 39:299; private, 13:450, 18:117, 25:302; Ohio, 14:227; Indiana, 14:341; local, 14:461, 17:68, 23:10-15, 25:101, 26:377; residential, 15:229, 34:213, 35:150; industrial, 16:446, 17:491, 18:102, 344, 472, 20:92, 24:362, 364, 25:303, 34:43, 35:201, 36:282; administration, 17:93, 24:260, 25:83, 39:209, 40:364; functions, 17:472, 20:436, 23:16, 47, 278, 279, 24:70, 25:95, 26:49, 101, 377, 31:15; post office, 18:472; financing, 21:48, 27:158; buildings, 21:49, 26:180; Canada, 21:421, 23:93, 186, 24:186; Wisconsin, 23:286, 24:378, 26:385; Washington State, 26:164; Louisiana, 26:283; fur trade, 34:353, 40:196, 197; steamboat, 36:283, 327. See also Historical societies, various community museums and historic residences
Historical Records Survey, see Works Progress Administration
Historical societies, functions, 11:53, 20:365-376, 436, 21:320, 22:200, 24:70, 360, 26:30, 73, 269, 27:158, 251, 30:365, 31:11-17, 34:219, 36:150, 37:85, 39:75; U.S. and Canada, 18:214, 24:377, 25:

390, 403, 26:163, 34:263, 36:30, 38:287; growth, 19:9, 25:294; in wartime, 23:278, 24:39; Swedish, 23:380; use of radio, 24:362, 25:46; relation to schools, 25:190; legislation for, 25:296; Indiana, 25:301; Michigan, 25:302; discard problem, 26:148; Catholic, 26:266; Wisconsin, 26:271, 385, 34:313; staff qualifications, 27:59; publications, 28:276, 32:58; libraries, 37:348; tour planning, 39:212; founders, 39:336. See also American Association for State and Local History, Historical museums, individual state and community societies

Local, progress, 11:12-24, 52, 12:22, 36-40, 313, 13:62, 70, 14:68, 15:65, 80, 16:58, 17:60, 64, 18:56, 62, 64, 19:58, 63, 20:41, 46, 291, 25:389; functions, 11:26, 13:109, 113, 286, 431, 14:122, 16:63, 17:91, 391, 19:10, 348, 21:49, 23:16-19, 285, 376, 25:190, 295, 379, 26:62, 377, 382, 29:163; financing, 11:46, 21:48, 26:176, 27:349, 34:267, 35:292; activities, 13:71, 16:237, 22:49, 23:188, 25:51, 187, 38:240; in wartime, 23:10-23, 47, 278, 389, 24:71; Iowa, 23:90; Minnesota, 23:187, 26:40, 27:145, 30:45, 321; junior, 26:78, 183, 253, 367, 27:66, 145, 147, 148, 353, 28:46, 160-166, 175, 187; Wisconsin, 26:271, 385; problems, 37:44

Historical Society of Berks County, Pa., publication, 26:168
Historical Society of Pennsylvania, Philadelphia, 21:86, 320; history conference, 29:258
Historical Society of St. Boniface, Man., 14:444, 15:70, 17:476, 18:246, 247, 280, 27:260
Historiography, techniques, 12:89, 14:222, 15:314, 19:435, 20:176-179, 26:60, 382, 28:73, 30:257, 33:226, 36:32, 84-88, 277, 37:182, 39:44; scholarship, 14:3-29, 88-90, 192-194, 15:207, 18:4, 20:1-6, 34:262, 298, 35:87, 243, 37:305; in literature, 21:1-4, 199, 25:191, 389, 28:369, 36:236
History, teaching, 12:169-171, 13:432, 14:112, 16:233, 25:68, 85, 168-170, 190, 389, 26:78, 266, 267, 383, 27:147, 148, 162, 257, 348, 28:71, 176, 353-359, 364, 29:77, 163, 30:149, 263, 34:311, 35:154, 38:196; source material, 13:417, 16:70-75, 18:15, 24:111, 26:72, 27:29-32, 29:57, 35:44, 36:150, 38:42; bibliographies, 16:220, 21:91, 322, 24:173, 30:64; business, 22:326, 25:391, 26:72, 27:64, 252, 28:331, 30:64, 33:92; in motion pictures, 23:83, 385, 27:158; cultural, 23:178; graduate degrees, 23:377, 40:314; defined, 24:68, 172, 360, 26:161; on radio, 24:362, 25:191, 201, 26:276; pictorial, 26:270, 358-360, 28:69, 278, 345-352, 30:53-55, 31:53, 248, 32:123, 33:133; periodicals, 28:102, 32:58, 34:352, 39:298; oral, 32:57, 33:137; urban, 33:

201-207. See also Economic history, Minnesota history
Local, study, 12:174, 39:265-271; use of newspapers, 13:45-54; importance, 13:431, 15:69-74, 19:1-20, 30:386, 31:118, 249; bibliographies, 21:88, 198, 318, 418, 22:91, 198, 325, 427, 23:79, 173-175, 276, 24:67, 171, 250, 25:189, 293
History Book Club, program, 28:173
Hitchcock, D. L., pioneer physician, 16:252
Hitchcock, Dr. E. D., author, 17:220
Hitchcock, H. M., author, 11:216, 12:97
Hitchcock, Ida J., author, 12:331
Hitchcock, R. W., author, 13:213, 17:91
Hitler, Adolf, autograph, 25:64
Hitterdal, history, 21:448
Hixon, Mrs. Minerva, author, 30:271
Hjelm, Anton, postmaster, 34:186
Hjelm-Hansen, Paul, career, 12:258-260; author, 12:270, 24:79; immigration promoter, 12:277, 278, 17:478, 19:234, 20:337, 31:27, 35:33
Hjermstad, Dr. Bengdt, 17:228
Hjermstad, J. M., speaker, 15:136
Hlady, Walter M., author, 33:227
Hoag, C., 17:214
Hoag, Charles, Minneapolis pioneer, 19:454, 22:260, 31:182
Hoag, Lindley M., Quaker minister, 18:250
Hoag, R. D., 22:344
Hoar, George F., Senator, 18:142, 145
Hoard, Hiram E., farmer, 33:224
Hoard, William D., dairyman, 12:99, 20:82, 22:267, 33:224; Wisconsin governor, 19:150
Hobart, Charles H., 15:238
Hobart, Rev. Chauncey, 13:103, 454, 19:214; diary, 15:60, 110
Hobbie, S. R., postmaster, 31:176
Hobbins, Dr. and Mrs. Joseph, genealogy, 33:85
Hobbs, Miss ---, English traveler, 11:166
Hobe, Engebreth H., Norwegian consul, 20:466, 22:322, 25:79; papers, 22:40, 24:34, 34:339
Hoblit, John T., publisher, 13:150
Hobson, James A., 39:117
Hockett, Homer C., work reviewed, 13:94; author, 34:352
Hockey, pictured, 40:386
Hodap, Adolph, trapper, 30:132
Hodder, Frank H., speaker, 13:327
Hodge, Frederick W., anthropologist, 16:476; author, 33:21, 37:84; editor, 37:84
Hodgedon, Irene, 33:16
Hodgedon, S. H., steamboat owner, 33:15, 16
Hodges, Leonard B., quoted, 29:24
Hodges, S. P. and P. F., farm machinery merchants, 24:301
Hodges, W. R., 11:332; author, 20:449
Hodgkins, Henry H., 27:346
Hodgman, Amison J., 12:54n
Hodgson, Bob, author, 30:264
Hodgson, James G., 18:448
Hodgson, Laurence C., 11:196; author, 13:113; mayor, 20:209
Hodgson, Laurence K., author, 20:209
Hodgson, Patricia, speaker, 15:138

Hodgson, R. E., 19:232; speaker, 20:99; author, 25:214
Hodgson, T. C., agrarian leader, 16:365, 36:117, 118
Hodgson, Thomas C., author, 21:340
Hodnefield, Jacob, head of accessions, 11:46, 17:55; compiler, 13:206, 16:108; speaker, 17:65, 19:65, 25:43; survey director, 18:49, 19:51; author, 18:458, 22:103, 24:243, 25:287, 26:153, 30:391; newspaper curator, 23:366; retires, 27:140
Hoebel, E. Adamson, review by, 34:301; author, 39:259
Hoeffern, Antonia, letters, 17:95
Hoeffler, Adolf, "Minnesota 100 Years Ago," 33:114-125; artist, 33:112-116, 119-124, 264, 34:121
Hoeffler, Heinrich, 33:112
Hoegh, Dr. Knut, 17:169; author, 39:135
Hoekman, Steven, author, 34:131
Hoeltje, Hubert H., "Ralph Waldo Emerson in Minnesota," 11:148-159; author, 11:327, 12:326, 18:325, 23:285
Hoeschen, John, 33:54
Hoevet, Albert, speaker, 13:343
Hofacker, Erich, author, 33:187
Hoff, Olaf, 29:294
Hoffman, Miss ---, cholera victim, 14:294
Hoffman, Agnes T. (Mrs. Veggo Anderson), 28:243, 245, 246
Hoffman, Alex., author, 19:219
Hoffman, Arnold, author, 37:41
Hoffman, Ben, 33:354
Hoffman, Charles W., sutler, 34:328n
Hoffman, Daniel C., work reviewed, 33:265; author, 32:187
Hoffman, Frank, 35:379
Hoffman, Mrs. Frank L., pianist, 39:61-63
Hoffman, George, 28:246; characterized, 38:247
Hoffman, Mrs. George, 28:247-249
Hoffman, John P., 29:364; editor, 25:97
Hoffman, M. J., highway commissioner, 25:379; speaker, 26:43
Hoffman, Mrs. R. D., speaker, 15:241
Hoffman, Virginia C., see Garrard, Mrs. George W.
Hoffman, Col. William, 25:226
Hoffmann, M. M., review by, 15:104; works reviewed, 12:76, 18:436; author, 11:106, 217, 14:349, 15:213, 531, 20:339, 33:356; editor, 11:324, 19:460
Hoffstrom, Piercy J. ("Hawf & Hawf"), speaker, 21:83; author, 27:47; cartoonist, 30:366
Hofkamp, G., 28:129
Hofman, Paul, musician, 33:100
Hofmann, Charles, author, 27:161, 29:86
Hofmann, Josef, musician, 39:55, 56
Hofstadter, Richard, works reviewed, 35:30, 89; author, 34:250, 37:261; quoted, 38:387
Hofstead, John A., author, 13:206
Hofstrom, Charles, speaker, 25:286
Hog Lake, Cook County, forest fire, 36:136, 137
Hog raising, Minnesota, 26:106, 114-118. See also Livestock industry

Hogan, Genevieve, stenographer, 24:30
Hogan, John, postmaster, 34:186
Hogges, James W., author, 29:73
Hoglund, A. William, work reviewed, 37:129
Hognander, Marjorie, 28:195
Hogue, O. E., 17:240
Hohl, Henry L., publisher, 18:226, 21:221
Hoidale, Einar, "The Study of Pioneer Life," 11:63-70; author, 11:185-187, 339, 21:222, 342; speaker, 16:483
Hokah, history, 16:249, 17:486, 25:183; directory, 19:235; minstrel show, 28:106; bank, 37:87, 40:110
Hokah Chief, history, 14:397, 404, 16:249, 18:226, 21:221
Hokanson, Nels, work reviewed, 24:156
Holabird, Gen. Samuel B., 28:222
Holand, Hjalmar R., 13:102, 33:216; "Radisson's Two Western Journeys," 15:157-180; "Concerning the Kensington Rune Stone," 17:166-188; "The Climax Fire Steel," 18:188-190; works reviewed, 12:179-181, 13:182-184, 21:302-304, 28:58-60, 35:141, 36:33, 38:193, 383; in rune-stone controversy, 13:278, 443, 15:355, 17:20-26, 28-35, 206, 18:40, 186, 20:85, 200, 24:257, 28:378, 29:175, 30:154, 31:250, 32:56, 33:314, 354, 34:265, 302, 35:294, 36:146, 238, 39:134, 137n, 139, 140, 40:47; author, 14:447, 18:203, 22:68, 25:193, 29:349, 30:169, 39:171, 40:95
Holberg, Richard, author, 20:450
Holberg, Ruth, author, 20:450
Holbert, Sue E., work reviewed, 40:255; compiler, 40:314
Holbo, Paul S., "The Farmer-Labor Association," 38:301-309
Holbrook, Bertha A., author, 26:385
Holbrook, Franklin F., 11:46; works reviewed, 11:195-198, 13:184, 14:318-322; editor, 11:202, 12:25; author, 13:192, 14:61, 23:390
Holbrook, Stewart H., "Some Unwritten Minnesota Novels," 33:45-52; reviews by, 29:70, 30:242, 31:50, 33:183, 219, 34:35, 35:326; works reviewed, 19:197, 21:183, 24:345, 28:54, 31:180, 34:38, 263, 348, 35:38, 37:36; author, 21:56, 23:98, 24:374, 25:398, 26:380, 28:371, 29:84, 104, 165, 30:292, 31:64, 124, 33:313, 35:153, 36:102, 39:82; editor, 28:173
Holbrook and Co., Minneapolis, meat packers, 26:17
Holcomb Dancing Academy, Minneapolis, 33:100
Holcombe, Return I., historian, 34:236, 237, 38:100, 113n, 114, 126-128, 39:272; librarian, 39:280
Holcombe, William, 19:146, 249, 26:110; land officer, 12:389; postmaster, 36:207, 208, 210; house, 38:339
Holcombe, Mrs. William, 28:313
Holdahl, Olaf, 16:492
Holden, George D., 16:255
Holden, Dr. Levi H., 32:84
Holden, Michael, author, 12:201, 18:229
Holden, S. G., speaker, 17:481

Holden, Goodhue County, Norwegian settlement, 11:286, 12:271; Lutheran school, 26:166
Holdingford, Congregational church, 29:358
Hole-in-the-Day I (Pagonageria), Chippewa leader, 24:20, 21, 23, 129, 27:170; grave, 20:97, 28:293; warfare, 21:32n, 337; characterized, 21:285, 24:15, 16; career, 29:270
Hole-in-the-Day II, Chippewa leader, 21:337, 22:85; warfare, 15:114, 285, 21:337, 28:215, 30:387, 31:216, 35:269, 38:275; at treaty councils, 15:289, 19:384, 35:105, 39:259; described, 21:285, 30:213, 214; in St. Paul, 29:35, 123, 30:215; career, 29:270; portrait, 30:212
Holidays, see individual occasions
Holl, Mrs. Caroline N., 18:110
Holladay, Ben, stage owner, 25:277, 38:226n
Holland, Don, 20:96
Holland, George, comedian, 23:307
Holland, J., and Co., St. Paul, merchants, 15:85
Holland, John, banker, 40:114, 118
Holland, Josiah, author, 28:361
Holland, Samuel, cartographer, 40:356
Holland, Stanford C., 35:14
Holland, Dutch settlement, 28:128; Lutheran church, 28:129
Holland (country), see Netherlands
Holland Land Co., 18:87
Hollandale, farming, 11:289, 28:247, 30:271; German settlement, 28:245
Hollanders, see Dutch
Hollaren, Mike, reminiscences, 20:361
Hollenstein, Gene H., author, 38:203
Holley, Henry W., publisher, 20:270; editor, 32:23
Holley, Horace, 15:12
Holley, L. G., commission merchant, 24:100
Holley, Marietta, poet, 26:298
Holliday, J. S., work reviewed, 38:238
Holliday, J. W., speaker, 11:219
Holliday, Ruth, author, 12:208
Hollingsworth, J. Rogers, work reviewed, 39:29
Hollinshead, William, lawyer, 39:45, 148n
Hollister, Byron L., author, 26:387
Hollon, W. Eugene, work reviewed, 30:376; speaker, 29:257; author, 30:258
Holloway, Jean, work reviewed, 37:129
Holloway, M. Maxson, author, 23:181
Holloway, Mark, author, 33:228
Holm, Erick, pioneer, 24:321, 325
Holm, Mary, 14:428
Holm, Mike, speaker, 18:278, 21:50, 28:298
Holm, Ole, pioneer, 24:321, 324
Holm, Wilhelm, 29:275
Holm, Mrs. Wilhelm, author, 29:271
Holman, Dr. Carl J., papers, 19:451
Holman, Charles ("Speed"), aviator, 33:241, 242, 34:44
Holman, Dr. Madge T., 19:451
Holman, Mary L., author, 19:466
Holmberg, A. R., author, 34:173
Holmberg, Nathaniel J., legislator, 33:158, 160

Holmes, Dr. Bayard T., career, 13:441
Holmes, Dorothy P., editor, 24:361
Holmes, Edward A., surveyor, 16:469
Holmes, Fred L., works reviewed, 27:134, 31:187; author, 19:351, 21:429
Holmes, George E., singer, 39:53
Holmes, Henry, politician, 34:222
Holmes, J. B., 14:273
Holmes, Jack D. L., work reviewed, 39:337
Holmes, John H., 34:173
Holmes, Joseph T., 29:365
Holmes, Mrs. Joseph T., 29:365; speaker, 28:88
Holmes, Kenneth, speaker, 29:164
Holmes, Oliver W., review by, 12:416; author, 14:399, 20:84, 24:70; archivist, 36:218
Holmes, Dr. Oliver Wendell, author, 22:201, 23:185, 27:16, 28:273; letters, 22:201, 34:132; poet, 23:185
Holmes, Justice Oliver Wendell, Jr., in Civil War, 28:373
Holmes, Robert S., army surgeon, 36:42n
Holmes, Thomas A., townsite promoter, 11:168, 331, 12:202, 14:232; emigrant leader, 13:436, 23:184, 38:58, 61, 62; trader, 20:443, 29:218
Holmes, Thomas J., author, 21:417
Holmes, William, author, 36:34
Holmes, William H., anthropologist, 16:1
Holmes City, Finnish settlement, 22:392n, 25:318, 320; history, 30:161
Holmes Landing, Wis., state boundary, 33:117n. See also Fountain City, Wis.
Holmes's Landing, Minn., see Shakopee
Holmgren, Charles E., 16:362, 18:112, 19:120; author, 18:224; speaker, 19:64
Holmquist, A. M., author, 20:98
Holmquist, Arthur, author, 16:132
Holmquist, Donald C., "Pride of the Pioneer's Parlor," 39:312-326; review by, 40:144; photographer, 34:133 (cover), 37:225 (cover), 254n; author, 40:96
Holmquist, Mrs. Donald C. (June Drenning), 30:290, 35:204, 40:316; "Century Day," 30:363-369; "Joseph Le Conte's Early Geological Excursion," 32:81-99; "Minnesota Newsboys' Greetings," 33:164-168; "Fishing in the Land of 10,000 Lakes," 33:252-259; "Commercial Fishing on Lake Superior," 34:243-249; "Convention City," 35:64-76; reviews by, 31:51, 244, 32:185, 33:310, 34:351, 35:240, 36:320, 37:79, 259, 301, 38:380, 39:33, 78, 207, 254, 40:259, 312; works reviewed, 38:86, 379, 39:123, 335, 40:255; author, 30:412, 31:64, 125, 256, 32:128, 191, 192, 35:156, 36:72; editor, 34:176, 35:100, 37:44; compiler, 40:314
Holst, Lars, editor, 20:402
Holstad, Agnes, 15:488
Holt, Edgar A., author, 12:441
Holt, Maj. John R., author, 19:354
Holt, Joseph W., missionary, 17:96
Holt, W. Stull, 22:328; author, 34:262

Holt Township, Fillmore County, Norwegian settlement, 12:268
Holte, Mrs. H., 24:188
Holte, Halvor, pioneer physician, 37:135
Holte, Jean L., author, 25:91
Holte, Rev. Raymond, author, 17:118
Holte Memorial Pioneer Museum, Crookston, 38:92
Holter, Anton M., lumberman, 36:98
Holterhoff, Robert, educator, 34:104, 105
Holtman, Flora, author, 27:174
Holton, David P., 28:134
Holton, John, Red Rock pioneer, 17:286
Holton, John, missionary, 31:82, 83n
Holtz, William V., author, 40:362
Holtzerman, Louis, merchant, 16:249
Holtzermann, Jacob D., 33:333, 337; publisher, 21:424
Holway, Mrs. E. W. D. (Mary Mortenson), 15:138, 19:118, 20:98
Holway, Edward W. D., career, 12:447
Holy, Lt. Antonín, 15:41
Holy Angels Church (Catholic), St. Cloud, 14:360
Holy Cross Church (Catholic), Minneapolis, 17:479
Holy Redeemer Church (Catholic), Marshall, 16:120; Minneapolis, 17:479
Holy Rosary Church (Catholic), Grand Portage, 39:301 (cover), 305, 309, 310
Holy Trinity Church (Catholic), Litomysl, Steele County, 21:457; Winsted, McLeod County, 25:315; New Ulm, 26:181
Holyland, John, photographer, 38:216
Holyoke, Will, diary, 21:315
Holzinger, J. M., 20:162n
Hölzlhuber, Franz, artist, 39:297
Homan, Sister Mary David, author, 36:107
Homar, Roman, missionary, 23:402
Home Economics Club, Stewartville, 21:454
Home for Children and Aged Women, Minneapolis, 38:82
Home for the Friendless, St. Paul, history, 38:77-85
Home Life Insurance Co., 18:362
Home missionaries, see American Home Missionary Society
Home of the Friendless Association of the City of St. Paul, program, 38:79-85
Home Owners' Loan Corporation, Washington, D.C., correspondence, 24:69
Home Society for Aged Women, 16:242
Homeopathic Medical Society of Southern Minnesota, 21:330
Homeopathy, 20:236; Minnesota, 22:334, 434, 435, 23:96; New England, 39:8, 9; Minneapolis, 39:10, 12, 15
Homer, Louise, singer, 39:59
Homer, population, 12:63; described, 19:342; museum, 39:139, 140
Homestead Act, provisions, 12:56; results, 12:265, 19:200, 23:358; proposed, 13:280, 17:416, 22:242, 246, 28:20, 21, 23, 25, 27, 30
Homestead Building and Loan Association, Duluth, 37:123

Hompe, John B., speaker, 13:120, 14:357, 17:357, 483; legislator, 32:142, 35:306-309, 36:114
Hone, David, 20:448
Honeycutte, Prince, lawyer, 38:14, 15
Honeyman and Andyke, Cannon City, Rice County, plow manufacturers, 23:324
Honeywell, Inc., Minneapolis, 33:244; history, 36:283, 37:346, 39:131
Honningstad, Paul, skier, 17:228
Hood, Lt. Robert, journal, 21:93
Hood, W. P., 29:87
Hoohamaza, Sioux Indian, 13:409
Hooker, Gen. Joseph ("Fighting Joe"), Union officer, 25:36, 131, 132, 234, 246, 344n, 347, 348n, 359, 38:246, 39:282, 40:271; replaces Burnside, 25:244; speaker, 25:245; described, 25:251; superseded by Meade, 25:360; at Chattanooga, 38:271, 272
Hooper, William H., steamboat captain, 13:234, 22:15, 20, 21, 28, 32:12n
Hoosaneree, Sioux Indian, 22:135
"Hoosier Schoolmaster," see Eggleston, Edward
Hoover, Herbert, 34:41; relief administrator, 11:350
Hope, Henry, governor of Canada, 15:95
Hope Academy, Moorhead, history, 38:382
Hope Engine Co., St. Paul, 38:290
Hopewell phase, Indian culture, 25:334, 341
Hopkins, Andrew W., author, 36:190
Hopkins, Mrs. C. E., author, 14:358
Hopkins, C. Howard, author, 33:228
Hopkins, Charles H., memorial marker, 11:456
Hopkins, Cyril G., biography, 13:441
Hopkins, Daniel, stock raiser, 26:110, 121
Hopkins, E. D., Freeborn County pioneer, 14:314
Hopkins, Edward M., trader, 28:282, 40:167n
Hopkins, Mrs. Edward M. (Frances Ann), artist, 28:282, 29:167, 33:187, 37:308, 40:165
Hopkins, Frank, author, 15:370; speaker, 21:108, 445
Hopkins, George B., steamboat captain, 12:333
Hopkins, Harley, postmaster, 16:365
Hopkins, Joseph G. E., work reviewed, 30:53-55; author, 28:278
Hopkins, Murat W., 18:124
Hopkins, Robert, missionary, 11:316, 16:137, 21:171, 32:71, 72; letters, 16:333, 469
Hopkins, Mrs. Robert (Agnes), 15:280, 16:137, 18:94
Hopkins, Vincent C., author, 33:138
Hopkins, Finland Swedes, 12:436; schools, 16:129, 23:101; post office, 16:365; Presbyterian church, 25:410; trolley line, 36:150
Hoppe, Muriel, library assistant, 23:367, 24:31
Hopper, William B., taxidermist, 20:348; speaker, 24:80
Hopper, Mrs. William B., speaker, 21:445
Hoppin, Charles A., author, 15:469

Hopwood, V. G., author, 35:378
Horan, James D., works reviewed, 31:50, 34:209, 35:92, 37:31; author, 35:130, 132
Horicon, Martin County, post office, 22:441
Horicon Church, Martin County, Fowler settlement, 11:463
Horine, Dr. Emmet F., work reviewed, 29:338
Hormel, George A., 18:471, 23:108
Hormel, George A., Co., Austin, meat packers, 15:250, 18:470, 23:108, 33:353, 35:203, 40:315; wage system, 23:388, 34:266
Horn, Charles L., 27:141, 282
Horn, Charles L., Jr., author, 35:294
Horn, H. Harcourt, author, 13:111
Horn, Henry J., pioneer, 33:4
Horn, Mrs. Henry J., 29:121, 33:4
Horn, Lenore, 33:4
Horn, Stanley F., author, 25:197
Hornaday, W. T., naturalist, 30:125
Hornby, St. Louis County, railroad, 34:184
Horne, Harry, Jr., 17:358
Horneman, W., steamship agent, 20:249, 250, 257, 258
Horner, William E., author, 21:364
Hornung, Clarence P., work reviewed, 36:232
Horowitz, Murray, editor, 22:331
Horowitz, Vladimir, pianist, 39:59, 60, 63
Horse Portage, Lake County, Basswood Falls, 37:244-246, 38:29
Horse racing, U.S., 14:421; Mankato, 16:126; state fair, 18:294; opposed, 19:79; St. Paul, 20:201, 37:43; New Ulm, 26:287; Ely, 40:61. See also Dan Patch
Horse thief detective society, Fergus Falls, 26:121. See also Waseca County Horse Thief Detectives
Horses, for hunting, 14:421, 422, 14:423; in American life, 20:205, 21:425; frontier Minnesota, 22:255, 24:305, 26:118-121; mustangs, 33:225; breeding, 34:124, 346; use by Indians, 35:88. See also Horse racing
Horsetail Falls, Cook County, underwater archaeology, 38:24, 25
Horticulture, Minnesota, 19:96, 20:79, 81, 301, 21:85; Iowa, 26:273. See also Agriculture, Apple raising
Horton, George E., 30:183
Horton, Gerald S., author, 16:101, 253
Horton, Henry, pioneer, 30:20, 183
Horton, William, 30:22, 183
Horton and Chase, cheese manufacturers, 27:112
Horwitz, A. B., author, 22:349
Hosford, Amanda, pioneer teacher, 28:139
Hosie, John, work reviewed, 13:302-304
Hosmer, George L., author, 14:352
Hosmer, James K., papers, 11:42, 12:85, 26:69, 29:189; author, 13:253; career, 13:441, 14:352, 21:113
Hosmer family, genealogy, 14:352
Hospes, Adolphus C., surveyor general, 31:34-39
Hospes, Ernest L., lumberman, 31:37

Hospes, Louis, Stillwater pioneer, 17:314, 25:210, 31:35
Hospitals, Minnesota, 12:104, 15:485, 16:219, 17:341, 21:114, 23:387, 38:377; Twin Cities, 15:456, 20:88, 466, 30:8, 405, 39:14–17; group care, 24:182, 27:160, 33:294; frontier, 24:272, 29:58; in Civil War, 25:117, 142–145, 347n; St. Cloud, 33:291–297
Hotaling, Herbert C., publisher, 19:364
Hotchkiss, Louise, author, 11:221
Hotchkiss, W. O., geologist, 15:131, 17:168
Hotchkiss, William A., publisher, 16:128, 25:93
Hotel Heinrich, Mankato, 17:234
Hotel Lafayette, Lake Minnetonka, 33:62, 63, 35:73
Hotel, Restaurant, and Bartenders Union, 35:379
Hotels, Minnesota: southern, 11:111, 398, 12:58, 13:213, 15:133, 198, 252, 365, 371, 16:367, 368, 17:234, 487, 488, 18:227, 19:95, 20:302, 356, 21:213, 24:189, 190, 25:314, 27:328, 28:260, 265, 381, 30:15, 181, 278, 400, 32:173, 33:323, 324, 35:112; St. Croix Valley, 11:225, 14:239, 16:377, 17:283, 284, 24:196, 197, 30:398, 35:363, 364, 36:214, 38:296; Mississippi River Valley, 12:47, 191, 343, 401, 13:145, 148, 150, 151, 15:113, 253, 467, 16:257, 18:353, 19:163, 451, 20:306, 307, 22:448, 24:332, 26:177, 35:255, 265, 36:93; northern, 12:107, 14:360, 16:268, 17:375, 22:225, 23:25, 37:107, 110n, 117; Minneapolis and suburbs, 12:343, 399, 402, 403, 13:195, 17:380, 18:30, 226, 19:84, 403, 407, 20:328, 393, 21:417, 23:220, 224, 297, 25:3, 4, 315, 27:295n, 29:32, 33n, 215, 32:18, 33:52, 62, 63, 95, 175, 34:99n, 173, 35:67, 68, 72–76, 36:71, 91, 327, 37:18, 38:273, 40:14, 15, 63, 100n, 135; St. Paul and suburbs, 12:392, 403, 14:300, 16:37, 71, 72, 231, 272, 377, 17:372, 375, 382, 18:106, 19:134, 164, 166, 407, 22:57n, 100, 24:332, 26:184, 27:366, 28:322, 29:35, 126, 128, 30:197, 200, 301, 31:96, 33:1–3, 197n, 34:96–98, 99n, 101, 102, 333, 35:355, 356, 36:264–266, 283, 304, 37:53, 38:176, 187, 294–296, 39:53, 144–146, 149, 282, 283, 40:15, 16, 135, 221, 265, 276, 331; central, 20:349, 23:64, 300, 40:100, 334
Non-Minnesota, 17:301, 430, 21:430, 24:331, 25:38, 33:56, 58, 34:23n
Houck, Clarence, 18:257n
Houdini, Harry, 26:170
Hough, Ardelle J., compiler, 37:37
Hough, Donald, author, 35:51
Hough, Dr. Franklin B., author, 34:294
Hough, Jack L., work reviewed, 36:188
Hough, Samuel C., 13:30
Hough, Walter, author, 11:109, 16:349
Houghton, C. C., hunter, 16:269
Houghton, Dr. Douglass, surgeon-explorer, 23:355, 356, 35:247, 40:

141; vaccination program, 11:58, 13:288, 16:353, 37:182; with Schoolcraft expedition, 12:226, 13:173, 441, 17:392, 18:180, 182, 19:226, 30:268, 31:190, 32:85n, 35:241; papers, 13:172, 320, 14:65, 35:153, 36:184, 40:409; map maker, 21:83, 23:243n; death, 26:266; career, 34:207
Houghton, George H., steamboat captain, 11:138, 139, 33:9–11, 13
Houghton, Horace H., editor, 22:24n
Houghton, Maria, author, 13:216
Houghton Line, steamboat company, 33:13
Houk, Norman, author, 30:406, 31:61
Houl, ———, trader, 32:230, 233, 235, 237
Houle, E. A., 13:214
Houlton, W. H., lumberman, 16:73
House, Col. Edward M., 17:165
House, Francis E., career, 24:375
House, Ruth, 12:407
House of David, Mich., communitarian colony, 25:369
Houser, Albert H. P., author, 24:81
Houses, sod, 11:308, 12:136–144, 440, 15:124, 18:464, 19:78, 21:99, 24:321, 26:93, 27:159, 28:248, 31:57, 221, 37:208, 211; log, 12:145, 13:136, 213, 14:276, 304, 15:43–49, 492, 16:126, 17:414, 18:65, 464, 19:473, 20:144, 21:450, 22:436, 448, 23:403, 25:395, 27:61, 86, 159, 28:55, 122, 30:271, 31:57, 92, 32:495, 34:357, 37:64, 71–77, 39:132, 203; Greek revival, 12:402, 25:1, 5; furnishings, 14:264–282, 15:134, 181–193, 252, 16:498, 17:189, 19:114, 335, 474, 20:215, 21:203, 27:69, 29:115, 33:47, 34:54–57, 35:322, 323; frontier styles, 15:49–55; building materials, 15:50–52; costs, 15:52, 35:106; immigrant influences, 24:259, 27:258; frame, 27:89–92, 28:311; Gothic revival, 27:125–127; historic, 29:72, 30:273, 34:219, 314; cottages, 30:193. See also Architecture, individual historic houses
Illustrated, 33:208–210, 37:138, 38:17, 337 (cover), 40:104; I. Garrard, 14:35, 37:64; log, 14:270, 15:44, 29:200, 30:115, 32:67, 34:5, 37:72–77, 40:70; H. H. Sibley, 15:45, 20:6, 33:208; Densmore, 15:48; A. Fuller, 15:52; H. Thompson, 15:52; I. Donnelly, 15:53, 37:65, 233; W. G. Le Duc, 15:53, 34:293, 36:108, 37:189, 192–194, 197–199; O. H. Kelley, 33:51; W. W. Mayo, 33:209; R. D. Hubbard, 33:210; H. R. Gibbs, 33:210; A. Faribault, 33:210, 35:320, 37:69; bunkhouses, 34:64, 275; S. Lewis, 34:89; J. H. Stevens, 34:144; A. Ramsey, 35:354, 37:65; W. Bunnell, 36:140; Mrs. B. Foster, 36:216; J. B. Faribault, 37:58; C. A. Lindbergh, 37:68; sod, 37:208, 211; St. Croix Valley, 38:338–342, 344–348, 350–352; J. R. Brown, 39:277; J. L. Merriam, 40:98; S. C. Gale, 40:99; G. W. Van Dusen, 40:105
Houston, George, editor, 25:165
Houston, history, 12:102, 268, 16:

217, 17:486; Baptist church, 14:451, 19:473; ethnic settlements, 28:121, 33:138
Houston County, roads, 11:397; ethnic groups, 12:265, 266, 15:367, 19:123, 211, 234, 28:379, 31:26, 35:90; Baptist records, 14:436; history, 17:361, 486, 22:86, 23:107, 25:383, 30:273; farming, 18:408, 20:163n, 359, 29:2n, 18n; archives, 23:93; historic sites, 24:265; land values, 25:183; medicine, 26:397, 27:80, 168; poorhouse, 38:373
Houston County Agricultural Society, fairs, 21:450
Houston County Historical Society, 17:223, 29:92, 362; meetings, 29:274, 30:76, 166
Houston County War History Committee, 24:82
Hovde, Brynjolf J., editor, 11:103; author, 19:459
Hove, David, lumberman, 18:167
Hove, Elling, career, 13:441
Hove, Pearl, 13:317
Hoverstad, T. A., speaker, 16:482, 21:436
Hovgaard, William, author, 17:27
Hovland, Gjert G., letter, 12:181
Hovland, described, 35:49
How, Jared, author, 24:189
Howard, Gen. Benjamin, 23:346n
Howard, Brice J., author, 36:35
Howard, Bronson C., letter, 29:284
Howard, Sister Celestine, 23:191
Howard, Clarence C., architect, 33:334
Howard, E. T., potter, 33:234
Howard, Ellen, 33:38
Howard, Helen Addison, work reviewed, 39:169
Howard, Rev. James, 23:191
Howard, James H., review by, 37:336; author, 34:213
Howard, Capt. John, at Mackinac, 11:247, 250
Howard, John R., "The Sioux War Stockades," 12:301–303
Howard, John T., author, 17:477, 25:305
Howard, Joseph K., work reviewed, 33:182; editor, 28:288
Howard, Julius D, postmaster, 34:185
Howard, Mark, 39:90
Howard, Gen. Oliver O., Union officer, 25:238, 38:250
Howard, Winifred M., author, 21:326
Howard Lake, archaeological site, 15:364, 25:334; school, 16:499; Quaker group, 18:254, 258
Howatt, Mrs. W., 20:353
Howay, F. W., author, 15:120, 21:93, 22:99
Howe, Albion P., 25:353
Howe, E. W., author, 19:437, 23:114, 157, 31:137
Howe, Elias, inventor, 35:92
Howe, Frederick C., 14:200
Howe, George F., speaker, 13:227; author, 26:85; editor, 37:342
Howe, Henry, missionary, diary, 15:237
Howe, Isola, 18:256n
Howe, James B., 31:100
Howe, John J., farmer, 31:100

Howe, Jonas H., pioneer, 20:431, 31:
92; artist, 22:440, 31:99-104
Howe, Julia Ward, feminist, 39:4
Howe, Judge Orlando C., papers, 15:
356
Howe, Mrs. Orlando C., author, 15:356
Howe, Will D., author, 24:173
Howell, David H., author, 21:424
Howell, James, 27:34
Howells, William D., 12:85, 18:32,
28:56; editor, 17:369; author, 23:
113, 26:75, 27:335, 31:101; let-
ters, 29:189
Hower, Ralph M., author, 22:326
Howitt, Mary, translator, 20:138, 31:
148
Howitz, E., and Co., St. Paul, music
store, 39:319
Howitz and Co., St. Paul, merchants,
15:184
Hoy, W. J., Co., construction firm,
39:158
Hoyme, Gjermund, career, 13:441
Hoyt, Benjamin F., papers, 14:100
Hoyt, E. S., pottery manager, 28:291,
33:235
Hoyt, F. M., 33:235
Hoyt, Henry F., author, 11:108
Hoyt, John F., papers, 14:100
Hoyt, Lorenzo, pioneer, 11:108
Hoyt, Dr. Otis, publisher, 25:301;
house, 38:340
Hoyt, William D., Jr., author, 26:376
Hoyt, William G., work reviewed, 34:
306; author, 17:230
Hoyt Lakes, taconite plant, 36:35,
382, 37:41, 39:131
Hrdlička, Aleš, author, 19:348; ar-
chaeologist, 28:181
Hubach, Robert R., author, 34:169,
216, 35:43, 38:41
Hubachek, Frank B., 22:177, 23:134,
38:29-31; speaker, 29:282
Hubbard, Asahel W., Congressman, 38:
61
Hubbard, Bela, author, 40:141
Hubbard, Frank G., 21:67
Hubbard, Freeman H., author, 26:379
Hubbard, G. S., 19:305
Hubbard, Henry, excursionist, 15:406
Hubbard, J. H., author, 19:121
Hubbard, Lucius F., career, 13:441;
newspaper publisher, 13:449, 28:
381, 35:382; pictured, 14:335, 15:
117, 35:317; governor, 16:83, 31:
34, 35, 37:148, 40:148; letters,
17:337, 35:313-319; grain merchant, 35:14, 15; politician, 36:
306, 307
Hubbard, Rensselaer D., house, 21:
104, 33:210
Hubbard, Stanley E., 16:483
Hubbard, Theodora K., author, 11:217
Hubbard, William, author, 26:215
Hubbard family, genealogy, 27:56
Hubbard County, summer resorts, 17:
487; history, 18:339, 469, 22:332,
23:401; wild-rice harvest, 22:103;
archives, 22:332; co-operative,
22:374; logging, 29:137, 138; Finnish settlement, 36:34; nursing
home, 38:377
Hubbard County Historical Society,
organized, 14:236, 328, 354, 16:
240, 30:277; activities, 16:360
Hubbard County Old Settlers Association, 16:494

Hubbard County War History Committee,
24:82
Hubbard, Wells and Co., grain mer-
chants, 35:14
Hubbart, Henry C., author, 23:83, 30:
386
Hubbell, Charles H., lawyer, 21:196
Hubbell, J. B., hotel owner, 28:381
Hubbell, James B., papers, 34:325-
329; speculator, 39:90; trader,
39:230-240, 255
Hubbell House, Mantorville, register,
15:198, 28:381, 30:181, 400
Hubbs, Ronald M., "The Civil War and
Alexander Wilkin," 39:173-190
Huber, Albert, author, 17:472
Huber, Leonard V., work reviewed, 35:
39
Huber mound, Scott County, excavated,
25:336
Huck, Virginia, work reviewed, 35:37
Huckins, J. M., 12:185
Hudnut, Joseph, author, 26:376
Hudson, ---, steamboat captain, 21:
159
Hudson, Arthur P., work reviewed, 36:
93; author, 28:281
Hudson, Charles, excursionist, 15:
406, 411, 413
Hudson, "Doc," mail agent, 27:3
Hudson, Edward, trader, 11:467
Hudson, Henry, explorer, 22:302, 305
Hudson, Samuel A., panoramist, 17:
138, 18:319, 33:287, 36:101
Hudson (Willow River), Wis., history,
15:237, 21:430, 24:165, 28:81, 34:
129, 312, 35:48, 38:239; July 4
celebration, 16:173; described,
17:277, 387, 19:320; newspapers,
17:314, 29:100; baseball club, 19:
176, 180, 181; churches, 20:400,
24:165, 27:344; name, 21:159n;
fire, 22:207, 330, 432, 39:83;
hospital, 23:185, 34:132; bridge,
23:290; mission, 28:395; architecture, 34:219, 314, 38:340-344,
347, 348, 350, 351; railroad, 37:
113n; land office, 40:312; road,
40:387
Hudson Bay, explored, 12:91, 24:340,
30:57; fur trade, 12:175, 16:423-
426, 21:423, 24:149, 40:162, 188,
189; trade route, 16:416, 417, 17:
27, 170, 173, 24:277, 36:191, 40:
156, 157, 170-172, 179n, 183; map,
16:421n; Eskimos, 28:282; wildlife, 31:238
Hudson River, trade route, 28:310,
40:184
Hudson (Wis.) Star-Observer, history,
21:430; anniversaries, 25:301, 34:
129
Hudson Strait, Norse exploration, 40:
94
Hudson's Bay Co., 34:80, 40:149,
179n; competition, 11:252, 262,
12:82, 18:183, 19:353, 22:277-281,
28:2, 3, 40:43, 185n, 186; in Minnesota, 11:354, 358, 361, 362,
366, 14:154, 17:96, 130, 18:183,
21:449, 22:270-289, 24:319, 320n,
26:284, 27:67, 29:176, 34:357;
posts, 11:363, 364, 13:300, 17:
171, 21:99, 432, 23:93, 24:284n,
328, 345, 370, 26:154, 27:37, 28:
283, 31:238, 33:130, 35:48, 261,
36:243, 40:188-191; relations with

North West Co., 11:365, 425, 12:
91, 441, 14:98, 338, 15:120, 16:
201, 17:75, 18:278, 20:17, 21:399,
22:178, 275, 23:186, 256, 24:41,
28:2, 143n, 281, 34:344, 35:141,
36:63, 64, 38:328, 39:166, 40:144,
157, 164, 165, 183; traders, 11:
451, 12:235, 372, 14:229, 15:286,
16:374, 17:445, 18:356, 20:70-72,
119, 27:67, 32:249, 33:139, 36:
241-249, 324; at Red River Settlement, 12:82, 240, 327, 438, 13:
241, 19:353, 22:148, 284, 24:45,
333n, 26:171, 28:61, 31:106-108,
217, 34:132, 317-324, 35:202, 282,
379, 36:37-53, 191, 38:63, 199,
200, 40:43, 83, 145; history, 12:
437, 13:298, 14:449, 15:177, 16:
230, 17:74-76, 94, 18:81-83, 20:
327, 23:92, 26:273, 28:61, 32:249,
35:44, 242, 36:272, 37:217, 40:
144, 157n; charter, 13:91, 16:397,
424n, 22:3, 61, 24:149, 30:63, 36:
102; use of steamboats, 13:241,
14:154, 21:249-253, 24:333n, 30:
70, 38:200; employees, 14:435, 18:
216, 21:398, 26:55, 27:62, 131,
28:282, 29:247, 30:259, 31:240,
34:174, 35:143, 36:315, 316, 37:
85, 38:1, 40:202; archives, 15:
231, 356, 477, 16:106, 200, 348,
394, 479, 18:277, 19:216, 394,
455, 20:39, 22:309, 24:340, 27:70,
28:169, 29:153, 30:375, 33:261,
35:154, 36:150; shareholders, 16:
396, 399, 415, 17:223, 31:184;
merged with North West Co., 22:
287, 309, 40:162, 165, 166-177,
184, 358; museum, 23:186, 24:363,
25:83; retail stores, 24:285; magazine index, 34:263; trade goods,
35:196, 37:254, 38:30, 40:200.
See also Fort Garry (Upper), Fur
trade
Hudson's Bay House, London, Eng., 24:
285n
Hudson's Bay Record Society, organized, 19:109; publications, 19:
455, 20:69, 21:399, 24:43-45, 340,
26:55, 27:37, 33:130, 182, 261
Huevelmann, William, 26:287
Huff, C. E., author, 15:240
Huff, Henry D., pioneer, 36:4n;
house, 36:144
Huff-Lamberton House, Winona, 36:139,
144
Hufford, Harold E., compiler, 36:278
Huff's Hotel, Winona, 15:253
Huggan, Mrs. Charles G. (Nancy Mc-
Clure Faribault), interpreter, 38:
126, 127
Huggard, J. T., author, 17:223
Huggins, Alexander G., letters, 12:
83, 16:333; house, 15:43, 21:207,
435, 22:211, 27:360; missionary,
16:70, 133-139, 142, 143, 145,
303, 21:31n, 170, 171, 23:50, 26:
77, 32:71
Huggins, Mrs. Alexander G. (Fanny),
21:31; teacher, 16:137, 145
Huggins, Amos W., letters, 39:344
Huggins, Gen. Eli L., letter, 13:427;
author, 28:287
Huggins, Jane S., missionary, 11:94
Hughes, Maj. ---, 32:155, 156, 159
Hughes, B. D., author, 12:448
Hughes, Justice Charles E., quoted,

17:78, 20:420, 37:171, 172; let-
ter, 18:316
Hughes, Charlotte, author, 26:266
Hughes, Daisy E., author, 11:466
Hughes, E. Raymond, 21:442, 22:215,
23:193; speaker, 21:215
Hughes, Edward J., author, 15:473
Hughes, James, pioneer printer, 15:19
Hughes, Bishop John, 25:373
Hughes, Martin, speaker, 14:463, 21:
287, 30:83
Hughes, Thomas, 11:54, 13:341, 14:79,
15:76, 17:62, 21:49; "The Mankato
Independent," 15:89; work re-
viewed, 11:87-89; author, 11:18,
52, 12:103, 14:115; speaker, 12:
448, 452, 13:342, 444, 15:130
Hughes, Thomas, park superintendent,
19:310
Hughes, Twiford E., papers, 17:467,
18:48
Hughes family, musicians, 22:114, 124
Huguenots, 18:387; immigration, 18:
384, 385, 397
Huhtala, J. W., attorney, 40:395
Huizinga, Albeertis, 28:125
Hujanen, Helen, author, 30:409
Hulbert, Archer B., works reviewed,
11:194, 12:172-174; author, 11:
429; editor, 12:93, 16:344
Hulbert, William D., work reviewed,
31:113
Hulette, Luke, townsite interests,
11:274
Hull, Cordell, secretary of state,
28:305, 40:371
Hull, Herbert A., author, 15:243
Hull, Rev. Joseph, 31:82n
Hull, Gen. William, surrender, 23:
182, 32:117, 36:67; governor of
Michigan Territory, 24:234
Hull, Eng., emigrant port, 20:250,
251
Hull, Que., founded, 28:9n
Hullinger, Warren L., author, 18:471
Hullsiek, John G., cholera victim,
14:298
Hulme, Edward M., author, 25:191, 33:
206
Hulst, Felix van, author, 28:200
Hultberg, Nels O., missionary, 33:43
Human Resources and Skills Advisory
Committee, 23:150
Humboldt, Alexander von, climatolo-
gist, 38:54
"Humboldt," steamboat, 17:280, 281
Humboldt High School, St. Paul, 40:
249
Hume, Edgar E., author, 22:92, 24:256
Humiston, J. D., 20:464
Hummel, August, 11:332, 17:120, 29:
282
Hummel, C. E., speaker, 27:363
Hummel, Edward A., speaker, 18:205,
281, 283; author, 19:107
Hummel, Mathilda, speaker, 12:453
Hummel, William, autobiography, 21:
111
Hummelbaugh, Jacob, 25:360
Humphrey, Constance H., compiler, 12:
316
Humphrey, David, pioneer, 12:419
Humphrey, Edward F., 14:331
Humphrey, Evy M., 20:315
Humphrey, Helena, 20:316
Humphrey, Hubert, 37:84
Humphrey, Hubert H., speaker, 27:172,

30:84, 172, 36:72; mayor, 34:190,
191, 38:41, 40:91; Senator, 34:
193, 194, 35:290, 40:407; presi-
dential candidate, 36:151, 37:343;
biographies, 37:84, 39:258; au-
thor, 39:172
Humphrey, John, 35:340
Humphrey, John A., in Sioux Outbreak,
23:295
Humphrey, Laura, 20:314
Humphrey, Mark, 20:316
Humphrey, Mary J., 20:315
Humphrey, N. Marcus, 20:314-316; pa-
pers, 20:190
Humphrey, Mrs. N. Marcus (Mrs. Eliza-
beth A. Young), 20:314, 315
Humphrey, Dr. Otis M., 21:194
Humphrey, Dr. Philander P., in Sioux
Outbreak, 34:234
Humphrey, Seth K., work reviewed, 12:
419
Humphrey, Silas, 20:315, 316
Humphrey, Stephen, 20:314
Humphrey family, papers, 20:314-316
Humphrey family, Sioux victims, 23:
295
Humphrey, Faribault County, prehis-
toric village, 26:387
Humphreys, Alice, papers, 19:388
Humphreys, Col. David, 19:36
Humphreys, William J., author, 17:
477
Hundred Associates, fur trade monopo-
ly, 15:158, 18:387
Huneke, E. F., 14:31n, 33, 42
Hungarians (Magyars), 29:261; Minne-
sota, 17:364; Detroit, Mich., 20:
202
Hungerford, Edward, author, 32:48
Hungerford, Sir Edward, grants, 16:
423-426
Hungerford, William S., 17:283
Hungry Hall, Ont., trading post, 11:
362, 24:280
Hunkins, Ralph V., author, 13:438
Hunnewell, James, papers, 13:180
Hunt, Lt. ---, 23:137
Hunt, C. C., speaker, 24:255
Hunt, C. J., author, 21:115
Hunt, Daniel H., 18:321; diary, 18:
204, 314, 19:49, 28:297, 39:132;
trader, 18:270; house, 27:228,
230, 28:383
Hunt, Dr. F. N., 17:237
Hunt, Frances M., author, 22:445, 24:
182, 25:411
Hunt, George B., blacksmith, 16:336
Hunt, Myron, architect, 40:107
Hunt, Nehemiah, settler, 24:182
Hunt, Oliver W., 16:336
Hunt, Dr. Roscoe C., author, 24:79,
25:307, 399; receives award, 35:
336
Hunt, Capt. Thomas, 18:406
Hunt, Thomas W., pioneer, 17:486
Hunt, William F., lawyer, 14:333
Hunt, Wilson D., trader, 15:422
Hunt, Dr. Winslow, 25:411
Hunt family, in Blue Earth County,
24:182
Hunter, Lt. ---, 18:405
Hunter, A. F., editor, 14:228
Hunter, Beatrice J., work reviewed,
31:110
Hunter, Dr. Charles H., 24:347
Hunter, Gen. David, Union officer,
25:150, 352; emancipation order,

20:275, 25:131, 132, 32:26, 27, 29
Hunter, Don L., author, 33:137
Hunter, Rev. James, Presbyterian min-
ister, 37:308
Hunter, John, banker, 37:121, 122
Hunter, Louis C., work reviewed, 31:
110; author, 25:88
Hunter, Rhoda, speaker, 19:361
Hunter, Robert, 11:238n
Hunter, Sam, lumberjack, 30:68
Hunter, William C., author, 38:385
Hunter family, piano owners, 39:323n
Hunter Island, Ont., ownership, 11:
331, 13:297
Hunterdon County, N.J., history, 28:
80
Hunter's patent well, use in Minnesota, 24:304
Hunting, by Indians, 11:302, 14:423,
15:272, 23:330, 339, 30:101, 36:
15, 40:158, 160; frontier, 14:385,
421-423, 15:385-394, 16:188-190,
259-271, 17:388, 20:102, 191, 193,
26:288, 27:87, 29:202, 32:85, 87,
97; of fowl, 15:386, 16:189, 28:
229, 32:97, 220, 33:70, 36:52; in
Minnesota, 16:253, 18:117, 159,
22:194, 23:110, 25:92, 35:50, 36:
91, 104, 195; regulated, 16:264,
18:415, 30:222, 224, 226, 33:141n,
144n; use of dogs, 16:265-267;
Wisconsin, 22:294; commercial, 26:
169, 373; Canada, 32:59; Kandiyohi
County area, 33:141-154; Rocky
Mountains, 35:153; Red River Valley, 38:4; prehistoric, 38:160,
162. See also Birds, Wildlife
Huntington, Collis P., railroad
builder, 39:31
Huntington, Henry E., philanthro-
pist, 39:336
Huntington, Henry M., letter, 25:383
Huntington, Margaret E., 15:243; ca-
reer, 13:441, 14:104
Huntington, Samuel P., author, 31:124
Hunziker, Otto F., dairyman, 12:99
Huot, Red Lake County, treaty monu-
ment, 14:350, 15:282
Hupmobile automobile, 38:206, 207,
211, 213-215
Hurd, Dr. Annah, 27:153
Hurd, Dan, 14:314
Hurd, Erastus, papers, 27:153
Hurd, Dr. Ethel E., papers, 15:113
Hurd, J. F., 26:361
Hurd, Mary Ann C., 14:313, 314
Hurd, Tyrus I., 27:153
Huré, Mme. Sebastien, publisher, 11:
8, 9
Hurlburt, Mrs. H. W., speaker, 26:183
Hurlbut, Gen. Stephen A., Union offi-
cer, 40:283
Hurley, Sister Helen A., "The Sisters
of St. Joseph," 30:1-13; work re-
viewed, 33:37; author, 18:89, 30:
94, 182, 266, 273
Huron Indians, warfare with Iroquois,
13:250, 260, 261, 397, 399, 15:
161, 176, 317, 318, 19:273; Radis-
son's visits, 13:259, 262, 265,
15:163, 165-167, 170, 171; in fur
trade, 15:157, 158, 40:205, 208;
culture, 37:174
Huron Island, see Washington Island
Huron River, Mich., described, 23:237
Hurst, James W., author, 40:357
Hurst, John S., author, 37:85

Hurt, Wesley R., author, 35:246
Husband, Joseph, author, 26:308
Huse, Bert, 16:362, 18:112, 19:120, 20:458
Huse family, pioneers, 30:199
Hushasha, see Red Legs
Husher, F. A., editor, 12:268
Huske, John, author, 35:340
Huss, Charlie, author, 25:310
Huss family, Scott County, pioneers, 11:118
Husser, John, author, 18:344
Hussey, Mrs. James, music teacher, 21:116
Hussey, John A., author, 37:85
Hussites, in Bohemia, 15:26; emigration, 31:28
Huston, Charles E., pioneer, 31:125
Hustvedt, Lloyd, work reviewed, 40:351
Hutcheson, Charles R., promotes alfalfa, 19:31, 32
Hutchins, Arthur, 21:350
Hutchins, Clyde, 21:350
Hutchins, James S., author, 38:238
Hutchinson, ---, mate on "Anson Northup," 18:357
Hutchinson, Abby, 19:343; diary, 19:449; musician, 22:116, 127, 27:233, 234; letter, 23:298
Hutchinson, Asa B., 20:347, 22:54, 292; papers, 19:343, 449; townsite promoter, 22:52, 113, 24:187; musician, 22:116, 26:54, 27:233, 234
Hutchinson, Jesse, musician, 22:123, 131; farmer, 27:233
Hutchinson, Mrs. Jesse, 27:233
Hutchinson, Jesse, Jr., musician, 22:123, 131, 27:233, 234
Hutchinson, John W., 20:347, 22:292; letters, 19:449; townsite promoter, 22:52, 113; musician, 22:116, 127, 129, 26:54, 27:233, 234
Hutchinson, Judson, 20:347, 22:292; townsite promoter, 22:52, 113; musician, 22:116, 26:54, 27:233, 234
Hutchinson, Paul H., 22:217
Hutchinson, S. F., speaker, 11:118
Hutchinson, William T., works reviewed, 19:435, 36:33
Hutchinson family, 21:87, 30:182; musicians, 11:115, 333-335, 13:147, 14:140, 16:238, 17:335, 18:208, 325, 444, 20:81, 347, 431, 21:108, 409, 452, 22:52-54, 113-132, 431, 23:160, 24:36, 120, 25:200, 26:53, 65, 27:80, 233, 256, 28:274, 302, 29:98, 265, 30:174, 301, 33:169, 318; in Minnesota, 11:134, 23:36; papers, 19:341, 343, 449, 20:33; history, 30:156, 34:356, 36:106
Hutchinson, historical meeting, 11:37; industries, 11:111, 19:124; anniversary, 11:115, 219, 333; stage line, 11:133, 12:339; history, 11:220, 334, 16:240, 17:128, 19:449, 21:452, 27:80, 28:274, 33:228, 34:356; in Sioux Outbreak, 11:463, 15:28, 18:210, 20:192, 38:98, 137n, 150, 151, 276, 281, 283; railroad, 18:116, 24:187; hotel, 20:349; town plan, 23:102; telephone service, 24:192; newspaper, 26:398; fort, 38:282
Hutchinson Co., organized, 22:113
Hutchinson Historical Society, organized, 11:14; activities, 11:26,

333, 16:240, 306, 488, 19:469, 20:455, 21:108, 444; museum, 11:219, 462, 12:208, 20:96, 212, 347-349, 21:216. See also McLeod County Historical Society
Hutchinson Leader, anniversary, 21:452
Hutchinson Township, McLeod County, plats, 20:348; records, 20:349
Hutchison, Adele S., physician, 39:9
Hutchison, Bruce, work reviewed, 35:35
Hutter, Catherine, translator, 39:342
Hutterian Brethren (Hutterites), American colonies, 23:183; history, 44:40
Hutton, Graham, author, 27:251
Hutton, Henry, surveyor, 19:425, 426
Huxman, Mrs. O. F., author, 33:192
Huyck, Sherman G., postmaster, 34:186
Huygens, Constantin, 20:423
Hyat, Gilbert, speaker, 34:222
Hyatt, Mrs. Grace G., speaker, 13:327
Hybels, Robert J., author, 31:190
Hybertson, Martin, 29:308
Hyde, Dr. A. T., 20:235
Hyde, Andrew, descendants, 18:462
Hyde, Edith D., author, 18:462
Hyde, Francis E., author, 16:115
Hyde, George E., works reviewed, 35:288, 36:316, 37:303; author, 15:232
Hyde, Henry W., Jr., author, 21:421
Hyde, L. Mel, author, 26:294
Hyde, Orson, 13:111
Hyde, Mrs. Walter, 16:117, 18:55; speaker, 16:64
Hyde, Warren C., author, 12:332
Hyland, Julia, 17:483, 18:110, 465, 19:231
Hylle, Knud J., author, 17:343
Hyma, Albert, author, 29:79
Hyman, Ray, author, 36:324
Hynes, John F., banker, 39:246
Hynes, Mrs. John F., speaker, 11:112
Hynes, Sister Mary C., author, 26:373
Hynson, Mason, settler, 35:78, 79, 86
Hyskell, Charles, 33:321n
Hyslop, Mrs. John, 15:250
Hyslop, Robert, 15:250, 16:124, 241, 542

I.W.W., see Industrial Workers of the World
Iberia, Brown County, ghost town, 23:195; grist mill, 26:282
Iberville, sieur d', colonizer, 13:85, 18:389, 19:393, 20:439; explorer, 16:199, 19:396, 397n
Ibsen, Henrik, interview, 13:315; author, 16:109, 18:199, 21:426
Iceboating, 25:299, 30:142, 40:384, 386
Iceland, sagas, 39:170
"Icelander," ice train, 25:299
Icelanders, settlements, 13:208, 17:343, 24:79, 26:397, 30:396, 34:164, 265; almanac, 15:447; churches, 18:469; Canada, 21:269, 27:166; in fiction, 23:118. See also Scandinavians
Icimani, pseud., see Northrup, George
Ickes, Harold, 27:133
"Ida," steamboat, 28:189

"Ida Campbell," steamboat, 28:92
Idaho, gold mining, 19:390, 39:230, 40:94; fur trade, 29:58-61; Fisk route, 38:218, 220, 229, 386
Ide, J. C., 14:47
"Ideal," steamboat, 37:296
Iden, Raymond J., author, 28:397
Idington Station, St. Louis County, Finnish settlement, 40:392
"Idle Prindle," steamboat, 34:239
Iglesias, Roberto, ballet manager, 39:64
Ile àla Crosse Lake, Sask., fort, 11:264
Ilinimek Indians, Illinois, 36:191. See also Illinois Indians
Illgen, Rudolph, hotel owner, 34:181
Illingworth, W. H., photographer, 21:95, 38:45 (cover)
Illinois, French regime, 11:78, 21:395, 29:337; British regime, 11:320, 19:393; Scandinavian settlements, 12:249, 251, 15:473, 17:401, 19:200, 24:156, 27:256, 29:278, 37:177; archives, 12:329, 19:351, 36:280; parks and memorials, 14:228; periodicals, 15:13, 26:293; counties, 15:473; transportation, 15:474, 37:90; environmental study, 16:229; pioneer life, 16:345, 449, 25:11, 395, 26:259; agriculture, 17:133, 18:196, 37:159; census, 17:221; health conditions, 17:256, 432; fur trade, 19:287, 32:227, 40:215; state fair, 22:261; history, 23:63, 25:85, 27:257, 31:47, 240, 34:81, 82; in literature, 23:114, 117, 28:276; constitution, 24:234; Indian villages, 24:236, 36:191; war records, 25:401; mineral survey, 26:223; hunting, 26:373; territorial boundaries, 27:128; architecture, 27:141, 32:109; sawmills, 27:190, 34:35; Yankees, 31:181; gazetteer, 34:360, 40:147; Mormon migration, 36:46; land office, 37:332; agrarian movement, 38:235, 39:130; atlas, 40:128, 129; forts, 40:146
"Illinois," steamboat, 34:10
Illinois Central Railroad, colonizing program, 11:325, 13:111, 206, 15:332, 35:133, 205; built, 15:474, 27:283n, 34:18n; archives, 26:264, 33:42; land grant, 35:358, 36:177, 37:158
Illinois Historical Survey, 39:165
Illinois Indians, 32:229, 231; relations with French, 19:274, 32:227
Illinois River, bluffs, 17:435; history, 22:73
Illinois State Geological Survey, 26:225n
Illinois State Historical Society, Springfield, 26:265; publications, 13:436, 25:85; library, 16:346, 18:428
Illinois State Library, Springfield, archives division, 13:207
Illinois State Normal University, Bloomington, history workshop, 27:257
Illinois War Council, records program, 25:93, 311
Illsley, David, speaker, 29:365
Illsley, Mrs. H. A., author, 23:302
Iltis, Mathias, actor, 32:166

Imholte, John Q., work reviewed, 38:
330; author, 39:129
Immaculate Conception Church (Catholic), Minneapolis, 13:313; 33:95;
New Munich, 17:479, 36:35; Faribault, 19:475; St. Peter, 21:453;
Fort William, Ont., 39:309
Immanuel Lutheran Church, Gaylord,
14:360; Ironton, 14:452; Courtland Township, Nicollet County,
15:480
Immigration and emigration, promoted
by railroads, 11:206, 13:25-44,
15:333, 16:25, 129, 26:372, 33:29-
34, 61, 35:133, 205, 37:158, 184;
agents, 11:217, 325, 12:255, 256,
13:356, 15:239, 488, 20:192, 31:
250, 35:248, 36:237; Catholics,
11:316, 325, 21:73-76, 25:194, 35:
155, 193, 213, 325, 37:133, 40:
352; Canada, 11:327, 14:284, 23:
357, 15:142; overland route, 11:
395, 396, 12:154-156, 395; causes,
12:252, 16:344, 30:186, 188, 282;
promoted by newspapers, 12:260,
14:205, 40:248; religious aspects,
13:304-307, 24:73, 33:80, 38:381;
relation to politics, 13:435, 36:
237; Mennonites, 14:114, 224, 15:
478, 18:456, 21:269, 23:88, 29:
166, 31:119, 37:184; Mexico, 14:
333; songs and folklore, 16:108,
17:463, 18:198-201, 20:428, 22:
328, 27:178-189, 28:280, 302, 36:
78, 37:83; Mississippi Valley, 16:
109, 293, 33:125; official encour-
agement, 16:332, 22:227, 235, 36:
163, 180, 181, 37:44; guides, 16:
339, 18:72-74, 251, 20:245, 25:
301, 31:105, 115, 33:187, 35:248,
36:102, 40:147; sociological aspects, 17:328, 27:38-40, 276, 29:
58; language controversy, 18:381;
effect of Civil War, 21:237; history, 22:67, 70-72, 95, 33:80, 37:
184, 299, 346, 39:167, 40:305,
410; in literature, 22:327, 27:
328, 34:163; effect on mining
areas, 27:204-215; remigration 27:
282; student research, 27:319-326;
Minnesota, 31:18-32, 108, 38:74;
nativist aspect, 34:343; geographical distribution, 35:292; re-
stricted, 35:326, 327, 373. See
also America letters, Emigrant
journey, Emigrant ships, various
countries and ethnic groups
Immigration Restriction League, 34:
343
Imperial Railway of Japan, 38:322
Impink, Mary D., author, 26:168
Improved Order of Red Men, Walker
branch, 17:468
Inabnit, Robert E., author, 37:185
Incarnation Church (Catholic), Minneapolis, 33:305
Independence, territorial postmark,
15:487
"Independence," steamboat, 23:356,
30:187, 34:10, 39
Independence Co-operative Dairy Association, 18:443
Independence Day, see Fourth of July
Independence Rock, Wyo., covered wag-
on centennial, 11:452
Independence Township, Hennepin Coun-
ty, archives, 18:443; Christian

church, 21:85; history, 34:128,
36:36
Independent baseball club, Lake City,
19:180
Independent Citizens Committee of the
Arts, Sciences and Professions,
34:189
Independent Order of Good Templars,
see Good Templars
Independent Order of Odd Fellows, see
Odd Fellows
Independent Voters' Association, 28:
42
"India," steamboat, 17:375
Indian Emergency Conservation Work,
16:225
Indian Forest Service, clears Grand
Portage trail, 27:358, 28:375
"Indian John," Sioux Indian, at Kaposia, 28:138
Indian mounds, studied, 12:75; St.
Paul, 12:201, 36:33; Minnesota,
12:449, 14:358, 15:148-151, 244,
485, 16:3, 15-18, 152, 251, 253,
307-312, 358, 18:472, 24:78, 25:
156, 329, 26:321, 27:267, 28:193,
29:83, 94, 34:170, 37:61-63, 70,
103, 347, 38:163, 164; age, 15:
153; Mississippi Valley, 15:471,
16:156; excavated, 16:12, 13, 117,
310, 25:336-341, 26:316-321, 323-
327, 27:261; Iowa, 16:112, 37:307;
U.S., 26:79; St. Croix Valley, 26:
286; Wisconsin, 28:2, 37:183, 39:
83; Rainy River, 31:163-171, 231-
237
Indian office, see United States Bureau of Indian Affairs
Indian Reorganization Act, 37:278
Indian reservations, maps, 21:83, 32:
180; problems, 23:163; Minnesota,
28:374. See also individual reservations and tribes
Indian Rights Association, 23:163
Indian treaties, negotiated by Cass,
11:208; listed, 30:388; in art,
33:89, 286; influence of traders'
claims, 40:216, 262. See also individual tribes and treaties
Indiana, art guide, 14:228; early
printing, 15:13, 18:454; boundaries, 15:124, 22:75; architecture,
16:228, 32:109; laws, 16:346;
agriculture, 18:196; Quakers, 18:
250, 255, 259; constitution, 18:
325, 34:82; frontier life, 19:461,
32:45, 254, 33:308, 34:81; territorial limits, 20:18, 21:423; historical societies, 25:95, 301;
geological survey, 25:175, 26:223;
history, 28:78, 186, 35:239; bibliography, 28:276; Indians, 29:
335; politics, 30:382; imprints,
34:350; Blacks, 36:101; atlas, 40:
128; forts, 40:146; gazetteer, 40:
147; fur trade, 40:186, 215, 216
"Indiana," steamboat, 13:224
Indiana Historical Bureau, 15:124,
16:346, 18:325
Indiana Historical Society, Indianapolis, 13:432
Indiana History Conference, 27:158
Indiana Magazine of History, anniversary, 34:311
Indiana State Library, Indianapolis,
22:191

Indiana War History Commission, 25:
94, 402, 27:352
Indiana University, Bloomington, bureau of government research, 26:82
Indianapolis, Ind., first press, 15:
14; immigration convention, 35:134
Indians, relations with whites, 11:
78, 80, 189, 240, 13:92, 15:239,
258, 20:260, 23:161, 28:288, 31:
115, 32:58, 243, 36:30, 279; Wisconsin, 11:104, 32:253; annuities,
11:136, 15:297, 16:150, 295, 21:
280; relations with British, 11:
179n, 13:99, 15:97, 17:197, 19:
302, 20:16, 22:306, 33:37; living
conditions, 11:208, 12:434, 27:
284; U.S. policy, 11:208, 18:305,
30:99, 100, 32:180, 34:313, 35:
151, 200, 36:72, 38:191; bibliographies, 11:214, 35:380; warfare,
11:299-304, 16:89, 27:296, 34:205,
35:235, 38:41, 40:143, 147; in agriculture, 12:90, 13:330, 15:122,
263-271, 16:472, 17:70, 21:91, 28:
366; industries, 12:177, 332; music, 12:199, 326, 22:138, 23:236,
24:71, 26:275, 27:65, 161, 253,
28:176, 29:86, 32:58, 123, 33:311,
34:161, 213, 35:244, 36:190, 37:
345, 39:129; Minnesota, 12:331,
15:221, 462, 16:452, 476, 18:85,
22:110, 29:363, 35:338, 37:31, 38:
335, 40:41; health conditions, 12:
436, 13:320, 14:330, 15:110, 478,
34:34; North Dakota, 13:335, 40:
193; pictured, 13:408-412, 15:262,
19:105, 123, 355, 20:136, 21:185,
25:297, 26:138, 150, 27:254, 28:
70, 277, 278, 29:60, 78, 349, 30:
139, 260, 31:54, 32:61, 107, 157,
158, 161, 162, 238, 33:200, 34:30,
126, 129, 137, 168, 174, 213, 215,
35:144, 242, 244, 287, 379, 36:69,
277, 309, 37:32, 262, 306, 322,
38:40, 40:177, 272; in U.S., 14:
91, 22:201, 33:344, 34:216; medicines, 14:109, 15:271, 16:353, 26:
302; food, 14:112, 385, 15:270,
40:47, 158; upper Missouri River,
14:223, 23:330-332; Canada, 14:
337, 26:76, 28:282, 37:86, 40:48,
145, 149 (cover); in literature,
14:337, 15:261, 16:105, 20:134,
378, 380, 406, 26:211-221, 37:306,
38:191; legends, 14:434, 15:262,
20:442, 22:338, 25:166, 393, 26:
170, 27:17, 28:12, 31:201-203, 35:
142, 153; prehistoric, 15:151-153,
483, 20:154, 24:236, 25:153-157,
303, 329-341, 26:312-329, 27:261,
28:181, 270-272, 30:374, 31:163-
171, 231-237, 32:222, 34:354, 35:
339, 36:33, 37:86, 174, 38:157-
165, 40:203-209; artifacts, 15:
154, 16:14-19, 117, 476, 21:424,
24:78, 25:260, 36:101, 38:161,
162; culture, 15:255-272, 33:303,
34:116, 35:244, 293, 344, 376, 37:
78; place names, 15:259, 16:476,
26:248, 28:374; hunting, 15:386,
23:330; medals, 16:321-323, 25:
265-270; in holiday celebrations,
16:373, 375, 379, 386, 22:10; education, 17:200, 35:135; liquor
question, 18:90, 22:21, 279, 27:
295, 32:36, 40:155, 160, 162, 164,
170, 180, 186, 201, 202; as

slaves, 19:290, 20:68; leaders, 19:330; characterized, 20:52, 40: 161, 198-202; women, 20:136, 27: 289, 34:174, 35:143, 40:159, 201, 208; fishing, 20:334, 23:144, 240, 330, 40:158; apparel, 22:143, 24: 370; censuses, 23:145, 329, 331, 40:160; burials, 23:237, 25:156, 329, 330, 333, 335-339, 398, 31: 165-171, 232-236; dances, 23:241, 27:237, 290; linguistics, 24:71, 31:238; trails, 26:394, 28:146; Southeast, 27:336, 32:108; use of catlinite, 31:194-196, 199, 201, 202; use of horses, 35:88; white captives, 36:100, 38:384; source materials, 37:84, 182, 40:261, 409; assimilation question, 38: 329, 39:292; religions, 39:128, 40:41. See also Fur trade, Missions and missionaries, United States Bureau of Indian Affairs, various tribes
Indrebö, Gustav, 17:178
Industrial Exposition and Home Appliance Show, Minneapolis, 17:348
Industrial Resources and Production Advisory Committee, 23:150
Industrial Township, St. Louis County, history, 23:302
Industrial Workers of the World, oppose war, 14:319, 35:368; founded, 25:220n, 40:341; Finnish members, 25:325; songs, 36:83; history, 38: 334, 40:362
Industry, importance of stone, 17:85; pulp manufacture, 19:358; Minnesota, 20:447, 34:217, 265; canneries, 20:470, 33:353; leaders, 35:44; building, 35:156. See also Business, Manufacturing, Meat packing, individual companies
Influenza, at Hamline University, 39: 218
Informal Club, St. Paul, 30:23
Ingalls, N. P., piano tuner, 39:319
Ingebriktsen, P. O., letter, 12:260n
Inger, Itasca County, Chippewa settlement, 26:81
Ingersoll, D. W., and Co., St. Paul, 11:227, 35:98
Ingersoll, Daniel W., businessman, 18:321, 363, 37:316
Ingersoll, Mrs. Daniel W., 38:76n
Ingersoll, Frederick G., 11:200, 12: 23, 13:74, 14:79, 15:313, 20:427; MHS president, 11:53, 54; speaker, 15:485
Ingersoll, Paul B., author, 25:185
Ingersoll, W. E., author, 19:109, 21: 326, 27:70
Ingersoll, William P., 14:116; author, 36:327
Ingersoll Hall, St. Paul, 11:147, 18: 362, 29:118, 33:192, 36:304, 306, 307
Inglenook Reading Club, St. Paul, 20: 330
Inglis, Ellice, and Co., London, Eng., 40:172
Inglis, John, trader, 40:177
Ingman, Lt. Samuel H., Union officer, 39:195n
Ingmanson, John E., author, 37:307
Ingraham, Capt. Duncan N., 25:245, 246

Ingraham, Mark H., speaker, 27:356, 30:72
Ingram, Leone, see Brower, Leone Ingram
Ingram, O. H., lumberman, 27:198, 199
Ings, Marvel Y., work reviewed, 26: 365; compiler, 25:85; author, 26: 271
Ingstad, Helge, archaeologist, 39: 170, 342; author, 40:94
Ingstad, Mrs. Helge, archaeologist, 39:170
Inkpaduta, Sioux leader, 19:385; leads massacre, 12:116n, 14:248, 257, 16:169-171, 17:235, 26:67, 28:288, 38:88, 95, 123, 124
Inkster, Colin, author, 15:357
Inland Steel Co., steamboat operations, 34:15
Inland Waterways Corporation, 16:79, 22:202; archives, 22:211
Innes, Col. James, 14:108
Innis, George S., professor, 39:214
Innis, Harold A., 18:82; works reviewed, 11:424-428, 13:181, 36:32; author, 14:339, 15:120, 16:229, 22:309, 28:362, 38:199, 40:202; editor, 15:125
Innis, Mrs. Harold A. (Mary Q.), editor, 36:32
Inspiration Peak, Otter Tail County, 37:4, 7
Institute for Scandinavian Studies, 18:324
Institute of Early American History and Culture, Williamsburg, Va., 27:349
Institute of Jesuit History, 23:57
Institute of Medical Technique, Minneapolis, 40:105
Insurance business, Minnesota, 12: 210, 20:346, 357, 22:87, 24:109; Canada, 22:99; frontier, 22:213, 23:404, 36:70
Inter Nos Study Club, Minneapolis, 15:467
Interim Committee on State Administration and Employment, 26:80
"International," steamboat, 15:357, 478, 19:110, 21:247, 250-254, 256, 259n, 261n, 262, 264-266, 269, 24: 333n, 32:60, 34:324
International Boundary Commission, 13:296, 39:128
International Brotherhood of Bookbinders, 18:445
International Conference on Documentation, 19:347
International Congress of Geologists, 32:222
International Congress of Historical Sciences, 19:347
International Falls, history, 16:366, 17:361, 21:204, 23:107, 31:184; schools, 19:473, 28:356; newspaper, 21:451; Junior Historians, 27:50, 147, 28:163; industries, 29:358, 30:407, 32:61; railroad, 31:183; river port, 33:17
International Folklore Congress, 25: 306
International Harvester Co., 12:323; mine, 28:251; history, 29:85
International Hotel, St. Paul, 19: 164, 166, 37:53, 38:294, 295, 39: 282, 283, 40:265, 276
International Institute, St. Paul,

22:202, 26:398, 27:280, 28:75, 31: 14, 39:56; Festival of Nations, 21:62, 22:336, 23:95, 25:306, 27: 39, 30:282, 31:32
International Joint Commission, activities, 16:230, 19:223, 20:441, 23:205-208, 270, 385, 24:176, 25: 196, 28:72, 29:135, 34:217
International Lumber Co., 27:302
International Milling Co., New Prague, anniversary, 23:388
International Order of Good Templars, see Good Templars
International Stock Food Co., 28:192, 36:65
International Woman Suffrage Alliance, 20:192
Interstate Commerce Act, 21:194
Interstate Commerce Commission, 12: 16, 13:19, 15:338, 20:83, 22:211, 23:372
Interstate Park, Minn., Wis., 16:192, 27:127; described, 15:237, 19:351; pageant, 16:359; historical meeting, 17:315, 18:42; guide, 19:228
Interstate Power Co., Chatfield, 24: 108
Interstate Transfer Railway, 40:245
Inver Grove Heights, Lutheran church, 14:53; Democratic convention, 39: 49
Inverarity, Robert B., archaeologist, 38:244; author, 39:209
"Invincible," lake schooner, 12:376, 28:6n
Invincible Vibrator thresher, 24:302
Iona, Catholic colony, 35:136, 137, 139
Iosco Community Club, New Richland, 12:211
Iota Study Club, Minneapolis, 27:249
Iowa, travel account, 11:106; Catholic church, 11:210; history, 11: 211, 12:416, 439, 13:208, 336, 435, 14:112, 226, 15:125, 16:478, 17:222, 20:338, 21:404-406, 430, 23:359, 27:355, 28:79, 30:160, 31: 122, 33:188, 34:40; roads, 11:394, 395, 397n, 398, 402, 21:233; ghost towns, 12:95; ethnic groups, 12: 180, 249-251, 17:401, 19:200, 25: 299, 26:273, 27:256, 29:174, 278, 30:28, 35:32, 33, 36:286-290; historic sites, 13:129, 15:475, 25: 89; surveys, 14:113, 25:175, 26: 223; industries, 14:447, 16:228, 22:184, 27:69, 190, 34:35, 39:211; conservation plan, 15:236; boundaries, 15:304n, 19:107, 222, 425, 426, 21:328, 25:396, 26:272, 27: 69, 128, 28:284; name, 16:227; schools, 16:346, 22:159, 23:184, 25:89; state fair, 16:478; described, 17:427, 22:22; health conditions, 18:155, 26:146; colleges, 18:184; Quakers, 18:255, 259; centennial, 19:106, 222, 460, 21:307, 26:272, 27:163, 257, 28: 184, 29:174; census, 19:350, 21: 326; election, 20:78; social life, 20:86; authors and artists, 20: 114, 21:431, 23:115, 119-122, 28: 287, 34:175; agriculture, 20:157, 22:19, 23:91, 28:186, 29:253, 33: 91; public lands, 20:198, 23:357-359, 24:368; guides, 20:203; merchants, 20:335; capitol, 20:338;

transportation, 21:226, 305, 28:
185, 39:66; Indian affairs, 21:
425; manuscript guides, 22:97;
pioneer life, 22:329, 23:91, 24:
261; rivers, 22:410; forts, 24:
239, 40:146; explored, 25:396, 34:
310; war records, 25:402; holiday
celebrations, 26:169, 273; hunting, 26:169, 373; mail service,
26:170, 30:268; politics, 26:209,
35:42; pioneers, 26:375; post offices, 30:174; emigrant guide, 31:
115, 36:102; medicine, 33:44;
Grange, 36:238, 39:130; Winnebago
Indians, 36:267, 38:353; in Civil
War, 36:279, 37:255, 38:202; promotes immigration, 37:184; in
Sioux Outbreak, 38:278-280; ciga-
rette ban, 39:25; archaeology, 39:
339; atlases, 40:124; gazetteer,
40:147; fur trade, 40:180, 186
"Iowa," steamboat, 22:13
Iowa and Minnesota Townsite Co., 27:
355
Iowa Association of Local Historical
Societies, 23:71, 90
Iowa Catholic Historical Society, 18:
436
Iowa City, Iowa, pioneer life, 12:94;
history, 20:338, 22:99; centen-
nial, 27:355
Iowa County, Wis., records, 24:178
Iowa Emigration Society, Hull, Eng.,
28:78
Iowa Historical, Memorial, and Art
Department, newspaper collection,
12:199; Minnesota items, 15:463
Iowa Historical Records Survey, pub-
lication, 22:97
Iowa Historical Society, see State
Historical Society of Iowa
Iowa Indians, 34:313; earthworks, 16:
312
Iowa National Guard, 15:420, 24:240
Iowa River, Iowa, mills, 22:185
Iowa State College of Agriculture and
Mechanic Arts, Ames, 22:326, 23:
91; history, 25:89. See also Iowa
State University
Iowa State Department of Agriculture,
history, 24:260
Iowa State Department of History and
Archives, 22:329, 23:90, 285, 25:
402
Iowa State Horticultural Society,
publication, 23:91
Iowa State University, Ames, 20:114;
anniversary, 19:107
Iowa University, see University of
Iowa
Irber, Andrew, Jr., photographer, 35:
205 (cover)
Ireland, Archbishop John, 11:347,
462, 13:313, 15:31, 77, 104, 16:
119, 19:350, 23:96, 24:92, 26:266,
373, 29:354, 30:255, 33:54, 305,
35:206, 37:61, 234, 39:153-155,
158, 162; colonizer, 11:436, 12:
103, 13:333, 419, 14:110, 335, 15:
113, 456, 19:440, 20:463, 23:191,
24:177, 31:21-23, 35:133, 135,
139, 205-213, 325, 326, 37:184,
39:128, 40:352; honored, 12:331;
career, 13:95, 440, 20:75, 92,
185, 22:334, 30:69, 33:38, 223,
304, 34:313, 38:243, 39:210; attitude toward Cahenslyism, 15:105,

27:161, 28:72, 37:133; author, 15:
213; speaker, 16:103, 17:325, 26:
304; educator, 17:349, 24:366, 25:
372-374, 27:271, 31:187, 35:134,
136-138, 243; papers, 18:316, 19:
213, 20:372, 30:2, 34:212; centennial, 19:464; liberalism, 22:382,
30:266, 38:91, 39:11; diplomat,
29:79; chaplain, 34:129
Ireland, Richard, 32:61
Ireland, Mother Seraphine (Ellen),
15:127, 23:191, 33:38; biography,
32:61
Ireland, Tom, author, 15:354
Ireland, W. W., merchant, 21:214
"Irene," steamboat, 33:16
"Irene No. 2," steamboat, 33:10, 13,
16-18
Irish, Frank, 13:345
Irish, Fred, author, 29:73
Irish, Lon, pioneer, 24:320
Irish, Lucy W., letter, 26:66
Irish, Ross A., compiler, 38:242
Irish, immigration, 11:110, 21:299,
27:40, 30:186, 188, 31:173, 32:81,
35:326, 36:237, 37:133, 38:91, 40:
352; Minnesota communities, 12:
210, 21:203, 22:220, 348, 23:96,
24:79, 27:210, 28:75, 84, 31:21-
23, 38:121, 39:49; U.S., 13:207,
14:117, 35:193, 39:210; colonies,
12:103, 13:418, 21:74, 75, 22:98,
458, 23:7, 191, 24:177, 35:205-
213, 325; St. Paul, 16:169, 28:
110, 33:5; newspaper, 16:338; Canada, 16:339; educational activities, 19:68; Wisconsin, 20:86, 27:
134, 34:210; Red River Settlement, 22:331, 24:41, 31:108; in
sports, 24:259; in Civil War, 25:
133, 253, 31:241, 33:84; in politics, 28:31, 34, 32:15, 22, 35:61,
36:304, 308, 39:260; humor, 33:
327, 328; in U.S. Army, 36:17
Irish-American Colonization Co., records, 16:74; organized, 19:92, 31:
22
Irish Catholic Colonization Association of the United States, 13:418,
40:352; founded, 23:191, 31:22
Irish Emigrant Aid and Land Colonization Society, 19:450
Irish Folklore Commission, 26:104
Irish Immigrant Aid Society, 21:75
Irish Standard (Minneapolis), file
acquired, 12:431, 13:59
Iron, use in architecture, 23:224,
230
Iron City Commercial College, Pittsburgh, 27:100
Iron Cloud, Sioux leader, 25:270
Iron Exchange Bank, Duluth, 37:124,
125
Iron Face, see Frazer, Joseph Jack
Iron Hawk, Sioux Indian, 38:123
Iron Hill, Wis., described, 17:298
Iron Lake, St. Louis County, 32:245,
34:279
Iron mining, Minnesota, 11:216, 12:
68, 15:140, 482, 16:26, 18:331,
19:85-87, 20:449, 22:180, 446, 25:
308, 26:77, 27:72, 263, 358, 28:
375, 30:267, 36:70, 103, 192, 283,
40:46; ore shipping, 11:414, 12:
178, 285, 14:321, 16:479, 26:380,
28:251, 33:24, 27, 226, 34:11,
266, 36:281, 39:262, 263; taxa-

tion, 14:208, 24:374; labor situation, 18:473, 27:205-215, 40:340,
342; Lake Superior region, 20:201,
29:259, 375, 32:148, 222, 34:179,
180, 36:276, 37:93-99, 38:42, 40:
141; place names, 21:349, 350;
Finns in, 22:96; school-land income, 25:306; Syracuse Lake, 26:
255; underground, 27:211, 36:82;
open-pit, 27:212, 28:70, 36:240;
mechanization, 27:215, 33:355; on
Chippewa lands, 31:97; U.S., 32:
46; living conditions, 32:201; museum, 34:43, 35:99; in fiction,
36:81; land laws, 38:329; historic
sites, 39:131. See also Taconite,
various ranges
Iron Mountain Railroad, 30:237
Iron River, Mich., located, 23:242
Ironside, George, Indian storekeeper,
18:37
"Ironsides," steamboat, 24:330
Ironton, Crow Wing County, Lutheran
church, 14:452
"Ironton," schooner, 34:266
Iroquois Indians, in fur trade, 11:
234, 16:408, 35:31, 40:159, 166,
205; wars, 13:399-401, 14:370, 15:
158, 161, 165-167, 173, 174, 318,
19:281, 288, 28:9, 12; Radisson's
visits, 15:178, 16:407; relations
with whites, 15:257, 16:403-406,
19:278, 280, 282-284, 286, 34:310;
Wisconsin, 15:471; removal, 23:
126; medals, 25:266; Ontario
lands, 39:338; prehistory, 40:47,
206, 208
Iroquois Trail, N.Y., 15:256
Irvine, Caleb, trader, 35:31
Irvine, Dr. Harry G., 34:316
Irvine, J. C., at Red Rock, 31:91
Irvine, Javan B., in Civil War, 39:
178
Irvine, John R., 36:265; donates park
land, 12:458; house, 15:45, 28:136
Irvine, M. Bell, author, 22:193, 23:
40
Irvine, Robert, artist, 31:56
Irvine, Cpl. William N., 25:237, 238
Irvine Hall, St. Paul, 32:101, 240n
Irvine Park, St. Paul, 33:4, 5; his-
tory, 27:271, 36:239; located, 33:
3
Irving, Henrietta, actress, 23:313
Irving, Peter, 21:398
Irving, Washington, 21:398; work re-
viewed, 35:239; author, 19:437,
20:109, 23:113, 26:165, 29:166,
40:152, 304; house, 38:343
Irwin, Harry A., 20:98
Irwin, Inez H., author, 15:230
Irwin, Leonard B., work reviewed, 21:
406; author, 23:53
Irwin, W. W., politician, 36:114
"Isaac L. Elwood," steamboat, 36:282
"Isaac Staples," towboat, 18:177
Isaak Walton League, Winona, 19:239
Isabella, Finnish settlement, 18:324
"Isabella," steamboat, 38:360
Isanti, Baptist churches, 16:355;
settled, 30:271; Sioux village,
37:272
Isanti County, pageant, 13:450; pio-
neer life, 17:487, 30:271; Swedish
settlement, 19:123, 20:359, 38:92;
library, 31:61; Mormon mission,

36:288; politics, 36:308; Farmer-Labor club, 38:303
Isanti County War History Committee, 23:391
Isbister, James, trader, 11:358
Ise, John, editor, 18:454
Isely, Bliss, work reviewed, 20:422
Isham, James, work reviewed, 31:238; trader, 40:202
Ishpeming, Mich., ski club, 17:228; mining, 25:197, 32:245
Island Lake, Carlton County, railroad, 34:184
Island No. 10, Tenn., in Civil War, 17:222, 25:36, 120
Isle, history, 28:292, 30:296
Isle aux Cerfs, Mich., 23:137n
Isle of Man, see Manxmen
Isle Pelée, see Prairie Island
Isle Royale, Mich., mining, 14:448, 35:247, 40:358; national park, 16:345, 27:351, 28:72; history, 22:431, 28:78, 37:43; fisheries, 27:262, 33:258, 34:248; lighthouse, 34:351; shipwrecks, 35:280, 281, 292; archaeology, 35:339
Islington, Ont., mission, 12:318
Isolationism, analyzed, 23:215, 40:410; Minnesota, 38:41, 40:366-369, 374; North Dakota, 38:331, 387
Italians, Minnesota, 13:83, 26:388, 28:75, 34:174; U.S., 16:118; Michigan, 20:202, 27:205; immigration, 20:467, 24:259, 27:322, 37:133; Catholic colonies, 21:74; on iron ranges, 27:204, 208-213, 215, 40:341, 343, 344, 347; New England, 35:326
Itasca, Indian girl, 13:167, 18:180; legend, 12:215-225, 13:169; name, 12:225-229, 13:163-174, 20:65
Itasca, Anoka County, ghost town, 29:216; settled, 40:332, 335; Grange office, 40:333
Itasca, Clearwater County, ghost town, 16:493
Itasca, Freeborn County, county seat fight, 14:79, 314, 15:346, 20:357; settled, 14:304-315
"Itasca," steamboat, 11:323, 16:173, 17:207, 36:279, 38:293, 295, 40:411
Itasca County, history, 11:114, 414, 15:487, 22:415, 445, 27:172, 37:260; name, 13:118; geology, 15:143; summer resort, 15:487; band, 16:249; county agent, 20:359; fair, 23:402; transportation, 24:191; Liberty Loans, 24:383; Finnish settlement, 25:319; mail service, 26:94, 34:185; shingle mills, 26:183; economic conditions, 26:288; archaeology, 26:321, 324; logging, 27:302, 29:137; wildlife, 30:127; library, 31:61; Farmer-Labor club, 38:303; poorhouse, 38:370
Itasca County Agricultural Association, 23:402
Itasca County Historical Society, organized, 29:275; meetings, 29:362, 30:79, 166
Itasca County War History Committee, 23:391
Itasca Lake, see Lake Itasca
Itasca Press, St. Paul, publication, 27:330, 340

Itasca State Park, historical meetings, 13:286-293, 18:182, 205, 282; forest experiment station, 14:104; pageants, 14:346, 450, 15:56, 126, 241, 359, 490, 16:358, 487, 498, 17:347, 18:281, 333, 30:281; saddle trail, 17:159n; established, 17:220, 24:372, 27:359, 30:313, 36:93, 37:60, 61; history, 19:214, 35:98, 36:235, 39:130; marker, 20:344; wildlife, 22:214, 25:203, 30:127; museum, 28:394; archaeology, 29:83, 37:87, 39:344; guide, 39:82
Iten, Lucille, 24:167
Iten, Michael, papers, 24:167
Iuka, Miss., in Civil War, 17:222
Iverslie, P. P., 21:426
Iverson, Marion D., work reviewed, 36:67
Iverson, Noel, work reviewed, 40:309
Ives, Brayton, letters, 28:395
Ives, Gideon S., 27:22, 35:303
Ives, James M., lithographer, 19:458
Ives, John H., legislator, 35:349, 350
Ivett, Daniel, 15:137
Ivett, Mrs. Daniel, 15:138
Ivory, archaeological item, 16:3, 7, 11,
Izatys, see Kathio

"J. B. Bassett," steamboat, 24:139
"J. J. O'Dill," steamboat, 25:72
"J. L. Grandin," steamboat, 21:259n, 260n, 262, 268
"J. S.," steamboat, 37:296
"J. W. Van Sant II," towboat, 39:167
Jacker, Father Edward, author, 36:32
Jackins, Israel, 25:226
Jacklin, Daniel C., 29:172; taconite interests, 34:272, 273, 279, 280, 37:41
Jacklin, Rudolph, miller, 24:326
Jackman, Henry A., legislator, 35:360; prison official, 37:146, 147
Jacks, L. V., author, 12:435
Jackson, ———, Scottish pioneer, 17:422
Jackson, Alice F., work reviewed, 33:84
Jackson, Andrew, President, 16:325, 17:76, 22:75, 27:309, 32:117; career, 22:313; farmer, 40:295
Jackson, Rev. Andrew, 39:81; educator, 33:309
Jackson, Bettina, work reviewed, 33:84
Jackson, Charles T., at Isle Royale, Mich., 35:339
Jackson, Donald, review by, 40:254; works reviewed, 40:138, 254; editor, 35:87, 38:240
Jackson, Elizabeth C., work reviewed, 31:111
Jackson, Francis J., 18:134
Jackson, Helen Hunt, author, 23:114, 39:240
Jackson, Henry, 20:128, 25:412, 29:218; pioneer merchant, 18:372; MHS founder, 20:367; house, 36:42; politician, 36:265, 266; postmaster, 40:83, 84, 88
Jackson, Mrs. Henry, 18:372

Jackson, J. A., review by, 28:64; author, 28:96
Jackson, Marjorie G., "British Trade at Michilimackinac," 11:231-270; author, 13:112, 16:200
Jackson, Mathew J., postmaster, 34:186
Jackson, Dr. Mercy B., feminist, 39:6
Jackson, Mitchell Y., pioneer farmer, 16:22, 17:393, 18:287, 290, 293, 295; diaries, 11:59, 457, 17:394n, 20:323, 417, 22:258, 27:61, 32:30n
Jackson, Preston T., 11:457
Jackson, Raymond A., speaker, 16:115; author, 21:176, 187
Jackson, Sheldon, missionary, 12:209, 24:72; papers, 34:212
Jackson, Gen. Thomas J. ("Stonewall"), Confederate officer, 25:37, 138, 140, 141, 143, 348
Jackson, William H., artist, 35:290, 39:298
Jackson, William Turrentine, author, 23:282, 383, 26:79, 27:67
Jackson, elections, 11:333, 14:250; G.A.R. post, 16:431, 434; Indian massacre, 38:95, 122
Jackson County, history, 11:333, 14:244, 457, 22:224, 26:259, 32:62; Norwegian settlement, 12:261, 274, 14:444, 25:411; Indian massacre, 14:248, 257; politics, 14:250, 262; census, 14:254, 256, 258, 259, 261; name, 20:368; archives, 21:327; wildlife, 22:214, 30:221; farming, 23:402, 37:210; Lutheran churches, 25:411, 29:275
Jackson County, Wis., history, 30:72
Jackson County Historical Society, 16:240; organized, 12:338, 13:71, 28:86; activities, 14:120, 28:296, 387, 29:92, 179, 362, 34:259; museum, 26:393, 29:275, 30:79
Jackson County Pilot (Jackson), anniversary, 20:461
Jackson County War History Committee, 24:82
Jackson Lake, Blue Earth County, Norwegian settlement, 18:465; Lutheran church, 18:466
Jackson Rifles, volunteer unit, 16:172, 173n
Jackson Street, St. Paul, name, 18:372, 20:369
Jackson Street Methodist Church, St. Paul, built, 16:274n
Jacksonport, Ark., in Civil War, 40:292
Jacksonville, Wilkin County, post office, 18:224
"Jacob Traber," steamboat, 36:251-258
Jacobs, Frank R., author, 20:465, 21:115
Jacobs, John M., Montana pioneer, 35:31
Jacobs, Peter, missionary, 15:463, 35:282; journal, 31:105
Jacobs, Royal, pioneer, 20:465
Jacobs, Wilbur R., author, 32:58, 40:198; editor, 38:200
Jacobs Prairie, Stearns County, Catholic church, 20:364, 32:40, 34:171
Jacobsen, Gertrude A., review by, 19:199-201; author, 19:207
Jacobsen, J. E., author, 29:361
Jacobsen, Mrs. J. E., speaker, 29:361
Jacobsen, Jerome V., author, 25:88

Jacobson, A. M., author, 17:117
Jacobson, Rev. Abraham, 24:94; author, 11:212
Jacobson, Charlotte, 26:369
Jacobson, Chester, aviator, 33:242
Jacobson, J. N., 12:106; translator, 11:212; speaker, 12:38, 210; author, 13:428
Jacobson, Jacob F., legislator, 28:73, 35:348
Jacobson, O. P. B., speaker, 16:491
Jacobson, Stanley W., speaker, 22:48
Jacobus, Sgt. Holder, in Civil War, 38:272
Jacquin, Ferdinand, 13:116
Jaeger, Mr. and Mrs. Luth, papers, 20:192
Jaffa, Harry, criminal suspect, 37:165
Jaffa, Harry V., editor, 36:323
Jaffe, Bernard, author, 26:165
Jaffray, Clive, banker, 19:113
Jager, H. J., speaker, 14:124; author, 18:119
Jaggard, Judge and Mrs. Edwin, pioneers, 33:4
Jaher, Frederic C., author, 39:260
Jahn, Raymond, author, 34:169
Jaklič, Franc, author, 15:122
Jallings, Jack K., compiler, 40:96
James, Dr. Edwin, editor, 31:105, 35:199; explorer, 34:284-286; author, 40:306
James, Mrs. F. L., 20:435
James, Frank, robber, 11:117, 23:40, 31:182, 35:202, 39:262; escape, 12:176; career, 12:335, 31:50, 40:307; effect on politics, 23:381; in Civil War, 34:305
James, Henry, author, 20:107, 23:113
James, Henry C., lawyer, 12:322
James, Mrs. Henry C., 21:112
James, James A., 39:220; speaker, 13:326
James, Jean, author, 29:278, 30:406
James, Jesse, robber, 11:85, 117, 14:461, 23:40, 31:182, 35:202, 39:262; 40:362; escape, 12:176; career, 12:335, 13:441, 31:50, 62, 34:125, 40:307; effect on politics, 23:381; railroad holdup, 34:83; in Civil War, 34:305; injured, 35:241
James, Marquis, 26:166
James, Thelma, speaker, 25:397
James, Thomas, author, 33:181
James, William, 14:28
James Bay, Que., Ont., Norse at, 40:95
"James Means," towboat, 18:177
"James P. Pearson," steamboat, see "Julius C. Wilkie"
James River, S.D., trading post, 11:380
Jameson, Lt. ---, commissary officer, 18:401
Jameson, Anna, 25:273
Jameson, Horatio G., author, 21:365
Jameson, John Franklin, 14:88, 91; career, 39:336
Jameson, Mrs. Wesley J., 15:79; author, 15:467, 16:233
Jamestown, Va., founded, 18:386; archaeological site, 40:205-207
Jamet, Lt. John, 12:357
Jamison, Alma H., author, 18:453

Jamison, James K., work reviewed, 28:62
Jamme, Anna, 21:114
Janauschek, Fanny, actress, 28:117, 118, 32:105
Janes, Alex L., memorial, 36:327
Janes, Mrs. Alex, pioneer, 33:5
Janesville, Civil War marker, 11:119; centennial, 35:152
Janesville, Wis., electric utilities, 36:99
Janney, Frances W., author, 17:230
Janney, Semple, Hill and Co., Minneapolis, hardware merchants, 34:113
Janowitz, Henry D., author, 30:259
Jansenists, refute Hennepin, 19:99, 20:424
Janson, Erik, colonizer, 17:401; career, 11:103, 13:305, 307, 21:98
Janson, Florence E., work reviewed, 12:413-416
Janson, Kristofer, Unitarian minister, 13:441, 20:400, 406, 407; poet, 26:301, 37:265; lecture tour, 40:357
Janson, Mrs. Kristofer, 20:400, 407
Jantz, Harold, essay reviewed, 39:198-200
Janvier, Matilda, letters, 31:185
Janvier, Sarah, letters, 31:185
Janvier family, genealogy, 31:184
Janzen, Cornelius, Mennonite, 17:466; diary, 18:47, 20:160
Japan, Copeland's visit, 38:311, 316-324
Japanese, U.S., 22:96, 29:261; resettlement, 29:262
Jaques, Francis Lee, author, 13:113; artist, 19:463, 24:371, 29:132, 135, 192, 282, 30:47, 31:58, 123, 33:310, 37:216, 305
Jaques, Mrs. Francis Lee (Florence P.), author, 19:463, 24:371, 31:123, 35:240
Jaques, S. H., 20:208
Jaques family, horse thieves, 17:235
Jarchow, Ila R., speaker, 27:174
Jarchow, Merrill E., 35:340, 36:240; "Agricultural Societies," 22:249-269; "Farm Machinery," 23:316-327; "Farm Machinery of the 1860's," 24:287-306; "Livestock in Frontier Minnesota," 26:107-125; "Beginnings of Minnesota Dairying," 27:107-121; "King Wheat," 29:1-28; "Red Rock," 31:79-92; "Exploring Local History," 39:265-271; "Charles D. Gilfillan," 40:221-232; reviews by, 22:181-183, 23:256, 24:50-52, 157, 25:170, 375, 26:360-362, 28:366, 29:70, 30:252-254, 32:119, 33:81, 224, 34:36, 203, 349, 35:91, 92, 286, 375, 37:220, 38:332; works reviewed, 18:87, 30:370, 40:256; author, 12:320, 14:438, 22:187, 316, 320, 23:271, 369, 24:60, 164, 352, 25:181, 379, 383, 26:150, 153, 370, 27:152, 242, 28:331, 399, 29:103, 30:39, 292, 340, 358, 406, 31:127, 128, 32:128, 33:91, 37:134, 39:311; speaker, 22:293, 35:201
Järnefelt, Akseli, author, 16:339
Jarrell, Myrtis, translator, 19:105
Jarvis, Dr. ---, 20:91
Jarvis, Clarence S., author, 17:230

Jarvis, Edward, journal, 34:254
Jarvis, Nathan, army surgeon, 16:22; art collector, 39:261
Jasper, history, 26:284
Jaspert, Mrs. Hilde, 33:113n, 114n
Jaxon automobile, 26:22
Jay, Justice John, 18:127n, 19:303, 311. See also Jay's Treaty
Jay, John, the younger, diplomat, 18:127; lawyer, 35:101
Jay Cooke State Park, historical aspect, 12:281; established, 13:80; pageant, 16:359, 487; portages and trails, 16:472, 17:233; mill, 23:300
Jay Lake (Town Lake), Cook County, forest fire, 36:135
Jay Township, Martin County, history, 12:103, 339, 35:156
Jay's Treaty, 12:295, 20:14, 40:163, 180
"Jeanette Roberts," steamboat, 11:126, 31:83, 34:240
Jeanne Marie, Sister, author, 17:478
Jeffers petroglyphs, Cottonwood County, 40:263
Jefferson, Alice, speaker, 14:124
Jefferson, Joseph, actor, 14:38, 23:307n, 28:117, 118
Jefferson, Robert, author, 11:107
Jefferson, Robert E., postmaster, 34:185
Jefferson, Thomas, 22:66, 313, 34:203, 40:409; western policy, 11:101, 24:3, 26:75, 36:220-225, 38:240, 40:178; President, 16:204, 39:165, 40:179, 180n; secretary of state, 19:303; Indian medals, 25:78, 268-270; agrarian, 25:84, 40:293-295, 298; author, 25:295; papers, 31:179, 32:248, 33:260, 34:118, 252, 35:144, 285, 36:231, 38:90, 39:295, 40:133; architect, 38:340, 40:133
Jefferson Barracks, St. Louis, army post, 24:2, 26:205, 28:16
Jefferson City, Mo., in Civil War, 39:184, 185
Jefferson County, Iowa, Swedish settlement, 17:401
Jefferson National Expansion Memorial, St. Louis, 21:423
Jefferson School, St. Paul, Czech class, 13:270-272; history, 36:239
Jefferson Township, Winona County, German settlement, 28:33
Jefferson Transportation Co., Chatfield, 24:109
Jeffery, J. B., author, 15:468
Jefferys, Charles W., author, 16:231, 17:472, 23:83
Jeffreys, Mrs. Ruth O., author, 26:175
Jeffries, Mrs. Frank M., 26:383
Jeffries, Joseph, trader, 22:283
Jejewigigic, George, Chippewa leader, 33:60
Jelinek, Vaclav, 13:270
Jemne, Elsa, artist, 26:251
Jemtland, Goodhue County, cemetery, 12:450, 14:428
Jenison, Ernestine, work reviewed, 21:395
Jenkins, Frederick E., 19:362, 24:87, 25:99, 408, 26:92; author, 21:446; speaker, 27:146
Jenkins, Sylvanus, farmer, 24:302

Jenkins, Rev. Thomas J., 21:210, 35:137; author, 20:331
Jenkins, W. T., speaker, 13:454
Jenkins, William S., author, 31:53
Jenkins, name, 21:349
Jenks, Albert E., "Discoveries in Minnesota Prehistory," 16:1-21; author, 14:222, 17:50, 18:104, 19:111, 348, 21:100, 22:210, 35:244; archaeologist, 14:451, 15:156, 364, 483, 16:55, 117, 221, 481, 25:154n, 330, 26:312, 28:181, 31:163, 38:157, 160; speaker, 15:457, 16:68, 17:49
Jenks, Capt. Austin T., house, 38:348
Jenks, Maj. Downing B., author, 27:57
Jenks, J. Ridgway, author, 13:99
Jenks, T. B., 25:96
Jenks, William L., work reviewed, 13:186
Jenks Archaeological Research group, 12:331
Jenness, Diamond, author, 14:337
Jenney, Col. W. L. B., 19:458
"Jennie Hayes," towboat, 18:177
Jennings, H. S., 14:22
Jennings, Jesse D., work reviewed, 40:47; editor, 29:166, 39:262
Jennings, John, author, 21:9, 33:227
Jennison, Gen. Samuel P., 25:79; politician, 37:327, 328
"Jenny Lind," steamboat, 15:409, 25:117, 29:204n, 34:135
Jensen, Alma M., 25:49, 26:39; manuscript assistant, 24:31; school service director, 25:49, 73, 381, 26:40
Jensen, Mrs. Alvah H., speaker, 12:208
Jensen, Andrew F., "Trouping in Minnesota," 28:97-119; author, 20:432, 21:103, 28:203, 393
Jensen, Mrs. Dana O., editor, 33:352
Jensen, George M., career, 19:126
Jensen, Mrs. Gudrun A., 18:59, 19:61
Jensen, Hans P., in co-operative movement, 15:486, 19:155, 27:119
Jensen, Harvey D., 25:73
Jensen, L., 19:468
Jensen, Merrill, 29:174; reviews by, 29:152, 32:247; author, 29:192, 32:256
Jensen, Petrine J., 28:244
Jensen, Vernon H., author, 26:166
Jensen, William H., discovers Browns Valley man, 16:7-9, 38:160
Jenson, J. A., 21:336, 444
Jenswold, John D., speaker, 14:456
Jerabek, Esther, "Antonín Jurka," 13:269-276; "A New-World Bohemia," 15:26-42; "Almanacs as Historical Sources," 15:444-449; genealogical notes, 22:195-199, 23:274-277; "Early Geography Textbooks," 24:229-233; work reviewed, 17:194; head of accessions department, 11:46; speaker, 14:328; author, 15:342, 16:331, 17:61, 24:244, 25:43, 26:167, 28:333, 34:356, 35:204; compiler, 17:51, 18:44, 57, 19:45, 430, 27:242; editor, 26:38; career, 38:244
Jerabek, John J. (Jan), Bohemian pioneer, 15:29n, 30, 34; papers, 11:318
Jerabek, Milan W., author, 22:320
Jeremy, John, bodyfinder, 39:262

Jermane, W. W., author, 39:101, 105
Jernegan, Marcus W., tributes, 19:435
Jerome brothers, mixed-bloods, 32:61
Jerpeland, A., 18:316
Jerrard, E. H., author, 15:244
Jerrard, Mrs. Frank H., author, 12:321
Jerrard, Leigh P., author, 35:202
Jerrold, Douglas, 27:233
Jesness, Oscar B., work reviewed, 16:206; speaker, 25:412; author, 32:118
Jespersen, Otto, 17:319
Jesser, Clinton J., author, 37:85
Jester, Jim, 24:321
Jesuit missions, Northwest, 11:305-307, 18:384, 386; Minnesota, 20:84, 39:301, 302, 308, 310; service to colonies, 21:74, 26:147; Wisconsin, 23:285; to Sioux, 38:385; Fort William, Ont., 39:309
Jesuits, explorations, 12:349, 355, 18:387, 19:275, 25:296, 32:112, 37:37; association with fur trade, 14:229, 19:279, 284, 287, 21:396, 38:329; "Relations," 15:160, 162, 18:448, 31:109, 188, 37:222, 38:200, 40:312; German, 17:113; excavate Fort St. Charles, 18:244-247, 31:52, 37:62; controversy with Recollects, 20:67; in Indian wars, 40:143
Jevning, Ole, 17:183
Jewell, D. B., 20:359
Jewell, Phineas A., 15:372
Jewell Nursery, Lake City, history, 15:372
Jewett, Charles H., 25:29
Jewett, Sarah Orne, author, 20:110, 111
Jewish Family Welfare Association, 16:248
Jewish Joint Distribution Service, 39:260
Jewish Relief Society, St. Paul, 17:99
Jewish Tercentenary Committee, 34:220
Jewish Welfare Board, 12:193, 14:320, 23:393, 27:352
Jewitt, John, captured by Indians, 17:438
Jews, Twin Cities, 13:217, 323, 20:216, 22:348, 25:394, 28:294, 30:163, 31:44, 35:49, 293, 40:46; Minnesota, 15:467, 27:213, 28:75, 31:29, 32:197, 198, 34:220, 36:319, 37:87; immigration, 24:259, 30:31; war records, 27:352; Russia, 33:223; U.S., 34:220, 353, 35:45, 39:128; relations with gentiles, 35:326, 378, 38:203, 335; genealogies, 36:236; North Dakota, 40:46. See also Anti-Semitism, individual synagogues
Jiránek, Rev. František, Bohemian priest, 15:31
Jirka, Frank J., author, 23:95
Job Printers Protective Association, 22:379
Jock's Island, Ont., Saganaga Lake, 37:235n, 254
Joerg, W. L. G., author, 25:305
Joesting, Herb, career, 35:335
Jogues, Father Isaac, explorer, 12:283, 15:321, 18:387, 19:198, 25:273

Johannes, Rev. Oswald, 25:96, 405, 28:386; speaker, 23:397
Johannsen, Robert W., work reviewed, 35:93; author, 33:92; editor, 35:242, 36:323, 38:202
Johansen, Dorothy O., reviews by, 36:315, 38:326; author, 33:313, 37:183, 38:199
Johansen, Johannes, pioneer, 24:348
Johansen, John P., author, 19:222
Johansen, Krøger, journalist, 20:407
Johanson, Isak, pioneer, 25:318
John, D. C., 21:184
John, DeWitt, author, 27:367
"John B. Alley," locomotive, 19:193-196
"John Brooks," steamboat, 25:152
"John C. Davis," locomotive, 19:196
"John Ericsson," steamer, 34:12
"John Jacob Astor," schooner, 39:304
Johns, H. T., author, 37:100n
Johns, Harry, compiler, 28:397
Johns, Rev. John R., speaker, 24:187
Johns Hopkins University, Baltimore, medical school, 24:209
Johnsburg, Mower County, history, 15:490
Johnsen, Arne Odd, 21:86
Johnsen, Erik K., theologian, 14:230
Johnsen, Paul A., Mormon, 36:293
Johnsen, R. V., Mormon, 36:293
Johnshoy, Rev. M. Casper, 16:241, 18:61; speaker, 17:232, 21:53; author, 23:198
Johnson, Dr. A. E., 21:101; skier, 17:228
Johnson, A. W., speaker, 17:358
Johnson, Abraham, lumberman, 16:73, 99, 36:158; papers, 16:217; mail contractor, 36:214
Johnson, Adolph E. L., lawyer, 19:214
Johnson, Aili K., author, 28:378, 32:188
Johnson, Albert W., author, 17:480, 34:128
Johnson, Alice M., 28:170; works reviewed, 30:375, 31:238, 33:130, 261, 34:80, 254, 35:141, 282, 38:199; archivist, 22:311, 32:250; author, 26:273; editor, 32:249, 36:150
Johnson, Allen, editor, 11:109, 216, 328, 12:200, 442
Johnson, Alvin W., work reviewed, 19:201; editor, 14:339
Johnson, Alvira, 25:11
Johnson, Amandus, author, 33:314; speaker, 16:108
Johnson, Andrew, mill worker, 34:3
Johnson, Andrew, 37:50; President, 22:408, 26:156, 36:175, 300, 38:114, 229, 287, 39:86, 87, 89, 40:337; characterized, 11:157, 297, 18:319; impeachment, 16:454, 33:330; inauguration, 20:431; in Civil War, 25:32, 39:192
Johnson, Mrs. Andrew, 34:3
Johnson, Arthur M., work reviewed, 40:405
Johnson, Mrs. Arthur W., author, 21:184
Johnson, Dr. Asa E., 39:111, 112n, 114-116
Johnson, Beverly M., author, 40:42
Johnson, Birger J., 16:491
Johnson, Brita, 14:428
Johnson, Gen. Bushrod R., 25:28

Johnson, C. E., 33:242
Johnson, C. S., Northampton colonist, 22:170
Johnson, Carl A., 17:231, 18:334
Johnson, Carl F., 25:184
Johnson, Caryl, manuscript assistant, 23:168, 24:31
Johnson, Charles, mail carrier, 16:244
Johnson, Charles A., review by, 35:372; author, 31:189
Johnson, Charles F., papers, 21:414, 22:41, 111, 24:65; career, 26:256, 365
Johnson, Charles W., politician, 35:66, 69
Johnson, Chris, deputy sheriff, 38:12
Johnson, Christian, Lutheran minister, 16:471
Johnson, Clarence, author, 17:237
Johnson, Mrs. Clarence, 17:465
Johnson, D. S., at Red Rock, 31:84
Johnson, Mrs. David, author, 22:112
Johnson, David B., attorney, 18:149
Johnson, Davis, 28:300
Johnson, Donald B., author, 35:291
Johnson, Donna, 27:147
Johnson, Dorothy E., author, 26:373
Johnson, Dorothy M., author, 36:279
Johnson, E. Bird, 28:286; author, 12:68
Johnson, E. E., Hutchinsons' agent, 11:334
Johnson, E. Gustav, author, 31:253; editor, 37:178
Johnson, E. H., author, 11:110
Johnson, E. W., speaker, 20:213
Johnson, Mrs. E. W., speaker, 24:188
Johnson, Eastman, 13:196, 21:429, 23:196, 30:176, 392; Duluth collection, 12:107, 19:355, 20:453, 21:149-157, 22:443, 23:14, 24:188, 25:313, 27:77, 173, 28:182, 37:263; works depicted, 29:152, 153, 33:75, 108, 37:235, 39:308
Johnson, Ebba, librarian, 37:188
Johnson, Edith, author, 15:369
Johnson, Edward, editor, 34:170
Johnson, Edward, opera singer, 39:62
Johnson, Edward A., 15:490, 16:491
Johnson, Edwin, postmaster, 34:186
Johnson, Edwin M., author, 22:439
Johnson, Elaine, author, 16:337
Johnson, Elden, reviews by, 34:160, 257, 35:376, 36:148, 191, 230, 37:30, 174, 38:87, 157-165, 39:340, 40:407; works reviewed, 35:199, 36:33; author, 36:282, 37:247, 40:47; archaeologist, 36:326, 37:86, 136, 282, 39:344
Johnson, Emeroy, works reviewed, 16:207, 29:255, 34:167; author, 24:90, 36:193, 39:299, 40:353, 412
Johnson, Mrs. Emil, 21:223
Johnson, Mrs. Emma, house, 38:344
Johnson, Esther, cataloger, 11:46, 24:243, 36:284
Johnson, F. H., author, 17:110
Johnson, Fred W., 11:332, 13:447, 16:240, 17:120, 18:109, 222, 19:115, 20:324, 454, 21:215, 23:13, 390, 25:312, 26:88; speaker, 12:335, 16:126, 19:359, 21:111, 23:193; picture collection, 14:234, 20:93, 350; author, 14:459, 15:137, 16:357, 493, 17:125, 210, 235, 20:356, 23:187, 295, 24:379, 36:70

Johnson, Fredericka, 14:428
Johnson, G. S., house, 37:76n, 77
Johnson, Gates A., engineer, 37:315
Johnson, Mrs. Gates A., 22:425
Johnson, George, Chippewa Indian, 13:393
Johnson, George W., 18:319, 19:99, 20:35; speaker, 18:320
Johnson, Gerald W., work reviewed, 36:31; author, 30:263
Johnson, Gilbert R., author, 29:165
Johnson, Gustaf A., 14:428
Johnson, H. C., Rothsay pioneer, 11:226
Johnson, H. Nat, work reviewed, 36:25; author, 35:204, 36:193
Johnson, Dr. H. P., 17:237
Johnson, H. T., 23:374
Johnson, Harry, speaker, 21:217
Johnson, Hattie I., 19:470, 25:98
Johnson, Henry, 19:438, 32:119; work reviewed, 25:67-69; author, 14:6, 28:172; career, 29:82
Johnson, Henry A., legislator, 12:430
Johnson, Hildegard B., "The Carver County German Reading Society," 24:214-225; "The Election of 1860," 28:20-36; "Eduard Pelz," 31:222-230; review by, 21:97; author, 22:335, 24:244, 258, 25:298, 26:79, 150, 276, 27:163, 167, 268, 28:96, 29:80, 31:243, 256, 34:214, 35:381, 36:69, 239
Johnson, Hollis L., author, 25:403
Johnson, Hugh S., backs farm bill, 38:179, 180
Johnson, Mrs. J. H., 19:360
Johnson, J. K., author, 13:116, 25:406
Johnson, J. L., speaker, 27:74
Johnson, J. N., 11:332
Johnson, Rev. J. W., speaker, 11:103
Johnson, Jack T., author, 19:460, 20:86, 203
Johnson, James, portrait, 11:322
Johnson, James, miner, 22:26n
Johnson, Sir John, British emissary, 19:298; letter, 14:228
Johnson, John, Ottawa Indian, see Enmegahbowh, John Johnson
Johnson, John, trader, 37:80
Johnson, John A., emigrant agent, 35:248
Johnson, John A., student, receives awards, 18:459, 19:357
Johnson, John Albert, papers, 11:319, 14:217, 20:83; political leader, 11:435, 15:338, 18:446, 19:440, 21:98, 203, 24:55, 34:187, 35:152; career, 14:230, 28:73, 183, 31:61; governor, 16:122, 22:296, 24:266, 30:148, 34:217, 37:84, 39:97, 40:148, 346; grave, 16:301; portrait, 20:185; house, 22:295; biography, 31:42; publisher, 35:310; legislator, 35:347, 348
Johnson, John H., Civil War draftee, 21:222
Johnson, John P., inventor, 24:90
Johnson, John R., steamboat captain, 12:333, 29:292
Johnson, John W., author, 12:211
Johnson, Joseph S., house, 14:269
Johnson, Kathryn A., compiler, 34:315; author, 34:337n
Johnson, L. A., horse trader, 24:383
Johnson, L. H., inventor, 24:290

Johnson, Laurence A., work reviewed, 38:39
Johnson, Lenora I., author, 36:34
Johnson, Leonard, livestock breeder, 22:265, 26:120, 124
Johnson, Capt. Leonard, Confederate officer, 25:253
Johnson, Lewis, Goodhue County farmer, diary, 26:281
Johnson, Lewis, Willmar pioneer, author, 15:488, 17:236
Johnson, Lovisa, papers, 21:222
Johnson, Lucien, miller, 24:101
Johnson, Lurtz, 29:182
Johnson, Luther A., Congressman, 27:349
Johnson, Luther G., St. Anthony pioneer, 17:336
Johnson, Lyndon B., President, 39:170, 172
Johnson, Magnus, 17:160n, 231; Equity president, 21:202; politician, 28:74, 34:187, 36:103
Johnson, Manville A., author, 35:200
Johnson, Marcus, autobiography, 35:200
Johnson, Martin N., politician, 35:68
Johnson, Mrs. Martinus, 16:363
Johnson, Mathilda, 18:125
Johnson, Matt, speaker, 12:207
Johnson, Maynard D., speaker, 34:314
Johnson, N. C., letter, 11:317
Johnson, N. I., diary, 22:192
Johnson, Neoma, author, 38:204
Johnson, O. J., educator, 23:301, 33:309
Johnson, Ole, Vasa pioneer, 14:428
Johnson, Olof, mill operator, 34:3
Johnson, P. O., Kandiyohi County pioneer, 30:272
Johnson, Parsons K., 11:172; founder of Mankato, 12:335, 18:337; diary, 16:489; legislator, 36:266
Johnson, Paul C., speaker, 23:386, 24:380
Johnson, Rev. Peter L., 11:317, 12:83; speaker, 13:105; author, 23:285, 24:76
Johnson, R. J. R., author, 37:188
Johnson, R. W., relief commissioner, 36:56
Johnson, Rachel, actress, 28:109, 33:173, 174
Johnson, Ralph, author, 14:457
Johnson, Rev. Richard, author, 19:475
Johnson, Col. Richard M., 22:26n
Johnson, Gen. Richard W., 14:231, 27:311
Johnson, Robert, 22:26n
Johnson, Robert C., author, 31:62, 32:126
Johnson, Robert Cummings, author, 17:221
Johnson, Robert J. R., review by, 40:306
Johnson, Mrs. Rollin G., 23:104
Johnson, Roswell B., prison official, 37:140
Johnson, Roy P., author, 17:359, 33:356, 34:357, 35:97, 295, 339, 378, 40:145; speaker, 36:284
Johnson, Ruby E., author, 12:211
Johnson, Russell L., author, 23:295
Johnson, Mrs. S. B., 20:96; museum owner, 20:303
Johnson, Samuel, author, 21:365
Johnson, Dr. Samuel, house, 38:350

Johnson, Lt. Samuel H., journalist, 38:220, 221
Johnson, Sarah, 21:150
Johnson, Stanley E., author, 11:110
Johnson, Syvert H., author, 22:448
Johnson, T. Walter, author, 21:203
Johnson, Violet, work reviewed, 24:52
Johnson, Mrs. W. H., 20:95
Johnson, Walter, author, 36:185
Johnson, Walter, politician, 34:192
Johnson, Sir William, 40:198, 202; Indian superintendent, 11:81, 266, 17:439, 19:77, 29:65, 33:37; fur-trade policy, 11:235, 244, 247, 250, 253, 254, 256, 19:291; career, 13:439
Johnson, Col. William C., prison official, 37:141
Johnson, Big Stone County, Lutheran church, 13:341
Johnson family, genealogy, 15:469
Johnson Land Co., St. Paul, 14:239
Johnson Township, Red Lake County, history, 38:204
Johnson-Wentworth Lumber Co., 27:302
Johnston, ---, schoolmaster, 20:399
Johnston, Gen. Albert S., Confederate officer, 29:64, 38:260, 264
Johnston, Anna Maria, 14:93
Johnston, Charles M., work reviewed, 39:338
Johnston, Clarence H., architect, 33:317, 38:80
Johnston, George, explorer, 13:288, 14:93, 18:180; papers, 13:426, 14:65, 21:93; trader, 14:98, 99, 20:78, 23:144, 146, 147, 36:242, 245, 249
Johnston, George H., colonizer, 16:432
Johnston, J. L., author, 33:89
Johnston, J. R., artist, 17:142
Johnston, James, pioneer printer, 15:7
Johnston, Jane, see Schoolcraft, Mrs. Henry R.
Johnston, John, trader, 11:385, 14:92, 98, 19:37, 23:144, 24:378
Johnston, Mrs. John (Susan), Chippewa woman, 23:144
Johnston, John C., insurance executive, 35:336
Johnston, Joseph E., 25:240
Johnston, Scott D., review by, 35:96
Johnston, William, trader, 11:371, 14:93
Johnston, William F., governor of Pennsylvania, 35:353
Johnston family, history, 14:92-94, 34:219
Johnston reaper, 24:290
Johnstone, Edward, work reviewed, 33:310; author, 33:268
Johnstone, Paul H., author, 23:180
Jolliet, Adrien, voyageur, 12:352, 30:56
Jolliet, Louis, explorer, 12:76, 13:254, 14:371, 16:449, 453, 17:176, 299n, 18:233, 20:67, 22:56, 73, 26:75, 268, 28:370, 29:77, 30:375, 32:112, 35:151, 36:70, 37:128; career, 13:439, 26:165, 30:56; trader, 18:388; map, 27:350
Jonas, Manfred, author, 40:410
Jonas, Maryla, pianist, 39:64
Jonason, Erick, pioneer, 14:427

Jonasson, Jonas A., author, 15:477, 18:216
Jones, ---, baseball player, 19:174
Jones, Maj. A. B., author, 19:113
Jones, Judge A. C., 14:259
Jones, A. J., Nininger investor, 13:132
Jones, Alexander C., Fort Ripley sale agent, 28:219-222
Jones, Arthur L., lawyer, 19:214
Jones, Carl W., author, 28:173; MHS president, 34:144n, 220, 35:52, 204, 37:222; tributes, 35:247, 296
Jones, Catherine, author, 15:245
Jones, Clifton Clyde, author, 30:393, 31:58
Jones, D. C., machinery merchant, 24:304
Jones, Rev. David, author, 16:153n
Jones, David, Union soldier, 25:128
Jones, E. J., 27:362; speaker, 29:363
Jones, Edith H., 18:249n
Jones, Mrs. Edwin J., 14:460, 16:241; speaker, 16:66
Jones, Elizabeth M., author, 30:74
Jones, Evan, reviews by, 37:335, 39:290; works reviewed, 37:30, 38:193, 40:138
Jones, George, papers, 15:463
Jones, George M., author, 26:168
Jones, George W., Senator, 31:178
Jones, Gwyn, author, 39:170
Jones, H. Millard, Quaker minister, 18:249n, 262
Jones, Harry W., architect, 19:213
Jones, Mrs. Harry W., 19:213
Jones, Herschel V., bequest, 11:447, 12:33, 23:40, 26:31, 30:319, 33:247; collector, 12:26, 14:231, 20:198, 27:41, 32:125, 33:314, 37:222
Jones, Ivan T., 39:221
Jones, J. Glancy, 13:434
Jones, J. W., author, 25:88
Jones, James A., 25:165; author, 20:442, 36:76
Jones, James C., Tennessee governor, 39:143
Jones, Jeanette L., 20:58
Jones, Jefferson, 11:54, 315, 13:199, 14:79, 15:62, 17:70, 18:249n, 19:360, 20:50, 23:50, 26:45; author, 14:196, 30:174; speaker, 16:67; compiler, 26:174; publisher, 28:398
Jones, John, Welsh minister, 24:94
Jones, Capt. John, in Sioux Outbreak, 12:117, 15:224, 18:209, 311, 321, 19:48, 38:97, 144n
Jones, John D., legislator, 35:348
Jones, Mrs. L. R., author, 15:372
Jones, Louis C., "Folk Culture and the Historical Society," 31:11-17; reviews by, 31:187, 34:121; author, 31:63, 192, 34:316, 35:150
Jones, Maldwyn A., author, 37:184
Jones, Mary H., labor organizer, 40:344
Jones, Robert A., author, 37:41
Jones, Robert F., career, 27:168
Jones, Robert Huhn, work reviewed, 37:255; author, 36:326; editor, 40:354
Jones, Robert Leslie, work reviewed, 28:366; author, 31:128
Jones, Mr. and Mrs. Robinson, murdered, 38:134
Jones, Roy, 26:151

Jones, Samuel M., reformer, 33:41
Jones, Sarah, speaker, 12:342
Jones, Mrs. Sarah, author, 28:280, 29:284
Jones, Stephen B., author, 14:109
Jones, Thelma, work reviewed, 36:25
Jones, Dr. William A., biography, 21:209
Jones Harrison Home, Minneapolis, 38:82
Jones Township, Beltrami County, history, 15:132
Jongh, L. J. de, author, 21:370
Jönsdotter, Ingar, 20:244
Jönson, Bengt, 15:116
Jönson, Henrik, see Johnson, Henry
Joppa, Livy E., author, 23:106
Joralemon, Edgar E., architect, 40:104
Joralemon, Ira B., author, 16:110
Jordahl, S. A., author, 14:358
Jordan, Charles B., letter, 26:201n
Jordan, Charles M., educator, 12:457
Jordan, David S., 17:160n, 18:265
Jordan, Emil L., author, 21:98
Jordan, Fred A., mineralogist, 34:273, 277, 280, 283
Jordan, George C., speaker, 25:97
Jordan, Dr. Lewis, collector, 30:402
Jordan, Michael A., biography, 19:214
Jordan, Moses D., pioneer, 30:393
Jordan, Philip D., 26:370, 27:240, 243, 340, 28:47, 49, 75, 165, 335, 29:370, 30:329, 405, 38:92; "The Hutchinson Family," 22:113-132; "Minnesota Sheet Music," 26:52-54; "Toward a New Folklore," 27:273-280; "A Minnesota Melting Pot," 28:241-268; "A Wit Looks at Old Fort Ripley," 28:339-344; "Rural Minnesota," 30:111-121; "Proctor Knott's Speech," 34:67-77; reviews by, 21:307, 404-406, 22:104, 23:359, 26:59, 144-146, 365, 27:137, 236, 237, 28:55-57, 65, 273, 362-364, 29:248-250, 338, 30:247, 379, 31:112, 32:44, 33:82, 215, 308, 34:121, 201, 35:95, 142, 194, 239, 37:300; works reviewed, 23:159, 27:233, 29:150, 30:372, 34:34, 37:299; editor, 14:352, 16:111, 542, 28:183, 37:183; author, 17:225, 18:325, 21:98, 310, 22:97, 23:370, 24:261, 25:84, 89, 26:170, 27:152, 341, 342, 28:69, 92-94, 177, 199, 287, 306, 307, 29:170, 30:76, 263, 393, 31:11, 191, 251, 33:350, 355, 34:176, 213, 266, 316, 35:381, 36:78, 105, 277, 37:182, 38:333; speaker, 22:52-54, 28:286, 29:98, 36:72, 152, 323, 37:40; receives fellowship, 25:200; research associate, 27:247
Jordan, Thomas, pioneer merchant, 14:463
Jordan, museum, 12:454; churches, 15:128, 20:218, 25:213, 28:395; business, 15:347; German theater, 34:242
Jordan Country, Montana, described, 12:198, 497
Jordan Junior High School, Minneapolis, murals, 27:148, 28:165
Jordy, William H., editor, 39:35
Jorgens, Ole, career, 30:278
Jørgensen, Mads, Mormon missionary, 36:290

Jorgensen, Margareth, author, 11:446
Jorgenson, Rev. H. G., author, 19:234
Jorgenson, Rev. Lars, 15:486
Jorgenson, Lloyd P., work reviewed, 35:198
Jorgenson, Theodore, work reviewed, 20:179-181; author, 20:86, 21:426; speaker, 24:270
Jorns, Byron C., artist, 26:271, 365
Jorstad, Erling, "Personal Politics in Minnesota's Democratic Party," 36:259-271; "Minnesota's Role in the Democratic Rift of 1860," 37: 45-51; reviews by, 35:94, 197, 330; author, 37:186; speaker, 40: 48
Josefson, Mrs. J. A., author, 18:469
Joseph, Nez Percé leader, 19:330, 34: 346, 35:333
Joseph, I. S., author, 16:248
Joseph, Sister Mary, hospital super-intendent, 21:114, 22:407
"Joseph H. Thompson," freighter, 34: 16
"Josephine," steamboat, 18:405, 35: 335
Josephites, religious sect, 36:290
Josephson, Bertha E., work reviewed, 26:60; author, 27:59
Josephson, Matthew, author, 21:199, 35:379
Josephy, Alvin M., Jr., work re-viewed, 40:93; author, 35:153, 37: 183, 40:156; editor, 38:40
Josten, H. Margaret, author, 23:384
Journal (Farmington), history, 15:245
Journal-Lancet, history, 20:85, 21: 209, 37:135. See also North-western Lancet
Journal of Education, established, 23:185
Journalism, women writers, 17:474; bibliographies, 19:456; frontier, 25:93, 203, 27:1-20, 142, 40:257; Minneapolis, 25:305; in fiction, 26:379; pictorial, 28:278; ama-teur, 28:397, 29:375, 35:378; med-ical, 33:312; Norwegian-American, 33:348; U.S., 34:202; dairying, 36:190; "yellow," 37:161-173; Ohio, 37:262; relation to poli-tics, 39:45, 46, 327-334; agri-cultural, 40:295. See also News-papers
Journeymen Cigar Makers' Protective Union, 21:379
Journeymen Tailors Self-Protection Society, 21:387
Joutel, Henri, 16:199
Joy, Charlie, pioneer motorist, 26:24
Joy, James F., railroad executive, 30:151, 33:308
Joy, James R., author, 12:201
Joy, Thomas, pioneer, 23:25
Joyce, Bishop Isaac W., 14:230
Joyce, M. M., letter, 30:93
Joys family, genealogy, 11:89
"Juanita," towboat, 18:177
Juchereau family, genealogy, 34:313
Judd, Burritt S., 20:141
Judd, Charles H., author, 12:418
Judd, Clarence E., publisher, 28:397
Judd, Dr. Edward Starr, 22:405, 407, 24:347; career, 25:305, 28:371, 40:309
Judd, Mrs. G. A., author, 13:454

Judd, George B., lumberman, 18:167, 176
Judd, Lewis S., lumberman, 18:167, 344, 20:448
Judd, Norman B., politician, 35:115
Judd, Samuel, postmaster, 36:213
Judd, Sarah L., pioneer, 24:203
Judd, Walter, speaker, 26:399, 37:343
Judd, William S., 20:141
Judd, Walker and Co., Marine on St. Croix, lumber firm, 17:285, 24: 245, 25:42, 40:243
Judson, Adoniram, missionary, 12:166
Judson, Ann, missionary, 28:135
Judson, Clara I., author, 24:89
Judson, Harry P., educator, 14:231, 18:132, 137, 139, 145, 147, 149, 150, 28:286
Judson, Leander, cartographer, 11:360
Judson, R. C., 22:265, 26:124
Judson, in Sioux Outbreak, 12:82, 448, 16:170, 171, 38:280
Judson Memorial Baptist Church, Min-neapolis, 16:121
Jugoslavs, see Yugoslavs
"Julia Dean," steamboat, 29:204n
Julien House, Dubuque, Iowa, 34:23n
Julien Theater, Dubuque, Iowa, 23:313
Juliopolis, bishop of, see Proven-cher, Rev. Joseph N.
"Julius C. Wilkie," steamboat museum, 35:202, 36:139, 142-144, 283, 327, 37:66
Jumer, Dr. J. A., 23:101, 24:86
June, Jenny, 17:474
Juneaux's Post, Mont., settlers, 13: 427
Juni, Benedict, in Sioux Outbreak, 34:237, 238, 38:92
Junior Historians, essay contests, 27:145-148, 29:283; publication, 28:52; activities, 28:160-166, 29: 40, 51, 91, 95, 96, 178, 30:328; name, 29:373. See also Gopher Historians
Junior Livestock Show, South St. Paul, 28:377
Junior Pioneers Association, Ramsey County, 15:254; New Ulm, 16:126
Junkin, Tom P., journalist, 34:227
Juno Lake, Cook County, forest fire, 36:133
Jurisch, C. P., author, 28:290
Jurka, Antonín, teacher, 15:446, 28: 334; career, 13:269-276
Jury, Wilfrid, author, 27:357
Justis, Lyle, artist, 29:159

Kabekona Lake, Hubbard County, log-ging, 34:153
Kabekona River, Hubbard County, In-dian mounds, 26:321
Kabetogama Forest, St. Louis County, 16:237
Kabetogama Lake, St. Louis County, archaeology, 28:373
Kacmarcik, Frank, artist, 33:310
Kaddatz, C. W., speaker, 14:122
Kaddatz, Mrs. C. W., author, 11:336
Kadlets, John, farmer, 24:99
Kagaw Chestin, see Little Crow (Tao-yateduta)
Kagin, Edwin, speaker, 19:237; au-thor, 36:192

Kahboka (The Drifter), Sioux leader, 21:169, 38:147
Kahler, Ardella, speaker, 22:441
Kahler Corp., history, 40:315
Kahn, Herman, author, 30:389
Kahn, Howard, author, 23:198, 26:368
Kaikkonen, Hjalmer, editor, 25:160
Kaiser, Albert, author, 15:251; pub-lisher, 30:273
Kaiser, Rev. Edward, 14:363
Kaiser, Peter, 12:342
Kaisersatt, Frank, 11:117, 13:121, 23:392; author, 12:209; speaker, 26:91
Ka-Ka Gesick, Chippewa Indian, 28:375
Kakabeka Falls, Ont., 36:309, 314
Kakima, Potawatomi woman, 19:299
Kalar, Joseph A., 34:359
Kalemeyn, M., 28:129
"Kalevala," Finnish epic, 24:228, 237
Kalevala Society, Finnish cultural group, 22:97
Kalevala Township, Carlton County, Finnish settlement, 25:320, 28:82
Kalm, Peter (Pehr), author, 16:338, 17:52, 19:216; scientist, 23:180
Kalmar Township, Olmsted County, frontier life, 11:186; politics, 21:214
Kalmoe, Mrs. George, author, 13:117
Kaltenborn, Hans V., papers, 40:258
Kamigichkang, Manebane, Chippewa In-dian, 39:304
Kaministikwia River, Ont., post, 11: 233, 234, 258, 12:364, 376, 13: 203, 17:111, 18:103, 19:287, 24: 277, 28:13, 14n, 35:140; trade route, 11:264, 357, 12:362, 365, 372, 15:92, 20:88, 29:132, 166, 37:345; suggested boundary, 23: 208, 24:342
"Kamloops," steamboat, 35:281
Kammerer, John J., 28:285, 31:163n, 231n; author, 24:78, 28:373
Kampesca, Sioux Indian, 13:410
Kampff, Louis, potter, 33:229, 231, 235
Kanabec County, history, 11:114, 14: 354, 15:368, 18:340, 19:365; log-ging, 18:172, 24:273, 36:195; name, 20:343; agriculture, 21:212, 22:110; archives, 22:332
Kanabec County Historical Society, 16:240; organized, 12:450, 13:71; meeting, 15:368
Kanabec County Times (Mora), anniver-sary, 15:368
Kanabec County War History Committee, 24:82
Kandiyohi, proposed capital, 16:306, 30:272, 40:67, 68; plat, 40:66
Kandiyohi County, pageant, 11:461; railroads, 12:254, 21:450, 36:104; described, 12:260; ethnic settle-ments, 12:261, 265, 276, 18:338, 23:107, 26:364, 28:121, 124, 33: 146, 153, 35:33, 90; historic sites, 13:450, 40:263; officials, 15:197; hunting, 16:264, 26:169, 33:141-154; townsite promotion, 17:214, 38:388; literary society, 19:236; archives, 20:212, 26:87; creamery, 22:346; history, 23:187, 30:272, 36:107, 39:212; in Sioux Outbreak, 28:375, 38:281, 286; centennial, 30:285; name, 30:331;

library, 31:61; map, 33:147; politics, 36:308
Kandiyohi County Historical Society, meetings, 21:336, 22:339, 23:297, 24:270, 26:393, 27:342, 362, 29: 363; activities, 21:444, 22:340, 34:359; museum, 23:14, 101, 26:26, 86-88, 254; publication, 38:242
Kandiyohi County Old Settlers Association, 11:12; museum, 11:16, 461, 12:37, 20:212; activities, 12:40, 16:304, 305, 21:444
Kandiyohi County War History Committee, 23:391, 24:185
Kandiyohi Town Site Co. (Whitefield Exploring Association), 15:210, 17:214, 30:112, 33:249, 40:65, 67, 71, 75
Kandota Township, Todd County, history, 16:131, 40:71; townsite, 18: 354; pictured, 20:364
Kane, Elisha K., explorer, 27:16, 35: 227
Kane, Lucile M., 27:340; "Touring with a Timber Agent," 31:158-162; "The Sioux Treaties and the Traders," 32:65-80; "The Autograph Collection," 33:298-300; "The Papers of John Harrington Stevens," 34:144-148; "New Light on the Northwestern Fur Company," 34:325-329; "Governing a Frontier City," 35:117-129; "Rivalry for a River," 39:309-323; reviews by, 28:361, 30:149, 376, 31:116, 184, 32:55, 180, 253, 33:88, 131, 34:40, 119, 35:146, 196, 237, 287, 36:29, 98, 189, 37:300, 340, 38:194, 39:127, 165, 40:305, 357; works reviewed, 32:243, 36:149, 37:219, 40:137; manuscript curator, 29:282, 30:41, 181, 39:164; speaker, 30:364; author, 30:388, 32:190, 33:92, 185, 226, 34:176, 220, 315, 35:52, 340, 37:188, 348, 38:329, 39:212, 40: 361; editor, 31:122; translator, 32:56; discovery of Clark Papers, 33:268, 34:315, 35:51, 36:216, 217; honored, 36:108; receives grant, 40:316
Kane, Paul, 11:363, 13:439, 25:273, 26:386; author, 14:334, 33:187; artist, 14:449, 15:357, 17:456, 18:95, 216, 21:185, 23:183, 26: 359, 380, 28:70, 31:54, 33:264, 35:282, 295, 36:277, 37:133, 134, 38:386; works depicted, 36:285 (cover), 309-314; buffalo hunter, 36:309-314
Kane, Thomas R., 17:101
Kane, Mrs. Thomas R., 17:101
Kanesville, Iowa, see Council Bluffs, Iowa
Kangas, J. Emil, 20:210
Kankakee River, Ind., Ill., raccoon trapping, 40:215
Kansas, agriculture, 12:430, 23:114, 117, 25:375; pioneer printing, 13: 109; immigration, 13:136, 17:323, 19:79, 27:256; history, 13:435, 34:307, 35:383, 40:129; in slavery controversy, 14:132, 164, 167, 175n, 189, 18:453, 27:14, 34:304; Mennonite settlement, 14:225, 18: 99, 20:181; pioneer life, 15:124, 18:454; baseball, 21:426; Yankee influx, 24:367, 31:182; in art,

25:278, 27:159, 29:266; statehood, 27:5, 39:70; dust storms, 28:79; bibliography, 28:276; Civil War publications, 38:202; political movements, 39:83; public lands, 39:92
Kansas City, St. Joseph & Council Bluffs Railroad, see Burlington Lines
Kansas Historical Society, 15:462, 531, 24:368
Kansas-Nebraska Act, controversy, 14: 132, 19:254, 23:261, 32:16, 34: 304, 307
Kansas Stock Yards Co., Kansas City, 27:354
Kantor, MacKinlay, work reviewed, 38: 88
Kaomdeiyeyedan, Sioux Indian, 38:134
Kaplan, Louis, author, 23:377
Kaplan, Milton, work reviewed, 33:216
Kaposia, Dakota County, Sioux village, 11:184, 13:192, 295, 15: 304n, 17:288n, 19:135, 23:341n, 28:272, 320, 30:198, 294, 31:79n, 153, 33:118, 35:99; battle, 11: 455, 13:443, 15:306n, 21:182; mission, 13:195, 16:136, 314, 333, 18:375, 20:123, 127, 135, 30:397, 31:82, 40:2; pictured, 13:409, 17: 207, 289, 290, 19:421, 35:29, 36:1 (cover); farming, 15:274, 301, 21: 22, 23, 38:93; river port, 18:372, 28:135, 136; marker, 21:439, 22: 440; school, 22:430, 28:133; medical service, 33:91; post office, 36:207, 40:82. See also South St. Paul
Kapplin, A. B., author, 14:359
Kapsner, Oliver, author, 40:361
Karjenaho, Matias, Finnish pioneer, 25:318
Karlstad, Kittson County, Lutheran church, 14:452; railroad village, 14:458
Karlstrand, Einar, author, 20:340
Karmany, Uriah S., diaries, 20:195
Karni, Michael G., "Otto Walta," 40: 391-402
Karns, S. D., pioneer, 40:65
Karns City, McLeod County, ghost town, 40:65-67, 75
Karpinski, Louis C., works reviewed, 13:186; author, 26:384, 27:66, 34: 303
Karstad, Ruby G., 16:469; "The New York Tribune," 17:411-420; author, 16:100, 17:459, 28:334; speaker, 17:317
Kaser, David, author, 38:333
Kaskaskia, Ill., hunting, 14:422; press, 15:14; history, 18:389, 394, 19:218, 29:337; fur trade, 19:293
Kaslo, Helen, author, 31:58
Kasota, founded, 11:171, 181; mill, 12:104
Kašpar, Jan, Bohemian pioneer, 15:27; in Sioux Outbreak, 15:29
Kašpar, Václav, Bohemian pioneer, 15: 27
Kasparek, Val E., 17:483, 19:117; speaker, 14:121, 26:179; author, 14:332, 19:360, 20:212, 21:337, 453, 23:197, 298, 24:167; compiler, 29:363
Kasper, Frank, speaker, 16:488

Kasper, T. Cyril, athlete, 39:20
Kassel, J. L., author, 18:71
Kasson, mill, 18:467; railroad, 37: 157; centennial, 39:344
Kašťánek, Josef, 15:34
"Kate Kearny," steamboat, 17:431, 31: 210
Kathio (Izatys), Mille Lacs County, Sioux village, 35:292, 36:284; historic site, 16:18, 37:67-69, 308; name, 21:348
Katikitegon, Mich., Chippewa village, 29:66
Katkov, Norman, novelist, 31:129, 134, 142, 146
Katz, Helen T. (Mrs. Arthur A.), 12: 197; compiler, 38:241
Katz, Maj. Morton S., 25:311
Katz, R. N., papers, 26:69
Katz and Hertz, packing firm, 16:471
Katzer, Archbishop Frederick, career, 34:313
Kaufert, Frank H., 34:316, 39:84
Kauffer, Henry B., potter, 33:230
Kauffman, Henry J., work reviewed, 33:134
Kauffman, J. W., author, 17:109
Kaufman, Mrs. H. L., 18:336
Kaul, Bert, speaker, 25:98
Kaul, Eberhard, brickmaker, 25:98
Kaups, Matti, author, 40:358
Kavanaugh, Rev. Benjamin T., missionary, 25:212, 31:80
Kavesh, Robert A., author, 35:44
Kay, Alexander, trader, 11:261, 20: 10, 11
Kay, Hillis G., editor, 34:355
Kazeck, Melvin E., work reviewed, 35: 331
KDAL, Duluth, radio station, 28:78, 181
Keane, Archbishop James J., career, 14:230
Keane, John J., life, 34:214
Kearny, Gen. Philip, Union officer, 25:132, 136
Kearny, Stephen W., 13:207, 30:103, 35:290; expeditions, 12:438, 13: 369, 16:232; journal, 23:339n; papers, 34:212; biography, 38:201
Keating, M. C., 15:114
Keating, William H., work reviewed, 37:31; author, 12:238, 327, 13: 368, 372, 374, 418, 16:157, 158, 17:305, 22:155n, 26:165, 30:125, 126, 223, 31:105, 34:284, 40:306; geologist, 14:215, 230; explorer, 30:124, 35:242, 378, 36:294-299
Keating Hotel, Graceville, history, 11:111
Keatley, Clarence E., 27:346
Keaveny, Rev. T. Leo, author, 12:456
Kebker, Vant W., work reviewed, 22: 314
Keck, Mrs. A. J. (Mary E.), speaker, 17:484; author, 23:399
Keckley, Elizabeth, 17:107, 216, 18: 319
Kedron, Fillmore County, Quaker meeting, 18:256, 257n
Keefe, Jack, author, 18:94, 107, 344
Keegan, Andrew, papers, 28:395
Keegan, W. Edward, author, 24:361
Keelboats, 29:260; Mississippi River, 14:150, 16:78, 23:61, 62, 36:46; Wisconsin River, 18:154; depicted, 22:142, 26:142; Minnesota River,

22:144-147, 32:76; in mail serv-
ice, 40:78, 79
Keeler, Herbert L., war hero, 12:100
Keeler, Bishop Stephen E., 36:319
Keeley, Col. Harry J., 23:167, 27:
262; speaker, 23:267, 27:250
Keen, Edwin L., 25:27
Keenan, Agnes, speaker, 16:235
Keenan, Anna M., author, 15:105
Keenan, Rev. Edward, author, 17:129,
349
Keenan, Jerry, author, 40:410
Keenan, Melvin, 22:440
Keene, C. A., 19:472
Keene, Laura, actress, 33:169, 175
Keenleyside, Hugh L., work reviewed,
11:191-194; author, 33:315
Keewatin, name, 20:343; mining town,
28:251
"Keewatin," steamboat, 21:247, 259n,
264, 32:60, 34:14
Kegley, Charles V., 16:101; author,
22:111
Kegley, Mrs. Charles V., author, 22:
111
Keinath, H. O. A., author, 29:79
Keiser, Albert, author, 16:105
Keith, Arthur M., biography, 16:249
Keith, Ellen (Mrs. Irvin W. Rollins),
39:201
Keith, Mr. and Mrs. Henry C., at St.
Anthony, 15:140
Keith, Joseph J., poet, 25:176
Keith, Walter J., biography, 16:249
Keith family, genealogy, 16:249, 21:
313
Keithahn, Rollo C., author, 11:98
Keithsburg, Ill., Henry Lewis' visit,
17:426
Keiwel, Mr. and Mrs. Charles E.,
house, 42:266
Keleva Lodge, Finnish society, 16:320
Kellar, Herbert A., 14:11, 28, 20:
325; review by, 18:79; work re-
viewed, 17:326, 18:195; author,
18:91, 31:128; speaker, 18:322,
32:123; memorial essays, 36:149
Keller, A. F., brewer, 37:263
Keller, Father George, at Faribault,
35:321
Keller, Henry, legislator, 35:304
Keller, Lulu, speaker, 24:188
Keller, Oscar, speaker, 34:222
Keller, Ralph, 36:103; speaker, 35:
247, 296
Kellett, Clark, review by, 39:208
Kellett, Mrs. Clark (Leota M.), 35:
50; work reviewed, 38:86; author,
36:70, 39:132, 40:263
Kellett, Thomas P., merchant, 12:318,
16:73
Kelley, Etna M., author, 35:241
Kelley, Fanny, 40:335
Kelley, Garaphelia, 40:335
Kelley, George W., 19:33; author, 16:
253, 28:83
Kelley, Grace, 40:335
Kelley, Julia, 40:335
Kelley, O. M., journalist, 34:146
Kelley, Oliver H., 33:310; agrarian
leader, 13:340, 14:137, 169, 230,
15:113, 253, 16:455, 18:410, 20:
448, 21:436, 22:251, 319, 26:170,
27:255, 352, 28:54, 30:253, 31:99,
33:50, 35:55, 284, 36:238, 39:83,
129; memorial marker, 13:382;
house, 16:487, 20:86, 26:82, 33:

51, 34:172, 36:95, 37:136, 40:336;
letters, 22:85; quoted, 24:298;
author, 26:297n, 38:295, 40:297;
postmaster, 40:89; journal, 40:
360. See also Granger movement
Kelley, Mrs. Oliver H., I (Lucy E.),
40:331, 332
Kelley, Mrs. Oliver H., II (Temperance L.), 30:253, 40:334, 335
Kelley, William, 40:335
Kelley, William D., Congressman, 34:
73
Kelley, William H., historian, 30:302
Kelley family, in Minnesota, 40:332
Kelley's Landing, Tenn., depicted,
38:272
Kelliher, history, 15:132, 33:356;
railroad, 29:147; school, 34:63
Kellog School, Renville County, 25:
102
Kellogg, Clara M., 39:56
Kellogg, Edward, radical leader, 27:
334
Kellogg, Frank B., 15:100, 17:160n,
20:185, 21:69, 22:80, 24:168, 36:
103; speaker, 13:83, 14:211, 344,
15:56; biographies, 18:423-428,
22:104; lawyer, 19:66; memorial,
20:36; papers, 20:372, 23:371, 33:
300, 34:212, 339, 37:44, 135; Senator, 24:373, 25:195, 39:205, 40:
90; career, 28:74, 35:285; bust,
30:40, 91; concept of history, 35:
157-166; secretary of state, 38:
35, 240, 39:80
Kellogg, Mrs. Frank B., 20:36, 24:168
Kellogg, Joseph, explorer, 28:68
Kellogg, Louise P., 13:291, 15:101,
18:193, 19:445, 24:76; "The French
Régime," 12:347-358; reviews by,
11:430-432, 15:90-92, 19:198, 20:
66-68, 22:60; work reviewed, 17:
196-198; author, 11:104, 105, 110,
211, 328, 12:201, 325, 328, 13:
210, 245, 252, 331, 14:220, 348,
15:358, 474, 476, 16:112, 115,
239, 350, 17:225, 477, 21:429, 23:
185, 24:337; editor, 11:309, 12:
94; speaker, 12:282, 13:56, 105,
326, 19:310-312, 20:30; Radisson
theory, 15:163, 324; research as-
sociate, 20:74
Kellogg, M. N., 21:316
Kellogg, Mark, 22:175
Kellogg, Paul U., papers, 39:300
Kellogg Boulevard, St. Paul, history,
18:118
Kellogg-Briand Treaty, 23:372
Kelly, A. A., song writer, 26:52
Kelly, A. R., author, 21:327
Kelly, Charles, 40:334
Kelly, Fanny, captured by Indians,
38:385
Kelly, Frank, logger, 36:133, 134
Kelly, Henry C., letters, 30:160
Kelly, Dr. Howard, author, 24:239
Kelly, James, 20:86; speaker, 19:316
Kelly, Mary, 16:336
Kelly, Sister Mary G., work reviewed,
21:73-76
Kelly, Monroe P., author, 17:115
Kelly, Patrick H., 39:329, 330, 40:
229
Kelly, Philip J., 11:413
Kelly, Robert O., author, 38:91
Kelly, William H., 24:27
Kelly Block, St. Paul, design, 23:221

Kelsay, Laura E., author, 34:212;
compiler, 40:146
Kelsey, A. Edward, Quaker minister,
18:261
Kelsey, Dr. C. C., author, 39:264
Kelsey, Mrs. Elizabeth W., 29:276,
271
Kelsey, Frank W., 20:349
Kelsey, Henry, 36:150; explorer, 17:
75, 35:243
Kelsey, Porter, 17:120
Kelsey, Vera, 24:371; work reviewed,
32:112-114; author, 35:243
Kelso Lookout, Cook County, ranger
station, 36:134, 136
Kelso Township, Sibley County, Nor-
wegian settlement, 12:275; co-op-
erative, 22:374
Kelson, Lt. John C., 11:168, 183
Kemble, E. C., agency inspector, 35:
175-177
Kemble, E. W., artist, 40:13, 16-20
Kemble, Gouverneur, 20:78
Kemp, Francis H., 21:108, 22:106, 23:
104, 27:30n, 26:178
Kemp, George E., author, 20:447
Kemp family, genealogy, 20:447
Kemper, Henry, 16:250
Kemper, Bishop Jackson, 17:350, 21:
450, 23:132; missionary, 14:111,
230, 27:368, 28:190; centennial,
16:477; letters, 36:35
Kempfer, Hannah, speaker, 17:122;
legislator, 32:121
Kenanites, religious sect, 36:290
Kendall, Harry T., MHS president, 32:
57
Kendall, Mrs. Juliana N., 13:213
Kendall, Rita, teacher, 32:195
Kendrick, Benjamin B., work reviewed,
14:429
Kenerson, Mrs. R. H. E., author, 26:
294
Kenfield, Charles T., lawyer, 21:196
Kenkel, F. P., author, 30:159
Kenly, R. G., 38:312
Kennan, George F., author, 36:236
Kennedy, Rev. Alvah A., 11:115
Kennedy, Charles J., review by, 21:
71; author, 20:443, 21:80
Kennedy, D. R., trader, 11:180
Kennedy, Duncan L., author, 28:74
Kennedy, E. H., road boss, 16:11
Kennedy, Lt. Ebenezer H., escorts In-
dians, 38:363
Kennedy, J., trader, 40:167n, 168n
Kennedy, Jeremiah C., cathedral com-
mitteeman, 39:154n
Kennedy, John F., President, 37:343,
38:92
Kennedy, John P., 14:268
Kennedy, Robert, tavern keeper, 11:
168, 30:295; town board president,
21:343
Kennedy, Roger G., 39:84; "Houses of
the St. Croix Valley," 38:337-352;
"Joseph R. Brown's House," 39:272-
277; "The Long Shadow of Harvey
Ellis," 40:97-108
Kennedy, Walter, 27:48
Kennedy, William, publisher, 26:304
Kennedy, Capt. William, letter, 21:
251n
Kennedy, William P., author, 27:241
Kennedy family, gunmakers, 38:197
Kennedy, history, 21:451

Kennedy Land and Town Co., Kittson County, 21:451

Kennedy Milling Co., Glencoe, 35:47

Kennedy's Own, literary magazine, 26: 304, 310

Kennerson, Fred, reminiscences, 16: 101

Kenneseth Israel Congregation, Minneapolis, 20:216

Kenney, James F., review by, 24:152-154; work reviewed, 13:300; author, 24:164; speaker, 25:84

Kenney, Nathaniel T., author, 36:280

Kenney, Seth H., farmer, 20:448, 34: 289

Kenney, William P., biography, 22:104

Kennicott, Dr. John, editor, 23:370

Kennicott, John A., journalist, 24: 246

Kennicott, Robert, naturalist, 23: 370, 24:58, 246, 370, 31:183; papers, 24:61; diary reviewed, 24: 344

Kenning, Charles, 19:22

Kenny, Sister Elizabeth, 24:181, 25: 309

Kenny, Thomas, letters, 27:345

Kenora (Rat Portage), Ont., trading post, 11:363; map, 15:239; canoe route, 24:276, 279, 25:204; resort, 24:278; railroad, 28:179; mills, 31:183, 34:4; lake port, 35:272, 275

Kenosha, Wis., in World War II, 26: 278

Kenosha County (Wis.) Historical Society, publication, 29:356

Kensington, located, 17:27-29, 31, 173-176

Kensington rune stone, 21:92, 22:439, 28:78, 29:168, 175, 349, 30:69, 154, 170, 34:215, 36:95; literature, 12:421, 13:442, 16:234, 349, 453, 19:356, 20:85, 200, 21:202, 302-304, 28:58-60, 176, 31:249, 32:56, 33:47, 34:53, 265, 302, 35: 47, 141, 294, 36:33, 146, 238, 38: 43, 193, 383, 39:133-140, 300, 40: 95; authenticity question, 13:182-184, 278, 15:355, 17:20-37, 166-188, 18:40, 102, 188-190, 19:106, 23:378, 24:257, 28:272, 301, 378, 33:88, 314, 354, 39:342; language, 13:197; source material, 14:437; inscription, 40:58, 59

Kent, Rev. Aratus, 21:18-20, 22

Kent, William, lumberman, 18:176

Kent, William, speaker, 34:222, 224

Kent, Catholic church, 24:94

Kent and Mahoney, lumber firm, 29: 205n

Kenton, G. M., publisher, 28:385

Kentucky, early printing, 15:10-12; geological survey, 25:175; pioneer life, 29:338; government, 34:82

Kentucky Historical Society, 24:367, 34:357

Kenway, Mary M., author, 29:350

Kenwood Armory, Minneapolis, 28:190

Kenwood Monday Club, Minneapolis, 25: 185

Kenyon, Methodist church, 14:354; newspapers, 22:423; history, 34: 127, 35:203

Keokuk, Fox leader, 20:56, 57, 29: 350, 34:41

Keokuk, Iowa, cholera epidemic, 14:

291; river port, 17:377, 431n, 22: 17, 31:247

"Keokuk," steamboat, 38:291

Keokuk & St. Louis Railroad, 30:233

Kercher, Alice C., lawyer, 17:213

Kercher, Leonard C., work reviewed, 22:314

Kerfoot, Samuel F., college president, 21:185, 39:214, 215, 225

Kerker, John, theater director, 34: 240, 241

Kerkhoven, school research project, 12:169-171, 210; churches, 12:170, 211, 15:481; anniversary, 29:359; hunting, 33:154n

Kerkhoven Baptist Church, 15:481

Kerlinger, Callie, 11:94, 205, 448, 12:83, 427

Kerlinger, Mrs. Mary H., reminiscences, 11:94

Kern, Benjamin, artist, 38:201

Kern, Charles, speaker, 27:78

Kern, Edward, artist, 38:201

Kern, Ray G., 22:219

Kern, Richard, artist, 38:201

Kerns, John, Methodist minister, 26: 243

Kerntz, Joseph, 38:29-31

Kerr, Mrs. Alma B., 17:346; speaker, 17:67, 68

Kerr, Chester, author, 36:190

Kerr, Duncan J., speaker, 20:336

Kerr, George, 35:340

Kerr, Jack, author, 34:129, 218

Kerr, James E., author, 15:473

Kerr, Joseph, 13:133

Kerr, Robert F., author, 13:253

Kerr, Robert S., Senator, 40:293

Kerr, Robert Y., review by, 34:256

Kerr, Walter C., engineer, 14:231

Kerst, Joseph A., 30:290

Kerst, Lena, student, 27:99, 103

Kerst, Margaret, student, 27:99

Kessenich, Henrietta W., author, 12: 444

Kessler, ---, 18:149

Kessler, Lillian, work reviewed, 23: 159; author, 22:187, 23:370

Ketchum, Richard M., work reviewed, 36:95

Keto, Helmi S., author, 40:48

Ketten, Sister Philomene, missionary, 18:269, 33:60, 36:24

Kettering, Charles F., industrialist, 39:30

Kettle River (Finland), Carlton County, name, 16:246; Johnson's camp, 21:151, 156; Finnish settlements, 22:392n, 25:318; fur trade, 28: 157n; history, 35:382

Kettle River, Pine County, logging, 18:166

Kettler, Elsa S., 27:49, 148

Kettles, trade goods, 40:200, 205, 206, 209

Keveny, Owen, 36:242

Keweenaw Bay, Mich., Lake Superior, 13:400; described, 23:238

Keweenaw Peninsula, Mich., copper mines, 23:355, 34:10, 35:247

"Key City," steamboat, 28:92, 37: 154

Keye, Elsie, 27:48

Keyes, Charles R., author, 11:326, 16:112; educator, 18:326

Keyes, D. W., 11:146

Keyes, Dency E., 25:343

Keyes, Gen. Erasmus D., 25:36, 137

Keyes, John A., legislator, 35:309

"Keyes," steamboat, 16:292

Keys, Thomas E., "Medical Books of Dr. Charles N. Hewitt," 21:357-371; author, 21:408, 23:167

Keyser, Charles, 28:262

Keyser, E., sculptor, 27:346

KFAM, St. Cloud, radio station, 30: 173, 284

Kiala, Fox leader, 19:288

Kickapoo Indians, 19:274, 36:191

Kickapoo River, Wis., 23:344

Kidd, Kenneth E., works reviewed, 38:87, 40:407; author, 28:70; speaker, 40:149

Kidder, Rev. ---, 13:148

Kidder, Homer R., author, 12:199

Kieffer, Stephen A., work reviewed, 36:150

Kiehle, David H., educator, 35:371

Kiekenapp, Marian R., author, 17:480

Kienitz, John F., author, 26:385

Kiessling, O. E., author, 21:439

Kiester, Norwegian settlement, 23:290; Evangelical church, 29:176

Kiewiet, C. W. de, editor, 34:357

Kihlstrum, Milton B., author, 25:308

Kilbourne, Byron, railroad magnate, 30:138

Kilbride, Thomas B., lawyer, 17:213

Kildahl, John (Johan) N., college president, 13:324, 14:231, 31:51

Kilde, Lois, 27:147

Kilen Hills, Jackson County, road, 23:403

Kiley, Edward C., 15:487

Kilkenny, Catholic church, 11:462

Killam, Edgar L., author, 27:68

Killdeer Mountain, N.D., historic site, 39:33

Killen, John, author, 34:355

Killing Hawk, Sioux leader, 38:149

Killorin, John F., lumberman, 24:375

Kilmer, Joyce, poet, 26:308

Kilmiste family, musicians, 22:115

Kilpatrick, Carroll, author, 37:343

Kilpatrick, Hugh J., cavalry leader, 25:353

Kilpatrick, Gen. Judson H., speaker, 35:227

Kimball, Mrs. Alden S., author, 17: 125

Kimball, C. Margaret, review by, 40: 47; author, 40:412

Kimball, Charles D., biography, 11: 432-434; house, 14:269

Kimball, Mrs. Emily S., papers, 28: 304

Kimball, Moses, excursionist, 15:413, 414

Kimball, Sarah Jane, diaries, 33:92

Kimball, Willis M., author, 13:340

Kimball, history, 19:117

Kimber, Alta, 13:344; "The Coming of the Latter Day Saints," 13:385-394; author, 12:340; speaker, 13: 281, 16:491

Kimber, Ben, speaker, 22:340

Kimber, Martha, 19:416

Kimberly, Arthur E., author, 19:455

Kimberly, Mrs. Mary R., 15:459

Kimberly-Clark Corp., history, 40:47

Kimmerle, Marjorie M., author, 23: 381, 24:74

Kincaid, Robert L., author, 28:279

Kincaid family, genealogy, 21:195

Kinder, Gertrude S., artist, 13:420
Kinder, Judge L. B., 11:218, 315, 15:
245, 17:120, 346, 20:95; speaker,
16:489; author, 18:333
King, ———, English traveler, 28:317
King, A. F., 20:352
King, Arthur W., author, 33:354, 34:
266
King, Gen. Charles, 14:38
King, Charles, speaker, 17:481
King, Charles B., artist, 19:420,
422, 20:174, 29:336, 34:213, 35:88
King, Clarence, surveyor, 28:348
King, Dan M., librarian, 30:410, 34:
220; author, 34:42
King, Daniel S., stage operator, 17:
465
King, David, missionary, 20:123, 124,
25:212
King, Edgar W., author, 25:401
King, Eleanor, 21:59
King, Ernestine, author, 31:121
King, Franklin A., compiler, 35:49
King, Grace, 20:110; author, 14:442
King, Maj. Henry L., paymaster, 25:
124, 245, 344
King, James S., author, 21:185
King, Mrs. James S., author, 15:467
King, John, journalist, 14:447
King, John E., speaker, 12:296
King, Josias R., in Civil War, 25:
119, 228, 39:77, 175; artist, 38:
257n; statue, 40:48
King, Judson, speaker, 34:222
King, Lawrence W., author, 34:314
King, Mackenzie, 35:35
King, Mary B. A., author, 15:115
King, Nancy, author, 24:93
King, Mrs. Otis H., 21:430
King, Rufus, 25:36
King, Ruth, author, 24:93
King, Samuel, landowner, 17:465
King, Samuel A., balloonist, 24:264
King, Shepherd H., 39:237
King, Stafford, poet, 16:81; speaker,
19:316, 26:386
King, William S., 30:371; farmhouse,
15:55; livestock breeder, 19:407,
22:261, 265, 26:117, 121-124; edi-
tor, 32:19; papers, 33:299; poli-
tician, 35:66, 70, 37:319, 329
King, Winifred, author, 24:93
King George's War, 18:392, 19:289
King Midas Mill, Hastings, 18:114
King Philip, Wampanoag leader, 19:330
King William's War, 18:391, 19:281-
283
Kingman, Eugene, author, 34:168, 36:
185
Kingman, Joseph R., author, 27:72
King's Grove, Stearns County, camp
meeting, 31:82
King's Retreat House, Buffalo, 40:100
Kingsbury, Arthur M., author, 33:314
Kingsbury, Felicia D., author, 31:249
Kingsbury, W. W., 14:249
Kingsley, Charles, author, 16:4
Kingsley, Cyrus M., 15:116
Kingsley, Lt. Gerald, 24:374
Kingsley, Ira, pioneer physician, 21:
101
Kingsley, Lydia W., author, 20:446
Kingston, C. S., author, 31:253, 33:
313
Kingston, William H. G., author, 34:
355
Kingston, mill, 11:116; history, 19:

117; in Sioux Outbreak, 20:192,
38:280, 281, 283; Finnish settle-
ment, 20:214
Kingston, Wis., history, 20:79
Kinietz, W. Vernon, 23:134n; work re-
viewed, 29:66
Kinkead, Alexander, founds Alexan-
dria, 30:161, 31:184
Kinkead, Clara J., work reviewed, 31:
184
Kinkead, George, founds Alexandria,
31:184
Kinkead, Mary A., letters, 31:185
Kinkead, William, founds Alexandria,
30:161, 31:184
Kinkead family, genealogy, 31:184
Kinkel, Gottfried, author, 24:222
Kinkeldey, Otto, 16:331
Kinmount, St. Louis County, wild-rice
processing, 33:354
Kinney, J. P., works reviewed, 18:
305, 32:180
Kinney, Rudolphus D., missionary, 11:
220; postmaster, 34:170
Kinnickinnic River, Wis., mills, 16:
229
Kinnugton, Sgt. ———, 28:209
Kinscella, Hazel G., author, 36:190
Kinsey, Ruth, author, 28:375
Kinyon, William R., banker, 22:350
Kinzie, ———, baseball player, 19:174
Kinzie, John H., 15:405; trader, 15:
432, 19:299; Indian agent, 23:
348n; house, 26:385
Kinzie, Mrs. John H., author, 12:94,
14:108, 15:423; house, 26:385
Kiowa Indians, 16:89, 40:47
Kipp, O. L., author, 13:115
Kirby, Miss ———, pioneer teacher, 15:
116
Kirby, Lt. Edmund, 25:125
Kirby reaper, trial, 24:290
Kircher, William H., author, 30:264
Kirchner, Capt. Albert, contractor,
37:283, 285, 290, 295, 297
Kirchner, Edward, contractor, 37:283,
285-287, 289, 292, 294, 295, 297
Kirchner, Mrs. Edward, 37:292, 293,
295
Kirchner, William H., Jr., author,
12:320
Kirk, H. H., speaker, 14:123
Kirk, John, land grants, 16:423-426
Kirk, Loren O., autobiography, 19:365
Kirk, W. H., 40:128
Kirker, John N., 16:137
Kirkland, Edward C., 23:256; author,
24:155
Kirkland, Joseph, 22:157; author, 21:
96, 23:114, 157
Kirkpatrick, George E., editor, 22:88
Kirkpatrick, K. A., speaker, 26:179
Kirkpatrick, William, editor, 26:398
Kirkup, Mrs. C. E., recollections,
13:209
Kirkwood, Edith B., author, 16:130,
28:383, 29:83
Kirkwood, William P., author, 26:307,
28:77, 32:118
Kise, John, 21:447
Kise, Joseph, author, 26:81, 29:352
Kittanning Path, Pa., Indian trail,
15:256
Kittle, Maria, Indian captive, 28:90
Kittleson, Ole, lumberjack, 13:364
Kitto, Reuben, missionary, 16:303

Kittredge, Charles P., pioneer, 23:
102
Kittredge, George L., author, 15:445
Kittson, Rev. Henry, 11:96
Kittson, Norman W., 14:205, 28:80,
30:70, 33:89, 35:252, 37:43, 39:
330, 332; raiload interests, 11:
308, 21:97, 25:187, 28:372, 31:55;
trader, 11:366, 13:224, 241, 278,
14:230, 15:285, 16:73, 19:109,
382, 20:79, 22:4, 148, 156, 278-
280, 289, 27:311, 28:337, 32:250,
35:282, 36:37, 260, 38:5-7, 9, 10,
63; hunter, 16:260; career, 21:99;
steamboat owner, 21:252-257, 32:
60; descendants, 25:78; legislator, 27:166, 33:121n; property,
29:89, 37:43, 39:21, 154; postmaster, 40:84
Kittson, William, diary, 32:250
Kittson County, history, 14:458, 16:
129, 495, 21:415, 22:110; pageant,
16:237; agriculture, 21:212; bonanza farms, 21:451; schools, 24:
323; Swedish collections, 26:364;
wildlife, 30:127, 33:142n
Kittson County Enterprise (Hallock),
historical edition, 15:488; anniversary, 16:495
Kittson County Historical Society,
18:62; organized, 20:46, 96; publication, 22:110; meetings, 23:
297, 27:172
Kittson County War History Committee,
23:391
Kittsondale, St. Paul race track, 37:
43, 39:21
Kiwanis Club, Anoka, 20:215; Wor-
thington, 25:208
Kjellberg, Isidor, journalist, 11:102
Kjorlaug, M. U. S., 16:351
Klacel, Ladimir, freethinker, 13:275
Klaeber, Frederick, 21:70
Klammer, A. A., pioneer, 37:71
Klammer, K. K., archaeologist, 37:71
Klammer, Paul W., "Collecting Log
Cabins," 37:71-77; author, 36:193,
39:132
Klapp, S. D., biography, 19:214
Klaragard, Sever, author, 19:213
Klaveness, Dr. E., author, 14:124,
24:374
Klavestad, Osborne, 27:48
Klaw, Marc, theater agent, 28:104
Klee, Loretta E., author, 29:77
Kleffman, Clarence, 22:218, 341
Klein, Alexander, author, 34:358
Klein, Earl E., review by, 35:289
Klein, Karl M., author, 13:117
Klein, Philip S., author, 38:202
Kleinhuizen, Albert K., 28:125
Klement, Frank, "The Abolition Move-
ment," 32:15-33; reviews by, 31:
243, 33:217, 38:330; work re-
viewed, 37:126; author, 31:256,
32:64, 38:384, 39:260
Klemer, Carl H., pioneer, 22:348
Klemer, Frank H., speaker, 22:107
Klepper, Franz, speaker, 24:219
Kleven, Bernhardt J., "The Mississip-
pi River Logging Company," 27:190-
202; author, 11:321, 12:85, 27:246
Klieforth Canadian-American History
Prize, 25:295
Klima, Stanislav, author, 13:199
Klingaman, O. E., speaker, 19:424n;
author, 19:460, 29:174

Klinsmann, Hermann J., bicycle racer, 33:315
Klock, George, 33:37
Klondike, Yukon Ter., gold mining, 29:300-315, 32:60, 35:199, 39:341
Klondike, Yukon, and Copper River Co., 29:303n
Kloos, John H., railroad official, 37:154, 155, 160
Kloss, Heinz, author, 21:97
Klostermann, Henry, 32:41
Klovstad, J. H., "The Study of Pioneer Life," 11:70-74; author, 11:185, 186
Klune, Frances M., author, 24:376
Knabe and Co., Baltimore, piano makers, 39:318, 323
Knaplund, Paul, review by, 36:98; work reviewed, 39:81; author, 13:206; speaker, 17:110; professor, 39:220
Knapp, Joseph G., author, 18:323
Knapp, Oscar, steamboat captain, 36:212
Knapp, Mrs. W. A. (Synneva), 20:96, 21:109, 22:106
Knapp, Stout and Co., lumber firm, 36:161
Knatvold, Thorvald V., legislator, 35:346
Knauer, Josiah, surveyor, 40:233, 239, 241
Knauss, James O., author, 15:125
Kneale, Orrin C., 18:123n, 142-144
Kneeland, Abner, 28:54
Kneisel String Quartet, 39:63
Knickerbacker, Rev. David B., 12:400, 21:450, 26:94
Kniett, H. F. J., topographer, 21:332
Knife Lake, Kanabec County, 15:176, 37:272
Knife Portage, St. Louis River, 23:246, 247, 249, 251; name, 31:95
Knife River, Lake County, 16:298; history, 22:242, 30:407, 34:177; railroad, 34:181, 183
Knife River, N.D., 40:193
Knight, Augustus F., architect, 37:193, 194, 38:187, 188
Knight, Eleanor, author, 35:152
Knight, Harold V., author, 29:267
Knight, Capt. James, journal reviewed, 13:300
Knight, Joseph, letters, 14:102
Knight, Ralph, author, 38:42
Knights of Columbus, Minnesota, 11:351, 14:230, 320, 30:163, 32:62, 37:62, 38:193
Knights of Labor, 30:254, 36:274, 40:353; Minnesota, 21:315, 384, 389, 392, 394, 22:367-390, 35:58, 36:33, 40:362; political aspect, 32:130, 35:59-61, 298, 327
Knights of Pythias, St. Paul, 14:124
Knights of the Forest, Mankato, 38:354
Knopp, Mary Fitz Gibbon, 18:59, 22:45
Knot, Gerrit, Dutch pioneer, 28:125
Knott, H. W. Howard, author, 11:216, 217
Knott, J. Proctor, speech on Duluth, 34:70-77; speaker, 25:392, 28:78, 279, 32:154, 33:65; Congressman, 32:150n, 34:67-70; bibliography, 34:78
Knotts, Elmer E., pioneer, 24:93
Knowles, C. R., author, 36:103

Knowles, Marjorie, author, 22:334
Knowlton, Evelyn H., work reviewed, 35:286
Knowlton, Hiram, surveyor, 40:387
Knowlton, Joseph E., postmaster, 34:185
Know-Nothing movement, 22:72, 28:26, 31:243; history, 16:88; policies, 21:192, 28:21, 35:291; among Republicans, 28:27, 32:15
Knox, F. W., steamboat captain, 33:12
Knox, G. W., steamboat captain, 33:12
Knox, George, editor, 37:40
Knox, Harold C., speaker, 18:277; author, 30:150, 262
Knox, Mrs. Henry M., 37:107n; singer, 29:119, 33:4, 39:52, 321
Knox, John J., financier, 14:231
Knox, Olive, author, 34:132
Knox, Philander, attorney general, 32:175
Knox, Mrs. T. J., 14:120
Knox College, Galesburg, Ill., collections, 14:337, 19:216; history, 24:113, 114
Knox County, Ill., settled, 24:113
Knudsen, Rev. A., author, 17:239
Knudson, Minnie M. L., author, 18:342
Knuth, Priscilla, review by, 40:143
Knutson, Harold, Congressman, 40:369, 410
Knutson, Helge O., author, 13:453
Knutson, Knute, 11:119
Knutson, Paul, explorer, 17:23-26, 29, 35, 171, 176, 21:304, 33:216, 34:353, 35:294, 36:238, 40:95
Knutson, Thomas, author, 12:211
Kobenas, Jim, Chippewa Indian, 24:320
Koch, Henry C., translator, 35:292
Koch, Karl, 32:102n
Koch, Theodore F., autobiography, 13:427; colonizer, 18:338, 28:130, 131, 35:33, 295, 36:104
Koch, Mrs. Theodore F., author, 18:339
Kodiak Indians, customs, 28:287
Koefod, Paul E., author, 22:224
Koehler, Betsy, author, 35:50
Koehler, Frank O., 33:228
Koehler, Robert, artist, 14:231, 19:365, 22:333
Koempel, Henry J., 20:185
Koeper, H. F., work reviewed, 39:124
Koeplar, Josephine, 28:259
Koepper family, 26:238
Kofron, Frank, typographer, 30:89, 33:19
Kohl, Johann G., 35:335; author, 16:102, 19:216, 35:156, 292, 36:74
Kohlbeck, Andreas, author, 19:219
Kohlepp, Harold, 21:334; author, 22:210
Kohler, Ruth de Y., author, 29:356
Kohlmeyer, Fred W., reviews by, 37:258, 39:163, 40:405
Kohlsaat, H. H., publisher, 26:20
Kohn, Clyde F., author, 36:282
Kohn, Henry G., house, 37:76n
Kohn, Otto, author, 17:118
Kohn, Theodore, author, 17:118
Kohr, Mrs. A. N. (Ida S.), 17:231, 23:100, 27:265; author, 23:100; speaker, 25:406, 28:85
Kohs, S. C., author, 27:352
Kolar, Frank J., 15:40
Kolchak, Adm. Alexander V., 38:324
Kolehmainen, John I., 27:162; "Fin-

nish Temperance Societies," 22:391-403; "The Finnish Pioneers," 25:317-328; reviews by, 27:38-40, 35:333; works reviewed, 29:347, 32:184; author, 22:418, 431, 25:301, 382, 393, 27:49, 55, 142, 30:404; speaker, 25:378, 26:391, 31:121
Kolko, Gabriel, author, 39:298
Koll, Mathias N., papers, 19:48, 98
Koller, Larry, work reviewed, 37:35
Kolliner, S. A., speaker, 23:195
Komensky, McLeod County, Bohemian settlement, 16:488
Komensky Klub, University of Minnesota, 15:39
Kondiaronk, Huron leader, 19:283
Konga, Tyyne E., work reviewed, 35:333
Konga, Vaino, speaker, 18:465
Konig Township, Beltrami County, history, 15:132
Koochiching County, business, 13:118; geology, 15:143; mail service, 16:366; name, 20:343, 30:332; newspapers, 21:451, 29:356; history, 22:415, 23:107, 30:162, 407, 33:315, 35:246; transportation, 24:191; schools, 25:177, 285, 27:50; logging, 27:302; wildlife, 30:132; nursing home, 38:377
Koochiching County Historical Society, 16:240; organized, 15:488, 16:63, 30:80; meetings, 16:124, 17:121, 356, 483, 18:464, 30:166, 277, 34:359
Koochiching County War History Committee, 23:391
Koochiching Falls, see International Falls
Kooistra, Jan, 28:131
Kool, Barent J., 17:88
Koon, Judge Martin B., 33:332, 333, 337
Koon family, genealogy, 20:346
Koop, Mrs. Madge, 22:216
Koos, Leonard V., educator, 35:371
Kopas, Clifford R., author, 17:110
Kopietz, Edmund, typographer, 35:196, 38:43
Kopperud, Eimer, author, 39:130
Kopperud, Linda, author, 39:130
Kops, Mr. and Mrs. Jacob de Bruyn, 37:160
Korean War, 39:208, 263
Koren, Rev. U. V., 18:114
Korista, František, 15:36
Korsrud, A. C., author, 22:221
Kortesmaki, W. J., 34:350
Koshkonong, Wis., Norwegian settlement, 12:270, 28:381
Kossuth, Louis, 28:321
Kostka, Sister Mary, 14:31n, 40
Kots, Jan Willem, 28:128
Kottenkamp, Frans, author, 12:86
Koukkari, Mikki, 32:195
Kountz, William J., steamboat owner, 38:236
Kovář, Frantisek, author, 14:123
Kovarik, J. J., author, 23:388
Kowalski family, 34:182
Kozlak, Chester, artist, 31:204, 33:310, 35:384, 36:152; author, 33:268; cartographer, 34:2, 179, 283n; museum curator, 36:108
Kozlowski, Otto, 19:238

Kraenzel, Carl F., work reviewed, 35: 148
Kragero Township, Chippewa County, Norwegian settlement, 12:275n
Krahn, B. J., 21:438
Kramer, Dale, work reviewed, 35:284; author, 23:197
Kramer, Frank R., work reviewed, 39: 76
Kramer, Rev. Frederick F., 12:106, 18:335; speaker, 17:232, 20:213; author, 23:194
Kramer, Horace, author, 23:123, 157
Kramer, Ida, 24:351; manuscript assistant, 23:367, 24:31, 34, 243, 25:40
Kramer, Reginald, speaker, 29:93
Krans, Olaf, artist, 24:256, 29:278
Krapp, George P., 17:319
Krauch, Elsa, 21:329; author, 22:99
Kraus, H. C., author, 27:365
Kraus, J. A., 16:363
Kraus, Lili, pianist, 39:64
Kraus, Michael, work reviewed, 40: 305; speaker, 29:348; compiler, 37:342
Krause, Herbert, reviews by, 29:73, 247, 31:113, 238, 32:52, 39:293; works reviewed, 20:183, 34:123; author, 20:117, 22:365, 23:122, 157, 28:392, 29:103, 287, 30:272, 31:128, 129, 133, 136, 146, 256, 32:64, 35:242, 378, 36:80
Krause, Lebrecht F. E., 14:50; career, 14:53-55
Kraushaar, R. W., author, 18:327
Krausnick, Gertrude, librarian, 27: 23; author, 12:81, 22:36; speaker, 15:218, 26:367
Krautkremmer, Edward K., editor, 38: 193
Kreage, Beulah P., author, 35:154
Krebs, Albert, author, 33:316
Krehbiel, Henry E., speaker, 39:52
Kreidberg, Irving, 33:19
Kreidberg, Mrs. Irving (Marjorie), work reviewed, 36:189; author, 40: 46
Kreidler, Dr. H. W., 25:250
Kreisler, Fritz, violinist, 39:62
Kremer, E. G., 26:322
Kremer, George F., 26:322
Kremer, Josephine, author, 26:183
Kremmeter, Sister Evangelista, 35: 264, 266, 271
Křenek, Rev. Josef, 15:41
Krengle, Alvin, library page, 25:41
Kreun, Jan, 28:129
Kreuter, Joseph, author, 19:219
Krey, August C., 19:70, 20:50, 23:50, 25:55, 73, 191, 26:45, 151, 27:26, 27, 28:75, 29:53, 97, 98, 30:180, 39:226; "History in the Machine Age," 14:3-29; reviews by, 18:83-86, 19:71-73, 427-430, 25:168-170, 35:145; works reviewed, 19:437, 34:298; author, 12:456, 15:59, 18: 91, 219, 19:91, 444, 25:181, 294, 26:170, 29:164; speaker, 13:327, 14:80, 15:57, 27:145, 146, 29:82, 348, 30:177, 34:115; educator, 32: 6, 10; quoted, 32:37
Krieger, Justina, author, 40:147
Krieghoff, Cornelius, artist, 23:78, 26:286, 36:318, 40:149 (cover)
Kriekaard, Rev. Cornelius, 28:126
Krist, E. D., artist, 11:335

Krit automobile, 38:205 (cover), 206-208, 214
Krit Motor Car Co., Detroit, Mich., 38:207
KROC, Rochester, radio station, 30: 81, 177
Kroeger, Frederick, author, 12:108
Krog, H. P., author, 23:107
Krogstad, Helene, author, 13:212
Krol, Dr. Marie, author, 13:435
Krollpfeifer, A. F., 20:249
Kron, Clemens, pioneer, 24:189
Kron, G. A., author, 19:233
Krout, John A., author, 11:100, 19: 347
Krueger, Edward, 13:286
Krueger, Leonard B., work reviewed, 16:91
Krueger, Lillian, author, 20:86, 203, 339, 27:68, 164, 29:355
Krug, Merton E., work reviewed, 27: 238
Krukemeyer, Ethel, author, 36:107
Krum, Mrs. Alburn H., 12:408, 497
Krum, Gracie B., 13:194; "Chauncey Niles Brainerd," 12:407-409
Krussow, William, author, 20:461
Krutch, Joseph Wood, speaker, 38:91
KSTP, St. Paul, radio station, 16:483
KSTP-TV, St. Paul, 39:172
KTCA-TV, St. Paul, 39:172, 40:364
Ku Klux Klan, educational program, 15:120
Kubelik, Jan, violinist, 39:59
Kučera family, Czech settlers, 15:30
Kuebelbeck, Joseph, 29:277
Kueker, William L., 19:238
Kuehl, John R., editor, 40:95
Kuehl, Warren F., compiler, 40:314
Kuenzli, Mr. and Mrs. Gottlieb, recollections, 16:252
Kugler's Musical Instrument Museum, Roseville, 39:313, 314
Kuhlman, Augustus F., author, 15:229; editor, 20:74, 26:161
Kuhlmann, Charles B., reviews by, 14: 206, 207, 16:82, 91, 33:132; author, 12:89, 16:114, 21:182, 28: 331, 29:9; speaker, 14:213
Kuhm, Herbert W., author, 33:186
Kuipers, F. H., 29:67
Kullberg, H. F., author, 36:103
Kulmala, Antti, 40:391, 399
Kulmala, Hilma M., 40:395
Kulmala, Laurie, 40:394
Kulmala, Otto, see Walta, Otto
Kulmala, Sofia, 40:394
Kummer, Julius, artist, 30:74
Kumro, G. M., author, 17:240
Kún, Rev. František, Czech missionary, 15:32-35
Kundig, Martin, missionary, 23:285
Kuno, Alfred, 20:359
Kunz, Virginia B., author, 30:267, 34:130, 36:152, 194, 40:364
Kunz Oil, Minneapolis, 38:308
Kunze, W. F., speaker, 12:96, 99
Kunzman, Oscar A., 19:470, 20:456
KUOM, Minneapolis, radio station, 28: 75, 184, 286, 30:171, 177
Kurenko, Maria, singer, 39:60
Kurikka, Matti, labor leader, 25:324
Kurtz, Wilbur G., author, 35:153
Kurz, Rudolph Friederich, diary, 19: 104; artist, 19:105, 32:155, 33: 264, 35:242, 40:403; trader, 37: 262

Kuske, Dorothy, author, 14:450
Kutz, George, speaker, 25:210
Kvale, Ole J., Congressman, 29:102, 38:177, 181, 40:367, 368
Kvale, Paul, Congressman, 12:449, 15: 62, 40:410
Kvande, Severt, author, 16:247
Kvernstoen, E. L., 17:238
Kviteseid Lutheran Church, Milan, history, 29:86
Kwiat, Joseph J., work reviewed, 37: 83
Kyner, James H., author, 37:262
Kyyhkynen, Alex, 26:88; speaker, 29: 273

La Balme, Col. Mottin de, 19:296
La Bar, O. C., author, 15:249
Labaree, Leonard W., author, 17:216
La Barre, Sieur de, 19:278, 280
La Bathe, François, trader, 11:384
La Bathe, Joseph, trader, 11:383
Lablanc, see Provençalle, Louis
LaBlanc, Therese, 28:253
Labor, U.S., 11:79, 35:97, 36:274, 37:127, 185, 38:334; Minnesota, 12:446, 13:444, 21:36, 195, 315, 372-394, 22:40, 367-390, 35:194, 40:362; organizations, 13:19, 16: 494, 18:332, 445, 20:432, 25:324, 325; immigrant influence, 13:20, 35:193, 326; of prisoners, 14:453; political aspect, 16:455, 32:130-134, 138, 34:222, 224, 232, 39:97, 101, 40:91; Minneapolis, 18:106, 23:197; strikes, 18:191, 327, 21: 380, 388, 389, 22:368, 377, 379, 23:197, 27:42, 211, 331, 30:383, 35:379, 36:105, 120-122, 326; women and children in, 21:374, 33:42, 39:12; Colorado, 23:264; publications, 23:292; wages, 23:396, 39: 71; war shortage, 24:287, 288; songs, 25:218-223, 28:378; padrone system, 27:211; on railroads, 27: 305; in agriculture, 29:21; in lumber industry, 29:141, 32:252, 36:153-166; maritime, 32:51; on Mississippi, 33:92; at Hormel plant, 34:266; Wisconsin, 36:29; records, 40:258, 409. See also Farmer-Labor party, Workman's Compensation Act, various labor organizations
Labor (St. Paul), newspaper, 38:305
Labor Day, celebrated, 18:332, 22:372
Labor Volunteers for Victory, 23:292
Labrie, Joseph, voyageur, 28:13
La Bruère, Montarville B. de, author, 17:114
Lac Blanc, wildlife, 15:389
Lac Court Oreilles, Wis., Huron village, 15:176, 318, 319, 321; Chippewa reservation, 34:355, 35:235, 244
Lac des Puants, see Lake Winnebago
Lac des Serpents, trading posts, 12: 369
Lac la Biche, see Lake Itasca
Lac la Coquille (Clam Lake), Burnett County, Wis., 28:225, 227
Lac la Croix, border lake, portage, 13:298; pictographs, 15:240, 24: 262, 29:130, 36:102; canoe route,

21:121, 29:132, 134, 32:242, 37:
248, 250, 253
Lac la Folle, Clearwater County,
trading post, 11:369
Lac la Pluie, see Rainy Lake
Lac la Ronge, Ont., trading post, 28:
2
Lac Plat, see Shoal Lake, Man.
Lac qui Parle, Lac qui Parle and
Chippewa counties, mission, 11:94,
183, 216, 316, 12:82, 83, 242,
243, 13:195, 15:129, 136, 222,
275, 16:133-151, 231, 239, 303,
333, 483, 18:94, 20:351, 21:30-32,
158, 170, 274, 412, 23:50, 97,
272, 27:259, 263, 28:180, 334, 30:
281, 38:147n, 154, 39:300; history, 11:102, 14:353, 18:339; trading post, 11:378, 12:231, 236; Indians, 12:241, 18:157, 21:171, 22:
136, 27:154, 32:66, 39:344; archaeology, 21:207, 434, 443, 22:
105, 210, 27:261, 359; school, 22:
430; restorations, 22:436, 445,
23:100, 296, 398, 24:80; post
office, 40:83, 87
Lac qui Parle County, pioneer life,
11:66, 21:222; Norwegian settlements, 12:275n, 14:444; county
seat fight, 12:320, 444; Lutheran
church, 20:360; politics, 21:342;
interest rates, 35:307; history,
36:107; agriculture, 37:207; sod
house, 37:208
Lac qui Parle County Agricultural Society, 22:260, 28:382
Lac qui Parle County Historical Society, 16:243; organized, 29:180,
30:87; meetings, 29:275, 361, 363,
30:80; centennial celebration, 30:
277, 281; museum, 35:381; publication, 39:300
Lac qui Parle County Old Settlers
Association, 16:366, 27:266
Lac qui Parle Indian Mission Centennial Commission, 16:303n, 483
Lac qui Parle River, Lac qui Parle
and Yellow Medicine counties,
floods, 11:68, 69
Lac qui Parle State Park, 12:339, 23:
97, 26:89, 37:60
Lac St. Louis, Que., 40:188
Lac Traverse, see Lake Bemidji
Lac Vieux Desert, Wis., Mich., In-
dians, 29:66
Lacey, A., author, 28:176
Lacey, Mrs. Joy M., author, 27:159
La Chaise, Father François de, Jesu-
it, 19:279
La Chapelle, Mrs. Antoine, 21:27,
160, 277
Lacher, J. H. A., author, 14:111
La Chesnaye, Charles Aubert de, mer-
chant, 22:60
Lachine, Que., fur trade, 28:6
Laclède, Pierre de, founder of St.
Louis, 20:203, 39:337
Lacomb, Stella, student, 27:103
Lacombe, Father Albert, missionary,
11:308, 13:439, 21:264
La Coquille River, Burnett County,
Wis., 28:159
La Corne, chevalier de, 12:364
La Corne, St. Luc de, trader, 32:
236, 238
Lacourcière, Luc, author, 37:345
La Crescent, transportation, 11:402,

37:157n; history, 15:466, 17:486;
apple culture, 20:301; river port,
36:3, 37:4
La Croix, Carry, 11:281
La Croix, Edmund N., millwright, 11:
276, 277, 279, 281, 12:80, 19:227,
26:361
La Croix, Joseph, millwright, 11:276,
281
La Croix, Nicholas, millwright, 11:
276, 281
La Croix, Mrs. Nicholas, 11:276
Lacroix, Paul, trader, 32:229-237
La Croix, Mich., mission, 15:110
La Crosse, Wis., mail service, 11:
407, 37:223; railroad, 12:63, 37:
157; river port, 12:162, 15:411,
17:296, 24:331, 29:126, 30:199,
31:247, 36:256-258, 37:53, 87,
154, 160, 38:293, 40:273, 275;
schools, 15:237; industries, 16:
347; immigrant home, 19:123, 28:
292; history, 20:340, 23:384, 27:
69, 32:253; ferry, 21:211; pioneer
life, 22:98, 24:177, 26:307; architecture, 22:99; bridge, 23:290,
24:177; Dutch settlement, 27:135;
described, 33:116; power company,
35:381, 36:99; Mormon mission, 36:
291-293
Lacrosse, Indian ball game, 13:410,
411, 24:19n, 32:71, 235, 33:116,
35:151
La Crosse and La Crescent Bank, Hokah, 37:87, 40:110, 114, 116, 118
La Crosse and Milwaukee Railroad, 34:
100n, 36:256, 37:154
La Crosse and Minnesota Steam Packet
Co., 36:258, 37:185
La Crosse County, Wis., history, 18:
97, 35:296; Dutch settlement, 28:
379
La Crosse County (Wis.) Historical
Society, 21:193, 30:76; publica-
tions, 20:340, 22:98, 24:176, 32:
254; history, 29:273
La Crosse Lumber Co., 36:155
La Crosse Medical School, 15:237, 20:
340
La Crosse Plow Co., 20:340
La Crosse Tribune, influence, 40:322
Lacy, Dan, author, 24:70
Lacy, Mary G., compiler, 16:235
Lacy House, Austin, 16:368
Lacy House, Fredericksburg, Va.,
Union headquarters, 25:345-347;
prayer meetings, 25:349, 351, 353,
354
Ladd, Edward F., 40:140
Ladd, George T., author, 21:368
Ladd, Sumner, politician, 36:60
Ladies Christian Union of the City of
St. Paul, 38:75
Ladies College, Davenport, Iowa, 16:
276n
Ladies' Floral Club, Austin, 12:452,
26:183
Ladies Musicale, see Schubert Club
Ladies Relief Association of the City
of St. Paul, history, 38:76-79
La Durantaye, Olivier M. de, 19:282
"Lady Elgin," steamboat, 21:156
"Lady Ellen," steamboat, 21:259n,
263, 266
"Lady Franklin," steamboat, 15:409,
417, 25:112, 33:198n, 34:135
"Lady Hamilton," steamboat, 34:15

La Fantaisie, ---, explorer, 32:230,
231
La Farge, Christopher G., 14:38
LaFarge, John, author, 13:443
La Farge, Oliver, work reviewed, 35:
287; author, 20:116, 35:244
Lafayette, Marquis de, 15:358, 18:396
Lafayette, Clay County, river port,
21:248
Lafayette, Ind., W. W. Mayo's practice, 20:442
"Lafayette," steamboat, 35:278, 279,
36:282
Lafayette Bay, Lake Minnetonka, 36:71
Lafayette Hotel, Minnetonka Beach,
33:63, 34:173, 35:73, 36:71, 327;
pictured, 33:62
Lafayette Park, St. Paul, 12:458
Lafferty, James, steamboat captain,
13:231
La Fittau, Joseph François, author,
34:301
La Follette, Philip F., politician,
36:29, 187
La Follette, Robert M., 15:338, 35:
291; reformer, 14:201, 21:68, 326,
22:79, 23:263, 285, 27:133, 30:
248, 380, 33:41, 34:189, 36:98,
187, 37:39, 39:96, 40:140, 147;
Senator, 18:314, 40:322; career,
21:306, 35:203, 236, 241; papers,
21:416, 36:29; autobiography, 37:
185
La Follette, Robert M., Jr., 36:187
La Forest, G. V., author, 39:128
Lafot, Edward, author, 26:259, 393,
27:154; speaker, 28:387
La Fountaine, Capt. Lloyd L., author,
27:57
Laframboise, Joseph, the elder, trader, 11:175, 178, 377, 378, 380,
13:224, 14:84, 459, 19:468, 20:78,
22:137, 25:182, 30:30, 31:198;
guide, 19:192
Laframboise, Mrs. Joseph (Julia), 11:
448, 20:193; trader, 12:440, 19:
305
La France, Baptiste, raft pilot, 21:
99
La Galissoniere, Marquis de, 22:63,
64; trader, 18:276
Lager, Martin P., legislator, 12:430
Lagerstedt, John, author, 35:336
Lagerstrom, J. G., educator, 33:309
Lagimonière, Jean B., 21:399
Lagimonière family, 35:282
La Grange, Mo., river town, 17:431n
La Harpe, Bernard de, explorer, 14:
215
Lahontan, Baron de, 13:439, 23:137n;
author, 11:447, 12:26, 14:367,
370, 15:234, 19:271, 20:67, 22:39,
23:185, 29:99, 30:90, 291, 36:100,
39:199; explorer, 11:451, 12:76,
16:453, 18:46, 318, 20:439, 23:
239n, 32:215, 33:88, 187, 36:277,
279; in Minnesota, 14:220-222,
367-377, 432; map maker, 14:373;
career, 34:216
Lahr, Nicholas, 26:238
Lahti, Matthew, author, 30:164, 404
Lahti, Peter, Finnish pioneer, 25:318
Laidlaw, William, trader, 22:285
Laidlow, ---, artist, 17:142
Laidlow, ---, trader, 17:304
Laing, George, author, 22:332
Laingen, T. P., editor, 12:108

Laird, Mrs. Blanche, 24:107n
Laird, Charlton, author, 34:219
Laird, John C., travel letters, 12:
158-168, 190, 31:109; career, 12:
157, 427
Laird, Matthew J., author, 12:157,
158
Laird, Robert H., 16:334
Laird, Scott, speaker, 40:327
Laird, William H., 12:157; career,
39:131
Laird family, in lumber industry, 12:
157, 30:242; papers, 12:158n
Laird Norton Co., lumber firm, 31:
109, 34:315, 36:142
Laivell, P. H., 24:107n
Laivell, Mrs. P. H., 13:448; author,
12:337, 13:215
La Jémeraye, Christophe D., 35:140;
trader, 11:361, 39:301; career,
12:326, 13:439; explorer, 12:363,
364, 369, 18:235-237, 25:96, 38:
26; death, 17:476, 18:239
La Jeunesse, ---, French soldier, 13:
203
La Jonquière, Marquis de, governor of
Canada, 32:227, 229
Lake, Sir Bibye, 36:273
Lake, Debs T., 24:96n
Lake, Mrs. E. C., 14:236, 16:240
Lake, James A., author, 38:240
Lake Abigail (Augusta Lake), Dakota
County, 35:24
Lake Abigail (Diamond Lake or Mother
Lake), Hennepin County, 35:24; on
map, 35:26
Lake Addie, McLeod County, garrison,
38:281
Lake Agassiz, Canada and U.S., gla-
cial lake, 24:321, 32:221; geolo-
gy, 12:150, 39:171; marker, 14:
350; archaeology, 16:3, 12-14, 37:
87, 135, 38:157-165, 204; maps,
38:159
Lake Amelia, see Lake Nokomis
Lake Athabasca, Alta., Sask., fur
trade, 11:361, 13:181, 16:106, 20:
70, 35:141, 240, 251, 258, 40:163,
170, 173, 174, 178; pass, 17:476
Lake Auburn, Carver County, antique
boat discovery, 14:349
Lake Belt Township, Martin County,
history, 22:441, 35:156
Lake Bemidji, Beltrami County, trading post, 11:369, 23:24, 24:230;
name, 23:27; steamboating, 23:31,
28:189; fishing, 23:330; logging,
29:138, 140, 146
Lake Benton, baseball teams, 15:489;
Congregational church, 19:49, 97
Lake Benton Times, 19:236
Lake Bronson State Park, Kittson
County, log cabin, 27:172; pageant, 30:281, 404
Lake Calhoun, Minneapolis, mission,
11:216, 15:242, 274, 16:135, 21:
23, 24, 27, 167, 35:29, 38:147;
Sioux village, 12:98, 443, 15:280,
18:157, 21:167n, 24:20n, 35:24,
28; pictured, 13:413, 15:469, 30:
117, 39:253, 271, 40:34; trails,
21:227, 29:87; settled, 29:242,
33:251; streetcar service, 35:284,
36:150
Lake Carribeau, Sask., Man., 40:173,
174

Lake Champlain, N.Y., Vt., explored,
18:386; boundary, 23:203, 204
Lake City, schools, 11:224, 16:318,
21:330, 33:22; history, 11:339,
17:366, 33:154n; stage line, 11:
402, 406; county seat fight, 13:
215, 16:372, 36:74n; Methodist
church, 13:454; business, 15:372,
16:362, 17:241, 28:285; hotel, 16:
257; telephone company, 18:344;
baseball club, 19:168, 170, 178,
180; physicians, 21:114; fire department, 21:342; unions, 21:380;
museum, 26:176-178; river port,
33:198, 34:25n
Lake City Bank and Trust Co., history, 15:372
Lake Como, St. Paul, sports, 29:89;
water level, 40:224, 229
Lake County, population, 11:414; history, 12:283, 17:359, 23:187, 27:
75, 30:407, 34:177, 178, 37:347;
boundary, 15:370; roads, 16:298;
politics, 16:488, 17:102, 123;
Finnish settlement, 25:323; trade
routes, 26:284; land grants, 37:
96, 97, 99
Lake County Historical Society, 12:
186, 13:442, 16:101, 240, 18:462,
19:452, 20:454, 23:396, 26:174,
27:75; organized, 11:13; meetings,
11:15, 115, 460, 14:346, 455, 15:
492, 16:488, 17:482, 22:442, 23:
101, 24:86, 27:266, 34:314; museum, 11:16, 26:90, 284; members,
11:19; finances, 11:20, 26:176;
collections, 36:193
Lake County War History Committee,
23:391, 24:268
Lake County, Ind., history, 18:196
Lake Crystal, cheese factory, 27:
112n; farmers' club, 30:161
Lake Duluth, glacial lake, 16:3
Lake Eliza, Hennepin County, 35:23n
Lake Elmo, Lutheran church, 12:211,
18:443, 19:49; resort, 36:92
Lake Elysian, Waseca County, Winneba-
go camp, 38:362
Lake Elysian Stock Farm, Janesville,
26:121
Lake Erie, names, 12:349; history,
26:76; car ferries, 38:237; de-
scribed, 40:271. See also Great
Lakes
Lake Franklin, Otter Tail County,
fishing, 33:255
Lake Fremont Township, Martin County,
history, 16:367, 491, 35:156
Lake Frontenac, see Lake Ontario
Lake George, Austl., levels, 17:303
Lake George, N.Y., Eggleston library,
26:242
Lake George, Stearns County, grasshopper subsidy, 36:61
Lake Hanska Township, Brown County,
Norwegian settlement, 12:273, 20:
459; in Sioux Outbreak, 14:455,
38:283; history, 21:111; Lutheran
church, 26:94. See also Hanska
Lake Harriet, Minneapolis, pictured,
13:413, 33:123, 124n; mission, 15:
275, 280, 17:224, 236, 20:123,
126, 443, 21:27, 28, 31, 73, 160,
166n, 168, 35:29; historical meeting, 15:315; summer resort, 16:33;
trails, 21:227, 29:87; settled,
29:242; described, 32:98; pavil-

ion, 33:325; on map, 35:23, 26,
28; Sioux village, 35:24; streetcar service, 35:284, 36:150; concerts, 39:271
Lake Hendricks, Lincoln County, Norwegian settlement, 13:340
Lake Henry, grasshopper subsidy, 36:
61
Lake Hiawatha, Minneapolis, name, 27:
288n
Lake House, Stillwater hotel, 35:363,
364
Lake Huron, fur trade, 11:259; discovered, 12:282, 347; names, 12:
349, 350; islands, 17:81, 18:184n,
23:143; explored, 19:272, 23:137-
144, 27:216, 31:93; history, 23:
143, 355, 25:272-274; rafting, 31:
62. See also Great Lakes
Lake Irving, Beltrami County, store,
23:24; logging, 29:138-140, 146
Lake Itasca, Clearwater County, discovered, 12:77, 217, 225, 13:191,
277, 287, 14:60, 16:118, 193, 17:
224, 18:180, 21:93, 22:274, 23:
130n, 30:269, 281, 31:96, 36:184,
37:62; legend, 12:215-225, 18:280;
name, 12:225-229, 13:69, 163-174,
286, 15:101, 18:180-185, 282, 23:
234n, 26:250, 36:73; pictured, 19:
421, 33:45 (cover); explored, 25:
401, 27:350; archaeology, 26:321;
wildlife, 30:129; historic site,
37:308
Lake Johanna, Ramsey County, Norwegian settlement, 18:472; name, 29:
89
Lake Josephine, Ramsey County, name,
29:89
Lake Julia, Beltrami County, discovered, 15:101, 132, 29:168, 351;
monument, 29:279
Lake Kasota, Kandiyohi County, 33:
149n; pictured, 33:247; townsite,
40:67
Lake Koronis, Stearns and Meeker
counties, hunting, 16:189, 33:142;
steamboating, 26:398; student
camp, 31:63
Lake Koronis Assembly Grounds, 23:388
Lake Leavenworth, Hennepin County,
name, 35:23n, 24
Lake Lillian, history, 39:212; name,
40:66
Lake Lucy, Hennepin County, 35:23n
Lake Manitoba, Man., trading post,
18:390; steamboating, 21:261; located, 29:259
Lake Michigan, fur trade, 11:259;
discovered, 12:282, 348; names,
12:349, 15:163; history, 23:355,
25:368-370; steamboating, 26:266;
car ferries, 34:14, 38:237; missions, 34:174, 36:32. See also
Great Lakes
Lake Minnetaga, Kandiyohi County,
pictured, 33:247
Lake Minnetonka, Hennepin County,
history, 11:95, 14:352, 27:176,
29:289-299, 32:55, 34:128, 351,
36:25, 327; settled, 11:171n, 20:
140, 22:172, 27:293-296; steamboating, 11:206, 12:333, 13:60,
14:351, 26:272, 27:176, 361, 29:
292, 33:63, 34:128, 170, 36:151;
summer resort, 11:340, 22:222, 36:
92; transportation, 15:367, 29:

292, 30:236, 33:65, 36:150, 204; pictured, 15:469, 28:392, 33:247, 250; proposed university site, 16: 182; G.A.R. encampment, 16:441; levels, 17:304; maple-sugar camp, 19:135-138; yachting, 19:365; described, 19:408, 28:377, 29:100, 30:117, 31:92, 33:63; roads, 21: 234; name, 22:173; mounds, 25:336; legends, 27:357; archaeology, 28: 374; historical meetings, 28:386, 390-392; map, 29:291; Lutheran churches, 29:294-296; explored, 30:113; fishing, 30:118, 120, 33: 251; orchards, 31:162; YWCA camp, 34:130; utilities, 35:337, 381

Lake Minnewaska (Lake Whipple), Pope County, described, 19:125; mounds, 25:336-338; pictured, 26:391, 40: 123

Lake Nipigon, Ont., fur trade, 11: 262, 18:234; legends, 40:358

Lake Nokomis (Lake Amelia), Hennepin County, name, 27:288n, 35:24; army camp, 29:318n

Lake of the Isles, Minneapolis, pictured, 33:123, 124n

Lake of the Woods, border lake, fur trade, 11:362, 363, 12:82, 13:98, 17:445, 18:276, 390, 19:78, 22: 276, 279, 289, 35:282; boundary, 12:443, 13:296-298, 15:239, 18: 231, 272, 277, 20:441, 22:179, 23: 60, 208, 24:176, 341, 25:182, 26: 385, 28:375, 36:242; name, 15:357; history, 15:477, 18:232, 20:440, 31:183; resorts, 16:366; massacre, 17:224, 473, 18:279, 28:77, 375, 31:52, 32:233, 34:130, 37:37, 39: 302; described, 18:216; maps, 18: 231, 34:2, 35:275; discovered, 18: 272n, 24:279, 281; historical meeting, 18:270; steamboating, 18. 279, 24:278, 25:316, 33:71; levels, 19:223; lumbering, 20:341; water route, 21:245, 433, 22:274, 24:276, 277, 345, 26:228, 33:187, 40:313; fishing, 25:316, 27:272, 35:272-277; explored, 33:89, 36: 295, 296, 37:31; geology, 38:158. See also Fort St. Charles, Northwest Angle

Lake of the Woods County, history, 23:108, 28:84; dairying, 23:197

Lake of the Woods County Historical Society, 30:80

Lake Onamia, Mille Lacs County, name, 21:347, 348; archaeology, 25:330

Lake Ontario, discovered, 12:282, 348; names, 12:349; car ferries, 38:237. See also Great Lakes

Lake Osakis, Douglas and Todd counties, settlement, 30:161; pictured, 33:247; resorts, 35:336

Lake Owassa (Hazeltine Lake), Carver County, name, 20:143n

Lake Owasso, Ramsey County, 38:242

Lake Park, Norwegian settlement, 12: 277; Indian scare, 15:244; school, 21:219; Lutheran church, 22:343

Lake Pelican, glacial lake, Otter Tail County, "Minnesota Man" discovered, 14:222, 451

Lake Onondaga, N.Y., French fort, 16: 404

Lake Pepin, Mississippi River, travel on, 11:141-144, 15:307, 413, 17:

155, 290-292, 20:384, 21:403, 25: 112, 299, 27:7, 28:314, 33:194, 198, 34:25, 35:104; trading posts, 11:382, 383, 13:433; reservation, 15:344; pictured, 15:469, 33:248, 36:73, 93; earthworks, 16:152-155; name, 16:476, 35:99; described, 20:390, 22:28, 23:342, 343, 27: 284n, 29:221, 30:141, 159, 31:151, 34:26, 138, 35:245; missions, 21: 102, 33:90; road, 21:231; steamboat race, 27:8; ethnic settlements, 27:135; legend, 27:357, 34: 137, see also Maiden Rock; rafting, 29:266; button industry, 35: 46; hotel, 36:93; steamboat wreck, 36:253, 255

Lake Pepin Valley Historical Society, 16:240, 20:305; organized, 15:371, 16:63, 256; meetings, 16:125, 244, 362, 489, 17:124, 18:111, 19:116, 20:99, 212, 353, 21:216, 342, 22: 106, 217, 23:104, 25:208; museum, 21:108, 336, 23:297, 26:176-178, 254, 27:29-32, 141; reorganized, 29:94

Lake Pepin Valley Old Settlers' Association, history, 16:256

Lake Phalen, Ramsey County, water source, 16:370, 40:224, 226-229

Lake Prairie Township (Scandia Grove), Nicollet County, Norwegian settlement, 12:275; Lutheran church, 14:356; mission school, 18:375

Lake Puzah, Martin County, ghost town, 22:441

Lake Rush Nutt, on Nicollet map, name, 25:77

Lake Sagaigan, see Basswood Lake

Lake St. Clair, Mich., Ont., crossed by Cass expedition, 23:136

Lake St. Croix, St. Croix River, bateau racing, 17:367; early trails, 21:227; lumbering, 24:199, 203, 206; portage, 28:149, 232; resort, 36:92; steamboating, 36:212. See also Point Douglas, Stillwater

Lake Shetek, Murray County, massacre, 13:100, 18:461, 22:89, 30:16, 38: 242; military trail, 30:276; marker, 37:59, 38:154; grasshopper plague, 37:205

Lake Sibley, Cass and Crow Wing counties, name, 21:349

Lake Side Hotel, Frontenac, 36:93

Lake Snelling (Cedar Lake), Hennepin County, 30:117, 35:24, 27

Lake Stewart, name, 21:349

Lake Superior, travel on, 11:258, 15: 160, 472, 28:6, 29:133, 32:59, 34: 357, 40:273-275, 316, 359; harbors, 12:190, 36:177; shipping, 12:200, 14:233, 15:92, 16:479, 25: 78, 34:216; maps, 12:348, 353, 355, 17:357; explored, 12:350-358, 372, 13:257, 17:345, 19:37-39, 216, 22:233-244, 27:216-218, 35: 156, 37:183; fur trade, 12:352-357, 15:160, 21:135, 28:1, 10, 29: 351, 31:93; portage routes, 12: 362; boundary, 13:296-298, 24:341, 36:242; fishing, 14:384, 20:72, 24:79, 25:401, 28:349, 33:66, 34: 221 (cover), 243-249, 265; geology, 15:142-144, 26:224, 225, 231; lumbering, 15:203, 21:211; road

connections, 16:286, 293, 294, 21:234, 37:104, 40:274; climate, 18:155; wildlife, 18:451; copper mines, 20:78, 26:260, 35:247; pictured, 21:84, 149-157, 25:54, 37:79, 308; folklore, 21:353-356, 23:379, 36:74, 75; history, 21: 401, 25:368-370, 34:311; length, 22:245; arches, 23:235, 236; missions, 23:366, 34:174, 36:32; cooperatives, 24:174; described, 25: 53, 34:132; iron mining, 25:196, 27:160, 204, 205; picture rocks, 29:131; discovered, 31:54, 37:86; caves, 32:88; lighthouse, 33:355; resort, 36:92; railroads, 36:179, 37:89, 90, 93, 156; islands, 37: 116n; shipwrecks, 37:186, 345. See also Great Lakes, North Shore

Lake Superior and Mississippi Railroad, encourages immigration, 12: 255, 13:29-31, 35, 37, 41; built, 17:98, 19:113, 35:338, 37:160n, 40:243, 247; financing, 17:218, 34:68, 37:113n, 119; land grant, 18:172, 34:67, 37:89-100; route, 19:406, 37:95, 104, 156; depots, 35:249 (cover), 37:96, 101; Donnelly holdings, 36:179; mail service, 36:214; excursions, 37:102-118

Lake Superior Copper Co., 32:86n

Lake Superior Iron Co., 14:462

Lake Superior Land District, geological survey, 26:224

Lake Tetonka, Le Sueur County, resort hotel, 33:323, 324

Lake Traverse, Traverse County, trading posts, 11:379, 12:116, 127, 128, 236, 237, 428, 15:473, 22: 282-286, 27:67; Indian school, 16: 146; levels, 17:302-310; wildlife, 17:303, 442n, 23:168, 30:126; boundary, 19:424, 425; engineering project, 20:448; Sisseton village, 22:136, 35:168; mounds, 25:339, 37:347; watershed, 32:161

Lake Traverse Reservation, white settlement, 24:207, 208, 261

Lake Vadnais, Ramsey County, fishing, 40:34; acreage, 40:226n

Lake Vermilion, see Vermilion Lake

Lake Washington, Nicollet County, settled, 33:318

Lake Wilson, history, 16:130, 18:471

Lake Wilson Literary Society, 16:130

Lake Winnebago, Wis., Indian villages, 23:346, 27:69

Lake Winnibigoshish, Itasca and Cass counties, trading post, 11:258, 370, 20:72; mission, 20:80; name, 20:343, 30:332; fishing, 23:330; explored, 26:230; logging, 33:14

Lake Winnipeg, Man., fur trade, 12: 82, 18:390, 28:1, 2, 40:174; canoe route, 16:416, 417, 29:133, 36: 295, 296, 37:31; Icelandic settlement, 17:344; steamboating, 21: 247, 261; described, 33:186; mooring stone, 35:294

Lake Winnipegosis, Man., steamboating, 21:261

Lakehead Pipeline Co., Superior, Wis., 40:245

Lakeland, history, 16:132, 27:154; farming, 17:393; river port, 19: 319; post office, 36:211; archi-

tecture, 38:344, 345, 347; Baptist church, 38:348
Lakeland Creameries, 35:334
Lakeland Township, Washington County, German settlement, 23:404
Lakers, basketball team, 36:93
Lakeside Hotel, see Frontenac Inn
Lakeside Press, see Donnelley, R. R., and Sons
Laketown Township, Carver County, Grimm farm, 19:21
Lakeview, St. Louis County, post office, 34:186
Lakeville, economic conditions, 15:112, 39:250; Junior Historians, 27:49, 144, 147, 28:161, 163
Lakewood, St. Louis County, post office, 34:186
Lalemant, Father Jerome, 15:171; author, 13:250, 253, 254, 264, 395, 15:161, 162, 324, 16:199; missionary, 18:386
Lamar, Howard R., work reviewed, 35:238
Lamar, Lucius Q. C., 18:125
La Mar (Lamare), Seraphim, trader, 21:147
Lamare-Picquot, F. V., naturalist, 28:180
Lamarque, Sieur de, 13:209
"Lamartine," steamboat, 37:310, 311
Lamb, Chauncy, lumberman, 27:198
Lamb, Mrs. Elton, speaker, 16:362; author, 21:342
Lamb, John, 21:392; labor commissioner, 21:381, 22:388
Lamb, P., author, 26:155
Lamb, R. E., work reviewed, 36:64
Lamb, Thomas, pork dealer, 26:114
Lamb, W. Kaye, author, 19:462, 24:43, 26:55, 27:37, 36:280; speaker, 40:149
Lambert, ---, St. Paul physician, 14:297
Lambert, David, letter, 36:261, 40:86
Lambert, George C., memorial, 15:467
Lambert, Ira M., 24:106n
Lambert Lake, Ramsey County, acreage, 40:226n
Lambert Township, Red Lake County, history, 38:204
Lamberton, Gretchen L., author, 38:244
Lamberton, Henry W., 39:90; banker, 36:144
Lamberton, Lutheran church, 15:481
Lambie, Morris B., review by, 17:201-204; author, 17:206
Lamborn, Robert H., railroad official, 37:97, 102
Lamborn Hotel, Bismarck, N.D., 33:56, 58
La Mer Douce, see Lake Huron
La Mer d'Ouest, trading area, 11:233, 261, 262, 19:290
Lameth, Alexander, 18:396
Lameth, Charles, 18:396
L'Amirant, Louis, voyageur, 16:161
Lammers, Albert J., logging contractor, 29:145; house, 38:337, 350-352
Lammers, Claude C., author, 14:438, 15:134
Lammers, George A., logging contractor, 29:145
Lammers Township, Beltrami County, name, 29:145

Lammon, L. D., author, 22:345
Lamon, Ward H., author, 27:335, 28:361
LaMont, J. B., career, 27:168
Lamoose, Charles, settler, 35:31
LaMothe, Rev. Arthur, speaker, 22:439
Lampard, Eric E., work reviewed, 39:31
Lampe, Arthur, 25:158; speaker, 13:454
Lampe, Father Simon, missionary, 18:331, 23:402, 33:60
Lampert, Leonard, Jr., MHS president 36:108, 240
Lamphere, George N., 15:134
Lampman, Clinton Parks, author, 21:103; speaker, 22:447
Lampman, H. S., speaker, 16:302
Lampson, C. M., and Co., London, Eng., 40:211n, 216, 218
Lampson, Sir Curtis M., fur trade official, 34:103n
Lamson, Chauncey, slays Little Crow, 38:150-153
Lamson, Frank B., author, 16:499, 17:130, 242, 18:345, 19:470, 20:463, 24:383, 384; editor, 19:117
Lamson, John B., 30:393
Lamson, Nathan, slays Little Crow, 38:150-153
Lanahan, Frances Fitzgerald, editor, 37:184
Lancaster, history, 34:170
Lancaster, Wis., early printing, 15:16
Lanctot, Gustave, work reviewed, 38:328; author, 16:480; editor, 23:185, 24:179
Land claim associations, 28:331; procedures, 11:161, 162, 14:137, 235
Land O' Lakes Creameries, Inc., marketing co-operative, 11:290, 17:348; history, 15:482, 24:174, 27:168, 366, 29:158
Land offices, see Public lands, United States land office
Land speculation, U.S., 14:197-200; Minnesota, 39:85-92, 211; Nebraska, 39:261
Land warrants, in frontier economy, 29:225-229
Landberg, L. L., 23:390; speaker, 24:188
Lander, Gen. Frederick W., 25:29
Landers, Col. J. C., 11:457
Landes, Ruth, author, 19:457
Landis, Paul H., work reviewed, 19:334; author, 16:486
Landis, R. E., reminiscences, 21:451
Landmann, ---, German immigrant, 12:126
Landon, Alfred M., pictured, 40:373
Landon, Fred, 12:427, 19:445; works reviewed, 23:357, 25:272-274; editor, 14:115; author, 25:178, 26:266, 28:366, 30:261; speaker, 26:178
Landon, R. H., author, 20:334, 21:424, 26:275; speaker, 21:335
Landquist, John, translator, 37:266
Lands, see Public lands, United States land office
Land's End, Hennepin County, trading post, 11:124, 376, 13:224
Landsverk, O. G., author, 38:43
Landy, J. R., 21:218; journalist, 23:403, 33:48

Lane, A. P., 16:492
Lane, D. H., 16:492
Lane, Eugene E., 20:215
Lane, Franklin K., 39:241, 242, 251
Lane, James H., in Civil War, 19:387, 34:305
Lane, Joseph, Senator, 35:94
Lane, Rose Wilder, author, 23:122, 157; editor, 38:198
Lanesboro, banks, 15:112; roadside park, 20:303; band, 40:324
Lanesburg Township, Le Sueur County, Lutheran church, 12:451
Lang, Mrs. Anton, 20:82
Lang, Earl, 12:223n, 13:289; speaker, 13:286
Lang, Frank S., author, 35:246
Langbein, Walter B., work reviewed, 34:306
Langdon, Robert B., contractor, 26:371, 35:70
Langdon, William C., work reviewed, 23:60
Langdon Butter and Cheese Factory Co., Cottage Grove, organized, 17:311, 27:113; methods, 27:114
Lange, Dietrich, 27:351; author, 13:108, 36:75n; papers, 24:356
Lange, Lauritz M., papers, 14:101
Langeland, Knud, historian, 22:68
Langen, William J., 13:450, 16:249
Langevin, ---, voyageur, 28:13
Langevin, Edward, hotel owner, 14:300
Langford, George, 22:193
Langford, Mrs. George (Chloe Sweeting), 33:6
Langford, Nathaniel P., I, 36:279, 319; papers, 12:85, 20:432, 22:40, 23:40; interest in Yellowstone area, 14:225, 230, 20:346, 23:383, 33:4, 37:134; career, 20:323; MHS president, 21:35; explorer, 23:282, 36:279, 38:58, 226, 39:262, 40:262
Langford, Mrs. Nathaniel P., I (Clara), 33:4
Langford, Nathaniel P., II, 15:217, 16:60, 17:70, 20:50, 21:409, 22:45, 23:35
Langford, Nathaniel P., III, 22:193, 26:31
Langford family, genealogy, 22:193
Langham, Elias T., Indian agent, 14:423; postmaster, 40:82
Langhei Township, Pope County, school, 30:401
Langlade, Charles de, trader, 17:196, 32:233; in Revolutionary War, 20:8
Langland, Carl G., author, 34:128
Langland, Harold S., author, 34:265
Langmack, George A., speaker, 20:47
Langola, Benton County, history, 11:96, 220
Langrishe Comedy Co., theatrical troupe, 28:110
Langsam, Miriam Z., work reviewed, 39:125
Langton, H. H., 19:104; author, 25:200
Langum, Capt. Otto, 18:148
Lanier, James, house, 29:72
Lankford, John, author, 39:171
Lankford, William C., Congressman, 40:297
Lanman, C. T., author, 14:358
Lanman, Charles, author, 12:219, 222,

19:217, 20:50, 391, 22:154, 155n, 40:141; artist, 32:88, 34:121

Lannestock, Gustaf, translator, 32:250, 34:163

L'Anniau, Pierre, trader, 12:368, 369

La Noue, Zacharie R. de, explorer, 12:361

Lanpher, R. A., and Co., St. Paul, 33:2

Lanphier, Charles H., editor, 37:127

Lansdale, Dr. Richard H., 35:31

L'Anse, Mich., mission, 15:122

Lansing, Abraham, 12:76

Lansing, Robert, 17:165, 38:314, 316

Lansing, Iowa, mail station, 40:87

Lantsheere, Viscount de, 11:343n, 12:97

Lantz, Charles E., editor, 22:447

La Perrière, Sieur de, explorer, 13:439, 16:453, 18:233

Lapham, Frances, speaker, 29:274

Lapham, Increase A., 19:124, 24:246; career, 21:429, 26:170

La Pierre, Dr. J. W. B., 19:235

LaPlant, Mrs. W. H., 20:210

La Plant Co., millers, 11:280

La Pointe, Pierre, interpreter, 21:27n

La Pointe, Wis., trading post, 11:385, 12:356, 357, 380, 19:41, 32:186, 226, 227, 229, 231, 233, 236, 238n, 35:154; Indian agency, 12:190, 16:215, 24:165, 32:88, 89; mission, 13:187, 195, 437, 15:122, 16:214, 17:96, 464, 18:47, 19:457, 21:73, 22:354, 33:185, 39:303, 308; Indian payments, 16:216, 24:17-21; surveyed, 19:37-39; described, 19:96; pioneer life, 19:357; census, 20:452; treaty, 34:177, 39:309; history, 37:216

Laporte, history, 16:494

Lappala, Risto, pioneer pastor, 25:324

Lappala, Mrs. Risto (Milma), pioneer pastor, 25:324

Laprairie, ---, trader, 28:155, 225, 227, 229, 232

Laprairie, Mrs. ---, 28:226

Larance (Larence), Jacques, guide, 28:6, 10

Laraway, Perrine and Co., Minneapolis, plow factory, 24:297

Lardner, Ring, 39:35

La Ribourde, Father Gabriel de, 20:68

Larimore, Newel G., bonanza farmer, 32:112

Larkin, Mrs. A. E., 15:224

Larkin, Edmund, 12:453

Larkin, Floyd, speaker, 19:233

Larkin, Oliver W., author, 31:55

Larkin, Sarah, work reviewed, 20:73

Larned, William L., 38:228

La Rock, Robert B., author, 18:452

La Rocque, ---, trader, 22:288

La Roque, Henri, trader, 17:440, 442

Larpenteur, Auguste L., pioneer, 11:322, 14:289, 17:213, 40:148; family, 14:438; merchant, 19:378

Larpenteur, Charles, author, 15:353, 429, 38:199; trader, 37:262, 40:314

Larpenteur, E. L., stock raiser, 22:255

Larpenteur, E. N., 14:289; house, 15:53

Larpenteur, J. D., artist, 22:333

Larpenteur, L. B., cholera victim, 14:289, 290

Larrabee, Maj. ---, 18:401

Larrabee, Judge Charles H., in Minnesota, 28:323

Larrowe Milling Co., 34:204. See also General Mills

Larsen, Arthur J., 23:6, 149; "Roads in the Minnesota Triangle," 11:387-411; "Early Transportation," 14:149-155; "Admission to the Union," 14:156-165; "Early Dakota Newspapers," 15:200-202; "Theodore C. Blegen and the Minnesota Historical Society," 20:287-295; MHS reports, 21:33-46, 22:35-46, 23:35-45, 27:21-28, 28:45-53; "Roads and the Settlement of Minnesota," 21:225-244; "The Air Transport Command," 26:1-18; "How the Junior Historians Work," 28:160-166; reviews by, 11:309, 12:310, 13:302-304, 16:463, 17:322-324, 328, 457, 18:433-435, 19:201, 205, 441, 20:61-63, 23:61, 25:276, 29:342, 30:251, 36:96, 37:302; work reviewed, 16:76-78; newspaper curator, 11:46, 288, 16:55; author, 12:430, 13:112, 14:347, 23:187, 27:340; speaker, 13:73, 195, 14:213, 328, 15:107, 16:65, 17:317, 21:49, 290, 22:50, 341, 23:48, 90, 27:145, 166; editor, 13:438, 15:462; receives doctorate, 19:209; MHS superintendent, 20:322, 21:53, 30:326-328; military service, 23:268, 24:58, 25:73, 30:329; career, 26:64, 27:46, 28:298; return to MHS, 26:367; resignation, 29:47; professor, 37:41

Larsen, Mrs. Arthur J. (Selma Press), editorial assistant, 11:443; "Sporting Magazines," 16:187-191; speaker, 15:107; author, 16:358; editor, 26:278

Larsen, Erling, work reviewed, 36:100; author, 34:358, 35:99; speaker, 37:40, 40:368

Larsen, Ernest T., author, 29:87

Larsen, Gilbert I., 29:4

Larsen, Hanna A., 20:412

Larsen, John, Mormon missionary, 36:288

Larsen, John G., Episcopal minister, 15:363; author, 16:120, 17:240

Larsen, Karen, 11:103; reviews by, 19:331, 29:255; work reviewed, 17:457; speaker, 17:110, 18:324; author, 18:199, 432, 19:337, 20:293, 29:288, 30:65

Larsen, Laurentius, Lutheran pastor, career, 11:103, 17:457, 18:199, 20:293

Larsen, Lawrence H., author, 36:280

Larsen, Mel, author, 37:42

Larsen, Rev. Peter L., career, 14:349, 356

Larsen, Mrs. Ruth M., research assistant, 27:340, 28:47

Larson, Agnes M., 24:370; "On the Trail of the Woodsman," 13:349-366; "When Logs and Lumber Ruled Stillwater," 18:165-179; reviews by, 14:209, 19:197; work reviewed, 30:242; speaker, 13:283, 14:213, 345, 443, 15:244, 16:212, 234, 236, 17:313, 18:335, 27:267; au-

thor, 16:108, 17:334, 18:203, 19:207, 28:331, 31:13, 34:263, 37:134

Larson, Alice, author, 34:43

Larson, Andrew, farmer, 22:446

Larson, Andrew, speaker, 16:305

Larson, Anna J., author, 12:103, 339, 497

Larson, Cedric, author, 21:200, 29:82

Larson, Constant, 15:135, 16:240, 17:121; speaker, 13:73, 278, 16:365; author, 19:356

Larson, E. J. D., author, 24:369

Larson, Elsye D. D., author, 34:315, 36:193

Larson, Esther E., compiler, 39:81

Larson, F. J. A., author, 11:337, 12:340; speaker, 18:110, 335; career, 20:457

Larson, Ferdie L., 14:427

Larson, Gordon R., house, 38:343

Larson, Henrietta M., 18:316; "The 'John B. Alley,'" 19:193-196; reviews by, 16:78-80, 29:156-158; work reviewed, 18:76-79; editor, 11:103; speaker, 13:327; author, 13:330, 17:111, 19:207, 23:53, 24:69, 26:163, 29:192, 30:64

Larson, Hilding, 23:298

Larson, Mrs. Ida, speaker, 27:362

Larson, Ingabret, 11:321

Larson, J. Edor, author, 34:175

Larson, J. P., establishes co-operative, 15:486

Larson, Kenneth, 26:291

Larson, Laurence M., 17:463, 18:41, 21:304; "The Kensington Rune Stone," 17:20-37; review by, 13:182-184; works reviewed, 18:431-433, 21:64-68; speaker, 15:119, 17:109, 18:324; author, 16:108, 17:90, 20:293, 21:303, 24:257; estimate of Kensington stone, 17:167, 169-173, 176-179, 181, 183, 185, 187

Larson, Mrs. Laurence M., 21:68

Larson, Lewis, speaker, 29:274

Larson, Lorayne, 13:279, 15:246, 17:356, 21:335

Larson, Louis, Nobles County pioneer, 16:368

Larson, Louis, Willmar pioneer, 20:360, 21:341

Larson, Louis, Wisconsin pioneer, 24:176

Larson, Mrs. M. A., 12:185

Larson, Marjorie S., author, 21:456

Larson, Nels, farmer, 29:14

Larson, O. J., speaker, 25:378

Larson, Olaf, pioneer, 11:115

Larson, Ole, cooper, 35:18

Larson, Mrs. Oscar, speaker, 29:363

Larson, P. M., 18:109

Larson, R. H., author, 21:451

Larson, Ralph, author, 36:195

Larson, Roy, speaker, 16:124

Larson, Mrs. Sarah A., 21:116

Larson, Swend, author, 11:468, 17:238

Larson, T. A., historian, 36:87

Larssen, Edward, legislator, 29:10

Larsson, August, emigrant agent, 36:237

La Salle, Robert Cavelier, Sieur de, explorer, 11:348, 12:410, 14:215, 371, 15:472, 16:453, 17:176, 342, 18:389, 21:100, 22:63, 92, 23:57, 25:273, 28:200, 30:375, 32:112,

248, 35:379, 36:325; career, 12: 435, 13:439, 14:348, 19:276; author, 16:199, 448, 38:41; in fur trade, 19:286; boat, 23:256, 25: 274, 40:141; pictured, 35:334; house, 40:188

La Salle, Nicolas de, 13:85

Laskianin Day, Finnish festival, 24: 73; in Minnesota, 30:145

Lasley, George, hotelkeeper, 32:84

Lass, William E., 39:264; "The Removal of the Sioux and Winnebago," 38:353-364; "The 'Moscow Expedition,'" 39:227-240; review by, 39: 296; work reviewed, 38:236; author, 35:246, 40:409

Lassallieur, Baptiste, Winnebago leader, 38:360, 361, 363

Lasson, Nelson B., author, 27:352

Lasswitz, Emil, actor, 32:103, 171, 34:241

Lathrop, Alfred C., 16:317n

Lathrop, Barnes F., work reviewed, 31:116; author, 29:258

Lathrop, Glenn H., author, 25:311

Lathrop, Harold W., author, 17:227, 23:192, 291, 24:80, 262, 27:359, 36:193; speaker, 18:204, 273, 20: 343, 344, 21:415, 22:339, 23:46, 296, 398

Lathrop, John, politician, 35:307

Lathrop, Noah, Methodist minister, 19:114, 31:82n

Latimer, Thomas E., Minneapolis mayor, 18:191; career, 19:214

Latin Americans, Catholic, 37:133

La Tourette, Claude Greysolon, Sieur de, 12:307; career, 13:439

Latourette, Kenneth S., author, 16: 239, 24:72

Latsch, John A., career, 35:46

Latta, S. N., Indian agent, 39:256

Latter-day Saints, Minnesota, 11:222, 12:340, 13:280, 281, 385-394, 17: 211; Utah, 13:111, 28:378, 39:71; Swedish, 13:305; Illinois, 15: 307n, 17:150, 429, 22:15n, 17, 19, 20, 25:275, 32:98, 36:46; U.S., 16:339, 24:235; Wisconsin, 22:98, 23:356; archives, 27:252; westward movement, 29:61, 36:98; Yankee, 31:181; missionaries, 36:285-293

Latterell, Mrs. Felix, 23:390

Latterell, Samuel, author, 19:366

Lattin, George, speaker, 13:342

Latto, Rudolph, 15:485

Latto Hospital, Hastings, history, 15:485

Latvians, U.S., 20:442

Laubin, Gladys, work reviewed, 35:376

Laubin, Reginald, work reviewed, 35: 376

Lauer Brothers Construction Co., St. Paul, 39:155

Lauermann, Leo, speaker, 36:283

Laughead, William B., 28:93, 372; quoted, 21:177; author, 21:187, 23:379, 24:176, 265, 25:393, 27: 255, 32:126, 33:91, 265, 37:39; editor, 26:380

Laughing Fish River, Mich., described, 23:237

Laughton, W. H., steamboat captain, 11:143

Laughton's Island, Lake St. Clair, 23:136

Laumann, Laura S., 11:221, 12:103; speaker, 11:53

Laumet, Antoine, see Cadillac, Antoine de la Mothe, Sieur de

Laurel, Koochiching County, see Smith Mounds

Laurens, Henry, 18:397

Laurent, Sister, 27:319n

Laurent, Francis W., work reviewed, 36:275

Laurie, Dr. James A., author, 11:112

Laurie, Rev. James A., 11:112

Lauritsen, Wesley, author, 14:438, 39:131

Lauson, Jean de, 15:158, 19:273

Laustrup, Margaret, author, 30:276

Laut, Agnes C., author, 11:103, 13: 298, 15:238

Lautishar, Father Lawrence, missionary, 15:455, 33:185, 36:192

Laval, Monsig. François de, 15:160

Lavalee family, genealogy, 11:110

La Vallée, Jacques, voyageur, 18:240

La Vega, Garcilasco de, author, 35: 248

Laveille, Auguste, 22:16n

Laveille, Bertrand, 22:16n

Laveille, Eugene, 22:16n

Laveille, Joseph C., architect, 22: 16n

Laveille, Theodore, 22:16n

Lavender, David, "Characteristics of the American Fur Company," 40:178-187; reviews by, 38:193, 40:39; work reviewed, 39:254

Laverdiere, Joseph, guide, 21:120n

La Vérendrye, Pierre Gaultier de Varennes, Sieur de, explorer, 11: 308, 12:357, 359, 362-364, 435, 14:444, 15:477, 16:116, 230, 349, 453, 480, 17:114, 18:273, 20:84, 21:99, 401, 432, 24:77, 256, 25: 96, 26:171, 27:260, 33:187, 34: 352, 35:97, 38:26, 27, 39:81, 40: 145; trader, 11:361, 362, 364, 12: 82, 13:209, 17:224, 18:237, 241, 24:318, 28:285, 29:133, 31:52, 183, 37:236, 39:301, 302; bicentennial, 12:186, 288-296, 13:345, 19:461; career, 12:295, 342, 13: 439, 14:226, 348, 15:238, 18:234, 243, 24:384, 35:140; at Lake of the Woods, 12:307, 15:477, 18:232, 236, 272, 21:328, 27:70, 32:62, 37:62; writings, 15:232, 18:275, 22:429, 24:60, 152, 30:223, 38:41; monuments, 18:238, 244; farmer, 18:238, 276; plaque, 18:242, 32: 226, 40:193; ancestry, 35:242; map maker, 36:277. See also La Vérendrye family

La Vérendrye, François, 18:234; trader, 37:237. See also La Vérendrye family

La Vérendrye, Jean-Baptiste, 18:234, 24:318; death, 17:224, 18:239, 28: 77, 29:133, 32:233, 39:302; skeleton found, 18:246. See also La Vérendrye family

La Vérendrye, Louis-Joseph, 18:239, 37:253; explorer, 32:226; trader, 32:232-234, 37:236-240, 243, 249

La Vérendrye, Pierre, 18:234

La Vérendrye family, 18:234; explorers, 16:230, 231, 17:114, 32:112, 33:88, 36:279; genealogy, 35:242,

36:191; traders, 37:239, 253, 38: 386

La Vérendrye stone, inscription, 38: 384

Lavergne, Joseph, voyageur, 32:235

Laverne, ---, Spanish trader, 19:78

Laviolette, Gontran, author, 27:161

Lavocat, Nicolas Joseph, pioneer, 11: 110, 14:104

Lavocat family, genealogy, 11:110, 13:116, 14:104, 332

Lavocat-Martin, Anne C. J., pioneer, 11:110, 13:116, 14:332

Lavocat-Martin Family Association, 14:332

Lavorie, Mrs. Grace D., 16:341

Law, James M., 14:332

Law, Laura T., author, 34:84

Law, William, 25:344

Lawe, John, trader, 22:285, 30:248

Lawler, Daniel W., lawyer, 22:98; politician, 35:61, 312, 36:124, 39:26

Lawler, J. Earle, 27:330

Lawler, John, journalist, work reviewed, 31:245

Lawler, John D., bridge builder, 22: 98, 23:286, 27:258

Lawler, Bishop John J., 19:464, 39: 154n

Lawrence, Donald, editor, 33:90

Lawrence, James, frigate captain, 40: 348

Lawrence, James G., miller, 35:15

Lawrence, John H., farmer, 17:99

Lawrence, M. D., 20:457

Lawrence, Maude L., author, 20:208

Lawrence, Mrs. O. P., author, 20:102

Lawrence, Percy J., musician, 33:101

Lawrence, Mrs. Percy J., 13:311; author, 14:110

Lawrence, Mrs. Ruth, speaker, 28:390

Lawrence, William B., lawyer, 18:130

Lawrence, William M., translator, 16: 109

Lawrence, Kan., social life, 19:80; museum, 27:178

Lawrence (Wahkon), Mille Lacs County, history, 28:292

"Lawrence," steamboat, 11:210, 13: 231, 40:79

Lawrence College, Appleton, Wis., lecture series, 26:73

Law's Mississippi Co., 18:390

Lawshe, Fred E., 21:334, 23:100; collector, 34:267; author, 35:99

Lawson, Eben E., author, 24:90, 26: 364, 398; editor, 26:95

Lawson, Edward, forester, 23:189

Lawson, George W., work reviewed, 35: 194

Lawson, Marcus J., artist, 37:151n

Lawson, Murray G., author, 29:258, 36:34

Lawson, Paul, author, 35:49

Lawson, Thomas, army surgeon, 28:15, 19

Lawson, Victor E., 22:50, 447, 23:48, 50, 100, 26:45, 29:97, 37:136; speaker, 21:218, 22:340, 23:193, 297, 26:393; author, 23:107, 187; editor, 26:95

Lawson, Victor F., journalist, 33:349

Lawyers, Minnesota, 32:63; women, 32: 120

Lax Lake, Lake County, resort, 34:181

Laxey, Wis., Methodist church, 27:84, 28:188

Layman, Martha, review by, 23:163; author, 23:170

Layman, Martin, 21:417, 22:223

Layman, Mrs. Martin, 21:417

Layman's Cemetery, Minneapolis, 23:296; history, 22:222

Lea, Maj. Albert M., diary, 11:291; explorer, 16:227, 453, 19:217, 21:340; career, 16:228, 28:184; centennial, 16:232, 365, 478, 494; author, 20:203, 29:253

Lea, Homer, 39:260

Lea, Luke, 28:320, 321; Indian commissioner, 32:65, 69, 71, 74, 77, 39:45

Leach, Albert R., 11:117, 12:106, 13:121, 15:138, 16:125, 19:118

Leach, Calvin F., lumberman, 18:169, 24:197, 198

Leach, George E., Minneapolis mayor, 37:165, 166

Leach, Mrs. Paul J., 15:133; "A 'Haunted Windmill,'" 12:65-67

Leach, William B., Union officer, 28:326

Leachman, J., and Son, publishers, 29:107

Leacock, Stephen, 33:88; "Lahontan in Minnesota," 14:367-377; author, 14:221, 15:59, 234, 476, 16:453, 18:318, 19:352, 35:240; speaker, 14:432, 15:57

Lead mining, Iowa, 12:77, 14:445; Wisconsin, 12:158, 13:334, 14:445, 27:83, 258; Galena, Ill., area, 13:223, 18:434, 22:23-26, 25:272, 34:135; Dubuque, Iowa, 18:434, 23:344n, 34:40; Missouri, 23:130; Owen's survey, 26:223

Leaf, Martin, 21:336, 26:26, 86; speaker, 22:339, 24:270

Leaf City, Otter Tail County, marker, 19:361

Leaf Lake (East Leaf Lake), Otter Tail County, 36:40; trading post, 11:373, 13:222

Leaf Mountains, Otter Tail County, described, 37:4, 7

Leaf River, Otter Tail County, trading posts, 11:373; trails, 21:229

Leaf Shooter, Sioux leader, see Wacouta

League for Independent Political Action, history, 40:360

League of American Wheelmen, Minnesota branch, 36:89-94

League of Minnesota Municipalities, publications, 12:98, 16:356; anniversary, 19:356; function, 23:266

League of Minnesota Poets, 18:47, 98

League of Nations, 23:272, 35:163, 166, 40:368, 369, 371

League of Protestant Women, 13:101

League of Women Voters, Minnesota, 18:97, 19:228, 23:266, 292, 35:201, 38:308; national, 23:393

Leahy, Adm. W. O., 24:240

Leaming, Alonzo, plowmaker, 24:295, 297

Leaping Rock, Pipestone County, Pipestone Quarry, 31:203, 204

Learned, Mrs. C. E., author, 15:467

Leary, B. P., 23:392

Lease, Mary Elizabeth ("Ellen"), 39:260; agrarian leader, 13:19, 35:284, 291

Leavenworth, Frederick P., letters, 15:111, 16:470, 17:53; surveyor, 16:334

Leavenworth, Col. Henry, 21:83, 23:339n, 24:195, 35:179, 40:262; founds Fort Snelling, 14:349, 15:311, 17:81, 311, 19:354, 30:211n; family, 18:400, 30:212n; letter, 23:74; characterized, 33:263

Leavenworth, Brown County, ghost town, 23:195, 39:236, 237

Leavitt, Charles T., speaker, 15:119; author, 15:353

Leavitt, T. H., 29:324

Leavitt's Swiss Bell Ringers, 33:319

Lebanon, Conn., Beaumont monument, 15:234

Leberman, J. E., author, 28:289

Le Blanc, George, mixed-blood, 38:136

Le Blanc, Louis, see Provençalle, Louis

Le Blancell, ---, trader, 11:264n

Le Boeuf, Pierre, voyageur, 18:241

Le Caron, Father Joseph, missionary, 25:273

Le Center, county seat fight, 12:444; history, 16:101, 22:110, 28:266

Le Center Leader, anniversary, 22:110

Le Clair, E. T., 35:273

Le Clair, Lake of the Woods County, post office, 35:273, 277; fishing, 35:275, 276

Le Claire, Antoine, Iowa pioneer, 13:111, 23:91; interpreter, 13:330, 35:88; papers, 20:89; trader, 20:123

"Lecompton constitution," 14:175

Le Conte, Maj. John E., 32:87

Le Conte, John L., in Minnesota, 32:81-99, 33:252

Le Conte, Joseph, 33:252; "Frontier Vacation," 32:82-99

Lecuyer, Joseph, trader, 21:142, 144, 146-148

Ledie, Charles, 13:148, 19:162

Ledon, Father Louis, 33:38

Le Duc, Alice, 37:200; author, 28:373

Le Duc, Rev. Charles S., 12:208, 17:229, 19:264, 37:192, 197, 199

Le Duc, Florence, 37:192, 198

Leduc, Jean B., trader, 11:236

Le Duc, Mary, see Gardner, Mrs. Augustine V.

LeDuc, Thomas, review by, 30:244; author, 30:292, 40:46

Le Duc, William B., son of William G., 37:192, 198

Le Duc, William G., 11:174, 12:445, 25:198, 32:80, 37:201; house, 11:459, 15:53, 54, 28:373, 29:73, 34:293, 314, 36:34, 107, 108, 196, 37:67, 189-203, 38:187; papers, 12:312, 28:373; commissioner of agriculture, 14:217, 18:449, 23:283, 27:351, 34:287-295, 35:243; career, 14:349, 26:66, 37:190, 200, 39:78; store, 16:32, 73, 34:120, 37:192, 39:318, 319; railroad promoter, 18:444, 19:193-196, 21:87, 39:88, 92; family, 22:89, 35:336; death, 37:203; in Civil War, 38:42, 271

Le Duc, Mrs. William G., 37:192, 193, 199-201, 203

Le Duc and Rohrer, St. Paul, merchants, 15:184, 185

Ledyard, Edgar M., author, 13:107, 433, 14:110, 231

Lee, Mrs. ---, Civil War nurse, 25:347

Lee, Alfred M., author, 18:451

Lee, Benjamin G., in Sioux Outbreak, 11:115

Lee, Charles H., author, 26:31

Lee, Mrs. Earl, pioneer, 33:5

Lee, Edward J., biography, 19:214

Lee, Ezra, 28:54

Lee, Col. Francis, 11:163, 29:319n, 30:213n, 33:263

Lee, Mrs. Francis, 30:213n

Lee, Franklyn W., author, 26:300, 31:130

Lee, James M., author, 12:442

Lee, Jason, missionary, 29:59

Lee, John J., author, 15:244

Lee, John J., Jr., author, 15:244

Lee, Mildred B., "The Pioneer," 33:246; author, 30:402, 33:354

Lee, Mrs. Minnie E., mill owner, 13:214

Lee, Minnie Mary, pseud., see Wood, Mrs. Julia A. S.

Lee, Morris, 29:308

Lee, Judge N. J., speaker, 20:456

Lee, Judge Orris E., 11:225

Lee, Richard H., 19:35

Lee, Robert, author, 39:344

Lee, Gen. Robert E., 16:53, 103, 29:344; Confederate officer, 11:318, 25:225n, 344-347, 352n, 355n, 358, 35:313, 318, 38:245, 246, 251, 257, 293; biography, 21:10; engineer, 21:428

Lee, Mrs. Robert E., house, 25:345n

Lee, Robert Edson, work reviewed, 40:304

Lee, Rudolph A., speaker, 28:388; editor, 38:305

Lee, Mrs. Susan, speaker, 21:108

Lee, Mrs. T. M., speaker, 24:85

Lee, Dr. Thomas G., 21:330, 24:347

Lee, Capt. Thomas J., surveyor, 24:368

Lee, William, businessman, 40:225

Lee, Judge William, 26:392, 30:402

"Lee," steamboat, 33:15, 18, 19

Lee Co-operative Creamery, Norman County, history, 24:273

Leech, Esther G., author, 16:227

Leech, Margaret, author, 23:179

Leech Lake, Cass County, posts, 11:111, 370, 13:195, 222, 15:366, 16:193, 17:72, 207, 342, 20:11-15, 72, 23:94, 251, 28:144, 30:258, 31:125, 35:151; historic sites, 11:112; uprising, 11:455, 18:333, 22:88, 109, 24:142-148, 180, 26:303, 28:77, 30:395, 35:235; steamboating, 12:310; missions, 15:184, 16:216, 375, 376, 19:431, 20:310, 313, 21:21, 40:146; Indians, 17:229, 21:182, 23:329, 331, 36:249, 37:347; climate, 17:245n; fishing, 23:330, 33:253; archaeology, 26:321; health conditions, 27:351, 33:91

Leech Lake Indian Reservation (Chippewa), 24:142, 29:169, 35:293; agency, 20:312, 23:93; historic sites, 40:148

Leech Lake River, Cass County, archaeology, 26:323
Leechman, Douglas, 29:167; author, 24:262, 26:76, 33:227
Leedy, Edwin C., career, 26:72
Leekley, Richard, review by, 21:68; author, 21:80
Leent, Chisago County, Grange, 17:481
Leenthrop Township, Chippewa County, Norwegian settlement, 12:275n
Lees, James H., author, 14:226
Le Fevre, Louis, author, 27:351
Lefler, Hugh T., author, 15:476
Lefroy, Capt. John H., 35:82; surveyor, 40:359
Leger, Charles, 21:131
Legg, Frederick C., auto driver, 38:207, 209
Leggett, William F., author, 30:55
Legislatures, unicameral, 19:201.
  See also Minnesota legislature
Le Hillier City, Nicollet County, ghost town, 17:238
Lehman and Duval, Philadelphia, lithographers, 33:20
Lehmann, Florence, 20:212; author, 11:453, 12:99, 20:101
Lehrke, Mrs. George W., author, 26:398
Lehtenen, Emil, 40:394
Lehtijärvi, Otter Tail County, Finnish settlement, 25:320
Le Huray and Co., 29:225, 227, 228
Leibbrandt, Georg, author, 14:224
Leicher, F. A., 12:106
Leidy, W. Philip, work reviewed, 33:303
Leifur, Conrad W., author, 23:382
Leighton, Benjamin G., "Pioneer Reunions," 25:158-164; author, 25:181, 191
Leighton, Fred, author, 35:336
Leighton, George R., author, 20:336
Leighton, Louise, work reviewed, 25:371
Leighton, Hennepin County, post office, 40:88
"Leila D.," steamboat, 12:310
Lein, Mrs. Ida, author, 22:346
Lein, Malcolm E., 36:108
Lein, Mrs. Olaf, author, 18:224
Leinonen, Matt, 21:110
Leip, William, hotelkeeper, 34:102
Leip Hotel, White Bear Lake, 34:102, 36:283
Leipold, L. Edmond, author, 27:63, 167
Leipzig, Germany, fur market, 40:213n, 219
Leisman, Gilbert A., author, 36:282
Leith, Andrew, author, 17:108
Leith, C. K., author, 17:108
Leith, James, trader, 24:262
Le Jeune, L. P. L., author, 13:439
Le Jeune, Paul, Jesuit, 16:199, 27:216, 217, 220
Leland, Charles G., editor, 30:204
Leland, J. A. C., author, 27:65
Leland, Waldo G., 17:8; work reviewed, 13:417; author, 23:178, 279
Leland, Wilfred C., work reviewed, 22:314
Le Lay, Mrs. Paul, speaker, 16:485
Le Manoir Lachine, Que., depicted, 40:188
Lemay, Jean Baptiste, 15:212

Lemay, P. Hugolin, work reviewed, 20:423
Lemay, Paul, musician, 27:367
Le May, Dr. Ray B., 18:112; speaker, 23:386
Lemke, William, politician, 36:187, 40:360; career, 39:79
Lemmer, George F., work reviewed, 33:307
Le Moine, Father Simon, 15:175
Lemmon, John T., speaker, 11:283
Lemmon, Robert S., author, 33:227
Lemond Township, Steele County, Norwegian settlement, 12:269
Lemons, William E., review by, 34:161
Le Moyne, Jacques, artist, 33:264
Lendrum, Frederick C., review by, 27:135; author, 27:152
L'Enfant Perdu, Ont., legend, 28:12
Lenfest, Mrs. C. E. (Fannie), 23:100; speaker, 19:229, 22:338
Lengby, history, 14:358
Lengyel, Emil, author, 29:261
Lenhart, John M., author, 17:473, 25:198
Lenmon, J. G., 22:255
Lenora, Fillmore County, Methodist church, 29:354; camp meeting, 31:82
Lent, D. Geneva, work reviewed, 38:326
Lenz, Paul, farmer, 37:73
Leo XIII, Pope, school decision, 25:373
Leon Township, Goodhue County, Lutheran church, 14:354
Leonard, Charles F., 40:228
Leonard, D. A., 11:442
Leonard, Gertrude, 39:115
Leonard, Herbert G., Methodist minister, 39:226
Leonard, J. A., 20:228
Leonard, L. O., 15:407
Leonard, Sarah M., teacher, 22:442
Leonard, Dr. William E., 12:427; "Early College Silhouettes," 16:178-186; author, 17:94
Leonard, Dr. William H., pioneer physician, 17:258, 260, 23:78, 39:112n, 40:224; papers, 12:427
Leonard, Zenas, diary, 36:317
Leonhaeuser, Col. Harry, 12:324
Leonhart, Rudolph, author, 38:86
Leonidas Mine, Eveleth, 21:289
Leopoldine Society, missionary activities, 14:339, 21:74, 25:193, 26:147, 33:185, 39:303, 306
Leota, settled, 28:129, 130, 36:104
Lepeltak, Pieter, Dutch Reformed minister, 28:123
Leppard, H. M., author, 25:305
Leprosy, among Scandinavians, 31:190
Le Ray Township, Blue Earth County, library association, 17:234
Lerdahl, Freeborn County, settled, 28:248
Lerner, Max, author, 17:477
Leroi-Gourhan, André, work reviewed, 28:361
Leroux, Laurent, 12:368
LeRoy, N., lumberman, 24:201
Le Roy, telegraph office, 19:343; bank, 24:273; architecture, 40:359
Leshall, Josephine, 35:264
Le Sieur, Toussaint, trader, 11:364
Leslie, ---, artist, 17:142
Leslie, Mrs. F. R., author, 15:137

Leslie, Frank, 39:190n
Leslie, Shane, author, 19:350
Leslie Township, Todd County, history, 16:131
Lesquereux, Charles Leo, explorer, 27:253
Lesser, Simon O., author, 24:73
Lester, Clarence B., author, 24:337
Lester, Henry C., military career, 39:179n, 191-197, 40:282
Lester, Mr. and Mrs. John, 18:469
Lester, S., 14:245
Lester Prairie, history, 18:469, 21:452
Lester Prairie News, history, 26:397
Le Sueur, Arthur, politician, 28:72, 35:155
Le Sueur, Mrs. Arthur (Marian), politician, 35:155
Lesueur, Charles A., artist, 19:458, 21:94, 26:359, 33:264, 316
Le Sueur, Meridel, 27:243; "North Country Folkways," 25:215-223; review by, 25:375; work reviewed, 27:41-43; author, 15:364, 16:481, 21:61, 24:371, 25:175, 287, 383, 26:84, 28:281, 35:155, 36:78, 83, 105; speaker, 25:397
Le Sueur, Pierre C., 15:100; explorer, 11:126, 383, 452, 12:76, 14:116, 215, 16:453, 18:233, 22:181, 23:85, 280, 32:186, 37:86; fort, 11:377, 381, 36:240; trader, 11:385, 12:356, 13:85, 19:282, 286; mine, 11:454; journal, 13:417; career, 13:439, 14:348
Le Sueur, industries, 11:111, 182; platted, 11:162; described, 11:170, 29:210; river port, 11:331, 12:60, 16:366, 37:226; county seat fight, 12:444; politics, 15:224; G.A.R. post, 16:431; climate, 17:253n; Catholic church, 17:479; agriculture, 18:408; history, 21:222, 33:353; railroad, 21:239; Mayo house, 33:209; garrison, 38:280
Le Sueur Center, see Le Center
Le Sueur County, history, 12:201, 14:120, 18:227, 21:103, 222, 22:111; county seat fight, 12:444, 16:101, 19:95, 28:266; agriculture, 13:176, 15:252, 17:127, 33:318; surveyed, 15:223; politics, 28:31, 32; Catholic church, 28:84; resort, 33:323; grasshopper bounty, 36:57; poor farm, 38:367, 369
Le Sueur County Old Settlers Association, 11:461
Le Sueur County War History Committee, 24:82, 185
Le Sueur River, Blue Earth, Waseca, and Freeborn counties, ferry, 12:51
Le Sueur Valley, Norwegian settlements, 12:269
Letcher, John, 25:149
Letellier, Man., marker, 17:476
Letofsky, Irvin, author, 37:43, 307
Letterman, Dr. Jonathan, 21:358; author, 21:371
Lettermann, Edward, compiler, 38:204
Lettsom, John C., Carver's physician, 11:325; author, 34:154
Leue, Gustav, 32:102n
Leuthold, Jacob, 19:358
Leuthold-St. Clair stores, clothing outlets, 19:358

Leutze, Emanuel, artist, 21:150
LeVander, Harold, governor, 40:411
Levasseur, Father ———, 13:203
Leven Lake, Pope County, 24:333
Levenson, Adeline, clerk typist, 25: 41, 26:39
Leverett, Frank, geologist, 16:5, 310
Levering, Albert H., pseud., see Ellis, Harvey
Levi, Sister M. Carolissa, work reviewed, 35:235
Levi, Werner, reviews by, 30:144, 31: 117; author, 30:184, 31:127
Levi, Mrs. Werner (Ilse), indexer, 25:43
Levik, Betty, author, 20:462
Levine, Norman, author, 25:412
Levins, Mrs. Bert, 22:107, 23:103, 194
Levinson, S. O., career, 25:195
Lewenhaupt, A., report, 24:258
Lewes, J. L., trader, 40:168n
Lewin, Evans, author, 14:222
Lewis, Abner, 26:195, 199, 200
Lewis, Addison, author, 26:308
Lewis, Amy A., speaker, 12:38
Lewis, Mrs. Anna, 35:105, 106
Lewis, Audrey, author, 17:360
Lewis, Benjamin M., author, 36:276
Lewis, Dr. C. B., 33:297
Lewis, Mrs. Charles E., author, 19: 124
Lewis, Charles H., house, 38:343, 344
Lewis, Dr. Claude B., 34:86, 88, 37: 2; letter, 34:176; journal, 37:40
Lewis, Donald K., 15:340, 16:56, 28: 394; author, 16:117
Lewis, Mrs. Donald K., 15:340
Lewis, Edmonia, sculptress, 20:328
Lewis, Edwin H., "Wholesalers' Catalogues," 34:106-113; reviews by, 35:36, 37:256; work reviewed, 33: 226; author, 33:355
Lewis, Dr. Edwin J., 34:85, 88, 89, 176, 35:234, 37:1-3, 5, 13; papers, 30:290
Lewis, Mrs. Edwin J., 37:2
Lewis, Eleanor, artist, 30:75
Lewis, G. H., 19:471
Lewis, George T., 17:132, 39:286; house, 39:289
Lewis, Grace Hegger, 37:2, 5; work reviewed, 35:234; author, 37:135
Lewis, Henry, "Journal of Canoe Voyage," 17:150-158, 288-301, 421-436; author, 14:338, 340, 15:111, 17:144-146, 392, 32:188, 202-213, 37:188; panorama, 14:340, 17:131-133, 136-143, 456, 18:319, 20:339, 380, 381, 25:275, 30:15, 201, 31: 46, 55, 32:202; career, 14:340, 17:131, 132, 432; diary, 15:61, 110, 17:332, 460, 19:217, 20:382, 31:210, 36:145; artist, 15:211, 350, 470, 17:146-148, 154, 155, 290, 291, 296, 297, 300, 301, 424, 425, 433, 19:458, 21:151, 186, 26: 359, 29:265, 350, 30:85, 152, 157, 176, 388, 31:56, 209, 33:89, 284, 285, 34:21, 35:29, 182, 379, 36: 22, 23, 233, 39:37 (cover), 200, 264, 265 (cover), 286-289; portrait, 17:432
Lewis, Herbert, speaker, 26:395
Lewis, James O., artist, 16:472, 17: 55, 456, 475, 21:151, 26:359, 28:

277, 29:350, 31:54, 33:20, 21, 264, 35:369, 37:78, 80
Lewis, Janet, work reviewed, 14:92-94
Lewis, Mrs. Janet D., 18:211
Lewis, John A., 17:143n, 332
Lewis, John G., 15:111, 17:138
Lewis, John L., labor leader, 20:318; career, 36:274
Lewis, Lloyd, works reviewed, 17:324-326, 30:379; author, 23:283, 32:57
Lewis, Lucy M., see Lewis, Mrs. William
Lewis, Mary E., speaker, 16:301, 18: 224
Lewis, Capt. Meriwether, author, 14: 423, 22:154; explorer, 14:430, 20: 84, 26:165, 28:184, 29:61, 34:303, 39:164, 169. See also Lewis and Clark expedition
Lewis, Oscar, author, 25:194
Lewis, Richard J., banker, 39:246, 247
Lewis, Robert P., accounts, 16:72
Lewis, Russel, 18:460
Lewis, Sinclair, 15:100, 25:69, 27: 141, 30:47, 34:357, 37:222; works reviewed, 30:142, 33:221; author, 18:330, 20:117, 438, 23:121, 27: 331, 28:279, 392, 29:172, 30:62, 149, 267, 358, 31:129, 130, 133, 137, 140-143, 146, 33:51, 34:42, 173, 36:237; career, 28:370, 34: 85-95, 35:234, 37:335; use of backgrounds, 34:126, 36:74, 76, 37:1-13; name, 34:176; anniversary, 37:40, 87, 135; birthplace, 37:66; evaluated, 37:345, 38:387, 40:411
Lewis, Mrs. Sinclair, see Lewis, Grace Hegger; Thompson, Dorothy
Lewis, Theodore H., archaeologist, 11:326, 13:374, 15:109, 148, 16: 21, 162, 22:210, 332, 25:336, 338, 339, 29:162, 32:229, 38:157, 164
Lewis, Warner, surveyor-general, 12: 385
Lewis, William, missionary, 15:43
Lewis, Mrs. William (Lucy M.), 16: 376; frontier cabin, 15:43, 44, 184; artist, 15:44
Lewis, Wilmarth S., author, 28:172
Lewis and Clark expedition, 12:435, 15:424, 428, 17:438, 28:57, 32: 112, 34:346, 36:236, 277, 40:312; members, 14:204, 33:180; route, 32:45, 40:179; records, 33:268, 34:315, 360, 36:216-229, 38:91, 240; political aspect, 33:302, 303; place names, 33:311; journals, 34:79, 40:304; scientific discoveries, 34:215, 35:241; health conditions, 37:183. See also Lewis, Capt. Meriwether; Clark, William
Lewis Bluff, Winona County, name, 32: 212
Lewis Society, Duluth, 21:195
Lexington, Le Sueur County, county seat fight, 12:444; school district, 14:100
Lexington Park, St. Paul, athletic field, 39:18-20
Leyburn, James G., author, 16:477
Leyde, Samuel, 25:27
Leyhe, Henry, steamboat captain, 22: 94

Leyhe, William, steamboat captain, 22:94
L'Herault, Napoleon A., career, 18: 211
Liancourt, Duc de, 12:82, 19:37, 40
Libbey, R. C., 23:105
Libby, Frederick W., 40:372, 374
Libby, Mark, trader, 21:349
Libby, Orin G., 12:223n, 27:67; speaker, 12:294, 13:56; author, 16:115, 24:152, 336, 40:145
Libby, Mrs. R. J., 23:390
Libby Prison, Richmond, Va., 17:98, 337, 25:144n
Libby Township, Aitkin County, name, 21:349
Libera, Paul, author, 35:51
Liberty Loan, in Minnesota, 14:320, 321, 24:383, 28:349
Liberty Township, Beltrami County, history, 15:365
Liberty Township, Itasca County, settlement, 22:415
Libraries, Minnesota, 17:468, 24:272, 26:386, 27:71, 78, 28:384; Twin Cities, 18:363, 19:403, 20:88, 411, 21:113; St. Louis, 20:202; Duluth, 21:456; frontier, 22:351-366, 26:242-247; Finnish, 22:398; county, 23:84, 294, 397, 25:91; functions, 23:279, 24:376, 28:173, 30:175; South, 26:162; war records, 26:175; historical, 26:377, 29:163; public, 29:58; school, 30: 70. See also individual libraries
Library of Congress, collections, 13: 47, 27:161, 188, 28:351; exhibits, 27:348, 28:378, 29:174, 268, 30: 84, 172, 403; copying projects, 39:165
Lie, Jonas, 18:200
Lieb, John, speaker, 14:237
Lieber, Francis, author, 29:154
Liebling, Jerome, photographer, 36: 106, 40:412
Lien, Mr. and Mrs. P. O., 28:195
Lien, Petra M., 23:105; author, 23: 400; translator, 26:94
Lienau, Charles H., publisher, 26:206
Lienhard, John, author, 11:215, 13: 433
Liesenfeld, Jacob, speaker, 17:126
Liesenfeld, John P., autobiography, 12:428
Liestøl, Aslak, "The Runes of Bergen," 40:49-58
Lieurance, Thurlow, musician, 36:190
Liggett, Walter W., career, 25:305
Light, Paul, pseud., see Kahn, Howard
"Lightfoot," steamboat, 36:46, 47
Lighthouse Service, history, 34:351
Lighthouses, Minnesota Point, 16:113, 21:157, 26:276, 33:355, 37:110, 111; Great Lakes, 24:175, 39:82; light keepers, 34:351
Lightner, Adam, 17:285
Lightner, William H., 11:54, 14:79, 17:70, 27:22
Lightning Blanket, Sioux Indian, 38: 128, 136n; "Lightning Blanket's Story," 38:144-146
Lighty, Kent, author, 11:453
Lighty, Margaret, author, 11:453
Ligne, Prince Albert de, 12:96; "Father Louis Hennepin," 11:343-351; author, 12:24
Ligne, Jean de, 11:344

Lignite deposits, Redwood Falls, 40:
   336n
Liguori, Mother, 14:40
Lilius, A., author, 18:71
Lillard, Richard G., work reviewed,
   29:68; author, 28:182
Lillegard, G. O., author, 24:258
Lillie, Leo C., author, 12:440
Lilly, Eli, author, 34:160
Lilly, Josiah K., 15:115
Lilly, Richard, airline executive,
   33:242
Lilly Dale, Dakota County, described,
   36:239
Limburger, Abraham, letter, 11:318
Lime kilns, frontier, 22:346
Lime Lake, Murray County, school, 35:
   138
Lime Township, Blue Earth County,
   pioneer house, 24:88
Limon, José, dancer, 39:64
Linch, Lyle K., 29:263
Lincoln, Abraham, 25:256, 34:81, 38:
   109, 220, 221, 39:282, 40:270n,
   271; characterized, 11:59, 16:77,
   354, 20:269-286, 22:408, 33:218,
   347; writings, 11:328, 12:429, 28:
   63, 29:77, 283, 34:126; biographies, 13:204, 21:12, 28:171, 360,
   40:313; presidential candidate,
   13:444, 14:77, 25:298, 28:323, 35:
   115, 39:85; Sioux execution order,
   14:453, 21:201, 25:179, 28:327,
   33:77-79, 38:98, 112, 113, 354,
   39:183; evaluated, 15:221; death,
   15:402, 33:167, 34:358, 35:313,
   318, 38:230; policies, 22:129, 24:
   157, 27:168, 29:342, 31:243, 32:
   20, 23, 26-28; elected, 22:227,
   234, 23:281, 24:308, 309, 315,
   316, 28:20-36, 324, 32:32, 33:180,
   34:333, 35:316, 36:171, 172,
   37:51, 54, 224; Emancipation Proclamation, 25:225, 243, 32:15, 29,
   36:169, 39:260; birthday celebrated, 26:169; bibliography, 27:
   335; property, 28:186; pictured,
   29:124, 33:77, 217, 34:212; Congressman, 30:189, 35:353; papers,
   30:309, 36:229; speaker, 36:280,
   323, 38:245; patronage, 37:325,
   326, 332, 333
Lincoln, Mrs. Abraham, 35:115
Lincoln, Robert P., author, 20:444
Lincoln, Robert T., 35:75; papers,
   29:283, 30:40, 33:79
Lincoln, S. D., author, 20:217, 360;
   speaker, 20:456
Lincoln family, genealogy, 13:197
Lincoln, Blue Earth County, Lutheran
   church, 15:490
Lincoln County, county seat fight,
   12:444; fair, 14:458, 23:403; history, 16:366, 17:127, 18:340; ethnic settlements, 17:344, 18:469,
   31:27, 38:42; archives, 22:332;
   wheat raising, 29:4; in Sioux Out-
   break, 38:281; poor relief, 38:373
Lincoln County Historical Society,
   29:275, 30:80, 400
Lincoln-Douglas debates, 24:113
Lincoln Freie Presse (Lincoln, Neb.),
   16:338
Lincoln Guard, Minneapolis, 16:177
Lincoln Mill, Anoka, 12:90, 14:234
Lincoln National Life Foundation,

Fort Wayne, Ind., 14:454, 17:216,
   19:217
Lincoln Township, Blue Earth County,
   Norwegian settlement, 12:273
Lincoln Township, Washington County,
   organized, 17:490
Linctot, René G. de, trader, 11:384,
   18:193
Lind, Jenny, singer, 20:450, 30:187,
   188, 192
Lind, John, 17:340, 19:440, 441, 21:
   203, 22:104, 29:147, 32:180, 36:
   109; governor, 11:213, 13:205, 28:
   183, 35:62, 63, 344, 39:97, 108,
   109, 332, 40:148; politician, 11:
   435, 15:339, 28:73, 31:206, 35:
   298, 312, 36:125, 37:260, 38:334,
   39:99, 103-107; honored, 12:322;
   career, 13:95, 14:349; biographies, 16:456-460, 31:42; Mexican
   mission, 16:459, 17:164; papers,
   17:53, 68, 159-165, 19:47, 20:83,
   288, 370, 23:8, 34:339, 37:44;
   teacher, 30:274; author, 30:372
Lind, Mrs. John, 17:53, 68, 159n
Lind, Melva, 35:340; singer, 35:52,
   156; author, 36:151; speaker, 37:
   136
Lind, Samuel C., author, 26:84
Lind Saddle Trail, Itasca State Park,
   17:159n
Lindall, Peter, author, 12:340
Lindberg, C. O., author, 28:373
Lindberg, Folke, "Organizing Research," 33:201-207
Lindbergh, August (Ola Månsson),
   20:246; migrates, 12:447, 20:244,
   434; career, 18:207, 26:256; characterized, 20:243, 247, 22:335
Lindbergh, Charles A., 15:338, 20:
   244, 21:98, 203, 22:79, 104, 36:
   83, 40:140; biographies, 11:443,
   13:188-190, 14:349, 16:482, 18:
   445, 22:44; letters, 12:192, 13:
   323, 14:65, 21:416; politician,
   13:188, 18:191, 20:434, 22:80,
   335, 26:256, 378, 28:72, 33:159,
   34:187, 221-232, 37:82, 40:362,
   410; house, 15:229, 18:269, 35:
   293, 37:64, 67, 68; portrait bust,
   21:294; papers, 17:164, 18:56,
   207, 19:47, 57, 67, 20:288, 304,
   370, 372, 40:132
Lindbergh, Mrs. Charles A. (Evangeline Land), 18:207, 37:82
Lindbergh, Col. Charles A., Jr., 15:
   100, 17:59, 18:207, 19:48, 22:313,
   37:68; aviator, 13:188, 30:383,
   33:238, 34:42, 175, 217, 222, 35:
   155, 293, 37:83, 38:335, 39:343;
   letter, 19:67; career, 22:335, 37:
   133, 40:410; author, 34:84; biography, 37:81; kidnapping case, 37:
   343; conservationist, 40:132
Lindbergh, Mrs. Charles A., Jr. (Anne
   Morrow), 17:59, 37:82
Lindbergh, Eva, see Christie, Mrs.
   George W.
Lindbergh, Frank, 18:207
Lindbergh, Måns Olsson, emigrant
   leader, 20:243-258; America letter, 20:249-258; author, 20:434
Lindbergh, Perry, 18:207, 20:244
Lindbergh family, 19:48; history, 12:
   447, 13:188, 19:445, 20:38
Lindbergh State Park, Morrison Coun-
   ty, 18:269, 23:301, 37:68

Lindblom, Ernst, author, 18:72
Lindegard, Axel, 16:129, 21:341; pa-
   pers, 21:415, 22:40
Lindeke, Mary P., author, 26:279
Lindeke, William, politician, 36:56
Lindeman, Marvin, author, 29:175
Lindemann, Mark, office assistant,
   25:41
Linden, Lawrence, speaker, 35:99
Linden Grove Township, St. Louis
   County, history, 23:302
Linden Township, Brown County, Nor-
   wegian settlement, 12:273, 23:105;
   Mormon mission, 36:288; log house,
   37:75
Linden Township, Iowa County, Wis.,
   farm life, 27:83-95
Linder, E. A., author, 25:316
Lindergreen, H. W., publisher, 13:150
Linderman, Frank B., author, 38:202
Lindesmith, Emery, author, 16:255
Lindesmith, Orlando, 16:255
Lindgren, J. R., 19:308
Lindholm, Algot, 27:178
Lindi, Elenita, author, 37:262
Lindley, Dr. Alfred H., Quaker, 18:
   252
Lindley, Mrs. Clarkson, 20:50, 24:
   279n, 27:176
Lindley, Mrs. Eliza, 18:263
Lindley, Mrs. Erasmus C. (Clara
   Hill), 30:268; work reviewed, 30:
   60
Lindley, Harlow, author, 13:109, 14:
   227, 24:70, 27:349
Lindquist, Rev. E. F., 14:456, 16:
   240; speaker, 15:492, 19:360
Lindquist, Emory, author, 34:175
Lindquist, Mrs. Eugene, author, 22:
   350
Lindquist, James, speaker, 11:224
Lindquist, Maude L., 11:223, 38:336;
   reviews by, 34:167, 35:35; work
   reviewed, 15:98-102; author, 18:
   327, 24:78, 28:357, 31:191; speak-
   er, 24:378; teacher, 35:204
Lindquist, Oscar E., author, 24:273
Lindsay, Lt. Andrew J., artist, 12:
   440
Lindsay, Effie G., author, 15:130
Lindsay, George F., 12:207
Lindsey, ---, Garrioch's companion,
   20:122
Lindsey, John C., author, 13:438
Lindsley, Col. D. C., 19:406
Lindsley, Pearle M., author, 13:445
Lindstrom, church, 14:353; ordi-
   nances, 15:466; main street, 16:
   364; teachers' training school,
   19:451; hotel, 25:96; Swedish set-
   tlement, 34:164, 35:337, 38:243
Lines, Charles B., excursionist, 34:
   137n, 139
Lingard, William, 28:110
Lingelbach, William E., editor, 19:
   347
Link, Arthur S., work reviewed, 34:
   342
Linn, Mrs. Rachel A., author, 13:322
Linnell, O. M., pioneer, 24:190
Linnevold, Rev. John, 27:77, 28:88;
   speaker, 27:266
Linney, Joseph, mining engineer, 34:
   277n
Linney, Robert, mining engineer, 34:
   277n
Lino Lakes, government, 39:299

Linquist, O. E., pioneer, 22:446
Linton, A. H., 26:371
Linton, Mr. and Mrs. Joseph W., farmers, 38:22
Linton, Dr. Laura A., career, 38:21-23
Linton, Dr. Sarah, career, 38:22, 23
Linton, Dr. William, 38:22
Lintonite, named, 38:21-23
Linwood, Lake Minnetonka, settled, 29:274
Linwood Lake, Anoka County, settled, 16:492
Lipove, Irving, author, 28:80, 29:84
Lippincott, Edward, alderman, 35:120
Lippincott, Gertrude L., "A Minnesota Saga," 21:58-62; author, 21:80
Lippincott, J. B., and Co., publishers, 19:422
Lippincott, Sara J. C., feminist, 30:251
Lippman, Eugene J., editor, 38:335
Lippmann, Walter, reformer, 14:201
Lippmann, Rosenthal and Co., Amsterdam, bankers, 37:153, 157n, 158n
Liquor traffic, in fur trade, 12:92, 18:395, 19:42, 21:125, 131, 134, 140, 141, 143, 146, 147, 22:277n, 288, 28:7, 143, 149, 40:155, 160, 162, 164, 170, 180, 186, 201, 202, 262; with Indians, 12:396, 16:317, 18:83, 19:279, 304, 21:397, 22:31, 279, 288, 24:21, 143, 28:149, 32:36, 38:26, 27, 121, 39:81; legislation, 14:138, 33:155-163, 38:121; Stillwater, 19:265-267; St. Paul, 22:3, 8; social aspect, 36:197-200, 205. See also Prohibition movement, Temperance movement
Lisa, Manuel, trader, 15:421, 426, 20:84, 39:255; career, 14:226, 35:243; on upper Missouri, 15:431; warehouse, 29:175, 40:192
Lisbon Township, Yellow Medicine County, Norwegian settlement, 12:275n
Lismer, Arthur, artist, 29:167
Lismore, Catholic settlement, 35:139
Lister, John H., author, 18:323
Listug, Carl, 19:362
Litchfield, Electus B., railroad executive, 14:349, 37:156, 157, 40:350
Litchfield, historical meeting, 11:37; immigrant house, 13:41; growth, 13:101, 19:408; Lutheran church, 14:451; Christmas celebration, 16:389, 31:221; G.A.R. post, 16:430, 37:42; pioneer life, 19:357; anniversary, 28:382; wheat raising, 29:10
Litchfield and Co., New York, 37:157
Litchfield Cemetery Association, records, 18:227, 19:344, 20:35
Litchfield Independent, anniversary, 17:361
Litchfield Livestock Shipping Association, records, 18:47, 97
Literary Digest, quoted, 37:170
Literary Northwest, reprint from, 24:276-286; history, 26:299-303; format, 26:310
Literary societies, Kandiyohi County, 19:236
Literature, anthologies, 19:436, 20:440, 25:297, 26:356-358, 37:218; regional, 20:105-118, 27:71, 28:

69, 276, 37:339, 40:304; criticism, 20:406, 21:3-14, 22:365, 30:149, 37:83, 39:291; periodicals, 24:235, 26:293-311, 28:185, 37:338; history, 30:62; juvenile, 33:340-343; use of folklore, 36:73-83, 95, 39:262; Minnesota authors, 36:147, 194; bibliography, 40:311. See also Fiction, Poetry
Lithuanians, Detroit, Mich., 20:202; Minneapolis, 20:216; U.S., 20:442; iron range, 23:387, 27:204, 211-213; remigration, 27:215
Litomysl, Steele County, name, 13:199; Catholic church, 21:457
Litschke, Gerald, author, 18:469
Little, Arthur D., Inc., consulting firm, 40:134
Little, Mrs. B. A., 14:331
Little, Frank E., residence, 23:229
Little, George, bookseller, 19:382n
Little, Dr. J. P., author, 35:218
Little, Nina F., author, 35:150
Little, Thomas, J., 14:217
Little American Island, Rainy Lake, gold mining, 15:489, 17:361
Little automobile, 38:207
Little Bighorn River, Mont., battle, 12:177, 302, 22:175, 33:57, 34:39, 131, 355, 39:342; national monument, 31:251
Little Canada, founded, 14:386; Catholic church, 15:480, 21:454; dairy farm, 27:110; history, 30:401; road, 36:209; in Sioux Outbreak, 38:275
Little Chute, Wis., Dutch settlement, 28:368
Little Corporal (Evanston, Ill.), juvenile paper, 18:366
Little Cottonwood River, Cottonwood County, garrison, 38:285
Little Crow (Big Thunder), 15:274, 21:23, 24:22n; portrait, 33:21
Little Crow (Taoyateduta), Sioux leader, 11:455, 12:335, 16:43, 17:215, 20:171, 21:23n, 22:152n, 28:315, 29:318n, 35:99, 37:228, 38:124, 129-143, 147-149; "Taoyateduta Is Not a Coward," 38:115; described, 12:119, 14:349, 38:96; career, 13:95; Mayer portrait, 13:412, 35:197, 39:198; death, 14:331, 38:150-153, 284; in Sioux Outbreak, 19:84, 218, 34:319, 38:98, 102, 103, 106-108, 144, 146, 148, 274, 280, 357, 39:85, 40:282; pictured, 30:66, 38:93 (cover); village, 38:138. See also Kaposia
Little Falls, banking, 14:356; business, 14:436; archaeology, 16:1; described, 17:225, 36:237; historical meeting, 18:204, 267-269; lumbering, 18:315, 23:197; Franciscan convent, 20:446; road, 21:234; music, 22:115; Pike's post, 23:298; history, 23:301, 29:270, 34:84, 40:38; Lutheran church, 24:90; school, 25:12, 14; ration board, 26:175; frontier settlement, 28:211, 213; dam, 28:293; depot, 28:396; mission, 33:90; museum, 35:293; in Sioux Outbreak, 38:276, 280; politics, 39:106
Little Falls, Hennepin County, see Minnehaha Falls

Little Falls and Dakota Railroad, 11:413, 415
Little Falls Daily Transcript, history, 23:301
Little Falls Guard, organized, 16:172
Little Falls Sun, 17:469
Little Fork, business, 13:118; history, 23:107, 26:397, 27:176, 33:315; logging railroad, 28:376
Little Fork River, Koochiching County, navigation, 24:192; mounds, 31:231
Little Giants, Democratic club, 16:175n, 39:175
Little Hill, Winnebago leader, 31:211, 213, 39:315
Little Kandiyohi Lake, Kandiyohi County, hunting, 33:146, 149, 152
Little Leaf, Sioux leader, 34:322
Little Prairie, Rice County, Methodist church, 12:106, 23:302
Little Priest, Winnebago leader, 38:137, 148, 360, 361, 363
Little Rapids, Minnesota River, 11:169, 38:361; post, 11:376, 20:263-265; Sioux village, 21:170, 171
Little Rock, Chippewa leader, at Old Crossing treaty, 15:289-291
Little Rock, Ark., in Civil War, 17:217, 40:281-291
Little Rock, Nicollet County, post, 11:175, 377, 378, 19:108, 468, 21:32n, 22:137n, 30:30, 36:40
Little Rock River, Renville and Nicollet counties, 11:176
Little Roebuck, Cree Indian, 32:236
Little Sauk Township, Todd County, history, 16:498
Little Sisters of the Poor, homes for aged, 38:82
Little Six, Sioux leader, see Shakopee
Little Thunder, Winnebago leader, 38:363
Little Vermilion Lake, St. Louis County and Ontario, post, 11:360, 22:275
Little White Cloud, Chippewa leader, author, 35:47
Littlejohn, Mr. and Mrs. Abram N., excursionists, 34:140
Littlejohn, Bruce M., author, 40:48, 144
Litton, Abram, surveyor's assistant, 26:227, 228
Litton, Gaston, author, 34:354
Litt's Grand Opera House, St. Paul, 39:53
Litwack, Leon F., author, 37:344
Livdahlen, Ole C., pioneer, 11:289
Live Topics Club, Faribault, 16:242, 19:467
Livermore, Mary A., feminist, 28:54, 35:227, 228, 39:5
Livermore, Shaw, Jr., author, 36:230
Liverpool, Eng., emigrant port, 20:251, 252; Catholic school, 35:134, 135
Livestock industry, Middle West, 11:324, 15:353, 28:276; hog raising, 18:409; Minnesota, 19:121, 22:255, 24:105, 27:357, 29:27n, 91, 201, 30:264, 406; state fair exhibits, 22:257, 261, 263; U.S., 24:157; frontier, 26:106-125, 27:88, 29:151; statistics, 27:107, 119; Kansas City, 27:354; historic sites,

40:404. See also Cattle industry,
  Dairy industry, Sheep raising
Ljungmark, Lars-Olov, author, 37:134
Lloyd, Harriet, 23:391
Lloyd, Henry D., 17:100, 27:334
Lloyd, Herbert M., editor, 37:78
Lloyd, J. J., author, 17:361
Lloyd, Marshall B., biography, 14:349
Lloyd, Trevor, author, 21:100, 22:432
Lobb, Albert J., 23:50, 26:45, 29:97
Lobdell, Mrs. Julia E. F., author,
  14:450, 20:449
Lobingier, Charles S., author, 16:
  115, 349
Lochead, Dr. D. C., author, 12:204
Lochren, William, 14:246; judge, 18:
  96, 128; author, 25:18, 38:251,
  252; papers, 36:328
Locke, John, 19:397n
Locke, Mrs. Tracy, author, 36:282
Locker, Mary, 22:52
Locker-Lampson, Frederick, quoted,
  27:41
Lockwood, James H., trader, 11:378,
  20:262, 40:186
Lockwood, Norman, house, 27:230
Lockwood, Sarah, work reviewed, 34:
  309
Locofoco party, 16:326
Locomobile automobile, 38:208, 214
Lodeon, Iver N., author, 20:346
Lodge, Henry C., 18:140
Loeb, Isidor, editor, 12:330
Loehr, Rodney C., 19:69, 23:393, 28:
  47, 50, 29:52, 186, 257, 30:46,
  89, 329, 39:84; "Minnesota Farmers' Diaries," 18:284-297; "Caleb
  Dorr," 24:125-141; "Franklin
  Steele," 27:309-318; "Jason C.
  Easton," 29:223-230; "Portrait of
  a Pioneer Home," 39:201-204; reviews by, 21:300-302, 22:186, 314,
  23:165, 179, 27:138, 234-236, 331-
  333, 338, 29:68, 155, 251, 345,
  30:60, 255, 389, 31:113, 247, 37:
  305, 38:196, 382, 39:127; works
  reviewed, 20:417, 33:219; speaker,
  18:205, 20:302, 29:98, 30:88, 180;
  author, 19:44, 93, 20:74, 21:310,
  323, 22:188, 316, 23:170, 24:164,
  255, 27:152, 247, 342, 343, 28:
  276, 331, 332, 29:104, 192, 287,
  376, 30:90, 95, 292, 391, 31:61,
  127, 256, 33:91; editor, 20:31,
  323, 21:40, 328, 30:327, 358; research associate, 27:340
Loehr, Mrs. Rodney C. (Nancy S.), review by, 18:309
Loemans, Alexander, artist, 27:270
Loenholdt, Wilhelmina P., author, 34:
  170
Loevinger, Judge Gustavus, 13:198,
  23:392, 35:289; author, 30:266
Loevinger, Lee, author, 38:92
Lofgren, Mrs. C. J., speaker, 30:167
Lofthus, Mrs. Anna, speaker, 20:351
Loftness, Serena, author, 13:206, 212
Loftus, George S., 15:338, 26:382;
  biography, 21:68
Log cabins, see Houses
Log marks, depicted, 17:490, 22:416;
  recorded, 23:395, 24:135, 25:92;
  function, 26:126-137, 27:195, 287
Logan, Frank B., author, 11:220
Logan, Gen. John A., 16:436, 441
Logan, Wilfred D., review by, 39:339;
  author, 37:307

Logan Township, Aitkin County, name,
  21:347
Logging, see Lumber industry
Loichot, Louis, 17:273; postmaster,
  13:132, 139
Loken, Hjalmar J., author, 20:85
Lokhorst, E., 28:128
Lokke, Carl L., "From Minneapolis to
  the Klondike," 29:300-315; "Roose-
  velt, Nelson, and Alaska," 32:174;
  reviews by, 32:53, 33:43; work re-
  viewed, 39:341; author, 29:376,
  30:93, 31:58, 32:60, 64, 191, 34:
  169
Lokken, Harry M., author, 36:105
Lokken, Roscoe L., work reviewed, 23:
  357-359
Loman, history, 30:162
Lomasney, Patrick J., author, 14:229
Lomasney, W. O., 19:308
Lomax, Alan, compiler, 24:367
Lomax, John A., author, 27:72
Lombard, Geraldine L., author, 20:208
Lomen, G. J., work reviewed, 11:89
Lomen family, genealogy, 11:89
Lomker, Dorothy, author, 24:273
Lommen, E. E., Senator, 35:306, 307
Lommen, George H., Senator, 24:356
Lommen, Georgina, author, 34:128
Lomoe, Orville E., author, 22:349,
  23:199
London, George, singer, 39:63
London, Jack, assessed, 39:260
London, Eng., Radisson's stay, 16:
  391-413; fur market, 24:149, 40:
  211, 213n, 215, 216, 218, 219;
  business center, 40:176, 179
London, Freeborn County, railroad
  station, 34:181
London Conference, achievements, 18:
  425
London String Quartet, 39:63
Lone Tree Lake, ghost town, 19:465,
  38:107. See also Battle Lake
"Lone tree prairie," Mo., river set-
  tlement, 17:431n
Long, Birch, architect, 40:107
Long, E. John, author, 37:186
Long, Frank, speaker, 21:215
Long, George S., Jr., author, 32:125
Long, Harold M., author, 29:77
Long, Huey P., politician, 12:10; in
  fiction, 37:5
Long, James, steamboat captain, 33:12
Long, John, trader, 11:262
Long, Dr. L. V., 18:108
Long, Lily A., author, 20:73, 26:307
Long, Mary A., author, 32:190
Long, Stephen H., engineer and explorer, 15:370, 16:26, 278n, 453,
  28:184, 30:209, 36:236, 296, 37:
  37; expeditions, 11:81, 205, 361,
  444, 12:238, 327, 13:367, 368,
  418, 14:430, 16:155-158, 17:305,
  307, 308, 438, 19:447, 458, 20:34,
  22:154, 288, 24:75, 26:165, 30:
  220, 31:105, 33:89, 34:284, 285,
  35:241, 242, 292, 378, 36:69, 103,
  294, 295, 298, 37:31, 40:144; biographies, 14:348, 40:305; author,
  15:429, 17:480, 19:217, 34:286,
  35:44; journals, 23:7, 27:61, 35:
  43, 38:41, 40:316; inventor, 25:
  88; map maker, 35:97, 36:277
Long family, in Minneapolis, 32:190
"Long Branch," steamboat, 25:127

Long Island Lake, Cook County, forest
  fire, 36:137
Long Lake, Hennepin County, history,
  36:106
Long Lake, Meeker County, stockade,
  12:302, 303
Long Lake, Watonwan County, Norwegian
  settlement, 12:182, 274; history,
  22:443; grasshopper plague, 37:207
Long Lake Farmers' Club, Echols, 20:
  218
Long Point, Lake of the Woods County,
  fishing, 35:275
Long Prairie, pioneer life, 11:224,
  15:253; Winnebago reservation, 11:
  316, 12:160n, 205, 13:216, 17:210,
  293n, 18:474, 22:191, 25:183, 29:
  101, 30:2, 5, 11, 12, 31:210, 33:
  118n, 36:267, 40:332; ethnic settlements, 12:263, 29:182; mission,
  13:321, 339; Indian agency, 13:
  447, 15:371, 17:154n, 156n;
  churches, 14:124, 24:94; early
  roads, 19:103, 40:233; history,
  23:111; dairying, 27:110; post office, 40:83
Long Prairie Leader, anniversary, 15:
  139; politics, 38:305
Long River, imaginary river, identi-
  fication question, 11:451; Lahontan's description, 14:220-222,
  375; map, 14:373
Long Sault, Ottawa River, Ont., Que.,
  portage, 28:8, 150
Long Siding, Mille Lacs County, name,
  21:349
Longbotham, Eileen, 26:256; manuscript assistant, 24:243, 25:40
Longfellow, Henry W., 20:135, 200,
  282, 27:16, 37:154; "Hiawatha"
  poem, 15:261, 27:288, 31:193, 203,
  32:107, 34:213, 35:153, 36:23, 75;
  promotes tourism, 16:33, 280n;
  poet, 16:105, 351, 36:21; evaluated, 21:13, 24:238; family, 21:
  149; influences, 24:237, 25:54,
  300, 28:323, 29:335, 34:32, 35:
  143, 380
Longfellow, Levi, papers, 12:191
"Longfellow," steamboat, 31:88
Longfellow Club, Mankato, 19:333
Longhway, Madeline V., author, 19:239
Longlac, Ont., post, 40:149
Longstreet, Gen. James, Confederate
  officer, 38:267, 269, 270
Longyear, Edmund J., work reviewed,
  32:244-246; mineralogist, 34:216,
  273
Longyear, Mrs. Edmund J., pioneer,
  32:245, 246
Longyear, John, surveyor, 14:462
Lonn, Ella, work reviewed, 33:83
Lonnrot, Becker County, Finnish set-
  tlement, 25:320
Lonsdale, history, 21:115
Looft, Carl, author, 21:365
Loomis, A. G., 23:296
Loomis, Ann H., see North, Mrs. John
  W., II
Loomis, David B., MHS founder, 20:367
Loomis, George, in Minnesota, 35:111,
  112, 114, 116
Loomis, Dr. George S., 35:101-116
Loomis, Gorton, 35:105
Loomis, Gustavus, army officer, 12:
  397, 21:159

Loomis, Maj. John, at Fort Snelling, 33:353
Loomis, Noel M., author, 35:199, 38:41
Loon Lake, border lake, portage, 13:298
Loper and Rumery, logging firm, 31:159
Loran, Erle, author, 17:228
Loras, Bishop Mathias, 15:81, 17:475, 18:436, 19:107, 461, 21:102, 28:184, 31:240; career, 11:105, 106, 14:339, 341, 349, 15:212–214, 33:356; in Minnesota, 11:210, 20:339, 22:51, 23:286, 24:12
Loras College, Dubuque, Iowa, history, 28:184
Lord, Clifford, 27:164, 258, 39:265; work reviewed, 39:336; author, 24:363, 25:390, 29:355, 30:72, 31:118, 187, 32:254, 34:219, 37:85, 39:209; speaker, 36:69; editor, 40:364
Lord, Elizabeth H., author, 25:390
Lord, J. A., Dramatic Co., 28:110
Lord, John, 35:195
Lord, Livingston C., author, 12:418; educator, 18:329, 25:68; biography, 19:332
Lord, Mrs. Livingston C., 19:333
Lord, Orville M., 31:162
Lord, Samuel, legislator, 27:346, 35:347, 349
Lord, Samuel, Jr., legislator, 27:346
Lorénzen, Lilly E., author, 34:172, 36:106
Loretto Hospital, New Ulm, 15:184
L'Orignal Portage, Alta., described, 20:327
Lorimer, Frank, author, 23:178
Loring, Albert C., 27:176; estate, 20:195
Loring, Justice Charles, 28:200
Loring, Charles E., publisher, 22:23n
Loring, Charles M., papers, 14:333, 15:60; biography, 14:349
Loring, Geneviève, 13:429
Loring, Dr. George B., 34:290
Loring Park, Minneapolis, 26:68, 284, 27:75, 270, 28:296
Lorne, Marquis of, at Rat Portage, Ont., 31:184
Lorrain, Claude, artist, 38:345
Los Angeles, Norwegians, 22:70
Loss, B. J., speaker, 20:306
Lothrop, Cass County, village ordinances, 17:468
Lott, Bushrod W., 39:148n; papers, 16:215; career, 21:343
"Lotta Lee," steamboat, 14:219
Lottinville, Savoie, essay reviewed, 38:238
Lotze, Marie L., author, 11:324
Louchheim, Aline B., author, 33:311
Loudon, Earl of, collector, 21:395
Loudon, W. J., author, 12:199
Loughrea, Mildred, review by, 36:66
Louis XIV, king of France, 19:275, 280; medals, 25:265
Louis XV, king of France, 18:234; medals, 25:265
Louisiana, French colony, 11:78, 15:472, 18:397, 19:393, 396, 23:161, 34:117; under Spain, 11:451, 18:394; laws, 12:9; boundaries, 12:410, 28:281; U.S. regime, 18:384, 23:258; resources, 18:390; fur

trade, 18:430, 19:292–295, 34:80; explored, 23:84; history, 25:193; archives, 30:57–59, 31:48; pictorial record, 34:253; 1763 revolution, 39:337
Louisiana Historical Association, publication, 37:39
Louisiana Purchase, explored, 11:189; extent, 22:100, 433; resources, 24:230; maps, 24:252; evaluated, 34:352
Louisiana Purchase Exposition, St. Louis, 39:155
Louisiana State Museum, New Orleans, guide, 26:383
Louisiana State University, Baton Rouge, press, 20:113
Louisville, Carver County, paper town, 13:141
Louisville, Scott County, trading post, 11:169; ghost town, 18:343; politics, 28:36
Lounsberry, Col. C. A., career, 22:174–176
Lounsbury, Thomas R., 12:191
Louraine, Dorothy M., compiler, 24:173
Louvigny, Louis de la Porte, Sieur de, 19:282
Lovatt, Mrs. John S., author, 16:233
Love, Peggy M., author, 34:116; editor, 37:176
Lovejoy, Allen F., author, 23:285
Lovejoy, Elijah, abolitionist, 20:430, 33:218
Lovejoy, George W., musician, 27:173
Lovejoy, James A., lumberman, 26:135, 136, 37:319
Lovelace, Delos, works reviewed, 15:450, 18:309; author, 16:238, 31:130, 146
Lovelace, Mrs. Delos (Maud H.), 32:64; reviews by, 13:295, 32:54; works reviewed, 15:450, 18:309, 30:246; author, 13:314, 436, 16:238, 21:448, 30:247, 31:129, 130, 146, 36:76; speaker, 15:457, 16:48
Lovelace, Francis, 16:401n, 406
Lovell, John W., speaker, 11:294
Lovell, William K., publisher, 17:300n
Lovell, William R., in Civil War, 18:210
Lover's Leap, see Maiden Rock
Lovett, Charles E., diaries, 34:359
Lovett, Libbie, author, 36:394
Lovness, Donald, house, 38:352
Low, Bartlett, settler, 14:85, 459
Low, Lt. G., 18:405
Low, John, settler, 14:85, 459
Lowater, Ninette M., poet, 26:298, 301
Lowden, Frank O., biography, 36:33
Lowe, Mrs. Alex, 15:250; speaker, 16:66
Lowe, Rev. Arnold H., 29:88
Lowe, Barrett, author, 14:226
Lowe, Edith J., author, 18:102
Lowe, Mrs. Inez K., 22:338
Lowe, John H., author, 31:58
Lowe, Kelsey, author, 17:120
Lowe, Lora L., speaker, 20:349
Lowe, Margaret, author, 11:321
Lowe, Marshall, 15:250
Lowe, Thaddeus S., aeronaut, 25:23n, 39:283
Lowe, Dr. Thomas, speaker, 15:250

Lowell, Edwin B., 25:356; steamboat owner, 33:12
Lowell, James Russell, 20:130, 37:154; letter, 18:139; author, 27:16
Lowell, Maria, 20:130
Lower, Arthur R. M., author, 12:88, 20:341, 28:282; editor, 15:125
Lower Fort Garry, Man., trading post, 11:364, 20:122, 36:38; social life, 15:477; history, 22:99; pictured, 24:262, 40:190. See also Fort Garry
Lower Rapids, see Des Moines Rapids
Lower Red Cedar Lake, see Cedar Lake, Aitkin County
Lower Red Lake, see Red Lake
Lower Sioux (Redwood) agency, 19:84, 37:348, 38:135; ferry, 11:29, 34:233–238; freight traffic, 11:132, 133, 136, 137, 139, 184, 36:256; established, 11:177, 183, 12:121; agent, 11:179; post, 11:378; mission, 11:455, 12:114, 118, 38:136n, 144n; in Sioux Outbreak, 12:297, 298, 18:461, 28:327, 29:123n, 35:288, 37:330, 38:95–97, 111, 113, 132n, 133, 137, 147, 148; Indian councils, 16:39, 43, 29:122n, 37:225–228; described, 16:42; map, 34:236; site, 37:60; agriculture, 38:93, 94, 130, 38:107n; sawmill, 38:112; courthouse, 38:112; function, 38:122; ferry, 38:154, 156
Lowery, Woodbury, geographer, 34:303
Lowie, Robert H., work reviewed, 34:255
Lowitt, Richard, work reviewed, 39:28
Lowland mounds, Minnesota, 16:307–312
Lowman, Mrs. ---, teacher, 39:318
Lowry, Mrs. ---, artist, 35:370
Lowry, David, Indian agent, 16:470, 21:425; missionary, 20:443, 21:20
Lowry, Rev. S. G., 16:496
Lowry, Gen. Sylvanus B., 11:454, 17:335, 21:412; trader, 11:374, 36:260–262; politician, 13:147, 32:17; colonizer, 15:139; slaveholder, 18:119, 25:202; letters, 19:343, 20:33
Lowry, Thomas, 23:197, 40:15n; career, 14:349, 29:88; transportation executive, 22:379, 36:150; author, 27:242; politician, 35:66–68, 70, 71; financier, 39:113, 115; monument, 40:409
Lowry, history, 11:337
Lowry Hill, Minneapolis, architecture, 40:104, 106
Lowth and Howe, Owatonna, seeder manufacturers, 24:304
Lowville Township, Murray County, post, 14:85; history, 14:459
Loyalists, characterized, 15:96; emigration, 22:71
Loye, Mrs. Jens, speaker, 12:338
Loyhed, Mrs. E. H., speaker, 16:361, 19:118, 21:109
Lucas, Eva L. (Mrs. Frank E. Higgins), 31:68, 77
Lucas, Frank, labor leader, 40:344
Lucas, Henry S., "Early Dutch Settlement," 28:120–131; review by, 29:67; works reviewed, 28:367, 35:33, 90; author, 28:204, 29:103; editor, 28:379, 29:174
Lucas, Robert, papers, 15:463
Luce, Edward S., author, 31:251

Luce, Evelyn S., author, 31:251
Luce, Robert, Congressman, 38:182
Luce, Sidney, Duluth settler, 12:384, 37:112; postmaster, 34:185
Luckhardt, Arno B., author, 20:337
Lucy Wilder Morris Park, Minneapolis, 40:48
Ludden, John D., 38:82, 40:229
Ludington, Harrison, 19:150
Ludington, James, banker, 40:112-114
Ludington, N., and Co., Chicago, 40:113
Ludlow, Mrs. H. J., speaker, 14:460
Ludlow, Israel, 14:32
Ludlow, Milton, 21:446
Ludlow, William, scientist, 32:219, 220; author, 34:304
Ludlum, David M., work reviewed, 40:312
Ludolph, Mrs. Carrie, 24:341; author, 11:465; speaker, 19:471
Ludvigh, Samuel, author, 24:222, 33:188; speaker, 26:67, 28:30; editor, 28:22, 23, 26
Ludwig, Emil, author, 28:360
Ludwig, Mary C., author, 30:268
Ludwig-Missionsverein, European society, 15:354, 21:74, 25:193, 33:138
Lue Gim Gong, horticulturist, 24:259
Lueders, Frederick G. J., botanist, 24:77
Lueders, H. F., author, 20:357
Luedke, William, 16:243, 17:358, 18:336
Lueg, Henry, journal, 31:253
Luelling, Henderson, nurseryman, 23:91
Luers, Herbert F., 17:241; author, 16:255, 372
Luethge, George M., memorial, 12:194
Luger, J. B., 18:405
Lugol, J. G. A., 21:367; author, 21:365
Luhrsen, Frederick, music dealer, 39:319, 320
Luihhunen, Oscar, labor leader, 40:344
Lukey, M., tavernkeeper, 19:133
Lull, Abram C., postmaster, 16:97, 36:208
Lull, C. P. V., steamboat captain, 21:249
Lull, Louis, 31:50
Lum, Leon E., bequest, 11:20
Lumber Exchange, Minneapolis, 18:143
Lumber industry, Minnesota, 11:95, 218, 13:341, 365, 14:102, 16:251, 21:211, 22:102, 25:309, 26:182, 27:312-314, 29:363, 30:272, 32:61; pine forests, 11:105, 13:349, 20:440, 30:242, 36:132; in fiction, 11:215, 14:209, 35:196, 37:12; Mississippi Valley, 12:108, 13:357, 15:253, 484, 22:416, 27:312-314; firms, 12:319, 428, 13:101, 14:112, 15:346, 464, 16:52, 73, 101, 19:360, 21:344, 27:165, 190-202, 29:177, 375, 31:109, 183, 32:60, 188, 34:263, 35:382, 36:28, 39:211; equipment, 13:99, 356, 24:130; Wisconsin, 13:438, 15:475, 16:217, 347, 479, 20:340, 22:312, 24:261, 30:71, 159, 31:113, 190, 32:252-254, 39:298, 40:357; Mille Lacs County, 13:452, 27:154, 28:292; logging methods, 15:203-206,

20:329, 25:197, 27:286, 28:188; Anoka area, 15:244, 28:379; Itasca County, 15:487, 22:445; St. Croix Valley, 16:131, 17:130, 282-286, 313, 390, 396, 18:165-179, 420, 474, 21:430, 24:166, 196-203, 27:310, 28:380, 31:33-39, 34:44; Canada, 16:366, 20:341, 23:385; museums, 16:486, 490, 17:491, 18:344, 21:330, 24:364, 25:303, 34:43, 35:201, 336, 36:282; log drives, 17:116, 238, 491, 23:197, 24:129, 137, 25:199, 211, 29:146, 31:62, 34:35, 45 (cover); executives, 18:97, 20:441, 22:94, 95, 206, 23:273, 24:125-141, 192, 28:182, 29:85, 142, 144, 39:129; employees, 21:378, 458, 22:154n, 23:99, 387, 26:166, 27:207, 208, 29:141-143, 30:73, 36:153-166; railroads, 21:439, 24:264, 25:102, 27:300-308, 28:376, 33:226, 34:180, 36:153-166, 37:90, 185, 40:361; periodicals, 22:437, 35:156; river transportation, 24:245, 33:7-19, 36:250, 38:348; lake shipping, 25:77, 34:12; in art, 27:262; Beltrami County, 29:137-149, 33:356, 35:202; effect on wildlife, 30:129, 132, 226; on Indian lands, 32:180, 36:69; Northwest Angle, 34:1-8; pictured, 34:59, 64, 66, 149-153, 40:126; labor problems, 36:156, 157, 162, 165, 166. See also Boom companies; Bunyan, Paul; Forestry; Log marks; Lumberjacks; Rafting; Sawmills
Lumber Manufacturers National Bank, Stillwater, 18:178
Lumberjacks, characterized, 11:101, 13:360, 366, 25:276, 30:68, 243; camp life, 12:99, 13:334, 352, 358, 364, 14:219, 462, 15:205, 18:332, 19:197, 24:194, 29:70; from Maine, 12:164, 16:26, 45, 479, 18:168, 21:56, 176, 23:99, 24:125, 127, 27:312, 30:242, 36:159, 37:41; ethnic origins, 13:284, 350-352, 365; food, 13:353-355, 360, 361, 24:383, 29:142; pictured, 13:356, 357, 15:368, 17:130, 36:78, 40:400, 401; amusements, 13:361-364, 17:367; songs and legends, 13:362, 16:236, 21:353-356, 23:382, 36:194, 39:129; language, 13:364, 21:453, 24:74, 25:219, 220, 35:335, 36:278; wages, 16:99, 17:400, 19:324, 29:143, 30:275; smallpox epidemic, 24:265, 34:34; missions, 31:65-78; duties, 34:62, 149-153; in fiction, 36:77. See also Bunyan, Paul; Lumber industry
Lumberman's Building, Winona, museum, 36:142, 144
Lumberman's National Bank, Stillwater, 18:173, 178, 31:34
Lumbermen's Board of Exchange, Stillwater, 31:36-38
Lumbermen's Board of Trade of the St. Croix Valley, 31:33, 35, 37
Lumbertown USA, Brainerd, established, 35:201; receives award, 35:336; historical meeting, 35:340; described, 36:282
Lumley, John, cholera victim, 14:289, 290

Lund, C. N., Mormon missionary, 36:288
Lund, Charles A., speaker, 11:117
Lund, Charles C., papers, 26:155
Lund, Doniver A., review by, 35:373; works reviewed, 38:382
Lund, N. L., Mormon missionary, 36:292
Lund, Richard J., author, 17:108
Lund Academy, Melby, 38:382
Lund Press, Minneapolis, receives award, 31:255
Lundeberg, Olaf K., author, 31:146
Lundeen, Ernest, author, 16:482, 17:478; speaker, 17:348; politician, 28:74, 38:302, 40:369-371, 373, 374, 410; papers, 29:350
Lundeen, Col. John A., 11:465, 20:353; speaker, 16:301, 18:329; author, 17:353
Lundgren, Paul, 20:97
Lundie, Edwin H., architect, 37:186, 38:189
Lundmark, Leon, artist, 25:54
Lundquist, Adolph, editor, 30:77
Lundquist, C. R., farmer, 37:77
Lundquist, G. A., speaker, 11:103
Lundquist, L., Swedish immigrant, 20:258
Lundstrom, R., labor leader, 40:344
Lunt, W. E., 14:194
Luoma, Everett E., work reviewed, 40:354
Luomala, Katherine, 33:45, 46
Luraas, John, pioneer, 24:348
Lurie, Mollie, librarian, 37:188
Lurie, Nancy O., work reviewed, 37:343; author, 34:215
Lutes, Della, author, 23:182
Luther, E. J., prospector, 24:383
Luther, E. L., author, 27:356
Luther, G., 37:16
Luther, Manton H., author, 23:310
Luther, Sally, author, 30:157, 181
Luther Academy, Albert Lea, 19:357
Luther College, Decorah, Iowa, 15:235, 39:135; outdoor museum, 12:328; history, 14:332, 15:361, 17:457, 38:37
Luther College, Wahoo, Neb., 37:40
Luther-St. Paul Hospital, history, 20:466
Luther Theological Seminary, St. Paul, 27:256, 31:126, 40:383; Muskego church, 38:231-233
Luther Valley, Wis., Mormon mission, 36:278
Lutheran Book Concern, Columbus, Ohio, 15:448
Lutheran Brotherhood, Minneapolis, 36:239
Lutheran church, Muskego, Wis., 11:209, 12:257, 14:54n, 24:348, 33:85, 38:231-233; Norwegian, 11:216, 15:114, 235, 16:471, 17:457, 18:472, 20:200, 345, 24:323, 348, 25:195, 26:296, 29:160, 36:98, 37:183; educational institutions, 11:226, 24:55, 264, 26:166, 167, 27:270, 28:286, 30:377, 391, 31:50, 32:51, 34:91, 35:98, 38:382; Iowa Synod, 11:320, 12:329, 19:211; Norwegian-Danish, 12:85; records, 12:194, 195, 13:429; German (and the Missouri Synod), 12:332, 13:114, 14:45-58, 324, 15:27, 16:335, 17:457, 21:427, 28:126, 29:79, 31:

25, 35:98, 201; Finnish, 12:436, 22:97, 25:324; Chippewa County, 13:116; Swedish (and Augustana Synod), 13:305, 306, 308, 14:95, 17:398, 24:323, 29:255, 30:263, 32:50, 53, 34:167, 175, 36:192, 37:40, 177, 38:92, 381, 39:81, 299, 40:353; East Ohio Synod, 14:46, 47; Minnesota Synod, 14:47-50, 53, 15:361; English, 14:47, 24:73; Buffalo Synod, 14:51, 54; Concordia Synod, 14:55; Hauge's Synod, 15:235; publications, 15:484; policies, 16:107, 22:193, 381, 32:16n, 36:287; history, 16:219, 35:200; Icelandic Synod, 17:343; lay movement, 18:432; frontier, 20:27, 25:396, 29:354; Slovak Synod, 24:73; Free church, 24:366, 29:296; children's home, 27:78; in politics, 28:36, 32:15, 22, 39:96; North Dakota, 29:354. See also individual communities and church bodies

Lutheran missions, Dakota Territory, 11:212; among Chippewa, 12:332, 14:55-58, 19:96, 28:291; Middle West, 19:211; Minnesota, 21:453, 24:373, 383, 27:271

Lutheran Normal School, Madison, 36:327

Lutheran Publishing House, Decorah, Iowa, 15:448

Luthin, Reinhard H., author, 36:326

Lutsen, pioneer days, 12:207; name, 12:287

Luttig, John C., journal, 39:261

Lutz, Josephine, see Rollins, Josephine Lutz

Luverne, history, 15:252; churches, 16:337, 27:344; G.A.R. post, 16:434

Luverne automobile, 40:148

Luxemburg, Stearns County, Catholic church, 16:484, 17:229

Luxemburgers, Rollingstone, 38:243

Luxon, Norval N., work reviewed, 29:62; author, 22:429

Luxton, William F., editor, 39:333

Lyback, Johanna R. M., author, 13:204

Lybe, Capt. A. Smith, 39:77

Lybrand, Jacob, 19:122, 473

Lyceum Theater, Minneapolis, 33:104n, 322

Lyceums, on frontier, 12:400, 13:146, 15:135, 16:317, 17:240, 388, 394, 466, 490, 18:293, 19:251, 20:26, 144, 22:360, 23:301, 27:9, 30:200, 35:112; Webster City, Iowa, 15:475; history, 35:194, 40:12-20

Lydon, J. W. (Jim), author, 31:62, 38:335

Lyell, Sir Charles, 39:167

Lyford, Carrie A., author, 23:181, 25:87

Lyksett, S. L., 23:392

Lyle, history, 16:368; railroad, 33:43

Lyman, C. W., farmer, 29:27n

Lyman, Clara C., "The World and Minnesota," 30:185-201; author, 30:291

Lyman, Cornelius, house, 38:338

Lyman, Dr. George D., work reviewed, 11:430-432; author, 11:210, 12:29, 190, 14:439

Lyman, H. M., 20:141, 145; postmaster, 20:144

Lyman, Theodore, 18:131

Lymanhurst Health Center, Minneapolis, history, 25:307

Lynch, Edward, speaker, 17:484

Lynch, Fred, 23:274

Lynch, Isidore, 11:237n, 238n

Lynch, John M., biography, 12:322

Lynch, Thomas, with Nobles expedition, 35:252

Lynch, Will, grain merchant, 24:103

Lynch, William O., author, 23:83, 27:158, 34:311

Lynchburg, Va., Confederate prison, 25:147

Lynd, Helen, author, 33:206

Lynd, James W., trader, 11:380, 12:119, 130, 133, 21:220; characterized, 12:131; editor, 14:262; author, 18:210, 19:386n; career, 18:461

Lynd, Robert, author, 33:206

Lynd, trading post, 11:380; history, 13:450, 15:489; county seat, 20:360; newspaper, 27:344

Lyndale Avenue, Minneapolis, farms, 16:385

Lynde, J. W., politician, 36:4n

Lynde, John, 14:233

Lyngblomsten Home for the Aged, St. Paul, 15:363

Lynn Township, Day County, S.D., scout camp, 40:313

Lynn Township, McLeod County, records, 20:349

Lynx, in fur trade, 30:134

"Lynx," steamboat, 13:233-235, 238, 239, 14:142, 18:372, 28:135, 136, 32:12

Lyon, ———, baseball player, 19:179

Lyon, Bessie L., author, 15:475

Lyon, D., 20:249

Lyon, E. Wilson, work reviewed, 23:258; author, 15:472

Lyon, H. R., 19:184n

Lyon, John, steamboat captain, 33:13, 14

Lyon, Lucius, Senator, 14:215, 40:23, 24, 80, 81

Lyon, Gen. Nathaniel, 19:387

Lyon, William H., work reviewed, 40:257

Lyon County, pioneer life, 13:119, 450, 17:87, 30:396, 37:20, 26; Lutheran church, 14:121; history, 15:489, 16:366, 30:407; Icelandic settlement, 17:344, 18:469, 26:397; courthouse, 20:360; mound, 24:78; library, 31:61; Catholic colony, 35:134, 325

Lyon County, Iowa, in 1879, 29:266

Lyon County Historical Society, 13:118, 16:241, 490, 30:80, 277; organized, 15:343, 368, 16:63

Lyons, Lord, career, 25:37n

Lyons, John L., 23:66

Lyons, T. D., author, 21:425

Lyons, Iowa, river town, 17:423; sawmill, 27:190

Lyons Township, Lyon County, trading post, 11:380

Lytle, A. D., photographer, 33:217

Ma, Gioh-Fang Dju, work reviewed, 30:245

Maailmasta, Unhotetujen, poet, 27:42

Maas, Melvin, Congressman, 40:374

Mabane, Adam, 15:96

Mabee, Carleton, work reviewed, 37:259

Mabel, schools, 13:342; pioneer life, 23:400, 24:89, 191

Mabel Creamery Association, 22:221

Mabey, Nell, "Fort Beauharnois," 30:122; author, 30:184

Mabrey, Fred J., 39:245, 246, 248, 249

McAfee, William J., 18:130

McAffee, Robert, engineer, 34:277

Macalester, Charles, biography, 14:349

Macalester College, St. Paul, 16:335, 18:375, 379, 19:68, 237, 30:88, 198, 202, 297, 34:94, 36:281, 38:285, 40:3; history, 11:458, 14:147, 16:276n, 17:239, 27:167, 30:244, 31:63, 34:131; air corps program, 25:403; anniversary, 30:265; athletics, 31:63, 39:21; religious aspect, 34:91, 93; kindergarten, 34:217. See also Baldwin School

McAllister, Henry E., 18:97

McAllister, Phosa, actress, 33:176

MacAllister Co., dramatic troupe, 28:113

McAlpin, Joseph, in Civil War, 38:264

McAlpine, Mrs. Grace, speaker, 19:119, 23:299, 399, 28:196

McAlpine, Michael, lumberjack, 13:352n, 362n, 363

MacArthur, Gen. Arthur, 30:40

MacArthur, Judge Arthur, lecturer, 18:365

McArthur, D. S., author, 22:98

MacArthur, Gen. Douglas, 30:40

McArthur, Lewis A., author, 26:383, 32:250

MacArthur, P., steamboat owner, 21:259n

Macaulay, Gordon, author, 34:311

Macaulay, Thomas B., author, 29:154

McAuliff, Kathryn, author, 30:86

McAvoy, Thomas T., work reviewed, 37:339; author, 34:216; editor, 37:133

McBean, John, fur trader, 20:14, 28:144

Macbeth, Florence, singer, 18:450

Macbeth Gallery, New York, 16:339

McBride, Jack, author, 21:456, 22:112, 213, 349

McCaffrey, Frank, 12:440

McCain, William D., author, 24:70, 253

McCall, Clayton W., author, 25:396

McCall, George A., 25:36, 140

McCall, John, printer, 13:110

McCall, Thomas M., author, 17:227, 38:204; speaker, 21:436, 27:81

McCallum, Daniel, railroad director, 33:218

McCallum, Ian, author, 37:38

McCallum, James B., editor, 13:329

McCallum, John, author, 34:358

McCallum, Mabel, 17:124

McCann, Elizabeth, author, 23:85

McCann, Franklin T., author, 21:100

McCann, Helen, see White, Helen McCann

McCann, James H., author, 14:117

McCannel, James, author, 12:200; speaker, 14:456

McCarriel, L. E., miller, 11:218, 13:214

McCart, M. H., speaker, 24:186

McCarthy, D'Alton, 17:455

McCarthy, Eugene J., speaker, 37:343; author, 39:172

McCarthy, Hugh, author, 35:49

McCarthy, Jane, artist, 18:309, 22:70, 25:66, 27:129, 29:161, 32:55

McCarthy, Margaret, author, 29:77, 272

McCartney, Dr. Clarence E., speaker, 16:355

McCarty, H. H., author, 16:228

McCarty, Dr. Paul D., 34:280

MacCarty, Mrs. William C., author, 21:115

McCauley, Rev. Lester, author, 14:237

McCauleyville, Wilkin County, history, 18:224, 35:382; Catholic church, 24:94; geology, 38:158

McCausland, Elizabeth, author, 31:248

McChesney, Mildred F., author, 27:66

McChord family, 28:296

McClain family, genealogy, 15:469

McClanen, Capt. ---, 15:428

McClellan, Gen. George B., diary, 20:80; Union officer, 22:129, 25:23n, 27, 36, 38, 119, 121, 127-129, 132, 135, 138, 139, 148-150, 152, 225, 230-232, 238, 29:64, 32:29, 31, 35:317n; in St. Paul, 29:118; presidential candidate, 33:192, 35:316, 36:171

McClellan, Mrs. George B., in St. Paul, 29:118

McClellan, Robert, fur trader, 15:422, 40:179n

McClelland, Mrs. Florence B., 13:104

McClernan, P. A., speaker, 18:464

McClernand, Gen. John A., 25:241n, 243; papers, 24:166, 36:229

McCliesh, Thomas, trader, 40:200

McClintock, Harry K., editor, 26:379

McClintock, Hugh, 22:161

McClintock, Inez, work reviewed, 37:342

McClintock, Marshall, work reviewed, 37:342

McCloud, Edward, pioneer printer, 15:13

McCloud, Robert, pioneer printer, 15:13

McCloy, William A., artist, 29:355

McCluer, Judge and Mrs. William M., house, 25:412

McClung, ---, artist, 28:317

McClung, John W., 24:298n; lawyer, 40:225

McClung, Mrs. John W., 38:81

McClure, Charles, 14:249

McClure, Ethel, "The Protestant Home of St. Paul," 38:74-85; "County Poor Farms in Minnesota," 38:365-377; reviews by, 39:27, 125; author, 37:41; award and grant, 39:84, 212

McClure, Mrs. Grace S., folklorist, 21:296-298

McClure, Harlan E., author, 34:314

McClure, Lt. James, 32:71

McClure, Col. John D., 39:190

McClure, Nancy, see Faribault, Mrs. David; Huggan, Mrs. Charles G.

McClure, Thomas, 18:332

McColley, Rev. Charles E., author, 24:382, 25:99, 210, 314, 409, 26:93, 181, 287

McCollough, Alameda, author, 27:158

McCollum, Catherine A., author, 24:261

McCollum, E. J., speaker, 18:336

McCollum, Elmer V., dairyman, 12:99

McCollum, Verna, author, 16:247

McConkey, John, 28:140

McConkey, Mrs. John, author, 26:294n; marriage, 28:140. See also Bishop, Harriet E.

McConnell, Harold G., 14:416

McConnell, James E., 14:416

McConnell, James M., 11:54, 59, 315, 14:79, 15:217, 16:60; portrait, 14:416; career, 14:416-420, 432; tributes, 15:467

McConnell, Mrs. James M., 14:416

McConnell, John, pioneer, 11:467, 20:464

McConnell, John R., educator, 14:416

McConnell, Rebecca M., 14:416

McConnell, S., 14:271

McConnell, William, 14:416

McConnon, J. R., 19:239

McConnon, Mrs. J. R., 22:342

McConnon, Jeannette M., author, 16:352

McConville, Constantine J., 39:154n

McCook, Robert L., Union officer, 38:260, 261, 263-266, 39:181

McCooks, Alexander M., 25:242

McCord, Louisa S., feminist, 30:251

McCord National Museum, Montreal, 17:184

MacCormack, John, singer, 39:58

McCormick, Cyrus H., inventor, 15:464, 23:316, 321, 322, 24:292, 294, 26:82, 260, 29:85, 31:55, 33:221

McCormick, Dell, author, 21:296

McCormick, R. P., author, 30:149

McCormick, Col. Robert R., publisher, 26:357, 37:167-169, 172, 173

McCormick, Washington J., trader, 35:31

McCormick, Willard F., author, 24:361

McCormick Harvesting Co., 15:464, 16:53, 23:322

McCormick Historical Association, Chicago, 15:464, 16:277n, 474, 18:411n

McCormick reaper, 24:288-290

McCosh, Edward M., 14:251

McCoskry, Bishop Samuel A., 32:83, 97

McCoy, Al, boxer, 30:383

McCoy, Donald R., work reviewed, 36:187

McCoy, James C., 18:448

McCoy, Raymond, author, 20:202

McCracken, H. L., Quaker minister, 18:262

McCracken, Harold, review by, 37:78; works reviewed, 33:263, 36:101, 37:32; author, 29:79

McCracken, Paul W., author, 26:166

McCrady, John, artist, 24:54

McCraney, Orlando, 17:300n

McCray Brothers, lumber contractors, 34:149, 152

McCrea, Willard F., author, 34:170

McCrory, William, politician, 35:66, 70, 72, 73

McCubrey, G. D., 13:286, 14:119, 219

McCulloch, Walter F., author, 36:278

McCullough, John, actor, 28:117, 118

McCumber, Porter J., Senator, 32:175

McCune, George, reviews by, 30:384, 33:262; author, 28:365, 30:412; editor, 29:53, 30:38, 32:10

McCurdy, C. J., 34:139

McDade, Thomas M., review by, 38:234; work reviewed, 38:39

McDaniel, Dr. Orianna, 19:111

McDavid, Raven J., Jr., author, 36:278

McDermot, Thomas, postmaster, 24:320n

McDermott, Andrew, smuggler, 22:281; trader, 38:327

McDermott, Clara A., author, 34:218

McDermott, John Francis, 28:79, 393; "An Upper Mississippi Excursion," 22:13-34; "A Journalist at Old Fort Snelling," 31:209-221; "J. C. Wild and Fort Snelling," 32:12-14; "The J. O. Lewis Port Folio," 33:20; "Minnesota 100 Years Ago," 33:112-125; reviews by, 19:436, 23:160, 28:167, 32:243, 35:143, 146, 36:62, 317, 37:31; works reviewed, 30:249, 33:131, 35:239, 36:233, 38:36, 333, 39:337, 40:144, 403; author, 19:445, 20:202, 22:82, 23:84, 169, 281, 28:204, 277, 29:104, 260, 349, 30:152, 153, 259, 260, 31:256, 32:61, 63, 125, 155, 188, 256, 33:89, 34:215, 36:69, 37:38, 38:384, 40:149; editor, 26:165; speaker, 36:323, 328, 40:411

McDermott, Thomas, trader, 22:288

McDermott, Thomas J., speaker, 13:444

McDiarmid, E. W., librarian, 31:246

Macdona, Rev. J. Cumming, 33:147n

McDonald, A. W., editor, 13:132, 135, 137, 138, 150; speaker, 13:146

McDonald, Bill, author, 40:411

Macdonald, C. F., editor, 17:365

Macdonald, Mrs. Charles F., 15:252

Macdonald, Colin F., author, 39:187

Macdonald, Dora M., work reviewed, 31:246

McDonald, Forest, work reviewed, 36:98

McDonald, G. H., forester, 36:136

McDonald, Sister Grace, 29:94, 366; "A Finishing School of the 1880's," 27:96-106; "The Benedictine Sisters," 33:291-297; "Pioneer Teachers," 35:263-271; reviews by, 15:455, 17:83-85, 18:89, 27:43, 33:38, 305; work reviewed, 36:24; author, 13:339, 14:443, 16:119, 234, 472, 17:113, 18:91, 107, 27:55, 151, 169, 30:265, 33:138; editor, 15:105; speaker, 16:234, 17:70, 355, 358, 18:268, 20:355

MacDonald, Helen L., author, 28:183, 30:172, 36:35

McDonald, John, lumberman, 24:127, 129

McDonald, John, trader, 12:370, 373, 13:432, 20:327

Macdonald, Sir John A., statesman, 33:183, 35:35, 47, 153, 283, 36:65

McDonald, John F., 17:101

McDonald, John L., politician, 36:119

McDonald, John S., properties, 17:101

McDonald, Sister M. Justible, work reviewed, 34:210

Macdonald, Norman, author, 21:432

McDonald, Philip B., author, 18:218

MacDonald, Thomas H., speaker, 29:85

McDonald, Rev. William, at Red Rock, 31:89

Macdonaldville, Norman County, post office, 23:109

McDonell, Alexander, governor of Red River colony, 17:335, 27:165

Macdonell, John, trader, 11:212, 358, 363, 364, 15:91, 22:432, 23:272; diary, 12:290, 14:223, 15:90-92; marriage, 15:92n

Macdonell, Magdeleine, 15:92n

Macdonell, Miles, trader, 11:212, 12:437, 21:399, 22:331, 24:179; governor of Assiniboia, 40:164

McDonnell, J. P., speaker, 14:452

McDonnell, Father Martin, educator, 35:136, 137

McDonnell, Michael, 35:136

McDonnell, Patrick, 35:136

Macdonnell, William J., letters, 22:331

McDougal, Alexander, lumberjack, 21:458

McDougal, Dr. Charles, army surgeon, 29:319n, 30:213n

McDougal, Mrs. Charles, 29:319

McDougall, Alexander, 34:216; ship captain, 14:232, 33:316; ship-builder, 15:122, 127, 34:12, 249, 36:32

McDougall, William, politician, 33:183, 35:283

MacDowell, Mrs. Edward, 17:101

McDowell, Mrs. Elma S., folk singer, 27:72, 180-182, 186

McDowell, Gen. Irvine, 25:36, 121

McDowell, Maj. Robert M., engineer, 22:322

McDowell, Tremaine, 26:74, 27:243, 37:83; "Regionalism in American Literature," 20:105-118; reviews by, 17:450-452, 20:179-181, 21:70, 95, 25:65; works reviewed, 19:436, 30:55; author, 17:459, 20:186, 323, 21:80, 421, 25:76, 26:274, 27:243, 29:261, 371

McDuff, James, 16:470

Mace, George, 21:110

McEachern, Margaret, author, 11:460

MacEachran, Clinton E., 17:160n

Macedonians, Detroit, Mich., 20:202; immigration, 27:214

McElroy, Robert, work reviewed, 24:341-343

McElwain, Frank A., author, 18:331

McEnery, Father Daniel, 26:90

MacEwan, Mrs. Theresa C., 19:377, 33:281n

McEwen, William C., labor leader, 35:379

McEwen, William E., postmaster, 34:185

McFadden, Hugh, lumberman, 24:201

McFadden, Molly, author, 32:60, 33:89, 35:295

MacFarland, A., theater manager, 28:109, 110, 33:173, 174

McFarland, Lt. Col. Earl, 20:54

McFarland, Franklyn, teacher, 17:87

McFarland, Col. O., 16:492

McFarland and Pickett, lumber company, log mark, 26:135

Macfarlane, Agnes, 39:323n

McFarlane, Charles T., author, 15:240

MacFarlane, Janet R., author, 26:266, 27:353

McFarlane, Peter, author, 40:141

MacFarlane, R. O., author, 26:273, 28:372

MacFarlane, Roderick, 35:240

McFarling, Lloyd, work reviewed, 34:303

MacGaheran, Joe, author, 16:248, 22:337

McGaheran, Paul E., biography, 19:214

McGann, James, speaker, 22:108

McGannon, James, murdered, 38:151

McGaughey, Edward W., politician, 30:104-108, 110, 39:38

McGaughey, J. P., labor leader, 21:315, 22:40, 372, 375, 379, 388

McGee, Gale W., work reviewed, 37:339

McGee, Mrs. Marjorie, house, 38:345

McGee, Thomas D'Arcy, 21:75

McGehee, E. J., letter, 34:146

McGhee, Flora, author, 23:301

McGhee, Fred L., career, 30:266

McGhee, J. C., author, 18:112

McGiffert, Mrs. J. R., speaker, 11:118, 13:216

McGill, Andrew, trader, 40:200

McGill, Andrew R., governor, 14:101, 16:443, 22:295, 296, 386, 387, 35:60, 297, 37:148, 149, 205

McGill, George M., diary, 19:349

McGill, James, trader, 11:261, 262, 372, 14:228, 40:200

McGill, John, trader, 11:261, 262

McGill University, Montreal, 15:90

McGill-Warner Co., St. Paul, growth, 18:450

McGillicuddy, V. T., Indian agent, 35:289

McGillin, John, speaker, 25:210

McGillis, Hugh, trader, 17:245n, 20:15, 18

McGillivray, Duncan, trader, 18:215, 19:302, 20:327, 28:144, 147, 38:28, 40:171; litigation, 21:117-148

McGillivray, James, author, 37:39

McGillivray, Simon, trader, 21:119n, 40:169, 177

McGillivray, Simon, Jr., trader, 22:275, 310

McGillivray, William, trader, 12:369, 13:439, 21:119n, 23:203, 272, 29:166, 36:64, 38:42, 40:167; career, 38:327

McGillivray family, traders, 28:12

McGilvrey, J. W., 27:72

McGlumphy, Dr. Samuel B., career, 17:220

McGolrick, Bishop James, 13:313, 22:379, 28:72

McGonagle, Agnes M., 11:413

McGonagle, Dr. E. H., author, 34:218

McGonagle, Joseph S., 11:419

McGonagle, Robert E., 11:419

McGonagle, William A., 11:54, 438, 12:184, 34:266, 35:38; career, 11:413-420, 15:243, 17:119; portrait, 11:414; author, 26:174

McGonagle, Mrs. William A. (Sarah L. Sargent), 11:419

McGonagle, William A., Jr., 11:419

McGovern, Francis E., politician, 35:241

McGovern, John, career, 35:335

McGovern, S. H., author, 15:240

Macgowan, Ernest S., 17:302; author, 15:140, 26:275, 30:158

McGowan, John T., legislator, 35:349

McGrade, Francis, author, 30:163

McGrane, Reginald C., 39:220; author, 16:356

McGrath, Mrs. Charles M., 38:77n

McGrath, James E., author, 17:491

McGrath, John S., author, 18:327

McGrath, Ralph, author, 16:236

McGrath, Robert B., author, 23:196, 30:407

McGrath, Aitkin County, veterans' colonies, 39:243, 245

McGraw, C. V., pioneer, 22:444

McGray, Frank, 18:179

MacGregor, A. L., author, 25:310

MacGregor, Della, 27:241

MacGregor, Effie, educator, 35:371

MacGregor, John, compiler, 40:212

MacGregor, Rob R., 16:349

McGregor, railroad, 33:10

MacGregor, Iowa, described, 12:180; ferry, 14:304, 312; bridge, 22:98

McGregorie, Maj. Patrick, 19:280

McGrew, C. L., 28:291

McGrew, Sgt. James G., in Sioux Outbreak, 38:144n

McGrorty, Charles, politician, 39:49

McGrorty, Eugenie F., author, 17:84

McGrorty, John, 39:49, 50

McGrorty, Capt. William B., 17:84; in Civil War, 29:101

McGuire, ---, jeweler, 16:242

McGuire, Arthur J., 15:115, 29:158

McGuire, Flora, speaker, 26:181

M'Guire, Fred B., 20:56

McGuire, J. C., 20:175

McGuire, Michael J., architect, 38:352

McHale, E., labor leader, 40:344

McHale, J. J., 18:321

McHale, Michael, prison official, 37:140, 141

Machek Lumber Co., 29:177

Machelosse, Gérard, author, 33:352

McHenry, Myron, jockey, 36:66

McHugh, Mother Antonia, 21:70, 33:38; speaker, 15:127, 313; author, 15:348, 456, 17:84, 349

McHugh, Carol H., lawyer, 21:196

McIlrath, Mrs. Charles, 39:52

McIlwain, Charles H., 14:194, 17:106

McIlwaine, Shields, author, 35:40

McIlwraith, T. F., author, 37:86

McInnis, Edgar W., work reviewed, 24:45-48

McIntire, Dr. George W., 22:425

McIntire, Marian, author, 12:208

McIntosh, Donald, 29:267

McIntosh, George B., 18:123n

McIntosh, history, 14:358, 37:64; museum, 21:115

McIntosh County, N.D., history, 23:92

McIntyre, Mrs. Sara W., speaker, 16:125

McIntyre, Thomas A., broker, 39:109

McIver, W. R., author, 17:115

Mack, Peter, author, 36:327

Mack, Stanley L., author, 21:223

MacKaniff, Nancy, 31:173

Mackay, Lt. Aeneas, with Cass expedition, 23:135, 248, 251, 336, 347, 348n

Mackay, Alexander, author, 29:154

McKay, Alexander, trader, 21:120n

Mackay, Corday, author, 27:260, 29:166

MacKay, Douglas, work reviewed, 18:81; author, 19:462, 35:240, 36:272

Mackay, Jack, author, 27:168

McKay, John, trader, 16:374, 22:270, 275, 31:183
MacKay, Kenneth C., author, 28:372
MacKay, Roderick, teacher, 36:204
MacKay, Sheridan K., tomb, 39:268; described, 39:269, 311
McKay, Valentine, speaker, 40:149
McKay, W. A., author, 40:144
McKay, William, trader, 35:261, 262
Mackaye, Steele, dramatist, 23:310
McKean, Elias, lumberman, 18:169, 24: 197, 198, 202
McKee, Maj. David, 19:350
McKee, Rev. James A., 19:268
McKee, Rose, author, 15:122, 131, 254
McKee, Russell, work reviewed, 40:141
McKee family, genealogy, 21:195
McKee Rankin Co., theater troupe, 28: 110
McKeel, Mr. and Mrs. Scudder, 11:443
McKellar, Archibald M., pioneer, 14: 99
McKellar, Kenneth D., Senator, 17:15
McKellar, Peter, frontier farmer, 14: 99
McKellar, Peter D., 14:99, 23:295, 24:186
McKelvey, Blake, author, 19:112
McKelvey, Mrs. Harriet, teacher, 11: 206
McKelvey, Susan D., author, 35:241
McKenney, Charles R., editor, 22:88
McKenney, John H., sutler, 40:88
McKenney, Thomas L., work reviewed, 37:79; author, 16:105, 19:38, 23: 155, 28:277, 29:61, 32:93, 33:20, 21, 40:409; explorer, 26:380; Indian commissioner, 36:323
McKenny, John S., editor, 32:23, 27, 31
McKenny, Mary, manuscript assistant, 24:162; cataloger, 24:243, 25:40, 27:240, 28:48
Mackenroth, Ida, 26:66
McKenty, Henry, 11:171-173, 29:89
McKenzie, Alexander, politician, 27: 97, 28:169, 32:174
Mackenzie, Sir Alexander, trader, 11: 246n, 267, 358, 12:294, 369, 371, 13:432, 16:200, 20:12, 326, 21: 124n, 28:12, 13, 58, 34:344, 352, 40:172, 175, 176; writings, 12: 364, 373-375, 13:106, 298, 24:364, 38:380, 40:170; explorer, 12:368, 370, 372, 13:182, 14:82, 84, 115, 15:232, 21:124n, 24:230, 28:57, 29:79, 130, 34:174, 35:35, 47, 36: 64, 38:30; papers, 40:150
McKenzie, Carl H., author, 24:173
McKenzie, Donald, trader, 15:422
McKenzie, H., trader, 40:168n
McKenzie, Henry, testimony, 21:141-144
McKenzie, Hugh, photographer, 34:1 (cover)
McKenzie, J., trader, 40:167n
McKenzie, John, Union soldier, 25:247
McKenzie, Kenneth, trader, 15:336, 20:119n, 32:76, 36:38, 39:255
McKenzie, Margaret, 20:119n
McKenzie, P., trader, 40:167n
Mackenzie, Roderic, trader, 11:357, 21:141n, 38:381, 40:168n; at Grand Portage, 12:367-369, 371, 373; diaries, 15:90, 29:166
McKenzie, Roderick, Jr., trader, 22: 309

McKenzie, Simon, 11:250
Mackenzie, William, 11:246n
Mackenzie and Oakes, Quebec, Que., merchants, 11:238
Mackenzie River, N.W.T., explored, 12:370, 13:182, 14:84; history, 38:386
McKern, William C., author, 24:371; speaker, 27:356
Mackey, Andrew, house, 38:343
Mackey, Mrs. Andrew, pioneer, 24:203
MacKim, Mead, and White, New York, architects, 39:155
Mackinac, Mich., British regime, 11: 231-270, 16:223, 17:196, 19:291, 297, 36:273, 40:21, 164; American post, 11:451, 17:335, 19:198, 301, 306, 20:14, 77, 23:142, 233, 347, 348, 33:316, 34:155, 35:383, 36: 67, 40:23n, 183, 185, 186; history, 11:452, 25:272, 274, 26:171; Indian agency, 12:317, 24:164; French regime, 12:356, 13:203, 14: 370, 376, 18:390, 19:282, 285-287, 290, 32:229; Indians, 13:260, 401, 25:396, 32:231; Beaumont memorial, 15:234, 33:316, 36:324; Nicolet tercentenary, 15:475; fur trade, 19:277, 295, 299; pictured, 19: 423, 23:89; mission, 20:262, 25: 13; medical experiments, 21:95; artifacts, 39:262, 297
Mackinac boats, St. Croix River, 17: 282
Mackinac Co., in Northwest, 15:462
Mackinac Island, Mich., Lake Huron, described, 15:320, 23:142, 32:84; lake port, 34:14; museum, 40:145
Mackinbines, David, teacher, 39:306
Mackinder, Halford J., author, 29:71
McKinlay, A., trader, 40:167n, 168n
McKinlay, D. A., land commissioner, 13:33
McKinley, Silas B., author, 27:253
McKinley, William, 35:73, 74; President, 17:12, 29:79, 30:147, 35: 300, 301, 39:85 (cover), 110, 120; candidate, 30:54, 234, 35:75, 39: 93, 94, 105, 107, 169, 332
McKinley, Rev. William, Methodist minister, 12:453, 18:350, 367, 23: 302
McKinley, mining town, 32:194
McKinney, Isabel, work reviewed, 19: 332-334
McKinstry, Archibald W., publisher, 25:187
McKinstry, Azro P., dairyman, 27:115, 119, 39:271
McKinstry, Grace E., artist, 25:187
McKinstry Mounds, Koochiching County, excavated, 31:231-237
Mackintire, Edmund, letters, 25:183, 383
Mackintire, Eliab P., letters, 16: 111, 542, 17:224
McKitrick, T. G., author, 33:315
McKnight, William L., 35:1; career, 35:38
McKnight Foundation, 40:49, 293; grants, 36:281, 37:43, 38:43, 336, 39:36, 212, 40:316
Mackubin, Charles M., pioneer banker, 34:99n
McKusick, D. Webster, 24:201
McKusick, Ivory E., house, 38:348, 349

McKusick, John, lumberman, 13:355, 16:73, 17:277, 18:168, 169, 176, 19:252, 24:193, 198-200, 204, 205, 30:195, 35:364, 38:187; marriage, 24:203
McKusick, Mrs. John, 24:203
McKusick, Jonathan E., portrait, 19: 454
McKusick, Judson, log surveyor, 31: 34-39
McKusick, Marshall, work reviewed, 39:339
McKusick, Tom, 28:194
McKusick, William, lumberman, 19:454, 24:200
McKusick Lake, Washington County, explored, 24:196; canal, 24:199
McLagon, Edward, steamboat captain, 11:134
McLaird, Mrs. C. A., speaker, 16:234
McLane, J. W., steamboat owner, 21: 254n
McLaren, Dr. ---, at Fort Snelling, 22:155
McLaren, Gen. Robert N., Fort Snelling commandant, 15:397; letters, 20:330
McLaren, Mrs. Robert N., artist, 39: 173 (cover)
McLarty, Capt. Samuel, at Fort Pomme de Terre, 38:66-70
McLarty, Mrs. Samuel, 38:68
McLaughlin, Andrew C., author, 14:231
McLaughlin, Glenn E., author, 23:87
McLaughlin, Jack, author, 39:83
McLaughlin, James H., Indian agent, 27:97, 154
McLaughlin, Melda, student, 27:97
McLaughlin, W. M., author, 24:369
McLaury, J. L., author, 11:337
McLean, Mrs. ---, at Red Rock, 31:84
McLean, Mrs. C. P., 15:483, 17:119, 20:349
McLean, Charles, author, 15:213
McLean, David, author, 11:208
McLean, Mrs. Effie M., 11:460, 12:86, 87, 14:456, 20:454, 21:443; speaker, 12:292
McLean, Henry, 11:162
McLean, Mrs. J. E., author, 17:123
McLean, Judge John, 14:35, 20:308
McLean, John, trader, 14:114
McLean, Mrs. John, biography, 33:188
Maclean, M. C., author, 25:199
McLean, Gen. N. C., dairyman, 27:119
McLean, Nathaniel, 19:214; Indian agent, 11:179, 24:354, 32:76; pioneer printer, 15:19
McLean, R., author, 17:359
McLean, R. B., prospector, 34:177
MacLean, Ray B., 18:329, 334; work reviewed, 18:201; speaker, 11:11n, 13:285; author, 16:117
McLean, Mrs. Sarah B., 20:308; house, 20:309
McLean County, N.D., pioneer women, 14:225; place names, 36:325
MacLeish, Archibald, quoted, 24:39; speaker, 25:197
McLeister, Ira F., author, 16:345
McLellan, Mrs. Elleine, author, 12: 325
McLellan, Hugh, 20:77
MacLennan, Hugh, author, 37:245, 38: 386
MacLennan, William L., 21:195
McLeod, Alexander, testimony, 21:145

McLeod, Archibald N., trader, 21:124, 126-129, 132, 31:2; diary, 14:223, 15:90-92; witness, 21:122
M'Leod, D., author, 16:102
McLeod, Dan, mill manager, 34:4-6
MacLeod, G. B., author, 21:369
McLeod, George, 11:180, 182, 19:390; trader, 11:180n
McLeod, John, in Sioux Outbreak, 11:467
McLeod, John, trader, 13:432, 22:281; explorer, 17:75
MacLeod, LeRoy, author, 23:157
MacLeod, Margaret A., work reviewed, 29:247; author, 16:231, 17:113, 20:204, 21:205, 206, 432, 433, 22:331, 27:70, 30:259, 261, 32:155, 35:202, 295; compiler, 38:200
McLeod, Martin, 12:240, 14:144, 16:31, 18:219, 19:446, 30:298, 31:173, 32:72; townsite promoter, 11:131, 219; interest in education, 11:329, 16:149, 17:478, 20:127, 22:357; trader, 11:376, 378, 379, 13:224, 15:127, 22:4, 32:66, 68, 38:147n; diary, 15:337, 17:445, 20:369, 36:26, 316; MHS founder, 20:368, 30:345; career, 21:99, 452, 28:337, 36:195
McLeod, Peggy, 28:256
McLeod, Walter S., Indian agent, 37:275, 38:147n
McLeod County, agriculture, 11:116, 17:128, 18:408, 19:226; politics, 11:331, 13:215; in Civil War, 11:462; history, 12:201, 21:452, 23:187, 35:47; prairie fire, 12:209; ethnic groups, 14:452, 15:27-42, 16:331, 17:128, 237, 21:97, 31:28, 34:356; district court, 15:348; pageant, 16:306; historical tour, 16:488; pioneer life, 20:102, 23:102; dairying, 20:360; name, 20:368; school, 26:183; townsite promotion, 33:251, 38:388, 40:65; grasshopper plague, 36:57, 61; in Sioux Outbreak, 38:276, 281, 283, 284; geology, 39:132
McLeod County Agricultural Society, 22:253
McLeod County Historical Society, 25:403, 29:275; museum, 12:37, 19:116, 23:11-14, 35:246; collections, 21:336, 22:224, 24:187, 26:53; meetings, 21:444, 22:106, 217, 339, 440, 23:101, 194, 279, 398, 24:86
McLeod County Public Health Association, 20:102
McLeod County War History Committee, 23:391
McLeod Farm Bureau, 21:452
McLeod, Gregory, and Co., traders, 12:367
McLoughlin, Dr. David, career, 36:315
McLoughlin, John, frontier physician, 11:58, 16:478, 19:226; career, 11:451, 13:439, 16:223, 26:164, 36:315; trader, 11:360, 361, 12:326, 17:220, 444, 445, 19:309, 21:399, 428, 22:179, 180, 271, 275, 276, 309, 29:248, 339, 31:1, 183, 32:250, 33:88, 261, 35:282, 290, 36:244-247; writings, 17:111, 18:103, 278, 24:43-45, 26:55, 27:37; explorer, 23:282
McLoughlin, Mrs. John, 33:261

McLoughlin, John, Jr., 33:261; with Dickson expedition, 17:444-447; death, 26:55, 27:38; career, 36:315, 316
McLoughlin, Marie Louise, career, 36:315
McLowery, Frank, 35:241
McMahon, Rev. John, 20:460
McMartin, Mrs. James D., author, 18:120
McMartin, Lewis, 19:336
McMaster, Clara M., 15:88
McMaster, John B., historian, 18:148, 149, 19:9, 40:313
McMaster, Joseph, 15:86
McMaster, S. W., 13:237
McMaster, Thomas, 15:87
McMaster, William C., 15:86, 88
McMaster, William J., 15:86-88
McMasters, Mrs. Julia R., letters, 29:188
McMath, Elizabeth, 18:462
McMath, Frank M., author, 18:462
McMath family, genealogy, 18:462
McMicken, Ham, tugboat captain, 21:266
McMillan, Edwin, speaker, 12:452
McMillan, Emily, artist, 27:346
McMillan, Mrs. Phebe H., 18:263
McMillan, Samuel J. R., 35:363; letters, 14:101, 15:223
McMillan family, genealogy, 11:321
McMillen, Loring, author, 23:376, 24:260
McMillen, Wheeler, author, 40:298
McMillen, Col. William L., 39:186, 187
McMiller, P. R., author, 17:487, 21:212, 24:193
McMunn, Dorothy, author, 40:411
McMurray, Thomas, trader, 20:71, 22:310
McMurry, Donald L., author, 11:104
McMurtrie, Douglas C., 16:454, 19:431, 21:199; "The Printing Press Moves Westward," 15:1-25; author, 12:439, 13:109-111, 205, 211, 335, 336, 436, 14:447, 15:121, 475, 16:479, 34:350; editor, 16:111, 24:361; speaker, 15:85, 16:48; bibliographer, 26:72
McMurtry, R. Gerald, review by, 28:171; author, 27:80, 28:204
McNair, Miss ---, missionary, 38:76
McNair, Henry C., 39:154n
McNair, John, labor leader, 40:344, 346
McNair, William E., businessman, 37:319
McNally, Judge Carlton F., 35:289
McNally, William J., work reviewed, 13:422; author, 11:452, 24:182, 31:129, 133, 146; speaker, 24:86
McNamee, Richard S., legislator, 35:347
McNanney, Mrs. Helen C., in Sioux Outbreak, 12:97
McNary-Haugen bills, 12:15, 32:181, 182
McNaught, Kenneth, work reviewed, 37:80
McNeal, George C., 36:213, 214
McNeal, Mrs. Sarah E., prison matron, 37:149
McNeal, Violet, author, 38:39
McNeall, ---, trader, 11:261, 262
McNeil, Donald R., review by, 34:307;

works reviewed, 35:146, 36:149; author, 34:175
McNeil, George, steamboat captain, 13:233
McNeill, W. H., trader, 40:168n
McNelly, C. L., work reviewed, 37:221
McNickle, D'Arcy, work reviewed, 30:374
McNicol, Donald M., author, 19:218
McNicol, Robert, architect, 40:100n
McNiff, John, farmer, 31:173
McNous, Mrs. ---, 18:406
McNulty, Father Ambrose, author, 30:2, 39:154n
McNutt, Paul V., 16:346
Macomb, Gen. Alexander, 28:18, 19
Macomber, Esther, 17:337
Macomber, John H., in Civil War, 17:337, 18:47, 25:289
McPhail, Lt. ---, 24:22n
McPhail, Samuel, settlement promoter, 17:486, 18:342, 20:467; in Sioux Outbreak, 38:102n, 103n, 139n, 280
MacPhail, William S., musician, 33:101
McPherson, Aimee Semple, in fiction, 37:5
McPherson, Donald, trader, 22:275
McPherson, Murdock, trader, 20:71
McPherson County, S.D., Garland's claim, 22:161
McPherson Township, Blue Earth County, settled, 17:125
McQuarrie, Dr. Irvine, author, 31:124
McQueston's addition, Le Hillier City, Nicollet County, plat, 17:238
McQuillan, E. J., 27:364
McRae, A.D., 16:497
Macrae, Alexander, author, 21:195
McRae, Gen. Dandridge, Confederate officer, 40:288, 290
McReynolds, Edwin C., author, 34:357
McReynolds, Sam D., Congressman, 40:373
McSherry drill, use in Minnesota, 24:304
McTavish, Donald, trader, 37:175, 40:167n
Mactavish, Dugal, clerk, 20:71
McTavish, John G., trader, 20:71
McTavish, Simon, trader, 12:369-371, 373, 16:200, 20:326, 21:119n, 123, 28:5, 34:344, 36:64, 37:175, 38:381
MacTavish, William, 21:252n, 34:317
McTavish family, traders, 28:12n
McTavish, Fraser, and Co., Montreal, 40:172
McTavish, Frobisher, and Co., Montreal, 12:376, 16:200, 21:139, 142, 143, 145
McTavish, McGillivray and Co., Montreal, 28:12n, 40:181
McVey, F. L., tax commissioner, 34:309
McWilliams, Carey, author, 30:66, 31:44
McWilliams, Margaret, work reviewed, 11:307-309
McWilliams, Richebourg G., works reviewed, 34:117, 39:337
Macy, Jesse, 16:218, 33:356
Macy, Roscoe, speaker, 21:110; author, 24:374, 28:192
Macy, William, artist, 29:260

220; mounds, 25:333, 26:325, 327, 328; pioneer life, 35:50
Malmquist, Mrs. Bert, 19:470, 20:456
Malmros, Oscar, 13:112; author, 25: 349; expansionist, 35:47
Malone, Dumas, work reviewed, 34:199; editor, 11:216, 328, 12:200, 442, 13:210, 440, 14:230, 348, 15:127, 357, 16:114, 238, 349, 17:114, 225, 476
Malone, Kemp, 21:70
Maloney, Mrs. J. J., speaker, 29:363
"Malta," steamboat, 13:226, 233, 238
Malvern Hill, Va., battle, 29:64
Maly, Josef, pioneer, 15:27
Mammen, Edward W., author, 28:179
Mammoth Hotel, Nininger, projected, 13:128, 130, 150
Mammoths, Grant County, 38:157
Mamre, Kandiyohi County, name, 31:253
Manaco, Adriano, speaker, 13:83
Manahan, James, 18:446, 21:68, 69; work reviewed, 15:337-339; career, 13:324; papers, 17:164, 213, 18: 46, 19:47, 34:339; politician, 26: 170, 37:181, 40:140
Manahan, Kathryn, 15:339
Manannah, Meeker County, in Sioux Outbreak, 12:302, 303, 18:461, 20: 192, 38:279-281, 283, 285; marker, 25:407
Manarini, F., labor leader, 40:344
Manassas, Va., battle, 25:150
Manchester, William D. Montagu, Duke of, 17:371
Manchester & Oneida Railway, built, 36:33
Manchester Township, Freeborn County, Norwegian settlement, 12:269
Mandan, S.D., flood, 11:69. See also Fort Mandan
"Mandan," steamboat, 13:224
Mandan Indians, in fur trade, 11:265, 33:302; culture, 13:60, 103, 18: 242, 22:93, 32:244, 34:161, 255, 35:244, 339, 40:47; archaeology, 17:216, 18:102, 25:155, 27:259, 37:347, 40:193; characterized, 32: 56; artists, 35:380
Mandigo, James W., papers, 13:320
Mandt Lutheran Church, Chippewa County, 14:451
Maney, Dr. James, house, 39:194, 197
Maney, Mr. and Mrs. Lewis, 39:196, 197
Maney, Ruth, artist, 38:192
Manfred, Frederick (Feike Feikema), review by, 27:41-43; works reviewed, 34:210, 39:208; author, 27:55, 71, 31:129, 145, 36:237, 37:3n
Manganese, Crow Wing County, ghost town, 19:464
Mangard, Carl, author, 23:88
"Manhattan," steamboat, 21:156
Manifest destiny, historical concept, 38:48, 53-62, 326
"Manila," steamboat, 36:282
Manion, Leo E., author, 29:167
Manitoba, links with Minnesota, 11: 307-309, 15:125, 18:277, 21:247, 29:263, 36:284; pioneer life, 12: 330, 33:315; archaeology, 14:342, 29:78, 165, 37:61, 38:158n; place names, 15:357; Mennonites, 15:478, 18:99, 456, 21:269, 29:166, 37: 184; archives, 16:230, 34:352;

doctors, 16:480; steamboat era, 21:245, 253, 255, 258, 262, 267, 268, 32:126; railroad, 21:260; immigration, 21:269, 433; in fiction, 23:118; explored, 27:70, 29: 259, 33:88, 186, 37:62; history, 28:283, 29:99, 36:63, 40:93; wheat farming, 33:64, 35:48; Icelandic settlement, 34:164; wild rice processing, 35:295; buffalo hunt, 36:311; folk songs, 38:200; Hutterites, 40:44; historic sites, 40:189, 190. See also Riel rebellions
"Manitoba," steamboat, 21:247, 255-257, 259n, 261-263, 264n, 268n, 271, 24:166
Manitoba Historical and Scientific Society, Winnipeg, Man., 36:284
Manitoba Museum, Winnipeg, Man., collection, 28:70
Manitoba Railroad, lands, 31:22
Manitou Island, White Bear Lake, history, 36:70
Manitou Rapids, Rainy River, 24:283
Manitou River, Lake County, 12:287
Manitoulin Historical Society, Ont., 35:153
Manitoulin Island, Lake Huron, Ottawa village, 13:401, 15:165; Radisson landing, 15:320
Manitowoc, Wis., cultural history, 15:355
Mankato, Sioux leader, 38:137, 138, 140, 142, 143, 147-149
Mankato, floods, 11:68, 17:230, 234, 34:306; trade center, 11:132, 21: 238, 24:272, 302n, 304, 34:325; river port, 11:171, 36:252, 255-258, 37:226, 227; roads, 11:392, 19:103, 21:233, 234; mail service, 11:400, 40:87; stage lines, 11: 402, 403, 12:58; population, 12: 51; execution of condemned Sioux, 12:59, 14:453, 495, 17:336, 21: 201, 274, 22:103, 425, 28:327, 29: 354, 30:68, 33:78, 38:98, 114, 136, 39:183, 184; churches, 12: 100, 16:120, 18:375, 379, 35:81, 82; pioneer life, 12:335, 15:484, 17:125, 29:357; schools, 14:416, 26:47, 166; mills, 14:455, 27:174, 29:354; volunteer guards, 16:169, 176; cemetery, 16:493, 17:234; Germans, 17:473, 21:98, 24:381, 28:36; history, 18:337, 35:293; lecture series, 18:366n, 19:217, 416; bells, 18:374, 379; circuses, 19:120; baseball club, 19:167, 169, 170, 472; clinic, 19:451; Jesuit residence, 20:84; Indian prison, 21:273n, 38:353, 354, 356, 357, 360-366; in fiction, 21:448; hotels, 24:189; industry, 24:297, 33:230; source material, 26:282, 30:150; German theater, 32:100, 102, 127, 169, 34:240; building stone, 35:65, 39:160; power company, 35:381; brewery, 36:200; gold fever, 38:53; in Sioux Outbreak, 38:125, 280, 285; name, 38: 137; Civil War barracks, 39:127; G.A.R. post, 39:190; supply depot, 39:227, 230-236, 238
"Mankato," locomotive, 38:295
Mankato Art History Club, 27:171
Mankato Claim Co., 12:202

Mankato Commercial Club, 16:489
Mankato Driving Park Association, 16: 33
Mankato Fair Association, 17:125
Mankato Free Press, history, 15:89, 18:337
Mankato Independent, 37:330n, 38:354; history, 15:89
Mankato Musical Society, 16:489
Mankato Normal School, 14:416; history, 14:149, 18:112. See also Mankato State Teachers College
Mankato Record, history, 18:337; politics, 36:301, 39:88
Mankato Rifle Co., 16:172
Mankato Settlers Association, records, 26:282
Mankato State Teachers College, 21: 106, 26:47, 34:93; history, 11: 458, 21:49, 25:100
Mankato Union, history, 13:214, 18: 337
Mankato War History Committee, 23:391
Mann, Dr. A. T., 24:347
Mann, Arthur T., author, 15:358; editor, 38:387
Mann, Dr. Eugene L., 21:317
Mann, George R., architect, 40:103; house, 40:104
Mann, Horace, educator, 34:93
Mann, Mrs. Horace (Mary Peabody), letters, 20:173, 22:433
Mann, Horace, Jr., 16:35, 36; in Minnesota, 16:40, 45, 20:171, 22:433, 35:215, 37:225-228, 38:335
Mann, Dr. T. T., newspaper correspondent, 11:163n
Mann, Thomas, steamboat captain, 20: 352
Mann, William, railroad executive, 36:66
Mann-Elkins Act, effects, 12:16
Manney, Solon W., chaplain, 28:209, 213; teacher, 28:210
Manni, John, author, 16:246, 18:338
Manning, Eileen, author, 40:99n
Manny, John H., 22:257
Manny reaper, 23:322, 24:288, 290
Manomin County, see Anoka County
Manomin Township, see Fridley Township
Manomonie, Anoka County, ghost town, 40:88
Mansfield, Helen C., author, 26:306
Mansfield, J. B., author, 25:369
Mansfield, Richard, actor, 33:1
Mansfield Township, Freeborn County, history, 30:405
Manship, Paul, sculptor, 16:110, 31: 55, 35:70
Manson, D., trader, 40:167n, 168n
Manson, Col. Mahlon D., Union officer, 38:261, 262, 39:180, 182
Månsson, Evelina, author, 18:69
Månsson, Ola, see Lindbergh, August
Manti, Iowa, Mormon settlement, 13: 386
Mantor, S. J., 22:170
Mantorville, Masonic lodge, 13:215; churches, 14:236, 19:122, 30:400, 35:246; pioneer life, 14:276, 438, 15:134, 35:52; hotel, 15:198, 28: 381, 30:181, 400; described, 19: 96; museum, 35:246; courthouse, 38:189n
Mantorville Express, subscription lists, 11:95, 16:72; history, 13:

448, 14:397, 404, 24:355, 27:141;
    source material, 15:135; analysis
    of contents, 27:5-20
Mantorville Press, history, 34:358
Mantouek Indians, Radisson's visit,
    13:261, 262
Manufacturers Bank of West Duluth,
    37:122
Manufacturing, Great Lakes basin, 16:
    113, 222; fluctuation, 21:373,
    384; Minneapolis area, 23:87. See
    also individual products and firms
Manuscript Society, publication, 35:
    51
Manuscripts, guides, 16:94, 197-199,
    17:51, 34:220, 337, 35:52, 36:280,
    37:340, 38:89; copying rules, 17:
    51, 93, 449, 450; preservation,
    17:59, 448, 459, 20:74, 25:282,
    30:65, 32:190, 37:219, 40:361;
    cataloging, 17:59, 448-450, 459,
    21:82; selection, 20:74, 32:123,
    35:146; display, 33:92, 351. See
    also MHS: Manuscript division
Manville, Helen A., poet, 26:298
Manweiler, J., author, 21:212
Manxmen, Greenvale, 26:285, 27:173;
    Wisconsin, 27:84
Manyaska Township, Martin County,
    school, 23:197; history, 28:387,
    35:156
Manzey, John, author, 13:216
Maple, Lake County, ghost town, 34:
    182
Maple Grove Township, Hennepin Coun-
    ty, Evangelical church, 17:479;
    plat, 23:171, 36:36
Maple Hill Township, Cook County,
    history, 11:217
Maple Plain, church, 27:344
Maple Plain Co-operative Creamery
    Co., 18:443
Maple Plain Fruit Growers' Associa-
    tion, 18:443
Maple Ridge Township, Isanti County,
    Swedish settlement, 20:359
Maple sugar, early manufacture, 14:
    383, 18:287, 288, 19:136, 22:331,
    24:92; made by Indians, 28:235,
    30:261; trade item, 38:71; syrup
    harvest, 40:47, 158
Maplebay automobile, 40:148
Mapleton, pioneer life, 14:455, 18:
    337, 25:210, 35:381; hotels, 15:
    133; library, 17:125; churches,
    19:344, 20:34, 25:211; history,
    21:106; Scottish colony, 24:382
Mapleton House, Mapleton, 15:133
Mapleton Woman's Study Club, 21:215
Maplewood Park, Waseca County, re-
    sort, 36:194
Maplewoods (Woodland), Hennepin
    County, history, 27:176
Maps, local history activities, 11:
    13; river towns, 11:167; fur
    trade, 11:355, 17:75, 18:235, 21:
    83, 22:272, 32:228, 40:173, 189,
    194, 195; roads, 11:391, 16:286,
    21:83, 228, 236, 37:104, 40:234,
    236-243, 389; Mississippi River,
    12:82, 13:405, 14:337, 27:350, 29:
    220; by Peter Pond, 12:82, 14:83,
    35:334; Deadwood, S.D., trails,
    12:93; Norwegian settlements, 12:
    267; Great Lakes, 12:348, 351,
    355, 13:186, 17:357, 25:302; his-
    toric markers, 12:441, 13:379;

Nininger, 13:137; Michigan, 13:
    186; Lake Pepin, 14:35; U.S., 14:
    91, 24:252, 25:374, 33:186; Minne-
    sota, 14:117, 349, 18:446, 19:453,
    22:433, 26:178, 36:278, 40:274;
    Long River, 14:373; boundaries,
    15:239, 18:430, 36:2; Old Cross-
    ing Treaty cession, 15:293; Hudson
    Bay, 16:421n; Fort St. Charles,
    18:245; Wadsworth Trail, 19:227;
    Fort Ridgely, 20:148; Indian
    reservations, 21:83, 37:273, 39:
    87; Cass expedition, 23:138; In-
    dian villages, 24:236; Madison,
    Wis., 25:185; German settlements,
    26:277; Beef Slough, Wis., 27:192,
    193; Lake Minnetonka, 29:291; St.
    Paul, 30:8; Burnett area, 33:107;
    Kandiyohi County lakes, 33:147; by
    David Thompson, 33:181; Lake of
    the Woods, 34:2, 35:275; Carver,
    34:158; railroads, 34:179, 37:104,
    156; American West, 34:219, 302,
    35:97, 36:277, 38:386; Lower Sioux
    Agency, 34:236; Babbitt area, 34:
    270, 279; Forest Mills, 35:17;
    Fort Snelling, 35:23, 26, 179,
    366; Nobles expedition, 35:253;
    Sawbill area, Cook County, 36:132;
    Duluth-Superior harbor, 37:95;
    border lakes, 37:244; Ramsey ex-
    pedition, 38:3; routes to Montana
    gold fields, 38:59, 224; Lake
    Agassiz, 38:159; Civil War, 38:
    261, 266, 268, 39:83, 177, 40:284,
    289; frontier forts, 38:282; In-
    dian removal route, 39:235; Grand
    Portage, 39:304; Canada, 40:355;
    Augsburg Park, 40:381; Finnish
    folklore area, 40:393
Maquoketa River, Iowa, located, 32:
    232
Maracci, Carmelita, 39:64
Marathon County, Wis., dairying, 29:
    268
Marble, Ella M. S., feminist, 39:10n
Marble, Jerome, hunter, 16:269
Marble, Manton, with Nobles expedi-
    tion, 18:274, 35:252-254, 258,
    261; author, 23:186, 34:335; art-
    ist, 35:249, 250, 255-257, 259,
    260, 262
Marble, Margaret Ann, Sioux cap-
    tive, 23:273, 38:123
Marble family, theatrical troupe, 28:
    111, 40:363
Marble, churches, 11:115, 16:485
Marburg, Theodore F., author, 35:154
Marcaut, ---, trader, 11:262n
March, Enoch C., sutler, 40:24
March, Frank, 16:241
Marchand, Ernest, author, 12:326
Marchant, George W., 35:70, 71
Marchesi, Blanche, singer, 39:55
Marchesseaux, ---, trader, 19:293
Marchman, Watt P., author, 31:252
Marclay, Jessie M., 18:263n
Marcley, Mrs. Walter, speaker, 11:120
Marcot, Hyacinthe, voyageur, 21:135
Marcus, Jacob R., 33:195n; editor,
    34:353
Marcy, Ellen M., 29:118
Marcy, Gen. Randolph B., 29:118
Marcy, William L., 11:318
Marden, Luis, review by, 39:123
Mareck, Titus, actor, 32:172

Margaret Barry Settlement, Minneapo-
    lis, 14:110
Margeax, ---, timber agent, 31:162
Margry, Pierre, 38:200; author, 13:
    202; editor, 36:30
Margulies, Herbert F., author, 35:241
Marias Pass, Mont., history, 12:93;
    discovered, 16:463, 21:97
Marietta, Ohio, Northwest Territory
    celebration, 18:101, 19:314
Marijuana, trade item, 40:204
Marin, Sam, 12:136
Marin, William A., "Sod Houses and
    Prairie Schooners," 12:135-156;
    parents, 12:135; speaker, 13:283;
    author, 18:116, 228, 20:466
Marin de la Malgue, Charles-Paul, ca-
    reer, 13:439
Marin de la Malgue, Joseph, trader,
    12:307, 18:193, 32:226-238; ca-
    reer, 13:439
Marin de la Malgue, Paul, trader, 11:
    382, 384, 12:307, 13:433, 18:193,
    32:226, 227, 229, 235n; career,
    13:439
Marin de la Perrière, Claude, 13:203,
    18:193
Marine, see Marine on St. Croix
Marine Bank, St. Paul, 20:257; his-
    tory, 40:109-119
Marine Engineers Beneficial Associa-
    tion, 21:380
Marine House, Marine on St. Croix,
    17:284, 36:214
Marine Lumber Co., 38:339; organized,
    18:167, 29:205n; store, 18:420,
    36:197 (cover), 213; mill, 20:448.
    See also Walker, Judd, and Veazie
Marine Mills, see Marine on St. Croix
Marine National Bank, Duluth, 37:122
Marine on St. Croix, lumber industry,
    15:346, 17:278, 285, 313, 392, 18:
    167, 20:448, 21:271, 24:126, 29:
    205, 30:195, 242, 35:382, 38:333,
    39:315; stores, 16:97, 18:420-422;
    mail service, 16:97, 36:206-215,
    40:83, 86; mission, 16:313, 316;
    river port, 17:280; hotel, 17:284,
    36:214; historical meeting, 17:
    316-318; Swedish settlement, 17:
    398, 399; centennial, 18:344, 19:
    363, 472; July 4 parade, 26:253;
    fire department, 36:107; pictured,
    37:137 (cover); architecture, 38:
    337, 339, 340; described, 39:208
Marinette River, Wis., pineries, 21:
    55
Marion, Gen. Francis, 18:397
Marion, Olmsted County, ghost town,
    11:399, 35:12, 121
Marion, Otter Tail County, townsite,
    15:465, 18:117
Marion County, Ind., probate records,
    17:189
Marion Lake, McLeod County, paper
    town, 40:65
Marion Township, Olmsted County, poor
    farm, 38:368
Mariposa Battalion, discovers Yosemi-
    te Valley, 15:233
Mark, H. F., druggist, 23:198
Mark, P. M., druggist, 23:198
"Mark Bradley," towboat, 18:177
Markers, see Monuments and markers
Market House (Hall), St. Paul, 18:30,
    23:306, 33:196, 197n, 36:239

Market Street Baptist Church, Minneapolis, 17:337
Marketing, co-operative, 17:474, 21:202, 28:37, 39, 304, 29:76; Middle West, 20:335; transportation problem, 22:230; survey, 30:265, 34:214; wholesale, 34:106-113. See also Dairy industry, Grain marketing, Livestock industry, Wheat raising
Markham, Edwin, 11:447
Markham, J. M., steamboat owner, 33:12
Markham, James E., speaker, 14:218
Markham, R. H., author, 21:310
Markham, Col. William, Union officer, 38:43, 258
Markoe, Francis A., speaker, 16:115
Markoe, James, 38:167n, 176n
Markoe, Ralston J., 19:451
Markoe, William, balloonist, 12:202, 22:9, 38:166-176, 39:280; alderman, 14:300
Markoe, Mrs. William, 38:172
Markoe, William F., author, 16:251
Marloue, Pope County, mill, 21:218
Marmaduke, Gen. John S., Confederate officer, 40:283
Marmata, Lake County, settled, 34:177
Marmon automobile, 38:207, 210, 211, 213
Marogna, Father Demetrius, missionary, 32:37-41; prior, 35:263-265, 268
Marpiwecaxta, Sioux leader, see Cloudman
Marquand, J. P., author, 20:116
Marquette, C. L., speaker, 24:255
Marquette, Father Jacques, explorer, 12:76, 13:254, 14:339, 371, 16:453, 17:299n, 18:233, 300, 19:190, 27:350, 30:57, 32:112, 35:151, 199, 36:70, 37:128; cartographer, 12:353, 26:164; missionary, 13:401, 35:43; author, 14:448, 22:56, 26:165, 33:344; death, 15:100; pictured, 19:461
Marquette Avenue, Minneapolis, 30:332, 384
Marquette Range, Mich., ethnic groups, 27:205
Marquis, A. S., author, 11:451
Marqusee, John E., author, 39:211
Marryat, Capt. Frederick, author, 13:222, 29:154, 36:74; in Minnesota, 18:152-164, 20:380; traveler, 18:215, 25:273
Mars, J. R., publisher, 26:294
Marsden, Ralph W., author, 36:103
Marsh, Lt. Adolphus, 25:225, 254
Marsh, Rev. Cutting, explorer, 16:134
Marsh, John, career, 11:210, 430-432, 14:439, 15:128, 479, 18:193, 22:205, 36:68; letters, 12:190, 18:439, 19:95; teacher, 14:143, 144, 17:478, 18:219, 26:362, 35:290; Indian agent, 20:78, 25:89, 40:24n
Marsh, Capt. John S., in Sioux Outbreak, 11:29, 18:209, 27:341, 34:234, 235, 35:288, 38:96, 136, 148
Marsh, Col. Josiah F., 39:186, 189
Marsh, Ruth, author, 24:71
Marsh harvester, described, 24:291
Marsh Hotel, Forest Lake, 30:398
Marsh River, Norman County, Norwegian settlement, 12:278

Marshall, Mrs. ---, mixed-blood, 24:324
Marshall, Albert M., work reviewed, 34:167; author, 35:245
Marshall, C. B., storekeeper, 34:280
Marshall, Douglas, 30:406
Marshall, John, 13:345; biography, 20:418-420
Marshall, Joseph M., banker, 35:363
Marshall, Lawrence W., author, 12:441
Marshall, Morgan, 22:133
Marshall, R. D., lawyer, 27:198
Marshall, Rebecca, see Cathcart, Mrs. Alexander H.
Marshall, Robert, author, 11:101
Marshall, Roujet D., autobiography, 14:112
Marshall, Thomas R., 21:98
Marshall, William R., 14:132, 39:317; encourages immigration, 12:259, 13:27, 20:246, 28:222, 29:244; land officer, 12:389, 37:98; career, 15:127; papers, 19:342, 21:86, 33:220; travels, 20:432; house, 23:221; military service, 26:206, 33:191, 38:104, 110n, 113, 293, 386; governor, 26:208, 36:304, 305, 37:143, 38:297, 40:67, 148, 223; speaker, 33:172, 35:359; publisher, 34:336, 37:328; businessman, 37:92
Marshall, Mrs. William R., 33:6
Marshall, blizzard, 11:187n; Catholic church, 16:120; pioneer life, 17:237; county seat, 20:360; railroad, 21:243, 24:177; wheat market, 29:4; parochial schools, 35:139
Marshall, Wis., college, 40:375
Marshall and Illsley, bankers, 16:91
Marshall County, history, 12:451, 16:250, 35:47; pageant, 16:237; archives, 21:101; agriculture, 21:212; cart trails, 36:107; mound, 38:164; electric service, 40:315
Marshall County Historical Society, 16:241, 36:104; organized, 15:71, 137; activities, 15:249, 369, 16:124, 361, 20:456, 37:67; pageant, 15:369, 16:64; meetings, 16:490, 17:64, 122, 483, 18:110, 464, 19:116, 469, 20:96, 21:108, 445, 22:106, 441, 23:102; newspaper collection, 17:66
Marshall County Old Settlers Association, 20:456, 22:441
Marshall House, Alexandria, Va., 25:38
Marston, Anson, 14:113
Marston, Moses P., 16:181, 182
Marston, Thomas E., author, 39:342
Marteau, Henri, violinist, 39:53
Martell, Charlie, ferryman, 34:233-238
Martell, Oliver, ferryman, 34:234, 235, 237, 238
Martell, Mrs. Oliver, fugitive, 34:237
Martell, Peter, ferryman, 34:233-238
Marten, Mrs. F. M., 11:443
Marten, Humphrey, trader, 33:261
Marten, in fur trade, 23:330, 30:131, 134, 38:190, 40:212
Marth, Sophia, author, 29:269
Marthaler, Sister Theresa, 35:271
Marti, Donald B., "The Puritan Tradition," 40:1-11

Martin, Anne J. L., letter, 13:116
Martin, Asa E., author, 13:329
Martin, Charles, author, 19:455
Martin, Chester, speaker, 13:105; author, 13:209, 20:69, 21:432; editor, 13:300
Martin, Father Claude, 13:417
Martin, Deborah B., editor, 12:329
Martin, Emmanuel, pioneer, 35:31
Martin, Ethyl E., 28:378; compiler, 23:90
Martin, Father Felix, 37:128
Martin, François, author, 12:322
Martin, Franklin H., surgeon, 15:131
Martin, George R., 11:54, 14:79, 15:116, 17:70; speaker, 11:461, 13:424, 16:491
Martin, Helen M., author, 21:325
Martin, Homer D., artist, 15:100, 128, 16:339, 18:106, 20:185
Martin, Mrs. Homer D., author, 16:339
Martin, Rev. J. W., 31:82n, 84
Martin, James A., biography, 14:333
Martin, John, compiler, 30:388
Martin, John, lumberman, 21:316, 37:319
Martin, John B., work reviewed, 25:276
Martin, Lorene, author, 23:281
Martin, Mamie, 12:332; work reviewed, 19:430; compiler, 26:72
Martin, Michael, work reviewed, 33:261
Martin, N. B., "Letters of a Union Officer," 35:313-319
Martin, O. B., 22:328
Martin, Paul S., work reviewed, 28:270-272
Martin, Ralph G., author, 34:265, 356
Martin, Thomas P., 16:95; author, 15:228
Martin, William J., author, 34:130
Martin County, ethnic groups, 11:295, 12:274, 16:496, 18:309, 21:98, 37:185; settled, 13:102, 14:244, 20:462, 29:74; anniversaries, 13:343, 451, 28:195, 30:162; politics, 14:247-249, 251, 259, 262, 35:307; census, 14:254, 256, 258, 259, 261; food shortage, 14:379; Indians, 14:453; agriculture, 17:212, 18:47; schools, 20:102, 23:197, 25:411, 36:193; archives, 20:445; post offices, 22:441; physicians, 24:79; horse thievery, 25:97; war veterans, 26:289; pictured, 28:387; pageant, 30:408; library, 31:61; history, 36:107, 239; grasshopper plague, 37:204; in Sioux Outbreak, 38:284
Martin County Atlas (Fairmont), founded, 22:174
Martin County Business Men's Association, 22:225
Martin County Historical Society, 16:241; organized, 11:14; meetings, 11:15, 463, 13:451, 14:459, 15:71, 489, 17:64, 121, 18:464, 19:64, 116, 470, 20:97, 456, 21:110, 445, 23:399; museum, 11:16, 293, 463, 16:445, 29:87, 35:155; members, 11:19, 20, 12:39; activities, 11:296, 14:449, 17:483, 28:194, 30:408; publications, 12:339, 13:343, 22:441, 23:15, 26:394, 27:172, 29:74, 34:315; Covered Wagon Club, 16:397; collections, 16:447, 20:

81, 24:270, 25:97, 28:296; build-
ing, 35:336
Martin County War History Committee,
23:391
Martin Lake, Martin County, in Sioux
Outbreak, 38:125
Martin Township, Rock County, Norwe-
gian settlement, 12:274
Martindale, John, 25:128
Martindale, Joseph, author, 27:100
Martindale, L., farmer, 24:301
Martineau, Harriet, 28:275; author,
18:152, 28:321, 29:154
Martini, Peter, artist, 26:238
Martinson, Embret, author, 13:324
Martinson, Flora, work reviewed, 36:
66
Martinson, Lorraine, author, 24:192
Martinsville, Ohio, Quaker settle-
ment, 18:255
Marty, Adam, G.A.R. commander, 16:438
Marty, Bishop Martin, missionary to
Sioux, 15:128, 23:383, 33:57
Marvin, C. F., author, 34:264
Marvin, Charles E., dairyman, 22:267,
27:120, 121
Marvin, J. B., 35:269
Marvin, Luke, 24:354; postmaster, 34:
185
Marvin, Mabel L., 11:446-448, 14:240,
22:342, 25:206; author, 15:349
Marvin, Sgt. Matthew, papers, 11:42,
25:31n, 38:249-253, 257
Marvin, Richard, merchant, 15:188
Marvin, Richard F., postmaster, 34:
185
Marx, Paul S., work reviewed, 35:372
"Mary Blane," steamboat, 33:131
"Mary C," steamboat, 19:138
"Mary Hatch," steamboat, 33:71
Mary Virginia, Sister, "The Study of
Family History," 27:319-326; au-
thor, 27:343, 28:165, 242n, 303
Maryland, Victor, bus line operator,
35:338
Maryland, early printing, 15:4; his-
toric sites, 17:112; in Civil War,
25:359; schools, 29:163; atlas,
40:122
Maryland Historical Society, Balti-
more, 26:376; centennial, 25:88,
197
Maryland Transfer Line, bus oper-
ations, 35:338
Maryland War Records Division, 27:352
Marzolf, William H., critic, 39:60
Mascouten Indians (Prairie Potowato-
mi), 32:230; Wisconsin, 13:253,
15:167, 170, 171; Illinois, 36:191
Maseres, Francis, 15:96
Masi, Eugenia C., author, 11:452
Mason, Bernard S., author, 33:227
Mason, Charles, jurist, 22:87
Mason, Lt. Charles H., 25:246
Mason, David T., work reviewed, 33:
219; author, 27:358, 36:159, 40:
405
Mason, Gen. E. C., Fort Snelling com-
mandant, 35:186-189
Mason, Eldon W., 18:204; review by,
18:201
Mason, Emily, letter, 24:182
Mason, George C., author, 33:316
Mason, J. Alden, "The Dickeson Pano-
rama," 23:352-354; author, 23:369,
29:261
Mason, J. D., author, 14:358

Mason, Rev. J. M., speaker, 17:355
Mason, J. R., miller, 35:17, 20
Mason, Leonard, review by, 24:54; au-
thor, 24:60
Mason, Philip P., work reviewed, 36:
184; editor, 34:263; author, 35:
153
Mason, Rachel C., diaries, 17:211
Mason, Capt. Richard B., 14:423
Mason, Stevens T., 18:153
Mason, William, shoemaker, 13:393
Mason, William F., papers, 17:211
Mason and Hilton, Fergus Falls, law
firm, 38:13
Mason, Olson and Engelhart, Forest
Mills, milling firm, 35:18
Masonic Hall, St. Paul, 16:274n, 26:
82, 33:196
Masonic order, see Freemasons
Masonic Temple, Minneapolis, archi-
tecture, 23:223n
Masonic Women, St. Paul, 16:370
Masqueray, Emmanuel L., architect,
26:173, 39:155-162
Massachusetts, migration from, 19:
132-141, 20:140-145, 22:169-173;
board of health, 21:358; labor
bureau, 22:387; voting laws, 28:
21, 22, 25-27; historic sites, 37:
30; atlas, 40:122
Massachusetts Historical Society,
Boston, organized, 19:9, 39:336
Massachusetts Homeopathic Hospital,
Boston, pictured, 39:7
Massachusetts State Library, Boston,
17:97
Massachusetts Woman Suffrage Associa-
tion, 39:4, 6
Massacre Island, Lake of the Woods,
murders, 18:239-241, 279, 28:77;
chapel, 18:244
Massen, Joseph, 11:238n
Massey, Louis, 15:238; mail carrier,
40:81
Massicotte, E.-Z., work reviewed, 12:
306; author, 11:327, 13:432, 23:
280; artist, 13:440
Massie, Homer, speaker, 16:488
Massie's Landing, Mississippi River,
settlement, 20:122, 123
Massillon farm machines, 24:290, 301
Massmann, John C., author, 37:87
Masson, Louis R., author, 12:367, 16:
200
Massopust, Janet, storekeeper, 36:193
Massopust, Rudolph, 18:471, 20:464
Masterman, Albion, lumberman, 24:200
Masterman, J. N., lumberman, 24:200
Masterman, Mrs. W. C., 15:372, 16:241
Masters, D. C., author, 25:200
Masters, Edgar Lee, 34:200; author,
28:360, 32:5
Masterson, Henry F., lawyer, 39:148n
"Mataafa," steamboat, 23:356, 34:14,
39, 35:278, 36:237, 282
Matawan, St. Louis County, railroad,
34:180
Maternity Hospital, Minneapolis, 20:
101, 39:1; history, 39:3n, 14-17
Mather, Cotton, bibliography, 21:417
Mather, Frank J., Jr., author, 15:
128, 17:477
Mather, Increase, 26:215
Mather, John C., speculator, 27:315;
Fort Ripley report, 28:218, 219
Mather, Ralph J., 26:185, 186, 335,
27:26, 27, 50; speaker, 26:367

Mather, Samuel L., manufacturer, 32:
46
Mather, William G., manufacturer, 32:
46
Mather, Lt. William W., career, 15:
128; explorer, 16:159-162, 232
Matherson, Miss J. L., teacher, 13:
140, 146
Mathes, Jacob, 14:298
Matheson, ---, Red River settler, 31:
108
Matheson, John P., 16:231
Mathews, Mrs. M. E., author, 20:449
Mathews, V. J., 17:235
Mathushek piano, 39:323n
Matinée Musicale Club, Duluth, 30:
175, 39:55
Matlon, John C., author, 40:360
Matonabbee, Chipewyan leader, 40:160
Matonenock Indians, 13:398
Matson, Frank W., 23:48; papers, 37:
44
Matt, Joseph, speaker, 14:229; au-
thor, 17:85; editor, 19:219
Mattawa River, Ont., canoe route, 11:
233, 40:165; located, 28:11n
Matter, F., 19:211
Matterson, Clarence H., author, 22:
326
Mattes, Merrill J., "Fur Trade
Sites," 40:192-197; review by, 39:
338; works reviewed, 38:238, 40:
403; author, 26:165, 33:181, 39:
209
Matteson, David M., compiler, 35:334
Matthews, Brander, 20:82
Matthews, Harold J., artist, 16:111
Matthews, William, compiler, 27:61
Mattinen, J. A., author, 23:300
Mattingly, Garrett, author, 27:348
Mattison, Ray H., review by, 38:379;
author, 35:200, 380, 37:262, 38:
385; editor, 40:314
Mattocks, Dr. Brewer, educator, 13:
272; author, 16:29, 26:297n, 302,
35:218, 220, 221
Mattocks School, St. Paul, 15:360,
27:231, 36:240
Mattoon, George, 33:18
Mattson, E. Neil, author, 36:107
Mattson, Edgar L., 24:57, 26:40
Mattson, Col. Hans, 15:351, 21:203,
26:378; promotes immigration, 12:
256, 13:28, 356, 15:127, 20:245,
247, 30:65, 31:125, 225, 250, 33:
48, 137; honored, 12:331; pioneer,
14:136, 37:262; papers, 20:33,
191; autobiography, 20:192; politician, 30:157, 36:326; in Civil
War, 33:84, 38:291, 39:196, 40:
286, 290, 291; publisher, 34:43;
diary, 37:134; author, 39:81; portrait, 40:292
Mattson, Mrs. Hans, 15:351, 16:53
Mattson, John P., journalist, 12:451
Mattson, Oliver M., 19:116, 20:96,
21:109, 22:106
Mattson, Selma E., author, 14:352
Matwakonoonind, Chippewa leader, 15:
284, 292, 294
Maud, Big Stone County, postal station, 17:485
Maudada, Traverse County, ghost town,
29:366
Mauerle, Jacob, killed in Sioux Out-
break, 34:237
Maule, Harry E., editor, 34:42

Maulevrier, Count Colbert, work reviewed, 18:86
Mauley, ---, see Millier, Hubert
Maumee River, Ind., Ohio, British post, 19:296
Maunder, Elwood R., 34:316, 39:84; reviews by, 33:134, 184, 266, 34: 38, 263; work reviewed, 40:405; author, 34:176, 220, 35:49
Maurepas, Count de, 18:241, 243
Maury, Matthew F., 15:330
Mauvais River, Ashland County, Wis., 23:242
Mavit, A., 11:238n
Maxfield, George, steamboat owner, 33:15
Maximilian, Prince of Wied, 15:429, 22:155n, 39:261
Maxwell, Capt. ---, 20:12
Maxwell, Dorothy, author, 39:342
Maxwell, G. E., author, 14:231, 16: 352
Maxwell, Moreau S., author, 31:171
Maxwell, Robert S., work reviewed, 35:236
Maxwell, William, pioneer printer, 15:12
Maxwell Land Grant Co., 20:192
May, Earl C., author, 26:268
May, Edward K., cholera victim, 14: 294
May, Gerhard, journalist, 12:342, 17: 365
May, Grace L., author, 34:170
May, Henry, author, 26:73
May, Joseph, excursionist, 37:228n
May, Capt. Rodolphe de, immigrant agent, 22:203, 32:160
May, Rev. Samuel, 37:228
May, William M., contractor, 38:187, 188
"May Queen," steamboat, 12:433
May Township, Washington County, school, 26:181
Mayall, Ada L., 38:85
Maybee, Rolland H., work reviewed, 37:132
Mayer, Charles, 28:295; author, 35: 203
Mayer, Frank A. R., author, 17:116
Mayer, Frank B., artist, 13:302, 26: 359, 30:176; "Diary," 22:142-156; work reviewed, 13:295; diary and sketches, 11:87, 12:425, 13:58, 191, 196, 314, 14:61, 16:25, 17: 109, 18:44n, 20:268, 290, 22:133-136, 27:61, 28:335; water colors, 13:408-414, 14:66, 107, 30:179, 289, 406; letters, 14:102; portrait work, 14:425, 35:197, 38: 198, 39:199n; memorial to legislature, 15:206; career, 19:459; at Traverse des Sioux, 22:133-156, 32:67, 70, 71, 73, 75, 80; Minnesota drawings, 26:140-142, 38:2, 98n, 115n, 40:161; portrait bust, 27:346; paintings, 30:157, 31:121, 32:188, 33:89
Mayer, George H., review by, 33:41; work reviewed, 32:246; speaker, 29:257
Mayer, Harold M., speaker, 34:176; author, 36:69
Mayer, Josephine J., author, 16:224
Mayer, Leopold, author, 34:353
Mayer, museum, 21:333, 22:105, 23: 293-295

Mayfield Township, Red Lake County, history, 38:204
Mayflower Descendants, Minnesota society, 19:47
Mayhew, Henry, founds Grand Marais, 31:191
Maynard, Theodore, author, 23:191
Mayne, Dexter D., letters, 28:396; professor, 39:243, 246
Mayo, Charles E., 18:363; papers, 11: 318
Mayo, Dr. Charles H., 13:443, 15:100, 24:347, 33:44, 34:170, 37:66; papers, 17:100, 34:212; estate, 20: 300, 40:316, 362; influence, 21: 437; career, 22:104, 404-408, 23: 364, 28:371, 40:309. See also Mayo Clinic
Mayo, Mrs. Charles H. (Edith Graham), 40:362
Mayo, Dr. Charles W., estate, 40:316, 362
Mayo, Frank, actor, 28:117, 33:175
Mayo, Joseph, 20:300
Mayo, Robert J., works reviewed, 13: 420-422; author, 13:338, 23:101, 28:357; speaker, 21:216
Mayo, William, engineer, 33:241
Mayo, Dr. William J., 14:79, 15:100, 20:232, 24:347, 33:44, 34:170; speaker, 11:199, 284, 14:117; author, 13:443, 15:254; papers, 17: 160n, 330, 20:82, 34:212; career, 18:227, 22:104, 404-408, 23:364, 28:371, 40:309, 362; influence, 21:437; house, 33:209, 37:66; office, 36:239. See also Mayo Clinic
Mayo, Dr. William W., 16:353, 17:478, 18:228, 20:435, 21:222, 22:386, 34:170, 37:187; career, 11:284, 15:127, 17:330, 20:442, 22:404-408, 23:364, 35:216, 221, 304, 381, 40:309; during Sioux Outbreak, 13:443, 23:365; speaker, 20:241, 242; library, 21:357; papers, 25:183; house, 33:209, 353; descendants, 40:362. See also Mayo Clinic
Mayo, Mrs. William W. (Louise Wright), 23:365; in Sioux Outbreak, 13:443
Mayo Association, Rochester, sponsors publication, 34:34, 176
Mayo Civic Auditorium, Rochester, 20: 300
Mayo Clinic, Rochester, 15:131; tours, 11:286, 20:187, 296; history, 16:118, 17:329, 22:405, 406, 23:96, 34:203, 218, 36:34, 282, 40:309, 362; library, 21:357; laboratories, 24:211; influence, 28:179; aviation tests, 35:155
Mayo Foundation, 24:211; history, 16: 119, 21:182, 23:289; affiliation with University of Minnesota, 17: 330
Mayo Foundation Museum of Hygiene and Medicine, Rochester, 16:353, 20: 297
Mayo Properties Association, grant, 26:367, 27:27, 240, 340, 341, 28: 49, 30:47, 329
Mayock, Thomas J., compiler, 24:337
Mayowood, Rochester, Mayo estate, 20: 300, 40:316, 362
Maypuck, Chippewa leader, 24:325

Mazakutemani, Paul, Sioux leader, 38: 106n, 123
Mazardhamani, Sioux Indian, 21:26n
Mazawakinyanna, Louis, Sisseton Indian, 35:173
Mazeppa, lands, 24:354; volunteer firemen, 27:76; camp meeting, 31: 82; mill, 35:18
Mazourka Hall, St. Paul, 12:402, 22: 10, 23:307, 28:320, 30:388
Mazzei, Phillip, 19:35
Mazzuchelli, Father Samuel C., missionary, 17:475, 18:437, 21:429, 28:184
Mdewakanton band, Sioux Indians, name, 13:249; Minnesota River, 13: 373, 31:213n, 35:29; lands, 21: 163; cattle, 21:166; missions, 21: 274; treaties, 32:76, 77, 231, 38: 129; Prairie Island, 35:24, 37: 271-282; in Sioux Outbreak, 38: 130-143, 147-149. See also Sioux Indians
Mead, Alden C., in Civil War, 16:359
Mead, David, author, 35:195, 38:333
Mead, George, letter, 11:331
Mead, J. F., publisher, 26:294
Mead, Sidney E., author, 36:185
Meade, Gen. George G., Union officer, 25:246, 359, 360, 29:344, 38:245, 251
Meade, Owen, 17:240
Meader, George, singer, 18:450
Meading Township, Koochiching County, history, 30:162
Meagher, John B., 39:154n
Meagher, Gen. Thomas F., Union officer, 25:133, 251-253; biography reviewed, 31:241
Meagley, Wilbur E., Indian agent, 37: 278
Mealey, Howard C., 20:469
Means, Florence C., author, 13:213
Means, Philip A., author, 24:257, 28: 59
Means, W. E., Methodist minister, 31: 82n
Mearns, David C., review by, 37:219; author, 30:257, 37:188
Mearns, Edgar A., naturalist, 15:128
Mears, Daniel, lumberman, 18:176; house, 38:342, 343
Mears, Louise W., author, 15:238
Measles, among Indians, 37:182
Meat packing, Iowa, 16:228; Austin, 18:470, 23:108, 388, 33:353, 34: 266, 40:315; Albert Lea, 22:445
Mechanic Arts High School, St. Paul, 40:146
Mechanics Hotel, Belle Plaine, 25: 260, 265
Mechanics Library, St. Anthony, 35: 222
Mechanicsville, Va., battle, 25:140n
Méchingan, Mich., Potowatomi village, 13:262, 15:167, 175; located, 13: 398, 15:168
Medals, 40:412; presidential, 16:321-323, 22:143, 25:78, 267-270; Columbian Exposition, 24:102; French, 25:265; British, 25:266, 267, 40:201, 204; Spanish, 25:267
Medary, Samuel, 26:357; territorial governor, 12:441, 14:164, 249, 252, 255, 256, 16:171, 34:100n, 37:141; journalist, 14:112; messages, 14:163, 27:6; career, 15:

127, 25:198, 28:183; papers, 16:
216, 34:40; Copperhead, 31:244,
37:127, 262
Medary House, Chatfield, 24:191, 27:
9
Medary House, Rochester, register,
18:117
Medborgaren (Lindstrom), Swedish paper, 16:246, 29:176
Medelman, John, author, 38:243
Medford, platted, 17:130; statistics,
28:305
Medical Library Association, 17:350
Medicine, history, 11:56-59, 19:225,
23:95, 24:181, 34:175; physicians'
biographies, 11:108, 284, 316, 12:
328, 14:445, 16:477, 21:95, 24:
347, 382, 25:100, 27:80, 28:83,
36:70, 327, 37:348, 38:92; service
to Indians, 11:283, 13:320, 16:
147, 22:102; Minnesota communities, 12:104, 211, 16:250, 252,
17:100, 20:103, 21:114, 329, 22:
212, 334, 24:182, 263, 25:307, 26:
96, 173, 287, 397, 27:80, 168,
269, 365, 28:83, 29:265, 33:353-
356, 34:312, 35:294, 381, 36:104;
frontier, 12:106, 440, 15:488, 16:
119, 245, 17:237, 19:463, 20:442,
21:101, 437, 25:200, 400, 26:143,
144, 29:338, 32:44, 36:100, 193,
324, 37:183; preventive, 12:204;
education, 12:204, 328, 17:220,
18:459, 21:101, 26:143, 27:135,
31:124, 33:312, 36:282, 40:362;
societies, 12:204, 16:29, 353, 17:
220, 19:357, 20:344, 21:210, 22:
330, 23:190, 387, 24:382, 26:397,
33:312, 36:29, 282; pediatrics,
12:204, 19:112, 31:124, 36:282;
among ethnic groups, 12:306, 18:
338, 20:466; epidemic diseases,
13:203, 14:288-302, 15:436-438,
16:147, 22:330, 24:265, 29:151,
30:9, 34:173, 37:348; Indian practices, 13:330, 14:109, 15:291, 21:
165, 325, 22:102, 135, 24:262, 33:
91, 38:151; patent remedies, 14:
413, 28:104, 34:121, 127, 38:39,
40:406; surgery, 14:439, 17:474,
20:241, 24:121, 123, 181, 27:164,
31:124, 34:173, 37:133; Ramsey
County, 15:254, 20:91, 206, 344,
446; journals, 15:353, 21:209, 22:
435, 31:124, 37:135; Canada, 16:
480, 17:111, 18:103, 22:273, 27:
260; equipment, 17:69, 27:273; licensing, 17:220, 19:97, 20:237,
29:353, 30:405, 37:135; home remedies, 19:205, 369-375, 25:400, 28:
231-233, 29:151, 34:195-197; mortality statistics, 19:226; Rochester, 20:221-242; quackery, 20:236,
35:294, 37:36, 40:406; fees, 21:
194, 26:96; libraries, 21:357-371;
urbanization, 24:79; prison service, 24:181; Walter Reed's career,
24:210-213; progress, 26:173;
group practice, 28:179; Red River
Valley, 30:259; ophthalmology, 31:
124; Iowa, 33:44; Detroit, Mich.,
33:87; childbirth, 35:108; derma-
tology, 36:282. See also Health
conditions, Homeopathy, Hospitals,
Mayo Clinic, Nursing, Public
health, various diseases
Medicine Bottle, Sioux leader, 14:

438, 15:399, 20:216, 21:339, 38:
98, 128, 131, 144, 146; village,
32:212; pictured, 34:322, 38:130
Medicine Lake, Catholic church, 15:
480, 16:484; pageant, 17:361; camp
meetings, 31:92
Medill, Joseph, publisher, 34:203
Medina Township, Hennepin County,
history, 34:128, 36:36
Medora, N.D., ghost town, 14:205, 27:
357
Meeker, Judge Bradley B., 19:135, 29:
219n, 30:109, 35:357, 39:39, 144,
151; speaker, 12:392, 400, 22:252,
30:200; MHS founder, 20:367, 368;
pictured, 28:348, 35:131; water
power interest, 37:311-323
Meeker, Ezra, 11:452
Meeker, Jotham, printer-missionary,
13:109, 15:20
Meeker County, mills, 11:116; pioneer
life, 11:220, 14:236, 19:440, 24:
112, 114-124; railroad, 12:254;
ethnic groups, 12:265, 277, 25:
318, 30:401; newspapers, 13:197,
17:361; archives, 13:311, 22:100;
agriculture, 18:408, 19:474, 22:
446, 24:90; history, 19:117, 344,
470, 20:463, 36:104; name, 20:368;
dairying, 21:452, 29:158; wildlife, 30:221, 33:141; grasshopper
plague, 36:57; in Sioux Outbreak,
36:234, 38:150, 281, 283; Mormon
mission, 36:292; politics, 36:308
Meeker County Historical Society, 14:
346, 16:241, 19:344, 22:106; organized, 13:216, 22:217; publications, 19:117, 470; meetings, 22:
340, 23:399, 24:87; activities,
25:407, 35:156
Meeker County News (Litchfield),
politics, 38:305
Meeker County Old Settlers Association, 11:12, 13:216; marking project, 11:17, 116, 335; minute book,
19:344. See also Meeker County
Historical Society
Meeker County War History Committee,
24:82
Meeker Island, Mississippi River,
Hennepin County, located, 37:309n;
dam, 37:312, 315-323
Meeks, Leslie H., author, 14:445
Megraw, Thomas, 26:242
Mehegan family, genealogy, 30:60
Mehegen, Mother Mary X., 16:340
Mehlhorn, F. D., 18:336
Meidell, Ditmar, author, 25:393
Meier, Prisca, 35:264
Meighan, Daniel, pioneer, 24:320
Meighen, Felix, pioneer merchant, 16:
367, 21:220
Meighen, John F. D., 11:289, 298, 12:
184, 14:79, 15:136; speaker, 11:
291
Meighen, Thomas J., 15:80, 485, 16:
240; store, 16:367, 20:302; pa-
pers, 21:324; politician, 32:144n,
222, 39:104
Meighen, William, gubernatorial can-
didate, 35:58
Meighen family, newspaper collection,
21:34
Meigs, Cornelia, work reviewed, 14:
209; author, 19:104, 31:132, 146
Meigs, Montgomery C., quartermaster
general, 38:221, 222, 287, 39:204

Meile, Adolph G., 29:282
Meilicke, Emil J., career, 32:62
Meinberg, Father Clodoald, author,
26:388
Meine, Franklin J., 35:40; author,
17:226; speaker, 29:83
Meinig, Donald W., author, 34:353,
35:152
Meixell, Mrs. William D., author, 30:
161
Mejakigijig, Chippewa leader, 21:285
Mekeel, Scudder, author, 25:86
Melander, C. W., 14:120
Melander, Henry, 29:182
Melander, J. B., 14:120
Melander, Leonard W., 20:159n
Melby, Dr. Benedik, 16:255
Melby, C. A., speaker, 14:346
Melby, John O., papers, 26:156
Melby, Methodist church, 20:35
Melchin, A. I., historian, 38:325
Melendy, Peter, career, 25:71
Melendy, Samuel W., pharmacist, 28:65
Melgard, Lloyd G., author, 35:203
Melland, Mrs. A. C., author, 11:117
Mellon, Andrew, depicted, 35:161
Meloy, John C., 27:345
Melrose, L. J., 27:48
Melrose, townsite, 12:85; history,
17:366, 35:336; court cases, 17:
467; churches, 18:119; Swedish
colony, 20:248; railroad, 21:241,
242, 393
Melville, Emilie, actress, 33:173,
174, 178n
Melville, Herman, author, 20:106, 23:
113, 30:188
Melvin, Grace, 25:393
Membré, Father Zénobe, 11:348, 15:
472, 20:67
Memler, Henrietta L., author, 14:438,
16:253
Memmler, H., Civil War veteran, 32:
102n
Memorial Day, observances, 14:117,
16:372, 435, 26:169, 28:287, 39:23
Memorial Lutheran Church, St. Paul,
17:118
Memphis, Tenn., river port, 19:185,
24:53; surrender, 25:137
Memphis Burlesque Opera House, 23:314
Menage, Louis F., 16:249; Philippine
collection, 39:116-120
Menahga, name, 20:343, 30:331
Menard, ---, trader, 11:262n
Menard, Mary A., 15:428
Menard, Pierre, trader, 40:194;
house, 29:72
Ménard, Father René, 13:248, 400;
missionary, 12:352; explorer, 14:
339, 18:388, 19:198
Menasha, Wis., history, 18:326
Mencken, August, work reviewed, 36:66
Mencken, H. L., work reviewed, 17:
319; author, 21:4, 427; 30:267;
influence, 28:55, 39:35
Mendelsohn, Eric, architect, 35:293
Mendenhall, Mrs. Abby, 18:263
Mendenhall, Alice, 14:276, 15:45
Mendenhall, Hiram W., cabin, 14:276,
15:45
Mendenhall, Luther, banker, 37:122
Mendenhall, Richard J., banker, 18:
251, 257n, 21:192, 22:424
Mendenhall, Mrs. Richard J., diary,
21:192

Mendenhall family, in Minnesota, 25: 292

Mendokaycheenah, Sioux Indian, 17:439

Mendota (St. Peter's), treaties, 11: 161, 12:248, 15:284, 18:44n, 22: 134, 140, 149, 151, 152, 414, 24: 382, 27:239, 28:343n, 30:25, 32: 65, 76, 34:360, 35:321, 36:3, 37: 271, 272, 38:1, 119, 129, 39:47; trading post, 11:375, 13:224, 14: 85, 19:192, 20:121, 262, 28:311, 29:174, 30:195, 35:24, 28, 356, 36:15n, 44, 259-264, 40:80, 262; roads and trails, 11:389, 390, 392, 12:61, 19:103, 21:227, 229, 233, 27:344, 36:37-39, 40:233; schools, 11:445, 14:331, 15:313, 348, 367, 16:337, 17:84; county seat, 13:141; Indian agency, 14: 215, 15:305n, 343, 16:215, 332, 18:157-159, 27:142, 35:23-27; Catholic church, 15:104, 195, 467, 19:190, 28:319, 29:206; located, 15:304n, 23:340, 29:206, 35:22, 23; bridge, 15:312, 35:189; history, 16:233, 23:214, 40:316; map, 18:108; river port, 18:154, 32: 12n, 97, 35:356, 36:46n; climate, 18:155; historic houses, 19:235, 20:342, 23:192, 29:206n, 36:95, 37:61; railroad, 21:239, 37:160, 38:295; name, 22:18n, 23:337n, 25: 114, 36:42n; rafting, 24:137; cantonment, 30:210, 211n; pictured, 33:120; historic site, 37:60, 64; judicial district, 39:145. See also Faribault House, Mendota; Sibley House

"Mendota," steamboat, excursion, 22: 15-21

Mendota-Big Sioux Road, see Dodd Road

Meneely, Andrew, bell manufacturer, 18:376, 377

Menefee, F. N., author, 21:422

Menefee, Selden C., author, 31:44

Menell, ---, arsonist, 28:209

Meng, John J., author, 27:161, 28:72

Menke, Bill, showboat captain, 33:39

Mennonites, Mountain Lake colony, 11: 294, 14:114, 16:344, 17:466, 18: 47, 445, 19:48, 213, 20:181-183, 459, 23:88, 24:365, 26:287, 27: 222-227, 365, 31:29, 37:184, 38: 243; Russian, 14:103, 18:99; Kansas, 14:114, 225; Canada, 14:224, 15:478, 18:456, 21:269, 29:166, 35:247; Minnesota, 14:224, 22:335, 31:119; immigration, 18:99, 23:88, 37:184; Iowa, 20:424; customs, 30: 161; Cottonwood County, 36:195

Menominee Indians, 32:229; Wisconsin, 12:435, 25:267, 32:189; in War of 1812, 19:304; dances and music, 28:176, 34:161; annuities, 32:186; pictured, 33:20; Illinois, 36:191; culture, 37:174

Menomonie, Wis., fire, 23:256; architecture, 40:101-103, 412; mills, 40:390n

Menominee River Boom Co., history, 28:188

Mentholatum Co., publisher, 22:433

Menzel, Louise F., author, 36:282

Mercantile Library Association, St. Paul, 18:363, 29:177

Mercer County, N.D., place names, 36: 325

Merchants Bank, Winona, architecture, 40:359

Merchants Bank of Duluth, 37:124

Merchants Bank of West Duluth, 37:124

Merchants' Hotel, Hutchinson, register, 20:349

Merchants Hotel, St. Paul, 16:71, 231, 272, 24:332, 35:355, 356n, 36:304, 38:187, 296

Merchants International Steamboat Line, Red River, 21:255-257, 269, 270, 32:60

Merchants National Bank, Duluth, 37: 122

Merchants National Bank, St. Paul, 20:59, 33:313

"Mercury," steamboat, 11:206

Meredith, Mamie, editor, 12:445

Meredith, William M., 39:38

Mereness, Newton D., archival agent, 11:205, 444, 12:83, 190, 317, 13: 195, 14:98, 330, 15:343, 16:96, 202, 215, 333, 17:95, 18:94, 209

Meriam, Lewis, 11:208

Meriden Iron Co., Minneapolis, 39:78

Meriwether, Robert L., editor, 37:37

Merk, Frederick, work reviewed, 38: 326; author, 23:52

Merkle, George, letter, 31:174

Merkle, Lorenz, 27:171

Merling, Bert, 23:398; author, 23: 400, 24:190

Merriam, John L., 26:63; house, 15: 54, 40:98-100, 135; Burbank agent, 39:233

Merriam, William P., real-estate agent, 18:142, 144, 146

Merriam, William R., 12:175, 36:70; papers, 11:445, 14:217; governor, 15:127, 17:162, 18:122, 32:133, 134, 138, 35:60, 61, 67, 68, 297, 300, 301, 36:113, 37:151, 38:16, 18, 20n, 39:94, 96, 101

Merriam family, genealogy, 27:56

Merriam Park, St. Paul, history, 21: 77

Merrick, George B., author, 18:373; steamboat captain, 29:3

Merrick, Martin, author, 36:325

Merricks, Osborn, 25:241

Merril, M. G., 18:401

Merrill, Mr. and Mrs. ---, stage station owners, 40:389, 390

Merrill, A. E., house, 25:407

Merrill, Adelaide K., author, 16:249

Merrill, Bertha E., author, 26:94

Merrill, Daniel D., 33:2; publisher, 26:301, 38:61, 386

Merrill, E. A., mayor, 33:332

Merrill, Ethel O., author, 14:110

Merrill, Galen A., author, 18:119

Merrill, George C., 19:184n

Merrill, George P., author, 13:441, 15:128, 16:115, 18:218

Merrill, H. L., 11:330

Merrill, Horace S., works reviewed, 34:37, 166; author, 33:314

Merrill, James A., author, 15:238

Merrill, Levi W., 25:143

Merrill, Mrs. Martha, speaker, 20: 456, 23:399

Merrill, Mrs. Mary A. K., author, 15: 140

Merrill, Lt. Michael R., 38:362

Merrill, Moses, missionary, 35:380

Merrill, Olive P., 27:250

Merrill, Pauline S., author, 26:273

Merrill, W. O., journalist, 15:41

Merrill and Ring Lumber Co., 27:302

"Merrimac," ironclad, 18:372, 25:34, 129, 130

Merriman, O. C., author, 11:226

Merrington, Marguerite, author, 31: 251

Merritt, Andrus R., autobiography, 16:336, 17:54

Merritt, Callie, author, 28:83

Merritt, Cassius C., 13:428

Merritt, Glen J., speaker, 15:492, 17:357; postmaster, 34:185

Merritt, H. Clay, author, 26:373

Merritt, Howard A., author, 20:194

Merritt, Jesse, author, 27:66

Merritt, Leonidas, 15:127, 16:296, 17:478

Merritt, Lewis H., 17:465, 21:292

Merritt, Lucien, 16:360

Merritt, Thomas H., speaker, 14:238, 18:465

Merritt, Gen. Wesley, 17:88

Merritt family, mining activities, 12:333, 14:462, 16:114, 116, 21: 183, 292, 23:361, 24:265, 25:185, 27:263, 33:106, 355, 34:216, 36: 192; pictured, 14:360; bankers, 37:124; piano owners, 39:323n

Merry, Robert, 12:445

Merryman, John, 17:77, 78

Merserve, Frederick H., author, 34: 212

Mershmann, Father Francis, 33:54n

Mershon, W. B., 21:297

Merton Township, Steele County, pioneer life, 19:127

Merz, Wendelin, settler, 35:265

Mesaba, St. Louis County, ghost town, 20:468, 34:178, 39:131; Finnish settlement, 22:392n, 40:341; railroad, 27:203, 32:245; post office, 33:258; trail, 34:274-276; bus service, 35:338

Mesaba Iron Co., organized, 19:309

Mesaba Transportation Co., bus line, 22:102, 36:190

Mesabe Electric Railway, 37:342

Mesabi Iron Co., 34:279, 282, 283, 37:41

Mesabi Range, ore shipping, 12:178, 27:359, 33:226, 34:11, 36:276; iron discovered, 12:333, 14:462, 15:127, 16:114, 336, 21:292, 25: 196, 28:70, 33:106, 36:192; mining, 13:115, 15:487, 18:332, 24: 93, 29:171, 259, 30:267, 34:44, 35:337; explored, 13:213, 16:371, 37:347, 39:78, 40:412; geology, 15:131, 143, 21:288, 32:222, 38: 203; developed, 16:116, 343, 23: 361, 25:185, 196, 411, 26:84, 29: 89, 32:244-246, 34:216, 36:196, 37:122, 124; towns, 16:193, 486, 19:334, 464, 21:290, 32:46; roads, 16:299, 32:244, 245; bibliography, 18:460; pioneer physicians, 19: 357; output, 21:102, 439, 27:203, 263, 33:67n; frontier life, 21: 183, 22:345; anniversaries, 21: 188, 33:226; bus line, 21:291, 22: 102, 27:272, 33:353, 35:338; ethnic groups, 23:387, 25:319, 320, 27:204-215, 28:251; pine lands, 24:134; importance, 26:268, 31:55; churches, 27:213; labor activities, 27:352, 40:340-347; in fic-

tion, 31:134, 34:309, 36:81; map, 34:270; schools, 40:402n. See also Iron mining, Taconite
Mesabi Syndicate, 34:273-275, 279
Mesabi Trail, built, 32:244, 245
Mesaiger, Father Charles M., Jesuit missionary, 12:363, 18:235, 239, 37:37, 39:301, 302
Mesick, David O., author, 36:326
Messein family, see Bailly family
Messer, Mrs. Emma N., 14:219, 331; author, 13:444; birth, 35:108
Messer, Reuben, 18:224
Messick, George N., 16:472
Messick, Capt. Nathan S., at Gettysburg, 16:472, 38:254
Messmer, Archbishop Sebastian, career, 34:313
Metcalf, A. L., letters, 16:242
Metcalf, Clarence S., 25:296
Metcalf, Cornelius, Jr., 20:162n
Metcalf, G. W., Sr., 20:162n
Metcalf, George, author, 38:41
Metcalf, Isaac S., letters, 11:95
Metcalf, Ralph, 35:378
Metcalf, Mrs. Richard, author, 30:272
Metcalfe, Ransom, 17:364
"Meteor," whaleback, 34:12
Meteorology, see Climate
Methodist church, Conshohocken, Pa., 11:417; Wisconsin, 12:158, 27:84, 94, 28:188; Minnesota, 12:320, 14: 438, 452, 15:110, 346, 17:397, 465, 18:208, 21:86, 203, 415, 28: 167, 29:354, 31:66, 33:81, 189-193, 35:77-86; ethnic groups, 13: 305, 14:353, 19:212, 464, 25:324, 31:25, 38:75, 332; educational institutions, 14:148, 224, 16:345, 17:465, 34:91; clergymen, 15:110; policies, 16:451, 33:319; conferences, 18:350, 359, 361, 364, 366, 19:114, 130, 132, 221, 26:242, 27: 9, 39:35; Massachusetts, 19:130-132; camp meetings, 25:212, 31:79-82, 189; Iowa, 28:184; Canada, 33: 315; in lumber camps, 34:67; newspaper, 36:291, 292; anniversary, 36:326. See also Hamline University, various Minnesota communities, individual church bodies
Methodist Ministers Association, 35: 347
Methodist missions, 15:130; Minnesota, 11:321, 21:430, 29:354, 33:90, 40:147; Canada, 12:427, 14:115, 15:240, 463; Kaposia, 14:363, 20: 123, 127, 21:274, 31:82, 40:82; Elk River, 15:344; Sandy Lake, 20: 80, 32:95; frontier, 21:71; Wisconsin, 21:430; Nebraska and Dakotas, 35:380
Methua-Scheller, Maria, actress, 32: 103, 104, 171, 34:241
Methy Portage, Sask., 40:163, 174; located, 12:361; discovered, 13: 182
Métis, see Mixed-bloods
"Metropolis," steamer, 40:359
Metropolitan Building, St. Paul, 40: 135
Metropolitan Hotel, St. Paul, 17:372, 19:407, 29:126, 128
Metropolitan Life Building, Minneapolis, early skyscraper, 16:249
Metropolitan Municipal Ski Club, Minneapolis, 16:249

Metropolitan Museum of Art, New York City, 20:334, 21:196, 26:266
Metropolitan Opera Co., tours, 36:33
Metropolitan Theater, Minneapolis, 33:97, 98; history, 18:468
Metropolitan Theater, Rochester, 18: 227
Metropolitan Theater, St. Paul, 23: 199
Metz, Lt. Charles E., 26:374
Metz, Charles W., auto driver, 38:207
Metz automobile, 38:206, 207, 209, 212-215
Metzdorf, Robert F., 36:218; author, 36:101
Metzger, Walter P., work reviewed, 35:30; author, 39:34
Metzner, Lee W., author, 24:176
Metzroth, John W., tailor, 35:265
Metzroth, Mrs. Otto, 22:108, 27:73
Meuli, Karl, author, 37:306
Mevig, A. M., 14:236
Mexican War, effect on army, 22:410; diary, 23:75; soldier vote, 26: 187n; soldiers' land bounties, 36: 16n
Mexicans, Twin Cities, 22:348, 24: 384, 31:30, 34:266; Mesabi Range, 27:214; in industry, 30:66; in Civil War, 33:84
Mexico, history, 11:77, 37:44, 40: 313; relations with U.S., 16:457, 17:164, 18:425; commerce with Twin Cities, 35:245
Mexico City, early printing, 15:3
Meyer, A. C., author, 30:154
Meyer, A. J., photographer, 20:215
Meyer, Ernest, author, 18:466, 28:380
Meyer, Eugene, 15:490, 16:491
Meyer, H., work rviewed, 14:324; author, 17:118
Meyer, Herbert W., author, 35:98, 337, 380
Meyer, John B., author, 34:265
Meyer, Julia, 18:59
Meyer, Robert, Jr., author, 33:91
Meyer, Roy W., "The Story of Forest Mills," 35:11-21; "The Prairie Island Community," 37:271-282; reviews by, 38:329, 39:208, 339, 40: 304; work reviewed, 39:293; receives award, 38:92; author, 39: 261
Meyerding, Henry, 13:273
Meyers, Cecil H., "Financing a Frontier City," 37:119-125
Miami Co., Detroit, Mich., traders, 19:299
Miami Indians, pictured, 29:335, 336; Illinois, 36:191; culture, 37:174; in fur trade, 40:208
Michaelis, Richard, author, 24:36
Michaelson, Rev. J. H., pioneer minister, 25:324
Michel, Gen. J., letter, 11:97
Michel, Virgil, career, 35:372
Michelet, Robert H., biography, 24: 263
Michelet, Simon, career, 24:263; papers, 36:36
Micheli, G. A., artist, 13:83
Michels, Aloysius, author, 18:173
Michels, Mrs. Joseph E., 40:99n
Michener, Carroll K., 11:282n, 22: 202; author, 14:119, 495, 26:308, 33:315
Michener, Daniel K., career, 14:119

Michener, Mrs. Daniel K. (Ida L. B.), career, 14:119
Michener, John L., pioneer, 14:119
Michigan, ethnic groups, 12:251, 16: 339, 22:96, 25:299, 301, 32:1n, 27: 256, 28:368, 29:174, 32:185, 35: 33; markers, 12:329; heroes, 12: 440; early printing, 13:110; atlas, 13:186; archaeology, 13:207; aborigines, 14:112; history, 15: 125, 26:270, 31:57, 32:117, 34: 207, 35:154, 36:100, 37:301; leaders, 15:236; pageant, 16:112; plat book, 17:101; wildlife, 18:451; Paul Bunyan legends, 21:177, 296-298; British regime, 21:182; mining, 21:183, 25:276, 27:153, 160, 30:269, 36:276; folklore, 21:354, 26:381, 28:186, 378, 33:183, 35: 95, 37:39; constitutional conventions, 22:73-76; boundaries, 22: 74, 75; co-operatives, 22:314; in fiction, 23:117; Indian affairs, 23:133; imprints, 24:75; agriculture, 24:259, 35:45, 36:278; architecture, 25:173, 32:109; lumbering, 25:276, 26:166, 34:35, 36: 153-166, 37:132; automobile laws, 26:26; geological surveys, 26:224, 32:215, 34:207; maps, 26:384, 27: 66; bibliography, 28:276; missions, 29:79, 33:185; Yankees, 31: 181; geographic names, 33:49; fishing, 34:265; politics, 35:332; source material, 35:383; in Civil War, 38:202; railroads, 39:263; forts, 40:146; gazetteer, 40:147
Michigan, N.D., country stores, 35: 200
"Michigan," steamboat, 18:154
Michigan Agricultural College, Lansing, 23:164
Michigan Central Railroad, conflict with farmers, 33:308; built, 40: 356
Michigan Folklore Society, 28:378
Michigan Historical Commission, Lansing, publications, 19:348, 25: 302, 26:169, 30:160; collections, 24:376; museum, 26:169
Michigan Territory, boundaries, 24: 234, 27:128, 163; papers, 25:271, 26:362; post offices, 30:174; explored, 31:93; fur trade, 36:247
Michigan Territory Medical Society, founded, 33:87
Michigan University, see University of Michigan
Michilimackinac, see Mackinac
Michilimachinac Co., 11:379, 16:200, 201, 19:300, 40:170, 180, 181; dissolved, 19:301
Michipicoten, Ont., post, 11:233, 262, 263, 16:360, 20:452, 34:254; legend, 25:372
Mickelson, C. N., 27:147
Mickelson, Siegfried, author, 22:93
Mickelson, Walter K., author, 21:333, 28:375
Mickinock, Chippewa Indian, 24:325
Micmac Indians, culture, 34:257
Microfilm, uses, 23:368, 24:69, 266, 26:271, 28:68, 29:50, 30:42, 46, 89, 167, 32:123
Mid-Continent Airlines, 25:195, 33: 240

Middle Border, defined, 22:157; in
literature, 22:158
Middle Creek, Redwood County, Evangelical church, 17:117
Middle Island, Mich., Lake Huron, 23:
141
Middle River, history, 17:483
Middle River Co-operative Creamery,
18:470
Middle States Association of History
and Social Science Teachers, 22:
329
Middle States Council for the Social
Studies, 29:163
Middle West, frontier, 12:419, 16:
477, 18:304; development, 16:196,
20:114, 24:74, 29:163, 36:185;
medicine, 22:404-408, 26:143-146;
democratic aspect, 23:83; literature, 23:113-125, 156-158, 25:175,
26:356-358, 27:71, 28:185, 30:62,
149, 37:218; culture, 26:73, 39:
76; holiday celebrations, 26:170;
farm life, 27:83-95; influence,
27:251; bibliographies, 28:276,
373, 34:169, 216; historic houses,
29:72; centennials, 29:164; pictured, 29:167, 30:55, 141, 39:82;
folk art, 31:46; utopian communities, 31:112; dialects, 34:127;
country towns, 34:200; defined,
37:85; economic history, 37:133;
evaluated, 37:339
Middlestadt, Vincent, 25:238
Middleton, Gen. Sir Fred, author, 30:
63
Middleton, William, lumberman, 24:
201, 202
Middleton, William D., work reviewed,
37:341
Middlings purifier, early use, 11:
276-278, 23:284; patented, 11:281
Mide, Chippewa religion, 39:04
Midland Cooperatives, 24:174, 30:67,
35:334, 38:203
Midland Monthly, literary magazine,
26:300, 302, 28:185
Midland Railway Co. of Manitoba, 23:
93
"Midora," steamboat, 11:134
Midway River, Carlton County, mill,
22:220
Midwest Heritage Conference, 35:43
Midwest Museums Conference, 11:313,
12:31, 24:58, 29:258, 30:66
Miers, Earl S., work reviewed, 29:344
Miessler, ---, missionary, 14:56
Miesville, Catholic church, 15:128,
20:460
Mihin, J. J., farmer, 16:496, 24:299,
301
Mikesell, Marvin W., author, 37:182
Milaca, described, 13:452; town hall,
19:366; name, 21:350; history, 24:
192; community study, 25:57-61,
28:163
Milan, Lutheran church, 29:86; his-
tory, 40:47
Milbank, Jeremiah, Jr., author, 24:
264
Milburn, W. H., lecturer, 11:157
Milch, Mrs. Louis, musician, 39:54n
Milch family, musicians, 39:56
Miles, Charles, author, 39:129
Miles, Col. Dixon S., 25:225
Miles, Gen. Nelson A., 40:94
Miles, R., trader, 40:168n

Miles, R. E., author, 36:105
Miles, R. E. J., actor, 23:313
Miles, Wyndham D., "A Verstile Ex-
plorer," 36:294-299; review by,
37:31
Milford, Brown County, monument, 11:
456, 23:192, 37:60; population,
20:93; settled, 30:30
Milhollen, Hirst D., works reviewed,
33:216, 37:33
Military Bounty Land Act, 29:225
Military Intelligence Service Lan-
guage School, Fort Snelling, 27:
261
Military Order of the Loyal Legion of
the U.S., 19:349, 22:193
Military Railway Service, 23:293
Military Reserve Claim Association,
19:449
Militia, see Minnesota Home Guard,
Minnesota National Guard
Mill Disaster Relief Fund, 11:316
Mill Pond Lake, Grant County, stage
route, 38:64
Mill Springs, Ky., battle, 11:317,
25:23, 38:258, 261-265, 270, 273,
39:179, 180
Millam, Elizabeth, 36:144
Millard, Glen E., house, 38:352
Millard, Dr. Perry H., 24:211, 30:405
Millay, Edna St. Vincent, author, 21:
3, 4
Mille Lacs, Ont., post, 36:242, 243
Mille Lacs aspect, prehistoric culture, 25:329-341, 26:313, 314,
322, 324, 325, 327-329, 31:163n,
167
Mille Lacs band, Chippewa Indians,
reservation, 13:452, 37:347; census, 21:285; massacre, 26:23
Mille Lacs County, anniversary, 13:
452; place names, 21:286, 345-352;
fair, 22:446; archives, 23:188;
lumbering, 27:154; politics, 36:
308
Mille Lacs County Historical Society,
29:180, 30:277
Mille Lacs County Times (Milaca),
politics, 38:305
Mille Lacs County War History Committee, 23:391
Mille Lacs-Kathio State Park, established, 35:292; archaeology, 39:
344, 40:363
Mille Lacs Lake, name, 11:335, 13:
249, 14:118, 21:346, 30:332; post,
11:374; history, 15:467, 35:50;
Sioux village, 16:18, 19:277, 20:
67; roads, 16:293, 294, 21:234;
battle, 21:182; resorts, 28:292;
mission, 29:168, 39:308n; steamboating, 30:396; fishing, 33:237;
museum, 36:284, 328, 37:44, 45
(cover), 66, 68, 70, 135, 188
Miller, Mr. and Mrs. ---, innkeepers,
40:388
Miller, Mr. and Mrs. A. O., theater
managers, 28:109, 110
Miller, Alden E., 20:345; author, 23:
286
Miller, Alfred J., artist, 22:154n,
155n, 25:278, 26:165, 29:58-61,
31:55, 32:188, 33:89, 264, 34:121,
35:144, 153, 379, 36:236
Miller, Mrs. Anna, 11:459
Miller, Archie, speaker, 21:216, 25:
378

Miller, Betty M., "The Waterville
Junior Historians," 27:122-125;
speaker, 27:146; author, 27:152
Miller, Dr. Clarence H., author, 11:
453
Miller, Clell, bank robber, 34:125
Miller, Mrs. Cornelia H., 27:83n, 151
Miller, Don C., author, 28:375, 36:
283
Miller, E. B., author, 17:480; speak-
er, 18:464
Miller, Emily C. H., educator, 15:128
Miller, Ernest I., author, 35:291
Miller, Fred, at St. Anthony, 17:154n
Miller, Fred, author, 20:334
Miller, Fred C. E., German pioneer,
25:211
Miller, Fred G., newspaper editor,
38:305
Miller, Genevieve, work reviewed, 27:
236
Miller, George H., author, 35:241
Miller, Gerrit S., author, 15:128;
papers, 28:370
Miller, Mrs. H. W., 19:320
Miller, Harmon J. B., author, 22:98
Miller, Herbert J., on war history
committee, 23:150
Miller, Herbert J., legislator, 35:
347
Miller, James E., Jr., author, 39:263
Miller, Jens P., 29:364
Miller, John, Jr., author, 30:389
Miller, John A., 13:117
Miller, Joseph, fur trader, 15:422
Miller, Joseph A., bibliographer, 37:
187; historian, 39:84
Miller, Joseph P., cattle breeder,
26:109
Miller, Judith, 27:30
Miller, Magdalena, 27:30, 31
Miller, Magnus, Dakota County pio-
neer, 24:190
Miller, Maria O., 27:30
Miller, Martin, postmaster, 34:186
Miller, Marvin A., 26:382
Miller, Matthew A., 13:147; at Ninin-
ger, 13:133; speaker, 13:146
Miller, Mildred, author, 24:247
Miller, Niels, author, 29:271
Miller, Norine, 27:144
Miller, Orange S., author, 11:227,
17:125
Miller, Peter, 27:30
Miller, Ruth, singer, 39:59, 60
Miller, Samuel, 34:41
Miller, Samuel R., in Civil War, 13:
115
Miller, Stephen, 35:221; land of-
ficer, 12:389; poet, 14:140, 16:
81, 26:294n; speaker, 16:434, 26:
202, 34:324, 36:172; railroad
agent, 17:485; correspondence, 18:
365, 19:96, 29:283, 30:91, 348;
governor, 22:109, 26:203, 36:171,
38:288-290, 293, 297, 39:190; military service, 25:25, 26, 28:325,
35:132, 38:280, 283, 356, 39:177,
178; depicted, 25:187; politician,
37:314, 326, 327, 329, 39:195
Miller, Stephen, Jr., 35:269
Miller, Thomas, trader, 11:366, 22:
277
Miller, Thomas, hunter, 30:228
Miller, W. F., 35:269
Miller, Ward I., author, 27:66
Miller, William, 19:176, 177, 181

Miller, William A., banker, 11:318
Miller, Dr. William S., author, 14:
    223, 15:237, 20:340
Miller, Willis H., "The Biography of
    a Piano," 19:319-321; author, 19:
    337, 21:430, 22:330, 432, 25:301,
    30:71; editor, 28:81, 34:132, 312,
    35:48, 38:240; speaker, 29:360
Miller Hospital, St. Paul, 20:59, 60
Miller-Humiston colony, see National
    Colony
Millers baseball team, Minneapolis,
    36:93
Millers' Belgian Relief movement,
    14:118, 233
Millers' International Exhibition,
    Cincinnati, 11:329
Miller's Island, Lake of the Woods,
    trading post, 11:363
Millers' National Association, 23:225
Miller's Station, Wilkin County, post
    office, 18:224
Millersburg, Rice County, Swedish
    settlement, 20:98
Millerville, church, 13:117
Milles, Carl, sculptor, 19:106, 22:
    438
Millet, Antoine, voyageur, 18:241
Millet, Frank D., artist, 13:296
Millette, Father Brian, author, 37:
    348
Millier, Hubert, ferryman, 34:233,
    236-238
Millington, Francis, 16:425n
Millis, Walter, 20:421
Mills, Alfred, author, 17:237
Mills, C. E., speaker, 16:304
Mills, E. P., 35:110
Mills, George A., "My French and
    Scotch Ancestors," 28:253-258
Mills, Helen M., compiler, 26:384
Mills, J. C., 15:485; author, 29:27n
Mills, John, pioneer, 30:165
Mills, Mrs. John, speaker, 18:223;
    pioneer, 30:165
Mills, John C., 18:109, 20:96, 21:
    335; speaker, 20:300
Mills, Mrs. John C., 26:89, 179, 393,
    28:194; author, 21:443; bequest,
    25:406
Mills, Joseph T., diary, 22:319
Mills, Mrs. Margaret, 15:486
Mills, Peggy, the younger, 28:258
Mills, Mrs. Peggy M., 28:256
Mills, Randall V., author, 26:383
Mills, Robert, cartographer, 40:120
Mills, Rolf, author, 14:116, 15:251
Mills, Sidney, Jr., 19:170
Mills, Walter T., speaker, 34:222
Mills, Wilbert R., 28:257
Mills, Mrs. Wilbert R. (Alma Rabish-
    ung), 28:254, 257
Mills, Capt. William H., Union offi-
    cer, 39:195n
Millspaugh, Dr. Joseph G., biography,
    17:220
Millstein, Gilbert, author, 35:200
Milne, Mrs. A. A., 12:84, 21:52;
    speaker, 14:363
Milne, Mrs. Winifred C. M., author,
    20:208
"Milo," emigrant ship, 20:250, 251
Miloma, Jackson County, name, 17:320
Milor, ---, guide, 17:305, 21:163,
    164n
Milroy, Robert H., 25:355

Milton, George F., author, 16:224,
    24:155, 34:81
Milton, Viscount, 16:113, 21:204
Milton House Museum, Milton, Wis.,
    39:299
Milton Mills, see Afton
Milwaukee, trading post, 11:258; im-
    migrant transfer point, 13:40, 20:
    256; history, 15:238, 25:299, 30:
    138, 40:129; market center, 22:
    430, 24:100, 26:118, 29:7; Ger-
    mans, 24:331, 25:301, 32:104, 105,
    173; railroad, 24:331n; German
    newspapers, 27:343; gardens, 28:
    377; pictured, 30:394, 34:353;
    lake port, 32:126, 35:355; social
    life, 32:149; banking, 40:112,
    114, 117, 118
"Milwaukee," steamboat, 12:61, 13:
    177, 14:173, 178, 180, 182, 15:420
Milwaukee and La Crosse Railroad, 15:
    419, 26:110
Milwaukee and Mississippi Railroad,
    see Milwaukee Road
Milwaukee County Historical Society,
    Milwaukee, Wis., 29:86
Milwaukee Lithographic and Engraving
    Co., 29:169
Milwaukee Public Museum, 15:453, 27:
    143
Milwaukee Road, 20:256, 24:331, 40:
    47, 235; snow blockade, 11:66;
    history, 12:93, 17:110, 345, 19:
    50, 21:196, 24:175, 26:371, 29:
    251, 34:214, 36:105; colonizing
    activities, 13:29, 30, 18:338, 24:
    177; construction, 14:37, 16:463,
    18:116, 29:117n; advertising, 17:
    214; merger, 33:15n, 21, 36:71;
    excursion, 33:61, 62; in Civil
    War, 33:219; Red Wing, 33:234;
    lawsuit, 35:309; growth, 35:355n;
    locomotives, 36:321
Mimms, John, pioneer, 15:30
Mimms, Theodore, pioneer, 15:30
Mims, Edwin, Jr., author, 11:100
Minden, Henning von, 32:102n
Mindoro Island, Philippines, gover-
    nor's report, 15:466
Miner, H. J., 15:488; author, 21:451
Miner, John R., letter, 30:182
Miner, Julius E., biography, 19:214
Miner, Dr. Kenneth W., author, 23:188
Mineral Point, Wis., Cornish houses,
    27:258; law firm, 35:287
Mineralogy, Keating's work, 36:297,
    298
Miners River, Lake Superior, 23:236
Minette, Frank E., legislator, 33:156
Mineville, N.Y., ore plant, 34:277
Mine Workers of America, 13:19
Minikahda Club, Minneapolis, 36:89,
    90
Mining, methods, 26:174; Michigan,
    28:63; U.S., 30:54; Minnesota, 30:
    55, 33:355, 34:9, 10; Wisconsin,
    38:240; historic sites, 40:404.
    See also various minerals
Minion, Mrs. Lewis, speaker, 28:86
Ministers' Life and Casualty Union,
    Minneapolis, 24:356, 25:63
Mink, John, Chippewa Indian, 35:244
Mink, in fur trade, 30:133, 34:103,
    40:212, 217, 220
Minneapolis, pioneer life, 11:95, 18:
    65, 19:83-85, 449, 450, 20:216,
    24:86, 26:155, 27:79, 168, 34:145,

35:154, 202, 40:6; literary visi-
    tors, 11:147, 16:31, 37-39, 17:39,
    42-45, 374, 378, 380-382, 18:30,
    33, 19:402-404, 407, 415, 22:162-
    164, 28:191; Universalist
    churches, 11:147, 16:120, 35:326;
    politics, 11:213, 35:300, 301, 36:
    307; railroads, 11:215, 24:165,
    30:379; Catholic churches, 11:320,
    13:312, 313, 15:128, 16:121, 17:
    118, 351, 479, 22:222, 27:176, 30:
    395, 33:95, 305; Methodist
    churches, 12:191, 15:362, 16:120,
    17:230, 338, 18:352, 19:266, 267,
    21:415, 33:104, 39:214, 217, 225,
    226; ethnic groups, 12:279, 436,
    18:70, 453, 19:112, 211, 464, 20:
    403-408, 447, 21:426, 23:68, 290,
    24:226, 25:319, 327, 28:121, 29:
    105-113, 33:188, 34:130, 39:168;
    Baptist churches, 12:343, 16:121,
    17:337, 18:331, 19:266, 267; Epis-
    copal churches, 12:343, 16:485,
    18:141n, 21:450, 33:196, 314; post
    office, 12:343, 17:467, 40:89; ho-
    tels, 12:402, 17:42, 380, 18:30,
    226, 19:84, 407, 21:417, 23:220,
    224, 25:3, 4, 33:52, 95, 175, 34:
    99n, 35:67, 68, 72-76, 37:18, 40:
    14, 15, 100n, 135; land office,
    12:445, 14:330, 436, 19:95;
    Lutheran churches, 12:457, 14:362,
    15:373, 21:221, 23:401, 26:182,
    28:291, 29:270, 294; Congregation-
    al churches, 13:123, 15:481, 16:
    74, 17:212, 229, 468, 18:115, 211,
    339, 19:262-267, 21:195, 28:91,
    40:6; platted, 13:198, 40:125;
    name, 13:332, 26:250, 31:182;
    first fire department, 13:346;
    pictured, 14:240, 335, 20:193, 22:
    333, 29:167, 30:112, 33:207, 331,
    333, 34:32, 165, 35:53 (cover),
    98, 228, 341 (cover), 37:3, 40:
    381; Evangelical Covenant church,
    15:129; history, 15:479, 21:308,
    27:361, 28:382, 30:406, 40:412;
    architecture, 16:110, 249, 19:112,
    23:220, 221, 226, 290, 25:4; Pres-
    byterian churches, 16:121, 129,
    355, 17:468, 18:33, 19:262, 20:
    101, 29:87, 30:23, 40:359; street-
    cars, 16:182, 17:360, 21:341, 34:
    130, 35:284, 36:233, 37:308;
    bridges, 16:182, 18:468, 23:290,
    27:79, 288, 28:70, 29:32, 34, 34:
    29; archives, 16:211, 26:176;
    grain market, 16:247, 23:225, 29:
    17, 35:210, 39:328, 40:147; wel-
    fare activities, 16:248, 351, 26:
    155; ski clubs, 16:249, 17:228,
    29:169; G.A.R. post, 16:434;
    parks, 16:494, 22:385, 23:225, 30:
    75; climate, 17:260; schools, 17:
    469, 26:166, 28:90, 29:354, 30:
    154, 39:12; Quakers, 17:478, 18:
    249, 254, 256, 20:358, 21:192;
    labor union activities, 18:106,
    191, 327, 21:376, 378, 380-382,
    388, 394, 22:368, 375-379, 382,
    383, 385, 389, 390, 23:197, 36:
    326, 37:185; social life, 18:226;
    Russian church, 19:123, 39:168;
    baseball clubs, 19:165, 166, 169,
    170, 179, 180, 36:93; river port,
    19:183-189; church activities, 19:
    262-270, 341; directory, 19:432;

guides, 20:64, 30:384, 36:239;
Jews, 20:216, 25:394, 31:44, 36:
320, 40:46; banking, 20:345, 21:
114, 29:88, 40:111; Unitarian
churches, 20:400, 23:228, 363, 37:
265, 40:357; characterized, 20:
410, 27:251; ferries, 20:413, 28:
286, 29:208; centennial, 20:455,
460, 21:62, 113, 35:196; mail-or-
der business, 21:103, 24:373; medicine, 21:194, 210, 24:372, 34:
312, 39:1, 9, 10, 12-17; roads,
21:234, 40:133; lumber industry,
21:314, 22:437, 24:137, 29:140,
208, 31:33, 71, 40:137; population, 21:329, 372, 23:219, 27:299,
35:222, 40:376; fairs, 22:255,
259, 261, 262; industries, 22:373,
23:87, 35:245, 36:106; co-operatives, 22:375, 26:381; economic
conditions, 23:97, 219-232, 29:
188, 32:190, 39:71, 74; hiring
center, 25:219, 36:162-164; air
service, 26:10, 33:241, 242; book
trade, 27:40; telephone service,
27:169; theaters, 28:99, 109, 111-
113, 115, 117, 119, 30:388, 32:
102, 127, 164-168, 172, 33:169-
178, 34:242; opera, 28:111; gardens, 28:377; local government,
30:144, 36:239; county seat, 30:
219n; wildlife, 30:223, 228; music, 31:61, 33:93-104, 37:306, 39:
321, 322; Benedictine mission, 32:
42; aquatennial, 33:91; city plan,
33:331-339; Republican convention,
35:64-76; power company, 35:381;
in fiction, 36:79, 80; real-estate
exchange, 36:189; Mormon mission,
36:290; farmers' market, 36:327;
yellow journalism, 37:163-166,
172; Whitefield exhibit, 40:71.
See also Flour milling, St. Anthony, Twin Cities
"Minneapolis," steamboat, 17:370
Minneapolis Advertising Forum, 14:437
Minneapolis and Cedar Valley Railroad, 17:110, 35:109, 112, 113,
115
Minneapolis and Manitoba Railroad,
16:359
Minneapolis and Rainy River Railroad,
22:416, 27:301
Minneapolis & St. Louis Railway, Sibley County, 13:122; officials, 18:
134n; passenger trains, 30:232-
241, 33:324; history, 32:47;
freight line, 33:43; employees,
35:44, 49, 38:312; locomotives,
36:321
Minneapolis Aquatennial, 35:196, 36:
91
Minneapolis Athenaeum, 20:411; history, 13:123, 17:127, 20:358, 35:
222-232, 37:308; building, 19:212.
See also Minneapolis Public
Library
Minneapolis Athletic Club, 36:91
Minneapolis Board of Park Commissioners, 30:75, 33:332, 35:190, 192,
37:223; maintains Godfrey House,
27:231
Minneapolis Board of Trade, 22:263,
23:219, 35:66, 37:319
Minneapolis Centennial Committee, 35:
196
Minneapolis Chamber of Commerce, 23:

225, 26:382, 28:304, 29:17, 33:
332, 35:66, 39:100
Minneapolis City Hall, architecture,
39:35
Minneapolis Civic and Commerce Asso-
ciation, 33:337, 339; study of
river navigation, 19:183-188
Minneapolis Civic Commission, 33:331,
333, 334, 336-338
Minneapolis Civic Council, 21:114
Minneapolis Civic Opera Association,
summer festival, 33:325
Minneapolis College Women's Club, 12:
98, 284
Minneapolis Commercial Club, 33:332,
337
Minneapolis Committee on Civic Im-
provements, 33:332, 339
Minneapolis Co-operative Mercantile
Co., 22:374
Minneapolis Council of Social Agen-
cies, 20:88
Minneapolis Engineers Club, 33:332
Minneapolis Exposition, 23:226, 227
Minneapolis Family Welfare Associa-
tion, history, 16:248
Minneapolis, Faribault and Cedar Val-
ley Railroad, 17:110
Minneapolis Friendly Visitors' Con-
ference, 33:334
Minneapolis Grain Exchange, 37:18
Minneapolis Grand Opera House, 28:99,
100, 394
Minneapolis Harvest Festival, 35:70
Minneapolis High School, 12:192, 18:
211, 35:154
Minneapolis Homeopathic Institute,
39:14
Minneapolis-Honeywell, see Honeywell,
Inc.
Minneapolis Improvement League, 39:13
Minneapolis Industrial Exposition,
35:70
Minneapolis Institute of Arts, 21:
202, 23:271, 24:242, 26:156; exhibits, 15:359, 22:332, 23:42, 28:
302, 29:369, 30:23, 176, 283, 36:
106, 194; beginnings, 16:248, 20:
185, 33:337, 339; collections, 17:
147, 456, 25:304, 29:265; bequest,
30:268; grounds plan, 33:335
Minneapolis Journal, radio station,
18:333; anniversary, 20:216; illustrations, 20:461, 22:320, 39:
107, 252; politics, 38:305, 39:93,
101, 107
Minneapolis Lutheran Mission Auxiliary, 24:383
Minneapolis Lyceum, 19:251n, 257, 38:
53
Minneapolis Mill Co., 35:98; water
power, 37:312-315
Minneapolis Millers' Association, 29:
10, 40:147
Minneapolis-Moline Power Implement
Co., 21:341
Minneapolis Municipal Airport, history, 19:49
Minneapolis Municipal Art Commission,
33:332
Minneapolis Municipal Ski Club, 16:
249
Minneapolis Musical Union, 30:17, 33:
172, 39:323
Minneapolis, Northfield and Southern
Railroad, 40:378

Minneapolis Pioneers and Soldiers'
Cemetery, 22:223
Minneapolis Planning Commission, 33:
339
Minneapolis Press Club, entertains
Mark Twain, 17:382
Minneapolis Public Library, 13:123,
20:39, 22:336, 39:120, 122; anniversaries, 11:120, 17:127, 20:358,
21:113; collections, 16:55, 17:
147, 19:212, 423, 20:82, 430, 27:
270, 358, 37:38; staff, 19:67, 20:
426, 35:231; buildings, 23:220,
227, 35:232, 37:187, 39:35, 116,
117; children's room, 23:284; history, 37:308. See also Minneapolis Athenaeum
Minneapolis Publicity Club, 33:332,
337
Minneapolis, Red Lake and Manitoba
Railroad, logging line, 27:301,
29:147
Minneapolis Retailers Association,
33:332
Minneapolis, St. Paul and Sault Ste.
Marie (Soo) Railroad, 19:113; organized, 17:345, 31:62; bridge,
33:18; promotes immigration, 35:
248; mail contract, 36:214; pictorial history, 38:335
Minneapolis, Sault Ste. Marie and At-
lantic Railway Co., 23:40
Minneapolis School of Art (Minneapolis School of Fine Arts), 14:231,
16:248, 21:114
Minneapolis School of Design and
Handicraft, 26:79
Minneapolis Six O'Clock Club, 33:332
Minneapolis Society of Fine Arts, 11:
55, 16:248, 19:123, 23:225, 26:
156, 33:337, 39:116
Minneapolis Star and Tribune, picture
collection, 37:38
Minneapolis Stock Yards and Packing
Co., 35:70
Minneapolis Street Railway Co., history, 21:341, 37:308
Minneapolis Study Club, 30:185
Minneapolis Symphony Orchestra, 31:
121; conductors, 16:359, 17:101,
477, 34:339, 39:55; history, 18:
330, 28:382, 30:174, 31:61, 33:93-
104, 222; affiliation with University of Minnesota, 20:92; organized, 23:192, 25:305, 30:354; programs, 36:106
Minneapolis Tidende, established, 14:
402
Minneapolis Times, politics, 39:106
Minneapolis Trades and Labor Assembly, 20:433, 21:392, 22:379, 33:
332, 334, 339
Minneapolis Traffic Association, 33:
337
Minneapolis Tribune, founded, 11:318;
radio programs, 16:116; false armistice edition, 18:99; history,
18:226, 20:461, 40:315; policies,
26:309, 36:301, 38:305; advertising, 28:382; microfilmed, 35:384;
legislative reporting, 37:162, 169
Minneapolis Union Card and Labor
Council, 20:433
Minneapolis War History Committee,
23:391, 26:176
Minneapolis Women's Club, 33:332

Minnehaha (St. Paul), early newspaper, 14:397, 405
"Minnehaha," Lewis' boat, 17:158n,
297, 298n, 301, 31:209, 218, 219
Minnehaha Academy, Minneapolis, 34:
172
Minnehaha baseball club, Northfield,
19:169, 170, 176, 179
Minnehaha County (S.D.) Historical
Society, 19:424n, 426, 20:87
Minnehaha Creek, Hennepin County,
mills, 14:440, 16:248; map, 35:23n
Minnehaha Engine Co. 2, St. Paul, 38:
290; records, 30:163
Minnehaha Falls, Minneapolis, described, 11:95, 15:478, 16:279,
19:407, 20:126, 22:32, 153, 25:
113, 27:288, 28:323, 29:208, 30:
216, 31:156, 32:98, 33:122, 123,
40:359; pictured, 15:350, 17:460,
19:215, 422, 20:35, 191, 22:333,
29:316, 30:21, 215, 33:113, 34:31-
33, 36:22, 40:39 (cover), 75; pub-
licized by Longfellow, 16:33, 351;
in panorama, 17:137; literary visitors, 17:374, 376, 20:133, 22:
433; names, 22:31n, 154n, 23:338n,
26:250, 28:318, 32:98n, 33:124;
city park, 23:225; tourist attrac-
tion, 29:87, 35:180, 181, 37:53;
located, 35:23, 24; bird life, 35:
242; legends, 36:22, 23, 75
Minnehaha Grange, 21:436; records,
17:98, 19:49, 97, 22:41
"Minnehaha Warblers," singing group,
20:329
Minnehoma Oil Co., 23:388
Minneiska, settled, 18:344; described, 30:159
Minneola Township, Goodhue County,
Norwegian settlement, 12:271;
Lutheran church, 20:358
Minneopa Creek, Blue Earth County,
settled, 14:116
Minneopa Falls, Blue Earth County,
camp meeting, 35:81-84
Minneopa State Park, Blue Earth County, 16:192; history, 14:115; grist
mill, 15:484, 27:174
Minneota, Catholic colony, 12:102,
35:139, 325; Lutheran churches,
18:469; Icelandic settlement, 26:
397
Minnesota, place names, 11:102, 214,
16:350, 31:253; histories, 12:68-
70, 15:98, 102, 16:114, 452-456,
36:100; maps, 13:186, 14:117, 349,
18:446, 19:453, 22:433, 26:178,
36:278, 40:274; described, 13:337,
26:250, 28:277, 30:112, 390, 34:
357; flag, 13:445; diamond jubilee, 14:115, 127, 165-171, 211,
343-348, 393n, 449, 15:56, 72,
109, 241; statehood, 14:156-165,
173-191, 15:99, 18:453, 22:101,
39:71, 40:31; mythical cities, 14:
243-262; school texts, 15:98-102,
16:481, 18:201; authors, 15:243,
16:80-82, 18:330, 19:225, 20:445,
25:400, 28:279; tourist traffic,
16:33, 114, 272-281, 351, 366, 17:
214, 228, 18:83, 20:396, 22:446;
land policies, 16:206, 235, 23:
189, 25:306, 37:258; county archives, 19:88-90, 462, 20:89, 445;
statistics, 19:226, 22:331, 36:
103; guidebooks, 19:462, 20:64-66,

35:184; dance theme, 20:347, 21:
58-62; state seal, 21:50, 22:7,
33:126-129; imaginary animals, 21:
353-356; names, 21:412, 27:183,
286, 30:204n, 32:211, 35:48; counties, 21:422; manuscript sources,
22:184; motion picture, 23:51, 93,
192; judicial districts, 23:188;
military leaders, 23:367; song
topic, 25:310, 328; in poetry, 25:
400, 32:163; proverbs, 27:33-36;
pictorial records, 27:330, 339,
28:51, 36:99, 105, 145, 40:412;
calendar, 30:145; distinguished
citizens, 30:171, 369, 36:105;
state flower, 33:229 (cover); governors, 34:217, 39:300, 40:148;
centennial, 36:105-107, 194-196;
community life, 37:180; state
bird, 37:308. See also Minnesota
Territory
"Minnesota," balloon, 38:170-176
"Minnesota," Civil War frigate, 12:
333; bell, 14:441, 18:372
"Minnesota," Mississippi steamboat,
22:15n
"Minnesota," Red River steamboat, 21:
255, 256, 259n, 261-263, 268
Minnesota Academy of Medicine, 19:
345, 20:35, 21:195, 29:353
Minnesota Academy of Science (Minne-
sota Academy of Natural Sciences),
16:58, 32:222, 223, 39:122n; his-
tory, 39:111-122
Minnesota Agricultural and Mechanical
Association, 22:262
Minnesota Agricultural Experiment
Station, St. Paul, 19:156, 20:164
Minnesota Alumni Weekly, 14:434
Minnesota and Alaska Development Co.,
29:303n
Minnesota and Dakota Cattle Co., 17:
112
Minnesota and Dakota Realty Co., 22:
320
Minnesota and International Railroad,
27:301, 29:147
Minnesota and Northwestern Railroad
Co., 15:112, 28:330, 36:5; land
grant, 22:231n, 35:359, 360
Minnesota and Ontario Paper Co., 28:
393, 30:44, 47, 329; history, 21:
452, 30:395, 31:183, 32:61; logging railroad, 28:376; publication, 29:358
Minnesota and Pacific Railroad, 12:
254, 17:110, 28:325, 35:249, 361,
363, 364, 38:45n
Minnesota and Western Railroad, 28:
127
"Minnesota Annals," described, 24:35,
63
Minnesota Anti-defamation Council,
23:292
Minnesota Archaeological Society, exhibits, 16:233, 27:240; publication, 17:115, 22:93, 28:77; meetings, 28:301, 373, 29:55
Minnesota Arrowhead Association,
meeting, 19:355; publication, 26:
276; founded, 36:92
Minnesota Art Project, 23:43
Minnesota Association for Retarded
Children, 39:28
Minnesota Association of Cooperatives, 36:108

Minnesota Association of Deans of
Women, 25:90
Minnesota Atlantic Transit Co.,
freighter operations, 34:13
Minnesota Bankers Association, his-
tory, 20:345; publications, 30:39,
174
"Minnesota Belle," steamboat, 12:393,
32:38
Minnesota Bible College, Minneapolis,
history, 33:354
Minnesota Bible Society, 18:352
Minnesota Boat Club, St. Paul, 19:
440; pictured, 23:173, 25:386, 36:
90
Minnesota Bookstore, St. Paul, 16:32
Minnesota Boom Co., 27:201
Minnesota Bureau of Labor Statistics,
22:387
Minnesota Butter, Cheese and Dairy
Stock Association, 27:108, 115,
117
Minnesota Canal and Harbor Improvement Co., organized, 37:95; land
grant, 37:96-100
Minnesota capital, removal controversy, 11:454, 12:205, 421, 14:159-
161, 15:111, 16:306, 18:105, 31:
178n, 40:67, 68, 332; territorial,
14:130, 18:106. See also Minnesota State Capitol
Minnesota Centennial Train, 36:106
Minnesota Central Railway, 35:338,
38:295; route, 37:157n. See also
Milwaukee Road
Minnesota Central University, Hastings, Baptist school, 13:143, 14:
146, 148, 18:45, 99
Minnesota Cheese Producers Association, 17:486
Minnesota Child Labor Committee, 29:
49, 102
Minnesota Child Welfare Commission,
30:246
Minnesota Children's Aid Society, see
Children's Home Society of Minnesota
Minnesota Chronicle (St. Paul), established, 14:400, 15:19
Minnesota Chronicle and Register (St.
Paul), established, 15:20; politics, 39:45, 46
Minnesota City, pioneer settlement,
12:108, 194, 18:230, 23:320; described, 19:342; Fourth of July
celebration, 23:172; advertisement, 27:19; mail station, 40:87
Minnesota Civil War and Sioux Uprising Centennial Commission, 37:44,
224
Minnesota Claim Association, 11:171n,
22:170, 31:20
Minnesota Club, St. Paul, 40:15
Minnesota College, Minneapolis, 38:
382
Minnesota College of Law, Minneapolis, 39:132
Minnesota Commission of Administration and Finance, history, 23:265
Minnesota Commission of Public Safety, in World War I, 14:319, 15:
338; functions, 17:163, 23:151,
25:64, 30:321, 35:368
Minnesota Commission of Statistics,
history, 34:330-336
Minnesota Committee for the Preserva-

tion of Historic Buildings, 27:
228-232
Minnesota Committee to Defend America, records, 27:249
Minnesota Congress of Parents and
Teachers, 15:467
Minnesota constitution, ratified, 14:
162, 167; amendments, 14:164,
189n, 35:57n, 201; published, 25:
78, 27:337; history, 36:1-12; interpreted, 37:166, 167
Minnesota constitutional conventions,
16:470, 17:97, 18:95, 29:84, 30:
272, 33:356, 35:49, 38:202, 360n;
delegates, 14:161, 245, 28:284,
38:121, 39:272; dual character,
14:162, 167, 244, 348, 35:114
Minnesota Co-operative Creameries
Association, 15:482
Minnesota Council of Catholic Women,
15:77
Minnesota Council of Religious Education, 15:130
Minnesota Cricket Club, St. Paul, 29:
89
Minnesota Crop Improvement Association, 19:31, 40:96
Minnesota Daily (Minneapolis), 40:
367; history, 21:208
Minnesota Dairymen's Association, 27:
114, 115
Minnesota, Dakota and Western Railroad, logging road, 27:300
Minnesota Democrat (St. Paul), founded, 30:300; politics, 39:45, 48
Minnesota Department of Conservation,
15:114, 28:377; publications, 14:
349, 15:241, 22:103, 26:277, 28:
183, 35:98; forestry division, 17:
117, 28:376, 34:182, 36:134, 37:
223; archives, 19:49, 98, 20:434,
21:36; historic sites project, 23:
192; lands and minerals division,
28:376; state parks division, 35:
190, 191, 293, 37:68, 69, 88, 223,
38:388; functions, 40:37, 316
Minnesota Department of Education,
15:98, 27:145, 242, 28:354
Minnesota Department of Highways,
marking project, 11:30, 202, 313,
12:30, 40, 13:63, 340, 14:68, 73,
15:79, 16:195, 18:459, 19:220, 21:
433, 33:209, 35:382, 38:388; maps,
12:194; history, 26:43, 44; Fort
Snelling plan, 35:190, 191
Minnesota Department of Rural Credit,
39:245, 251
Minnesota Department of Taxation,
history, 34:308
Minnesota Deutsche Zeitung (St.
Paul), 33:180, 37:87; established,
14:401, 405, 27:327. See also
Minnesota Staatszeitung
Minnesota Drug Store, St. Anthony,
14:266
Minnesota Editorial Association, organized, 14:394, 35:50; anniversary, 22:212; publications, 23:
187, 27:142, 30:85
Minnesota Editors and Publishers Association, 18:451. See also Minnesota Editorial Association
Minnesota Education Association, 14:
417, 17:469; history, 18:105, 37:
186
Minnesota Emigrant Aid Association,
13:136

Minnesota Epilepsy League, 39:84
Minnesota Equal Franchise League, 13:
101
Minnesota Eugenics Society, 17:16,
25:63, 64, 38:243
Minnesota Falls, Yellow Medicine
County, Norwegian settlement, 12:
275n
Minnesota Farm Bureau Federation, 21:
212
Minnesota Farmer and Gardener (St.
Paul), pioneer farm journal, 18:
407-410
Minnesota Farmers' Exchange, records,
21:412
Minnesota Federal Savings and Loan
Association, history, 30:175
Minnesota Federal Writers' Project,
publications, 20:218
Minnesota Federation of Architectural
and Engineering Societies, 15:140
Minnesota Federation of Women's
Clubs, 14:437, 17:347; papers, 11:
97, 12:429, 14:104, 17:101; histo-
ry, 15:243, 363, 21:221, 22:101,
25:399; war activities, 23:150,
292
Minnesota Field and Track Associa-
tion, 39:21
Minnesota Finnish-American Historical
Society, 26:88, 379, 391
Minnesota Fire Insurance Co., Chat-
field, 24:109
Minnesota Folk Arts Foundation, 25:
178, 305, 26:97, 153, 29:40, 371;
organized, 25:380, 397, 26:37; activities, 26:384, 386, 27:35
Minnesota Folklore Society, 25:305
Minnesota Forestry Association, 35:98
Minnesota forestry division, see Minnesota Department of Conservation
Minnesota Fruit Growers Association,
22:259, 260, 40:334
Minnesota Geographic Board, 19:59,
20:42
Minnesota Geological and Natural History Survey, 21:315, 35:154
Minnesota Geological Survey, 17:226,
30:314; publications, 33:138;
iron-range studies, 34:276, 358,
37:93, 38:203, 39:132
Minnesota Grimm Alfalfa Growers Association, 19:30
Minnesota Historic Sites and Markers
Commission, 22:209, 23:43, 46, 24:
163
Minnesota Historical Building, 20:
325, 22:189, 25:363, 27:144, 32:2;
dedicated, 12:312, 13:159, 23:10;
redecorated, 12:425, 28:394;
cornerstone, 16:168, 274n; alter-
ations, 16:330, 17:57, 18:53, 19:
55, 28:48, 30:42, 325, 37:88; described, 20:207, 429, 21:310; completed, 24:27, 27:22, 32:7; space
problem, 25:50; auditorium, 25:
381; guards, 26:368; history, 30:
299-302, 311, 315; pictured, 33:
317 (cover)
Minnesota Historical Records Survey,
see Works Progress Administration:
Historical Records Survey
Minnesota Historical Society, 17:90,
27:47, 141, 28:302, 39:172; historic sites program, 11:30, 34,
202, 313, 314, 13:63, 317, 340,
377-384, 14:68, 73, 329, 16:195,

18:459, 21:433, 37:135, 38:44,
388, 40:36, 37, 138, 263, 314,
316, see also individual sites;
picture collection, 11:43, 15:440,
461, 16:53, 17:54, 18:48, 52, 19:
50, 419n, 20:35, 54, 215, 289,
370, 21:36, 417, 22:43, 88, 332,
23:42, 71, 24:34, 28:398, 29:102,
30:290, 410, 32:13n, 34:42, 35:
247, 37:308, 38:37; information
bureau, 11:45, 12:29, 13:62, 14:
68, 15:65, 16:58, 17:60, 18:56,
19:58, 20:41, 21:38, 30:319;
staff, 11:46, 443, 13:63, 425, 14:
69, 70, 434, 15:67, 17:62, 18:58,
20:43, 76, 21:43-46, 22:42, 45,
421, 23:43, 168, 269, 366, 367,
24:28, 30-32, 162, 173, 243, 25:
40, 26:36, 39, 256, 368, 369, 27:
23, 26, 140, 340, 28:47, 29:47,
187, 281, 372, 30:43, 44, 180,
181, 290, 304-315, 410, 34:173,
220, 35:52, 100, 339, 384, 36:108,
152, 284, 37:43, 44, 188, 224, 38:
204, 244, 39:132, 212, 40:48, 412;
directors, 11:48, 55, 315, 442,
12:31, 81, 104, 311-314, 16:59,
19:60, 208, 224, 20:287-295, 322,
21:39, 45, 53, 187, 322, 23:268,
366, 26:63, 255, 27:46, 28:298,
29:47, 186, 281, 30:39, 316-329,
32:10, 34:175, 315, 36:108, 284,
37:88, 136, see also individual
directors; finances, 11:48, 12:32,
186, 13:65, 14:70, 15:68, 16:61,
17:63, 18:59, 19:61, 20:44, 21:42,
22:46, 23:44, 26:367, 27:26, 27,
240, 28:49, 196, 30:300, 302, 303,
307, 311, 312, 315, 323, 33:268,
35:296, 36:284; executive council,
11:54, 438, 12:184, 424, 13:57,
423, 14:78, 432, 15:217, 17:460,
18:205, 20:50, 187, 21:42, 53,
408, 22:45, 188, 23:35, 50, 24:57,
25:378, 26:45, 367, 27:22, 26, 46,
28:46, 29:97, 30:310, 311, 316,
318, 326, 32:6, 35:296, 39:36, 40:
349; exhibits, 11:61, 311, 442,
12:425, 13:63, 96, 194, 424, 14:
80, 433, 15:63, 109, 340, 359, 16:
214, 17:58, 71, 463, 491, 18:52,
54, 441, 19:54, 20:38, 372, 21:37,
190, 22:208, 23:42, 71, 27:32n,
48, 141, 240, 242, 28:394, 29:49,
30:179, 283, 288, 289, 367, 411,
31:123, 33:142, 37:188, 224; be-
quests and gifts, 11:200, 30:47,
319, 328, 329, 32:13n, 34:78, 220,
268, 35:296, 339, 383, 36:196,
327, 37:44, 136, 224, 264, 38:43,
336, 39:36, 172, 212, 40:48, 96,
316; radio talks, 13:97, 194, 14:
69, 127n, 211, 213, 328, 344, 434,
15:65, 107, 108, 127, 141n, 148n,
219, 16:57, 65, 232, 19:94; sponsored projects, 14:211, 343-345,
15:56, 277, 382n, 457-459, 16:143,
17:349, 21:207, 25:336, 27:125,
228, 28:47, 302, 29:55, 98, 34:
316, 37:44, 58-70, 39:264, see also Civil Works Administration,
Federal Emergency Relief Administration, Works Progress Administration; educational program, 16:
104, 25:49, 55, 73, 381, 28:389;
archaeological investigations, 17:
347, 18:328, 456-458, 19:53, 20:

146, 152, 27:359, 35:24-34, 244,
336, 340, 384, 36:36, 152, 230,
37:282, 39:123, 130, 40:150, 261,
262; history, 20:323, 366-372,
436, 21:409, 23:1-10, 25:390, 30:
196, 202, 293-330, 363-369, 32:1-
11, 36:240, 39:75, 40:3; reports,
1939, 21:33-46, 1940, 22:35-46,
1941, 23:35-45, 1942, 24:26-40,
1943, 25:40-52, 1944, 26:29-41,
1945, 27:21-32, 1946, 28:45-53,
1947, 29:46-56, 1948, 30:36-49,
1949, 31:17; women's organization,
30:88, 89, 170, 286, 288, 365,
366, 369, 35:248, 36:36, 152;
tours, 36:36, 139, 152, 196, 240,
284, 37:43, 88, 135. See also
Forest History Society, Inc.; Minnesota State Archives; Minnesota
Territorial Centennial
   Meetings, 11:37, 27:143-146,
28:301, 373, 30:298; annual, 11:
51-61, 12:35-41, 13:69-75, 14:73-
80, 15:75-85, 16:63-69, 17:64-72,
18:61-68, 19:63-70, 20:46-53, 21:
47-54, 22:47-54, 23:46-51, 24:56,
25:53-56, 26:42-46, 27:45, 28:197,
29:55, 97, 30:86-88, 31:11n, 32:
1n, 33:236, 34:90n, 35:99, 247,
36:71, 196, 37:88, 188, 224, 38:
244, 40:4, 49; summer, 11:283-298,
441, 12:281-296, 13:277-294, 424,
14:59, 15:309-316, 16:300-306, 17:
311-318, 464, 18:267-283, 19:308-
317, 338, 20:296-309, 21:284-293,
22:290-296, 23:267, 24:349, 25:41,
28:390-392, 29:371, 30:287, 31:
193n, 34:267, 35:100, 340; 90th
anniversary, 20:426-428
   Library, accessions, 11:41, 12:
25, 312, 13:58, 14:63, 15:59, 16:
51, 17:52, 18:45, 19:46, 20:32,
288, 21:33, 22:38, 23:40, 25:41,
26:30, 27:23, 29:48, 30:40; attendance, 12:312, 425, 13:61, 193,
315, 14:67, 15:64, 16:57, 465, 18:
55, 207, 19:57, 20:38, 40, 429,
22:38, 420, 23:39, 24:37, 25:40,
26:33, 27:24, 29:48; collections,
13:324, 15:445-449, 18:69-75, 23:
190, 24:229-233, 26:42, 31:251,
35:248; collecting policy, 30:308-
310, 318
   Manuscripts division, inventories, 11:44, 12:28, 14:66, 16:63;
attendance, 12:425, 13:62, 193,
16:57, 465, 17:59, 462, 18:55,
206, 441, 19:57, 446, 20:40, 21:
37, 311, 410, 22:38, 189, 420, 23:
71, 167, 24:37, 25:40, 26:33, 27:
24, 35:340; guides, 16:49, 94,
197-199, 467, 17:51, 19:455, 34:
315, 337-340; organized, 30:41,
319
   Publications, 16:221, 22:316,
27:60, 241, 330, 28:52, 67, 29:51,
30:289, 300, 34:176, 220, 35:204,
36:196, 37:264, 38:336, 39:300,
40:48, 316, 364; reviewed, 12:68-
70, 13:295, 314, 14:318-322, 15:
462, 16:76-78, 197-199, 17:194,
448-450, 20:417, 22:177-181, 24:
41-43, 27:128, 29:254, 30:50, 370,
see also Gopher Historian, Minnesota History, individual authors
   Newspaper department, 18:323;
collections, 11:203, 206, 13:46,

442, 15:200-202, 16:51, 338, 17:
52, 102, 469, 18:99, 20:331, 21:
33, 22:39, 88, 194, 423, 23:76,
372, 24:34, 35, 27:343, 29:100,
30:40; attendance, 12:29, 425, 13:
315, 14:67, 212, 15:64, 16:57, 17:
59, 333, 18:55, 206, 19:57, 446,
21:38, 22:38, 23:39, 24:37, 25:40,
29:50; accessions, 18:45, 19:46,
20:32, 24:58, 26:30, 27:24, 29:50;
preservation policy, 19:56, 29:50
   Museum, 30:320; accessions, 11:
42, 13:60, 14:65, 15:62, 16:53,
17:54, 18:48, 19:50, 20:35, 21:36,
37, 22:41, 23:41, 24:36, 25:42,
26:31, 27:24, 28:49, 29:50, 30:40;
attendance, 11:45, 202, 313, 12:
29, 312, 13:62, 14:67, 212, 15:64,
460, 16:57, 330, 18:55, 206, 311,
19:50, 57, 58, 92, 20:40, 289,
324, 21:37, 310, 22:37, 189, 23:
39, 71, 24:37, 25:40, 26:33, 27:
24, 48, 243, 29:49; special collections, 12:27, 13:212, 18:372,
374, 20:334, 21:416, 22:424, 27:
155, 29:83, 34:268, 36:284
Minnesota Historical Survey, report
on sites and monuments, 11:314,
12:30, 188, 313, 315, 447, 14:68,
73, 15:65, 16:218
Minnesota history, publications, 12:
68-70, 188, 284, 308-310, 13:420-
422, 15:98-103, 16:213, 232, 452-
456, 17:81-83, 463, 18:83-86, 218,
307-309, 327, 19:427-430, 462, 20:
294, 23:187, 24:78, 29:95, 254,
30:155, 173-175, 203, 328, 405,
31:105-109, 36:25, 62, 100, 106,
107, 189, 195, 37:176, 38:378; radio talks, 13:194, 17:60; teaching, 13:338, 16:481, 18:56, 25:45,
57-61, 73, 258-264, 362-367, 26:
47-51, 234-241, 330-333, 27:26,
122-125, 221-227, 319-326, 28:160-
166, 241-268, 303, 353-359, 386,
31:191, 38:388, 39:263, 40:364; in
fiction, 15:457, 34:42; drama-
tized, 15:479; correspondence
courses, 20:204, 22:317; war program, 23:1-23; popularized, 23:49,
25:49; value, 24:39; bibliographies, 24:173, 25:398, 28:172; relation to folklore, 26:100; in
pictures, 26:138, 27:25, 330, 28:
69, 348-350, 34:42, 36:105, 145,
39:211; sources, 28:68, 284; pageant, 29:279; in advertisements,
30:85; calendar, 30:145; statistics, 36:103; military, 36:194
Minnesota History: A Quarterly Magazine, content, 11:40, 12:24, 80,
13:57, 14:62, 16:50, 17:50, 19:44,
20:31, 21:39, 22:36, 23:36, 24:32,
25:42, 177, 26:34, 27:25, 28:67,
329-338, 29:51, 30:43, 32:62, 33:
28, 268; indexes, 11:201, 311, 12:
78, 315, 13:57, 24:161, 25:43, 26:
150, 27:141, 28:199, 29:186, 30:
179, 31:254, 33:139, 34:41, 125,
35:139, 36:196, 37:36, 38:185, 39:
226, 40:143; articles cataloged,
12:27; characterized, 12:312, 14:
96, 327, 20:289, 27:22, 30:91-94,
32:8; functions, 15:58, 18:43, 25:
47, 30:320; contributors, 17:90,
206, 331, 459, 18:91, 203, 440,
19:91, 207, 347, 444, 20:74, 186,

322, 426, 21:80, 187, 310, 408,
22:82, 187, 316, 418, 23:72-74,
168-170, 270, 287, 369, 24:59,
163, 244, 352, 25:75, 180, 287,
382, 26:64, 153, 257, 370, 27:54,
151, 243, 246, 342, 28:95, 203,
307, 399, 29:103, 191, 287, 375,
30:94, 183, 291, 411, 31:63, 32:
63, 127, 191, 255; format, 21:188,
23:70, 24:28, 32, 350, 26:150, 27:
45, 28:51, 299, 29:186, 30:89, 31:
40, 33:19, 225, 38:43, 336; re-
prints, 28:75; editors, 29:323,
325, 37:188, 224; jubilee number,
30:324; development, 33:35; Buck
awards, 34:175, 220, 35:51, 296,
36:71, 109, 240, 37:88, 264, 38:
92, 336, 39:29n, 36, 84, 93, 125,
264, 40:96, 316; questionnaire,
37:298; subscription rate, 37:348;
anthology, 39:172, 335, 40:264
Minnesota Home Guard, 12:193, 27:57.
See also Minnesota National Guard,
Minnesota State Guard
Minnesota Homeopath (St. Paul), 20:
206, 22:435
Minnesota Homeopathic Medical College, Minneapolis, 22:435
Minnesota Hospital Association, 12:
342
Minnesota Hospital College, Minneapo-
lis, 18:460
Minnesota Hospital for the Insane,
St. Peter, see St. Peter State
Hospital
Minnesota Hospital Service Associa-
tion, 24:372; records, 19:51, 24:
356; organized, 24:182
Minnesota House, St. Paul, 33:197n
Minnesota House, Stillwater, 16:377,
35:363
Minnesota Industrial Commission, 20:
434, 21:195, 374n
Minnesota Institute of Governmental
Research, 19:358
Minnesota Irish Immigration Society,
14:110, 31:21
Minnesota Iron Co., 12:285, 27:205,
40:412
Minnesota Kennel Club, 16:268
Minnesota Labor Relations Act, 35:194
Minnesota Lake, windmill, 12:65-67,
15:133
Minnesota Land Agency, St. Paul, 40:
75
Minnesota Leader (Hokah), established, 21:221. See also Hokah
Chief
Minnesota Leader (St. Paul), 38:304
Minnesota League of Credit Unions,
30:158
Minnesota legislature, road program,
11:395, 396, 408-410; territorial,
12:205, 14:131, 157, 18:105, 22:
100, 28:284, 29:31n, 30:196, 293,
36:7, 8, 40:331; 1931, 12:430;
1857, 14:133, 162-164; special
sessions, 14:161, 26:188-193; game
laws, 16:264; makeup, 19:202;
state fair established, 22:264;
history, 24:263; 1945, 26:80, 176;
evaluated, 26:82; regulates railroads, 29:8, 11; relation to University of Minnesota, 32:177;
geological survey legislation, 32:
217-219; nonpartisan aspect, 33:
155-163; members characterized,

34:313; biennial system, 35:57n; 1891, 35:297-312; grasshopper relief program, 36:54-61; gag law, 37:161-173

Minnesota Library Association, 16:95; anniversary, 23:386

Minnesota Light Artillery, 18:210

Minnesota Light Cavalry, 16:172

Minnesota man, 26:75; discovered, 14: 222, 451, 16:5, 221, 21:100, 28: 77, 180, 35:201, 38:159; age, 15: 156, 16:2; described, 16:6, 18: 104, 19:348

Minnesota Manpower Commission, 24:28

Minnesota Masonic Home, Bloomington, history, 33:310

Minnesota Methodist Conference Historical Society, 31:82n

Minnesota Midland Railway Co., 11: 445, 35:14-16, 21

Minnesota Mining and Manufacturing Co., St. Paul, 34:179, 35:1; history, 34:266, 35:37

Minnesota Missionary (Minneapolis), history, 19:112

Minnesota Monthly, agricultural periodical, 18:409, 26:295, 310, 30: 254

Minnesota Motor Car Co., Minneapolis, 38:207

Minnesota Municipal and Commercial League, 20:83

Minnesota Municipal Commission, 39: 299

Minnesota Museum of Mining, Chisholm, 34:43

Minnesota Museum of Natural History, Minneapolis, 23:50, 30:176, 228, 230n

Minnesota Mutual Life Insurance Co., St. Paul, 17:354, 23:292, 394, 25: 94; history, 35:46, 382

Minnesota Mutual Life Insurance Co. of St. Paul, see Northwestern Mutual Life Insurance Co.

Minnesota National Demokrat (St. Paul), politics, 28:22, 24, 26

Minnesota National Guard, 14:438, 15: 225, 465, 466; history, 12:193, 14:104, 25:205; at Fort Ripley, 13:340, 28:224; Duluth unit, 24: 84; in World War II, 26:389; in World War I, 28:349. See also Minnesota Home Guard, Minnesota State Guard

Minnesota Newspaper Association, 40: 48. See also Minnesota Editorial Association

Minnesota Nurses Association, history, 34:217, 35:46

Minnesota Office of Civilian Defense, 23:149, 151, 153, 24:37, 83, 26: 279

Minnesota Office of Military Defense, 23:149

Minnesota Old Settlers' Association, 12:427

Minnesota Outdoor Recreation Resources Commission, publications, 38:388, 39:264, 40:48, 92; archaeological work, 39:344, 40:263, 363; activities, 40:35-38, 316

Minnesota Packet Co., 12:159n, 13: 235, 15:405, 409n

Minnesota Peace Society, records, 26: 372

Minnesota Pioneer (St. Paul), estab-

lished, 13:45, 14:400, 15:18, 27: 2, 28:342; first issue, 16:370; indexed, 17:57; microfilmed, 23: 368; excerpts, 29:193-222; politics, 39:45, 46; characterized, 39:268. See also Pioneer and Democrat

Minnesota Pioneer Guard, 16:166-177; organized, 16:166; regulations, 16:167; uniforms, 16:168, 169; social activities, 16:168, 173; companies, 16:169-172; in Indian skirmishes, 16:170; band, 16:174; in Civil War, 16:175. See also Minnesota Home Guard, Minnesota National Guard

Minnesota Point, Duluth, lighthouse, 16:113, 21:157, 26:276, 33:355, 37:110, 111; canal, 20:363, 24:62; located, 28:146n; pictured, 37:89 (cover), 91, 111

Minnesota Posten (Red Wing), established, 14:402; policies, 15:473

Minnesota Power Co., Minnetonka, 35: 337. See also Northern States Power Co.

Minnesota Press Women, history, 28: 184

Minnesota Protective Association, 22: 370

Minnesota Public Health Association, 13:446, 18:371n, 23:96, 27:82

Minnesota Railroad and Warehouse Commission, 17:340; history, 25:201, 29:11; functions, 35:298, 309

Minnesota Register (St. Paul), established, 14:400, 15:19. See also Minnesota Chronicle and Register

Minnesota Republican (St. Anthony), newsboys' greeting, 16:386

Minnesota Resources Commission, 20: 447, 26:172

Minnesota Retail Hardware Association, history, 23:87; essay contest, 30:86

Minnesota River, floods, 11:68, 69, 17:230, 21:344, 34:306, 39:251; steamboating, 11:123-144, 163, 165n, 12:59, 113, 210, 455, 13: 176, 224, 342, 443, 14:151, 15: 130, 134, 16:40-42, 44, 333, 366, 18:337, 20:173, 21:215, 27:296, 28:92, 378, 29:122, 30:211, 32:71, 33:9, 34:26n, 53, 36:251-258, 37: 225-228, 39:91, 92; navigation, 11:126, 127, 12:190, 26:272, 29: 195; freight rates, 11:133n, 135; fur trade, 11:375-377, 380, 13: 181, 225, 15:462; bridges, 12:455, 16:279n; explored, 14:372-376, 16: 453, 21:92, 25:396, 26:165, 27:62, 30:124, 33:88, 352, 34:156, 36: 294-296, 37:31, 40:316; geology, 15:143, 26:224, 225, 38:158; excursion, 16:39-42; ferries, 16: 279, 20:100, 30:119, 121, 34:233-238; described, 17:343, 20:169, 30:24; 29, 120, 32:122; maps, 21: 83, 35:22, 24, 28, 29; connecting road, 21:232; keelboat voyage, 22: 142, 144-147; name, 22:312, 33: 114, 124n; mounds, 25:336; forest, 30:117; sources, 32:230; pictured, 36:191, 37:226, 38:154; history, 38:193; charted, 39:130; pollution, 40:132

Minnesota Sandstone Co., 21:194

Minnesota Scenic Highway Association, 19:98

Minnesota School for the Blind, Faribault, 35:321n

Minnesota School for the Deaf, Faribault, 17:227, 19:238, 467, 20: 104, 21:115; history, 15:480, 31: 100, 39:131

Minnesota School of Missions, papers, 21:194, 22:41

Minnesota Seminary, Wasioja, 35:12; depicted, 13:215; history, 14:147

Minnesota Settlement Association, Mankato colony, 17:323

Minnesota Sharpshooters, see First Minnesota Volunteer Infantry

Minnesota Society for the Prevention of Blindness, 39:84

Minnesota Staatszeitung (St. Paul), 27:327; politics, 28:21-23, 28, 31, 33:180, 36:303. See also Minnesota Deutsche Zeitung

Minnesota Stage Co., 14:153, 16:284, 38:64; lines, 12:50n, 51n, 35:258, 37:157n

Minnesota State Advisory Council on Indian Affairs, 11:320

Minnesota State Agricultural Society, 14:277, 18:409, 19:25, 169, 22: 262, 24:290, 26:113, 40:334; incorporated, 22:256; finances, 22: 259, 261-263

Minnesota State Archives, legislation, 22:209, 23:42

 Records, inventories, 11:48, 15:198, 16:54, 211, 17:55, 461, 18:50, 19:52, 66, 88-90, 20:89, 205, 445, 21:100, 207, 327, 434, 22:100, 211, 332, 434, 23:93, 188, 288, 24:361, 30:321; governor, 11: 319; attorney general, 11:446, 12: 322; secretary of state, 13:198; local, 14:103; department of education, 15:198; conservation department, 19:49, 20:434, 21:36; boundary commission, 19:425; industrial commission, 20:434, 21: 36, 195; surveyor general, 23:368; disposal, 24:29, 26:81, 27:261

Minnesota State Archives Commission, 29:47; organized, 26:80, 28:198; program, 28:301, 30:46, 33:227, 34:68, 39:35; members, 29:52; archivist, 34:68, 35:100

Minnesota State Art Society, 14:436

Minnesota State Association of Base Ball Players, 19:169, 170, 339

Minnesota State Automobile Association, history, 35:382, 38:244

Minnesota State Bar Association, 13: 78, 28:200, 29:281, 368, 30:289, 32:62

Minnesota State Board of Control, 15: 123, 20:83, 38:374; Emergency Relief Administration, 16:211, 213, 218, 338, 351, 364, 17:349. See also Civil Works Administration, Federal Emergency Relief Administration, Works Progress Administration

Minnesota State Board of Corrections and Charities, established, 38: 369; activities, 38:370-374

Minnesota State Board of Education, established, 14:416, 418

Minnesota State Board of Fish Commissioners, 33:253

Minnesota State Board of Health, 12:
427, 19:111, 213, 21:362, 24:212;
history, 11:458, 22:102, 29:84,
33:312, 34:34; report on climate,
17:256-260; established, 21:358,
359, 29:170
Minnesota State Board of Immigration,
13:27; activities, 12:256, 17:260,
18:74
Minnesota State Board of Medical Ex-
aminers, 33:312
Minnesota State Butter and Cheese Association, activities, 22:266-268
Minnesota State Capitol (first),
site, 14:330; history, 14:452;
pictured, 27:271, 30:316, 34:330,
36:9, 37:57; arms depot, 29:121;
fires, 30:302, 312, 317, 383, 33:
126, 128; MHS headquarters, 30:
313; appropriation, 31:177; described, 34:138, 142; fenced, 37:
139; burned, 40:223
Minnesota State Capitol (second),
pictured, 35:297 (cover), 308, 311
Minnesota State Capitol (third), described, 17:118; architect, 17:
342, 28:396, 29:264, 36:328, 37:
41; murals, 19:114; guides, 20:
207, 39:84; built, 22:422, 26:173;
commission, 23:273, 25:384; MHS
headquarters, 30:317; pictured,
35:248; Ripley plaque, 39:17
Minnesota State Dental Association,
16:219
Minnesota State District Judges'
Association, 27:249
Minnesota State Eclectic Medical Society, organized, 20:238, 22:435
Minnesota state fair, 17:214; MHS
displays, 11:311, 442, 12:425, 13:
63, 382, 424, 14:69, 433, 30:43,
411; grounds, 12:445; exhibits,
13:35, 14:388, 23:172, 24:288,
295, 297, 298, 301, 302, 304, 350,
26:118, 29:369, 30:76, 283; first,
14:137, 38:43; events, 16:190,
267, 271, 496, 20:201, 22:262, 29:
128, 31:253; manager, 17:354; Owatonna, 21:332; Fort Snelling, 22:
256, 259; site acquired, 22:261,
263; weather, 22:438; history, 29:
230, 39:300; institute hall, 37:
25; piano exhibit, 39:323
Minnesota State Federation of Labor,
17:338, 22:389, 35:194, 379; influence on legislation, 12:99,
446, 13:444, 14:453; organized,
18:332, 22:384; anniversary, 21:
436. See also American Federation
of Labor
Minnesota State Forestry Association,
14:332, 17:220
Minnesota State Geographic Board, 18:
463, 21:351, 22:337, 26:37, 35:100
Minnesota State Grange, 30:254
Minnesota State Guard, 23:268, 270,
25:312. See also Minnesota Home
Guard, Minnesota National Guard
Minnesota State Homeopathic Institute, 15:61, 113, 22:334, 434
Minnesota State Horticultural Society, 16:235, 19:48, 96, 31:162
Minnesota state hospitals, conditions, 12:427
Minnesota State Medical Association,
history, 11:56-58, 14:288n, 23:
190, 289, 387, 24:347, 33:268,

294, 312, 35:220, 221; organized,
16:29, 21:209, 23:190, 30:405, 36:
282; legislative activity, 20:237,
21:359; publication, 21:209, 23:95
Minnesota State News (Minneapolis),
subscription lists, 11:444, 16:72;
in Civil War camps, 25:253
Minnesota State Office Building, described, 20:207
Minnesota State Pharmaceutical Association, 14:432
Minnesota State Planning Board, 16:
114, 233, 452
Minnesota State Poultry Association,
22:265
Minnesota State Prison, 27:127, 35:
107, 122; Stillwater era, 11:85,
17:280, 285, 29:205, 37:137-151;
history, 11:339, 23:273; library,
11:458; publication, 17:386, 481,
18:462, 29:321; evaluated, 19:112;
contract labor, 22:387, 38:187;
first physician, 24:181; Chautauqua Circle, 29:321-333, 31:57
Minnesota State Public School, Owatonna, history, 18:119
Minnesota State Reform School, St.
Paul, 40:48
Minnesota State Reformatory for Men,
St. Cloud, 12:456, 19:112, 35:194
Minnesota State Sabbath School Association, 18:118, 352
Minnesota State Wool Growers Association, 22:263, 266, 26:114
Minnesota Statehood Centennial Commission, 34:265, 35:48, 339, 340,
365, 383, 384; publications, 36:
31, 62, 66, 71, 99, 194; activities, 36:36, 106, 108, 139, 152,
196, 230, 240, 37:67, 203, 38:87
Minnesota State-wide Archaeological
and Historical Research Survey,
22:332, 436
Minnesota Stock Breeders' Associ-
ation, 22:261, 265, 26:124
Minnesota Stoneware Co., see Red Wing
Potteries
Minnesota Supreme Court, 18:122, 27:
84; decisions, 16:468, 19:432, 23:
180, 24:100, 27:120, 35:7-10; history, 19:441; territorial, 30:266,
267, 39:141-152
Minnesota Surveyor General of Logs
and Lumber, 26:126
Minnesota Tax Survey, 14:207
Minnesota Taxpayers Association, 23:
266
Minnesota Teacher's Retirement Fund
Act, 14:420
Minnesota Territorial Agricultural
Society, 22:254, 255, 266, 26:110
Minnesota Territorial Centennial,
plans, 27:27, 45, 144, 349, 28:52,
196-198, 388-390, 29:36-45, 183-
185, 279-281, 368-370, 30:38, 76,
84-88; publications, 27:128, 330,
28:299, 388, 29:187, 254, 368, 30:
85, 162, 173, 175, 328, 31:58;
staff, 28:300, 29:38, 95, 30:172,
329, 410; art committee, 28:302,
389, 29:40, 30:43; history, 28:
329; agricultural committee, 28:
390, 29:39; local celebrations,
29:41, 90, 96, 367, 30:86, 164-
168, 276-279, 388-402; appropriation, 29:54; pageants, 29:95,
184, 279, 369, 30:87, 165, 281,

282, 285, 288, 398, 400, 402, 404,
407-409; in schools, 30:86, 87;
significance, 30:161, 264, 267;
Establishment Day, 30:170-172; exhibits, 30:172, 176, 282-284;
events, 30:176-178, 280-286, 368,
403-409
Minnesota Territorial Fair, 40:71
Minnesota Territorial Pioneers Association, 26:156, 259, 30:268, 35:
190
Minnesota Territorial Pioneers' Museum, state fair grounds, 39:316
Minnesota Territorial Temperance Society, 19:214
Minnesota Territory, organized, 11:
339, 14:127-134, 161, 15:467, 16:
27, 17:393, 18:373, 20:366, 22:5,
24:60, 26:368, 28:208, 310, 329,
30:195, 33:120, 35:352, 36:261;
settled, 11:387, 28:277, 30:24,
115-117; mail service, 11:399-401,
26:174, 30:174, 31:176, 40:78-89;
roads, 11:408-410, 31:176, 36:210,
278, 40:233-247; population, 12:
191, 14:134, 21:225, 22:229, 236,
34:139n, 36:250; advertised, 12:
255, 13:26, 17:411; newspapers,
13:45, 14:396, 24:309, 27:2-20,
28:342n; politics, 13:433, 35:105-
109, 114-116, 36:1-12, 259-271,
39:37-48; pioneer life, 14:134-
142; land speculation, 14:243;
bibliography of documents, 17:194,
18:44; boundaries, 19:424, 28:284,
32:65, 36:3; governors, 22:414,
25:198, 28:310, 30:104-108, 266;
maps, 24:252, 26:387, 30:173, 174;
described, 28:280, 309-328, 29:
195-222, 349, 30:50-52, 33:114,
350; history, 28:329-338, 388, 30:
162; seal, 29:185, 30:267, 33:126-
128, 38:37; officials, 30:108, 31:
172; background, 30:185-201; supreme court, 30:266, 267, 39:141-
152; legislature, 30:293, 40:331;
congressional delegate, 31:172-
178; government buildings, 31:177;
social life, 39:51. See also
Minnesota Territorial Centennial
Minnesota Thalbote (Carver), politics, 28:24
Minnesota Thresher Co., prison labor
contractors, 37:144, 145, 151
Minnesota Tourist Bureau, 18:333;
guide, 26:63
Minnesota Town Association, 15:223
Minnesota Transfer Railway Co., activities, 34:130, 172, 35:49
Minnesota Trunk Highway, bonds, 12:85
Minnesota Union (St. Cloud), established, 17:364
Minnesota Union Advocate (St. Paul),
34:264, 38:305
Minnesota University, see University
of Minnesota
Minnesota Valley, settled, 11:131,
144, 162, 15:129, 21:226, 22:172,
447, 30:29, 38:94, 118, 39:85-92;
described, 11:161-184, 30:24, 33:
316; map of townsites, 11:167;
politics, 11:206; roads, 11:392,
14:153, 21:229, 231; stage line,
11:402, 404; ethnic groups, 12:
264, 274, 28:22, 266, 31:23, 27,
39:299; pioneer life, 15:345, 16:
340, 24:79; travel, 15:478, 16:

192, 19:447; wildlife, 16:42, 263, 30:225; railroads, 17:267, 18:220, 21:239, 36:179; business conditions, 24:272; archaeology, 26:387, 27:261, 28:76; source material, 28:305; plant life, 35:241; natural resources, 36:69; pictured, 36:253, 37:60; log buildings, 37:71; historical tour, 37:88; Sioux reservation, 37:271, 272, 274, 38:93, 119; in Sioux Outbreak, 38:242, 274-286

Minnesota Valley Canning Co., 33:353

Minnesota Valley Historical Society, 20:354; marking project, 11:31, 37:59, 60, 40:232

Minnesota Valley Pageant Association, 20:449

Minnesota Valley Railroad, 26:68, 35:338; built, 12:59n, 60n, 22:112, 37:160; first locomotive, 38:295. See also St. Paul and Sioux City Railroad

Minnesota Veterans Home, Minneapolis, 38:82

Minnesota Volksblatt (St. Paul), 32:239

Minnesota War History Committee, program, 23:149-153, 291-293, 392-394, 24:244, 25:401; local units, 23:390-392, 24:81-83, 185, 268; director, 24:31, 37; accessions, 24:83-85, 183, 268, 376, 25:206, 311, 403, 26:86

Minnesota War Records Commission, 15:69, 23:18; publication, 11:195-198, 30:321; archives, 19:56, 20:38, 23:18, 151

Minnesota Western Railroad, 15:41

Minnesota Wheat Growers' Association, 28:38

Minnesota Woman Suffrage Association, 13:101, 15:61, 113, 18:47, 97, 39:10

Minnesota Women's Relief Corps, pageant, 12:334

Minnesota Writers' Project, 21:308, 27:330

Minnesotian (St. Paul), handbill, 14:173; editorials, 14:178, 40:387; politics, 39:46, 49

Minnetonka, territorial postmark, 15:487; history, 36:106

"Minnetonka," locomotive, 20:374

Minnetonka Beach, history, 27:176, 34:173, 351, 36:71; historical meeting, 28:391; hotel, 33:63, 34:173, 36:71, 327

Minnetonka Fruit Growers' Association, 18:443

Minnetonka Hotel, Wayzata, 27:295n

Minnetonka Mills, Minnetonka, history, 27:176; furniture factory, 36:327

Minnetonka Township, Hennepin County, settled, 36:36

Minnetonka Yacht Club, 19:365

Minnetrista, settled, 36:36; government, 39:299

Minnewashta Lake, Carver County, name, 22:173

Minnewawa, Stearns County, ghost town, 22:447

Minnie Township, Beltrami County, history, 15:132

"Minnie Will," towboat, 18:177

Minogue, Adelaide E., work reviewed, 25:282

Minot, N.D., electric service, 35:381

"Minute Men," frontier defenders, 38:285

Mire River, Man., trading post, 11:365

Mirer, Alexander S., postmaster, 40:82

Miro, Estevan, author, 11:451

Mirsky, Jeannette, reviews by, 32:111, 33:301-303; works reviewed, 28:57, 33:266; author, 28:174, 32:128

Miska, Mrs. Josephine, speaker, 23:398

Missabe Mountain Township, St. Louis County, mine, 13:428

Mission Covenant church, among Swedes, 13:305

Mission Creek, Crow Wing County, name, 14:58

Mission Friends, among Swedish immigrants, 13:305; Roseau Valley, 24:323

Mission Lakes, Crow Wing County, name, 14:58

Mission Township, Crow Wing County, name, 14:58

Missionary Ridge, Tenn., battle, 38:258, 269, 271-273; depicted, 38:259

Missions and missionaries, Red River Valley, 11:42, 18:44, 22:36, 23:366, 24:41, 94; Minnesota, 11:94, 12:207, 15:247, 16:454, 17:210, 18:94, 22:353, 28:210, 277, 32:216; Dakotas, 11:212, 19:379-381, 20:193; to Sioux, 11:317, 12:190, 330, 13:339, 14:330, 359, 15:225, 16:133-151, 335, 345, 483, 20:123, 21:15-32, 158-175, 272-283, 425, 22:30, 23:272, 24:72, 27:259, 28:133, 29:173, 30:156, 32:71; to Chippewa, 13:187, 14:330, 15:20, 488, 16:97, 375, 21:414, 26:275, 388, 28:62, 181, 191, 29:101, 168; functions, 16:28, 335, 20:27, 21:397; schools, 16:214, 17:84, 25:13; finances, 16:217; publications, 17:342; bells, 18:375, 20:204; Slovenian, 22:200; Northwest, 23:366, 24:41-43; Wisconsin, 24:178, 32:186; to Winnebago, 29:173; among lumberjacks, 31:65-78; camp meetings, 31:79-92. See also individual denominations, mission stations, and missionaries

Missisauga Indians, in fur trade, 40:208

Mississippi, voting laws, 12:9; territorial papers, 19:217

Mississippi and Rum River Boom Co., 16:340, 24:139; history, 24:134-137

Mississippi Boom Co., 24:135, 26:126

Mississippi Bote (Winona), 16:338

Mississippi Headwaters Museum, Itasca State Park, exhibits, 28:394

Mississippi pattern, defined, 25:154; pottery, 25:156, 330; village sites, 26:387

Mississippi River, steamboating, 11:84, 104, 126, 130, 210, 212, 323, 340, 12:45-47, 61-63, 77, 92, 159-161, 164, 165, 319, 13:321, 330, 435, 14:100, 150, 379, 15:121,

134, 307, 346, 409-414, 467, 475, 481, 16:37, 79, 116, 335, 345, 454, 478, 17:150-158, 335, 369-374, 413, 18:433, 452, 19:74, 75, 355, 458, 20:194, 304, 377-396, 21:99, 403, 22:94, 108, 448, 23:183, 305, 24:128, 25:72, 393, 27:63, 69, 28:92, 342, 29:126, 213, 30:4, 199, 205, 409, 31:80, 83, 85, 88, 149-153, 209, 212n, 32:12n, 38, 98, 33:7-19, 90, 115-119, 125, 194, 198, 34:24-26, 50, 239, 35:44, 335, 355, 356, 36:15, 46, 250-258, 37:154, 185, 196, 265 (cover), 283-297, 38:74, 384, 39:66, 68, 90, 316, 40:62, 184, 263, 359, 411; depicted, 11:85, 12:47, 63, 13:60, 14:228, 337, 440, 16:36, 44, 276, 277, 17:147, 369-374, 18:154, 19:400, 21:92, 22:159, 24:331, 25:166, 27:63, 283-285, 28:70, 136, 30:62, 31:55, 149, 33:1 (cover), 90, 34:32, 136, 35:334, 36:20, 22, 69, 73, 90, 93, 139, 191, 237, 241 (cover), 250, 254, 37:1 (cover), 4, 38:357, 40:72; posts, 11:371-373, 375, 381, 382, 384, 13:98, 14:362, 18:195, 24:230; houseboat journey, 11:453; maps, 12:82, 25:87, 33:186, 35:22-29, 39:212; traffic on, 12:447, 16:78-80, 21:226, 227, 22:202, 26:272, 27:8, 28:313, 31:246; history, 13:212, 24:53, 25:174, 31:250, 38:384; Radisson visit, 13:247, 249-252, 264, 15:160, 171, 16:453; name, 13:254, 30:331; geology, 13:404, 406, 15:145, 26:224, 225; source, 13:405, 16:118, 234, 349, 18:180, 184, 21:415, 22:439, 23:233n, 328, 333n, 24:230, 371, 372, 25:77, 27:241, 350, 29:83, 30:141, 258, 31:96, 32:234, 33:345, 34:264, 36:184, 235, 37:40, 62; panoramas, 14:340, 15:111, 17:115, 131-143, 148, 149, 332, 427, 456, 20:200, 380, 23:349-354, 24:63, 178, 26:260, 28:70, 33:284-290, 316, 35:279, 36:23, 101, 190, 233, 39:286; explored, 14:370, 20:439, 21:201, 403, 22:327, 23:58, 30:57, 31:188, 202, 33:89, 34:285n, 35:44; drainage areas, 15:234; reached by railroad, 15:405, 23:64, 25:103, 26:272, 29:29; lumber industry, 15:484, 23:198, 24:127-131, 134-137, 26:132, 133, 27:190-192, 195-202, 29:138, 140, 146, 148, 33:125, 34:35, 39:72; ports, 16:26, 17:273, 20:126, 22:226, 416, 26:272, 28:16n; tours, 16:33, 272, 20:131, 377-396, 22:13-34, 56-59, 24:369, 25:104-116, 28:272, 34:133, 35:180, 181; channel, 16:79, 19:182-189, 355, 27:63, 35:337, 37:283-285; connecting roads, 16:283, 293; discovered, 16:453, 18:388, 24:252, 26:75, 27:62; lower rapids, 17:150, 430; upper rapids, 17:151n; floods, 17:230, 343, 34:306; canoe trips, 17:288-301, 421-436, 23:328, 333-345, 32:81, 83, 90, 95-97, 34:48; islands, 17:294, 28:190; boundary, 18:232, 20:8, 24:234; locks and dams, 18:452, 19:103, 182, 24:93, 130, 27:63, 28:293, 37:275, 286,

288, 290-295, 321, 322; fishing,
19:142, 34:260; tributaries, 23:
236, 343, 345n, 24:232; folk songs
and folklore, 23:382, 27:182, 35:
39; in Civil War, 25:130, 131,
144, 40:281, 306; winter traffic,
25:299, 28:313, 38:157; naviga-
tional aids, 34:351; importance to
Twin Cities, 37:309-323; pollution, 40:133; recreational aspect,
40:263, 386. See also Barges,
Bridges, Ferries, Keelboats, Rafting
Mississippi River Improvement and
Manufacturing Co., history, 37:
311-323
Mississippi River Logging Co., 39:211;
history, 27:190-202; activities,
29:266, 30:71, 32:252, 37:185; organized, 32:125, 188
Mississippi River Lumber and Boom
Co., log marks, 26:136
Mississippi River Slackwater Navigation Co., 37:318
Mississippi Transportation Co., 33:
16-18
Mississippi Valley, earthquakes, 12:
198; French in, 12:325, 23:84,
161, 39:337, 40:259; history, 13:
417, 16:188, 32:248; maps, 14:338,
18:446, 19:214, 24:236, 27:350,
35:292; archaeology, 15:148, 16:
152, 25:154; population, 16:109;
agriculture, 16:474, 28:39; depicted, 17:144-146, 294, 21:94,
25:110-113, 30:158, 31:250, 32:12-
14, 125, 202-213, 33:112-125, 316,
35:248, 36:23, 40:76, 77; climate,
17:248, 255n; settled, 19:80, 31:
23, 33:214, 35:46; fur trade, 19:
95, 21:423, 32:226-238; roads, 21:
231; in fiction, 23:124; explored,
25:296, 26:379, 28:200, 30:62, 37:
128; geography, 26:73; wildlife,
27:63, 36:278; natural resources,
27:253; railroads, 30:380; historical significance, 30:387; urbanization, 31:119; historic
sites, 35:151
Mississippi Valley Historical Association, 14:434, 16:60, 25:168;
meetings, 12:315, 13:105, 326-328,
14:328, 339, 15:66, 118, 119, 227,
16:212, 21:311, 22:327, 428, 23:
83, 24:162, 242, 254, 25:178, 294,
26:37, 28:370, 29:257, 30:180,
317, 35:383, 36:36, 84n; committees, 20:294, 26:161; publications, 24:41-43, 30:327. See also
Alvord Memorial Commission
Mississippi Valley Historical Review,
index, 13:329; topical guide, 16:
220
Mississippi Valley Lumberman, anniversary, 22:437
Mississippi Valley Lumbermen's Association, 12:193
Mississippi Valley Press, organized,
21:98
Mississippi Valley Sanitary Fair, 21:
193
Missouri, politics, 12:330, 15:331,
23:381, 26:209, 40:308; population, 13:435; place names, 16:227;
boundary, 16:478; dairying, 17:
101; climate, 18:155; agriculture,
18:196; history, 19:10, 28:79;

pioneer merchants, 20:335; frontier life, 21:402; in World War
II, 25:311, 26:279; traffic laws,
26:26; business records, 26:384;
sawmills, 27:190, 34:35; in Civil
War, 34:304, 40:291; atlas, 40:
122; gazetteer, 40:147; newspa-
pers, 40:257
Missouri Compromise, 11:60, 23:261,
24:312, 314
Missouri Expedition, reaches Fort
Snelling, 23:339
Missouri Farmers' Association, 28:44
Missouri Fur Co., 39:261; records,
15:463, 29:175; post, 40:194
Missouri Gazette (St. Louis), file
acquired, 13:199
Missouri Historical Review, index,
16:220
Missouri Historical Society, St.
Louis, 29:350, 40:152
Missouri Pacific Railroad, 30:237
Missouri River, flood, 11:68; steamboating, 15:121, 16:335, 19:391n,
25:72, 32:244, 33:131, 34:265, 35:
44, 38:236, 40:409; traffic, 16:
102, 18:390, 26:165; panoramas,
17:136, 36:190; fur trade, 21:
136n, 29:260, 34:325-329, 39:255,
261, 40:152, 155, 178, 179, 184,
186, 192-195, 220, 314, 410; depicted, 24:178, 40:192, 193; in
Montana, 28:288; history, 33:301-
303; voyageur songs, 34:126; dam,
39:213 (cover); map, 40:194
Missouri Territory, history, 30:57-
59, 31:48
Missouri Valley, settled, 15:200, 19:
206; explored, 23:170, 26:379; archaeology, 25:297, 27:259; depicted, 27:254; plant life, 35:241
Mistaken Lake, Cook County, forest
fire, 36:137
Mitau, G. Theodore, "The Democratic-
Farmer-Labor Party Schism," 34:
187-194; reviews by, 34:258, 35:
332, 39:258; work reviewed, 37:
131; author, 34:316, 36:70; receives award, 35:51; compiler, 37:
135; speaker, 37:136; editor, 39:
210
Mitchell, Alexander, railroad builder, 39:31
Mitchell, Alexander M., MHS founder,
20:367, 368; territorial marshal,
30:109, 35:357n, 36:266, 39:39,
44, 148; politician, 36:268-270,
39:42, 43, 45
Mitchell, Alma C., editor, 36:326
Mitchell, Ben, engineer, 34:280
Mitchell, Broadus, author, 16:349
Mitchell, C. C., speaker, 37:135
Mitchell, Elaine A., "International
Buying Trip," 36:37-53; author,
34:352, 38:199
Mitchell, Henry, potter, 33:232
Mitchell, Henry Z., I, letters, 12:
84; postmaster, 19:96
Mitchell, Henry Z., II, 16:98; speak-
er, 18:280; editorial, 28:92-94
Mitchell, J., 35:269
Mitchell, J. H., author, 16:225
Mitchell, Jennie, 35:268
Mitchell, John, map, 28:68
Mitchell, Margaret, novelist, 21:7
Mitchell, Mary, 35:268

Mitchell, Mary A., work reviewed, 22:
186
Mitchell, Nelson, 40:75
Mitchell, Peter, prospector, 19:309,
34:216, 273, 275, 36:192, 37:42,
39:163
Mitchell, R. C., pioneer journalist,
18:473, 25:307, 27:72
Mitchell, Dr. Ross, author, 16:480,
20:88, 21:204, 30:259
Mitchell, S. Augustus, geographer,
24:232
Mitchell, Samuel, mining interests,
34:275
Mitchell, Stewart, author, 19:456
Mitchell, Mrs. W. F., author, 37:85
Mitchell, William, 11:146; judge, 15:
358
Mitchell, William B., 35:269; pioneer
journalist, 11:223, 14:395, 17:
365, 28:197; papers, 12:84, 456,
16:98, 19:96; author, 40:84
Mitchell, William D., portrait, 28:
199, 29:55
Mitchell, Iowa, mail service, 11:400;
stage lines, 11:402
Mitchell Building, St. Cloud, 33:292
Mitchell County, Iowa, Norwegian settlement, 12:258
Mitchell "Moose" automobile, 38:208-
211
Mitchill, Samuel L., scientist, 23:
342
Mitman, Carl W., author, 11:328, 12:
201, 14:349, 15:127
Mitropoulos, Dimitri, orchestra conductor, 33:222
Mittelbiberach, Germany, castle, 40:
269, 270
Mittelholtz, Erwin F., review by, 40:
41; speaker, 35:50; author, 35:380
Mix, Col. ---, railroad official, 25:
112
Mix, Catherine (Cassie), 12:120n;
pictured, 12:120
Mix, Charles E., clerk and Indian
commissioner, 12:120n, 38:362, 39:
230, 231
Mix, Maj. John, 25:33
Mix, Monnie, pictured, 12:120
Mixed-bloods, White Earth, 11:206,
15:196, 21:315; Red River Settlements, 11:308, 13:176, 428, 15:
303, 357, 477, 21:84, 22:148, 156,
280, 24:41, 26:76, 27:285, 28:61,
36:46n, 241, 38:69, 71; scrip, 11:
462, 14:435, 15:296; depicted, 13:
410, 413, 21:89, 28:314, 32:61,
94, 33:199, 200, 227, 36:248, 310,
311, 313, 40:161; Pembina, 15:289,
19:411, 29:235; characterized, 15:
336, 36:48; in fur trade, 15:422,
423, 18:384, 28:282, 38:327, 40:
160, 162-164, 167, 183; as guides,
15:478, 23:247, 32:87, 97n, 38:3,
7, 40:265 (cover); land claims,
17:335; schools, 21:30n, 22:287;
beadwork, 22:148, 23:288; women,
22:152; family life, 24:282, 34:
142; Canada, 25:200, 28:60-62, 32:
60, 33:89; annuities, 38:7; in
Sioux Outbreak, 38:98, 106, 131,
139, 143, 280; songs, 38:200; Fort
Snelling, 38:357; Grand Portage,
39:303, 305, 307, 308, 310. See
also Bonga family, Riel rebellions, Voyageurs

Mizener, Arthur, work reviewed, 32:
115–117; author, 28:279
Mizpah, history, 23:107; newspaper,
29:356
Mladineo, Ivan, author, 19:219, 508
Moberg, J. E., 18:471
Moberg, Vilhelm, 30:181; works re-
viewed, 32:250, 34:163, 38:38; au-
thor, 30:65, 39:341
Mobile (Alabama) Daily News, Union
paper, 22:422
Moccasin Democrats, in Minnesota Ter-
ritory, 14:246; decline, 14:262.
See also Democratic party
Mock, James R., author, 21:200
Modern Dance Group, "Minnesota Saga,"
20:347, 21:58–62
Modern Life Insurance Co. of Minneso-
ta, St. Paul, publications, 13:290
Modern Medicine Foundation, grant,
39:264
Modern Samaritans, Walker, 17:468
Modern Woodmen, Bemidji, 23:32
Modjeska, Helena, actress, 28:117,
118
Modley, Rudolf, work reviewed, 19:90
Moe, Mrs. Lester, letter, 30:183
Moe, Wesley S., editor, 18:226, 21:
221; author, 27:69
Moehlman, Arthur H., editor, 13:334
Moeller, Hubert L., author, 18:218
Moen, Esten, author, 14:358, 25:212,
34:359
Moen, Henry, 40:58
Moen, John, blacksmith, 34:359
Moen family, 19:366
Moepels and Co., emigrant agents, 20:
251
Moes, Josephine, see Alfred, Mother
Moffat, Judge John S., house, 38:348
Moffet, George H., 40:16
Moffet, Lot, 14:292; house, 27:177
Moffet, Col. William P., author, 28:
80
Moffet's Hotel, St. Paul, 16:377
Moffitt, James W., author, 25:190
Mohawk Indians, 13:400; capture
Radisson, 15:163; relations with
English, 16:404
Mohawk Valley, trade route, 40:184
Mohawk Valley plow, advertisement,
24:296
Mohm, Rev. James, speaker, 19:361
Mohn, Thorbjørn N., author, 30:391;
college president, 31:51
Mohr, Carolyn C., work reviewed, 33:
42
Mohr and Danber, Mankato, plow manu-
facturers, 24:297
Moilanen, Henry, 22:392n
Moir, Ann, 21:110
Moiseiwitsch, Benno, pianist, 39:59
Moland Township, Clay County, Nor-
wegian settlement, 12:278
Molander, O. Morris, author, 18:72
Molander, S. B., author, 18:340, 19:
365
Molasses, 17:238, 20:80
Molbach, C. A., emigrant agent, 20:
256
Moley, Raymond, speaker, 16:498
Moline, Ill., pictured, 17:423; plow
factory, 23:323; river port, 26:
381; sawmill, 27:190
Moline plow, 23:323; use in Minneso-
ta, 24:296
Moll, Judge Henry, 12:103, 15:80, 16:

491; recollections, 12:104; speak-
er, 13:122; actor, 33:318
Moll, Herman, map maker, 25:41
Möllhausen, Heinrich B., artist, 29:
350
"Mollie Mohler," steamboat, 12:210
Moltke, Erik, author, 33:314, 354
Moltke Township, Sibley County, German settlement, 36:197, 199
Mommsen, Theodor, historian, 19:6
Monaghan, Jay, reviews by, 22:408,
28:63; works reviewed, 29:61, 31:
47, 34:304; author, 22:418, 23:
281, 25:395, 28:96; editor, 28:
279, 39:129
Monarski, Rev. Paul J., author, 23:
286
Monday Club, Faribault, history, 20:
363
Monday Literary Club, St. Paul, rec-
ords, 27:249
Monday Study Club, Stewartville, 21:
454
Money Creek, Houston County, Norwe-
gian settlement, 12:268; pioneer
life, 22:223
Monfort, Charles, hotelkeeper, 33:1,
6
Monfort, George, pioneer, 33:1
Monger, Frieda J., author, 34:44
Mongrain, Mrs. Nelson W. (Claribel
O.), 20:211, 29:180, 275
Monière, Alexis le Moine, trader, 12:
82, 18:276
"Monitor," ironclad, 25:118, 129, 241
Monitor Gold Mining and Trading Co.,
32:60; history, 29:302–315, 39:241
Monitor Plow Works, Minneapolis, 24:
297
Monk, George H., farmer, 26:106
Monk, James, 15:96
Monker, Claus C., speaker, 12:283
Monnier, Mrs. ———, 14:283
"Monona," steamboat, 22:18
Monongahela River, Pa., navigation,
19:184, 185
Monongalia, territorial county, Nor-
wegian settlements, 12:265, 276;
historic sites, 13:450; county
seat, 21:341. See also Kandiyohi
County
Monroe, Cecil O., "The Rise of Base-
ball," 19:162–181; author, 19:207,
338
Monroe, James, secretary of state, 12:
82, 92; President, 22:67, 35:23,
40:261
Monroe, Capt. James, Jr., 11:168,
177, 183, 29:319n
Monroe, John A., author, 30:149
Monroe, Mrs. W. G., author, 20:218
Monson, Anna L., 17:123; author, 16:
362
Monson, M. O., cabin, 21:450
Monson, Reub, author, 34:131
Monson Lake, Swift County, in Sioux
Outbreak, 15:488, 16:365, 38:154
Monson Lake Memorial Association,
historic tour, 13:450
Monson Lake Memorial Park, 23:291,
30:281, 37:60
Monsoni Indians, warfare, 24:318
Montagnais-Naskapi Indians, 40:158;
conjuring, 24:54
Montague, Judge James E., 25:54, 26:
45, 27:173, 29:97; speaker, 26:91
Montague, W. K., speaker, 28:385

Montana, livestock industry, 12:177;
press, 13:336; immigration, 13:
436, 33:31; medical association,
17:220; Norwegian settlement, 19:
200; highway markers, 20:203; mining, 20:432, 23:184, 31:253, 34:
328, 40:94, 254; 50th anniversary,
21:428; frontier era, 24:158, 26:
80; history, 28:288, 33:182, 35:
34, 36:279; fur trade, 29:58–61;
in art, 35:295; conservation, 40:
38; aeronautics, 40:146
Montana Historic Landmark Society,
25:385
Montana Society of Equity, 27:165
Montana Territory, gold rush, 38:53–
62, 71, 216, 219, 386, 39:261
Montana Wheat Growers Association,
38:181
Montauban, see St. Paul, Pierre
Montcalm, Marquis de, 18:383
Montenegrins, Mesabi Range, 22:180,
27:204, 210–213, 40:341, 347; remigration, 27:214; in lumber industry, 36:162. See also Yugoslavs
Monterey, Martin County, history, 34:
315
Monteur, George, settler, 35:31
Montevideo, flood, 11:68, 69, 17:230;
settled, 16:127; historical meeting, 16:303; county seat fight,
17:235; historical exhibit, 17:
481; driving club, 18:466; newspapers, 18:466; railroad union, 21:
393; seminary, 22:444; Norwegian
settlement, 24:79; anniversary,
26:392; museums, 27:263, 359; log
cabins, 27:265; library, 29:357;
farmers' institute, 33:224; power
company, 35:381
Montevideo American, anniversary, 22:
445; politics, 38:305
Montevideo Choral Club, 16:303
Montevideo High School, yearbook, 12:
100
Montevideo Junior Association of Com-
merce, 17:481
Montezuma, St. Louis County, ghost
town, 15:370, 16:298, 34:177
Montezuma, Winona County, see Winona
Montfort, Delos A., 40:16
Montgomery, Misses ———, 25:251, 256
Montgomery, Edmund T., speaker, 27:75
Montgomery, Florence M., author, 35:
150
Montgomery, Dr. Frank H., author, 36:
282
Montgomery, H. C., compiler, 25:83
Montgomery, James, 19:387
Montgomery, Col. Milton, in Sioux
Outbreak, 38:125, 279
Montgomery, Morton L., author, 25:88
Montgomery, Capt. Norris, 25:151
Montgomery, Richard G., author, 16:
223
Montgomery, Mrs. Sarah P., reminis-
cences, 19:450, 21:213
Montgomery, Thomas, Civil War let-
ters, 23:170
Montgomery family, genealogy, 25:182
Montgomery, threshing party, 25:187
Montgomery Pioneer Historical Associ-
ation, 16:241, 25:403, 26:90, 27:
75; organized, 11:14; museum, 11:
16

Montgomery Ward and Co., St. Paul
store, 37:43
Monticello, history, 13:115, 16:257,
28:385, 30:398; volunteer guards,
16:175; G.A.R. post, 16:431; sawmill, 17:368; Methodist church,
17:479; Mormon mission, 36:291;
described, 37:159; in Sioux Outbreak, 38:275
Monticello Academy, established, 14:
147
Monticello Times, established, 14:
397, 404; history, 28:385
Montman, Henry, 21:430
Montreal, Que., fur trade, 11:231,
232, 259, 12:357, 13:259, 15:157,
19:109, 271, 291, 28:1, 5n, 6,
142, 40:157, 163, 164, 168, 170,
174, 175, 178, 180, 181, 188, 200,
358; settled, 18:386, 29:78;
court, 21:120-148
Montreal Lacrosse Club, 35:151
Montreal-Michilimackinac Co., 19:301,
40:170, 181
Montreal Ocean Steamship Co., Liverpool, Eng., emigrant agents, 20:
249, 258
Montreal River, Wis., Mich., 23:242
Montreal River Lumber Co., Eau
Claire, Wis., 12:319
Montreuil, ---, mixed-blood, 36:48,
49
Montrose, Iowa, river town, 17:431n
Monuments and markers, 14:349, 20:97,
25:203, explorers, 11:4, 12:96,
443, 13:83-85, 110, 15:472, 476,
19:461, 26:388; Minnesota communities, 11:111, 222, 225, 335, 336,
12:341, 453, 13:345, 449, 14:357,
457, 15:138, 17:482, 20:344, 464,
21:445, 22:108, 26:43, 398, 27:
363, 30:400; military, 11:119,
330, 333, 12:438, 14:97, 15:359,
35:245; highway project, 11:202,
313, 12:40, 13:63, 377-384, 14:68,
15:79, 18:107, 459, 21:433, 33:
314; Sioux Outbreak, 11:456, 12:
342, 448, 20:449, 23:291, 35:156;
Indians, 12:98, 13:442, 20:97, 21:
339, 22:440; Indian treaties, 12:
203, 14:350, 15:116, 282, 23:291;
missions and missionaries, 12:332,
15:242, 362, 21:415, 22:346; iron
ranges, 12:333, 15:481, 482, 16:
371; fur trade, 12:437, 13:339,
16:498, 19:109, 361, 21:438; immigration, 12:450, 14:428, 19:106,
30:401; agriculture, 13:340, 19:
32, 161, 20:86, 21:110, 218; roads
and trails, 14:350, 453, 16:298,
485, 17:476, 21:433, 35:
382; prehistoric, 14:350, 27:267;
to medicine, 14:446, 15:234, 20:
446; Twin Cities area, 23:296, 26:
387; selection policy, 26:376; See
also Historic sites
Mooar brothers, buffalo hunters, 37:
79
Mood, Fulmer, 17:223, 19:432; "The
Radisson Problem," 16:391-413; "An
Unfamiliar Essay by Frederick J.
Turner," 18:381-398; review by,
24:149-151; work reviewed, 24:336;
author, 18:440, 21:200, 24:164,
255, 360, 26:265, 274, 29:258, 31:
251

Moody, Dwight L., speaker, 18:118,
40:12
Moody, Mrs. L. H., 20:352
Moody, Lowell H., speaker, 27:266,
361, 28:386
Moody, V. Alton, author, 22:326
Mooers, Calvin, in Sioux Outbreak,
35:337
Mooers, Edmund, genealogy, 35:337
Mooers, Hazen, 21:99, 458, 27:259;
government farmer, 11:184, 21:175;
trader, 11:377-379, 381, 19:108,
468, 20:351, 21:32, 438, 23:383,
27:67, 35:335; family, 14:438, 35:
337; county commissioner, 24:160;
papers, 30:320
Mooers, Josiah P., genealogy, 35:337
Mooers family, genealogy, 35:337
Mooers Prairie, Wright County, name,
35:337
Moon automobile, 38:207
Moonan, John, legislator, 33:157
Moore, ---, lumberman, 17:278
Moore, Judge Alfred S., in Alaska,
32:174, 191, 192
Moore, Allen L., author, 13:343, 14:
453
Moore, Mrs. Altah, 27:345
Moore, Augustus O., artist, 11:43;
letter, 20:307
Moore, Mrs. Augustus O., 20:308
Moore, Cecil, 21:70
Moore, Charles W., author, 11:338,
455, 467
Moore, Curtis B., 25:143
Moore, E. R., 21:337
Moore, Geoffrey, author, 38:387
Moore, Mrs. George F., author, 27:362
Moore, George W., editor, 14:179n,
39:46
Moore, Mrs. George W., author, 22:223
Moore, Hannah, 20:141n
Moore, Henry R., account books, 23:76
Moore, Dr. James E., 24:347; career,
15:358
Moore, Jennie D., 18:211
Moore, John Basset, 25:68
Moore, John W., 35:16
Moore, Joshua, 20:141
Moore, Mrs. Julia, pioneer, 12:212
Moore, Nathaniel F., work reviewed,
28:272
Moore, Nina, see Tiffany, Mrs.
Francis
Moore, R. A., agronomist, 33:224
Moore, Royal S., author, 35:384
Moore, Vivian L., author, 12:440
Moore Lake, Anoka County, wildlife,
30:228
Moore School, Bismarck, N.D., 15:125
Moorehead, S. P., author, 31:249
Moorhead, William G., investor, 37:92
Moorhead, settled, 11:220, 15:134;
fire department, 12:101; ethnic
groups, 12:278, 16:344; anniversary, 12:336; historical meeting,
13:283-286; newspapers, 15:201,
21:448; log cabin, 15:366; telegraph line, 16:100; Episcopal mission, 20:431; railroads, 21:239,
253, 29:13, 30:70, 31:122, 37:93;
river port, 21:254, 267, 270, 29:
73; printers' union, 21:393;
schools, 23:95, 25:68, 26:166;
post office, 28:82; wheat raising,
29:14; commerce, 30:91; wildlife,
30:223; history, 34:357, 35:295

Moorhead Daily News, history, 15:134
Moorhead Rod and Gun Club, 28:190,
30:75
Moorhead State Teachers College, 25:
312, 34:93; history, 12:337, 15:
134, 18:329, 19:333, 25:68; mu-
seum, 17:231, 23:193, 25:258
Moorhead Transportation Co., 21:259
Moos, Malcolm, work reviewed, 35:285;
author, 37:185, 186
Moose, Clearwater County, ghost town,
16:493; baseball team, 23:26
Moose, Wyo., museum, 40:197
Moose, depicted, 12:350, 40:385; Minnesota, 18:451, 21:440, 30:125,
128, 35:48; in fur trade, 23:330,
40:210; hunted, 28:179, 37:238.
See also Wildlife
Moose Dung, Chippewa leader, 15:84;
receives land, 15:294
Moose Fort, Ont., fur trade, 34:254
Moose Lake, Carlton County, monument,
11:111; trading post, 11:358;
growth, 15:133, 35:382; fire, 15:
225, 16:116, 24:346, 30:74, 33:46,
92, 37:223; road, 16:292; schools,
17:235; Finnish settlement, 22:
392n, 25:324; located, 37:107n;
veterans' colony, 39:243, 244,
246-249
Moose Lake, Ont., trading post, 22:
278n
Moose Lake State Hospital, 40:395,
397
Moose Lake Township, Beltrami County,
history, 15:483
Moose Mountain, Sask., ore plant, 34:
272, 273, 280, 283
Moose River, Beltrami County, history, 15:132
Moose River, Ont., map, 34:255; fur
trade, 40:171
Moose School, Clearwater County, his-
tory, 16:247
Mootz, A. P., speaker, 22:340
Mora, history, 15:368, 18:340, 36:
193, 195; Swedish settlement, 34:
61; logging, 34:62
Moran, Mrs. Flora, speaker, 14:124
Moran, Joe A., author, 24:261
Moran, Thomas, artist, 33:264
Moravec, Frank D., 19:239
Moravia, immigration from, 15:26-30
Moravian Brethren, 15:26, 31; in Min-
nesota, 14:451, 20:330, 31:28
Moravian College and Theological Sem-
inary, Bethlehem, Pa., 20:100, 330
Moravians, Carver County, 15:114.
See also Czechs
Morcom, Elisha, mining interests, 35:
338
More, Dr. C. W., author, 17:241
More, Margaret E., author, 28:383
Morehead, Col. Turner G., 25:238, 349
Morehouse, D. B., steamboat captain,
15:409
Morehouse, Frances, author, 35:193
Morehouse, Legrand, steamboat cap-
tain, 15:409, 417, 25:112
Morès, Antoine de Vallombrosa, Mar-
quis de, 16:116; in North Dakota,
22:207, 27:357, 28:169, 31:122
Morey, C. R., 14:194
Morgagni, John B., author, 21:363
Morgal, Louis, speaker, 29:274
Morgan, Fox leader, 20:56
Morgan, ---, church trustee, 19:267n

Morgan, Capt. ---, 17:156, 293
Morgan, Caleb, papers, 23:273
Morgan, Charles A., papers, 23:273
Morgan, Dale L., "The Fur Trade and
    Its Historians," 40:151-156; re-
    view by, 39:164; work reviewed,
    38:238; author, 34:219, 40:149,
    201, 312; editor, 39:128, 261, 40:
    147; speaker, 40:411
Morgan, David P., works reviewed, 36:
    321, 39:30
Morgan, Edward J., newspaper editor,
    37:164
Morgan, Frank, 17:483, 18:465
Morgan, Fred, author, 37:183
Morgan, George, Indian agent, 19:295
Morgan, Col. George N., Union offi-
    cer, 25:19n, 238, 255, 343, 349;
    career, 18:96
Morgan, George T., review by, 37:132
Morgan, George W., author, 12:344
Morgan, J. E., 14:461, 18:465, 19:471
Morgan, J. Pierpont, railroad mag-
    nate, 18:424, 39:110
Morgan, Col. John H., Union cavalry
    leader, 25:241n
Morgan, Gen. John Hunt, Confederate
    officer, 38:266
Morgan, Lewis Henry, work reviewed,
    37:78
Morgan, M. F., author, 36:34
Morgan, Richard G., work reviewed,
    29:161
Morgan, Robert, farmer, 24:334
Morgan, Stephen W., jeweler, 18:344
Morgan, William T., author, 12:437
Morgan, Youngs L., diary, 39:82
Morgan, pageant, 14:359, 15:491; li-
    brary and museum, 20:98, 354, 466
Morgan Messenger, anniversary edi-
    tion, 20:363
Moriarty, J. J., speaker, 24:85
Moriarty, Lawrence, teacher, 15:37
Morice, Father Adrian C., 15:92n;
    work reviewed, 16:460-462; author,
    11:212, 33:183
Morin, Rev. ---, 28:321
Morin, William, 14:314
Morison, Bradley L., author, 40:315
Morison, Elting E., editor, 32:146,
    192
Morison, Samuel E., 23:256; works re-
    viewed, 12:74, 34:298; author, 13:
    307, 19:102, 29:348, 34:251;
    speaker, 22:326
Morken, H. N., speaker, 25:316
Morlan, Robert L., "The Nonpartisan
    League," 34:221-232; review by,
    35:368; work reviewed, 34:347
Morley, Christopher, speaker, 21:113;
    poet, 26:308
Mormon Coulee, Wis., described, 22:98
"Mormon War," 17:430n, 39:71n
Mormons, see Latter-day Saints
"Morning Star," steamboat, 37:296
Morning Sun, Iowa, mail service, 30:
    268
Morphy, Edward H., biography, 16:337
Morrell, John & Co., Ottumwa, Iowa,
    28:185
Morrill, Ashley C., Indian agent, 15:
    288, 25:183
Morrill, James L., 27:262, 36:186;
    work reviewed, 37:175; speaker,
    30:155; honored, 30:171
Morrill, Justin S., Congressman, 35:
    379

Morrill, Mrs. Medora, 17:151n
Morrill, Miron, author, 21:185
Morrill, True, diary, 18:444
Morrin, ---, trader, 28:226, 230
Morris, A. B., speaker, 11:117
Morris, Abbie, diary, 26:156
Morris, Mrs. Annie B., 23:100
Morris, Clara, actress, 23:309, 310,
    28:117
Morris, D. A., author, 30:397
Morris, Frank, 11:320, 27:171; ballad
    collector, 13:323, 27:186; speak-
    er, 19:120, 20:100
Morris, George, 17:355
Morris, Gouverneur, 18:397
Morris, H. S., author, 18:456, 19:
    108, 21:99
Morris, J. L., author, 23:186, 26:76
Morris, J. T., author, 11:101
Morris, James M., 14:333
Morris, Mrs. James T. (Lucy Wilder),
    11:54, 14:78, 79, 17:62, 19:47;
    speaker, 11:330; honored, 14:97;
    editor, 15:483; memorial, 17:208,
    18:46, 24:36, 25:41; park memori-
    al, 40:48
Morris, Kenton W., author, 35:292
Morris, Lloyd, author, 34:42
Morris, Mrs. Martha R., 18:210; let-
    ters, 23:272
Morris, Owen, memorial, 12:194; pa-
    pers, 12:320
Morris, Richard B., author, 24:70,
    253, 38:387
Morris, Robert, land speculator, 18:
    87; letter, 12:429
Morris, Robert L., author, 31:251
Morris, Mrs. T. B., author, 22:108
Morris, W. C., cartoonist, 34:223,
    231
Morris, William, diary, 26:156
Morris, Wright, editor, 38:384
Morris family, settlers, 34:183
Morris, flood, 11:68; banking, 11:
    467; immigrant house, 13:41; his-
    tory, 16:99, 28:384; Episcopal
    church, 16:381; stage service, 18:
    225, 19:408; common council, 18:
    474; railroad, 19:408, 35:207,
    208; unions, 21:393; agricultural
    school, 22:413, 28:384 Irish colo-
    ny, 35:211, 212; prairie fires,
    37:204
Morris and Morse, Minneapolis, in-
    surance company, accounts, 22:320
Morris River, Man., trading post, 11:
    365
Morriseau, Norval, author, 40:358
Morrison, Addison, 19:476
Morrison, Allan, trader, 11:220, 26:
    362, 28:313, 35:337, 36:40, 41
Morrison, Mrs. Allan, 36:40
Morrison, Don, author, 40:412
Morrison, Dorilus, 37:312, 318, 320;
    mayor, 12:457; lumberman, 16:479,
    24:133, 32:180; career, 29:88
Morrison, George, dairy farmer, 27:
    113
Morrison, Irma, author, 29:278
Morrison, J. G., interpreter, 15:287
Morrison, James C., author, 28:375
Morrison, Bishop James D., 13:325,
    22:321, 36:319
Morrison, John G., 35:340; collector,
    18:464, 22:440, 35:50
Morrison, Kenneth D., author, 21:440,
    24:80, 182

Morrison, Lee, farmer, 25:338
Morrison, Lt. Pitcairn, 28:18
Morrison, William, 12:225; trader,
    11:369, 12:92, 13:99, 20:78, 22:
    274, 23:233, 24:372, 25:386, 28:6,
    30:259, 36:246, 40:185n
Morrison, William B., author, 18:103
Morrison family, genealogy, 21:195
Morrison County, trading post, 11:
    374; history, 14:121, 34:359; for-
    est fires, 18:97; pioneers, 18:
    212; commissioners, 18:223, 227;
    post offices, 19:231; officers,
    19:470; Lutheran church, 20:361;
    ethnic groups, 21:98, 453, 24:90;
    archives, 21:327; historic sites,
    28:292, 29:363; geology, 37:307;
    poor farm, 38:369
Morrison County Historical Society,
    19:470; organized, 17:483, 18:62;
    projects, 18:223, 19:231, 20:97,
    23:298, 29:363; meeting, 19:117;
    museum, 20:212; accessions, 23:446
Morrison County War History Commit-
    tee, 23:391
Morristown, trading post, 11:382;
    churches, 14:123, 339; G.A.R.
    post, 16:431; pageant, 18:342;
    history, 21:115
Morrow, Anne, see Lindbergh, Mrs.
    Charles A., Jr.
Morrow, Dwight, 18:426
Morrow, Col. J. C., 40:301
Morrow, Ralph E., work reviewed, 40:
    403
Morrow, Stanley J., photographer, 35:
    246
Morrow, W. V., author, 16:226
Morse, Abner, 20:339
Morse, Ann, 24:125
Morse, Eric W., author, 37:345;
    speaker, 40:149
Morse, Frank P., author, 22:202
Morse, Hermann N., author, 16:345
Morse, Horace T., 21:188, 25:73, 27:
    26, 147, 29:54, 283; speaker, 27:
    143, 29:184, 274; quoted, 27:339;
    author, 28:365, 30:86; editor, 29:
    53, 30:38, 32:10
Morse, Irl, poet, 16:81
Morse, J. W., speaker, 20:456
Morse, Jedidiah, 23:132; geographer,
    23:169, 24:229
Morse, Mrs. R., 17:231
Morse, Samuel F. B., inventor, 19:75,
    25:308, 35:92
Morse, W. W., 19:184n
Morse, William D., businessman, 22:
    320
Mortensen, A. R., work reviewed, 38:
    237
Mortensen, Rev. Enok, 27:256; author,
    30:400, 38:42
Mortenson, August, pioneer, 20:98
Mortimer, E. D., speculator, 35:245
Morton, ---, stage driver, 40:390
Morton, Arthur S., work reviewed, 27:
    131; author, 15:238, 17:476, 18:
    215, 21:432, 24:154, 25:67, 31:
    184, 33:182, 183, 36:272, 40:166,
    176
Morton, Louis, author, 34:251
Morton, Oliver P., career, 30:382
Morton, W. L., 29:81; "The North West
    Company," 40:157-165; reviews by,
    32:112-114, 33:182, 34:305, 344,
    35:148, 36:29, 37:126, 337, 38:

328, 40:142; works reviewed, 28:
64, 35:282, 36:63, 40:93; author,
31:56, 32:60, 128, 36:191, 38:200;
speaker, 40:262
Morton, Zylpha S., "Harriet Bishop,"
28:132-141; author, 28:204, 39:51
Morton, monuments, 12:299, 38:149n;
history, 13:453, 17:240; mission,
14:359; newspapers, 17:103;
schools, 17:240, 38:144n; Indian
settlement, 27:358; railroad, 30:
240; settled, 34:131; historical
society, 40:232
Morton County, N.D., place names, 36:
325
Morton Enterprise, history, 17:240
Mosboek, Ludvig, author, 17:239
Mosby, Capt. John S., 25:252
"Moscow Expedition," history, 39:227-
240
Moscrip, W. S., 27:48
Mose, Carl C., 14:350, 15:62, 116
Moser, Sister Gregoria, 35:264
Möser, Justus, historian, 19:8
Moses, Barr, see Moses, W. J. B.
Moses, Montrose J., author, 26:308
Moses, W. E., farmer, 15:487
Moses, W. J. B., author, 16:250, 305,
468
Mosier, Grace, 18:111, 19:119, 20:99
Moss, Henry L., 17:393, 27:271, 33:4,
36:4n; territorial official, 30:
109, 35:357, 39:39, 145; Still-
water pioneer, 36:208
Moss, Mrs. Henry L., 33:4
Mote, Marcus, panoramist, 33:316
Mother Lake, Hennepin County, 35:24
Motion pictures, Austin, 11:116;
forerunners, 17:115, 132, 21:422;
historical, 17:472, 23:51, 83, 93,
192, 27:158, 29:102; preservation,
21:400; documentary, 23:385; in
education, 25:59, 84, 28:357, 29:
77; Lake Minnetonka, 30:92
Motley, Maude, author, 14:227
Motley, settled, 34:64
Motschenbacher, George, 11:459
Mott, David C., author, 12:95
Mott, Frank L., 26:161; author, 11:
323, 20:85, 25:176, 26:74
Mott, Louise, speaker, 29:365; au-
thor, 30:168
Mott, R. A., pioneer lawyer, 30:168
Mott, Valentine, surgeon, 21:369
Mouer, Thomas, lawyer, 21:196
Mould, Charles T., architect, 40:100n
Mound, history, 11:227, 14:352; Cath-
olic churches, 15:362, 480, 481;
historical meeting, 28:391
Mound Bayou, Miss., Black settlement,
24:54
Mound builders, see Indian mounds
"Mound City," ironclad, sunk, 25:131n
Mound Prairie Township, Houston Coun-
ty, Norwegian settlement, 12:278
Mound Township, Rock County, Norwe-
gian settlement, 12:274
Mounds Park, St. Paul, Indian burial
ground, 15:149, 30:209n; historic
site, 40:48
Mounds View Township, Ramsey County,
drainage, 40:230
Mount Ida Female College, Davenport,
Iowa, 16:276n
Mount Josephine, Grand Portage, 21:
156
Mount Rose, Grand Portage, 21:156

Mount Rushmore, S.D., monument, 33:86
Mount Stephen, George Stephen, Lord,
railroad builder, 11:308, 14:449,
17:218, 40:142, 316
Mount Vernon, Va., Washington estate,
25:118, 39:336
Mount Vernon Township, Winona County,
churches, 14:48; Germans, 28:33
Mount Zion Temple, St. Paul, 17:99;
anniversaries, 13:217, 28:294, 35:
293; welfare work, 22:348; history, 30:163, 36:320
Mountain, N.D., Icelandic community,
17:344
Mountain Iron, monument, 12:333; mining, 12:334, 13:428, 21:289, 292,
23:361, 24:265, 27:203, 359, 29:
89, 32:245, 33:27, 67n, 226, 355,
34:12, 44, 36:192; historical
meeting, 21:289-293; Finnish settlement, 22:392, 396, 398, 400,
401, 25:319; history, 40:48;
strike, 40:342, 346. See also
Mesabi Range
Mountain Lake (town), Mennonite settlement, 11:294, 14:114, 16:344,
17:466, 18:47, 445, 19:48, 213,
20:181-183, 459, 23:88, 24:365,
26:287, 27:221-227, 365, 31:29,
37:184, 38:243; schools, 12:101,
20:459; first newspaper, 20:215;
library, 21:220; Junior Historians, 27:49, 144, 146, 148, 245,
28:162, 163; agriculture, 29:189
Mountain Lake, border lake, pictured,
37:239
Mountain Lake Preparatory School, 20:
459
Mountain lion, in Minnesota, 30:130,
33:354
Mountain Meadows Massacre, Utah, 39:
71n
Mountain men, in fur trade, 40:145,
149, 152, 155, 157, 182, 184, 186,
201, 218, 219
Mountain Wolf Woman, Winnebago Indian, autobiography reviewed, 37:343
"Mounted Minute Men," in Sioux Outbreak, 38:285
Mountfort, Mrs. Herbert, speaker, 19:
115
Mousseau, Charles, St. Paul pioneer,
15:301
Mouw, D., Dutch pioneer, 28:128
Movern, John, labor leader, 40:344
Movers, D. S., 28:221
Mowat, Farley, author, 40:94
Mower, John E., house, 38:338, 339,
352
Mower, Martin, lumberman, 31:34, 35,
38; builder, 37:138; house, 38:
338, 339
Mower County, Norwegian settlements,
12:265, 269, 14:444, 31:27; courthouses, 12:444, 15:249, 250; newspapers, 16:368; agriculture, 16:
496, 18:462, 20:159, 23:319, 39:
81; automobile traffic, 20:463;
pioneer life, 21:222, 453; history, 23:108, 36:107; soldier vote,
26:200; creameries, 27:116; village histories, 33:353; iron mining, 36:70; convention delegates,
37:42; poor farm, 38:369n, 373
Mower County (Pioneer and) Historical
Society, founded, 29:180; build-

ing fund, 30:81, 167; museum, 30:
400, 35:202, 37:42
Mower County War History Committee,
23:391
Mowry, George E., work reviewed, 27:
132-134
Mowry, George H., 13:140
Moyer, Sumner L., author, 15:366
Moyle, John B., author, 23:99, 25:
309, 35:98
Moynahan, James H. S., author, 35:44
Moyne, Ernest J., translator, 34:163
Moynihan, Monsig. Humphrey, 17:349,
33:304; speaker, 14:230; author,
15:104, 456, 26:303, 35:213
Moynihan, Monsig. James H., work re-
viewed, 33:304; speaker, 15:241;
author, 15:467
Mozart Hall, St. Paul, 39:53
Mozeemlek Indians, 14:375
Mrak, Father Ignatius, missionary,
33:185
Muckenthaler, Benno, missionary, 32:
38
Muckraking, history, 14:200-202
Mud Creek Mine, St. Louis County, 34:
180
Mud Lake, Cass County, archaeology,
26:321, 323, 327
Mud Lake, Hennepin County, see Lake
Hiawatha
Mudge, Bill, mine superintendent, 34:
280
Mudgett, Helen P., speaker, 24:376;
editor, 34:355
Muehlberg, Hermann, journalist, 24:
215n
Muelder, Hermann R., author, 16:234,
25:196
Muelken, Walburga, 35:271
Mueller, Agnes H., review by, 35:149;
work reviewed, 34:349; author, 36:
69, 239
Mueller, Franz H., author, 33:188
Mueller, Herbert L., author, 23:404
Mueller, Herman, politician, 34:231
Mueller, John H., work reviewed, 33:
135
Mueller, Rev. R. J., speaker, 24:85
Muench, J. F., speaker, 21:290
Muggah, Mary G., author, 26:170
Muhlenberg, Maj. Peter, at Fort Craw-
ford, Wis., 23:343
Muir, John, naturalist, 23:356, 25:
221
Muirhead, Frank, 23:100
Mulcahy, James, artist, 29:260
Mulder, Arnold, work reviewed, 29:67
Mullan, Lt. John, road builder, 38:58
Mullan Road, Montana to Washington,
24:159, 38:58
Mullen, Ada W., author, 29:272
Mullen, James, author, 15:245
Mullen, John H., 26:43
Mullen, Michael, 17:113
Muller, Dr. Alfred, 15:137, 32:240n
Muller, Mrs. Alfred (Elizabeth), 15:
137; pianist, 32:240n, 39:322
Muller, Alice B., author, 13:439
Muller, Charles, author, 38:251, 253,
256
Muller, Capt. Lewis, 25:231, 251,
252, 256, 357
Miller family, genealogy, 26:177
Müller-Freienfels, Richard, author,
29:154
Mullett, Charles F., author, 17:107

Mulligan, Ed, woodsman, 21:355
Mulvahill, Morris, speaker, 11:338
Mulvany, John, artist, 28:79
Mulvey, Sister M. Doris, author, 17:
  473
Mumey, Nolie, author, 15:234
Mumford, Lewis, quoted, 24:95, 40:134
Mumm, Marguerite, review by, 37:342
Mumps, among Indians, 14:330
Munch, Gen. Emil, in Sioux Outbreak,
  21:88, 33:84, 38:283
Münch, Friedrich, 31:230
Munch, Paul, house, 38:343
Mundale, Charles, author, 36:105
Munden, Kenneth W., work reviewed,
  38:382
Mundua Indians, 27:216, 218, 219
Munger, Dell H., author, 23:157
Munger, R. S., musician, 23:310
Munger, Russell C., 15:483, 19:164,
  33:2; musician, 23:310
Munger, W. H., 39:320; musician, 23:
  310
Munger Brothers Music Store, St.
  Paul, 15:483, 23:310, 33:2, 318,
  39:319, 320
Municipal Electric Co., Twin Cities,
  incorporated, 37:323
Munk, Jens, navigator, 17:25; expedi-
  tion, 17:170, 20:337
Munro, Dr. ---, frontier physician,
  11:58
Munro, William, testimony, 21:145
Munroe, Mrs. James, 29:319
Munsingwear Inc., Minneapolis, his-
  tory, 37:346
Munson, Augustus A., 28:89
Munson, O., army surgeon, 25:143
Munson, Raymond, author, 19:475
Munsterberg, Hugo, author, 29:154
Munzer, Clarence I., auto driver, 38:
  207, 214
Munzer, Rudolph W., and Sons, Minne-
  apolis, car distributors, 38:207
Munzer, Warren W., auto driver, 38:
  207, 214, 215
Murchie, R. W., work reviewed, 18:87
Murder, see Crime
Murdoch, Angus, author, 40:141
Murdock, George P., compiler, 37:346
Murdock, Hollis R., 11:318
Murdock, Hyrum, 13:392
Murdock, Mrs. J. W., author, 15:243
Murdock, Victor, politician, 21:416,
  22:79
Mure, John, 14:338
Murfree, Mary, 20:110
Murfreesboro, Tenn., in Civil War,
  17:222, 25:240, 241, 39:191-197,
  40:282
Murphy, Bob, author, 28:393, 33:313,
  314, 34:256, 35:201, 39:39
Murphy, Charles, 28:291
Murphy, Donald R., work reviewed, 37:
  340
Murphy, Edmund R., author, 22:327,
  432
Murphy, Edward, businessman, 37:318,
  319, 40:376
Murphy, Mrs. Frank, 40:146
Murphy, Frederick E., 25:154n, 38:
  205, 207
Murphy, Harold, 16:368
Murphy, John, letter, 24:166
Murphy, Dr. John H., pioneer physi-
  cian, 11:108, 21:101, 22:405, 33:
  312, 35:108, 220, 221

Murphy, Lawrence E., author, 24:178
Murphy, Sister Mary, author, 26:171,
  27:166
Murphy, Maj. Richard G., Indian
  agent, 17:296n, 20:328, 34:130
Murphy, Rowley, author, 35:153, 292
Murphy, S. C., speaker, 11:217
Murphy, Thomas D., author, 27:61, 28:
  73
Murphy, Sister Ursula, letters, 30:
  2, 11; teacher, 30:10, 13
Murphy, William, farmer, 29:99
Murphy family, in Todd County, 22:89
Murphy Park, Minneapolis, 40:376
Murray, Mrs. Agnes, 19:116, 21:107,
  22:216
Murray, Alexander H., trader, 15:350,
  356; explorer, 17:75; artist, 18:
  216
Murray, Byron D., 18:330
Murray, Charles A., 22:154
Murray, Elsie M., author, 23:384, 28:
  179
Murray, Mrs. Francis H., letter, 30:
  182
Murray, Genevieve, author, 12:93
Murray, Gilbert, 18:101
Murray, J. Buxton, author, 35:248
Murray, J. M., author, 13:113
Murray, Gen. James, 11:234, 247, 250;
  governor, 15:95, 96
Murray, John, actor, 18:137n, 28:113,
  33:175-178
Murray, Archbishop John G., 19:475,
  20:92, 39:160; speaker, 14:230,
  16:234, 19:464, 22:51, 347, 436,
  23:36; author, 15:104; career, 33:
  223, 35:202
Murray, John J., work reviewed, 36:
  185
Murray, John W., diary, 20:34, 81
Murray, L. C., author, 16:245
Murray, Paul, author, 34:312
Murray, Robert A., author, 40:96
Murray, Stanley N., author, 36:69
Murray, William P., 14:363, 21:52;
  lawyer, 12:84; politician, 14:245,
  26:199; family, 20:208; quoted,
  28:312
Murray, Mrs. William P., 14:255
Murray, Clearwater County, ghost
  town, 16:493
Murray-Cartland, theatrical company,
  33:176-178
Murray County, grasshopper plague,
  11:335; established, 14:244, 16:
  130; politics, 14:247-251, 256,
  261, 262; population, 14:252, 254,
  256-259; agriculture, 16:496, 37:
  205; archives, 22:332; history,
  23:109; plat book, 25:101; pageant, 30:408; Irish settlement,
  31:22; Sioux in, 34:355; Catholic
  colony, 35:134, 136, 137, 325
Murray County Historical Society, 16:
  241; organized, 15:250, 16:63;
  meetings, 15:369, 16:124, 17:122,
  19:361; activities, 16:64, 30:278;
  museum, 36:34
Murray County War History Committee,
  24:82
Murtha, Edwin, work reviewed, 35:370
Muscalus, John A., compiler, 30:263
Muscatine, Iowa, prairie described,
  17:425, 426; lumbering, 29:85
"Muscatine," steamboat, 38:289

Museum of Modern Art, New York, Indian exhibit, 22:189
Museums, administration, 11:202;
  functions, 13:431, 432, 14:337;
  Twin Cities, 29:259; St. Louis,
  29:260. See also American Association of Museums, Historical museums
Musgrove, Jack W., author, 26:169
Mushroom cave, St. Paul, pictured,
  40:252
Music and musicians, bands, 11:319,
  15:39, 370, 16:40, 249, 255, 497,
  17:389, 19:325, 23:310, 403, 26:
  282, 33:3, 36:199, 263, 37:306;
  Minnesota, 12:451, 16:333, 351,
  18:335, 446, 20:94, 21:101, 23:
  302, 30:173, 174, 36:147, 194;
  Twin Cities, 13:114, 16:238, 17:
  102, 20:188, 21:193, 24:191, 26:
  155, 298, 29:119, 30:406, 31:61,
  32:239, 240, 33:1, 175; singing
  groups, 13:213, 16:251, 255, 19:
  449, 22:52-54, 113, 132, 402, 26:
  59, 27:256, 35:203; in schools,
  13:271, 35:266, 268, 269; scores,
  15:115, 16:102, 22:431, 23:171,
  24:63, 26:52-54, 29:98; frontier,
  16:32, 19:312-321, 25:207, 26:378,
  27:179-189, 28:320; symphony or-
  chestras, 17:101, 18:330, 19:333,
  20:92, 24:78, 33:93-104, 135, 222,
  36:106; University of Minnesota,
  20:92; Duluth, 21:116; anthology,
  23:159; on river boats, 24:72; St.
  Olaf College, 24:258, 26:59; war
  songs, 25:311; criticism, 26:306,
  39:59, 60, 63, 64; transportation
  songs, 26:379; Wisconsin, 30:72;
  for dancing, 32:200; emigrant
  songs, 37:83. See also Folk music
  and songs, Opera, Pianos, individual performers and organizations
Musical Art Society, Faribault, 19:
  467
Muskego, Wis., Norwegian settlement,
  11:209, 19:107, 24:366, 28:381,
  33:85; history, 24:348; church,
  25:195, 27:256, 38:231-233
Muskegon River, Mich., logging, 34:35
Muskrat, in fur trade, 13:237, 23:
  330, 30:133, 34:103, 35:295, 38:
  190, 40:180, 209, 212, 213, 215,
  217, 220; Michigan, 18:451; trapping, 22:194
Muskrat Portage, see Kenora, Ont.
Musser, Joseph, miller, 25:101
Musser, R. D., 18:269
Musser, Samuel, miller, 25:101
Mussey, H. E., author, 11:222
Mussgang, Margaret, author, 15:224
Muus, Rev. Bernt J., missionary, 18:
  466; career, 14:356, 20:345; au-
  thor, 26:167
Myer, Dr. Jesse S., author, 21:95
Myers, Alice V., author, 23:184
Myers, Frank A., author, 35:153
Myers, Col. Henry, aviator, 26:15
Myers, Dr. J. Arthur, work reviewed,
  31:43; author, 12:334, 25:307, 35:
  220, 37:135
Myers, James, 15:112
Myers, Leonard, Congressman, 34:73
Myers, Mrs. Mary, teacher, 15:112
Myers, R. S., author, 11:222; speak-
  er, 11:336
Myers, Theodore B., jeweler, 33:2

Myhers, Jim, author, 35:156
Myhrman, Anders M., author, 39:131
Myrick, Andrew, murdered, 38:135
Myrick, Nathan, trader, 11:181, 374,
    18:209, 29:218, 32:253, 38:135n;
    businessman, 22:98, 40:224, 225,
    228
Myrold, Don, author, 37:135

Nachbar, C. A., 12:454, 18:334
Nachtrieb, Henry F., 21:209, 28:286;
    photographer, 35:272-274, 277;
    biologist, 37:29
Naegele, Henry, diary, 21:204
Naegele, Lambert, in Sioux Outbreak,
    14:217; newspaper publisher, 34:
    130
Naeseth, Franz, author, 20:468
Naeseth, Henriette C. K., review by,
    33:349; work reviewed, 33:40
Naftalin, Arthur, 25:191; "The Tradi-
    tion of Protest," 35:53-63; review
    by, 35:41; author, 25:202; editor,
    33:312; speaker, 36:108, 37:135
Nafziger, Ralph O., author, 27:270
Nagasaki, Japan, Russian railway
    corps in, 38:316-324
Nagel, Arend J., Dutch pioneer, 28:
    121, 123, 124
Nagel, Mrs. Arend J., Dutch pioneer,
    28:122
Nagel, Mr. and Mrs. Berend, Dutch
    pioneers, 28:122
Nagel, Derk, 28:122
Nagel, Diana, 28:122
Nagel, Gerrit, 28:122
Nagel, Dr. Gunther W., work reviewed,
    40:309
Nagiwicakte, Sioux Indian, 38:134
Nagle, Mary D., editor, "The Noxious
    Weed," 39:24; author, 40:144; art-
    ist, 40:150n
Nagonabe, Chippewa leader, 21:285
Nagurski, Bronko, career, 35:335
Nahbahgahdoway, Chippewa leader, 12:
    296
Nairn, John, engineer, 39:239
Namakan Lake, border lake, 21:433;
    archaeology, 28:373; steamboat
    route, 34:178
Namakan Lumber Co., log mark de-
    picted, 26:128
Namew Lake, Man., Sask., 40:172
Nanabazhoo, Indian hero, legends, 25:
    54
Nanaimo, Vancouver Island, B.C.,
    bastion, 40:191
Nance, Joseph M., author, 22:432
"Nangatuck," ironclad, 25:129
Nannestad, Dr. Jonas R., 11:289
Nantouagan River, route, 12:362. See
    also Pigeon River
Napoleonic Wars, effect on fur trade,
    40:180, 182, 212
Napolska, Sister Mary R., author, 27:
    257
Narveson, B. H., author, 26:166
Nasatir, Abraham P., work reviewed,
    33:301-303; author, 11:451, 39:
    261; editor, 28:79
Nasby, Petroleum V., lecturer, 11:
    158, 21:326, 28:56
Nasett, Lars I., 15:249
Nash, Edgar, storekeeper, 37:111n

Nash, Helen L., author, 18:224
Nash, Howard F., Jr., work reviewed,
    36:187
Nash, Jean, author, 25:198
Nash, Joshua W., 35:70
Nash, Mrs. O. J., author, 19:239
Nash, William C., 18:341
Nash, Z. E. B., 24:139
Nashotah House, Nashotah Lakes, Wis.,
    theological seminary, 14:111, 18:
    326
Nashville, Iowa, river town, 17:431n
Nashville, Tenn., literary group, 20:
    113; battle, 38:245 (cover)
Nashville & Chattanooga Railroad, in
    Civil War, 39:192
Nashville Township, Martin County,
    history, 18:465
Nashwauk, Yugoslav settlement, 28:
    251-253; strike, 40:346. See also
    Mesabi Range
"Nasmyth," barge, 34:14
Nason, E. L., 25:22
Nason, Joel F., house, 38:346
Nason, John, author, 40:256
Nast, Thomas, 18:30; speaker, 35:227,
    228
Natchez, Miss., in Civil War, 11:206
Natchez Trace, 23:61
Nathan, George Jean, author, 21:4
Nathan, Hans, author, 30:152, 39:84
Nathanson, Copenhagen, Den., banking
    house, 20:249
National Academy of Sciences, publi-
    cation, 26:84
National Archives, collections, 11:
    41, 15:62, 22:307, 26:265, 27:161;
    building, 15:228, 16:104, 17:1, 9,
    14-16, 19, 71, 216; publications,
    16:329, 18:58, 93, 24:70, 25:310,
    391, 26:147, 30:388, 389; estab-
    lished, 16:342, 17:9-15; impor-
    tance, 17:1-10, 71; survey, 17:7,
    460, 18:49; staff, 17:18, 29:259;
    guides, 18:214, 21:399, 28:68, 30:
    149, 39:127, 170, 210, 40:360;
    training programs, 19:218, 26:162;
    preservation methods, 19:455; Min-
    nesota material, 21:83, 314, 22:
    422, 29:284, 36:85; military rec-
    ords, 22:297, 298, 25:282, 296,
    398, 39:204, 279; photograph file,
    28:347-349, 351, 34:242-249, 35:
    131; inventories, 32:189; Conti-
    nental Congress papers, 34:169;
    microfilms, 34:212; Indian materi-
    al, 34:354; in Clark papers case,
    36:218, 226, 228; function, 36:236
National Archives Act, provisions,
    17:15, 18
National Association for the Advance-
    ment of Colored People, Minnesota,
    38:88
National Association of Importers and
    Breeders of Norman Horses, 22:265,
    26:124
National Association of Real Estate
    Boards, history, 36:189
National Bank of Commerce, Duluth,
    37:122
National baseball club, Lake City,
    19:170
National Board for Historical Serv-
    ice, 23:178
National Board of Missions of the
    Presbyterian Church, 16:354
National Building Loan and Protective

Union, Minneapolis, 18:123, 136,
    140, 142n, 144, 147, 211
National Capital Sesquicentennial,
    Minnesota exhibit, 31:121; publi-
    cation, 31:248
National Cigarmakers Union, 20:433
National Citizens Political Action
    Committee, 34:189
National Colony, Worthington, 24:90,
    29:271; described, 17:337; estab-
    lished, 18:471, 20:465, 27:362;
    site, 24:91
National Colony Journal (Toledo,
    Ohio), 20:217
National Committee on Militarism in
    Education, 40:366n
National Conservation Congress, 40:
    322, 324
National Co-operative Council, 18:323
National Council for Historic Sites
    and Buildings, inventory, 30:258;
    program, 33:137
National Council for Prevention of
    War, 15:120, 40:372
National Council for the Social
    Studies, 25:168
National Council of State Superin-
    tendents and Commissioners of Edu-
    cation, 14:417
National Dairy Union, 40:324
National Demokrat (St. Paul), German
    paper, 27:127
National Editorial Association, 14:
    393, 18:451
National Education Association, 14:
    393, 25:373; Washington, D.C., 23:
    393; history, 27:61, 35:371; Wino-
    na, 35:98
National Farmers Bank, Owatonna, ar-
    chitecture, 35:242, 37:344, 38:91
National Federation of Settlements
    and Neighborhood Centers, 39:300
National Gallery of Art, Washington,
    D.C., Minnesota material, 30:85,
    173
National Grange, 16:487, 17:467, 20:
    86, 31:190, 37:136, 39:83, 40:330.
    See also Granger movement
National Herbart Society, publica-
    tions, 19:433
National Highway Users Conference,
    19:102
National Historical Publications Com-
    mission, 34:212, 37:340, 40:96,
    261
National Institute of Mental Health,
    grant, 39:300
National Labor Relations Board, ar-
    chives, 22:211
National Labor Union, organized, 21:
    378
National League of American Pen Wom-
    en, Minnesota branch, 17:340
National Lutheran Council, 15:449
National Monetary Commission, 12:12,
    22:422
National Museum, see Smithsonian In-
    stitution
National Park Service, 18:458, 27:60;
    staff, 16:330, 18:281; projects,
    16:487, 17:105, 18:66, 311, 328,
    20:146, 21:327, 423, 24:252, 31:
    249, 37:63, 66, 85, 308; publica-
    tion, 39:33; functions, 39:337,
    40:35; records, 40:361
National parks, 39:336, 40:38

National Planning Association, Washington, D.C., 23:393
National Popular Education Board, National Popular Education Society, see Board of National Popular Education
National Producers' Alliance, 28:304; history, 28:37-44, 72. See also Farmers Union
National Recovery Administration, records, 26:265
National Resources Planning Board, 23:9, 16, 188, 279
National Road, history, 28:279, 29:150, 30:142; trade route, 40:184
National Society of Autograph Collectors, 29:164, 30:65, 257
National Society of the Colonial Dames of America, see Colonial Dames of America
National Teachers' Association, see National Education Association
National Trust for Historic Preservation in the United States, 30:258, 33:311, 35:150
National Union Labor party, 35:59
National Voters' League, 18:313
National War Labor Board, 18:314
National Weeklies, Inc., Winona, 16:338, 17:52
National Woman Suffrage Association, program, 39:4
National Woman's Party, 20:192
Nationalbund, Catholic society, 17:85
Natural history, Nerstrand Woods, 22:291; Mendota area, 23:340; Minnesota, 24:246
Natural resources, Minnesota, 36:67, 69, 105, 193
Natural Resources Fund, 40:314
Nau, Anthony, map maker, 12:82
Nauvoo, Ill., Mormon settlement, 15:306n, 307, 463, 17:429, 22:19, 20, 98, 32:98, 36:46, 285; Lewis' visits, 17:150
"Navigator," steamboat, 19:249
Navratil, Antonín, Bohemian pioneer, 15:27
Navratil, František, 15:31
Nawajibigokwe, Chippewa Indian, 21:285
Nawench-Marawski, Dr. A., author, 13:435
Naylor, Mrs. E. H., speaker, 12:107
Nazareth Unitarian Church, Minneapolis, 20:400
Nazism, interpretation of history, 18:2, 4
Nea, St. Louis County, post office, 34:186
Neal, Robert M., author, 27:258
Neal, W. E., boatbuilder, 33:13
Neal, William H., author, 22:112
Neale, Dr. M. Gordon, author, 12:418
Neale, William, 11:238n
Nealis, Rev. John W., 16:341
Neall, Henry L., 21:177
Near, Jay M., lawsuit, 24:373; newspaper editor, 37:161-173
Neary, Robert, speaker, 19:316
Neatby, Hilda M., author, 19:352
Nebelthau, Jessie H., editor, 15:237
Nebergall, Ralph, author, 15:245
Nebish Township, Beltrami County, history, 15:132; logging railroad, 29:147
Nebraska, train exhibit, 11:107; pioneer life, 12:440, 19:79; ethnic groups, 13:419, 14:225, 18:99, 19:200, 20:181, 21:75, 98, 27:256, 29:278, 37:39; population, 13:435; lumber market, 18:175; land policies, 19:81-83; legislature, 19:202, 33:155; poets, 19:225; in fiction, 23:116, 124; pictured, 27:159; bibliography, 28:276; history, 34:307; Catholic colonies, 35:212, 40:352; geological survey, 35:242; missions, 35:380, 36:286, 289; in Civil War, 37:255; Indian reservations, 39:240, 261; atlas, 40:128; forts, 40:146; fur trade, 40:193, 196; drought, 40:409
Nebraska and Lake Superior Railroad Co., see Lake Superior and Mississippi Railroad
Nebraska State Historical Society, Lincoln, publications, 19:81; photograph collection, 28:346; activities, 40:193
Necedah, Wis., history, 33:314
Neche, N.D., wheat raising, 29:14
Needler, G. H., editor, 30:63
Neely, Wayne C., work reviewed, 16:327
Neenah, Stearns County, platted, 22:447
Neenah, Wis., Nicolet pageant, 15:474; history, 18:326
Nef, John U., author, 25:389
Neff, George W., 13:214
Neff, Paul, 13:214
Neff, Wanda F., author, 11:459, 31:146
Negroes, see Blacks
Negus, Nathan, artist, 31:100
Neiderheiser, Clodaugh, "Wallpaper Newspapers," 33:211-213; review by, 36:235; work reviewed, 35:237; research assistant, 27:340, 28:47
Neighborhood House, St. Paul, 28:293; history, 22:348
Neihardt, John G., author, 19:437
Neil, William M., author, 35:200
Neile, Sir Paule, 16:425n
Neill, Edmund P., journalist, 24:247
Neill, Edward D., pioneer minister, 19:214, 262-264; "St. Paul and Its Environs," 30:204-219; papers, 11:42, 318, 16:332, 19:341, 20:370, 33:77-79, 299; educator, 11:329, 14:144, 145, 16:274n, 275n, 17:239, 18:219, 19:446, 27:167; career, 11:458, 15:357, 16:276, 30:202, 244, 265, 40:3-9; church founder, 12:105, 397, 18:379, 26:289; author, 13:166, 204, 20:142, 35:184, 36:72, 37:59, 38:200, 39:150; MHS activities, 15:75, 16:387, 23:5, 30:294, 297, 303, 310, 37:55; speaker, 15:131, 30:198, 38:49-51; army chaplain, 16:215, 24:27, 25:32, 235n, 30:303; missionary, 16:315, 22:58n; state seal designer, 33:127, 128; portraits, 38:50, 40:3
Neill, Mrs. Edward D., 11:315
Neill, Minnesota, 11:318, 322; author, 11:315
Neils, J., Lumber Co., 29:148
Neilson, Eleanor, author, 36:106
Neligan, J. M., author, 21:370
Nelles, Father Felix, missionary, 23:402

"Nellie Kent," stern-wheeler, 24:332, 31:85, 86, 90, 38:188
Nelligan, Francis J., author, 37:37
Nelligan, John E., author, 11:105, 13:334
Nelsen, Ancher, speaker, 30:275
Nelson, ---, wagon driver, 20:310-312
Nelson, Dr. A. C., 22:217; author, 25:407
Nelson, A. Herbert, 20:448
Nelson, A. M., 19:116
Nelson, A. W., 21:110
Nelson, Aileen, author, 12:211
Nelson, Alfred, 28:4
Nelson, Alfred H., legislator, 22:50
Nelson, Alfred L., author, 14:450, 30:157, 32:63
Nelson, Alfrey, 2:4, 6
Nelson, Arthur, 28:4
Nelson, Arthur M., 11:298, 17:121; work reviewed, 29:74; speaker, 11:294, 13:451, 14:457, 459, 15:489, 20:456, 21:445, 23:399; author, 26:394
Nelson, August, speaker, 17:483
Nelson, Benjamin N., editor, 33:312
Nelson, Bruce, 24:371, work reviewed, 28:168
Nelson, C. A. A., author, 30:128
Nelson, C. G., pioneer farmer, 13:346
Nelson, C. L., 22:217
Nelson, C. N., Lumber Co., Cloquet, 25:102
Nelson, Carl L., author, 16:357
Nelson, Charles, 28:4
Nelson, Charles, author, 19:123
Nelson, Charles, speaker, 11:458; author, 23:106
Nelson, Clara W., 24:371
Nelson, Cornelius J., 17:235
Nelson, Daniel, 17:355, 18:108
Nelson, David T., work reviewed, 38:37
Nelson, Donald M., author, 27:352
Nelson, Doris, author, 12:211
Nelson, E. Clifford, work reviewed, 37:183
Nelson, E. M., author, 19:113, 21:342
Nelson, Edwin H., author, 34:130
Nelson, Eugene, 28:4
Nelson, Frank G., author, 25:85
Nelson, George, trader, 28:1-3, 29:99; "A Winter in the St. Croix Valley," 28:3-14, 142-159, 225-240; author, 28:95, 29:355
Nelson, Gilbert, author, 16:366
Nelson, Gust T., author, 12:207
Nelson, Col. Harold S., speaker, 12:343
Nelson, Helge, work reviewed, 26:56-59
Nelson, Henry, 28:4
Nelson, Herman G., author, 26:167
Nelson, Horace, 28:4
Nelson, Isabelle, 12:263
Nelson, Lt. Col. J. E., author, 12:202; speaker, 15:219
Nelson, Jacob, pioneer, 24:320, 324
Nelson, Jake, author, 16:498, 17:130
Nelson, Johannes, pioneer, 20:360
Nelson, John, diary, 11:114
Nelson, John M., insurgent, 22:79
Nelson, John P., career, 18:211
Nelson, Gen. Joseph E., speaker, 35:340, 384
Nelson, Knute, 19:152, 20:75, 32:180, 36:103; governor, 11:319, 25:298,

35:61-63, 312, 36:116-118, 122-
124, 39:95-98, 100, 332, 40:148;
papers, 11:445, 14:437, 17:337,
20:81, 22:319, 23:273, 370, 24:61,
25:290; boyhood home, 14:448; career, 15:357, 19:213, 459, 28:73,
30:271, 35:99, 285; politician,
17:161, 28:74, 32:138, 145, 146;
photograph, 18:321, 36:119; Senator, 29:301, 34:217, 328, 36:237,
39:25, 98, 101, 104-106, 108, 205,
40:323, 324; interest in Alaska,
32:174
Nelson, Lawrence W., 29:280; author,
30:39, 174
Nelson, Lowry, works reviewed, 34:
251, 37:180; author, 24:79, 27:
176, 40:363
Nelson, Luella, 22:217
Nelson, Mabel, 12:450
Nelson, Mrs. Mamie B., artist, 26:276
Nelson, Marcus, lumberman, 33:19
Nelson, Mrs. Marcus, 33:19n
Nelson, Marion John, author, 40:357
Nelson, Markus, bank cashier, 36:201
Nelson, Martinus, Methodist mission-
ary, 36:292
Nelson, Milton O., author, 26:306
Nelson, N. L. T., speaker, 12:338
Nelson, N. P. R., speaker, 16:491
Nelson, Mrs. Naomi, postmistress, 34:
6
Nelson, Neal, author, 18:329
Nelson, Nils, 12:340
Nelson, O. J., 23:390
Nelson, Dr. O. N., speaker, 11:336
Nelson, Orvis M., author, 26:276
Nelson, Oscar, speaker, 28:388
Nelson, Paul W., 19:308
Nelson, Peter, 26:291
Nelson, Mrs. Peter A., speaker, 11:
219
Nelson, Mrs. R. F., 21:334
Nelson, Rensselaer R., 21:150; jur-
ist, 15:357, 37:55; lawyer, 39:
148n
Nelson, Richard, 23:301
Nelson, Robert, 28:4
Nelson, Roberta J., author, 34:264
Nelson, Mrs. S., pioneer, 24:203
Nelson, Samuel, postmaster, 20:361
Nelson, Socrates, 17:393; lumberman,
18:176, 38:187
Nelson, Soren, creamery operator, 11:
457
Nelson, Stanley E., 22:442, 23:399
Nelson, Theodore A. E., 18:221, 19:
114, 22:104, 23:100; author, 18:
108
Nelson, Verna E., author, 15:369
Nelson, Walter, 28:4
Nelson, Walter, speaker, 11:114
Nelson, Dr. Wolfred, 28:2, 4
Nelson family, 19:366
Nelson Act, 15:300, 24:281n
Nelson and Gunderson, Rochester, plow
manufacturers, 24:297
Nelson River, Man., 24:231; naviga-
tion, 17:26, 27, 171, 175
Nelson's Landing, see Wabasha
Nemacolin's Path, Pa., trade route,
15:256
Nemadji River, Minn., Wis., lumber
camps, 15:203; fur trade, 20:12,
13
Nerstrand, Methodist church, 14:354;

history, 21:115; Norwegian settle-
ment, 26:272; name, 30:332
Nerstrand Woods State Park, Rice
County, 20:343, 21:440, 22:103,
23:191, 24:183, 27:359, 29:263;
historical meeting, 22:290-292
Nesheim, Lars N., 13:206
Nesmith, James W., Senator, 38:56
Nesmith Cave, Minneapolis, 11:74, 32:
191
Ness, George T., Jr., author, 22:349
Ness, J. O., author, 20:214
Ness, Zenobia B., author, 21:431
Nessel Township, Chisago County, his-
tory, 36:195
Nessell, C. W., author, 37:346, 39:
131
Netherlands, emigration from, 28:120-
131, 35:90; stock exchange, 37:
152, 155, 157. See also Dutch
Netherlands Museum, Holland, Mich.,
28:120
Netherly, Winifred, author, 22:334
Netley Creek, Man., 21:266; trading
post, 11:364
Nett Lake Indian Reservation (Chip-
pewa), medicine society, 15:121;
roads, 16:296, 297, 19:103; his-
torical meeting, 17:121; agency,
23:93; smallpox epidemic, 27:351;
wild-rice harvest, 34:44
"Netta Durant," raftboat, 31:36
Nettels, Curtis, author, 15:228
Nettleton, Alvred B., 15:358, 35:67
Nettleton, Claude F., author, 36:194
Nettleton, E. M., 11:466
Nettleton, George E., 22:352; town-
site owner, 12:384, 37:114n
Nettleton, Mrs. George E., 22:352
Nettleton, William, townsite owner,
12:384, 37:114n
Neu, Irene D., work reviewed, 35:237
Neubauer, August, speaker, 17:484
Neuberger, Richard L., work reviewed,
35:41; author, 34:211
Neudecker, Rev. R. A., author, 21:453
Neumeier, Catherine, speaker, 17:314
Neumeier, Frederick C., papers, 11:42
Neumeier, Karl G., legislator, 24:
349; speaker, 22:342
Neumeier, Mrs. Karl G., 25:210
Neunaber, Rev. H. W., speaker, 13:343
Neuse, Eloise, author, 34:219
Neutson, K., 16:100; memoirs, 20:208
Nevada, settled, 28:284; surveyed,
28:348
Nevada Township, Mower County, Nor-
wegian settlement, 12:269
Neveaux, Damase, pioneer, 22:345
Nevers, John N., in Leech Lake upris-
ing, 24:144-146
Nevers, Mrs. John N., 24:145
Nevers Dam, St. Croix River, 40:357
Neville, Mrs. Arthur C., author, 15:
236
Neville, Jay, 22:405
Neville, Morgan, career, 20:202
Nevins, Allan, 18:44, 217, 20:31,
289, 26:166; review by, 14:88-90;
works reviewed, 20:176-179, 33:
266, 346, 38:379; author, 12:442,
14:327, 15:59, 124, 20:333, 23:
377, 27:335, 28:54, 95, 32:57, 34:
42, 81, 158, 164, 251, 37:185; review analyzed, 14:192-194; editor,
40:313
Nevius, Aaron C., 16:334

Nevius family, genealogy, 16:334
Nevue, Wilfrid, "A Winter in the
Woods," 34:149-153
New, J. W., speaker, 11:118
New Albin, Iowa, boundary point, 21:
328
New Amsterdam, see New York (city)
New Amsterdam, Wis., Dutch settle-
ment, 28:121, 379
New Auburn, history, 13:122, 34:129
New Boston, Ill., described, 17:426
New Brunswick, Can., fur trade, 20:
452; boundary, 23:205
New Canada, see Little Canada
New Century Club, St. Paul, records,
14:137, 16:74
New Deal, program, 23:162, 32:182,
36:187, 38:203, 39:80; evaluated,
35:89, 90; history, 38:387
New Diggings, Wis., lead-mining district, 12:157
New Duluth, St. Louis County, development, 21:116; post office,
34:186
New Duluth Land Co., 37:123
New Duluth National Bank, 37:124
New England, emigration from, 11:287,
13:284, 32:15, 109, 33:84, 34:81;
settled, 12:173; influence in Minnesota, 14:137; roads and trails,
14:340; English in, 16:402; literature, 20:109, 110, 30:192; culture, 24:48, 49, 34:82; source material, 24:112; merchants, 24:150;
folklore, 27:238; depicted, 40:62,
65, 76; county maps, 40:120. See
also Yankees
New England Boot and Shoe Shop, St.
Paul, 15:190
New England Colony and Bureau of Migration, settles Detroit, 16:432
New England Emigrant Aid Co., 17:323,
324, 24:367
New England Furniture Co., Minneapolis, 18:226
New-England Magazine, publishes Snelling's tales, 17:438
New England Mutual Life Insurance
Co., 22:213
New England Society of Minneapolis,
12:402
New England Society of the Northwest,
31:20
New England Woman Suffrage Association, 39:4, 6
New Englanders, see Yankees
New Era (Sauk Rapids), 16:234. See
also Sauk Rapids Frontierman
New France, maps, 12:348, 24:252;
forts, 13:203; described, 13:418;
wars with British, 14:370, 24:150;
fur trade, 16:410, 32:226-238;
census schedules, 16:448; history,
18:383-398, 30:56, 40:145; explored, 19:272; boundaries, 22:63;
bibliography, 40:312
New Germany, history, 18:338
New Glarus, Wis., history, 28:188
New Hampshire, emigration from, 17:
336, 18:250; Hutchinsons' home,
22:116; song, 22:116-118
New Hampshire War Records Committee,
publication, 26:389
New Harmony, Ind., utopian community,
19:459, 21:94; David Dale Owen's
home, 25:174, 26:223, 233
"New Haven," steamboat, 24:202

New Hope, cantonment, 23:213. See also Mendota

New Hope mission, Yellow Medicine County, 16:150

New Iceland, Man., history, 27:166

New Independence Township, St. Louis County, history, 23:302

New Jersey, early imprints, 12:316; war history program, 25:94; proverb collection, 27:34; atlas, 40: 122; fur industry, 40:219

New Jersey Sisters of Charity, history, 16:340

New Kent Court House, Va., in Civil War, 25:131

New London, mill, 20:359; anniversary, 21:341; newspapers, 21:444; Lutheran church, 26:95; Morman mission, 36:290

New Madrid, Mo., earthquake, 12:198, 17:474, 28:281; in Civil War, 25: 35, 36

New Munich, Catholic church, 17:479, 36:35; name, 30:332; bank, 33:54

New Nation (Winnipeg, Man.), 16:465

New North West Co., 21:138n

New Orleans, port, 11:144, 23:61; founded, 18:390; French settlement, 18:394, 395, 397; flour market, 18:409; fur market, 19:293, 40:213, 214, 220; battle, 24:53; in Civil War, 25:124, 125; army post, 28:16, 17; historic sites, 40:134

"New Orleans," steamboat, 14:150

New Orleans Minstrels, 28:111

New Prague, anniversary, 12:450, 13: 114; Catholic church, 12:451, 13: 450; flour mills, 12:451, 23:388; name, 13:199; Czech settlement, 13:270, 23:381, 28:266, 35:152, 38:243; history, 16:219, 22:224

New Prague Flouring Mill, 12:451

New Prague Foundry Co., 12:451

New Prague Times, history, 12:451, 20:462

New Richland, Norwegian settlement, 12:269; Lutheran church, 13:340; schools, 35:51

New Rome, Sibley County, German theater, 32:100, 34:242

New Salem (Ill.) State Park, outdoor museum, 27:143

New Sweden Township, Nicollet County, ethnic settlements, 12:275, 19: 220, 36:201

New Trier, history, 17:118; Catholic church, 17:117, 20:460; name, 30: 332

New Ulm, founded, 11:174n, 16:363, 18:109, 19:472, 27:268, 30:24-35, 74, 188, 31:243, 36:327; in Sioux Outbreak, 11:303, 12:335, 13:443, 15:133, 18:460, 23:75, 295, 365, 28:374, 36:240, 38:86, 97, 113, 116-118, 125, 136, 138, 144-146, 275, 279-281, 283, 285, 39:33; settled, 12:430, 16:126, 20:351, 21:202; roller mills, 12:449, 27: 78, 28:202; water system, 14:353; churches, 14:353, 451, 26:181, 30: 34, 32:172; hotel, 15:365, 25:314; hospital, 15:484; German settlement, 16:42, 18:112, 453, 19:214, 31:24, 35:294, 36:255, 38:120, 243, 40:263, 309; volunteer guard, 16:171, 176; law office, 16:458;

fire department, 16:493, 19:120; military encampment, 17:360; museum, 17:481, 20:92-95, 454; plat, 18:466; newspapers, 19:230, 27: 327, 343, 28:201, 34:130; schools, 20:356, 21:111; breweries, 20:459, 24:189, 36:200, 204; unions, 21: 381; library, 23:193, 26:88; Pfaender house, 24:259; implement trade, 24:302n; river port, 26: 181, 39:120; veterans, 26:287; monuments, 27:328, 35:294, 38:155; politics, 28:36, 323; Christmas celebrations, 28:81; history, 28: 202, 34:170; name, 30:30, 267, 332; social life, 31:46, 33:91, 35:245; German theater, 32:100, 102, 127, 168-173, 33:188, 34:239, 240, 37:227, 228; in Civil War, 33:84; log buildings, 37:72, 76; pictured, 37:226; post office, 38: 121

New Ulm Battery, 18:466, 27:269

New (Neu) Ulm Pionier, 27:327; politics, 24:23, 30; history, 33:187

New Ulm Post, founded, 27:327, 33:180

New Ulm Review, founded, 19:234

New Ulm Roller Mill Co., records, 28: 202

New Ulm Transportation Co., 26:181

New Ulm Turnverein, 18:112; history, 13:116

New Ulm Women's Literary Club, history, 27:78

New Upsala, Pine Lake, Wis., Swedish settlement, 16:479, 30:159, 32:49

New Year's, balls, 12:401, 13:148, 14:140, 16:377, 387; social calls, 12:402, 14:141, 16:385, 17:129, 31:237; excursion, 16:247, 387; frontier celebrations, 16:373-390, 20:339, 22:10, 26:169, 28:186, 30: 67, 31:37, 40:70; Indian celebrations, 16:375, 18:238, 19:380; newsboys' greetings, 16:387, 33: 164-168; traders' celebration, 23: 93; parade, 29:32; among Mennonites, 29:161

New York (city), politics, 12:192; immigrant agents, 13:40; port, 17: 89; Norwegians, 22:70; manuscript collections, 22:328; theater center, 28:103, 107; depicted, 30: 193; arts and crafts, 34:312; child welfare, 39:125; banking, 40:111, 113; fur market, 40:163, 213n, 214; draft riots, 40:271

New York (state), historic sites, 11: 32; colonial period, 11:234, 16: 402-411; history, 14:341, 17:111; first printer, 15:6; agriculture, 15:123; emigration from, 23:404, 40:10; soldier franchise, 26:188, 209; proverb collection, 27:34; cheese production, 27:121; ethnic groups, 31:14; folklore, 34:316; arts and crafts, 36:322; capitol, 40:99, 100; atlas, 40:120, 122; Indian sites, 40:204, 206-208; fur industry, 40:219

"New York," steamship, 37:15

New York Academy of Medicine, 14:446

New York Central Railroad, route, 15: 256; history, 35:354n

New York Custom House, architect's plans, 28:396

New York Evening Mirror, articles on Minnesota, 29:29, 31-35

New York Folklore Society, 31:14

New York Grain Exchange, 33:332

New-York Historical Society, New York City, 11:450, 20:436, 25:394, 26: 63; Catlin collection, 23:181; history, 34:206

New York Institution for the Deaf and Dumb, Washington Heights, 12:408

New York Lyceum Co., 28:105

New York Mills, frontier life, 11:221; ethnic groups, 14:239, 21:342, 22: 392n, 25:318, 327; lime industry, 22:346

New York Public Library, 17:96, 214; care of newspapers, 13:47; collections, 15:210, 16:112, 26:140-142; publication, 16:111, 542

New York Restaurant, Minneapolis, 18: 124, 128, 138, 143

New York State Agricultural Society, 15:123

New York State Association of County Historians, 26:168

New York State Historical Association, Cooperstown, 12:434, 26:267, 377; publications, 14:341, 17:111, 27:66, 162, 35:150; museum, 24: 363, 27:353; collections, 27:252; history, 28:187; seminars, 29:348, 30:150, 33:228

New York State Library, Albany, manuscript holdings, 22:329

New York State Normal School, Albany, 28:132

New York Times, American history survey, 25:44, 168, 294, 28:364; on freedom of press, 37:168, 170

New York Tribune, in frontier Minnesota, 16:32, 17:317, 411-420, 18: 409, 19:404, 22:336, 361, 27:11, 30:192

Newbern, Robert, 39:132

Newberry, John S., geologist, 32:215

Newberry Library, Chicago, Ayer collection, 12:425, 13:192, 408, 14: 425, 17:464, 18:438, 19:423, 22: 133, 26:140, 376; Burlington records, 24:253; fellowship, 28:393; manuscripts, 36:280

Newburg Township, Fillmore County, Norwegian settlement, 12:268; Lutheran church, 14:119; history, 23:400, 24:89, 191

Newby family, genealogy, 21:195

Newcomb, Dr. E. B., 16:334

Newcomb, Rexford, work reviewed, 32: 109; speaker, 27:66

Newcomb, Simon, astronomer, 18:352-358, 33:191, 271

Newcombe, L. C., 22:341

Newcomer, Mabel, work reviewed, 35:36

Newdahl, Axel, lawyer, 17:213

Newell, F. S., 14:270

Newell, Harriet, missionary, 28:135

Newell, L. D., 12:319, 14:100

Newell, Lyman C., author, 16:115

Newell, Martin E., author, 12:333, 25:308

Newell, Stanford, career, 15:358

Newell, Stephen, politician, 39:49

Newfolden, history, 12:452, 20:456, 38:163

Newfoundland, fisheries, 22:64; place names, 30:67; Norse settlement, 39:170, 342, 40:94

Newgren, Andrew J., 17:70, 20:51, 23:
50, 26:45, 27:46, 29:97
Newhall, Beaumont, "Minnesota Daguer-
reotypes," 34:28-33; author, 29:
164
Newhall, C. W., author, 12:209, 16:
370
Newhall, Corp. Gene, 23:393
Newhall, Maj. John B., author, 20:
203, 36:102
Newhall Hotel, Milwaukee, 24:331
Newman, Cecil, journalist, 36:36
Newman, Dr. D. B., pioneer physician,
23:31
Newman, Harry S., 28:70
Newman, Ralph, work reviewed, 29:63
Newman, W. A., speaker, 13:454
Newmarket Township, Scott County,
Norwegian settlement, 12:271
Newport, Mary M., 14:436
Newport, Reese M., 14:436
Newport, G.A.R. post, 16:430; agri-
culture, 17:465; library, 21:112;
historic sites, 21:339
Newport, R.I., stone tower, 24:257,
27:350, 28:59, 60, 29:349, 33:88,
35:141
Newsboys, New Year's greetings, 16:
387, 33:164-168
Newsome, Albert R., author, 20:197
Newson, Hattie, 15:396
Newson, Mary J., "Fort Snelling in
Civil War Days," 15:395-404; author, 15:224; speaker, 15:311, 16:
122
Newson, Nellie, 15:396
Newson, Thomas M., publisher, 13:100;
author, 14:86; journalist, 14:406,
495, 21:375, 376, 23:307, 34:140,
35:363, 38:187; in Civil War, 15:
311, 395-404; portrait, 15:396
Newson, Mrs. Thomas M., 15:396
Newspapers, Twin Cities, 11:41, 22:6,
25:211, 28:197, 29:31n, 34:50n,
140n; ethnic, 11:206, 12:260, 14:
401, 15:473, 16:338, 18:71, 22:
399, 424, 23:373, 25:326, 27:327,
343, 28:21-24, 26, 31, 201, 33:
180, 187, 188, 34:43, 130, 35:328,
37:87, 38:91; Wisconsin, 11:326,
12:439, 36:67; historical value,
11:441, 12:391-403, 441, 13:45-50,
72, 14:408, 17:92, 314, 385-390,
23:22, 179, 24:272, 25:409, 26:74,
376; Minnesota communities, 12:
108, 456, 14:360, 17:123, 19:118,
467, 20:94, 299, 21:106, 214, 332,
24:326, 27:270, 28:265, 30:271,
34:44, 35:382; Iowa, 12:199, 16:
479, 17:427n; weekly, 12:434, 13:
211, 442, 14:74, 102; Minnesota
bibliography, 13:58, 14:63, 15:
340, 16:54, 55, 65, 17:56, 29:51,
30:325; preservation, 13:73, 17:
91, 21:312, 30:295; frontier, 14:
139, 173-191, 393-415, 15:1, 16-
25, 86-89, 16:332, 18:99, 450, 24:
309, 27:1-20, 345, 28:342n, 40:
302; Dakotas, 14:205, 15:200-202,
475, 35:383; in westward movement,
15:1-25; union list, 15:120, 341,
16:55, 65, 331, 17:56, 18:322; Red
River, 16:230; newsboys, 16:387,
33:164-168; indexes, 17:93, 362,
20:39, 21:214, 22:442, 27:349; St.
Croix Valley, 17:385-390, 29:100;
influence, 17:427; Philippines,

18:99; editors' association, 18:
451; socialist, 19:346; Republican, 20:270; labor unions, 21:375,
385; early press, 21:441; northern
Minnesota, 21:451, 29:356; in Civil War, 22:86, 422, 25:129, 130,
144, 147, 149-151, 232, 234, 239,
248-250, 253, 256; army periodicals, 22:194, 23:292, 393, 24:83,
184, 25:33; microfilmed, 23:368,
26:271, 29:50, 30:42, 89; in slavery controversy, 24:310, 32:16-33;
Catholic, 27:169; Ontario, 28:179;
publishers' association, 31:119;
Ohio, 31:186; on wallpaper, 33:
211-213; history, 34:83; relation
to folklore, 36:101; dailies, 36:
103; Farmer-Labor, 38:304-308.
See also Journalism, individual
newspapers
Newton, A. Edward, 27:41
Newton, E., 16:318n, 20:225n
Newton, Earle W., 30:368; review by,
31:47; author, 28:135n, 30:258,
31:64; editor, 30:386
Newton, Isaac, 40:335, 336
Newton, O. W., author, 17:240
Newton, Stan, author, 28:177
Newton, Walter H., 12:96, 17:160n
Newton, William H., townsite pro-
moter, 21:150; house, 21:152; at
Superior, Wis., 21:153
Newton, Mrs. William H., 21:150; por-
trait, 21:156
Newton Township, Otter Tail County,
frontier life, 11:221
Nez Percés Indians, 32:249; warfare,
12:420, 16:89; mission, 29:59;
history, 34:346, 40:93; in fur
trade, 40:156
"Niagara," steamboat, 28:310, 35:355
Niagara Cave, Harmony, described, 24:
265
Niagara Falls, 13:395; described, 16:
36; customs station, 40:180
Nicaragua, earthquake, 17:2
Nichol, John P., author, 21:371
Nicholas of Lynne, friar, 35:294, 38:
383
Nichols, ---, automobile designer,
26:21
Nichols, Austin R., 21:349
Nichols, Browning, county commis-
sioner, 37:207
Nichols, Charles L., postmaster, 37:
327
Nichols, Charles W., 19:341; "Henry
Martyn Nichols," 19:129-147, 247-
270; "The Northampton Colony," 20:
140-145; "New Light on the Northampton Colony," 22:169-173; author, 19:207, 337, 20:186, 22:187,
29:163; speaker, 20:190
Nichols, Frances S., compiler, 34:216
Nichols, Frederick D., author, 35:150
Nichols, George, 16:215
Nichols, Harriet S., missionary, 19:
132
Nichols, Henry, 19:267
Nichols, Rev. Henry M., in New England, 19:129-133; marriage, 19:
130; abolitionist, 19:131, 132,
260, 32:16; Northampton colonizer,
19:132-141, 20:140-143, 22:169-
171, 173, 31:20; maple-sugar maker, 19:135-137; farmer, 19:141-
143, 145; home missionary, 19:141-

147; in Stillwater, 19:145-147,
247-262, 35:362, 363; temperance
lecturer, 19:146, 265; in Minneapolis, 19:262-270; death, 19:267;
tributes, 19:269; papers, 19:341,
20:33, 327, 28:336; house, 38:344
Nichols, Mrs. Henry M. (Nancy Sikes),
19:251; marriage, 19:130; letters,
19:139, 142; death, 19:267
Nichols, Capt. J. A., 12:333
Nichols, Jeannette P., works re-
viewed, 23:256, 24:50-52, 25:170;
author, 23:83
Nichols, L. Nelson, author, 12:98
Nichols, Marcus P., papers, 11:444
Nichols, Phebe J., author, 12:435
Nichols, Roger H., work reviewed, 39:
338
Nichols, Roy F., works reviewed, 23:
256, 24:50-52, 25:170; author, 13:
433, 19:347, 34:168, 39:34
Nichols, Samuel N., biography, 19:214
Nichols, Thomas, 12:54n
Nichols, William H., 16:9
Nichols, Aitkin County, name, 21:349
Nichols and Chisholm Lumber Co., 27:
302
Nicholls, Henry, lecturer, 11:157
Nicholsen, Mrs. J. N. (Annie M.), au-
thor, 13:452, 14:218
Nickells, Dorothy J., author, 13:429
Nickerson, Clifford, papers, 15:464
Nickerson, John Q. A., lumberman, 16:
73; papers, 15:463, 16:52, 71, 72
Nickerson, William B., 29:162
Nickerson, Dr. Winfield S., 24:347
Nickey family, in Todd County, 22:89
Nicklin, Myrtle A., author, 13:336
Nicolay, Helen, author, 30:387
Nicolay, John G., treaty commissioner, 15:285; author, 28:361,
30:387, 39:259, 40:313
Nicolet, Jean, explorer, 12:283, 348,
13:253, 439, 15:159, 358, 17:114,
299n, 342, 18:233, 387, 19:198,
272, 23:355, 25:273, 27:216-220,
32:238; tercentennial, 15:236,
474, 16:113
Nicoli, Julius, saloonkeeper, 36:197,
199
Nicollet, Joseph N., 15:383, 21:99;
diaries, 11:87, 23:170; explorer,
11:381, 444, 12:239, 13:173, 14:
220, 15:82, 110, 16:453, 478, 19:
192, 475, 30:209, 35:204, 36:235,
37:62; papers, 12:83, 15:61, 18:
314, 23:40, 25:76, 34:338; author,
12:218, 17:306, 307, 33:132; career, 15:358, 27:350; centennial,
17:224, 348; map maker, 27:69, 33:
186, 36:277, 39:212, 314; at Pipestone, 31:196, 200, 202, 207, 40:
96
Nicollet Avenue, Minneapolis, 16:385;
name, 20:65, 27:366
Nicollet County, ethnic settlements,
12:265, 275, 14:356, 17:399, 22:
335, 28:31, 36:201, 40:412; pioneer life, 13:119; courthouse, 14:
161; ghost towns, 17:238; county
agent, 19:113; archives, 20:89;
early printing, 21:223; 4-H club
work, 21:342; fair, 23:75; election, 28:32; grasshopper bounty,
36:57; log houses, 37:73, 76; in
Civil War, 38:259; in Sioux Outbreak, 38:283; poor farm, 38:369n

Nicollet County Farm Bureau Association, 21:342
Nicollet County Historical Society, 12:37, 16:241, 17:122, 20:456, 22: 188, 290, 23:36; organized, 11:14, 464, 12:36; museum, 11:16, 12:103, 19:231, 21:217, 337, 25:98, 209, 404, 405, 26:77, 90, 27:76, 28:87, 29:276; activities, 11:18, 53, 221, 12:340, 15:80, 16:301; members, 11:19; finances, 11:20, 25: 407; meetings, 12:452, 15:250, 490, 16:491, 19:117, 470, 26:179, 27:342, 362, 30:81; building fund, 20:353; collections, 22:107
Nicollet County War History Committee, 24:268
Nicollet Hotel, Minneapolis, 25:315, 35:73
Nicollet House, Minneapolis, 19:84, 407, 33:175, 34:99n, 35:73
Nicollet Island, proposed capital site, 14:160; flora, 16:38; dam, 24:130; bridges, 27:79, 29:32n, 35:101 (cover), 205 (cover); sawmills, 27:288n; ferry, 28:286; caves, 28:291; depicted, 30:218, 33:338, 34:29, 33; park plan, 33: 336; settled, 35:103, 104, 106, 39:316; access, 39:317
Nicolls, Col. Richard, British commissioner, 16:395; association with Radisson, 16:400-411
Nicols, John, papers, 19:449, 20:33
Nicols, Mrs. John V., 38:77n, 78, 79
Nicols and Berkey, St. Paul, wholesale firm, 34:355
Nicols and Dean, St. Paul, wholesale hardware firm, 24:355
Nicols, Dean and Gregg, St. Paul, wholesale firm, 34:355
Niebler, John, 35:268
Niebuhr, Reinhold, quoted, 40:365, 366
Nielsdatter, Gro, 19:97
Nielsen, C. M., Mormon missionary, 36:290-293
Nielsen, Etlar L., author, 23:99
Nielsen, "Little Ole," 19:97
Nielsen, Ole, Sr., 18:316, 19:97
Niemela, John, author, 28:82
Niemeyer, Mrs. James C., 39:56
Niemi, Matti, Finnish pioneer, 25:318
Nietz, John A., author, 37:344
Nigger Coulee, Hudson, Wis., name, 21:430
Nightingale, Mrs. J. A., 29:363, 30: 81; author, 30:408
"Nightingale," battleship, 27:57
Nikander, J. K., pioneer pastor, 25: 324
Nikander, V. K., college president, 27:162
Nikiforoff, C. C., author, 21:212
Niles, Hezekiah, publisher, 29:62
Niles, Nathaniel, composer, 22:130
Niles, O. J., author, 26:288
Niles, Sanford, 18:105; geographer, 24:233
Niles Weekly Register, evaluated, 22: 429; history, 29:62
Nilsen, Laila, author, 15:114
Nilsen, Nils, 12:264
Nilsen, Rev. Ole, papers, 16:471, 17: 212, 18:47
Nilson, N. A., pioneer merchant, 28: 384

Nilsson, Alex, author, 18:73
Nilsson, Christine, 16:238
Nilsson, Fredrik O., in St. Croix Valley, 17:398, 402
Nilsson, Isak, Swedish immigrant, 20: 258
Nilsson, Svein, 22:68
"Nimrod," steamboat, 13:233, 234
Nine Mile Creek, Lake County, island, 34:182
Nineteenth Century Club, Minneapolis, records, 17:339
Nininger, Alexander R., scrapbooks, 25:183
Nininger, Lt. Alexander R., Jr., World War II hero, 25:394, 26:158
Nininger, John, 32:240, 241n, 242, 34:97; townsite promoter, 13:128, 129, 134, 17:264, 266, 22:99, 38: 229
Nininger, Mrs. John, 34:97
Nininger family, in Minnesota, 25:292
Nininger, Dakota County, townsite, 11:454, 32:239, 241n; history, 13: 69, 127-151, 17:263-275; churches, 13:148; founded, 14:135, 20:80, 22:99, 25:275, 33:48, 39:132; newspaper, 14:403, 17:272, 29:84; fair, 15:246; boom town, 16:481, 39:240; baseball club, 19:162; citizens' petition, 26:190
Nininger and St. Peter Railroad, see Nininger, St. Peter and Western Railroad
Nininger Reading Room Society, 13:147
Nininger, St. Peter and Western Railroad, 13:141, 143, 150, 17:270, 274, 275
Ninth Federal Reserve District, 25: 279, 280
Ninth Minnesota Volunteer Infantry, in Sioux Outbreak, 12:302, 18:210, 38:280, 281; in Civil War, 13:427, 26:197n, 205, 27:153, 38:43, 245 (cover), 287, 39:183-190; homecoming, 38:289, 291, 292
Niobrara River, Neb., post, 34:327; Sioux reservation, 39:261
Nipigon, Ont., trading post, 11:233, 258, 35:140; fishing, 30:387
Nipigon River, Ont., road, 16:299
Nipissing Indians, 13:400
Nisbet, Ralph, poet, 26:302
Nisbeth, Hugo, author, 11:106, 18:73, 31:221; traveler, 16:383n, 388
Nix, Else M., editor, 12:334
Nix, Capt. Jacob, author, 30:394, 38: 81
Nix, Richard, actor, 32:172
Nix, Robert, poet, 12:334
Nixon, Anna M., "An Elementary School Project," 26:47-51; author, 26:65
Nixon, J. H., author, 18:339, 469
Nixon, John, report, 28:170
No, Yong-Park, author, 29:154
No Mans Land, Mass., Atlantic island, runic inscription, 25:193
Noah, Jacob J., career, 35:49
Noble, David W., reviews by, 33:136, 348, 39:76, 40:303; works reviewed, 36:97, 37:83, 39:335; speaker, 40:303
Noble, Frederick A., biography, 15: 358
Noble, Mrs. Frederick A., 38:75, 76n
Noble, Mrs. Lydia, murdered, 38:123, 124

Noble Order of the Knights of Labor, see Knights of Labor
Noble plow, 24:297
Nobles, Rev. Johnson, at Red Rock, 31:90
Nobles, William H., 28:81, 30:266, 36:4n, 38:221; expedition, 11: 169n, 13:177n, 16:215, 18:274, 35: 251-262, 38:57, 217; surveyor, 27: 344, 39:238
Nobles County, marker, 11:335; records, 13:311, 21:207; ethnic settlements, 13:419, 28:121, 129, 35: 90; established, 14:244; county seat, 14:250; settled, 14:252, 18: 471, 20:217; census, 14:254, 256, 258, 259; militia, 14:261; politics, 14:262; churches, 14:357; fair, 14:460, 15:491; oldest house, 15:250; history, 16:368, 20:361, 465, 36:104; pioneer life, 17:237, 26:90, 35:325; agriculture, 17:337, 20:464, 37:205, 209; schools, 18:227; library, 31:61; Catholic colony, 35:134; townships, 36:105
Nobles County Historical Society, 16: 241, 19:361, 22:217, 23:399; organized, 14:459, 15:71; activities, 16:66; essay contest, 16: 243, 361; meetings, 16:491, 17: 483, 18:465, 20:456, 21:446, 22: 441, 24:380, 25:408, 26:394, 29: 363; members, 18:110; collections, 19:117, 28:195; museum, 19:231, 25:209, 26:90; pageant, 19:470; exhibits, 21:217, 337; publications, 25:97, 26:179, 27:76, 173, 362, 28:87, 296, 29:92; centennial plans, 30:278
Nobles County War History Committee, 23:391
Nobles Pass, Calif., discovered, 11: 169n, 35:251
Noecker, Mary F., author, 35:154
Noel, Milton P., 12:456, 14:435
Noetzel, Gregor, artist, 11:190
Nohl, Lessing H., Jr., essay reviewed, 38:238
Nohman, Clarence, 22:292
Nokasippi River, name, 21:348
Nokay, Chippewa leader, 21:348
Nokay Lake, Crow Wing County, name, 21:348
Nokes, ---, traveler, 28:317
Nolan, W. I., legislator, 33:159
Nolin, Angelique, teacher, 40:313
Nolin, Augustin, trader, 22:288
Nolin, Louis, 21:399
Noll, Victor H., author, 12:419
Nollen, John S., author, 33:356
Nolte, Julius M., 25:305, 28:300, 388, 29:54, 30:37, 38, 287, 329; "The Territorial Centennial," 29: 36-45; review by, 29:159; speaker, 28:390, 393, 29:97, 185, 372, 30: 83, 166, 170, 285, 364, 398; author, 29:103, 192, 280, 30:75, 85, 34:355
"Nominee," steamboat, 11:123, 130, 226, 12:159, 393, 13:234, 14:379, 17:278, 20:131, 132, 134, 137, 21: 96, 27:187, 28:314, 317, 318, 321, 29:203, 212, 30:198, 31:149, 34: 31, 37:311, 40:4; excursions, 11: 126, 127; pictured, 13:235, 34:33
Nonnweiler, Mary, author, 30:270

Nonpareil Mill, Chatfield, 24:100-102
Nonpartisan Leader (Fargo, N.D.; St. Paul), established, 19:108
Nonpartisan League, 18:323, 21:91, 22:335, 23:363; Minnesota, 11:435, 17:164, 21:94, 32:247, 35:53, 63, 36:151, 38:178, 39:299, 40:147, 362; in World War I, 12:193, 14: 319; 1918 campaign, 13:188; organized, 15:338, 20:65, 23:284; records, 16:52, 100, 218; newspapers, 16:219, 17:52, 19:108; activities, 16:341, 35:155, 334, 368; development, 16:482, 18:459; significance, 21:93; North Dakota, 26:171, 27:259, 32:182, 35:247, 37:39, 38:178, 331, 40:360; South Dakota, 27:356, 36:88; effect of depression, 28:43; history, 28:72, 74, 30:66, 31:124, 32:182, 34:221-232, 347, 36:101, 38:301-309, 39:79; Canada, 29:342. See also Agrarian movement, Farmer-Labor party
"Nonsuch," ketch, 16:399, 419-422, 18:82
Noonan, P. H., 13:279
Nootka Indians, songs, 34:161
Noquet Indians, 27:216, 218, 219
Norbeck, Edward, editor, 39:262
Norbeck, Peter, governor of South Dakota, 27:356; biography, 30:60
Norberg, Carl, review by, 40:353
Norby, Charles H., compiler, 16:220; author, 22:326
Norcross beach, Lake Agassiz, geology, 38:158
Norcutt, Mrs. B., 15:190
Nord Lake, Aitkin County, name, 21: 350
Nordberg, E. U., Swedish pioneer, 17: 401, 402
Nordberg, Ruth, author, 19:345
Nordbye, Judge Gunnar H., 35:51, 204, 248, 340, 36:218, 219n, 227; speaker, 26:392
Nordecht Publishing Co., New Ulm, records, 28:202
Norden Theater, see Pence Opera House
Nordica, Lillian, singer, 16:238, 39: 55
Nordin, Elsa R., 18:213; cataloger, 26:39; translator, 32:106-108; author, 32:128
Nordin, Gustaf A., author, 25:309
Nordin, Vilhälm, author, 18:70
Nordine, Marian, speaker, 18:111
Nordisk Folkeblad (Rochester, Minneapolis), 12:280
Nordland Township, Aitkin County, name, 21:350
Nordlie, Herman C., 13:286, 16:240, 242, 17:231; speaker, 13:285; author, 23:95
Nordlin, George, legislator, 38:376n, 39:26
Nordquist, Frank A., speaker, 20:95
Nordre Immanuel Church, Pelican Rapids, 12:340
Nordrum, G. H., Rothsay pioneer, 11: 226
Nordstern (St. Cloud), German paper, 12:342
Nordstrom, O. L., author, 17:329
Nordström-Bonnier, Tora, "In Fredrika Bremer's Footsteps," 32:106-108
Nordyke, Lura B., compiler, 14:110

Norelius, Rev. Eric, 14:47, 28:76; journalist, 11:454, 25:203, 34:43; characterized, 13:307, 309; author, 13:308, 32:53, 38:92; religious leader, 14:452, 22:222, 24:190, 373, 30:263; centenary, 15:123; biographies, 15:358, 34: 167; journals, 16:207, 40:353; in St. Croix Valley, 17:396-398; educator, 18:329, 33:309
Norelius, Theodore A., 23:398; author, 33:315, 35:337, 36:240
Norfolk, Va., in Civil War, 25:130
Norlie, Olaf M., author, 22:68, 24: 74, 90; biography, 23:192
Norman, Dr. J. F., author, 35:381
Norman, Rev. O. A., speaker, 12:105
Norman County, Farmers' Alliance, 12:430; railroad, 14:357, 28:383; agriculture, 15:491, 21:212, 29: 14; pageants, 16:237, 30:408; fairs, 16:251; mail service, 23: 109; dairying, 24:273; buffalo, 30:126; history, 36:107; bonanza farm, 37:267
Norman County Historical Society, organized, 30:81; meeting, 30:167
Norman County Index (Ada), history, 11:335
Normania Township, Yellow Medicine County, Norwegian settlement, 12: 275n
"Noronic," steamboat, 34:39
Norquist, Carla, author, 39:344
Norquist, John, 13:345; miller, 31: 161
Norris, Frank, author, 14:201, 16:106
Norris, George W., Senator, 14:218, 37:39, 40:147; biographies, 21:68, 39:28, 40:140; Congressman, 22:79
Norris, J. S., convention delegate, 14:245
Norris, James, frontier farmer, 23: 321
Norris, Joe L., editor, 14:448, 35: 243
Norris, Sullivan, 22:336
Norrish, Gertrude, 22:192
Norrish, John F., merchant, 21:413
Norse-American Centennial, 18:98, 26: 269
Norseland, Nicollet County, Lutheran church, 14:356; Swedish settlement, 36:201
Norsemen, see Vikings
North, Clara, 35:109
North, Emma B., see Messer, Mrs. Emma N.
North, George L., 35:109
North, John G., shipbuilder, 36:98
North, John Greenleaf, 35:111
North, John W., 11:322, 14:219, 19: 138, 475, 36:10; townsite interests, 11:274; milling interests, 11:275, 15:251; founder of Northfield, 11:337, 13:120, 22:111, 31: 182, 39:316; in politics, 13:444, 14:162, 35:285, 36:9, 37:55, 326; interest in education, 19:446; papers, 28:283; St. Anthony house, 28:317, 31:154; career, 34:359, 35:101-116; lawyer, 39:148n; biography, 39:291
North, Mrs. John W., I (Emma Bacon), 35:101
North, Mrs. John W., II (Ann H. Loomis), portrait, 11:322, 35:103;

St. Anthony house, 20:133, 39:316; letters, 28:283, 35:101n, 102, 104, 105, 110, 112; piano teacher, 39:317
North, Sterling, author, 23:117, 157
North (Minneapolis), Henrik Ibsen interview, 13:315
"North American," steamboat, 34:14
North American Fur Co., post, 35:320
North American Fur Trade Conference, 40:149
North American Gymnastic Union, 13: 116
North American Telegraph Co., 35:67
North Baptist Church, Isanti, 16:355
North Branch, railroad station, 24: 372, 34:181; founded, 30:271
North Branch Mill, Chatfield, 24:108
North Carolina, politics, 12:8, 9; first printing, 15:7; history, 15: 476; lands, 17:452, 18:435; in fiction, 23:114; folk music, 27: 188
North Carolina Department of Archives and History, 34:132
North Carolina Folk Lore Society, 20: 112
North Carolina Historical Commission, 17:90
North Carolina Historical Review, history, 34:311
North Central Airlines, 33:240
North Central School of Agriculture (North Central School and Experiment Station), Grand Rapids, 15: 487, 22:446, 27:358
North Dakota, historic sites, 11:32, 40:316; railroads, 11:320; ethnic settlements, 11:321, 19:200, 34: 265; handbook, 11:453; map, 13: 112; pioneer printing, 13:335; population changes, 13:435, 23: 287; capital fight, 14:113; authors, 14:114, 36:102, 37:306; first senator, 16:115; medicine, 17:220; climate, 17:253; frontier life, 18:113, 19:79, 29:354; newspapers, 19:108; anniversaries, 20: 444, 21:99; immigration promoted, 22:93, 35:248; state parks, 22: 207; history, 23:382, 35:331, 36: 279, 40:257; explored, 24:60; bonanza farming, 25:300, 39:206; political movements, 26:171, 27:259, 34:221, 222, 348, 35:247, 40:360; capitol building, 26:173; place names, 28:80, 36:325, 37:40, 38: 385; boundaries, 29:85; co-operatives, 29:158, 267; emigration from, 31:158, 160; mineral resources, 34:265; Indians, 35:339, 380, 40:47; isolationism, 35:383, 38:331, 387; in Civil War, 37:255; archaeology, 38:158, 161, 39:212; agrarian movement, 38:178; frontier, 38:201; geography, 39:83; Jewish colonies, 40:46; fur trade, 40:145. See also Dakota Territory
North Dakota Agricultural Experiment Station, Fargo, 19:26
North Dakota Farmers' Elevator Association, 21:69
North Dakota Grimm Alfalfa Seed Producers' Association, 19:30
North Dakota Historical Society, see

State Historical Society of North
Dakota
North Dakota State Medical Associa-
tion, history, 12:204
North Dakota State Outdoor Recre-
ational Agency, 40:316
North Dakota State University of
Agriculture and Applied Science
(North Dakota Agricultural Col-
lege), Fargo, 38:385
North Dakota University, see Univer-
sity of North Dakota
North East Neighborhood House, Min-
neapolis, 21:450
North Fork, Stearns County, Norwe-
gian settlement, 24:94
North Hero Township, Redwood County,
in fiction, 38:43
North High School, Minneapolis, ath-
letics, 39:20
North Hudson, Wis., history, 34:129
North McGregor, Iowa, bridge, 23:286
North Methodist Church, Minneapolis,
anniversary, 16:120
North Oaks, Ramsey County, history,
40:231n
North Prairie, Fillmore County, Norwegian settlement, 18:114
North Redwood, history, 13:453, 35:
44; mail order business, 21:103,
24:373
North St. Paul, boom town, 16:364;
Presbyterian church, 20:433
North St. Paul Courier, 12:195
North Salem, N.Y., history, 27:162
North Shore, Lake Superior, place
names, 12:287; land sales, 12:384;
roads, 16:298, 25:91; history, 17:
123, 18:216, 24:354, 35:49; explored, 22:319; depicted, 22:341,
33:257, 259, 34:133 (cover); fishing, 24:79, 26:174, 27:262, 33:
256, 39:303; historical societies,
24:377, 34:314; watershed, 25:309;
in verse, 25:371; mail service,
26:83; summer resort, 27:72; logging, 27:302; wildlife, 30:128;
geology, 32:216; shipwrecks, 35:
278-281, 292, 36:192, 282; MHS
tour, 37:88; lintonite discovered,
38:21-23
North Shore Advocate (Buchanan, St.
Louis County), 14:403
North Shore Historical Assembly, 23:
99; meetings, 11:15, 460, 12:281,
13:442, 14:346, 455, 15:70, 492,
16:488, 17:482, 18:462, 19:308-
310, 20:430, 454, 22:442, 23:201n,
396, 24:32, 85, 377, 25:95, 405,
28:335, 34:314
"North Star," steamboat, 14:151, 18:
270, 21:248, 24:139, 33:9, 35:264
North Star (Hudson, Wis.), 34:129
North Star (St. Paul), campaign
sheet, 23:372
North Star baseball club, St. Paul,
19:162-170, 173, 175, 176, 181
North Star Boot and Shoe Co., Minneapolis, fire, 35:69
North Star College, Warren, 12:452;
history, 38:382
North Star Creamery, McIntosh, history, 14:358
North Star Grange, 19:49, 24:120n;
history, 15:61, 113, 18:410, 19:
98, 30:254
North Star plow, 24:297

North Star Stoneware Co., see Red
Wing Potteries
North Star Woolen Mills, Minneapolis,
23:225
"North West," steamboat, 17:378
North West Co., 18:183; in fiction,
11:102, 32:122; name, 11:240n;
partners, 11:260-265, 21:137, 138,
22:3, 23:255, 28:12, 34:352;
posts, 11:354-372, 374, 19:305,
24:75, 230, 28:154, 229, 29:166,
40:163; relations with Hudson's
Bay Co., 11:425, 426, 12:92, 14:
98, 338, 15:120, 16:201, 17:75,
20:70, 21:399, 22:178, 275, 23:
186, 256, 28:281, 35:141, 243, 36:
63, 241, 40:144, 164, 166-177,
183, 184; records, 11:451, 16:201,
19:445, 20:38, 117, 326, 24:78,
27:55, 34:344; China trade, 12:91;
monopoly, 12:295, 21:119; employees, 12:372, 15:424, 16:223,
17:476, 21:143-145, 147n, 148, 22:
271, 28:144, 233, 31:1, 56, 35:
143, 36:242, 243, 37:185, 38:26,
328, 40:162; boat builders, 15:92,
16:340; history, 14:220, 16:200-
202, 36:64, 40:157-165; communi-
cation system, 16:23; relations
with XY Co., 16:200, 19:300, 21:
118, 24:77, 28:1, 2, 40:170, 171,
178-181; founded, 19:299, 300n,
28:5n, 33:130; relations with
Indians, 19:302, 28:149; trade
goods, 22:204, 35:151, 196; characterized, 40:166, 169, 179; relations with American Fur Co., 40:
180, 182. See also Fur trade;
Selkirk, Thomas Douglas, Earl of;
individual posts
North West Emigration Society, Huron,
Ont., 32:126
North West Fur Co., see Northwestern
Fur Co.
North West Territory, Canada, 35:34,
148, 283
North Western Druggist, history, 24:
175
North Western Gazette & Galena Ad-
vertiser, 24:14
North Western Line, organized, 39:298
North Western Manufacturing and Car
Co., 37:144
North Western Packet Co., 38:295; or-
ganized, 39:298
North Wisconsin Railroad, built, 34:
69
Northampton Colony, settlers, 11:171,
19:141; planned, 19:132-138, 210,
341; Chanhassen settlement, 20:
140-145, 329, 22:169-173
Northampton (Mass.) Courier, 22:169
Northeast Experiment Station, Du-
luth, 19:356, 508
Northeastern land district, Minneso-
ta, 12:381, 382, 386
"Northern," steamboat, 38:358, 359
"Northern Belle," steamboat, 15:419,
420, 20:377, 27:183, 186, 38:291
Northern Boom Co., 24:136
Northern Coal and Dock Co., advertising, 38:308
Northern Herald (Little Falls), 13:
322, 27:2
"Northern Light," steamboat, 15:419,
38:289, 292

Northern Light Lake, Ont., portages,
38:25
Northern Line Packet Co., 29:2, 38:
358
Northern Lumber Co., Cloquet, 27:302
Northern Minnesota Development Association, 19:98
Northern Minnesota Sheep Growers
Association, 19:98
Northern National Bank of Duluth, 13:
78
Northern Navigation Co., boats described, 30:272
Northern Pacific Railroad, expansion,
12:73, 341, 435, 14:200, 37:93,
118; routes, 12:276, 278, 30:233,
33:62, 37:38; completed, 13:332,
15:224, 24:373; constructed, 14:
446, 16:106, 360, 17:100, 25:277,
26:371, 28:70, 223, 34:263; used
by hunters, 16:268, 269; Stampede
Tunnel, Wash., 17:102; routes, 19:
450, 29:306, 313, 30:233; trips,
20:193, 29:87, 33:61-71, 36:66;
freight rates, 29:17; history, 30:
70, 31:120, 34:214; in fiction,
31:132. See also Pacific railroad
surveys, St. Paul and Pacific
Railroad
Northern Pacific Railway Co., promotes settlement, 12:73, 254, 277,
13:27, 30-43, 18:324, 22:93, 23:
371, 31:227, 228, 33:29-34, 49,
55, 56, 61, 35:33, 205, 36:68, 37:
184; first president, 16:115; archives, 18:76, 23:94, 31:223n, 35:
152; financing, 18:78, 315, 19:
404, 28:395, 37:120, 39:31; control, 22:202, 34:216; anniversary,
26:387; publication, 33:29-34;
lands, 36:179, 37:96, 100, 39:206,
211; merger, 39:233
Northern Pacific Refrigerator Car
Co., St. Paul, 27:357
Northern Pine Manufacturers' Association, 12:193, 22:437
Northern Power Co., Minnetonka, 35:
337. See also Northern States
Power Co.
Northern Securities Co., 12:17, 35:
39, 39:94, 110, 333, 334
Northern States Cooperative League,
20:434, 21:36, 30:66
Northern States Power Co., Minnesota
division, 15:41; history, 20:92,
35:98, 380, 36:99; Minnetonka, 35:
337; projected plant, 37:86, 136,
282; dam, 40:240, 357
Northern Steamship Co., 22:202
Northern Tribune (Brainerd), 15:366
Northfield, bank robbery, 11:85, 117,
12:176, 335, 14:461, 15:224, 16:
116, 253, 371, 20:355, 23:381, 29:
93, 31:62, 34:125, 35:97, 202, 36:
73, 39:262, 40:362; mills, 11:274,
275, 280, 36:281; history, 11:337,
14:462, 15:251, 16:498, 22:111,
28:284, 30:408, 31:182, 33:228,
34:359, 35:111-116; pageant, 11:
338; churches, 12:341, 13:120,
121, 311, 312, 24:72; name, 13:
120, 30:332; frontier life, 13:
444, 19:114, 24:92; museum, 16:
131, 252; Indian mounds, 16:307-
312, 18:472; G.A.R. post, 16:431;
lyceum, 17:240, 466, 18:47; old
settlers' association, 17:484;

baseball club, 19:169, 170, 176, 177, 179; library association, 22: 359; school, 26:166; dairying, 27: 242; hotels, 27:363; Norwegian settlement, 28:286; in fiction, 39:267

Northfield, Tex., founded, 13:120

Northfield Association, 16:253

Northfield, Kasota and Western Railway Co., 11:206

Northfield News, 14:461; historical articles, 13:51; anniversary, 16: 497

Northfield Township, Rice County, Norwegian settlement, 12:271

Northland, St. Louis County, ghost town, 19:464

Northland Greyhound Lines, Inc., see Greyhound Bus Lines

Northman, Father Ulric, 33:55

Northome, history, 27:176; logging, 29:145

Northrop, Cyrus, 14:231, 22:101, 23: 185, 25:68, 26:372, 28:76, 32:4; university president, 14:452, 16: 184, 18:150, 151, 19:71, 32:176, 36:318; career, 15:358, 28:66, 31: 52; letters, 17:100, 19:96, 451, 20:82; author, 26:300; editor, 34: 134n; characterized, 36:186

Northrop School, Rochester, museum, 24:188

Northrup, George, scout, 33:190, 39: 83; papers, 15:61, 111, 350, 16: 349; career, 15:370, 19:377-393, 28:337, 33:193, 269-281; characterized, 18:357; handcart trip, 25:309

Northrup, Jesse E., seed merchant, 27:79

Northrup, King and Co., Minneapolis, history, 27:78

Northup, Anson, 15:344, 16:225, 19: 390, 29:74, 34:357, 35:154, 37: 115n; steamboat operations, 13: 241, 14:154, 21:234, 248, 30:70, 33:9, 35:250; lumberman, 24:200; solicits enlistments, 25:14

Northup, Mrs. Anson, 24:203

Northup, E. W., editor, 26:294

Northup, George, death, 37:115n

Northwest Airlines, 27:168; Pembina airport, 12:437; mail service, 19: 238; history, 25:195, 33:240-242, 38:335; army contract, 26:7, 10

Northwest Angle, 22:193, 439; boundary point, 12:443, 13:297, 18:231, 272, 279, 20:441, 23:255, 270, 24: 176, 277, 28:375, 33:315, 37:86, 183; history, 14:338, 21:328, 23: 404, 25:90, 27:270, 28:178, 37:62, 39:300; map, 15:239; located, 18: 204; felspar mine, 23:108; wildlife, 30:128, 132; stage line, 32: 242; logging, 34:1-8; homesteading, 34:5; MHS tour to, 34:267; proposed national monument, 36: 325, 37:308

Northwest Association of Ice Cream Manufacturers, 17:116

Northwest Automobile Co., Minneapolis, 38:207

Northwest Bancorporation, Minneapolis, 19:113, 25:279, 34:166, 205, 35:49

Northwest Coin Club, 28:394

Northwest Co., see North West Co.

Northwest Construction Co., 26:371

Northwest Crop Improvement Association, 14:207, 23:86

Northwest Dairymen's Association, 22: 267

Northwest Electric Construction and Supply Co., St. Paul, 36:99

Northwest Experiment Station, see Northwest School and Experiment Station

Northwest Farmers Union, history, 18: 323, 19:104

Northwest Farmstead, promotes alfalfa, 19:31, 32

Northwest Fur Co., see Northwestern Fur Co.

Northwest Good Roads Association, 22: 213

Northwest Junior Live Stock Show, South St. Paul, 19:121

Northwest Life (Minneapolis), 26:311

Northwest Magazine (St. Paul), 20:85; history, 33:29-34

North-west Mounted Police Memorial and Indian Museum, Battleford, Sask., 29:167

Northwest Ordinance, see Ordinance of 1787

Northwest Paper Co., Cloquet, Brainerd, 19:358, 22:337; history, 15: 358

Northwest Passage, sought, 11:107, 14:84, 16:453, 18:390, 19:76-78, 461, 20:337, 31:238, 32:229, 231, 34:155, 158, 159, 36:273, 37:62, 40:314; discovered, 16:418, 34:80

North-West Sanitary Fair, Chicago, 33:190

Northwest School and Experiment Station, Crookston, 37:26; pageant, 16:237, 337; anniversaries, 16: 482, 21:436; history, 17:227, 27: 80, 38:204; weather records, 18: 107

Northwest Territory, documents, 14: 336, 16:205; laws, 16:346; sesquicentennial, 16:474, 18:101, 322, 19:59, 103, 311, 314-317, 446; pageant, 19:224, 308; state boundaries, 19:351; name, 24:76; partitioned, 27:128; history, 28:55-57; railroads, 30:146; settled, 35:291

Northwest Territory Celebration Commission, 19:314, 315, 20:42, 295

Northwest Transportation Co., steamboat operators, 38:236

Northwest Underwriters, insurance agency, 24:109

Northwestern Agriculturist (Minneapolis), policies, 20:336, 39:109

Northwestern Architect (Minneapolis), 20:85

Northwestern Bell Telephone Co., 24: 108

Northwestern Chronicle (St. Paul), 17:229, 27:161

Northwestern College, Fergus Falls, history, 38:382

Northwestern College of Commerce, Mankato, 19:357

Northwestern Express, Stage, and Transportation Co., 13:112, 16:71, 34:18n

Northwestern Farmer, founded, 34:173. See also Farmer

Northwestern Farmer and Breeder, see Farmer

Northwestern Farmers Alliance, see Farmers' Alliance

Northwestern Female College, Evanston, Ill., 23:281

North-Western Freedman's Aid Commission, 11:206

Northwestern Fuel Co., St. Paul, 38: 308

Northwestern Fur Co., 34:325-329, 39: 255

Northwestern Gazette and Galena (Ill.) Advertiser, 22:23n

Northwestern Guaranty Loan Co., Minneapolis, 39:116, 118

Northwestern Hospital, Minneapolis, 38:22; organized, 18:263

Northwestern Interscholastic Association, 39:20

Northwestern Lancet, history, 21:209, 22:435. See also Journal-Lancet

Northwestern land district, 12:382

Northwestern Lumber Co., Eau Claire, Wis., 12:319, 13:101

Northwestern Lumbermens Association, history, 22:437

Northwestern Medical and Surgical Journal, founded, 21:209, 22:435, 26:173, 35:221

Northwesten Mill, Minneapolis, 12:333

Northwestern Miller, 20:82, 85, 26: 311

Northwestern Minnesota Educational Association, 17:100

Northwestern Minnesota Historical Association, 13:191, 289, 15:114, 126, 241, 359, 16:358, 18:333; publication, 13:290; pageant, 14: 347; essay contest, 14:450

Northwestern Minnesota Singers' Association, 14:358, 16:251

Northwestern Monthly Magazine (St. Paul), history, 26:299

Northwestern Motor Vehicle Co., Minneapolis, 26:23

Northwestern Mutual Life Insurance Co., Milwaukee, history, 29:171, 35:336, 36:70

Northwestern National Bank, Minneapolis, 18:462, 33:54; history, 25: 279, 29:88

Northwestern National Life Insurance Co., Minneapolis, publication, 30: 174

Northwestern Passenger and Express Co., stage operators, 11:405

Northwestern Pediatric Society, 19: 112

Northwestern Publishing House, Milwaukee, 15:448

Northwestern Storage Warehouse, Minneapolis, design, 23:220

Northwestern Telegraph Co., 18:120

Northwestern Trust Co., St. Paul, 11: 439, 20:59

Northwestern Union Packet Co., St. Paul, 12:426, 39:129, 40:119

Northwestern University, Evanston, Ill., 21:415; museum, 23:370

Northwood, Wright County, post office, 40:88, 89; ghost town, 40: 334, 335

Norton, ---, baseball player, 19:174

Norton, ---, Peter Garrioch's companion, 20:122

Norton, Charles E., letters, 38:200

Norton, Clark F., author, 34:355
Norton, Daniel S., Senator, 16:454, 37:314, 39:86-88
Norton, Eunice, 15:100
Norton, Floyd J., speaker, 12:210
Norton, Frank E., biography, 19:214
Norton, H. Wilbert, author, 37:42
Norton, John, real-estate agent, 34:266
Norton, Margaret C., editor, 17:221; speaker, 18:322, 25:84, 26:74; author, 19:351
Norton, Sister Mary A., review by, 13:187; work reviewed, 11:305-307; author, 12:437, 15:455
Norton, Slunkey, chimney sweep, 33:188
Norton, W. I., legislator, 33:159
Norton family, in lumber industry, 30:242
Norton and Hempsted, Chicago, merchants, 23:321
Norton and Peel, Minneapolis, photographers, 40:365 (cover)
Norway, emigration from, 12:262, 20:247, 21:65, 23:105, 290, 400, 26:374, 27:65, 207, 30:373, 32:51, 63, 177-179; labor unions, 18:315
Norway, Ill., Norwegian settlement, 15:473
Norway House, Man., mission, 15:240, 463; history, 19:223; post, 31:105, 35:259, 36:37; described, 33:186; pictured, 40:190
Norway Lake, Kandiyohi County, Norwegian settlement, 12:276; in Sioux Outbreak, 15:488, 16:365, 38:280, 286
Norway Township, Fillmore County, Norwegian settlement, 12:268
Norwegian America Line, history, 26:252
Norwegian Baptist Conference, 21:76
Norwegian Evangelical Lutheran Church, Norseland, 14:356
Norwegian Grove, Mower County, settled, 12:269
Norwegian Hospital Society, 20:466
Norwegian Lutheran Church, Bergen, McLeod County, 14:452
Norwegian Lutheran Church, Richwood, Becker County, 14:451
Norwegian Society, Minneapolis, 39:135
Norwegian Total Abstinence Society, 20:404
Norwegian-American Historical Association, 18:57, 25:86; publications, 11:47, 12:304-306, 14:444, 16:108, 17:221, 457, 18:431-433, 19:199-201, 20:293, 21:64-68, 22:68-70, 24:258, 26:251, 29:156-158, 160, 32:52, 121, 38:241, 40:351, 357; meetings, 17:109, 18:206; history, 19:350, 21:426; grants award, 20:287; archives, 24:270; library, 26:369
Norwegian-American Historical Museum, Decorah, Iowa, 18:452
Norwegians, Wisconsin, 11:82, 13:205, 17:343, 24:177, 348, 27:135, 28:381, 29:160, 32:54, 33:85, 35:296, 37:177; immigration, 11:89, 103, 12:179-182, 304-306, 13:206, 15:234, 19:199-201, 459, 20:337, 22:40, 29:58, 31:26, 32:51, 177-179, 36:98; Dakotas, 11:212, 321, 12:

95, 19:204, 222, 32:52; Minnesota communities, 11:219, 226, 285, 12:247-280, 13:116, 340, 18:228, 465, 19:106, 366, 20:459, 21:193, 455, 22:291, 23:191, 290, 400, 24:352, 25:411, 28:278, 29:177, 289-299, 31:126, 35:203, 38:243, 39:130, 212; lags, 11:454, 14:217, 437, 17:213; Canada, 12:95, 17:110; source material, 12:199; in lumber industry, 13:284; literature, 14:444, 16:107, 18:432, 20:180, 23:119, 36:79, 39:126, 40:351, 357; Illinois, 15:473, 26:251; emigrant songs, 16:108, 17:463, 18:58, 198-201, 20:428; schools, 17:457, 25:166, 30:377, 34:91, 38:37, 40:375-383; Iowa, 18:431, 23:92; pioneer life, 18:452, 20:200, 24:79; acculturation, 21:64-68, 22:68-70, 104, 25:85; skiing, 21:422, 29:169, 36:91; Pennsylvania, 23:88; surnames, 23:381, 24:74; folklore and folk songs, 24:260, 32:126, 36:79, 194, 39:129; folk museum, 24:364; physicians, 24:374; lodges, 26:269, 36:35; in politics, 27:13, 36:237, 38:177-185; engineers, 29:156-158; in gold rush, 29:301-315; attitude toward slavery, 32:16; influence, 33:187; newspapers, 33:348; language, 33:349; fishing, 34:246; bibliography, 38:241. See also America letters, Emigrant journey, Emigrant ships, Lutheran church, Scandinavians
Nor'west Angle, Lake of the Woods County, Canadian settlement, 26:290, 28:178
Nor'wester (Fort Garry, Man.), 16:465, 18:442
Norwood, Joseph G., geologist, 19:309, 25:175, 26:225, 227, 30:267, 32:216, 37:93; survey, 26:229-232
Norwood, Percy V., author, 18:331
Norwood, history, 18:466, 28:380; Catholic churches, 15:480, 20:218
Norwood Times, history, 21:339
Notestein, Wallace, 32:7; critic, 26:307
Nothstein, I. O., editor, 28:75
Notman, William and Son, Montreal, photographers, 26:385
No-Tobacco League of America, 39:24
Nott, W. S., 38:308
Nottage, J. P., 13:117
Nottage, Mrs. Jessie, 26:392, 27:170, 361, 29:361
Nourse, Ethel, 14:331
Nourse, George A., 14:331
Nourse, W., trader, 40:167n, 168n
Nova Scotia, history, 23:254; folk music, 27:188
"Nova Scotia," emigrant ship, 20:252-254
Nova Trebon, Le Sueur County, name, 13:199
Novak, Adele, actress, 13:273
Novak, Antonín, publisher, 13:274
Novotny, Frank, gunmaker, 33:307
Nowell, James A., 22:320; biography, 23:192
Nowell, Reynolds I., work reviewed, 16:206
Noya, Haydée, author, 28:284

Noyelles, Nicolas-Joseph de, trader, 37:253
Noyes, ---, baseball player, 19:174
Noyes, Alfred, poet, 26:308
Noyes, Arthur H., in Alaska, 32:174
Noyes, Charles P., 27:22
Noyes, Dr. Helon F., 37:142
Noyes, Dr. J. L., 19:238
Noyes, Winthrop G., letters, 18:210
Noyes Brothers and Cutler, St. Paul, wholesale drug firm, 18:210, 34:113
Noyon, Jacques de, explorer, 40:145
Nugent, Father James, colonizer, 31:22, 35:206-208; school founder, 35:134-136
Nugent, John, speaker, 16:360
Nugent, Walter T. K., author, 39:83
Nunda Township, Freeborn County, Norwegian settlement, 12:269
Nunis, Doyce B., Jr., speaker, 40:149
Nunnally, Mrs. Earl G. (Helen), speaker, 15:359
Nunns, William, piano maker, 19:318
Nunns and Fischer, piano manufacturers, 19:318
Nunvar, Antonín, pioneer, 15:28
Nurmijärvi, Pine County, Finnish settlement, 25:320
Nursing, pioneer, 22:11; organized, 26:94; Ohio, 33:44; education, 37:300. See also Hospitals
Nushka Club, St. Paul, 17:215, 23:173
Nute, Grace L., 28:393, 30:171; "Posts in the Fur-Trading Area," 11:353-385; "A Western Jaunt," 12:157-168; "Frederick Jackson Turner," 13:159-161; "The Radisson Problem," 13:255-267; "A Peter Pond Map," 14:81-84; "Peter Rindisbacher," 14:283-287; "Minnesota County Archives," 15:194-199; "Fort Beauharnois," 16:323; "Radisson and Groseilliers' Contribution," 16:414-426; "John McLoughlin, Jr.," 17:444-447; "Some Early Galtier Letters," 19:190-192; "Father Hennepin's Later Years," 19:393-398; "Rindisbacher's Minnesota Water Colors," 20:54-57; "The Lindbergh Colony," 20:243-258; "A British Legal Case," 21:117-148; "The Lindbergh Bust," 21:294; "Hudson's Bay Co. Posts," 22:270-289; "A Rindisbacher Water Color," 23:154-156; "Indian Medals and Certificates," 25:265-270; "Letters of John McLoughlin," 27:37; ed., "A Winter in the St. Croix Valley," 28:1-14, 142-159, 225-240; "The Picture Rock," 29:130-136; "Marin versus La Vérendrye," 32:226-238; reviews by, 11:87-89, 305-307, 424-428, 12:306, 410, 13:179-181, 417, 14:92-94, 15:211, 335-337, 16:448-450, 17:74-76, 196-199, 204, 18:86, 193, 196, 428-430, 438, 19:76-78, 442, 20:69-73, 422-424, 21:72, 183, 398, 399, 22:76, 184, 309-311, 24:43-45, 152, 340, 344, 25:282, 371, 26:55, 363, 27:131, 134, 28:60-62, 169, 29:153, 339-341, 30:375, 31:52, 32:46, 249, 33:130, 181, 220, 261, 34:39, 80, 254, 305, 351, 35:141, 282, 377, 36:25, 150, 37:128, 38:238, 40:313; works reviewed,

13:87–92, 16:197–199, 17:448–450,
22:177–181, 24:41–43, 149–151, 25:
368–370, 31:183, 32:244–246, 36:
147; speaker, 11:58, 13:194, 288,
14:76, 328, 15:78, 219, 17:67, 18:
277, 20:190, 306, 22:49, 23:49,
25:53; author, 11:328, 12:188, 13:
64, 210, 291, 398, 14:223, 15:90,
92, 319, 327, 16:114, 238, 480,
17:225, 18:89, 218, 312, 328, 19:
102, 20:66, 74, 324, 21:82, 182,
22:83, 317, 420, 23:168, 187, 268,
367, 24:58, 262, 352, 370, 25:287,
26:35, 63, 152, 255, 273, 364, 27:
70, 129, 242, 341, 28:282, 292,
362, 29:52, 164, 167, 262, 266,
282, 30:273, 359, 31:58, 32:59,
33:88, 355, 34:132, 213, 215, 216,
360, 35:242, 245, 340, 36:102, 37:
86, 39:212, 40:359; translator,
13:85n, 28:370; fellowships, 15:
218, 16:60, 24:370, 25:380; manuscripts curator, 16:412n, 17:93,
20:38, 26:55; interview, 16:468;
editor, 17:94, 23:366, 29:99; professor, 21:44, 22:44; honorary degree, 24:162; career, 26:36, 35:
384; research associate, 27:140
Nuthead, William, pioneer printer,
15:4
Nutt, Rush, 25:76
Nuttall, Thomas, botanist, 35:241
Nutter, E. J. M., author, 11:109
Nutter, Frank H., author, 15:349
Nutting, Elijah G., 22:218
Nutting, Mrs. F. B., speaker, 18:343
Nutting, Rev. Freeman, 19:129, 133,
136–138, 20:140, 22:170, 171;
founds Northampton Colony, 19:135,
22:169, 31:20; death, 20:141n
Nutting, Levi, 19:135, 20:140, 141,
22:170, 172
Nutting, Marcella, author, 18:12
Nutting, Porter, 22:170, 172, 35:110
Nutting, Walter M., 22:218; author,
13:212
Nutting family, genealogy, 13:212;
concert troupes, 13:213
Nutting Hotel, Faribault, 13:213
Nutting Truck Co., Faribault, 22:218
Nuttle, Charles W., 22:341
Nyberg, John, author, 36:106
Nydahl, J. L., 29:295
Nydahl, Theodore L., 17:120, 36:71;
"The Pipestone Quarry," 31:193–
208; reviews by, 27:333, 28:364,
35:284, 40:404; work reviewed, 37:
176; author, 12:320, 27:343, 28:
399, 31:256, 40:96; speaker, 35:
202
Nye, Bartlett, 20:77
Nye, Edgar W. (Bill), papers, 20:82,
193, 21:35
Nye, Frank M., attorney and Congress-
man, 17:213, 28:73; papers, 20:
193, 21:35; speaker, 26:304
Nye, Gerald P., Senator, 38:331
Nye, Russel B., works reviewed, 33:
41, 37:339; author, 23:285, 36:
278; editor, 40:313
Nye, Wallace G., 33:332
Nye, Willis, pioneer, 23:25
Nye Normanden (Minneapolis), reports
on Yukon gold rush, 29:302, 303,
305, 308
Nygaard, J. P., author, 15:132
Nygaard, Norman E., author, 31:146

Nygard, I. J., author, 20:359
Nygren, Andrew, pioneer, 34:62, 63
Nyhammer, Louis, steamboat captain,
32:51
Nylin, V. E., 16:129
Nyman, Mel R., 12:223n
Nyquist, J. P., educator, 33:309
Nystuen, Mrs. Oscar, speaker, 17:357;
author, 17:484
Nyvall, Ernest E., author, 18:333

Oak Glen, see Belle Plaine
Oak Grove, Hennepin County, mission,
14:362, 15:222, 16:314, 333, 21:
274, 276; Ponds' residence, 21:
172; Sioux at, 35:29; post office,
40:88
Oak Grove House, Minneapolis, 25:184;
health resort, 35:214, 36:91
Oak Grove Tennis Club, Minneapolis,
records, 25:184
Oak Hall, St. Paul, school, 14:147
Oak Hill, Todd County, history, 15:
371
Oak Hill Cemetery, Excelsior, 17:336
Oak Island, Lake of the Woods, 28:77;
store, 34:7
Oak Island, Wis., Lake Superior, 23:
243
Oak Lake, Jackson County, mythical
city, 14:256
Oak Park, Washington County, road,
40:236
Oak Point, Lake of the Woods, fish-
ing, 35:272–276; Chippewa settle-
ment, 35:277
Oak Port, see Oakport, Clay County
Oakdale Avenue Community Church, St.
Paul, 20:330
Oakdale Township, Washington County,
Germans, 23:404
Oakes, ---, ballplayer, 19:174
Oakes, Charles H., 22:420, 28:320,
36:70; house, 16:377; banker, 22:
4; trader, 26:362, 32:186, 39:
182n; Indian agent, 32:88, 89
Oakes, David, steamboat agent, 11:39;
death, 39:182
Oakes, Forest, trader, 11:258, 261,
262n
Oakgrove, Brown, singer, 35:50
Oakland, Baptist church, 14:237
Oakland Cemetery, St. Paul, records,
17:54, 97
Oakland Township, Freeborn County,
first settlement, 18:225
Oakland-Moscow settlement, Freeborn
County, Welsh community, 16:496
Oakley, Annie, biography, 34:169
Oakport, Clay County, 19:410
Oaks, Capt. H. A., speaker, 25:405
Oaks, James, 13:392
Oakwood settlement, S.D., trading
post, 11:380
Oasis, Murray County, election pre-
cinct, 14:250, 256, 258
Oastler, J. A., author, 21:433
Oat raising, history, 13:436; Paynes-
ville, 19:324; yield, 24:334
Oates, Mrs. James A., 28:110
Ober, Edgar B., career, 35:38
Oberg, Mrs. Grace L., author, 26:93
Oberg, Paul, compiler, 30:85
Ober Hoffer, Johann, musician, 33:94

Oberhoffer, Emil, 20:66; papers, 17:
53, 34:339; orchestra conductor,
17:101, 18:330, 23:192, 25:305,
30:354, 31:61, 33:94–104, 122, 39:
54, 55; pictured, 33:94
Oberhoffer, Mrs. Emil, singer, 33:95,
100
Oberholtzer, Ellis P., author, 11:217
Oberholtzer, Ernest C., review by,
13:296–298; author, 12:335, 16:
236, 25:92; conservationist, 40:
145
Oberlin College, Oberlin, Ohio, described, 19:130; missionaries, 20:
80; history, 31:181
Oblates of Mary Immaculate, missions,
13:440; at Red River, 36:48n, 37:
183
O'Brien, Sister Antonine, author, 17:
349
O'Brien, Christopher D., lawyer, 19:
357, 440, 39:154n, 40:15
O'Brien, Dillon, colonizer, 13:419,
19:450, 31:21, 23, 35:207–211,
213, 325; career, 15:105, 244, 19:
357, 439
O'Brien, Dillon J., 15:217, 17:70,
20:51
O'Brien, Frank G., author, 11:74
O'Brien, Mrs. H. J., author, 17:229
O'Brien, Dr. Harry, 19:357, 440
O'Brien, Cpl. Henry D., Union sol-
dier, 25:247
O'Brien, John, lawyer, 19:440
O'Brien, John B., author, 31:62
O'Brien, Joseph A., auto driver, 38:
207
O'Brien, Thomas D., work reviewed,
19:439; speaker, 12:96, 14:229;
author, 15:105, 244, 19:357; law-
yer, 17:160n, 19:440
O'Brien, Mrs. Thomas J., house, 38:
340, 341
O'Brien, W. S., 19:470
O'Brien, William, Lumber Co., 27:302
Obst, Janis, author, 40:364
"Ocean Wave," steamboat, 18:373, 39:
175, 40:63
"Oceanic," steamboat, 25:72
Ochagach, see Auchagah
Ochs, A. C., 11:332
Ochs, Adolf S., memorial, 25:295;
publisher, 34:203
O'Connell, Donald, author, 27:330
O'Connell, Marvin R., author, 35:155
O'Connell, Millett V., speaker, 20:
343
O'Connell, Mrs. Minnie, speaker, 16:
256
O'Connell, Samuel, author, 13:428
O'Connor, Agnes, author, 30:75
O'Connor, J. C., Indian agent, 35:173
O'Connor, Bishop James, 40:352; immi-
gration promoter, 31:22, 35:206,
208, 212
O'Connor, John P., 35:135
O'Connor, Richard T., 15:338
O'Connor, Rose A., author, 14:226
O'Connor, Thomas F., author, 27:252
O'Connor, William V., 35:340; work
reviewed, 36:147
O'Connor, Neb., Catholic colony, 35:
135
Octagon House, Afton, 15:468, 21:211,
27:231, 34:129
Odd Fellows, Independent Order of,
16:215, 242, 18:142, 144; Hutchin-

son, 17:237; Minnetonka, 18:96;
Bemidji, 18:112; Minneapolis, 18:
125; St. Paul, 19:134, 33:196,
197n; records, 34:339
Odegard, J. T., work reviewed, 12:182
Odell, Thomas E., editor, 29:267
Odell, Thomas S., 22:151n
Odell, Mrs. Thomas S., 22:151
Odeon Building, St. Paul, 39:53n
"Oder," steamship, 20:398
Odin Township, Watonwan County, Nor-
wegian settlement, 12:274; grist
mill, 21:219
Odland, Martin W., speaker, 12:292;
author, 13:46, 14:445, 25:201
O'Donnell, Emmett, author, 17:102
O'Donnell, Rev. J. P., author, 12:102
O'Donnell, Thomas, 20:218
O'Donoghue, William B., letter, 12:95
O'Dowd, Mike, boxer, 30:383
Oehler, C. M., works reviewed, 29:70,
36:234; author, 30:47
Oehler, Ira C., 11:54, 12:184, 14:79,
16:466, 17:59, 70, 71, 316, 18:55,
23:50, 26:45, 27:26, 29:97; "Fred-
eric Augustine Fogg," 11:438;
speaker, 17:209, 18:320, 20:306,
427, 21:287; MHS president, 20:51,
300, 303, 304, 21:50, 53, 22:50,
52, 293, 23:48, 49
Oehlerts, Donald E., work reviewed,
36:67
Oerting, Mrs. Harry, author, 27:81
Oeste, George I., editor, 29:163
Oestlund, Oscar W., scientist, 39:122
O'Fallon, Maj. Benjamin, Indian
agent, 34:126, 285n
O'Farrell, Margaret G., 28:300; au-
thor, 16:350, 29:368; speaker, 29:
184
O'Ferrall, Ignatius F., 24:96
Office of Indian Affairs, see United
States Bureau of Indian Affairs
Officer, Harvey, lawyer, 35:5-7
Ofsterdahl, Lucille, speaker, 25:286
Oftedal, Sven, 29:294; biography, 15:
358
Ogaard, L. A., author, 19:473
"Ogantz," lake steamer, 16:288
Ogden, Dr. B. H., 18:212
Ogden, Capt. Edmund A., 12:397, 21:26
Ogden, H. A., artist, 36:17n
Ogden, Isaac, letter, 14:81
Ogden, Peter S., journals, 32:249,
38:199; trader, 32:250, 35:141,
38:42, 40:167n, 170, 177
Ogden, Warren C., work reviewed, 35:
39
Ogden, William B., railroad builder,
30:146
Ogden, Dr. William B., at Nininger,
13:132
Ogechie Lake, Mille Lacs County,
name, 21:348; archaeology, 40:363
Ogg, David, speaker, 13:449
Ogier, P., 11:238n
Ogilvie, David, 19:364
Ogilvie, Kanabec County, history, 24:
273
Ogilvy, John, trader, 21:132
Oglala band, Sioux Indians, 34:355,
39:339
Oglebay, Norton and Co., mining ac-
tivities, 34:179n, 275
Ogley, Dorothy C., author, 31:134,
146, 36:81
O'Gorman, Edmundo, author, 23:377

O'Gorman, Bishop Thomas, career, 16:
114
O'Grady, Don, author, 28:303, 30:163,
34:128, 36:240
O'Grady, John, author, 13:333, 14:110
Ohage, Dr. Justus, pioneer surgeon,
12:204, 16:353, 21:437, 33:312
O'Hara, Rev. Edwin, author, 30:69
O'Hara, Fiske, actor, 26:291
O'Hara, John, author, 32:115
O'Harra, Cleophas C., author, 11:106
O'Hearn, Thomas L., 22:211
Ohio, 18:126; politics, 12:441, 30:
147, 40:318; history, 14:227, 15:
356, 16:220, 25:89, 34:121, 37:
301; archaeology, 16:153n; early
printing, 15:12; Quakers, 18:250,
255, 259; boundary dispute, 22:74,
75, 34:119; proverb collection,
27:34; bibliographies, 28:276, 29:
161; architecture, 32:109; early
government, 34:82; Civil War
press, 37:262; atlases, 40:122,
124; gazetteer, 40:146; climate,
40:312
Ohio and Mississippi Railroad, in
Civil War, 33:219
Ohio Land Co., Boston, Mass., 16:204
Ohio Journalism Hall of Fame, Columbus, 14:112
Ohio Life Insurance and Trust Co.,
New York, 29:227; failure, 40:225
Ohio River, route to West, 15:13, 82;
navigation, 15:82, 19:185, 21:17,
28:135, 32:38, 99, 36:251, 255,
37:245; panoramas, 17:137, 36:101,
190; discovered, 22:63; boatbuild-
ing, 36:253
Ohio State Archaeological and His-
torical Society, Columbus, collec-
tions, 26:384, 27:354
Ohio State Medical Association, cen-
tennial, 27:341
Ohio State University, Columbus,
naval recognition school, 26:85
Ohio Territory, politics, 16:204
Ohio Valley, settlement, 23:62; fur
trade, 40:214, 215
Ohio War History Commission, 25:402,
26:175; publications, 26:85, 389
Ohiyesa, see Eastman, Dr. Charles A.
Ohlson, O., Swedish immigrant, 20:258
Ohman, Arthur, 38:43
Ohman, John N., lawyer, 19:214
Ohman, Olof, discoverer of Kensington
rune stone, 17:21, 170, 33:314,
34:265, 36:146, 238, 39:139; farm,
33:47
Ojard, Hans, speaker, 22:442
Ojibway Indians, see Chippewa Indians
Ojibway, Cass County, land office,
12:382
Ojibway language, 12:316, 13:165, 18:
46, 28:278, 37:243; grammars, 17:
53, 96, 19:96, 39:303n; dictionaries, 20:430, 21:36, 205, 424,
25:87, 35:248; bibliography, 24:
71; geographic names, 25:304;
glossary, 26:81. See also Chippewa Indians
Ojibway-Dakota Research Society, 25:
304, 28:374
Ojibwe, Chippewa Indian, 21:285
Okabena, Lutheran church, 22:223
Okarpe, Sioux Indian, 40:79
O'Kelly, Father H. A., immigration
promoter, 35:212

Okerson, Olaus, missionary, 15:235
Oklahoma, ranching, 12:177; military
posts, 18:103; guide, 23:89; his-
tory, 34:357
Oklahoma Historical Society, Oklaho-
ma City, history, 13:336, 28:81
Oklee, history, 38:204
Okoboji Lake, Iowa, settlement, 13:
335; Indian massacre, 16:169, 38:
95, 122, 123
Okwanin, St. Louis County, see Wyman
Olafson, Rev. K. K., author, 17:343
Olafsson, Jon, colonizer, 34:165
Olander, William, 25:208
Olcott, William J., mining official,
38:42
Old Bets (Old Betsy), Sioux woman,
38:131
Old Catholics, sect, archives, 20:423
Old Connecticut Path, Indian trail,
15:256
Old Crossing, Otter Tail River, gar-
rison, 38:286
Old Crossing, Red Lake River, monu-
ment, 14:350, 15:66, 84, 116, 23:
291; treaty, 15:84, 282-300, 38:
204
Old Folks Concert Troupe, itinerant
musicians, 22:115
Old Gent's Band, St. Paul, 23:310,
313
Old Home Building, University of Min-
nesota, historic monument, 27:228,
230, 232
Old Kuskuskies, Pa., archaeological
site, 40:204
Old Main, University of Minnesota
building, 16:178, 179, 183, 23:1
Old Mill State Park, Marshall County,
36:104, 37:67
Old Mission Mill, St. Lucas, Iowa,
11:106
Oldenburg, Henry, secretary of Royal
Society, letter, 16:418
Oldenburg, Henry, of Carlton, papers,
24:246
Older, James A., editor, 20:462
Older, M. De Witt, memoirs, 20:462
Olds, L. M., speaker, 29:34
Olds, Gen. Robert, organizer of fer-
rying command, 26:2, 8
Olds, Robert E., lawyer, 25:304
Oleana, Pa., Norwegian colony, 12:
180, 25:86, 26:167, 29:267, 35:32
"Oleana," ballad, 36:80
O'Leary, James, 19:475
O'Leary, Johanna M., author, 19:475,
20:213
Oleson, Everett, author, 16:496
Oleson, John, cabin, 21:447
Oleson, John, Wisconsin pioneer, 32:
54
Oleson, Thurine, pioneer, 32:54
Oleson, Tryggvi J., reviews by, 35:
141, 36:146; author, 34:353, 35:
47, 40:95
Olguin, Jose, author, 35:245
Olin, Rollin C., baseball player, 19:
169, 170, 172, 174, 175, 177, 178;
in Sioux Outbreak, 38:110n
Olin, Col. Salathiel, cattle raiser,
26:110
Oliphant, Laurence, traveler and art-
ist, 25:273, 34:42, 45-53, 355
Olive, Gregory, 11:238n
"Olive Branch," steamboat, 13:232,
18:372

Oliver, Dr. Clarence P., author, 25:
91
Oliver, Dr. Clifford I., author, 20:
208
Oliver, Edmund H., author, 12:198,
330
Oliver, Eula B., author, 14:462
Oliver, Henry W., biographies, 16:
114, 23:361; mining pioneer, 34:
216, 36:192
Oliver, James, inventor, 24:298
Oliver, John W., review by, 24:239;
author, 23:389, 24:245
Oliver, Wis., road, 40:245
Oliver County, N.D., place names, 36:
325
"Oliver Kelley," Liberty Ship, 30:254
Oliver Mining Co., 18:332, 28:189;
Minnesota holdings, 23:361, 362;
employees, 27:210; Trout Lake
plant, 29:172, 36:35; history, 32:
46; strike, 40:341-347. See also
United States Steel Corp.
Oliverius, Jan A., 13:269
Oliver's Grove, see Hastings
Olivet Methodist Church, Minneapolis,
17:338; St. Paul, 17:479
Olivia, history, 13:453; anniversary,
14:347; Dutch settlement, 28:125
Olivia Times, anniversary, 13:453
Olivier, Willem, Dutch pioneer, 28:
129
Olmanson, Albert, translator, 39:263
Olmanson, Bernt, letters, 39:263
Olmstead, Gen. S. B., aids Nobles expedition, 35:251, 252
Olmsted, A. J., author, 17:114
Olmsted, David, 12:209, 20:368; MHS
founder, 20:367; portrait, 21:214;
papers, 22:191; trader, 32:74, 77,
36:263; politician, 36:268-270,
39:42, 45
Olmsted, Loring, 17:160n
Olmsted County, schools, 11:17, 18:
105; name, 12:209, 20:368; Norwegians, 12:265, 270, 14:444, 31:27;
medical practice, 16:250, 33:355,
35:381; historical museum, 17:362;
pioneer life, 18:208, 408, 26:288;
hotel, 18:227; archives, 20:445;
court, 21:215; in fiction, 22:167;
mills, 24:89; population, 24:97;
wheat raising, 24:97, 103, 29:2n,
13, 16, 24, 26, 27, 36:69; history, 24:192, 26:394, 29:364, 34:
218; sheep raising, 26:112; politics, 28:32, 40:324; wildlife
protection, 30:224; county seat,
35:21; poor farm, 38:368
Olmsted County Historical Society,
11:199, 283, 13:344, 16:241, 26:
284, 30:177, 36:193, 40:316; organized, 11:13; activities, 11:17,
28:387, 29:180, 276, 30:167, 34:
171, 267, 359; museum, 17:232, 18:
334, 19:64, 20:187, 297, 298, 21:
217, 22:219, 442, 23:11, 12, 14,
26:91, 27:76, 178, 35:50, 202,
246; finances, 21:48, 22:217, 25:
98; collections, 21:213-215, 446,
27:362, 29:364, 30:278; meetings,
22:340, 23:102, 24:87, 27:173, 28:
195, 29:92, 30:81; war records,
24:186; publications, 26:394, 28:
87, 296, 33:315, 40:362; history,
34:218, 36:194

Olmsted County Medical Society, 20:
240; organized, 20:241
Olmsted County Merchants' Associa-
tion, 21:202
Olmsted County War History Committee,
23:392, 24:185; records, 27:363
Olness, Patricia, author, 34:217
Olney, Jesse, geographer, 24:231
Olsen, George T., speaker, 16:491
Olsen, Peter O., mail carrier, 28:83
Olsen, Mrs. Sigurd (Emily Veblen),
reminiscences, 26:372
Olsen, Tinius, engineer, 29:157
Olson, Mrs. Abe, author, 16:366
Olson, Adolf, author, 28:83, 33:138
Olson, Al, author, 30:165
Olson, Albert T., 17:121
Olson, Alice C., author, 20:98
Olson, Andrew, 14:458
Olson, C. W., Iron Works, Minneapo-
lis, 38:308
Olson, Christine, speaker, 27:364
Olson, Erick, 13:122
Olson, Ferdie, speaker, 12:338
Olson, Floyd B., 14:347, 27:155, 34:
217, 40:148; "The Heritage of Min-
nesota," 14:165-171; speaker, 12:
336, 343, 448, 13:83, 14:345, 15:
115, 16:498; governor, 14:211,
343, 18:219, 38:303; author, 15:
56; characterized, 16:482, 19:223,
26:251, 36:83; policies, 18:191,
19:202, 37:170, 172, 40:366; career, 18:211, 327, 21:203, 28:74,
183, 32:246; papers, 20:33, 34:
339; politician, 34:187, 188, 36:
187, 37:84, 38:308, 309; county
attorney, 37:165, 166; law
teacher, 39:132
Olson, Gole, 14:428
Olson, Harold, speaker, 22:217
Olson, Henry, postmaster, 36:214
Olson, Herman T., author, 36:282
Olson, James, pioneer, 19:230
Olson, James C., review by, 39:335;
works reviewed, 34:307, 39:339;
speaker, 36:36
Olson, John, pioneer, 34:61
Olson, Mrs. John G., speaker, 20:351
Olson, Julius E., professor, 21:67,
31:252, 39:138; speaker, 14:448
Olson, Judge Julius J., 16:468
Olson, Karin, 14:428
Olson, Leone, author, 19:122
Olson, May E., compiler, 38:91
Olson, Nels, stage owner, 14:458
Olson, Nels L., pioneer, 22:346
Olson, Nels M., miller, 35:18
Olson, Olof, 13:307
Olson, Olof E., author, 20:359
Olson, Orville, politician, 34:190,
192
Olson, Oscar N., work reviewed, 32:53
Olson, P., merchant, 20:249
Olson, Pehr, 14:428
Olson, Russell L., author, 34:130
Olson, S. E., Co., Minneapolis,
store, 26:396
Olson, Samuel, in rune-stone contro-
versy, 17:21, 23, 169
Olson, Sigurd F., 38:29; review by,
37:216; works reviewed, 37:305,
39:34; author, 30:69, 31:123, 36:
192, 39:130; conservationist, 36:
325, 38:91, 40:145; speaker, 37:43
Olson, Søren, pioneer, 12:263

Olson, Mrs. Thomina G., pioneer, 25:
406
Olson, Virgil A., author, 28:83
Olson (Floyd B.) Memorial Associa-
tion, papers, 27:155
Olsson, Jöns, author, 27:72
Olsson, Måns, see Lindbergh, Måns
Olsson
Olsson, Nils W., 29:80; "The Swedish
Pioneer Centennial," 29:182; work
reviewed, 37:177; author, 29:80,
31:54, 37:262; editor, 32:49;
translator, 36:195
Olympic baseball club, St. Paul, 19:
162, 164
Omaha, Neb., lumber market, 18:175;
Populist convention, 22:162; Mor-
mon mission, 36:289, 290
Omaha Indians, legend, 37:62; Nebras-
ka, 39:228
Omaha Railroad, see Chicago, St.
Paul, Minneapolis, and Omaha Rail-
road
Oman, Anders P., Swedish immigrant,
16:365; writings, 39:81
O'Meara, Walter, "Adventure in Local
History," 31:1-10; works reviewed,
32:122, 35:196, 37:174, 38:191;
author, 31:63, 134, 146, 32:33,
36:75, 77; quoted, 39:207; speak-
er, 40:149
"Omega," steamboat, 13:231
Omich, Dr. J. P., pioneer physician,
23:27
Ominsky, Alan, designer, 38:86; pho-
tographer, 39:277, 326n
Omro Township, Yellow Medicine Coun-
ty, Lutheran church, 13:454, 24:94
Onahan, William J., aids immigrants,
35:207, 208, 211, 212
Onalaska, Wis., sawmills, 32:254
Onamia, history, 11:464; Crosier Or-
der, 29:67; Dutch settlement, 37:
222; veterans' colony, 39:243-249
Onan, D. W., and Sons, Inc., Minne-
apolis, trade with Mexico, 35:245
One Hundred and Second Illinois In-
fantry, 25:18
One Hundred and Sixtieth Pennsylvania
Cavalry, 25:242n
One Hundred and Thirty-fifth Infan-
try, Minnesota National Guard,
Company B, 14:233, 26:389
One Hundred and Twenty-seventh Penn-
sylvania Volunteer Infantry, 25:
346, 348, 349
Oneida, N.Y., utopian community, 31:
181, 37:83
Oneida County, Wis., reforested, 36:
236
O'Neil, Marion, author, 12:91
O'Neill, Charles, Congressman, 34:73
O'Neill, Mrs. James E., speaker, 13:
121
O'Neill, Capt. John, in Sioux Out-
break, 28:261
O'Neill, Gen. John, colonizer, 40:352
O'Neill, William, settler, 35:213
Oneland, see Ulen
Oneota, Duluth neighborhood, 14:238;
mail service, 16:285, 287, 34:186;
roads, 16:291, 298; pioneer life,
16:336; town council, 18:95; saw-
mill, 21:150, 212; platted, 22:
349; church, 28:83
Ongstad, S. H., speaker, 13:344

Onigum, Cass County, Chippewa settlement, 26:81
Onnela, St. Louis County, Finnish settlement, 25:320
"Onoko," steamboat, 35:280
Onondaga Indians, Radisson's visit, 15:178
Ontario, wildlife, 18:451; relations with U.S., 23:357; forestry, 23:385; Indians, 26:76, 27:65, 39:338; medicine, 27:260; newspapers, 28:179; agriculture, 28:366; historical guide, 34:357; history, 37:86
"Ontario," steamboat, 24:166
Ontario Historical Society, activities, 13:113
Ontario Mineral Lands Co., 35:153
Ontonagon Pool, prospecting syndicate, 34:275
Ontonagon River, Mich., explored, 23:126, 239, 240, 26:380
Oostburg, Wis., Dutch settlement, 28:128, 368
Oosterhoff, Rev. Albert, 28:123
Opdal Norwegian Lutheran Church, Renville County, 22:348
Ope-en-dah (Two Quills), Sioux leader, 31:215, 216
Opera, 19:344, 29:125, 33:135; Twin Cities, 12:84, 193, 14:140, 15:254, 17:40, 32:166, 167, 33:96, 97; Crookston, 20:466; traveling troupes, 28:107; Minnesota, 28:110, 111; New Ulm, 32:171; Andrews family, 33:317-325. See also Metropolitan Opera Co., Music
Opera Companion, first issue, 12:84
Opjorden, Gudren, author, 29:87
Opossum, in fur trade, 30:134
Oppegaard, John E., legislator, 35:348
Oppegard, Ray W., author, 18:446
Oppenheim, Ansel, 39:329
Oppenheim, James, novelist, 16:115
Opstead, Mille Lacs County, school, 11:464; name, 21:350
Optional Drill League, University of Minnesota, 40:365
Oraas, Telford V., 21:447
Oram, William H., letters, 37:183
Orange City, Iowa, academy, 28:130
Orcadians, in fur trade, 33:261
Orchard Gardens, Dakota County, veterans' colony, 39:243
Orcutt, Wright, reminiscences, 15:483
Order of Sovereigns of Industry, founded, 35:56
Order of the Holy Cross, see Crosier Order
Ordeson, Vincent, "Planning a City," 33:331-339
Ordinance of 1787, 35:1; sesquicentennial, 16:474, 18:101, 322, 455; history, 19:103, 311; marker, 20:342. See also Northwest Territory
Ordway, Sgt. John, diary, 34:79
Ordway, Lucius P., 35:38
Oregon, railroads, 12:72; fur trade, 12:326, 26:56, 35:143, 40:179; place names, 13:109, 26:383, 34:159; boundary dispute, 15:306n, 17:345, 19:353, 29:339; Quakers, 18:259; British regime, 24:44; war records, 25:402; forts, 26:273; proverbs, 26:383; explored, 29:61,

38:199, 327; overland journey, 31:253; politics, 35:41, 94
Oregon and Western Colonization Co., 34:268
Oregon Central Railroad Co., land grant, 25:277
Oregon Historical Society, Portland, manuscript collections, 21:428
Oregon Railroad and Navigation Co., promotes immigration, 34:68
Oregon Territory, geography, 16:344
Oregon Trail, 27:247, 35:242; landmark, 11:453; Indian path, 15:256
Oregon Trail Museum, Scott's Bluff, Neb., 40:196
Orehek, Frederick A., author, 25:194
O'Reilly, Alexander, 24:53
O'Reilly, Charles D., emigrant agent, 13:28
Oreland, Crow Wing County, ghost town, 19:464
O'Rell, Max, pseud., see Blouet, Leon Paul
Orff, Fremont D., architect, 40:104
Orient, fur market, 40:208. See also China
"Oriole," steamboat, 22:109, 33:7, 14, 17-19
Orlando, Sherburne County, Mormon meeting, 36:289
Orloff, Nikolai, pianist, 39:59
Orman, James A., novelist, 31:130
Ormandy, Eugene, orchestra conductor, 33:222; career, 36:106
Ormsby, M. P., stage operator, 11:403
Ornithology, Minnesota, 19:96, 35:242, 36:108; in army medical corps, 22:92, 24:256. See also Wildlife
Orono, history, 11:118, 27:176, 36:36; pioneer life, 36:327
Oronoco, mill, 11:111; industries, 21:214; stage line, 30:70
Orphean family, musicians, 22:114
Orpheum Theater, St. Paul, 20:363, 23:76
Orr, Bernice, 29:365
Orr, Charles N., legislator, 33:159; papers, 35:340
Orr, Judge Grier M., 35:289; author, 12:85
Orr, James L., interest in Nininger, 13:132
Orr, L. W., speaker, 16:125, 26:286
Orr, Leslie W., guide, 13:289
Orr, history, 17:364; farmers' cooperative, 25:326
Orrock, Sherburne County, farming center, 11:119; Lutheran church, 15:129; Swedish settlement, 20:258n
Orth, Heinrich, 27:30
Orth, Jacob, 26:177, 27:30
Orth, Johannes, 27:30
Orth, John, alderman, 35:120
Orth, Maria K., 27:30
Orth, Peter, 26:177, 27:30
Orthmann, Dr. Adolph, theater director, 32:164, 165
Orthwein, Friedrich, newspaper editor, 27:327, 28:22, 24, 37:87
Orton, C. K., 16:246
Orton, Clark, author, 16:246
Ortonville, early history, 16:246; churches, 16:337, 355, 356, 20:447; mail service, 17:485; unions, 21:393; granite quarries, 37:87

Orwig, Louise, author, 21:431
Osage, Iowa, land sales, 17:418-420; crop failure, 20:162; school, 22:159
Osage Indians, agent, 20:78; in fur trade, 40:216
Osakis, history, 35:336; stage route, 38:64; Glidden tour, 38:208, 210
Osbelt, Brother William, 35:135
Osborn, Chase S., work reviewed, 24:237, 31:113; author, 20:441, 23:185
Osborn, Edward B., businessman, 39:211
Osborn, James E., song writer, 26:52
Osborn, Merritt J., businessman, 39:211
Osborn, Stella B., author, 20:441, 23:185
Osborn, Stellanova, work reviewed, 24:379, 31:113
Osborn, William, railroad official, 13:111, 15:333
Osborne, Frank O., lawyer, 13:324
Osborne brothers, 17:278
Osborne Township, Pipestone County, Indian mounds, 17:119
Oscar, Ole, 25:227
Osceola, Wis., sawmill, 17:283, 29:205; newspapers, 17:385, 387; log boom, 18:176; bridge, 23:290; postal service, 36:211, 214; architecture, 38:341, 342, 346
"Osceola," steamboat, 31:86
Osceola Lumber Co., 29:205n
Oschwald, Father Ambrosius, colonizer, 23:286
Osgood, Rev. E. Phillips, speaker, 11:330
Osgood, Ernest S., 13:65, 15:227, 36:219; reviews by, 12:72, 176, 13:92-94, 14:429, 16:450, 18:303-305; work reviewed, 39:164; speaker, 13:328, 14:74, 29:82; author, 21:182, 29:164, 34:169; editor, 33:268, 36:217, 222, 39:267
Osgood, James R., publisher, 17:370
Osgood, Mrs. Millie H., speaker, 17:481
Oshawa Township, Nicollet County, history, 11:464; Norwegian settlement, 12:275
O'Shea, Dennis, in Sioux Outbreak, 38:144n
O'Shea, Michael V., educator, 16:115
Oshkosh, Menominee leader, 32:186, 189
Oshkosh, Wis., history, 18:326; museum, 27:178; Welsh settlement, 29:85
Oshkosh Township, Yellow Medicine County, pioneer life, 13:346
Osland, Birger, work reviewed, 26:251; author, 23:381
Osler, Edmund B., art patron, 21:186, 36:314
Osler, Sir William, in Minnesota, 29:353, 30:144
Oslo, name, 30:332; history, 35:46
Oslo, Norway, panorama showing, 17:133; museum, 18:189
Osnaburgh House (Albany House), Ont., Hudson's Bay Co. post, 34:254
Osseo, first settlement, 15:487; G.A.R. post, 16:431; Catholic church, 16:484; German drama, 32:100, 34:242; post office, 40:89

Osseo, Wis., frontier road, 40:383
Ostenso, Martha, poet, 16:81; author, 20:115, 22:104, 23:118, 157, 25:309, 31:129, 132, 146
Østergaard, Kristian, author, 13:324
Ostrander, Hiram, journalist, 18:226, 21:221
Ostrem, Walter M., "Track and Field Sports in Minnesota," 39:18-23
Ostrom, John E., 15:249
Osufsen, William, 26:316-321
O'Sullivan, Timothy H., photographer, 28:347, 35:93
Oswald, Gottlieb, author, 15:133
Oswald, John C., author, 18:450
Oswald, Capt. William L., 25:134
Oswego, N.Y., fort, 20:14
Otakle, ---, mulatto, sentenced, 38:110n
Other Day, John, Sioux Indian, 12:133n, 15:383, 27:328, 29:123; frees whites, 37:160, 38:123
Otherington, ---, trader, 19:78
Otis, Arthur, resort owner, 33:228
Otis, Benjamin F., farmer, 40:238
Otis, Charles E., jurist, 16:115
Otis, George L., 12:120n, 40:229; St. Paul mayor, 40:225
Otis Township, Yellow Medicine County, Norwegian settlement, 12:275n
Otisco Township, Waseca County, Norwegian settlement, 12:269
Otisville, Washington County, frontier road, 40:233, 234, 238
Oto Indians, 32:230
Ott, George, 13:116
Ottawa, Le Sueur County, river town, 12:60
Ottawa County, Mich., history, 12:440
Ottawa Indians, 13:397, 15:165; at Prairie Island, 13:248, 15:318; visited by Radisson, 13:258, 259, 262, 15:163, 171, 317; mission, 13:400; Lake Superior, 13:401; in fur trade, 15:157, 158, 160, 19:274; Washington Island, 15:167, 170, 171, 175; Chequamegon Bay, Wis., 15:176; relations with Sioux, 15:320; with Cass expedition, 23:135; Illinois, 36:191
Ottawa River, Ont., Que., fur trade route, 11:233, 15:91; described, 15:163; portages, 28:8-10; history, 38:386
Otten, Mrs. J. S., author, 20:340
Otter, 30:134; in fur trade, 13:237, 23:330, 38:190, 40:179, 212, 218; trapped, 22:194
"Otter," sailing vessel, 12:376, 16:348, 20:13; built, 15:92
"Otter," steamboat, 13:233, 235, 237, 238, 17:155, 24:202, 26:181
Otter Lake, Ramsey County, acreage, 40:226n
Otter Tail City, in Sioux Outbreak, 13:385, 38:279; resettled, 13:392; frontier life, 14:216, 332; marker, 14:357; townsite companies, 14:435, 18:117; state park site, 30:278
Otter Tail County, Latter-day Saints, 11:222, 13:281, 385-394; ethnic groups, 12:259, 277, 16:251, 19:124, 23:26, 24:241, 25:318, 319, 36:34; history, 12:340, 16:250, 368, 30:273, 36:107; settlement, 13:344, 27:363; county seat, 14:

357; Indian mounds, 14:358; survey, 15:464; pageant, 16:237; hunting, 18:117; medicine, 20:103, 34:360; in literature, 20:183, 31:136, 37:7; archives, 22:100; pioneer life, 22:436; architecture, 24:259; agriculture, 24:259, 29:26; politics, 28:32, 32:145, 35:306, 307, 36:114, 308; grasshopper plagues, 36:55, 61; Catholic colony, 37:222; Finnish place names, 40:358
Otter Tail County Farmers' Alliance, 20:194
Otter Tail County Historical Society, 12:38, 15:73, 16:241; organized, 11:13; meetings, 11:15, 12:104, 204, 13:120, 344, 14:122, 16:124, 491, 17:122, 483, 18:110, 335, 19:117, 20:353, 21:337, 22:107, 340, 23:103, 298, 30:82; museum, 11:16, 465, 12:37, 15:137, 369, 19:471, 20:97, 457, 23:12, 26:91; publications, 11:18; members, 11:19; finances, 11:20, 25:408; markers, 11:26, 222, 12:341, 13:280, 14:357, 19:361, 27:363; essay contest, 11:221, 12:340, 13:71; collections, 16:492, 18:465, 19:124, 231, 455, 21:109, 218, 22:442, 24:87, 28:297, 29:93; marks territorial centennial, 30:278
Otter Tail County War History Committee, 24:82, 185
Otter Tail Lake, Otter Tail County, fur trade, 11:373, 20:11, 31:125; Indian mounds, 14:358, 25:338; Mormons at, 17:211; history, 18:117; described, 19:384, 26:227; Red River Trail, 21:229; explored, 35:335
Otter Tail Point, Leech Lake, trading post, 11:370
Otter Tail Power Co., history, 35:41
Otter Tail River, log drive, 17:116; archaeological work, 39:344
Otter Tail Valley, pictured, 30:273
Otteson, Bertha, author, 18:224
Ottinger, Tobias, 19:24
Ottis, Francis J., career, 23:192
Ottman, Reuben, 15:286
Otto, Clement, speaker, 23:194
Otto, Gustavus, letters, 36:13-17
Otto, William T., 39:86, 91
Otto Lake, St. Louis County, railroad, 34:184
Ouiatanon, Wea, Ohio, trading post, 11:234
Our Lady of Lourdes Church (Catholic), Minneapolis, history, 30:395
Our Lady of Perpetual Help Catholic Church, Clayfield, Wis., 15:481
Our Lady of the Lake Catholic Church, Mound, 15:362, 480
Ouse, Melvin, 20:458, 21:110; speaker, 21:53
Outdoor Recreation Resources Review Commission, 40:35
Outhwaite, Leonard, author, 16:349
Outing, summer resort, 13:115
Overbeck, Barney, hotelkeeper, 35:265
Overland Stage Line, 38:220, 223, 225, 226
Overland Trail, history, 29:61
Overman, William D., 24:183; review by, 34:82; compiler, 16:220; au-

thor, 21:422, 26:389; speaker, 26:74
Overseas Lunch Club, Minneapolis, 18:98
Overton, Capt. George A., real-estate dealer, 37:159
Overton, J. B., 21:88
Overton, Richard C., "Railroad Archives," 23:52-56; reviews by, 21:406, 32:47, 40:405; work reviewed, 21:305, 23:63-65, 40:356; author, 20:374, 21:408, 23:73, 28:276, 30:151, 393, 32:64, 35:45; speaker, 23:380, 26:75
Owatonna, historical convention, 11:286-289; churches, 11:328, 14:123, 20:345; roads, 11:393; stage lines, 11:403, 12:50n; railroads, 12:46; agricultural fairs, 12:445, 22:263; Czech community, 13:216; beginnings, 16:131; quarries, 16:255; history, 16:372, 28:172; G.A.R. post, 16:431; climate, 17:260; ordinances, 18:343; baseball, 19:168-170, 180; chain store, 19:358; social development, 20:61-63; horticulture, 20:79; pioneer life, 20:450; farm machinery, 24:304; cheese factory, 27:112; minstrel shows, 28:107n, 111; German theater, 32:100, 34:242; pottery, 33:230; centennial, 34:170; bank, 35:242, 37:38, 344, 38:91, 40:107, 108; state school, 38:372
Owatonna Journal-Chronicle, history, 17:241
Owatonna Public Library, history, 28:384
Owatonna Township, Steele County, history, 19:127
Owen, Amy, speaker, 13:449
Owen, David D., surveys, 12:381, 15:344, 467, 17:139, 26:78, 222-233, 30:83, 273, 36:296; biography, 16:115, 21:323, 25:174; explorer, 27:253; geologist, 30:267, 32:216, 39:288
Owen, Harry N., author, 30:264
Owen, Horatio R., publisher, 18:411, 36:110
Owen, J. H., 13:140
Owen, John, trader, 35:31
Owen, Julius, memoir, 22:425
Owen, Maj. Richard, geologist, 26:231
Owen, Robert, colonizer, 26:223, 31:112
Owen, Sidney M., editor, 18:411, 36:240; politician, 22:388, 32:138-141, 145, 146, 35:60-62, 298, 300, 312, 36:109-126, 39:96, 100, 101, 104, 107, 332
Owen, Thomas M., Jr., 26:166; author, 36:236
Owens, Dr. Jay, 21:209
Owens, John P., 14:292; "A Winter's Journey," 40:387-390; author, 11:164; newspaper editor, 11:183, 15:19, 17:276; quoted, 17:278, 280-284
Owens, Gen. Joshua T., 25:251, 350
Owens, Thomas, engineer, 19:236, 34:314, 36:281; speaker, 12:285, 13:442, 15:492; author, 16:101; career, 19:451
Owre, Dr. Alfred, papers, 17:53, 58, 100, 18:55, 20:288, 34:339; biography, 19:71-73, 25:305

Owre, Oscar, flutist, 29:298
Owsley, Frank L., historian, 34:81
Oxcarts, 22:213, 31:92; in immigrant travel, 12:253, 279; caravans, 15: 357; in farm work, 29:4. See also Red River carts
Oxenstierna, Eric, archaeologist, 39: 342
Oxford community, Isanti County, established, 19:123, 30:271
Oxford House, Man., post, 36:37
Oyaas, Joanna, editor, 36:66
Oyen, J. J., author, 12:207, 14:353, 18:339
Oyens, H. I., Dutch investor, 37:153
Ozawindib (The Yellowhead), Chippewa Indian, 12:216, 227, 18:180, 181
Ozmun, Edward H., legislator, 35:342, 343

Pabody, E. Fitch, 17:302, 18:91; "Mark Twain's Ghost Story," 18:28-35
Pabst Brewing Co., Milwaukee, Wis., history, 27:252
Pace, C. Robert, author, 18:105
Pace, Charles N., 24:162; work reviewed, 21:184, 33:81
Pachot, ---, explorer, 12:361
Pacific Coast, route to, 29:61; fur trade, 40:164
Pacific Fur Co., 15:421, 40:181, 182; in Oregon, 35:143
Pacific Historical Review, 13:328
Pacific Hose Co., St. Paul, 21:314
Pacific railroad, envisaged, 38:46-51; financed, 39:31; link to shipping, 39:334. See also Northern Pacific Railroad
Pacific railroad surveys, 24:166, 33: 313, 38:55; authorized, 13:177n; source material, 14:435, 17:335, 19:210, 34:213; surgeon, 16:97, 26:380; leaders, 17:114, 20:80, 81, 21:96, 22:330, 29:317n, 34: 353; accounts, 21:401, 22:86, 28: 69, 330, 33:273n, 35:242, 39:36, 169; personnel, 22:155, 23:183, 24:256, 33:90, 38:58; evaluated, 37:39; route, 38:4n, 60
Pacific Steam Marble and Granite Works, St. Paul, depicted, 40:126
Pacifici, Sergio J., translator, 35: 151
Packard, Rev. ---, 16:28
Packard, Francis R., author, 16:119
Packet ships, described, 30:187
Pactons, use in fur trade, 21:140, 141, 144, 145
Padrone system, on Mesabi Range, 27: 211
Paganini Quartet, St. Paul concert, 39:64
Page, H. R., and Co., Chicago, publishers, 40:128
Page, James M., diary, 15:464
Page, John H., speaker, 11:116
Page, Kirby, letter, 18:314
Page, Mrs. Leroy A. (Edna May Ripley), 39:1n, 5
Page, Sherman, impeached, 15:224
Page, Zeno B., house, 14:276
Page, Mille Lacs County, name, 21:349
Pageants, G.A.R., 12:334; Minneapo-

lis, 17:348; territorial centennial, 29:95, 184, 279, 369, 30: 281, 282, 285, 288, 398, 400, 402, 404, 407-409; Madelia, 29:272; Stillwater, 29:367; costumes, 30: 85; Macalester College, 30:265
Pagel, Louis, author, 23:404
Paget, Sir James, author, 21:369
Pagnac, Mrs. Georgia, 21:109
Pagnac, Mrs. J. J., 22:106
Pagonagerig, see Hole-in-the-Day I
Pahlas, Clark J., 36:193; author, 40: 315
Paige, James, compiler, 13:211
Paige, Mabeth H., biography, 32:120
Paige "36" automobile, 38:208
Paine, ---, baseball player, 19:164, 174, 175
Paine, Albert B., author, 17:377
Paine, Mrs. Clarence S., speaker, 13: 326
Paine, Frederic W., biography, 24:375
Paine, Halbert E., letters, 23:371; Congressman, 34:72
Paine, Parker, 31:83, 84; banker, 25: 212, 33:313, 34:43
Paine, Rodney, 12:207
Paine, Thomas, 19:256
Paine and Lardner, Duluth, bankers, 37:122
Painted Rock, Crooked Lake, 33:310; Lac la Croix, 36:102
Painted Woods, N.D., Jewish colony, 40:46
Painter, Adam, author, 11:227
Painter, Clara, work reviewed, 18: 307-309; author, 28:357
Painter, George D., author, 39:342
Painter, "Ike," 25:225, 254
Painter, L. O., speaker, 18:320
Painter, Samuel J., career, 15:370
Paist, William, 24:120
Pajutazee, Yellow Medicine County, mission, 14:436
"Palace" ("Walter Taylor"), steamboat, 33:14, 15
Palestine, Hennepin County, post office, 40:89
Palestine (Gladstone), Man., agricultural settlement, 28:64
Palin, Harriett, 23:44
Palisade, Aitkin County, railroad, 33:18
Palisade Mill, Minneapolis, 12:90
Palkie, Eric, miller, 22:220
Palliser, Capt. John, explorer, 20: 88, 34:304, 39:211
Palm, Ernest A., author, 12:105
Palm, Gunnar, 34:183
Palm, H. M., author, 25:186
Palm, Jonas, author, 30:397
Palmer, ---, teacher, 13:141
Palmer, Alice F., author, 26:301
Palmer, Ben W., work reviewed, 20: 418-420; author, 12:443, 32:62
Palmer, C. B., author, 35:245
Palmer, Edward C., judge, 35:5-10
Palmer, Elizabeth, author, 20:450
Palmer, Rev. Francis L., 16:52, 19: 47, 24:36; speaker, 14:461; author, 16:119, 17:350, 18:331, 19: 112
Palmer, George A., author, 12:320
Palmer, George M., speaker, 15:365; author, 16:235
Palmer, H. H., miller, 35:13, 14

Palmer, Harry, steel manufacturer, 35:203
Palmer, Howard, author, 12:447
Palmer, Mrs. Jake, author, 13:454
Palmer, John E., 12:207
Palmer, Joseph, 28:54
Palmer, L. R., editor, 34:171
Palmer, Ralph S., author, 31:60
Palmer, Robert R., author, 39:34
Palmer, Rev. and Mrs. Walter, at Red Rock, 31:89
Palmer's Stock Co., theatrical troupe, 28:117
Palmes, Mary E., chief clerk, 23:44, 367, 24:30, 32; memorial fund, 34: 268
"Palmyra," steamboat, 11:124, 16:33, 17:392, 18:161, 27:310
Palmyra Township, Renville County, Norwegian settlement, 12:275n
Palo, St. Louis County, Finnish settlement, 22:392n, 25:319, 320
Palsson, Hermann, translator, 40:95
Pan American Airways, in World War II, 26:4; army contract, 26:7
Pan automobile, 40:148
Panamá, Pan., seaport, 15:307
Panama Canal, 16:464; effect on Minneapolis trade, 19:185
Pancake Island, Beaver Bay, Lake Superior, 33:355
Pangman, "Bastonnais," interpreter, 22:281
Pangman, Peter, trader, 11:258, 12: 367, 368, 14:229
Panics, see Depressions
Pankratz, Theodora, 27:144, 148
Panoramas, 18:443, 35:379; Mississippi Valley, 17:131-149, 456, 18: 319, 20:200, 23:349-354, 24:178, 26:260, 29:261, 30:153, 201, 260, 32:188, 202, 33:284-290, 316, 36: 101, 190, 233; Ohio River, 18:319, 36:101; Battle of Atlanta, 18:453; influence on tourist trade, 20: 380-383; Battle of Gettysburg, 23: 198; Sioux Outbreak, 24:180, 30: 14-23, 36:234, 38:105; accompanying music, 26:53; in cartoons, 30: 406; Great Lakes, 36:324; Civil War, 37:38
Panzram, Herman A., 19:232, 20:214, 21:110, 218, 22:219, 25:99, 210
Papago Indians, songs, 34:161
Paper manufacturing, 18:408n; International Falls, 21:452; Minnesota, 22:337
Papineau, Louis Joseph, leads rebellion, 28:2, 32:151n
Pappas, Paul J., hotelkeeper, 28:381
Paquette, P. M., author, 13:122
Pardee, John S., portrait, 12:433; papers, 20:452
Pardee, Walter S., 16:384
Parent-Teacher Associations, Silver Lake, 15:40; Mendota Township, Dakota County, 15:115; council, 17: 469
Pargellis, Stanley, 24:253, 26:161; work reviewed, 18:194, 28:272, 30: 379; speaker, 24:255, 25:83; author, 26:162, 27:64, 34:257, 36: 280; editor, 28:276
Paris, France, treaty, 11:232; archives, 13:417
Paris Conference, Frank B. Kellogg's participation, 18:425, 25:195

Parish, Rev. Earnest C., author, 14:
363
Parish, John C., review by, 12:70-72;
author, 11:429; editor, 13:328
Parish, Richard J., 36:284
Park, Herbert T., 26:284
Park, Dr. James D., auto driver, 38:
208, 214
Park Congregational Church, St. Paul,
18:96, 39:53, 58
Park Place, St. Paul, history, 27:271
Park Rapids, trails, 16:492, 23:28,
29, 29:138; early theater, 23:26;
supply headquarters, 23:28; rail-
road, 33:256
Park Region, Norwegian settlements,
12:247, 265, 276
Parker, Mrs. A. F., 38:77n
Parker, Albert, letter, 38:265
Parker, Alton B., presidential candi-
date, 39:332
Parker, Arthur C., 27:162; author,
13:431, 24:70, 28:187, 30:257, 34:
213
Parker, Asa, lumberman, 18:167;
house, 38:339, 340
Parker, Barton L., author, 11:211
Parker, Benjamin, 24:138
Parker, Chad, comedian, 33:323
Parker, Charles A., 33:177; papers,
35:340
Parker, D. G., lawyer, 14:314
Parker, D. W., author, 16:203
Parker, Donald Dean, work reviewed,
26:60, 40:139; author, 31:60,
197n, 252
Parker, Gen. Ely S. (Donehogawa),
Union officer, 25:267
Parker, Frances, speaker, 26:180
Parker, George A., 12:341
Parker, George F., work reviewed, 21:
404-406
Parker, Sir Gilbert, in St. Paul,
33:1
Parker, Glenn C., author, 30:281
Parker, J. H., 13:117
Parker, Judge Joel, excursionist, 15:
406
Parker, John, librarian, 33:352; com-
piler, 35:151; author, 36:70, 40:
314; speaker, 40:149
Parker, Nathan H., author, 20:449,
40:147
Parker, Dr. Owen W., author, 19:357
Parker, Rodney, hotel manager, 39:
145, 149
Parker, Mrs. Rodney, hotel manager,
39:145, 147
Parker, Samuel, missionary, 24:44,
29:59
Parker, Samuel M., Union soldier, 38:
265
Parker, Truman, election commissioner, 26:205
Parker, Watson, work reviewed, 40:354
Parker, Gerrard and Ogilvy, traders,
21:132n, 28:1, 6
Parker's Prairie, history, 11:222,
336, 12:340; hunting, 16:262; Indian mounds, 25:338
Parkhurst, Col. John G., 39:192
Parkman, Francis, historian, 14:368,
15:431, 24:48-50; work reviewed,
34:298; author, 13:252, 397, 19:
437, 23:133, 25:265, 35:334, 38:
384, 387, 40:133, 304, 313; letters, 38:200

Parks, David, trader, 12:341
Parks, Gordon, author, 40:146
Parks, Joseph, interpreter, 23:135n
Parks, Capt. Maynard E., author, 27:
57
Parks, William, pioneer printer, 15:
6, 7
Parks, St. Paul, 12:458, 15:149, 17:
311, 23:403, 26:388, 27:271, 30:
209n, 404, 33:3-5, 36:239, 40:45,
253; Minneapolis, 16:494, 22:385,
23:225, 26:68, 284, 27:75, 270,
28:296, 29:352, 30:75, 35:23, 40:
48; international, 22:178. See
also Interstate Park, Minnehaha
Falls, State parks, individual
national parks
Parley, Peter, 17:437
Parlor Opera Troupe, 28:110
Parmalee, Philander, 21:413
Parnell, C., author, 23:92, 26:274
Parnell, Charles S., lecturer, 21:326
Parr, Samuel S., 16:371
Parrant, Pierre ("Pig's Eye"),
trader, 12:421, 17:311, 374; in
radio dramatization, 15:479; in
fiction, 30:247
Parrington, Vernon L., author, 21:14,
29:264, 39:335; quoted, 35:54, 36:
276, 38:387
Parrish, Philip H., author, 12:326
Parry, Charles C., botanist, 35:241
Parsons, E. Dudley, works reviewed,
13:95, 15:214-216, 30:384; speak-
er, 13:444, 20:92; author, 19:227
Parsons, John E., works reviewed, 35:
89, 39:32; author, 33:89, 37:135
Parsons, Lewis B., in Civil War, 33:
219
Parsons, Philip B., artist, 37:174
Parsons, William, speaker, 35:227
Parton, James, speaker, 35:227
Partridge, G. H., 19:184n
Partridge, R. A., pioneer, 18:224
Partridge, Mrs. Stanley, author, 27:
176
Partridge, Thomas C., 18:229
Partridge, Danish settlement, 17:239.
See also Askov
Parvin, Josiah, 23:77
Pary, Olaf, speaker, 12:105
Pary, Mrs. Olaf, Jr., author, 12:340
Passavant, Rev. William A., 14:49;
missionary, 12:333, 24:73, 373;
letters, 15:361
Passenger pigeons, 20:171, 29:223
Pasteur, Louis, chemist, 12:99, 21:
361
Patch, Edith, speaker, 29:178
Patch, Harry L., author, 20:201
Patchatchanban, Itasca County, trad-
ing post, 11:370
Patchin, S. A., speaker, 34:218
Pate, Miner, 18:299, 300
Paterson, Rev. A. B., meteorological
research, 17:251, 258, 259
Paterson, Mrs. M. J., author, 34:170
Pathfinder (Gotha, Carver County),
emigration paper, 31:227
Patience, operetta, 17:40, 325
Patriotic Americans of German Origin,
Minnesota branch, 14:437
Patriotic organizations, history, 35:
197
Patrons of Husbandry, see Granger
movement
Pattee, Alma J., 13:77

Pattee, Edward S., diaries, 35:52
Pattee, Lynus R., author, 23:281
Pattee, William S., 14:231, 452, 17:
213; letters, 20:81
Patten, Alice M., artist, 19:377
Patten, F. J., author, 38:243
Patten, George W., poet, 22:97, 126;
army officer, 28:214
Patten, James, lumberman, 24:201
Patten, Jerry, in Sioux Outbreak, 38:
243
Patten, Katharine, author, 13:123
Patten, Nevada (Mrs. Edmund J. Long-
year), pioneer, 32:245, 246
Patterson, Ada, 17:474
Patterson, Charles, trader, 11:182n,
261, 262, 378, 382, 19:104
Patterson, Charles S., businessman,
34:226
Patterson, Darwin, 16:340
Patterson, Frank M., bequest, 23:285
Patterson, H. S., author, 17:345, 20:
88
Patterson, Helen M., author, 27:242
Patterson, J. B., editor, 13:330, 35:
88
Patterson, J. W., "The Post Office in
Early Minnesota," 40:78-89
Patterson, Margaret K., compiler, 24:
173
Patterson, R. M., editor, 35:141
Patterson's Rapids, Minnesota River,
name, 11:182n; post, 11:378
Patti, Adelina, 25:86; singer, 14:
140, 16:32, 30:192, 39:321
Pattie, James O., explorer, 14:430
Pattie, Sylvester, explorer, 14:430
Pattison, Granville S., editor, 21:
364
Pattison, J. B., 22:108
Pattison, Murdock, 25:141
Pattison and Benson, stage line, 12:
394, 29:204n
Patton, Dr. George R., 21:114
Patton, James W., author, 15:124
Patton, Willard, musician, 33:93, 94
Patton, William, 14:42
Paul, Amasa C., 18:211
Paul, Clarence J., 19:214
Paul, Dorothy, author, 13:429
Paul, Prince of Württemberg, ex-
plorer, 34:285
Paul, William G., compiler, 40:96
"Paul Anderson," steamboat, 32:38
Paullin, Charles O., work reviewed,
14:91
Paullin, William, balloonist, 38:168,
169, 176
Paul's Reformed Church, Hamburg, 14:
451
Paulsen, Rev. O., author, 14:235
Paulson, Al, station agent, 36:204
Paulson, Arthur, author, 21:426
Paulson, P. A., 21:448
Paulson Mines, Cook County, ghost
town, 34:179
Pauly, Gus J., 18:123n
Pauly, James, hotelkeeper, 12:192,
343
Pauly House, Minneapolis, 12:343
"Pavilion," steamboat, 13:232, 236
Pavlish, Adolph, 24:103; millwright,
24:101
Pawnee Indians, as slaves, 19:290;
songs, 34:161
Paxson, Frederic L., 12:328, 17:51,
18:305; review by, 11:421; work

reviewed, 11:422-424; author, 11: 428, 429, 12:70, 13:332, 17:106, 477, 28:80; professor, 39:218-220, 226

Paxson, Dr. Joseph A., diary, 28:80

Paxton, J. W., speculator, 39:90

Paxton, Redwood County, ghost town, 19:465

Pay, B. F., 21:442

Pay, Byron E., in Sioux removal, 34: 328

Pay, William H., 12:38, 39, 448, 14: 234, 15:76; speaker, 11:52; author, 13:116

Payne, D. L., 21:378

Payne, Mrs. Harry, author, 18:120

Payne-Aldrich tariff, 22:79, 40:321

Payne Avenue Baptist Church, St. Paul, 29:359

Paynesville, in Sioux Outbreak, 12: 302, 303, 20:192, 28:192, 38:279, 280, 283, 286; Methodist church, 16:355; frontier life, 18:444, 19: 114, 321-327; history, 36:107

Payte, William P., engineer, 37:160n, 40:235n

Pazoiyopa, Sioux Indian, 38:134

Peabody, E., whaleback captain, 34:11

Peabody, William B., 26:154

Peak bell ringers, 33:174

Peak family, musicians, 22:114

Peake, Rev. Ebenezer Steele, missionary, 16:380, 21:35, 27:289n, 28: 210; papers, 20:431

Peake, Mrs. Ebenezer Steele, missionary, 16:380, 36:35

Peake, John, lumberman, 24:127

Peake, Ora B., work reviewed, 34:310

Peake's Opera, Wadena theater, 28:99

Peale, Charles W., artist, 26:359, 36:296, 299n

Peale, Titian R., artist, 33:21, 40: 144

Pearce, Roy H., work reviewed, 33: 303; compiler, 27:61

Pearl Harbor, Hawaii, attacked, 26:6

Pearson, Mrs. A. H., speaker, 13:121

Pearson, Doris, author, 23:171

Pearson, Emil C., speaker, 14:120

Pearson, Ezra G., Quaker minister, 18:256n

Pearson, Floyd, compiler, 36:239

Pearson, Hilma, author, 37:223

Pearson, M. Winston, author, 17:351

Pearson, T. Granville, 18:314

Pearson, Trued G., Swedish immigrant, 37:262; writings, 39:81

Pearson, William L., Quaker minister, 18:261n

Pease, Arch G., author, 37:348

Pease, Granville S., pioneer journalist, 14:395, 24:381

Pease, T. G. J., journalist, 24:381; author, 26:286, 28:290, 379

Pease, Theodore C., 39:166; review by, 21:182; works reviewed, 16: 448-450, 18:428-430, 21:395, 31: 47; author, 21:187

Peasley, George, 15:95

Peat, Wilbur D., author, 29:336

Peavey, Frank H., career, 16:114, 40: 147; grain merchant, 37:14, 15, 17, 18

Peavey family, 25:93, 40:147

Pecatonica River, Wis., source, 27:87

Pecheto, mixed-blood, 19:381

Pecinovsky, Renata K., author, 11:446

Peck, A. R., papers, 27:153

Peck, Anne M., work reviewed, 25:66

Peck, C. K., steamboat owner, 38:236

Peck, F. B., convention delegate, 14: 261

Peck, Frank W., author, 32:118

Peck, George W., 19:152

Peck, Mrs. N. A., author, 22:443

Peck, S. L., diary, 16:335

Peckham, Howard H., 26:169; works reviewed, 29:65, 34:205, 350; compiler, 24:69; author, 25:310, 28: 78, 29:336, 38:333

Peckham, Joseph, 14:231

Peckham, Stephen F., chemist, 16:115, 38:21, 22

Peckham, Wheeler H., house, 15:55; lawyer, 16:29, 115

Peckhamp, William P., scrapbook, 16: 360

Peddlers Grove, Waseca County, stage line, 12:50n

Pedersen, A. B., author, 11:226

Pedersen, Rev. John U., author, 14: 445

Pedersen, Knut, see Hamsun, Knut

Pedersen, Per, 20:399

Pederson, A. M., 16:219

Pederson, Kern, artist, 30:173, 40: 31n, 48; work reviewed, 40:92

Pederson, Ole, 11:226

Pederson, Thomas, recollections, 18: 48, 96, 19:107, 465, 20:86; author, 18:113

Peebles, Thomas, lawyer, 21:196

Peek, George N., backs farm bill, 38: 179, 180, 182, 183

Peel, Bruce B., compiler, 35:295, 39: 128

Peel, Roy V., author, 19:459

Peerson, Cleng, 12:180, 16:115; immigrant leader, 19:81, 201, 21:98, 25:274

Peet, Emerson W., 22:104

Peet, Rev. James, diaries, 16:360, 29:49; missionary, 17:465, 28:83, 34:249; papers, 18:47; at Stillwater, 31:80

Peet, Stephen, missionary, 24:178

Peet, William F., 22:104

Peffer, William A., politician, 36: 122

Pehrson, Selma, author, 21:101

Peik, Wesley E., 38:385; author, 12: 418, 18:105, 35:371

Pelamourgues, Abbé Anthon, 18:437; missionary, 20:338

Pelan, Charles, 14:458

Pelan, history, 14:457

Pelcher's Crossing, see Roseau

"Pelee," steamboat, 34:14

Pelee Island, see Prairie Island

Pelican Lake, Grant County, settled, 24:272; stage line, 38:64

Pelican Rapids, frontier days, 11: 117, 12:341, 13:118; schools, 11: 221; church, 12:340; history, 20: 465, 21:115, 23:298; prehistoric skeleton, 25:153, 38:159; map, 26: 91

Pelicans Nest, Jackson County, mythical city, 14:256

Pell, Capt. John H., 25:34

Pella, Iowa, Dutch settlement, 28:368

Pelland, Koochiching County, mounds, 31:231

Pellant, Joseph Frequette, guide, 28: 7

Pellegrini, Ernest, sculptor, 39:161

Pellet, Kent, author, 23:90

Pelletier, Jean B., 15:423

Pelling, Henry, work reviewed, 37:127

Pelly, A. C., trader, 40:167n

Pelton, E. A., 17:238, 530; author, 12:99, 16:368, 17:116, 18:332

Pelton, Rev. George S., author, 14: 113

Peltoperä, Elias, Finnish pioneer, 25:318

Pelz, Eduard, emigration promoter, 31:222-230, 250

Pelzer, Louis, 16:220, 25:69, 26:161; author, 12:94, 177, 14:226, 15: 475; speaker, 16:301, 23:380

Pemberton, Gen. John C., Confederate officer, 40:286

Pembina, N.D., described, 11:102, 14: 284, 18:357, 19:411, 20:88, 38: 199; missions, 11:305, 12:205, 13: 440, 15:111, 17:113, 18:68, 19: 379, 20:327, 21:205, 22:149n, 286, 23:97, 31:240; trading posts, 11: 366, 12:433, 13:278, 19:353, 378, 22:148, 274, 276-281, 288, 289, 36:37, 52, 38:63, 40:145; military post, 12:317, 19:457, 22:280, 29:233, 236, 237, 34:321, 35:260, 39:129; weather records, 12:437, 17:245n; politics, 14:248, 16:359, 33:121n, 36:4; treaty, 1851, 15: 283, 22:150, 28:315, 31:18, 38:1-10; customs office, 15:479, 24: 333; travel routes, 16:231, 20: 122, 21:229, 35:262, 36:39n, 107, 38:63, 66, 40:332; mail service, 19:387, 33:278, 35:260, 37:56, 38: 65, 40:83-85, 87; frontier life, 20:79, 84, 37:175; stage line, 20: 444; river port, 21:235, 247, 255, 262, 26:228, 35:251; railroad, 21: 260, 36:7, 37:156n; history, 21: 432; Selkirk grant, 24:41; included in Iowa Territory, 25:396; pictured, 26:171; St. Paul trade, 27:285, 32:34, 34:53, 38:69; mixed-bloods, 28:61; wheat crop, 29:19; wildlife, 30:126, 35:242; telegraph, 30:262, 36:176; Hatch's Battalion in, 34:320, 324, 35:337, 38:284

Pembina, territorial county, population, 14:253n, 31:59; cattle, 26: 108

Pembina County, N.D., Icelandic settlement, 13:208, 17:344, 34:164, 265; place names, 38:385

Pembina Mountain, N.D., trading post, 11:366

Peminan, ---, trader, 32:231, 235

Pemmican, 26:76, 35:97, 38:7, 40:47; price, 14:386; described, 22:149; in fur trade, 28:281, 40:163, 164; preparation, 36:310, 37:78

Pemmican War, 38:328, 40:175

Penasse, Northwest Angle, post office, 18:279, 34:6, 7n

Pence, George, author, 15:124

Pence, John W., financier, 33:169-178

Pence Automobile Co., Minneapolis, 26:23

Pence Opera House, Minneapolis, 18: 137n, 28:112, 113; history, 33: 169-178

Pendel, Joseph, 33:292
Pendergast, J. H., pioneer farmer, 22:446
Pendergast, Mrs. Judith M., 21:336
Pendergast, Lloyd G., in Civil War, 11:462
Pendergast, Solomon, diary, 19:342
Pendergast, Timothy H., in Civil War, 11:334, 19:341, 38:269
Pendergast, Warren W., 19:341
Pendergast, William W., 11:334, 19:341, 20:456; educator, 21:452
Pendergast family, papers, 13:114, 19:341, 20:33
Pendergast Academy, Hutchinson, history, 11:334
Pendleton, Kearney & (Childs), Co., Philadelphia, lithographers, 20:174
Penetanguishine, Ont., post, 18:184
Penetion, Sioux leader, see Good Road
Penfield, Clara M., cataloger, 13:66, 425
Pengilly, John, 35:338, 40:61
Penicaut, Jean, 16:199, 23:84; work reviewed, 34:117; author, 13:85, 18:439, 25:193
Peninsula campaign, Civil War, 25:38n, 117-148
"Penn Wright," towboat, 18:177
Pennel, Richard B., 25:37n
Pennell, Joseph, Minnesota sketches, 17:352
Penniman, Clara, work reviewed, 34:308
Pennington, William S., 30:106, 108, 110, 39:38
Pennington County, pageant, 16:237
Pennington County Historical Society, organized, 20:46, 97; meeting, 19:471; museum, 20:354, 457
Pennington County War History Committee, 24:82
Pennock, Rev. A. C., 19:249
Pennock's wheat drill, 24:304
Pennoyer, James, 11:94
Pennsylvania, historic sites, 11:33; ethnic groups, 12:304, 26:168, 177, 27:29-32; politics, 13:99, 17:211, 30:107, 35:353, 354; records survey, 16:110, 18:325; bibliography, 16:220; history, 21:179, 26:383; in World War II, 24:267, 26:278; in Civil War, 25:360; soldier suffrage, 26:188, 192, 209; university, 36:298; crafts, 36:322; atlas, 40:122; fur industry, 40:200, 219; Indian sites, 40:204
Pennsylvania Central Railroad Co., promotes emigration, 31:224
Pennsylvania Historical and Museum Commission, 28:289
Pennsylvania Railroad, 30:378; in Civil War, 33:218
Penny Press (Minneapolis), politics, 39:106
Penobscot Indians, 40:47
Penobscot River, Me., lumbering, 24:125
Pentecostal church, in lumber camps, 34:61
People (New York), file acquired, 20:194
Peoples, George W., Sr., speaker, 19:229
People's Bank, St. Peter, 40:110

People's Church, St. Paul, records, 17:339; lecturers, 17:382, 40:15
People's party, 12:192; history, 12:3-20, 411-413, 20:341; conventions, 17:100, 20:433; in Minnesota, 17:162, 31:99, 35:53, 76, 312, 36:109, 39:100; founded, 35:65, 291. See also Populist movement, Third-party movements
Peoples Savings Bank, Duluth, 37:122
People's Theater, Minneapolis, 18:137, 144
People's Theater, St. Paul, 23:199, 32:101; history, 23:312-314; fire, 30:163
Pepin, Pierre, 13:439
Pepperton, Stevens County, Methodist church, 16:121
Pepys, Samuel, 16:406
Pequette, Rev. F. H., speaker, 12:454
Pequot, archaeology, 12:207, 28:193
Perala, Elsa, 21:289
Perch Lake, Polk County, winter sports, 40:384
Percival Mine, Wis., 35:202
Percy, Mary C., author, 16:248
Percy, William A., poet, 26:308
"Percy Swain," steamboat, 37:283, 285, 289, 293, 295, 296
Péré, Jean Baptiste, 16:418n
"Pereosa," emigrant ship, 25:262
Perham, Mrs. G. A., author, 17:240
Perham, Josiah, railroad official, 16:115
Perham, churches, 14:452, 16:369; logging, 16:368; schools, 19:124; history, 29:88, 36:196; German theater, 32:100, 34:242
Perkins, A. H. S., journalist, 25:101
Perkins, Charles E., railroad official, 30:151, 40:356
Perkins, Dexter, work reviewed, 38:196
Perkins, Dwight H., architect, 40:107
Perkins, Edward R., letters, 11:317, 12:319
Perkins, Fred D., 16:257
Perkins, T. H., 15:88
Perkins, W. G., speaker, 12:210
Perkinsville, Hennepin County, post office, 40:88
Perl, Lila, author, 40:47
Perley, flour mill, 18:341
Perley Co-operative Creamery Association, 24:273
Perosa, Sergio, author, 40:95
Perra, Elaine M., 16:61
Perranteau, ---, mixed-blood, 36:48
Perrault, J.-Alfred, author, 24:255
Perrault, Jean Baptiste, trader, 11:359, 368, 370-372, 375, 382, 13:443, 19:109, 24:179; builds Fort St. Louis, 11:359, 19:314; at Fond du Lac, 20:10-13, 28:147n
Perreault, Elzear, 33:23, 24
Perreault, "Le Blanc," French-Canadian settler, 33:23-26, 74, 76, 105, 107, 111
Perret, Abram, pioneer, 22:203
Perret, Jules, 24:77
Perrigault, ---, millwright, 11:276
Perrine, C. K., plow manufacturer, 24:297
Perro, Joseph, river pilot, 40:236
Perrot, Nicolas, 13:439, 16:114, 24:255; posts, 11:383, 384, 450, 452, 17:114, 19:103, 456; explorer, 12:

307, 15:166, 318, 18:233; author, 13:255, 265, 15:166; trader, 19:274, 283, 286; career, 28:184, 33:352; source material, 28:370
Perrot State Park, Wis., 15:237
Perry, Abraham, pioneer, 22:203
Perry, Bliss, author, 21:71
Perry, Charles, 29:89
Perry, Dora, 17:123; speaker, 29:181
Perry, Dorothy D., "Fourth of July," 40:60; compiler, 40:314
Perry, Comm. Matthew C., 40:348n; expedition to Japan, 38:55, 322
Perryville, Ky., battle, 17:222, 20:277, 38:266
Perseverance City, Stearns County, paper town, 22:447
Person, Avis, author, 36:105
Persons, Frederick T., author, 11:217
Persons, Irene, 18:55
Persons, Thomas, farmer, 40:235
Perth, Ont., Presbyterian church, 15:469
Perunovich, Petar, folk singer, 34:297
Peshtigo, Wis., forest fire, 25:275, 35:153
Pestalozzi, F. O., author, 32:155
Peter, James B., 21:297
Peterkin, Julia, author, 20:113, 116
Peters, ---, hunter, 35:258
Peters, G. S., printer, 27:31
Peters, J. L., music publisher, 26:53
Peters, John A., Congressman, 34:72
Peters, Mrs. Orville, author, 35:47
Peters, Samuel, at Prairie du Chien, 18:193; upholds Jonathan Carver's claim, 34:157, 158
Peters, Victor, work reviewed, 40:44
Petersburg, Jackson County, Norwegian settlement, 12:274
Petersen, Erik L., career, 30:391
Petersen, Eugene T., compiler, 39:262
Petersen, Harold F., author, 39:211
Petersen, Hjalmar, 20:465
Petersen, Karen D., author, 39:171, 259
Petersen, N. F., 29:308
Petersen, William J., 30:369; "Steamboating on the Minnesota River," 11:123-144; "Steamboating in the Fur Trade," 13:221-243; "Rock Island Railroad Excursion," 15:405-420; "Veritas Caput: Itasca," 18:180-185; reviews by, 12:76, 15:208, 24:53, 25:72, 31:115; work reviewed, 18:433, 22:410, 23:359, 34:40; author, 11:104, 210, 211, 12:92, 438, 13:208, 330, 336, 435, 14:226, 446, 15:236, 16:109, 228, 478, 17:222, 18:203, 215, 282, 19:222, 460, 20:86, 21:203, 22:97, 24:60, 369, 25:76, 299, 26:169, 273, 28:79, 185, 276, 331, 378, 29:253, 30:62, 160, 268, 31:122, 34:265, 310, 36:102, 184, 279, 37:222; speaker, 13:326, 15:227, 18:205, 20:187, 304; compiler, 33:188
Petersens, Gösta af, 36:106
Peterson, Alfred, farmer, 25:338
Peterson, Alice, work reviewed, 36:66
Peterson, Alvin M., author, 30:158
Peterson, Andrew, diaries, 16:340, 21:35, 85, 26:256, 39:270; pioneer farmer, 24:292n, 26:113
Peterson, Mrs. Anna S. B., author, 15:488

Peterson, Arthur G., 14:354; author, 11:114, 23:179, 27:60, 37:134
Peterson, Mrs. Bernard N., 23:391
Peterson, C. R., museum collection, 11:116, 21:440-442
Peterson, C. Stewart, author, 21:224, 26:269; compiler, 25:394
Peterson, Lt. Carl D., author, 25:312
Peterson, Carl J., author, 21:97
Peterson, Charles E., 28:79; author, 28:288, 29:175
Peterson, Clarence S., author, 31:59, 37:345; compiler, 36:195
Peterson, Conrad A., 16:491, 19:470; work reviewed, 24:55, 33:309; speaker, 11:464, 15:123, 16:300; author, 12:104, 23:201, 29:278
Peterson, E. J., speaker, 22:108
Peterson, Edward P., legislator, diary, 22:211
Peterson, Edwin, farmer, 25:338
Peterson, Elmer T., author, 27:277
Peterson, Elmer W., author, 13:115
Peterson, George F., speaker, 11:120; career, 20:216
Peterson, George L., 24:89; author, 23:386, 24:79, 176, 265, 25:93, 312, 36:103
Peterson, H. C., work reviewed, 35:368
Peterson, H. E., speaker, 29:363
Peterson, H. I., 17:361, 22:106, 217; author, 13:197
Peterson, Harold, author, 20:219
Peterson, Harold F., "Early Minnesota Railroads," 13:25-44; review by, 21:63
Peterson, Harold L., 37:135; author, 39:209
Peterson, Harry, speaker, 18:221
Peterson, Herman, 23:195, 24:188; speaker, 17:489; author, 17:490
Peterson, Hilberg, 18:110
Peterson, John, speaker, 13:454
Peterson, John, 19:184n
Peterson, John H., 20:361
Peterson, Lena, speaker, 17:124
Peterson, Mabel C., author, 15:114
Peterson, Mrs. Magnus, 15:490, 16:491, 17:122
Peterson, Mendel, work reviewed, 40:263
Peterson, N. E., speaker, 15:249
Peterson, N. M., author, 17:174
Peterson, Mrs. O. H., editor, 24:269
Peterson, Ole, politician, 14:306
Peterson, Ole, cabin, 26:391
Peterson, Rev. P. Alfred, author, 20:346
Peterson, Peter, speaker, 18:329
Peterson, R. M., 23:14, 29:277; museum worker, 21:344, 440, 442
Peterson, Mrs. R. M., 23:14; museum worker, 21:344, 440, 442
Peterson, Rhoda, author, 12:341
Peterson, Mrs. S. O., pioneer, 25:411
Peterson, Sam G., 14:236
Peterson, Theodore, author, 36:32
Peterson, Virgil V., author, 26:278, 27:160, 252
Peterson, W. C., 15:368
Peterson, Dr. William J., author, 27:355
Peterson Lake, Beltrami County, county seat fight, 23:30
Peterson Lake, Cook County, copper mine, 34:179

Petit, Gertrude, 35:271
Petit, Jonathan E., 14:124
Petit Ouinipique, see Lake Winnibigoshish
Petite Chute, see Little Falls
Petran, Mrs. H. J., speaker, 16:494
Petran, Wenzel, 39:67; letters, 26:371, 39:65-74
Petran, Mrs. Wenzel, settler, 39:65-67, 73, 74
Petran family, 26:371
Petrell, Edwin, editor, 25:160
Petrell, St. Louis County, Finnish settlement, 25:320
Petrich, Frank J., author, 19:99
Petriella, Teofilo, labor leader, 40:341-346
Petroglyphs, Cottonwood County, 40:263
Petrov, Eugene, author, 29:154
Petschow, H. A., 21:218, 22:341, 23:299
Pettengill, George E., author, 26:168
Petterson, G. S., 38:43
Petterson, K. P., 17:181
Pettigrew, Richard F., reformer, 40:140
Pettijohn, Eli, 17:235; family, 14:438
Pettijohn, Jonas, at Lac qui Parle, 16:137; missionary, 22:211, 27:360
Pettijohn, Mrs. Regina, reminiscences, 21:223
Pettingill, Olin S., naturalist, 30:221
Pettit, Curtis H., papers, 11:315, 12:26
Pettit, Louis W., 16:199
Pettit, W. F., pioneer, 20:61
Pettit, William, letters, 11:316
Pettit Mill, Minneapolis, 12:333, 497
Petun Indians (Tobacco Hurons), 13:397
Petzet, Walter, 39:56
Pew, Marlen, author, 13:201
Pew, Mrs. S. C., author, 18:340
Pewter, trade items, 40:204, 206, 207
Peyla, Peter, pioneer, 25:160
Peyote cult, 37:343, 347
Peyton, B. Murray, banker, 37:125
Peyton, Hamilton, banker, 37:119, 122
Peyton, John L., author, 33:350
Peyton, Theresa D., papers, 13:101
Pfaender, Albert, speaker, 15:129; author, 21:333; legislator, 33:159
Pfaender, William, 13:28, 34:170, 37:146; letter, 19:214; house, 24:259; founds New Ulm, 27:268, 30:74, 31:24, 29, 243; German immigrant, 28:28, 30:24-35; in Civil War, 33:84
Pfaender, Mrs. William (Catherine), 34:170
Pfaller, Rev. Louis, author, 38:385, 39:83
Pfeiffer, Ida, Minnesota tour, 20:308, 388, 390
Pfeiffer, Josie W., author, 37:348, 38:92
Pfeiffer, Mrs. Peter, author, 12:341
Pfeil, Anna, actress, 33:40
Pfeil, Carl, actor, 33:40
Pfeil, Walter, 36:394
Phalen, James M., author, 13:441, 16:350, 24:76
Phalen Creek, Ramsey County, water supply, 40:226, 227

Pharmacology, Minnesota, 14:432, 28:65, 35:381; education, 24:175, 30:143; businesses, 30:154
Phelan, R. A., lawyer, 39:50
Phelan, William, 16:124
Phelps, Dorothy K., artist, 21:79
Phelps, E. J., pioneer motorist, 26:21
Phelps, Edith M., 31:245
Phelps, Ethel L., editor, 27:249
Phelps, Fred T., printer, 14:196, 19:83, 21:79
Phelps, Judge J. O., excursionist, 34:139
Phelps, Dr. Robert M., 38:23
Phelps, Roswell, 17:370
Phelps, Ruth, poet, 16:81
Phelps, Rev. Sylvester N., 13:449
Phelps, William F., 16:115, 35:371
Phelps, William Lyon, 22:164; author, 21:71
Phelps, William W., Congressman, 12:389, 14:164, 191, 254n, 37:47, 48, 50
Phelps, Winthrop H., diary, 27:249
Phenix House, Prairie du Chien, Wis., 19:33
"Phil Sheridan," steamboat, 15:420, 31:160; bell, 18:374
Philadelphia, cholera epidemic, 14:299; directories, 24:63; Presbyterian church, 40:1, 4; freeways, 40:134; fur market, 40:200, 213n, 214
Philately, Civil War covers, 38:298-300
Philathea Literary Society, Mankato, 19:333
Philbrook, Rufus, letters, 31:60
Philharmonic Club, Minneapolis, 20:66, 30:175; history, 33:93-104
Philharmonic Hall, Winona, 18:34, 28:98, 32:102
Philharmonischer Verein, Winona, records, 25:207
Philip, George, author, 17:112
Philip, James, cattleman, 17:112
Philipp, Anton, New Ulm founder, 12:451, 22:224
Philippine Insurrection, 16:336, 23:171, 24:247. See also Spanish-American War
Philippine Islands, newspapers, 18:99; supreme court, 18:122; annexation, 39:108, 120; scientific expedition, 39:116, 118, 119, 122
Philips, James, 20:142
Philleo, Dr. Addison, journalist, 18:183; mail contractor, 40:81
Philleo, William M., potter, 33:232
Phillipps, Gerald R., author, 28:399
Phillips, A. C., speaker, 17:121
Phillips, B. W., author, 18:468
Phillips, David, 13:147
Phillips, E. W., lumberman, 24:201
Phillips, Eleazer, Jr., pioneer printer, 15:7
Phillips, Eugene M., "James Moore McConnell," 14:416-420
Phillips, George L., author, 33:188
Phillips, Gerald R., "A Survey of Methods and Material," 28:353-359
Phillips, J. E., speaker, 16:125
Phillips, J. Philip L., geographer, 34:303
Phillips, Paul C., 13:425; review by,

11:80; work reviewed, 38:190; author, 12:442, 15:128, 40:151, 157n
Phillips, Stephen, poet, 26:308
Phillips, Ulrich B., author, 26:265
Phillips, W. J., author, 18:216
Phillips, Wendell, 19:436, 22:127; lecturer, 11:157, 158, 21:326, 32: 15, 35:195
Phillips, William D., lecturer, 16: 31; lawyer, 20:368, 29:219, 39: 148n; politician, 36:265; in fiction, 37:5
Philolectian Society, Anoka, essay contest, 16:245
Philomathian, University of Minnesota, literary society, 16:182
Phinney, Charles H., 19:360; author, 15:486, 16:247, 17:236, 20:358, 21:113; speaker, 16:365
Phlughoeft, H. A., author, 17:227
Phoenix Athletic Club, White Bear Lake, 39:23
Photography, historical value, 15:78, 439, 471, 22:91, 28:345-352, 31: 188, 35:246; frontier, 21:95, 39: 294; on Red River boat, 21:262; Civil War, 33:216, 34:212, 35:93; Minnesota, 34:28-33. See also Daguerreotypes, Microfilm
Phyn, Ellice, and Co., Schenectady, N.Y., fur traders, 14:228
Pianos, on frontier, 15:187, 19:318-321, 39:312-326
Pic River, Ont., fur post, 28:1, 29: 266, 267
Piccard, Jean F., balloonist, 33:244
PICK Electric Cooperative, 37:347
Pickands Mather and Co., mining firm, history, 36:276
Pickard, Madge E., work reviewed, 26: 143
Pickerel Lake Township, Freeborn County, history, 30:405
Pickett, Eli K., 14:303n, 306, 309; in Sioux and Civil wars, 14:310-313, 315; letters, 17:336, 18:48
Pickett, Milton, 14:312
Pickett, Philena, 14:303n, 311, 312, 315
Pickett, Victor G., 14:79, 303n; work reviewed, 14:206
Pickett family, on Minnesota frontier, 14:303-315
Pickford, Arthur, author, 23:91
Pickwick, Winona County, mill, 14: 124, 34:129
Picotte, Mrs. Ebba, 25:96
Picture Rock, Crooked Lake, history, 29:130-136
Pictured Rocks, Lake Superior, described, 23:235
Pictures, as historical sources, 15: 439-444, 37:37; cataloging, 15: 441-443. See also Minnesota Historical Society: picture collection
Piegan Indians, Montana, 34:76n
Piel, Gerard, speaker, 38:91
Pier, Ella, 19:99
Pierce, Judge Allen, 31:173
Pierce, Bessie L., reviews by, 21: 179, 23:60; editor, 14:448; author, 15:120, 19:221, 21:187, 23: 74, 31:119
Pierce, E. B., 20:206; author, 27:262
Pierce, Franklin, biography, 13:433; presidential candidate, 27:14;

President, 36:3, 39:47; investigates Alexander Ramsey, 39:48
Pierce, G. H., 16:363
Pierce, Gilbert A., 16:115, 35:70; publisher, 35:66
Pierce, J. W., 18:465
Pierce, Maj. James O., Union officer, 15:112
Pierce, Capt. John S., Union officer, 23:144, 347
Pierce, Mrs. L. N., 17:231, 482, 20: 95, 21:107, 22:105; speaker, 18: 463, 19:115, 22:339, 29:273
Pierce, M. Frances, author, 25:315
Pierce, Mabel, 22:107, 23:104
Pierce, Thomas W., 20:435
Pierce County, N.D., ranching, 21:99
Pierce County, Wis., history, 19:352, 36:280; boundaries, 23:384
Pierce County (Wis.) Historical Society, 29:360
Piercy, Frederick, artist, 30:74
Pierotti, Venanzio, 20:413
Pierre, S.D., flood, 11:68, 69; capital, 26:270, 36:3
Pierre-Deadwood Trail, S.D., map, 12: 93
Pierse, Allen, lawsuit, 35:4-10
Pierson, Father Francis, Jesuit missionary, 11:345
Pierson, George W., speaker, 23:82; author, 23:283, 24:76, 29:76
Pierz, Bartholomew, 30:392
Pierz, Father Francis X., 13:117, 23: 402, 24:263, 25:186, 34:171, 38: 193; missionary, 11:205, 12:83, 205, 14:454, 15:446, 22:200, 24: 354, 25:193, 194, 26:146, 27:367, 31:25, 32:35-37, 39, 39:304-308; letters, 11:316, 15:61, 110, 233, 354, 472, 16:106, 225, 17:84, 20: 90, 33:138; stations, 12:107, 456, 14:361, 18:375, 19:464, 20:446, 28:219, 33:188, 35:46, 263, 269, 36:192; biographies, 16:114, 33: 185; author, 28:277, 29:168, 349; depicted, 39:303
Pigeon River, border river, mission, 11:306, 39:306-309; name, 12:361; road from Duluth, 16:298; falls, 20:205, 37:241; boundary, 23:209; explored, 26:231; trade route, 29:132, 34:358, 37:253, 39:82
Pike, Alonzo, 22:103
Pike, Charles B., 17:221
Pike, F. H., and Co., St. Paul, piano dealers, 39:320
Pike, Frederic A., author, 17:475
Pike, Marcia Doughty, 22:103
Pike, Robert, Jr., 23:172, 27:19; diary, 21:313
Pike, William A., speaker, 39:115
Pike, Lt. Zebulon M., 15:221, 25:79, 30:67, 31:62, 37:37; fort, 11:28, 13:433, 16:374, 28:293; expeditions, 11:101, 111, 12:238, 13: 210, 14:166, 333, 15:366, 16:26, 155, 193, 20:15, 84, 22:220, 23: 234n, 298, 25:288, 26:106, 29:270, 30:131, 258, 35:151, 37:347; maps, 12:82, 33:186, 35:292, 36:97, 277; journals, 13:367, 40:138, 147, 409; explorer, 15:370, 16:349, 24: 372, 28:184, 32:216, 37:62; memorials, 15:472, 17:230, 473; biographies, 16:115, 30:376, 35:200; author, 19:217, 36:76; treaty ne-

gotiator, 19:354, 23:85, 213, 24: 382, 25:269, 29:231, 30:210, 34: 312, 35:179
Pike family, musicians, 22:120
Pike Bay, Lake Vermilion, mound, 31: 164-168
Pike Island, Dakota County, Mississippi River, 15:397; trading post, 11:376; Faribault claim, 12:190, 317, 15:344; map, 35:23
Pike Lake, border lake, 21:347, 351
Pilcher, H. M., 19:184n
Pilcher, Joshua, author, 34:304
Pilger, Celina M., author, 12:430
Pilger, Rev. John M., author, 14:355
Pilgrim Baptist Church, St. Paul, 23: 110
Pilgrim Congregational Church, Duluth, 11:416, 17:230, 26:262
Pilkey, A. M., author, 17:227
Pillager, newspapers, 14:235
Pillsbury, Alfred F., 25:154n
Pillsbury, Charles A., 25:308, 29:88, 139, 31:252, 39:15, 115, 298; miller, 16:114, 19:466, 23:223, 33: 133, 39:99, 106
Pillsbury, Charles S., career, 19:466
Pillsbury, Mrs. Charles S., 12:207; author, 17:230
Pillsbury, Fred C., career, 19:466; house, 23:229, 40:100
Pillsbury, George A., Minneapolis mayor, 19:466, 22:385; house, 23: 229; miller, 33:63, 64
Pillsbury, John S., 19:152, 446, 466, 25:154n, 28:66, 29:128, 37:22; letters, 14:101, 19:96, 27:248; portrait, 15:117, 20:209; miller, 16:114, 31:252; statue, 20:415; university benefactor, 23:231, 32:176; lumberman, 26:136; governor, 26:366, 34:217, 35:58, 325, 36:54, 58, 59, 37:210, 40:148; house, 29:72
Pillsbury, Philip W., author, 31:252
Pillsbury family, 25:93, 31:252, 35: 248; in lumber industry, 30:242
Pillsbury, Todd County, ghost town, 15:371; wildlife, 30:223
Pillsbury A Mill, Minneapolis, design, 23:222-224, 40:100n; preserved, 27:231, 232; described, 33:63
Pillsbury Academy, Owatonna, 16:235, 20:32
Pillsbury Building, Minneapolis, 37: 18
Pillsbury Baptist Bible College, Owatonna, athletics, 39:20
Pillsbury Co., Minneapolis, 19:466, 39:127; products, 14:234, 40:47; publication, 17:343; anniversary, 25:308
Pillsbury Hall, University of Minnesota, 23:231
Pillsbury House, Minneapolis, 18:339
Pilot Grove Township, Faribault County, Scottish settlement, 14:456, 15:112, 19:364
Pilot Knob, Dakota County, view, 22: 151, 33:122
Pilot Mound Township, Fillmore County, Norwegian settlement, 12:268
Pinchot, Gifford, 40:322, 323; work reviewed, 29:155; letters, 18:314, 21:416
Pine, Leslie G., author, 38:42

Pine Bend, Dakota County, 20:216; ghost town, 21:339

Pine City, Methodist church, 16:484; centennial exhibit, 30:178; county seat, 34:217; railroad, 37:90, 105n, 40:243; in Sioux Outbreak, 38:277, 286

Pine County, soil survey, 24:91; ethnic groups, 28:130, 29:271, 35:90, 39:130; wildlife, 30:125; history, 30:168; roads, 34:218, 40:242; forests, 34:267, 39:264; quarries, 35:295, 338; historic sites, 35:338; politics, 36:308; poorhouse, 38:375; archaeology, 40:412

Pine County Historical Society, organized, 29:364; meetings, 30:82, 34:218, 220, 360; publication, 30:167; exhibit, 30:178; historic sites project, 35:338

Pine County War History Committee, 24:268

Pine Creek, see Browns Creek

Pine Creek, Iowa, mills, 22:185

Pine Grove Village, Wis., stump fences, 21:429

Pine Island, cheese industry, 17:186; history, 34:127

Pine Lake, Clearwater County, archaeology, 26:321

Pine Lake, Cook County, logging railroad, 36:132

Pine Lake, Wis., Episcopal church, 11:83; Swedish settlement, 20:131, 30:159, 32:49

Pine Mountain Lookout, Cook County, fire watch, 36:133, 137

Pine Point, Leech Lake, mission school, 11:332; trading post, 11:370

Pine Ridge (S.D.) Indian Reservation, 24:324, 35:289, 293, 39:342

Pine River, Crow Wing County, trading post, 11:372, 20:11, 13; described, 23:335; steamboating, 33:13. See also Crow Wing River

Pine Tree Lumber Co., Little Falls, history, 23:301; log marks, 26:136

Pinechon (Pinisha), Sioux leader, see Good Road

Pinecreek, Lutheran church, 11:466; settlement, 21:455

Pink Sheet (Minneapolis), weekly, 37:172

Pinkerton, John, geographer, 24:230

Pinkerton, Robert E., work reviewed, 13:298

Pinkerton National Detective Agency, St. Paul branch, 22:377

Pinkham, Patricia N., compiler, 25:299

Pinkham, Rev. Victor E., speaker, 12:341, 14:461

Pinney, Charles N., 16:471

Pinney, Ovid, 11:171n

"Pioneer," steamboat, 21:249n, 250, 252n, 265, 268, 37:53, 56. See also "Anson Northup"

Pioneer and Democrat (St. Paul), statehood extra, 14:173, 179; politics, 28:29, 30, 37:330-332, 39:49

Pioneer Building, St. Paul, architecture, 39:35

Pioneer Club, Northfield, history, 24:168

Pioneer Hall, University of Minnesota, 12:331, 17:477

Pioneer Hook and Ladder Co., St. Paul, 30:301; welcomes veterans, 38:290

Pioneer Independent Rifles, St. Paul, 17:336

Pioneer life and conditions, on prairies, 11:63-74, 185-187; clothing, 12:141, 146, 27:93; fuel, 12:144, 146, 16:499; democratic aspect, 13:11, 22:67; housekeeping, 14:263-282, 438, 24:241, 27:92, 39:201-204; diaries and letters, 14:303-310, 24:245, 39:82; furnishings, 15:181-193, 21:441, 22:204, 27:160; evaluated, 16:22-34, 17:411-420, 19:203-205; Indiana, 19:461; rural institutions, 20:19-28, 335; Minnesota communities, 21:340, 22:109, 111, 334, 36:104; Mesabi Range, 22:345; Iowa, 23:92, 27:163; reunions, 25:158-164; in art, 25:278, 26:359; literature, 26:293-311, 35:329, 37:306, 38:387, 39:291; culture, 26:378; Wisconsin, 27:68, 69, 31:187; speech customs, 28:371, 31:53. See also Food, Frontier, Houses, Social life

Pioneer Mill, Minneapolis, 35:341 (cover)

Pioneer Mine, Vermilion Range, 25:320, 35:338, 40:361

Pioneer Rivermen's Association, papers, 20:194, 21:36

Pioneer Savings and Loan Co., Minneapolis, 18:211

Pipe Lake, Meeker County, in Sioux Outbreak, 12:302, 38:283

Piper, Carson F., speaker, 19:360, 23:295

Piper, G. W., cattleman, 26:110

Piper, Henry Dan, author, 40:95

Pipes, manufacturing methods, 15:453, 31:196; trade item, 25:202; ceremonial aspect, 31:194, 33:344, 351, 40:199, 201; depicted, 33:345; materials, 40:203n, 206, 207

Pipestone, name, 14:250n; founded, 14:449, 31:205; baseball team, 15:489; churches, 16:121, 27:344, 28:395; power company, 35:381; railroad center, 36:71. See also Pipestone National Monument

Pipestone (mineral), see Catlinite

Pipestone Civic and Commerce Association, 22:293

Pipestone County, established, 14:244; politics, 14:250, 262, 17:119; boundaries, 14:253n; census, 14:254, 256, 258, 259; militia, 14:261; anniversary, 14:449; pioneer life, 15:492, 21:454; archives, 21:100; Dutch colony, 28:128, 35:90; topography, 31:193; settled, 31:205

Pipestone County (Old Settlers) Historical Society, 16:241, 21:218, 23:103; meetings, 11:465, 14:460, 18:465, 19:471, 22:340, 23:299, 26:284; reorganized, 12:37; anniversary program, 14:449; manuscript collections, 17:119, 24:87

Pipestone County Star (Pipestone), history, 20:362

Pipestone County War History Committee, 23:392

Pipestone Indian Shrine Association, 31:207

Pipestone National Monument, Sioux reservation, 12:434, 14:450, 27:154, 31:204-207; quarry, 15:156, 454, 16:225, 17:224, 18:458, 19:213, 20:334, 27:357, 28:286, 31:178, 193-208, 36:95; established, 15:369, 18:458, 31:207, 37:62, 63; Indian agency, 23:93; custodian, 29:263; pageant, 31:208; guides, 34:314, 39:82; MHS tour, 35:100; depicted, 36:18, 19, 21, 75, 37:186; museum, 37:66; history, 40:96

Piquadinaw Township, Aitkin County, name, 21:350

Pirrie, William, author, 21:368

Pitcher, Dr. Zina, 19:226

Pitt, William, the elder, foreign policy, 22:62

Pittenger, William A., Congressman, 40:368

Pittman, Mrs. Dora H., author, 28:83

Pittman, Edward F., author, 12:199

Pittman, Key, Senator, 40:373

Pittman-Robertson Wildlife Survey, 30:229n

Pitts, William S., pioneer physician, 14:227

Pitts thresher, 23:324, 325, 24:301

Pittsburgh, Pa., river port, 11:144, 19:184, 20:383; early printing, 15:8, 9; manufacturing, 23:87; ethnic settlements, 27:210, 213

Pittsburgh Saturday Visiter, 16:76

Pittsburgh Steamship Co., Lake Superior, 35:279

Pitz, Henry C., artist, 26:366

Pius X, Pope, message, 39:158

"Pizarro," play, 23:306

Pizer, Donald, author, 37:344

Place names, see Geographic names

Placide, Henry, actor, 32:97

Placide's Varieties, theatrical troupe, 23:307

Pladsen, Emil, 28:42

Plains Archaeological Conference, 12:426; publication, 29:165

Plains Indians, in art, 34:213; culture, 34:255, 301, 40:44; art work, 35:380; history, 36:316, 37:132; decline, 39:242

Plainview, history, 13:217, 35:152; creamery, 22:226; camp meeting, 31:82; July 4th celebration, 38:72; settled, 39:201

Plan of Union Church, St. Anthony, 40:7, 8

Plankerton, Ray E., lawyer, 17:213

Plasterers Protection and Benevolent Union, 21:387

Plath, Herman, 26:282

Platt, Rutherford, author, 33:227

Plattdütsche Claus Groth Guild, 26:79

Platte Lake, Morrison County, trading post, 11:373

Platte River, lumbering, 15:464; trade route, 40:195, 196

Plattes, Cyril W., speaker, 22:292

Plattsburgh, N.Y., Beaumont monument, 15:234; battle, 27:236

Plaut, W. Gunther, work reviewed, 36:319; author, 33:351, 35:49, 293, 40:46

Player, Preston, 14:337

Pleasant Grove, Olmsted County, church, 16:355; hotel records, 21:214; camp meeting, 31:82; history, 35:336, 38:42

Pleasant Hill, Winona County, Methodist meetings, 21:86

Pleasant Lake, Ramsey County, acreage, 40:226n; water supply, 40:228, 230; farm, 40:231n

Pleasant Mound Township, Blue Earth County, history, 23:399

Pleasant Prairie Township, Martin County, organized, 12:54; town meeting, 12:56; settled, 12:57n

Pleasant Valley Township, Olmsted County, history, 35:336

Pleasonton, Gen. Alfred, 25:234, 40:271

Plenty-Coups, Crow leader, 38:202

Plessis, Bishop Joseph O., missionary, 11:306, 24:42; papers, 11:42, 94, 307, 12:82, 13:426

Pletcher, David M., 39:84

Pletcher, N. M., speaker, 18:111

Pletcher, Dr. Nuba, 27:363, 28:88, 195, 29:93; speaker, 27:364

Pletsch, W. H., 15:372, 19:116, 20:99

Pletsch, Mrs. W. H., speaker, 16:362

Plimpton, Russell A., 15:83; speaker, 28:390

Plischke, Elmer, 23:392

Plouff Creek, Cook County, forest fires, 36:138

Plowman, George T., etcher, 16:239, 18:227

Plows, manufacture, 24:292-298

"Pluck," steamboat, 11:104

Plumb, G. W., author, 17:337

Plumb, Ralph G., author, 12:94, 26:266

Plumbe, John, Jr., work reviewed, 29:253

Plummer, Florence, author, 24:259

Plummer, Henry, 16:226

Plummer, Dr. Henry S., 20:300, 22:405, 407

Plummer, Sgt. John W., letter, 38:254

Plummer, Samuel F., author, 30:162; speaker, 30:277

Plummer, William T., 19:390

Plummer, history, 34:171

Plunkett, Charles, theater manager, 28:109, 110, 33:174, 175

Plunkett Co., theatrical troupe, 40:363

Plymouth, J. H. B., author, 14:337

Plymouth Congregational Church, St. Paul, 11:120, 12:318, 23:221, 38:75; Minneapolis, 17:229, 18:339, 19:262, 264-267

Plymouth Home Guards, in Sioux Outbreak, 31:99

Plymouth Township, Hennepin County, plat, 23:171; settled, 31:92, 36:36; history, 34:128

Plympton, Maj. Joseph, commandant at Fort Snelling, 18:159, 161, 162, 20:122, 21:23, 166-168, 172, 24:13, 19, 22n, 27:311

Plympton, Mrs. Joseph, at Fort Snelling, 39:312-314, 326

Poage family, genealogy, 21:195

Poatgieter, A. Hermina, "Yesterday's Books for Children," 33:340-343; "A Dutch Investor," 37:154-160; work reviewed, 36:62; reviews by, 33:137, 36:25, 189, 37:260; author,

thor, 35:204; translator, 37:188, 39:264, 286n

Pochmann, Henry A., works reviewed, 35:327, 37:299; compiler, 34:42; speaker, 37:40

Poe, Edgar Allan, 20:109, 406; editor, 30:203

Poehler, August L., 22:108, 23:104, 25:210

Poehler, Henrietta, 39:275

Poehler, Henry, memoirs, 13:426; house, 39:275, 276

Poehler, James A., letter, 39:275-277

Poehler, Mathilda, 39:276

Poetker, Rev. Albert H., author, 15:475

Poetry, on frontier, 26:293n, 298, 301; in Bellman, 26:307, 308; Schiller's use of Sioux theme, 39:198-200

Poferl, John, 29:287

Poggi, Edith M., author, 16:229

Pohl, Frederick J., work reviewed, 33:216

Pohl, Joseph, potter, 33:231-233

Poindexter, Miles, Senator, 22:79, 38:238

Point, Father Nicholas, 16:90

Point Abbaye (Point aux Baie), Mich., located, 23:238n

Point au Chene, Lake Huron, 23:140

Point aux Pins, Ont., Lake Superior, 23:147

Point Douglas, Washington County, roads, 16:282-284, 288, 17:317, 19:103, 36:210, 37:103n, 40:233-247; beginnings, 16:315, 17:279, 29:205; depicted, 17:148n, 392; population elements, 17:393; described, 17:394, 40:9; post office, 36:207, 208, 40:82, 83, 87; church, 37:277

Point du Sable, Baptiste, 15:424, 432

Point du Sable, Jean B., trader, 15:423, 432

Point du Sable, Suzanne, 15:423

Point Levis, Que., port, 20:255

Point Roberts, Wash., boundary, 23:255

Pointe au Sable (Sand Point), Goodhue County, 20:306

Pointe aux Barques, Mich., Lake Huron, 23:139-141

Poissant, Joseph, voyageur, testimony, 21:131

Pokegama, name, 20:343

"Pokegama," steamboat, 33:10, 11

Pokegama Bay, Superior, Wis., Lake Superior, 21:153; log cabin, 21:152

Pokegama Creek, Pine County, dam, 39:264

Pokegama Falls, Itasca County, road, 16:295, 299; river port, 29:213, 33:7, 8, 10, 11

Pokegama Lake, Itasca County, boys' camp, 19:451; dams, 24:93, 33:11

Pokegama Lake, Pine County, trading post, 11:371, 374, 16:214; mission, 17:351, 37:105; road, 40:233, 241

Poker Fleet, Minnesota-Atlantic Transit Co., ship names, 34:13

Pokorny, Rev. Francis, 15:33n

Poland, Henry, compiler, 40:211, 212, 214, 216, 217

Poland, St. Louis County, post office, 34:186

Polar Star Mills, Faribault, 11:275

Poles, Minnesota, 12:444, 28:75, 31:29; Minnesota communities, 13:108, 15:31, 16:372, 24:79, 26:235, 35:51; Michigan, 20:202, 27:205, 257; U.S., 20:442, 21:74, 25:86, 27:40, 37:344; bibliographies, 24:259, 25:299, 26:167; Mesabi Range, 27:204, 207, 208, 211, 213, 215, 40:341; Milwaukee, 30:139; New England, 35:326; religion, 37:133; in politics, 40:328; Nebraska, 40:352

Polish language, taught, 13:435

Polish National Alliance, 37:344

Polish National Catholic Church of the Sacred Heart, Minneapolis, 17:351

Polish Roman Catholic Union, 37:344

Polish Roman Catholic Union Archives and Museum, Chicago, 27:257

Political Action Socialists, 27:334

Political Equality Club of Minneapolis, records, 15:61, 113

Political Equality Club of St. Paul, 13:101, 17:468

Politics, Wisconsin, 11:82, 12:94, 200, 23:285, 35:295, 36:188; Minneapolis, 12:332; Ohio, 12:441, 36:323; frontier, 13:8-11, 17, 14:131-133, 15:209, 22:85, 413-415, 27:5, 6, 13-15, 35:105-109, 114-116; among ethnic groups, 13:434, 16:108, 17:85, 20:20-36, 36:237, 326, 40:328n; third-party movements, 14:339, 27:334, 32:129-146, 36:187, 40:139; Minnesota, 15:99, 16:100, 456, 458-460, 17:161-164, 21:416, 28:73, 74, 183, 321, 323, 324, 33:155-163, 34:129, 35:341-351, 36:1-12, 70, 173-183, 282, 37:131, 135, 39:37-48, 141-152, 344; Missouri, 15:331, 23:381, 40:308; national campaigns, 16:27, 30:189, 33:329, 330, 35:291, 36:151, 37:186, 307, 39:169; totalitarianism, 20:437, 23:216; labor activities, 21:383, 389, 22:384, 40:91; in land policy, 22:227-248; veterans' activities, 23:165, 35:197, 38:296, 297; military officeholders, 24:240, 35:313, 314; Middle West, 26:73, 36:185, 40:90, 353; soldier vote, 26:187-210, 36:167-172; governors, 28:183, 32:246, 35:352-357, 39:257; Indiana, 29:252, 30:382; historical aspects, 29:258, 34:352; women in, 32:120; patronage, 33:314, 37:324-334, 40:87; Oregon, 35:41; campaign songs, 35:200; Dakota Territory, 35:238; Iowa, 35:246; Michigan, 35:332; Pennsylvania, 35:353; Canada, 36:65; among Sioux, 38:130; theory, 39:172, 40:407; dynasties, 40:359. See also various parties and movements, individual politicians

Polk, Asa D., lawyer, 24:375, 25:384

Polk, Grace E., 13:103

Polk, James K., President, 16:326, 30:190, 191, 196, 39:38n

Polk, R. L., and Co., 27:64

Polk County, grasshopper plague, 12:263, 37:207; Norwegian settlements, 12:278; Lutheran church,

12:452; archives, 13:311; history, 15:369, 19:474, 38:204; boundaries, 15:491; mounds, 16:13; pageant, 16:237; fairs, 16:251; settled, 17:128; frontier life, 18:228; newspapers, 19:125, 30:273; organized, 20:207; agriculture, 21:212, 29:26; divided, 29:89; politics, 35:306, 307; physicians, 35:381

Polk County, Wis., Swedish settlement, 17:404; boundaries, 23:384

Polk County Fair Association, 14:358

Polk County Historical Society, 16: 241; organized, 14:358, 15:71; meetings, 17:484, 18:110, 22:107, 23:103, 299, 25:209, 26:91, 257, 285, 27:173, 30:168; museum, 19: 117, 23:194, 24:188, 270, 37:135; publication, 37:42; Junior Historians, 38:92

Polk County Hospital, Crookston, history, 35:381

Polk County War History Committee, 24:188

Polkton, Mich., Dutch settlement, 28: 120

Pollack, Norman, work reviewed, 38: 235; author, 37:261, 39:343

Pollard, James E., author, 17:218

Pollard, Mrs. Sophia, in Sioux Outbreak, 11:334; speaker, 23:298

Polley, A. D., author, 30:71

Polley, Arthur, steamboat owner, 33: 15

Pollock, Duncan, 12:368

Pollock, Hester M., 24:354

Pollock, J. D., architect, 15:54

Pollock, Mrs. Martha M., letters, 24: 354

Pollution, of water, 12:145, 35:45, 40:132

Polo, on frontier, 20:441

Pomarede, Leon, panoramist, 17:137, 143, 20:380, 382, 24:178, 28:278, 29:78, 30:15, 260, 33:286, 316, 35:379, 36:233; break with Henry Lewis, 17:139

Pomerantz, Sidney I., author, 30:63

Pomeroy, Earl, author, 34:262

Pomeroy, Earl N., author, 18:468

Pomeroy, Capt. George, Union officer, 25:29, 28:326

Pomeroy, Jesse H., carpenter, 11:177

Pomeroy, Marcus M. ("Brick"), newspaper editor, 37:127

Pomeroy, Milo, 17:119, 19:114; speaker, 18:333

Pomeroy, Robert D., cartoonist, 34: 359

Pomeroy, S. C., Congressman, 32:22

Pomeroy, Dr. Seth, 17:236

Pomfret, John E., author, 35:193

Pomme de Terre, Grant County, stockade, 12:302; stage line, 19:408, 20:432; described, 19:409; platted, 38:63. See also Fort Pomme de Terre

Pompe, Johann, 39:65, 72

Pompe, Theresia, 39:65, 72, 73

Ponca Indians, 35:177

Poncet, Father Joseph, letter, 13:417

Poncin, Sophie, cholera victim, 14: 290

Pond, Alonzo W., author, 19:228

Pond, E. J., author, 13:443; reminiscences, 14:116

Pond, Elnathan J., genealogy, 15:469, 25:80

Pond, F. Wilson, speaker, 23:101

Pond, George A., speaker, 15:316, 27: 266

Pond, Mrs. George A., speaker, 19:65

Pond, Gideon H., at Lac qui Parle, 12:210, 339, 16:136, 38:147n; Presbyterian missionary, 12:331, 16:22, 216, 239, 314, 345, 454, 17:236, 336, 18:460, 19:249, 21: 15-32, 163, 164, 167, 273, 282, 23:97, 24:4, 20n, 25:399, 27:264, 35:28, 36:192, 195, 37:85, 39:300, 40:8, 11; editor, 12:396, 26:138; letters, 13:169, 15:222, 16:469; sermons, 14:101, 20:209; cabin, 15:43; Bloomington house, 15:51, 468; centennial, 15:126, 242, 309, 315, 316, 16:105; career, 15:273-281, 383, 21:15, 28:337; portrait, 15:275; Dakota studies, 15: 276-278, 16:140-148, 21:160, 276-280, 29:58, 30:298; memorials, 15: 362, 16:354; government farmer, 16:135, 149, 17:70, 21:165, 169, 22:256, 40:139; papers, 17:53, 30: 320, 39:344; diaries, 18:47, 94, 21:108; author, 21:17; salary, 21: 166n; in fiction, 30:247, 37:10; educator, 36:35

Pond, Mrs. Gideon H., I (Sarah Poage), 15:280, 21:165; teacher, 16:134, 137; missionary, 16:145

Pond, Mrs. Gideon H., II (Mrs. Robert Hopkins), 15:280, 18:94

Pond, H. H., 12:445

Pond, Maj. James B., impresario, 17: 378, 379, 383, 384, 18:34, 40:13, 18, 19

Pond, Mrs. James B., 17:379, 383

Pond, Jennette, diary, 18:47, 94

Pond, Peter, 18:193; trader, 11:236, 261, 264, 15:100, 17:222, 19:95, 109, 294, 22:433, 33:130, 261, 34: 344, 35:243; map maker, 12:82, 14: 81-84, 16:230, 453, 35:97, 36:277; career, 13:181, 15:238, 16:239, 35:334; diary, 14:223, 15:90-92, 20:7, 31:195, 40:313; explorer, 28:71, 31:196, 33:187, 36:279

Pond, Ruth Hine, 21:18n

Pond, Samuel W., "Narrative," 21:17-32, 158-175, 272-283; map maker, 12:99; Presbyterian missionary, 12:190, 331, 13:321, 16:22, 148, 216, 345, 387, 454, 17:236, 18: 460, 23:97, 24:4, 20n, 25:399, 35: 28, 36:192, 195, 38:147n, 39:300, 40:139; letters, 13:170, 14:226, 15:222, 16:333, 469, 18:94; cabin, 15:43; centennial, 15:126, 242, 309, 315, 16:105, 239; career, 15: 273-281, 21:15-17, 28:337; portraits, 15:274, 25:187; ordained, 15:275, 21:158; Dakota studies, 15:275-278, 16:140-143, 21:160, 276-280, 29:58, 30:298; memorials, 15:362, 16:354; quoted, 20:260, 261, 267, 24:12; government farmer, 21:163; author, 30:219n; in fiction, 30:247, 37:10; papers, 30:320

Pond, Mrs. Samuel W., I (Cordelia Eggleston), 15:281, 21:165, 172

Pond, Mrs. Samuel W., II (Rebecca Smith), 15:281

Pond, Samuel W., Jr., author, 21:16

Pond family, 21:18n; history, 12:444; reunions, 14:362; missionary services, 16:345; records, 18:47, 19: 65

Pond Family Association, 15:281, 16: 354, 25:80; organized, 14:454; celebrates Pond centennial, 15: 126, 242, 362

Ponemah, Chippewa settlement, 26:81, 31:274

Ponomarew, ---, Russian officer, 40: 265 (cover), 273n

Ponsford, J. J., author, 11:332

Ponsford, Orville D., 11:332

Ponsford, history, 11:331; Chippewa settlement, 26:81

Pontchartrain, Louis P., 13:418, 19: 284, 294, 295, 20:423

Pontiac, Ottawa leader, 19:330, 20:7, 23:355, 29:65, 33:37, 344; death, 22:73

Pontiac's War, 11:240, 40:199

Pony express, route, 14:431

Pool, Roy, speaker, 16:130

Poole, S. Alicia, author, 12:327

Poor, A. C., 13:140

Poor, Albert, 13:147

Poor Handmaids of Jesus Christ, Catholic order, 15:484

Pooter, --- de, Jesuit missionary, 39:308

Pope, Alice, pioneer, 33:3

Pope, Elsie, pioneer, 33:3

Pope, Gussie, pioneer, 33:3

Pope, J. C., 12:450

Pope, Rev. J. D., 18:361

Pope, Gen. John, 39:233; expedition, 11:367, 368, 12:83, 190, 16:239, 22:148n, 281, 282, 40:363; Union officer, 25:137, 146, 149, 150; in Sioux Outbreak, 38:106, 110, 112, 274, 278-281; portrait, 38:279

Pope, R. M., journalist, 15:368

Pope, Rev. William C., 40:349; papers, 11:96, 16:336, 23:76

Pope County, schools, 11:223, 16:243, 17:239, 18:64, 445, 26:183, 390, 398; courthouses, 11:337, 38:189n; history, 11:466, 40:363; described, 12:259; Norwegian settlement, 12:277, 24:92; press, 19: 125; Lutheran church, 19:125, 23: 198, 24:92; in fiction, 20:354; milling, 21:218; centennial program, 30:285; pioneer farming, 37: 204; electric utility, 40:315

Pope County Fair, history, 22:442

Pope County Historical Society, 16: 241, 20:354, 21:109, 218, 22:442; projected, 13:120, 453; organized, 14:237; activities, 16:243, 18:64, 110, 445, 19:361, 20:457; WPA projects, 17:122, 232, 530, 20:97, 213; museum, 19:471, 20:458, 21: 338, 24:380, 26:389-391, 27:76, 28:88, 297; meetings, 19:471, 27: 266, 28:195, 29:181; finances, 25: 209; collections, 30:401

Pope County War History Committee, 23:392, 24:185

Popelka, Josef, 15:31

Popelka family, Bohemian settlers, 15:30

Popham, Earle C., author, 15:477

Poplar, Mont., stop on Glidden tour, 38:214

Poplar Creek, Northwest Angle, 34:7n
Poplar Lake Lutheran Church, Polk County, 19:125
Poplar River Township, Red Lake County, history, 38:204
Popovich, Peter S., 28:300; speaker, 35:384, 36:108
Poppe, Forrest R., biography, 16:337
Popper, Samuel H., work reviewed, 35:289
Popple, Charles S., work reviewed, 25:279
Popple, Beltrami County, in county seat fight, 23:30
Poppleton, ---, Missouri pioneer, 17:434
Population, Midwest, 13:435, 16:109; distribution, 14:91; growth, 14:170, 253, 407, 16:428, 17:276, 21:225, 372, 438, 23:87, 24:308; Minnesota, 16:469, 18:87, 19:358, 23:87; Michigan Territory, 25:271. See also Census
Populist movement, leaders, 14:169, 35:61, 378, 36:109-126, 183, 37:181, 39:260, 343; origins, 18:106, 32:129-146, 36:101; economic aspect, 21:94; influence, 22:78, 35:89, 97, 39:98, 293; conventions, 22:162, 39:100, 101; ideology, 23:283, 37:261, 38:235, 236, 39:83, 40:46, 95; history, 25:298, 26:171, 34:354, 36:34, 37:262, 38:387, 39:94. See also People's party
Porcupine Mountains, Mich., 23:241, 242
Pork Bay, Lake County, fur trade route, 26:284
Porlier, ---, Montreal merchant, 11:237n
Porlier, Jacques, trader, 12:233, 15:421
Port, Walter C., 16:347
Port Arthur (Thunder Bay), Ont., lake port, 24:166, 25:54, 35:48; Dawson Trail, 32:242, 40:359
Port Austin, Mich., located, 23:140n
Port Hudson, La., in Civil War, 25:353
Port Huron, Mich., customs station, 20:255
Port Louisa, Iowa, river town, 17:426
Port McNicoll, Ont., lake port, 34:14
Port Nelson, Man., explored, 16:418n; post, 40:174
Port Royal, N.S., post, 40:188
"Port Royal," gunboat, 25:129
Portage, Wis., history, 11:452, 29:173; Indian agency, 26:385
Portage de L'Isle Fort, Ont., trading post, 11:363
Portage des Chênes, Ont., 12:375
Portage des Sioux, Mo., treaty, 12:317
Portage Entry, Keweenaw Peninsula, Mich., 34:248
Portage La Prairie, Man., 33:71; river port, 21:261
Portage Point, Lake Huron, 23:141
Portage River, Mich., 23:238
Portage St. Croix, Upper Lake St. Croix, 28:149, 232, 233, 235
Portages, in fur trade, 12:293, 360, 33:130; prehistoric, 15:155; used by Indians, 15:255; Big Stone Lake to Lake Traverse, 17:304, 307; le-

gal aspect, 21:118; Sault Ste. Marie, 23:147; crossing methods, 23:239, 245, 246, 252; St. Louis River, 23:245, 32:92, 94; Falls of St. Anthony, 23:338, 32:96; La Loche, 25:90; Lake St. Croix, 28:149, 232; Rove Lake, 29:134; Brule-St. Croix, 32:90, 186; on Dawson Trail, 32:242. See also individual portages
Porteous, ---, trader, 11:261
Porter, Carrie L., 15:345
Porter, Charles W., author, 24:252
Porter, David D., 25:243
Porter, Edward D., agriculture professor, 16:352, 33:224, 37:22
Porter, Gen. Fitz John, 25:36, 128, 132, 244
Porter, George F., diary, 26:380
Porter, H. H., capitalist, 33:221
Porter, Henry H., author, 21:365
Porter, Dr. Horace P., journalist, 19:336, 24:264
Porter, Howard F., art dealer, 24:180, 30:20
Porter, J. A., 15:345
Porter, J. Henry, author, 26:380
Porter, Rev. Jeremiah, letter, 12:226, 18:182; missionary, 12:229, 13:173; diary, 18:47, 94, 34:219
Porter, John J., politician, 38:361
Porter, Kenneth W., "Negroes and the Fur Trade," 15:421-433; work reviewed, 13:179-181; author, 12:91, 15:352, 531, 16:475, 18:76, 24:261, 26:73, 27:131, 39:254
Porter, Kirk H., author, 35:291
Porter, Mae R., author, 29:58, 60, 61
Porter, Rufus, inventor, 38:168, 169, 171
Porter, William A., speculator, 39:90
Porter, William T., editor, 14:424, 15:384, 16:187, 28:340n, 35:330
Portland, land office, 12:387; roads, 16:291, 298; settled, 21:151; townsite, 37:112-114. See also Duluth
Portland, Me., immigrant port, 20:252
Portland, Ore., schools, 25:191
Portland Prairie, Houston County, agriculture, 20:162
Portman, John, 16:400n, 425n
Portugal, trade with India, 35:151
Posey, Walter B., author, 12:198
Posner, Ernst, 28:69; author, 37:136
Post, Albert, work reviewed, 24:338-340
Post, Mary C., author, 15:252
Post offices, Duluth, 15:467, 34:185; Minnesota communities, 17:485, 18:341, 23:25, 109, 28:82, 34:170, 35:16, 18, 112, 36:209, 210, 214, 215; Crow Wing County, 22:344; Martin County, 22:441; territorial, 26:174, 30:174, 40:79, 83, 84; Cook County, 35:246; Chicago, 40:87. See also Mail service
Post War Council, New York, donor, 23:393
Postl, Karl, author, 14:334
Potgieter, ---, Dutch minister, 28:126
Potomac River, Va., navigation, 14:108
Potosi, Stevens County, post office, 19:239
Potowatomi Indians, 13:400, 19:304;

Radisson's visit, 13:260, 262, 399, 15:167, 171; Wisconsin, 13:397, 402, 33:351; warfare, 13:401, 15:176; in fur trade, 19:274; Indiana, 29:335; depicted, 29:336, 33:20; Nebraska, 34:285; Illinois, 36:191; culture, 37:174
Potsdam Flouring Mill, Olmsted County, 40:126
Potter, D. D., teacher, 18:227
Potter, Daniel C., quarrying operations, 16:255
Potter, David M., author, 31:243, 34:310, 39:34
Potter, Israel, Revolutionary War prisoner, 33:346
Potter, Joshua, missionary, 20:447
Potter, L. E., 14:459
Potter, Marion E., 31:245
Potter, Merle, review by, 13:422; work reviewed, 12:420-422; author, 11:454, 12:202, 203, 333, 444, 13:215, 314, 446, 14:113, 117, 35:155; speaker, 13:73, 15:82, 219
Potter, William H., 16:217
Potter Co., Aitkin, 33:14
Pottery, prehistoric, 16:3, 14-19, 481, 24:78, 25:156, 329-335, 26:387, 28:193, 31:166-171, 232-236; Minnesota factories, 33:229-235
Pottgieser, Maria L., 18:321
Pottgieser, Nicholas, hotelkeeper, 33:197n
Potts, Dr. Thomas R., 14:295, 20:368, 28:311n, 31:173, 174; health officer, 14:299, 301; papers, 16:71, 20:91, 30:298; career, 17:220, 21:343, 437, 36:282; MHS founder, 20:367
Potts, Mrs. Thomas R. (Abbie A. Steele), 28:311n, 31:173
Pouchot, François, 32:233
Poulin, Narcisse, account book, 17:119
Poultry industry, Minnesota, 22:265
Pound, Arthur, author, 25:273
Pound, Ezra, author, 20:107
Pound, Louise, author, 28:186
Poussin, Nicolaus, artist, 38:345
Powderhorn Lake, Minneapolis, 35:23
Powderly, Terence V., labor leader, 21:315, 22:326, 371, 382, 27:334
Powell, Arthur, pictured, 35:84
Powell, Dr. Ernest S., speaker, 22:347
Powell, John H., author, 23:326
Powell, John Walker, pioneer preacher, 31:82n, 35:77, 83
Powell, Mrs. John Walker, 35:77, 86
Powell, John Walker, the younger, "A Summer in the Big Woods," 35:77-86; author, 28:76, 286; career, 35:77; pictured, 35:84
Powell, Maj. John Wesley, surveyor, 24:62; geologist, 32:223
Powell, Dr. Lester D., author, 23:289
Powell, Louis H., "Around a Geologic Clock in Minnesota," 15:141-147; review by, 34:116; work reviewed, 36:33; speaker, 15:220, 17:315; author, 20:207, 26:164, 34:354, 35:244
Powell, Mary M., author, 30:74
Powell, Peter, trader, 22:282, 285; family, 22:287
Powell, Ransom J., 11:206; career, 19:214; papers, 20:33, 83, 21:316

Powell, Mrs. Rose, 20:95
Powell, Walter D., author, 18:102
Power, Mrs. Charles E., 18:321
Power, George, farm, 26:90
Power, James B., land agent, 36:68
Power, Richard L., work reviewed, 34:81
Power, Victor L., 33:51
Powers, ---, colonist, 19:41
Powers, Dr. F. W., 19:360, 23:296
Powers, George M., 20:141, 142, 144, 329
Powers, Joseph L., author, 31:58
Powers, Le Grand, labor leader, 14:153, 22:388
Powers, Simon, stage owner, 40:387, 388
Powers, William H., editor, 14:448
Powers Dry Goods Co., Minneapolis, 26:396
"Powhatan," steamboat, wrecked, 15:413
Powhatan Indians, in fur trade, 40:205
Powicke, F. M., author, 13:431
Prahl, Augustus J., author, 31:242
"Prairie Bird," steamboat, 17:151, 18:372
Prairie City, Ill., post office, 25:11n; academy, 25:12
Prairie du Chien, Wis., trade center, 11:98, 13:223, 225, 226, 15:343, 16:37, 19:294, 20:335; Indian agency, 11:105, 431, 17:96, 25:89; Catholic churches, 11:108, 17:475, 23:286, 30:5; post, 11:384, 451, 15:379, 380, 17:335, 19:292, 456, 20:16, 205, 259, 261n, 262, 23:344n, 25:267, 31:212, 34:284, 286, 36:67, 40:23, 78, 81, 184, 186, 261; stage line, 11:404; history, 11:452, 17:196, 18:193, 21:98, 25:271, 272, 26:233, 29:173; described, 12:159, 17:153, 18:154, 326, 33:116; in War of 1812, 12:234, 13:208, 16:223, 31:189; river port, 13:228, 231, 16:45, 17:486, 20:128, 394, 21:20, 22:27, 28:311, 29:126, 175, 35:355, 36:43-47, 40:79; geography, 13:437; treaty, 14:98, 16:472, 17:55, 475, 18:207, 404, 23:85, 28:277, 33:20, 35:24, 27, 36:148, 280; sports, 14:222; in verse, 14:227; mail service, 15:311, 30:196, 36:206-208, 40:78-80, 85, 86; depicted, 16:53, 17:296, 298, 26:359, 28:277, 40:80; Dousman house, 17:344, 20:76, 339, 24:242, 25:409; business, 17:389; frontier life, 18:327; archaeology, 20:188; railroad, 20:256, 29:116; Presbyterian church, 20:443; health conditions, 21:95; trail, 21:227, 22:203, 23:288; census, 21:428; land titles, 23:128, 24:176; pontoon bridge, 23:286, 25:198, 27:258; French settlement, 23:343, 27:135; historic sites, 25:409, 37:40; newspaper, 29:359; showboat performances, 33:39; in fiction, 34:219; MHS tour, 36:240; road, 40:387, 388. See also Fort Crawford
Prairie du Chien, Hudson, and St. Paul Packet Co., 12:426, 13:234
Prairie du Chien Patriot, 15:467

Prairie Farmer (Chicago), centennial, 22:201, 23:283
Prairie fires, 11:69, 72, 14:99, 37:204; Red River Valley, 12:151-153; described, 20:145
Prairie Island, Goodhue County, Mississippi River, post, 11:381; history, 11:452; archaeology, 13:245, 25:398, 37:86, 136; Radisson's landing isle, 13:245-255, 265, 395-402, 15:172, 318, 319; fort, 19:214; MHS tour, 36:240; map, 37:273
Prairie Island Indian Community (Sioux), 37:271-282
Prairie La Crosse, see La Crosse, Wis.
Prairie Lake, St. Louis County, fur trade, 20:11
Prairie Portage, Lake County, Minn., Ont., post, 11:372, 12:375; geology, 13:406; canoe route, 38:29
Prairie Queen, Fillmore County, church, 13:448
Prairie River, Aitkin and St. Louis counties, geology, 13:406; log drives, 33:19
Prairie River, Itasca County, log drive, 24:192
Prairie Rose Bud, mission magazine, 11:94
Prairie schooners, Pembina trail, 12:153-156. See also Covered wagons
Prairies, pioneer life, 11:63, 71; floods, 11:67-69; described, 12:48-51, 272, 23:337; breaking process, 12:55, 57; Canada, 12:198; advantages for farming, 12:247; travel account, 35:239. See also Prairie fires
Prairieville (Shakopee), mission, 12:190, 16:333, 21:175
Prairieville, Wis., frontier life, 27:153
Prang, Louis, lithographer, 33:351
Pratt, Albert H., speculator, 37:87
Pratt, Albert W., 15:195
Pratt, Mrs. Albert W. (Agnes V.), 15:195
Pratt, Alice D., work reviewed, 35:42
Pratt, Anne S., 19:35n
Pratt, Fletcher, work reviewed, 35:35
Pratt, Henry P., cholera victim, 14:297
Pratt, Mrs. Jennie, speaker, 22:106
Pratt, Julius W., author, 16:223, 22:307
Pratt, Martin V., 35:225n
Pratt, Richard, work reviewed, 40:45
Pratt, Gen. Richard H., biography, 17:200
Pratt, Mayor Robert, 17:382
Pratt, Sophia C., teacher, 11:220
Pratt, Col. William M., settler, 35:42
Pratte, Bernard, and Co., 40:185
Pratte family, in fur trade, 15:421
Praus, Alexis, author, 38:385
Pray, Otis A., millwright, 18:208
Preble Township, Fillmore County, Norwegian settlement, 12:268
Predmore, Olmsted County, railroad, 35:12
Pre-emption laws, relation to frontier, 13:106; effects, 19:200, 23:358; extended, 22:229, 235, 23:

162; provisions, 22:234, 237, 239n, 27:293; defended, 22:241
Prehistory, see Archaeology
Premier automobile, 38:207, 208
Prendergast, Harold, author, 15:456
Presbrey, Paul W., author, 15:130
Presbyterial Institute, St. Paul, 14:147
Presbyterian church, Minnesota Synod, 11:41, 25:186, 399, 34:91; educational program, 14:330, 30:244; Minnesota, 15:223, 28:395, 34:266; history, 18:196; Wisconsin, 24:178, 28:395, 34:266; German, 24:366, 28:126; archives, 27:252; frontier, 27:344, 36:192; Dutch, 28:123, 129; camp meetings, 31:79; Hennepin County, 37:308. See also Macalester College, Presbyterian missions, individual cities and church bodies
Presbyterian College, Jamestown, N.D., described, 20:444
Presbyterian missions, Lac qui Parle, 12:339, 15:136, 16:483, 21:171n, 412, 434; records, 16:313; Minnesota Valley, 16:357; women's society, 17:100; Orr, 17:364; Fort Snelling, 18:197; Traverse des Sioux, 20:260, 21:171n; Wisconsin, 20:443, 28:395; Minnesota, 20:447, 21:457, 40:1-11; ideology, 21:71; Dakotas, 23:383, 35:167, 168, 170, 380; to lumberjacks, 31:65-78; Nebraska, 35:380. See also individual missionaries
Prescott, Mrs. Carrie, 11:96
Prescott, Mary, teacher, 13:140
Prescott, Philander, 21:163, 22:147, 152, 223, 31:207; interpreter, 11:184, 31:215; trader, 12:119, 130, 164, 21:161n; death, 12:133n; house, 22:155; papers, 30:320; author, 31:196, 202, 203, 208, 252, 40:139; career, 35:197; postmaster, 36:207, 40:87; town founder, 36:280
Prescott, William H., author, 40:313
Prescott, Wis., history, 11:452, 36:280; described, 17:279, 394; newspaper, 17:314; trail, 21:227; ethnic groups, 27:134; river port, 34:74n, 132; mail service, 36:212; band, 37:202; architecture, 38:341, 343-346; lumbering, 40:9
Prescott Journal, established, 17:385
Prescott Township, Faribault County, poor farm, 38:368
"President," steamboat, 18:452
Presley, Mrs. ---, piano owner, 39:319
Presque Isle, Mich., Lake Huron, 23:141
Presque Isle, Mich., Lake Superior, 23:237
Presque Isle River, Mich., 23:242
Press, Selma, see Larsen, Mrs. Arthur J.
Press (Farmington), history, 15:245
Press Club, St. Paul, 12:344
Pressly, Thomas J., work reviewed, 34:81
Pressnell, Thomas H., author, 22:87
Prestgard, Kristian, 29:314
Presto, see Staples
Preston, C. P., 18:128n

Preston, Dr. Harriet, pioneer physician, 33:312
Preston, John B., Union officer, 39:195n
Preston, William, Jr., author, 38:334
Preston, pageant, 11:333; churches, 14:451, 15:128, 21:449; county seat fight, 16:127; band, 18:467; scarlet fever epidemic, 20:225n
Preston Lake, Renville County, in Sioux Outbreak, 12:302, 303, 38:279n
Preston Lake Township, Renville County, school, 25:102
Preston Republican, anniversary edition, 16:127
Preston Township, Fillmore County, Norwegian settlement, 12:268
Prettyman, William, 16:425n
Preus, Jacob A. O., governor, 14:437, 36:239, 40:148; papers, 15:61; politician, 36:103
Pribilof Islands, Alaska, seal fisheries, 40:217
Price, D. C., author, 16:493
Price, E. V., 17:366
Price, James, pioneer, 23:401
Price, Leontyne, singer, 39:63
Price, Dr. Milo B., speaker, 11:286
Price, Robert, work reviewed, 34:201
Price, Mrs. Sadie R., author, 29:176
Price, Gen. Sterling, Confederate officer, 25:28, 29, 34:305, 40:283-286, 290, 291
Price, Warwick J., author, 26:306
Price, Willard, author, 36:237, 38:384
Prichard, Walter, review by, 31:48; author, 31:64
Priest, Loring B., work reviewed, 23:163
Priestley, Thomas, diary, 17:98
Priestly, Herbert I., work reviewed, 11:77
Prignitz, Christian, surveyor, 18:466
Prim, Gen. Juan, 25:137
Prime, W. C., excursionist, 15:406, 413, 414
Primm, Wilson, author, 33:132
Primmer, George H., "Pioneer Roads Centering at Duluth," 16:282-299; speaker, 15:138; author, 15:482, 16:482, 18:343, 19:110, 113, 20:83
Prince, A. E., author, 25:199
Prince, John S., 14:272; mayor, 14:299, 38:290, 293, 40:223; house, 34:101, 102, 215
Prince Edward Island, colony, 24:41, 39:166
Prince of Wales Fort, Man., 40:190
"Prince Rupert," steamboat, 21:259n
Princeton, history, 13:452, 15:152; clubs, 16:367; G.A.R. post, 16:431; Methodist church, 17:230; garrison, 38:286
Princeton Civic Betterment Club, 16:367
Princeton Rod and Gun Club, 16:367
Pringle, Mrs. Henry, Hastings hostess, 37:201
Pringle, Henry F., author, 27:133, 29:258
Pringle family, in Hastings, 22:89
Prins, A. J., author, 18:339
Prins, D., 28:129
Prins, Martin W., 18:338, 36:104

Prins and Koch, colonizers, 18:338, 28:124, 126
"Prins Willem IV," motor ship, 34:356
Prinsburg, Dutch settlement, 28:126, 127, 36:104
Printing, pioneer, 12:98, 13:109-111, 211, 317, 335, 336, 14:447, 15:1-25, 18:454, 19:431, 26:178, 293, 30:327, 36:189, 276; newspapers, 13:107, 20:461; bibliographies, 13:436, 26:72; by deaf, 17:227; in Americas, 18:450; unions, 21:376, 378
Prior Lake, mounds, 15:149; resort, 36:92
Prison Mirror (Stillwater), established, 17:386; policies, 29:322, 324
Pritchard, Hugh, 16:231
Pritchard, John, letter, 12:437
Pritchard, Sam, 16:231
Pritchett, John P., reviews by, 11:85-87, 12:419, 13:186, 298, 300, 14:204, 15:333-335, 16:460-462; works reviewed, 24:152-154, 31:239; editor, 12:95, 437, 22:331, 25:200, 27:62; author, 12:200, 441, 24:179; speaker, 12:287, 13:105
Pritz, Mrs. William H., 38:81
Probtsfield, Randolph M., Clay County pioneer, 20:454, 34:357; diary, 29:357, 35:97; hunter, 30:126
Proclamation of 1763, 11:243, 15:95
Proctor, Ellen, author, 31:146
Proctor, John S., surveyor general of logs, 31:33; prison official, 37:142, 143, 146; house, 38:339, 352
Proctor, Richard A., astronomer, 39:115
Proctor, post office, 34:186
Proctor Journal, history, 35:152
Proehl, Wilhelm, journalist, 12:195
Progressive Age, 36:119
Progressive Citizens of America, 34:189
Progressive Education Association, 21:62
Progressive League, Minneapolis, 40:321
Progressive movement, Colorado, 23:263-265; history, 27:132-134, 28:372, 33:41, 40:46; evaluated, 35:89, 36:97; Wisconsin, 35:236, 241; North Dakota, 36:34; financial policy, 39:293
Progressive party, platform, 11:446; Minnesota, 17:213, 33:158, 34:193, 194; leaders, 18:316, 423, 21:69
Prohibition movement, amendment repealed, 28:55; opposed, 30:26; Minnesota, 33:156-163; Iowa, 34:22n. See also Liquor traffic, Temperance movement
Prohibition party, 18:110; platform, 35:291
Prosser, Richard S., work reviewed, 40:315
Prosser, Thomas, 11:94
Protestant church, among ethnic groups, 15:26, 31-36, 31:29, 31, 112, 35:33; Fort Snelling, 16:354; Canada, 17:454; frontier, 20:27, 29:81, 33:373; interfaith cooperation, 38:335. See also individual denominations

Protestant Episcopal church, see Episcopal church
Protestant Home, St. Paul, history, 38:74-85, 370
Protestant missions, in West, 11:429; schools, 15:111; to Sioux, 15:126, 273-281; history, 15:211; Minnesota communities, 15:242, 16:129, 17:224, 27:263; to Chippewa, 16:216, 17:351, 391, 31:54; Red River Valley, 20:327; Oregon, 26:56; Canada, 28:61; attitude of Indians, 39:292. See also individual denominations
Protestant Orphan Asylum, St. Paul, 21:343, 455, 39:56
Prouleau, Charles, 39:304
Prout, Briton C., miner, 25:411; author, 27:82
Prout, Clarence, 13:289; author, 35:98
Prouville de Tracy, Alexandre de, 12:282, 349, 16:404, 405
Provanché, François, voyageur, 18:240
Provençalle, George, portrait, 11:88
Provençalle, Louis, cabin, 12:452, 20:268; trader, 16:73, 300, 20:259-268, 430, 21:44, 162, 31:198, 32:71, 37:33
Provencher, Father Joseph N., missionary, 11:307, 20:204, 24:42, 179, 35:282; papers, 12:82, 13:426, 21:205, 34:352; bishop, 21:432, 24:43, 29:81, 267, 40:313
Proverbs, Minnesota, 27:33-36; frontier, 28:371, 30:135-137; Wisconsin, 30:248
Provincial, see Provençalle
Provost, Paulette, lumberman, 24:201
Prucha, Father F. Paul, "Minnesota's Attitude toward Secession," 24:307-317; "Fort Ripley," 28:205-224; "The Settler and the Army," 29:231-246; "Minnesota 100 Years Ago," 34:45-53; "An Army Private at Old Fort Snelling," 36:13-17; "Army Sutlers," 40:22-31; reviews by, 34:38, 35:35, 37:34, 338; works reviewed, 33:262, 36:148, 38:191, 39:254; author, 24:352, 28:307, 29:287, 33:316, 34:42, 220, 40:42; speaker, 40:150
Prucha, Jan, 15:35
Prussians, see Germans
Public Archives of Canada, 15:94; art collection, 14:284, 18:216, 28:282; documents, 15:90, 16:200, 22:306, 429; described, 16:480; organized, 17:7, 21:433; copying projects, 23:272, 39:165
Public health, North Dakota, 12:328; Minnesota, 19:111, 213, 21:358-362, 29:170, 34:316, 39:84; McLeod County, 20:102; legislation, 21:358, 367; literature, 21:365-371; history, 26:367, 27:27, 240, 340, 341, 28:49, 29:53, 34:34, 176; pollution problem, 39:114, 40:132. See also Medicine, various diseases
Public lands, administration, 12:286, 379-389, 34:354; policies, 12:379, 22:227-248, 23:161-163, 25:69, 35:381; surveys, 12:380, 22:228, 237, 240, 23:86, 24:252; sales, 17:416-420, 22:234, 236-243, 245-247, 39:85-92; Nebraska, 19:81-83, 39:261;

iron ranges, 19:85-87; railroad grants, 22:229-233, 34:67; speculation, 22:236; Minnesota, 23:189, 24:174, 28:330, 29:222; Iowa, 23:358; value, 25:183; school grants, 25:306; settled, 27:292-295; military reservations, 28:216-224, 29:241-246; veterans' grants, 34:4, 67, 39:241, 242; history, 38:201, 329; bibliography, 38:388. See also Pre-emption laws

Public Ownership party, 33:158, 159
Public Records Office, London, Eng., 17:7, 9, 94, 454
Pueblo Indians, music, 12:326; social organization, 40:358
Puget Sound, Wash., mail service, 40:89
Puget Sound Agricultural Co., 27:38
Pugh, Rev. T., 13:148
Pugh, Zeke, speaker, 19:316
Pulitzer, Joseph, publisher, 34:203
Pulli, E. A., speaker, 30:77
Pullman, George M., 36:66, 122
Pullman Co., strike, 39:94, 101
Pulozky, Francis, author, 29:154
Pulozky, Therese, author, 29:154
Pumpelly, Raphael, author, 40:141
Punderson, Carolyn E., speaker, 11:51, 15:241; author, 15:466
Punteney, William F., steamboat captain, 33:16, 18
Puposky, Polish settlement, 13:108
Purcell, Dr. Edward, army doctor, 14:98, 16:353, 18:400, 19:354, 21:101, 437, 25:399; letters, 21:93
Purcell, Richard J., author, 12:442, 13:213, 441, 14:230, 15:128, 16:114, 17:114, 115, 25:305, 30:69
Purcell, William C., architect, 40:97, 98, 108, 359; work reviewed, 40:310
Purdy, Daniel, 15:484
Purdy, Ellison R., Quaker minister, 18:261
Purdy, G. A., county commissioner, 37:209
Purdy, Samuel, 15:484
"Puritan," steamboat, 29:292
Puritanism, among immigrants, 22:72; influence, 24:48, 33:80; Minnesota, 40:1-11
Purmort, Abner, letters, 21:415
Purmort, Mrs. Abner, letters, 21:415
Purmort, John E., diaries, 21:415
Purnell, Edmund, 19:450
Purple, Charles W., 18:128, 129, 145, 146
Purrington, Rev. Robert, speaker, 12:453
Pursell, Carroll W., Jr., compiler, 40:360
Pusey, Pennock, papers, 14:101, 17:211, 466
Puthuff, William H., Indian agent, 19:305
"Put-in-Bay," steamboat, 34:15
Putnam, Frank E., speaker, 11:292
Putnam, Henry C., 25:70
Putnam, Herbert, librarian, 21:113, 35:231, 232
Putnam, Jackson, author, 35:247
Putnam, James L., "The Yellow Medicine County Museum," 30:402
Putnam, Jay L., 18:337; speaker, 16:302; collector, 30:404
Putnam, Katherine, 17:62

Putnam, S. Newton, speaker, 18:110
Putnam, Samuel M., diary, 13:321, 14:65
Putnam, W. H., speaker, 11:219
Pye, James, 18:468
Pye, Watts O., missionary, 16:239
Pye, William W., 12:106; author, 11:337, 29:96; speaker, 28:388
Pyle, Howard, 20:82; artist, 37:308, 38:245 (cover)
Pyle, Joseph G., editor, 39:333

Quadna Township, Aitkin County, name, 21:350
Quaife, Milo M., 16:96, 18:190, 23:134; "A Footnote on Fire Steels," 18:36-41; "Paul Bunyan Tales," 21:296-298; review by, 21:302-304; works reviewed, 25:368-370, 32:184, 35:199; author, 11:108, 14:108, 15:353, 17:22-26, 29, 166, 18:68, 91, 188, 21:187, 310, 24:72, 28:276, 378, 29:175, 34:311, 35:243; editor, 11:326, 13:106, 23:182, 24:77, 25:178, 272, 26:270, 34:215; speaker, 15:118, 17:20; quoted, 15:423, 21:178, 188, 27:129
Quakers (Society of Friends), 33:81; Minneapolis, 17:478, 20:358, 21:192; Minnesota, 18:249-266; Iowa Meeting, 18:250; activities, 18:262-265; Anoka County, 24:189; as Indian agents, 37:273
Qualey, Carlton C., "Pioneer Norwegian Settlement," 12:247-280; "Territorial History," 28:329-338; "The Minnesota Historical Society in 1947," 29:46-56; "Some National Groups in Minnesota," 31:18-32; "John Wesley North," 35:101-116; "A Pioneer Businessman," 39:65-74; reviews by, 12:179-183, 21:76, 24:156, 348, 26:251, 28:269, 367, 29:154, 30:250, 31:50, 180, 32:51, 33:218, 34:163, 199, 343, 35:33, 90, 193, 290, 36:275, 319, 37:129, 256, 39:167, 291, 40:305; works reviewed, 19:199-201, 37:299; author, 11:321, 21:426, 22:68, 27:49, 28:276, 308, 365, 34:359; professor, 21:80, 193, 28:399; compiler, 21:193; MHS superintendent, 28:299, 29:47, 186, 30:39, 329; speaker, 29:95; career, 31:63; editor, 40:357
Qualla Reservation, N.C., 37:271
Quam, Halvor, 29:308
Quamme, John R., author, 23:298
Quammen, Rev. A. G., 14:359
Quammen, Rev. N. A., 14:359
Quant, Rachael, 22:52
Quantrill, Charles, guerilla leader, 34:304
Quarfoth, Hal, author, 36:239, 37:44, 223, 308, 38:43
Quarries, Minnesota, 16:255, 17:85, 25:308, 35:295, 338, 36:69, 37:87, 117, 194-196, 227, 263, 290, 291. See also Pipestone National Monument
Quayle, William A., Methodist bishop, 16:239
Quebec (city), traders licensed, 11:

259-265; fur trade, 19:271, 40:157; immigrant port, 20:252; settled, 29:78
Quebec (province), history, 15:94-98; folk songs, 17:204; emigration from, 27:207; politics, 36:65; climate, 40:312
Quebec Act, 11:269, 13:331, 20:8; effects, 11:446, 18:384, 19:352; preliminaries, 15:95
Queen Anne's War, 18:392, 19:288
"Queen of the West," war vessel, 25:343
Quetico Provincial Park, Ont., 13:297; established, 16:236, 36:192; forests, 23:385; history, 25:92, 40:48, 144; pictographs, 29:130, 135, 36:102, 38:87, 91, 40:407
Quetico-Superior area, see Quetico Provincial Park, Superior National Forest
Quetico-Superior Council, established, 16:358
Quetico-Superior Wilderness Research Center, 38:29
Quick, Birney, artist, 35:51, 382
Quick, Herbert, 22:158; author, 16:106, 23:118, 158, 28:287
Quids, political party, 14:339
Quiett, Glenn C., author, 16:343
Quigley, Harold S., author, 21:182; professor, 39:215, 216, 224-226
Quigley, Mrs. Harold S., 39:225
Quigley, Rev. John, temperance lecturer, 13:147; at Red Rock, 31:90
Quigley, Walter E., author, 22:335; politician, 34:226
Quileute Indians, songs, 34:161
Quill, James E., compiler, 34:311
Quiller-Couch, Arthur, author, 26:308
Quimby, George I., works reviewed, 28:270-272, 37:174, 40:259; author, 34:126
Quimby, Maynard W., author, 15:364
Quin, Peter, 25:255
Quincy, Josiah, 17:10
Quincy, Ill., described, 17:431, 22:16
Quincy, Olmsted County, maps, 15:464
"Quincy," steamboat, 37:265 (cover), 296
Quinlivan, Wilfred A., lawyer, 21:196
Quinn, Clement K., and Co., 34:282
Quinn, George, reminiscences, 38:128, 136n, 147-149
Quinn, Germain, 33:177
Quinn, James H., autobiography, 11:445
Quinn, Michael, 26:381
Quinn, Peter, 13:374, 21:166, 172n; interpreter, 12:117, 24:22n; death, 12:133n, 38:136; career, 36:195
Quinn, William B., St. Paul pioneer, letter, 24:119, 120
Quinn, William J., lawyer, career, 14:333
Quinn, William L., scout, 39:237
Quinney, John W., Mohican Indian, 22:150
Quist, Oval, author, 29:278
Quist, Peter P., Swedish pioneer, 24:291; author, 11:457, 13:212, 14:449, 26:167; speaker, 13:122
Qvale, George, 12:185

"R. G. Coburn," steamboat, 19:405
Raaen, Aagot, work reviewed, 32:52; author, 33:228
Raaen, Kjersti, 32:52
Raaen, Tosten, 32:52
Raattaamaa, Isaac, pioneer, 23:300
Rabbit Lake, Crow Wing County, mission, 12:84, 14:55, 56
Rabinovich, Joseph, speaker, 14:350
Rabishung, Alma (Mrs. Wilbert R. Mills), 28:254, 257
Rabishung, George, 28:255
Rabishung, Laura, 28:256
Rabishung, Louis, 28:254-257
Rabishung, Mrs. Louis (Martha Thiers), 28:254-256
Raccoon, 40:150; in fur trade, 30: 133, 40:180, 210, 212-216, 220
Rachie, Elias, author, 31:146
Rachlis, Eugene, work reviewed, 37: 132; author, 39:311
Racine, Norwegian settlement, 12:269
Racine, Wis., Bohemians, 15:27; thresher factory, 23:324; settled, 32:185
Racine Township, Olmsted County, history, 35:336
Radcliff, Abraham M., architect, 14: 279, 23:221, 33:171, 37:194
Radcliff Lumber Co., 27:302
Radcliffe-Brown, A. R., anthropoligist, 34:301
Radermacher, V., editor, 17:366
Radical movement, U.S., 27:334, 28:94
Radio, history dramatizations, 15: 479, 16:67, 25:260-263, 26:276, 27:357, 367, 28:75, 78, 181, 29: 180, 276, 30:81, 171, 173, 177, 284, 291; Northwest, 16:483; early broadcast, 18:333; Ames, Iowa, 23: 285; pioneer songs, 27:181-187; war news, 27:332; sports, 28:184; folklore, 28:286

    Stations: KDAL, Duluth, 28:78, 181; KFAM, St. Cloud, 30:173, 284; KROC, Rochester, 30:81, 177; KSTP, St. Paul, 16:483; KUOM, Minneapolis, 28:75, 184, 286, 30:171, 177; WAMD, Minneapolis, 16:483; WBAD, Minneapolis, 18:333; WCAL, Northfield, 30:291; WCCO, Minneapolis, 34:207, 35:340, 384, 36:105; WTCN, Minneapolis, 15:479
Radisson, Pierre Esprit, sieur de, work reviewed, 25:371; source material, 11:204, 14:64, 98, 435, 15:61, 17:94; explorer, 11:307, 385, 12:91, 350, 13:245-267, 395-402, 14:115, 15:317-327, 16:349, 391-426, 17:75, 114, 342, 18:388, 19:273, 24:340, 26:255, 273, 30: 375, 32:112, 186, 37:337; author, 12:350, 352, 16:391-413, 26:151; memorial, 13:110; letters, 13:417, 14:215; biographies, 13:439, 15: 238, 16:239, 24:149-161; western journeys, 15:157, 180, 368, 479, 16:453; in verse, 20:73, 25:372; portrait, 29:79; trader, 29:153; career, 36:150
Radisson Hotel, Minneapolis, built, 37:18
Rae, Dr. John, explorer, 17:75, 29: 248, 34:80
Rae, William G., 20:71, 24:45
Raeder, Ole Munch, work reviewed, 11: 82; author, 12:252, 20:293, 29:154

Rafinesque, Constantine S., 13:418, 34:160
Rafn, C. C., author, 28:59
Rafting, Mississippi River, 11:83-85, 16:37, 79, 345, 21:98, 24:127, 137, 25:275, 393, 27:8, 200, 28: 306, 29:266, 30:71, 37:222; depicted, 15:253, 26:136, 28:182; St. Croix River, 16:345, 17:367, 18:177-179, 24:202, 206, 27:201; procedure, 26:132; Chippewa River, Wis., 27:192, 196, 201. See also Lumber industry
Ragueneau, Father Paul, letter, 13: 418
Raguet, Lt. Samuel, Union officer, 25:29
Rahilly Museum, Mower County, 35:202
Rahmlow, H. J., author, 26:170
Raihala, Michael W., author, 35:295
Raihle, Paul H., 22:206; author, 26: 170
Raikes, Arnold, speaker, 19:316
Raikes, C. F. G., author, 14:233
Railroads, transcontinental, 11:104, 12:72, 16:344, 18:306, 20:80, 21: 96, 406, 37:38; Twin Cities, 11: 215, 12:394, 15:367, 27:299n, 34: 130, 36:280; need for, 11:397, 21: 238, 373, 38:45-52; iron ranges, 11:414, 415, 467, 12:285, 19:451, 30:158; government regulation, 12: 15-17, 29:11, 32:130n, 35:56, 308, 39:96, 98, 298; effect on settlement, 12:253, 254, 13:25-44, 14: 225, 20:61, 21:239-244, 30:158, 35:12, 205, 325, 36:68, 37:184; finances, 12:262, 16:289, 356, 18: 76, 21:97, 34:169, 37:82, 40:405; grants, 13:16, 14:155, 156, 161, 22:229-232, 27:6, 28:185, 36:4, 6, 7, 177-180, 38:329; rolling stock, 13:332, 19:193-196, 211, 236, 20: 255, 24:91, 29:117, 271, 35:338, 36:66, 321; gauges, 13:336, 15: 493, 35:14, 15, 237; excursions, 14:99, 16:469, 19:343, 25:104-116, 34:133-143, 36:204, 37:103; trackage, 14:169, 17:340, 20:374, 21: 239, 374; taxed, 14:208, 39:110, 257; employees, 15:140, 18:445, 452, 20:257, 25:196; rates, 15: 224, 18:106, 21:194, 29:7, 8; Minnesota communities, 15:245, 16: 100, 292, 18:111, 175, 337, 24:96, 26:332; Red River Valley, 15:370, 16:225, 32:112, 38:241; Illinois, 15:474; use by sportsmen, 16:268-271, 33:141, 143, 253; names, 17: 340, 33:311; Wisconsin, 17:345, 19:107, 30:138; bridge collapse, 18:120; in literature, 19:104, 21: 423, 31:132; importance to marketing, 20:222, 29:5, 13; unions and strikes, 21:382, 385, 393, 36:274; source material, 23:52-56, 393, 24:69, 26:371; Canada, 23:93; logging, 24:264, 25:102, 27:300-308, 28:376, 29:138, 147, 30:391, 33: 226, 35:49, 37:185, 40:361; glossary of terms, 25:83; songs, 26: 379, 27:181, 34:214; Freedom Train, 28:369; construction, 28: 375, 40:315; U.S., 30:378, 33:314, 35:237, 39:343; bibliography, 31: 250; in Civil War, 33:218; lake freighter connections, 34:13; de-

picted, 34:22, 75, 37:101, 38:45 (cover); St. Croix Valley, 35:358-364; maps, 37:104, 156, 38:261; interurban, 37:131, 341; car ferries, 38:237; Russia, 38:310-325. See also Five million loan, Pacific railroad survey, Transportation, various railroads and railway companies
Railway and Locomotive Historical Society, Twin City chapter, 20:345; publications, 19:107, 21:423
Railway Express, in Minnesota, 18:220
Rains, Maj. W. K., 19:198
Rainy Lake, border lake, trade route, 11:263, 264, 29:133, 33:187, 37: 253, 254; posts, 11:361, 451, 12: 364, 16:230, 374, 18:277, 390, 19: 78, 20:71, 22:270, 273, 274, 309, 23:94, 24:44, 77, 342, 28:170, 33: 88; mission, 12:82, 427, 20:327, 23:366; map, 15:239; gold mining, 15:489, 17:361, 24:265, 30:272, 34:178; proposed park, 16:236; resorts, 16:366; water levels, 20: 441; waterfall, 24:284; name, 24: 285; history, 29:52; trade competition, 36:242-249, 40:185n
Rainy Lake City, Koochiching County, gold-mining center, 15:489, 16: 366, 17:361, 30:272, 34:178
Rainy River, boundary river, fur trade, 11:239, 240, 35:282; post, 11:362, 22:178, 270, 271, 273, 274, 34:254; trade route, 15:92; mounds, 15:155; lumbering, 20:341, 23:385, 31:159; boat travel, 23: 206, 24:192, 276, 280-286, 33:17; described, 24:278, 281; map, 25: 239; archaeology, 26:316, 322, 327, 31:163-171, 231-237, 39:262; frontier life, 30:277, 33:315; history, 31:183; watershed, 35: 194; fishing, 35:272, 273, 275. See also Fort Frances
Rainy River aspect, prehistoric culture, 26:316, 327, 31:163-171, 231-237
Rainy River Improvement Co., history, 29:358
Rakestraw, Lawrence, author, 40:358
Raleigh, O. H., author, 27:163
Ralston Act, passed, 16:202
Ramaley, David, career, 24:273
Ramaley Printing Co., St. Paul, history, 24:273
"Rambler," steamboat, 11:124, 13:240, 18:372
Ramdall, Charles E., author, 19:466
Ramer, Sgt. James T., diary, 38:386
"Ramon de Larrinaga," ship, 36:281
Ramsay, A. C. Lamothe, St. Cloud physician, 33:291, 292, 294, 295
Ramsay, J. R., engineer, 34:277
Ramsay, John, author, 33:89
Ramsay, Robert L., author, 16:227
Ramsdell, Charles W., speaker, 17: 105; author, 34:81
Ramsey, Alexander, 17:340, 18:409, 22:182, 191, 23:85, 34:216, 38:82, 39:281, 284; diary, 11:205, 14: 291, 16:382, 20:79, 32:107; historical interests, 12:37, 20:366, 30:295, 303; state governor, 12: 116, 14:133, 16:454, 25:234, 255, 26:191, 195, 28:30, 29:283, 34: 332, 335, 336, 35:2, 36:167, 169,

170, 37:45, 324-334, 38:354, 40:
148; property, 12:161; papers, 13:
59, 16:332, 19:96, 21:83, 414, 26:
67, 155, 27:248, 28:202, 30:91;
Senator, 13:113, 20:320, 33:315,
37:90, 97-100, 315, 319, 38:61,
221, 39:86, 88; territorial governor, 13:211, 14:130, 15:20, 131,
16:469, 30:214n, 33:119-121, 35:
105, 352-357, 359, 36:262, 267,
268, 37:137, 39:37-48, 145, 147-
151; secretary of war, 14:117;
pictured, 14:117, 425, 26:141, 28:
348, 30:266, 35:131, 352, 36:169,
182, 302, 37:213, 324, 39:37; interest in education, 14:144, 19:
446, 23:189; politician, 14:162,
246-249, 35:47, 99, 297, 36:300-
308; Civil War policies, 14:168,
16:176, 37:212-214, 39:175, 176,
178, 179; treaty negotiator, 15:
283, 286, 288-292, 297, 22:138,
149, 32:65, 68, 69, 74, 79, 38:1-
10, 70; social activities, 15:347,
16:40, 174, 386, 20:132, 29:119,
129, 31:153, 32:102, 37:53;
quoted, 16:182, 26:29, 209, 30:
348; career, 16:239, 22:413-415,
28:183, 309-328, 30:107, 108, 110;
memorial, 17:230; MHS president
and founder, 20:369, 30:296, 297;
business interests, 23:94, 28:74,
35:336; religion, 28:334; in Sioux
Outbreak, 29:343, 38:99, 113n,
274, 275, 277, 281; attitude toward slavery, 32:20, 24, 29; first
house, 35:354. See also Ramsey
House
Ramsey, Mrs. Alexander (Anna E.
Jenks), 16:40, 386, 20:132, 133,
28:310, 312, 326, 29:117, 128, 30:
198, 31:153, 35:355, 37:53, 38:81,
39:39, 317; papers, 13:99; portrait, 33:112
Ramsey, Alexander, Jr., 28:310, 313,
35:355; death, 14:290, 28:399
Ramsey, Justus C., MHS founder, 20:
367; Freemason, 33:310; career,
35:354n; Winnebago agent, 38:361
Ramsey, Marion, see Furness, Mrs.
Charles E.
Ramsey, Dr. Walter R., author, 33:
187, 34:314
Ramsey, William, 28:399
Ramsey family, genealogy, 21:195
Ramsey County, in World War I, 11:
195-198, 202, 12:25; schools, 11:
438, 18:97, 35:125; courts, 12:85,
15:197, 35:289; census, 12:191,
14:262, 290; archives, 14:65, 103,
15:196; mortality records, 14:289;
medicine, 15:254, 20:91, 206, 344,
446; agriculture, 18:408; abstract
office, 20:103; name, 20:368;
fair, 22:258, 263; courthouses,
22:438, 35:4, 340; atlas, 23:40;
history, 23:187; first auto license, 26:26; boys' homes, 27:56,
35:290; politics, 28:31, 32, 34,
35:344, 347, 349, 36:305, 40:223;
scrip, 30:263; boundaries, 30:397,
35:119; library, 31:61; poor farm,
38:82, 366, 368; in Civil War, 38:
259, 296; established, 39:146;
maps, 40:125n; lakes, 40:226, 229
Ramsey County, N.D., place names, 38:
385

Ramsey County Agricultural Society,
organized, 14:137, 22:252, 29:201n
Ramsey County Bar Association, 14:
218; deceased members, 12:194,
322, 13:324, 14:333, 15:349, 467,
16:337; records, 26:156
Ramsey County Board of Commissioners,
22:447
Ramsey County Historical Society, 30:
397, 35:190; meetings, 30:168,
401, 34:220, 35:52, 39:265; officers, 30:279; museum, 33:210, 34:
130, 172, 359, 36:239, 38:204;
publications, 39:132, 40:364
Ramsey County Medical Society, 11:
448; library, 15:353; anniversary,
16:353; history, 20:344; meeting,
24:210
Ramsey County War History Committee,
24:186, 268, 26:278
Ramsey County War Records Commission,
12:321; publication, 11:195, 202,
12:25; minutes, 17:339
Ramsey House, St. Paul, 37:64, 39:36,
40:46; located, 27:271, 33:4, 39:
325; described, 34:314; pictured,
37:65, 308, piano, 39:324-326,
visitors, 40:36; historic site,
40:48
Ramsey mill, Vermillion River, 18:114
Ramsey Street, St. Paul, name, 20:369
Ranching, see Livestock industry
Ranck, James B., author, 18:453
Rand, Mrs. Alice, translator, 11:226
Rand, Judge Lars, speaker, 20:408
Randall, ---, at York Factory, 29:248
Randall, Andrew, geologist, 17:99;
letters, 35:335
Randall, Maj. Benjamin H., sutler,
11:168, 12:115, 117; map, 20:148;
author, 27:343; letters, 34:237
Randall, Mrs. Benjamin H., 12:115,
117
Randall, Clarence B., author, 29:259
Randall, E. W., author, 17:353
Randall, Horace, 25:230
Randall, James G., editor, 23:83; au-
thor, 34:81, 251
Randall, John J., prison official,
29:324, 37:149, 150
Randall, Samuel J., Congressman, 34:
73
Randall, Thomas E., author, 16:163
Randall, Mrs. W. G., author, 17:361
Randall, pioneer life, 18:97, 19:465,
20:86; Catholic church, 29:176
Randel, William P., "Edward Eg-
gleston's Library," 26:242-247;
"Edward Eggleston's Minnesota Fic-
tion," 33:189-193; "The Kit Carson
of the Northwest," 33:269-281; re-
views by, 28:272, 30:55, 34:309;
work reviewed, 28:167; editor, 26:
257; author, 26:277, 27:167, 28:
308, 337, 30:95, 34:311
Randin, Capt. Hughes, map maker, 12:
353, 27:350
Randolph, Edmund, 16:205, 19:303
Randolph, John, 14:339
Randolph, Vance, author, 31:251
Randolph County, Ill., census, 17:221
Raney, Dr. M. L., speaker, 17:350
Raney, William F., work reviewed, 21:
306; author, 16:479, 17:345, 26:73
Rangman, R., author, 18:71
Ranke, Leopold von, historian, 35:87
Rankiellour, Caroline, career, 34:217

Rankin, Albert W., speaker, 13:341;
author, 13:428; educator, 23:363
Rankin, Belle, author, 13:441
Rankin, Jeanette, letter, 18:316
Rankin, Lois, author, 20:202
Rankin, Mrs. Silas H., 14:331
Ransom, Charles R., grocer, 21:221
Ransom, John C., 20:113
Ransom Brothers Co., Albert Lea, gro-
cers, 21:221
Rant, Rev. Francis S., author, 14:455
Rantoul, Robert, 18:444; lumberman,
24:127, 130, 25:396, 27:312
Ranville, Joseph, see Renville,
Joseph
Raphael, Ralph B., work reviewed, 34:
116
Rapid Canyon Line, S.D., history, 39:
298
Rapid City, S.D., Catholic diocese,
39:299
Rapidan, grasshopper bounty, 36:56;
poor farm, 38:363
Rappahannock River, Va., Civil War
campaign, 25:234-237, 244, 247,
253
Rappahannock Station, Va., cavalry
fight, 25:354
Rappites, religious sect, 36:278
Rarig, Frank M., Jr., 16:351
Raschick, Walt, author, 27:366
Rascoe, Benton, author, 35:97
Rask, Lt. Olaf H., Union officer,
diary, 12:429
Rasles, Father Sébastien, 16:199
Rasmussen, C. A., 13:118, 15:136, 16:
240, 17:486, 20:309, 21:391, 392,
27:171; "A Pioneer Cemetery," 14:
426-428; speaker, 11:114, 12:102,
15:372, 17:121, 20:306; author,
15:247, 17:126, 18:468, 20:211,
345, 352, 21:222, 22:216, 222, 24:
272, 379, 26:282
Rasmussen, Mrs. Geraldine, publisher,
16:254
Rasmussen, H. E., reporter, 16:254
Rasmussen, Knud, in Arctic, 17:171
Rasmussen, Louise, author, 23:183
Rasmussen, Wayne D., works reviewed,
36:150, 37:178
Rastoute, ---, trader, 21:123
Rat Portage, see Kenora, Ont.
Rat Portage House, Ont., Lake of the
Woods, trading post, 11:363
Rat River, Man., trading post, 11:365
Ratchen, Edna, author, 25:309
Ratcliff, Mrs. Zalia, 18:208
Rath, Frederick L., Jr., author, 39:
209
Rathbone, Perry T., work reviewed,
34:253; author, 28:278, 29:78, 31:
56, 250; receives award, 34:353
Rathbun, Hoxie, 27:7
Ratigan, William, work reviewed, 37:
179
Rauch, George, speaker, 21:339
Raudenbush, Mrs. Webb R., 39:62
Raudenbush Hall, St. Paul, 39:53n
Rausch, Father Jerome, work reviewed,
37:221
Rauschenbusch, Walter, philosopher,
36:97
Ravary, Viateur, author, 33:88
Ravel, Marietta, singer, 30:17
Raven River (Creek), Itasca County,
archaeology, 26:322
Ravenswaay, Charles van, work re-

viewed, 30:249; author, 31:56,
250; editor, 35:335
Ravoux, Father Augustin, missionary,
11:105, 12:83, 337, 13:215, 17:
475, 18:437, 21:454, 24:4, 160;
activities, 13:313, 14:121, 17:
473, 20:460, 21:102, 30:395; ca-
reer, 16:239, 22:334, 38:193; in
Faribault, 19:475, 35:321; in St.
Paul, 22:51, 27:166, 39:153; map
maker, 30:8; in fiction, 37:5, 10
Rawley, James A., author, 26:74
Rawlings, Marjorie K., author, 20:
116, 23:120n
Rawlins, Cora M., 14:283n
Rawson, Carl, artist, 26:43
Rawson, Marion N., author, 14:340
Ray, G. R., photographer, 33:207
Ray, James B., Indiana governor, pa-
pers, 34:175
Ray, John, 27:34
Ray, P. O., author, 15:128
Ray, Verne F., author, 34:215
Rayback, Joseph G., work reviewed,
36:274
Rayer, Pierre F., author, 21:370
Rayford, Julian L., 35:40; author,
26:381
Raymbault, Father Charles, 15:321,
531, 18:387; explorer, 12:283
Raymond, Ebenezer, 38:369
Raymond, Evelyn, sculptor, 36:151
Raymond, Henry, journalist, 27:1
Raymond, Rev. V. H., 17:363
Raymond, William L., author, 15:243
Raymond, history, 19:365; Dutch set-
tlement, 28:126; church, 28:127
Rea, Alice, 21:134n
Rea, Dr. Charles E., author, 21:437
Rea, Marjorie, author, 30:260
Read, Allen W., author, 11:187n, 16:
227
Read, Charles R., trader, 11:467, 36:
241; pioneer, 14:362, 22:226, 27:
345
Read, Donald A., author, 12:430
Read, Eve, author, 20:443
Read, Evelyn P., author, 24:362
Read, Opie, author, 23:114, 158
Read, Ralph, 27:345
Read, Thomas T., author, 15:127
Reader's Digest, history, 27:353, 36:
32, 281
Reading, Pa., theater, 26:168
Reading Railroad Co., finances, 36:
299
Reading Room Association, Faribault,
19:416
Reads Landing, post, 11:383; roads,
11:393, 21:232, 233; history, 11:
467, 14:362, 15:360; hotels, 12:
343; newspaper, 15:86; river port,
15:130, 22:226, 26:177, 27:8, 30:
71, 34:25n; G.A.R. post, 16:431;
in Civil War, 17:112; name, 27:
345; theater, 32:100; pictured,
36:241 (cover); post office, 40:83
Ready, William, work reviewed, 36:
237; author, 29:81
Reagan, Albert B., author, 15:121,
16:343
Real estate, agents, 36:189; Mora,
36:193; speculation, 36:260, 264;
St. Anthony, 39:67-69; Minneapolis, 39:69, 73, 74
Reames, O. K., speaker, 19:316
Reapers, use in Minnesota, 23:321-

323, 24:287; self-raking, 24:288-
290, 292
Reardon, Monsig. James M., 12:87;
works reviewed, 13:312, 33:223,
34:205; speaker, 14:230, 30:69,
177; author, 16:309
Reaume, Charles, trader, 19:302
Reaume, Joseph, trader, 11:369, 28:
233; post, 11:373
Reciprocity Agreement of 1911, 20:336
Reck, Franklin M., author, 25:394
Reck, Rev. Michael, letters, 16:335
Recktenwald, Anna K. D., pioneer, 30:
135-137
Recktenwald, Lester N., "A Pioneer
Woman's Songs," 30:135-137; "More
Than History," 31:98; author, 30:
184, 31:127
Recollect Order of Franciscans, 11:
344, 345; explorers, 11:348; con-
troversy with Jesuits, 16:449, 20:
67. See also Franciscans
Reconstruction era, reaction in
North, 31:58
Record, J. L., 19:184n
Record (Mankato), 38:353, 354
Recreation, see Amusements, Sports
Rector, S. M., speaker, 17:357, 483
Rector, William G., "Lumber Barons in
Revolt," 31:33-39; reviews by, 30:
378, 31:110, 37:337; work re-
viewed, 34:35; speaker, 30:180;
author, 30:391, 412, 31:62, 63,
127, 190, 33:226, 35:382
Red and White Stores, established,
22:437
Red Bear, Chippewa leader, 15:294
Red Bird, Winnebago leader, sur-
render, 11:431
Red Cedar Lake, see Cass Lake
Red Cedar Quarterly Meeting (Quaker),
Iowa, 18:250
Red Cliff, Wis., Chippewa reservation, 35:235
Red Cloud, Sioux leader, 11:209, 35:
289, 39:339
Red Clover Township, Carlton County,
history, 38:243
Red Cross, see American Red Cross
Red Iron, Sioux leader, 12:121, 30:78
Red Jacket, Seneca leader, portraits,
19:420, 422, 29:350; medal, 25:267
Red Lake, Beltrami and Clearwater
counties, posts, 11:368, 369, 13:
322, 16:31, 18:277, 20:72, 22:
280n, 281; missions, 15:455, 16:
216, 375, 376, 18:331, 20:90, 328;
fur trade, 18:271, 20:11, 13;
wildlife, 20:66, 30:127, 128, 132,
134; maple-sugar making, 22:331;
Indian agency, 23:93; agriculture,
26:230; archaeology, 26:321; logging, 29:146, 147, 34:8; chronology, 30:274
Red Lake County, agriculture, 21:212;
organized, 21:223, 29:89; township
histories, 38:204; nursing home,
38:277
Red Lake County Historical Society,
15:71, 29:365, 30:82
Red Lake Falls, post, 11:368; sawmill, 29:137
Red Lake Fisheries Association, 30:
274, 35:380
Red Lake Indian Forest, established,
15:300; described, 17:220
Red Lake Indian Reservation (Chip-

pewa), 14:359, 19:450, 29:169;
mission, 15:354, 34:131, 35:338,
36:192, 38:335; cemetery, 16:321;
crafts, 16:476; logging, 27:302,
31:160, 36:69; tribal life, 30:
161, 274, 35:293, 380, 37:347, 40:
42; diagramed, 40:146. See also
Red Lake
Red Lake River, 15:283; post, 11:209,
368; "Old Crossing," 11:216, 12:
203, 15:282; flood, 17:230; described, 18:358; logging, 29:37,
146
Red Lake Transportation Co., Beltrami
County, 29:147
Red Legs, Sioux leader, 38:138, 139;
village, 38:148n
Red Middle Voice, Sioux leader, 38:96
Red River, steamboating, 11:104, 220,
308, 15:357, 478, 16:117, 240,
495, 17:128, 18:356, 19:109, 410,
20:207, 21:204, 234, 245-271, 23:
110, 186, 24:328, 329, 334, 28:
282, 372, 29:73, 30:70, 262, 31:
253, 32:60, 112, 126, 33:89, 270-
273, 277, 34:132, 324, 357, 35:
250, 251, 258, 38:64, 65, 241;
posts, 11:364, 366-368, 12:438;
mission, 12:82; trade, 12:175, 14:
444, 40:163, 173, 190; floods, 14:
286, 16:469, 17:305, 21:205, 326,
28:190, 34:306, 35:295; depicted,
14:287, 18:357, 19:410, 26:359,
33:70, 36:243, 38:386, 40:144;
name, 15:357; flatboats, 16:100,
33:277; logging, 17:116, 238, 29:
137; wildlife, 18:358, 33:138;
hunts, 19:105, 381; boundary, 19:
424; 1870 expedition, 23:40; fishing, 23:403; geological survey,
26:224, 226; boatbuilding, 32:124;
mail route, 33:89; canoeing, 33:
187; explored, 36:295, 40:316
Red River carts, 11:102, 21:253, 23:
187, 24:273, 29:32, 31:253, 35:
250; routes taken, 12:153, 395,
27:71, 34:103n, 38:63; depicted,
12:437, 13:176, 23:186, 24:256,
335, 25:275, 28:286, 33:199, 200,
35:259, 268, 36:49, 310, 311, 38:
3, 5, 7, 9, 70; caravans, 14:152,
15:463, 16:231, 17:225, 19:84, 28:
136, 341n, 30:200, 31:174, 34:103,
36:38; disappearance, 14:154;
trade, 14:205, 15:120, 291, 16:
495, 19:109, 25:196, 27:285n, 37:
158, 38:69; museum exhibit, 20:372
Red River Junction, Polk County, in
1860 census, 15:370
Red River Lumber Co., 27:302; publications, 21:177, 23:379, 25:393,
26:380, 27:255, 28:93, 372, 32:
127, 33:91, 265; mill, 29:139
Red River rebellions, see Riel rebellions
Red River Settlement, missions, 11:
94, 306, 307, 13:426, 21:432, 24:
41, 27:166, 29:81, 31:240, 37:53,
57; annexation question, 11:97,
20:320, 30:387, 37:258; colonists,
11:212, 308, 13:206, 337, 14:115,
351, 15:303, 20:123, 337, 22:203,
331, 23:154, 24:179, 28:372, 31:
106-108, 240, 32:160, 161, 33:187,
36:63; struggle with North West
Co., 12:287, 21:399, 38:328, 39:
166, 40:164, 183; history, 12:330,

Reed, Dr. Walter, army surgeon, 19:111, 24:207-213; biography, 24:238; papers, 34:212
Reed, Gen. Walter L., 24:209
Reed Lake, see Roseau Lake
Reeder, D. F., steamboat captain, 13:231
Reedfield, Mrs. Mora, 16:360
Reeds Landing, see Reads Landing
Reedy, David, 31:160
Reedy, William M., editor, 29:331
Rees, Charles, potter, 33:231
Rees, John M., lawyer, 21:196
Reese, ---, in fur trade, 15:430
Reeside, James, career, 29:150
Reeve, Charles, swine raiser, 26:117
Reeve, Gen. Charles M., 29:324; collector, 13:60, 74, 102
Reeve, G. J., author, 15:238
Reeves, Budd, poet, 26:84
Reeves, Mrs. Ernest H., speaker, 28:385
Reeves, Richard S., 18:142
Reeves, Will, 30:76; author, 28:191, 293, 29:177, 30:163, 34:44
Reff, E. H., 19:468
Reformed Church in America, Dutch, 28:120-131, 35:34; German, 31:25
Regan, W. M., 23:226
Reger, Rev. Walter, 17:233, 19:119, 22:108, 29:94; speaker, 20:355
Regier, C. C., work reviewed, 14:200-202; author, 14:114
Regina, Clearwater County, ghost town, 16:493
Register Cliff, Wyo., trading post, 40:196
Regli, Adolph, work reviewed, 23:364; author, 18:343
Regnault, ---, explorer, 24:285
Rehan, Ada, actress, 28:117
Rehse, George W., cartoonist, 35:342, 347, 351n
Rehse Brothers, merchants, business records, 20:349
Reichardt, Ferdinand, artist, 30:157, 31:56, 35:369
Reichardt, Konstantin, review by, 28:58-60; author, 28:96, 373; speaker, 28:301, 30:69
Reichers, Col. Louis T., aviator, 26:5
Reichert, Joseph, 35:268
Reichmann, Felix, author, 25:88
Reid, Bill G., "Colonies for Disabled Veterans," 39:241-251
Reid, J., 21:130n
Reid, J. H. Stewart, work reviewed, 37:80
Reid, L. F., author, 20:104
Reid, Mary J., author, 26:301, 302; editor, 26:303
Reid, Robie L., author, 24:77
Reid, Russell, author, 22:207, 40:145; editor, 24:77; speaker, 34:267
Reid, Capt. Tom, career, 36:237
Reid, Walter, see Reed, Dr. Walter
Reid, Whitelaw J., journalist, 34:344; vice-presidential candidate, 35:64, 75
Reid Lake, see Roseau Lake
Reiersen, Johan R., colonizer, 16:239
Reiersgord, O. E., author, 17:485
Reiff, Ernest R., 21:190, 23:154, 26:64, 27:48, 141
Reilly, Daniel F., work reviewed, 25:372-374
Reilly, Edward C., author, 26:85
Reilly, Nina B., author, 13:452
Reilly, Robert A., steamboat captain, 22:15-17
Reim, Victor P., speaker, 20:351, 21:438; author, 23:295
Reindahl, Knute, violin maker, 15:235
Reindeer Lake, Sask., Man., 40:173
Reineke, H. W., 19:119, 24:380, 26:92, 395, 27:364, 29:366
Reiner, Jacob, 26:371; translator, 39:65
Reinertson, Thomas, 18:336
Reinhardt, C. J., 14:116
Reinmuth, Allen, author, 16:499
Reishus, Gunder, author, 28:381
Reishus, Mrs. Sondre, pioneer, 28:381
Reitan, Norman, speaker, 23:193
Reiter, Arthur, speaker, 20:297
Reitinger, Rev. Filip, 15:35
"Relief," steamboat, 36:251
Religion, frontier, 12:70, 397, 18:294, 40:403; denominations, 18:409; in lumber camps, 34:59-66; communal sects, 36:278; Indian, 37:85, 273, 277, 40:40; interfaith co-operation, 38:335; archives, 39:35; atlas, 39:128. See also Missions and missionaries, various denominations and orders
Remer, Lutheran church, 17:469
Remer Record, file acquired, 16:103
Remey, Adm. George, 22:87
Remey, Mrs. George, 22:87
Remington, E., and Sons, typewriter manufacturers, 16:446
Remington, Franklin, author, 35:240
Remington, Frederic, 38:238; artist, 17:109, 22:410, 29:79, 266, 33:264, 34:210, 36:232; letters, 20:82, 38:200
Remington, G. W., speaker, 16:129
Remington, Harry, author, 13:346, 15:479, 16:116, 227
Remington Rand, Inc., 16:446
"Remnica," steamboat, 33:16, 17
Remore, J. F., pioneer, 25:25
Remsberg, Mrs. O. Z., 12:185
Remsburg, George J., author, 13:331
Remsburg, John E., author, 13:331
Remy, H. H., lumberman, 24:201, 202
Renaud, Jean Baptiste, voyageur, 18:241, 24:285n
Renaudot, Eusèbe, 13:417, 418
Rene, K. A., work reviewed, 12:181
Renfro, William C., 36:42n
Rennebohm, Oscar, Wisconsin governor, speaker, 29:268
Reno, Gen. Jesse L., 21:349, 40:148
Reno, Milo, 21:68; agrarian leader, 23:91, 35:284, 285, 40:354
Reno Lake, Crow Wing County, name, 21:349
Rensch, Ethel G., author, 14:228
Rensch, Hero E., author, 14:228
Renville, Misses ---, teachers, 12:242
Renville, Evangeline, 12:131
Renville, Gabriel, 39:261; farmer, 12:131; speaker, 12:132; organizes rangers, 19:450; Sisseton leader, 35:168, 170-177; scout, 38:280, 40:313; family, 38:357
Renville, Rev. John B., 35:171, 174
Renville, Joseph, 18:157, 21:99, 412, 24:179, 26:106; trader, 11:378, 18:339, 20:259, 21:107, 207, 22:282, 283, 285, 310, 23:272, 27:67, 263; career, 12:231-246, 28:337; relations with missionaries, 16:134, 135, 143, 147, 148, 21:162, 170, 274; translator, 16:142, 18:158, 21:31, 275; hymn writer, 21:280; descendants, 24:80
Renville, Joseph, Jr., 12:127, 131; guide, 12:239
Renville, Mary B., Sioux captive, 18:46
Renville, Victor, scout, 40:313
Renville, history, 13:453, 17:488, 19:126; newspaper, 17:103; football team, 20:104; Dutch settlement, 28:124-127; pioneer life, 34:173
Renville County, ethnic groups, 12:275n, 18:338, 21:102, 22:348, 25:318, 28:121, 124, 35:33, 90; settled, 12:444, 30:274, 39:273; history, 13:453, 16:218, 19:126; organized, 14:347, 488; newspapers, 17:102; churches, 17:240, 18:257, 258, 22:348; archives, 22:100; in Sioux Outbreak, 26:200, 38:281, 283; central committee, 29:185, 30:87; grasshopper plague, 36:57, 37:209, 211
Renville County Farm Bureau, 22:111
Renville County Historical Society, organized, 21:218; collection, 21:338; museum, 28:297
Renville County Times (Beaver Falls), established, 19:126
Renville Rangers, 26:200; in Sioux Outbreak, 38:131
Renz and Karcher, St. Paul, confectioners, 27:327
Repentigny, Louis de Gardeur, sieur de, 11:242n, 18:325, 19:198
Reporter (St. Paul), founded, 37:163. See also Twin City Reporter
Republican Eagle (Red Wing), 27:270
Republican party, ethnic groups, 13:435, 26:373, 28:20-36, 31:31, 33:180; organized, 14:77, 132, 15:331; Minnesota Territory, 14:131-133, 156-159, 161, 162, 244, 27:13, 36:3, 5-11; policies, 14:164, 183n, 187, 191, 15:123, 333-335, 20:270, 22:234, 241, 245, 24:310, 312, 313, 315, 26:191-208, 27:14, 32:15-33, 36:168-172, 38:178, 40:368, 369, 374; in elections, 14:246-253, 24:308, 309, 37:45, 51, 38:297, 39:82, 40:362; conventions, 16:226, 19:96, 262, 20:280, 281, 25:77, 78, 26:189, 27:7, 28:284, 382, 30:234, 33:1, 126, 35:64-76, 156, 39:172; Minnesota, 17:161, 162, 18:128, 24:311, 28:183, 34:188, 35:61-63, 114, 115, 297, 298, 301, 304, 305, 307, 309, 312, 36:113, 116, 122, 173-183, 300-308, 37:52-57, 324-334, 39:93-110, 234, 327n, 40:317-329; leaders, 19:456, 26:155; Wisconsin, 21:306, 31:113; relation to third parties, 22:78-80, 32:130-146, 34:221, 347, 38:301, 308; platforms, 22:386, 35:291; G.A.R. support, 23:166; symbol, 25:395; Ohio, 30:147; dissension, 31:42, 32:246; history, 33:34, 35:285; in legislature, 33:

155-163; characterized, 34:37; Iowa, 34:41, 35:42; Oregon, 35:94. See also Politics, Whig party
Reque, Rev. Peter S., missionary, 18:472; diary, 19:125
Reque, Sigurd S., author, 19:460
Rerat, Eugene A., career, 39:132
"Rescue," steamboat, 11:143
Rescue Hook and Ladder Co., Winona, 25:207
Research, Inc., Minneapolis, 33:244
Research Associates, St. Paul, 33:244
Reser, Sister Johanna, 35:271
Reservation River, Cook County, trout fishing, 33:256
Reserve Mining Co., Beaver Bay, 33:255; activities, 34:269-283, 35:245; organized, 39:163. See also Babbitt, Silver Bay
Reserve Town, Ramsey County, history, 15:456
Resler, George E., artist, 40:221 (cover), 249-253
"Resolute," launch, 18:279
"Restoration," sloop, 19:199, 22:70
Retrum, C. E., 27:266; speaker, 30:80
Retzek, Rev. Henry, author, 16:481, 21:100; speaker, 30:169
Reunick, Selma M., author, 11:102
Reuther, Charles, 28:23
"Reveille," steamboat, 11:135, 140, 142
Revere, Paul, inventor, 35:92
Revolutionary War, causes, 11:79, 22:66; influence on Canada, 11:193, 15:95; in Wisconsin, 17:196; relation to land question, 18:435; effects, 19:295-307, 22:306, 23:258; soldier vote, 26:187n; personal narratives, 33:346; weather data, 40:312
Rexford, Eben E., poet, 26:298
Rexford, Orcella, author, 25:400
Rexroth, Kenneth, poet, 35:244
Reyling, August, editor, 37:128
Reymert, James D., journalist, 24:348; colonizer, 25:396
Reynold, Capt. Ira B., 17:234
Reynolds, Anna, 39:15
Reynolds, Arthur R., work reviewed, 36:28; speaker, 29:257; author, 30:71, 31:59, 32:60
Reynolds, Charles, 21:221; journalist, 18:226
Reynolds, Charley, scout, 13:331
Reynolds, George, 11:465
Reynolds, Horace, author, 24:72
Reynolds, Joseph, 24:369
Reynolds, Quentin, author, 26:5
Reynolds, Dr. R. M., pioneer physician, 20:103; papers, 34:360
Reynolds, William M., 25:233
Reynolds Township, Todd County, history, 16:372
Rezac, W. J., 19:127
Rhindesberger, Peter, see Rindisbacher, Peter
Rhinelander, Wis., logging museum, 16:486, 24:364
Rhoads, James B., "The Fort Snelling Area," 35:22-29; review by, 36:26; compiler, 36:278
Rhode Island, first printing, 15:6; atlas, 40:122
Rhodes, Charles D., author, 12:442, 14:231, 17:115
Rhodes, James F., autho
313; historian, 19:6
Rhodes, William, 36:254
Rholl, Arthur, editor,
Ribourde, Father de la,
11:345
Rice, Mrs. A. J., speak
Rice, Allen Thornton, e
Rice, Ann E., author, 3
Rice, Charles S., elect
sioner, 26:208
Rice, Charles S., work
322
Rice, Daniel B., letter
Rice, Maj. Ebenezer O.,
217, 475, 17:54
Rice, Edmund, 16:130, 2
career, 16:239; port
politician, 35:58, 3
speaker, 35:105; rai
cial, 35:359, 37:156
Rice, Mrs. Edna, 18:334
Rice, Ellen, pioneer, 3
Rice, Frank, 18:134, 1
Rice, George, author, 3
Rice, Harvey, 38:385
Rice, Henry M., 12:458,
22:58n, 26:361, 30:
35:152, 321; trader,
191, 278, 23:94, 32
er, 12:392, 40:301;
196, 16:224, 21:412
183, 26:209, 258, 2
374, 30:40; busines
21:429, 33:221, 35:
237, 39:144, 145, 1
13:433, 14:132, 20:
36:259-271, 38:120,
39:41-46, 148, 150,
225, 362; territori
14:129, 158, 182, 1
27:314, 28:216, 35:
4, 6, 7, 10; Senato
190, 191, 20:320, 2
29:84, 32:24, 29, 3
37:46, 54, 156n, 32
house, 15:54, 30:74
cy, 15:297; career,
197; hunter, 16:260
removal, 16:333, 17
28:205, 31:214, 36:
er and president, 2
427, 30:87, 296, 34
287; social life, 2
owner, 22:57n; stat
372; portrait, 27:
33:310
Rice, Mrs. Henry M.,
26:258; biographica
267
Rice, Martha Ellen, p
Rice, Ora R., 27:68
Rice, Mrs. R. S., 18:
Rice, Mrs. S. E., 13:
242, 17:231, 19:35
Rice, Rev. W. A., aut
Rice family, in Minne
genealogy, 26:258
Rice, Catholic church
Rice and Myrick, stag
Rice County, census,
groups, 12:265, 27
settled, 12:430, 1
archives, 13:312,
fair, 14:461; surv
historical exhibit
life, 16:244; agri

Richard, Father Gabriel
cator, 13:110
Richards, Amasa, papers
Richards, Bergmann, 25:
253, 28:200, 29:97;
34:351; author, 25:2
speaker, 26:284, 27:
30:87, 170, 171, 363
403, 36:217; MHS pres
282, 371, 30:37, 330
Richards, Mrs. Carmen N
400
Richards, Ella, musicia
Richards, Eva L. Alvey,
Iron Land," 32:147-1
Country Post Office,
"Child Pioneer," 33:
"Schoolgirl of the Ir
tier," 33:105-111; au
Richards, Thomas, 13:209
Richardson, Mrs. A. D. (
Young), 19:319, 320
Richardson, Ahira, 14:2
Richardson, Brad, author
Richardson, C. W., chees
turer, 27:112
Richardson, Daniel, sett
Richardson, Edgar P., au
35:379, 38:333
Richardson, Edward E., a
Richardson, F. A., speak
Richardson, H. W., speak
papers, 20:452
Richardson, Henry H., ar
223, 231, 40:99, 101,
Richardson, Israel B., U
25:36, 131
Richardson, J. T., autho
Richardson, James O., in
25:355
Richardson, James P., au
Richardson, John ("Jock"
owner, 37:235; storyt
236-253; guide, 38:33
Richardson, Sir John, 35
Richardson, Nathan, 20:9
Richardson, T. J., artis
Richardson, Mrs. W. D.,
Richardson, Dr. W. J., 1
Richardson, William H.,
16:71
Richelot, Louis G., autho
Riches, Arthur W., 16:10
Richfield, developed, 13
churches, 13:346, 24:
planting, 29:264; name
Augsburg Park site, 4
Richfield Baptist Church
sary, 13:346
Richfield Lake, see Grass
Richfield Methodist Chur
sary, 13:346
Riching, Mr. and Mrs. ---
28:326
Richland County, N.D., h
104
Richland Township, Rice
wegian settlement, 12
Richman, Irving B., work
12:416; author, 13:21
Richmond, George A., 22:
Richmond, Gordon, author,
Richmond, churches, 18:1
Outbreak, 20:192, 2 :1
281, 283
Richmond, Va., in Civil W
286

16:348, 462, 495, 23:92, 272, 24:
153, 262, 28:177, 282, 29:99, 35:
242, 243, 37:224, 40:43, 93; depicted, 12:437, 14:284, 18:216,
20:71, 21:186, 33:227, 35:261,
295, 36:309, 37:306; founded, 12:
441, 14:283, 338, 16:454, 24:328;
Minnesota trade, 13:239–242, 17:
217, 19:109, 210, 22:148, 149, 31:
174, 217, 32:34, 36:37, 38:241,
278; in Fenian raids, 15:239;
hunting, 15:357, 36:309–314; fur
trade, 20:71, 84, 26:171, 35:282,
36:191, 241, 247, 249, 39:318;
livestock, 21:205, 24:45; steamboat transportation, 21:245, 30:
70; refugees from, 22:3, 51, 29:
232, 35:25, 335; troops, 24:77,
35:202; Indians, 27:161, 34:317–
324; frontier life, 30:259, 38:
199; agriculture, 31:56, 35:48;
survey, 33:139, 36:324; folk
songs, 38:200; mail service, 40:
83, 84. See also Selkirk, Earl of
Red River Star (Moorhead), established, 15:134
Red River trails, history, 14:101,
16:128, 19:361, 20:207, 28:330;
traffic, 12:153, 13:340, 28:372;
routes, 12:188, 447, 14:152, 17:
116, 20:469, 21:229, 23:107, 32:
63, 33:210, 35:256, 335, 36:107,
38:4n, 63; length, 12:437; mapped,
16:218, 17:57, 207, 360, 18:52,
19:54, 21:228; depicted, 17:359,
18:270, 314, 24:167, 27:165, 35:
257, 36:39, 38:4, 5, 40:358; impact on settlement, 21:230, 33:353
Red River Transportation Co., rates,
21:247, 255, 270; monopoly, 21:
254, 257–260; decline, 21:261
Red River Valley, missions, 11:42,
20:79, 23:366, 24:41, 94; pioneer
life, 11:220, 12:135, 183, 330,
14:444, 35:97; explored, 12:83,
22:85, 33:316, 35:378; geography,
12:150, 18:355, 39:171; Norwegian
settlements, 12:248, 259, 266,
278, 19:234, 20:337, 24:258, 31:
27; railroads, 12:254, 21:239, 29:
13, 36:68; agriculture, 12:258,
14:434, 17:227, 21:212, 32:119,
33:69–71, 314, 39:201; grasshopper
plague, 12:263, 37:210; bonanza
farms, 13:205, 29:14, 31:122, 33:
70, 39:206; history, 14:205, 16:
251, 465, 17:128, 18:443, 20:207,
21:448, 24:152–154, 25:200, 26:31,
27:81; land cessions, 14:350, 15:
84, 283, 36:2, 38:1–10, 70; wildlife, 14:386, 16:262, 30:123, 126,
131; wheat raising, 15:134, 29:14,
36:69; settled, 15:201, 19:409,
23:186, 24:41, 32:112–114; archaeology, 15:232, 17:128, 38:157–
165; pageant, 16:237, 337; Indians, 17:128, 32:238; climate, 18:
107; flour mill, 18:341; advertised, 19:126; fur trade, 20:17,
22:270, 277–288, 309, 24:319, 28:
281, 30:131, 133, 37:37; surveys,
22:193, 26:228, 28:172, 37:183;
Selkirk grant, 22:283, 24:41; maple-sugar industry, 22:331; in
fiction, 23:117, 31:132; flora,
24:246, 35:241; mixed-bloods, 28:
61, 31:253; architecture, 28:179;

lumbering, 29:146; freight line,
30:91; agrarian movement, 30:151,
38:177–185; theater, 31:121, 138;
described, 33:69, 186; drainage,
35:45; historical tour, 36:240;
Knut Hamsun's account, 37:265–270;
maps, 38:3, 159; transportation
problems, 38:241
Red Rock, Lake Superior, 33:257
Red Rock, Washington County, depicted, 17:286, 31:151, 36:22, 23;
mission, 17:311, 29:354; legend,
22:337; agriculture, 23:316, 26:
66; name, 31:79n; camp meetings,
31:82–92; post office, 40:83
Red Rock Camp Ground Association, 31:
83, 85n
Red Rock Park Association, 31:84
Red Wing, Sioux leader, 12:190, 317,
13:369, 15:247, 16:239, 20:171,
22:30, 23:342n, 25:396, 32:114,
35:377, 37:271; medal, 25:79, 269
Red Wing, river port, 11:142, 14:100,
33:198, 35:14, 38:292; churches,
11:219, 461, 14:451, 15:111, 27:
176, 37:277, 39:223; mission, 11:
316, 13:321, 16:214, 18:375;
roads, 11:393, 395, 21:233, 26:28,
34:25; mail service, 11:400, 40:
83, 89; stage line, 11:402; ethnic
settlements, 12:271, 25:318, 34:
167; fairs, 12:445, 22:259; Sioux
village, 13:99, 17:290, 291, 21:
163n, 22:29, 29:174, 221, 37:271,
272; grain market, 13:212, 14:387,
20:160, 24:272; Cutlerites, 13:
387; newspaper, 14:174–177, 189,
23:95, 27:270, 28:381, 35:314,
382; history, 15:247, 24:168; industries, 15:249, 35:319; archaeology, 15:367, 25:269, 27:261, 29:
83; surveyed, 15:464, 16:469; depicted, 16:44, 17:221, 22:160, 30:
159, 33:203, 35:315, 40:77; volunteer guards, 16:177; place names,
16:476; skiing, 17:228, 21:422,
29:169, 36:91; fire department,
18:468; baseball club, 19:165,
166, 168–170, 178, 180, 37:277;
pageant, 19:364; Hamline University site, 21:51, 28:303; medicine, 21:361, 26:287, 34:34; county museum, 22:440, 23:194, 296,
24:380, 26:280–282, 35:50; sawmills, 24:127, 27:190; schools,
26:166, 33:309; in World War II,
26:278, 27:365; social life, 26:
307; art in, 27:137; camp meeting,
31:80; German theater, 32:100, 34:
240, 242; post, 32:229; railroad,
33:166; potteries, 33:231–233; hotel, 34:26; power projects, 34:84,
35:381; centennial, 34:127; politics, 34:229, 35:350; historical
meeting, 36:240; octagonal house,
38:348; geology, 39:132
Red Wing Art History Club, 27:137
Red Wing Collegiate Institute, history, 29:87
Red Wing Potteries, 27:138, 345, 28:
84, 91; depicted, 33:232, 233,
235; history, 33:233–235, 34:127
Red Wing Republican, history, 13:449;
established, 14:397, 404; content
analyzed, 27:5–20
Red Wing Rifles, organized, 16:169,
172

Red Wing Seminary, 15:235, 20:200,
25:314, 26:298, 29:87, 39:81; his-
tory, 13:444
Red Wing Stoneware and Potters Union,
16:494
Red Wing Stoneware Co., see Red Wing
Potteries
Red Wing War History Committee, 23:
392
Redby, history, 30:274
Redding, J. Saunders, work reviewed,
31:244
Redding, P. G., 19:116
Redens, Rev. Sysko, 28:123
Redfield, Capt. David, Union officer,
19:390
Redfield, Capt. Davis R., 38:356
Redfield, Robert, author, 34:301
Redstone, Nicollet County, plat, 17:
238; name, 37:227
Redwood agency, see Lower Sioux
agency
Redwood County, Norwegians, 12:275n,
23:290; explored, 13:453; politics, 14:262; settled, 15:491, 37:
223; history, 16:130, 39:208; pioneers, 16:252; agriculture, 19:32,
40:231; archives, 23:93; grasshopper plagues, 37:210; Indians, 37:
275; travel guide, 38:243; poorhouse, 38:374
Redwood County Historical Society,
20:354, 38:43
Redwood County War History Committee,
24:82
Redwood Falls, fire department, 13:
344; explored, 13:453; Quaker
meeting, 18:255, 258n; history,
18:342; anniversary, 20:467;
Catholic settlement, 21:210; pioneer life, 26:290; sawmill, 36:
154; hanging, 38:18n; lignite deposits, 40:336
Redwood Falls Patriot, first issue,
37:264
Redwood Ferry, Minnesota River, see
Lower Sioux (Redwood) agency
Redwood Gazette (Redwood Falls), his-
tory, 30:397, 37:264
Redwood River, Redwood County, trad-
ing post, 11:380
Redwood Valley, history, 11:216
Ree Indians, customs, 32:244
Reed, Mrs. Arthur, speaker, 26:178
Reed, Charles A., architect, 28:293
Reed, Dorinda R., author, 37:86
Reed, Mrs. Edward W., 22:440
Reed, George, convention delegate,
14:245
Reed, George, with Nobles expedition,
35:252
Reed, George P., music publisher, 22:
127, 131
Reed, J. B., at Nininger, 13:132
Reed, James, government farmer, 17:
296
Reed, James Allen, founder of
Trempealeau, Wis., 12:212
Reed, John, steamboat captain, 34:10
Reed, John, trader, 15:422
Reed, John A., prison official, 37:
147–149
Reed, Robert R., 25:305; author, 16:
352
Reed, Thomas B., politician, 35:75
Reed, W. B., at Nininger, 13:132;
speaker, 13:146

Reed, Dr. Walter, army surgeon, 19:
    111, 24:207-213; biography, 24:
    238; papers, 34:212
Reed, Gen. Walter L., 24:209
Reed Lake, see Roseau Lake
Reeder, D. F., steamboat captain, 13:
    231
Reedfield, Mrs. Mora, 16:360
Reeds Landing, see Reads Landing
Reedy, David, 31:160
Reedy, William M., editor, 29:331
Rees, Charles, potter, 33:231
Rees, John M., lawyer, 21:196
Reese, ---, in fur trade, 15:430
Reeside, James, career, 29:150
Reeve, Charles, swine raiser, 26:117
Reeve, Gen. Charles M., 29:324; col-
    lector, 13:60, 74, 102
Reeve, G. J., author, 15:238
Reeves, Budd, poet, 26:84
Reeves, Mrs. Ernest H., speaker, 28:
    385
Reeves, Richard S., 18:142
Reeves, Will, 30:76; author, 28:191,
    293, 29:177, 30:163, 34:44
Reff, E. H., 19:468
Reformed Church in America, Dutch, 28:
    120-131, 35:34; German, 31:25
Regan, W. M., 23:226
Reger, Rev. Walter, 17:233, 19:119,
    22:108, 29:94; speaker, 20:355
Regier, C. C., work reviewed, 14:200-
    202; author, 14:114
Regina, Clearwater County, ghost
    town, 16:493
Register Cliff, Wyo., trading post,
    40:196
Regli, Adolph, work reviewed, 23:364;
    author, 18:343
Regnault, ---, explorer, 24:285
Rehan, Ada, actress, 28:117
Rehse, George W., cartoonist, 35:342,
    347, 351n
Rehse Brothers, merchants, business
    records, 20:349
Reichardt, Ferdinand, artist, 30:157,
    31:56, 35:369
Reichardt, Konstantin, review by, 28:
    58-60; author, 28:96, 373; speak-
    er, 28:301, 30:69
Reichers, Col. Louis T., aviator,
    26:5
Reichert, Joseph, 35:268
Reichmann, Felix, author, 25:88
Reid, Bill G., "Colonies for Disabled
    Veterans," 39:241-251
Reid, J., 21:130n
Reid, J. H. Stewart, work reviewed,
    37:80
Reid, L. F., author, 20:104
Reid, Mary J., author, 26:301, 302;
    editor, 26:303
Reid, Robie L., author, 24:77
Reid, Russell, author, 22:207, 40:
    145; editor, 24:77; speaker, 34:
    267
Reid, Capt. Tom, career, 36:237
Reid, Walter, see Reed, Dr. Walter
Reid, Whitelaw J., journalist, 34:
    344; vice-presidential candidate,
    35:64, 75
Reid Lake, see Roseau Lake
Reiersen, Johan R., colonizer, 16:239
Reiersgord, O. E., author, 17:485
Reiff, Ernest R., 21:190, 23:154, 26:
    64, 27:48, 141

Reilly, Daniel F., work reviewed, 25:
    372-374
Reilly, Edward C., author, 26:85
Reilly, Nina B., author, 13:452
Reilly, Robert A., steamboat captain,
    22:15-17
Reim, Victor P., speaker, 20:351, 21:
    438; author, 23:295
Reindahl, Knute, violin maker, 15:235
Reindeer Lake, Sask., Man., 40:173
Reineke, H. W., 19:119, 24:380, 26:
    92, 395, 27:364, 29:366
Reiner, Jacob, 26:371; translator,
    39:65
Reinertson, Thomas, 18:336
Reinhardt, C. J., 14:116
Reinmuth, Allen, author, 16:499
Reishus, Gunder, author, 28:381
Reishus, Mrs. Sondre, pioneer, 28:381
Reitan, Norman, speaker, 23:193
Reiter, Arthur, speaker, 20:297
Reitinger, Rev. Filip, 15:35
"Relief," steamboat, 36:251
Religion, frontier, 12:70, 397, 18:
    294, 40:403; denominations, 18:
    409; in lumber camps, 34:59-66;
    communal sects, 36:278; Indian,
    37:85, 273, 277, 40:40; interfaith
    co-operation, 38:335; archives,
    39:35; atlas, 39:128. See also
    Missions and missionaries, various
    denominations and orders
Remer, Lutheran church, 17:469
Remer Record, file acquired, 16:103
Remey, Adm. George, 22:87
Remey, Mrs. George, 22:87
Remington, E., and Sons, typewriter
    manufacturers, 16:446
Remington, Franklin, author, 35:240
Remington, Frederic, 38:238; artist,
    17:109, 22:410, 29:79, 266, 33:
    264, 34:210, 36:232; letters, 20:
    82, 38:200
Remington, G. W., speaker, 16:129
Remington, Harry, author, 13:346, 15:
    479, 16:116, 227
Remington Rand, Inc., 16:446
"Remnica," steamboat, 33:16, 17
Remore, J. F., pioneer, 25:25
Remsberg, Mrs. O. Z., 12:185
Remsburg, George J., author, 13:331
Remsburg, John E., author, 13:331
Remy, H. H., lumberman, 24:201, 202
Renaud, Jean Baptiste, voyageur, 18:
    241, 24:285n
Renaudot, Eusèbe, 13:417, 418
Rene, K. A., work reviewed, 12:181
Renfro, William C., 36:42n
Rennebohm, Oscar, Wisconsin governor,
    speaker, 29:268
Reno, Gen. Jesse L., 21:349, 40:148
Reno, Milo, 21:68; agrarian leader,
    23:91, 35:284, 285, 40:354
Reno Lake, Crow Wing County, name,
    21:349
Rensch, Ethel G., author, 14:228
Rensch, Hero E., author, 14:228
Renville, Misses ---, teachers, 12:
    242
Renville, Evangeline, 12:131
Renville, Gabriel, 39:261; farmer,
    12:131; speaker, 12:132; organ-
    izes rangers, 19:450; Sisseton
    leader, 35:168, 170-177; scout,
    38:280, 40:313; family, 38:357
Renville, Rev. John B., 35:171, 174
Renville, Joseph, 18:157, 21:99, 412,

24:179, 26:106; trader, 11:378,
    18:339, 20:259, 21:107, 207, 22:
    282, 283, 285, 310, 23:272, 27:67,
    263; career, 12:231-246, 28:337;
    relations with missionaries, 16:
    134, 135, 143, 147, 148, 21:162,
    170, 274; translator, 16:142, 18:
    158, 21:31, 275; hymn writer, 21:
    280; descendants, 24:80
Renville, Joseph, Jr., 12:127, 131;
    guide, 12:239
Renville, Mary B., Sioux captive, 18:
    46
Renville, Victor, scout, 40:313
Renville, history, 13:453, 17:488,
    19:126; newspaper, 17:103; foot-
    ball team, 20:104; Dutch settle-
    ment, 28:124-127; pioneer life,
    34:173
Renville County, ethnic groups, 12:
    275n, 18:338, 21:102, 22:348, 25:
    318, 28:121, 124, 35:33, 90; set-
    tled, 12:444, 30:274, 39:273; his-
    tory, 13:453, 16:218, 19:126; or-
    ganized, 14:347, 488; newspapers,
    17:102; churches, 17:240, 18:257,
    258, 22:348; archives, 22:100; in
    Sioux Outbreak, 26:200, 38:281,
    283; centennial committee, 29:185,
    30:87; grasshopper plague, 36:57,
    37:209, 211
Renville County Farm Bureau, 22:111
Renville County Historical Society,
    organized, 21:218; collection, 21:
    338; museum, 28:297
Renville County Times (Beaver Falls),
    established, 19:126
Renville Rangers, 26:200; in Sioux
    Outbreak, 38:131
Renz and Karcher, St. Paul, confec-
    tioners, 27:327
Repentigny, Louis de Gardeur, sieur
    de, 11:242n, 18:325, 19:198
Reporter (St. Paul), founded, 37:163.
    See also Twin City Reporter
Republican Eagle (Red Wing), 27:270
Republican party, ethnic groups, 13:
    435, 26:373, 28:20-36, 31:31, 33:
    180; organized, 14:77, 132, 15:
    331; Minnesota Territory, 14:131-
    133, 156-159, 161, 162, 244, 27:
    13, 36:3, 5-11; policies, 14:164,
    183n, 187, 191, 15:123, 333-335,
    20:270, 22:234, 241, 245, 24:310,
    312, 313, 315, 26:191-208, 27:14,
    32:15-33, 36:168-172, 38:178, 40:
    368, 369, 374; in elections, 14:
    246-253, 24:308, 309, 37:45, 51,
    38:297, 39:82, 40:362; conven-
    tions, 16:226, 19:96, 262, 20:280,
    281, 25:77, 78, 26:189, 27:7, 28:
    284, 382, 30:234, 33:1, 126, 35:
    64-76, 156, 39:172; Minnesota, 17:
    161, 162, 18:128, 24:311, 28:183,
    34:188, 35:61-63, 114, 115, 297,
    298, 301, 304, 305, 307, 309, 312,
    36:113, 116, 122, 173-183, 300-
    308, 37:52-57, 324-334, 39:93-110,
    234, 327n, 40:317-329; leaders,
    19:456, 26:155; Wisconsin, 21:306,
    31:113; relation to third parties,
    22:78-80, 32:130-146, 34:221, 347,
    38:301, 308; platforms, 23:386,
    35:291; G.A.R. support, 23:166;
    symbol, 25:395; Ohio, 30:147; dis-
    sension, 31:42, 32:246; history,
    33:34, 35:285; in legislature, 33:

155-163; characterized, 34:37;
Iowa, 34:41, 35:42; Oregon, 35:94.
See also Politics, Whig party
Reque, Rev. Peter S., missionary, 18:
472; diary, 19:125
Reque, Sigurd S., author, 19:460
Rerat, Eugene A., career, 39:132
"Rescue," steamboat, 11:143
Rescue Hook and Ladder Co., Winona,
25:207
Research, Inc., Minneapolis, 33:244
Research Associates, St. Paul, 33:244
Reser, Sister Johanna, 35:271
Reservation River, Cook County, trout
fishing, 33:256
Reserve Mining Co., Beaver Bay, 33:
255; activities, 34:269-283, 35:
245; organized, 39:163. See also
Babbitt, Silver Bay
Reserve Town, Ramsey County, history,
15:456
Resler, George E., artist, 40:221
(cover), 249-253
"Resolute," launch, 18:279
"Restoration," sloop, 19:199, 22:70
Retrum, C. E., 27:266; speaker, 30:80
Retzek, Rev. Henry, author, 16:481,
21:100; speaker, 30:169
Reunick, Selma M., author, 11:102
Reuther, Charles, 28:23
"Reveille," steamboat, 11:135, 140,
142
Revere, Paul, inventor, 35:92
Revolutionary War, causes, 11:79, 22:
66; influence on Canada, 11:193,
15:95; in Wisconsin, 17:196; rela-
tion to land question, 18:435;
effects, 19:295-307, 22:306, 23:
258; soldier vote, 26:187n; per-
sonal narratives, 33:346; weather
data, 40:312
Rexford, Eben E., poet, 26:298
Rexford, Orcella, author, 25:400
Rexroth, Kenneth, poet, 35:244
Reyling, August, editor, 37:128
Reymert, James D., journalist, 24:
348; colonizer, 25:396
Reynold, Capt. Ira B., 17:234
Reynolds, Anna, 39:15
Reynolds, Arthur R., work reviewed,
36:28; speaker, 29:257; author,
30:71, 31:59, 32:60
Reynolds, Charles, 21:221; journal-
ist, 18:226
Reynolds, Charley, scout, 13:331
Reynolds, George, 11:465
Reynolds, Horace, author, 24:72
Reynolds, Joseph, 24:369
Reynolds, Quentin, author, 26:5
Reynolds, Dr. R. M., pioneer phy-
sician, 20:103; papers, 34:360
Reynolds, William M., 25:233
Reynolds Township, Todd County, his-
tory, 16:372
Rezac, W. J., 19:127
Rhindesberger, Peter, see Rindis-
bacher, Peter
Rhinelander, Wis., logging museum,
16:486, 24:364
Rhoads, James B., "The Fort Snelling
Area," 35:22-29; review by, 36:26;
compiler, 36:278
Rhode Island, first printing, 15:6;
atlas, 40:122
Rhodes, Charles D., author, 12:442,
14:231, 17:115

Rhodes, James F., author, 16:86, 40:
313; historian, 19:6, 436, 34:81
Rhodes, William, 36:254, 40:119
Rholl, Arthur, editor, 13:444
Ribourde, Father de la, missionary,
11:345
Rice, Mrs. A. J., speaker, 14:460
Rice, Allen Thornton, editor, 28:63
Rice, Ann E., author, 30:167
Rice, Charles S., election commis-
sioner, 26:208
Rice, Charles S., work reviewed, 36:
322
Rice, Daniel B., letter, 22:89
Rice, Maj. Ebenezer O., diary, 16:
217, 475, 17:54
Rice, Edmund, 16:130, 21:150, 38:46;
career, 16:239; portrait, 26:261;
politician, 35:58, 37:46, 39:148;
speaker, 35:105; railroad official, 35:359, 37:156, 157
Rice, Mrs. Edna, 18:334
Rice, Ellen, pioneer, 30:7
Rice, Frank, 18:134, 135, 141, 143
Rice, George, author, 34:265, 355
Rice, Harvey, 38:385
Rice, Henry M., 12:458, 17:95, 338,
22:58n, 26:361, 30:7, 8, 34:357,
35:152, 321; trader, 11:372, 22:4,
191, 278, 23:94, 32:77, 79; speaker, 12:392, 40:301; papers, 13:
196, 16:224, 21:412, 22:192, 25:
183, 26:209, 258, 29:49, 101, 283,
374, 30:40; businessman, 13:234,
21:429, 33:221, 35:109, 113, 36:
237, 39:144, 145, 147; politician,
13:433, 14:132, 20:284n, 24:309,
36:259-271, 38:120, 121, 218, 297,
39:41-46, 148, 150, 151, 40:224,
225, 362; territorial delegate,
14:129, 158, 182, 17:317, 18:372,
27:314, 28:216, 35:337, 363, 36:1,
4, 6, 7, 10; Senator, 14:163, 164,
190, 191, 20:320, 24:311, 28:74,
29:84, 32:24, 29, 34:145, 35:116,
37:46, 54, 156n, 325, 326, 329;
house, 15:54, 30:74; Indian policy, 15:297; career, 16:239, 30:
197; hunter, 16:260; in Winnebago
removal, 16:333, 17:156n, 18:223,
28:205, 31:214, 36:278; MHS founder and president, 20:367, 368,
427, 30:87, 296, 345; author, 21:
287; social life, 22:10; hotel
owner, 22:57n; statue, 24:263, 26:
372; portrait, 27:240; Freemason,
33:310
Rice, Mrs. Henry M., 22:10; portrait,
26:258; biographical sketch, 30:
267
Rice, Martha Ellen, pioneer, 30:7
Rice, Ora R., 27:68
Rice, Mrs. R. S., 18:273
Rice, Mrs. S. E., 13:286, 14:119, 16:
242, 17:231, 19:359
Rice, Rev. W. A., author, 18:333
Rice family, in Minnesota, 22:89;
genealogy, 26:258
Rice, Catholic church, 17:118
Rice and Myrick, stage owners, 34:17n
Rice County, census, 11:317; ethnic
groups, 12:265, 270-272, 30:162;
settled, 12:430, 19:475, 35:321;
archives, 13:312, 15:196, 22:100;
fair, 14:461; surveyed, 15:223;
historical exhibits, 16:131; wildlife, 16:244; agriculture, 17:129,

18:408, 24:92, 29:2n, 35:322;
newspaper index, 17:357, 484, 18:
223, 19:118, 467; churches, 18:
118, 30:408; county seat, 18:368;
name, 20:368; history, 21:115, 23:
187, 30:408, 37:187; state park,
23:191, 29:263; soldier vote, 26:
200; grist mill, 29:4; poor farm,
38:369n
Rice County Agricultural and Mechanical Association, 16:242
Rice County Farm Bureau, 21:115
Rice County Historical Society, 13:
52; organized, 11:13; meetings,
11:15, 18, 337, 12:105, 209, 341,
453, 13:121, 344, 14:122, 237,
461, 15:138, 251, 370, 16:100,
124, 243, 361, 17:123, 357, 484,
18:111, 223, 335, 19:118, 232,
361, 20:98, 213, 354, 458, 21:109,
338, 446, 22:107, 218, 341, 23:
103, 194, 299, 24:87, 270, 25:98,
26:91, 285, 27:77, 173, 267, 342,
28:88, 287, 387, 388, 29:93, 276,
365, 30:82, 168, 279, 34:218, 359;
quarters, 11:16, 52, 466; essay
contest, 11:17; members, 11:19;
finances, 11:20, 25:408, 26:395,
27:146; officers, 11:117; museum,
12:37, 19:466, 23:11, 13, 14, 26:
180, 33:210; activities, 14:346,
347, 27:231, 363, 35:50, 322, 37:
67; exhibits, 14:461, 16:119;
manuscript collection, 16:241; anniversary, 17:232
Rice County War History Committee,
23:392
Rice Creek, Anoka County, 24:332
Rice Creek, Redwood County, Sioux
village, 38:243
Rice Hotel, St. Paul, 20:393
Rice Lake, Aitkin County, Chippewa
village, 23:330
Rice Lake, Anoka County, Indian bat-
tle, 24:2
Rice Lake (Lac La Folle), Clearwater
County, trading post, 11:369
Rice Lake, Freeborn County, see Hol-
landale
Rice Lake, Hennepin County, 35:24
Rice Lake, Itasca County, Indian
mounds, 26:316
Rice Lake, St. Louis County, 40:392,
397, 398
Rice Lake, Wis., archaeology, 37:183
Rice Park, St. Paul, 33:3, 40:253;
history, 12:458
Rice School, St. Paul, 16:130
Rice Street, St. Paul, name, 20:369
Riceland Township, Freeborn County,
Norwegian settlement, 12:269
Rich, E. E., works reviewed, 20:69-
72, 21:398, 24:43-45, 340, 26:55,
27:37, 28:169, 29:153, 339-341,
30:375, 31:238, 32:249, 33:130,
261, 34:80, 254, 35:141, 282, 36:
150, 272, 37:217; author, 19:455,
40:157n, 358
Rich, H. S., stoneware manufacturer,
33:235
Rich, John H., stoneware manufac-
turer, 28:291, 33:235
Rich, William W., legislator, 35:347
Rich family, genealogy, 27:56
Rich Valley Township, McLeod County,
Bohemian settlement, 15:28

Richard, Father Gabriel, 20:262; educator, 13:110
Richards, Amasa, papers, 24:165
Richards, Bergmann, 25:54, 26:45, 253, 28:200, 29:97; work reviewed, 34:351; author, 25:204, 36:71; speaker, 26:284, 27:75, 28:391, 30:87, 170, 171, 363, 369, 401, 403, 36:217; MHS president, 29:98, 282, 371, 30:37, 330, 366, 32:13n
Richards, Mrs. Carmen N., editor, 25:400
Richards, Ella, musician, 39:53
Richards, Eva L. Alvey, "Pioneers in Iron Land," 32:147-154; "North Country Post Office," 33:22-28; "Child Pioneer," 33:72-76; "Schoolgirl of the Indian Frontier," 33:105-111; author, 32:191
Richards, Thomas, 13:209
Richardson, Mrs. A. D. (Elizabeth Young), 19:319, 320
Richardson, Ahira, 14:219
Richardson, Brad, author, 25:97
Richardson, C. W., cheese manufacturer, 27:112
Richardson, Daniel, settler, 40:339
Richardson, Edgar P., author, 33:36, 35:379, 38:333
Richardson, Edward E., author, 17:115
Richardson, F. A., speaker, 27:108
Richardson, H. W., speaker, 11:118; papers, 20:452
Richardson, Henry H., architect, 23:223, 231, 40:99, 101, 104, 107
Richardson, Israel B., Union officer, 25:36, 131
Richardson, J. T., author, 27:160
Richardson, James O., in Civil War, 25:355
Richardson, James P., author, 37:186
Richardson, John ("Jock"), resort owner, 37:235; storyteller, 37:236-253; guide, 38:33
Richardson, Sir John, 35:282
Richardson, Nathan, 20:97, 21:446
Richardson, T. J., artist, 25:313
Richardson, Mrs. W. D., 14:298
Richardson, Dr. W. J., 17:237
Richardson, William H., shoemaker, 16:71
Richelot, Louis G., author, 21:370
Riches, Arthur W., 16:103, 21:87
Richfield, developed, 13:115; churches, 13:346, 24:90; tree planting, 29:264; name, 40:89; Augsburg Park site, 40:378, 382
Richfield Baptist Church, anniversary, 13:346
Richfield Lake, see Grass Lake
Richfield Methodist Church, anniversary, 13:346
Riching, Mr. and Mrs. ---, actors, 28:326
Richland County, N.D., history, 18:104
Richland Township, Rice County, Norwegian settlement, 12:271
Richman, Irving B., work reviewed, 12:416; author, 13:210
Richmond, George A., 22:147
Richmond, Gordon, author, 28:293
Richmond, churches, 18:119; in Sioux Outbreak, 20:192, 28:192, 30:280, 281, 283
Richmond, Va., in Civil War, 20:275, 286

Richter, Dan E., lawyer, 17:213
Richter, Francis, 14:345
Richter, Mrs. Helen V., 16:61, 17:62
Richtmann, Jacob, contractor, 37:283, 284n, 285
Richwood, Becker County, Lutheran church, 14:451; grasshopper plague, 37:208
Rickaby, Franz, author, 21:56; compiler, 36:77
Rickard, T. A., author, 14:445
Rickenbacker, Capt. Edward V., 24:240
Ricker, A. W., author, 18:323, 19:104; editor, 28:44
Ricker, Celestia A., 24:132
Ricketson, Daniel, 16:45
Ricketts, Capt. James B., 39:176
Ricketts' Battery, in Civil War, 25:30n
Riddell, William R., author, 11:107
Rideau Falls, Ottawa, Ont., 28:10
Ridenour, A. C., speaker, 12:342
Rideout, Walter B., review by, 38:235; work reviewed, 37:81
Ridge, Martin, "The Humor of Ignatius Donnelly," 33:326-330; "Ignatius Donnelly, Minnesota Congressman," 36:173-183; reviews by, 31:49, 33:350, 34:162, 37:81; work reviewed, 38:235; author, 31:58, 64, 35:98, 378
Ridgeville, Man., history, 34:132
Ridley, Gen. Clarence S., 24:5
Riebe, John, journalist, 23:403
Ried, Rev. J. M., 31:89
Riedell, Henry, miller, 11:275
Riedesel, George M., house, 38:348
Riegel, Robert E., review by, 18:306; work reviewed, 12:70-72; author, 11:421; speaker, 13:367
Riel, Louis, I, rebel leader, 22:281
Riel, Louis, II, career, 33:183, 34:356, 35:151, 36:64, 37:86; métis leader, 33:315; at Fort Garry, 35:34
Riel rebellions, history, 12:330, 16:460-462, 495, 17:128, 453-455; 1869-70, 13:209, 15:356, 477, 17:217, 19:218, 20:207, 23:186, 287, 24:329, 28:61, 281, 31:56, 35:148, 36:63, 102, 40:93; source material, 15:232, 20:80, 34:352, 35:282, 36:325, 37:80; suppressed, 16:297, 348, 21:433, 24:277n, 30:63, 34:242, 36:192; amnesty, 18:216; 1885, 19:218, 23:186, 287, 25:200, 28:61, 281, 35:148; American involvement, 30:150, 35:34, 47, 151
Rienow, Leona T., 27:72
Riepp, Mother Benedicta, 35:263, 264, 270
Ries, H., author, 21:200
Ries, Jakob, Bottling Works, Inc., Shakopee, history, 28:294
Riese, Elizabeth, author, 18:106
Rieser, Carl, author, 36:283
Riesman, David, work reviewed, 33:348
Riess, Father Bruno, 35:265
Rietbrock, Fred, 29:268
Rife, Clarence W., 40:96; reviews by, 18:438, 20:319-321, 23:58-60, 257, 26:363, 39:166; author, 14:230, 18:440, 20:322, 23:74, 271, 26:370, 35:282; speaker, 15:241, 29:164
"Rifle Grays," Ottawa, Ont., 16:471

Rigand de Vaudreuil, François de, 32:232
Rigand de Vaudreuil, Philippe de, Marquis de, governor of New France, 19:288
Rigand de Vaudreuil de Cavagnial, Jeanne Charlotte, Marquise de, 11:246, 19:289, 290, 32:237
Rigand de Vaudreuil de Cavagnial, Pierre de, Marquis de, trader, 11:246, 19:289; surrender, 15:94; map, 18:430; papers, 21:395; governor of New France, 32:232, 237, 238
Riggle, Alma E., author, 18:341
Riggs, Rev. Alfred L., 13:333, 23:97, 35:177, 380
Riggs, Anna J., 20:351
Riggs, Dr. C. Eugene, 21:330
Riggs, G. Oliver, 19:474
Riggs, Harry, ferryman, 33:19
Riggs, Isabella, 12:130
Riggs, J. W., author, 29:73
Riggs, Martha, 12:130, 13:100
Riggs, Mrs. Mary B., author, 12:330
Riggs, Stephen R., missionary, 12:190, 245, 16:357, 21:99, 275, 27:264, 35:168, 380, 38:357; papers, 11:317, 12:26, 318, 428, 13:100, 15:222, 16:333, 469, 18:210, 444, 20:454, 23:272, 25:183, 29:283; Dakota studies, 12:244, 13:165, 171, 15:277, 16:140, 141, 19:448, 21:160, 278-280, 22:102, 25:390, 30:298, 35:48; at Lac qui Parle, 12:339, 16:136-151, 39:344; travels, 13:232, 21:170-172, 425; author, 13:374, 375, 16:335, 20:193, 30:156, 35:340, 39:340; portrait, 16:137; quoted, 16:142; career, 16:239; at Traverse des Sioux, 20:260; in fiction, 37:10
Riggs, Mrs. Stephen R. (Mary), 21:170, 39:300; letters, 18:376, 25:183, 27:154, 264; author, 19:448
Riggs, Thomas, work reviewed, 24:341-343; editor, 25:182
Riggs, Rev. Thomas L., 18:444, 20:351, 21:425; speaker, 16:425
Riggs, Mrs. Thomas L., 16:301
Riggs family, 12:133n; missionary work, 16:345, 35:380; papers, 23:272
Riheldaffer, Rev. John G., 36:192; speaker, 19:254; educator, 36:238
Riis, Frithjof, 37:209
Riis, Paul B., author, 16:358
Riker, Dorothy, works reviewed, 24:343, 35:239; editor, 16:346, 34:175
Riley, A. Dale, 15:83
Riley, Alice K., author, 25:211
Riley, Edward M., author, 39:209
Riley, James W., letter, 20:193
Riley, Robert J., review by, 38:327
Rimer, Lenore E., author, 31:118
Rindisbacher, C. H., 26:261, 27:70
Rindisbacher, Peter, I, emigrant, 32:160, 161
Rindisbacher, Peter, II, artist, 17:456, 22:154n, 23:169, 25:54, 33:264, 35:369; career, 14:283-287, 27:70, 30:260, 32:155-159; works, 14:284-287, 423n, 20:71, 434, 21:432, 23:154-156, 26:261, 28:372, 29:61, 32:238, 33:21, 227, 36:249n, 318, 37:306, 39:261, 40:144;

Minnesota water colors, 19:445, 20:39, 54-57, 21:37, 23:189; Indian portraits, 20:173-175, 22:203, 29:350, 35:242; showings, 22:317, 434, 23:94, 30:176

Rindisbacher family, travels, 14:286

Rines, Henry, legislator, 33:156, 158n, 159, 160

Ring, Nancy, author, 13:339

Ringdahl, Matthias P., pioneer, 12:264, 271, 21:449

Ringdahl, Mrs. Matthias P. (Ingeborg), 21:449

Ringdahl, Olive, author, 21:449

Ringer, C. W., author, 16:492

Ringgold County Historical Society, Mount Ayr, Iowa, publication, 23:90

Ringling, Al, circus master, 21:429

Ringling, William, fisherman, 34:2

Ringling brothers, career, 26:170; circus, 23:185, 24:76, 28:266

Ringstad, Ivan, author, 18:342

Ringstad family, genealogy, 11:89

Rintala, Edsel K., work reviewed, 34:207

Rio Grande Railroad Co., tracks, 30:237

Ripley, Abigail, 39:5

Ripley, Judge C. G., career, 30:53

Ripley, Clara, 39:5

Ripley, Edna May (Mrs. Leroy A. Page), 39:1n, 5

Ripley, Dr. Frederic N., career, 29:265

Ripley, Dr. Martha G. (Mrs. William W.), pioneer physician, 20:101, 446; career, 30:405, 39:1-17

Ripley, William W., rancher, 39:3; mill owner, 39:5, 9, 13

Ripley Memorial Hospital, Minneapolis, 39:16, 17

Rippe, Henry, 20:361

Ripple, Stanley, 16:308

Risedorph, John E., diary, 15:224, 16:52

Rishworth, Thomas D., 14:345; author, 11:330; speaker, 16:67

Rising, Henry G., 17:239; author, 20:354, 458

Risley, John, panoramist, 17:133, 20:380, 382

Riss, Father Bruno, missionary, 32:38-40

Rissanen, Juho, artist, 25:317, 378, 26:31, 378, 27:142, 30:404; speaker, 26:392

Rister, Carl C., work reviewed, 22:181-183; speaker, 13:327; author, 25:190

Ristine, Col. Ben F., 24:5

Ristow, Walter W., "Alfred T. Andreas," 40:120-129; review by, 40:355

Ritchey, Charles J., 18:54; reviews by, 12:68-70, 13:94; editor, 12:191; speaker, 18:204, 269; author, 28:331

Ritchie, Mrs. H. B., author, 22:102

Ritchie, Dr. Harry P., 12:207, 18:92

Ritchie, Dr. Parks, 24:347

Ritchie, Mrs. S. S., 12:444; author, 15:469

Ritchie, Thomas, editor, 30:106

Ritchie, Thompson, 15:210; letter, 21:192

Ritchie, Mrs. William, 14:452, 18:399

Ritchot, Rev. N.-J., 40:93

Ritter, Johann, and Co., Reading, Pa., printers, 27:31

Ritter, L. B., author, 34:264

Ritzema, Derk, Dutch pioneer, 38:125

Ritzenthaler, Robert E., author, 33:351

Rivard, Father John T., author, 35:152

River Falls, Wis., frontier life, 20:339; history conference, 29:360; Congregational church, 34:264; power company, 35:381

River Falls (Wis.) Academy, history, 39:171

River Falls (Wis.) State Teachers College, history, 14:342, 39:171

River Warren, glacial river, 38:158

Riverdale-Lake Hanska Junior Pioneer Club, 21:111

Riverdale Township, Watonwan County, frontier life, 17:491

Rivers, Don, author, 17:360

Riverside, Redwood County, ghost town, 19:465

Riverside Chapel, Minneapolis, 15:480

Riverside House, Wabasha, hotel, 15:113

Riverside Press (Appleton), history, 21:344

Riverview Civic Club, St. Paul, history, 24:356

Rivière au Sable, see Sandy River

Rivière Jaune, see Yellow River

Rivière la Chaudière, see Kettle River, Carlton County

Rivington, James, printer, 23:172

Roach, Elinor, author, 25:311

Roads and highways, territorial, 11:205, 333, 14:153, 17:115, 18:315, 21:83, 30:173; builders, 11:215, 26:42; maps, 11:309, 391, 12:194, 16:286, 21:228, 236, 37:104, 38:58, 224, 40:234, 236-243, 388; legislation, 11:320, 407; Minnesota Triangle, 11:387-411; military, 11:389-392, 14:153, 17:317, 19:102, 31:176, 38:58, 40:233-247; markers, 12:30, 13:378-384, 18:459, 19:220, 35:382, 40:314; surfaces, 12:52, 16:288, 19:122; stage routes, 14:153, 18:354, 35:258, 38:55; source material, 14:218, 15:346, 23:74, 27:344, 35:52; New England, 14:340; state, 15:243, 19:345, 22:213, 26:43-45, 28:381, 30:274, 34:172, 35:189, 190, 379, 36:102; Duluth axis, 16:282-299; Lac qui Parle area, 18:339; Cottonwood County, 19:121, 234; federal, 21:83, 230, 231, 28:211n, 38:229; effect on settlement, 21:225-244, 23:28, 36:97; Wisconsin, 28:290, 31:176; wagon, 35:256, 37:35, 106-109, 38:61; auto club interests, 35:382, 38:205, 214; international, 36:325; freeways, 40:133; Canada, 40:358. See also Mail service, various roads and trails

Roanoke Valley, Va., N.C., Siouxan sites, 40:206

Roback, Dr. C. W., 18:74; career, 11:103

Robards, Mrs. O. J., speaker, 15:246

Robb, James T., Sr., 16:257

Robb, John S., artist, 17:140; trav-

els with Henry Lewis, 17:291, 295, 297, 300, 424, 430, 32:212; journalist, 30:152, 31:209-211; letters, 31:211-221

Robbins, Howard C., author, 15:129

Robbins, Roland W., work reviewed, 37:30

Robbins, Roy M., work reviewed, 23:161-163; author, 13:106, 24:52, 38:201

Robbins, Mrs. Samuel, pioneer, 33:4

Robbins Island, Mille Lacs Lake, Aitkin and Mille Lacs counties, donated to MHS, 36:328

Robbinsdale, beginnings, 15:249

Roberdeau, Maj. Isaac, letters, 34:285

Robert, Francis, cholera victim, 14:290

Robert, J., author, 37:224

Robert, Louis, 17:335, 21:99; family, 11:98; steamboat captain, 11:142, 181n; trader, 11:169, 12:119, 130, 210, 14:233, 238, 18:209, 29:218, 32:76, 35:356; career, 30:163

"Robert Dodds," towboat, 18:177

"Robert Harris," steamboat, 37:296

Roberts, Arthur L., 20:217

Roberts, Lt. Benjamin, at Mackinac, 11:257, 19:291

Roberts, Benjamin F., postmaster, 34:186

Roberts, Charles, journalist, 31:191

Roberts, Charles G. D., editor, 16:113

Roberts, Edward F., 13:207

Roberts, Elizabeth, author, 20:116

Roberts, Horace W., 14:234, 455, 16:240, 19:358, 21:106, 107, 22:215, 23:193, 24:187; speaker, 15:72, 75, 21:49, 53, 24:88; author, 20:350, 23:197

Roberts, John, diaries, 27:248

Roberts, Mrs. John, diaries, 27:249

Roberts, Kenneth, 26:166; work reviewed, 19:76-78; author, 19:312, 21:7

Roberts, M. Emma, artist, 27:250

Roberts, Marion, 21:61

Roberts, Nathan, 21:417

Roberts, Mrs. Nathan, 21:417

Roberts, Nelson, steamboat captain, 11:139

Roberts, Mrs. Pearl K., speaker, 24:381

Roberts, T. M., Supply Co., Minneapolis, 36:205

Roberts, Thomas O., farmer, 17:190

Roberts, Thomas P., author, 16:102

Roberts, Dr. Thomas S., 24:347; naturalist, 19:463, 20:170n, 21:209, 23:330n, 340n, 30:129, 130, 221, 224, 227, 228, 230, 35:154, 36:26, 103; author, 21:208, 22:213, 24:80, 26:277; papers, 27:248, 34:339

Roberts, William P., legislator, 35:343

Roberts and Throp, Three Rivers, Mich., thresher manufacturers, 24:302

Roberts County, S.D., frontier life, 18:456, 19:108, 27:259; place names, 27:260

Roberts County National Bank, Sisseton, S.D., 27:259

Roberts Township, Wilkin County, history, 18:224
Robertson, ---, trader, 21:148
Robertson, Mrs. Amy E. M., memorial, 26:151
Robertson, Andrew, government farmer, 11:184; trader, 11:381
Robertson, Angus M., mixed-blood, 18:209
Robertson, Archibald, diaries, 17:213
Robertson, Mrs. Cecil, author, 23:106
Robertson, Colin, 20:69; correspondence, 21:398; trader, 40:166, 168, 169, 175
Robertson, Daniel, 20:326; British commandant, 15:425
Robertson, Daniel A., 14:219, 18:363, 30:310, 36:237; letters, 16:224, 28:202; agricultural leader, 18:410, 20:448, 26:170; horticulturist, 19:357, 22:259, 40:335; townsite promoter, 21:150, 40:243; library, 23:3; house, 25:2, 9, 56, 27:231; editor, 26:295, 30:254, 39:45, 48; career, 30:300; promotes immigration, 31:224; politician, 33:330, 37:46, 47, 50; St. Paul mayor, 40:225n
Robertson, David A., 13:408
Robertson, Francis A., mixed-blood, 18:209
Robertson, George O., 13:140, 150, 17:268; promotes Nininger, 13:131, 135; speaker, 13:146
Robertson, H. A., letters, 27:153
Robertson, H. C., 22:219; speaker, 24:189
Robertson, H. E., author, 18:218
Robertson, James A., editor, 14:443
Robertson, M. C., 15:365
Robertson, Mrs. M. C., 15:365
Robertson, Margaret, 21:137n
Robertson, Mrs. Nellie A., work reviewed, 24:343
Robertson, Sidney, editor, 24:260
Robertson, Thomas A., mixed-blood, 34:235, 38:141n, 143; interpreter, 35:176
Robertson, Victor, 11:54, 14:79, 15:60
Robertson, William, trader, 21:135
Robertson family, genealogy, 14:218, 332, 438, 22:193
Robey, Mark E., author, 26:183
Robichaux, Michel, testimony, 21:127-129
Robidoux, Joseph, Jr., trader, 40:196
Robin Hood Flour Mills, Ltd., New Prague, 23:388
Robindeau, ---, guide, 32:89
Robinson, A. D., jeweler, 29:206n
Robinson, Anna, 12:421
Robinson, Doane, 13:368, 375, 14:226; author, 11:324, 35:44
Robinson, Edgar E., 17:385; speaker, 17:105
Robinson, Edward V., career, 16:349; author, 19:102
Robinson, Elwyn B., review by, 37:304; work reviewed, 40:257; author, 36:191, 279
Robinson, George W., speaker, 18:320
Robinson, J. L., author, 26:274
Robinson, James L., career, 23:192
Robinson, James H., historian, 11:450, 25:68, 33:207
Robinson, Jesse S., 39:269

Robinson, Sir John, land grants, 16:423-426
Robinson, Mortimer, career, 20:329
Robinson, Percy J., author, 22:64
Robinson, Perry, author, 26:306
Robinson, Solon, works reviewed, 17:326, 18:195
Robinson family, house, 37:76
Robinson's minstrels, 28:111
Robison, Mabel O., author, 36:69, 103
Robison, Sophia M., editor, 25:394
Robson, Albert H., work reviewed, 21:185
Robson, Joseph, author, 31:238
Roch, John, dairy promoter, 35:18
Roche, Owen W., ranch, 23:402
Roche, T. C., photographer, 35:93
Rocheau, Napoleon de, guide, 12:175
Rocheblave, Pierre de, trader, 15:421
Rochejacquelin, Comtesse de la, supports Indian missions, 30:3
Rochester, Anna, author, 25:298
Rochester, Nathaniel, portrait, 21:214
Rochester, historical meetings, 11:199, 283-286, 20:187, 296-300; medical center, 11:285, 17:330, 20:233-242, 298, 22:404-408, 23:95, 24:372; roads, 11:393, 394, 397, 398, 21:233; stage lines, 11:398, 402, 405, 406, 30:70; depicted, 12:49, 20:64, 193, 34:267, 35:161; churches, 12:209, 13:334, 14:451, 17:230, 21:330, 24:193, 28:293, 29:176; fairs, 12:445, 19:178, 20:223, 22:261, 262; statehood celebration, 14:185, 187; cyclone, 14:460; school, 16:368; G.A.R. post, 16:431, 440; museum, 18:117; baseball, 19:168-170, 178-180; growth, 20:221-223; health conditions, 20:224-232, 35:381; newspapers, 21:214, 22:442; airports, 21:454; music, 22:115, 125, 30:20; parks, 22:447; history, 23:301, 25:183; businesses, 24:108, 373, 29:8n; ration board, 26:175; private collections, 26:383; traveling show, 28:105; pioneer life, 29:358; panorama shows, 30:15, 18-20, 22; wildlife, 30:124, 223; art festival, 30:278; camp meeting, 31:82; German theater, 32:100, 34:242; bicycle clubs, 33:315; centennial, 34:170, 218; county seat, 35:21; politics, 40:321, 324. See also Mayo Clinic
Rochester, N.Y., milling center, 14:227, 33:132
Rochester and Northern Minnesota Railroad, 35:15, 21
Rochester Business and Professional Women's Club, 13:120, 19:64, 21:48, 213
Rochester Commercial Club, 21:214
Rochester High School, mural, 20:299
Rochester Infirmary, early clinic, 20:239
Rochester Junction, N.Y., archaeological site, 40:207
Rochester Junior College, 23:302
Rochester (N.Y.) Museum of Arts and Sciences, 13:431, 20:430, 28:187
Rochester Normal School, 26:298
Rochester Old School Boys' and Girls' Association, reunion, 12:452
Rochester Public Library, history,

11:465, 27:177; museum, 20:299, 21:213
Rochester State Hospital, 23:387, 38:22, 23
Rock, Augustin, see Rocque, Augustin
Rock, William, surveyor, 40:242, 245
Rock Bend, see St. Peter
Rock County, ethnic settlements, 12:274, 19:211, 28:121, 129, 35:90; courthouses, 12:341; agriculture, 14:102, 24:299n; established, 14:244; politics, 14:247-251, 262; name, 14:253n; census, 14:254, 256, 258, 259, 261; Methodist church, 17:363; newspaper, 21:343; archives, 21:434; welfare problem, 37:205; poorhouse, 38:370
Rock County Historical Society, 12:37, 38, 210, 314, 14:346, 16:241; organized, 12:106; meetings, 12:342, 15:252
Rock County War History Committee, 23:392
Rock Dell Township, Olmsted County, Norwegian settlement, 12:270; history, 35:336
Rock Island, Ill., frontier post, 15:379, 380; Henry Lewis' visit, 17:423, 424; depicted, 22:22; lumber industry, 22:94, 26:132, 27:190, 194; river port, 25:103, 109, 26:381, 34:134, 135; bridge, 30:160
Rock Island Lines, built, 12:253, 36:5, 71, 38:55, 40:85; excursion, 1854, 12:392, 14:440, 446, 15:405-420, 16:27, 18:434, 20:384-386, 25:103-116, 29:29, 170, 34:133-143, 35:181, 183, 37:101, 38:45; tracks, 30:232, 237; St. Paul, 30:233, 236; history, 34:83
"Rock Islander," keelboat, 18:403
Rock Lake Colonization Co., 33:315
Rock Prairie, Wis., Norwegian settlement, 12:252
Rock River, Ill., trading post, 13:222; ferry, 21:18n
Rock River Valley, Wis., described, 24:76
Rock Valle Lutheran Ladies' Aid Society, 30:164
Rockefeller, John D., 23:381; mining interests, 21:292, 23:361, 27:263, 32:148, 33:221
Rockefeller, John D., Jr., career, 39:336
Rockefeller, Nelson, politician, 40:293
Rockefeller Foundation, grants, 15:120, 24:163, 254, 353, 361, 370, 383, 25:43, 90, 168, 200, 380, 27:61, 29:173, 32:255, 37:44
Rockford, established, 13:115; church, 14:451; G.A.R. post, 16:431; sawmills, 37:159
Rockne, A. J., legislator, 33:156, 157, 159, 160
Rockstad, see Thief River Falls
Rockton, Mantorville Township, Dodge County, mill, 18:467
Rockwell, John A., excursionist, 15:416, 34:143
Rockwell, John G., commissioner of education, 19:237, 40:368
Rockwood, B. L., pioneer farmer, 23:316
Rockwood, Chelsea J., lawyer, 17:213
Rockwood, Capt. William T., 38:66

Rocky Mountain Fur Co., 15:426, 40:
201, 218; influence on exploration, 14:430; relations with
American Fur Co., 29:58-61; history, 38:199
Rocky Mountains, explored, 16:463;
fur trade, 29:260, 35:31, 36:317,
39:261, 40:145, 152, 154, 155,
184, 220; hunting, 35:153; expedition, 35:292, 36:294, 295, 40:144;
trade sites, 40:194-197
Rocque (Rock), Augustin, trader, 11:
383, 467, 14:253n, 362, 18:193,
20:263, 22:226, 40:81
Rocque, Joseph, trader, 18:193
Rodabaugh, James H., works reviewed,
29:161, 33:44; editor, 26:278, 34:
121; author, 29:81
Rodabaugh, Mary J., review by, 33:87;
work reviewed, 33:44
Rodberg, Ivan, 26:42
Rodda, Dr. F. C., speaker, 19:112
Roddis, Louis H., 18:321; review by,
35:288; work reviewed, 35:235; au-
thor, 14:226
Roden, Carl, 14:374
Roden, Rev. Eugene M., essay re
viewed, 38:193
Rodgers, Andrew D., III, author, 24:
371, 27:253
Rodgers, Brad, death, 13:215
Rodgers, Rev. George, colonizer, 25:
261, 29:87
Rodgers, J. K., 19:170
Roe, Frank G., work reviewed, 35:88;
author, 15:238, 17:476, 33:138,
34:260
Roe, Herman, "The Frontier Press in
Minnesota," 14:393-410; speaker,
14:74, 450, 15:219; author, 15:89,
28:333; publisher, 16:497
Roe, Ludwig I., speaker, 16:304
Roedocker, Louise, author, 31:146
Roehm, Marjorie C., work reviewed,
40:311
Roelker, William G., author, 26:73
Roemer, Rev. Theodore, author, 14:
339, 15:354, 25:193
Roepke, Howard G., author, 36:278
Roetter, Paulus, artist, 30:74
Rogen, Mrs. Ingeborg, pioneer, 11:336
Rogers, ---, artist, Henry Lewis'
assistant, 17:140, 301, 421, 423,
424, 433
Rogers, ---, Peter Garrioch's com-
panion, 20:122
Rogers, A. R., airline executive, 33:
242
Rogers, Anthony A. C., Congressman,
34:72
Rogers, Ben F., "William Gates Le
Duc," 34:287-295
Rogers, Bruce, typographer, 33:309
Rogers, Dr. C. E., 39:112n
Rogers, C. H., author, 24:175
Rogers, Dr. Clara, 39:7
Rogers, Earl M., compiler, 40:360
Rogers, Edward L., speaker, 14:350
Rogers, Edward S., work reviewed, 39:
34
Rogers, Francis, farmer, 39:1, 3;
house, 39:2
Rogers, Mrs. Francis, 39:1, 3; house,
39:2
Rogers, Fred, pioneer, 12:209
Rogers, H., hide dealer, 14:299
Rogers, Harold, author, 30:74

Rogers, Jessaline, actress, 33:176
Rogers, Joe, speaker, 17:483
Rogers, Lester D., career, 18:211
Rogers, Martha G., see Ripley, Dr.
Martha G.
Rogers, N. P., quoted, 22:129
Rogers, Maj. Robert, 13:109, 17:196,
18:439, 29:65; at Mackinac, 11:
107, 266, 267, 19:291; career, 11:
204, 13:439, 19:76-78; tried for
treason, 11:268; trader, 16:224;
exploration plan, 16:453, 18:194,
33:261, 34:155; papers, 34:157n;
author, 36:100; biography, 36:273
Rogers, Samuel P., lumberman, 24:265,
30:68
Rogers, William Allen, artist, 31:253
Rogers, William C., compiler, 36:103
Rogers, William K., papers, 18:444;
land speculator, 21:414, 35:150
Rogers, Winfield H., 19:436
Rogin, Leo, author, 13:204
Rognlie, W. P., author, 23:196
Rogstad, Einar A., 22:108, 23:104;
speaker, 27:174
Rogstad, Dr. F. J., 27:170
Rogue River, Ore., Indian war, 27:161
Rogue's Island, Renville County,
Preston Lake, name, 13:215
Rohan, William J., contractor, 35:337
Rohne, J. Magnus, author, 11:216,
328, 13:441, 14:231, 349, 15:129,
358
Rohr, Rev. Heinrich von, 37:187
Rohr, Philip, musician, 13:131, 135,
32:239-242, 39:322
Rohr, Rev. Philip von, 37:187
Roi, Jean Baptiste, voyageur, 23:243
Rolet, François, family, 23:287
Rolette, (Jean) Joseph, 23:287, 288,
24:179, 37:40; trader, 11:376, 12:
236, 16:156, 350, 18:193, 19:95,
20:262, 263, 265, 22:205, 278, 40:
23n, 81; death, 13:224; source material, 17:95, 25:272; Prairie du
Chien, Wis., post, 40:80
Rolette, Joseph, Jr., 18:275, 23:309;
in capital controversy, 11:454,
12:205, 421, 14:160, 15:479, 18:
105, 22:437, 29:84, 35:155, 36:6,
283; trader, 13:241, 20:79; legislator, 14:158, 248, 27:166, 271,
33:121, 34:84; marker, 15:479, 19:
109; described, 35:260, 261;
source material, 35:282
Rolette family, genealogy, 23:287
Rolette County, N.D., history, 34:84
Rolfe, A. O., author, 11:336
Roll, Charles, work reviewed, 29:252
Rollag, Clay County, Norwegian settlement, 12:278; cemetery, 21:112
Rolling Forks Township, Pope County,
schools, 26:398
Rolling Stone Industrial Association,
21:313
Rollingstone, roads, 11:392, 21:232;
Yankee colony, 18:230, 21:313, 25:
207; crop failure, 20:159; de-
scribed, 30:159; Luxemburger set-
tlement, 38:243; townsite, 39:82
Rollins, C. B., 21:403
Rollins, Irvin W., farmer, 22:41;
diary, 21:313, 35:152, 39:201-204
Rollins, Mrs. Irvin W., 39:201
Rollins, John, steamboat captain, 12:
164n, 24:138, 29:215
Rollins, Josephine Lutz, "Exploring

with Brush and Palette," 33:208-
210; speaker, 22:434, 27:365; art-
ist, 24:194, 350, 25:50, 56, 30:
157, 367, 411, 31:201, 33:189
(cover), 310
Rollins, Laban, settler, 39:201
Rollins, Mrs. Laban, settler, 39:201
Rollins, Richard, 24:350
Rollins family, genealogy, 21:313
Rollins, St. Louis County, railroad
station, 34:180
Rollins, Eastman, and Upton, millers,
12:393
Rollitt, Charles, I, diaries, 16:470
Rollitt, Charles C., II, diaries, 16:
470; records, 17:212, 18:47
Rølvaag, Ella V., author, 17:350
Rolvaag, Karl F., governor, 38:378,
39:257
Rølvaag, Ole E., 15:100, 19:437, 21:
203, 23:381, 25:86; works dis-
cussed, 11:63-74, 185, 14:444, 18:
330; author, 11:100, 13:324, 16:
106, 20:86, 117, 438, 23:119, 123,
125, 158, 30:149, 378, 31:135,
144, 146, 32:250, 35:11, 234, 36:
79, 237, 37:86, 38:387; career,
13:49, 16:349, 17:350, 20:179-181,
21:426, 22:104, 37:184, 39:126;
letters, 16:218; characterized,
22:365; influence, 33:187
Romaine, Lawrence B., work reviewed,
37:256
Romanians, South St. Paul, 26:181;
Mesabi Range, 27:212, 214, 215;
reverse migration, 27:214
Rome Township, Faribault County, Norwegian settlement, 12:270
Romick, Charles J., family, 27:29, 30
Romick, Mrs. Louisa E., 27:29, 30
Romick, Robert, pioneer, 27:29; city
assessor, 27:30
Ronchi, Umberto, author, 34:264
Ronellenfitsch, Rev. Victor, speaker,
29:277
Roney, Betty, author, 25:412, 37:43
Roney, E. L., 17:124, 18:111, 19:119,
20:99, 21:110, 447, 23:104, 392,
396, 24:161, 349, 26:151, 28:298,
332, 29:95; "An Old Store at Ma-
rine," 18:420-422; author, 13:445,
18:440; speaker, 25:210, 27:78,
29:360
Ronnenberg, Harold A., author, 30:68
Rønning, Rev. H. N., at Red Wing, 25:
314
Rønning, N. N., 29:276, 295; work re-
viewed, 24:348; author, 13:424,
444, 15:460, 25:314; autobiogra-
phy, 20:200; speaker, 29:93; edi-
tor, 29:177
Ronningen, Col. Otto I., speaker, 17:
482
Rood, Florence, teacher, 35:371
Rood, John, sculptor, 33:354; review
by, 33:86; work reviewed, 32:55
Rood, Mrs. John, 33:354
Rood, Rev. John, 35:20
Rookey, Peter, log mark, 26:136
Roos, Alford, house, 38:341
Roos, Carl, pioneer, 16:125
Roos, Charles, papers, 28:202, 29:49
Roos, Frank J., Jr., editor, 25:298
Roos, Hugo G., 14:234; papers, 28:202
Rooseboom, Capt. Johannes, 19:280
Roosevelt, Franklin D., 15:474, 16:
329, 358, 17:15, 18:302, 25:273;

President, 20:318, 23:217, 35:90,
36:134, 187, 40:298, 369; characterized, 20:319; Hyde Park library, 21:322, 22:326, 23:10; career, 22:313; letters, 28:305, 40:
350; reformer, 35:89
Roosevelt, Nicholas J., 14:150
Roosevelt, Theodore, 18:302, 303,
423, 22:313, 30:54, 147, 39:110,
40:319; career, 11:446; reformer,
14:201, 35:89; characterized, 16:
326; letters, 18:316, 19:213, 23:
371, 32:146, 175, 192; President,
20:421, 22:174; in St. Paul, 22:
164; conservationist, 23:162, 29:
156, 40:321, 322, 324; Progressive
leader, 23:263, 26:309, 27:132-
134, 33:41, 156n, 158; presidential medal, 25:79; author, 40:348
Roosevelt College, Chicago, 26:377
Roosevelt International Highway Association, 19:98
Root, Elihu, 29:84; letter, 18:316
Root, George F., publisher, 22:123
Root, Henry, 18:229
Root and Cady, music publishers, 26:
53
Root River, Fillmore, Mower, and Olmsted counties, mills, 16:128, 24:
101, 35:12; steamboating, 18:223
Root River State Bank, Chatfield,
presidents, 16:364, 28:203, 29:
223-230; records, 24:107n, 29:49
Root River Valley, pioneer life, 20:
184, 22:448, 30:90; described, 20:
303, 22:292
Root River Valley and Southern Minne-
sota Railroad Co., 40:110; incor-
porated, 24:96; history, 25:183
Rooth, Signe A., work reviewed, 35:
95; author, 33:351
Rosché, Louis, steamboat captain, 25:
72
Roscoe, railway suit, 11:445
Rose, Anson H., 31:83
Rose, Arthur P., 15:368, 16:241, 17:
492; author, 16:368, 31:205, 36:
104
Rose, B. A., musician, 33:93
Rose, Benjamin, 35:293
Rose, D. L., author, 17:125
Rose, David, 26:321
Rose, Edward, mixed-blood, 15:428,
432; career, 15:426; interpreter,
15:429
Rose, Immanuel, 35:293
Rose, Isidore, 35:293
Rose, Mrs. Johanna, 11:463
Rose, Margaret, author, 39:35
Rose Creek Township, Mower County,
agriculture, 16:496
Rose Lake, border lake, trade route,
29:134, 37:237; railroad connec-
tion, 36:132
Rose Township, Ramsey County, schoolhouse, 16:130; poll tax, 25:290
Roseau, historical meeting, 18:204,
231n, 271-278; border community,
21:204; settled, 24:321, 326;
railroad, 24:327; boundary survey,
37:86
Roseau County, trading posts, 11:366;
Lutheran churches, 11:466, 22:349;
first school, 13:345, 18:274;
pageant, 16:237; anniversaries,
16:244, 362, 18:272, 26:285; history, 16:498, 17:129, 18:273,

274n, 278, 21:455, 23:104, 24:326;
agriculture, 24:193; wildlife, 30:
127, 230n; census, 31:161; medicine, 34:173; post office, 34:185;
power service, 40:315
Roseau County Historical Society, 17:
130, 23:104, 26:285, 29:181; organized, 11:13; museum, 11:16, 18:
223, 274, 335, 21:109, 336, 447,
456, 23:11-13, 25:409, 26:180, 29:
93, 30:82; members, 11:19; finances, 11:20; meetings, 11:223,
17:64; marking project, 11:466,
22:341, 28:298; celebrations, 13:
345, 14:346; publication, 14:237,
18:272n; officers, 16:241, 492,
19:362, 22:341, 24:271, 27:364,
29:365; pageants, 16:362, 19:471
Roseau County War History Committee,
24:82
Roseau Electric Cooperative, Inc.,
40:315
Roseau Lake, Roseau County, trading
posts, 11:366, 17:96, 22:276, 279,
280n, 288, 289, 319, 320n
Roseau River, Roseau County, trading
post, 11:365, 366; name, 15:357,
18:278; course, 24:318; floods,
24:322; archaeological site, 38:
162
Roseau Route, marker, 17:476
Roseau Valley, history, 16:498, 17:
129, 24:318, 26:290; fur trade,
24:319; settled, 24:320-324;
churches, 24:323; Indian scare,
24:324-326
Roseboom, Eugene H., work reviewed,
34:121; author, 15:356, 36:151
Rosebud, Polk County, see Fosston
Rosebud Indian Reservation (Sioux),
S.D., 13:107, 35:289, 293
Rosebud River, Mont., battle, 27:161
Rosecrans, Gen. William S., Union of-
ficer, 25:240-242, 38:266n, 267,
270, 271
Roseland, Ill., Dutch settlement, 28:
125-127, 368
Rosemount, railroad, 38:295
Rosen, Joseph A., career, 39:260
Rosenau, Sadie M., 27:49, 122; "An
Eighth-Grade Project," 26:330-333;
review by, 30:385; editor, 26:260;
author, 26:370, 30:412
Rosenbach, A. S. W., bookseller, 37:
222
Rosenbaum, Crane, author, 21:334
Rosenberg, B. G., author, 37:345
Rosenberger, Balthasar, pioneer, 32:
37, 35:265
Rosenberger, Henry, pioneer, 32:37,
35:268
Rosenberger, Homer T., author, 26:168
Rosenberger, Lizzie, 35:268
Rosenberry, Marvin B., speaker, 27:
356
Rosendahl, Carl O., botanist, 17:126,
18:107, 23:332n; work reviewed,
34:308
Rosendahl, Paul H., diaries, 22:86
Rosendale, Meeker County, creamery,
21:452
Rosendale Township, Watonwan County,
Norwegian settlement, 12:273
Rosenholtz, Jennie, novelist, 31:146
Rosenkrantz, Frederick A. U., 40:271n
Rosenthal, Francis J., career, 14:333
Rosenthal, Moriz, pianist, 39:55

Rosenthal, Dr. Robert, reviews by,
30:245, 40:309; author, 30:292,
33:312, 35:381, 36:327, 37:186,
348, 38:92
Rosenwald, Julius, museum founder,
11:100
Rosenwald, Walter F., 11:30, 13:380,
15:79
Roseville, Kandiyohi County, Mormon
colony, 36:290
Roseville, Ramsey County, musical mu-
seum, 39:313, 314
Rosewood Township, Chippewa County,
Norwegian settlement, 12:275n
Rosholt, Thorman W., equipment firm,
38:308
Rosing, Leonard A., papers, 20:33, 83
Rosing, Morrison County, name, 31:253
Rosness, Rev. A. W., speaker, 14:122
Ross, Mrs. ---, housekeeper, 35:85
Ross, Alexander, work reviewed, 35:
143; trader, 16:350, 38:42; au-
thor, 33:227, 35:242
Ross, C. M., speaker, 23:397
Ross, Carl, author, 36:105
Ross, D., trader, 40:168n
Ross, David, attorney, 21:122
Ross, Donald, trader, 11:358, 20:71
Ross, Earle D., author, 12:442, 14:
108, 339, 22:326, 24:52, 174, 25:
89, 27:351, 28:172, 284; speaker,
13:327, 24:255
Ross, Mrs. Elizabeth, 13:425, 14:70
Ross, Frank E., "The Fur Trade," 19:
271-307; author, 19:337, 20:84
Ross, Hamilton N., review by, 34:206;
works reviewed, 32:186, 37:216
Ross, Harlow, publisher, 35:44, 199
Ross, Ishbel, 17:474
Ross, John, at Grand Portage, 12:368
Ross, Malchom, trader, 16:106
Ross, Martin, work reviewed, 22:80
Ross, Marvin C., work reviewed, 36:
222; editor, 33:90; author, 36:69
Ross, Philip, letter, 19:449
Ross, Robert F., speaker, 11:112
Ross, Samuel, cabinetmaker, 20:348
Ross, W. E. C., 11:298; speaker, 11:
292
Ross, settled, 21:455; Indian vil-
lage, 28:298
Rosser, J. Travis, politician, 37:47,
48
Rossignol, François, 21:130
Rossing, T. H., author, 22:348
Rossman, Allen, author, 35:245
Rossman, George A., 35:204; author,
35:245
Rossman, Grant, athletic director,
39:21
Rossman, Lawrence A., 22:188, 23:35,
50, 25:55, 26:45, 27:147, 29:97,
30:171; reviews by, 23:361, 25:
276; author, 13:118, 20:216, 22:
102, 446, 23:370, 24:265, 25:288,
29:169, 30:68, 85, 31:54, 33:228,
35:204, 245, 36:195; speaker, 21:
291, 26:84, 28:198, 29:55, 30:166
Rost, Arnie, author, 22:442
Rost, Jackson County, Lutheran meeting, 29:275
Rostovtzeff, Michael I., 14:90;
speaker, 17:105; author, 23:280
Rostropovich, Mstislav, cellist, 39:
64
Rosvold, Martin, speaker, 21:337
Rotary International, educational

program, 15:120; Minneapolis, 17: 236; Fairmont, 28:292
Roth, E. G., 26:89
Roth, Franz, pianist, 39:321, 322
Roth, Gordon, author, 16:249
Roth, Rev. J. W. P., 28:123
Roth, Rev. J. W. P., Jr., 28:123
Roth, Paul H., author, 24:73
Rothe, Emil, politician, 28:29, 30
Rothenburg, Dr. J. C., 21:107
Rothfuss, Hermann E., "Early German Theater," 32:100-105, 164-173; "Plays for Pioneers," 34:239-242; author, 32:127, 128, 173, 191, 33: 91, 188, 315, 34:99n, 130, 36:239
Rothkopp brothers, land claims, 32: 39-43
Rothrock, Dr. John L., author, 15: 254, 21:102
Roths, Daniel, printer, 27:31
Rothsay, railroad, 11:119, 226, 468; school, 21:458; Lutheran church, 29:359
Rothstein, Morton, author, 37:261
Rotten Foot, Wichita Indian, 40:199
Rottsolk, James E., work reviewed, 37:260; author, 36:195
Roubadeau Pass, Neb., 40:196
Roucek, Joseph S., editor, 19:459; author, 20:442, 26:167; compiler, 25:299
Rouillard, Thomas H., author, 37: 274n; minister, 37:277
Rouleau, Charles, mail carrier, 36: 207
Rouleau, Joseph, 18:212
Rouleau, Mrs. Joseph, 18:212
Roulston, Reyburn, author, 35:294
Roulstone, George, pioneer printer, 15:14
Roumanian Orthodox church, St. Paul, 15:481
Round Lake, Becker County, Indian outbreak, 11:332
Round Lake, Ont., Chippewa colony, 11:332
Round Prairie Norwegian Lutheran Church, Freeborn County, history, 21:449
Round Prairie Township, Todd County, history, 23:111
Round Tower, Fort Snelling, 27:262; described, 15:360, 16:249, 23:290; restored, 20:342, 35:189; pictured, 33:189 (cover), 34:314, 35: 188, 36:89, 39:279; highway problem, 35:191; balloon ascensions, 39:279. See also Fort Snelling
Round Tower Museum, Fort Snelling, 24:56, 59, 81, 35:367, 36:36; exhibits, 20:342, 22:434, 23:41, 94, 189, 268, 24:374, 25:286, 26:64, 27:242, 30:289, 36:230; dedicated, 21:327; sponsored by MHS, 21:408, 23:38, 267, 37:67; described, 22: 207-209; murals, 22:208, 317, 35: 197; visitors, 23:12; function, 23:14; collection, 24:354, 25:311; maintenance, 28:53, 35:190
Rourke, Constance, 27:275
Rourke, Francis E., author, 37:185
Roussain, ---, trader, 11:359
Roussain, Eustache, 12:431; trader, 26:362
Roussain, François (Francis), 12:431; trader, 24:354

Rousseau, Dominique, legal case, 21: 117-148
Rovainen, Antti, Finnish pioneer, 25: 318
Rove Lake, Cook County, portage, 29: 134
Rover's Club, Excelsior, 19:344, 20: 35
Rowan, Carl T., author, 33:188, 35: 293
Rowand, John, trader, 20:71, 72, 36: 51, 40:167n
Rowberg, A. A., speaker, 17:357
Rowe, C. W., 31:171
Rowe, Miles, author, 29:272
Rowena, Redwood County, ghost town, 19:465
Rowland, Buford, compiler, 36:278
Rowland, Maj. Thomas, 32:132
Rowland, William S., 13:27, 28
Rowley, Timothy, speaker, 18:341
Rowsome, Frank, Jr., work reviewed, 35:283
Roy, ---, trader, 11:367
Roy, Francis (Frank), 15:292; trader, 18:209
Roy, J. E., author, 14:368
Roy, Peter, 15:292
Roy, Pierre-Georges, author, 12:431, 13:432; career, 25:200
Roy, Vincent, trader, 11:368, 20:71, 26:174
Royal Canadian Mounted Police, 17:154
Royal Empire Society, London, 14:222
Royal Fredrik University, Oslo, 19: 208
Royal Library, Stockholm, 20:248
Royal Norwegian Air Force, training camp, 25:311
Royal Ontario Museum, Toronto, archaeology, 20:199; collections, 21:186, 28:70, 36:314, 317; underwater research, 39:130, 171
Royal Society of Canada, 12:293, 15: 477
Royal Township, Lincoln County, cabin, 23:403
Royalton, trading post, 11:220; post office, 34:170; museum, 34:218
Royer, Catherine, author, 31:255
Roy's Addition, Superior, Wis., 20:13
Roy's Fort, Dak. Ter., trading post, 11:367
Rozwenc, Edwin C., author, 40:360
Ruane, James, speaker, 16:124
Rubins, W. H., artist, 24:248
Rubinstein, Anton, pianist, 39:325
Rubinstein String Quartet, 39:53
Ruble, George S., Albert Lea pioneer, 15:136, 16:494, 21:340; lumberman, 23:106; horse breeder, 26:118
Ruble, Kenneth D., work reviewed, 29: 158; author, 20:430, 40:147
Ruble Brothers, Albert Lea, horse breeders, 26:118
Ruble Brothers, McGregor's Landing (McGregor), Iowa, farm machinery merchants, 24:301
Ruckman, Mrs. Charles, 13:197
Rudd, Albert, musician, 33:101
Rudd, Velva E., author, 34:215
Rudh, Casper, pioneer, 11:226
Rudolf, Paul O., author, 17:110
Rudolph, John C., speculator, 39:91
Rudstrom, Rosemary, author, 30:407
Rue Hennepin, Ath, Belgium, 11:2, 4
Ruede, Howard, author, 18:454

Ruedy, A., author, 16:226
Ruehle, Leo H., author, 18:343
Rueping, F. J., translator, 25:301
Rueping, William, German immigrant, 25:301
"Rufus Putnam," steamboat, 11:124, 13:224, 230
Ruger, Gen. Thomas H., 17:88
Rugg, Betty, 15:459
Rugg, Mrs. George C., 15:459
Rule, Edith, author, 13:208
Ruley, Gus, steamboat captain, 31:85
Ruliffson, Mrs. Albert G., 38:75
Rum River, Mille Lacs, Isanti, and Anoka counties, name, 11:325, 14: 118, 21:348; trading posts, 11: 374, 375; traffic, 12:447, 35:50; lumbering, 13:284, 354, 355, 366, 15:484, 18:166, 24:126, 129-131, 134, 29:137; battle, 15:280, 21: 167n, 24:11, 12, 23-25; archaeology, 25:330, 40:363; settlements, 25:364, 35:167; ferry, 35:255; forests, 36:70
Rumanians, Detroit, Mich., 20:202
Rumble, Wilfrid E., 28:200
Rumson, N.J., history, 26:267
Runals, D. E., author, 17:119
Rundell, Walter, Jr., work reviewed, 38:238
Rundlett, Joseph, 22:104
Rundquist, Myrtle T., author, 31:61
Runeberg, Becker County, Finnish settlement, 25:320
Runes, in Kensington inscription, 17: 179-181, 40:49, 58; Bergen, Norway, 40:50-58
Runick, Robert, 11:332
Runions, L. F., pioneer farmer, 22: 346
Runk, John, photograph collection, 18:344
Runnerstrom, Arnold, 20:214, 23:195
Running Walker (The Gun), Sioux leader, 11:178n
Ruohonen, Mrs. Hilma, pioneer, 25:161
Rupert, Prince of Bohemia, 16:399, 419, 423, 424n, 24:340, 29:154; characterized, 16:396; governor of Hudson's Bay Co., 16:398; career, 26:273
Rupert House, Que., canoe factory, 34:174
Rupert's Land, Canada, bishopric, 20: 431, 24:262, 30:387, 37:53, 57; northern department, 22:309-311; Swiss settlement, 32:160; in Sioux Outbreak, 34:317-324; history, 35: 34, 202, 36:272; ownership, 35: 243, 36:241, 37:56; fur trade, 36: 37; mail service, 37:55; route to Minnesota, 37:134
Ruppius, Otto, author, 24:222
Rural Electrification Administration, 34:84, 264
Rush, Dr. Benjamin, 37:183; author, 21:363
Rush, N. Orwin, work reviewed, 38:238
Rush City, railroad, 16:292; museum, 20:101; commercial club, 27:177; settled, 28:395, 40:411; history, 36:195; described, 37:103n
Rushford, village and township, Norwegian settlement, 12:268; centennial, 34:128; Bible school, 37:42
Rushseba Township, Chisago County, history, 36:195; name, 37:103n

Rusk, Jeremiah M., 19:150
Rusk, Ralph L., author, 12:201
Ruskin, John, quoted, 38:343
Russel, B. S., bank manager, 37:120
Russel, Fred, 17:238
Russell, Lt. ---, at Fort Snelling, 40:79
Russell, Arthur J., author, 11:74, 24:90, 25:211, 315; poet, 26:308
Russell, C. M., and Co., Massillon, Ohio, thresher manufacturers, 24:301
Russell, Carl P., work reviewed, 35:376; author, 15:233; editor, 29:260
Russell, Charles E., author, 11:83, 39:82
Russell, Charles M., artist, 26:307; career, 36:101
Russell, D. M., 19:326
Russell, Capt. E. U., Union officer, 33:211n
Russell, Falsum, author, 25:186, 311
Russell, Frank, 14:122
Russell, Horace H., 18:410n, 19:148n; "Wendelin Grimm and Alfalfa," 19:21-33; author, 18:324, 19:69, 91
Russell, Jeremiah, 19:143, 28:210; journalist, 14:439, 21:412; papers, 22:40; farm, 29:219
Russell, Lord John, 18:81
Russell, Rev. Joseph A., 19:131, 250
Russell, L. F., 16:471
Russell, Morris C., 18:467
Russell, Nelson V., 25:408; review by, 21:78; work reviewed, 21:182; author, 19:218, 21:80; speaker, 21:53, 26:91
Russell, Peter, correspondence, 14:228
Russell, Roswell P., reminiscences, 19:95; lumber agent, 24:130; papers, 26:155
Russell, Capt. W. F., court martial, 25:246
Russell, newspaper, 27:344
Russell House, Sauk Rapids, stage stop, 34:170
Russell-Miller Milling Co., Minneapolis, 40:147
Russell Sage Foundation, 39:300
Russia, Mennonite settlements, 14:103, 18:99, 20:181, 27:222; railways, 16:464, 38:310-325; emigration from, 27:65, 213; agriculture, 39:260; fur trade, 40:144, 181n, 208, 216, 217; suppresses Polish insurrection, 40:274n
Russian Orthodox Cemetery Association, Minneapolis, 13:323
Russian Orthodox church, Minneapolis, 24:72; Bramble, St. Louis County, 27:82
Russian Orthodox Greek Catholic church, Minneapolis, 19:123, 39:168
Russian Railway Service Corps, history, 38:310-325
Russian War Relief, 23:21, 152, 292
Russians, Mountain Lake, 11:294, 23:88, 24:365, 31:29, 38:243; in lumber industry, 13:365; immigration, 16:344, 27:40, 37:184; Minneapolis, 19:123, 39:168; Detroit, Mich., 20:202; Canada, 20:342, 35:247; North Dakota, 23:92; source material, 25:299, 26:167; Wisconsin, 27:135; in iron mining, 27:204, 208, 213; contributions, 28:75
Rust, George H., miller, 35:16
Rust, Henry, trader, 11:374
Rust, John R., miller, 35:16-18
Rustad, Edward, legislator, 33:161
Rustvold, Bertha, 19:234
Ruth, Kent, author, 39:129
Ruth, Peter S., memorial, 35:246
Ruth, Mrs. Peter S., memorial, 35:246
Ruthenians, Mesabi Range, 27:213
Rutherford, Edward, boom foreman, 23:395, 26:172
Rutherford, William, 20:81
Rutland, Robert, editor, 33:315
Rutledge, Ann, 11:60
Ruud, Martin B., reviews by, 18:431-433, 21:64-68; work reviewed, 18:198-201; editor, 16:59, 17:463, 18:58, 440, 19:93, 20:293, 21:80, 22:328, 26:167, 30:359, 36:80
Ryan, Dennis, 27:366
Ryan, George, photographer, 22:439
Ryan, J. C., "Minnesota Logging Railroads," 27:300-308; author, 24:264, 27:342, 28:376
Ryan, John, papers, 16:366
Ryan, Father John A., career, 23:96, 39:26, 40:359
Ryan, Lawrence F., author, 39:153n, 155
Ryan, Michael, author, 21:371
Ryan, Mrs. Thomas D., speaker, 14:229
Ryan Hotel, St. Paul, 17:375, 382, 27:366, 40:15, 16; concert, 39:53; razed, 40:135
Ryberg, Hugo, 15:447
Rybot, Francis, 11:238n
Rydell, A. E., 14:461
Ryden, Einar R., author, 26:364
Ryden, George H., author, 19:220
Ryder, Franklin J., author, 40:315
Ryder, Israel, trader, 24:321
Ryder, Walter S., author, 15:140
Rydh, Hanna, author, 31:121
Ryding, Reuben, author, 27:158
Rygh, Oluf, archaeologist, 39:134
Ryland, William J., work reviewed, 22:413-415
Ryley, James, interpreter, 23:135n, 248
Rynda, Joseph T., Jr., 14:458; author, 16:218, 241
Rynning, Ole, 18:74; author, 16:108; immigrant leader, 16:350; centennial, 18:325
Rynning, Rolf S., author, 35:296
Rypins, Rabbi Isaac L., 28:294; career, 35:293
Rysgaard, G. N., author, 22:337, 23:99
Ryswick, Netherlands, treaty, 19:283

Saari, Matt, author, 35:245, 36:70
Saatoff, Leona, author, 30:75
Sabatier, I., 11:238n
Sabin, Dwight M., Senator, 35:297; labor contractor, 37:143, 144, 149
Sabin, Joseph, compiler, 18:213, 25:395, 36:297
Sablé, Marie-Anne Dandonneau du, 18:234

Sac Indians, pictorial record, 33:20; in Black Hawk War, 35:87
Sacagawea, Shoshone woman, 11:81, 14:204, 16:226, 39:169, 40:193
Sacco and Vanzetti case, 21:401
Sachs, Bertram, author, 19:126
Sacket, Edward, cranberry grower, 25:198
Sackett, Leonard, author, 33:226
Sackett, Richard R., 27:48, 28:300, 29:54, 187; WPA adviser, 18:57n; archaeologist, 19:354, 20:42, 29:365; speaker, 20:51, 23:50, 29:178; author, 23:188, 25:202, 29:263; field director, 27:26, 140
Sacred Heart, Scandinavian settlement, 12:275n, 21:223; history, 13:453, 19:126; J. R. Brown house, 25:213, 28:191, 29:185, 36:283, 37:60, 39:273, 274
Sacred Heart Cathedral (Catholic), Duluth, 16:355, 17:117
Sacred Heart Catholic Church, Heron Lake, 16:121
Sacred Heart Industrial School, Iona, 35:136
Sacred Heart School, Owatonna, established, 20:62
Saerchinger, Cesar, speaker, 24:362
Safford, Dr. Mary J., 39:9, 14
Safford, R. W., journalist, 15:368
Saga Hill, Lake Minnetonka, 28:392, 29:55; history, 29:289-299, 30:91-93
Saga Hill Association, Lake Minnetonka, 29:294, 295
Saganachens family, Chippewa Indians, 39:305n
Saganaga Lake, border lake, 37:245; geology, 15:143; underwater archaeology, 35:281, 37:254, 38:24, 25; trail, 35:295, 37:248, 250; resort, 37:235n, 38:33; Chippewa village, 37:238, 242, 253; canoe route, 37:246; pictured, 37:252
Sage, Henry W., 25:71
Sage, Leland L., author, 35:246
Sage, Russell, letters, 18:444
Sage, Walter N., author, 11:107; editor, 11:451
Sagean, Mathieu, 39:337
Sageng, Ole, speaker, 21:337; legislator, 35:348
Saginaw, Mich., lumbering, 23:356, 32:126
Saginaw, St. Louis County, logging, 30:180; railroad station, 34:184
Saginaw Bay, Rainy Lake, 23:139, 141n; described, 23:140
Saginaw River, Mich., 21:296; logging, 34:35
Sagnes, John H., author, 25:213
Saguenay, Que., French settlement, 23:385
Sailor, Moses, pioneer, 11:292
St. Adalbert Church (Catholic), Silver Lake, 15:37
St. Agnes Church (Catholic), St. Paul, 39:131
St. Agnes School (Catholic), St. Paul, 20:345
St. Alexis Hospital, Bismarck, N.D., 33:56, 58
St. Andrew's Catholic Church, Fairfax, 15:128
St. Andrews Society, St. Paul, 15:226

St. Anne des Chenes, Man., marker, 21:433

St. Anne's Church (Catholic), Le Sueur, 17:479; Montreal, Que., 28:8; Somerset, Wis., 35:152

St. Ansgar, Iowa, Norwegian settlement, 12:258, 270, 27:164

St. Ansgar's Academy, see Gustavus Adolphus College

St. Ansgar's Hospital, Moorhead, history, 11:460

St. Anthony, stage lines, 11:401, 405, 28:190, 29:206, 33:200; described, 12:162-164, 13:335, 14:100, 19:401, 21:415, 29:206-208, 214, 30:91, 219, 34:48, 49, 35:102, 104, 39:67-69; mail service, 12:343, 27:248, 40:86, 89; schools, 12:398, 14:144, 18:226, 30:2, 13, 35:102; hotels, 12:403, 13:195, 19:84, 403, 20:328, 32:18, 36:91, 38:273, 40:63; cholera outbreak, 14:295; early printing, 15:22, 19:431, 432; buildings, 15:49, 27:291, 35:106, 37:192, 38:343, 39:73; volunteer guard, 16:176; settled, 16:315, 21:309, 22:154, 24:132, 26:155, 27:299, 30:195, 199; sabbath school, 16:317; medicine, 17:220, 35:221; pictured, 18:468, 30:112, 35:98, 39:69, 74, 40:6, 64, 75; Henry Nichols mission, 19:141-147, 341; churches, 19:249n, 27:291n, 30:395, 40:6, 7; roads, 20:140; railroads, 20:374, 21:239, 35:364, 36:7, 37:153, 38:45-52, 295; summer resort, 20:393, 23:196, 33:125; population, 21:225, 27:286; dentistry, 21:437; lumber industry, 21:450, 23:273, 27:286, 29:199, 31:109, 34:50, 37:197, 39:71; politics, 24:139, 35:105, 107, 117-129, 36:3, 6, 9, 40:223; business, 24:295, 26:371, 27:248, 289, 291, 28:284, 291, 35:104, 105, 109, 39:67-74; map, 25:41; trails, 27:71; bridges, 27:288, 28:70, 29:30-34; founded, 27:311, 30:219n, 32:96n, 40:137; steamboating, 28:342n, 33:9, 37:109, 38:2, 40:332; German theater, 32:102, 127, 164-168, 173; merges with Minneapolis, 35:229, 40:376; rivalry with St. Paul, 37:90, 310-323; judicial district, 39:145; singing school, 39:320. See also Minneapolis

St. Anthony Agricultural Association, 22:251

St. Anthony Boom Co., 24:135

St. Anthony Brewery, 35:120

St. Anthony Commercial Club, 33:332; history, 11:216, 35:46

St. Anthony Express, established, 14:400, 15:23; New Year's greeting, 16:387

St. Anthony Falls, see Falls of St. Anthony

St. Anthony Falls Bank, 19:207

St. Anthony Falls Water Power Co., history, 35:98; activities, 37:312, 321, 323

St. Anthony-Fort Ridgely Road, route, 11:392

St. Anthony Hill, St. Paul, 33:195, 199, 200

St. Anthony Iron Works, 16:71

St. Anthony Library Association, 26:386, 35:359

St. Anthony Literary Society, 35:222

St. Anthony Lumber Co., 26:136

St. Anthony Park, St. Paul, beginnings, 18:460

St. Anthony Park Area Historical Society, organized, 26:257, 285; preserves historic buildings, 27:228-232, 28:71, 383, 29:364; meetings, 27:266, 28:88, 195, 297, 29:93, 276; publications, 29:181, 30:168; program, 30:77. See also Ramsey County Historical Society

St. Anthony Park Congregational Church, St. Paul, 18:460

St. Anthony Pottery, 33:229

St. Anthony Turnverein, Minneapolis, history, 13:217; records, 16:335

St. Anthony Zouaves, in Civil War, 16:176

St. Anthony's Benevolent Society, St. Paul, 39:131

St. Augusta, Stearns County, townsite, 16:334; German settlement, 31:25

St. Augustine (Fla.) Historical Program, 22:316, 23:85

St. Barnabas Hospital, Minneapolis, 24:372, 26:94

St. Benedict's Academy, St. Joseph, history, 27:96-106, 151; archives, 27:169. See also College of St. Benedict

St. Benedict's Church (Catholic), St. Benedict, Scott County, 17:117, 118

St. Benedict's College, see College of St. Benedict

St. Benedict's Hospital, St. Cloud, 33:59, 291-294

St. Benedict's Mission School, White Earth Reservation, 26:275

St. Bernard's Church (Catholic), St. Paul, history, 22:111

St. Boniface, Man., church bells, 18:376, 20:204; growth, 19:353; riot, 19:412; church archives, 20:35, 79, 430; railroad, 21:260, 24:329; mission, 26:171, 27:166, 31:240, 35:270, 37:183, 40:313; schools, 29:81

St. Boniface Church (Catholic), Minneapolis, 15:128; Hastings, 15:197, 27:269

St. Boniface College, Man., 18:244

St. Bonifacius, sorghum mill, 35:201

St. Bonifacius Catholic Church, Mound, 15:480

St. Bonifacius Verein, Minneapolis society, 32:167

St. Bridget's Church (Catholic), Rochester, 14:451

St. Canice Church (Catholic), Kilkenny, 11:462

St. Casimir Catholic Church, Wells, 16:355

St. Catherine's College, see College of St. Catherine

St. Charles, described, 12:48; Methodist church, 14:240; history, 20:364, 34:171; wildlife, 30:223; museum, 36:14

St. Charles Hotel, St. Anthony, 12:399, 402, 20:393, 29:32, 33n, 215, 40:63; Winona, 12:401

St. Clair, Gen. Arthur, governor of

Ohio Territory, 16:204, 20:17, 32:44

St. Clair, George A., mining interests, 34:270, 271n, 272, 275

St. Clair, Harry, actor, 34:85

St. Clair, Rev. Henry Whipple, letters, 16:242; career, 35:248

St. Clair, Sallie, actress, 23:308-310, 313

St. Clair, located, 12:51n; Indian agency, 15:468; Winnebago reservation, 35:293

St. Clair River, Mich., 23:136, 137

"Ste. Claire," excursion steamer, 34:15

St. Clement's Episcopal Church, St. Paul, 27:81, 28:396

St. Clement's Parish (Catholic), Duluth, 33:59

St. Cloud, churches, 12:106, 107, 456, 14:239, 360, 15:119, 16:371, 28:254, 30:156, 33:393n, 35:46, 267; in Sioux Outbreak, 12:446, 16:253, 38:204, 276-278, 283; anniversaries, 12:455, 29:272; pioneer life, 14:276, 15:139, 17:489, 30:275; history, 14:438, 16:334, 18:119, 21:344; in World War I, 15:115; stage line, 15:135, 18:353, 32:63, 33:277n; land office, 16:65, 24:134n, 39:90; newspapers, 16:76, 17:358, 365, 39:260; volunteer guard, 16:176; Red River trail, 16:231, 17:225, 21:253n; granite industry, 16:234, 21:393, 29:171, 37:263; roads, 16:293, 299, 21:234, 235, 241, 35:258, 291, 38:55, 59, 63, 69, 70, 40:69, 71; schools, 16:371, 17:465, 23:110, 24:93, 27:180, 32:40, 42, 33:53, 36:107; climate, 17:260, 261; trolley line, 17:365; in Civil War, 17:489, 18:119, 38:43; ethnic groups, 18:89, 453, 21:98, 28:254, 30:292, 31:25, 32:37; flour milling, 18:208; baseball, 18:343, 19:169, 170, 173, 175; hotels, 18:353, 24:332, 35:255; mail service, 19:196, 30:262, 40:84; described, 20:64, 30:112; railroads, 21:239, 240, 22:379, 24:332, 32:126, 35:208, 37:155, 156n, 38:71; labor unions, 21:393, 22:379, 380; circus history, 23:199; river port, 24:138; history surveys, 26:234-241, 28:164; parks, 26:398; Junior Historian chapter, 27:147, 28:163; government, 30:144; art, 30:284; county seat, 32:36; in fiction, 33:356; depicted, 35:265, 267; direct primary, 35:350; power company, 35:381; gold fever, 38:53; Glidden tour, 38:211; mission, 39:308n; music, 39:321

St. Cloud and Lake Traverse Railroad, 35:208

St. Cloud Cyclone Relief Committee, 16:74

St. Cloud Daily Times and Daily Journal-Press, history, 14:397, 405, 17:364

St. Cloud Democrat, 16:76, 98, 30:181, 32:17

St. Cloud Hospital, history, 33:291-297

St. Cloud Journal, 14:405, 16:98, 36:301

St. Cloud Opera House, 28:99
St. Cloud Printing Co., 16:98
St. Cloud Rifle Co., volunteer unit, 16:172, 173n
St. Cloud State Teachers College, history, 12:456, 14:149, 26:83, 34:93; depicted, 34:90
St. Cloud Street Car Co., history, 14:361
St. Cloud Technical High School, local history survey, 26:234-241
St. Cloud Visiter, finances, 14:404; name changes, 14:405; controversies, 14:406, 16:76, 27:2, 30:252, 32:17
St. Cloud War History Committee, 23:392
St. Columba mission, Gull Lake, Cass County, 14:55, 57, 27:289n, 28:190
St. Columba Parish, Iona, Iowa, 35:136, 137
St. Coutourier, Hyacinth, trader, 28:380
"St. Croix," steamboat, 22:13
St. Croix and Lake Superior Mining Co., 25:396
St. Croix and Lake Superior Railroad, land grants, 34:67-69
St. Croix Ball Club, Stillwater, 19:169, 173, 175, 177-179, 181
St. Croix Boom Co., 14:99, 17:313, 367, 31:33, 34, 36, 38, 35:282; charter, 17:282, 18:176, 26:126; production figures, 18:177; records, 23:395, 26:132, 30:391; charges, 26:133
St. Croix Collegiate and Military Academy, Hudson, Wis., 19:451
St. Croix County, Wis., pioneer life, 12:94, 15:344; organized, 15:237, 25:198; county seat, 17:277; history, 21:430; board, 21:458; boundaries, 23:384, 24:159, 349; livestock, 26:107; census, 30:195; courthouse, 38:351
St. Croix County (Wis.) Bible Society, 24:165
St. Croix County (Wis.) Historical Society, 36:152, 39:83
St. Croix Falls, Wis., trading post, 11:375, 13:222; land office, 12:381; pioneer life, 16:359, 23:164; mills, 17:283, 24:196, 27:310, 29:205; newspaper, 17:314, 385; power company, 35:381, 40:357; logging, 36:159; mail service, 36:207, 209, 214, 40:84, 86; described, 36:281; architecture, 38:341, 344-346
St. Croix Falls Lumber Co., 18:168, 27:302, 310
St. Croix Inquirer (Hudson, Wis.), 17:385, 389, 22:189
St. Croix River, steamboating, 12:319, 17:277-279, 19:249, 24:245, 27:310, 28:92, 29:196, 34:132, 35:355, 36:252, 38:188; dalles, 15:237, 18:359, 19:228, 26:225; flood, 15:346; projected ferry, 17:269-271; falls, 17:282, 313, 25:396; fishing, 22:337; described, 23:342, 28:235; lumbering, 26:130, 132, 133, 27:194, 30:391, 31:62; source, 28:147; depicted, 29:265, 39:265 (cover); water level, 36:46, 47; mail boat, 36:213; history, 39:290. See also Rafting

St. Croix River Association, 24:385
St. Croix State Park, Pine County, established, 24:262; historical exhibit, 29:50
St. Croix Union, established, 14:401, 17:385
St. Croix Valley, fur trade, 11:375, 385, 24:195, 28:1-14, 142-159, 225-240, 32:234; lumber industry, 13:284, 366, 15:346, 16:479, 17:277, 313, 18:165-179, 344, 420, 468, 20:448, 24:126, 130, 166, 194, 245, 27:191, 310, 313, 29:199, 30:195, 31:33-39, 33:226, 35:49, 243, 36:70, 159, 40:357; archaeology, 15:151; pioneer life, 15:344, 23:164; explored, 17:139; described, 17:276-287, 37:3, 39:286-289, 40:310; historical meeting, 17:312-318; Swedes, 17:396-405, 34:163, 38:38, 39:341; roads, 21:227, 230, 231, 40:233, 246; history, 23:394, 24:79, 165, 28:185, 395; railroad, 35:358-364; mail service, 36:206-215; depicted, 37:4, 39:287; in Sioux Outbreak, 38:275, 276; architecture, 38:337-352
St. Croix Valley Academy, Afton, 17:389
St. Croix Valley Historical Society, organized, 22:331
St. Croix Valley Old Settlers Association, history, 34:129
St. Cyril's Church (Catholic), Minneapolis, 22:222
St. Denys, Charles J. de, 12:307
St. Edward's Church (Catholic), Minneota, 12:103
St. Elizabeth Convent, Morris County, N.J., 16:340
St. Eloi Church (Catholic), Ghent, 14:356
St. Felix Catholic Parish, Wabasha, 15:128
St. Francis, history, 12:455, 18:333; mill, 14:454
St. Francis de Sales Catholic Church, St. Paul, 15:481
St. Francis High School, Little Falls, 16:372
St. François du Lac, Que., Indian village, 19:76
St. François Xavier, Man., 21:206
St. François Xavier Mission, Pembina, N.D., 22:286
St. Gabriel's Church (Catholic), Prairie du Chien, Wis., 11:108, 17:475, 23:286
St. George, Nicollet County, log houses, 37:73, 75
St. George Catholic Church, New Ulm, 14:451; West Newton, 36:193
St. George's Island, see Sugar Island, Mich.
St. Germain, Venant, 20:16, 23:379
St. Hubert's Lodge, Frontenac, 35:245; described, 14:34; depicted, 14:35, 37:64; historic building, 15:467, 36:95; name, 20:307
St. Ignace, Mich., mission, 13:401; directory, 35:383
St. James, history, 11:111, 12:108, 19:362, 26:399; railroad, 22:112; anniversary, 22:443; historical meeting, 26:395
St. James African Methodist Episcopal

Church, St. Paul, anniversary, 15:362
St. James Church (Catholic), Jacobs Prairie, history, 20:364; Randall, 29:176
St. James School for Boys, Faribault, 21:115, 446
St. Jefferson, Clearwater County, ghost town, 16:493
St. John Nepomucene's Parish, Prairie du Chien, Wis., 23:286
St. John River, Que., 38:386
St. John the Baptist Catholic Church, Dayton, 16:484
St. John the Evangelist Church (Catholic), Little Canada, 15:480, 21:454; Derrynane, Le Sueur County, 28:82
St. John the Evangelist Episcopal Church, St. Paul, 33:95
St. John's, Neb. Terr., Catholic colony, 21:74
St. John's Abbey and University, Collegeville, 39:310; history, 12:99, 16:372, 18:473, 20:446; established, 14:147, 15:354, 31:25; publications, 18:229, 26:388, 35:338, 339; army training, 25:312, 27:368; churches, 26:275, 37:187, 347, 39:128; abbots, 27:105, 32:37, 41, 43, 33:53, 55, 57-60, 114n, 35:372; territorial centennial program, 30:284; locations, 32:42, 43, 33:53; described, 33:138, 34:93, 131; centennial, 35:46; biographical directory, 35:155; Indian school, 35:338, 38:335; architecture, 36:100, 37:38; microfilm project, 40:361
St. John's Church (Catholic), St. Paul, 18:117; Union Hill, Scott County, 21:456; Grand Marais, 39:310
St. John's Evangelical Lutheran Church, Omro Township, Yellow Medicine County, 13:454, 24:94; Elmore, 15:481
St. John's Hospital, St. Paul, 34:356
St. John's in the Wilderness Episcopal Church, White Bear Lake, 17:350
St. John's Lutheran Church, Baytown, 14:52, 53; Minneapolis, 14:362; Red Wing, 14:451; Wykoff, 15:481
St. John's Seminary, see St. John's Abbey and University
St. John's Society, Sleepy Eye, 14:455
St. Joseph, trading post, 11:233, 258; Catholic churches, 15:38, 27:367, 31:25, 36:35; Indian school, 17:84; Benedictine convent, 17:219, 27:96-106, 32:42, 33:53, 58-60, 292; monastery, 33:53; in Sioux Outbreak, 35:271, 38:276
St. Joseph, Mich., history, 13:110, fort, 19:298
St. Joseph, Mo., Sioux stopover, 38:359, 362, 363; architecture, 40:103
St. Joseph Island, Ont., history, 19:198
St. Joseph of Carondelet, Sisters of, see Sisters of St. Joseph of Carondelet
St. Joseph River, Mich., post, 13:203, 19:286, 287, 296

St. Joseph's, N.D, mixed-bloods' settlement, 18:357, 35:261
St. Joseph's Academy, St. Paul, history, 33:38
St. Joseph's Catholic Church, Silver Lake, 15:31; Miesville, 15:128; Medicine Lake, 15:480, 16:484, 17:479; Waconia, 16:120; Appleton, Wis., 25:193; Minneapolis, 27:176; St. Joseph, 27:367
St. Joseph's Hospital, St. Paul, 17:69, 21:437, 35:264, 38:366; founded, 14:110, 293, 30:405; in cholera epidemic, 14:297-301; history, 15:456, 24:372, 33:312; site, 30:7; described, 30:9
St. Joseph's Mission (Catholic), Ball Club, 23:402
St. Joseph's Provincial House, St. Paul, archives, 30:2
St. Lawrence, Clara, 17:121
St. Lawrence, Rev. James G., papers, 16:336
St. Lawrence River, route to interior, 18:383, 384, 34:159; source, 24:231, 28:146; panorama, 33:290, 36:324; traffic, 34:356, 35:292, 38:386; fur trade, 40:157, 165, 178, 183; archaeological site, 40:205
St. Lawrence Seaway, 39:210; history, 12:95, 21:422, 34:265, 36:324, 37:259; described, 15:354, 24:175, 34:356, 36:280, 37:39; bibliography, 18:102; source material, 20:452, 37:41; economic aspect, 35:292, 36:69, 39:262; negotiations, 37:302, 39:128
St. Louis, trade center, 11:144, 23:321, 29:2, 3, 7, 30:154, 34:17, 18, 35:356, 357n, 36:37-53, 38:355, 356, 39:68, 230, 40:334; river port, 11:181n, 14:273, 18:175, 20:383, 387, 22:13-15, 94, 26:155, 32:12n, 36:251, 252, 257, 38:358-360, 40:78, 79, 195; fur trade, 13:225, 226, 240, 15:421, 431, 18:394, 19:293, 29:78, 36:260, 262, 40:145, 152, 155, 183, 185, 201, 212, 214, 218, 220, 410; theater, 14:114, 23:305, 306, 310, 31:116; first printing, 15:13; army post, 15:379; fire, 17:137; panorama exhibit, 17:142; depicted, 17:433, 25:114, 30:269, 32:13, 14, 36:47; Frederick Marryat's visit, 18:160, 161; lumber center, 18:169, 174, 177, 24:127, 202, 26:132, 27:190; libraries, 20:202; school, 25:108; frontier life, 28:288; art center, 30:74, 34:253, 353; German colony, 32:155, 156; cholera epidemic, 36:17; architecture, 40:103, 104, 107, 108, 134, 192
St. Louis and San Francisco Railway Co., 18:150n
St. Louis County, authors, 12:322; history, 12:454, 22:87, 23:187; logging, 13:366, 25:102, 26:156, 27:302, 29:137, 40:401; geology, 15:143, 39:132; boundary, 15:370; roads, 16:291; 4-H clubs, 18:473; marriage records, 20:194; schools, 21:48, 24:73; pioneer reunions, 21:116, 456, 22:302, 25:158-164; ethnic celebrations, 22:225; judicial district, 23:387; Finnish settlements, 25:318, 319, 323, 31:28, 40:392; health conditions, 27:82; census, 28:303; depicted, 28:350; biographies, 29:94; library, 30:61; newspapers, 34:44; post offices, 34:175; elections, 35:344, 349, 39:107; railroad, 37:90n; mineral lands, 37:99, 347; poorhouse, 38:368; baseball, 40:61
St. Louis County Historical Society, 16:241; founded, 11:12, 418, 30:321; meetings, 11:15, 18, 118, 223, 338, 460, 12:186, 13:121, 216, 442, 454, 14:123, 346, 15:138, 492, 16:488, 17:357, 482, 484, 18:462, 465, 20:213, 22:442, 23:396, 24:85, 26:92, 286, 28:385, 30:83, 279, 34:218, 314, 35:99; members, 11:19, 419, 13:81, 27:77, 29:94, 366; finances, 11:20; collections, 12:322, 15:252, 16:125, 244, 360, 362, 17:357, 18:223, 19:355, 20:363, 450-453, 21:149, 155, 156, 22:341, 443, 23:14, 28:182, 29:91, 34:359, 35:279, 37:41, 39:323n, 40:146; officers, 17:123, 19:118, 21:290, 24:380, 25:99; museum, 24:188, 25:313, 27:267; activities, 26:180, 33:356, 34:44; quarters, 27:146, 28:88; publication, 27:173
St. Louis County Medical Society, 19:226, 357
St. Louis (Mo.) Historical Documents Foundation, publications, 28:79, 30:249
St. Louis Hotel, Duluth, 17:375
St. Louis on the Lake, see St. John's Abbey and University
St. Louis Park, Jewish population, 37:87
St. Louis River, Minn., Wis., geology, 13:404-406; trade routes, 16:193, 20:8, 11-13, 23:249n, 251, 28:146, 32:234; portages, 16:472; source, 18:462; proposed boundary, 20:15, 23:208; described, 22:319, 33:68, 106, 107, 37:116, 117, 40:273, 274; explored, 23:233, 244-248, 26:225, 31:94, 95, 32:90-95, 34:46; steamboating, 37:109; road to, 40:233-247
St. Louis Varieties, theatrical troupe, 23:310, 312n
St. Luke's Catholic Church, St. Paul, 20:103
St. Luke's Episcopal Church, Willmar, 13:343; Hastings, 19:121
St. Luke's Hospital, Fergus Falls, 18:228; Duluth, 26:96; St. Paul, 35:46, 38:79
St. Lusson, François Daumont, sieur de, French envoy, 16:227, 231, 18:388, 19:274-276
St. Mark's Catholic Church, Shakopee, 12:454; St. Paul, 21:77
St. Mark's Episcopal Church, Minneapolis, 16:485
St. Martin, Alexis, voyageur, 14:446, 15:234, 19:105, 20:337, 21:428, 27:236, 30:259, 36:324
St. Martin family, genealogy, 11:110
St. Martin, Catholic church, 14:361; history, 36:107
St. Martin Islands, Mich., Lake Huron, 23:142

St. Martin's Church (Catholic), St. Martin, 14:361
St. Martin's Lutheran Church, Winona, 14:50, 55, 218
St. Mary's Academy, Graceville, history, 16:363
St. Mary's Academy, Church, and Convent, Bismarck, N.D., 33:56, 36:58
St. Mary's Basilica (Catholic), Minneapolis, 13:312
St. Mary's Cathedral (Catholic) of St. Cloud, 12:106, 33:293n, 35:46
St. Mary's Church (Catholic), Bird Island, 11:117; Chatfield, 12:337, 13:215; St. Paul, 15:456, 16:369, 17:84, 38:187; Ellsworth, 16:485; New Trier, 17:117, 118; Rice, 17:118; Stillwater, 17:391n
St. Mary's College, Winona, history, 29:354
St. Mary's Hall, Faribault, girls' school, 17:363, 21:115
St. Mary's Home for Girls, St. Paul, 15:456, 16:369
St. Mary's Hospital, Rochester, 17:69, 18:227, 20:465, 21:114, 34:218, 37:186; Duluth, 33:59
St. Mary's Hospital and Junior College, Minneapolis, 23:227, 40:383
St. Mary's Memorial Church (Catholic), Warroad, 34:130
St. Mary's River, Mich., see Sault Ste. Marie
St. Mary's Roumanian Orthodox Church, St. Paul, 15:481
St. Mary's Russian Orthodox Greek Catholic Church, Minneapolis, 19:123, 39:168
St. Mary's Select School, St. Anthony, 17:478
St. Matthew's Church (Catholic), St. Paul, 18:117, 21:210
St. Matthew's Evangelical Lutheran Church, St. Paul, 14:362, 19:126
St. Michael, Wright County, spa, 28:192
St. Michael's Catholic Church, Buckman, 13:119; Madison, 15:243; St. Paul, 26:182
St. Nazianz, Wis., German settlement, 23:286
St. Nicholas, Freeborn County, frontier village, 19:122, 473, 20:357
St. Nicholas Catholic Church, Stearns County, 14:451
St. Olaf College, Northfield, 17:94; presidents, 13:324, 26:95, 30:377, 391; "Old Main" building, 14:359; founded, 15:251; anniversary, 15:361; journalism studies, 18:229; faculty, 20:86, 179, 25:86; music, 20:438, 24:258, 25:86, 26:59; history, 21:115, 24:270, 31:50; naval school, 25:312; library, 26:369, 39:35; theater, 29:271; student life, 32:127; characterized, 34:91, 93; depicted, 34:92, 131
St. Olaf Township, Otter Tail County, history, 11:221
Saint-Onge, Jean Garau, and Co., 32:235n
St. Patrick's Catholic Church, Cedar Lake Township, Le Sueur County, 12:451; St. Paul, 16:121; Kandiyohi, 16:355; Shieldsville, Rice County, 22:348
St. Patrick's Day, celebrations, 17:

325, 19:450, 21:191, 25:253, 30:18
St. Patrick's Society, Chicago, 35:
207
St. Paul, Pierre, voyageur, 32:233
St. Paul, pioneer life, 11:95, 13:
303, 14:99, 16:98, 19:357, 22:55-
59, 26:66, 27:17, 28:314, 319,
322, 29:114-129, 188, 222, 283,
34:96-105, 267, 37:200; health department, 11:108, 14:290-292, 297,
298; real estate, 11:109, 13:321,
17:211, 23:97, 273, 25:212, 412,
34:268, 39:150; Congregational
churches, 11:120, 12:318, 13:176,
15:35, 17:351, 18:96, 460, 23:97,
221, 38:75, 39:53, 57, 58, 60-63;
business, 11:130, 143, 14:278,
386, 17:214, 24:287, 297, 26:132,
29:88, 199, 30:154, 34:106-113,
329, 35:245, 37:190, 192; river
port, 11:132, 137, 138, 143, 13:
223, 14:100, 379, 17:269, 20:386,
387, 22:94, 24:331, 369, 27:8,
283, 285, 28:212, 310, 29:198,
219, 33:194, 199, 34:133, 138, 35:
102, 118, 181, 381, 36:251-258,
326, 37:53, 87, 154, 160, 196,
225, 226, 38:74, 39:66, 68; literary visitors, 11:147, 149, 151,
155-157, 16:31, 37, 17:38, 45,
371, 373, 375, 376, 18:30, 19:400-
402, 407, 414, 20:393, 34:48, 49,
51-53, 40:12-20; in World War I,
11:195-198, 202, 12:25; railroads,
11:215, 14:102, 20:373, 374, 21:
239, 24:373, 28:375, 29:13, 170,
30:158, 379, 35:364, 36:179, 37:
102, 153, 38:45-52, 40:247; Catholic churches, 11:217, 12:397, 13:
123, 15:104, 254, 361, 456, 481,
16:121, 274n, 369, 17:84, 102, 18:
117, 19:115, 335, 20:92, 103, 446,
21:77, 210, 22:51, 111, 347, 24:
72, 90, 92, 264, 25:9, 10, 26:173,
182, 29:209, 30:7, 9, 206, 207,
266, 38:187, 39:131, 40:4; Episcopal churches, 11:340, 12:105, 397,
398, 13:346, 15:481, 18:444, 23:
76, 25:9, 27:81, 28:396, 30:207,
33:5, 95, 38:75; roads, 11:388,
398, 12:61, 16:283, 285, 287-291,
293, 21:229, 233, 234, 40:148,
358, 388; mail service, 11:400,
404, 407; stage lines, 11:401-403,
405, 13:335, 16:284, 28:190, 33:
277; Lutheran churches, 11:468,
12:344, 13:323, 14:52, 53, 362,
16:235, 484, 17:97, 118, 19:126,
20:193, 21:223, 22:88, 23:371, 24:
373, 25:213, 26:69, 28:203, 34:
356, 38:75; musical center, 12:84,
16:32, 497, 22:115, 26:155, 32:
239, 240, 34:240, 242, 39:51, 319-
322; Presbyterian churches, 12:
105, 15:373, 481, 16:74, 276n,
485, 18:96, 378, 379, 19:213, 20:
35, 21:314, 22:58n, 26:289, 27:
320, 28:396, 29:115, 118, 211,
212, 30:202, 207, 274, 297, 33:4,
38:49, 74-76, 78, 85, 39:35, 53,
40:1, 4, 9, 10; described, 12:161,
175, 391, 15:414, 16:274, 17:129,
225, 394, 20:193, 21:193, 25:110,
113, 28:311, 29:167, 211, 30:195,
204-210, 31:19, 109, 153, 33:119,
36:41, 42, 239, 39:316, 40:359;
streets, 12:212, 29:272, 33:141

(cover), 37:307; ethnic groups,
12:279, 16:338, 18:453, 22:2, 23:
290, 25:319, 27:256, 29:105-113,
31:23, 29, 35:209, 212, 213; hotels, 12:392, 16:37, 251, 272, 22:
57n, 30:197, 200, 301, 34:96, 97,
101, 36:264-266, 39:144-146, 149,
40:15, 135, 331; celebrations, 12:
392, 16:382, 17:325, 22:372, 26:
67, 31:237, 36:130, 38:287-297;
Unitarian church, 12:397; Baptist
churches, 12:397, 398, 15:254, 16:
120, 18:331, 20:330, 23:110, 28:
320, 29:359, 38:75; schools, 12:
398-400, 14:330, 16:123, 275, 18:
229, 25:109, 28:133-141, 356, 29:
354, 30:154, 175, 40:146; parks,
12:458, 17:363, 21:194, 39:132,
154; Methodist churches, 13:100,
14:363, 15:254, 362, 16:274n, 17:
118, 467, 39:151; city planning,
13:115, 19:342, 36:328; population, 13:175, 14:225, 290, 20:190,
21:329, 29:319, 32:211, 35:356n,
37:154, 38:82, 39:67, 327; charter, 13:198, 20:362, 24:62; Jewish temples, 13:217, 17:99, 22:
348, 28:294, 30:163, 35:293, 36:
320; surveys, 13:218; Red River
trade, 13:240, 241, 15:120, 291,
16:231, 17:217, 21:249, 258, 22:
148, 156, 281, 23:186, 24:328,
333, 33:199, 36:37, 39n, 47, 38:
63, 71; capital, 14:130, 15:111,
35:106, 107, 182, 36:283; statehood celebration, 14:178-187;
utilities, 14:267, 269, 270, 15:
140, 16:370, 40:223-231; cholera
epidemic, 14:291-301; printing,
15:18; cemeteries, 15:105; manu-
factures, 15:186, 39:329; depicted, 15:210, 17:146, 147, 221,
22:333, 26:359, 27:271, 30:157,
291, 33:90, 113, 114n, 121, 134,
141 (cover), 197, 34:27, 30n, 85
(cover), 98, 35:249 (cover), 357,
36:4, 43, 250, 37:308, 39:37 (cover), 316, 40:221 (cover), 250-253;
Indian battle, 15:306n, 19:140;
history, 15:479, 21:310, 22:193,
225, 26:184, 30:202; Romanian Orthodox church, 15:481; banks, 16:
24, 20:345, 33:31, 40:109-119;
climate, 16:116, 18:130, 33:195,
198; volunteer guard, 16:176, 177;
archives, 16:211; maps, 16:215,
18:50; summer resort, 16:273, 29:
122; directories, 16:332, 19:432,
27:252; winter carnivals, 16:341,
17:214, 18:118, 20:203, 332, 21:
317, 23:173, 27:141, 177, 30:145,
163, 33:91, 35:156, 36:91; G.A.R
post, 16:432n, 434-437; in Civil
War, 17:112, 39:175; medicine, 17:
220, 20:206, 344, 24:182, 35:221;
ski club, 17:228, 33:187; recreation, 17:362; fire department, 18:
317, 19:49, 50, 30:163; libraries,
18:362-364, 29:177; Catholic diocese, 18:436, 19:460, 21:102, 33:
56, 34:313, 35:139, 39:35, 153,
299; post office, 18:472, 36:70,
206-208, 212, 40:82-84, 86-89;
sports, 19:162-176, 178, 180; centennial, 19:190, 237, 21:409, 22:
50-52, 346, 347, 436, 29:96, 30:
177, 34:128; police department,

19:238; social life, 19:440, 22:8-
11, 26:307, 28:313, 317, 320, 33:
1-6, 196, 200, 39:145; Sioux village, 21:163n; city government,
21:342, 28:23, 30:144; unions, 21:
376, 378, 381, 385-387, 394, 22:
377, 382, 385; characterized, 22:
1-12, 27:251; fur-trade center,
22:3, 30:133, 34:102-104, 36:260,
262, 263, 40:219; fairs, 22:256;
theater, 23:76, 305-315, 369, 26:
373, 28:99, 103, 107, 109, 110,
115, 117, 118n, 32:100-105, 127,
166, 168, 172, 33:188, 315, 34:
240; welfare, 25:212, 377; livestock market, 26:110, 125, 27:357;
name, 26:250; dairy market, 27:
113, 114, 120; German newspapers,
27:327, 28:22, 24, 34:130; in
World War II, 29:102; floods, 34:
306; rivalry with Minneapolis, 35:
65, 119; outfitting center, 35:
249-251; historic sites, 37:64,
263, 39:124. See also Twin Cities
"St. Paul," Lake Superior steamer,
37:118
"Saint Paul," Mississippi River
steamboat, 29:203, 37:296
St. Paul Academy, history, 20:362;
publication, 40:95
St. Paul Academy of Medicine and Surgery, 16:353
St. Paul Alumni Association of the
University of Minnesota, 12:193
St. Paul and Chicago Railroad, papers, 16:217, 26:371; excursions,
31:86; finances, 37:157
St. Paul and Duluth Railroad, 17:399,
33:65; promotes settlement, 13:42,
28:124, 130
St. Paul and Milwaukee Railroad,
freight rates, 29:8
St. Paul and Pacific Railroad, survey, 11:108; routes, 12:276, 278,
339, 14:169, 15:291, 16:254, 19:
408, 20:373, 21:239, 242, 243,
451, 24:333, 29:13, 35:207, 382,
37:155, 38:45; St. Cloud branch,
21:240, 241, 24:332n; transports
hunters, 33:143, 148; river ship-
ments, 35:338; map, 37:156
St. Paul and Pacific Railroad Co.,
promotes settlement, 12:253-255,
13:31n, 35, 36, 38, 39, 42, 43,
31:21, 225, 226, 35:133, 135; records, 15:464; bonds, 37:153, 157,
158; officials, 37:154. See also
Great Northern Railway Co.; St.
Paul, Minneapolis and Manitoba
Railway
St. Paul and St. Anthony Plank Road
Co., 29:206n
St. Paul and St. Croix Co., steamboat
excursions, 31:86
St. Paul and Sioux City Railroad,
snow blockades, 11:187; colonization projects, 12:254, 255, 445,
13:29, 31n, 38, 17:485, 31:221,
35:133, 136; routes, 12:272, 39:
92; beginnings, 18:173; excursion,
37:102. See also Minnesota Valley
Railroad
St. Paul and Southern Railway, 21:339
St. Paul and Winona Railroad, route,
12:46n
St. Paul Area Chamber of Commerce
(St. Paul Association of Com-

merce), history, 12:344; anniversaries, 14:347, 20:426, 22:50, 30:170; projects, 20:374, 38:84; promotional activities, 21:248, 249, 22:263, 30:70, 35:249, 37:320, 38:221; policies, 29:10, 39:110; centennial observance, 29:96, 30:170

St. Paul Association of Public and Business Affairs, papers, 12:193

St. Paul Athletic Club, 39:23

St. Paul Auditorium, 39:58, 61, 62; architecture, 28:293

St. Paul Automobile Club, White Bear clubhouse, 36:283

St. Paul Book and Stationery Co., 33:2

St. Paul Boom Co., 24:137

St. Paul Bridge, see Wabasha Street Bridge

St. Paul Bridge Co., 17:211

St. Paul Building, 40:101; depicted, 40:100

St. Paul Cathedral, see Cathedral of St. Paul

St. Paul Chamber of Commerce, see St. Paul Area Chamber of Commerce

St. Paul City Planning Board, 16:338, 17:362

St. Paul College, see College of St. Paul

St. Paul College Club, records, 14:217, 25:185; centennial show, 30:284. See also American Association of University Women

St. Paul College of Law, founded, 17:115

St. Paul Commercial Club, 21:69

St. Paul Community Chest, 17:239, 26:289

St. Paul Congregational Union, 18:96

St. Paul Council of Arts and Sciences, 39:64, 40:149

St. Paul Daily News, politics, 32:139

St. Paul Daily Press, 25:250, 40:335, 336, 338; editor, 14:406, 16:215, 34:330, 336; carriers' greetings, 16:387, 388; merger, 22:212; politics, 36:300, 301, 307, 308, 37:328, 330-333. See also St. Paul Pioneer Press

St. Paul Daily Times, founded, 15:395; politics, 28:24

St. Paul Daily Union, politics, 37:332

St. Paul Dramatic Club, 11:97, 19:440

St. Paul Female Seminary, established, 14:147

St. Paul Fire and Marine Insurance Co., history, 20:346; in Canada, 22:99; expansion, 28:74; first president, 29:358, 39:173, 174; centennial, 33:268, 312

St. Paul Fire Insurance Patrol, archives, 20:330, 21:36, 22:87, 24:34, 62; equipment, 21:37

St. Paul Foundry Co., history, 15:140

St. Paul Gallery and School of Art, 28:302, 29:370; exhibits, 23:42, 71, 36:108

St. Paul Gas Light Co., 12:426; serves balloonists, 39:278, 279, 284, 285

St. Paul Globe, politics, 39:102, 108; history, 39:327-334

St. Paul Grand Opera House, see Grand Opera House, St. Paul

St. Paul High School, Walter Reed at,

24:209, 211, 239; athletics, 39:19. See also Central High School, St. Paul

St. Paul Hotel, 40:221 (cover)

St. Paul House, 35:356; located, 39:144

St. Paul Housing Committee, papers, 29:102

St. Paul Institute of General and Applied Science, see Science Museum, St. Paul

St. Paul Junior Association of Commerce, 30:170

St. Paul Library Association, 16:332; lecture series, 11:146, 147, 157, 16:31, 19:415; organized, 18:363, 33:189

St. Paul Light Cavalry, volunteer unit, 16:170, 172, 173n, 27:8

St. Paul Medical College, 35:221, 39:114

St. Paul, Minneapolis and Manitoba Railroad, hunters' car, 16:270; route, 20:373, 30:262; expansion, 28:376

St. Paul, Minneapolis and Manitoba Railway Co., promotes settlement, 13:31n, 33, 16:129; monopoly, 38:241, 39:100; history, 40:142. See also Great Northern Railway Co.

St. Paul Municipal Chorus, 18:47, 97

St. Paul Musical Society, 16:497, 21:193, 32:240n, 33:172

St. Paul Mutual Insurance Co., 29:358

St. Paul Opera House, see Grand Opera House, St. Paul

St. Paul Park, developed, 35:340

St. Paul Philatelic Society, 11:206

St. Paul Phrenological Society, 15:225

St. Paul Pioneer, carriers' greeting, 16:388; politics, 36:303, 304, 308

St. Paul Pioneer Press, history, 12:457, 14:404, 406, 30:383; founded, 14:397; editors, 22:211, 26:95, 30:198, 34:330, 39:333; centennial, 28:197, 30:273; politics, 38:305, 39:101. See also St. Paul Daily Press, St. Paul Pioneer

St. Paul plow, 24:297

St. Paul Printing Pressmen and Assistants' Union No. 29, 27:178

St. Paul Protestant Orphan Asylum, 18:317, 19:49, 26:260

St. Paul Public Library, built, 26:173; building fund, 39:55; fire, 39:58

St. Paul Real Estate Exchange, organized, 25:213

St. Paul Rod and Gun Club, 29:89

St. Paul School of Fine Arts, 40:249

St. Paul Seminary, 23:96; history, 17:84, 349; bell, 18:379

St. Paul Society for the Relief of the Poor, 18:210, 38:79, 81

St. Paul Soldiers' Home, 38:289, 295

St. Paul, Stillwater, and Taylors Falls Railroad, 18:173

St. Paul Structural Steel Co., 35:203

St. Paul Symphony Orchestra, 39:57

St. Paul Trades and Labor Assembly, 21:387, 34:264; organized, 18:332, 22:368; papers, 21:36; activities, 21:390-393, 37:144

St. Paul Turnverein, anniversary, 15:140; records, 17:338, 18:47

St. Paul Union Depot, first, 33:29, 32; second, 37:187

St. Paul Volkszeitung, German newspaper, 35:328

St. Paul War History Committee, 23:392; activities, 26:278; archives, 29:49, 102

St. Paul Water Co., history, 40:223-231

St. Paul Workingmen's Association, 21:388

St. Paul Yacht Club, Raspberry Island, 33:4; history, 38:336

St. Paul's Church (Catholic), Brainerd, 28:190

St. Paul's Church on the Hill (Episcopal), St. Paul, 13:346, 38:75

St. Paul's Episcopal Church, Owatonna, 11:338; Duluth, 26:96, 37:110n

St. Paul's Evangelical Lutheran Church, Preston, 14:451; Chatfield, 15:481

St. Paul's Lutheran Church, Fairmont, 14:452

St. Paulus Evangelical Church, South St. Paul, 14:104

St. Peter, industries, 11:111; river port, 11:132, 133n, 135, 12:60, 38:361; townsite, 11:171n, 38:118, 119; roads, 11:399, 40:148; stage lines, 11:402; anniversary, 12:36, 103; ethnic settlements, 12:275, 24:79, 25:318, 31:42, 39:263; schools, 12:398, 15:345, 19:333, 36:201; pioneer life, 12:402, 17:353, 26:67; banks, 13:174, 19:465, 40:110; churches, 14:121, 21:453, 23:109, 37:262; proposed capital, 14:159-161, 15:111, 27:271, 31:178n, 36:6, 7, 283; volunteer guard, 16:170; historical meetings, 16:301, 22:292-296; lyceum, 167:470; cemeteries, 17:122; climate, 17:260; hotel, 17:488; agricultural trade, 18:409, 24:302n, 27:111, 39:233; baseball, 19:169, 172; unions, 21:393; founded, 22:295; described, 23:75, 37:262; German theater, 32:100, 102, 171, 34:242; music, 33:319, 321; ginseng trade, 34:146n; literary visitors, 37:226-228; in Sioux Outbreak, 38:94, 96, 97, 100-102, 116, 124, 125, 276, 280, 283; land office, 39:86, 87, 89-91; in Civil War, 39:127, 184

St. Peter and Paul's Catholic Church, Mankato, 18:375; Blue Earth, 25:410

St. Peter Claver's Church (Catholic), St. Paul, history, 24:92, 30:266

St. Peter Co., capital removal attempt, 12:104, 205, 14:159, 161, 27:271, 36:6

St. Peter Guards, organized, 21:313

St. Peter State Hospital, 17:341, 39:328

St. Peter Tribune, politics, 28:30

St. Peter's, see Mendota

St. Peter's Cathedral, Rome, 39:161, 162

St. Peter's Catholic Church, St. Peter, 14:121; Mendota, 15:195, 467

St. Peter's River, see Minnesota River

St. Philip's Church (Catholic), Mankato, 17:473

St. Pierre, Jacques le Gardeur, sieur de, 12:364; fort commandant, 11:383, 16:154, 18:240, 32:231, 238

St. Pius the Fifth Catholic Church, Cannon Falls, 15:481

St. Raphael's Hospital, St. Cloud, 33:292, 295-297

St. Raphael's Rest Home, St. Cloud, 33:292, 296

St. Rose of Lima Church (Catholic), Argyle, 20:217

St. Scholastica's Catholic Church, Heidelberg, 14:120

St. Stephen, Slovene settlement, 25:194

St. Stephen's Catholic Church, Minneapolis, 11:320, 17:118

St. Thomas Church (Catholic), Kent, history, 24:94

St. Thomas College, see College of St. Thomas

St. Thomas Military Academy, see College of St. Thomas

St. Vrain, Col. Ceran, 15:430

St. Wenceslaus Catholic Church, New Prague, 12:451, 13:450

St. Wendelin's Church (Catholic), Luxemburg, Stearns County, 16:484, 17:229

Saints baseball team, St. Paul, 36:93

Sakolski, A. M., work reviewed, 14:197-200

Sakry, Cliff, speaker, 30:83, 87, 279; author, 30:173, 32:63, 36:70

Sale River, Man., trading post, 11:365

Saleesh House, Mont., trading post, 24:74

Salem Covenant Evangelical Church, Minneapolis, 15:129

Salem Lutheran Church, St. Cloud, 14:238; Karlstad, 14:452; Mahtowa, 15:481

Salem Mission Church, Swift County, 12:171, 211; Kandiyohi County, 12:208; West Duluth, 22:112

Salem Township, Olmsted County, Norwegian settlement, 12:270

Sales, Raoul de Roussy de, author, 29:154

Salisbury, Albert, work reviewed, 32:45

Salisbury, Jane, work reviewed, 32:45

Salisbury, Susan E., missionary, 11:455

Salisbury, W. R., author, 14:236

Sallet, Richard, author, 16:344

Salmon, Lucy M., work reviewed, 15:207; author, 13:201, 14:408

Salmon Trout River, Mich., 23:237

Salmore, Mrs. Theresa, speaker, 34:174

Salo, Ruth, author, 18:340

Salo, Carlton County, Finnish settlement, 25:320, 28:82

Saloutos, Theodore, "The National Producers' Alliance," 28:37-44; reviews by, 30:60, 40:91; work reviewed, 32:181-183; author, 21:326, 26:381, 27:165, 259, 28:72, 96, 304, 29:76, 30:95

Salsich, L. R., 22:346

Salt Lake City, Utah, Mormon settlement, 28:378, 36:286

Salt shakers, history, 37:134

Salter, Rev. Charles C., 16:28

Salter, Robert H., author, 27:175

Salter, Rev. William, missionary, 16:111, 542, 17:224, 21:98

Salter family, pioneer farmers, 27:175

Salvation Army, Mora, 34:62; history, 35:94; Minneapolis, 36:130

Salverson, Laura G., author, 34:3

Salvini, Tommaso, actor, 28:117, 118

Salvus, Frank J., author, 21:426

Salzmann, C. G., 19:16

"Sam Ward," steamboat, 35:102

"Sam Young," steamboat, 11:143

Samatchi, Joseph, 39:305n

Sample, Dr. C. H., 21:297

Sample, Rev. Robert F., 22:162

Samson, Verne L., author, 17:477

Samuel, C. L., pseud., see Clemens, Samuel L.

Samuel, Maurice M., trader, 11:375

Samuel, Ray, work reviewed, 35:39

Samuelson, H. E., author, 11:320

Samuelson, Mrs. Hanna, 32:195

Samuelson, Oscar W., author, 11:112

San Francisco, Jewish population, 25:394; freeways, 40:134; fur trade, 40:219

San Francisco Township, Carver County, log house, 37:77

Sanborn, Edward P., 11:54; biography, 16:337

Sanborn, Franklin B., 16:41, 44, 46, 37:227; editor, 20:169, 171

Sanborn, John A., businessman, 33:230

Sanborn, Gen. John B., 29:97, 30:310, 353; in St. Paul, 12:344, 26:67, 155; G.A.R. commander, 16:438; Union officer, 28:326, 30:91, 33:211, 212, 39:77

Sanborn, Mrs. John B., 38:77

Sanborn, Ruth E., author, 13:113

Sanborn, Walter H., circuit judge, 16:349

Sanborn Sentinel, history, 16:497

Sanchez, Nellie V., author, 13:210

Sand, George, author, 20:137

Sand, Rose, editor, 17:366

Sand Beach Sanatorium, see Sunnyside Rest Home

Sand Creek, Colo., massacre, 38:223

Sand Hill River, Polk County, 12:278, 35:249

Sand Point Lake, St. Louis County, archaeology, 28:373; steamboat route, 34:178

Sandberg, Mrs. Carl, teacher, 20:213

Sandberg, G. H., speaker, 28:86

Sandburg, Carl, author, 13:62, 20:116, 21:12, 201, 24:156, 28:63, 171, 361, 33:265

Sander, Arthur, 22:108, 27:174

Sanders, A. H., traveler, 32:12

Sanders, J. H., pioneer, 24:326

Sandford, Philander, 15:248

Sandheim, Ole, 29:308

Sandnes Township, Yellow Medicine County, Norwegian settlement, 12:275n; history, 36:194

Sandow, Erich, author, 35:294

Sandoz, Jules, pioneer, 24:208

Sandoz, Mari, work reviewed, 34:345, 39:207; author, 23:124, 158, 25:176, 34:355, 37:262, 40:305

Sandridge Trail, Kittson and Roseau counties, 24:321

Sandro, Gustav O., author, 13:340

Sands, Darlyne, author, 16:250

Sands, J. W., speaker, 22:441

Sandstedt, Frank G., postmaster, 34:186

Sandstone, history, 26:183, 34:61, 39:212; school, 28:131; fire, 34:62, 218; frontier road, 40:243, 244

Sandstrom, Alexander, speaker, 40:61

Sandstrom, Mrs. Phyllis, chief clerk, 23:367, 24:31, 162, 25:41; stenographer, 24:30

Sandum, K. O., 20:460

Sandusky, Ohio, fur trade, 19:296

Sandusky Fish Co., Oak Point, Lake of the Woods County, 35:272-275

Sandusky River, Ohio, massacre, 40:204

Sandy Lake, Aitkin County, trading posts, 11:371, 12:92, 13:210, 222, 443, 14:231, 16:213, 17:72, 207, 19:349, 20:14, 21:346, 23:188, 249n, 333, 26:106, 276, 30:275, 31:95, 33:19, 34:18, 35:155, 382, 36:249, 39:82; Indians, 13:339, 443, 16:214, 18:404, 23:329-331; history, 14:116, 27:130; Indian school, 16:333; trade route, 20:8, 11, 21:84; archaeology, 23:188, 34:268; explored, 23:247-251, 328, 31:96; climate, 23:332; surveyed, 23:334; wildlife, 30:132; described, 32:95; steamboating, 33:9, 10, 14-17, 19; dam, 33:14, 15

Sandy Point, Lake Pepin, trading post, 11:382

Sandy River, Aitkin County, trading post, 11:371; described, 23:140; trade route, 32:234; steamboating, 33:8, 15, 18, 19

Sanfacon, ---, trader, 28:144

Sanford, Dr. A. H., speaker, 17:350

Sanford, Albert H., work reviewed, 32:253; author, 16:347, 22:98, 29:273, 35:296

Sanford, Frank, speaker, 16:360

Sanford, Gen. Henry S., 13:427, 25:135, 38:243

Sanford, J. N., author, 16:248

Sanford, Maria L., educator, 14:231, 333, 452, 16:184, 350, 25:68, 31:52; statue, 24:263, 36:151, 37:187; reformer, 39:11

Sanger, Margaret, 25:64

Sanitary Fair, Chicago, Minnesota exhibit, 18:365

Sann, Paul, work reviewed, 34:209

Sanstead, Rev. J. W., author, 12:450, 19:125

Santa Fe Railways, 30:237; promotes immigration, 16:344

Santa Fe Trail, route to West, 15:256; historic site, 40:195

Santee (Neb.) Normal Training School, 12:330, 23:97

Santee Reservation, Neb., 37:271-275, 281

Santiago, history, 12:455

Sapiro, Aaron, 28:38, 39, 43

Sarasohn, Stephen B., work reviewed, 35:332

Sarasohn, Vera H., work reviewed, 35:332

Saratoga Springs, Lyon County, proposed townsite, 14:250, 251

Sarbach, Louis N., author, 22:347

Sardeson, Frederick W., paleontologist, 39:114
Sardis, Big Stone County, postal station, 17:485
Sarff, Ezra, author, 30:397
Sarff, Manus, pioneer, 30:397
Sargent, Dr. A., cholera victim, 14:293
Sargent, Charles S., 25:71
Sargent, Epes, excursionist, 15:406, 413, 20:384
Sargent, George B., 16:360; land officer, 12:286, 389; speaker, 22:362; Jay Cooke's agent, 26:96; career, 28:284; banker, 37:92-94, 110n, 120
Sargent, George H., editor, 16:350
Sargent, Julia A., see Wood, Mrs. William H.
Sargent, Julian, author, 11:209, 218
Sargent, Mary F., author, 11:463
Sargent, Sarah L., 11:419
Sargent, T. T., steamboat captain, 11:115
Sargent, William C., 12:281
Saroni, Herman, automobile manufacturer, 26:19
Sarpy's Post, Neb., store, 40:193
Sartell, Joseph B., 26:238
Sartell, Mrs. William, 19:119
Sarvela, Heikki, pioneer pastor, 25:324
Sarver, C. E., speaker, 20:99
Saskatchewan, fur trade, 16:106; Riel Rebellion, 1885, 17:454; caribou herds, 21:212; hunting, 32:59; explored, 32:238n, 35:339, 37:54, 39:171; described, 34:126; anniversary, 35:45; wheat farming, 35:48; government, 35:148; Hutterite colony, 40.44
Saskatchewan River, in fur trade, 11:261, 13:181, 33:130, 40:163, 173, 174; explored, 12:293, 32:231; surveyed, 17:476; steamboating, 21:260; gold mining, 35:249; history, 38:386
Sasse, Fred A., work reviewed, 36:65
"Satellite," steamboat, 26:132
Saterstrom, A. J., author, 14:358
Satre, Mrs. A. G., 23:399
Satterlee, L. D., work reviewed, 33:307
Satterlee, Marion P., historian, 34:237
Satterlee, W. W., at Red Rock, 31:90
Saturday Evening Post (Burlington, Iowa), 14:439
Saturday Press (Minneapolis), history, 37:164-173
Saturday Visiter (Pittsburgh, Pa.), abolitionist newspaper, 32:16
"Saturn," steamboat, 26:132
Saucier, Jean Baptiste, house, 29:72
Sauer, Carl, author, 11:428, 430
Sauer, Elfrieda von R., biography, 37:187
Sauer, Emil, pianist, 39:55
Sauer, Philip von R., author, 37:187
Sauers, Ernest, pioneer, 36:235
Saugstad, John, 14:358, 18:110, 22:107, 23:103; author, 14:351
Sauk Centre, in Sioux Outbreak, 12:302, 318, 20:364, 38:276, 277, 279-281, 284-286; depicted, 15:139, 20:363, 28:172, 37:7, 12; literary society, 15:253; dog

trials, 16:267; churches, 17:337, 18:119; hunting, 20:191; roads, 21:235; pioneer life, 25:67, 69; Sinclair Lewis' home, 28:370, 30:267, 34:42, 85-89, 126, 35:234, 37:1n, 6, 13, 40, 66, 88, 135; Norse "chapel site," 30:169; growth, 30:275; in fiction, 31:137; history, 34:173
Sauk Centre Board of Trade, 23:199
Sauk City, Stearns County, ghost town, 22:447
Sauk City, Wis., nickname, 23:66; German settlement, 24:77
Sauk Indians, 32:227, 229, 232, 235; history, 12:76; Wisconsin, 15:176, 189; Illinois, 36:191; culture, 37:174
Sauk Lake, Stearns and Todd counties, fishing, 37:2
Sauk Rapids, trading post, 11:375, 23:94; roads, 16:293, 21:234; missions, 16:316, 28:210, 33:90; cyclone, 16:365; described, 19:96; pioneer life, 21:412; river port, 24:138, 28:342n, 29:204, 218, 32:34, 33:9, 10, 40:332; cemetery, 25:316; on Red River Trail, 27:165, 38:2; railroad, 27:181; German settlement, 31:25, 32:36; Catholic church, 32:34; mail route, 33:89; centennial, 34:170; post office, 40:83
Sauk Rapids Frontierman, 16:234, 19:215; established, 14:403; file, 14:439, 15:60; subscribers, 21:412; farm column, 40:334
Sauk River, Benton County, described, 24:332
Sauk Trail, Rock Island, Ill.-Detroit, Mich., 23:248n
Sauk Valley, described, 18:355, 22:86, 40:69, 75; survey, 21:192; travel route, 21:229; German settlements, 31:253, 32:35, 37, 35:263; claim shanties, 35:256, 257
Sauk Valley man, discovered, 21:100, 35:201
Sault Rapids, Rainy River, 24:283
Sault Ste. Marie, Mich., Ont., trading post, 11:233, 242, 263, 21:146, 22:285, 29:351, 36:242, 248, 37:80, 241; described, 11:242n; explored, 11:452, 12:348, 13:261, 15:170, 18:387; names, 12:349, 16:227; fort, 13:99, 15:379, 19:290, 299, 40:184; mission, 15:110, 122, 18:47, 29:168, 33:185, 34:219; Nicolet celebration, 15:475; history, 18:325, 19:198, 34:206; canal and locks, 19:199, 21:234, 23:355, 24:175, 28:54, 33:67, 34:263, 311, 355, 38:55; land claims, 23:128, 145; Cass expedition at, 23:144-147; ship traffic, 23:355; Indian agency, 24:164, 238, 25:271; fishing, 34:245
Saulteaux Indians, 36:39, 49, 52; conjuring customs, 24:54
Saum, Lewis O., work reviewed, 40:39
Saum, school, 36:104
Saunders, Frank E., 13:120
Saunders, Rev. J. A., 17:363
Saunders, Jefferson, forest ranger, 19:121
Saunders, Capt. John, 25:21n
Saunders, Lt. T. M., 39:204

Sauntry, William, house, 37:43, 38:351, 352
Savage, D. R., author, 12:101, 19:234; speaker, 27:75
Savage, Rev. Edward P., 38:82
Savage, John, house, 27:267
Savage, Marion W., horse owner, 20:201, 28:192, 36:65
Savage, mission site, 21:167n; shipbuilding, 27:63
Savage's Station, Va., battle, 25:141; hospital, 25:142, 143
Savanna Portage, described, 13:339, 23:251, 26:229, 32:95; geology, 13:403-407; used by travelers, 14:116, 16:288, 26:276, 35:155, 40:275n; trade route, 20:11; trail opened, 21:328, 22:438; trading post, 23:188
Savanna River, see East Savanna River, West Savanna River
"Savannah," steamboat, 38:288, 291, 292
Savard, Joan, contest winner, 27:147
Savelle, Max, work reviewed, 22:62-65; author, 36:32
Saveth, Edward N., work reviewed, 34:250; author, 33:92
Savoyard, Toussaint, trader, 28:144, 145, 148, 150, 230
Savre, B. K., 28:88, 297
Savs, Rev. Mathias, author, 12:454, 15:315
Sawbill area, Cook County, forest fires, 36:131-138; map, 36:132
Sawbridge, Charles J., speaker, 12:104
Sawmills, Minnesota River, 11:171, 181; Falls of St. Anthony, 12:163, 22:153, 29:208, 31:109; Mississippi River, 16:469, 27:190, 28:207; St. Croix Valley, 17:278, 279, 18:167, 170, 359, 19:319, 20:447, 24:193, 29:199, 205, 30:391, 31:62, 36:215, 37:333; technology, 18:171; Rum River, 19:236; Staples, 20:469; Bemidji, 23:25, 32, 34; Iowa, 23:184, 27:190; Indiana, 31:61; Redwood Falls, 36:154; Brown County, 36:193
Sawyer, James A., expedition leader, 23:184
Sawyer, P. H., author, 39:170
Sawyer, Philetus, politician, 31:113, 34:72
Sawyer, Robert W., historian, 32:250
Sawyer and Austin, La Crosse, Wis., mill, 35:296
Sawyer and Heaton, Stillwater, mill, 24:205
Sawyer Goodman Co., lumber firm, 13:365
Sawyer House, Stillwater, 24:200, 35:364
Sawyer ranch, Glenwood, described, 11:337
Sawyers, Mott R., speaker, 29:91
Saxhaug, O. E., 23:391
Saxon, C. R., 18:465, 19:470; speaker, 14:460
Saxon, Wallace, 18:110
Saxon baseball club, St. Paul, 19:164, 167, 170, 173, 175, 178-181
Saxton, Thomas, 11:415
Saxton, Cook County, ghost town, 34:177
Say, Thomas, naturalist, 12:327, 16:

156, 19:458, 31:112, 35:241, 378,
36:295, 296, 37:31; career, 26:165
Sayer, Guillaume, mixed-blood, 22:281
Sayer, J. C., trader, 21:120n
Sayer, John, trader, 20:12, 18
Sayer's House, Cass Lake, trading
post, 14:231
Sayles, Charles N., 19:118, 20:98,
21:109
Sayles, Mrs. Charles N., speaker, 16:
243
Saylor, John, author, 14:462
Scallan, Joseph, 13:346
Scallen, Raymond, author, 37:135
Scambler, Otter Tail County, history,
23:298
Scammon, Dr. Richard E., quoted, 24:
347
Scandia, Lutheran church, 29:371;
historical meeting, 37:88; Swedish
settlement, 38:243
Scandia Building and Loan Associ-
ation, Duluth, 37:123
Scandia Grove, see Lake Prairie Town-
ship
Scandia Swedish Baptist Church, anni-
versaries, 11:459, 16:340, 17:117;
history, 12:206
Scandinavian-American Publishing Co.,
Minneapolis, 20:191
Scandinavian Dramatic Society, Duluth, 21:414
Scandinavian Evangelical Lutheran
Church, East Union, 14:451
Scandinavian Immigration Society, 12:
277
Scandinavian Ladies Emigrant Society,
38:79
Scandinavian National Society, Winnipeg, Man., 18:72
Scandinavian Relief Society, Moorhead, 13:214
Scandinavian Woman Suffrage Association, 20:192
Scandinavians, place names, 11:102,
16:350, 21:350; characterized, 11:
103, 19:408, 20:226, 30:243, 31:
182; immigration, 11:325, 19:81,
31:126, 34:85; Wisconsin, 12:328,
18:383, 27:134, 31:252; literature, 13:324; influence, 14:438,
18:219; Minnesota communities, 15:
245, 18:421, 21:223, 22:348, 23:
25, 107, 24:241, 258, 25:213, 26:
281, 28:243, 35:203, 36:240; in
politics, 16:459, 17:161, 328, 25:
192, 385, 35:61, 36:111, 238, 308,
37:12, 39:95, 96, 40:321, 328; religion, 18:360, 361, 365, 21:112,
36:285-293, 37:42, 38:332; Canada,
20:342, 21:269; dances, 21:60; in
agriculture, 21:91, 441, 23:14;
leaders, 21:98, 27:56; on iron
range, 21:290, 27:204-206, 209,
212, 215, 40:341; loan words, 21:
427; fraternal societies, 22:394n,
436; in lumber industry, 23:99,
27:208, 34:7, 36:153; newspapers,
24:257; cooking, 24:259, 40:47;
folklore, 28:280; in gold rush,
29:300-315, 32:174, 39:341; leprosy victims, 31:190; in Civil War,
33:84; Minneapolis, 33:169, 175;
theater, 33:176, 178; in fiction,
37:11. See also various Scandinavian groups
Scandrett, Mrs. B. W., 23:41

Scandrett, Henry A., 19:50
Scanlan, Dr. Peter L., 17:462, 530;
work reviewed, 18:193; author, 11:
105, 17:475, 22:98, 25:89
Scanlon, Sister Ann E., author, 31:58
Scanlon, Marion S., author, 35:151
Scanlon, William, author, 18:105
Scanlon-Gipson Lumber Co., 29:140
Scannell, Bishop Richard, 35:135, 136
Scantlebury, Thomas, diary, 11:334
Scarbo, George, artist, 26:270
Scarborough, Mrs. Mae, speaker, 14:
119
Scarlet Eagle Tail, Sioux Indian, 35:
172
Scarlet fever, at Fort Snelling, 33:
91
Scarlet Plume, Sioux leader, 12:121
Schadle, Dr. Jacob E., laryngologist,
16:350
Schaefer, Mrs. Alvin C., speaker, 11:
118
Schaefer, Edward, author, 36:283
Schaefer, Rev. Francis J., author,
15:104, 455
Schaefer, Mrs. Fred C., 25:311
Schafer, Joseph, 14:75, 344, 31:116;
review by, 11:82; work reviewed,
18:79; author, 11:11, 103, 211,
430, 13:334, 15:355, 17:114, 18:
326, 19:35; career, 12:328, 24:
337; editor, 12:440; quoted, 13:
91, 27:83; speaker, 13:106, 326,
14:448, 15:119, 17:344
Schafer Brothers Logging Co., Aber-
deen, Wash., 27:165
Schaff, Philip, author, 29:154
Schaffer, H. J., politician, 39:49
Schaft Lake, Lake County, resort, 34:
81
Schall, Anna, 18:143
Schall, Thomas D., Senator, 11:331,
25:305, 40:369; lawyer, 17:213;
career, 28:74
Schaller, Albert, legislator, 35:348
Schaller, Celestine M., 11:318, 14:
31n, 19:451
Schantz, Jacob Y., author, 29:166
Schantz-Hansen, T., work reviewed,
22:183
Schaper, William A., professor, 35:
368, 39:205
Schappes, Morris U., review by, 31:
44; author, 31:64
Scharwenka, Xaver, pianist, 39:53
Schaub, Mrs. B., author, 18:333
Schauffler, Rev. Henry A., 15:35
Schauinger, J. Herman, review by, 40:
352
Scheben, Joseph, author, 15:447
Scheele, Carl A. A., author, 18:74
Scheer, Luke, author, 26:270
Scheers, Charles F., author, 23:402,
30:76
Scheers, Mrs. Charles F., author, 30:
76
Scheffer, Albert, 39:329; politician,
28:23, 27, 32:132-134; banker, 31:
35
Scheffer, Charles, 25:21, 29:171, 40:
231
Scheider, Rev. Cyrinus, 12:96
Schell, Herbert S., "Writing State
History," 36:84-88; reviews by,
35:238, 38:378, 40:257; work re-
viewed, 37:304; author, 14:114,

19:108, 24:369, 34:312, 313;
speaker, 36:36
Schell, Rev. James P., 15:22n
Schell, Richard, 27:315
Schell Brewing Co., New Ulm, history,
20:356, 24:189
Schellbach, Louis H., legislator, 35:
348
Schellenberg, T. R., author, 35:335
Schelling, Ernest, pianist, 39:59
Schem, Alexander T., editor, 12:195,
24:222
Schenectady, N.Y., burned by French,
19:282
Schenk, Carl A., forester, 34:176;
work reviewed, 34:256
Schennach, Emmanuel, 14:39
Schennach, John, 14:3ln, 39, 42
Scherbauer, Sister Willibalda, 35:
264, 266, 269, 271
Scherfenberg, Mrs. Martha, 12:106
Scheunemann, Leona, 20:428
Schiavo, Giovanni, author, 16:118
Schick, Joseph S., author, 32:59, 35:
195
Schiffman Building, St. Paul, 39:53n
Schiffrer, Father Vincent, artist,
33:60n
Schiller, Friedrich, poet, 39:198-200
Schiller, Hans von, aeronaut, 40:268
Schilling, Mrs. Cecelia O., 12:446
Schilling, Mrs. H. F., speaker, 16:
244
Schilling, William F., 21:452; au-
thor, 20:360, 33:228; speaker, 21:
336; collector, 27:81
Schilplin, Fred, publisher, 17:365;
sheriff, 28:85
Schilplin, Mrs. Fred (Maude C.), 20:
445; work reviewed, 16:80-82; au-
thor, 12:455, 16:232, 24:183;
speaker, 15:241, 16:115
Schjeldahl, G. T., Co., balloon research, 38:334
Schlebecker, John T., essay reviewed,
38:238; author, 33:352, 36:190
Schlegel, Marvin W., author, 26:85,
278, 27:61, 28:73, 30:257
Schleiden, Rudolf, ambassador, 40:
270, 271, 277, 278
Schlener, John A., politician, 35:345
Schlener, John A., and Co., Minneapolis, 31:148
Schlenk, Hugo, accountant, 40:405
Schlesinger, Arthur M., 17:51, 20:
289, 23:389; reviews by, 12:304-
306, 22:68-70; work reviewed, 21:
299; author, 19:347, 21:321, 22:
82, 96, 23:52; editor, 22:70, 71
Schlesinger, Arthur M., Jr., review
by, 33:214; editor, 28:173; author, 29:258, 34:250, 38:387
Schlicher, J. J., author, 24:76
Schlick, Lena, student, 27:99
Schlinkert, Leroy, work reviewed, 29:
159
Schlitgus, Ernest H., 20:397, 22:340,
28:88, 195, 387; speaker, 29:180
Schlueter, Dr. Robert E., author, 17:
475
Schlusnus, Heinrich, singer, 39:63
Schmahl, Alexander, 26:290
Schmahl, Julius, state treasurer, 11:
315; author, 11:467, 12:85, 13:
287, 390, 18:474, 19:474, 23:189,
25:306; speaker, 12:452, 16:483,

19:66, 471, 21:409, 22:294, 23:
396; editor, 30:397
Schmeckebier, Laurence E., 24:350,
25:381, 26:150, 27:26, 125, 247,
262, 279, 28:47; "Art on Main
Street," 25:1-10; review by, 22:
77; works reviewed, 25:278, 27:
137; speaker, 21:209, 25:56, 397,
26:39, 27:228; author, 22:82, 24:
194, 25:75, 26:172, 387; fellowship, 25:200; compiler, 38:42
Schmerler, Robert M., 29:269
Schmid, Calvin F., 20:88; work reviewed, 19:202; author, 19:226,
23:97
Schmid, H. C., 23:149
Schmidt, Albert, essay reviewed, 36:
185
Schmidt, Dr. E. C., 22:216
Schmidt, Edward W., 15:367, 26:280;
"Minnesota Lowland Mounds," 16:
307-312; speaker, 15:370; author,
16:242, 17:126, 18:472, 22:332,
29:83
Schmidt, Friedrich A., theologian,
16:350
Schmidt, George P., author, 35:379
Schmidt, Gottlieb, author, 16:126
Schmidt, Hubert, review by, 19:85-87;
author, 19:91
Schmidt, Joseph, 33:293
Schmidt, Karl M., author, 38:41
Schmidt, Father Lawrence, 39:310
Schmidt, Louis B., author, 16:107,
22:92, 326, 31:190
Schmidt, Mrs. Mary S., see Schwandt,
Mary E.
Schmidt, O. W., Saddlery Co., Man-
kato, history, 16:126
Schmidt, Paul, author, 12:333
Schmiedel, Oscar, 17:238
Schmitt, A., Jr., miller, 16:127
Schmitt, Hubert, in Sioux Outbreak,
28:264
Schmitt, John, author, 18:224
Schmitt, Martin F., works reviewed,
33:86, 34:345; editor, 27:161; au-
thor, 30:66
Schmitz, Mrs. C. J., author, 20:102
Schmitz, Henry, 28:50
Schmitz, Lorene L., author, 12:320
Schmitz, Rev. P., author, 24:90
Schmitz, Mrs. Peter M., compiler, 36:
36
Schneider, Albert, bacteriologist,
16:350
Schneider, Allan F., author, 37:307
Schneider, Carl E., author, 21:427
Schneider, Don, author, 21:204
Schneider, Joseph, in Sioux Outbreak,
34:234
Schneider, Father Roman, author, 26:
388
Schneider, Walter S., reminiscences,
15:136
Schocker, William, 26:312, 313
Schoen, E. N., 23:390
Schoenberger, J. H., author, 16:106
Schoening, Herbert F., lawyer, 21:196
Schoepf, Gen. Albin, Union officer,
25:24, 38:261, 262, 39:180
Schofield, George B., gunmaker, 36:68
Schofield, Gen. John M., Union offi-
cer, 39:185
Scholes, France V., essay reviewed,
38:238

Scholljegerdes, Mrs. F. D., 28:196;
speaker, 27:364
Scholte, Hendrik P., colonizer, 35:33
Schön, August, actor, 32:171
Schön, Mrs. August, actress, 32:171
Schoolcraft, Henry R., 18:94, 20:78,
202, 22:277n, 24:379, 25:297, 33:
49, 34:219, 37:33, 38:201; works
reviewed, 33:345, 35:142; explorer, 11:58, 12:216, 14:342, 16:215,
453, 24:372, 25:273, 26:363, 30:
372, 37:80, 302; discovers Lake
Itasca, 12:215, 13:287, 288, 16:
118, 18:180-185, 23:233n, 30:281,
36:184, 37:62; poet, 12:220, 14:
339; influence on Longfellow, 12:
221, 24:237, 35:380; names Itasca,
12:226, 228, 13:163, 166, 168,
169, 292; Indian agent, 13:195,
14:92, 15:344, 23:356, 25:271;
centennial, 13:277, 289-291, 15:
241; author, 13:301, 369, 16:96,
18:162, 19:420, 23:130, 247n, 26:
359, 27:254, 29:131, 30:209, 31:
220n, 34:213, 216, 36:74, 75, 78n,
323; letters, 13:426, 18:183-185,
21:93, 23:75, 38:200, 40:409;
marker, 17:230; quoted, 17:248,
256; career, 18:215, 28:184, 36:
148; with Cass expedition, 23:129,
135, 140, 239, 248, 251, 340, 344,
348, 31:94, 96; interest in education, 23:185; bibliography, 24:
238; portrait, 27:241; draftsman,
40:145
Schoolcraft, Mrs. Henry R., I (Jane
Johnston), 23:144n, 24:379
Schoolcraft, Mrs. Henry R., II (Mary
Howard), diary, 16:96
Schoolcraft, James, murdered, 14:93,
35:199n
Schoolcraft family, 18:215
Schoolcraft Island, Lake Itasca, 36:
326
Schoolcraft River, Beltrami and Hub-
bard counties, 23:29; sawmill, 29:
138; logging, 29:139, 140, 146
Schooling, William, author, 13:298
Schools, see Education, individual
communities and institutions
Schöpflin, F. Wilhelm, printer, 27:31
Schorer, Mark, work reviewed, 37:335;
author, 30:394, 37:345, 38:387
Schorger, A. W., work reviewed, 34:
259
Schostag, Gustaf, miller, 27:174
Schouler, James, historian, 18:128
Schouler, William, excursionist, 15:
406, 413
Schouweiler, Sara, author, 28:84,
291, 293, 373, 29:83, 87
Schrader, Christian, artist, 32:45
Schrader, Eileen, author, 28:297
Schrader, Thomas A., author, 35:45
Schrader family, 28:388
Schramm, Jacob, letters, 17:79
Schreeven, William J., author, 24:70
Schreiber, Theodore, author, 24:259
Schreiner, Charles, Co., Kerrville,
Tex., 26:168
Schreiner, Jacob, letter, 34:146
Schreyer, Lowell, editor, 38:43
Schrier, William, author, 29:175
Schrimper, Richard J., author, 36:195
Schrøder, Johan, journalist, 12:256,
273

Schroeck, Alfred, author, 16:493, 19:
120
Schroeder, John, clerk, 13:29
Schroeder, Mrs. John, 33:15
Schroeder, Leslie L., "Fifty Years of
Flight," 33:237-239
Schroeder, Louella, speaker, 28:387
Schroeder, W. G., author, 16:492
Schubert Club, St. Paul, 17:363, 30:
175; archives, 13:323, 14:218, 17:
102, 26:372; activities, 13:444,
33:95, 35:382; origin, 20:323;
concerts, 28:302, 336, 29:55, 98,
265, 30:179, 36:194; history, 39:
51-64
Schugens, Ed, musician, 33:100, 101
Schuknecht, H. E., author, 23:301
Schulberg, Budd, author, 37:222
Schuldt, Louis J., author, 27:56
Schulenberg, Raymond F., author, 35:
339
Schulenburg, Frederick, lumberman,
17:286, 18:174, 24:271
Schulenburg and Boeckler Lumber Co.,
Stillwater, 24:205, 31:37
Schultz, A. C., 17:121
Schultz, Arthur R., editor, 34:42,
35:327
Schultz, Dorothy, librarian, 37:188
Schultz, Ferdinand P., review by, 20:
424; work reviewed, 20:181-183;
author, 19:213, 20:426
Schultz, Rev. J. H., 28:126
Schultz, Mrs. J. W., 28:295
Schultz, Mrs. Jack, speaker, 25:313
Schultz, James W., author, 14:204
Schultz, John Christian, politician,
35:283
Schultz, John R., editor, 19:217
Schultz, Rev. Otto C., 14:50n
Schulze, E. A., 19:309
Schumacher, Matthias, pioneer, 24:88
Schuman, Henry, publisher, 27:237
Schumann-Heink, Ernestine, singer,
39:61-63
Schünemann-Pott, Friedrich, journal-
ist, 24:222
Schurman, Charles S., papers, 20:331
Schurman, Mrs. Charles S., 20:331
Schurz, Carl, 15:331; letter, 12:429;
Wisconsin pioneer, 15:355, 26:170,
34:219; politician, 16:27, 19:456,
28:24, 26, 28-30, 32:102, 33:180,
39:152; Missouri Senator, 29:127
Schussler, Peter, 14:440
Schütz, Fritz, career, 24:217-219;
author, 24:222
Schütz, Mrs. Fritz, 24:219
Schutz Lake, see Goldschmidt Lake
Schuyler, Montgomery, author, 39:35
Schuyler, Robert L., author, 23:82,
26:84
Schwab, John, house, 39:73
Schwacker, William, farm, 16:14
Schwalen, Mrs. R. F., 25:316
Schwandt, Mary E., Sioux captive, 12:
446, 38:109n; monument, 23:192
Schwandt family, monument, 23:192,
37:60
Schwartz, Aaron, murdered, 29:219n
Schwartz, George M., works reviewed,
34:116, 36:320; speaker, 30:176;
author, 30:267, 38:204
Schwartz, Mrs. R. F., 19:321
Schweiger, ---, labor union member,
22:371

Schweikert, Rev. George, speaker, 28: 387
Schwendeman, Joseph R., author, 15: 240
Schwenderer, Norma, author, 24:367
Schwendinger, Alexander, artist, 36: 240, 38:105, 118, 125n
Schweppe, Carl, author, 21:333
Schwerdtfeger, August, 26:282
Schwerdtfeger, Henry, 26:282
Schwieso, Harriet, song writer, 26:53
Schwyzer, Dr. Arnold, 15:254
Science Museum, St. Paul, 36:108; collections, 15:121; described, 17:363, 20:207; building, 40:99
Scofield, Anna J., 15:487
Scofield, Dr. C. L., 11:119, 16:241; author, 11:339
Scofield, Mrs. C. L., 26:290
Scofield, Edward J., 15:487
Scofield, Mrs. George, speaker, 27: 267
Scofield, Dr. John L., career, 27:267
Scofield, Mary, pioneer teacher, 28: 139
Scofield, Robert L., author, 27:267
Scofield Memorial Auditorium, Elbow Lake, 15:487
Scoles, John, engraver, 36:276
Scotch-Irish, immigration, 24:259; folk songs, 24:261
Scotland Township, Day County, S.D., Indian scout camp, 40:313
Scots, Wabasha County, 12:211; in lumber industry, 13:351; Faribault County, 14:456, 19:364; in fur trade, 15:421, 423, 23:155, 33: 261; Canada, 15:469, 24:285, 28: 256; in granite industry, 16:234; Pipestone County, 17:99; Red River Settlement, 20:342, 22:145, 24:41, 31:108; Minnesota communities, 23: 136, 24:385, 27:204, 209, 210, 33: 227; immigration, 24:259; in Civil War, 33:84; characterized, 40:308; introduce curling, 40:384, 386. See also British
Scott, A. W., 18:130
Scott, Alma S., work reviewed, 31:45; receives award, 25:201
Scott, Beryl H., author, 35:153
Scott, Charles, plasterer, 15:184
Scott, D. L., theater manager, 23:313
Scott, Donald, 20:98, 21:109, 22:107, 23:104, 25:408
Scott, Dred, 20:89, 30:265; court decision, 15:331, 17:76-78, 466, 20: 420, 23:262, 28:26, 37:45; at Fort Snelling, 16:350, 19:354, 21:165, 25:202, 27:167, 39:299; marriage, 29:351, 33:138
Scott, Mrs. Dred (Harriet), marriage, 29:351, 33:138
Scott, Duncan C., letters, 34:126
Scott, Franklin D., work reviewed, 37:299; author, 34:353; speaker, 37:40
Scott, George, religious leader, 13: 310, 18:75
Scott, George E., logger, 26:183; Cass County resident, 26:321
Scott, Sir George Gilbert, architect, 38:343
Scott, H. Y., mill owner, 20:217
Scott, Harvey E., Union soldier, 25: 141
Scott, Hiram, trader, 28:273

Scott, J. G., mill owner, 20:217
Scott, Jack D., work reviewed, 39:297
Scott, Louis N., theater manager, 15: 254, 28:103, 35:156; papers, 35: 340
Scott, Capt. Martin, 27:311; with Stephen H. Long expedition, 16: 156; hunter, 18:159, 32:85, 86, 97; Fort Snelling commandant, 20: 122; biography, 26:298
Scott, R. H., miller, 11:280
Scott, Robert E., 19:231, 360, 20:96, 22:216, 23:391, 25:55, 26:179; speaker, 20:212, 352
Scott, Roy V., "Pioneering in Agricultural Education," 37:19-29; review by, 36:276; work reviewed, 38:235; author, 39:83
Scott, Thomas, death, 36:65
Scott, William E., 12:184, 14:79, 17: 67, 70, 23:93, 101, 391, 25:405; speaker, 14:73, 15:492, 16:101, 488, 17:482, 18:462; author, 17: 102, 123, 23:187, 26:174, 27:75, 262, 36:282; compiler, 18:318, 36: 193
Scott, William W., house, 38:341, 342
Scott, Gen. Winfield, 28:19; biography, 18:203, 449; at Fort Snelling, 18:450, 25:289, 30:211; border operations, 23:59; in Mexican War, 24:2; in Black Hawk War, 35: 88; presidential candidate, 39:46
Scott, Winfield T., author, 27:350
Scott County, history, 11:118, 467, 12:201; ethnic settlements, 12: 271, 14:451, 19:475, 21:98, 28:31; pioneer life, 15:492, 19:449; road, 17:241; grasshopper plague, 17:364; agriculture, 18:408, 24: 296; archives, 20:205; election, 28:32, 34; medicine, 29:265, 353; Indians, 37:274, 275
Scott County, Iowa, German settlement, 21:98
Scott County Historical Society, 15: 71, 34:130; organized, 20:46, 98, 213
Scott County War History Committee, 24:82
Scott-Graff Lumber Co., 27:302
Scott Guards, Belle Plaine, 16:171
Scott-James, R. A., author, 26:308
Scottish Rite Building, St. Paul, see Masonic Hall, St. Paul
Scott's Corner, Carlton County, see Twin Lakes Township
Scottsbluff, Neb., museum, 40:196
Scottsboro case, 21:401
"Scout," steamboat, 18:279
Scovell, Bessie L., author, 20:450
Scovell, H. M., banker, 11:219
Scranton family, 39:305n
Scratching River (Morris River), Man., trading post, 11:365
Scribner, M. V. B., editor, 26:373
Scrip, 25:33n, 30:263; half-breed, 11:462, 14:435, 15:296; in depression of 1857, 14:238
Scriven, Margaret, author, 36:280
Scriver Block, Northfield, 22:111
Scroggs, Claud L., editor, 35:334
Scruby, L. E., 20:435
Scuba diving, see Archaeology: underwater
Scudder, Samuel, with eclipse expe-

dition, 18:352, 33:191, 271, 279, 34:132; author, 18:353n
Scudder, Townsend, author, 28:173
Scull, Gideon D., work reviewed, 25: 371; editor, 16:394
Scull, John, pioneer printer, 15:10
Sculley, Clement F., Co., Minneapolis, advertising, 38:308
Scullin, John, railroad builder, 16: 350
"Sea Wing," steamboat, wrecked, 16: 116
Seaborn, Edwin, author, 27:260
Seabrook, William, author, 18:219
Seabury, Bishop Samuel, 14:461
Seabury Divinity School, Faribault, 11:329, 35:321; archives, 13:427, 14:101, 21:86; established, 14: 112; history, 14:461, 17:115, 18: 331, 23:194, 25:102
Seabury University, Faribault, 11: 329, 19:367
Seabury-Western Theological Seminary, Evanston, Ill., history, 18:331
Seal, Mrs. Joseph, 18:207
Seal, 18:131; in fur trade, 40:210, 214, 217-220
Sealock, Richard B., compiler, 30:67
Searle, Dolson B., diary, 18:96
Searle, Frank E., legislator, 35:303
Searles, A. L., 32:13n
Searles, Colbert, 21:70
Searles, Jasper N., papers, 11:42, 95
Searls, Adah W., author, 29:279
Searls, Harold, 30:81; pageant director, 29:95, 365, 30:77; author, 29:184, 279, 352, 30:85, 157, 281; speaker, 29:370, 30:167, 176
Searls, Ida S., poet, 26:301
Sears, B. F., 22:170
Sears, David, Jr., surveyor, 30:392
Sears, Louis M., author, 11:110, 19: 435
Sears, Oscar W., 25:23
Sears, R. W., and Co., Minneapolis office, 24:373
Sears, Richard W., company founder, career, 13:95, 16:350, 21:103, 24: 372, 35:44
Sears Roebuck and Co., beginnings, 16:350, 21:103, 24:372, 35:44; automobile dealers, 26:23; first store, 38:243
Seashore, Carl E., author, 22:329, 23:184
Seattle, Wash., transportation, 16: 343, 20:337; Norwegians, 22:70; pioneer school, 25:191
Seattle Chamber of Commerce, records, 29:300
Seavey, Samuel L., in Civil War, 25: 385
Seaway Port Authority, 39:210
Seay, Virginia, author, 25:385
Sebeka, name, 20:343; anniversary, 29:272; industries, 36:34
Sebo, Mildred, 16:363; speaker, 17:65
Seccombe, Charles, missionary, 16:28, 317, 19:144, 249, 268; in St. Anthony, 16:315, 18:115, 40:6-10; speaker, 19:134, 269; diary, 28:91
Seccombe, Mrs. Charles, death, 40:8
Séchelles, Mme. Hérault de, 13:203
Secombe, David A., lawyer, 35:110, 111
Second Congregational Church, Minneapolis, 17:212

Second Connecticut Heavy Artillery, 27:249

Second Corps, Union Army, Army of the Potomac, 25:250, 361

Second Indiana Volunteer Infantry, 23:75

Second Louisiana Infantry Regiment, 25:353

Second Minnesota Battery of Light Artillery, 16:471, 25:18, 242, 245, 26:205, 38:291

Second Minnesota Cavalry Regiment, 12:302, 16:217, 25:100, 26:208, 38:284, 294

Second Minnesota Volunteer Infantry, 32:171, 39:179; battles, 11:317, 12:319, 38:258-273, 287, 39:182; memorial, 11:333; personal accounts, 17:466, 39:263; soldier vote, 26:196, 201, 206; personnel, 33:84, 318, 35:49, 38:43, 39:178, 181; in Sioux Outbreak, 37:226n; homecoming, 38:289, 291

Second National Bank, St. Paul, 18: 173, 37:154, 155, 40:116, 117; Winona, 20:58

Second New Hampshire Volunteer Infantry, 15:347

Second U.S. Infantry, 22:97, 28:214

Sectionalism, incited by slavery question, 22:193, 24:307, 32:15, 36:3

Security Bank, Duluth, 37:122; Owatonna, 40:107, 108

Security Mutual Fire Insurance Co., Chatfield, 24:109

Security Savings and Loan Association, Minneapolis, 29:301, 303

Sedgwick, Catharine M., 25:103; "The Great Excursion," 25:104-116; excursionist, 15:406, 409n, 410, 412, 417-419, 20:384; author, 25: 180

Sedgwick, Gen. John, Union officer, 25:27, 32, 36, 122, 125, 126, 130, 132, 134, 241, 344, 346, 352, 353, 355; occupies Fredericksburg, 25: 345n

Sedgwick, Dr. Julius, career, 36:282

Sedweek, T. M., author, 21:423

Seeburger, Vernon R., author, 24:369

Seefried, Irmgard, singer, 39:64

Seeger, Charles, author, 23:179

Seeger, Walter F., speaker, 22:50

Seeger, William, promotes immigration, 31:29

Seehausen, Paul, author, 13:432

Seeley, Mabel, author, 31:129, 133, 138, 140, 147, 36:77, 79

Seely, Pauline A., compiler, 30:67

Seely Township, Faribault County, Norwegian settlement, 12:270

Seemann, Joseph, 24:259

Segall, Julius G., art teacher, 40: 249

Seglem, Charles, founds Grand Marais, 31:191

Sehlin, Andrew, 11:464

Sehlin, Mrs. Peter, author, 11:464

Seib, Charles B., author, 37:343

Seibert, George, musician, 16:497, 21:193, 32:103, 33:95, 34:240, 242

Seidel, Toscha, violinist, 39:59

Seidel's Addition, Minneapolis, 18: 138n

Seidenbusch, Bishop Rupert, 27:105, 32:43, 33:53, 56-59, 34:313

Seidl, Edward H., author, 28:182, 29: 88

Seigel, Cooper and Co., Chicago, merchants, 29:67

Seip, Didrik A., author, 13:315

Seiter, Adolph (Adolf), 28:81; hotel owner, 15:365, 25:314; theater director, 32:168, 169, 173

Seiter, Adolph (Adolf), Jr., actor, 32:172

Seitzinger, Lavinia, nurse, 35:355

Selbulaget, Norwegian club, 14:445

Selby, Jeremiah W., 22:89; house, 29: 200

Selby, Samuel S., 14:259

Selby, Stella, 39:154

Selby Avenue, St. Paul, name, 22:89

Selden, George B., automobile manufacturer, 26:19

Selden, Samuel, author, 24:254

Selective Service Act, adopted, 24:4

Selfridge, Thomas O., Union naval officer, 40:306

Seligman, Edwin R. A., editor, 14:339

Selke, Mrs. Esther A., "Pioneers of German Lutheranism," 14:45-58; author, 12:332, 13:114

Selke, George A., conservation commissioner, 35:191; speaker, 36:35, 71, 283; author, 36:105

Selkirk, George, Chippewa leader, author, 27:358, 35:49

Selkirk, Lady Jean, letters, 24:42, 40:166, 168; characterized, 39:166

Selkirk, Thomas Douglas, Earl of, 20: 69, 21:433, 25:200; papers, 11:94, 307, 12:82, 17:334, 24:42, 153, 27:165; in fur trade, 12:91, 14: 98, 17:95, 18:193, 20:17, 22:283-287, 23:256, 24:154, 40:166, 175; colonies, 12:441, 13:209, 14:283, 16:495, 17:75, 24:41, 28:61, 40: 174, 176; author, 19:37, 40:168; death, 39:166. See also Red River Settlement

Selkirk, Man., railroad, 21:260; river port, 21:261, 263

"Selkirk," steamboat, 11:308, 18:463, 19:410, 412, 21:253, 254, 259n, 260, 261n, 262, 268-270, 32:60, 126; pictured, 20:208

Selkirk colony, see Red River Settlement

Sell, Mrs. E. F., author, 13:454

Sell, O. D., 21:333, 22:105, 339, 23: 100, 293, 390, 24:85, 214n, 26: 283, 27:74, 146, 30:78, 276, 399; author, 34:264

Sellards, Elias H., author, 17:477

Selle, Erwin S., work reviewed, 17: 458; author, 16:352

Sellers, James L., speaker, 15:119; author, 31:128

Sellie, Rev. J. H., author, 18:227

Selover, Mrs. George W., 15:372, 19: 116, 20:99

Selvig, Conrad G., 14:350, 358, 16: 241; work reviewed, 33:119; Congressman, 11:216, 33:120, 38:184; speaker, 16:482, 21:436

Semans, Nadine E., 18:108

Semat, Jerome, trader, 11:366

Sembrich, Marcella, singer, 33:102, 103

Seminole Indians, removal, 15:121

Semmingsen, Ingrid Gaustad, 19:446; works reviewed, 32:177-179, 37:

299; editor, 36:237; speaker, 37: 40

Semple, Annie, pioneer, 33:4

Semple, Ellen C., author, 29:250

Semple, Robert, 40:183

"Senator," steamboat, 13:233, 240, 17:151n, 152n, 22:58n, 28:313, 29: 212; depicted, 29:350

Sencerbox, Charles E., steamboat captain, 11:34, 140

Seneca Falls Declaration, 1848, 16: 451

Seneca Indians, archaeological sites, 40:204, 206-209

Senkler, Dr. Albert E., 17:258, 260

Senn, Judge Fred W., 20:214; speaker, 22:108

Sennett, George B., ornithologist, 16:350

Seppman, Louis, miller, 27:174

Seppman Mill, Minneopa State Park, Blue Earth County, 14:116, 15:484, 26:50

Serbs, iron range, 22:180, 23:387, 27:204, 210-213, 40:341; reverse migration, 27:214

Sergeant, Elizabeth S., author, 11: 459, 31:147

Serkin, Rudolf, pianist, 39:64

Serle, Harry M., speaker, 11:199, 295, 14:459; author, 16:496

Serpent Lake, Crow Wing County, name, 21:348

Serum, A. O., author, 14:444

Service, C. M., author, 14:228

Sessions, Henry H., railroad builder, 16:350

Seton, Ernest Thompson, artist, 20: 199; author, 21:201

Seton, Julia M., author, 20:199, 21: 201

Setrum, J. E., 17:124, 18:111, 20: 100, 22:219; speaker, 19:362

Setser, Vernon G., author, 25:310

Settle, William A., Jr., work reviewed, 40:307; author, 23:381

Setzer, Henry W., author, 34:215; prison official, 37:141, 142

Sevareid, Eric (Arnold E.), work reviewed, 27:331-333; author, 16: 347, 31:191; career, 36:102; student, 40:365-367

Sevareid, Paul A., author, 39:132

Sevastopol, Goodhue County, ghost town, 35:12

Seven Hundred and First Military Police Battalion, 23:267

Seven Hundred and Tenth Military Police Battalion, 23:167, 267

Seven Oaks, Winnipeg, Man., battle, 14:115, 15:477, 21:206, 40:163

Seven Pines, see Fair Oaks

Seven Years' War, see French and Indian War

Sevenich, Joseph M., author, 19:219

Seventeenth of May, celebrated, 20: 403, 408

Seventh Congressional District, history, 11:338

Seventh-day Adventists, Roseau Valley, 24:323; Nebraska, 36:209

Seventh Minnesota Volunteer Infantry, 18:209, 23:170, 26:205, 206, 258, 38:356, 386, 39:183; in Sioux Outbreak, 38:103, 104n, 110n, 280, 283, 286n; at Nashville, 38:245

(cover); homecoming, 38:287, 291–293, 296

Seventh New York Volunteer Infantry, 25:344

Seventh Ohio Volunteer Cavalry, 14:36

Seventh Street Church (Methodist), Minneapolis, 17:338

Seventh U.S. Cavalry, in Little Big Horn battle, 34:131

Seventh U.S. Infantry, in World War I, 11:97

Seventy-Second Pennsylvania Volunteer Infantry, 25:239

Severance, Cordenio, 17:48n, 22:158, 164

Severance, M. J., 13:77

Severance, Maidie, 22:164

Severance, Mrs. Mary H., editor, 26:301

Severance Township, Sibley County, history, 30:274, 35:336

Severe, Mrs. Blanche K., accessions assistant, 22:45; reference assistant, 26:369, 27:46, 28:48; cataloger, 27:340

Severson, Harold, author, 40:315

Severtson, S. T., author, 18:114

Sevey, A. C., blacksmith, 13:99, 16:71, 17:393

Sevier, John, 18:397

Sewall, Alfred, publisher, 33:190

Sewall, Mrs. S. L., author, 21:114

Sewall, Samuel, diary, 40:312

Seward, William H., 16:27, 25:238; in Minnesota, 15:419, 16:335, 20:394, 25:25, 324, 29:121, 33:180, 37:53; quoted, 17:250, 37:56; New York Senator, 33:308, 37:52, 39:38; cabinet officer, 34:319, 37:57; speaker, 37:118

Seward Township, Nobles County, grasshopper plague, 37:209

Sexton, Ethelyn, author, 16:112

Seymor, John, 40:79

Seymour, Adm. Edward H., 22:305

Seymour, Ephraim S., author, 18:118, 22:170, 33:114n, 36:209, 40:84

Seymour, Flora W., work reviewed, 11:80

Seymour, George M., contractor, 37:143, 145, 38:187

Seymour, H. S., baseball umpire, 19:173

Seymour, Horatio, speaker, 19:456, 25:241; politician, 36:303

Seymour, Samuel, artist, 13:368n, 371, 17:456, 29:336, 31:46, 54, 33:89, 264, 35:369, 36:69, 236, 295, 297, 299n, 37:31, 40:144; explorer, 35:378

Seymour, Sabin and Co., Stillwater, lumber firm, 18:175, 37:144

Shadrick, R. H., labor leader, 22:368, 385

Shafer, George F., author, 27:67

Shaffer, Dr. J. M., diary, 33:44

Shaffer, Kenneth R., author, 24:266

Shaffer, Virgil, author, 18:224

Shain, Charles E., speaker, 37:40; author, 38:203

Shakers, religious sect, 36:278; on frontier, 31:112

Shakespeare, William, 23:311

Shakopee (Little Six), Sioux leader, 24:24n, 34:322, 38:96, 134, 144, 148; characterized, 11:125, 15:400, 21:173n, 175; village, 15:

280, 21:163n, 170, 172, 174, 274, 283, 31:213n, 35:29; depicted, 19:135, 34:323, 38:130; capture, 20:328, 38:98; executed, 38:131

Shakopee, trade center, 11:132, 29:2, 3, 8n; river port, 11:139; land speculation, 11:331, 14:436; churches, 12:454, 17:98, 20:431; battle, 13:380, 443, 14:116, 27:296n; pioneer life, 14:99, 16:333, 387, 30:91; history, 14:238, 325, 37:180; name, 15:315, 30:332; school, 16:253; G.A.R. post, 16:432n, 433, 437, 441; bank, 19:465; archaeology, 25:398; industry, 28:294; first physician, 29:265; described, 30:120; Catholic mission, 32:42; German theater, 32:100, 34:242; store, 33:226; gold fever, 38:53; railroad, 39:92

"Shakopee," locomotive, 18:220

Shambaugh, Benjamin F., 18:435; speaker, 11:53, 59–61, 12:22, 13:326; author, 13:331, 15:236, 16:228, 19:107, 20:338

Shamburger, Page, author, 39:343

Shanahan, Rev. Emmett A., 34:131; works reviewed, 31:52, 38:193; speaker, 34:267

Shanahan, Rev. Thomas J., speaker, 14:229; translator, 18:89; author, 23:97

Shandrew, F. E., politician, 36:307

Shane, Ralph M., 32:250

Shankle, George E., author, 14:450, 23:379

Shanklin, Abraham, 18:298, 301

Shanklin, Arnold, 17:160n

Shanley, Bishop John, 17:229, 325, 18:89

Shannon, Don P., author, 11:441

Shannon, Fred A., works reviewed, 29:63, 40:353; author, 26:265, 29:104, 36:101

Shannon, James P., "Catholic Boarding Schools," 35:133–139; "Bishop Ireland's Connemara Experiment," 35:205–213; reviews by, 35:329, 36:24, 37:175; work reviewed, 35:325; author, 34:129, 37:133, 38:193, 241; speaker, 35:248, 36:72, 152, 37:223

Shannon, Rev. W. A., autobiography, 21:415

Shannon, William V., author, 39:210

"Shannon," frigate, 40:348, 350

Shapiro, Elliott, author, 22:431

Sharkey, Sister Mary Agnes, author, 16:340

Sharkey, Robert P., work reviewed, 37:130

Sharon, Thomas, author, 31:130

Sharon, Le Sueur County, agriculture, 17:127

Sharon Lutheran Church, Lamberton, 15:481

Sharp, Paul F., reviews by, 32:181–183, 33:347; work reviewed, 29:341, 35:34; speaker, 29:257, 30:180; author, 30:151, 31:119, 32:192, 33:139

Sharp, Robert P., work reviewed, 36:320

Sharpe, Anthony, 24:106

Sharpe, Mary G., author, 17:490

Sharpe, Peter, 11:320; author, 11:336

Shastag, Gottlieb, miller, 12:65

Shatola, E. G., 28:291

Shattuck, Frances, 18:256n

Shattuck, L. Hubbard, 26:265; author, 23:278

Shattuck, Mrs. N. B., speaker, 27:362

Shattuck School, Faribault, 35:321; anniversaries, 11:329, 16:370, 36:107; history, 12:209, 21:115; publications, 19:367; student life, 35:248; athletics, 39:1 (cover), 18, 20

Shave, Ed, speaker, 19:316

Shave, Harry, author, 30:387

Shaver, Craig H., speaker, 28:391

Shaver, Muriel, author, 11:110

Shaver, U. B., 22:344

Shaw, ——, baseball umpire, 19:168

Shaw, Albert, 18:138

Shaw, Alexander, 25:226

Shaw, Angus, trader, 20:327, 21:145

Shaw, Dr. Anna H., career, 39:7, 14

Shaw, Daniel, Lumber Co., Eau Claire, Wis., records, 12:319, 13:101, 32:253; activities, 30:71; history, 31:59, 36:28, 161; finances, 32:60

Shaw, Eugene, lumberman, 36:161, 166

Shaw, John, 17:119

Shaw, Joshua, artist, 29:61, 33:264

Shaw, Mrs. Louis F., 26:253

Shaw, Marcus, Cutlerite, 13:387, 393

Shaw, Mrs. Marcus, Cutlerite, 13:387, 388

Shaw, Mrs. Mary V., 20:97

Shaw, Percy M., lumberman, 25:77

Shaw, R. W., author, 14:337

Shaw, Dr. S. Wheeler, house, 24:266

Shaw, William B., author, 12:442

Shaw, Mrs. William B., 38:77n

Shaw, St. Louis County, history, 23:302

Shawano County, Wis., Stockbridge reservation, 22:150n

Shawe, Elsie M., music educator, 39:54, 55

Shawe, Lewis, 39:56

Shawnee Indians, legends, 35:143; Illinois, 36:191; sites, 40:209

Shay, John W., 29:185

Shea, John G., translator, 11:8, 20:67

Shea, Martin H., pioneer, 12:340

Shea, W. E., author, 18:218

Sheardown, Dr. S. B., 20:237

Shearman, H. F., colonizer, 11:296

Shearman, Thomas G., 21:315

Sheboygan, Wis., centennial, 28:289

Sheehan, Timothy D., legislator, 35:344

Sheehan, Col. Timothy J., memorial, 11:456; papers, 17:336, 18:48; in Sioux Outbreak, 38:94, 96, 148

Sheep raising, Minnesota, 22:266, 24:105, 26:110–114; breeds, 26:110, 112; Fort Snelling, 35:183, 184n; South Dakota, 35:331; historical aspect, 40:404

Sheffield, Jack, hunter, 35:258

Sheffield, Joseph E., railroad builder, 25:105, 107, 116, 29:170, 34:133

Sheffield and Farnam, railroad contractors, 15:405

Sheire, Mrs. E. R. (Catherine M.), speaker, 16:302; author, 20:344, 28:184

Shelburne, Lord William, trade policies, 11:252, 254, 255, 19:297

Shelby, Gen. Joseph O. ("Jo"), Confederate officer, 34:305, 40:283
Shelby automobile, 26:23
Shelby County, Mo., Norwegian settlement, 12:181
Shelbyville, Blue Earth County, stage line, 12:51n; in Sioux Outbreak, 15:484; beginnings, 25:211
Shelbyville Rifle Co., volunteer unit, 16:173n
Sheldon, Addison E., work reviewed, 19:81-83; author, 12:440
Sheldon, Rev. Charles B., 19:268
Sheldon, Jackson, career, 13:441
Sheldon, Lynn, county agent, 19:31
Sheldon, T. B., and Co., papers, 23:40, 24:61
Sheldon, Theodore B., papers, 24:34; businessman, 33:235
Sheldon, Mrs. Theodore B., pioneer motorist, 26:25
Sheldon Township, Houston County, Norwegian settlement, 12:268; ghost town, 35:12
Shell, Daniel, stage driver, 20:465
Shell Drake River, Mich., 23:147, 148, 234
Shell Oil Co., history, 36:27
Shell Rock (village and township), Freeborn County, settled, 12:269, 17:486; county seat fight, 15:346, 20:357
Shell Rock River, Minn., Iowa, dam, 23:106
Shelley, Capt. E. Y., 33:278
Shelley, Edward, farm, 21:111
Shelley, Fred, author, 34:212
Shelly (village and township), Norman County, history, 14:357, 28:383
Shelp, Mahlon H., publisher, 35:378
Shenandoah Valley, campaign, 25:17
Shenehon, F. C., 19:184n
Shepard, David C., papers, 26:371, 27:23, 34:339; grain dealer, 39:210
Shepard, Eugene S., biography, 21:429
Shepard, Irwin, educator, 35:98, 371
Shepard, Mrs. Mary N., author, 11:337
Shepard, Sgt. Myron, Union soldier, 25:227
Shepard, Roger B., promotes aviation, 33:242
Shepard, Rev. W. C., itinerant preacher, 19:122
Shephard, Esther, author, 21:57, 33:265, 36:77
Shepley, Lt. James H., Union officer, 25:17, 343
Shepley, Louis E., contractor, 24:375
Sheply, E. R., lawsuit, 18:133-136
Sheppard, ---, chief mate, 16:420
Sheppard, George, editor, 28:78; emigrant agent, 31:228, 230
Sheppard, Henry L., 18:131
Sheppard, L. W., 18:126, 137
Sheppard, M. B., 17:236
Sheppe, Walter, work reviewed, 38:380
Shepperson, W. S., work reviewed, 35:374
Shera, Jesse H., reviews by, 31:179, 32:248, 33:260, 34:118, 252, 35:144, 285, 36:231, 38:90, 39:295; author, 31:192, 32:256
Sherbrook, Calvin G., 25:141
Sherburn (city and township), creamery, 13:216; pageant, 19:470; history, 35:156

Sherburne, Moses, attorney, 39:272
Sherburne County, anniversary, 12:448; churches, 15:129; land deeds, 15:464; ethnic settlements, 17:364, 20:243; census, 20:258n; map, 31:62; medicine, 37:348; established, 40:334n
Sherburne County Farm Bureau, 12:448
Sherburne County Historical Society, museum, 12:37; meetings, 12:106, 30:279; organized, 30:169
Sherburne County War History Committee, 24:82
Sheridan, Charles M., author, 13:334
Sherman, C. A., author, 11:464
Sherman, Clyde G., Indian agent, 37:279
Sherman, E. A., papers, 26:68
Sherman, H. F., colonizer, 31:30
Sherman, John, Congressman, 14:183; opposes Minnesota's statehood, 14:164, 177, 179, 180
Sherman, John J., Civil War reminiscences, 20:81
Sherman, John K., "The Birth of a Symphony Orchestra," 33:93-104; review by, 33:135; works reviewed, 33:222, 36:147; author, 18:330, 28:86, 30:406; quoted, 39:54, 60
Sherman, Merle, author, 38:335
Sherman, Milton, editor, 40:47
Sherman, Gen. William T., 34:263; letter, 12:429; Civil War career, 17:466, 25:241, 29:124, 35:317, 38:260, 271-273, 287, 288, 39:179, 185, 40:123; inspects Fort Snelling, 27:317; in settlement of the West, 35:291; quoted, 40:286
Sherman, Zeruah, teacher, 13:393
Sherman, Rock County, history, 20:104
Sherman Antitrust Act, 18:424, 33:133
Sherman Township, Redwood County, history, 17:240
Sherping, Dr. O. T., 18:228
Sherry, Laura, poet, 14:227
Sherwin, Gracia, letter, 36:196
Sherwin, Sterling, editor, 26:379
Sherwood, Thomas R., 18:145n
Sheshepaskut, Chippewa leader, 11:209
Shetrone, Henry C., work reviewed, 12:75
Shevlin, Thomas H., pioneer motorist, 26:27
Shevlin, Mrs. Thomas, 31:75
Shevlin, pioneer life, 16:247
Shevlin-Carpenter Co., Minneapolis, log marks, 26:136; lumber interests, 29:147, 148
Shevlin Hall, University of Minnesota, 17:226
Shevlin-Mathieu Lumber Co., Minneapolis, log mark, 26:128
Sheyenne River, N.D., trading post, 11:380; Norwegian settlements, 20:337; buffalo hunt, 26:76; camp, 38:5, 7
Shideler, James H., author, 36:103
Shields, Capt. Charles, 14:441
Shields, Gen. James, 13:207, 14:441, 20:269, 36:4n; career, 11:214, 13:213, 17:114, 20:458, 21:191; land speculator, 11:274; milling interests, 11:275; land officer, 12:389; colonizer, 14:110, 31:23; Senator, 14:163, 164, 190, 191, 28:74; pictured, 19:467, 28:84; letters, 24:166; Union officer,

25:36, 37; railroad president, 35:113; author, 35:335
Shields, James M., politician, 34:192
Shields, Father Thomas E., career, 17:115
Shields Guards, St. Paul, 16:169
Shieldsville, Rice County, Irish colony, 20:458, 31:23; Catholic church, 22:348
Shiels, railroad station, 34:184
Shiely, Michael, 27:177
Shifferes, Justus G., author, 12:204
Shigley, ---, frontiersman, 35:85
Shilloch, John, speculator, 39:90
Shiloh, Tenn., battle, 25:120n, 38:265
Shimer, F. W., author, 14:235
Shimer, Ruth, 13:448, 14:235, 456, 16:242
Shindler, A. Z., photographer, 38:93 (cover)
Shingledecker, Simon, farmer, 40:235
Shipley, Nan, author, 35:295
Shippee, Elizabeth, 16:330, 17:55, 62, 26:321
Shippee, Lester B., 11:54, 12:32, 13:65, 14:79, 16:60, 349, 17:70, 20:428, 21:410, 23:38, 50, 32:6; reviews by, 11:428-430, 12:172-174, 14:200-202, 15:94-98, 328-330, 16:202-205, 17:452, 18:423-428, 24:234; works reviewed, 19:73-76, 20:319-321; author, 11:328, 12:442, 14:349, 15:127, 358, 16:114, 115, 17:114, 115, 226, 459, 477, 18:218, 440, 19:102, 20:51, 21:423, 23:8, 24:245; speaker, 15:228, 359, 16:62, 212, 23:267; editor, 15:355, 19:58; MHS president, 23:5, 167, 24:57, 25:49, 51, 79, 26:40, 30:330; death, 25:73
Ships, west coast, 15:307; packet, 30:187; clipper, 30:187. See also Emigrant ships, individual ships
Shipstead, Henrik, speaker, 13:83, 450, 14:449; letters, 17:100, 160n; career, 22:80; Senator, 24:374, 31:124, 207, 38:177, 40:368; politician, 32:247, 36:103; isolationist, 40:366, 369; quoted, 40:367, 371; depicted, 40:370
Shiras, George, III, author, 18:451
Shirley, H. L., 16:241, 362, 18:112, 19:120; author, 11:120, 226
Shisler, Mrs. Iliff, 29:273
Shoal Lake, Man., trading post, 11:363, 22:289, 24:320n
Shoankah Shahpah, Sioux Indian, 17:439
Shober, John H., papers, 35:52
Shoemaker, Floyd C., 17:332; editor, 12:330; author, 30:73
Shoen, Scott, author, 37:264
Sholes, C. Latham, inventor, 16:445, 25:198, 30:263
Shonkasha, Sioux leader, see White Dog
Shonkwiler, William F., compiler, 32:189
Shook, ---, steamboat captain, 33:12
Shoolman, Regina L., translator, 17:204
Shooter from the Pine Tree, see Wazikute
Shore, John, 20:456
Shore, Robert, 16:491

Shoreham Flats, Minneapolis, wild-
    life, 30:228
Short, C. M., author, 27:70
Short, Capt. Jerome E., reminis-
    cences, 14:224; career, 16:345
Short, John, mail carrier, 40:80, 81
Short, Lloyd M., works reviewed, 23:
    265, 34:308
Short, Thomas, pioneer printer, 15:6
Short Cut Trail, Silver Lake, McLeod
    County, 15:42
Short Line Park, St. Louis County,
    post office, 34:186
Shoshone Indians, 40:201
Shotley Township, Beltrami County,
    history, 15:110
Shotwell, Daniel, 19:124
Shotwell, James T., 18:427, 22:71,
    23:201, 26:363
Shove, Raymond H., compiler, 36:194
Shover, John L., work reviewed, 40:91
Showboats, see Theater
Shreve, Henry, influence on steam-
    boating, 23:183, 25:88
Shriners, papers, 12:193
Shriners Hospitals for Crippled
    Children, history, 37:187
Shrive, F. N., author, 36:325
Shrode family, genealogy, 27:58
Shryock, Richard, quoted, 26:144
Shuck, A. M., author, 22:345
Shugg, Mrs. Roger, see Clapesattle,
    Helen
Shull, George H., agronomist, 31:55
Shulman, Max, author, 31:129, 191
Shultz, Earle, author, 37:38
Shuman, Jesse W., "The Levels of Lake
    Traverse," 17:302-310; author, 17:
    331
Shumard, Benjamin, geologist, 26:225,
    226, 232, 233
Shumway, Royal B., author, 18:105
Shurick, E. P. J., author, 28:184
Shurtleff, Malcolm C., author, 13:102
Shutter, Rev. Marion D., author, 26:
    302, 304
Siberts, Bruce, work reviewed, 34:124
Sibiwisse, Lake County, name, 34:180
Sibley, Alexander, mining interests,
    35:153
Sibley, Alfred B., letter, 15:459
Sibley, Billings P., drummer boy, 38:
    43
Sibley, C. C., 11:304
Sibley, Catherine W. (Mrs. Charles C.
    Trowbridge), 23:132
Sibley, Fred, letter, 36:268
Sibley, Henry H., 31:199, 36:55, 40:
    229; "Buffalo and Elk Hunt," 15:
    385-394; "Game in the West," 18:
    416-419; work reviewed, 14:195-
    197; papers, 11:96, 13:196, 223,
    15:61, 464, 16:97, 332, 18:317,
    439, 20:79, 82, 25:183, 26:32, 27:
    130, 29:283, 30:90, 34:360, 35:
    246, 36:195; speaker, 11:157, 12:
    392, 22:254, 23:324, 25:114n, 30:
    194, 34:99n; territorial delegate,
    11:161, 390, 14:128, 129, 15:284,
    16:215, 17:317, 20:131, 21:230,
    28:316, 29:367, 30:195, 196, 31:
    149, 35:105, 107, 337, 352, 359,
    360, 38:10; trader, 11:180, 376,
    12:236, 13:224, 229, 230n, 231,
    16:24, 73, 18:193, 19:95, 192, 20:
    122, 123, 261, 335, 22:4, 191,
    205, 278, 27:63, 31:57, 172-178,

36:262-264, 39:315, 40:23-26, 28-
    31, 81, 262; quoted, 11:317, 30:
    126, 38:354, 40:80; autobiography,
    12:127n; military activities, 12:
    297, 298, 13:421, 14:168, 19:389n,
    28:327, 35:235, 38:66, 276, 279,
    285, 39:83, 234; church elder, 12:
    397; career, 12:426, 13:453, 15:
    358, 479, 17:114, 20:343, 21:99,
    220, 26:303, 31:41, 32:63, 33:3,
    36:260, 39:316; governor, 13:95,
    14:246-249, 16:172, 28:183, 323,
    33:127, 40:148; business inter-
    ests, 13:234, 235, 14:345, 16:73,
    21:28, 163, 22:420, 26:226, 29:
    171, 35:110, 36:70, 37:191, 316,
    39:329, 330; depicted, 13:416, 29:
    84, 36:269, 38:100, 40:27; poli-
    tician, 14:132, 22:235, 36:9, 169,
    259, 261, 265-271, 278, 37:46, 47,
    50, 51, 329, 39:41-43, 47, 147-
    150; sportsman, 14:421, 16:260,
    17:151, 152, 33:153; St. Paul
    houses, 15:55, 25:6, 34:101n; cen-
    tennial, 15:241, 309, 352, 359,
    457-459, 490, 16:48; family, 15:
    382, 35:154; author, 15:383-385,
    16:188, 18:163, 20:259, 260, 27:6,
    30:129, 372, 32:114, 33:139, 34:
    174, 35:331, 37:186; social life,
    15:415, 18:155, 19:414, 20:214,
    28:311, 317, 30:197, 31:237, 35:
    356, 39:39; characterized, 15:458,
    20:132, 27:164, 31:151, 221, 39:
    272; library, 16:31, 22:358; con-
    servationist, 18:415; baseball of-
    ficial, 19:170, 172, 174, 339; in-
    terest in education, 19:446; MHS
    founder, 20:367, 368, 427, 23:5,
    30:296, 345; marriage, 24:182, 38:
    100n; in fiction, 27:328; treaty
    negotiator, 32:65-80; designs
    state seal, 33:128; autograph col-
    lector, 33:299; legislator, 35:
    170; Indian commissioner, 35:175,
    176; campaign letters, 38:99-114.
    See also Sibley expeditions, Sib-
    ley House
Sibley, Mrs. Henry H. (Sarah Jane
    Steele), 15:459, 20:131, 28:311,
    31:173; marriage, 24:182, 38:100n;
    portrait, 38:103
Sibley, Maj. Henry H., inventor, 15:
    272
Sibley, Hiram, lumberman, 30:243
Sibley, Marjorie H., review by, 33:
    42; author, 33:42n
Sibley, Mulford Q., work reviewed,
    37:83; editor, 33:312
Sibley, Solomon, 35:154; westward mi-
    gration, 15:383; papers, 15:462;
    judge, 23:132
Sibley, Mrs. Solomon (Sarah W.
    Sproat), 15:383
Sibley, William, trader, 40:192
Sibley family, westward movement, 15:
    382; genealogy, 29:189, 35:154
Sibley County, history, 12:201, 13:
    122, 30:279, 34:219; ethnic set-
    tlements, 12:275, 14:360, 21:98,
    22:335, 28:31, 32; archives, 15:
    195; pioneer life, 17:335; agri-
    culture, 18:408; name, 20:368;
    grasshopper plague, 36:57, 61, 37:
    205, 207; in Sioux Outbreak, 38:
    281, 284
Sibley County Historical Society, or-

ganized, 22:107; appropriation,
    22:218, 25:299, 29:366; quarters,
    22:341; meetings, 23:104, 25:99,
    27:173, 29:276, 30:83; museum, 30:
    279, 35:99
Sibley County War History Committee,
    24:82
"Sibley Crossing," N.D., Sheyenne
    River, 28:80
Sibley expeditions, 12:191, 446, 18:
    104, 20:330, 36:234, 239, 38:116,
    137, 140-143; 1863, 11:330, 12:
    200, 17:336, 18:209, 20:191, 201,
    328, 22:86, 26:259, 34:131, 38:
    280, 281, 283, 39:36; 1862, 23:
    170, 272, 38:97, 148, 149, 274,
    39:183
Sibley House, Mendota, 15:467, 25:9,
    28:377, 29:206n, 30:195, 406, 36:
    95, 260; depicted, 14:110, 15:45,
    25:8, 33:208; built, 15:51; owner-
    ship, 15:195, 20:343, 37:61; mu-
    seum, 15:229, 313, 31:221n; de-
    scribed, 15:483, 19:235, 20:323,
    30:270, 34:314, 35:28, 36:239;
    history, 16:192; anniversary, 16:
    233, 487; school, 17:84; guides,
    20:342; restored, 22:231, 32:107,
    36:186
Sibley State Park, Kandiyohi County,
    exhibits, 15:76, 21:49, 105, 106,
    26:50; geology, 17:125
Sibley Street, St. Paul, name, 20:368
Sibley Tea House, Mendota, 19:235,
    20:343
Sibley Township, Sibley County, Nor-
    wegian settlement, 12:275
Sicard, Ray L., author, 12:107, 24:
    262
Sicilians, Mesabi Range, 27:211
Sickels, Alice L., work reviewed, 27:
    38-40; author, 22:202, 25:385, 26:
    398, 27:280, 31:14; receives
    grant, 24:371; speaker, 25:397
Sickles, Gen. Daniel E., Union offi-
    cer, 25:246, 29:345, 38:251
Sidle Block, Minneapolis, 23:225
Sidney-Deadwood Trail, Neb., S.D.,
    maps, 12:93
Sidons, C., pseud., see Postl, Karl
Sieber, George W., author, 39:211
Siebert, Fred S., author, 40:48
Siebert, George, Sr., musician, 23:
    310, 403
Siefert, Mrs. Julius, speaker, 12:208
Sielaff, Richard O., author, 35:294
Siems, Peter, 26:371
Sievers, Ferdinand, missionary, 12:
    333, 457, 14:52, 55, 28:291, 35:98
Sieverts, Mrs. Helmut J., 33:112n
Sigbjørnsen, Torsten, Mormon mission-
    ary, 36:287
Sigel, Gen. Franz, Union officer, 25:
    226, 234, 238, 246
Sigerist, Dr. Henry E., author, 16:
    118
Sikes, George W., editor, 39:333
Sikes, Nancy, see Nichols, Mrs. Henry
    M.
Silfvesten, Carl J., author, 12:436,
    13:108; speaker, 13:121, 14:238
Sill, Dr. Charles, 21:112
Silliman, ---, scientist, 40:226
Silliman, Arthur, author, 14:462
Silliman, Benjamin, diary, 29:170;
    excursionist, 15:406, 411, 413,
    20:384, 34:137, 140

Silliman, Mrs. Benjamin, excursion-
ist, 34:137, 140
Silliman, Mrs. S. V., speaker, 26:285
Silliman, Sage V. S., author, 27:173
Silliman, Sue I., author, 13:110
Silsbee, Henry, 24:104
Siltman, Minnie, teacher, 22:350
Silver, trade items, 22:93, 204, 24:
77, 33:351, 40:200, 201; demone-
tized, 36:111; free, 36:119, 123,
124; lost mines, 40:307
Silver Bay, taconite plant, 34:269-
283, 35:245, 36:35, 39:163; de-
picted, 36:282; scuba diving, 38:
24, 26
Silver Creek Cliff, Lake County, Lake
Superior, 12:286
"Silver Crescent," steamboat, 37:296
Silver Island Lake, Lake County,
trail, 34:178
Silver Islet, Ont., mine, 35:153, 37:
86
Silver Lake, Hennepin County, 16:129
Silver Lake (village), McLeod County, pioneer store, 11:220; ethnic
settlements, 15:30-42, 342, 21:
452, 23:297, 29:358, 31:28, 29;
schools, 15:36-38; highway, 15:43
Silver Lake, Martin County, Christmas
celebration, 16:381
Silver Lake, Ramsey County, Henry A.
Castle residence, 16:364
Silver Lake (McLeod County) Leader,
15:41
Silver Lake Milling Co., McLeod Coun-
ty, 15:41
Silver mining, Lake Superior region,
34:179, 35:153, 37:86
Silver Republican party, 15:337, 16:
459, 17:162; fusion with Populists and Democrats, 35:62, 63,
36:125; 1896 platform, 35:291
Silver Ridge, Hennepin County, his-
tory, 16:129
Silver Shirts, political group, 27:
331
Silver Springs, Dane County, Wis.,
dairy farm, 19:150, 151
Silver Star, Aitkin County, veterans'
colony, 39:243-245, 247, 248
Silverson, Charles, miller, 16:127
Silverson, William, miller, 16:127
Silvestro, Clement M., compiler, 37:
37; author, 38:240; editor, 39:209
Silvis, Capt. William L., diary, 23:
75
Simak, Clifford D., author, 27:71
Simard, Dunoid, 23:374
Simcoe, John G., 19:304
Sime, H. P., 18:335
Simek family, pioneers, 13:216
Simirenko, Alex, work reviewed, 39:
168
Simmons, Carroll B., 36:196, 37:67,
189, 190n, 203; speaker, 36:107,
108
Simmons, Frank A., 12:319
Simmons, Hezekiah, 20:335
Simmons, T. K., immigration agent,
12:256
Simmons, Walter, author, 37:38
Simmons, Rev. William, 11:220
Simms, J. E., author, 15:354
Simms, William G., 26:215
Simon, Donald J., "The Third Minneso-
ta Regiment," 40:281-292

Simon, Sir John, 21:367; author, 21:
365
Simon, Louis A., author, 25:391
Simon, Menno, Mennonite leader, 20:
181-183
Simonds, C., lumberman, 24:201
Simonet, Genevieve, author, 25:284
Simons, Mrs. John, 19:115, 21:107
Simons, Luman G., 18:315
Simons, Orlando, 16:488, 39:148n;
speaker, 11:116; portrait, 11:448
Simons, T. W., speaker, 22:439
Simonsen, Anker M., author, 29:271,
39:130
Simonsen, S. J., author, 31:147
Simonson, N. A., 21:447
Simonson, Rev. S. C., speaker, 16:130
Simonton, Dr. ---, at Nininger, 13:
132
Simonton, Joseph, publisher, 30:275
Simpson, Bishop ---, speaker, 11:157
Simpson, Alexander, 20:70
Simpson, Dr. Charles, 39:112n, 113
Simpson, Lady Frances, 11:361, 22:
273, 24:284n; diary, 34:132, 40:
359
Simpson, Sir George, 32:250, 35:282,
38:42; Hudson's Bay Co. official,
11:361, 364, 17:445, 18:83, 19:
353, 21:251n, 22:273, 24:284n, 31:
240, 35:202, 36:247-249, 316;
diary, 19:455, 20:69-72; biography, 27:131; characterized, 21:
398, 22:309, 26:55, 27:37, 29:247,
34:132, 35:141, 259; author, 22:
154, 155n, 23:255; quoted, 22:277,
35:154, 36:45n, 36:246; portrait,
26:385; travels, 29:339-341, 32:
59, 35:35, 36:47, 37:134, 40:359;
career, 35:243; pictured, 36:244
Simpson, Howard E., author, 12:437
Simpson, Capt. James H., engineer,
16:282, 283, 17:115, 317, 40:233,
235, 237-239, 241, 245; portrait,
40:246
Simpson, "Sockless" Jerry, 26:357;
agrarian leader, 35:284, 291
Simpson, Thomas, 29:248; Arctic explorer, 18:81, 19:462; death, 20:
71
Simpson, Thomas, banker, 18:360,
361n; quoted, 33:192
Simpson Logging Co., Shelton, Wash.,
27:165
Sims, P. K., author, 39:132
Sinclair, Daniel, pioneer journalist,
23:111, 25:203
Sinclair, Harold, author, 23:117, 158
Sinclair, Henry, explorer, 33:216
Sinclair, James, smuggler, 22:281;
career, 38:326
Sinclair, Capt. Patrick, 19:296
Sinclair, Upton, letter, 18:314
Sinclair, W., trader, 40:167n
Sinclair, William, chief factor, 38:
327
Singley, Grover, "Retracing the Mili-
tary Road," 40:233-247
Singmaster, Elsie, author, 26:308
Singstad, Ole, engineer, 29:157
Sinnissippi Valley, history, 24:76
Sinnott, Archbishop Alfred, 12:96
Sino-Japanese War, 40:369, 370, 372
Sioux-Chippewa boundary, 24:165; es-
tablished, 23:85
Sioux-Chippewa warfare, see Chippewa-
Sioux warfare

Sioux City, Iowa, history, 14:226;
meat-packing industry, 16:228;
ethnic groups, 26:273, 28:128;
panorama, 27:255
Sioux City and St. Paul Railroad, 16:
247, 268, 33:143, 148; connection,
37:90
Sioux City Railroad, see Sioux City
and St. Paul Railroad
Sioux Claims Commission, 39:229
Sioux County, Iowa, Dutch settlement,
28:128
Sioux County, N.D., place names, 36:
325
Sioux Falls, S.D., newspaper, 15:200,
475; power plant, 35:381; diocese,
39:299
Sioux Historic Trail, Minnesota Valley to Pembina, 17:480
Sioux (Dakota) Indians, agencies, 11:
136, 12:121, 27:97, 29:237, 35:23,
24; annuities, 11:137, 16:39, 19:
383, 23:76, 28:321, 29:122, 198,
37:225, 228, 38:94, 132n, 133n;
removals, 11:165, 12:121, 14:216,
18:209, 27:259, 29:173, 235, 34:
328, 36:176, 38:98, 122, 295, 353-
364, 39:227-240; Lac qui Parle
band, 11:178; hostilities, 11:299-
304, 431, 13:401, 18:240, 20:8,
260, 21:401, 24:324, 25:87, 28:
225, 228, 32:231, 233, 36:191, 38:
62, 95, 39:302; missions, 11:305,
15:211, 16:133-151, 303, 357, 17:
201, 18:197, 20:447, 21:15-32,
158-175, 272-283, 383, 24:72, 28:
133, 33:57, 34:123, 35:29, 38:385,
39:300; reservations, 11:323, 12:
121, 13:107, 16:358, 493, 21:333,
35:288, 37:348, 39:85-92, 261;
folklore, 11:324, 13:367-376, 15:
278, 23:282, 27:357, 30:219n, 31:
220, 32:126, 33:118, 35:143, 36:
18-23, 38:201, 39:129; culture,
11:443, 13:375, 15:278, 20:199,
22:334, 23:341, 25:329-341, 26:
378, 28:180, 181, 30:156, 34:255,
355; in War of 1812, 12:233, 19:
304, 36:67; Kaposia band, 12:234,
22:284, 32:71, 38:151; relations
with French, 12:354, 356, 19:282,
32:231, 36:15m; liquor problem,
12:396, 13:99; depicted, 13:409-
414, 18:156-158, 160, 19:134, 421,
20:134, 21:325, 22:58, 136, 26:
141, 30:208, 211, 31:150, 33:20,
34:159, 37:348, 38:93-98, 113,
149, 39:261, 40:364; dances, 13:
411, 16:43, 21:425, 22:143, 151,
23:287, 28:176; health conditions,
14:330, 16:147, 22:102; Canada,
14:337, 27:161, 33:183, 36:295;
name, 14:372, 15:465, 16:417;
source material, 14:435, 16:105,
332, 335, 18:209, 25:183, 33:131,
40:409; arts and crafts, 15:154,
19:218, 20:344, 23:181, 39:261;
Wisconsin, 15:471; burials, 16:15,
17:152, 22:30, 25:329, 33:118,
123, 38:163-165, 39:198, 200; history, 16:452, 21:161, 23:339, 28:
168, 34:128, 35:44, 339, 37:336,
40:42; religious practices, 16:
475, 22:135, 31:79n, 37:85; villages, 17:155, 290, 20:127, 21:
24n, 22:433, 23:341, 342, 30:294,
31:210, 211, 33:122, 35:29; inter-

tribal relations, 17:157, 27:358, 31:211-213, 215-217; in fiction, 17:439, 33:274-277, 35:288, 37:11, 12; education, 19:438, 35:138, 40:46; place names, 21:348, 28:374, 30:331; Iowa Territory, 21:425; lands, 23:213, 29:231, 233, 30:30, 210, 32:237, 238, 34:157, 158; Lake Calhoun band, 24:20, 21n; music, 24:71, 29:86, 32:124, 33:227, 312, 34:161, 39:315; characterized, 25:167, 27:42, 154, 29:202, 32:97, 35:335; councils, 28:311, 312, 29:318n, 30:214; dwellings, 30:121, 32:190, 33:123, 227, 38:132; artifacts, 30:403, 38:163; at Pipestone, 31:196, 198, 199, 203; agriculture, 35:28; in fur trade, 36:260, 263, 38:199; "winter count," 38:385. See also Chippewa-Sioux warfare; Dakota language; Mdewakanton, Oglala, Sisseton, Wahpekute, Teton, Wahpeton, and Yankton bands; Sioux treaties; Sioux Outbreak; various agencies
Sioux Land Commission, 35:289
Sioux language, see Dakota language
Sioux Outbreak, markers and sites, 11:29, 456, 12:297, 301, 342, 448, 20:449, 21:439, 23:192, 291, 25:407, 30:276, 31:62, 34:237, 35:156, 294, 37:59, 60, 38:154-156, 242, 40:232, 263; contemporary accounts, 11:92, 334, 12:97, 102, 14:310-312, 331, 15:114, 347, 371, 484, 488, 16:76, 365, 17:336, 18:210, 20:192, 330, 449, 21:212, 26:181, 29:364, 30:394, 31:184, 35:337, 36:239, 37:224, 38:126-149, 242, 243, 385, 39:73, 40:147; history, 11:191, 12:207, 309, 310, 420, 13:421, 443, 15:99, 479, 16:240, 454, 17:480, 21:201, 325, 27:161, 341, 28:285, 29:164, 34:358, 35:235, 36:234, 37:188, 255, 308, 335, 38:93-98, 204, 39:342; fighting methods, 11:299-304; Indian captives, 11:317, 15:399, 38:242; peace negotiation, 11:351; in fiction, 11:436, 12:331, 27:328, 31:131, 35:288, 39:208; white captives, 11:456, 12:133n, 446, 19:465, 38:92, 103n, 109, 127n, 128, 140n, 40:35; property claims, 11:462, 22:343; source material, 12:85, 317, 13:321, 322, 16:335, 470, 20:79, 25:183, 349n, 34:352; causes, 12:123n, 15:111, 19:84, 450, 20:276, 21:281, 28:375, 29:123, 34:358, 39:259; effects, 12:248, 261, 273, 16:254, 20:462, 21:237, 32:42, 34:131, 36:32, 37:262, 38:63-71, 219, 39:85, 86, 261; destruction, 12:274, 19:342, 20:104, 30:33, 35, 32:169, 36:283; battles, 12:297-301, 15:133, 17:337, 23:75, 25:383, 38:41, 39:197; casualties, 12:298, 18:361, 444, 33:191, 36:195; stockades, 12:301-303, 318, 342, 448, 15:28, 18:342, 35:156; execution of condemned prisoners, 14:453, 15:400, 21:201, 22:103, 425, 29:168, 283, 30:66, 67, 33:77-79, 299, 39:183; forts, 14:455, 22:298, 33:356, 35:339, 38:282; Chippewa participation, 15:114; panoramas, 15:221, 24:180,

30:14-23, 176, 180, 183, 31:248, 249, 36:240; refugees, 15:356, 18:315, 26:77, 34:233-238; depicted, 15:395, 26:95, 27:345, 28:327, 30:383, 38:62, 242; military units, 16:332, 17:207, 19:44, 25:250, 348, 38:274-287, 39:77; anniversaries, 18:460, 19:465, 21:439, 23:295, 399, 28:374, 38:242; soldier vote, 26:189, 196, 36:167, 168, 170; relief work, 27:248; political aspect, 37:329-332. See also Sibley expeditions, Wood Lake: battle
Sioux treaties, 38:132n, 133n; 1851, 11:161, 162, 12:121, 207, 15:284, 16:150, 20:82, 21:280, 22:134, 141, 294, 23:85, 26:66, 27:248, 28:315-317, 343n, 30:25, 162, 31:203, 32:34, 65-80, 211, 35:321, 37:271, 272, 38:10, 93, 123, 129, 39:47; 1858, 12:122, 31:204, 38:93, 96, 147, 39:85n; 1837, 15:305, 16:454, 18:161n, 215, 23:85, 32:76, 38:93; 1841, 16:332; 1863, 20:207; 1805, 23:213, 38:93; with Chippewa, 27:289; 1867, 35:168, 170; abrogated, 28:98, 152
Siqveland, Dr. I. E., pioneer motorist, 26:22
Sire, Joseph A., trader, 36:260, 263, 264
Sirjamaki, John, "The People of the Mesabi Range," 27:203-215; reviews by, 29:347, 32:184, 40:309; author, 27:247, 29:376, 32:192, 40:345n
Sissabagamah Lake, Aitkin County, 21:347, 348
Sisseton, S.D., founded, 23:383
Sisseton band, Sioux Indians, 13:204, 17:299, 32:235, 38:145; depicted, 11:178, 13:410, 413, 22:134, 136-138, 23:94, 35:176; lands, 22:143n, 38:129n; payments, 29:122n; at Traverse des Sioux, 32:69, 72, 75; education, 35:138; mission, 35:167-177; dwellings, 35:169. See also Sioux Indians
Sisseton (S.D.) Courier, historical edition, 23:383
Sisseton Reservation (Sioux), S.D., 16:363, 27:259, 35:167-177, 293; opened for white settlement, 23:383, 24:207
Sissons, Lynn, 15:240
Sisterhood of Bethany, founded, 18:263
Sisters of Charity, St. Boniface, 40:313
Sisters of Mercy, St. Paul, hospital, 30:207
Sisters of St. Joseph of Carondelet, schools, 17:84, 22:334, 32:61, 33:38, 35:138; on Minnesota frontier, 17:349, 30:1-13, 273; history, 33:37. See also College of St. Catherine, St. Joseph's Hospital
Sisters of St. Francis, Rochester, 22:405
Sisters of the Holy Child Jesus, Avoca, 35:137
Sitting Bull, Sioux leader, 27:97, 33:57, 35:289; death, 11:81, 324, 16:105, 21:425, 28:80; career, 13:95, 19:330, 34:345, 35:333; wars,

16:89, 226, 34:328; characterized, 28:169; flight to Canada, 35:34
Sitz, Mrs. Edward, 21:336
Siverts, Samuel A., bank official, 37:121
Sivesind, Raymond S., review by, 39:124; author, 30:270
Six Mile House, Stillwater road, hotel, 38:296
Sixteenth U.S. Infantry, 27:236
Sixteenth Maine Volunteer Infantry, 17:98
Sixth Independent Ohio Cavalry, 14:37
Sixth Minnesota Volunteer Infantry, 11:330, 20:209, 33:84, 38:291, 292, 39:234; in Sioux Outbreak, 25:383, 36:239, 38:99, 101, 103, 104n, 110n, 243, 280, 284; soldier vote, 26:205; in Civil War, 33:287
Sixth U.S. Infantry, 11:163, 24:5, 28:343, 36:14, 15n
Sixty-fifth U.S. Colored Infantry, in Civil War, 23:170
Sixty-seventh U.S. Colored Infantry, in Civil War, 23:170
Sizer, Theodore, author, 34:120
Sjöblom, Rev. P., 13:309
Sjogren, Oscar, 12:86
Sjoselius, George B., author, 26:81, 29:352
Sjostrand, John, postmaster, 36:215
Skadan, see Provençalle, Louis
Skandinaven (Chicago), Norwegian-language newspaper, 16:108
Skandinaven (New York), Swedish-language newspaper, 34:43
Skaro, Capt. Asgrim K., 39:184
Skating, in rural districts, 18:294; St. Paul, 29:88; Perch Lake, 40:384; Fort Snelling, 40:385
Skavlan, Einar, 20:402
Skelton, R. A., author, 39:342
Skiff, Smith, 14:305
Skiing, Pope County, 11:337, 20:213; clubs, 16:249, 33:187; Red Wing, 17:228, 21:422, 29:169, 36:91; equipment, 18:220; Minnesota, 36:195
Skijoring, Fort Snelling, 40:385
Skillings, David N., author, 29:89, 34:44
Skinnaway, Tom, Chippewa Indian, 22:109
Skinner, Constance L., review by, 13:87-92; author, 11:61, 12:201; editor, 19:80
Skinner, Col. George A., author, 12:436, 13:203
Skinner, George E., legislator, 39:131
Skinner, Dr. H. O., speaker, 16:115
Skinner, John S., author, 18:467n, 40:295
Skinner, Mrs. Miron W., 16:102, 26:53
Skinner, Roy, author, 26:398
Skinner Iron Foundry, Buffalo, N.Y., 39:142
Skins, defined, 40:210
Skjeberg Lutheran Church, Teien Township, Kittson County, 14:452
Sklar, Robert, author, 40:411
Skog, Frank A., 29:303, 304, 308
Skog, Louis, 17:235
Skoglund, Mrs. Victor, 21:335
Skogsbergh, E. August, portrait, 13:307

Skolla, Father Otto, missionary, 11: 306, 18:89, 33:185, 39:303n, 307–309

Skordalsvold, J. J., author, 13:315

Skovgard, H. D., 12:106

Skrefsrud, Lars O., missionary, 29: 297, 298

Skugrud, Kittel S., pioneer, 11:226

Skunk, in fur trade, 30:133, 40:217

Sky Top Conference, 1939, 29:71

Skyline Drive, Duluth, 19:313

Skyscraper, design developed, 19:458, 23:229, 230, 37:187

Slab Town, Anoka, 25:364

Slack, Hiram W., letters, 19:451, 20: 34

Slade, J. J., 17:160n

Slade, William, 25:109, 28:132, 138

Slater, Mrs. Florence C., speaker, 13:442, 16:488

Slater, George, settler, 40:339

Slattery, Charles L., 20:433; biographies, 15:129, 17:115

Slaughter, Dr. B. Franklin, army surgeon, 19:205; diary, 19:206

Slaughter, Mrs. B. Franklin (Linda W.), 19:205; author, 15:125, 19: 206

Slaughter, M. S., 21:67

Slaughter, Robert E., 37:224

Slave Lake (Great Slave Lake), N.W.T., 14:82, 84, 16:230

Slavery, relation to statehood, 14: 164, 167, 187; in literature, 16: 86, 30:193; history, 16:88, 33:81; Minnesota, 18:65, 443, 20:447, 25: 202, 32:18, 19; Bishop Whipple's appraisal, 19:74; in fur trade, 19:290; attitude of Lutheran church, 22:193; promotes sectionalism, 23:161, 24:307, 36:3; controversy in press, 24:310–317, 27: 5, 13–15, 33:180; Missouri, 25: 115; army policy, 28:17; political aspect, 28:25, 36:3, 174, 37:46, 54, 39:82, 40:223; expansion question, 30:110, 189, 191, 31:174, 37:45, 307, 40:223. See also Abolition movement; Scott, Dred

Slavs, see Yugoslavs, various Slavic groups

Slayton, sorghum mill, 17:238

Sleeper Opera House, Brainerd, 28:99

Sleepy Eye, first schoolhouse, 12: 100; diphtheria epidemic, 15:434–438; pioneer life, 16:246, 21:211; Catholic church, 20:218; name, 23: 400, 28:380, 30:332

Sleepy Eyes, Sioux leader, 20:266, 30:332; village, 11:173; career, 11:174n; depicted, 13:413; grave, 16:101, 23:400, 28:380; monument, 17:235; at treaty council, 32:74

Sleighs and sleighing, for travel, 11:145, 29:120, 40:387–390; recreational, 16:384, 18:294, 29:116, 40:385

"Sleipner," emigrant ship, 39:212

Slen, Theodor S., speaker, 16:130

Slensby, John, theater manager, 33: 176, 178

Slensby's Theater, see Pence Opera House

Sletto, Raymond F., 20:88

Slidell, John, Louisiana Senator, 37: 48

Sliney, Maurice, speaker, 20:214

Slingerland, Teems, 16:240

Slingerland, Ternis, 13:117

Slingerland, William H., homestead, 26:397

Sloan, Marion L., author, 18:208

Sloan, R., artist, 14:440, 15:62, 20: 59, 35:370

Sloan, William, letter, 16:216

Slocum, A. M., 22:437

Slocum, Charles H., publisher, 15:89, 26:203

Slocum, Frances, portrait, 29:336

Slocum, G. H., 11:218, 12:449, 13:117

Slogans, American, 23:379

Slogvik, Knut A., 12:181

Sloop's Cove, Man., depicted, 40:190

Slosson, W. E., artist, 18:212, 19:50

Slotte, O. E., farmer, 24:305

Slovaks, Minneapolis, 22:222, 23:68, 24:73; Wisconsin, 27:135; Michigan, 27:205; iron ranges, 27:207, 208, 210, 211, 215, 31:29; Morrison County, 29:358

Slovenes, almanacs, 15:446; background, 22:96; iron range, 22:180, 23:387, 25:186, 27:204, 207–209, 211–213, 28:384, 33:355, 40:341, 347; missions, 22:200, 25:194, 39: 303n, 304, 310; Wisconsin, 27:135; Michigan, 27:205; Minnesota, 30: 292

Slover, John, war prisoner, 33:346

Slude River, Que., map, 34:255

Småland, Sweden, agriculture, 16:457; emigration from, 17:398, 401, 40: 412

Small, Patrick, trader, 12:373

Smalley, Donald, editor, 33:90

Smalley, E. V., Publishing Co., St. Paul, 33:30

Smalley, Eugene V., 40:16; author, 17:115, 33:34; editor, 33:29–34

Smalley, George W., journalist, 34: 344

Smalley, Harvey, Jr., author, 16:250, 368

Smalley, Orange A., author, 36:70

Smalley, P. J., politician, 35:303, 36:124n

Smalley, Victor H., editor, 33:33, 34

Smalley's Magazine, see Northwest Magazine

Smallpox, among Indians, 14:216, 15: 110, 344, 478, 20:8, 21:164, 27: 351, 29:59, 30:30, 34:76n, 37:182, 274; Rochester, 20:225; epidemics, 20:226, 24:93, 33:261; prevention, 19:372, 21:361, 34:196, 35:126; in lumber camps, 24:265, 30:68, 34: 34; among immigrants, 38:74

Smallwood, Mrs. Blanche, 14:460

Smart, Burleigh, letters, 15:344

Smart, John F., author, 26:259, 30: 275

Smart, Murray, 17:234

Smart family, genealogy, 17:101

Smelser, Marshall, author, 33:311

Smertenko, Clara M., author, 13:210

Smiley, David L., work reviewed, 36: 150

Smiley, William, 25:27

Smit, J., 28:131

Smith, A. C., map maker, 40:125n

Smith, Albert, 24:114, 116–121, 124; characterized, 24:122

Smith, Albert W., author, 14:231

Smith, Alexander B., 12:159n

Smith, Alfred E., letter, 18:314

Smith, Alice E., 17:332; "Peter Rindisbacher," 20:173–175; reviews by, 13:418, 16:197–199, 22:313, 23:164, 26:147, 29:334; works reviewed, 26:148, 34:208, 40:308; author, 11:196, 15:355, 20:187, 22:205, 316, 23:170, 24:75, 25: 395, 26:154, 29:376, 30:159, 269, 35:147; editor, 28:1n

Smith, Mrs. Amanda, at Red Rock, 31: 89

Smith, Gen. Andrew J., Union officer, 39:189, 190

Smith, Arthur C., instructor, 39:246, 247

Smith, Ayscough, 27:84

Smith, B. M., pioneer, 24:288

Smith, Bradford, author, 29:261

Smith, Bruce, author, 18:342

Smith, C. A., educator, 33:309

Smith, C. F., expedition, 16:128

Smith, C. Henry, author, 24:365

Smith, C. R. F., author, 11:326

Smith, Cal P., publisher, 21:452

Smith, Caleb E., Indiana Congressman, 39:38

Smith, Carmen, 18:147

Smith, Caroline V., 16:363, 18:112; author, 16:352

Smith, Carric, student, 27:97

Smith, Mrs. Catherine G., pioneer, 13:196, 212, 34:174

Smith, Charles A., 19:424n

Smith, Charles A., lumberman, 29:147

Smith, Dr. Charles E., papers, 11:97; at cholera quarantine station, 14: 301

Smith, Charles H. F., 39:154n

Smith, Charles K., territorial secretary, 20:367, 30:109, 266, 345, 31:173, 35:182, 357, 39:39, 45; MHS founder, 20:367, 30:295; speaker, 30:298; Freemason, 33:310

Smith, Charles Wesley, compiler, 13: 207

Smith, Charles William, work reviewed, 17:76–78

Smith, Chauncey, letter, 20:173

Smith, Clarence T., author, 14:462

Smith, Maj. Clifton T., papers, 15: 466

Smith, D. D., National Guard member, 18:100

Smith, D. Y., publisher, 17:366

Smith, Dave, trader, 34:103

Smith, David, blacksmith, 23:320

Smith, Donald A., see Strathcona and Mount Royal, Lord

Smith, Donnal V., speaker, 13:105; author, 13:434

Smith, Dora V., author, 34:42

Smith, Dwight L., work reviewed, 38: 238

Smith, E. A. Cappelen, engineer, 29: 157

Smith, Lt. E. K., 20:123

Smith, E. P., Indian commissioner, 35:172

Smith, Gen. Edmund K., Confederate officer, 40:287

Smith, Edward E., biography, 13:333; legislator, 35:349, 350

Smith, Edward F., 20:98

Smith, Elizabeth, I, see Smith, Mrs. William

Smith, Elizabeth ("Bessie"), II,

student, 24:115, 118, 120, 124; letters, 24:121-123
Smith, Erle, 26:178
Smith, Ernest V., work reviewed, 24:347
Smith, Rev. Eugene K., diaries, 21:85
Smith, Mrs. Fannie B., author, 28:303
Smith, Francis M., politician, 34:192
Smith, Frank, 18:140
Smith, Frank, author, 14:339
Smith, Fred, farmer, 16:15
Smith, Fred L., pioneer journalist, 14:395
Smith, Frederick L., author, 33:188, 353
Smith, G. Hubert, 14:86, 17:197, 22:316, 23:47, 73; "The Winona Legend," 13:367-376; "Carver's Fortifications," 16:152-165; "Count Andreani," 19:34-42; "Excavating Old Fort Ridgely," 20:146-155; "The Archives of Military Posts," 22:297-301; "The Local Historical Society in Wartime," 23:16-19; "Minnesota Potteries," 33:229-235; reviews by, 18:104, 329, 19:88-90, 22:210, 23:85, 27:238, 336, 28:270-272, 29:66, 161, 337; archaeologist, 18:51, 19:54, 34:354; speaker, 18:66, 19:69; author, 19:345, 20:208, 27:341, 28:181, 285, 373, 29:263, 31:53, 36:151; museum curator, 27:140, 143, 28:394
Smith, Garnet, author, 26:90
Smith, George, author, 16:496
Smith, George, financier, 40:308
Smith, Rev. George, speaker, 22:439
Smith, Maj. George H., cattleman, 26:121
Smith, Corp. George L., Union soldier, death, 25:141
Smith, George M., railroad man, 28:303
Smith, George T., miller, 11:281
Smith, George W., letters, 21:193
Smith, Gerrit, reformer, 22:127, 28:371, 35:102
Smith, Glanville, review by, 29:253; author, 16:350, 18:330, 29:288, 31:62, 36:74; speaker, 29:181, 277, 30:83, 169, 279
Smith, Guy-Harold, author, 11:105, 12:328
Smith, H. E., banker, 37:124
Smith, Harrison, work reviewed, 33:221
Smith, Henry A., diaries, 24:354
Smith, Henry J., work reviewed, 17:324-326
Smith, Henry Ladd, work reviewed, 34:202; author, 25:195, 34:358
Smith, Henry Nash, work reviewed, 37:84; author, 28:174, 34:261, 35:330
Smith, Henry W., recollections, 13:208
Smith, Hilda, author, 12:430
Smith, Hiram, murdered, 32:98
Smith, Horace B., gunmaker, 36:68
Smith, Irwin F., 16:310
Smith, J. A., and Co., fur dealers, 34:326, 327
Smith, J. C., author, 27:100
Smith, J. George, pioneer motorist, 26:22; confectioner, 33:2
Smith, J. Harley, pioneer, 27:264, 265
Smith, J. L., author, 17:227

Smith, J. M., author, 11:109
Smith, J. T., 36:104, 195
Smith, James, Jr., legislator, 35:2, 37:333; investigator, 35:171, 172
Smith, Jedediah, 32:250, 40:152; explorer, 29:339, 34:219; mountain man, 38:199
Smith, Mrs. Jennie K., 26:3
Smith, Joe P., 11:97; work reviewed, 15:333-335; author, 15:123
Smith, John, Duluth pioneer, 21:116
Smith, John, Red River settler, 33:187
Smith, Capt. John, author, 16:105; founder of Virginia, 22:313
Smith, Judge John D., legislator, 12:457
Smith, John Rowson, panoramist, 17:115, 133, 148, 20:380, 32:188, 33:285, 287, 289, 35:379, 36:233
Smith, Jonathan, student, 24:113; farmer, 24:114-116, 118, 119, 122, 124
Smith, Joseph, Mormon leader, 13:281, 385, 15:307n, 17:150n, 429, 22:20, 31:115, 36:289; murdered, 17:430n, 32:98
Smith, Mrs. Joseph (Emma H.), 17:429, 430n
Smith, Joseph, the younger, 36:290
Smith, Justin, author, 31:147, 40:153
Smith, Katherine L., author, 18:108
Smith, Kendall, author, 34:42
Smith, Kirby, 25:150n
Smith, L. Herman, author, 19:216, 351
Smith, Rev. L. P., Methodist minister, 31:82n
Smith, Leathem D., author, 27:353
Smith, Lewis W., poet, 26:307
Smith, Lloyd L., Jr., author, 25:309
Smith, Louis B., storekeeper, 33:2
Smith, M. D., author, 19:235
Smith, Dr. M. W., 13:118, 27:171; speaker, 15:372
Smith, Mamie, pioneer teacher, 23:197
Smith, Margaret M., see Taylor, Mrs. Zachary
Smith, Mortimer, author, 23:88, 25:86
Smith, Morton W., author, 36:104
Smith, Mrs. Nora S., 19:111
Smith, O. E., speaker, 20:215
Smith, Mrs. Octavia, speaker, 29:178, 361
Smith, Orrin, steamboat captain, 12:159, 13:231, 234, 20:132, 22:226, 29:212, 31:149, 34:31; career, 11:225; memorial, 12:197
Smith, Orrin F., 12:158n, 159n, 197, 13:196, 212, 15:136, 19:221; author, 12:108, 427, 13:102, 18:230
Smith, Mrs. Pascal, 38:81
Smith, Patricia, "Oliver Hudson Kelley," 40:330-338
Smith, Peter, Astor partner, 28:371
Smith, Preserved, author, 11:450, 24:347
Smith, Rebecca, 15:281
Smith, Robert, Illinois Congressman, 27:317, 29:208
Smith, Rev. Robert, at Red Rock, 31:91
Smith, Robert A., businessman, 40:225
Smith, Rollin E., editor, 13:333
Smith, Russell, sheep raiser, 26:111
Smith, Samuel E., business executive, 22:104

Smith, Samuel G., steamboat captain, 22:94
Smith, Rev. Samuel G., portrait, 20:196
Smith, Seagrave, district attorney, 39:50
Smith, Seba, composer, 22:118
Smith, Sharon C., work reviewed, 36:29
Smith, Sidney, papers, 29:188
Smith, Maj. Simeon, Union officer, 38:258
Smith, Dr. Theobald, bacteriologist, 21:361
Smith, Mrs. Thomas, 14:235
Smith, Timothy L., work reviewed, 35:372; author, 40:48, 410
Smith, Truman, Connecticut Senator, 30:104, 109, 39:144
Smith, Truman, M., granger, 15:113; banker, 16:25, 19:48, 96
Smith, Villa B., author, 34:356
Smith, W. E., 14:456
Smith, W. L. G., author, 11:208
Smith, Dr. W. M., speaker, 11:114
Smith, Mrs. Walter F., author, 22:223
Smith, Mrs. Walter G., author, 30:392
Smith, Willard H., work reviewed, 33:267
Smith, William, fur trader, 28:144, 145, 148, 149, 155, 156, 158, 159
Smith, William, Illinois pioneer, 25:395; marriage, 24:111n; businessman, 24:113-117; letter, 24:120; illness, 24:121, 123; death, 24:124
Smith, Mrs. William (Elizabeth Stearns), papers, 24:57, 111, 113, 118, 121-124, 25:395; marriage, 24:111n; education, 26:78
Smith, William, Jr., businessman, 24:116
Smith, William ("Billy"), log driver, 27:201
Smith, William A., Union soldier, 13:445
Smith, William Calvert, Otter Tail County pioneer, 22:436
Smith, William E., Wisconsin governor, 19:150
Smith, William E., work reviewed, 15:330-332; author, 15:127
Smith, William F., Union officer, 25:36, 121, 122, 140, 246
Smith, Mrs. William I., 38:75
Smith, William R., author, 17:251n, 20:203
Smith and Griggs Manufacturing Co., Waterbury, Conn., 35:154
Smith, Jackson, and Sublette, fur-trading company, 40:152
Smith Mounds, Laurel, Koochiching County, 31:163, 231n, 37:61, 63, 39:262; excavated, 16:15-18, 31:168-171; described, 37:61
Smith Park, St. Paul, 12:458, 33:3
Smithson, Arthur, inventor, 21:109; boatbuilder, 26:398
Smithsonian Institution, Washington, D.C., 39:112-114, 40:339; publications, 15:277, 16:143, 30:298, 39:298; collections, 24:345, 27:254, 30:260, 33:131, 39:122; activities, 27:350; Minnesota material, 30:85, 173, 176; represented on Nobles expedition, 35:252, 253

Smithville, St. Louis County, post office, 34:186
Smokey, Mrs. Catherine, 14:232
Smol, Abel J., 28:129
Smolen, Joseph S., author, 40:362
Smurr, John W., author, 38:190
Smutka, Mrs. J. A., author, 20:102
Smyth, Mrs. Henry M., 38:81
Snake Indians, 32:249
Snake River, Kanabec and Pine counties, fur trade, 11:374, 15:92, 32:234; Chippewa village, 17:392; lumber industry, 18:166; name, 21:348, 28:150; bridges, 40:242
Snake River, Marshall County, trading post, 11:367; archaeological site, 38:165
Snana, Sioux woman, 12:446
Snarr, O. W., speaker, 25:100
Snell, Eleazer, 14:436
Snell, John L., work reviewed, 38:196
Snell, Silas, Hudson, Wis., pioneer, 21:430
Snell, Stephen D., 14:436
Snelling, Elizabeth R., grave, 18:400, 20:342, 22:208, 30:212n
Snelling, Henry H., work reviewed, 21:78; photographer, 17:114, 21:95; author, 17:464, 18:48, 20:56, 21:81
Snelling, James G. S., career, 22:349
Snelling, Col. Josiah, 22:321, 23:274, 25:272, 30:211n; fort commandant, 11:190, 15:473, 22:287, 27:261, 33:263, 40:262; papers, 14:452, 18:439, 19:448, 39:251; family, 15:234, 16:344, 17:114, 450, 469, 18:48, 400, 405, 406, 20:56, 342, 21:79, 95, 316, 22:208, 321, 23:41, 26:212, 30:212, 267; career, 17:114, 28:377, 35:197, 36:67, 37:302; diary, 18:399-406, 20:34; portrait, 21:316, 22:42, 208; in fiction, 22:205; builder, 23:213, 24:126; author, 35:376. See also Fort Snelling
Snelling, Mrs. Josiah, 18:405, 21:79, 30:212n; portrait, 21:316, 22:42, 208; biographical sketch, 30:267
Snelling, Mary, death, 18:406
Snelling, William J., 17:210, 20:78; "The Last of the Iron Hearts," 26:215-221; work reviewed, 17:450-452; author, 13:369, 15:234, 16:344, 19:437, 25:165, 26:213-215, 27:63, 30:373, 31:130, 36:74, 76, 77; career, 15:233, 17:437-443, 26:211-213; biography, 17:114; critic, 19:104
Snider, C. H. J., author, 35:153
Snider, Lizzie, see Eggleston, Mrs. Edward
Snively, Samuel F., speaker, 12:282
Snodgrass Hill, Ga., see Chickamauga
Snow, Chauncy H., surveyor, 19:425, 426
Snustad, Jacob, 16:492, 19:362, 22:341
Snustad, O. N., author, 14:358
Snyder, Alice L., author, 13:437
Snyder, C. L., plow manufacturer, 24:297
Snyder, Rev. Charles E., author, 20:89
Snyder, Fred B., 14:219, 333; university regent, 13:211, 29:172; au-

thor, 25:306; speaker, 29:179, 276, 372; career, 31:125
Snyder, Frederic B., legislator, 35:344, 349
Snyder, Fremont, speaker, 13:342; singer, 27:181
Snyder, Margaret, 24:370; "Chatfield," 24:95-110; review by, 30:138; work reviewed, 30:52; author, 14:333, 23:401, 24:89, 163, 191, 383, 26:150, 30:184, 33:353
Snyder, Martin P., author, 33:356
Snyder, Simon P., pioneer, 31:125
Snyder, Van Vechten and Co., Chicago, publishers, 40:128
Sobieski Building and Loan Association, Duluth, 37:123
Soby, Elizabeth, 28:268
Social Credit party, Canada, 29:341
Social life, 28:288; ethnic groups, 11:286, 12:398, 15:38-40, 16:319, 19:222, 20:86, 202, 22:399, 401-403, 25:300, 322, 323, 27:257, 32:46, 121, 36:201-203; church-centered, 11:286, 28:320; frontier travel, 11:309, 21:210, 23:60, 37:85; juvenile games, 12:149, 35:296, 37:345; organizations, 12:400, 13:146, 16:317, 17:87, 20:144, 23:26, 24:214-225, 26:93, 27:126, 39:51; described, 12:401-403, 14:205, 28:315, 29:117-121, 126-129, 284, 32:195-201, 33:1-6; recreation, 13:283, 14:140, 15:135, 17:362, 20:441, 27:94, 28:186, 34:7, 8; parties, 15:401, 26:273, 27:9, 28:313, 317, 320; on river boats, 15:412-418, 37:345; Fort Garry, Man., 16:480; rural, 18:293, 19:203-205, 461, 20:418, 28:190, 33:347; frontier, 19:210, 218, 22:110, 330, 415, 23:92, 24:261, 30:259, 32:49, 52, 54, 33:195-200; family, 27:79, 90, 32:152-154, 37:199, 200; publications, 30:193, 200, 406. See also Pioneer life and conditions, Sports, individual holidays
Social Science Research Council, committees, 11:93, 12:31, 18:91, 39:34; publications, 13:184, 26:60; projects, 15:229, 18:442, 19:159, 21:49, 82; grants, 25:204, 28:20n
Social Security Act, passed, 18:449, 38:376; amended, 38:377
Social studies, source material, 13:184; teaching methods, 19:437-439
Social welfare, see Welfare
Social Welfare History Archives, University of Minnesota, 39:300
Socialism, New Ulm, 27:268; South Dakota, 29:77
Socialist Labor party, source material, 20:194
Socialist party, 39:299; platforms, 25:63, 35:291; Mesabi Range, 25:325, 40:342, 344, 347; North Dakota, 27:259, 35:247; influence, 33:157; antiwar stance, 35:368
Socialist Publishing Association, Minneapolis, 13:323
Socialistic Labor Union, 22:378
Society for American Archaeology, 21:82
Society for the Preservation of New England Antiques, 31:249
Society for the Propagation of the

Faith, 17:102, 21:74, 25:193, 30:3, 10, 13
Society for the Propagation of the Gospel, 35:47
Society for Visual Education, 26:164, 267
Society of American Archivists, meetings, 18:322, 20:76, 22:428, 24:70, 25:84, 26:74, 264, 27:49, 30:46; publications, 19:216, 26:255; projects, 20:198, 25:281, 296; organized, 20:294; award, 36:108
Society of Colonial Wars in the State of Minnesota, 20:59
Society of Friends, see Quakers
Society of Heaven People, Chippewa cult, 40:358
Society of Jesus, see Jesuits
Society of Mayflower Descendants, 18:320, 21:411
Society of the Cincinnati, history, 35:197
Sociology, rural, 12:90; relation to history, 33:205
Sod houses, see Houses
Soderberg, Nathaniel F., author, 12:184
Soderberg, Olga, 28:386, 30:78; speaker, 24:378, 28:385; author, 30:288, 34:217, 267
Söderblom, Archbishop Nathan, 16:458
Soderquist, Harold O., author, 18:105
Sohlberg, Anders G., 18:313
Sohlberg, Mrs. Anders G., 18:313
Sohon, Gustavus, artist, 23:183, 40:403
Sokols, Czech gymnastic societies, 15:40, 25:300, 36:91
Solberg, A. M., speaker, 12:210
Solberg, K. K., speaker, 21:447
Solberg, Winton U., 36:240; "Martha G. Ripley," 39:1-17
"Soldiers' Rest," Washington, D.C., 25:37, 227
"Soldiers' Retreat," Washington, D.C., 25:37, 227
Solem Norwegian Evangelical Church, Douglas County, 14:451
Solheim, Oswald J., work reviewed, 38:239
Solisti di Zagreb, chamber orchestra, 39:64
"Solitaire," pseud., see Robb, John S.
Solitaire Peak, Winona County, 32:212
Solomon, Barbara M., work reviewed, 35:326
Solomon, Ezekiel, trader, 19:78
Solomon Lake, Kandiyohi County, garrison, 38:286n
Solomons, ---, trader, 11:261
Solseth, Rev. O. E., Lutheran pastor, 13:116
Solstad, Alfred, author, 31:126
Soluce, John M., 39:154n
Solum, Nora A., 27:34; work reviewed, 20:179-181; author, 21:426
Solway, logging, 29:141, 33:356; platted, 29:145; newspaper, 29:356; anniversary, 30:160
Somerndike, John F., speaker, 16:354
Somers, F., St. Paul piano dealer, 39:319
Somers, John W., author, 17:367
Somerset, Wis., French-Canadian settlement, 27:135; history, 34:129, 35:152

Somerville, George W., author, 16:246
Sommer, Carl H., author, 36:195; banker, 40:411
Sommereisen, Father Valentine, career, 17:473
Sommers, Charles L., sponsors Boy Scouts, 37:43
Sommers, G., and Co. (B., and Co.), St. Paul, 40:249; wholesale catalogs, 24:35, 64, 34:106-113
Sommers, Mrs. Helen, speaker, 28:88, 29:277
Sommerville, S. J., author, 27:166
Somsen, Henry N., Sr., speaker, 20:351
"Song of Hiawatha," Longfellow poem, 15:261, 16:279, 280n, 351, 24:237, 27:288, 28:323, 31:193, 203, 32:107, 34:32, 35:153, 36:21, 23, 75
Sons of Hermann, Minnesota, 35:294, 36:200
Sons of Malta, St. Paul, 33:196
Sons of Norway, history, 26:269
Sons of Temperance, Minnesota, 14:138, 31:90
Sons of the American Revolution, Pennsylvania, 14:111; Minnesota, 16:74, 35:190; South Dakota, 18:210
Sons of Veterans' Auxiliary, Knute Nelson camp, 18:98
Soo Line, see Minneapolis, St. Paul and Sault Ste. Marie Railroad
Soo Line Trafficgram (Minneapolis), house organ, 31:62
Soper, Hugh H., author, 23:200
Soper, Mrs. Hugh H., 11:287
Sorbel, Dr. A. O., 11:466
Sorbo, Mrs. Erling, 37:224
Sorden, L. G., compiler, 35:335
Sorem, Mrs. Milton, author, 30:282, 31:58
Sorensen, Martin, author, 29:271
Sorensen, Nels, 16:9
Sorenson, Floyd, author, 15:348, 486
Sorenson, O. C. F., 18:467
Sorenson, P. C., 11:290
Sorghum, frontier manufacture, 17:212, 238, 20:80, 102, 26:66, 35:201
Sorlie, A. G., 28:43
Sornberger, John W., evangelist, 31:78, 34:60
Sorokin, Pitirim A., editor, 12:90
Soth, Lauren, work reviewed, 35:375
Soudan, Finnish settlement, 25:319; history, 30:409, 34:171; bus service, 35:338
Soudan Mine, 11:414; investors, 12:285; monument, 15:481; history, 18:332, 36:282, 40:412; ore shipment, 19:236; state park, 40:35
Souders, Rev. J. F., 15:485
Soule, Sidney, papers, 21:106
Soule, Rev. W. H., Methodist minister, 31:82n
Soulen, Harvey, author, 21:424, 25:398
Sousa, John Philip, band leader, 37:307
South, hunting, 14:422; Bishop Whipple's visit, 19:73-75; literature, 20:109, 110, 37:83; regionalism, 20:112; country stores, 25:392; nationalism, 32:15; culture, 34:81; agriculture, 34:291, 40:337;

Reconstruction Era, 36:174-176; politics, 37:45, 48, 50, 51, 54
South Africa, frontier history, 37:182
"South American," steamboat, 34:14
South Atlantic Quarterly, 20:112
South Baptist Church, Isanti, 16:355
South Bend, Blue Earth County, sawmill, 12:273; volunteer guards, 16:171; pioneer life, 20:450; business, 24:72; located, 37:227n; in Sioux Outbreak, 38:113, 125, 276, 277, 280
South Carolina, franchise, 12:9; early printing, 15:7; Quakers, 18:258; secession, 24:317; atlas, 40:120
South Creek Township, Martin County, see Pleasant Prairie
South Dakota, statehood, 11:324, 21:99; population, 13:435; textbooks, 13:438, 14:226, 24:369, 40:146; newspapers, 15:475, 23:373, 24:35, 35:383; map, 17:88; medicine, 17:220; Mennonites, 18:99; ethnic groups, 19:200, 222, 23:183, 40:44; history, 21:401, 37:304; public domain, 23:382; economy, 24:124, 34:265; place names, 24:178; capital, 26:270, 30:146; co-operatives, 26:381, 29:158; politics, 27:356, 30:61, 35:238; publications, 29:173; manufacturing, 34:312; sheep raising, 35:331; Indian missions, 35:380; dry farming, 36:28; described, 36:86-88; Catholic church, 36:325, 39:299; woman suffrage, 37:86; in literature, 37:306; Indian battles, 38:41; archives, 39:35; archaeology, 39:212, 40:47; railroads, 39:298; fur trade, 40:180; scout camps, 40:313. See also Dakota Territory
South Dakota Educational Association, 18:327
South Dakota Historical Society, Pierre, 21:416, 35:100; publications, 17:112, 35:383
South Dakota State College, Brookings, 25:300; history, 14:448
South Dakota State College of Agriculture, Brookings, 28:40
South Dakota State Medical Association, history, 12:204
South Elmdale Congregational Church, Holdingford, 29:358
South Fork, Houston Township, Houston County, settlement, 28:292
South Fork Grange, Kanabec County, organized, 22:110
South Holland, Ill., Dutch settlement, 28:368
South Immanuel Lutheran Church, Rothsay, history, 29:359
South Pass, Wyo., discovered, 16:175, 40:196; wagon road, 38:57, 217
"South Point," relief ship, 11:350
South St. Paul, Lutheran church, 14:104; livestock industry, 19:121, 26:182, 29:76, 91, 33:226; Romanian colony, 26:181; stock show, 28:377. See also Kaposia
South St. Paul Union Stockyards, 19:121, 26:182, 33:226
South Side Commercial Club, Minneapolis, 33:332

South Side High School, Minneapolis, newspaper, 28:90; athletics, 39:19
South Slavonic Catholic Union of America, 14:445
South Stillwater, see Bayport
South West Co., 12:91, 21:401; rivalry with Hudson's Bay Co., 12:82, 92, 20:17; organized, 19:301, 20:15, 40:181; ownership, 19:305, 20:16, 40:184; operations, 40:182
"Southampton," steamboat, 30:188
Southdale, Edina, shopping center, 36:283
Southern Minnesota Medical Association, 15:129
Southern Minnesota Railroad, 24:96, 35:338; colonization activities, 12:254; lands, 13:37; wheat contract, 24:100, 29:223
Southern Minnesota Stock Breeders' Association, 22:265, 26:124
Southern Minnesotan, established, 12:97
Southern Pacific Railroad, 30:237, 379
Southern Review, 20:113
Southerners, St. Cloud, 15:139, 28:384, 35:265
Southesk, Earl of, traveler, 37:134
Southey, Robert, poet, 33:311
Southwest, regionalism, 20:113; agriculture, 29:76; mustang herds, 33:225
Southwest Review, regional periodical, 20:113
Southwest Territory, established, 17:452
Southworth, Cornelia A., 12:409
Southworth, Henry, 23:391
Southworth, Dr. Newton, letters, 12:106; author, 17:364
Spada, Cardinal Fabrizio, 19:398
Spaeth, G. Howard, tax commissioner, 34:309
Spaeth, Louise, 29:95; speaker, 29:178; author, 29:369, 30:86
Spahr, Walter E., author, 11:450
Spain, American colonies, 11:77, 350, 428, 451, 13:92, 18:303, 394, 395, 20:439, 22:98, 23:85, 40:42; archives, 17:7; medals, 25:267, civil war, 40:371, 372. See also Spanish
Spalding, Henry H., missionary, 29:59
Spalding, Bishop John, colonizer, 13:418, 31:22, 35:209; career, 13:419; author, 15:235
Spalding, Kate C., 25:173
Spalding, Neb., Catholic colony, 35:135
Spangler, Mrs. Barney A., author, 27:69, 35:296
Spangler, Earl, work reviewed, 38:87; author, 36:108; compiler, 39:260
Spangler, Theodore, 16:341
Spangler, Mrs. Theodore, 16:341
Spanier, Mrs. Francisca L., author, 18:229
Spanish, relations with Indians, 11:80, 248; in fur trade, 11:252, 268, 383, 19:78, 292-296, 25:267, 38:190; explorations, 15:93, 24:53, 32:112, 33:302, 303, 40:205n; influence on American language, 17:320, 23:84; place names, 26:248; on iron range, 27:214; architecture, 32:109. See also Spain

Spanish-American War, 20:421; Minnesota in, 12:100, 192, 15:99, 16:372, 28:349, 35:319, 36:195; depicted, 14:440, 16:340; service newspapers, 16:103, 17:469, 26:157; veterans' organizations, 19:452; source material, 23:20, 24:247; nurses, 26:94; peace efforts, 29:79, 33:305
"Sparhawk," steamboat, 34:135
Sparkes, Boyden, 32:13
Sparks, Jared, author, 36:296, 297; letters, 38:200
Sparta, St. Louis County, mining town, 32:194
Sparta, Wis., road, 40:387
Sparta Township, Chippewa County, Norwegian settlement, 12:275n
"Spartan," steamboat, 34:14
Spatten, St. Louis County, post office, 34:186
Spaulding, E. Wilder, author, 14:341, 17:226, 25:305
Spaulding, George, missionary, 16:316
Spaulding, Kenneth A., work reviewed, 35:143
Spaulding, Oliver L., Jr., author, 16:239
Spaulding, Thomas M., author, 11:328, 17:114
Spavin, Don, author, 36:327
Spear, Allan H., author, 37:346
Spear, Blanche D., author, 16:370
Spear, Maj. C. Treat, 38:315, 318
Spear, Jacob, 26:154
Spear, Katherine B., author, 16:338, 17:362
Spearin, S. B., horse breeder, 26:120
Specht, Raymond E., author, 36:282
Special Libraries Association, 25:179, 36:326
Speer, Ray P., author, 39:300
Speerschneider, Ethel D., work reviewed, 30:247
Spence, Thomas H., Jr., author, 27:252
Spencer, Benjamin, alderman, 35:120
Spencer, David, missionary, 16:216, 19:382
Spencer, Mrs. David, missionary, 19:381
Spencer, George H., Jr., hotelkeeper, 11:181; clerk, 19:378, 38:135
Spencer, H. H., 18:343
Spencer, Henry R., quoted, 14:409
Spencer, John W., reminiscences, 24:77
Spencer, Dr. Kirby, house, 35:228; bequest, 35:229
Spencer, Laurens, 27:293n
Spencer, R. M., steamboat captain, 11:137, 140
Spencer, Robert, architect, 40:107
Spencer, Robert F., review by, 40:40; work reviewed, 40:47
Spencer, Mrs. Rose, house, 38:345
Spencer, Rose H., author, 16:132
Spencer, Steven M., author, 28:180
Spencer, Truman J., author, 35:378
Spencer, William A., 17:120, 18:222
Spencer, Mrs. William A., 29:121, 33:5, 6
Spencer, Lt. William C., 28:209, 210
Spendlove, F. St. George, work reviewed, 36:317
Sperry, Albert A., speaker, 11:287; author, 19:223

Sperry, De Witt, Cutlerite, 13:387
Sperry, Esther, 32:205
Sperry, Dr. Lyman B., explorer, 19:223
Sperry Co., see General Mills
Spettel, Michael, 25:198; bridge builder, 23:286; architect, 27:258
Spicemaker, ---, trader, 11:259, 264n
Spicer, Lester W., 23:390, 27:175, 29:179; author, 18:114, 20:357, 21:340, 22:445, 23:106, 24:272; speaker, 23:300
Spielman, Jean, papers, 18:445, 19:48
Spiller, Robert E., work reviewed, 37:84
Spillman, William J., 19:25, 26
Spillville, Iowa, Bohemian settlement, 14:341; history, 19:460
Spirit Island, Hennepin County, Mississippi River, 34:33; described, 30:219
Spirit Knob, Lake Minnetonka, name, 34:128
Spirit Lake, Iowa, Indian massacre, 11:292, 13:335, 438, 14:113, 248, 257, 330, 342, 15:463, 16:470, 18:95, 19:385, 20:80, 94, 21:401, 23:273, 24:61, 26:67, 394, 28:288, 30:121n, 35:235, 38:88, 122-124, 40:147; road, 11:392; hunting, 15:386; legend, 15:393
Spirit of Liberty (Pittsburgh, Pa.), abolitionist newspaper, 32:16
Spirit of the Times (New York), sports magazine, 14:421, 424; Henry H. Sibley's contributions, 15:384, 16:188, 34:174; historical value, 16:187; influence, 35:330
Splady, Charles F., 19:184n
Split Rock, Lake County, lighthouse, 34:351; scenic area, 37:182
Spofford, Ainsworth R., 15:449
Sponberg, Evelyn, speaker, 17:489; author, 17:490
Sponberg, Harold, speaker, 20:458
Sponland, Ingeborg, autobiography, 19:459
Spooner, Mary, teacher, 16:137
Sports, American, 11:100, 21:422; boxing, 14:413, 30:406; periodicals, 14:421-423, 16:187-191, 36:195; Indian, 15:272; boating, 16:188, 36:90, 195, 40:33; at state fair, 16:190; basketball, 20:441, 22:221, 30:406; softball, 21:422; juvenile, 22:98; ethnic influence, 24:259, 36:91; equipment, 26:269; winter, 27:169, 39:91, 40:384-386; pioneer, 28:190; collegiate, 34:93, 40:377; Minnesota, 36:89-94, 103; tennis, 36:90, 40:32; track, 36:94, 39:18-23. See also Amusements, individual sports
Spotswood, Alexander, Virginia governor, 18:391
Spotted Tail, Sioux leader, 34:345, 35:174, 289, 37:303
Sprague, Frank J., 35:283
Sprague, Gen. J. W., G.A.R. commander, 16:438, 439; speculator, 39:89
Sprague, Philander, potter, 33:232
Spriggs, Mrs. Ann G., boardinghouse keeper, 35:353n
Spring, Mrs. C. E., speaker, 17:357
Spring, Mary, stenographer, 24:31; manuscript assistant, 24:162, 25:40

Spring Cave, St. Paul, 20:393
Spring Creek Lutheran Church, Yellow Medicine County, 14:452
Spring Garden Lutheran Church, Goodhue County, 14:354
Spring Grove, Norwegian colony, 12:268, 19:199, 211; Lutheran church, 15:367; history, 17:486, 28:382
Spring Grove Herald, origin, 28:382
Spring Grove Posten, Norwegian newspaper, 28:382
Spring Hill, Stearns County, grasshopper subsidy, 36:61
Spring Island, Blue Earth County, pioneer life, 35:77-86
Spring Lake, Dakota County, mill, 11:218, 18:114
Spring Lake, Isanti County, Lutheran church, 15:481, 19:123
Spring Lake, Itasca County, archaeology, 26:316, 34:354, 35:199, 36:282
Spring Lake Park, Freeborn County, history, 21:340
Spring Park, Lake Minnetonka, recreation area, 29:290, 292, 297, 30:92
Spring Valley, Lutheran church, 16:335; Methodist meetings, 21:86, 31:82; Indian mounds, 27:261; centennial, 34:356; iron mining, 36:283
Spring Valley Community Historical Society, 35:99
Spring Wells, Detroit, Mich., treaty, 23:145n
Springers, James D., 18:134n
Springer, Wesley J., boom master, 28:379
Springfield, Brown County, anniversaries, 12:449, 35:203; in Sioux Outbreak, 15:356; Catholic church, 20:218
Springfield, Jackson County, see Jackson
Springfield Advance, history, 15:365
Springfield Township, Cottonwood County, records, 17:231
Sproat, Florantha T., author, 13:437
Sproat, Granville T., missionary, 13:437, 22:353; artist, 14:330
Spruce, Roseau County, Lutheran church, 22:341
Spruce Park, Itasca County, established, 22:415
Sprung, Herman, author, 11:336
Spry, Irene M., author, 39:211
Squier, Ephraim G., 29:161
Squires, ---, telegraph operator, 19:163
Squires, Dr. D., speaker, 17:483
Squires, Monas N., author, 14:340
Srsen, Charles E., author, 13:216
Stacey, C. P., author, 19:353
Stacy, C. E., politician, 36:60
Stadtverband, St. Paul, Catholic federation, 17:85
Staffenson, Frank A., author, 36:104
Stafford Court House, Va., in Civil War, 25:355
Stagecoaching, companies, 11:133, 405, 12:394, 13:112, 14:351, 38:63, 64, 66, 40:387; freight transportation, 11:138, 18:221, 38:66; routes, 11:308, 402, 12:50n, 93, 339, 14:458, 16:128, 284, 291, 292, 296, 298, 17:360, 19:385, 23:297, 29:150, 30:69, 35:21, 258,

37:157, 40:387; social aspects, 11:309, 19:409; importance in road building, 11:401, 407; in mail service, 11:403-405, 17:353, 20: 465, 38:66, 40:85, 247; travel accounts, 12:50-53, 175, 203, 13: 334, 17:361, 18:353, 354, 19:139, 408, 20:432, 29:116, 213-215, 33: 277, 35:155, 201, 36:45, 37:157, 40:387-390; fares, 16:288-290, 20: 444; stations, 21:235, 241, 28: 190; depicted, 21:431, 28:310, 33: 276, 34:17, 35:102, 155, 355, 38: 63-71, 40:247, 387-390; hazards, 32:171, 35:102, 38:66; by sledge, 34:18-22

Stagg, Henry, 17:140

Stahl, Mrs. Anna, pioneer, 24:189

Stahl, Gen. Julius, Union officer, 25:357

Stahl, Mrs. LeRoy, 20:458, 21:110

Stahlberger, Andrew, 32:41

Stakman, Elvin C., professor, 20: 156n, 186, 21:53

Stambaugh, Samuel C., sutler, at Fort Snelling, 17:210, 23:288, 26:362, 40:26-31, 82; at Prairie du Chien, Wis., 18:193

Stambaugh, Mrs. Samuel C., at Prairie du Chien, Wis., 23:288

Stampede Tunnel, Wash., constructed, 17:102

Stampp, Kenneth M., works reviewed, 30:382, 31:243

Stanchfield, Bessie M., "The Beauty of the West," 27:179-189; author, 27:72, 246, 28:75, 199, 32:163n; speaker, 28:280

Stanchfield, Daniel, lumberman, 13: 350, 354, 15:344, 16:429, 18:97, 166, 27:312; alderman, 35:120

Stanchfield, William, 15:344

Stanchfield Baptist Church, 17:479

Standard Gas and Electric Co., 36:99

Standard Oil Co., 18:424, 28:95; Indiana, 35:91; New Jersey, 35:91, 286

Standing Bear, Sioux leader, 13:107

Standing Buffalo, Sioux leader, 12: 121, 19:391, 29:122

Standing Cedar, Chisago County, trading post, 11:375

Standing Rock, N.D., Indian agency, 27:97, 154; Sioux reservation, 33: 227, 35:289, 293, 40:46

Standish, Matt, in Civil War, 25:343

Stanford University, Stanford, Calif., publication, 16:85

Stanley, Gen. David S., author, 13: 100

Stanley, Edward, author, 21:369

Stanley, George F. G., work reviewed, 17:453; author, 16:113, 31:189, 33:183; translator, 22:303

Stanley, John Mix, artist, 17:114, 456, 475, 21:95, 151, 22:154n, 155n, 23:183, 25:278, 28:69, 30: 176, 31:54, 55, 32:188, 33:90, 264, 269 (cover), 35:369, 379, 38: 10n, 201

Stanley, Lake County, railroad station, 34:181

Stannard, B. A., steamboat captain, 32:86, 87

Stannard, Lucas K., papers, 37:42

Stannard, Capt. William, Hudson Bay expedition, 16:419-423

Stannard Rock, Mich., Lake Superior, lighthouse, 34:351

Stansbury, Howard, 35:242, 40:247; career, 17:115

Stansfield Hall, St. Anthony, 28:29

Stanton, Edwin M., secretary of war, 25:250, 347, 38:43, 56, 217, 227

Stanton, Elizabeth Cady, 39:4, 10

Stanton, W. S., author, 34:304

Stanton, mounds, 16:307

Staples, Cpl. Benjamin F., 25:238, 356

Staples, Fred, lumberjack, 21:176

Staples, Mrs. George H., speaker, 15: 367; author, 16:337

Staples, Isaac, 24:200; lumberman, 18:170, 172, 174, 21:176, 31:34, 37-39, 33:226; log mark, 26:136

Staples, King G., 20:469

Staples, Winslow, 21:176

Staples family, genealogy, 13:197

Staples, anniversaries, 20:469, 39: 263; labor unions, 21:382, 393

Staples Commercial Club, 17:241

Staples, Merritt, and Young, Lakeland, sawmill, 19:319

Staples School, Mendota Township, Dakota County, anniversary, 15:367

Star Granite Co., Albert Lea, 27:345

Star Lake, Cook County, forest fire, 36:133

Starbeck, Frank L., 21:107

Starbeck, Mrs. Frank L., 27:75, 265, 28:85; speaker, 25:313, 26:392

Starbeck, Robert, 27:265

Starbuck, Lutheran churches, 12:341, 23:198; history, 16:369

Stark, Mrs. H. L., 12:103

Stark, Harold, author, 17:107, 456

Stark, Mrs. Herman, author, 15:466

Stark, Bishop Leland, 35:245

Stark, Mrs. Leland (Phyllis), author, 35:245

Stark, Chisago County, name, 31:253

Starr, Chester G., author, 39:34

Starr, H. V., editor, 13:344

Starr, Harris E., author, 12:442, 13: 210, 14:230; editor, 25:304

Starr, Joshua, editor, 25:394

Starr, Louis, 36:216

Starr, Margaret Hammond, 36:218

Stars and Stripes, service newspaper, 26:175

Starved Rock, Ill., legend, 22:73

Stassen, Harold E., 35:57; governor, 21:101, 335, 22:294, 23:36, 149, 24:28, 25:291, 34:188; author, 21: 208; honored, 24:265; war service, 24:266; speaker, 26:31, 38:244; career, 28:74, 279, 35:285, 36: 151, 40:148

State Bank of Duluth, 37:122

State Bank of Minnesota, Minneapolis, 40:111

State Blue Label League, labor organization, 20:432

State Dairymen's Association, 22:263, 265, 268

State Eight Hour League, 22:383

State Historical Society of Iowa, Iowa City, 23:90, 35:100; publications, 13:331, 336, 16:227, 18: 433-435, 19:351, 20:338, 424, 21: 404-406, 22:184, 410, 23:357-360, 25:299, 33:188, 228, 356, 35:246; sponsors river cruise, 30:392

State Historical Society of Missouri,

Columbia, 21:403; publication, 12: 330; library, 23:379; history, 30: 73

State Historical Society of North Dakota, Bismarck, 34:267, 38:158; publications, 22:207, 40:316; library, 26:269

State Historical Society of Wisconsin, Madison, landmarks committee, 11:32; collections, 12:439, 15: 355, 16:334, 347, 474, 17:96, 100, 26:271, 30:159, 34:119, 35:147; publications, 12:440, 17:196-198, 18:326, 23:90, 25:85, 26:365, 385, 28:189, 387, 30:247, 270, 35:202; founded, 23:76; director, 24:337; guides, 26:148, 36:29, 40:96, 258, 409; art gallery, 27:164, 32:238; centennial, 27:356, 30:72; youth program, 29:269; medical records project, 34:175; functions, 34: 219, 313; building, 35:154

State parks, 17:220; Iowa, 12:239; Minnesota, 14:349, 16:114, 17:227, 18:273, 20:343, 22:337, 23:192, 291, 25:203, 28:183, 29:263, 279, 351, 34:314, 36:193, 38:388, 40: 35-38; Middle West, 15:236; Wisconsin, 15:237, 30:270; conferences, 20:344, 37:58n; North Dakota, 22:207; recreational areas, 24:80; guide, 38:239. See also individual parks

Stateler, Sylvester, lumberman, 24: 201

States' Rights movement, 1948 platform, 35:291

Staton, Frances, author, 13:210; editor, 17:223

Statuary Hall, capitol building, Washington, D.C., 26:372

Staude, Edwin G., inventor, 36:238

Stauffer, Alvin P., author, 24:252

Stauffer, William, homestead, 12:102

Stay, Mrs. Frank, diary, 18:222

Steadman, Alexander, cabin, 15:44

Steamboats and steamboating, ports, 11:101, 138, 142, 143, 12:46, 108, 13:139, 142, 177, 223, 225, 15: 307, 16:26, 17:277, 278, 19:410, 22:13, 22, 23:28, 25:114, 26:77, 181, 272, 29:203, 359, 35:118, 263, 264; advertisements, 11:134, 139, 20:389, 392, 29:205, 36:128; rates, 11:135, 142, 13:228, 238, 20:132, 383, 29:221, 33:11; cargoes, 11:136, 13:227, 230, 238, 239, 321, 18:434, 33:10, 15, 17, 19, 35:338, 38:295; seasonal travel, 11:138, 143, 13:236, 22:229; races, 11:323, 12:210, 19:349, 20: 394, 27:8, 36:279, 40:411; described, 12:45, 13:234, 20:386, 22:16, 24:138, 139, 331, 29:215, 33:11, 16, 17, 19; history, 12:70, 22:411, 25:72, 30:51; in fur trade, 13:221-243, 40:184; cholera cases, 14:291, 292, 298, 300, 16: 209, 19:343, 30:9, 39:67; excursions, 15:409-414, 16:387, 18:434, 20:384-386, 25:103-116, 29:29, 34: 133-142, 35:181; border lakes, 15: 489, 17:361; bells, 18:372-375; effect on settlement, 21:226, 237; inventors, 25:88; vessels listed, 25:88, 27:63, 36:32; in Civil War, 25:117, 151, 38:42, 260, 271n,

272, 290; glossary, 25:196; depicted, 25:386, 26:398, 33:7, 10, 13, 15, 194, 199, 251, 289, 34:1 (cover), 12-15, 36:213, 241 (cover), 250, 254, 37:66, 283, 286, 289, 291-294, 296, 38:272; records, 28:92, 29:175, 284; in lumber industry, 29:146, 33:8; technology, 31:110; labor conditions, 33:92; disasters, 33:289, 35:40, 292; in gold rush, 34:178, 37:135; museum, 35:202, 36:327, 37:66; mail carriers, 36:207, 208, 212, 213, 40:79, 86; Indian removals, 38:355-359, 361, 363. See also individual steamboats and steamboat companies, bodies of water

Stearn, Allen E., author, 27:351

Stearn, E. Wagner, author, 27:351

Stearns, Bertha-Monica, review by, 16:76-78; author, 13:106, 434, 17:225

Stearns, Charles T., carpenter, 28:207

Stearns, Elizabeth, see Smith, Mrs. William

Stearns, John, 24:112

Stearns, Malcolm, Jr., author, 34:120

Stearns, Nancy, 24:116

Stearns, Col. Ozora P., 29:188

Stearns, R. P., 28:170; author, 26:273

Stearns family, in New England, 24:112

Stearns County, ethnic groups, 11:205, 12:276, 277, 21:98, 30:392, 31:25, 32:37, 34:171; religious communities, 11:205, 15:354, 16:371, 32:43, 33:53, 35:46, 263-271; pioneer life, 12:310, 19:321-327; churches, 14:451, 18:119, 24:94, 36:35; in World War I, 15:61, 116; census, 17:358, 27:74; history, 17:365, 23:187; WPA survey, 18:98; agriculture, 18:408, 29:19; described, 19:476; archives, 21:434; paper towns, 22:447; politics, 28:26, 31, 32, 34-36, 85, 33:162, 35:350, 36:306; in Sioux Outbreak, 28:192, 38:283; library, 31:61; historic sites, 31:62; Red River Trail, 32:34, 63; county seat, 32:36; wildlife, 33:141, 142

Stearns County Historical Society, organized, 17:64, 123, 233; meetings, 17:357, 18:111, 19:119, 22:108, 27:77, 243, 28:388, 29:94, 181, 276, 366, 30:83, 169, 279, 32:34n, 33:291n; museum, 17:358, 18:336, 19:232, 362, 20:214, 355, 26:286, 27:73, 268; collections, 20:98; marking project, 32:63; reorganized, 35:51; publication, 35:152

Stearns County Old Settlers Association, 16:98, 30:279

Stearns County War History Committee, 24:82

Stearns House, St. Cloud hotel, 35:255

Steason, John, steamboat captain, 33:14

Stebbins, Columbus, pioneer journalist, 13:143, 448

Stebbins, Edward S., 14:99

Stecher, Theodore, fur dealer, 35:18

Steck, Daniel F., Iowa Senator, 24:240

Steck, Francis B., work reviewed, 37:128

Steckert, John, potter, 33:231

Steckler, Gerard G., author, 38:201

Stedman, Alfred D., author, 29:262, 33:353

Stedman, E. C., author, 26:302

Steefel, Lawrence D., 13:65

Steel industry, use of Minnesota ore, 21:102, 23:362; markets, 28:189; companies, 35:203, 36:103, 276

Steele, Mrs. A., artist, 22:21, 27

Steele, Abbie A., 28:311n, 31:173

Steele, Franklin, 15:344, 467, 16:454, 20:369, 22:182, 420, 24:195, 30:173, 35:103, 106, 36:261; business interests, 13:224, 234, 238, 354, 355, 20:336, 22:153n, 28:332, 29:208n, 243, 30:181, 35:108, 118, 183; promotes immigration, 13:356; lumberman, 13:366, 24:129, 130, 132, 135, 193, 36:159; papers, 14:99, 16:72, 30:320; politician, 14:163, 36:261, 266; career, 15:479, 18:468, 24:127, 27:309-318, 35:187; MHS founder, 20:367, 30:345; sutler, 27:310, 31:237, 34:145, 35:104, 36:260; family, 28:311n, 30:197; postmaster, 40:82

Steele, Gen. Frederick, Union officer, 40:281-286, 288, 290

Steele, J. P., gold seeker, 29:308, 309

Steele, Gen. James, 27:309

Steele, Mrs. James, 28:311n

Steele, Jules L., author, 24:384

Steele, Sarah Jane, see Sibley, Mrs. Henry H.

Steele County, ethnic groups, 12:270, 343, 14:123, 21:457, 31:27, 29; pioneer life, 13:213; organized, 17:130; newspapers, 17:241; paper towns, 20:218; name, 20:368, 24:127; World War II veterans, 26:389; dairying, 27:108; census, 28:303

Steele County Historical Society, 27:364; organized, 11:286, 287, 12:37, 107, 30:280

Steele County War History Committee, 23:392

Steen, H. A., railroad man, 12:171

Steen, Henry, legislator, 33:159

Steen, Herman, work reviewed, 39:127

Steen, Otto K., speaker, 12:342

Steenerson, Halvor, letters, 16:218; Congressman, 38:177, 178, 40:324

Steenerson Township, Beltrami County, history, 15:132

Steensma, Robert, author, 37:86

Steenson, Rev. James, speaker, 27:361

Steere, Isaac, letters, 30:90

Steere, Mrs. Isaac, letters, 30:90

Stees, Charles, 11:54, 13:74, 14:79, 80, 17:70, 18:67, 279n, 20:50, 51, 23:50, 26:45, 29:97; speaker, 11:283, 12:296, 16:302, 18:271

Stees, Mrs. Charles, speaker, 13:293

Stees, Capt. Charles J., 28:287; diary, 16:302

Stees and Hunt, St. Paul, furniture dealers, 15:186

Stefansson, Vilhjalmur, explorer, 25:221, 34:164; author, 28:176, 36:102

Steffen, P. W., 29:92, 274

Steffens, Charles H., papers, 22:423, 27:153

Steffens, Mrs. Charles H., papers, 27:153

Steffens, Lincoln, 14:200, 17:160n

Steffens, O. R., author, 28:373

Stefferud, Jacob, 25:79

Steglich, Eric W., house, 38:343

Stegner, Wallace, author, 35:378

Stehling, Kurt R., author, 38:334

Steidl, John, mill owner, 23:25, 32, 29:138

Steidle, Theodor, actor, 32:102; theater director, 32:127, 165, 169, 34:240

Steiger, William A., author, 34:175

Steinbeck, John, author, 20:116, 22:157, 23:124

Steiner, Frank M., career, 23:192

Steiner, John H., aeronaut, 39:279-281, 283-285, 40:265, 276, 277, 279, 314

Steinhauser, Albert, speaker, 28:81

Steinhauser, Gretchen, translator, 30:394

Steinmetz, Rollin C., work reviewed, 36:322

Steinway and Sons, New York, piano makers, 39:324-326

Stem, Allen H., architect, 28:293

Stemsrud, Mrs. M. A., 12:185

Stene, Gabriel, author, 11:219, 14:355, 15:488

Stenlund, Milton H., author, 35:48

Stennes, J. J., author, 17:235

Stenstrom, Andrew M., artist, 34:45 (cover), 59-66

Stenstrom, Mrs. Andrew M., 34:63

Stenstrom, John, farmer, 34:63

Stenstrom, Louis S., artist, 34:61, 62

Stenstrom, Mrs. Louis S., pioneer, 34:61

Stenvig, Ole, 29:308

Stephan, A. Stephen, 20:88

Stephan, Dr. E. L., speaker, 25:412

Stephan, John A., postmaster, 20:361

Stephanites, religious sect, 14:334

Stephen, history, 12:452; roller mill, 35:299

Stephens, A. D., speaker, 16:482

Stephens, A. J., 18:131

Stephens, Alexander A., letters, 11:318

Stephens, Ann S., author, 38:242

Stephens, George W., author, 12:95

Stephens, Henry M., 18:12, 133

Stephens, P. O., fisherman, 33:254-259

Stephens, Uriah S., 22:367

Stephenson, Col. B. F., founder of G.A.R., 16:439

Stephenson, George M., 16:466, 17:319, 19:81, 21:203, 25:191; "The John Lind Papers," 17:159-165; "Swedes in the St. Croix Valley," 17:396-405; "Swedish Immigration Material," 18:69-75; reviews by, 11:434-436, 12:413-416, 13:188-190, 308-311, 14:316-318, 325, 15:337-339, 16:86, 325-327, 17:79, 328, 18:302, 19:81-83, 90, 435, 20:317-319, 21:299, 22:70-72, 23:260-263, 362-364, 26:56-59, 27:132-134; works reviewed, 13:304-307, 16:456-460, 19:331, 20:420,

22:65-67, 33:80; author, 11:102,
103, 14:349, 15:127, 17:110, 206,
329, 331, 459, 18:91, 19:91, 444,
20:322, 21:182, 310, 22:82, 96,
327, 23:8, 271, 370, 26:65, 27:
152, 28:332, 29:278, 32:49, 34:
199; speaker, 14:328, 344, 15:219,
16:212, 17:208, 317, 18:324, 20:
85, 28:178
Stephenson, Jean, 18:214
Stephenson, Oscar, lawyer, 40:225
Stephenson, Wendell H., author, 17:
225
Sterling, Christina, 33:277n, 35:258
Sterling, Ellenora, 13:337, 33:277n,
35:258
Sterling, Everett W., "Moses N.
Adams," 35:167-177; reviews by,
35:288, 37:303, 39:255; author,
36:34, 39:261
Sterling, George, poet, 26:308
Sterling, William, actor, 33:176
Sterling Township, Blue Earth County,
pioneer life, 24:182; grasshopper
plague, 36:58
Stern, Henry, author, 34:353
Stern, Isaac, violinist, 39:63, 64
Stern, Madeleine B., work reviewed,
35:329; author, 22:431, 38:242
Stern, Malcolm H., author, 36:236
Sternberg, Col. George M., army phy-
sician, 24:210; surgeon general,
24:212
Sterrenberg, T., 28:129
Sterrenberg, Wolter, 28:129
Sterrett, Andrew J., diaries, 24:245
Sterrett, Frances R., author, 31:132,
147, 36:79
Sterrett, James M., career, 17:115
Sterritt, Mrs. Frank, 25:269
Sterry, De Witt, 16:318n
Sterry, William, artist, 33:172
Steube, Charles, 17:113
Stevens, Dr. A. E., author, 16:127;
speaker, 25:313
Stevens, Carl, forester, 33:219
Stevens, Charles L., author, 12:451
Stevens, Cornelia (Mrs. Daniel
Gavin), 21:160, 276
Stevens, E. A., letter, 32:28n
Stevens, Dr. F. A., pioneer phy-
sician, 28:89
Stevens, F. C., 20:83
Stevens, Francis W., author, 16:126
Stevens, Frederick C., 19:451
Stevens, Freling H., legislator, 37:
161
Stevens, Gardner, I, letter, 34:144,
145
Stevens, Gardner, II, 34:148
Stevens, George, trader, 35:48
Stevens, Harry R., author, 37:133
Stevens, Hazard, author, 21:96
Stevens, Hiram F., lawyer, 40:115;
biography, 17:115
Stevens, Isaac I., explorer, 12:435,
16:128, 20:191, 24:371; letters,
14:435, 16:224, 19:342, 21:96, 35:
242; Washington governor, 22:330,
33:273n, 313; author, 33:90; char-
acterized, 34:353, 39:169, 40:94.
See also Pacific railroad survey
Stevens, J. Walter, architect, 40:101
Stevens, James, art dealer, 33:2
Stevens, James, author, 21:296-298,
28:362, 32:151, 33:265
Stevens, Jedediah, missionary, 16:

134, 135, 18:157, 197, 24:20n,
21n; family, 15:242, 25:77; at
Lake Harriet, 15:275, 17:236, 20:
123, 443, 21:27, 73, 167, 35:29;
Dakota studies, 16:142; diary, 17:
391, 20:126, 28:3; cabin, 20:470;
characterized, 21:28, 158, 160,
162
Stevens, Jim, singer, 33:324
Stevens, John, artist, 35:369; Sioux
Outbreak panoramas, 24:180, 30:14-
23, 176, 180, 182, 411, 31:46,
121, 248, 249, 33:78, 34:316, 35:
52, 379, 36:234, 236, 38:108; portrait painter, 34:267
Stevens, John B., labor contractor,
37:143
Stevens, John F., engineer, 16:224,
21:97, 29:165, 38:311, 312, 314,
316; autobiography, 16:343, 463,
17:354
Stevens, John H., career, 11:219, 17:
114, 20:448; papers, 11:330, 13:
197, 19:342, 20:209, 30:320, 34:
144-148; pioneer, 14:238, 35:197;
author, 15:49, 16:22, 17:306, 308,
20:140, 416, 27:309; editor, 18:
408n, 25:93; colonizer, 19:135,
23:196; house, 20:415, 29:208, 31:
125, 34:145, 40:48; agricultural
leader, 22:252, 253n, 254, 260,
30:371; farmer, 26:109, 33:331;
quoted, 27:112; depicted, 34:145,
147; businessman, 34:312, 40:65,
75; army officer, 38:276
Stevens, Lucy C., teacher, 21:30
Stevens, Marion, speaker, 20:214
Stevens, N. E., publisher, 15:86
Stevens, Neil E., author, 25:198
Stevens, Nicholas, trader, 16:224
Stevens, S. George, speaker, 15:492;
author, 16:101
Stevens, Silas, cabin, 20:470
Stevens, Simon, 13:426, 18:97, 19:141
Stevens, Solon, scout, 39:237
Stevens, Sylvester K., author, 23:
376, 24:267, 25:310, 29:163;
speaker, 32:123
Stevens, Thaddeus, politician, 22:
409, 33:328, 36:183
Stevens, Wayne E., 17:197; review by,
27:129-131; compiler, 11:260; au-
thor, 27:152
Stevens, William R., 11:331
Stevens, O'Brien, Cole, and Albrecht,
St. Paul, law firm, 17:89
Stevens County, history, 11:467, 33:
192; railroads, 12:254; Norwegian
settlement, 12:277; schools, 15:
348; pioneer life, 16:256; place
names, 25:316; agriculture, 26:
291; census, 28:303; physicians,
36:327; electric service, 40:315
Stevens County Historical Society,
28:385, 29:366
Stevens County War History Committee,
24:268
Stevens House, Minneapolis, 15:229,
360, 467
Stevens House, Rochester, hotel, 30:
15
Stevens Point, Wis., industries, 35:
48; electric service, 36:99; centennial, 36:280
Stevens Seminary, Glencoe, 13:216,
14:121

Stevenson, Adlai, politician, 37:343,
39:102
Stevenson, Col. James, 15:432
Stevenson, St. Louis County, mining
town, 28:251
Steward, Ira, 21:379
Steward, Muriel, author, 11:340
Stewart, Dr. A. B., 11:286
Stewart, Alexander, 22:305
Stewart, Andrew, Methodist minister,
33:315
Stewart, Dr. C. A., author, 12:204
Stewart, Carl L., author, 29:276
Stewart, Charles, mill owner, 18:116,
21:115
Stewart, Charles, naval officer, 21:
349
Stewart, George, Union soldier, 25:
253, 255
Stewart, George R., work reviewed,
26:248-250
Stewart, Harland, Quaker minister,
18:261n
Stewart, J. A., author, 14:102
Stewart, Dr. J. Clark, 21:330
Stewart, Dr. Jacob H., 14:300, 301,
20:237, 35:221, 39:178
Stewart, James A., 22:105
Stewart, Jane, 15:459
Stewart, John Charles, testimony, 21:
139-141
Stewart, Levi M., career, 15:364;
philanthropist, 39:15
Stewart, Lillian K., work reviewed,
11:432-434
Stewart, M. S., banker, 37:122, 124
Stewart, Mary L., 14:331
Stewart, Maude G., 17:123, 20:98;
speaker, 20:355
Stewart, Nina, 15:459
Stewart, Omer C., author, 34:310
Stewart, Solomon P., career, 29:276
Stewart, Stanley, 22:225
Stewart, T. R., author, 11:114, 14:
331
Stewart, Rev. W. J., speaker, 12:103
Stewart, W. M., author, 17:476
Stewart, Sir William D., traveler,
15:110, 26:154, 29:59, 35:153;
letter, 17:96
Stewart, William J., "Settler, Poli-
tician, and Speculator," 39:85-92;
author, 39:261
Stewart, history, 21:452; school his-
torical society, 26:183
Stewartville, schools, 12:104, 18:
228; pioneers, 17:488; mill, 18:
116, 27:80; post office, 18:341;
founded, 21:115; history, 21:454,
26:398, 35:44; centennial, 35:336
Stewartville Co-operative Creamery
Association, 26:289
Stewartville Star, anniversary, 21:
454
Stiansen, P., work reviewed, 21:76
Stickles, Arnt M., author, 22:205
Stickley, Gustave, publisher, 40:106
Stickley, W. A., 16:241, 243, 17:358,
18:336
Stickney, Alpheus B., 26:20; career,
17:226; railroad executive, 19:
121, 27:352, 33:226, 356, 36:33,
39:298; papers, 21:194
Stickney, Charles A., automobile
builder, 26:20
Stiefel, Agnes C., author, 24:356

Stikine River, B.C., trading post, 26:55
Stiles, Bill, bank robber, 34:125
Stiles, Ezra, 19:35
Still, Bayrd, work reviewed, 30:138; author, 22:430
Stillwater, historic sites, 11:225; beginnings, 11:339, 12:160, 24:195–206; stage line, 11:404; newspapers, 11:468, 16:244, 17:385; land office, 12:381, 16:216; river port, 14:100, 17:153, 154n, 277, 30:199, 35:355, 36:46n, 37:94; schools, 14:144, 17:388, 24:366, 25:373, 28:72, 34:105n, 214, 39:19, 321, 40:222; hotels, 14:239, 16:377, 35:363, 364; Indian battle, 15:280, 21:167, 24:11, 13, 21–23; lumber center, 16:131, 17:130, 280, 313, 390, 396, 18:165–179, 474, 24:126, 193, 199–203, 205, 26:132, 136, 28:272, 30:195, 242, 31:33, 33:226, 35:382, 40:126, 357; volunteer guard, 16:173, 176; frontier life, 16:217, 17:54, 389, 20:190, 450, 29:205; Presbyterian churches, 16:313, 17:391n, 19:146, 247–257, 262, 35:362, 37:142, 38:344, 40:5; boatbuilding, 17:112; depicted, 17:139, 394, 19:253, 23:104, 25:50, 56, 31:182, 35:361; climate, 17:260; courthouses, 17:285, 38:186–189, 349, 40:135; historical meeting, 17:312, 18:42, 24:242, 29:367, 372; Episcopal church, 17:350, 19:250, 27:368; Catholic church, 17:391n; ethnic groups, 17:398, 29:182, 34:174; anniversaries, 17:490, 24:242, 381, 385, 25:41; railroads, 18:175, 34:174, 35:358–364; library, 18:344, 20:360; Methodist church, 18:352, 355–360, 24:204; baseball club, 19:169, 173, 175, 177–181; history, 19:252, 24:274, 29:368; land sale, 19:449; pioneer physician, 19:463, 23:95, 36:193; bank, 19:465; labor unions, 21:392, 22:370, 371; art colony, 22:434, 24:194; bridge, 23:290; business, 23:396; opera house, 24:189, 28:119; name, 24:199; streets, 24:203, 204; architecture, 25:412, 37:43, 38:337 (cover), 338–352; politics, 26:198, 33:329, 36:3; performing arts, 28:104, 32:59, 100, 34:241, 39:320–322; electric service, 35:381; street railway, 36:150; mail service, 36:206–210, 212–214, 40:82, 86, 87; judicial district, 39:145, 146; road, 40:237, 246. See also Minnesota State Prison, Stillwater Convention of 1848
Stillwater Association, 29:95, 182
Stillwater Convention of 1848, 16:469, 21:401, 39:273; activities, 14:128, 36:261; records, 17:393; centennial, 29:95, 182, 279–281, 367
Stillwater Democrat, established, 17:386
Stillwater Gazette, anniversaries, 11:468, 26:399; established, 17:386, 19:476
Stillwater Guard, volunteer unit, 16:172, 173, 175, 176

Stillwater High School, 17:314
Stillwater Lumber Co., established, 18:169, 24:199, 274; record book, 24:201, 202
Stillwater Lumberman, founded, 17:386
Stillwater Messenger, 16:332, 17:386, 490
Stillwater Post-Messenger, essay contest, 14:239; established, 14:397, 404; anniversary, 17:490
Stillwater Republican, established, 17:386
Stillwell, Mrs. Harry, 17:483, 19:117; speaker, 18:209
Stillwell, John, pioneer, 36:235
Stimson, Albert, lumberman, 24:200
Stimson, Emmor B., auto driver, 38:207
Stimson, Henry L., secretary of state, 39:80
Stinnett, Ronald F., work reviewed, 39:257
Stirling, Matthew W., 12:224; author, 34:216
Stites, Adam, 25:253
Stites, Cpl. Samuel, in Civil War, 25:226
Stivers, Edgar, newspaperman, 22:109
Stivers, H. C., legislator, 35:303
Stock, Frederick A., 17:101
Stock, Leo F., author, 15:352
Stockbridge Indians, land payments, 14:216; mission, 16:134, 22:150
Stockenstrand, J. L., author, 18:72
Stockholm, Sweden, depicted, 33:202
Stockholm, Wis., history, 24:369
Stockholm Township, Wright County, pioneer life, 21:344, 442
Stockinger, E. L., 35:51; speaker, 22:108
Stockton, Frank R., 20:82
Stockton, Lucius W., career, 29:150
Stockwell, Maud C., author, 27:79
Stockwell, Miss Missouri, name, 33:285; marriage, 33:290n
Stockwell, Samuel B., panorama painter, 17:137, 140, 20:380, 33:284–290, 35:279, 36:233
Stockwell, Sylvanus A., legislator, 16:127, 35:304; speaker, 16:489; memorial, 24:356; portrait, 25:80
Stockwell, Wilhelmina G., editor, 14:333
Stoddard, James, 13:32n
Stoddard, John, 21:418
Stoddard, Whitney S., author, 36:100
Stoddard piano, 39:320
Stoeckeler, Joseph H., author, 27:262
Stoick, Hazel T., artist, 27:262
Stokes, I. N. Phelps, work reviewed, 15:210
Stoll, Elmer Edgar, 21:70
Stoll, H. B., 19:133
Stolte, S. L., speaker, 17:346
Stoltz, Mildred K., author, 35:203
Stomberg, Andrew A., editor, 11:325; author, 22:438, 23:190; papers, 27:56
Stone, ———, church trustee, 19:267n
Stone, Dr. Alexander J., 24:347; editor, 21:209, 22:435, 26:173; career, 35:221
Stone, Carl F., 11:332
Stone, Maj. Carl L., letters, 15:466, 18:317
Stone, Gen. Charles P., Union offi-

cer, 25:16, 21; arrested, 25:24, 26
Stone, Clarence E., legislator, 33:159
Stone, David, trader, 40:182, 185, 186
Stone, Gen. David L., Fort Snelling commandant, 15:310, 312
Stone, E. D., farmer, 13:133
Stone, Edwin M., editor, diary, 17:464
Stone, Ferris D., 23:134
Stone, George C., financier, 12:285, 33:220, 36:192, 37:120, 40:412
Stone, Irving, author, 36:68
Stone, Jesse M., farmer, 17:266, 268, 22:100; papers, 16:216
Stone, Lucy, feminist, 28:54, 39:4–6, 10, 14
Stone, Mrs. M. E., 17:488, 19:470, 25:98, 404, 405, 26:90, 179, 28:87
Stone, Richard G., author, 29:62
Stone, Rigmor O., author, 36:69
Stone, Robert, author, 30:161
Stone, Justice Royal A., 17:70, 20:51, 21:410, 23:50, 24:57
Stone, Thomas J., 39:228
Stone, Dr. William T., 33:294, 295
Stone, quarrying and uses, 17:85, 35:65, 39:160
Stone, Bostwick and Co., St. Louis, 40:183, 185
Stone-Ordean-Wells Co., Duluth, wholesale grocers, 13:361
Stonehouse, Merlin, work reviewed, 39:291
Stoneman, George, 25:348n
Stoneman, Dr. Mark, dentist, 39:112n
Stoner, John E., author, 25:195
Stoney Brook, St. Louis County, history, 21:456, 23:302
Stong, Phil, author, 20:116, 201, 21:425, 430, 23:119, 122, 158, 25:325, 31:134, 147, 36:81, 82, 37:12
Stony Run, Yellow Medicine County, Norwegian settlement, 12:275n, 23:240
Stor, Paul W., speaker, 25:210
Storaker, Petra, 21:107, 22:105
Storck, John, work reviewed, 33:132
Storden Township, Cottonwood County, history, 17:231, 20:95, 101
Stordock, Halvur G., prison official, 37:148–150
Storer, Daniel M., diary, 16:333, 17:53, 33:225
Storey, Wilbur F., 26:357; editor, 37:127
Stork, Harvey E., speaker, 15:251; author, 22:103
Storm, Colton, 36:218; review by, 34:117; author, 30:65, 34:257
Storrs, Caryl B., music critic, 33:104
Stortroen, Anders, letters, 13:205
Stortroen, Ole J., letters, 13:205
Stott, C. B., author, 21:429
Stoughton, Gen. Edwin H., Union officer, 25:252
Stout, ———, St. Louis resident, 17:424
Stout, Elihu, pioneer printer, 15:13, 14
Stout, Wilfred O., Jr., reviews by, 22:80, 23:263–265; author, 17:102, 22:82, 23:271, 31:58

Stoutenburgh, John L., Jr., work re-
viewed, 37:84
Stovall, Bates M., author, 34:215
Stover, Helen, speaker, 17:357
Stover, John F., review by, 33:308
Stovring, Sigurd, author, 29:271
Stowe, Gerald C., 21:325
Stowe, Harriet B., 22:67, 28:54; in-
fluence, 16:86; author, 35:219
Stowe, Lewis, diaries, 19:48, 95
Stowe, Rev. Walter H., author, 16:
477, 24:72
Stowell, Mrs. William H., pioneer,
33:4
Stoylen, Sigvald, author, 25:285
Strachauer, Clarence, musician, 33:93
Strader, Mildred, author, 20:447
Strafford Western Emigration Co., 15:
111, 20:328, 35:198
Straight, Leonard A., biography, 15:
349
Straight River, Rice and Steele coun-
ties, mills, 11:276, 35:13; quar-
ries, 16:255; road, 21:233
Straker, Robert L., author, 22:433
Strampfer, Friedrich, theater direc-
tor, 32:105
Strand, Charles, 18:420
Strand, Mrs. Maybelle O., author, 19:
451
Strand, Roy E., 20:99, 21:110, 22:
219; store, 18:420; speaker, 19:
119, 232
Strand, Wallace, 18:420
Strandberg, Hilma A., author, 18:72
Strang, James J., 23:356
Strange, H. G. L., speaker, 25:397;
author, 35:48
"Strassburg," emigrant ship, 23:88
Strathcona and Mount Royal, Donald A.
Smith, Lord, railroad interests,
11:308, 31:55, 32:112, 35:153,
295, 40:143; J. J. Hill associate,
17:217, 28:372; papers, 19:445,
20:38, 326, 21:117; career, 35:
243; diplomat, 40:93
Strato Equipment Co., Minneapolis,
33:244
Stratton, Levi W., 17:392; author,
12:84; records, 16:72
Stratton, Robert, 18:126, 128, 144,
146
Stratton, William J., author, 12:329,
13:207
Strawberry Point, Iowa, stage stop,
34:21
Strawberry raising, Iowa, 26:273
Strawman, C. M., letter, 38:181
Strayer, George T., author, 12:418
Strayer, Joseph R., author, 24:360
Strayer, Martha, work reviewed, 36:
186
Streckfus Line, steamboat company,
37:265 (cover)
Street, Ida M., author, 11:105
Street, James, 26:166
Street, Joseph M., Indian agent, 11:
105, 21:425, 26:363, 40:261; pa-
pers, 15:463
Street, W. F., lawyer, 23:31
Street, W. P. R., 25:200
Street railways, Twin Cities, 13:123,
15:140, 338, 439, 16:182, 17:360,
18:445, 28:293, 34:44, 130, 36:
150, 233, 37:308; St. Cloud, 17:
365; interurban, 19:127, 36:150,
37:131; Duluth, 20:468; replaced

by buses, 34:44; horse-drawn, 35:
202; U.S., 35:283; Minnesota, 40:
316
Streighliff, Walton, author, 18:226,
21:213
Streitz, Sister Antonia, 35:271
Strettell, John, 11:238n
Stribling, Thomas, author, 20:116
Strickland, Miss E. H., teacher, 13:
140
Strickland, O. F., lumberman, 24:201
Strickler, Thomas M., career, 12:322
Striker, George W., career, 23:192
Strikes, see Labor
Strindberg, Gustaf, author, 18:70
Stringer, Arthur, author, 23:116, 158
Strobel, John, 13:116
Strobel, Mrs. John, 13:116
Strom, Rev. E. I., 19:115, 20:95;
speaker, 17:355, 19:231
Strom, Mrs. H. L., 12:338
Strømme, Peer O., journalist, 17:225
Stromness Island, Mich., Lake St.
Clair, 23:136n
Strong, Mrs. Charles D., 38:75, 76n
Strong, Fred H., author, 19:464
Strong, Freeman, 19:164
Strong, James W., 13:344; career, 17:
226
Strong, Mrs. Marcia, 19:236
Strong, Moses M., career, 34:313
Strong, Samuel M., author, 25:399
Strong and Miller, St. Paul, meat
packers, 26:115
Strong Earth (Strong Ground), Chippe-
wa leader, 18:404, 24:19, 20, 23
Strong, Hackett and Co., St. Paul,
33:259n
Stronks, James B., review by, 34:299
Stroud, St. Louis County, railroad
station, 34:184
Strout, Irwin C., budget commis-
sioner, 38:308
Strout, Capt. Richard, in Sioux Out-
break, 38:137n, 276
Strub, Father Augustine, author, 26:
388
Struck, Mrs. Vasilia T., 18:315
Strunk, Mrs. Synneva, 15:137, 16:124,
17:122, 18:110
Strunsky, Simeon, author, 21:5
Strupe, Henry, 14:31n
Struve, Gustav, author, 24:222
Stuart, Dr. A. B., climate reports,
17:258
Stuart, Mrs. Annis L., 18:263
Stuart, George H., 25:351
Stuart, Gilbert, 26:359
Stuart, Mrs. Hester H., 13:318
Stuart, Hulen, work reviewed, 33:216
Stuart, Gen. James E. B., Confederate
officer, 25:228n, 249, 38:247, 39:
282, 40:271
Stuart, Jerry, lumberman, 24:200
Stuart, Jesse, author, 25:176
Stuart, John, trader, 31:10
Stuart, R. Douglas, politician, 33:
306
Stuart, Robert, trader, 17:95, 210,
23:347, 29:61, 39:255, 40:183,
184, 196; diaries, 16:475
Stuart family, Linwood Lake settlers,
16:492
Stuart Lake, B.C., post, 40:191
Stub, Rev. Hans A., Muskego, Wis.,
settler, 24:348; portrait, 38:233

Stub, Rev. Hans G., church leader,
16:471; biography, 17:225
Stub, Rev. J. A. O., speaker, 13:450
Stubbs, Avery, author, 37:308
Stubbs, Charles H., author, 27:158
Stubbs, Don, "Pageant of the Past,"
30:343-362; author, 30:368, 412
Stubbs, Ellen B., author, 36:327
Stubbs, Roger A., compiler, 36:36;
author, 36:327
Stubbs, Rollo, 21:440
Stubbs, Roy St. George, author, 21:
433
Stubbs, William, historian, 18:3
Stubbs Bay, Hennepin County, Lake
Minnetonka, settled, 27:293n
Stubler, John N., 40:244n
Stuckert, Howard M., author, 16:477
Studdart, Ion F. A., 13:272
Students' Army Training Corps, pro-
gram, 39:219, 220
Stugo, Ole, 14:307, 313
Stuhr, Charles, 13:200
Stuntz, Albert C., diaries, 24:166
Stuntz, George R., land officer, 12:
286, 389; engineer, 14:453, 462,
21:183, 24:354, 30:267, 33:220,
36:192, 37:42, 40:412; monument,
16:371; papers, 19:355, 30:320; in
fiction, 33:51; career, 37:347
Stuntz, Stephen C., compiler, 18:
407n, 23:86
Stuntz Township, St. Louis County,
mining area, 37:347
Stur family, Scott County pioneers,
11:118
Sturgeon-Alango area, St. Louis Coun-
ty, pioneer life, 25:161
Sturgeon Lake, Goodhue County, trad-
ing post, 11:381
Sturgeon Lake, Man., Sask., fur
trade, 40:172
Sturgess, Harold G., inventor, 26:21
Sturgis, Gen. Samuel D., Union offi-
cer, 39:185-189
Stutsman, Enos, in Riel rebellions,
33:183
Stutz, Charles F., author, 26:95, 36:
283
Stutz automobile, 38:207, 209, 210,
213
Stuyvesant, Peter, governor of New
Netherland, 16:404
Sublette, Milton, trader, 29:59
Sublette, William L., trader, 29:59,
38:199
Sucker River, St. Louis County, set-
tled, 34:177
Suckley, Dr. George, with Isaac I.
Stevens expedition, 16:97; career,
24:256; letters, 26:380
Suckow, Ruth, author, 16:106, 20:115,
116, 23:119, 120, 158, 26:356, 28:
287
Sudbury, Ont., nickel deposits, 39:79
Sudduth, Dr. W. Xavier, speaker, 39:
114
Sudeith, William J., 19:50
Sudermann, Leonhard, author, 18:98
Sue, Eugène, author, 20:137
Suel, Cormac A., author, 20:462
Suel, John L., journalist, 20:462
Suelflow, August R., compiler, 39:35
Suemnicht, H. F., 27:364
Suffolk County, Mass., records, 16:
336
Suffrage, see Woman suffrage

Sugar Creek, Iowa, Norwegian settlement, 12:181
Sugar Island, Mich., St. Mary's River, acquired by U.S., 23:208
Sugar Lake, Itasca County, settled, 11:114; name, 21:347; resort, 33:228
Sugar Point, Cass County, Leech Lake, battle, 24:146-148, 180, 26:303
Sugden, Mrs. George W. (Mary), 22:215, 23:193
Sullivan, Sir Arthur, composer, 17:40
Sullivan, Daniel, 15:113
Sullivan, Edward, traveler, 34:42
Sullivan, George H., legislator, 11:225, 33:157, 161
Sullivan, Helen J., author, 11:453
Sullivan, J. J., 17:367
Sullivan, James, author, 16:115
Sullivan, Louis H., architect, 40:107, 108, 375; designer of Owatonna bank, 35:242, 37:38, 344
Sullivan, Mark, author, 24:50
Sullivan, Mike, lumberjack, 30:68
Sullivan, Oscar M., work reviewed, 33:350; author, 31:132, 147
Sullivan, Roger J., editor, 28:184
Sullivan, Thomas L., author, 12:434
Sully, Gen. Alfred, 14:459, 25:34, 125, 236-238, 245, 348, 39:77; artist, 22:333, 33:264, 35:369; intercedes for Winnebago, 39:228
Sully expeditions, 15:111, 20:330, 35:235, 36:239, 37:224; 1864, 16:217, 475, 17:54, 98, 19:390, 23:75, 34:320, 38:284, 39:77, 83; 1863, 20:192; Missouri River, 26:208, 34:131
Sulphur Creek, St. Louis County, name, 34:275; dam, 34:279, 280
Sulphur Mine, St. Louis County, taconite deposits, 34:274, 276; name, 34:275
Sulphur Siding, St. Louis County, taconite deposits, 34:270, 271, 279; depicted, 34:274, 275
Sulphur Springs, Cottonwood County, election precinct, 14:250
"Sultana," steamboat, 24:53
Sulte, Benjamin, author, 11:320, 13:247, 253
Sülter, Louis, 24:219
Summers, Mrs. Frank, pioneer, 33:1
Summers, Joseph, author, 30:74
Summit Avenue, St. Paul, 29:272, 33:141 (cover)
Summit Avenue Boulevard and Park Association, 29:272
Summit Hall, St. Paul, 39:53
Summit Township, Beltrami County, history, 15:132
Sumner, Charles, 23:261, 28:325; speaker, 11:157; Congressman, 16:281n; characterized, 22:409; Senator, 25:26, 27n; in Minnesota, 28:323
Sumner, Gen. Edwin V., Red River expedition, 19:353, 33:316; in Civil War, 25:36, 122, 125, 133, 135, 138, 228, 232n, 234, 243, 244; death, 25:254
Sumner Township, Fillmore County, Quaker meeting, 18:256; settled, 21:443; history, 35:336
Sunburg Township, Swift County, history, 12:170, 211
Sunday, Billy, career, 34:41

Sunde, Reinert, 29:294
Sundell, Edward, papers, 12:192, 13:59
Sunder, John E., work reviewed, 39:255; speaker, 40:150; author, 40:155, 220
Sundquist, Mrs. Anne, 20:454, 21:443
Sungigidan, Sioux Indian, 38:134
Sunken Lake, Itasca County, disappearance, 23:99
Sunny Slope, Minneapolis, 26:288
Sunnyside Rest Home, Lake Park, 38:376, 377
Sunrise, Chisago County, Indian problems, 12:202, 27:8, 38:275; described, 17:387; pioneer life, 36:282; garrison, 38:280; stage route, 40:247n
Sunrise River, Chisago County, post, 11:375, 32:234; lumbering, 21:227
Suomi, Itasca County, history, 11:114; anniversary, 18:340; Finnish settlement, 22:392n, 25:320
Suomi College, Hancock, Mich., Finnish library, 27:161
Superior, Wis., harbor, 11:433, 21:155, 24:62, 30:385, 397, 37:91, 100n; economic conditions, 12:387, 20:336, 37:98; projected state, 14:184; history, 16:113, 21:429, 37:91; roads, 16:283-290, 292, 294, 37:103n, 40:233-247; stage line, 16:284, 288, 292, 21:234; mail service, 16:285, 287, 21:151, 26:83; weather records, 20:152; anniversaries, 20:339, 34:129; frontier conditions, 21:150, 40:399; social life, 21:152; depicted, 21:155, 37:113, 116, 40:247; medicine, 22:330; rivalry with Duluth, 26:291, 27:72, 37:98; port, 28:69, 31:229, 35:294, 37:39, 91, 95, 98; Finnish colony, 32:185; first ore shipment, 34:11; railroad, 34:69; employment office, 36:163; located, 37:94, 111; Count Ferdinand von Zeppelin's visit, 39:282
Superior Brick Co., advertising, 38:308
Superior Central Co-operative Wholesale, 25:326
Superior National Forest, established, 16:237, 29:135; wildlife, 18:451, 30:130, 35:48; described, 23:67; history, 25:92, 34:264, 35:51; picture rock, 29:130, 169; preservation, 30:69, 31:123; survey, 30:262; extended, 36:134; legislation, 36:192. See also Quetico Provincial Park
Superior (Wis.) Tidende, Norwegian-language paper, anniversary, 19:106
Supple, Barry E., work reviewed, 40:405
Supple, Mrs. George, 17:124, 18:111, 22:219; speaker, 19:119
Suprey, Leslie V., author, 38:335
Surber, Thaddeus, 30:132; author, 21:440, 22:214, 26:277
Surgeons' Club, Rochester, depicted, 19:451; founded, 22:405
Survey Associates, records, 39:300
Surveyer, E.-F., author, 23:287
Surveyor General of Logs and Lumber, archives, 23:368

Surveys and surveying, public lands, 11:379-381, 383, 384, 22:228, 23:86, 24:368, 28:219, 39:85; roads, 11:389, 390, 15:346, 32:242, 37:35; personal accounts, 15:130, 223, 464, 16:334, 469; Des Moines River, 17:430n; ore lands, 19:309, 28:347, 39:78; soils, 21:212; Sandy Lake, 23:334; Winona township, 25:207; Michigan, 34:207; Sioux reservation, 37:348; cartographic, 40:125, 355. See also Boundaries, individual surveyors, various railroad companies
Susie Island, Cook County, Lake Superior, silver mine, 34:179
Susijärvi, Finnish settlement, 25:320
Susquehanna Indians, archaeological sites, 40:205-208
Susquehanna River, N.Y., Pa., Md., Indian settlement, 13:399
Susswein-Gottesman, Rita, author, 34:312
Sutherland, ---, Red River settler, 31:108
Sutherland, Daniel, testimony, 21:137-139; in fur trade, 21:146
Sutherland, Helen, 16:184
Sutherland, James, trader, 18:277
Sutherland, James B., broker, 24:375
Sutherland, James F., author, 18:102
Sutherlin, B. W., Winona plow manufacturer, 24:297
Sutley, Zach T., work reviewed, 12:174-176
Sutlief, Asa G., memorial, 17:490; farm, 21:110, 218
Sutter, Clara M., author, 30:264
Sutton, Alice T., author, 26:383
Sutton, C. C., steamboat captain, 33:9, 11, 12, 15
Sutton, C. Z., Worthington pioneer, 24:91
Sutton, Ernest V., author, 24:90, 29:271
Sutton, Glen, steamboat pilot, 33:12
Sutton, H. W., storekeeper, 24:326
Sutton, Lyman, Stillwater pioneer, 17:367, 24:204n
Sutton-Smith, B., author, 37:345
Suurmeyer, A. G., 23:392
Suydam, John V., pioneer printer, 15:16
Suzor, Jean-Renaud, author, 21:360, 361, 365
Svalander, Carl G., author, 18:74
Svea, Swedish settlement, 26:361
Svendsen, August, Mormon missionary, 36:288
Svendsen, Gro, letters, 32:121, 35:32
Svenska Amerikanska Posten (Minneapolis), Swedish-language paper, 26:308, 34:43
Svenskarnas Dag, Swedish holiday, 29:277, 278
Sverdrup, Georg, biography, 17:225; college president, 29:294, 297, 298, 40:377
Swahn, Charles, potter, 33:230
Swahn, J. G., Sons, potters, 33:230
Swahn, Jonas G., potter, 33:229, 230
Swain, David M., boatbuilder, 17:112
Swain, Frank O., collector, 13:447, 21:105
Swain, Thomas H., 35:48, 36:142
Swainson, John, pioneer, 40:65

Swainson, Kandiyohi County, name, 40:
68
Swales, Francis S., author, 40:98,
105, 106
Swallaw, Arthur C., lumberman, 24:375
"Swallow," steamboat, 21:259n, 264,
32:60
Swallow-Hopkins Lumber Co., St. Louis
County, 27:302
Swamp Portage, international bound-
ary, 13:298
Swan, Chauncey, letters, 30:160
Swan, Frank L., author, 18:120
Swan, Marshall W. S., author, 30:157
"Swan," steamboat, 33:12, 14, 15
Swan City, Nicollet County, plat, 17:
238; garrison, 38:280
Swan Lake, Cook County, logging, 36:
133
Swan Lake, Stevens County, bird life,
30:220, 35:242
Swan Lake Township, Stevens County,
sorghum mill, 17:212; agriculture,
26:291
Swan Land and Cattle Co., 12:177
Swan River (river), Itasca County,
steamboating, 33:8, 14, 17; log-
ging, 33:12
Swan River (river), Morrison County,
road, 19:103, 40:233; fur trade,
20:11; logging, 24:129
Swan River (river), Sask., Man., fur
trade, 40:174
Swan River (town), Morrison County,
ghost town, 26:179; lynching, 28:
213; German settlement, 31:25; de-
picted, 34:359; name, 36:327; post
office, 40:83, 87
Swan River Lumber Co., 29:177
Swaninger, Mrs. Elizabeth, 12:446
Swann, Clarence R., 12:185
Swann, Esther, 12:185
Swann, George W., 12:185
Swann, John R., 11:54; portrait, 12:
184; career, 12:184-186
Swann, Sophia Q., 12:185
Swann, Walter M., author, 22:445
Swanson, Rev. A. A., 14:359
Swanson, August, letter, 36:237
Swanson, C. J., speaker, 16:489, 17:
354
Swanson, Charles C., author, 27:269
Swanson, Mrs. Conrad, author, 30:405
Swanson, Gustav, speaker, 21:287; author, 22:103, 25:203, 26:227
Swanson, Mrs. Gustav (Evadene A. Burris), "Keeping House on the Minnesota Frontier," 14:263-282; "Frontier Food," 14:378-392; "Building
the Frontier Home," 15:43-55;
"Furnishing the Frontier Home,"
15:181-193; "Thoreau's Last Journey," 20:169-173; "The Dight Papers," 25:62-64; reviews by, 17:
86, 19:78-80, 203-205, 334, 20:64-
66, 22:311, 23:364, 25:173, 377,
26:366, 28:274, 29:160, 32:121;
author, 13:429, 14:438, 19:91,
207, 337, 20:74, 186, 22:316, 337,
23:99, 370, 25:76, 91, 92, 181,
383, 26:370, 28:308, 337, 29:192,
30:124n, 284, 31:13, 32:128, 34:
260, 39:260; speaker, 20:49
Swanson, Harold B., author, 30:264,
36:105
Swanson, Hilding, 22:216; speaker,
20:455

Swanson, Neil H., work reviewed, 15:
335-337; author, 17:444, 31:131,
147
Swanson, Peter, 14:428
Swanson, Roy W., 17:319, 29:185; "Ola
Värmlanning," 29:105-113; reviews
by, 12:420-422, 30:148, 36:100;
work reviewed, 30:145; author, 11:
102, 453, 12:81, 201, 212, 19:338,
29:191, 278, 282, 354, 30:184, 31:
14, 251, 36:106, 40:147; translator, 11:106, 31:221; speaker,
13:72
Swanston, J., trader, 40:168n
Swanstrom, Henry N., biography, 19:
214
Swanton, John R., work reviewed, 27:
336; author, 11:209
Swanton, Milo K., speaker, 27:356
Swanville, Lutheran church, 21:453
Swart, Walter G., mineralogist, 34:
272-283; depicted, 34:276
Swartwout, Egerton, author, 25:305
Sweatt, Charles B., businessman, 39:
131
Sweatt, Harold W., businessman, 36:
283, 39:131
Sweatt, William R., businessman, 39:
131
Sweatt family, 37:346
Sweatt Manufacturing Co., see Honeywell, Inc.
Swedberg, J. I., work reviewed, 39:
208
Swedberg, P. W., author, 35:50
Swede Grove Township, Meeker County,
history, 19:470; located, 33:144n
Swede Hollow, St. Paul, 23:69; depicted, 36:239, 40:252
Swede Town, Anoka, 25:364
Sweden, free-church movements, 12:
414, 13:310; press, 12:415, 20:
248; emigration from, 17:404, 18:
69, 19:331, 20:192, 247, 26:259,
378, 30:65, 32:49, 53, 34:199,
353, 37:177, 38:386, 39:260, 341;
state church, 32:53; urban history, 33:201-207; commentators on
America, 39:81
Swedes, pioneer life, 11:337, 18:225,
314, 25:394, 26:259; during colonial period, 11:453, 24:156, 27:
62, 28:55; Minnesota communities,
12:271, 450, 14:354, 427, 16:493,
17:316, 353, 399, 487, 489, 19:
125, 475, 20:243-258, 24:90, 190,
241, 352, 26:95, 31:160, 34:61,
35:50, 337, 36:201, 38:243, 40:
412; immigration, 12:413-416, 18:
69-75, 19:106, 20:98, 24:258, 30:
188, 31:26, 27, 37:262, 38:381;
organizations, 13:214, 19:112, 34:
172, 36:35, 106; occupations, 13:
284, 27:206, 207; religion, 13:
304-307, 14:94, 356, 17:328, 396-
398, 19:112, 28:75, 29:255, 354,
30:263, 32:53, 33:138, 35:201, 37:
177, 39:81, 40:353; almanacs, 15:
448; journals, 16:207, 21:35, 31:
54, 39:270, 40:353; celebrations,
16:389, 19:356, 22:225, 27:256,
29:80, 182, 277-279, 31:221; Wisconsin, 16:479, 19:331, 20:86, 24:
369, 27:135, 30:159; in politics,
17:161, 18:213, 22:104, 35:63, 36:
326; language, 17:320, 21:427, 26:
57, 27:175, 38:381, 39:36; St.

Croix Valley, 17:396-405, 36:195,
38:38, 39:131; newspapers, 17:403,
18:71, 19:219, 29:176, 34:43; contributions, 19:220, 33:187; South
Dakota, 19:222; agriculture, 23:
88, 24:79; in fiction, 23:118, 29:
105-113, 30:391, 33:137, 34:163,
36:80, 37:39, 38:38; Iowa, 23:184;
museums, 23:190, 24:256, 26:87,
167; in Civil War, 24:157; history, 26:56-59, 364, 31:111, 34:
199; co-operative movement, 26:
361; in iron mining, 27:206, 207;
biographies, 30:148, 32:49; place
names, 31:253; theater, 33:40;
schools, 33:309, 34:172, 38:382,
39:81; population, 34:175; bibliography, 35:290; Nebraska, 37:39;
ballads, 40:44. See also Finland
Swedes, Scandinavians
Swede's Forest Township, Redwood
County, settled, 12:275n, 13:453
Swedish American Bible Seminary, St.
Paul, 15:235
Swedish-American Line, essay contest,
29:80
Swedish-American Tercentenary, celebrated, 19:59, 20:42
Swedish Baptist Church, Brunswick,
Kanabec County, 15:481; Cokato,
22:350
Swedish Evangelical Lutheran Church,
Vista, Waseca County, 14:451, 452
Swedish Evangelical Mission Covenant
of America, St. Paul, 15:362, 19:
212, 20:34
Swedish Historical Society of Amer-
ica, meetings, 11:103, 12:93, 13:
107, 15:123, 16:108; collections,
11:202, 12:27, 81, 192, 13:59, 61,
23:190, 29:108, 31:251
Swedish Historical Society of Rockford, Ill., museum, 26:167
Swedish Methodist Church, Lindstrom,
14:353
Swedish Mission church, Duluth, 14:
452; Forest Mills, 35:20
Swedish Pioneer Centennial, celebrated, 29:80, 105n, 182, 277-279,
30:148, 152
Swedish Pioneer Historical Society,
31:54; publications, 31:251, 32:49
Swedish Saengerfest, meeting, 15:460
Swedish Tabernacle, Minneapolis, 33:
96
Swedish Young People's Hall, Marine
on St. Croix, 17:316
Sweeley, Phyllis, 23:367; author, 16:
349, 17:395n; speaker, 17:484;
manuscript assistant, 22:421, 23:
44, 24:31, 34
Sween, Milo I., author, 17:102
Sweeney, Gen. Thomas W., Union officer, 40:123
Sweeny, Robert O., papers, 21:35, 84,
312, 33:129n; artist, 29:200, 209,
211, 30:206n, 32:190, 34:98, 101,
35:182, 354, 355, 369, 36:1
(cover), 44, 40:11, 89; designs
state seal, 33:127
Sweepstakes thresher, 24:301, 302
Sweet, D. H., founder of Pipestone,
31:205
Sweet, Francis B., collector, 15:345
Sweet, Rev. Frank W., papers, 11:42
Sweet, George W., election commissioner, 26:195

Sweet, Jannette E., Sioux captive, 34:236, 38:107n, 140n
Sweet, Rev. Joshua, Fort Ridgely chaplain, 38:107n
Sweet, William W., reviews by, 24:41-43, 33:80; works reviewed, 18:196, 21:72; speaker, 13:327; author, 16:239, 24:60
Sweetcorn, Sioux Indian, 35:172
Sweeting, Chloe (Mrs. George Langford), 33:6
Sweeting family, 22:193
Sweetman, Fred, papers, 12:320
Sweetman, Honoria, 19:92
Sweetman, John, colonizer, 19:92, 23:7, 31:22
Sweetser, Mrs. H. B., author, 11:320
Sweetser, Madison, 34:360; traders' agent, 32:77-79; trader, 39:48
Swem, E. G., 16:220
Swendsen, Carl J., 15:123
Sweney, Dr. William M., archaeologist, 26:280, 29:83
Sweney, Dr. William W., 26:287; climate report, 17:258
Swenson, Anna, speaker, 19:117
Swenson, Rev. C. V., 24:190
Swenson, Charles E., farmer, 23:88
Swenson, David F., speaker, 12:93; author, 12:325
Swenson, Gunder, 15:488
Swenson, Harry S., papers, 29:286
Swenson, Jonas, pioneer, 23:403
Swenson, Laurits S., letters, 21:86
Swenson, Myrna, author, 16:337; speaker, 16:362
Swenson, Nels, speaker, 24:270
Swenson, Paul, author, 36:106
Swenson, Ralph, speaker, 19:316
Swenson, Rinehart J., author, 11:450
Swenson, S. O., author, 20:358
Swenson, Mrs. S. T., 20:358
Swift, Ernest, author, 28:290
Swift, Fletcher H., author, 12:418
Swift, Henry A., governor, 22:295, 26:199, 200, 36:170; land officer, 39:86, 91
Swift, Sarah, 18:263
Swift and Co., South St. Paul, 19:121
Swift County, history, 11:42, 339, 434-436; pioneer life, 12:211, 31:59; railroad, 12:254; ethnic groups, 12:275n, 277, 23:290, 31:21; anniversary, 17:366; homestead records, 21:224; school, 28:192; census, 28:303; Catholic colonies, 35:134, 325; Farmer-Labor members, 38:303; electric service, 40:315
Swift County Historical Society, 16:241; organized, 11:14, 119; dues, 11:20; activities, 11:224, 338, 12:169; publication, 11:434-436, 12:39; museum, 11:467, 12:37, 18:224, 336; reorganized, 30:280
Swift County Monitor (Benson), history, 17:366
Swift County News (Benson), politics, 38:305
Swift County War History Committee, 23:392
Swift Falls, Swift County, Norwegian settlement, 23:290
Swimming, Lake Calhoun, 40:34
Swinburne, John, army surgeon, 25:143
Swindlehurst, A. G., 18:109, 22:444; author, 30:394
Swindlehurst, Mrs. A. G., 22:444

Swineford, Alfred P., 21:375; pioneer journalist, 23:300
Swisher, Carl B., work reviewed, 17:76-78
Swisher, Jacob A., works reviewed, 22:184, 24:239; author, 12:329, 14:226, 15:236, 475, 16:346, 17:222, 21:203, 22:430, 26:170, 172, 27:69
Swiss, Red River settlers, 13:240, 14:283, 284, 286, 20:56, 175, 21:205, 22:3, 51, 203, 287, 23:94, 28:372; Wisconsin, 16:226, 28:188; in cheese industry, 17:486, 27:119; Minnesota, 21:203, 22:203, 28:333; in Civil War, 33:84; cooking, 40:47
Swiss-American Historical Society, publication, 22:203
Swisshelm, Jane G., 14:279, 389, 18:208, 30:406, 411, 35:265; controversies, 11:454, 16:98, 18:119, 19:343, 25:202; in fiction, 11:459; family, 12:84, 18:280; travels, 12:203; journalism career, 13:211, 14:404, 405, 16:116, 117, 17:365, 22:430, 25:93, 27:2, 38:204; reformer, 13:434, 14:139, 22:245, 29:238, 32:16-19, 21:23, 24, 29-31, 37:344; letters, 14:63, 15:58, 462, 16:50, 76-78, 467, 20:290, 28:299; quoted, 14:273, 276, 29:240, 30:268, 269; memorial, 15:476, 19:228; author, 17:107, 18:319; biography, 17:225, 26:237; war nurse, 18:319, 22:174, 176; source material, 18:443, 19:450, 20:81, 328; speaker, 20:329; characterized, 30:252, 35:255
Swisshelm, Nettie, 35:268, 269
Switzerland County (Ind.) Historical Society, 19:221
Swore, Rudolph, speaker, 15:246
Syberg, Arnold, engineer, 40:224, 226
Sybil Lake, Otter Tail County, name, 12:341
Sykes, Egerton, work reviewed, 31:49
Sykes, Sir Francis, 33:277n, 278; hunter, 19:385, 20:191, 35:258
Sykes, James, 12:190, 25:289
Sylvan, Wright County, Quakers, 18:254n
Sylvan Lake, Jackson County, ghost town, 14:256
Sylvania, proposed state, 20:9, 27:129
Sylvester, John, 13:196, 412n
Sylvester, Mrs. John, 13:196, 412n
Syme, Ronald, author, 32:124
Symmes, John C., 16:204
Symons, Charles, 14:272
Syndicate Building, Minneapolis, 33:177
Synsteby, Ole, 14:455; author, 20:459
Syracuse (Sabin) Lake, St. Louis County, iron deposits, 26:255
Syrians, Detroit, Mich., 20:202; Mesabi Range, 27:214
Syrjamaki, John, see Sirjamaki, John
Szarkowski, John, work reviewed, 36:99; author, 35:242

"T. H. Camp," steamboat, 34:247
Taaffe, Agnes, author, 27:47

Taaffe, Florence, author, 12:447, 452
Tabeau, Jean Baptiste, testimony, 21:136
Tabeau, Jean Baptiste Henri, trader, 21:136n
Tabeau, Father Pierre Antoine, missionary, 11:306, 21:136n, 399, 39:303, 305; letters, 12:82, 24:42
Taber, Irving, Quaker minister, 18:261n
Taber, Louis J., 20:86; speaker, 16:487
Tabor, Edward O., author, 27:255
Tabor, name, 13:199; Bohemian settlement, 17:128
Taché, Archbishop Alexandre A., 13:209, 19:412, 21:252, 432
Tacoma, Wash., land speculation, 24:124
Taconite, processing, 29:172, 30:155, 36:103; mines, 33:282; companies, 33:283, 34:216, 269, 35:245, 36:282, 37:41; name, 33:283, 34:270n; development, 33:355, 34:269-283, 314, 35:294, 36:35; economic aspect, 39:144; history, 39:163. See also Iron mining
Tadoussac, Que., history, 23:385; trade center, 40:157
Taeuber, Irene B., "Weekly Newspapers," 14:411-415; author, 13:211, 442, 14:103
Taft, Robert, reviews by, 29:335-337, 33:133; author, 21:95, 27:159, 254, 354, 28:79, 29:266, 350, 376, 31:253, 33:90, 134n, 264
Taft, Robert A., isolationist, 40:410
Taft, William H., 30:54; President, 18:122, 303, 22:78-80, 40:317, 318, 320, 321, 326; letter, 18:316; speaker, 21:401; presidential medal, 25:79; characterized, 27:133, 29:156
Taft, St. Louis County, railroad station, 34:184
Tainter, Andrew, lumberman, 40:102, 103
Tainter, Louis, house, 40:103
Tainter, Mabel, memorial, 40:97 (cover), 101-103, 108n, 412
Taintor Brothers and Merrill, New York, map publishers, 18:446
Tajiri, Cpl. Tom, author, 27:261
Takela, A., labor leader, 40:344
Talbot, Francis, 16:162
Talbot, Loretta T., 14:233
Talbott, C. C., Alliance organizer, 28:42, 44
Talcot Lake, Cottonwood County, trading post, 11:381
Talcott, Amelia, pioneer teacher, 23:111
Talcott, Capt. Andrew, at Fort Snelling, 23:339, 340; surveyor, 24:368, 30:392
Talcott, Orlando, 21:108
Taliaferro, Maj. Lawrence, 11:373, 375, 23:85; Indian agent, 11:372, 381, 13:222, 15:274, 275, 16:96, 135, 454, 18:404, 19:354, 20:121, 262, 21:24, 22:287, 23:339, 24:3, 18n, 19n, 21n, 23n, 40:79, 138, 139, 186n; source material, 12:190, 14:99, 330, 25:272; journals, 12:218, 232, 239, 13:230, 16:373, 18:154, 20:264, 23:7, 24:11, 12, 28:16n, 30:103, 31:197n, 40:146;

land claim, 12:317, 16:215, 34:
355; papers, 15:462, 16:73, 20:77,
21:93, 25:182, 26:362, 35:204, 40:
96; quoted, 16:138, 18:163, 28:
18n; career, 17:225, 35:23, 197,
40:261; politician, 19:460; map
maker, 21:83, 27:142, 35:22-29,
197; characterized, 21:163; slave
holder, 25:272, 29:351, 33:138;
portrait, 28:89; in fiction, 30:
247

Taliaferro, Mrs. Lawrence, portrait,
28:89; biographical sketch, 39:
267; piano owner, 39:314

Tallamy, B. D., author, 21:423

Tallmadge, Thomas E., architect, 40:
106

Tallman, D. N., reminiscences, 21:451

Talman, Capt. Byron, 11:185

Talman, James J., 24:330; author, 32:
126

Talman, John, "The Study of Pioneer
Life," 11:185-187; author, 11:447,
13:198, 16:122, 17:92; newspaper
librarian, 13:116; poet, 26:301

Talman family, genealogy, 13:198

Talmoon, Itasca County, name, 20:359

Talon, Jean B., intendant of New
France, 18:388, 19:274, 23:254,
25:265

Tamaha, Sioux Indian, 25:269

Tamarack House, Stillwater, hotel,
11:225, 24:196, 197

Tamarack River, Beltrami and Koochiching counties, log drives, 29:146

Tamaroa Indians, 30:249

Tanberg, Christian, homestead, 11:226

Tancig, A., author, 33:355

Tandy, Sara E., author, 23:402

Taney, Justice Roger B., 23:262, 25:
360, 28:310, 39:39; biographies,
17:76-78, 20:418-420

Tangen, Leland R., house, 38:350

Tanner, A. F., publisher, 25:327

Tanner, G. W., author, 22:443

Tanner, Rev. George O., career, 11:
338; author, 18:331

Tanner, James, 18:95; missionary, 19:
378, 381n, 382, 35:282

Tanner, Mrs. James, 19:378

Tanner, John, 14:93, 19:378, 24:342,
34:219, 36:151; trader, 11:361;
author, 14:423, 29:66, 30:123, 35:
199, 36:100; career, 15:238; Indian captive, 17:210, 22:180, 24:
44, 25:297, 26:362, 31:105, 34:
285, 39:191, 385

Tanner, Louise, author, 37:133

Tansill, Charles C., work reviewed,
25:171

Tantankamani, see Red Wing, Sioux
leader

Tanzer, Lester, work reviewed, 37:343

Taopi (Wounded Man), Sioux leader,
11:317, 38:96, 131, 136, 141n;
opposes outbreak, 38:106n

Taoyateduta, see Little Crow (Taoyateduta)

Tappan, Henry P., library, 23:3

Tapper, Capt. John, ferryman, 20:413,
414; statue, 20:413-416; career,
20:415, 28:286

Tapping, Mrs. A. E. (Minnie E.),
speaker, 21:335; author, 36:104

Tarbell, Elliott, author, 27:358, 28:
84

Tarbell, Ida, author, 14:200, 28:361

Tariff, political issue, 11:453, 40:
320-325; legislation, 22:79, 40:
321; Canada-U.S., 32:126, 39:93

Tarkington, Booth, author, 26:308

Tasa, Knut T., 12:328

Tasker, A. E., 16:366; speaker, 17:
122; author, 17:127, 18:340

Tate, Allen, essay reviewed, 37:83

Tate, Vernon D., speaker, 17:105

Tatepaha Golf Club, Faribault, records, 16:242

Tatley, Hans J., author, 12:336

Tattersall Hotel, High Forest, 16:
367, 18:227, 21:213

Taube, Edward, author, 33:90

Taube, Henning A., emigrant agent,
17:404, 18:74

Tavernier, Jules, artist, 27:159

Tawas Point, Mich., Lake Huron, 23:
140n

Tawney, James A., papers, 12:312, 13:
198, 14:64; Congressman, 17:226;
boundary commissioner, 23:207;
politician, 40:317-329; portrait,
40:318

Tax, Sol, author, 34:301

Taxes, inheritance, 12:17, 16:356;
income, 12:17, 21:300-302, 22:422,
24:52; Minnesota, 14:207, 16:82,
20:91, 24:374, 35:310; sales, 16:
357, 40:36; property, 22:241;
beneficiaries, 22:363, 35:127,
128, 40:37; study, 35:336. See
also Tariff

Taylor, Abraham M., 18:251

Taylor, Allen, author, 15:371

Taylor, Ann (Mrs. Robert C. Wood),
marriage, 28:177, 30:97, 98

Taylor, Arnold W., 24:127; characterized, 27:313

Taylor, Bayard, speaker, 12:94; letters, 19:217; lecturer, 19:399-
418, 21:326, 35:222; evaluated,
19:417; author, 23:114, 27:16

Taylor, Bert L., career, 17:226

Taylor, C. T., speaker, 12:208, 17:
121

Taylor, Judge Charles, 19:170

Taylor, Col. Charles W., author, 11:
209

Taylor, Clarence, speaker, 11:114

Taylor, Danford, 25:18, 225, 254

Taylor, David, letter, 16:217

Taylor, E. A., speaker, 16:243

Taylor, E. G. R., author, 30:375

Taylor, Edward, farmer, 25:13; Union
soldier, 25:131, 141

Taylor, Elizabeth, missionary, see
Ayer, Mrs. Frederick, I

Taylor, Elizabeth, traveler, 29:167,
262, 30:387, 31:56

Taylor, Emma R., 25:11n, 18

Taylor, Garland, 13:345

Taylor, George, boatbuilder, 33:17

Taylor, George R., works reviewed,
19:90, 35:237

Taylor, Mrs. H. J., author, 25:300

Taylor, H. Knox, 19:415

Taylor, Dr. H. Longstreet, medical
leader, 20:46, 23:96, 30:175

Taylor, H. S., theatrical agent, 28:
103

Taylor, Henry O., 14:90

Taylor, Isaac L., I, 18:96; career,
25:11-17; diary, 25:11-39, 117-
152, 224-257, 342-361; death, 25:
360; burial, 25:361

Taylor, Isaac L., II, 25:17

Taylor, James, boatbuilder, 33:14

Taylor, James, career, 23:75

Taylor, James, genealogy, 15:349

Taylor, James C., Jr., author, 30:268

Taylor, James W., 12:441, 33:1, 34:
333, 40:262; consul, 13:112, 337,
17:226, 19:412, 29:167, 30:150,
262, 387, 33:183; papers, 15:123,
17:464, 18:47, 315, 21:86, 34:352,
40:93; with William H. Nobles expedition, 18:274, 35:249, 252,
258, 260-262; speaker, 19:259, 35:
364; annexation advocate, 20:321,
33:139, 315, 35:47, 151, 36:32,
102; career, 23:75, 37:54, 57; author, 31:185, 35:253, 37:55, 56;
railroad interests, 35:363, 37:38;
depicted, 37:54, 38:56

Taylor, Jay, singer, 33:324, 325

Taylor, Jesse, pioneer, 27:127; lumberman, 17:283, 24:201

Taylor, Mrs. Jesse, pioneer, 24:203

Taylor, Jesse, Co., construction
firm, 37:138

Taylor, Jonathan, 25:13, 14, 18, 245

Taylor, Jonathan H., 25:11, 13, 20,
224, 289, 342, 344, 351

Taylor, Mrs. Jonathan H., 25:11

Taylor, Joshua L., 17:283, 35:257n;
lumberman, 27:125; house, 27:125-
127, 231; prison official, 37:
143-145

Taylor, Mrs. Joshua L. (Clarinda Wyman), 27:126, 127

Taylor, Judson, 25:18

Taylor, Knox, Jr., architect, 38:80

Taylor, Lucy P., author, 29:356

Taylor, Lute A., 15:88

Taylor, Lytton, author, 36:325

Taylor, Mary, 25:17, 18

Taylor, Mary Elizabeth (Betty), 30:
97, 98

Taylor, Nathan C. D., geologist, 32:
217; postmaster, 36:209

Taylor, Oscar, 12:318

Taylor, Patrick Henry, 18:96, 25:18;
education, 25:12; family, 25:13;
Union soldier, 25:14, 16, 38, 39,
117, 127, 225, 227, 228, 230, 232,
234, 240, 241, 247, 248, 250, 349,
350, 360n, 361; career, 25:19n;
letters, 25:126n, 134n; prisoner
of war, 25:141-152

Taylor, Philip S., work reviewed, 35:
199; author, 34:354

Taylor, Richard, 30:97, 98

Taylor, Col. Richard, death, 30:100n

Taylor, Richard B., author, 39:132

Taylor, Russell J., 25:18, 139

Taylor, Samuel, 25:18

Taylor, Mrs. Samuel S., 38:77n

Taylor, Sarah K., 25:15n, 29:335,
30:97

Taylor, Thomas B., 14:455

Taylor, W. L., speaker, 11:338; author, 14:462

Taylor, Will H., journalist, 20:462

Taylor, William, barber, 29:120

Taylor, Rev. William, at Red Rock,
31:89

Taylor, William A., author, 12:442

Taylor, Mrs. William D., author, 18:
118

Taylor, William L., lumberman, 12:448

Taylor, William R., Indian agent, 37:
40

Taylor, William R., Wisconsin governor, 19:150

Taylor, Zachary, 28:319, 343; "Zachary Taylor to Thomas Lawson," 28:15-19; army officer, 16:112, 22:206, 24:2, 30:103, 33:263, 39:174, 40:79; biography, 17:225, 27:253; at Fort Snelling, 28:177, 30:98-103; President, 28:206, 310, 30:104-110, 189, 196, 33:82, 35:353, 36:3, 267, 39:38, 143, 144; letter, 29:100; family, 30:97; death, 30:190, 191

Taylor, Mrs. Zachary, 28:16, 30:97, 101

Taylor family, in Minnesota, 25:13; in Civil War, 25:18

Taylor's Alarm Register, thresher accessory, 24:302

Taylors Falls, lumbering, 13:99, 39:273; newspapers, 13:315, 17:314, 385; library, 15:360; Methodist church, 15:468, 38:341; roads, 16:283, 36:210, 40:239, 245, 246; pageant, 16:359; G.A.R. post, 16:431, 447; river port, 17:282, 24:206, 36:212; described, 17:283, 284, 36:281; geology, 17:315; source material, 17:393, 394, 20:190, 315, 36:195; postmaster, 20:316; school, 23:164, 36:128; history, 23:400; architecture, 27:125-127, 232, 38:338, 339, 341-343, 350; railroad, 29:87; mail service, 36:209, 211-213, 40:83. See also Interstate Park

Teach, Edward ("Blackbeard"), pirate, 26:166

Teague, Guy E., cartoonist, 24:167, 30:160

Teague, Walter D., work reviewed, 33:132

Teasdale, Sara, poet, 26:308

Tebbutt, John T., author, 16:480

Tebishgobenais, Chippewa leader, 16:321

Technical High School, St. Cloud, history, 16:371, 23:110

Tecumseh, Shawnee leader, 19:330, 28:56, 33:344, 40:180

Teegarden, Wis., sorghum mill, 35:201

Teeple, Addison V., in Civil War, 26:67

Tegeder, Father Vincent, 31:256, 38:336; "The Benedictines in Frontier Minnesota," 32:34-43; "Pioneering Monks," 33:53-60; reviews by, 31:239, 38:193; author, 32:64

Teien Township, Kittson County, Lutheran church, 14:452

Teigan, Henry G., 28:38n; author, 18:459; papers, 23:40, 24:34; portrait, 38:304; Congressman, 40:369, 371-374

Teigen, Ferdinand A., author, 34:226

Teigen, Knut M., author, 13:324

Teigland, Martin A., author, 14:121

Telander, Mrs. Clara, speaker, 23:399

Telegraph, Winona, 18:120; early St. Paul, 25:307, 38:55; Atlantic cable, 26:67; Winnipeg, 30:262

Telephone, Itasca County, 15:487; museums, 18:102, 319, 19:50, 99, 28:89; Minnesota communities, 18:337, 344, 24:192, 27:169; La Crosse, Wis., 20:340; Carver County, 20:356; in business, 23:87; Iowa, 23:

285; in lumber industry, 27:306; North Dakota, 28:268

Television stations, historical programs, 36:323; KSTP, St. Paul, 39:172; KTCA, St. Paul, 39:172, 40:364

Temiskaming, Que., trading post, 11:233

Temperance House, St. Paul, hotel, 34:99n, 101

Temperance Lake, Cook County, 36:135

Temperance movement, 25:63; Wisconsin, 12:200; among Norwegians, 12:305, 16:219; support groups, 12:395, 14:138, 15:135, 16:317, 18:264, 19:214, 22:370, 23:76, 31:90; legislation, 14:138, 16:469, 29:220, 40:390n; Minnesota, 14:438, 20:80; periodicals, 16:219, 20:331, 35:120, 122; political action, 19:146, 35:114; leaders, 19:257, 265-267, 28:54, 35:109; songs, 22:123-125; among Finns, 22:391-403, 32:185, 40:48, 344; Iowa, 34:22n; relation to woman suffrage, 39:10. See also Liquor traffic, Prohibition movement

Temperance Reform Club, Minneapolis, 18:264

Temperance River, Cook County, name, 12:287

Temple, Wayne C., work reviewed, 36:191

Temple & Beaupre, St. Paul, farm machinery merchants, 24:288; steamboat agents, 37:227

Temple Baptist Church, Duluth, 15:243

Temple University, Philadelphia, founded, 14:394

Ten Lakes Township, Beltrami County, history, 15:132

Ten Mile Lake, Otter Tail County, resort, 16:492; stage route, 38:64

Ten Thousand Lakes of Minnesota Association, St. Paul, 36:92; publication, 16:259; activities, 19:98

Ten Eyck, J. C., excursionist, 15:406

Ten Hoor, Marten, author, 29:174

Tennant, Joseph F., author, 29:99

Tennelly, Rev. J. B., editor, 17:84

Tennessee, printing, 15:12, 14; travel in, 15:124; government, 34:82; politics, 39:143

Tennessee Coal and Iron Co., 27:133

Tenney, ---, church trustee, 19:264, 267n

Tenney, Col. Frank, speaker, 19:316

Tenney, Hiram B., 14:455

Tenney, William W., 12:450

Tennis, on frontier, 20:441; St. Paul, 40:32

Tennyson, Alfred, Lord, 26:302

Tenstrike, logging, 29:141; railhead, 29:147; newspaper, 29:356

Tenstrike Tribune, 29:356

Tenth Judicial District, judges, 15:250

Tenth Minnesota Volunteer Infantry, 14:310, 26:197n, 205, 206, 38:292, 362, 363; at Indian execution, 17:336; in Civil War, 38:245 (cover), 287; in Sioux Outbreak, 38:276, 280; homecoming, 38:291

Tenth U.S. Infantry, 12:61n, 116n

Tenvoorde, John W., hotelkeeper, 35:265-267

Terhaar, Herman J., 33:54

Terpstra, Bouke, Dutch pioneer, 28:125

Terrace, history, 11:337; mill, 21:218

Terre Haute, Ind., lyceum, 14:445; frontier post, 15:379, 380

Territorial party, in politics, 36:3, 265, 266, 270, 39:40, 42, 45, 48

Territorial Road, St. Paul-Minneapolis, 30:373, 33:331

Terry, Gen. Alfred H., 28:224; biography, 17:226

Terry, Elijah, murdered, 16:97, 19:379

Terry, R. W., author, 23:109, 25:101

Tesca, F. G., 11:113

Teske, Louis F., author, 16:255

Tessie, ---, trader, 11:262

Tessier, Abbé Albert, author, 17:113

Tesson, Louis, pioneer horticulturist, 23:91

Tête-au-Brochet, Man., Lake Winnipeg, trading post, 28:2

Teton band, Sioux Indians, 37:346; hostilities, 19:388, 33:274, 279n, 281; history, 25:86, 32:124; songs, 35:244; westward migration, 37:303; culture, 39:342, 40:47

Tetonka Lake, Le Sueur County, railroad, 30:236; hotel, 33:323, 324

Tetonka Park, Tetonka Lake, resort hotel, 33:323, 324

Tetonka Tonah, Rice County, Sioux village, 35:320

Tew, Martin E., journalist, 20:340

Tewksbury, Donald G., author, 14:224

Tews, Lorraine, author, 19:98

Texas, ranching, 12:176; history, 30:251, 31:116

Texas and Pacific Railway Co., history, 28:187

Texas State Historical Association, Austin, 25:190; junior branch, 28:175

Thain, Thomas, trader, 28:12

Thalbitzer, William, author, 33:314

Thalbote (Chaska), German-language paper, 27:327

Thalia Theater Society, St. Paul, 32:240

Thams, Dr. Tonnes, 20:401, 407

Thanksgiving Day, menus, 14:391, 16:378, 18:296; frontier celebrations, 15:131, 16:168, 18:378, 23:196, 26:93, 30:67, 37:223, 39:320; varied dates, 19:134, 248, 255, 30:145, 37:223; church services, 19:255; Wisconsin, 20:339; in Civil War camp, 25:234

Tharalson, D. N., 22:106

Thatcher, Mrs. Elizabeth, murdered, 38:123

Thatcher, Myron W., career, 35:203

Thatcher, Orville D., 25:21, 141n, 247, 251, 253

Thatcher, Roscoe W., career, 17:226

Thayer, Burton W., author, 17:115, 21:424, 22:210, 23:288, 25:304, 398, 37:307

Thayer, Mrs. Carl T., speaker, 15:313, 16:485, 487; author, 22:338

Thayer, Rev. Charles, 27:344, 37:308; papers, 28:395, 29:49

Thayer, Maj. Sylvannus, West Point commandant, 36:97

Thayer family, musicians, 22:114

Thayer and Co., Boston, music publishers, 26:53

Theater, traveling troupes, 11:100, 28:97-119; ethnic, 13:273, 15:39, 21:414, 22:402, 33:40; halls, 15:254, 468, 18:468, 23:109, 199, 311-314, 24:189, 25:101, 26:291, 28:98-101, 103, 113, 119, 32:170, 33:169-178, 34:99; amateur, 16:383, 29:271, 37:348; Minnesota communities, 17:490, 18:227, 20:94, 466, 23:26, 29:271, 40:363; Twin Cities, 18:137, 138, 294, 23:198, 305-315, 369, 26:373, 39:263; pioneer, 20:432, 27:94, 30:388, 31:116; vaudeville, 23:76, 33:177; German, 23:286, 32:100-105, 127, 164-173, 33:188, 315, 34:99, 239-242; performers, 23:305-308, 310, 314, 28:108-110, 112-115, 117-119, 179, 31:120, 33:173, 174, 176; stagehands' union, 26:291; management, 28:97-103, 109, 31:116, 33:173, 174, 177, 35:156; showboats, 32:59, 33:39, 36:106, 40:410; history, 36:147; bibliography, 40:311

Theatre Comique, Minneapolis, 28:99

Theissen, Henry, 19:120

Theissen, John (Jack), 27:170; speaker, 29:273

Theobald, Father Stephen L., 24:92; career, 30:260

Theony, Capt. M., 23:102

Theopold, H. C., speaker, 14:461, 18:335

Theopold, Mrs. H. C., 19:467, 22:107, 25:408, 29:93; speaker, 17:232, 21:446

Theosophical Society, Minneapolis, 19:235

Thexton, H. A., 22:195

Thibodo, Dr. Augustus J., with Nobles expedition, 35:253, 261

Thief, The, Sioux leader, 38:137, 148

Thief Lake, Marshall County, pageant, 17:483

Thief River, Marshall, Pennington, and Red Lake counties, trading post, 11:368; name, 14:122

Thief River Falls, creamery, 11:117, 18:470; name, 11:222; pioneer days celebration, 14:122; sawmills, 17:128, 29:137; lumbering, 29:146; library, 40:363

Thiegles, Betty L., 29:283

Thiel, George A., review by, 36:188; works reviewed, 17:85, 34:116; author, 18:104; speaker, 21:288

Thiel, Helen, author, 14:239

Thiele, Gilbert A., author, 35:201

Thiers, Louis A., 28:253

Thiers, Martha (Mrs. Louis Rabishung), 28:254-256

Thiers, Paul, 28:253

Thiers, Mrs. Paul, 28:253

"Thingvalla," steamboat, 20:408

Third Crossing, Man., agricultural settlement, 28:64

Third Illinois Cavalry, in St. Paul, 38:288, 289

Third Minnesota Volunteer Infantry, veterans, 14:427, 17:468; source material, 15:223; officers, 16:334, 25:204, 38:110n, 39:193, 194, 196, 197, 40:281-283, 291; depicted, 17:217, 39:197, 40:287; votes, 26:201, 205; Scandinavian

company, 33:84; surrender, 36:169, 39:191-197; in Sioux Outbreak, 36:234, 38:106, 107, 277, 278, 284; Arkansas campaign, 38:287, 40:281-292; homecoming, 38:291, 40:292; illnesses, 40:283

Third New York Cavalry, 25:22

Third Street, St. Paul, depicted, 29:116, 117

Third U.S. Cavalry, in Spanish-American War, 25:384

Third U.S. Infantry, 24:207; at Fort Snelling, 23:212, 267, 24:4; history, 23:268, 24:1, 5; archives, 23:271, 24:34, 25:398

Thirteen Towns, Polk County, anniversary, 14:358

Thirteen Towns (Fosston), 14:359; anniversaries, 15:251, 30:273

Thirteenth Avenue Church (Methodist), Minneapolis, 17:338

Thirteenth Minnesota Regimental Association, archives, 19:452, 20:35

Thirteenth Minnesota Volunteer Infantry, 14:219; in Spanish-American War, 12:192, 13:429, 15:466, 16:340, 473, 18:92, 99, 317, 19:97, 21:87, 25:78, 28:349, 29:265

Thirteenth Wisconsin Volunteer Infantry, 11:96

Thirtieth Wisconsin Volunteer Infantry, in Sully expedition, 17:98

Thirty-eighth Iowa Volunteer Infantry, 18:444

Thirty-fourth New York Volunteer Infantry, in Civil War, 25:345, 353

Thirty-ninth U.S. Colored Infantry, in Civil War, 29:188

Thirty-seventh Wisconsin Volunteer Infantry, 19:150

Thistlethwaite, Frank, work reviewed, 34:341

Thoburn, Rev. J. M., 17:379

Thoburn, Joseph B., 16:310, 311

Thole, Father Titus, author, 35:155

Thom, Emma M., author, 19:217

Thom, George, army engineer, 40:246, 247

Thomas, Benjamin P., work reviewed, 28:360; author, 40:296

Thomas, C. B., 22:293

Thomas, Charles H., author, 21:98

Thomas, Charles M., "Promoting Settlement," 18:298-301

Thomas, Cyrus, 29:70

Thomas, Dorothy, author, 20:116

Thomas, E. D., author, 15:373

Thomas, Sgt. E. K., artist, 35:182, 369

Thomas, Gen. George H., Union officer, 25:23n, 24, 33:280, 38:260, 261, 267, 270, 39:179, 181; quoted, 39:184

Thomas, H. L., author, 40:96

Thomas, Isaiah, editor, 16:153n; publisher, 34:203

Thomas, John, trader, 34:255, 355

Thomas, Joseph, 21:70

Thomas, Katharine G., author, 31:122

Thomas, L. G., author, 35:47

Thomas, Lewis F., author, 30:62, 32:14, 125, 33:314

Thomas, Lewis H., 26:39; reviews by, 25:66, 171; work reviewed, 35:148; author, 36:191

Thomas, Gen. Minor T., 39:179; in

Sioux Outbreak, 33:281n, 38:280, 283

Thomas, Norman, isolationist, 40:410

Thomas, Robert B., author, 15:445

Thomas, Robert D., translator, 21:370

Thomas, Theodore, orchestra conductor, 26:155, 33:96, 39:53, 54

Thomas, U. M., newspaperman, 21:451

Thomas, W. C. E., editor, 22:23

Thomas, W. Stephen, author, 29:77, 349

Thomas, William, letters, 30:150

"Thomas," transport ship, 38:313, 314, 316, 318

Thompson, Mrs. A. G., author, 21:222, 453

Thompson, A. W., speaker, 17:344

Thompson, Albert W., author, 17:473

Thompson, Judge Anton, 13:120, 16:124, 241, 17:122, 18:110, 20:353, 22:340, 23:103; speaker, 14:357, 16:369, 497, 17:357, 484, 19:361, 21:447

Thompson, Arthur T., author, 11:326

Thompson, Arvilla N., author, 13:346

Thompson, Benjamin, contractor, 11:181; at Old Crossing Treaty negotiations, 15:286, 292; land agent, 35:207, 209, 210; Indian agent, 38:357, 359

Thompson, Mrs. C. R., 22:442, 23:399

Thompson, C. W., author, 16:228

Thompson, Charles N., author, 15:125

Thompson, Charles T., author, 20:101

Thompson, Clark W., 21:221, 29:261; Indian agent, 25:183, 37:228n, 38:131, 355, 360, 363, 39:227-240; papers, 26:32; politician, 37:326

Thompson, D. O., author, 29:268

Thompson, David, 29:340, 31:183, 37:62; career, 11:107, 12:199, 13:439, 31:125, 37:183; explorer, 11:209, 12:294, 15:120, 238, 16:230, 349, 453, 18:215, 25:273, 27:259; author, 11:367, 15:239, 19:109, 26:276, 33:187, 34:174, 38:28, 39:171; trader, 12:326, 372, 373, 20:84; journals, 13:298, 18:94, 24:74, 29:133, 33:181; biography, 17:225; surveyor, 17:476, 18:232, 20:441, 22:179, 276; cartographer, 22:276, 26:268, 29:58, 132, 35:378, 36:277, 324; geographer, 36:64; described, 39:169

Thompson, David W., author, 30:280

Thompson, Denman, actor, 28:118

Thompson, Dorothy, 37:222

Thompson, E. A., author, 36:193

Thompson, E. Bruce, work reviewed, 34:209

Thompson, Earl, farmer, 34:64

Thompson, Edward, 21:221, 39:232, 233

Thompson, Edwin J., professor, 16:181

Thompson, Edwin S., lawyer, 14:333

Thompson, Eleazar, excursionist, 15:406

Thompson, Frank L., career, 23:192

Thompson, Fred, letters, 25:78

Thompson, George, portrait, 18:321; journalist, 26:95

Thompson, Mrs. George, portrait, 18:321

Thompson, Mrs. George R., 13:448, 14:456, 24:109n

Thompson, H. E., author, 15:484

Thompson, Harold W., author, 27:275, 34:213

Thompson, Helen J., speaker, 12:210
Thompson, Horace, 37:316; house, 15:
52, 54, 25:6; banker, 34:43, 99n
Thompson, J. E., medievalist, 14:194
Thompson, J. G., papers, 25:185
Thompson, J. Jørgen, speaker, 21:109
Thompson, James E., banker, 34:43,
99n
Thompson, James L., map maker, 35:23n
Thompson, James W., work reviewed,
24:157
Thompson, Jerome, artist, 33:21
Thompson, Jim, slave, 30:397
Thompson, John A. ("Snowshoe"), 12:
180; career, 36:98
Thompson, L. N., author, 15:140
Thompson, Lawrence S., author, 31:243
Thompson, Marjorie, 16:242
Thompson, Mark J., author, 19:356,
36:327
Thompson, Neil, speaker, 36:284
Thompson, Ole, farmer, 29:14
Thompson, Oscar, author, 18:450
Thompson, Paul J., letters, 18:98;
lawyer, 25:385
Thompson, Paul P., author, 11:225,
12:212, 14:124, 351, 15:253
Thompson, Ralph, author, 18:448
Thompson, Richard W., biography, 29:
252; traders' agent, 32:68, 69,
74; politician, 35:75
Thompson, Robert, author, 11:218
Thompson, Roy A., author, 37:42
Thompson, Ruth, 19:360, 20:96, 26:
151, 179; "The Statue of Captain
John Tapper," 20:413-416; author,
20:426, 21:182, 26:182, 27:168,
270, 358, 28:190, 286, 30:406
Thompson, S. A., 37:260
Thompson, Samuel M., 19:122, 473
Thompson, Stith, "Folklore and Minnesota History," 26:97-105; speaker,
25:306, 397; author, 26:153, 253,
368, 27:255, 35:153
Thompson, Thomas H., map publisher,
40:124, 127
Thompson, W. W., with Nobles expedi-
tion, 35:252
Thompson, Rev. William E., author,
12:106, 14:232, 18:225, 19:122,
364, 473; speaker, 12:453, 13:342;
editor, 17:486
Thompson Brothers, St. Paul, bankers,
40:111-114
Thompson Falls, Mont., trading post,
24:75
Thompson River, B.C., name, 29:340;
gold fields, 35:251
Thomsen, T. G., author, 30:396
Thomsen, T. H., craftsman, 15:470
Thomson, Cornelia, 14:46
Thomson, Don W., work reviewed, 40:
355
Thomson, Ezra, 14:46
Thomson, Hamilton, 14:46
Thomson, Helene M., career, 40:48
Thomson, Irving L., author, 15:358
Thomson, Joseph, 14:46
Thomson, Louisa, 14:46
Thomson, Luther, 14:46
Thomson, Mildred, work reviewed, 39:
27
Thomson, Mortimer S., career, 17:226
Thomson, Samuel, 14:46
Thomson, Rev. William, career, 14:46-
-48; speaker, 14:49
Thomson (Thomson's Junction), mill,

23:300; Finnish settlement, 25:
318; lumber center, 31:162; rail-
road, 37:93
Thorbeck, Margaret, author, 27:82,
178
Thordeman, Bengt, 17:183
Thoreau, Henry D., in Minnesota, 11:
327, 16:29, 35-46, 22:433, 35:215,
37:225-228; travels, 16:36, 38:
335; author, 16:105, 20:382; biog-
raphy, 17:226; journal quoted, 20:
169-173, 35:184
Thoreen, Reuben G., speaker, 29:368
Thoren, Helen M., speaker, 24:378
Thorgeirsson, Ólafur S., 15:447
Thorkelson, Willmar, author, 36:239
Thorkveen, Rev. L. P., biography, 12:
108
Thorlakson, Pall, author, 13:209
Thörn, Olof, author, 36:237
Thornbrough, Emma L., author, 36:101
Thornbrough, Gayle, review by, 32:
254; work reviewed, 35:239; au-
thor, 29:335, 32:256; editor, 34:
175
Thornburg, Opal, author, 33:316
Thorne, Harry D., 20:448; author, 16:
487, 19:463
Thorne, John L., banker, 21:413, 22:
89
Thorne, Sir Richard, author, 21:363
Thorne Norrish and Co., Hastings,
records, 21:413, 22:41, 192
Thornton, George, author, 26:179
Thornton, H. B., 18:120
Thornton, Harrison J., author, 13:
436, 14:226, 31:57
Thornton, M. J., 26:126n, 132
Thornton, R. S., 17:231; author, 30:
161, 271, 36:106
Thornton, Ralph, author, 36:36
Thorp, Col. Freeman, artist, 21:332
Thorp, Mrs. J. G., 29:335
Thorp, Margaret F., work reviewed,
30:251; author, 22:430
Thorp, Raymond W., author, 35:377
Thorp, Sara, 25:86
Thorp, Vivian, author, 20:216, 21:215
Thorp, Willard, editor, 28:279
Thorpe, Samuel S., 19:184n; career,
36:189
Thorpe Brothers, Minneapolis, real-
estate firm, 26:287
Thorson, Gerald, review by, 39:126
Thorson (Harold) Library, Elbow Lake,
15:487
Thorsten, Serine, 27:46
Thorton, John, map maker, 16:421
Thortvedt, Levi, 13:286; author, 19:
234; diary, 25:262
Thortvedt, Ola, pioneer, 21:219
Thott, A., 20:244n
Thousand Islands, N.Y., Ont., St.
Lawrence River, described, 29:218
Thoynard, Nicolas, 19:396
Thrall, Mrs. L. A., author, 27:173
Thrane, Marcus, 32:51, 40:140; ca-
reer, 18:315
Three Forks, Mont., depicted, 40:194
Three Hundred and Eighth Machine Gun
Battalion, 12:321
Three Hundred and Forty-sixth College
Training Detachment, history, 25:
312
Three Lakes, Redwood County, garri-
son, 38:285

3M, see Minnesota Mining and Manufac-
turing Co.
Three Maidens, Pipestone National
Monument, 31:201-203
Three Rivers, Mich., history, 13:110
Three Rivers, Que., see Trois
Rivières
"Three Spot," locomotive, 12:284, 19:
236, 26:276
Throckmorton, Joseph, steamboat cap-
tain, 11:210, 13:229, 231-236,
238, 18:154, 434
Throne, Mildred, author, 30:160; edi-
tor, 33:228, 36:279
Thuland, Conrad M., lawyer, 33:43
Thule culture, 40:95
Thullen, J. H., artist, 39:190n
Thunder, Jim, Chippewa Indian, 34:2
Thunder Bay, Mich., Lake Huron, 23:
141
Thunder Bay (bay), Ont., Lake Su-
perior, Chippewa legends, 40:358
Thunder Bay (city), Ont., see Fort
William, Port Arthur
Thunder Bay (Ont.) Historical Soci-
ety, 11:287, 23:99, 396, 25:403,
26:88, 34:314; publication, 12:
200; meetings, 13:337, 17:120, 18:
464, 19:354, 359, 20:454, 23:385,
26:178; museum, 23:93, 295, 24:186
Thunder Voice, Sioux leader, 38:148
Thurber, Charles, inventor, 16:445-
447
Thurber, Charles L., insurance agent,
24:109
Thurber, Cleveland, 23:134
Thurber, Herschel P., 24:109n
Thurber, Lewis M., 13:448, 14:456,
16:242, 24:109n
Thurn, Helen, editor, 36:107
Thurn, Karl, editor, 36:107
Thursday Musical, Minneapolis, 24:
191, 30:175, 31:61, 33:95, 39:55
Thursfield, Richard E., work re-
viewed, 28:364; editor, 28:300
Thurston, J. M., dairyman, 27:120
Thvedt, N. B., 16:471
Thwaites, Helene B., speaker, 12:210
Thwaites, Reuben G., 11:431, 39:166;
editor, 11:8, 14:220, 23:132, 26:
148, 36:225; biographies, 12:328,
39:336; author, 13:252, 40:312
Thwing, Alfred L., 24:191
Thwing, Charles F., author, 11:110
Thye, Edward J., governor, 24:242,
349, 25:286, 308, 379, 407, 26:43,
86, 399, 27:27, 250, 262, 272, 28:
52, 29:352; letter, 27:45, 29:36
Thyreen, G., author, 18:74
Tiahma, Sauk leader, 20:56
Tiarks, J. C., surveyor, 23:203
Tiarks, Dr. J. L., astronomer, 20:441
Tibbetts, Abner, New Ulm settler, 37:
207
Tibbetts, Mrs. Mary M., 11:419
Tibbetts Lake, see Great Oasis Lake
Tibbs, Anna B., 16:101
Tichenor, Lt. Isaac P., Union of-
ficer, 39:195n
Tichenor, Phil, author, 36:105
Tichý, Father František, 15:31
Tickner, Rev. W. A., 31:82n
Ticknor, Herman L., druggist, 25:365,
26:286
Tidball, J. C., artist, 19:420
Tidd, Mrs. Ann M., 16:471
Tidd, Tristam, 16:471

Tideman, Rev. Carl G., author, 12:206
Tideman, Philip L., editor, 39:299
Tietema, Rev. K., 28:123
Tiffany, ---, sportsman, 15:286, 16:210
Tiffany, Mrs. Francis B., speaker, 20:308; author, 33:188
Tifft, C. M., speaker, 11:334
"Tiger," steamboat, 11:130, 137, 164, 170, 171n, 172, 177, 181, 183
Tighe, Ambrose, 40:16
Tighe, Richard L., lawyer, 21:196
Tigrett, John B., author, 27:272
Tikkanen, Rev. Juhani, 25:324
Tilden, Floyd, author, 20:208
Tilden, Freeman, works reviewed, 38:239, 39:294
Tilden, Lt. James, murderer, 14:93
Tilden, Samuel J., presidential candidate, 15:405, 35:58
Till, John, 35:204
Tillenius, Anna, author, 35:295
Tiller, Carl W., work reviewed, 23:265
Tiller, Mrs. Edith W., author, 11:222
Tilley, Morris, editor, 27:34
Tillinger, John, 28:320
Tillman, Benjamin R., politician, 12:6, 9
Tillotson, Mrs. Henry B., editor, 12:430
Tillquist, Fred E., politician, 34:222
Tilman, Hannah B., author, 25:185
Tilton, Frank, author, 12:328
Tilton, Theodore, speaker, 11:156, 157
Tilton and Co., see Columbia Fur Co.
Timber Lake, Cook County, forest fire, 36:136
"Time," steamboat, 22:13-15, 19, 34n; excursion, 22:20-31
"Time and Tide," steamboat, 11:139, 141-143, 18:372, 20:377; depicted, 11:126
Timm, F. A., 15:368
Timm, Otto, aviator, 34:217
Timothy, Lewis, pioneer printer, 15:7
Timpe, George, author, 17:342, 19:219
Tindolph, Wiley, 18:138, 139, 143, 144, 150
Tingerthal, Father Rhaban, author, 37:187
Tingley, Benjamin W., art collector, 23:155
Tinker, E. W., forester, 36:133
Tinker, Ralph, steamboat engineer, 22:94
Tinkham, Miss ---, teacher, 13:140
Tinsley, Mrs. George W., 39:115
Tinsley, James A., work reviewed, 36:150
Tintah Beach, Lake Agassiz, geology, 38:158, 160
Tipi Wakan, Hennepin County, Lake Minnetonka, church conferences, 33:354
Tipperman, Elizabeth, pioneer, 22:222
Tipton, John, papers reviewed, 24:343; Indian agent, 40:186n
Tischer, H. G., author, 25:315
Tischler, John A., career, 29:90
"Tisiphone," gunboat, 40:278
Titlie, Rev. Joseph, speaker, 16:130
Titus, Mrs. Frances P., 21:15
Titus, Harold, author, 17:342, 31:147
Titus, Moses S., 15:222

Titus, William A., author, 12:328
Tjornhom, Rev. T., speaker, 18:335
Tjosvold, S. O., politician, 34:222
Tobacco, use by Indians, 15:453, 31:194; dictionary of terms, 34:169; health hazard, 39:24
Tobey, Stephen H., letters, 11:96
Tobin, Leslie J., speaker, 19:118
Tobogganing, 23:105, 40:384
Tocqueville, Alexis de, author, 29:154
Tod, J., trader, 40:167n, 168n
Todd, Andrew, trader, 11:258, 261-263, 19:294
Todd, Mrs. Anna, speaker, 16:360
Todd, Irving, pioneer journalist, 14:395; Masonic library, 26:82
Todd, Isaac, 11:264n
Todd, Capt. John B. S., 36:70; career, 22:213; Fort Ripley commandant, 28:343, 40:87, 88; land speculator, 35:238; politician, 38:148
Todd, Mabel O., 37:136
Todd and McGill, traders, 11:263
Todd County, Norwegian settlement, 12:277; pioneer life, 15:253; ghost towns, 15:371; townships, 16:131, 257, 372, 23:111; Quakers, 18:258; name, 22:213; school, 22:350; Baptist church, 24:94; grasshopper plague, 36:57; geology, 37:307
Todd County Historical Society, meetings, 19:119, 232, 21:238, 23:296, 24:380, 26:92, 369, 395, 27:342, 364, 28:388, 29:366, 30:401; exhibit, 21:447
Todd County Old Settlers' Association, 11:12; museum, 11:16; activities, 11:18
Todd County War History Committee, 25:95
Toensing, Waldemar F., librarian, 37:188; speaker, 40:150
Toews, W. J., 17:466
Tofte, name, 12:287; copper mine, 34:179; ranger station, 36:134, 137
Toftey, Adolph, 20:454
Tohill, Louis A., 18:194; author, 22:285
Toimi, Lake County, temperance society, 22:392n; Finnish settlement, 25:160, 319, 320, 323
Toivola, St. Louis County, Finnish settlement, 22:392n, 25:320
Toland, John, author, 35:333
Tolbert, H. Allan, reviews by, 40:45, 138, 404
Toledo, Ohio, marketing center, 40:272, 273n
Toledo Strip, Ohio, Mich., controversy, 25:369
Tollefson, John, 18:116
Tollefson, Ole, 12:263
Tollefson, Thomas, 18:124n
Toller, Ernest, 21:11
Tolman, R. P., author, 11:110, 17:114
Tolmie, W. F., trader, 40:167n
Toltz, Maximilian E. R., engineer, 13:446
Tomahawks, pipe, 40:199, 201
Tomazin, Father Ignatius, missionary, 13:117, 18:268, 331
Tomhave, William H., author, 32:118
Tomison, William, trader, 30:261

Tomkins, Charles H., quartermaster, 35:185
Tomlinson, Mrs. H. A., 12:429, 17:341
Tomlinson, Wilber F., 25:250, 353
Tompkin, John A., 25:228
Tompkins, Joseph, speaker, 19:466
Tonty, Henri de, 20:68; portrait, 12:87; explorer, 14:110, 215, 26:74; career, 17:225; author, 21:92, 23:57, 26:75; trader, 22:327
Toole, K. Ross, reviews by, 34:39, 209, 36:149; work reviewed, 38:237; speaker, 36:36; author, 36:279
Toole, Robert C., "Steamboat Pioneer," 36:250-258; reviews by, 37:82, 38:236; author, 37:185, 39:129, 298
Toombs, Robert, 14:190
Topelious, Otter Tail County, Finnish settlement, 25:320
Topping, A. Dale, editor, 40:268
Toqua, Big Stone County, described, 19:227
Torbert, Donald R., work reviewed, 36:147; author, 36:106
Tordenskjold, Otter Tail County, ghost town, 21:337
Torgerson, Arthur G., author, 11:323
Torgerson, Mrs. N. V., 23:391
Torguson, G. C., author, 11:337, 20:97, 213; speaker, 19:471
Torinus, Louis E., lumberman, 24:200
Torkelson, M. W., author, 35:380
Tornado thresher, 24:301, 302
Tornadoes, see Blizzards and storms
Tornell, Jacob, murdered, 17:154
Tornøe, J. K., author, 39:170
Toronto, Ont., battle, 15:472, 27:236; founded, 22:64; museum, 36:314, 317; balloon flight, 39:283
Toronto (Ont.) Public Library, 17:223
Torrance, Mrs. Bertha R., 13:318
Torrance, Dr. Charles M., 13:318
Torrance, Judge Ell, interview, 12:457; papers, 13:198, 319, 26:69; Civil War collection, 13:318-320, 14:63, 16:56, 27:80
Torrance, Graham M., 13:318
Torrence, ---, ballplayer, 19:174
Torrence, M. C., poet, 26:301
Torres-Lanza, Pedro, geographer, 34:303
Torrey, Charles T., abolitionist, 33:218
Torrey, John, botanist, 18:314, 24:371
Torrison, Alfred, author, 23:110
Torstenson, Joel S., 22:193
Torvik, Mrs. Clara C. J., translator, 28:382
Tostevin, ---, ballplayer, 19:174
Tostevin, J. F., 31:84
Totušek, Jan, Silver Lake pioneer, 15:30, 34
Tou, Erik H., missionary, 17:225
Touchmarks, pewter, 40:204
Touhy, Dr. E. L., author, 24:181
Touin, Roc, voyageur, 18:241
Tourism, historic sites, 16:192-195; publicity, 16:351; resorts, 21:449, 25:101, 27:176; influence, 23:31. See also Description and travel
Tourist Club, Minneapolis, 18:317, 25:290; papers, 19:49

Tourist Club, Worthington, women's study group, 28:298

Tourson, Alfred, author, 22:445

Tourtellotte, Col. John E., career, 29:356

Tourtillotte, Sylvanus, Yankee pioneer, 34:54-58

Tourtillotte, Mrs. Sylvanus (Lydia), Yankee pioneer, 34:54-58

Tousley, Albert S., work reviewed, 11:85-87

Tousley, Mortimer, family, 12:97

Tousley, O. V., educator, 35:371

Tow Head settlement, Freeborn County, name, 18:225

Tower, Charlemagne, mining activities, 12:285, 16:26, 27:205, 33:355, 34:216, 36:192, 40:412; career, 17:226, 33:220; ambassador, 37:17, 18

Tower, Mrs. Charlemagne, 37:18

Tower, Charlemagne, Jr., 12:285

Tower, George W., speaker, 28:192

Tower, Lt. Z. B., 29:318

Tower, mining center, 11:414, 12:285, 30:409, 34:171, 36:282; markers, 15:481, 35:382; road, 16:297; railroad, 19:451, 32:245, 34:180; temperance society, 22:391, 392n; Finnish settlement, 25:319, 30:156; bus line, 35:338; gold rush, 36:282; baseball club, 40:61; labor problem, 40:345. See also Vermilion Range

Tower-Soudan State Park, St. Louis County, 40:35

Towle, Charles, author, 35:338

Towler, Mrs. George H., 22:216; author, 13:346

Town, J. D., 16:433

Town and Country Club, St. Paul, 24:92, 29:88, 36:89

Town House, Marine on St. Croix, 38:337, 350

Town Lake (Jay Lake), Cook County, forest fire, 36:135

Towne, C. W., author, 21:428

Towne, Charles A., 12:35, 17:160n; Congressman, 13:205, 17:226, 39:103, 105, 107

Towne, Ellen, see Windom, Mrs. William

Towne, Oliver, pseud., see Hiebert, Gareth

Townley, Arthur C., 15:338, 32:247, 40:140; papers, 16:218; agrarian leader, 18:191, 28:37, 40, 42, 34:347, 36:34, 38:305; politician, 27:259, 28:72, 32:182, 35:247, 37:39, 38:178; speaker, 34:222, 224; portrait, 35:284; imprisonment, 35:368

Townsend, Ann, 28:267

Townsend, Archie, 28:267

Townsend, Clara, 28:267

Townsend, Daniel Charles, education, 28:267; editor, 28:268; marriages, 28:268

Townsend, Mrs. Daniel Charles, I (Genevieve Gillrup), 28:268

Townsend, Mrs. Daniel Charles, II (Pearl Forslof), 28:268

Townsend, Dorothy, 28:268; "My British Background," 28:258-268

Townsend, Edward, I, career, 28:258-260; in Sioux Outbreak, 28:261-264

Townsend, Mrs. Edward, I, marriages, 28:259, 264

Townsend, Edward, II, 28:267

Townsend, Edward, III, 28:268

Townsend, Grace, 28:267

Townsend, Jean, 28:268

Townsend, Joseph E., reminiscences, 13:454, 14:463, 15:138, 252, 370, 16:367, 28:261, 264, 266; newspaper publisher, 15:492, 16:253, 28:265-268; birth, 28:259; marriages, 28:266, 267; death, 28:267

Townsend, Mrs. Joseph E., I (Julia Harty), 28:266, 267

Townsend, Mrs. Joseph E., II (Josephine Mares), 28:267

Townsend, Josephine, 28:267

Townsend, Mary, 28:268

Townsend, Mary J., 28:267

Townsend, Mayme, 28:267

Townsend, Samuel P., archaeologist, 38:244

Townsend family, genealogy, 14:233

Townsend House, Belle Plaine, hotel, 28:260, 265

Townshend, Thomas, 19:297

Toyne, S. M., author, 30:65

Toys, 16:381, 382, 389, 17:242, 34:107; history, 37:342

Tozer, David, lumberman, 31:36; log mark, 26:135

Trabert, Rev. George H., 14:362; career, 21:221

Track meets, Minnesota, 39:18-23

Tracy, H. W., Co., St. Paul, merchants, 14:380

Tracy, Marquis de, see Prouville de Tracy, Alexandre de

Tracy, land office, 16:458; railroad, 24:194

Tracy High School, museum, 19:366

Trade, see Business, Fur trade

Trade goods, blankets, 11:101; importance, 11:241, 40:198, 202; exchange rates, 11:245, 21:131, 133, 146, 23:241, 333; varieties, 13:227, 229, 18:237, 395, 19:42, 20:12, 25:397, 38:26-28; wampum, 15:257; fire steels, 18:36-41, 188; weapons, 20:268, 29:199, 30:102, 33:89, 35:151, 196, 38:71; silver, 22:93, 204, 24:77, 33:351, 40:200; pipes, 25:202; archaeological finds, 25:398, 34:268, 38:24, 28-34, 40:203-209; embargo, 40:179-182; brass, 40:200

Trades and Labor Assembly, Twin Cities, 17:99, 19:451, 20:35, 22:385, 387; Minnesota, 22:377-379, 386, 35:59

Trading posts, see Fur trade, individual traders, companies, and posts

Trae, Cora, author, 22:221

Traill County, N.D., early settlers, 21:99

Train, Arthur, Jr., author, 23:284

Train, Mrs. G. L., speaker, 14:463

Train, George F., career, 25:176

Train Bay, Mich., Lake Superior, 23:237

Train River, Mich., 23:237

Transcontinental and Western Air Lines, 26:7

Transit Railroad, 14:182; proposed route, 11:397, 14:255; incorporated, 14:183n

Transit Township, Sibley County, history, 13:122

Transportation, frontier, 11:212, 17:365, 19:310, 22:85, 230, 24:131, 191, 27:85, 28:310, 330; in fur trade, 11:426, 33:130; steam wagon, 11:454, 12:115, 13:95, 21:86, 22:204, 34:306, 35:155; of freight, 12:178, 13:228, 16:75, 479, 19:349, 24:247, 38:386; immigrant, 12:253, 279, 13:8, 16:25, 24:128, 159, 329, 29:61, 30:199, 32:126; rates, 13:228, 15:126, 19:195, 28:312, 31:86; development, 14:149-155, 16:233, 17:359, 18:85, 337, 23:60, 32:44; relation to agriculture, 15:123, 26:332, 29:2-18, 30:264, 37:269; horse-drawn vehicles, 15:254, 19:139, 22:213, 25:302, 35:39-41, 48-53, 89; of livestock, 15:353; Canada, 15:356, 20:87, 342, 24:277, 30:262; Red River Valley, 15:357, 17:128, 19:109, 33:277, 35:154; Illinois, 15:474; recreational, 16:268, 19:385; North Dakota, 21:99, 23:92; history, 21:324, 30:406, 36:105, 106, 192, 39:124, 40:410; Oregon, 25:276; songs, 26:379; Pennsylvania, 26:383; impact on newspapers, 27:1-3; Iowa, 28:79; Montana, 28:288; function of army engineers, 36:96; legislation, 36:176-180; in pictures, 36:231. See also Horses, various bodies of water and means of transportation

Transportation Act, effects, 12:16

Trans-Siberian Railway, aided by U.S., 38:310-325

Transylvania University, Lexington, Ky., 15:12

Trapp, I., author, 34:128

Trappist Order, travels, 16:90

Traquair, Ramsay, author, 26:274

Trask, David F., author, 40:46

Trask, James, speaker, 40:48

Traub, Mrs. J. F., 13:446

Travel, see Description and travel

Traveler's Club, Faribault, records, 16:242, 19:467

Traveling Hail, Sioux leader, 38:130, 134, 147

"Traveller," steamboat, 40:273

Traver House, Mapleton, hotel, 15:133

Traverse County, county seat fight, 12:444; county agent, 19:113; archives, 20:89; agriculture, 22:212; centennial committee, 29:181; ghost towns, 29:366; land grant, 35:207; nursing home, 38:377

Traverse County Historical Society, projected, 20:98, 29:181, 366; organized, 30:169

Traverse County War History Committee, 24:82

Traverse des Sioux, Nicollet County, history, 11:87-89, 102; mission, 11:94, 183, 316, 12:83, 16:333, 18:350, 21:171, 274, 39:344; river port, 11:129, 133n, 136, 170, 171n, 184, 36:257; townsite, 11:162, 180, 29:209n; growth, 11:182, 32:80; posts, 11:376, 377, 13:102, 20:265-268, 21:161, 31:198, 32:71; depicted, 12:425, 13:192, 196, 295, 414, 14:425, 15:206, 38:119; frontier life, 14:391, 22:138;

volunteer guard, 16:171, 172; memorials, 20:464, 23:291, 37:61, 38:155, 39:299; Indian unrest, 21:170, 172; roads, 21:229, 233, 234; historical meeting, 22:293-295, 23:36; Indian agency, 22:422, 38:93; churches, 30:156, 32:72; in fiction, 37:10; name, 37:226, 227n; mail route, 40:87

Traverse des Sioux, treaty, 19:450, 20:94; ratified, 11:161, 28:343n; negotiations, 12:452, 16:149, 32:77, 38:2; source material, 13:195, 15:223, 16:332, 469, 18:44n, 26:66, 30:388; provisions, 16:140, 30:25, 38:121, 39:47; history, 21:401; Frank B. Mayer's observations, 22:133-152, 32:80; anniversary, 22:188; preliminaries, 28:315; relation to fur trade, 32:65-76, 36:44n; effect on Indians, 34:311, 37:272, 38:129, 130

Traverse des Sioux State Park, Nicollet County, 18:273; historical session, 16:300

Traverse House, Graceville, register, 23:300

Traverse Township, Nicollet County, Norwegian settlement, 12:275

Traves, Frederick W., German settler, 32:164

Travis, Capt. ---, marksman, 27:6

Travis, William B., 35:241

Treacy, Sister Leone, author, 18:89

Treadwell, John N., career, 13:174; letter, 13:175-178

Treanor, Glen R., author, 16:357

Treat, Selah B., 21:281, 35:170

Treaties, see individual treaties

Trecy, Father Jeremiah, colonizer, 21:75

Treloar, Alan E., author, 18:107

Trelogan, Mrs. Florence, stenographer, 23:44; chief clerk, 24:30, 162, 25:41

Tremaine, Marie, editor, 17:223

Trembly, Clifford, poet, 26:301

Tremont Hall, Nininger, social center, 13:142, 148; removal, 13:151

Trempealeau, Wis., post, 11:384, 19:456; founded, 12:212; name, 15:360; mission, 21:159; river port, 37:87

Trempealeau County, Wis., community study, 36:231

Trempealeau Mountain, Wis., Mississippi River, state park, 15:237; described, 17:294, 32:212

Trempealeau River, Wis., wildlife, 30:126

Trenerry, Walter N., "The Minnesota Rebellion Act," 35:1-10; "The Legislator and the Grasshopper," 36:54-61; "Votes for Civil War Soldiers," 36:167-172; "The Bray-Goheen Murder Case," 38:11-20; "The Shooting of Little Crow," 38:150-153; "When the Boys Came Home," 38:287-297; "Lester's Surrender," 39:191-197; reviews by, 36:275, 37:33, 38:39, 40:307; work reviewed, 38:234; honored, 35:296; speaker, 36:196, 219, 37:136

Trenton, Carlton County, platted, 40:244

Trenton, N.J., Jewish population, 25:394

Trescot, William H., 18:131

Trever, Karl L., 26:34

Trevor, J., 16:424, 426

Trevor, Joseph G., Union soldier, 25:247, 253

Trewartha, Glenn T., author, 13:437, 19:456, 22:98

Tribune Building, Minneapolis, design, 23:226

Trimble, Lyman, 18:39

Trimbo, Howard, house, 39:276, 277

Trimbo, Mrs. Howard, house, 39:276, 277

Trinity Episcopal Church, Anoka, 15:364; Excelsior, 27:232, 28:392

Trinity Evangelical Lutheran Church, St. Paul, 11:468, 16:484, 17:97, 20:193

Trinity Lutheran Church, St. Paul, 12:344, 14:53, 23:371, 24:373, 26:69, 28:203, 34:356, 38:75; Long Prairie, 14:124; Benson, 15:481; Welcome, 15:481

Trippe, Martin, ornithologist, 36:103

Trisco, Robert F., author, 38:202

Tri-State Telephone Co., 18:319

Trittabaugh, Oscar, 21:333

Triumph, Martin County, Covenant church, 15:481; history, 34:315

Trobec, Bishop Jacobus, biography, 26:303

Trobriand, Philippe Régis de, journal, 32:56, 128, 243, 33:131n, 34:304, 325, 38:386; artist, 32:244, 38:385, 40:314

Troien, C. N., author, 13:340

Trois Rivières (Three Rivers), Que., fur-trade center, 15:157, 19:271, 40:157; archives, 15:164, 28:370; garrison, 15:174; anniversary celebration, 15:476, 16:480, 17:113; settled, 29:78

Trollope, Anthony, river tour, 20:308, 391, 33:90

Trollope, Mrs. Frances, author, 36:45, 46, 40:18

Trommald, Crow Wing County, ghost town, 19:464

Troost, Gerard, letter, 17:96; geologist, 29:67

Trosky, history, 24:91

Trost, Mrs. A. A. (Ella K.), 15:137, 369

Trost, Albert, war veteran, 23:374

Trost, Charles, house, 38:347

Trost, Hermann, letters, 38:202

Trott, Gen. Clement A., 24:5

Trott, Hermann, colonizer, 31:224, 226; railroad official, 37:154, 155, 158, 160; portrait, 37:157

Trott, Mrs. Hermann, 37:160

Trotter, Reginald G., 15:334; work reviewed, 16:83-85; author, 16:230

Trout Lake, Itasca County, ore plant, 11:114, 29:172, 36:35

Trout Lake Lumber Co., 27:302

Trout Valley, Winona County, settled, 34:129

Trowbridge, Charles C., "Journal," 23:135-148, 233-252, 328-348; Union officer, 14:101; on Cass expedition, 23:75, 169, 271, 369, 26:363, 33:345; career, 23:132-134

Trowbridge, Mrs. Charles C. (Catherine W. Sibley), 23:132

Trowbridge, Frederick N., author, 24:176

Trowbridge, John T., "Railroad Route," 37:103-118

Troxel, Kathryn, author, 34:263

Troy, Winona County, mill, 25:101

Troyer, Howard W., author, 14:443

Truax, Abraham, 17:278

Truax, Emma, author, 16:127

Truax, Moses, farmer, 37:193, 195, 197

Truax family, Hastings, 35:336

Truck Drivers Union No. 574, Minneapolis, 18:191

Trucks, co-operatives, 18:460; in lumber industry, 27:308; antique, 40:148

Trudeau, Edward L., 35:215

Trudel, Marcel, editor, 40:145

True, Alfred C., author, 18:449

True, Norman T., speaker, 18:465

True, Webster P., author, 27:350

Truedson, E. P., reminiscences, 21:451

Trueman, G. Ernest, YMCA director, 38:317

Truesdale, Dorothy S., author, 24:71

Truesdell, Leon E., author, 25:199

Truman, Harry S, President, 34:189-191, 194, 342

Truman, history, 18:464, 20:462; creamery, 27:366

Trussell, Sumner L., 18:128

Truth, Sojourner, reformer, 25:65

Trygg, J. William, review by, 33:216; author, 36:69; forester, 38:29

Tryon, Charles J., memorial, 16:219

Tryon, Rolla M., Jr., author, 34:172

Tryon, Warren S., work reviewed, 33:350

Tuberculosis, Northwest, 12:334; Minnesota, 13:446, 20:230, 25:307, 27:82, 30:175, 31:43, 35:214, 216-219; sanatoriums, 38:377

Tuberg, Andres, homestead, 26:396

Tuck, Louis, teacher, 19:238

Tucker, G. R., 12:401

Tucker, Sara J., review by, 30:56; work reviewed, 24:236; author, 30:95

Tucker, William B., author, 34:313

Tucker, Willliam P., author, 27:352, 29:76

Tucker family, genealogy, 24:354

Tuckerman, Henry, 20:175

Tudor, Frederic, merchant, 28:54

Tuesday Study Club, Mountain Lake, 21:220

Tufte, Lt. Theodore B., 23:393

Tugwell, Rexford G., author, 19:347

Tuininga, John, career, 15:367, 35:90

Tuke, James H., 31:22

Tull, Charles J., author, 40:359

Tullis, Aaron W., sheriff, 34:19n

Tully, ---, boatbuilder, 33:16

Tully, Andrew, Sioux captive, 20:56

Tully, David, murdered, 20:55, 56

Tully, John, death, 18:399; Sioux captive, 18:400, 20:56

Tully family, in Sioux Outbreak, 11:224; murdered, 18:400, 20:56, 23:94

Tully, Mo., river town, 17:431n

Tulsa, Okla., schools, 29:77

Tumberg, Julia, author, 11:221

Tumuli Township, Otter Tail County, historic buildings, 17:238

Tungseth, E. L., speaker, 14:122

Tunnell, Arthur L., editor, 16:113

Tunsberg Township, Chippewa County, Norwegian settlement, 12:275n
Tuohy, Dr. Edward L., author, 31:124
Tuper, Frank, speaker, 13:118
Turbert, G. L., 16:31
Turck, Charles J., 25:403; review by, 21:184; author, 21:187; speaker, 25:403
Turkey, on frontier menus, 14:391, 16:378, 379, 18:296, 28:321
Turkey River, Iowa, mill, 11:106
Turkey River Valley, Iowa, ceded to U.S., 17:153n
Turks, Mesabi Range, 27:214
Turnblad, Mrs. Ed, 25:208
Turnblad, Swan J., publisher, 23:190, 26:21, 34:43, 39:133n; museum founder, 30:391, 34:172, 37:135
Turnbull, Andrew, author, 38:203; editor, 39:35
Turnbull, John G., author, 33:92
Turner, Amelia, author, 11:465
Turner, Asa, college founder, 33:356
Turner, Beatrice C., author, 15:473
Turner, Rev. Chester, 22:170
Turner, Florence, author, 11:465
Turner, Frederick J., historian, 24: 255, 360, 33:311, 34:81, 39:335; "Rise and Fall of New France," 18: 383-398; work reviewed, 14:316-318, 16:325-327, 19:432; quoted, 12:4, 88, 15:255, 19:306, 23:83; biography, 12:328, 17:477, 24:336; assessed, 13:159-161, 293, 17:198, 19:435, 23:283, 26:265, 29:76; author, 15:90, 18:381-383, 21:200, 23:52, 40:151, 156; frontier theory, 15:228, 16:197, 17:322, 324, 20:197, 22:62, 23:377, 28:269, 379, 29:71, 30:250, 34:82, 310, 35:43, 329, 36:230, 37:182, 261, 38:329, 40:303, 403; character-ized, 17:73; speaker, 23:10; honored, 23:82; letters, 25:85; newspaperman, 31:251; centennial, 38:201; in rune-stone controversy, 39:136-140; portrait, 39:137
Turner, Dr. George F., army surgeon, 16:147, 32:97, 98, 33:91, 36:42n
Turner, Howard H., author, 24:174
Turner, Capt. J. M., author, 21:98
Turner, John P., author, 14:444, 15: 357, 25:90
Turner, Jonathan, educator, 35:379
Turner, Katharine C., author, 32:189
Turner, Kathryn, review by, 34:300
Turner, Mrs. O. H., 12:102
Turner, R. A., author, 15:489
Turner Colonization Society, 18:109, 34:170
Turner Hall, Minneapolis, 20:408
Turner Settlement Association, Cin-cinnati, Ohio, 27:268, 31:24
Turney, Agnes, author, 33:265
Turney, Ida V., author, 23:379, 24: 367
Turnham, Mrs. Vivian, 22:216
Turnor, Philip, diaries, 16:105
Turnverein (Turner Clubs), 24:218, 367; St. Paul, 15:109, 17:54, 338, 18:47, 24:357, 25:77, 27:328; Min-neapolis, 16:335; New Ulm, 18:112, 19:214, 21:111, 190, 25:314, 28: 81, 202, 30:33, 34, 74, 33:84, 36: 91, 128, 200, 40:310; Davenport, Iowa, 27:163; in politics, 28:36; Cincinnati, Ohio, 30:25, 27, 28,

31, 36:255, 40:310; principles, 30:26, 32, 34, 31:242, 36:90; colonizing activities, 30:27-33; Chicago, 30:28, 29n, 31; halls, 30:33, 32:105, 164-172, 36:128; contributions, 33:179; Winona, 34: 239; Red Wing, 34:240; Duluth, 34: 242
Turpie, Mary C., work reviewed, 37:83
Turpin, Mrs. Amable, pioneer, 30:7, 182
Turrell, Orlando B., banker, 40:112-119
Turtle Creek Township, Todd County, history, 16:131
Turtle Mountain, N.D., post, 22:280n, 289
Turtle Mountain Indian Reservation (Chippewa), N.D., 35:293
Turtle River (river), Beltrami Coun-ty, trading post, 11:370; logging, 29:141, 145, 146, 148
Turtle River (river), N.D., trading post, 11:368, 22:276, 281
Turtle River (village), history, 16: 125; railhead, 29:147; newspaper, 29:356; logging center, 33:356
Turtle River Lake, Beltrami County, logging, 29:145
"Tuscania," steamboat, 11:322
Tute, Capt. James, explorer, 11:107, 33:261; trader, 14:229, 16:224, 20:10n, 33:130
Tuttle, F. G., publisher, 35:50
Tuttle, Fred C., 18:112
Tuttle, J. B., Baptist minister, 18: 112
Tuttle, J. M., author, 20:440
Tuttle, Rev. James H., 11:147
Tuttle, Philemon M., diaries, 18:314, 19:48
Tuttle, William G., 20:465
Tverberg, Rev. Svein, 13:206
Twain, Mark, pseud., see Clemens, Samuel L.
Tweed Hall, Duluth, depicted, 26:180
Tweedsmuir, Lady (Susan C. Buchan), author, 20:197
Tweet, Roald, 27:146; "The Mountain Lake Community," 27:221-227; au-thor, 27:245, 247
Twelfth Illinois Cavalry, 25:18
Twelfth Minnesota Volunteer Infantry, 32:119; in Spanish-American War, 17:159n, 39:108; roster, 18:320
Twentieth Century Club, Wadena, 17: 358, 20:99
Twentieth U.S. Infantry, 12:138
Twenty-eighth Wisconsin Volunteer In-fantry, 20:431
Twenty-fifth Wisconsin Volunteer In-fantry, 38:279, 280
Twenty-ninth Wisconsin Volunteer In-fantry, in Civil War, 15:112, 22: 86
Twenty-seventh Iowa Volunteer Infan-try, 38:279, 280
Twenty-seventh Wisconsin Volunteer Infantry, in Civil War, 40:285
Tweton, D. Jerome, author, 36:237
Twichell, Col. Heath, 25:291
Twichell, J. Fred, speaker, 11:338
Twichell, Rev. Joseph H., 17:369
Twichell, Luther, 14:330
Twichell, Rev. Royal, 19:144, 40:10
Twiford, E. M., 16:255
Twiford, Thomas B., Chatfield pio-

neer, 24:95, 96; miller, 24:101, 102; career, 30:53
Twiggs, David, 33:263
"Twilight," steamboat, 40:314
Twin Cities, metropolitan entity, 13: 441, 31:119, 37:346, 39:327; trade center, 16:351, 28:189, 33:226, 36:279, 39:105; rivalry, 17:354, 33:166, 35:301, 37:309-323, 40:14; social climate, 20:88, 185, 31: 114; transportation, 21:291, 28: 293, 331, 30:232-241, 32:47, 33: 43, 37:131, 308, 39:99; depicted, 22:332, 28:398, 32:106-108, 36: 237, 37:300; airport, 27:166; newspapers, 28:287, 39:106, 40: 302; parks, 30:77, 168; theaters, 33:41, 39:263; proposed consolida-tion, 37:320; history, 38:243; re-ligious communities, 38:335; eco-nomic conditions, 39:98, 40:146; water supply, 39:114; suburbs, 39: 299; Jewish population, 40:46; historic sites, 40:48, 255; ar-chitecture, 40:97-101, 104-106, 135. See also Minneapolis, St. Paul
Twin Cities Civil War Roundtable, 37: 87, 224, 39:173, 191
Twin Cities Metropolitan Planning Commission, reports, 37:187
Twin Cities Waves and Spars Mothers Club, 26:253
Twin City Book Round Table, 36:152
Twin City Cataloguers' Round Table, 24:32
Twin City Commercial Club, 37:321
Twin City Council on Fair Employment Practice, papers, 27:155
Twin City Federal Saving and Loan Association, Minneapolis, 38:44
Twin City History Club, 28:160n
Twin City Library Association, 26:63
Twin City Milk Producers Association, organized, 17:480; history, 40:315
Twin City Philetelic Society, 30:170, 368
Twin City Rapid Transit Co., 37:322; organized, 17:360; history, 36: 150; equipment, 37:342; Selby tun-nel, 39:156
Twin City Reporter (Minneapolis), characterized, 37:163; editors, 37:163, 164
Twin City Society of Artists and Art Directors, 33:19
Twin Lake School, May Township, Wash-ington County, history, 26:181
Twin Lakes Township, Carlton County, stage station, 16:287, 40:244; roads, 16:291, 296, 40:245; lo-cated, 37:107; described, 37:108
Twin Valley, removal, 17:261; mill, 17:362; mounds, 27:261
Twining, Alexander C., excursionist, 15:406, 34:139; speaker, 15:416, 34:143
Twitchell, ---, baseball player, 19: 174
Twitchell, Dr. Refine W., biography, 33:353
Two Harbors, historical meeting, 11: 15, 12:284-286; history, 11:115; railroad, 11:414, 27:203, 32:245, 34:180, 36:281; ore port, 12:283, 15:482, 19:113, 26:77, 33:355, 34: 177 (cover), 366; Finns, 12:436;

Presbyterian church, 18:318, 19:
49, 123; labor unions, 22:381;
sleigh road, 34:181; described,
35:49
Two Hearted River, Mich., 23:234
Two Stars, Solomon, Sioux scout, 35:
171, 40:313
Twohey Lake, Cook County, lumbering,
34:183; logging railroad, 36:132
Tyler, Alice F., "The Westward Movement as Reflected in Family Papers," 24:111-124; "William Pfaender," 30:24-35; reviews by, 11:78-
80, 12:74, 13:415, 14:197-200,
202, 15:330-332, 17:76-78, 106,
19:102, 24:48-50, 154-156, 338-
340, 34:200; work reviewed, 25:65;
speaker, 24:57; author, 24:60,
163, 351, 353, 25:304, 395, 26:78,
30:94
Tyler, Elmer, pioneer printer, 15:22
Tyler, Hugh, 32:68, 71, 79; treaty
agent, 38:1, 6
Tyler, John, President, 16:326, 17:
106
Tyler, Moses Coit, author, 40:313
Tyler, Robert, letters, 17:106
Tyler, Lutheran church, 38:42; Danish
settlement, 38:243
Tyler and Hewitt, music publishers,
26:53
Typewriter, invented, 16:445, 25:198;
history, 25:262
Typhoid fever, among immigrants, 35:
97
Tyra, Margaret, author, 16:349
Tyrell, Truman, diary, 22:86
Tyrell, William G., author, 29:77
Tyrrell, Joseph B., author, 11:107,
15:239, 18:215; editor, 11:209,
15:120, 16:105, 39:171; biography,
12:199, 34:132; quoted, 12:372
Tyson, Joseph, author, 16:252
Tyson, Nathaniel E., Co., St. Paul,
merchants, 14:380

Ubrechsen, J. H., Dutch pioneer, 28:
128
Udall, Stewart, speaker, 38:91
Udden, Johan A., geologist, 17:477
Ueland, A. O., author, 14:357
Ueland, Judge Andreas, 20:407, 29:
294; family, 32:63
Ueland, Mrs. Andreas, 29:294
Ueland, Brenda, author, 21:410, 32:63
Ueland, Ole G., 32:63
Ueland, Sigurd, 26:45, 29:97, 39:271
Uhl, Gen. F. E., 23:167, 267
Uhlenkott, George, 20:469
Uhler, J. P., educator, 24:55, 33:309
Ukrainians, in iron mining, 19:112,
27:213; Detroit, Mich., 20:202;
bibliography, 25:299, 26:167; in
agriculture, 39:260
Ulen, Ole, pioneer, 17:485
Ulen (Oneland), post office, 17:235;
anniversary, 17:485; history, 21:
448
Ulio, Gen. J. A., 24:209n
Ullmann, Charles, 33:194, 34:96, 100;
education, 34:104
Ullmann, Joseph, I, merchant, 12:175,
14:299, 30:131-134; life in early
St. Paul, 33:194, 195, 34:96-105;

houses, 33:197n, 34:97, 98, 101;
buying trip, 34:17-27; business
buildings, 34:97, 98, 103, 104;
career, 35:293
Ullmann, Mrs. Joseph, I (Amelia),
"Spring Comes to the Frontier,"
33:195-200; "Frontier Business
Trip," 34:17-27; "Pioneer Home-
maker," 34:96-105; author, 29:284,
34:353; early life, 33:194; por-
trait, 34:96
Ullmann, Joseph, II, 33:195
Ulloa, Antonio, 24:53
Ulloa, Berta, researcher, 37:44
Ulric, Father, see Northman, Father
Ulric
Ulrich, Christian, architect, 37:17
Ulrich, Dr. Mabel, 17:57, 19:59;
speaker, 17:66
Ulvigen, Thyge N., pioneer, 26:289
"Uncle Toby," steamboat, 11:136
Underhill, F. H., editor, 34:357
Underhill, Nettie, author, 16:494
Underhill, Ruth M., works reviewed,
33:344, 40:40; quoted, 37:343
Underhill, W. M., author, 13:436
Underhill family, genealogy, 16:102
Underleak, Mrs. G. H., 14:456, 16:242
Underwood, A. J., publisher, 13:453;
Union soldier, 25:139
Underwood, Joseph M., 15:372
Underwood, Oscar W., biography, 17:
477
Underwood, R. D., speaker, 11:224,
17:123
Underwood, founded, 16:369, 497
Ungava Bay, Que., Norse settlement,
40:94
Unger, Mrs. Muriel, catalog typist,
25:40
"Union," Astor Fur Co. supply boat,
21:156
Union army, records, 13:318-320; ethnic groups, 24:157, 33:83; diary
account, 25:11-39, 117-152, 224-
257, 342-361; use of balloons, 25:
22, 23n, 119, 120, 126n, 229, 242,
246, 345, 354, 35:184, 333, 39:
283, 40:276; in fiction, 33:82;
depicted, 38:247, 249, 250, 257,
270, 39:189; officers, 39:189; in
Virginia, 40:265, 267; veterans,
40:361. See also Civil War,
United States Army, various military units
Union baseball club, Lake City, 19:
168, 178, 180; Minneapolis, 19:
179, 180; Chester, 19:180
Union Building and Loan Association,
Duluth, 37:123
Union Center, Le Sueur County, in
county seat fight, 12:444
Union City, Nicollet County, plat,
17:238
Union Congregational Church, Winthrop, 15:243
Union for Democratic Action, 23:292
Union Grove Township, Meeker County,
history, 19:470
Union Hall, New Ulm, theatrical per-
formances, 32:172
Union Hill, Scott County, Catholic
church, 21:456; mail service, 22:
215; pioneer life, 22:334
Union Improvement and Elevator Co.,
Hastings and Stillwater, 37:94

Union Lake, Polk County, pioneer
life, 30:148
Union Lake, Rice County, family histories, 28:388
Union League, Minneapolis, 18:125,
126n, 128, 35:66
Union Mission, Minneapolis, 33:178
Union National Bank, Duluth, 37:122
Union National Bank, Rochester, pub-
lication, 29:358
Union Pacific Railroad, 23:64; rival-
ry with Northern Pacific, 12:73;
built, 18:307, 29:61, 34:263, 38:
62; records, 19:51n; finances, 33:
267; federal subsidy, 36:179, 180;
re-forms buffalo herds, 37:134
Union party, 1936 campaign, 36:187,
39:80, 40:360
Union Pass, Wyo., depicted, 40:197
Union School, New Ulm, 24:190; St.
Anthony, 33:126
Unitarian church, 24:112; St. Paul,
12:397; liberalism, 24:338; Fin-
nish, 25:324; influence, 33:81.
See also individual church bodies
United American Slavs of Minnesota,
23:292
United Brethren Church, Beauford
Township, Blue Earth County, 15:
362
United Charities, St. Paul, 21:343,
25:377
United Church of Christ, see Congre-
gational church, Reformed Church
of America
United Confederate Veterans, records,
13:319
United Daughters of the Confederacy,
20:33, 23:41, 24:36; records, 13:
319, 34:340
United Laborers Association of the
U.S., Winona branch, 21:393
United Lutheran Publishing House,
Philadelphia, 15:448
United Methodist Church, see Metho-
dist church
United Mine Workers, 40:344; history,
36:274
United Packinghouse Workers of
America, Local No. 9, 34:266
United Service Organizations, 23:22,
152, 26:387
United Servicemen's Organization, St.
Paul, 27:249
United Spanish War Veterans, 19:98
United States, colonial period, 11:
77, 32:247; relations with Canada,
11:191-194, 15:334, 16:230, 332,
20:319-321, 21:204, 22:306-308,
23:58-60, 201, 204, 357, 24:45-48,
25:171, 199, 26:363, 29:165, 30:
387, 34:317-324; territorial papers, 14:336, 16:202-205, 17:452,
21:423, 24:234, 25:271, 26:362,
30:57-59, 31:48, 240, 36:85, 323;
post-Civil War, 14:429, 20:420-
422, 24:50-52, 40:353; sectionalism, 16:325-327; source material,
16:450, 34:251; 20th century, 18:
302, 20:317-319; pre-Civil War,
18:438, 21:189, 23:256, 26:358;
bibliographies, 20:198, 26:72, 35:
334, 37:342; flag, 24:72; atlases,
24:252, 25:374, 390; as seen by
foreigners, 29:154; historical
geography, 29:248-250; place
names, 30:67; aid to France, 30:

179; historiography, 33:214, 34:
250, 38:200, 39:335, see also
Boundaries
  History, 11:78-80, 189-191, 13:
  415, 14:202, 25:170, 28:269, 34:
  342, 40:313; research, 13:94, 38:
  333; social, 19:347; dictionaries,
  21:180-182, 401, 33:261; popular,
  34:162; texts, 34:341, 36:62
United States Agricultural Society,
  17:327
"United States Aid," steamboat, 36:
  251
United States Air Corps, 12:193; officers' school, 23:269, 366;
  transport command, 26:1-18; in
  England, 26:279; history, 28:299,
  29:345; in Pacific Theater, 31:247
United States Army, relation to westward movement, 15:310, 375-381,
  16:26, 33:262, 316, 38:57, 61, 62,
  296, 40:409; cultural aspect, 15:
  381; frontier defense, 17:80, 321,
  29:231-246, 36:148; Department of
  Dakota, 17:88, 226, 24:209, 25:
  296, 28:187, 32:219, 243; supply
  system, 19:349, 39:240; medical
  corps, 22:92; posts, 19:457, 22:
  297-301, 39:129, 254, 40:42, 145,
  184; in Indian wars, 22:409; camp
  newspapers, 23:292; mobilization,
  24:8; viewed by travelers, 34:42;
  ranger battalion, 34:214; uniform,
  36:14; Corps of Engineers, 36:96,
  37:34, 284, 285, 288, 40:233, 315;
  chaplains, 36:238; in Vladivostok,
  U.S.S.R., 38:324, 325; sutlers,
  40:22-31. See also Sioux Outbreak, Union army, individual
  units and posts
United States Board of Equitable Ad-
  judication, function, 34:354
United States Bureau of Fisheries,
  survey, 28:349
United States Bureau of Indian Affairs, 37:275, 279, 39:44; archives, 14:65, 329, 435, 15:343,
  16:333, 17:95, 210, 335, 18:94,
  209, 20:77, 22:307, 23:163, 39:
  296; administration, 15:297-300,
  16:26, 23:163, 37:79; Minnesota
  agencies, 15:298, 23:93, 25:183,
  28:314, 321, 326, 327, 39:45, 47;
  Michigan superintendency, 23:133,
  24:164, 25:42; Fort Wayne agency,
  24:243; missionary agents, 35:167-
  177; use of trade guns, 35:196;
  role of territorial governors, 35:
  200; conference, 36:72; Sioux relocation project, 36:176, 38:354,
  39:41, 227-240; Winnebago removal,
  36:267, 268, 270
United States Bureau of Labor Statistics, poorhouse survey, 38:375
United States Bureau of War Risk Insurance, 39:242
United States Catholic Historical Society, 26:266
United States Christian Mission, in
  revival movement, 35:373
United States Civil Service Commission, archives, 22:211
United States Congress, appropri-
  ations for Minnesota Territory,
  11:389, 16:282, 283, 296; Minnesota admission controversy, 14:
  164, 175; archives legislation,

17:11, 12, 14-16; Senate, 24:373,
  35:290; Minnesota representation,
  28:74; foreign-born members, 36:
  34; House, 36:278, 40:407; trade
  regulations, 40:179-182, 184-187
United States Constitution, anniversary, 28:369; relation to state
  law, 37:161-173
United States Department of Agriculture, library, 16:328, 18:411n;
  alfalfa study, 19:27; archives,
  19:462, 29:81; established, 22:
  254; commissioner, 23:283, 34:287-
  295; bureau of animal industry,
  35:243; reforms, 36:182; history
  branch, 40:360
United States Department of Commerce,
  building code committee, 19:452
United States Department of Justice,
  sponsors "Freedom Train," 28:369
United States Department of Labor,
  Minnesota records, 21:434; women's
  bureau, 33:42
United States Department of State,
  archives, 26:79, 38:35; special
  agents, 32:189; policy toward
  fugitive Sioux, 34:319, 323; sec-
  retaries, 38:35, 240
United States Department of the Interior, archives, 26:79; conservation work, 30:274; timber agents,
  31:158-162
United States Department of the Navy,
  archives, 19:224, 40:349, 350
United States Dispatch (Teheran,
  Iran), Persian Gulf Command paper,
  26:175
United States Dragoons, at Albert Lea
  Lake, 16:494
United States Employment Service,
  records, 23:151
United States Fish and Wildlife Service, bird surveys, 30:221, 230
United States Food Administration, in
  World War I, 23:151
United States Forest Service, functions, 30:153, 33:219; history,
  34:264; fire-fighting activities,
  36:131-138; rangers, 36:135-137
United States Geographic Board, decisions, 15:354, 26:249
United States Geological Survey, publication, 13:404, 17:108, 230;
  Minnesota expedition, 14:215, 15:
  225; use of photographs, 28:347;
  director, 32:223
United States government, publications guides, 33:303, 38:42; sub-
  sidizes research, 36:26; suit
  against prison officials, 37:140;
  in navigation controversy, 37:311-
  323; co-operation with states, 37:
  347, 38:195, 39:209. See also
  United States Congress
United States Indian Service, reconstruction of Grand Portage, 17:
  347, 461, 18:51, 328, 457, 19:53,
  21:207
United States land office, records,
  11:447, 15:491, 20:452, 23:93, 40:
  124, 125, 146; administration, 12:
  286, 28:284, 39:87, 91; frontier,
  12:379-389, 17:418-420, 36:261;
  Minnesota districts, 22:228, 239n,
  23:30, 24:95, 96n, 29:284, 30:30,
  34:1, 5, 37:112n; auction sale,

39:89-92; filing procedure, 39:
  265. See also Public Lands
United States Marine Corps, histori-
  cal unit, 23:389
United States Military Academy, West
  Point, N.Y., cadet life, 17:353;
  Ordnance Museum, 20:54, 434, 22:
  317, 434, 23:94, 154, 155;
  founded, 36:96
United States Mint, Philadelphia, 16:
  322
United States Navy, officers, 24:240;
  ethnic groups, 33:83
United States Post Office Department,
  centennial stamps, 26:272, 28:185
United States Sanitary Commission, in
  Civil War, 25:37n, 39:3
United States Steel Corporation, Du-
  luth plant, 18:343, 36:103; ex-
  pansion, 27:133, 39:109, 40:412.
  See also Oliver Mining Co.
United States Steel Supply Co., St.
  Paul, 28:189
United States Supreme Court, jus-
  tices, 17:76-78, 20:318, 419, 39:
  205; decisions, 27:262
United States Topographical En-
  gineers, 27:345
United States Upper Mississippi River
  Wildlife and Fish Refuge, 20:66
United States Veterans Bureau, func-
  tions, 39:242-246, 248
United States Volunteers, history,
  39:77
United States War Department, ar-
  chives, 11:444, 21:207, 25:288;
  sells Fort Ripley Reservation, 28:
  219
United States Weather Bureau, 17:261
Universal Friends, religious sect,
  36:278
Universalist Church, Minneapolis, 11:
  147, 16:120, 35:226; Anoka, 17:
  466; St. Paul, 30:312
University Community Development
  Corporation, Minneapolis, 40:383
University of Alberta, Edmonton, 40:
  262
University of Arizona, Tucson, publi-
  cation, 27:65
University of Chicago, faculty, 18:
  132n, 33:136; anniversary, 23:381
University of Denver, folklore conference, 27:255
University of Illinois, Urbana, faculty, 21:65, 68
University of Iowa, Iowa City, Scandinavian department, 14:437; law
  school, 18:121; centennial, 28:287
University of Maryland, College Park,
  American studies program, 26:274
University of Michigan, Ann Arbor,
  Henry R. Schoolcraft's role, 23:
  185; Clements Library, 24:69, 29:
  65; war records, 25:310
University of Minnesota, Minneapolis,
  memorials, 11:213, 329; convoca-
  tions, 11:213, 14:231, 450, 15:56,
  22:165, 26:82; alumni, 11:215,
  328, 12:193, 24:184; college of
  education, 11:329, 12:417-419;
  student life, 11:459, 15:360, 480,
  16:118, 184, 20:200, 22:211, 25:
  67, 28:76, 286, 31:51, 32:190, 35:
  154; history, 12:68, 20:206, 22:
  336, 24:187, 29:207n, 31:41, 191,
  32:176, 34:94, 95, 36:185, 38:378;

established, 12:116, 13:212, 14:
131, 224; presidents, 12:191, 14:
323, 16:178-180, 182, 184, 22:101,
23:289, 27:262, 32:3; school of
forestry, 12:204, 33:353; buildings, 12:331, 16:178, 183, 17:226,
18:151, 23:231, 27:9, 26, 228,
230, 28:293, 396, 29:353, 35:108,
40:101; regents, 12:398, 17:163,
20:82, 25:306; legislation, 13:
211; languages, 13:435, 34:297;
faculty, 14:231, 452, 16:180-182,
184, 352, 18:122, 23:190, 287, 32:
7, 33:312, 39:113-115, 122, 243,
245, 246; college of engineering,
15:140; Base Hospital No. 26, 15:
225, 16:74; school of agriculture,
15:243, 22:412; publications, 15:
352, 16:185, 331, 18:121, 219, 25:
191, 40:412; libraries, 16:55,
186, 23:2-4, 190, 24:257; com-
mencements, 16:183, 18:150; enrollment, 16:185; agricultural experiment station, 16:352, 18:449,
19:26; college of dentistry, 17:
100, 19:71-73, 25:203; college of
agriculture, 17:101, 18:411, 19:
152-161, 32:118, 37:25, 39:83;
women's organizations, 17:226;
sports, 17:228, 35:335, 36:94, 39:
18, 20-22; graduate school, 18:
121, 132, 137, 32:6, 40:314; law
school, 18:122, 19:356, 25:203;
medical school, 18:460, 21:101,
330, 24:347, 31:124, 33:312, 35:
221, 36:282, 37:133; Institute of
Child Welfare, 19:111; school of
music, 20:92; natural history museums, 21:208, 27:248, 28:394, 32:
218, 222; school of public health,
21:359; status of women, 22:101;
co-operation with MHS, 23:1-10,
32:1-11; school of mines, 23:189;
extension division, 23:289, 37:87;
archives, 24:79; land grants, 24:
133, 167, 174, 35:107, 379; gifts,
24:140, 141, 25:63, 28:285; college of pharmacy, 24:175, 29:84,
30:143; in World War II, 24:268;
Dight Institute for Human Genet-
ics, 25:63, 91, 38:243; archaeological research, 25:154, 26:321,
323, 324, 31:163, 37:86, 38:158;
anniversaries, 26:82, 29:172, 32:
1n; American studies program, 26:
274, 28:280, 29:261, 348, 30:56,
35:201, 37:83; branch campus, 27:
358; radio station, 28:184, 30:
343n; special projects, 28:241,
285, 32:217, 219, 220, 38:334, 39:
300; University Gallery, 28:302,
29:370; drama, 30:280; book store,
31:245; geology department, 32:
215; Rosemount Research Center,
33:243, 244; James Ford Bell room,
33:352; depicted, 34:95; industrial relations center, 34:264;
mines experiment station, 34:269-
279, 39:163; religious education,
35:77; preparatory school, 35:108,
125; farmers' institutes, 37:22-
24, 28, 29; legal status, 37:185;
school of nursing, 37:300; hospitals, 39:84; pacifists, 40:365-
367. See also Mayo Foundation
University of Minnesota Press, Minneapolis, 12:308, 20:117; publications, 12:25, 15:67, 97, 16:460,
17:452, 463, 18:214, 19:94, 226,
228, 352, 463, 23:8, 101, 256, 27:
176, 30:246, 367; anniversaries,
18:219, 28:183; fellowships, 29:
371
University of Missouri, Columbia,
manuscript collection, 26:384
University of North Carolina Press,
Chapel Hill, 17:78
University of North Dakota, Grand
Forks, medical school, 12:328;
history, 36:318
University of Oklahoma Press, Norman,
17:201, 20:113
University of Oslo (Royal Fredrik
University), Norway, 19:208
University of Pennsylvania, Philadelphia, anthropological museum, 23:
349, 353
University of Pittsburgh, 12:94, 184;
history conference, 12:188
University of South Dakota, Vermillion, medical school, 12:328
University of Wisconsin, Madison, 19:
160; student life, 17:475; college
of agriculture, 19:152, 33:224;
graduate school, 21:65, 67; history department, 24:336, 39:81,
215, 216, 220; farmers' institutes, 27:356; subsidized, 28:81;
American civilization study, 29:
173; history, 30:380-382; Scandinavian studies, 32:52; agricultural experiment station, 37:134;
president, 37:262
University of Wisconsin Press, Madison, 18:311; publication, 19:433
Unonius, Gustaf, works reviewed, 32:
49, 37:177; pioneer pastor, 11:83,
13:307, 17:400, 28:76; career, 16:
479; promotes immigration, 17:402,
30:65, 31:27; letters, 19:331;
colonizer, 30:159; diaries, 31:54
Untermeyer, Louis, poet, 26:308
Untermeyer, Samuel, 17:160n
Unumb, P. H., 17:121
Upgren, Arthur R., review by, 34:165;
author, 30:406
Upham, Gladys, stenographer, 16:61,
17:62, 23:44
Upham, Henry P., 20:58; house, 23:221
Upham, Mrs. Lionel R., 23:150
Upham, Warren, 11:54, 12:428, 13:246,
247, 14:79, 16:1, 17:172; speaker,
11:120; author, 13:245, 14:220,
16:163, 24:28; quoted, 14:118, 17:
168, 38:128; archaeologist, 14:
434, 15:67, 16:310, 311; career,
15:106, 16:61, 359, 467, 17:476,
30:313-315; geologist, 15:225, 17:
167, 39:114, 134; bibliography,
17:61, 18:45, 20:32; papers, 21:
315; MHS secretary, 22:302, 30:
353, 32:82n, 33:129, 40:349
Upjohn, E. M., author, 19:458
Upper Fort Garry, see Fort Garry,
Winnipeg, Man.
Upper Midwest History Conference,
meetings, 29:82, 266, 30:66, 89,
264, 35:248, 36:237, 40:48, 364;
publication, 29:164
Upper Mississippi Barge Line Co., 16:
79
Upper Mississippi River Improvement
Association, papers, 22:41, 87,
24:34
Upper Mississippi River Wildlife and
Fish Refuge, 35:46
Upper Mississippi Valley Ethno-History Committee, 20:43, 325
Upper Mississippi Waterway Association, 16:78-80
Upper Missouri Trading Co., 33:302
Upper Red Cedar Lake, see Cass Lake
Upper Red Lake, see Red Lake
Upper Sioux, see Sisseton band, Wahpeton band
Upper Sioux (Yellow Medicine) agency,
mission, 11:182n, 14:330, 16:150;
post, 11:378; agents, 12:121, 428,
29:237, 38:94, 95, 122-124, 39:
273; smallpox epidemic, 14:216;
government farmer, 15:111, 38:93;
payments, 16:470, 19:383, 37:228n,
38:93, 94, 124; in Sioux Outbreak,
17:337, 29:123n, 37:185, 38:107,
110, 243; mission school, 18:375;
store, 19:450; reached by steamboat, 36:256; site, 37:60; boundary, 37:348; agriculture, 38:130,
143; depicted, 38:155
Upsala, Lutheran church, 20:361
Upson, Arthur, poet, 16:81, 18:330,
26:307, 27:41
Upson, Ralph H., "Aeronautical Science," 33:242-246; aeronautics
teacher, 33:242
Up-to-Date Club, Bemidji, 23:32
Upton, B. F., photographer, 21:95,
37:189 (cover), 309 (cover)
Upton, Rev. H. R., speaker, 16:366
Upton, Gen. La Roy, letters, 19:98
Urang, Olai, author, 37:42
Urban League, Minnesota, 38:88
Urevig, Frances, ed., "With Governor
Ramsey to Minnesota," 35:352-357;
review by, 35:372; editorial as-
sistant, 35:100
Urevig, M. S., farmer, 24:272
Urquhart, Kenneth T., author, 37:39
Urseth, H. A., 29:295
Ursuline Order, Frontenac, 14:39, 15:
480, 16:372, 22:445, 29:87; an-
niversary, 15:480, 16:372; Quebec,
36:315
Usher, John P., secretary of the in-
terior, 20:284, 38:354, 355, 363,
39:228, 229
Usher's Landing, see Fort Thompson
Utah, Latter-day Saints, 13:111, 28:
378, 36:285-293, 39:71; early
journalism, 20:204; proverb collection, 27:34; depicted, 27:159;
folk music, 27:188; surveyed, 28:
348
Utah Centennial Commission, publica-
tion, 28:378
Utah State Historical Society, Salt
Lake City, publications, 20:204
Ute Indians, 32:249; songs, 34:161
Utecht, Leo F., 29:324, 333
Utica Township, Winona County, depicted, 40:122
Utley, Robert M., work reviewed, 38:
237
Utrecht, Holland, treaty, 12:295, 18:
392
Utzman, Donald, 29:283

"Vacationland," steamboat, 34:15
Vaccination, see Smallpox
Vachon, André, editor, 40:145
Vagts, Alfred, author, 34:219
Vail, Mrs. Clarence, speaker, 27:268
Vail, Robert W. G., 25:394; work reviewed, 34:206; author, 16:110, 17:109, 21:94; editor, 18:213; librarian, 18:448, 25:395
Vaile, Roland S., reviews by, 18:87, 25:280; work reviewed, 14:206; speaker, 16:225; author, 18:91, 25:288, 26:279, 27:365; editor, 22:314
Vajen brothers, log house, 39:132
Valdres, Norway, described, 11:89
Valentine, Mrs. Daniel H., 38:77n
Valentine, G. T., speaker, 13:118
Valentine, Thomas, surveyor, 23:203
Valentines, early, 13:212; depicted, 35:248
Valinger, Leon de, Jr., author, 26:278
Vallandigham, Clement L., Copperhead, 20:283, 37:127; trial, 24:155, 25:350
Vallé, Ant., guide, 21:120n
Valle, Jean Baptiste, house, 29:72
Valley Chief reaper, 24:290
Valley City, N.D., mission, 20:431
Valley Creek, Washington County, architecture, 38:337, 343; road, 40:235, 236
Valley Herald (Chaska), 16:493; anniversary, 16:127, 18:113
Valley Ventilator (Montevideo), 18:466
Valois and Le Clerc, fur traders, 40:186
Van Akkeren, Jan, Dutch pioneer, 28:125
Van Alen's Cavalry, New York unit, 25:22
Van Alstine, Addie, reminiscences, 20:195
Van Alstyne, Richard W., author, 30:387
Van Arum, Willem, Dutch pioneer, 28:125
Van Beck, D., Dutch pioneer, 28:128
Van Beeck, August, diary, 12:445
Van Buren, Martin, 30:104; President, 16:326, 27:311
Van Buren, William H., author, 21:369
Vance, Maurice M., author, 37:261
Vance, R. W., author, 19:124
Vance, W. R., 13:211
Van Cleef, Eugene, author, 20:442
Van Cleve, C. E., "The Nesmith Cave Hoax," 11:74
Van Cleve, H. P., dairy farmer, 27:110
Van Cleve, Gen. Horatio P., 37:146; Union officer, 38:258, 260, 262, 264-266, 270, 39:176; portrait, 38:263; characterized, 39:181
Van Cleve, Mrs. Horatio P. (Charlotte Ouisconsin), 14:379; speaker, 35:187
Vancouver Island, B.C., granted to Hudson's Bay Co., 18:82; historic site, 40:191
Vandemark, Charles, 14:216
Van den Berg, G., Dutch pioneer, 28:128
Van den Einde, Corolas, Dutch pioneer, 28:125

Van Depoele, Charles, 35:283
Vanderbilt, Cornelius, Jr., work reviewed, 34:347
Vanderbilt, George W., 34:256
Vanderbilt, Paul, review by, 35:92
Vanderburgh, Judge Charles E., 40:376; papers, 19:450; pioneer, 25:313; speculator, 39:91
Vanderburgh, William H., lawyer, 21:196
Van Derlip, John, lawyer, 17:213
Van der Lippe, Rev. A., author, 14:105
Van der Meer, H., Dutch pioneer, 28:129
Van der Meulen, Rev. Cornelius, speaker, 28:368
Van der Ploeg, Rev. Harmen, 28:123
Vandersluis, Dr. Charles, author, 33:313, 356; editor, 34:131, 35:202; compiler, 38:388
Van Derveer, Col. Ferdinand, Union officer, 38:267, 269-272
Vandervoort, Paul, II, author, 37:39
Van Deventer, Fred, author, 37:187
Van Dooser, J. F., 20:435
Van Doren, Carl, author, 21:10-12, 51
Van Doren, Gen. Earl, 25:251
Van Doren, Harold L., author, 14:231
Van Dusen, George W., dairyman, 27:120; house, 40:105
Van Duzee, Charles A., auto driver, 38:207
Van Duzee, Fred, legislator, 35:302, 303
Van Dyke, Mrs. Fannie, pioneer, 30:271
Van Dyke, Mrs. Henry, speaker, 18:222
Van Dyke, J. H., speaker, 29:362
Van Dyke, John C., biography, 17:477
Van Dyken, Rev. William, speaker, 23:103
Van Essen, E., Dutch pioneer, 28:128
Van Etten, Mrs. Isaac, singer, 29:119, 39:321
Van Every, Dale, author, 40:39
Van Hee, Angelus, pioneer, 14:356
Van Heemskerk, Lawrence, explorer, 16:449
Van Hise, Charles R., university president, 30:381; biography, 37:261
Van Hise, Joseph, author, 36:230
Van Hoesen, H. M., journalist, 34:227
Van Horne, Sir William, 23:53; career, 31:120
Van House, John, author, 33:356
Van Inervan, ---, baseball player, 19:174
Van Ingen, Miss ---, cholera victim, 14:294
Van Ingen, Rev. John V., 14:294, 37:55
Van Kirk, Mrs. R. E., 39:58; author, 25:399
Van Koughnet, Donald E., "The 1932 Annual Meeting," 13:69-75; "The Historical Convention of 1932," 13:277-294; "The 1933 Annual Meeting," 14:73-80; "The Creation of the Territory," 14:127-134; "Minnesota Diamond Jubilee," 14:343-348; reviews by, 13:311, 312; research assistant, 12:424, 14:434; speaker, 13:70, 195, 14:213, 328
Van Lear, Thomas, speaker, 34:222

Van Liew, Henry, theater manager, 23:312-315
Van Ostrand, Ferdinand A., diary, 24:77
Vanous, Jan, Czech pioneer, 15:28
Van Pelt, J. Robert, author, 30:269
Van Pelt, John V., author, 14:337
Van Quickenborne, Father Charles F., 20:84
Van Raalte, Rev. Albertus C., colonizer, 28:368, 29:79, 35:33
Van Ravenswaay, Charles, 36:218
Van Rensalaer, George W., 17:278
Van Sant, Samuel R., 15:315, 17:313, 19:184n, 39:102; governor, 11:85, 33:129, 35:63, 346, 350, 351, 39:110; author, 11:212, 12:422; papers, 11:319; speaker, 11:330, 16:305; steamboat captain, 12:175; raftsman, 18:178, 179; interview, 12:457; career, 28:73
Van Schelven, Gerrit, 28:120
Van Schreeven, William J., author, 25:391
Van Slyke, W. R., speaker, 19:118
Van Slyke, William A., papers, 35:156
Van Steenwyck, E. A., 19:51; author, 24:356
Van Steenwyk, Gysbert, author, 27:69
Van Styke, W. A., merchant, 27:114
Van Tassell, David D., author, 36:150, 37:200
Van Tyne, Claude H., 39:220
Van Vechten, Carl, author, 26:308
Van Vorhes, Maj. Abraham, legislator, 35:360, 364
Van Vorhes, Andrew J., publisher, 17:490, 19:270
Van Wagenen, Jared, Jr., work reviewed, 33:347
Van Waters, George, geographer, 24:231
Vapaa, Ivar, 17:319
Vardaman, James K., 12:10
Varden, Dolly, pseud., see Slaughter, Linda W.
Värmlänning, Ola, tales, 29:105-113
Vasa, Goodhue County, Lutheran church, 11:333, 22:221, 33:49; Scandinavian settlement, 18:314, 24:89, 26:281, 30:148, 33:48, 34:167, 172, 37:262; historical meeting, 36:240
Vasa, Washington County, roads, 13:449; cemetery, 14:426-428; post office, 36:211; platted, 40:238
Vasa Children's Home, Goodhue County, anniversary, 27:78
Vasa Community Club, Goodhue County, 11:16, 12:338
Vasquas, Sister Scholastica, missionary, 30:3-5, 10, 13
Vassall, Irving, 35:215
Vaucel, Louis du, 20:423
Vaudreuil, François de Rigand, see Rigand de Vaudreuil, François de
Vaudreuil, Marquise de, see Rigand de Vaudreuil de Cavagnial, Jeanne Charlotte
Vaudreuil, Philippe de Rigand, see Rigand de Vaudreuil, Philippe de
Vaudreuil, Pierre de Rigand, Marguis de, see Rigand de Vandreuil de Cavagnial, Pierre de
Vaughan, J. P., author, 18:105
Vaughan, Maria, teacher, 21:453
Vaughan, Walter, author, 23:53

Vavasour, M., explorer, 17:345, 28:68
Veblen, Agnes, 14:217
Veblen, Andrew A., papers, 14:217, 436, 15:60; career, 14:332, 26:372
Veblen, Kari, pioneer, 15:235
Veblen, Oswald, 14:437
Veblen, Thomas A., pioneer, 15:235, 26:372
Veblen, Thorstein, 21:98, 36:105; career, 13:49, 28:278, 33:348; family, 14:437, 15:60, 26:372; biographies, 17:477, 28:270; economist, 28:54, 33:92, 36:97; author, 30:62; letters, 30:391; influence, 33:187, 34:352, 37:83
Veblen family, genealogy, 14:437
Velva, N.D., described, 27:331
Venn, Mary C., 15:22n
Venneman, Harry, author, 23:389
Vennerstrom, Jennie A., work reviewed, 24:240
Ventura, Viola, author, 18:458
Verboort, Ore., Dutch settlement, 29:68
Verbruggen, Henri, orchestra conductor, 16:359, 33:222; career, 17:477
Verdandi Study Club, Minneapolis, 29:160
Verdon Township, Aitkin County, river port, 33:16, 17; ferry, 33:19
Vérendrye, see La Vérendrye
Verhage, William, review by, 24:55; author, 24:60
Verill, A. Hyatt, work reviewed, 34:116
Vermilion Lake, St. Louis County, fur trade, 11:359, 17:111, 22:274, 23:330, 36:244-246, 39:82; roads, 16:295, 299, 17:233, 19:309, 34:178; fisheries, 25:185
Vermilion Lake Township, St. Louis County, pioneers' reunion, 21:116, 25:160
Vermilion Range, gold rush, 12:107, 13:176n, 14:453, 16:193, 295-297, 19:355, 442, 450, 20:193, 24:166, 32:217, 34:178, 36:282; history, 12:454; geology, 15:142, 32:222; iron discovery, 19:309, 27:160, 30:267, 37:93, 347; physicians, 19:357; entrepreneurs, 23:361, 35:338; ethnic groups, 25:319, 320, 27:205, 207, 210, 213; railroad, 27:203, 33:355, 36:281; labor situation, 27:209; bus line, 35:338; land-grant schemes, 37:97. See also Iron mining; Soudan Mine; Tower, Charlemagne; Tower
Vermilion Range Old settlers Association, 15:481, 35:382
Vermilion River, St. Louis County, described, 32:216
Vermilion Trail, St. Louis County, markers, 14:453, 35:382
Vermillion, Dakota County, churches, 20:440, 27:344
Vermillion, S.D., lumber market, 18:175
Vermillion baseball club, Hastings, 19:163, 173-175, 179
Vermillion Falls, Dakota County, 17:278; mill, 37:201
Vermillion River, Dakota County, bridge, 13:143; steamboating, 17:278; described, 17:279; mill, 18:114, 35:336

Vermont, schools, 28:137; dairying, 37:19, 20
Verndale, bank, 13:346
Verndale Mining Co., 29:303n
Vernon, Dodge County, creamery, 11:290, 19:157n, 20:357; Norwegian settlement, 12:270; pioneer life, 15:246, 367
Vernon Center, stage service, 12:51n, 52; in Sioux Outbreak, 38:285
Verrazano, Giovanni da, 18:385
Verwyst, Chrysostom A., missionary, 17:477
Veseli, Catholic church, 12:451; name, 13:199; history, 21:115
Veseth, Johannes O., 18:200
Vessel Point, see Pointe aux Barques
Vessels, Jerry, author, 22:214
Vestal, Stanley, pseud., see Campbell, Walter S.
Vetch, Joseph, 28:192
Veterans, see Civil War, Spanish-American War, World Wars I and II
Veterans' Administration, 37:133; archives, 21:327; Fort Snelling, 28:53, 77, 35:190
Veterans of Foreign Wars, 19:98, 23:292; Princeton, 16:367
Veteransville, Aitkin County, veterans' colony, 39:243-245, 247, 248, 250
Veterinary medicine, Finnish practice, 18:338; U.S. Department of Agriculture, 23:283; progress, 35:243
Vetter, Rev. Heinrich, missionary, 21:453
Vevray, Ind., Edward Eggleston's home, 18:349, 370, 454, 26:242
Vezina, Rosemarie, author, 40:357
Vialars, A., 11:238n
Vialars, Daniel, 11:238n
Vianney, Jean-Baptiste-Marie, 14:341
Vicchers, Dr. Charles L., cholera victim, 14:294
Vickers, Chris, author, 29:78, 165, 259, 263
Vicksburg, Miss., siege, 20:279, 25:241, 242, 33:211-213
Victor, Iowa, depicted, 39:289
"Victor," Minnetonka steamboat, 29:292
Victoria, queen of England, 17:135
Victoria, Carver County, agriculture, 27:175
"Victoria," Red River steamboat, 21:259n, 263
"Victory," Mississippi steamboat, 38:288
Victory Aides, organized, 23:21; importance, 23:23; Hibbing, 24:269
Viebahn, Charles D., steamboat captain, 33:16, 18, 19
Vieg, John A., author, 22:326
Vienna Exposition, 1873, Minnesota display, 13:35
Vienna Township, Rock County, Norwegian settlement, 12:274
Vigilantes, defined, 14:109; Montana, 16:226
Vigness, Lauritz A., college president, 31:51
Vik, Robert, office assistant, 25:41
Viking Township, Marshall County, anniversary, 35:47
Vikings, Greenland, 17:24, 171; Minnesota, 18:40, 102, 28:176; Cana-

da, 19:105, 20:85, 199; Great Lakes region, 21:92; explorations, 21:302-304; Newport, R.I., 24:257, 27:350, 29:349, 33:88, 35:141; in America, 28:271, 32:51, 33:216, 34:199, 214, 353, 37:30, 39:170, 171, 342. See also Vinland
Vilain, Marcel, artist, 33:334
Vilaine, Sister Philomene, missionary, 30:3, 5, 13
Vilas, Dr. Calvin D., 21:114
Vilas, William F., Wisconsin Senator, 19:310; biography, 34:166
Vilbon, --- de, trader, 32:237
Viles, Jonas, speaker, 15:227
Villa Louis, see Dousman, Hercules L.: house
Villa Maria Academy, Frontenac, land donated, 14:39; pageant, 15:480, 16:372; anniversary, 22:445; history, 29:87
Villard, Harold G., author, 14:231
Villard, Henry, work reviewed, 25:276; railroad executive, 12:72, 13:332, 445, 14:447, 21:97, 23:53, 33:30, 39:31; author, 13:331; career, 17:477, 33:316, 356; Minnesota visit, 24:374, 33:314; financier, 37:320, 321
Villard, Oswald Garrison, editor, 25:276; isolationist, 40:410
Villard, history, 11:337
Villiers, Baron Marc de, work reviewed, 12:410
Vimont, Father Barthélemy, 13:253, 27:218
Vincennes, Ind., first press, 15:13, 14; French settlement, 18:394
Vincent, Felix A., actor, 28:109
Vincent, George E., 27:41; papers, 17:100, 160n, 20:82; author, 19:328, 329; university president, 22:101, 23:289, 31:52, 32:176, 177, 36:186; quoted, 30:362
Vincent, Henry, 11:158
Vincent, Jean A., 25:2, 29:104; review by, 29:72
Vincent, Bishop John H., 29:321, 324
Vinde, Victor, author, 29:154
Vine, Earl A., 21:48, 213
Vine Street Society, Minneapolis, 17:212
Vinegar Hill, Jo Daviess County, Ill., lead mining, 22:24
Vineland, Mille Lacs County, homesteading, 27:154; Chippewa artifacts, 36:284
Vining, pioneer life, 11:117
Vinje, Aasmund O., poet, 20:382
Vinland, presumed location, 21:304; sagas, 23:378, 24:176, 40:94, 95; map controversy, 39:342, 40:94. See also Vikings
Vinton, Stallo, author, 16:475, 35:180
Violet Study Club, Minneapolis, 12:321
Virginia (city), ethnic groups, 12:436, 17:409, 19:112, 21:290, 25:319, 325, 30:156; lumbering center, 13:366, 21:212, 27:208, 31:71; mining town, 16:486, 19:334, 21:290, 32:245, 33:355; Finnish temperance society, 22:392, 395-397, 399, 400, 402; history, 30:409; bus line, 35:338; miners' strike, 40:345

Virginia (city) War History Committee, 23:392
Virginia (state), historic sites, 13:
382, 17:112; early press, 15:4, 6;
historical guide, 16:220; land
claims, 18:435, 20:9, 33:260; government, 32:248, 40:201
Virginia (state) Historical Society,
Richmond, centennial, 13:207
Virginia (state) Quarterly Review,
20:112
Virginia (state) World War II History
Commission, 26:85, 175
"Virginia," steamboat, on Minnesota
River, 11:123; first on upper Mississippi, 11:210, 455, 12:77, 13:
330, 435, 437, 14:150, 18:372,
433, 20:304, 378, 22:13, 27:355,
28:79, 30:211n, 212n, 40:79, 411
Virginia and Rainy Lake Lumber Co.,
operations, 14:106, 27:302, 29:70,
177, 375; camp depicted, 36:153
(cover); labor problem, 36:153,
156, 160
Virginia Warrior's Path, Indian
trail, 15:256
Virtue, Ethel B., 11:46
Vischer, Mrs. E. A., 30:79, 166
Visitation Convent, St. Paul, 16:369
Visscher, Dr. Maurice B., author, 21:
101
Vista, Waseca County, Lutheran
church, 14:451, 452; anniversaries, 17:489, 35:203; pageant, 28:
385
Vitalis, Earl, speaker, 28:196
Vitz, Carl, speaker, 19:67
Vivaldi, Father Francis de, mission-
ary, 14:121, 28:210; at Long
Prairie, 13:339, 18:107; letters,
15:105, 21:192; characterized, 30:
10; career, 33:38
Vivian Township, Waseca County, lo-
cated, 18:298n
Vizetelly, Frank H., author, 12:443
Vladivostok, U.S.S.R., depicted, 38:
310, 325; railway corps visit, 38:
314-316, 324
Voegeli, Jacque, author, 39:82
Voegelin, C. F., translator, 34:160
Voegelin, Ermine, author, 34:160
Voelker, Frederick E., editor, 34:
254; author, 39:337
Vogel, Louis G., 11:332, 17:120, 23:
296
Vogel, William, speaker, 12:341
Vogt, Evon Z., author, 36:324
Voight, Robert C., "Aaron Goodrich,"
39:141-152; receives award, 39:264
Vojta, Rev. Vaclav, author, 23:381
Vold, George, criminologist, 37:162n
Volk, Douglas, artist, 17:170, 38:
273n
Volksblatt des Westens (Winona), Ger-
man-language paper, 16:338
Volksfest Association of Minnesota,
36:239
Volkszeitung (St. Paul), German-lan-
guage paper, 15:468, 19:215
Vollharth, Henry, 16:255
Vollmer, George F. J., author, 24:194
Vollum, E. P., engraver, 26:225
Volney, Constantin François Chasse-
boeuf, comte de, 18:396
Volstead, Andrew J., Congressman, pa-
pers, 29:101, 34:339; sponsors
agricultural bill, 38:179

Volunteer guards, see Minnesota
Pioneer Guard
Volunteers of America, St. Paul chap-
ter, 27:177
Volz, Rev. John R., author, 16:371
Von Arx, H. A., 20:359
Von Corvin, Col. ---, emigration
agent, 13:35
Vondersmith, Archibald, farm, 16:12
Von Grueningen, John P., editor, 22:
203
Von Hagen, A. C., author, 23:400
Von Hamm's Bookstore, St. Paul, piano
sales, 39:320
Von Holst, Hermann E., historian, 19:
6, 436, 36:2
Von Koch, Sigfrid, author, 16:106
Von Kraemer, Henry, author, 18:70
Von Miklos, Josephine, 20:201
Vonnegut, Emma S., work reviewed, 17:
79
Von Scholten, Agnes, author, 18:226,
22:222
Von Steinwehr, Gen. Adolph, Union
officer, 25:357n
Voree, Wis., Mormon colony, 23:66
Vornholt, Dan E., editor, 24:260
Vorspan, Albert, editor, 38:335
Vosburgh, Frederick G., author, 30:
390
Vose, Maj. Josiah H., Fort Snelling
commandant, 19:448, 28:16n
Vosmek, Josef, Czech pioneer, 15:28
Vosmek family, Czech settlers, 15:30
Voss, Fred J., speaker, 34:171
Voxland, George H., legislator, 33:
158
Voyageur Press, Minneapolis, 14:196,
15:237
Voyageurs, tasks, 11:232, 241, 353,
22:135, 144, 23:246; roster, 12:
307, 13:432; life described, 12:
357, 13:87-92, 18:87, 241, 384,
395, 23:286, 30:206, 32:124, 40:
162, 359; source material, 13:59,
98; songs, 13:88, 89, 14:227, 17:
205, 20:72, 22:139, 147, 23:281,
29:136, 34:126, 35:339, 36:190,
194, 37:345, 38:238; holidays, 16:
374; engagements, 16:450, 32:233;
canoe races, 16:480, 33:91; depicted, 17:109, 18:239, 28:282,
36:127, 40:161; explorations, 20:
341, 23:135, 136n, 26:224, 31:93,
94, 34:46; Grand Portage lawsuit,
21:121-148; history, 21:401, 34:
360, 38:386, 40:182; routes, 22:
177-181, 439, 24:277, 25:90, 26:
172, 29:133, 134, 31:105, 32:122,
37:216, 236-254, 346; costume, 22:
320; food, 23:250, 28:281, 32:94,
pipes, 25:202, 38:34; legends, 28:
11, 12, 33:187; customs, 37:79.
See also French Canadians, Fur
trade, Mixed-bloods
Vriege, Willem, Dutch pioneer, 28:122
Vrooman, Carl, author, 34:222
Vyner, Sir Robert, trade and territorial grants, 16:423-426
Vytlacil, Mrs. Vaclav, 36:217

"W. D. Washburn," steamboat, 11:206
Wabash Railroad, route, 30:236; ferry, 38:237

Wabash Valley, history, 24:343
Wabasha I, Sioux leader, 13:373, 374;
family, 20:219; memorial, 40:21
Wabasha II (La Feuille), Sioux
leader, 12:234, 13:373, 374, 17:
153, 154n, 155, 157, 296, 21:167n;
career, 17:477; family, 20:219,
21:27n; treaty signer, 22:152n;
arrested, 31:214-216
Wabasha III, Sioux leader, 12:121,
38:131n; family, 20:219; in outbreak, 38:96, 106n, 130, 134,
141n, 144, 148; treaty signer, 38:
147
Wabasha (city), post, 11:383; roads,
11:389, 393, 407, 19:103, 27:344,
40:233; population, 12:62n; county
seat, 13:215, 16:372, 18:296;
French voters, 13:217; Catholic
church, 15:128, 21:330; railroad,
15:493, 35:14, 15n; volunteer
guard, 16:177; G.A.R. post, 16:
430; library, 19:239; described,
19:342; bridges, 22:98, 23:290;
button factory, 28:285; wildlife,
30:223; name, 30:332; German theater, 32:100, 34:242; located, 34:
25n; depicted, 36:191, 40:62, 77;
post office, 36:206, 207, 40:83,
87; river port, 38:72
Wabasha County, ethnic settlements,
12:211, 13:217, 21:98, 40:328;
county seat, 13:215, 16:372;
schools, 13:454; history, 20:218;
archives, 20:445; source material,
20:462, 26:178; pioneer life, 21:
313, 39:201-204; medicine, 26:96;
hog raising, 26:114; wheat production, 29:2n, 13, 18n, 36:69; Indians, 37:274, 275; poor farm, 38:
368; geology, 39:132; politics,
40:324-327
Wabasha County Herald-Standard
(Reads Landing), established, 14:
397, 404, 15:86; name, 15:87
Wabasha County Historical Society,
29:94
Wabasha County Medical Society, 17:
489
Wabasha County War History Committee,
23:392
Wabasha Prairie, Winnebago encampment, 17:153, 155, 30:211; Sioux
village, 21:163n, 29:174; located,
23:342n, 33:117n. See also Winona
Wabasha Reservation, Wabasha County,
Lake Pepin, mixed-blood allotment,
29:221n
Wabasha Roller Mill Co., 15:492
Wabasha Street, St. Paul, depicted,
33:197
Wabasha Street Bridge, St. Paul,
built, 13:178n
Wabassimong (White Dog), Islington,
Ont., mission, 11:306, 12:318, 13:
440
Wabasso, anniversary, 16:130, 252;
high school, 27:81
Wabegon, Lake County, railroad, 34:
180
Wabeke, Bertus H., author, 25:299
Wabeno, Wis., logging museum, 24:364
Wabiko-digingjo, Joseph, Chippewa
Indian, 39:304
Waconia, Carver County, churches, 12:
206, 16:120; fruit raising, 21:85;

German culture, 24:214, 32:100, 34:242
Waconia, Goodhue County, see Frontenac: resort
Waconia Creamery Association, 24:190
Waconia Lake, Carver County, described, 12:336; railroad, 30:236
Wacouta (Wakute, Leaf Shooter), Sioux leader, 12:121, 317, 15:247, 38: 101n, 106n, 144, 149; peacemaker, 38:134
Wacouta (village), Goodhue County, quarry, 37:290; post office, 40:89
Wadd, John A., logger, 29:177
Wadd, John C., author, 29:177
Wadden, Etienne, murdered, 34:344
Wade, Benjamin F., characterized, 22: 409
Wade, Henry H., mineralogist, 34:271, 273; author, 36:35
Wade, Mark S., work reviewed, 13:302-304
Wade, Mason, work reviewed, 24:48-50; author, 28:282, 35:151
Wade, Rex A., speaker, 40:364
Waden, Jean Etienne, trader, 33:261
Wadena, Chippewa leader, 21:285, 30: 396
Wadena (city), mission, 20:90; railroad colony, 23:371
Wadena County, soil survey, 12:343; name, 20:343; Finnish settlement, 25:318, 36:34; agriculture, 29:272
Wadena County Historical Society, 34: 359; planned, 17:358, 20:99; organized, 29:182
Wadsworth Trail, St. Cloud-Fort Wadsworth, Dak. Ter., marker, 16:485; history, 19:227
Waendelin, S., author, 15:355
Waggoner, Isaac N., steamboat interests, 13:233
Waggoner, Mat, author, 30:275
Wagner, A. H., politician, 28:28
Wagner, Corydon, 28:51
Wagner, Henry R., author, 18:451, 34: 303, 35:334
Wagner, Samuel T., 11:413
Wagner, Webster, 36:66
Wagnild, Rev. O. J., author, 25:411
Wagoner, Mrs. Nina, speaker, 28:88
Wahcic, Albina J., author, 13:333
Waheoka, Nicollet County, ghost town, 17:238
Wahkeeyah Hotonna, Sioux leader, 38: 148
Wahkon, logging town, 28:292
Wahkon Lake, Mille Lacs County, name, 21:348
Wahlgren, Erik, work reviewed, 36: 146; author, 36:238, 38:43
Wahlquist, Rev. E. A., speaker, 14: 353
Wahlquist, Judith J., author, 36:106
Wahlstrand, Harry L., speaker, 24:270
Wahnahta, territorial county, 29:182, 30:273
Wahpekute band, Sioux Indians, treaty, 32:76, 77, 37:272; in Spirit Lake massacre, 38:88, 123; reservation, 38:129; village, 38: 148n
Wahpeton band, Sioux Indians, 31:217, 220; treaty, 22:143n, 32:69, 72, 75, 76, 38:129n; allotments, 35: 177, 36:34; rescue captives, 38: 123; in outbreak, 38:137, 145

Waite, E. F., 12:207
Waite, Frederick C., work reviewed, 27:135
Waite Park, Evangelical church, 14: 361
Waite's Crossing, Sauk River, trail marked, 32:63
Waitley, Douglas, author, 39:82
Wakeeta, Rock County, election precinct, 14:250, 256
Wakefield, Edward G., colonizer, 35: 375
Wakefield, Harry B., speaker, 11:334; author, 11:335
Wakefield, Dr. J. L., 12:130
Wakefield, Mrs. J. L., 12:130
Wakefield, James B., house, 30:165; career, 35:216, 221
Wakefield, Jay T., letter, 15:345
Wakefield, Capt. John, 11:393
Wakefield, Mrs. Lyman E., 19:449
Wakefield, Mrs. William, 38:75, 76n, 77n
Wakefield, Sgt. William L., 25:251, 349
Wakelin, Edward W., postmaster, 34: 186
Wakin, Edward, author, 39:128
Walcott, Samuel, 20:467
Walcott, Rice County, Norwegian settlement, 12:271; fire, 20:467
Waldenmaier, Nellie P., author, 22: 203
Waldier, Michael, politician, 39:49
Waldo, Edna L., work reviewed, 14: 205; author, 12:446
Waldo, Lake County, railroad, 34:180
Waldorf Paper Products Co., St. Paul, 22:337
Waldron, Eli, author, 30:394
Waldron, George, pioneer farmer, 11: 186
Waldron, Lawrence R., agriculturist, 19:26, 32
Wales, C. R., collector, 14:335
Wales, H. Basil, author, 30:389
Wales, Thomas, diaries, 26:371, 27:23
Wales, William W., Quaker, 18:249; career, 18:250; papers, 27:248
Walker, Archie D., lumberman, 28:372, 32:127, 33:91
Walker, Mrs. Archie D., 27:48
Walker, Charles R., work reviewed, 18:191; author, 18:106, 218
Walker, Con, theater manager, 31:120
Walker, Cornelius, Sibley County settler, 11:170n
Walker, David, reformer, 25:65
Walker, F. A., Indian commissioner, 35:170
Walker, Fowler, merchants' agent, 11: 249, 254, 19:292; papers, 11:250, 261
Walker, Franklin, author, 34:126
Walker, G. M., 23:399
Walker, Hartwell, postmaster, 11:170n
Walker, Hudson, 17:139n
Walker, Mrs. J. W., 28:283
Walker, James B., author, 31:55
Walker, James C., author, 22:437
Walker, Dr. James R., 20:312
Walker, Joseph, Sibley County settler, 11:170n
Walker, Capt. Joseph R., trader, 36: 317
Walker, Leroy P., politician, 37:50

Walker, Lucius C., Indian agent, 14: 332, 28:214, 38:275
Walker, M. O., stage operator, 11: 404, 406, 30:70, 34:18n
Walker, Mary A., author, 18:454, 34: 350
Walker, Norman, translator, 21:365
Walker, O. A., speaker, 24:380
Walker, Orange, 36:211; lumberman, 17:278, 18:167, 176, 29:205n; house, 18:344, 38:339; postmaster, 36:208, 213
Walker, Platt B., 22:437
Walker, Porter E., postmaster, 36:211
Walker, R. J., letter, 16:224
Walker, Robert H., author, 37:261
Walker, Sears C., letter, 18:314
Walker, Thomas, trader, 11:236, 248
Walker, Thomas B., 35:67, 229, 231, 39:115-117, 121; art collector, 17:146, 147, 28:82; career, 17: 477; family, 25:93, 28:82; log mark, 26:135; lumber magnate, 26: 136, 29:139, 145, 147, 31:75, 32: 180, 37:41
Walker, Versal J., 16:181
Walker, Gen. William, 27:2
Walker family, genealogy, 28:82
Walker, in Chippewa uprising, 14:332, 24:145, 146, 28:78; market, 23:28; railroad, 23:33, 24:142, 29:138, 139
Walker and Akeley Lumber Co., operations, 27:302, 29:139, 140, 142, 34:153; Minneapolis mill, 34:149
Walker Art Center, Minneapolis, 26: 302, 28:82, 302; director, 21:216; publication, 28:76, 34:353; exhibits, 29:370, 30:176, 283, 34: 253; buildings, 39:122n
Walker Commercial Club, marking project, 11:112
Walker, Judd, and Veazie, Marine on St. Croix, lumber firm, records, 15:346, 23:395, 24:245. See also Marine Lumber Co.
Walker's Landing (Faxon), Sibley County, 11:169, 170n
Walking-bell-ringer, Sioux Indian, 21:272n
Walking Buffalo, see Red Wing, Sioux leader
Wall, Alexander J., 25:394; speaker, 23:82
Wall, Joseph F., reviews by, 35:30, 329; work reviewed, 35:151
Wall, Oscar G., author, 34:236
Wallace, Abithel, political candidate, 39:143
Wallace, Carleton L., legislator, 35: 343
Wallace, Dan A., 18:410
Wallace, David H., work reviewed, 35: 369
Wallace, DeWitt, career, 27:353, 36: 281; publisher, 36:32
Wallace, Elizabeth, work reviewed, 33:136
Wallace, Mrs. Grayce, 18:249n
Wallace, Henry A., quoted, 23:216; speaker, 25:84; house, 29:73; depicted, 29:189, 190; politician, 29:190-194, 40:140; 1948 crusade, 38:41
Wallace, Henry C., agriculturist, 40: 322
Wallace, Hiram B., sheriff, 20:217

Wallace, J. S., timber agent, 31:158
Wallace, James, author, 12:335;
    speaker, 19:237; Macalester presi-
    dent, 27:353; biography, 35:370
Wallace, Thomas F., 26:45, 29:97
Wallace, W. L., author, 13:208
Wallace, W. Stewart, works reviewed,
    16:200-202, 34:344; author, 13:
    209, 432, 14:229, 15:477, 19:109,
    20:200, 21:433, 24:262, 25:200,
    29:339, 31:56, 33:139; editor, 14:
    114, 16:480
Wallace, William, trader, 40:186
Wallace, William H., territorial
    delegate, 38:227
Wallace family, genealogy, 12:335
Wallack, James W., actor, 23:314;
    stock company, 28:117
Wallack, Mrs. James W., actress, 23:
    314; stock company, 28:117
Wallas, ---, mine operator, 34:274
Waller, Mrs. C. V., speaker, 17:481
Waller, George, work reviewed, 37:343
Wallin, Russell, author, 18:228
Wallis, F. J., artist, 29:286
Wallis, Ruth S., work reviewed, 34:
    257
Wallis, Wilson D., work reviewed, 34:
    257
Wallof truck, 40:148
Walnut Grove, first school, 18:118;
    pictorial account, 37:223; marker,
    38:43
Walnut Grove Tribune, anniversary,
    22:447, 37:223
Walon Lahde Hall, Eveleth, 32:199
Walquist, John, 33:333, 334, 337
Walsh, Gen. Ellard A., 23:149
Walsh, Timothy F., architect, 39:155,
    159, 160
Walsh County, N.D., boom towns, 21:
    99; place names, 38:385
Walsingham, Thomas, Lord, quoted, 19:
    297
Walston, Cragg, musician, 33:101
Walstrom, M., educator, 33:309
Walta, Antti, 40:399; depicted, 40:
    391
Walta, Edward, depicted, 40:391
Walta, Otto, folk hero, 40:391-402;
    depicted, 40:391, 400
Walter, Erich A., author, 39:82
Walter, Frank K., author, 14:231;
    compiler, 31:188
Walter, H. H., speaker, 20:351
"Walter Taylor," steamboat, 33:14, 15
Walters, Dorothy V., "Pioneering with
    the Automobile," 26:19-28; speak-
    er, 25:379, 26:44; author, 26:65,
    27:356
Walters, E. M., weaver, 15:189
Walters, Emile, artist, 34:164
Walters, Henry, collector, 13:409,
    22:133, 134
Walters, Horace, music publisher, 26:
    53
Walters, Thorstina, 25:201; work re-
    viewed, 34:164
Walters, Dr. Waltman, author, 40:309,
    362
Walther, Rev. C. F. W., defends slav-
    ery, 32:15, 22
Walther, Rev. E. H. T., speaker, 13:
    451
Walther, Rev. Paul, author, 21:453
Walther League, Minnesota district,
    14:105

Walton, Charles W., author, 31:123
Walton, Clyde C., 37:78; editor, 36:
    280, 37:222
Walton, Ivan H., author, 22:431, 24:
    175
Walton, Mrs. J. F., speaker, 17:356,
    483
Wambach, Xavier, author, 11:220
WAMD, Minneapolis, radio station, 16:
    483
Wanamingo, Norwegian settlement, 12:
    271; trade center, 34:127
Wand, Augustin C., author, 33:352
Wanda, Polish settlement, 13:108
Wanderer (St. Paul), German-language
    paper, 19:219
Wanderer Printing Co., St. Paul, pub-
    lication, 15:446
Waneta (Wanata, Wanotan), Sioux lead-
    er, 11:191, 21:79
Wangensteen, Dr. Owen H., author, 31:
    124
Wanigans, see Barges
Wanless, Lake County, name, 34:183;
    fire lookout, 36:136
Wanwig, D., emigrant agent, 12:256,
    13:28
Waples, Dorothy, author, 26:73
War Camp Community Service, in World
    War I, 14:320
"War Eagle," steamboat, races, 11:
    143, 12:393, 27:8, 33:198; crew,
    11:174n; described, 12:113; in fur
    trade, 13:233; excursions, 15:409-
    411, 419, 22:13, 34:135; used by
    writers, 16:45, 17:376, 377, 20:
    377, 22:160; signaling equipment,
    18:372, 19:249; depicted, 25:88;
    burned, 38:244
War Industries Board, 13:189
War of 1812, Indians in, 11:179n, 15:
    473, 31:189, 36:67; British
    forces, 12:233-235, 17:196, 22:
    283; finances, 13:180; American
    forces, 14:103, 40:348; effect on
    fur trade, 20:15, 38:328, 40:164;
    peace treaty, 22:306; memoirs, 23:
    182; in Canada, 24:46; on Lake On-
    tario, 24:71; history, 40:142
Waraju River, see Cottonwood River
Warba, history, 24:383
Ward, Artemus, author, 19:437, 28:56
Ward, B., 18:401
Ward, Charles A., career, 34:312, 35:
    245
Ward, Christopher, author, 19:220
Ward, D. E., 14:236
Ward, Edward, 14:443
Ward, Col. George H., 25:246
Ward, Harold R., 14:333
Ward, Henry A., scientist, 39:113
Ward, Mrs. Herbert, 23:297
Ward, J. Q. A., union official, 21:
    376
Ward, Jack, 26:205
Ward, Jacob C., artist, 15:211
Ward, James, steamboat captain, 29:
    204
Ward, Jesse, pioneer, 23:297
Ward, John, speaker, 19:316
Ward, John W., essay reviewed, 37:83
Ward, Mary Ann, speaker, 20:458
Ward, Mrs. Matt, speaker, 11:223
Ward, Sam, diary, 30:59
Ward, Seth E., trader, 40:196
Ward, W. T., author, 21:369
Ward, William, letter, 14:215

Ward Township, Todd County, history,
    16:131, 256
Ward's Lake Superior Line, steamboat
    company, 37:118n
Ware, Caroline F., editor, 23:178
Ware, Charles, 14:455
Ware, Joseph E., author, 13:331
Warehouse Act, provisions, 12:13
Warfel, Harry R., author, 25:305
Warfeld, Henry, immigration commis-
    sioner, 13:28
Warg, Lorin C., author, 36:106
Wargelin, Rev. John, speaker, 25:378
Warkentin, A., author, 24:366
Warming, Irene, reference assistant,
    23:366, 26:359; author, 18:58, 20:
    43, 21:45, 25:379
Warner, ---, cabinetmaker, 15:187
Warner, Mrs. Amos, speaker, 13:73,
    15:241
Warner, Anne R., biography, 17:477
Warner, Charles, publisher, 18:113
Warner, Charles H., legislator, 33:
    159
Warner, Donald F., "The James F. Bell
    Collection," 31:105-109; "Prelude
    to Populism," 32:129-146; reviews
    by, 31:42, 32:246, 34:37, 347, 35:
    236, 36:64, 37:80, 40:43; work re-
    viewed, 37:126; author, 30:63,
    151, 31:64, 127, 32:191, 256, 33:
    315
Warner, E. C., 19:184n
Warner, E. R., hunter, 16:268
Warner, Fred C., 27:162
Warner, Marjorie F., author, 28:180
Warner, Robert M., author, 34:310
Warner, William A., 17:141
Warner and Beers, Chicago, publish-
    ers, 40:128
Warnke, Roberta, author, 15:245
Warnock, Arthur W., author, 12:457,
    13:123
Warnson, Mrs. Gustava C. S., 35:313
Warntz, William, author, 35:291
Warre, Lt. Henry J., explorer, 17:
    345, 28:68; artist, 17:346, 25:
    302, 26:56, 35:144, 36:318
Warren, A. L., house, 38:352
Warren, Annie M., papers, 27:154
Warren, Arthur G., author, 19:345
Warren, Chester, 25:225, 254, 344
Warren, Dorothy, author, 22:94
Warren, Fitz Henry, postmaster, 40:88
Warren, Francis E., 22:80
Warren, George, lumberman, diaries,
    27:154
Warren, Mrs. George, 14:119
Warren, George P., 11:211
Warren, Gouverneur K., engineer, 17:
    477, 37:315
Warren, Irene, author, 16:128
Warren, John E., 14:158
Warren, Lyman, 22:206; Indian agent,
    11:326; trader, 22:355, 26:362,
    28:202, 29:58, 32:186; library,
    22:356
Warren, Robert P., author, 20:114
Warren, Mrs. S. H., 27:250
Warren, Truman, trader, 32:186
Warren, Tyler, 18:405
Warren, Whitney, architect, 39:159,
    160
Warren, William W., 14:337, 19:342;
    map maker, 11:361; author, 16:312,
    28:77, 181, 29:66, 35:384
Warren family, in fur trade, 11:326

Warren, marketing center, 12:451; county seat, 12:452; pageant, 15: 137; water supply, 15:249; Lutheran church, 17:229; first house, 21:445; Knights of Labor, 22:369; Indians, 24:246; anniversary, 35: 203

Warren Hospital, 12:452

Warren Sheaf, anniversary, 12:451

Warren Woman's Club, 15:137

Warrick, W. Sheridan, author, 35:151

Warrington, Joseph, author, 21:370

"Warrior," steamboat, 13:229, 230, 15:273, 17:296n, 21:21n

Warroad, post, 11:366, 13:345, 18: 279, 22:274, 276, 24:319, 36:246; located, 18:278; feldspar mining, 23:108; Indians, 24:325; railroad, 24:327; fishing station, 25:316, 35:275; chapel, 34:130; road, 36: 325

Warroad River, Roseau County, timber, 31:161

Warsaw, ethnic settlements, 12:271, 13:108; Methodist church, 14:123; G.A.R. post, 16:431

Warsaw, Ill., river town, 17:431n

Wartburg Federation of the Northwest, records, 11:319, 12:321

Wartman, Joseph, farmer, 35:201

Warville, Brissot de, author, 29:154

Wasastjerna, Hans R., author, 36:192

Waseca, railroads, 12:46n, 21:239; bank, 13:213; churches, 14:239, 452, 18:316, 19:49, 25:102; G.A.R. post, 16:431; labor unions, 21: 393, 22:380; Chautauqua, 29:321; German theater, 32:100, 34:242; baseball team, 36:94; resort area, 36:194

Waseca County, ethnic settlements, 12:269, 21:98, 31:27; history, 12: 320; county seat fight, 12:444; pioneer life, 18:298-301, 21:457; Catholic churches, 20:218; first settlement, 22:108; anniversary, 23:302; name, 30:331; library, 31: 61; politics, 40:327

Waseca County Bar Association, 18:211

Waseca County Historical Society, 23: 14, 25:403, 30:409, 35:156; organized, 19:232, 20:46; meetings, 19:362, 20:99, 23:104, 195, 24: 188, 25:99, 210, 26:92, 180, 27: 364; museum, 20:214, 355, 22:108, 219, 23:299, 24:87, 271; picnic, 20:458; marking project, 21:110, 218; finances, 21:447, 22:443; anniversary, 24:381; gifts, 25:409; incorporated, 27:78, 174; officers, 28:196; essay contest, 30: 280

Waseca County Horse Thief Detectives, 19:232, 350, 26:121; history, 12: 195, 13:153-157, 25:214; meeting, 15:253; picnic, 20:458

Waseca County Sunday School Association, 18:211

Waseca County War History Committee, 24:83

Waseca Farmers Club and Agricultural Society, fair, 21:458

Washburn, Abbott M., 13:77

Washburn, Algernon S., papers, 21: 314, 22:40

Washburn, Cadwallader C., miller, 11: 278, 12:203, 33:133, 34:204; pa-

pers, 12:99, 14:65, 102; career, 17:477, 478, 40:359; Wisconsin governor, 21:427; Congressman, 34: 71, 72; lawyer, 35:287; businessman, 37:312, 315

Washburn, Christopher C., 13:77

Washburn, Claude C., 13:77

Washburn, Edson, 20:192

Washburn, Edward A., 24:61

Washburn, Frederic L., scientist, 39: 113, 121

Washburn, Genevieve, 13:77

Washburn, Hope, 13:77

Washburn, Israel, Jr., letters, 21: 314; family, 21:427; Maine governor, 25:232; career, 40:359

Washburn, Mrs. Israel, Jr. (Patty), family, 21:427

Washburn, Jed L., 11:54, 12:424, 13: 57; career, 13:77-82; portrait, 13:78

Washburn, Mrs. Jed L., 13:77

Washburn, John L., 13:77

Washburn, Julia A., 13:77

Washburn, Lilian, author, 21:427

Washburn, Mildred, 13:77

Washburn, Dr. Walter L., author, 31: 190

Washburn, Wilcomb E., "Symbol, Utility, and Aesthetics," 40:198-202; compiler, 36:30

Washburn, Mrs. Will O., 20:330

Washburn, William, 24:61

Washburn, William, Jr., letter, 24:61

Washburn, William D., 35:378, 37:314; papers, 11:318, 12:99, 14:102, 15: 223, 21:314; Senator, 12:389, 21: 427, 32:134, 35:66-68, 70, 305, 39:93, 94, 98-100, 110; lumberman, 13:350, 16:479, 26:136, 37:41; career, 17:477; log mark, 26:135; railroad interests, 31:62; speaker, 33:172, 178; miller, 34:204; politician, 36:301, 306, 307, 39: 101, 103, 328, 40:359; businessman, 37:312, 319; surveyor general, 37:327

Washburn, William D., Jr., 33:332

Washburn A Mill, explosion, 11:330, 17:352, 27:270

Washburn and Woodman, Mineral Point, Wis., bankers, 16:91

Washburn B Mill, 11:278

Washburn-Crosby Co., Minneapolis, 12: 90, 14:234, 22:186; brands, 11: 329; litigation, 21:194; mills, 33:133. See also General Mills, Inc.

Washburn-Doane expedition, 23:282

Washburn Mill Co., see Washburn-Crosby Co.

Washburn sawmill, Anoka, 18:333

Washburne, Elihu B., letters, 21:314; Congressman, 33:329, 330, 36:181, 183, 301-304, 37:313, 314, 332, 40:359

Washington, Booker T., 31:244; author, 26:304

Washington, Justice Bushrod, 35:9

Washington, George, 20:371, 21:6, 10; bicentennial, 13:96, 14:105; papers, 14:108, 16:52, 19:36, 28:91, 33:186; President, 15:221; birthday celebrated, 19:326, 25:249, 26:169, 38:55; career, 22:313; church, 25:38, 227; Indian medals, 25:267; farmer, 40:294

Washington, George A., 28:91

Washington, J. E., letter, 17:108

Washington, Richard, 20:452

Washington family, genealogy, 15:469

Washington (state), source material, 23:84, 89; war records, 25:311; proverb collection, 27:34; boundaries, 38:219; timberland, 39:90

Washington, Conn., Congregational church, 23:97

Washington, D.C., in Civil War, 11: 205, 16:77, 25:37; treaty, 20:320; hotel, 28:323, 40:270; sesquicentennial, 31:248; Ferdinand von Zeppelin's visit, 40:270, 271

Washington, Fillmore County, Methodist meetings, 21:86

Washington, Nicollet County, ghost town, 17:238

Washington, N.C., in Civil War, 25: 343

Washington Avenue, Minneapolis, 30: 384

Washington Avenue Bridge, Minneapolis, 23:68

Washington County, archives, 14:76, 15:198, 20:89, 21:458; history, 14:239, 17:490; territorial census, 14:262, 17:393, 23:395; pioneer life, 15:347; railroads, 18: 336; Lutheran church, 18:443; medicine, 19:463; fair, 22:250; agriculture, 23:321, 24:126, 40: 235; logging, 24:194; hog raising, 26:114; Scandinavian settlement, 31:27, 36:240; courthouses, 38: 186-189, 348, 349, 40:135; in Civil War, 38:259; poor farm, 38: 367; road, 40:239

Washington County Historical Society, 16:241, 25:403, 28:89, 29:281; organized, 15:372, 16:63; members, 15:493, 26:92; meetings, 16:125, 244, 337, 362, 17:124, 233, 358, 484, 18:111, 336, 19:119, 232, 20: 99, 214, 355, 21:110, 22:108, 23: 195, 299, 24:189, 25:210, 26:180, 395, 28:196, 29:95, 182, 30:83, 401, 34:173; picnic, 19:472, 20: 458, 21:339, 23:399, 27:364; museum, 21:447, 22:219, 342, 23:12, 394-396, 24:271, 350, 381, 25:313, 26:286, 27:78, 174, 268, 29:277; collections, 23:104, 395, 26:133; marks Stillwater centennial, 24: 161, 349, 25:41; excursion, 25: 409, 28:298

Washington County Journal (Stillwater), file, 21:316

Washington County Light and Power Co., 20:92

Washington County Soldiers Monument Association, 11:225, 28:89

Washington County War History Committee, 23:392

Washington Island (Potawatomi Island), Wis., Lake Michigan, 15: 172, 174, 175; occupied by Potawatomi, 13:402; Radisson's visit, 15:166-171; Icelandic settlement, 34:265

Washington Lake, Sibley County, grasshopper plague, 36:61

Washington Light Artillery, volunteer company, 16:172, 173

Washington Seminary, Stillwater, 19: 250; curriculum, 17:388, 39:321

Washington State Historical Society, Tacoma, publication, 27:66
Washington Territory, governors' messages, 22:330; centennial, 33:313; politics, 35:93
Washingtonians, temperance society, 22:124
Wasioja, Dodge County, ghost town, 13:215, 16:367, 35:11; described, 14:276; Christmas celebration, 17:126; Baptist church, 19:122; wheat raising, 29:23
Wasioja Gazette, history, 13:215
Wasioja Institute, Methodist school, 16:345
Wasson, Chester R., author, 20:448
Wasson, Franklin, steamboat builder, 11:128
Wasson, George S., author, 27:238
Wasuihiyayedan (Traveling Hail), Sioux leader, 38:130, 134, 147
Watab, Benton County, trading post, 11:374, 29:219; treaty, 1853, 14:330; settled, 26:155; Chippewa name, 30:331
Watab Reveille, 16:332; established, 14:402
Watab River, Stearns County, logging, 24:131
Water power, Garden City, 12:52; Twin Cities, 37:109, 309-323; St. Louis River, 37:117; St. Croix River, 38:242. See also Dams
Water witching, in U.S., 36:324
Waterbury Township, Redwood County, Lutheran church, 24:193
Waterford, Dakota County, mounds, 16:308; post office, 35:111
Waterloo Historical Society, Kitchener, Ont., 15:473
Waterman Guards, volunteer unit, 16:173n
Waterous Co., St. Paul, history, 37:263
Waters, Alvin W., "The Last of the Glidden Tours," 38:205-215
Waterton-Glacier International Peace Park, Alta.-Mont., 22:178
Watertown, bell foundry, 16:364, 18:376; literary society, 24:214; anniversary, 35:293
Watertown, S.D., John Banvard's residence, 25:300
Watertown, Wis., German settlement, 34:219
Watertown Township, Crow Wing County, name, 21:347
Waterville, post, 11:382; horse thieves jailed, 13:156; history, 26:260, 330-333; junior historians, 27:49, 122-124, 144, 28:162; railroad, 30:236, 240; resort, 33:323; settled, 34:177; sawmill, 34:235
Waterville House, register, 19:95
Waterville (N.Y.) Times, 12:434
Watkins, Arthur V., Utah Senator, 28:378
Watkins, Harry, actor, 23:307
Watkins, J. R., Medical Co., Winona, architecture, 39:130
Watkins, Oscar, 18:136
Watkins family, in Minnesota, 25:386
Watkins, history, 19:117
Watonwan (Blaine), Blue Earth County, milling center, 27:365

Watonwan, Cottonwood County, election precinct, 14:250, 251
Watonwan County, Norwegian settlements, 12:273; pioneer life, 16:498, 17:491, 24:65; agriculture, 17:367; post offices, 18:65, 22:444; farmers' club, 20:218; library, 31:61; grasshopper plague, 37:207
Watonwan County Historical Society, 20:355; organized, 17:64, 124; meetings, 18:111, 224, 19:119, 233, 362, 472, 20:99, 214, 21:110, 445, 22:219, 24:88, 26:395; exhibit, 22:443; collections, 24:271
Watonwan County Plaindealer (St. James), 39:225
Watonwan County War History Committee, 23:392
Watonwan Farmers' Club, Lake Crystal, history, 30:161
Watonwan River, Blue Earth, Cottonwood, and Watonwan counties, 14:251; name, 12:52n; mills, 26:394
Watrin, Father Benno, 12:223n, 22:47; compiler, 11:332; speaker, 19:115
Watrous, Maj. John S., 24:354, 36:4n; town planner, 35:49
Watrud, Mrs. Harriet, author, 28:296
Watson, Capt. ---, artist, 25:166n
Watson, Brook, 11:238n
Watson, Elmo S., author, 11:451, 25:87
Watson, Isabella, speaker, 13:121, 345, 16:361, 23:299
Watson, Mrs. Louise H., speaker, 21:335
Watson, LuElla, author, 14:235
Watson, P. H., letter, 38:243
Watson, Robert, author, 12:326; diary, 17:54, 96
Watson, Thomas E., Georgia Senator, 12:10, 39:29
Watson, settlers, 12:207, 14:353; Lutheran church, 13:117
Watson, Dak. Ter., bonanza farm, 20:405
Watson and Eastman, St. Paul, commission merchants, 27:108
Watterson, Henry, 26:357; journalist, 35:151
Watts, ---, ship captain, 20:253
Watts, Florence, 12:286
Waubun, Congregational church, 16:485
Waud, Alfred R., artist, 33:217
Waud, William, artist, 33:217
Waugh, Frances, speaker, 11:112
Waugh, Harvey, composer, 30:173
Waukenabo Lake, Aitkin County, name, 21:348
Waukesha County, Wis., Welsh settlements, 24:176
Wau-kou (Spirit), Winnebago mixed-blood, 31:215
Waumadee Herald (Reads Landing), 15:86, 87
Waumidokiga, Sioux teacher, 16:146
Waverley automobile, 26:22
Waverly Township, Martin County, records, 34:131
Wawatosa Island, Hennepin County, Lake Minnetonka, name, 34:128
Wawiekumig, Chippewa Indian, 21:285
Waxlax, John, settler, 34:181, 182
Way, Frederick, Jr., author, 25:196; compiler, 25:393
Way, Ronald L., author, 31:118

Wayburne, Redwood County, ghost town, 19:465
Wayne, Ralph W., author, 19:474
"Wayne," steamboat, see "Anthony Wayne"
Wayzata, history, 14:352, 27:176; pageant, 14:457; school, 20:209; hotel, 27:295; historical meeting, 28:391; pioneer life, 30:407; centennial, 34:128, 170
Wazikute, Sioux Indian, 13:372-375; Stephen H. Long's guide, 13:368
WBAD, Minneapolis, radio station, 18:333
WCAL, Northfield, radio station, 30:291
WCCO, Minneapolis, radio and TV station, 36:105; name, 34:204; contest, 35:340, 384
Weagamow Lake, Ont., Chippewa colony, 39:34
Weasel, in fur trade, 35:295
Weasel Lake, Faribault County, settlement, 14:456
Weather, see Climate
Weatherhead, George, author, 16:496
Weatherhead, Harold, author, 12:430, 21:430
Weatherhead, Jason, author, 22:109
Weatherwax, Paul, work reviewed, 34:160
Weaver, Clarence L., compiler, 26:384
Weaver, Dorothy Ann, author, 16:245
Weaver, Elijah, 25:247
Weaver, George, author, 22:214
Weaver, Mrs. J. L., speaker, 19:229
Weaver, James B., politician, 35:58, 76, 291
Weaver, Robert B., author, 20:441
Webb, Mrs. E. O., 21:107
Webb, Edward A., 18:410
Webb, George, pioneer printer, 15:7
Webb, Rev. Harvey, 26:96, 31:83
Webb, L. E., Indian agent, 25:183
Webb, Walter P., works reviewed, 13:92-94, 33:215; speaker, 13:327; author, 24:68, 29:71, 40:151, 156; historian, 33:311; quoted, 36:87
Webb, Wayne E., work reviewed, 39:208; author, 38:242
Webb, William, Jr., legislator, 36:57
Webb Publishing Co., St. Paul, 27:353; history, 34:173
Webber, Capt. Alfred B., prison official, 37:145, 146
Webber, C. C., 19:184n
Webber, Dr. E. E., house, 37:3
Webber, Everett, author, 36:278
Webber, Rev. J. S., 17:388, 19:249, 250
Webber, Robert, 36:278
Weber, Bob, author, 39:344
Weber, Dr. Gustav, 27:136
Weber, H. G., 26:126n
Weber, Herbert Y., "The St. Paul Globe," 39:327-334
Weber, J. V., speaker, 18:465, 23:299
Weber, Max, artist, 28:76
Weber, Rev. Nicholas A., author, 30:395
Weber, Thomas, work reviewed, 33:218
Weber and Fields, comedians, 33:177
Webster, C. C., business leader, 33:233
Webster, Charles L., and Co., New York, publishing firm, 17:376n, 378

Webster, Daniel, 22:66, 23:60, 205, 28:275, 39:38; portrait, 21:149; letter, 21:412; politician, 39:46, 47, 150, 151. See also Webster-Ashburton Treaty
Webster, E. M., 11:223
Webster, Mrs. Florence G., recollections, 21:440
Webster, Mortimer, house, 38:347
Webster, Noah, lexicographer, 29:81
Webster, Sidney, 13:434
Webster, Viranus, murdered, 38:134n
Webster, W. H., 20:461
Webster, William, manufacturer, 37:143, 145
Webster, Capt. William W., Union officer, 39:195n
Webster, Norwegian settlement, 29:177
Webster-Ashburton Treaty, 23:60, 204, 205, 24:57, 29:132, 40:46; provisions, 18:232, 22:213, 23:270, 396, 29:135; background, 23:59; centennial, 23:201n, 396, 24:32. See also Boundaries
Webster City, Iowa, lyceum, 15:175
Wechsler, Rabbi Judah, 40:46
Weckman, Violet M., author, 35:338
Wecter, Dixon, work reviewed, 22:313; author, 28:67, 174, 34:261
Wedel, Waldo R., author, 39:262
Wedge, Dr. Albert C., 14:314; career, 21:340; army surgeon, 40:291
Wedum, Mrs. J. A., speaker, 15:246
Weed, Col. ---, hotelkeeper, 16:268
Weed, Thurlow, 14:280; excursionist, 15:406, 20:384, 25:103; papers, 30:104
Weekly Reveille (St. Louis), 22:14; travel accounts, 22:15-34, 31:209-221
Weeks, Edward, speaker, 33:352
Weeks, Kathleen, author, 26:385
Weeks, Mrs. L. C., 11:320; speaker, 18:334, 19:229
Weenaas, August, 20:401, 402
Weesh-koob, Narcisse, speaker, 13:442
Wefald, Harold, quoted, 38:178
Wefald, Jon M., "Congressman Knud Wefald," 38:177-185; review by, 40:354
Wefald, Knud, 40:367; Congressman, 38:177-185; portrait, 38:179; reformer, 40:140
Wegdahl, Chippewa County, political meeting, 34:229
Wegelin, Oscar, author, 27:252
Wegmann, Theodore, pioneer, 36:235
Wehle, Harry B., author, 20:334
Wehrle, Charles, 16:103
Wehrwein, George S., author, 13:438
Weibel, Jacob S., artist, 32:160
Weibel, Rodney, 22:52
Weibull, Jörgen, work reviewed, 34:199
Weicht, Carl L., 11:117, 17:232, 23:103; "The Local Historian," 13:45-54; author, 11:338, 12:453, 16:371, 497, 22:111, 218, 23:187, 191; speaker, 13:72, 15:251, 16:252, 17:240, 21:446, 22:107, 291, 292, 341, 23:299, 27:77, 144, 363
Weidman, Charles, 21:59
Weidner, Edward W., 28:285; author, 37:347
Weigert, Mrs. Lillian, speaker, 19:471
Weik, Jesse, author, 28:361

Weimer, David R., work reviewed, 37:83
Weinberg, Jack, author, 28:183
Weinfeld, William, work reviewed, 25:280
Weinmann, Joseph, politician, 28:28
Weisel, George F., work reviewed, 35:31
Weisenburger, Francis P., 24:183; work reviewed, 34:121; author, 15:356, 17:226, 25:401, 36:280
Weiser, Dr. George B., author, 22:212, 334
Weismiller, Edward, poet, 25:176
Weiss, A. C., career, 14:360
Weiss, Harry B., author, 12:327
Weiss, S., 21:427
Weisse, Harold, author, 22:98
Weitbrecht, George F., speaker, 39:114
Weitenkampf, Frank, author, 31:54, 32:123; librarian, 40:76n
Welch, Maj. A. Edward, 39:179n
Welch, Clarence H., farmer, 37:29
Welch, Douglas, author, 30:378
Welch, Dr. George, 12:105
Welch, Mrs. George (Phoebe L.), career, 12:105
Welch, Ita, actress, 28:113
Welch, Thomas W., pioneer, 24:205
Welch, historic site, 16:309, 36:240
Welcome, Mrs. Earl (Pauline), speaker, 28:387; author, 39:212
Welcome, Lutheran church, 15:481; history, 28:387, 39:212
Welcome Times, historical editions, 28:387
Weld, Angelina Grimké, 19:436
Weld, Burt I., author, 17:238
Weld, Charles, letters, 15:463
Weld, Daniel, 15:301
Weld, Eben, government farmer, 14:99, 15:222, 304, 344, 17:288; career, 15:301; letters, 15:302-308, 28:336; house, 15:305, 17:95, 289
Weld, Gladys I., 15:302
Weld, Isaac D., lumberman, 24:201
Weld, Dr. John F., 15:306n, 307; letters, 15:463
Weld, Mrs. Lydia F., 15:301
Weld, Martin, 15:304, 307
Weld, Mildred, 15:302
Weld, Theodore, abolitionist, 32:15, 33:218
Welden, Charles, journalist, 34:139n
Welfare, agencies, 16:114, 351, 19:98, 21:450, 25:377, 39:27; New York, 17:111; Quakers, 18:263; Minnesota, 18:449; bibliography, 20:88; Wisconsin, 27:69; old-age assistance, 37:41, 38:78-85, 39:26; poor farms, 38:365-377; issues, 39:26; medical aspect, 39:84. See also Child welfare, individual organizations
Welford, Walter, 18:104
Welin, S., 17:182
Welker, Mrs. Att, speaker, 16:132
Wellcome, Dr. F. H., 22:425
Wellcome, Sir Henry S., 12:436; biography, 34:127
Welles, A. M., author, 11:108
Welles, Edward L., author, 11:74
Welles, Gideon, 20:284
Welles, Henry T., politician, 26:201, 35:120, 36:4n, 171
Welles, John, trader, 11:236, 21:141

Welles, Sumner, quoted, 23:217
Welles family, genealogy, 35:248
Welles Memorial Park, Breckenridge, 18:104
Wellesley, Marie, actress, 33:176
Wellham, Hiram C., speaker, 18:333
Wellman, Mrs. C. H., speaker, 13:345
Wellman, Mrs. M. H., speaker, 23:103
Wellman, Mary A., teacher, 11:113
Wellman, Paul I., work reviewed, 16:89; author, 29:164
Wellner, Dr. George C., author, 17:100
Wellner, John, murdered, 12:91
Wellner, L. H., 17:100
Wells, ---, trader, 11:261
Wells, A. L., 16:491, 17:483, 18:465, 22:442
Wells, Charles K., banker, 40:113, 114, 116-118
Wells, Mrs. Cyrus, author, 22:102
Wells, Daniel, Jr., banker, 37:87, 40:110-119; grain dealer, 39:210; portrait, 40:111
Wells, Mrs. Eliza, author, 37:274
Wells, Frederick B., 25:154n, 32:13n
Wells, H. G., author, 14:10, 26:308
Wells, James, trader, 14:31, 19:95, 20:307, 29:267
Wells, Jane, 14:32
Wells, Rev. John A., 13:452
Wells, John G., 33:52n
Wells, Justus O., steamboat captain, 34:11
Wells, Leander, 13:142
Wells, Leonard H., bookseller, 26:396
Wells, Philip F., author, 29:267
Wells, Robert J., legislator, 35:348
Wells, Rosalie, author, 16:486
Wells, William S., miller, 35:13-16
Wells, Willoughby, 26:261
Wells, churches, 16:355, 17:117; history, 20:460; flour mill, 23:388; dairying, 27:111n, 112n, 113; theater, 28:119; railroad, 39:240
Wells Advocate, 17:469
Wells and Smith, Belle Plaine, plow factory, 24:296
Wells Memorial, Minneapolis, 33:315
Welp, Treumund, pseud., see Pelz, Edward
Welsh, Jeremy G., artist, 38:165n, 39:140n, 203n, 285
Welsh, Thomas J., "Logging on the Northwest Angle," 34:1-8
Welsh, Dr. William, 24:209
Welsh, Minnesota communities, 12:448, 16:170, 496, 19:464; Wisconsin, 24:176, 27:56, 29:85; immigration, 24:259, 37:256; in Civil War, 29:86, 33:84. See also British
Welter, Katherine, author, 12:340
Welter, Rush, author, 37:261
Welti, Jakob R., author, 35:242
Welty, Eudora, author, 25:176
Welty, Raymond L., author, 19:349, 457
Weltzin, Elmer, speaker, 27:145
Wemett, W. M., author, 39:36
Wemett, William W., 13:112
Wenberg, Jennie, author, 14:354
Wendago, Itasca County, settled, 22:223
Wendt, Father Pierin, speaker, 19:119
Wenger, John C., author, 22:335
Wengler, Jean B., artist, 11:43, 35:357

Wennerberg, Gunnar, composer, 39:322
"Wenona," steamboat, 36:252
Wenstrom, Otto, 16:498
Wenstrom, Ruth, author, 16:498
Went, Stanley, author, 26:308
Wentworth, Col. Edward N., author, 28:281, 35:97
Wentz, Abdel R., author, 35:200
Wentzel, Charles, memorial, 21:445
Wenzell family, genealogy, 17:101
Wergeland, Henrik, 18:199
Wergeland Lodge, Minneapolis, 20:408
Werneke, Edward, newspaper assistant, 18:58, 19:61, 24:162, 25:40
Werner, Raymond C., work reviewed, 16:448-450
Werrenrath, Reinald, singer, 39:59
Wertenbaker, Thomas J., work reviewed, 23:259; author, 29:163
Werthun, ---, fur dealer, 34:102
Wesbrook, Dr. Frank F., 24:347; career, 18:218, 21:330, 24:181; public-health leader, 19:111, 24:211
Wescott, Abbie, 20:456
Wescott, Mrs. Ethelyn M., 20:456
Wescott, Glenway, author, 23:158
Wescott, James, innkeeper, 20:456
Wesenberg, Michael F., 19:106
Wesley, Edgar B., 19:429, 21:49, 25:44, 73, 294, 27:243; "Historical Research," 14:192-194; "The Army and the Westward Movement," 15:375-301, "History at Home," 19:1-20; reviews by, 12:417-419, 15:214-216, 17:81-83, 321, 18:103, 19:202, 20:176-179, 21:306, 22:65-67, 26:60, 138; works reviewed, 17:80, 19:437-439, 20:61-63, 23:360, 25:168-170, 27:333, 35:371; author, 12:436, 13:329, 334, 17:331, 18:103, 19:91, 199, 207, 20:187, 21:182, 310, 22:82, 23:8, 24:174, 25:61, 26:65, 73, 153, 27:147, 28:172, 204, 29:77, 34:170; speaker, 13:327, 15:310, 18:441, 19:70, 20:29, 31, 48; quoted, 22:297; educator, 24:254
Wesley Methodist Church, Minneapolis, anniversary, 15:362
Wesleyan Methodist Seminary, Wasioja, 14:147
Wesselhoeft, Dr. Conrad, homeopath, 39:9
Wessen, Ernest J., 36:218
Wesson, Daniel, gunmaker, 36:68
West, Charles, author, 21:370
West, Col. Charles W., portrait, 21:417
West (Wert), Capt. D. Mortimer, Union officer, 28:326
West, Emily J., 12:119, 130, 133
West, George A., work reviewed, 15:453
West, Gordon H., author, 19:465
West, H. D., motorist, 26:22
West, Harry B., author, 14:359, 450, 15:492
West, J. D., manufacturer, 40:333
West, Rev. John, 20:204; teacher, 29:81
West, John T., hotel owner, 35:67
West, Lee, steamboat captain, 33:12, 14
West, Norbert D., author, 36:190
West, Mrs. Sarah, speaker, 20:100
West, William M., author, 35:233

West, Willis M., work reviewed, 11:78-80; honored, 13:341, 428
West, outlaws, 34:209, 39:262; mapped, 34:302; settled, 34:345; depicted, 35:146, 37:31, 33; interpreted, 38:237; historic sites, 39:33; source material, 39:128. See also Far West, Frontier, Middle West
West Albion, Wright County, Finnish settlement, 38:243
West Battle Lake, Otter Tail County, sugar camp, 13:390; name, 38:141
West Central School of Agriculture, Morris, history, 11:338, 28:384; archaeological collection, 26:321
West Concord, anniversary, 17:121
West Duluth, Salem Mission Church, 22:112; united with Duluth, 24:385; post office, 34:186. See also Duluth
West Duluth Bank, 37:124
West Duluth Building and Loan Association, 37:123
West Duluth Saw Mill Experts' Association, 36:162
West End Building and Loan Association, Duluth, 37:123
West End Herald (Minneapolis), 17:469
West Hennepin County Pioneer Association, 36:36
West Hotel, Minneapolis, 17:380, 18:30, 33.52, 35.67, 73, 40.15, 100n; name, 21:417; built, 23:220, 224; razed, 25:3, 4, 40:135; orchestra, 33:95; described, 35:68, 72, 75, 76; depicted, 35:74, 40:14
West India Co., Montreal, trading practices, 11:232
West Indians, Mississipi Valley, 23:84
West Lynne, Man., history, 34:132
West Newton, Nicollet County, prairie described, 11:172; pioneer store, 18:171, 20:464, 23:109, 36:193; logging company, 26:132, 27:196, 201, 29:266; Catholic church, 36:193; log house, 37:76
"West Newton," steamboat, 19:138; freight contract, 11:136, 137, 164-180
West Point, N.Y., see United States Military Academy
West Point, Va., in Civil War, 25:127
West Prairie, Yankton County, S.D., pioneer school, 24:370
West Publishing Co., St. Paul, lawbook firm, 36:190; building, 40:221 (cover)
West St. Olaf, Dodge County, Norwegian settlement, 12:270
West St. Paul, school district, 11:445; county seat election, 13:141; Presbyterian church, 27:344; founded, 34:287
West Saint Paul Times, anniversary, 19:366
West St. Paul Turnverein, 17:339
West Savanna River, Aitkin County, 23:251n, 33:15; canoe route, 31:95, 96, 32:95, 34:46
West Side Neighborhood House, St. Paul, music class, 39:56
West Side Turner Hall, Minneapolis, 32:167, 172
West Union, Iowa, described, 12:165

West Union, Scott County, Lutheran church, 19:475
West Union, Todd County, history, 16:131; archaeology, 28:181
West Virginia, historic markers, 19:220; in Civil War, 25:31, 228n; proxy vote, 26:209
"West Wind," steamboat, 38:363
West Yorkshire Pioneer (Skipton, England), reprint, 27:283-299
Westbrook Mutual Insurance Co., Cottonwood County, history, 20:357
Westchester County, N.Y., historical buildings, 14:443
Westergren, Charles, postmaster, 36:214
Westerheim, Lyon County, Icelandic settlement, 18:469
Western, Capt. H. H., Fort Ridgely commandant, 12:115n
Western, Iowa, Czech settlement, 15:33
Western Air Express, army contract, 26:10
Western Air Lines, 33:240
Western Classical Academy, Orange City, Iowa, 28:130
Western College, Western, Iowa, 15:33
Western Department, fur traders, 40:184-186
Western Farm and Village Advocate (New York), 12:194, 13:59, 23:321
Western Farm and Village Association, 17:324; colonies, 12:194, 17:323, 18:230, 23:321; records, 25:321
Western Federation of Miners, Mesabi Range, 40:340-347
Western Female Seminary, Oxford, Ohio, 23:272
Western Flotilla, in Civil War, 40:306
Western Folklore Conference, 27:255
Western Guard (Dawson), 21:342
Western History Association, publication, 39:209
Western Home and Foreign Missionary Association, in Minnesota, 19:141
Western Hygeian Home for Invalids, St. Anthony, 35:217, 36:91
Western Intercollegiate Championships, 39:22
Western Land Association, organized, 17:218, 37:92
Western League, baseball association, 39:331
Western Minnesota Seminary, Montevideo, see Windom Institute
Western Monthly Magazine, founded, 26:293
Western Pennsylvania Historical Society, Pittsburgh, 12:93, 184, 311, 16:329
Western Pennsylvania Historical Survey, 12:184, 311, 21:179
Western Railroad Co., lands, 28:224
Western Reserve Historical Society, Cleveland, Ohio, 30:314, 394
Western Reserve University, Cleveland, Ohio, school of medicine, 27:135
Western Theological Seminary, Chicago, 18:331
Western Union Telegraph Co., Winona office, 18:120
"Western World," steamboat, 15:307
Westervelt, Mrs. Everett, 14:31n

Westervelt, Evert V., at Frontenac,
14:31-33; house, 14:34
Westervelt, Mary, 14:34
Westervelt, Goodhue County, name, 14:
32; located, map, 14:35. See also
Frontenac
Westfall, Wilson P., businessman, 37:
318
Westford Township, Martin County,
frontier life, 18:465
Westgate, John W., agriculturist, 19:
27, 32
Westin, Gunnar, works reviewed, 13:
308-311, 38:381; author, 18:75
Westin, Leslie E., "Community His-
tory," 25:57-61; instructor, 24:
192; author, 25:76; legislator,
36:284, 37:44, 223
Westlake, E. G. ("Eddie"), portrait,
38:212
Westland (Heidelberg, Ger.), German-
language periodical, 33:187
Westlicher Herold (Winona), German-
language paper, 16:338
Westlund Monument Co., Fergus Falls,
19:361
Weston, George E., restaurant operator, 35:225n
Weston, J. M., speaker, 33:287, 288
Weston, Latrobe, author, 19:459
Weston and Curtis reaper, 24:290
Westover, Lake County, railroad station, 34:181
Westport, Mo., battle, 40:291
Westport Township, Pope County,
schools, 26:398
Westward movement, surveys, 12:70-72,
18:303-305, 20:440, 22:311, 33:
301, 36:275, 38:387; relation to
agriculture, 12:172-174; in song,
22:125-127, 25:211; effect of urbanization, 22:430; source material, 24:111-124, 27:247, 30:290;
in fiction, 25:192; of culture,
34:299. See also Frontier, Immigration and emigration
Wetherby, Isaac A., artist, 31:46
Wetherell, June P., author, 31:147
Wethern, Mrs. Rudolph J., author, 12:
207
Wey, Rev. William, speaker, 16:488
Weyer, Dr. C. N., 17:342
Weyer, Martin, German pioneer, 17:342
Weyerhaeuser, Frederick E., lumberman, 14:112, 16:479, 18:178, 218,
20:336, 441, 22:206, 23:99, 184,
24:134, 27:190, 194, 195, 198,
199, 30:242, 32:188, 36:132, 37:
185, 39:129; biography, 22:94;
timber appraiser, 27:196; career,
28:182, 32:125, 34:263, 38:379
Weyerhaeuser, Fredrick K., 28:51;
speaker, 32:188
Weyerhaeuser, Mrs. Frederick K., 30:
89, 170, 287, 366, 32:57; honored,
30:368, 31:11
Weyerhaeuser, Mrs. Louise L., author,
22:194
Weyerhaeuser, Mrs. Rudolph, 37:152,
38:83
Weyerhaeuser family, lumber interests, 25:197, 38:379; philanthropies, 28:50, 30:90, 329
Weyerhaeuser and Rutledge, log marks,
26:136
Weyerhaeuser Foundation, grant, 37:
187

Weyerhaeuser Timber Co., 32:125, 180
Weyl, Charles G., 11:225
Weyl, Walter, 14:201
Whalebacks, on Great Lakes, 15:122
Whaley, Charles, automobile manufacturer, 26:22
Whaley, John A., grain inspector, 24:
103n
Whaley, Samuel, biography, 16:337
Wharton, Gabriel C., 19:388
Wheat, Carl I., work reviewed, 34:
302; author, 34:219, 35:97, 36:
277, 38:386
Wheat raising, types, 11:273, 279,
23:86, 29:18, 19, 20n; transportation, 12:178, 329, 14:355, 16:344,
33:67, 35:295, 381, 37:94, 185,
39:328; Red River Valley, 13:205,
15:134; yields, 14:387, 24:99,
334, 37:103, 108, 159n, 40:296;
prices, 17:127, 19:324, 29:5, 7,
24, 37:159n; Canada, 18:217, 28:
366, 35:48; diseases, 20:156-164,
29:19, 20, 36:80; Rochester, 20:
222; regional pattern, 21:94; relation to population, 21:438;
source material, 22:223, 39:270;
relation to Populism, 23:283;
Kansas, 25:375; costs, 28:42, 29:
22, 23; Minnesota, 29:1-28; in
Catholic colonies, 35:209; depicted, 36:73 (cover); grading,
39:328, 329n. See also Agriculture, Flour milling, Grain marketing
Wheaton, Herbert E., author, 17:103,
18:226, 21:221
Wheaton, Capt. Lloyd, 12:438
Wheaton, anniversary, 18:474; his-
tory, 36:107; archaeology, 38:165
Wheeler, ---, Union soldier, 25:151
Wheeler, Alonzo, fisherman, 35:272
Wheeler, Bert N., speaker, 14:238
Wheeler, Charles N. B., author, 20:
362
Wheeler, Chester E., author, 14:443
Wheeler, Cleora C., author, 29:272
Wheeler, Col. E. S., speaker, 14:460
Wheeler, Edward, 23:107
Wheeler, Lt. George M., surveyor, 28:
348
Wheeler, Helen W., 19:446
Wheeler, Dr. Henry M., 40:362
Wheeler, Howard, biography, 13:324
Wheeler, Joseph, 19:388
Wheeler, Leonard H., missionary, 17:
464
Wheeler, Olin D., 13:331; author, 26:
303
Wheeler, Robert C., 35:339; "History
below the Rapids," 38:24-34; re-
views by, 37:35, 38:191, 39:256,
40:260, 263; work reviewed, 31:
186; author, 36:72, 105, 152, 284,
37:264, 38:336, 39:212; editor,
36:196, 37:264; MHS associate director, 37:348, 40:262
Wheeler, Mrs. Robert C. (Ardis H.),
work reviewed, 39:123
Wheeler, Rush B., 29:272; letters,
15:224
Wheeler, Thomas C., work reviewed,
39:207
Wheeler, William A., 18:295
Wheeler and Co., St. Paul, piano
dealers, 39:319

Wheeler and Son, St. Anthony, mer-
chants, 14:267
Wheeler House, St. Peter, hotel, 17:
488
Wheeler-Howard Act, 15:258
Wheeler's Point, Lake of the Woods,
name, 35:273
Wheelhouse, Mary, see Berthel, Mary
W.
Wheeling Township, Rice County, ethnic settlements, 12:271, 28:33
Wheelock, Arthur T., employment
agent, 29:141
Wheelock, Eleazar, 13:329
Wheelock, Ellen, 16:210, 18:275
Wheelock, H. M., 16:124
Wheelock, Joseph A., 35:47, 256, 260-
262; editor, 14:406, 15:284, 18:
274, 22:211, 23:309, 25:203, 26:
95, 149, 28:197, 33:315, 34:203,
36:304, 37:330, 38:56; quoted, 15:
286, 288, 289, 292, 16:210, 35:
254, 258; papers, 16:215, 332, 17:
53, 26:155, 37:333; biography, 18:
218; author, 26:67, 189, 35:253,
255, 37:56n, 38:70; statistics
commissioner, 34:330-336; illness,
34:333, 35:221, 252
Wheelock, Mrs. Joseph A. (Katharine
French), 34:331, 333-335, 38:77n;
papers, 16:215
Wheelock, Sarah, 16:445
Wheelock, Clearwater County, ghost
town, 16:493
Wheelwright, Edward, traveler, 36:44,
45n
Wherland, Capt. Fred, 14:232
Whetstone, Dan, "Printer's Appren-
tice," 36:197-205; portrait, 36:
198; author, 36:283
Whetstone, Kay, author, 36:284
Whig party, newspaper support, 15:20,
17:427; leaders, 29:252; Pennsylvania, 35:353, 39:38, 39; Minnesota Territory, 36:3, 4, 7, 259,
261, 266, 269, 270, 39:40-48, 147,
148, 151, 40:223, 407; Tennessee,
39:143
Whipple, Com. Abraham, 15:383
Whipple, E. P., speaker, 11:158
Whipple, Bishop Henry B., 12:117, 14:
454, 17:350, 18:295, 19:104, 475,
21:105, 349, 22:321, 28:190, 31:
87, 32:180, 35:248; work reviewed,
19:73-76; services to Indians, 11:
96, 455, 15:84, 111, 292, 294-297,
299, 363, 16:97, 357, 376, 20:95,
21:201, 24:72, 30:391, 35:170,
246, 36:34, 37:42, 38:136n, 357;
described, 12:114, 15:286, 16:210;
papers, 12:317, 429, 13:59, 16:94,
99, 217, 336, 17:54, 98, 19:467,
20:372, 433, 25:183, 28:203, 29:
49; memorials, 12:332, 15:129, 16:
119; career, 13:95, 15:130, 18:
217, 21:450, 26:96, 36:35; collector, 14:334, 17:104; injured, 15:
287; quoted, 15:298; diaries, 15:
355, 19:58; southern trip, 16:66;
sermons, 16:241; consecrated, 16:
477; houses, 17:363, 18:325; portraits, 17:471, 18:325, 19:467;
quarrel with Father Tomazin, 18:
268; speaker, 18:365, 19:268; author, 30:372
Whipple, Mrs. Henry B., death, 11:455

Whipple, J. C., in Sioux Outbreak, 38:144n
Whipple, John, land-office receiver, 12:382, 384–387
Whipple, W. J., journalist, 23:111
Whipple Lake, Clearwater and Crow Wing counties, name, 21:349. See also Lake Minnewaska
Whipple School, Moorhead, history, 15:134
Whiskey Flat, Anoka, 25:364
Whistler, George, topographer, 24:342
Whistler, Capt. William, Fort Howard commandant, 23:247
Whiston, Nathaniel, letter, 26:155
Whitaker, Ephraim, farmer, 29:89
Whitaker, Mrs. F. E. (Roxanne), 16:243, 17:358; speaker, 17:67
Whitall, Ellis G., lawyer, 39:148
Whitcomb, James, 26:223
Whitcomb, Orlen P., speculator, 39:91
White, ---, ship captain, 28:6, 7
White, A. W., pioneer, 15:136
White, Almond A., 20:82
White, Andrew D., university president, 12:191, 13:59, 16:30
White, Arthur, theater manager, 23:198
White, Mrs. Arthur C., 30:89, 288
White, Asa, trader, 11:374
White, Ashton S. H., at Traverse des Sioux, 22:139, 146; artist, 26:141
White, Bernice, author, 36:105
White, Clyde R., lawyer, 17:213
White, E. V., 35:16
White, Mrs. Emma C., memoirs, 13:100
White, Frank, speaker, 16:361
White, Gerald, author, 18:116
White, Mrs. Harry, 22:106
White, Harry H., 18:216
White, Helen McCann, 40:130; "Minnesota and Manifest Destiny," 38:53–62; "Captain Fisk," 38:216–230; reviews by, 22:183, 35:148, 38:326, 39:124, 169, 40:93, 263, 307, 354; work reviewed, 40:254; honored, 18:459, 38:336, 39:36; manuscript assistant, 19:61, 20:429, 22:190; author, 22:83, 26:256, 365, 35:49, 243; editor, 40:261
White, J. C., 18:109, 20:96
White, J. G., Engineering Corporation, New York, economic analysts, 26:172
White, J. W., pioneer merchant, 23:25
White, James, river pilot, 18:405
White, Maj. James C., at Fort Snelling, 24:6
White, Janet K., manuscript cataloger, reviews by, 40:96, 258
White, John, artist, 34:117
White, John W., lawyer, biography, 12:322
White, Langdon, author, 18:343
White, Laura A., author, 14:225
White, Leslie A., work reviewed, 37:78
White, Lyman P., 21:332
White, M. Catherine, reviews by, 33:180, 34:303; work reviewed, 33:181; author, 24:74
White, Milo, 24:96; wheat dealer, 24:100; merchant, 24:106, 108, 29:3
White, Peter, author, 34:311
White, Mrs. Sophie P., 20:96, 21:216, 444, 22:217, 440; speaker, 11:334,

21:108; author, 21:336, 22:224, 23:102, 187, 298
White, Stewart E., author, 13:298, 36:77
White, Theodore H., work reviewed, 37:343
White, William, work reviewed, 32:184
White, William Allen, quoted, 12:18; author, 14:201; letter, 18:314; editor, 22:408, 34:203
White, William S., work reviewed, 35:290
White, Father Xavier, author, 37:187
White Bear (Ramsey County) Historical Society, 16:241; organized, 16:243, 17:64; meetings, 17:358, 18:336
White Bear Lake (city), library, 15:137; fires, 15:137; Indian mound, 16:251, 37:103; depot, 16:370, 37:101; G.A.R. encampment, 16:441; churches, 17:350, 18:229; Boy Scouts, 18:228; hotel, 34:102, 36:283; railroad, 35:364; depicted, 36:196; road, 36:209; sports events, 39:23
White Bear Lake (lake), Pope County, Norwegian settlement, 12:277; described, 33:251
White Bear Lake (lake), Ramsey and Washington counties, depicted, 15:469, 33:247, 36:92, 37:103; legend, 17:374, 22:337, 36:75; summer colonies, 17:490; resort, 20:394, 25:101; picnic, 22:372, 34:102; gardens, 28:377; lands, 33:251; streetcar service, 36:150; sailing, 40:33; acreage, 40:226n; drainage question, 40:228, 229
White Bear Yacht Club, Dellwood, Washington County, 33:4; depicted, 36:196; history, 38:92
White Bull, Sioux leader, 35:333
White Cloud, Chippewa Indian, 21:337
White Dog (Shonkasha), Sioux leader, 15:363, 38:131, 136
White Dog, mission, see Wabassimong
White Earth, Chippewa agency, 17:336, 19:95, 23:93; missions, 18:331, 20:90; history, 18:470
White Earth Indian Reservation (Chippewa), 12:205, 16:193, 376, 19:450, 29:169; allotments, 11:206, 15:196, 18:306, 20:442; missions, 11:332, 15:354, 18:107, 268, 20:310, 26:275, 388, 33:58–60, 35:338; timber, 11:445; established, 15:114, 35:337; depicted, 15:117, 28:349; schools, 16:120, 27:169, 36:24, 38:335; rice camps, 16:225; source material, 20:83, 21:315; music, 24:71; festivals, 27:358, 33:91; white settlers, 35:47; living conditions, 35:293; historic sites, 40:148
White Elk Lake, Aitkin County, name, 21:348
White Face River, St. Louis County, course, 13:406
White Fisher, Chippewa leader, 21:285
White Oak Point, Itasca County, post, 11:371; archaeology, 26:321; mounds, 26:324–327
White Oak Township, Hubbard County, history, 18:469
White River, Ind., raccoon trapping, 40:215

White Spider, Sioux leader, 38:139
"White Swan," steamboat, 21:259n, 33:10
White Wood Lake, see Basswood Lake
Whitefield, Alfred, 40:65n, 70
Whitefield, Constance, 40:65n, 70
Whitefield, Cordelia, 40:65n, 70
Whitefield, Edwin, "A Trip to Lake Minnetonka," 30:114–121; artist, 14:270, 15:210, 469, 17:221, 18:455, 20:364, 28:392, 30:115, 116, 118, 119, 32:45, 33:89, 247–251, 34:138, 141, 144–147, 36:191, 318, 37:1 (cover), 40:49 (cover), 62–77; colonizer, 16:25; townsite promoter, 17:214, 22:333, 34:146, 38:388, 40:64–75; family, 20:191, 40:65n; career, 30:111–113, 35:369
Whitefield, Mrs. Edwin (Lillian Stuart), 40:65n, 70, 71, 77; depicted, 40:64
Whitefield, Wilfred J., 15:65n, 70, 71, 211; artist, 15:139, 20:150, 364, 21:35; papers, 20:191
Whitefield Exploring Association, see Kandiyohi Town Site Co.
Whitefield Township, Kandiyohi County, name, 33:249n
Whitefish Bay, Mich., Ont., Lake Superior, explored, 27:217, 220
Whitefish Lake (Bay), Ont., Lake of the Woods, posts, 11:363, 372, 22:310
Whitefish Point, Mich., Lake Superior, 23:234; fishing, 34:245
Whitehead, D. H., Pipestone settler, 31:206
Whitehead, James, Indian agent, 13:101, 17:338
Whitehead, James L., MHS assistant director, 30:410; review by, 31:114; author, 31:128
Whitehill, Walter M., work reviewed, 39:75
Whitehouse's New England Bards, singing group, 22:120
Whiteman, Alonzo J., swindler, 34:358
Whiteman, W. C., editor, 33:353
Whitestone Hill, S.D., historic site, 39:33
Whitewater Falls, Winona County, ghost town, 35:245
Whitewater River, Winona County, 35:13; floods, 39:36
Whitewater State Park, Winona County, 39:36; pageants, 14:450, 15:372, 16:359, 487, 30:281; described, 30:159
Whitewater Valley, wheat raising, 32:69; erosion, 36:70, 39:36
Whitford, Joseph, 13:452, 19:124
Whitham, Louise M., author, 29:77
Whiting, Carmelia, Cutlerite, 13:387
Whiting, Chauncey, Cutlerite leader, 13:386, 393; portrait, 19:232
Whiting, Mrs. Chauncey, portrait, 19:232
Whiting, E. K., publisher, 17:241
Whiting, Edmund, Cutlerite, 13:387
Whiting, F. L., Cutlerite, 13:386, 390
Whiting, Mrs. F. L., Cutlerite, 13:386, 390
Whiting, Frank M., "Theatrical Personalities," 23:305–315; author, 23:369, 26:373, 28:337
Whiting, Harry H., biography, 22:104

Whiting, Isaac, Cutlerite, 13:387
Whiting, Mrs. Isaac, Cutlerite, 13:387
Whiting, Lewis, pioneer farmer, 23:326
Whiting, Lurett, pioneer farmer, 23:317, 318, 325
Whiting, Nathan, 15:109
Whiting, S. J., Cutlerite, 13:387, 390, 392, 393
Whiting, Mrs. S. J., Cutlerite, 13:387, 388
Whiting, Capt. Sam, printer, 13:211; career, 14:405, 27:2; author, 26:294; editor, 27:12, 16, 20
Whiting, Warren, photographer, 13:391
Whiting, William W., 13:388
Whitlark, Frederick L., author, 37:39
Whitman, Mrs. F. E., author, 27:81
Whitman, Marcus, missionary, 11:429, 29:59, 35:241; career, 29:61
Whitman, Mrs. Marcus (Narcissa), missionary, 29:59
Whitman, Walt, 20:109; poet, 15:259; characterized, 20:107; quoted, 25:65
Whitmarsh, Thomas, pioneer printer, 15:7
Whitney, Andrew G., scientist, 23:129
Whitney, Asa, 39:31
Whitney, Charles, journalist, 23:371
Whitney, Daniel, career, 22:205; trader, 40:186
Whitney, Eli, biography, 33:266
Whitney, J. O., convention delegate, 14:261
Whitney, Joel E., picture gallery, 18:409, 34:31; photographer, 21:95, 29:286, 30:40, 33:142, 34:30-33, 36:328, 38:125n, 40:265 (cover); portrait, 34:28
Whitney, Mrs. Joel E., artist, 29:286
Whitney, John H., inventor, 20:242
Whitney, Joseph C., missionary, 16:313, 19:247n, 249, 36:192, 40:5, 6, 8; army captain, 39:235, 237, 238
Whitney, Pearl, author, 30:75
Whitney, Wheelock, author, 14:361
Whitridge, Grace B., 39:53n
Whittaker, ---, Pennsylvania financier, 28:323
Whittaker, Alfred H., author, 33:316, 36:324
Whittemore, Margaret, work reviewed, 34:307
Whittemore, Nathaniel K., pioneer physician, 38:92
Whittier, C. F., 22:265
Whittier, Ethlyn W., author, 25:313
Whittier, John G., poet, 18:376, 20:200, 382, 27:16, 238, 30:209, 32:15; letters, 20:338
Whittier College, Salem, Iowa, 20:338
Whittles, Rev. Thomas D., author, 31:76; missionary, 31:78
Whittlesey, Asaph, Wisconsin pioneer, 34:357
Whittlesey, Charles, geologist, 32:216, 217
Whooping cough, among Indians, 14:330
Wiard, Norman, inventor, 25:299, 30:142
Wiberg, Anders, Baptist leader, 17:403
Wichers, Willard, 28:120
Wichman, Mrs. E. W., speaker, 15:242

Wickenden, Arthur C., author, 26:389
Wickens, David L., 19:112
Wicker, George, author, 22:88
Wicker, Lillian, 22:88
Wickersham, Dr. M. R., 18:209
Wicklund, Gustaf, actor, 33:40
Wickman, Carl E., bus company operator, 21:291, 36:190
Wickman, Eric, bus company operator, 18:220, 27:272
Wickman, G. H., author, 23:89
Wicks, Judson L., career, 24:182
Wide Awakes, St. Paul, Republican club, 16:175n, 28:323
Widen, Albin, 25:194; work reviewed, 26:364; author, 23:380, 24:256, 25:394, 26:365, 28:280; speaker, 25:397
Widener, Harry E., 27:41
Widsten, Martin, 18:221; speaker, 18:64
Widstrand, C. A., piano tuner, 39:322
Wiechmann, Rev. Frederick, author, 17:229
Wiecking, Anna, author, 35:293
Wied, Mrs. Katherine, speaker, 12:210
Wiederhoeft, W. O., author, 23:399
Wiedman, ---, educator, 24:381
Wied-Neuwied, Maximilian A. P., explorer, 15:429, 29:59, 61, 34:303, 35:241
Wiegand, Karl H. von, journalist, 39:279, 281, 282, 40:265
Wieland, Christian, surveyor, 19:309; mill owner, 22:346
Wieland, Ernest, contractor, 19:309; mill owner, 22:346
Wieland, Fred W., career, 12:337
Wieland, Henry, contractor, 19:309; mill owner, 22:346
Wieland, Otto E., 19:118, 20:46, 48, 453, 21:154n; speaker, 18:462, 19:309, 316, 21:47, 290, 443, 22:442, 23:397, 24:86; author, 22:87, 23:187; death, 24:380
Wieneke, Henry J., papers, 36:279
Wier, Rev. F. W., career, 14:51-53, 58
Wiggins, J. Russell, speaker, 30:265
Wiggins, Lewis N., speaker, 29:348
Wighman, J. G., 20:399
Wigley, Earle J., 37:264
Wik, Reynold, reviews by, 34:251, 263, 348; work reviewed, 34:36
Wilberforce, William, 40:167
Wilbur, John, speaker, 16:125
Wilbur, Winifred, author, 14:123
Wilcox, Alvin H., lumberman, 12:448
Wilcox, Benton H., author, 21:93
Wilcox, C. W., missionary, 21:217
Wilcox, Charles P., lumberman, 12:448
Wilcox, Ella Wheeler, poet, 26:298
Wilcox, Jerome V., editor, 20:74
Wilcox, Ralph D., aviator, 34:44
Wilcox, W. A., field agent, 34:243
Wilcox, Walter W., author, 29:81
Wilcox, William, farmer, 33:144, 146, 148, 150
Wilcox, Mrs. William, farmer, 33:144, 146
Wilcox automobile, 40:148
Wilcox Lake, Meeker County, hunting, 33:144n, 145
Wilcox Lumber Co., Detroit Lakes, 12:448
Wilcoxson, Rev. T., 13:148
Wild, John C., artist, 22:22, 30:62,

33:89, 314, 35:182, 36:53n, 69, 37:308; career, 32:12-14, 125, 33:356
"Wild Boy," towboat, 18:177
Wild rice, processing, 14:381, 16:225, 22:204, 23:181, 26:172, 33:354, 34:44; in Indian diet, 14:381, 21:325, 22:59, 438, 23:180, 34:174, 40:47, 158; harvesting, 14:382, 423n, 17:472, 21:100, 440, 22:103, 23:250, 28:151, 33:72, 34:355, 37:183; marketing, 17:472, 35:155; in fur trade, 18:238, 23:330, 28:229, 36:242-244; historical account, 21:401; Wisconsin, 23:346, 35:244; importance, 26:230, 33:90, 35:98, 155; on canoe trail, 34:46; legislation, 34:172, 35:155; Manitoba, 35:295; Crystal Palace exhibit, 37:191
Wild Rice River, Clearwater, Norman, and Mahnomen counties, Norwegian settlement, 12:278; flour milling, 18:341; post, 22:282
Wilde, Norman, speaker, 13:341; author, 13:428
Wilde, Oscar, impersonated, 16:384, 17:48n; American tour, 17:38-48, 324-326; in Twin Cities, 17:42-48, 325, 20:65; in Iowa, 18:325
Wilder, A. H., and Co., St. Paul, failure, 19:326
Wilder, Amherst H., career, 29:177; businessman, 34:329, 38:236; house, 39:159, 40:135
Wilder, Amherst H., Foundation, 29:177, 33:139
Wilder, Laura Ingalls, work reviewed, 38:198; author, 30:247, 37:223; family farm, 38:43
Wilder, Lucy, work reviewed, 17:329
Wilder, Roy F., speaker, 18:320
Wilder, Burbank and Co., St. Paul, express company, records, 16:71, 98
Wilder Farm College, Windom, 14:416
Wilder Health Center, St. Paul, opened, 33:139
Wilderness Road, Va.-Ohio, history, 28:279
Wildlife, snakes, 16:38; conservation, 16:259, 264, 496, 18:415-419, 23:99, 30:75, 38:336, 40:38, 131-133, 135; photographic record, 18:451; legendary animals, 21:353-356, 23:379, 27:263, 31:191; taxidermist records, 24:246; Wisconsin, 28:290; mammals, 30:123-134, 33:354, 35:378; Minnesota, 30:264, 35:48, 36:72; Mississippi Valley, 36:278. See also Birds, Fishing, Hunting, individual animals
Wildwood, White Bear Lake, amusement park, depicted, 36:92; athletic meet, 39:23
Wiley, Alexander, Wisconsin Senator, speaker, 29:269
Wiley, Bell I., review by, 38:35; works reviewed, 33:82, 37:33; speaker, 37:188, 224
Wiley, Frank W., aviator, 40:146
Wiley, Jay W., essay reviewed, 37:339
Wiley, John, book dealer, 32:205, 206
Wiley, Litle, trader, 13:433, 15:343, 16:96
Wiley, S. Wirt, 33:228; author, 20:101

Wilford, Lloyd A., "The Prehistoric Indians of Minnesota," 25:153-157, 329-341, 26:312-329, 31:163-171, 231-237; author, 12:206, 21:100, 22:210, 25:180, 303, 398, 26:370, 387, 28:76, 285, 29:78, 83, 31: 192, 256, 34:354; archaeologist, 15:483, 25:382, 27:261, 28:374, 38:157, 163, 164

"Wilfred Sykes," ore carrier, 34:11, 15, 16

Wilgus, William J., author, 23:53

Wilkes, Charles, map maker, 34:219

Wilkes-Barre, Pa., ethnic settlements, 27:210, 213

Wilkeson, Samuel, businessman, 33: 221, 39:142

Wilkie, James, 36:142

Wilkie, Julius C., career, 36:142, 327

Wilkie, Leighton, 36:142, 143; speaker, 36:327

Wilkie, Robert, 36:142

Wilkie Foundation, aids Winona County Historical Society, 36:142-144

Wilkin, Col. Alexander, career, 18: 474, 29:358; in Civil War, 25:15, 38:259, 264, 266, 267, 39:173-190; businessman, 28:74, 39:173; in Sioux Outbreak, 28:280, 283; politician, 39:148; depicted, 39:173, 190

Wilkin, James W., Congressman, 39:174

Wilkin, Matilda J. C., author, 11: 328; papers, 34:339

Wilkin, Samuel J., Congressman, 39: 174, 180

Wilkin, Sarah, 39:175

Wilkin, Westcott, district judge, 33: 1, 39.174

Wilkin County, railroad, 12:254; history, 18:104, 19:233; place names, 18:474; agriculture, 21:212; poor relief, 38:373; name, 39:190

Wilkin County Historical Society, 16: 241; organized, 16:362, 17:64; museum, 17:358, 19:64, 363; meetings, 18:111, 19:120, 20:458, 21: 110, 219; essay contest, 18:224; activities, 18:336, 19:233

Wilkin County War History Committee, 23:392

Wilkins, C. W., 14:236

Wilkins, Daniel, 27:265

Wilkins, James F., 17:435

Wilkins, Robert P., work reviewed, 36:319; author, 35:383, 38:241, 387; speaker, 36:237

Wilkins, Wynona H., work reviewed, 36:319

Wilkinson, Francis, "Here and There in America," 27:283-299; author, 16:216, 27:168; letters, 21:108; career, 21:281

Wilkinson, H. C., 19:164

Wilkinson, Gen. James, 30:376; merchant, 23:61; letter, 25:288; governor of upper Louisiana, 30:57, 40:180

Wilkinson, Maj. Melville C., death, 24:146, 148; at Browns Valley, 24: 207

Wilkinson, Morton S., 17:393; MHS founder, 20:367, 368; letters, 25: 183; Senator, 28:25, 325, 31:60, 32:24, 29, 37:212, 325, 326, 330, 38:61, 217, 218, 227, 354, 355n,

39:85, 230-232; portrait, 35:130; lawyer, 35:363, 39:148n

Wilkinson, Mrs. Morton S., 25:140

Wilkinson, Norman B., author, 29:268

Wilkinson, Richard, shoemaker, 27: 289n

Wilkinson, Thomas, papers, 22:87

Wilkinson Lake, Ramsey County, water supply, 40:230

Will, Drake W., author, 37:183

Will, Elizabeth, student, 27:99

Will, Fred, musician, 33:101

Will, George F., author, 22:207, 25: 297, 26:269, 27:258

Willan, Robert, author, 21:370

Willand, Jon, author, 39:300

Willard, Miss A. E., speaker, 12:102

Willard, Daniel E., 38:311, 312, 316; author, 28:357

Willard, E. V., author, 16:237, 22: 337

Willard, Frances E., letter, 12:429; biography, 26:77

Willard, James F., work reviewed, 11: 428-430

Willard, John A., 33:230; author, 14: 277, 24:272; papers, 15:484, 20: 350, 21:106, 26:282; land speculator, 39:89, 90

Willard, Myron G., pottery owner, 33: 230

Willard, W. D., 20:350, 24:272, 27: 266, 29:273

Willcuts, J. Edgar, 13:361

Willett, Nels, 29:143n

Willey, Alma, teacher, 21:221

Willey, Dr. Samuel, 14:300, 20:237; St. Paul city physician, 14:297

Willging, Eugene P., compiler, 36:325

"William Crooks," locomotive, 11:338, 339, 18:274, 20:374, 30:158, 37: 159

"William Edenborn," steamboat, 35: 279, 36:282

"William J. Lewis," steamboat, 25:72

William Penn School, Minneapolis, war activities, 25:206

"William Robinson," steamboat, 21: 259n

"Wm. S. Nelson," steamboat, 13:145

Williams, ———, cholera victim, 14:301

Williams, Rev. A. D., lecturer, 12: 400

Williams, Alpheus S., 25:36

Williams, Amy M., editor, 35:337

Williams, Arthur B., mail carrier, 22:447

Williams, Mrs. Boyd T., house, 38:344

Williams, C. E., 12:450, 16:240

Williams, Dr. Cornelius D., 14:299, 33:1

Williams, Curt, author, 36:193

Williams, D. M., forest ranger, 36: 134-137

Williams, D. S., artist, 35:183

Williams, Daniel J., author, 19:464

Williams, Rev. Edwin S., author, 39: 311

Williams, Ezekiel, 15:427

Williams, Fred, 12:106

Williams, Fred J., author, 15:140

Williams, Col. G. H., 38:324

Williams, George F., 15:338

Williams, Mrs. H. O., author, 15:467; speaker, 15:242

Williams, Dr. Henry L., 36:94; biographies, 20:206, 35:335

Williams, Howard Y., papers, 40:360; political activities, 40:366n, 371, 373, 374

Williams, J. Fletcher, 22:212; author, 11:41, 22:193, 28:190, 40: 78, 84; letters, 13:196; quoted, 14:289, 15:439; hunter, 16:189, 33:142, 143, 147-152; career, 18: 218; MHS secretary and librarian, 27:22, 30:304, 306-313, 352, 34: 120; characterized, 30:307; journalist, 30:349; editor, 35:184

Williams, John G., "Jed L. Washburn," 13:77-82; speaker, 13:75; mining interests, 34:269-275

Williams, John G., journalist, 26:69

Williams, Mrs. Leonard A., museum curator, 26:286, 27:73

Williams, Lucille S., author, 16:111

Williams, Martin, pioneer journalist, career, 19:117; portrait, 25:404

Williams, Mary, teacher, 27:69

Williams, Mary Ann B., author, 14: 226, 36:325, 37:40, 38:385

Williams, Mattie, Sioux captive, 38: 109n

Williams, Mentor L., works reviewed, 33:345, 35:142; author, 31:120

Williams, Mollie, actress, 28:107, 109, 33:174

Williams, Montagu, 28:317

Williams, Nathan, 35:225

Williams, Ora, author, 23:285, 24:369

Williams, Richmond D., author, 38:240

Williams, Robert L., author, 23:94

Williams, Robert S., naturalist, 24: 80

Williams, Roger, map maker, 32:228

Williams, T. Harry, work reviewed, 22:408

Williams, Thomas H., librarian, 19: 212, 20:430, 35:224, 229-231; portrait, 35:225

Williams, W. Ben, 16:340

Williams, W. O., artist, 31:204

Williams, W. R., author, 35:292

Williams, William, Hudson's Bay Co. governor, 36:241, 40:166, 169

Williams, William A., author, 35:43

Williams Brothers, traders, 19:304

Williamsburg, Va., battle, 25:127n, 128, 129; restored, 39:336

Williamson, Andrew W., 12:130; author, 21:412

Williamson, Arthur S., reviews by, 11:195-198, 14:318-322, 35:370

Williamson, Dr. G. M., author, 17:220

Williamson, Harold F., author, 36:70

Williamson, Henry M., 16:183

Williamson, Jane, 12:130

Williamson, Rev. Jesse P., 16:301; speaker, 16:483

Williamson, Mrs. Jesse P., 16:301

Williamson, John P., papers, 11:317, 34:326; missionary, 35:380, 38: 357, 358, 364, 39:228, 230, 238, 239; portrait, 38:358

Williamson, Sareen, 29:182

Williamson, Thomas C., reminiscences, 21:413

Williamson, Dr. Thomas S., 11:58, 13: 321, 14:145, 21:29n, 163, 166, 278; at Yellow Medicine, 11:182, 183, 14:216, 330, 436, 16:150; papers, 11:317, 13:170, 195, 15:222, 16:333, 17:210, 18:314, 21:412, 25:183, 29:283, 39:344, 40:2; at

Lac qui Parle, 12:127, 128, 339, 15:43, 129, 16:133-142, 149, 21:30, 31, 207, 274, 23:97, 39:300; teacher, 12:242; missionary, 12:243, 331, 15:126, 275, 16:357, 20:124, 21:73, 170n, 171, 273, 25:399, 27:264, 30:156, 35:380; translator, 12:245, 16:142-145, 21:25, 160n, 279, 30:298; at Fort Snelling, 12:397, 16:354; at Kaposia, 14:142, 28:133, 136; implements treaty, 15:297; depicted, 16:103, 136; physician, 16:147, 20:91, 22:102; family, 16:301, 483, 30:169; career, 16:355

Williamson, Mrs. Thomas S., 11:183, 16:133

Williamson, William, pioneer pastor, 25:324

Williamson family, 15:129; captivity, 12:133n; missionary activities, 16:345

Willim, William, papers, 15:344, 16:71; legislator, 35:360; stonemason, 38:188

Willis, ---, with William H. Ashley expedition, 15:429

Willis, Mrs. Charles L., house, 33:5

Willis, Grove W., 24:95

Willis, Judge John, 33:5

Willis, John W., author, 26:304

Willis, Nathaniel P., author, 27:16

Willis, Sue, 33:5

Willis House, St. Cloud, hotel, 18:353, 35:255

Williston, N.D., Glidden tour, 38:213

Willius, Dr. Fredrick A., author, 33:44

Willius, Gustav, banker, 27:56

Willius, Henrietta W., author, 39:51

Willius Brothers and Dunbar, St. Paul, bankers, 38:221-223

Willmar, pageant, 11:461; schools, 12:208, 21:221, 26:166; immigrant house, 13:41; railroads, 13:41, 21:222, 450, 28:396; churches, 13:343, 16:305, 355, 484, 17:236, 23:107; wheat market, 14:355; hunting, 16:263; historical meeting, 16:304; pioneer life, 17:236; post office, 21:222; newspapers, 21:444

Willmar and Sioux Falls Townsite Co., 20:104

Willmar Daily Tribune, politics, 38:305

Willmar High School, history, 16:365

Willock, Roger, author, 36:192

Willoughby, Amherst, stage owner, 40:387, 388

Willoughby, William R., work reviewed, 37:302; author, 34:265

Willoughby and Powers, stage operators, 11:403-405, 12:394, 20:393, 29:204n

Willoughby University, Cleveland, Ohio, medical school, 27:135

Willow River, Roseau County, fishing, 35:275

Willow River, Wis., French regime, 15:237; Henry Lewis' visit, 17:139n; land office, 40:312. See also Hudson, Wis.

Wills, Bernt L., author, 39:83

Willson, ---, Peter Garrioch's companion, 20:122

Willson, Beckles, author, 13:298, 18:81

Willson, Mrs. Bunn T., 20:297, 21:213, 22:340, 442, 28:88, 296, 36:193; speaker, 19:64, 20:298, 21:48, 217, 25:97, 26:284; author, 33:315, 36:194

Willson, Charles C., 20:435; collector, 20:299, 21:214

Willson, David H., 29:164

Willson, Mrs. David H., research assistant, 27:340, 28:48

Willson, Mrs. Grace N., author, 34:218

Willson, Mrs. Lillian M., author, 29:373, 30:47

Willson, William, G.A.R. commander, 16:437

Wilmerding, Lucius, Jr., works reviewed, 38:90, 39:295

Wilmington, Del., landing of Swedish colonists, 19:106

Wilmington, Houston County, Norwegian settlement, 12:268; history, 17:486

Wilmot, Allen, trader, 11:376

Wilmot, Harold E., author, 35:294, 36:104

Wilmot Proviso, significance, 23:261

Wilno, Lincoln County, Polish settlement, 13:108, 24:79

Wilsey, F. W., colonizer, 22:93

Wilson, ---, ballplayer, 19:164

Wilson, A. A., author, 16:252

Wilson, Alice, speaker, 19:120

Wilson, Archie D., educator, 37:27

Wilson, Ben Hur, author, 13:336

Wilson, Bertha, teacher, 39:115

Wilson, Mrs. Bess M., 19:446; author, 15:137, 462; speaker, 19:228

Wilson, Blanche N., work reviewed, 32:55

Wilson, C., ballplayer, 19:174

Wilson, Dr. C. H., speaker, 13:121

Wilson, C. S., baseball official, 19:164

Wilson, Charles, baseball official, 19:164, 174, 175

Wilson, Chester S., 18:111; review by, 24:345; speaker, 16:362, 24:385; author, 24:353

Wilson, Clara D., murdered, 38:134n

Wilson, Clifford P., "Where Did Nicolet Go?" 27:216-220; review by, 31:183; work reviewed, 35:240; author, 17:222, 19:461, 23:92, 25:83, 302, 404, 27:70, 247, 31:192, 33:88, 35:47, 36:102, 39:81; editor, 27:166

Wilson, Edmund, author, 32:115; influence on F. Scott Fitzgerald, 39:35

Wilson, Rev. Edward A., medical quack, 20:234

Wilson, Mrs. Elsie, author, 11:223

Wilson, Eugene M., Congressman, 34:71, 36:183, 37:98, 319; politician, 36:307, 308; mayor, 40:376

Wilson, F. J., author, 24:179

Wilson, Fletcher, author, 22:332

Wilson, Frank E., author, 16:477

Wilson, Frank M., county attorney, 37:275

Wilson, Fred N., artist, 29:263

Wilson, George, author, 15:118, 29:272

Wilson, Rev. Gilbert E., collector, 13:60, 103; honored, 29:263

Wilson, Gordon, author, 27:160

Wilson, H., ballplayer, 19:174

Wilson, H. Clyde, author, 35:244

Wilson, H. W., Co., New York, publishers, 31:245

Wilson, Halsey W., publisher, 29:172; career, 31:245

Wilson, Herbert, 18:336

Wilson, J. D., 19:167

Wilson, J. E., founder of Lake Wilson, 18:471

Wilson, J. W., carpenter, 33:172

Wilson, Jack, steamboat captain, 34:10

Wilson, James F., Congressman, 38:61

Wilson, Mrs. John A., author, 22:345

Wilson, John L., St. Cloud founder, 15:139, 16:334, 32:32

Wilson, Joseph, missionary, 22:351; names Duluth, 22:352

Wilson, Joseph P., papers, 16:334

Wilson, Joseph S., land commissioner, 39:86, 87

Wilson, Leonard S., speaker, 19:307, 22:218; author, 20:207, 21:343, 438

Wilson, Dr. Louis B., director of Mayo Foundation, 11:286, 21:357n, 24:181, 347; speaker, 11:283; author, 15:127, 19:111, 21:330; scientist, 24:211, 239

Wilson, M. L., speaker, 20:86, 25:84

Wilson, Margaret, author, 23:158, 28:287

Wilson, Netta W., work reviewed, 19:71-73; speaker, 19:66; author, 23:8, 25:305, 33:312

Wilson, Mrs. Nettie, 16:360

Wilson, O. Meredith, university president, speaker, 37:135

Wilson, P., ballplayer, 19:174

Wilson, Mrs. P. L., 18:109, 25:97, 26:89, 27:75

Wilson, Quintus C., "Joseph A. Wheelock," 34:330-336; review by, 34:83; speaker, 28:197, 29:55

Wilson, Rev. R. Jay, author, 16:242

Wilson, Samuel, Jr., work reviewed, 39:337

Wilson, Samuel B., chief justice, 12:87, 37:166, 167, 169

Wilson, Sarah A., teacher, 25:386

Wilson, Mrs. Taylor, 12:449

Wilson, Thomas, chief justice, 26:382; politician, 35:61, 297, 36:4n, 11, 113n

Wilson, Thomas W., real-estate dealer, 40:228, 229

Wilson, Virginia M., compiler, 33:355

Wilson, Dr. W. F., 17:489; speaker, 20:212; author, 21:114

Wilson, W. L., speaker, 13:120

Wilson, William, ballplayer, 19:162, 174, 175

Wilson, William B., secretary of labor, 39:241

Wilson, Capt. Willis, 25:118

Wilson, Woodrow, 15:338, 24:336; politician, 14:201; letters, 14:437, 18:316; Mexican policy, 16:457, 459, 17:165; assessed, 18:302, 19:435, 22:313; President, 23:211

Wilson and Co., Chicago, meat packers, 22:445

Wilson High School, St. Paul, war veterans, 28:305

Wilson Steamboat Line, 20:250

Wilson Township, Winona County, Germans, 28:33
Wiltberger, Frank W., author, 28:296
Wilton, Beltrami County, railroad, 29:148
Wilton, Waseca County, stage line, 12:50n; county seat, 13:154n, 21:218; pioneer life, 21:457; ghost town, 35:12
Wilton and Northern Line, logging railroad, 29:148
Wiltroit, Dr. Irving D., 23:185, 34:132; author, 35:47
Wiltse, Mrs. Elmer, speaker, 20:456
Wiltse, Henry A., surveyor, 12:380, 385
Wily, Mrs. G. A., speaker, 14:456
Wimar, Carl (Charles), 17:456, 32:188, 33:264, 35:151; upper Mississippi trip, 17:137, 24:178, 28:278, 29:78
Wimberly, Lowry C., work reviewed, 25:175
Wimmer, Abbot Boniface, 32:37, 38, 35:46; visit to St. John's Abbey, 33:138
Winans, George, 18:179
Winans, W. K., 11:453
Winchell, Alexander, papers, 12:319; career, 32:214n; geologist, 32:217, 225, 40:358; editor, 32:224
Winchell, Horace V., geologist, 34:272, 39:116; biography, 18:218; described, 34:273
Winchell, Newton H., geologist, 16:1, 25:175, 30:314, 34:273, 35:154; papers, 11:97, 13:325, 19:451; author, 13:253, 373, 16:162, 163, 23:131, 29:162, 31:201, 32:94, 33:282; mounds survey, 16:309, 23:269, 336, 339; rune-stone studies, 17:167, 172, 39:134; career, 18:218, 32:214-225; portrait, 21:209; map maker, 38:386; Minnesota Academy activities, 39:111, 113-115; death, 39:121
Winchester, Alice, author, 36:67
Winchester, James, author, 36:280
Wind Mill (Claremont), pioneer newspaper, 19:336, 24:264
Windemere Township, Pine County, school, 15:348
Winder, Gen. John, Union officer, 25:145
Windmills, Dakota County, 24:190; depicted, 34:60, 62, 37:21. See also Seppman Mill
Windom, Florence, 25:286
Windom, Roger L., 24:246, 25:42; speaker, 25:286
Windom, William, 18:266n, 26:361, 28:24, 27; Senator, 14:101, 28:74, 34:290, 35:246, 297; career, 18:218, 24:373, 36:195; papers, 19:96, 21:86, 24:246, 355, 25:183; speaker, 22:39, 23:180; portraits, 23:247, 35:132; secretary of the treasury, 25:184; honored, 25:286; Congressman, 32:24, 29, 36:302, 37:325, 38:61, 217, 218, 354, 39:87
Windom, Mrs. William (Ellen Towne), portrait, 24:247; letters, 25:77, 184
Windom, William D., 25:77, 184
Windom, history, 11:111, 17:485; 1880 blizzard, 12:101; Norwegian set-

tlement, 12:274; farm college, 14:416; county seat, 15:245; public square, 16:247; G.A.R. post, 16:434; churches, 17:231, 30:395; schools, 21:112; railroad, 21:243; log cabin, 21:450
Windom Community Club, 26:283
Windom Hotel, Minneapolis, 35:73
Windom Institute, Montevideo, seminary, history, 18:113, 22:444
Windom School, Minneapolis, 25:286
Windrum, J. J., 18:132, 134, 141
Windsor Castle, Windsor, Eng., panorama presentation, 17:135
Windsor Hotel, St. Paul, 33:1, 3; depicted, 33:2; concerts, 39:53
Windsor Theater, St. Paul, 15:254
Winesky, Mrs. Frank, speaker, 28:89
Wing, Camilla, work reviewed, 26:366
Wing, Frank, artist, 29:102
Wing, George, 17:227
Wing, Isaac, Wisconsin pioneer, 34:357
Wingate, H. K., speaker, 12:341
Winge, C. S., Mormon missionary, 36:288; portrait, 36:289
Wingen, Joseph, reminiscences, 17:125
Winger, history, 14:358, 34:171
Wingfoot Lighter-Than-Air Society, Akron, Ohio, 40:268
Winks, Robin W., review by, 39:32; work reviewed, 37:257; author, 36:32, 38:199
Winnebago City, population, 12:53n; county seat fight, 12:450; history, 23:106, 30:277; business, 24:302n; creamery, 27:115; camp meeting, 31:82
Winnebago City Enterprise, file acquired, 17:469
Winnebago County, Iowa, Norwegian settlement, 18:431
Winnebago County, Wis., history, 18:326
Winnebago Indians, 39:41, 42; hostilities, 11:190, 25:272; Long Prairie agency, 11:224, 316, 13:216, 321, 17:210, 18:474, 25:183, 30:5, 40:332; missions, 11:305, 325, 12:205, 13:339, 21:20, 28:210, 30:2, 10; Winnebago agency, 12:51, 24:272, 28:216, 35:293, 37:327, 38:276, 39:92n, 127, 233; enrollment list, 12:83; removal from Wisconsin, 12:160, 14:215, 16:97, 333, 34:214, 38:201; culture, 12:326, 28:176, 29:86, 37:174, 343; debt to traders, 12:426; annuities, 14:435, 29:198, 36:257; trading activities, 14:436, 23:94, 29:101, 36:260, 262-264; source material, 16:332; depicted, 17:137, 20:55, 57, 33:20, 38:362; treaties, 17:153n, 23:400, 28:205, 36:280; removal from Iowa, 17:155-157, 22:191, 28:206, 208, 33:286, 36:267-269, 271; removal from Minnesota, 18:209, 38:98, 353-355, 360-364, 39:227-240; in War of 1812, 19:304, 31:189; history, 19:452, 21:425; dress, 20:199; names, 23:346, 27:218, 219; villages, 23:346, 32:189, 36:191; diseases, 27:351, 37:182; Nebraska agency, 28:80; maple-sugar making, 30:261; at Fort Snelling, 31:210, 211; relations with Sioux, 31:212-215,

217, 38:131, 137, 148, 275, 361, 364; at Prairie Island, 37:281; bibliography, 37:346; prehistoric, 38:197
Winnegge, Paul W., 17:102; author, 16:131, 218
Winnesheek, Isaac, portrait, 20:174
Winneshiek, Winnebago leader, 29:217, 31:214, 38:360, 39:229; depicted, 31:215, 38:362
Winneshiek, Iowa, see Hesper, Iowa
Winneshiek County, Iowa, Norwegian settlement, 12:278; history, 19:460, 39:2; schools, 39:3
Winnipeg, Man., located, 11:364, 36:53n; anniversary, 15:477, 30:261; log drive, 17:116; railroads, 17:218, 23:93, 24:329, 28:372, 35:153; consulate, 17:465, 19:412, 37:57; La Vérendrye celebration, 19:461; river port, 21:245, 247, 255, 261, 270, 271; growth, 21:246; steamboat line, 21:255-257; fur trade, 21:432; forts, 22:99; described, 23:186, 33:70; newspapers, 23:368; Selkirk grant, 24:41; founded, 27:166; dog race, 27:177; theater, 31:121; flood, 34:307; history, 36:307; strike, 36:64; MHS tour, 36:284. See also Fort Garry (Upper), Red River Settlement
Winnipeg and Western Transportation Co., organized, 21:260
Winnipeg Art Gallery Association, 25:302
Winnipeg Board of Trade, 21:255
Winnipeg Rifles, in Riel rebellions, 16:348
Winnipeg River, Man., posts, 11:363, 364, 19:78; mission, 20:327; portage, 21:186; travel on, 40:313
Winnipegon, see Fort St. Charles
Winnly, Charles K., 38:358, 362
Winona, Sioux woman, legend, 13:367-376, 33:118, 34:137, 36:22, 76; in poetry, 15:278, 29:100; feminist symbol, 20:136
Winona, literary visitors, 11:146, 153, 16:31, 18:34; plat, 11:226; road, 11:396n, 399, 407; stage lines, 11:398, 402, 405, 406; mail service, 11:400; railroads, 12:46, 21:239, 22:322, 36:105, 37:157; hotels, 12:47, 15:253, 22:448; history, 12:108, 20:64, 30:409, 35:46, 36:107; education problem, 12:400, 27:12; lumber industry, 12:427, 15:253, 24:127, 27:190, 30:71, 242; fairs, 12:445, 22:261, 26:120; townsite promotion, 13:59; churches, 14:50, 218, 18:120, 364-366, 19:221, 21:210, 33:189, 37:187; statehood celebration, 14:165, 182, 186, 348; grain market, 14:387, 18:409, 21:238, 24:99, 29:2, 6, 7, 37:87; volunteer guards, 16:177; pioneer life, 16:334, 379, 384, 27:7; newspapers, 16:338, 23:111, 34:130; pageant, 16:351; G.A.R. post, 16:431; in Civil War, 17:112, 38:273, 292, 293; source material, 17:212, 28:303; depicted, 17:221, 27:16, 28:70, 30:158, 39:131; mission, 17:224; climate, 17:260, 20:161n; bridges, 18:120, 23:290, 24:80, 177; busi-

ness, 18:344, 19:465, 20:219, 24:
287; baseball club, 19:165, 169,
180; historical meeting, 20:303-
305; ethnic groups, 21:98, 25:207,
28:36, 31:29, 35:51; labor unions,
21:393, 22:380; ferry service, 24:
80; social life, 26:307; river
port, 27:7, 37:296, 38:357;
schools, 29:354, 30:154, 34:93,
35:221; land office, 30:30, 38:
120; name, 30:332, 36:144, 40:89;
German theater, 32:100, 102, 127,
34:239; post office, 37:223; gold
fever, 38:53, 220; architecture,
39:130, 40:359; William H. Taft
speech, 40:320. See also Maiden
Rock, Wabasha Prairie
Winona Adler, German-language newspaper, 16:338
Winona and St. Peter Railroad, 16:
439; route, 11:181n, 12:46n, 272,
24:96, 37:157n; journey described,
12:47-51; promotes settlement, 12:
254, 13:31n, 35:133, 325; land
sale, 13:38; absorbed, 24:97; lawsuit, 29:8; built, 35:338; history, 36:105; encourages dairying,
37:21; depicted, 37:152
Winona Argus, established, 14:401
Winona Artillery, volunteer unit, 16:
173n
Winona Banner, 16:338
Winona Carriage Works, products, 24:
305
Winona Cottage, Frontenac, 14:35
Winona County, ethnic settlements,
12:269, 21:98; flour mills, 14:
124; tombstone records, 15:349;
pageant, 15:372; pioneer life, 17:
353, 23:200; physicians, 21:329,
437; wheat production, 23:318, 29:
2n, 13, 16, 18n, 36:69; mail service, 37:223; politics, 37:224,
40:325n, 327, 328; poor farm, 38:
369n, 374; mapped, 40:125n
Winona County Bank, Winona, 40:109,
110
Winona County 4-H Leaders Club, 15:
372
Winona County Historical Society, organized, 16:245, 363, 492; members, 17:124, 18:62; officers, 18:
112, 24:88; museums, 22:219, 342,
444, 24:271, 25:206-208, 34:174,
35:99, 202, 36:139-144, 283, 327,
37:43, 66; meetings, 24:58, 30:76;
reorganized, 30:169; activities,
34:219, 35:51, 38:244; gift, 34:
315; receives award, 34:360
Winona County Medical Society, organized, 21:330
Winona County Old Settlers Association, 12:194, 20:219, 304, 22:226,
342; meetings, 11:225, 12:212, 14:
240, 15:253, 16:257
Winona County Poultry Association,
22:265
Winona County War History Committee,
23:392
Winona Daily News, centennial, 35:46
Winona Gesang Verein, musical society, 25:207
Winona Herald, founded, 12:208
Winona Little Theatre, activities,
20:219, 37:348
Winona Parent-Teacher Association,
16:132

Winona Republican, 27:3; founded, 12:
108, 14:404; content, 27:4-20;
politics, 28:30, 39:106
Winona Republican-Herald, 14:404; anniversary, 12:108; founded, 14:
397, 405
Winona Review, founded, 12:108
Winona Savings Bank, architecture,
39:130
Winona State Normal School, 17:353,
18:409, 26:298, 35:98, 371; established, 14:148, 231, 18:219;
source material, 17:97, 22:423;
kindergarten, 19:110; first building, 25:207
Winona State Teachers College, 22:
226; anniversaries, 11:225, 16:
351; history, 17:458; museum, 22:
342, 444, 25:206
Winona Township, Winona County, records, 20:219; survey, 25:207
Winona War History Committee, 24:83,
25:95
Winser, Henry J., author, 33:34
Winship, P. D., 26:321
Winslow, C. A., house, 38:341, 342
Winslow, Charles C., 18:134, 136; career, 18:123n
Winslow, Edith, see Elliott, Mrs.
Charles B.
Winslow, Gen. Edward F., Union officer, 18:150
Winslow, Edwin M., 28:285
Winslow, James M., letter, 13:195;
builder, 17:487; water company director, 40:224
Winslow, Mary N., work reviewed, 33:
42
Winslow, Walter E., student, 18:124,
125, 142, 148, 150
Winslow Bank, Chicago, 20:249
Winslow House, St. Anthony, hotel,
19:84, 403, 36:91, 38:273; de-
picted, 12:403, 13:195; ghost
story, 20:328; abolitionist inci-
dent, 32:18
Winslow House, St. Paul, hotel, 16:
272, 30:301
Winslow House, St. Peter, hotel, 17:
488
Winsted, French cemetery, 16:488;
history, 21:452; ethnic settlements, 23:194, 25:315; Catholic
church, 25:315
Winsted Lake, McLeod County, settled,
25:315
Winston, Carleton (Mrs. John H.
Dietrich), work reviewed, 23:362-
364
Winston, Eliza, slave, 16:116, 19:
261, 32:18
Winston, Fendall G., contractor, 35:
337
Winston, Frederick, conservationist,
40:145
Winston, Philip B., contractor, 35:
337
Winston, Thomas B., 17:274
Winston, William O., contractor, 35:
337
Winston, Mrs. William O., author, 27:
176
Winston, St. Louis County, ghost
town, 34:178
Winston Brothers Co., Minneapolis,
railroad builders, 26:371, 35:337
Wintemberg, W. J., author, 24:371

Winter, Alice A., author, 26:302
Winter, Carl G., author, 34:217
Winter, Edwin W., 40:16
Winter, Frank, author, 20:340
Winter, George, artist, 29:335;
journals, 29:336
Winter, Mrs. James Douglas, author,
12:431; model maker, 19:228;
speaker, 21:333
Winter, Thomas G., 35:294
Winterbotham, William W., 17:112
Winterich, John T., author, 17:119
Winters, Henry C., 25:232, 243
Winther, Christian, 18:199
Winther, Oscar O., works reviewed,
24:235, 37:338, 38:238, 39:124;
author, 26:167
Winther, Sophus K., author, 32:250
Winthrop, Beekman, letter, 40:349
Winthrop, John, Jr., Connecticut
governor, 16:405
Winthrop, Mose S., biography, 18:211
Winthrop, anniversary, 13:122; Ger-
man-Russian settlement, 16:344;
railroad, 30:240; Lutheran church,
36:201
Winthrop News, anniversary edition,
13:122
Winton, David M., 28:51
Winton, Finnish settlement, 17:407;
history, 36:107
Winton automobile, 26:22, 38:208
Winzen Research, Inc., St. Paul, 33:
244, 38:334
Wion, F. E., editor, 37:173
"Wiota," steamboat, 22:17n
Wirt, pioneer life, 20:359
Wirth, Conrad L., author, 39:33
Wirth, Fremont P., work reviewed, 19:
85-87; author, 38:329
Wirth, Mrs. Sophie, 28:294
Wirth, Theodore, park superintendent,
16:494; author, 30:75
Wirtz, Father Othmar, 32:42, 43
Wisby, Herbert A., Jr., work reviewed, 35:94
Wisconsin, ethnic groups, 11:82, 89,
105, 12:180, 249-251, 328, 14:447,
15:26, 18:381, 19:200, 219, 20:86,
21:98, 24:176, 25:299, 301, 27:
134, 28:379, 29:160, 32:54, 185,
34:210, 37:177; government, 11:83;
boundaries, 11:211, 339, 14:184n,
19:351, 25:396; statehood, 11:326,
14:342; travel account, 12:44-46;
authors, 12:328; early printing,
12:439, 15:16; historic buildings,
13:110, 27:141, 32:109, 35:151;
maps, 13:186, 16:217; in fiction,
13:208, 23:117; mining, 13:334,
21:183, 27:160, 38:240; lumber industry, 13:438, 24:261, 364, 26:
166, 30:71, 31:181, 190, 32:252-
254, 34:35, 36:28, 153-166, 40:
357; schools, 14:342, 33:224, 35:
198; wildlife, 14:423, 26:373, 28:
290; geography, 15:238, 23:185;
historical celebrations, 15:474;
banks, 16:91, 34:165; pageant, 16:
113; roads, 16:285, 28:290, 40:
245; resources, 16:347; forests,
17:110; trails, 17:112, 21:227;
British, 17:196-198; pioneer life,
18:113, 20:86, 27:55, 68, 69, 83-
95, 164, 28:188, 31:187; climate,
18:155; agriculture, 20:157, 35:
45, 36:278; history, 21:306, 26:

365, 29:159, 173, 269, 334, 30:
247, 35:203, 37:301, 38:196, 40:
129; agrarian movements, 21:326,
28:42, 39:130; co-operatives, 22:
314, 29:158; guides, 23:65, 25:
301; circus beginnings, 23:184,
24:76; politics, 23:285, 31:113,
34:166, 208, 313, 35:236, 241,
295, 36:188, 39:46, 40:322; county
boundaries, 23:383; name, 24:75;
land titles, 24:176; archaeology,
24:371; land policy, 25:69-71, 36:
235; geology, 25:175, 26:223, 224;
in art, 25:278; horticulture, 26:
170; soldier vote, 26:209; described, 26:250, 30:394; historical societies, 26:271; centennial,
27:67, 28:379, 29:268, 355; cheese
production, 27:121; legislature,
27:192, 197, 199; composers, 30:
72; historic sites, 30:73; dairy
industry, 30:154, 39:31; paper industry, 30:159; social studies,
30:269; pipestone deposits, 31:
200; railroads, 34:67; cutover
lands, 34:176, 35:340, 38:194;
newspaper guide, 36:67; electric
utilities, 36:98; in Civil War,
37:255, 38:202, 275; biographies,
37:337; in Sioux Outbreak, 38:278-
280; atlas, 40:128; forts, 40:146;
gazetteer, 40:147
Wisconsin Archaeological Society, 11:
32, 15:471, 31:171
Wisconsin Centennial Art Exhibition,
17:455, 456
Wisconsin Central Airlines, 33:240
Wisconsin Central Railroad, pine
lands, 39:298
Wisconsin Folklore Society, publications, 26:170, 381, 27:165
Wisconsin Historical Records Survey,
25:198; publication, 23:383, 24:
159, 160
Wisconsin Land and Lumber Co., 32:
253, 36:156
Wisconsin Library Association, 23:66
Wisconsin Magazine of History, index,
16:220, 28:189
Wisconsin Marine and Fire Insurance
Company Bank, Milwaukee, 40:112
Wisconsin Medical Society, historical
project, 34:175
Wisconsin Public Service Commission,
papers, 26:69
Wisconsin Regional Planning Commit-
tee, 16:347
Wisconsin River, Wis., fur trade, 11:
384, 13:225; wildlife, 14:423;
lumbering, 16:479; explored, 23:
345, 24:76. See also Fox-Wiscon-
sin portage
Wisconsin Society of Equity, 21:326
Wisconsin State Centennial Committee,
publications, 28:289, 29:86
Wisconsin State Historical Society,
see State Historical Society of
Wisconsin
Wisconsin State Horticultural Socie-
ty, history, 26:170
Wisconsin State Medical Society, 14:
446, 22:330
Wisconsin State Normal School, see
River Falls (Wis.) State Teachers
College
Wisconsin State Telegraph Co., 14:182
Wisconsin Territory, St. Croix Tri-

angle, 14:128, 129, 35:352, 36:
260; centennial, 17:222, 344, 455;
artists, 17:455; geography, 19:
222; census, 19:350; guide, 20:
203; business, 20:335; county records, 25:198; diocese, 26:272;
maps, 27:128; post offices, 30:
174; roads, 31:176; pioneer life,
32:185, 35:382
Wisconsin University, see University
of Wisconsin
Wisconsin Valley Lumbermen's Association, 12:193
Wisconsin War Records Commission, 23:
392, 25:205
Wise, Evelyn U., novelist, 31:134,
147
Wise, Henry A., Virginia governor,
17:106
Wise, John, balloonist, 38:169-171
Wise, John C., editor, 15:89, 38:353,
354, 356, 39:234-236; engraver,
30:66
Wise and Clark, Mankato, printers,
29:169
Wish, Harvey, author, 33:187
Wishek, Nina F., author, 23:92
Wishkob, Joseph, Chippewa Indian, 39:
304
Wissakoda (Breda), St. Louis County,
railroad station, 34:180
Wissler, Clark, 22:133; author, 21:
325
Wistar, Casper, author, 21:364
Wister, Owen, author, 19:437, 38:238
Wistrom, Elof, 14:428
Wistrom, Helen C., 14:428
Wiswell, Mrs. Frances, 20:310
Witherspoon, Herbert, singer, 39:59,
62
Witt, Frank A., auto driver, 38:205
(cover), 207, 214
Witt, Mrs. Frank A., auto driver, 38:
207, 208, 214
Witte, Bernard, author, 28:380
Witthoft, John, "Archaeology as a Key
to the Colonial Fur Trade," 40:
203-209
Wittich, Mrs. Frederick W., 15:115,
38:308; author, 11:214; speaker,
13:70
Wittich, Walter, speaker, 27:356
Wittke, Carl, review by, 29:150;
works reviewed, 33:179, 35:193,
328, 39:167; author, 21:202, 22:
327, 29:192, 350; editor, 21:306,
34:122
Wittmann, Father Cornelius, mission-
ary, 32:38-40
Wittmar, Friedrich von, musician, 33:
100
"Wivenhoe," Radisson's ship, 16:393
Wiyaha, Sioux Indian, 35:172
Wobschall, Dana, 19:362
Woestemeyer, Ina F., 20:440
Wohlfohrt, Rev. K., speaker, 16:130
Wolcott, Dr. Alexander, explorer, 31:
94, 33:131, 135, 330, 348n
Wolcott, Edward O., Senator, 35:75
Wolcott, Steele County, statistics,
28:305
Wolcutt, Sylvester, 18:229
Wold, A. M., 16:103
Wold, Edwin M., 29:303
Wold, Mrs. Eva E., author, 12:194,
14:333
Wold, Josephine, author, 35:382

Wold, K. O., Drug Co., Austin, 30:167
Wold, Ole J., 29:308, 309, 312; letter, 30:93
Wold, Pauline, "The Leech Lake Uprising," 24:142-148; nurse, 24:164
Wold, Theodore, 19:184n
Wold-Chamberlain Field, Minneapolis,
35:190; statistics, 19:99
Wolf, Edwin, II, author, 37:222
Wolf, Hazel C., ed., "Campaigning
with the First Minnesota," 25:11-
39, 117-152, 224-257, 342-361;
work reviewed, 33:217; career, 25:
75; editor, 25:181, 287, 382
Wolf, John B., review by, 34:298
Wolf, in fur trade, 13:327, 35:295,
38:119, 40:212; hunts, 14:422,
423, 16:189; bounties, 17:117;
predator, 30:129; field study, 35:
48. See also Wildlife
Wolf Lake, Beltrami County, archaeology, 26:321
Wolf River, Wis., pineries, 21:55,
31:113; Menominee reservation, 32:
186, 190
Wolfe automobile, 40:148
Wolfer, Henry, 19:112; prison official, 29:323, 324, 37:151
Wolff, Albert, immigration commissioner, 13:28, 27:328, 31:226; au-
thor, 27:327-329, 33:188; editor,
28:21-23, 26, 28, 29:351, 33:180,
35:328
Wolff, Julius F., Sr., author, 34:358
Wolff, Julius F., Jr., "Some Vanished
Settlements," 34:177-184; "Skin
Diving and Research," 35:278-281;
"Some Major Forest Fires," 36:131-
138; review by, 37:179; speaker,
35:99; author, 36:192, 37:186,
345, 38:336
Wolfsberg, Vernie H., author, 28:74
Wolfskill, William, 14:430
Wollaston, Percy, house, 18:464;
mill, 20:361
Wolle, Sylvester, 20:100
Wollgate, ---, horse breeder, 26:118
Wolseley, Col. Garnet J., expedition
leader, 21:245, 24:277, 280, 28:
282, 32:242, 36:191, 192
Wolters, Mary, 35:264, 266
Woltman, Mrs. Henry L., 13:69, 22:201
Wolverine, in fur trade, 30:131, 35:
295
Woman suffrage, Populist support, 12:
5; background, 20:328; Donnelly's
support, 20:433; Minnesota, 28:74,
37:39, 39:10; Wisconsin, 35:203;
leaders, 35:228; South Dakota, 37:
86; Massachusetts, 39:4-6
Woman's Christian Association,
founded, 18:263
Woman's Christian Temperance Union,
26:156; Minnesota, 13:101, 20:450;
local units, 16:242, 18:340, 19:
122, 21:214; pledge, 16:451;
Quakers in, 18:264
Woman's Club, Mound, anniversary, 21:
221
Woman's Historical Society of Pennsylvania, 15:476
Woman's Home and Foreign Missionary
Society, 19:213
Woman's Indian Association, 25:289
Woman's Industrial Exchange, Minneapolis, 18:125

Woman's Presbyterial Missionary Society, St. Paul, 17:468, 18:318
Woman's Progress Club, Mendota Township, 15:115
Woman's Progressive Club, Reads Landing, 14:362
Woman's rights, background, 15:230; source material, 16:451; New York State, 17:111; Minnesota, 20:328, 22:114, 25:376, 39:11, 12; leaders, 28:54, 30:251, 32:120, 40:338
Women, pioneer, 14:225, 18:296, 22:9-11, 27:68, 164, 30:267; authors, 15:230, 17:474, 26:297-299; Masonic, 16:370; wages, 18:332; Indian, 19:457, 20:136, 27:289, 34:174, 35:143, 38:238, 40:159, 208; university, 22:101; library founders, 22:363; as drivers, 26:23-25; in World War II, 26:253; Wisconsin, 29:356; physicians, 30:405; lawyers, 32:20; in industry, 33:42, 39:26; in education, 33:136; careers, 38:242. See also individual women's organizations
Women's Airforce Service Pilots (WASPs), 26:16
Women's Business and Professional Club, Rochester, 20:299
Women's Christian Home, St. Paul, 38:79
Women's Civic League, Hills, 19:239; International Falls, 23:107
Women's clubs, local units, 12:338, 17:240, 18:470, 21:221, 23:32, 24:168, 30:349, 406. See also Minnesota Federation of Women's Clubs
Women's Institute, St. Paul, 22:336
Women's International League for Peace and Freedom, 40:366n
Women's Northwest Conference on Current Problems, 16:225
Women's Rescue League, Minneapolis, 39:12
Wood, A. DeLacey, journalist, 13:447, 19:120
Wood, A. P., publisher, 17:300n
Wood, Abel, Minnesota Valley pioneer, 15:133
Wood, B. F., steamboat clerk, 13:238
Wood, Charles E. S., 40:94
Wood, Clark, speaker, 15:134
Wood, Edward H., papers, 17:336
Wood, Eleanor, Quaker minister, 18:261
Wood, Eva, manuscript assistant, 24:31, 243
Wood, Mrs. F. A., author, 25:102
Wood, Fernando, 16:451
Wood, Fred B., adjutant general, 24:64
Wood, Grant, artist, 20:114, 438, 26:79
Wood, Harold E., "The Shape of Things to Come," 23:211-218; military career, 23:270
Wood, Rev. J. A., 31:87
Wood, James P., author, 36:281
Wood, Jane, 33:5
Wood, John K., farmer, 16:71
Wood, John T., 30:98
Wood, L. E., author, 19:355
Wood, Laura N., 24:209n; work reviewed, 24:238
Wood, Lorraine, research assistant, 27:340; reference assistant, 28:48
Wood, Mary, 27:84, 85

Wood, Nancy, 33:5
Wood, Owen, artist, 40:314
Wood, Richard G., "Dr. Edwin James," 34:284-286; review by, 36:148; work reviewed, 40:305; author, 16:479; compiler, 32:189; editor, 35:44
Wood, Dr. Robert C., army surgeon, 22:206, 28:177, 30:97, 98
Wood, Mrs. Robert C. (Ann M. Taylor), marriage, 28:177, 30:97, 98
Wood, Robert C., Jr., at Fort Snelling, 30:98
Wood, Robert S., explorer, 31:198
Wood, S. A., postmaster, 15:355
Wood, Mrs. Sally, letters, 27:345
Wood, Seward, pioneer, 24:321
Wood, Stella L., author, 19:110; educator, 34:217
Wood, Swete, 11:238n
Wood, T. D., Northampton colonist, 22:170
Wood, Truman D., student author, 30:285
Wood, Mrs. Wallace, author, 21:340
Wood, William H., publisher, 16:234, 19:215, 342, 27:345
Wood, Mrs. William H. (Julia A. Sargent), 18:107; author, 16:234, 19:342, 20:34, 27:170; portrait, 21:412
Wood, William H., surveyor, 15:130
Wood Lake, Hennepin County, 35:24, 40:378; drought, 17:304; Methodist church, 18:120
Wood Lake, Yellow Medicine County, 39:33; monument, 11:31, 23:291, 37:60; Norwegian settlement, 12:275n; battle, 16:302, 21:401, 36:234, 38:66, 98, 108, 131n, 137, 149, 152, 156, 279, 40:282; church, 18:120; name, 38:141
Woodall, Allen E., 25:305, 27:34; author, 15:233, 17:114, 26:211n
Woodbridge, Dwight E., mineralogist, 34:272
Woodbridge, Harriet, 16:120
Woodbridge, William, Michigan Senator, 14:215; Michigan territorial delegate, 23:127, 128
Woodburn, Tom, artist, 14:117
Woodbury Township, Washington County, German settlement, 23:404
Woodcock, George, author, 37:86
Woodcock, Mrs. Loretta C., author, 30:272
"Wooden Shoe" Railroad, see Duluth, Mississippi River and Northern Railroad
Woodfill, Virginia, 12:286
Woodford, Frank B., work reviewed, 32:117
Woodham-Smith, Cecil, author, 34:168
Woodhull, Victoria, speaker, 35:228
Woodland pattern, defined, 25:155; pottery, 25:156, 330-335; Mille Lacs aspect, 25:329-341
Woodlawn Cemetery, Winona, veterans' graves, 11:446
Woodley and Berry, St. Anthony, plow factory, 24:296
Woodman, Cyrus, 25:71; career, 35:287
Woodman's Hall, Minneapolis, 19:266, 32:165
Woodress, James, editor, 38:387
Woodrow Township, Beltrami County, history, 15:132

Woodruff, Al, author, 35:98
Woodruff, Mark W., author, 20:362
Woodruff, Theodore T., career, 36:66
Woodrum, Clifton A., speaker, 16:342
Woods, Capt. A. P., 12:334
Woods, Alfred F., 20:82
Woods, Donald Z., 31:128; "Playhouse for Pioneers," 33:169-178; reviews by, 31:116, 120, 33:40, 34:214, 36:147, 40:311
Woods, Maj. Samuel, 14:459, 33:263; expedition, 12:83, 190, 16:128, 17:480, 22:148n, 280, 281, 38:4n; letters, 20:328; Fort Snelling commandant, 35:357
Wood's reaper, 24:288, 290, 292n
Woodson, Carter G., 15:423n
Woodstock, pioneer life, 17:99
Woodward, Arthur, speaker, 40:150
Woodward, C. Vann, author, 34:168
Woodward, Ellen S., 18:214
Woodward, George W., 22:152
Woodward, J. S., author, 13:344
Woodward, James M., journalist, 34:139
Woodward, Kendal W., postmaster, 34:186
Woodward, Mary D., work reviewed, 19:203-205
Woodward, Rev. Walter C., author, 17:478
Woodward, William A., 25:70
Woodworth, John M., author, 21:365
Wool, prices, 26:111, 113; exports, 26:112. See also Sheep raising
Woolfries, A. G., author, 23:285
Woollcott, Alexander, 26:307
Woolley, John G., prohibitionist, 18:218
Woolnough, ---, train conductor, 29:292
Woolnough, James, 15:367
Woolsey, John E., author, 17:116
Woolson, Albert, Civil War veteran, 37:345; monument, 35:245
Woolson, Constance F., 20:82
Woolstencroft, B. W., 14:252n
Woolworth, Alan R., reviews by, 37:84, 132, 38:40, 39:259, 40:409; museum curator, 37:44, 38:25; author, 37:264, 39:212, 40:412; speaker, 40:150
Woolworth, Mrs. Alan R. (Nancy L.), "The Grand Portage Mission," 39:301-310; author, 38:386
Woolworth, Frank W., 37:38
Woolworth Building, New York, architecture, 37:38, 39:35
Worcester, Dean C., scientist, 39:116-118, 120; depicted, 39:119
Wordie, J. M., author, 34:80
Work, Henry C., composer, 22:123
Work, John, trader, 38:42, 40:168n
Work, John L., author, 40:315
Working, Win V., author, 11:116, 118, 220, 330, 334, 441, 467, 12:106, 209, 210, 342, 13:121, 215, 454, 14:238, 15:369, 479, 488, 491, 16:129, 251, 17:128; editor, 12:97, 16:240; speaker, 13:72
Working People's Nonpartisan Political League, see Farmer-Labor party
Workingmen's Association No. 1 of the United States, St. Paul, 21:382
Workingmen's Union, St. Paul, 21:389; organized, 21:388

Workman, Dr. Harper M., 14:252n; author, 13:100; speaker, 15:369
Workman, Leland, author, 16:245
Workmen's Compensation Act, administration, 12:206; cases, 20:434, 21:195
Works, George A., author, 24:73
Works Progress Administration (Work Projects Administration), MHS program, 17:55-59, 61, 62, 65, 207, 461, 18:49-56, 107, 206, 19: 51-55, 354, 20:37-39, 42, 21:207, 22:332, 24:34, 361, 30:325; writers' projects, 17:57, 66, 18: 56, 21:308, 342, 22:110, 347, 416, 23:65-69, 282, 24:35, 63, 80; local activities, 17:68, 122, 123, 207, 232, 238, 357, 358, 362, 18: 64, 98, 110, 221, 223, 281, 336, 445, 19:361, 366, 20:47, 213, 21: 207, 22:102; research methods, 17: 332; directors, 17:346, 18:57n, 21:44; federal archives survey, 17:461, 18:49; art projects, 18: 68, 22:208, 24:181, 256; reports, 18:460; ethnic studies, 21:102, 22:104, 23:68, 24:226; program terminated, 24:38

   Historical Records Survey, 18: 94, 214, 20:198, 292, 23:43, 36: 150; inventories, 17:461, 18:63, 19:52, 66, 110, 462, 20:36, 21: 200, 22:87; county surveys, 18: 119, 458, 19:88-90, 20:89, 205, 445, 21:41, 100, 207, 327, 434, 22:100, 434, 23:93, 188, 288; publications, 18:325, 19:88-90, 224, 430-432, 455, 462, 21:207, 327, 434, 22:43, 103, 184, 210, 211, 328, 331, 23:93, 188, 288, 24:361. See also Federal Emergency Relief Administration, Minnesota Historical Survey
World Court, The Hague, Neth., 40: 369; Frank B. Kellogg's participation, 18:427
World Industrial and Cotton Centennial Exposition, New Orleans, Minnesota exhibit, 22:269, 27:120
World War I, source material, 11:97, 12:193, 321, 14:104, 15:61, 16: 360, 17:6, 24:167, 375, 40:361; tactics, 11:304; effect on Nonpartisan League, 12:193, 16:218, 34:221-232; veterans, 12:212, 15: 115, 16:472, 20:452, 21:97, 24: 185, 189, 25:160, 39:241-251; history, 14:203, 16:455, 23:389, 24: 51, 36:195; Minnesota home front, 14:318-322, 462, 23:179, 40:365-369; attitude of ethnic groups, 15:40, 16:344, 26:269, 35:193; transportation in, 17:89; armistice, 18:99; service newspapers, 22:194, 25:311; songs, 23:172, 25: 311; opposed, 23:363, 35:368, 40: 365-369, 371, 374; war history committees, 23:390-392; Iowa in, 24:240; Michigan in, 24:376; federal agencies, 25:281; nurses, 26:94; soldier vote, 26:187n; effect on immigration, 27:214; photographic records, 28:349; effect on colleges, 39:218-220, 40: 378. See also Minnesota War Records Commission
World War II, home front, 23:9, 24: 184, 192, 25:366, 26:278, 27:367, 28:162, 29:81, 39:263; records, 23:19-23, 388-394, 24:58, 81, 183, 247, 267, 375, 376, 25:310, 311, 401, 402, 26:85, 27:160, 175, 352, 28:180, 29:81, 32:183, 189; political aspect, 23:214-218; history, 24:51, 26:269, 27:49, 61, 36:195; rationing, 24:56, 26:175; local committees, 24:81-83, 185, 268, 25:94, 95, 29:102; camp life, 24:83, 184, 25:94; Ohio activities, 24:183, 26:85, 175; Pennsylvania in, 24:267; effect on colleges, 24:268, 25:312, 403; civilian defense, 24:376; Illinois program, 25:93; letters, 25:94, 26:176, 28:305; salvage projects, 25:135n, 284; service newspapers, 25:311, 312, 403, 26:175; transportation, 26:77, 35:45; soldier vote, 26:187, 36:167; veterans, 26:253, 389; industry, 26:268, 27: 352, 353, 40:47; postwar planning, 26:279, 27:365; bond drives, 26: 372; memorials, 26:376; European Theater, 27:57; Red Cross work, 28:82; Pacific Theater, 30:389, 36:24; opposed, 33:306, 35:369, 40:410. See also Minnesota War History Committee, various military units
World's Fair (Columbian), Chicago, 40:353; medals, 24:102; architecture, 38:351, 352, 40:108
Worm, Ole, 18:185
Wormser, Jean, theater director, 32: 105
Worrall, Henry, artist, 27:354
Worrall, John E., 18:249n
Worrell Sisters, theatrical troupe, 28:110
Wortabet, Gregory M., speaker, 12:397
Worth, Edward, mail carrier, 36:207
Worthington, businesses, 11:111, 16: 121; churches, 14:357; G.A.R. post, 16:432, 434; land office, 16:433; shipping point, 18:341; agriculture, 20:464; county seat fight, 20:465; railroad, 21:243; in fiction, 22:166, 37:2n; pioneer life, 24:91, 27:362, 29:271; history, 26:179; anniversary, 28:87; award, 36:105. See also National Colony
Worthington Advance, file acquired, 17:469
Worthington Community Club, history, 27:173
Worthy, Mrs. Martha B., author, 18: 228
Wortman, Isaac, 25:358
Wounded Knee, S.D., battle, 26:303, 378, 35:289, 38:41, 39:342, 40:46
Wowinapa, Sioux Indian, captured, 38: 151; portrait, 38:153
WPA, see Works Progress Administration
Wraaman, Wilhelm W., speaker, 29:314
Wrabek, John F., journalist, 20:462
Wren, Sir Christopher, 29:154
Wrenshall, history, 35:382; school board, 38:334; road, 40:245
Wright, ---, hunter, 15:388
Wright, A. W., lumberman, 21:439
Wright, Arthur F., author, 39:34
Wright, Benjamin F., author, 16:196
Wright, Benjamin F., Jr., 17:198; author, 12:88; speaker, 15:119
Wright, C. D., collector, 14:357
Wright, C. R., 21:109; author, 18: 117, 19:124
Wright, C. S., author, 18:119
Wright, Carl, 19:116, 20:95, 21:107, 35:340; author, 35:337
Wright, Carroll D., labor commissioner, 22:387
Wright, Charles, St. Paul pioneer, 33:4
Wright, Charles D., papers, 23:171
Wright, Charles L., logger, 35:202
Wright, Charles R., 14:216, 358; author, 14:332; speaker, 17:357, 483
Wright, Cushing F., work reviewed, 34:204; author, 34:99n
Wright, Cyrus, career, 35:41
Wright, Dana, author, 28:80, 39:36
Wright, Mrs. Edith, author, 23:401
Wright, Edward R., 23:134
Wright, Mrs. Fanny, speaker, 16:360
Wright, Frances, reformer, 24:339, 25:65
Wright, Frank Lloyd, architect, 25:7, 37:264, 38:352, 40:104, 107, 375; career, 26:170, 385, 30:248
Wright, Dr. Franklin R., author, 18: 459
Wright, George B., career, 17:488; founder of Fergus Falls, 20:103, 29:358; papers, 23:171, 35:384; land speculator, 39:90; map maker, 40:125n
Wright, Helen, author, 16:239
Wright, I. P., health inspector, 14: 300
Wright, Isaac, house, 25:9
Wright, J. F. C., author, 35:45
Wright, Sgt. James A., 17:468; at Gettysburg, 38:246-248, 254-257
Wright, Jean, author, 16:361
Wright, John K., work reviewed, 14:91
Wright, John S., publisher, 22:201, 23:283
Wright, Lillian, 16:123
Wright, Louis B., work reviewed, 34: 299; author, 34:257
Wright, Luella M., work reviewed, 25: 71; author, 20:86, 21:326, 27:355, 28:185, 287
Wright, Mathiel, pioneer, 35:259n
Wright, Nellie B., author, 29:274; papers, 36:26
Wright, Mrs. Nellie G., 13:200
Wright, Orville, aviator, 33:236
Wright, Philemon, 28:9
Wright, R. C., pioneer motorist, 26: 26
Wright, Robert L., work reviewed, 40: 44
Wright, Mrs. Sela G., letter, 16:216
Wright, Susie W., compiler, 25:89
Wright, Thomas C., work reviewed, 35: 41; papers, 35:384
Wright, Vernon A., architect, 20:103; letters, 18:405; career, 35:41
Wright, Wilbur, aviator, 22:302, 33: 236; interviewed, 22:303-305
Wright County, railroad, 12:254; grasshopper plague, 12:456; in Civil War, 16:257; politics, 16: 499; history, 17:242; Quakers, 18: 254, 256, 258; agriculture, 18: 408; Finnish settlement, 21:102, 25:318, 30:401; archives, 21:434;

farmers' union, 22:112; in Sioux
Outbreak, 35:337. See also Wright
County War
Wright County Historical Society, 23:
195, 29:277
Wright County Journal-Press (Buffa-
lo), anniversary, 18:120
Wright County Medical Society,
minutes, 16:471
"Wright County War," described, 11:
455, 17:242; volunteer guards in,
16:175
Wright County War History Committee,
23:392
Wrong, George M., author, 22:64
Wroolie, Mrs. Dagny, reminiscences,
19:123
Wroolie, Melvin S., 14:120; speaker,
29:275, 30:87; editor, 36:107
Wroolie, Mrs. T. S. V., author, 28:
292
Wroth, Lawrence C., author, 18:448,
34:303
Wulff, Mrs. Walter, author, 37:87
Wulffenstein, B. P., Mormon mission-
ary, 36:288
Wulling, Emerson G., reviews by, 15:
451, 16:80-82; publisher, 16:129,
18:143
Wulling, Frederick J., 24:347; works
reviewed, 28:65, 30:143; author,
24:175; scientist, 39:121, 122
Wunderlich, Herbert J., author, 16:
344
Wyandot Indians, 18:197; village
site, 40:204
Wyeth, Capt. Nathaniel, 38:385; ex-
plorer, 29:59; career, 29:61, 38:
199
Wykoff, C. G., clerk, 39:233, 235
Wykoff, Lutheran church, 15:481;
politics, 40:327n
Wyllie, Irvin G., author, 28:81
Wyman, Clarinda, 27:126, 127
Wyman, Mrs. James C., author, 27:73
Wyman, James T., Senator, 35:342, 343
Wyman, O. S., author, 17:350
Wyman, Robert, tavernkeeper, 16:72
Wyman, Roger E., "Insurgency in Minnesota," 40:317-329; review by,
40:407
Wyman, Walker D., reviews by, 29:61,
33:86, 303, 34:79, 208, 35:331,
36:95, 230, 37:36, 38:196; works
reviewed, 33:266, 34:124; speaker,
15:227; compiler, 16:220; author,
29:104, 33:311, 34:264, 37:134,
39:262
Wyman (Okwanin), St. Louis County,
railroad station, 34:180
"Wyman X," steamboat, 36:213
Wyoming (town), road, 16:285; railroad, 16:289, 290, 29:87, 36:213;
centennial, 34:356; stage route,
40:247n
Wyoming (state), 19:211; ranching,
12:177; emigration from, 25:321n;
fur trade, 29:59, 40:196, 197; in
World War II, 36:87; in fiction,
37:306
Wyoming State Historical Department,
28:189
Wysor, Elizabeth, singer, 39:62
Wytrwal, Joseph A., author, 37:344

Xan, Erna O., work reviewed, 32:54
XY Co., 18:81, 21:129n, 28:6n; posts,
11:357, 358, 361, 363, 365, 366,
20:14, 22:270; source material,
14:338, 28:3; relations with North
West Co., 16:200, 19:299, 21:118,
24:77, 28:1, 2, 40:170, 171, 178-
181; partners, 21:124n, 132n,
137n; relations with Hudson's Bay
Co., 28:2; at Yellow Lake, Wis.,
28:142-159, 225-240. See also Fur
trade

Yale Township, Beltrami County, history, 15:132
Yandes, James W., career, 22:425
"Yankee," steamboat, 11:123, 137,
172, 29:210; excursions, 11:126,
127, 135, 20:388
Yankee Ridge, Stevens County, settled, 26:291
Yankees, Minnesota communities, 15:
134, 139, 253, 16:257, 492, 17:
486, 21:411, 23:14, 102, 24:93,
97, 98, 182, 25:395, 27:176, 28:
266, 35:265, 39:201; attitudes,
15:135, 19:247-270, 21:71, 22:360,
35:326, 37:268; travelers, 16:216,
275; social life, 16:384; colonization projects, 18:95; influence
on education, 19:68, 22:101, 25:
109, 28:132, 39:201; Northampton
Colony, 19:129-147, 20:140-145,
22:169-173; word usage, 19:241-
246; customs, 20:162; architecture, 27:126, 37:337-352; contributions, 29:163, 31:18-21, 41;
food, 34:54-58; religion, 34:264,
40:1-11. See also Mainites
Yankton, S.D., newspaper, 15:201;
Catholic church, 17:473
Yankton band, Sioux Indians, agent,
15:223, 39:229; hostilities, 27:
97, 32:233, 33:274, 279n, 38:280;
at Pipestone, 27:154, 31:203, 206,
36:21, 40:96; relations with Cree,
32:230, 235; relations with
whites, 33:272, 276, 38:123; bibliography, 37:346
Yantes, Ray, 23:392
Yaqui Indians, songs, 34:161
Yardley, Wade H., biography, 16:337
Yates, Fred, artist, 30:291
Yates, Norris W., work reviewed, 35:
330; author, 34:174
Yaw, Ellen B., singer, 39:55
Yaworski, N., author, 21:439
Yazoo Pass, Miss., 25:249
Yellow Bank Township, Lac qui Parle
County, Lutheran church, 11:461
Yellow fever, Walter Reed's discov-
eries, 24:213
Yellow Lake, Wis., trading posts, 11:
384, 28:142-159, 225-240, 39:297;
mission, 13:195, 28:3, 29:355; re-
sort, 28:2
Yellow Medicine agency, see Upper
Sioux (Yellow Medicine) agency
Yellow Medicine County, ethnic set-
tlements, 12:275n, 17:344, 23:290;
archives, 23:93; medical history,
33:354; in Sioux Outbreak, 38:243
Yellow Medicine County Historical So-

ciety, organized, 18:336; meet-
ings, 21:447, 30:280; reorganized,
30:169; museum, 30:402; tour, 35:
246
Yellow Medicine County War History
Committee, 23:392
Yellow Medicine Township, Yellow
Medicine County, Norwegian settlement, 12:275n
Yellow River, Wis., located, 28:149n;
explored, 28:151; source, 28:159n;
islands, 28:235
Yellow Wolf, Cheyenne leader, 34:345
Yellowhead, see Ozawindib
Yellowstone expedition, 17:473, 27:
161, 35:241; extent, 12:436, 17:81
Yellowstone National Park, 36:280;
history, 14:225; photographed, 23:
282, 35:295, 36:279; established,
23:383, 37:134; explored, 24:158,
40:263; discovered, 33:180
Yellowstone River, Mont., Wyo., dust
storms, 16:475; explored, 23:282
Yeovil Colony, Hawley, Clay County,
history, 12:336, 21:448, 28:190
Yetter, Mrs. H. I., 15:137, 16:124,
17:122, 18:110, 20:96; speaker,
18:464
Ylvisaker, Erling, author, 15:234
Ylvisaker, Rev. N. T., 26:182
Ylvisaker, Paul N., author, 35:201
"Yorick," pseud., "Queer Epistle from
Minnesota Territory," 28:339-344
York, slave, with Lewis and Clark expedition, 15:424
York, James Stuart, Duke of, 16:415,
419; proprietor of New York, 16:
406, 411
York, Ont., battle, 15:472, 27:236
York boats, 30:150; in fur trade, 11:
426, 33:130, 34:174; depicted, 12:
436, 20:208, 25:90; construction,
32:124
York Factory, Man., trade route, 16:
347, 33:130, 36:102, 40:83; his-
tory, 19:223; trading post, 20:71,
31:235, 238, 33:261, 34:132; set-
tlers, 24:179, 29:247; located,
32:161n; depicted, 40:189
Yorktown, Va., surrender, 13:213;
siege, 25:119n, 120n, 126
Yorktown National Military Park, 24:
168
Yosemite Valley, discovered, 15:233
Yoshpe, Harry B., editor, 22:329; au-
thor, 30:389
Yost, Edna, author, 12:201
Yould, Thomas, labor leader, 27:178
Youmans, E. L., speaker, 11:157
Young, Albert L., lawyer, 36:201
Young, Alexander, author, 27:62
Young, Antoin, miller, 11:182
Young, Archer, speaker, 12:210
Young, Mrs. Archer, 16:125
Young, Arthur, author, 40:294
Young, Brigham, Mormon leader, 13:
281, 386, 28:378, 32:98, 36:287,
289, 39:71
Young, Demos, 11:88
Young, Earl, author, 28:82
Young, Mrs. Edward B., 12:426, 15:
217, 16:60, 466, 17:70, 20:51, 76,
22:45, 23:35; author, 17:344
Young, Edward T., legislator, 35:348
Young, Elbert A., 15:459
Young, Mrs. Elbert A., 14:195
Young, Elizabeth, 19:319, 320

Young, Mrs. Elizabeth A., 20:314
Young, Francis M., author, 19:219
Young, Frank, 20:315
Young, Harry H., 18:74; journalist, 23:372; publisher, 26:299
Young, J. Tracy, composer, 23:172
Young, James C., collector, 27:41
Young, James M., works reviewed, 38: 39, 40:406; author, 34:127
Young, John, diary, 19:343
Young, Margaret A., lawyer, 17:213
Young, Mary B., author, 17:344
Young, Mary E., author, 22:103
Young, Mrs. Milo, speaker, 18:269
Young, Otis E., author, 34:214
Young, Pearl I., author, 40:268
Young, Mrs. Rachel Hardy, teacher, 22:220
Young, Richard M., politician, 39:48
Young, Russell S., compiler, 35:339
Young, Shebna S., 19:319, 320
Young, T. F., 17:366
Young, W. J., Lumber Co., Clinton, Iowa, 27:190, 39:211
Young, William B., and Co., Chicago, plow factory, 24:298
Young, Winthrop, letters, 28:304
Young family, genealogy, 28:304
Young America, Carver County, chronology, 20:459; literary society, 24:214; German theater, 32:100; singing society, 34:241, 242; platted, 34:264; centenary, 35:203
Young America Eagle, anniversary, 20: 459
Young and Lightner, St. Paul, law firm, records, 29:189
Young Men's Association, St. Anthony, 12:397
Young Men's Christian Association, camps, 11:417; St. Paul, 12:458, 13:101, 18:210, 363, 25:289, 35: 293, 384; in World War I, 14:320, 18:98; activities, 16:31, 19:258, 400; Northfield, 16:242; Winona, 17:242, 27:9; Minneapolis, 20:101, 21:411, 35:225, 226, 39:22; history, 25:298, 33:228; in Civil War, 25:351n; in revival movement, 35:373; Vladivostok, U.S.S.R., 38: 316, 324, 325; Nagasaki, Japan, 38:317, 319
Young Men's Library Association, Winona, 11:146, 18:365
Young Men's Library Association of Minneapolis, see Minneapolis Athenaeum
Young Men's Literary Association, Minneapolis, 19:403, 20:358
Young Naturalists' Society, Minneapolis, 24:80, 35:154
Young Women's Christian Association, in World War I, 14:320; at University of Minnesota, 17:226; St. Paul, 34:43; camps, 34:130
Youngdahl, Luther W., 30:287, 288, 400, 403, 409, 32:108; speaker, 23:194, 29:277, 362, 363, 30:170, 285, 369, 398; governor, 28:183, 196, 197, 30:84, 171, 32:107, 40: 148; author, 28:374; travels, 29: 182; biography, 35:96
Youngdahl, Oscar, author, 21:113
Youngdahl, Oscar F., Congressman, 22: 423
Youngdahl, Rosalie, 12:102, 13:118,

16:243; speaker, 14:120; author, 22:216
Youngdahl family, 36:106
Youngdale, James M., work reviewed, 40:139; politician, 34:194n
Younger, Edward, work reviewed, 35:42
Younger, James, robber, 11:117, 31: 182, 33:175, 35:202, 39:262; career, 12:335, 31:50, 35:97; capture, 20:355, 26:394
Younger, Dr. Lewis I., "The Winona County Historical Society," 36: 139-144; author, 37:43; underwater research, 38:244
Younger, Richard D., essay reviewed, 36:150; author, 35:241
Younger, Robert, robber, 11:117, 31: 182, 33:175, 35:202, 39:262; career, 12:335, 31:50, 35:97; capture, 20:355, 26:394
Younger, Thomas Coleman ("Cole"), robber, 11:117, 31:182, 33:175, 39:262; described, 11:85; career, 12:335, 18:218, 31:50, 35:97, 202; prisoner, 18:462; capture, 20:355, 26:394
Young-Quinlan Co., Minneapolis, mercantile firm, anniversary, 26:288
Youth Conservation Act, 39:210
"Ypsilanti," steamboat, 29:292
Ysaÿe, Eugène, violinist, 39:53, 56
Yugoslavs, on iron ranges, 19:219, 27:210, 28:251-253, 32:197, 40: 343; Detroit, Mich., 20:202; bibliography, 25:299, 26:167; immigration, 27:40, 35:292; folklore, 34:296; U.S., 38:241. See also various Balkan groups
Yukon and Copper River Mining Co., 29:303n
Yukon Territory, source material, 39: 128; gold rush, 39:341
Yuma-Folsom flints, archaeological find, 16:7-11
Yuma Indians, songs, 34:161
Yurka, Blanche, actress, 13:273
Yzermans, Rev. H., author, 14:239
Yzermans, Father Vincent A., work reviewed, 38:193

Zaar, Rev. Carl G., 20:448
Zackrison, Jens, pioneer, 14:426-428
Zackrison, John, 14:428
Zackrison, Julia, 14:428
Zackrison, Magnil, 14:428
Zackrison, Minnie, 14:428
Zackrison, Ole, 12:450, 14:426
Zackrison, Ramborg, 14:428
Zackrison, Zackri, 14:428
Zagel, Hermann H., author, 14:105
Zahler, Helene, work reviewed, 28:269
Zakrzewska, Dr. Marie E., feminist, 39:6
Zalusky, Joseph W., 23:391, 26:176, 29:179; speaker, 22:216; author, 37:308
Zanesville, Ohio, museum, 27:178
Zanger, Jules, essay reviewed, 40:403
Zapffe, Carl, work reviewed, 27:338; author, 15:131, 20:201, 27:269, 28:381
Zapffe, Mrs. Carl, 28:86
Zaplotnik, Father J. L., editor, 15: 455

Zapp, Edward, banker, 33:54
Zapp, John, banker, 33:54
Zavertnik, Joze, author, 25:186
Zavoral, James, 23:298
Zeeland, Mich., Dutch settlement, 28: 368
Zeilinger, G. J., author, 12:329
Zeisler, Fannie B., pianist, 39:56
Zeitlin, Jake, author, 24:360
Zeleny, Anthony, 15:37
Zeleny, Charles, 15:37
Zeleny, John, 15:37; author, 12:201
Zellers, John A., author, 30:262
Zenith Building and Loan Association, Duluth, 37:123
Zenith Mill, Minneapolis, 12:333
Zenith Mine, Vermilion Range, 25:320, 35:338
Zenzius, Conrad, musician, 32:240n
Zeppelin, Count Ferdinand von, 24: 266; Minnesota visit, 19:354, 39: 278-285, 40:265-276; balloonist, 35:184, 333, 39:278; passenger, 39:280, 285, 40:267, 276; depicted, 39:281, 40:265 (cover); airship, 39:285; aeronautical experiments, 40:278
Zetterstrom, John, author, 15:348
Zgonc, Louis, scuba diver, 38:29-31, 33
Zicha, Josef, Czech pioneer, 15:28
Zicha family, Czech settlers, 15:30
Ziebarth, E. W., 35:340
Ziegele, Albert, brewer, 40:273
Ziegler, Chauncey J., 12:409
Ziegler, Grace M., author, 12:327
Ziegler, John T., pioneer, 12:53, 58, 406, 407, 409
Ziegler, Nettie, 12:409
Ziegler, William H., Co., Minneapolis, anniversary, 34:217
Zieglschmid, A. J. F., author, 23:183
Zierke, Jean, 16:445
Zierke, Dr. R. H., 16:445
Zierke, Mrs. R. H., 16:445
Zigrosser, Carl, artist, 26:165
Zilliacus, Konni, author, 18:72
Zimbrick, Edward, speaker, 16:361
Zimmerman, Carle C., 11:445; editor, 12:90; author, 12:334
Zimmerman, Charles A., "The Kandiyohi Country," 33:141-154; artist, 33: 141, 143, 146, 149, 151-153; career, 33:142; photographer, 35:249 (cover), 37:89 (cover)
Zimmerman, Edward O., 33:142
Zimmerman, Dr. Harry B., 19:419n, 23: 50, 26:45, 29:97
Zimmerman, Johann G., 17:294
Zinc mining, Wisconsin, 38:241
Zink, Harold, author, 12:332
Zion Lutheran Church of North Effington, Otter Tail County, 15:481
Zippel, Wilhelm M., fisherman, 35: 272, 273
Zippel Bay, Lake of the Woods, 35: 272, 273, 275
Zoll, Rev. Joseph, 23:27
Zollicoffer, Gen. Felix K., Confederate officer, 25:24, 38:260-263, 39:179
Zollman, Frederick W., biography, 14: 333
Zon, Raphael, forestry official, 39: 241
Zorn, Anders, artist, 25:384
Zorn, Roman J., author, 31:60

Zornow, William F., author, 35:383
Zrust, Mrs. John (Isabelle), 13:197, 14:236, 16:240, 22:106, 440, 23:101
Zschokke, Herman, speaker, 27:105
Zubaran, Rafael, 17:165
Zucker, A. E., work reviewed, 31:242; author, 29:80
Zucker, Norman L., work reviewed, 40:140
Zuidema, Dutmur, Dutch pioneer, 28:125
Zumberge, James H., author, 33:138
Zumbro Falls, mill, 11:111; co-operative creamery, 19:157n; agricul-

ture, 26:177; railroad, 35:15n
Zumbro River, southeast Minnesota, floods, 11:186; trading post, 11:383; gold rush, 13:176n; covered bridge, 16:486, 20:296; mills, 35:11-21
Zumbro Valley, Norwegian settlement, 12:271; camp meeting, 31:82
Zumbro Valley Historical Society, publication, 35:198
Zumbrota, creameries, 11:290, 35:18; roads, 11:394, 398; founded, 14:134; settled, 15:111, 20:328, 21:449; railroads, 15:493, 35:15, 21;

described, 16:216; bridges, 16:486, 20:296, 23:290; anniversaries, 22:221, 35:198; library, 24:272; depicted, 26:281; stage routes, 30:70, 35:21; trade center, 34:127, 35:20, 21; telephone service, 34:264; mills, 35:13; churches, 35:19
Zumbrota Building Association, 12:318
Zuzek, Father John, 14:121
Zwaanendael Colony, Lewes, Del., 21:401
Zwakman, G., Dutch pioneer, 28:131
Zweiner, C. A., 23:149

Errata

11:58, line 33, for Douglas, read Douglass.
11:86, line 3, for polar, read poplar.
11:112, line 4, for Blue Earth County Post, read Blue Earth Post.
11:316, line 17, for John W., read Joseph W.
11:357, line 27, for McKenzie, read Mackenzie.
11:364, line 26, for Nettly, read Netley.
11:370, line 2, for Tongue, read Turtle.
11:381, line 1, for Lake Talcott, read Talcot Lake.
11:433, line 4, for A. W., read A. H.
11:448, line 24, for Erickson, read Ericksen.
11:483, column 1, line 19, for John J., read John E.

12:25, line 14, for History, read Records.
12:59, line 31, for December 27, read December 26.
12:96, line 34, for Earl, read Earle.
12:103, line 13, for Larsen, read Larson.
12:104, line 20, for Andreson, read Andresen.
12:127, line 4, for Frenier, read Frenière.
12:177, line 13, for Robert S., read Robert H.
12:198, line 15, for County, read country.
12:203, line 30, for Governor, read Cadwallader C.
12:207, line 30, for George C., read George G.
12:207, line 35, for Gustafson, read Gustavson.
12:226, line 16, for Douglas, read Douglass.
12:278, line 25, for Polk County, read Polk and Norman counties.
12:324, line 19, for Major, read Colonel.
12:318, line 8, for Wabissimong, read Wabassimong.
12:333, line 20, for Petit, read Pettit.
12:361, line 3, for Methye, read Methy.
12:367-373, for Roderick McKenzie, read Roderic Mackenzie.
12:408, line 12, for Album, read Alburn.
12:421, line 38, for Pioneer Press, read Dispatch.
12:433, line 12, for J. J., read J. G.
12:433, line 20, for Goodhue, read Fillmore.

13:141, line 22, for Carver, read Scott.
13:150, line 29, for Habbitt, read Hoblit.
13:182, line 9, for Methye, read Methy.
13:182, line 30, for The Kensington Rune Stone, read The Kensington Stone.
13:211, line 5, for Dudley E., read Dudley S.
13:293, line 34, for Gustafson, read Gustavson.
13:317, line 28, for Taope, read Taopi.
13:337, line 1, for Elleonora, read Ellenora.
13:427, lines 20, 22, for Kock, read Koch.
13:460, column 1, line 46, for Eric, read Erland.
13:483, column 2, line 24, for (Pa.), read (Va.).

14:55, line 24, p. 57, line 11, for St. Columbo, read St. Columba.
14:65, line 10, for Douglas, read Douglass.
14:75, line 16, for William S., read William E.
14:119, line 29, for her narrative, read his narrative.
14:158, line 11, for St. Andrew, read St. Andre.

14:238, line 34, for 1858, read 1857.
14:294, line 9, for Abbey, read Abbe.
14:332, line 28, for Lucius G., read Lucius C.
14:356, line 34, for Scandian, read Scandia.
14:359, line 24, for Hennman, read Hinman.
14:406, line 27, for Thomas N., read Thomas M.
14:452, line 12, for Iron Hub, read Ironton.
14:453, lines 36, 37, for thirty-eight Indians at New Ulm, read thirty-nine Indians at Mankato.
14:475, column 1, line 14, for Norwegian settlement, read Lutheran church.
14:482, column 1, line 49, for Anston, read Anson.

15:16, line 31, for Grant County, read Wisconsin.
15:90, line 31, for Roderick, read Roderic.
15:158, line 30, for Lauzon, read Lauson.
15:163, line 26, for Gareau, read Garreau.
15:171, line 3, for account of the second journey. This is plainly indicated by, read account of the experiences on both journeys, which together. . .
15:213, line 32, for Hoffman, read Hoffmann.
15:218, line 13, for Charles A., read Charles M.
15:243, line 32, for Hebert, read Herbert.
15:252, line 31, for Alexander, read Andrew.
15:254, line 7, for L. J., read John L.
15:258, line 20, for Larzaro Cardenas, read Lázaro Cárdenas.
15:309, line 14, for June, read July.
15:321, line 17, for Reymbault, read Raymbault.
15:336, line 20, for Mackenzie, read McKenzie.
15:352, line 27, for June, read June, 1933.
15:359, line 37, for Door, read Dorr.
15:460, line 8, for Case, read Case, Jr.
15:462, line 36, for Kansas City, read Topeka.
15:480, line 33, for Brown, read Nicollet.

16:111, lines 32, 33, for that institution's Bulletin, read Bulletin of the New York Public Library.
16:114, line 23, for Volume 16, read Volume 14.
16:150, line 21, for lower, read upper.
16:174, line 11, for Brigadier, read Surveyor.
16:178, line 16, for 1853-54, read 1856-58.
16:178, line 27, for Hobart College at Geneva, New York, read Kenyon College at Gambier, Ohio.
16:180, line 12, for Methodists, read Baptists.
16:183, line 18, for 1907, read 1904.
16:216, line 31, for Frances, read Francis.
16:222, line 25, for Bridgewater, read Bridgwater.
16:229, line 22, for Kinnikinnic, read Kinnickinnic.
16:241, line 8, for Hysloop, read Hyslop.
16:315, line 25, for Secombe, read Seccombe.
16:317, line 4, for Secome, read Seccombe.
16:332, line 28, for James M. Doty in 1842, read James D. Doty in 1841.
16:336, lines 8, 9, delete his widow; for New York, read Minnesota.
16:338, line 14, for Folksblat, read Volksblatt.

16:340, line 5, for Mehegen, read Mehagan.
16:341, lines 5, 6, for William T., read W. P.
16:341, line 22, for William C., read William B.
16:361, line 13, for Lake, read Lakes.
16:364, line 9, for ante, p. 21, read post, 19:21.
16:471, line 26, for John H., read John J.
16:483, line 32, for 1934, read 1935.
16:508, column 1, line 28, for Belle Plaine, read Blooming Prairie.

17:29, line 3, for used, read us.
17:54, line 1, for M. Chase, read W. Chase.
17:98, line 28, for George E., read George G.
17:122, line 34, for Glencoe, read Glenwood.
17:213, line 21, for August, read Auguste.
17:226, line 23, for Burt, read Bert.
17:226, line 22, for Thompson, read Thomson.
17:238, line 20, for E. H., read E. A.
17:313, line 35, for A. B., read W. E.
17:335, line 14, for Sylvanus P., read Sylvanus B.
17:349, line 23, for Antoine, read Antoine O'Brien.
17:357, line 36, for Sarah R., read Sarah T.
17:392, line 1, for Douglas, read Douglass.
17:393, line 17, for Douglass, read Douglas.
17:462, line 37, for Scanlon, read Scanlan.
17:489, line 37, for Asa A., read Asa G.
17:530 (errata), delete line 6.

18:134, line 25, for James O., read James D.
18:163, line 37, for 1:482, read 1:393.
18:180, line 7, for Douglas, read Douglass.
18:209, line 16, for Nacisse Frenier, read Narcisse Frenière.
18:224, line 36, for grandparents, read parents.
18:225, line 4, for grandfather, read father.
18:314, line 22, for daughter, Mrs. Claudia G. Perkins, read granddaughter, Miss Claudia Perkins.
18:325, line 14, for E. Clever, read F. Clever.
18:332, line 11, for Clark, read Clarke.
18:345, line 7, for Wright, read Meeker.
18:384, line 11 [corrected in part of the edition], for between the Allegheny Mountains and the Atlantic. In the course, read between the rivers; they made friends with the Indians, traded. . .
18:459, line 26, for Lorraine Blake, read Barbara Hall.
18:462, line 9, for pack, read back.
18:464, line 34, for Wolleston, read Wollaston.
18:492, column 1, line 22, for Casper M., read M. Casper.
18:493, column 1, line 1, for U. B., read U. V.

19:116, line 13, for J. A., read J. M.
19:120, line 1, for S. Hage, read George S. Hage.
19:219, line 16, for Marodni, read Narodni.
19:356, line 22, for Northwest, read Northeast.
19:389, line 1, for Crooks, read Crook.
19:446, line 28, for Everett M., read Everett N.
19:457, line 20, for Kansas, read Fort Hays Kansas.
19:489, column 2, line 50, for (St. Paul), read (Hastings).
19:492, column 2, line 30, for News, read Times.

20:116, line 27, for Edmunds, read Edmonds.
20:180, line 11, for Boyer, read Bojer.
20:195, line 17, for Oberamergau, read Oberammergau.
20:198, line 30, for Charles I., read Charles L.
20:325, line 24, for Historical, read Library.
20:329, line 12, for Hennepin, read Carver.
20:336, line 2, for Alexander, read Archibald.
20:337, line 37, for Cheyenne, read Sheyenne.
20:421, line 29, for "Mister Dooly," read "Mr. Dooley."
20:435, line 5, for George A., read George K.

21:27, line 37, for David, read Daniel.
21:36, line 11, for E. S., read E. G.
21:70, line 16, for Edgar Elmer, read Elmer Edgar.
21:83, line 23, for Douglas, read Douglass.
21:88, line 15, for Mahlon T., read Mahlon N.

21:98, line 25, for Jansen, read Janson.
21:141, line 37, for Roderick McKenzie, read Roderic Mackenzie.
21:167, line 25, for Wabasha III, read Wabasha II.
21:193, line 37, last line missing, read affairs and photographic copies of two letters that he received from. . .
21:248, line 16, for Cheyenne, read Sheyenne.
21:323, line 18, for Bernard, read Bernhardt.
21:330, line 13, for Westbrook, read Wesbrook.
21:333, line 23, for Walter W., read Walter K.
21:401, line 36, for Gallop, read Gallup.
21:417, line 17, for Marguerite, read Margaret.
21:429, line 11, for W. C., read W. W.
21:448, line 36, for Yoevil, read Yeovil.
21:472, column 1, line 54, for William, read Willis.
21:479, column 2, line 47, for Malhoit, read Malhiot.

22:10, line 25, for Mazurka, read Mazourka.
22:40, line 22, for James, read Joseph A.
22:106, line 13, for Bombach, read Bohmbach.
22:106, line 13, for Erikson, read Erickson.
22:200, line 2, for Julian K., read Julian P.
22:285, line 10, for Frénier, read Frenière.
22:333, line 11, for Peter Q., read Peter G.
22:347, line 16, for Sarback, read Sarbach.
22:379, line 29, for McGoldrick, read McGolrick.
22:431, line 34, for Madeline, read Madeleine.
22:445, line 8, for Frances W., read Frances M.
22:467, column 1, line 51, for Rudolphe, read Rodolphe.

23:24, line 12, for Aitkin, read Aitken.
23:40, line 11, for Teigen, read Teigan.
23:103, line 31, for Thomas E., read Thomas S.
23:104, line 31, for Miss, read Mrs.
23:106, line 21, for Gordonville, read Gordonsville.
23:143, lines 36-39, for this note, read The Drummond Island post was founded in 1815 and abandoned in 1828. See William F. Lawler, "Michigan Islands," in Michigan History Magazine, 22:286, 287 (Summer, 1938).
23:155, line 19, for McKenny, read McKenney.
23:183, line 33, for costumes, read customs.
23:192, line 32, for De Puis, read Du Puis.
23:249, lines 32, 40, p. 251, line 31, for Fairbank, read Fairbanks.
23:273, line 24, for House, read Home.
23:243, line 34, p. 355, line 23, p. 356, line 29, for Douglas, read Douglass.
23:274, line 20, for C. E., read E. C.
23:286, line 27, for Michel, read Michael.
23:298, line 29, for Scrambler, read Scambler.
23:322, line 37, for Constance, read Constans.
23:356, line 2, for "Griffin," read "Griffon."
23:385, lines 25, 27, for Historical, read Geographical.
23:391, line 27, for E. L., read E. R.
23:408, column 1, line 49, for Jean, read John J.
23:423, column 1, line 38, for James, read Jumer.

24:34, line 14, for Charles E., read Charles F.
24:36, line 3, for Ausiedler, read Ansiedler.
24:70, line 25, for William C., read William D.
24:73, line 33, for Laskianinen, read Laskianin.
24:175, line 37, for Wittemore, read Whittemore.
24:190, line 21, for Cederstrom, read Cederstam.
24:224, line 36, for M. J., read J. M.
24:258, line 35, for Charles, read Chr.
24:264, line 2, for Kasson, read Claremont.
24:268, line 25, for Thoreen, read Thoren.
24:276, line 22, for 2:221-218, read 2:211-218.
24:344, line 9, for Armstrong, read Robertson.
24:384, lines 17, 20, for Emmet, read Emmett.

25:54, line 26, for William E., read William W.
25:95, line 26, for R. E., read R. A.
25:192, line 34, for Anderson, read Andersen.
25:234, line 16, for Pleasanton, read [Alfred] Pleasanton.

25:241, line 36, for John J., read John A.
25:285, line 6, for Staylen, read Stoylen.
25:313, line 15, for Winslow W., read Winslow M.
25:314, line 24, for Eric Norelius, read Erland Carlson.
25:314, lines 26, 27, for The work inaugurated by
   Norelius . . ., read The work inaugurated by Carlson
   was continued in the same year by the Reverend Eric
   Norelius.
25:385, line 10, for Arlo, read Arlow.

26:89, line 18, for Gustafson, read Gustavson.
26:121, line 28, for N. R. Clark, read N. P. Clarke.
26:166, line 7, for Jonathan, read John.
26:189, line 7, for Joseph P., read Joseph A.
26:211, line 28, for Allan, read Allen.
26:222, line 10, for Featherstonehaugh, read Featherstonhaugh.
26:273, line 33, for MacFarland, read MacFarlane.
26:348, column 1, line 8, for Clarence C., read Clarence
   R.
26:370, line 28, for Carleton, read Carlyle.
26:372, lines 10, 12, for Leedly, read Leedy.
26:414, column 1, line 37, for Bertha D., read Bertha E.

27:38, line 30, p. 39, lines 6, 22, 29, p. 40, line 17,
   for Sickles, read Sickels.
27:198, line 24, for Lumber, read Logging.
27:268, line 30, for Ferdinand, read Frederick.
27:288, line 31, for Nakomis, read Nokomis.
27:344, line 18, for Plaine, read Plain.
27:355, lines 12, 27, for Peterson, read Petersen.
27:356, line 8, for Mark S., read Mark H.
27:361, line 8, for Miss, read Mrs.

28:34, line 19, for Breckenridge, read Breckinridge.
28:47, line 14, for Public, read University.
28:60, line 8, for G. F., read G. T.
28:69, line 4, for Ernest, read Ernst.
28:77, line 30, for Heibert, read Hiebert.
28:130, line 28, for T. Koch, read F. Koch.
28:180, lines 15, 19, 25, for Lamare-Piquot, read
   Lamare-Picquot.
28:181, line 2, for Alfred A., read Albert E.
28:193, lines 20, 26, 31, for Gustafson, read Gustavson.
28:206, lines 35, 36, for manuscript history of Fort
   Ripley, read "Fort Ripley Military Reservation,"
   p. 44.
28:281, line 8, for Jonathan, read John.
28:295, line 16, for Gustafson, read Gustavson.
28:300, line 33, for Robert N., read Robert M.
28:317, line 20, for Colville, read Colvile.
28:320, line 25, for William W., read Charles W. W.
28:326, line 14, for Wert's, read [D. Mortimer] West's.
28:348, line 36, for Benjamin, read Bradley.
28:371, line 7, for 1828, read 1928.

29:8, line 24, for 1870, read 1869.
29:83, line 6, for St. Anthony, read Anthony Wayne.
29:101, line 3, for Christ's, read Crist's.
29:166, line 8, for Roderick McKenzie, read Roderic
   Mackenzie.
29:172, line 1, for tonconite, read taconite.
29:206, line 40, for plant, read plank.
29:273, line 14, for Kyyhkonen, read Kyyhkynen.
29:277, line 29, for Svenskanras, read Svenskarnas.
29:362, line 17, for Ray, read Roy H.
29:364, line 27, for Levina, read Lavina.
29:382, column 1, line 26, for (Alaska), read (Yukon
   Ter.).
29:384, column 1, line 43, for Fort des Chartres, read
   Fort de Chartres.
29:391, column 1, line 22, for Macauley, read Macaulay.

30:70, line 21, for Blakely, read Blakeley.
30:70, line 25, for Carleton, read Carlton.
30:83, line 5, for Owens, read Owen.
30:157, line 26, for Prichardt's, read Reichardt's.

30:161, line 30, for Kinkaid, read Kinkead.
30:267, lines 7, 11, for Menchen, read Mencken.
30:269, line 6, for Cooper, read Copper.
30:369, line 23, for William L., read William J.
30:397, line 31, for Jonas, read Jones.
30:412, line 17, for A. Fritiof, read O. Fritiof.
30:438, column 2, line 14, delete Turpin, Marie R.

31:1, line 14, for Snare, read Snake.
31:1, line 26, for Frazer, read Fraser.
31:25, line 17, for Augusta, read St. Augusta.
31:55, line 36, for Adolph, read Adolf.
31:56, line 11, for Pritchard, read Reichardt.
31:98, line 25, for March, read June.
31:123, lines 22, 27, 31, for Olsen, read Olson.
31:196, line 15, for Charles, read John.
31:266, column 2, line 40, for 253, read 254.
31:266, column 1, line 44, for Mazzeppa, read Mazeppa.

32:138, line 20, for Samuel J., read Sidney M.
32:190, line 30, for Hall, read Long.
32:261, column 1, line 19, for 120, read 126.
32:261, column 1, line 44, for (Wis.), read (Minn.).

33:154, column 2, line 43, for Kirkhoven, read Kerkhoven.
33:337, column 2, line 18, for Association, read Society.
33:363, column 3, line 1, for C. W., read G. W.
33:372, column 3, line 20, for 355, read 356.
33:375, column 1, line 52, for 225, read 226.

34:128, column 1, line 47, for Watwatasso, read Wawatosa.
34:133, line 3, for Charles F. Babcock, read James M.
   Babcock.
34:174, column 2, line 5, for Rupert's, read Rupert.
34:174, column 2, line 31, for Yales, read Yates.
34:215, column 1, line 18, for Brønsted, read Brøndsted.
34:216, column 1, line 15, for Thomas F., read Thomas T.
34:267, column 2, line 10, for Fred N., read Fred E.
34:311, column 2, line 50, for William B., read William
   O.
34:339, column 1, line 40, for Engebret, read Engebreth.
34:362, column 1, line 20, for Charles F., read James M.
34:364, column 2, lines 13-15, delete Citizens Political
   Action Committee. See Progressive Citizens of
   America.
34:366, column 2, line 26, for Ewer, read Ewers.
34:377, column 2, line 23, for Shields, read Shiels.
34:378, column 2, line 24, for Sweeney, read Sweeny.
34:378, column 2, line 26, for Janette, read Jannette.

35:38, column 1, lines 25, 26, for William H., read
   William A.
35:46, column 1, line 43, for Erickson, read Ericksen.
35:60, column 2, line 46, for R. M., read R. J.
35:75, column 1, line 15, for Richard G., read Richard W.
35:87, column 1, line 9, for Henry, read Herbert.
35:94, column 1, line 42, column 2, lines 1, 25, for
   Wiseby, read Wisby.
35:151, column 1, line 36, for Joliet, read Jolliet.
35:151, column 2, lines 28, 29, for Carl Wimer, read
   Charles Wimar.
35:151, column 2, line 33, for F. Mason, read Mason.
35:152, column 2, line 5, for Wisconsin, read Minnesota.
35:242, column 1, line 53, for R. P. Ant., read Rev.
   Antoine.
35:303, column 1, line 3, for F. J., read P. J.
35:335, column 1, line 29, for Harry, read Henry L.
35:335, column 2, line 54, for J. B., read Joseph.
35:348, column 2, line 27, for Schellenbach, read
   Schellbach.
35:349, column 2, line 6, for Alan, read Alan [Allen].
35:369, column 2, line 51, for Pritchardt, read
   Reichardt.
35:389, column 2, line 56, for legislator, read
   publisher.
35:390, column 1, line 17, for 268, read 269.

35:390, column 3, line 61, for 247, read 246.
35:391, column 3, lines 48, 49, for 152, 153, read 180, 181.
35:394, column 1, line 10, for 383, read 382.
35:395, column 1, line 41, for 152, read 153.
35:396, column 1, line 12, for Sioux chief, read Nez Percé leader.
35:403, column 1, line 48, for 152, read 153.
35:403, column 1, line 27, for Carondolet, read Carondelet.
35:405, column 3, line 38, for Olmsted, read Fillmore.
35:408 (errata), delete line 11.

36:33, column 1, line 5, for Hjalmer, read Hjalmar.
36:33, column 2, line 1, for Frank B., read Frank P.
36:35, column 2, line 28, for Carson, read Carlson.
36:67, column 1, line 36, for Alex, read Alec.
36:91, column 1, line 26, for Hygiean, read Hygeian.
36:97, column 2, line 2, for Carl, read Walter.
36:103, column 2, line 19, for Thomas L., read Thomas S.
36:106, column 2, line 19, for Cottonwood, read Nobles.
36:107, column 2, line 41, for 1850s, read 1860s.
36:112 (caption), for W. R., read Nicholas R.
36:183, column 1, line 47, for p. 179, read p. 178.
36:185, column 1, line 13, for Arthur J., read Arthur E.
36:190, column 2, line 51, for Antonio, read Antoine.
36:193, column 1, line 31, for Harold J., read Harold W.
36:239, column 1, line 4, for Hermann R., read Hermann E.
36:306, column 1, line 14, for Lucius B., read Lucius F.
36:323, column 1, line 17, for Du Val, read Duval.
36:330, column 3, line 6, for 179, read 183.
36:332, column 1, line 27, for 132, read 131.
36:334, column 1, line 27, for Kan., read Neb.
36:337, column 1, line 52, for 174, read 175.
36:337, column 2, line 63, for Kellet, read Kellett.
36:343, column 3, line 25, for Rosebloom, read Roseboom.
36:345, column 2, line 10, for 324, read 325.
36:345, column 3, line 19, for 191, read 192.
36:346, column 1, line 15, for 267, read 268.

37:41, column 1, line 3, for Robert S., read Robert A.
37:44, column 1, line 24, for Marian, read Marion.
37:138, column 2, line 12, for John, read Jacob.
37:182, column 2, line 44, for Douglas, read Douglass.
37:262, column 2, line 41, for Troed, read Trued G.
37:308, column 2, line 8, for Francis, read Frances.
37:315, column 1, line 1, for George, read Gouverneur.
37:316, column 2, line 20, for Dominic, read Daniel.
37:316, column 2, line 21, for Blakely, read Blakeley.
37:327, column 1, line 34, for St. Andrew, read St. Andre.
37:350, column 1, line 18, for Rufus G., read Rufus J.
37:358, column 1, line 25, delete 154.
37:362, column 2, line 39, for 11, read 10.
37:363, column 1, line 29, for 11, read 10.

38:29, column 1, line 14, for William J., read J. William.
38:36, column 2, line 22, for Buckhalter, read Burkhalter.

38:55, column 1, line 21, for the same year, read 1859.
38:63, line 3, for William M. Goetzinger, read William H. Goetzinger.
38:131, column 1, line 23, for [William S.], read [William J.].
38:160, column 2, lines 4-6, for on the south edge of the town . . . of gravel spread, read and discovered a partially disturbed burial showing in the wall of the gravel excavation. He found that the pit contained . . .
38:178, column 1, line 10, for 1913 to 1915, read 1912 to 1916.
38:243, column 2, line 20, for Wilbur T., read Wilbur B.
38:293, column 2, lines 30, 32, for "Diamond Joe," read "Diamond Jo."
38:327, column 1, lines 6, 7, 32, for McDermot, read McDermott.
38:377, column 1, lines 39, 40, for 1919, read 1909.
38:381, column 1, line 12, for Roderick, read Roderic.
38:385, column 2, line 32, for William, read Wesley.
38:385, column 2, line 34, for Wright, read Rice.
38:386, column 1, line 54, for McLennan, read MacLennan.

39:59, column 1, line 15, for Gans, read Ganz.
39:91, column 1, line 8, for Rudolf, read Rudolph.
39:143, column 1, line 26, for f, read of.
39:158, column 1, line 24, for June 12, read June 3.
39:170, column 2, line 43, for Brønstad's, read Brøndsted's.
39:176, column 2, lines 14, 23, 30, for Rickett's, read Ricketts'.
39:200 (caption), delete German.
39:238, column 1, line 2, for Noble's, read Nobles'.
39:297, column 1, line 26, for in the United States, read in the continental United States.
39:302, column 1, lines 25, 26, for Claude Godfrey, read Claude-Godefoy.
39:350, column 1, lines 55-57, delete these lines and read
Flandrau, Charles E., quoted, 196; editor, 332
Flandrau, Charles M., critic, 58, 59
39:354, column 1, line 8, for N.W.T., read Yukon.
39:357, column 1, line 13, for singer, read pianist.
39:357, column 2, line 42, for 1930s, read source material.
39:359, column 1, line 42, for 174, read 175.
39:360, column 3, line 7, delete 175.
39:361, column 2, line 37, for 314, read 344.

40:16, lines 1, 2, for Montfort, read Monfort.
40:83, column 1, line 51, column 2, line 13, for Cavalier, read Cavileer.
40:108, column 1, line 17, for 1958, read April, 1952.
40:110, column 1, line 34, for Root River, read Root River Valley.
40:148, column 2, line 29, for Lucius B., read Lucius F.
40:163, column 2, line 19, for Versailles, read Paris.
40:168, column 2, line 44, for McKenzie, read Mackenzie.
40:418, column 2, line 43, for N.D., read Neb.